会计学精选教材·双语注释版

中级会计学

19E **INTERMEDIATE ACCOUNTING**

〔美〕詹姆斯·D.斯蒂斯（James D. Stice） 著
厄尔·K.斯蒂斯（Earl K. Stice）
杨有红 陈凌云 改编

第19版

北京大学出版社
PEKING UNIVERSITY PRESS

著作权合同登记号　图字：01-2016-9808

图书在版编目(CIP)数据

中级会计学：第19版／(美)詹姆斯·D.斯蒂斯(James D.Stice)，(美)厄尔·K.斯蒂斯(Earl K.Stice)著；杨有红，陈凌云改编．—北京：北京大学出版社，2018.6

（会计学精选教材·双语注释版）

ISBN 978-7-301-29256-3

Ⅰ.①中… Ⅱ.①詹… ②厄… ③杨… ④陈… Ⅲ.①会计学—双语教学—高等学校—教材 Ⅳ.①F230

中国版本图书馆 CIP 数据核字(2018)第 032251 号

James D.Stice，Earl K.Stice
Intermediate Accounting，nineteenth edition

Copyright © 2018 Cengage Learning Asia Pte Ltd.
Original edition published by Cengage Learning. All Rights Reserved.

本书原版由圣智学习出版公司出版。版权所有，盗印必究。

Peking University Press is authorized by Cengage Learning to publish, distribute and sell exclusively this custom reprint edition. This edition is authorized for sale in the People's Republic of China only (excluding Hong Kong SAR, Macao SAR and Taiwan). No part of this publication may be reproduced or distributed by any means, or stored in a database or retrieval system, without the prior written permission of Cengage Learning.

此客户定制影印版由圣智学习出版公司授权北京大学出版社独家出版发行。此版本仅限在中华人民共和国境内（不包括香港、澳门特别行政区和台湾地区）销售。未经出版者预先书面许可，不得以任何方式复制或发行本书的任何部分。

本书封面贴有 Cengage Learning 防伪标签，无标签者不得销售。

书　　　名	中级会计学（第 19 版） ZHONGJI KUAIJIXUE
著作责任者	〔美〕詹姆斯·D.斯蒂斯（James D.Stice）　〔美〕厄尔·K.斯蒂斯（Earl K.Stice）　著 杨有红　陈凌云　改编
责任编辑	黄炜婷
标准书号	ISBN 978-7-301-29256-3
出版发行	北京大学出版社
地　　　址	北京市海淀区成府路 205 号　100871
网　　　址	http://www.pup.cn
电子信箱	em@pup.cn　　QQ：552063295
新浪微博	@北京大学出版社　　@北京大学出版社经管图书
电　　　话	邮购部 62752015　发行部 62750672　编辑部 62752926
印　刷　者	涿州市星河印刷有限公司
经　销　者	新华书店
	787 毫米×1092 毫米　16 开本　65.5 印张　1 308 千字 2018 年 6 月第 1 版　2018 年 6 月第 1 次印刷
印　　　数	0001—3000 册
定　　　价	139.00 元

未经许可，不得以任何方式复制或抄袭本书之部分或全部内容。
版权所有，侵权必究
举报电话：010-62752024　电子信箱：fd@pup.pku.edu.cn
图书如有装印质量问题，请与出版部联系，电话：010-62756370

出版者序

作为一家致力于出版和传承经典、与国际接轨的大学出版社，北京大学出版社历来重视国际经典教材，尤其是经管类经典教材的引进和出版。自2003年起，我们与圣智、培生、麦格劳-希尔、约翰·威利等国际著名教育出版机构合作，精选并引进了一大批经济管理类的国际优秀教材。其中，很多图书已经改版多次，得到了广大读者的认可和好评，成为国内市面上的经典。例如，我们引进的世界上最流行的经济学教材——曼昆的《经济学原理》，已经成为国内最受欢迎、使用面最广的经济学经典教材。

呈现在您面前的这套引进版精选教材，是主要面向国内经济管理类各专业本科生、研究生的教材系列。经过多年的沉淀和累积、吐故和纳新，这套教材在各方面正逐步趋于完善：在学科范围上，扩展为"经济学精选教材""金融学精选教材""国际商务精选教材""管理学精选教材""会计学精选教材""营销学精选教材""人力资源管理精选教材"七个子系列，每个子系列下又分为翻译版、英文影印/改编版和双语注释版。其中，翻译版以"译丛"的形式出版。在课程类型上，基本涵盖了经管类各专业的主修课程，并延伸到不少国内缺乏教材的前沿和分支领域；即便针对同一门课程，也有多本教材入选，或难易程度不同，或理论和实践各有侧重，从而为师生提供了更多的选择。同时，我们在出版形式上也进行了一些探索和创新。例如，为了满足国内双语教学的需要，我们改变了部分图书之前单纯影印的形式，而是在此基础上，由资深授课教师根据该课程的重点，添加重要术语和重要结论的中文注释，使之成为双语注释版。此次，我们更新了丛书的封面和开本，将其以全新的面貌呈现给广大读者。希望这些内容和形式上的改进，能够为教师授课和学生学习提供便利。

在本丛书的出版过程中，我们得到了国际教育出版机构同行们在版权方面的协助和教辅资料方面的支持。国内诸多著名高校的专家学者、一线教师，更是在繁重的教学和科研任务之余，为我们承担了图书的推荐、评审和翻译工作；正是每一位推荐者和评审者的国际化视野和专业眼光，帮助我们书海拾慧，汇集了各学科的前沿和经典;正是每一位译者的全心投入和细致校译,保证了经典内容的准确传达和最佳呈现。此外,来自广大读者的反馈既是对我们莫大的肯定和鼓舞,也总能让我们找到提升的空间。本丛书凝聚了上述各方的心血和智慧,在此,谨对他们的热忱帮助和卓越贡献深表谢意!

"千淘万漉虽辛苦,吹尽狂沙始到金。"在图书市场竞争日趋激烈的今天,北京大学出版社始终秉承"教材优先,学术为本"的宗旨,把精品教材的建设作为一项长期的事业。尽管其中有探索、有坚持、有舍弃,但我们深信,经典必将长远传承,并历久弥新。我们的事业也需要您的热情参与!在此,诚邀各位专家学者和一线教师为我们推荐优秀的经济管理图书(em@pup.cn),并期待来自广大读者的批评和建议。您的需要始终是我们为之努力的目标方向,您的支持是激励我们不断前行的动力源泉!让我们共同引进经典、传播智慧,为提升中国经济管理教育的国际化水平做出贡献!

北京大学出版社
经济与管理图书事业部

前　言

现状 + 背景 = 动机

动机

从最小型的夫妻零售店到最大型的跨国公司，各种规模的企业已认识到会计专业人士不再只是简单的"数字计算器"，而是在实现组织根本目标的过程中必不可少的合作伙伴。当人们意识到会计在企业管理和商业决策中的重要作用时，他们开始有目的地学习会计。正是基于这样的背景，《中级会计学》（第19版）紧密联系会计和当前的企业实践，主要表现在：

商业战略案例　每章开篇的商业战略案例揭示了现实世界中的公司。例如，微策略公司（MicroStrategy）如何尽可能地在收入确认与管理层解读收入的压力中进行权衡。

涵盖一些广受关注的热点问题　在当前的商业环境下，会计深受一些热点问题的影响，如盈余管理、公允价值、国际财务报告准则等，本书对此进行了讨论。

美国财务会计准则委员会的准则汇编行为　通过对这些行为的描述将美国财务会计准则委员会的研究与现实的商业情境联系起来，以帮助读者研究和使用官方准则指南，并理解这些指南的重要性。

真实企业案例　每章结篇的案例说明了现实中企业（如华特迪士尼公司、波士顿凯尔特人队、惠普、戴尔等）的财务结果，以帮助读者将会计与商业联系起来。

现状：最新的、相关的范围

读者从任何报刊商业版面的阅读中可以获得一些貌似真实的、长期的成功经验，但过去的成功经验在当前的商业环境下可能很快就不再适用，这是我们在真实世界中将会计作用与商业活动联系起来的第一课。

国际财务报告准则(IFRS) 对国际财务报告准则的讨论贯穿于全书,有助于读者理解不同国家之间的会计实务差异,并反映商业活动中日渐增强的全球化趋势。

商业活动的国际化背景正在使会计环境发生翻天覆地的变化。美国财务会计准则委员会(FASB)和国际会计准则理事会(IASB)正在合作制定一套全球通用的企业会计准则。会计准则的制定不再是美国先行、其他国家紧随其后,取而代之的是FASB和IASB一起合作制定会计准则,这甚至在五年前都是难以想象的。

国际化的商业环境同样对本书影响深远,每一章节在讨论相关的会计准则及其发展时都会兼顾美国和全球其他地区的视角。对企业会计准则和程序的讨论都以美国公认会计原则为出发点,随后探讨美国公认会计原则与国际会计准则显著不同的地方,使读者理解会计准则在全球的趋同和差异。

这种方法的目的是培养读者了解美国之外世界的能力,并理解全球化的商业环境正在导致全球化的会计准则。读者将会发现,他们不但正在学习美国的公认会计原则,而且通过熟练地理解并运用国际会计准则和美国会计准则更加积极地参与全球化的会计环境中。

公允价值会计 这是另一个影响会计环境的重要问题。2008年的信贷危机被部分归因于对公允价值会计的不恰当运用。我们经常用一个模型描述为何、何时、何处、如何在财务报表中使用公允价值,由于公允价值会计的概念十分重要,影响本书中许多原则与专题的讨论,因此我们在结束了对财务报表的学习之后,马上进入公允价值会计的学习。

盈余管理 第6章"盈余管理"为会计学的其余部分构建了一个框架,通过最新的真实案例、美国证券交易委员会处罚公告节选、商业媒体分析以及大量的学术研究结论,读者可以理解盈余管理的重要性及其结果。

美国财务会计准则委员会的准则汇编 我们为读者提供了相关背景及问题,以帮助他们理解在研究中如何使用美国财务会计准则委员会的准则汇编。每一章的准则汇编包括一项现实问题的描述,对于给定背景下的特定问题和"搜索准则汇编"的建议,以引导读者沿着正确的方向展开研究。本书的参考文献也体现了美国会计准则委员会的会计准则汇编(FASB ASC)。

实时更新 《中级会计学》(第19版)进行了全新改版,以反映会计准则、实务和技术的最新变化。在现实中,这些变动已经在企业的财务报表和其他公司报告中得到体现,受其影响,公司的信息披露也已进行了相应修订。

背景:基于组织的商业活动

与其他教材不同,本书试图阐述会计对于组织决策制定能力的整体重要性,尽可能地围绕会计程序和商业活动的基本内在联系来组织相关内容,为读者提供会计业务之后的商业背景。在为读者提供针对商业实践的可靠建议时,这种创造性的结构是卓有成效的。本书的章节顺序更接近传统资产负债表上各项目的顺序,在涉及具体的商业活动时仍然保持相关项目的结构,例如,投资章节在筹资章节之前,为教师和学生提供一个他们更为熟悉的章节顺序。

第一部分——财务会计基础 提供财务会计的基本理论,包括盈余管理、货币时间价值模块和公允价值模块等内容。

第二部分——公司日常经营活动 着眼于商业活动,在讨论企业的经营及投资活动时,将会计与管理相结合。

第三部分——公司其他营运活动 主要讨论企业在筹资、租赁、所得税及员工薪酬计划中的会计处理。

第四部分——财务报告的其他视角 包括每股收益、衍生工具、或有事项、企业分部、中期报告、会计政策变更、财务报表分析等。

为何与如何处理 每章中都有学习目标,还对每一章的关键概念提供补充说明,包括会计程序的概括(说明如何处理)及其背景(说明为何这样处理)。当读者通读全章后,他们不仅能够深刻理解相关的会计要素,还能够理解这些会计处理的商业实质和逻辑。通过揭示每个关键概念的"为什么",培养读者意识到企业的不同决策和商业意义之间的关联,有助于更好地从事会计职业。

这样的框架是基于许多批判性思辨要素的,这些要素使得读者在分析相关主题时能够拓展思维,在学习和工作中应用这种批判性思维也是很关键的。

对现金流量表的"重新修订" 现金流量表贯穿于全书,使得这一重要主题的处理在各章均得到体现。

开放性情境问题 在每章开始提出一些针对公司最新实务的批判性思考问题,在每章结束时提供这些问题的解决方案。当业务处于相关情境时,读者可以与这些解决方案进行比较,思考相关的会计处理。

Stop & Think 在该栏目中,我们提供了一些多项选择题,读者可以测试相关的知识,章末提供相关问题的答案。

FYI 在该栏目中,我们为一些重要问题提供扩展性背景,介绍一些特定的知识点。

Caution　在该栏目中,我们提供在研究复杂概念与问题时的一些注意事项。

"反解"问题　一般出现在章节末,以一个 REVERSE SOLVABLE 图标列示,要求读者根据不完整信息,在完成相关处理前补齐缺失的信息,阐述对会计概念和会计关系的掌握与理解。

各章更新与强调的内容

第1章
- 准则制定程序的更新
- 修订的概念框架和一些最新讨论
- 对美国公认会计原则和国际会计准则理事会准则趋同的进一步解释
- 美国公认会计原则和国际会计准则异同点的延伸讨论

第2章
- 新专栏"使用美国财务会计准则委员会准则汇编"

第3章
- 开放式案例(可口可乐)的更新与修订
- 新专栏"使用美国财务会计准则委员会准则汇编"
- 对提议中的新资产负债表格式的分析

第4章
- 更新表格
- 新专栏"使用美国财务会计准则委员会准则汇编"
- 对提议中的新利润表格式的分析

第5章
- 新专栏"使用美国财务会计准则委员会准则汇编"
- 总结修订的美国财务会计委员会及国际会计准则理事会汇编

第6章
- 更新表格
- 体现次贷危机和经济危机相关内容的修订

货币时间价值模块(删)

公允价值模块(删)

第 7 章
- 更新章节引例以反映全球经济危机
- 新的美国财务会计准则委员会会计准则汇编指南
- 新专栏"使用美国财务会计准则委员会准则汇编"
- 更新表格

第 8 章
- 学习目标修订
- 对美国财务会计委员会和国际会计准则理事会联合项目中收入确认的资产负债方法的更新及延伸讨论
- 新专栏"使用美国财务会计准则委员会准则汇编"
- 更新数据和表格

第 9 章
- 新专栏"使用美国财务会计准则委员会准则汇编"
- 更新数据和表格

第 10 章
- 对美国财务会计准则委员会会计准则汇编指南的全面更新
- 新专栏"使用美国财务会计准则委员会准则汇编"
- 更新数据和表格

第 11 章
- 对美国财务会计准则委员会会计准则汇编指南的全面更新
- 新专栏"使用美国财务会计准则委员会准则汇编"
- 对商誉减值估计的最新讨论
- 更新数据和表格

第 12 章
- 对美国财务会计准则委员会会计准则汇编指南的全面更新
- 新专栏"使用美国财务会计准则委员会准则汇编"
- 更新数据和表格
- 对报告金融资产和金融负债时采用公允价值选择权的最新讨论

第 13 章
- 对美国财务会计准则委员会会计准则汇编指南的全面更新
- 新专栏"使用美国财务会计准则委员会准则汇编"

- 对报告综合收益的最新讨论
- 更新数据和表格

第 14 章

- 对美国财务会计准则委员会会计准则汇编指南的全面更新
- 新专栏"使用美国财务会计准则委员会准则汇编"
- 更新数据和表格
- 对国际财务报告准则和美国公认会计原则下投资性证券分类的最新讨论
- 对采用权益法核算证券采用公允价值选择权的最新讨论

第 15 章

- 对美国财务会计准则委员会会计准则汇编指南的全面更新
- 新专栏"使用美国财务会计准则委员会准则汇编"
- 对未来准则允许多数租赁适用融资租赁的可能性的最新讨论
- 更新数据和表格

第 16 章

- 对美国财务会计准则委员会会计准则汇编指南的全面更新
- 新专栏"使用美国财务会计准则委员会准则汇编"
- 对不确定性税收条款会计处理的延伸讨论

第 17 章

- 对美国财务会计准则委员会会计准则汇编指南的全面更新
- 新专栏"使用美国财务会计准则委员会准则汇编"
- 国际财务报告准则下养老金会计的新范畴
- 关于通用汽车及公司破产对养老金和其他退休后计划的影响的最新讨论

第 18 章(删)

第 19 章

- 对美国财务会计准则委员会会计准则汇编指南的全面更新
- 新专栏"使用美国财务会计准则委员会准则汇编"
- 关于"放弃美国财务会计准则委员会关于增加或有负债披露"提案的最新讨论

第 20 章

- 对美国财务会计准则委员会会计准则汇编指南的全面更新
- 新专栏"使用美国财务会计准则委员会准则汇编"
- 更新数据和表格

第 21 章(删)

第 22 章(删)

第 23 章

- 在权益估值中使用会计数据的示例更新
- 对美国财务会计准则委员会会计准则汇编指南的全面更新
- 新专栏"使用美国财务会计准则委员会准则汇编"

增强学生的理解

丰富的章末资料 在提供多样化、广泛的系列内容安排的基础上,《中级会计学》(第 19 版)继续将内容质量提升到一个新高度,在传统练习、问题和案例上具备了多样化特征:

- 每章设置了 15—25 个问题
- 编排了 400 多个实践练习
- 设置了供课堂讨论或家庭作业的案例讨论
- 提供了习题以加强对关键概念的理解或应用
- 整合了概念和技术的综合性问题
- 针对 CPA 考试中常见的问题,提供了样题以供学习参考

案例资料 为了增强读者在批判性思考、交流、研究和团队工作等方面的基本技能与发展,本书提供了大量的案例资料,基于关键概念的根植和应用而成长的未来会计师与从业者可以用到的很多工具均可以在此找到。这些案例满足了美国注册会计师核心能力框架所支持的以技能为主的课程设置,并得到会计教育改革委员会的推荐。

解读实际的财务报表案例 使读者能够基于公司(如华特迪士尼、可口可乐、波士顿凯尔特人队等)近期的年度报告分析财务数据。

职业道德困境的安排 有助于培养读者的批判性思考能力,这些能力是在真实商业世界中面临一些"灰色"情境所必需的。

欲获得本书相关教辅资料的教师,请填写并反馈"教学支持服务"表格。

简明目录

第一部分　财务会计基础

　　第1章　财务报告
　　第2章　会计循环回顾
　　第3章　资产负债表与财务报表附注
　　第4章　利润表
　　第5章　现金流量表与勾稽关系
　　第6章　盈余管理

第二部分　公司日常经营活动

　　第7章　收入/应收账款/现金循环
　　第8章　收入确认
　　第9章　存货与销售成本
　　第10章　非流动性营运资产的投资——取得
　　第11章　非流动性营运资产的投资——使用和处置

第三部分　公司其他营运活动

　　第12章　债务融资
　　第13章　股权融资
　　第14章　负债和权益类证券投资
　　第15章　租赁
　　第16章　所得税
　　第17章　雇员福利——工资、养老金及其他福利

第四部分　财务报告的其他视角

　　第18章　每股收益(本章删除)
　　第19章　衍生工具、或有事项、企业分部与中期报告
　　第20章　会计变更与差错更正
　　第21章　重温现金流量表(本章删除)
　　第22章　国际会计(本章删除)
　　第23章　财务报表分析
　　附录

CONTENTS

PART ONE: FOUNDATIONS OF FINANCIAL ACCOUNTING

1 FINANCIAL REPORTING 1-1
  Accounting and Financial Reporting 1-4
  Development of Accounting Standards 1-8
  Other Organizations Important to Financial Reporting 1-14
  International Accounting Issues 1-18
  A Conceptual Framework of Accounting 1-20
  Careers in Financial Accounting and the Importance of Personal Ethics 1-32
  Overview of Intermediate Accounting 1-34

2 A REVIEW OF THE ACCOUNTING CYCLE 2-1
  Overview of the Accounting Process 2-3
  Recording Phase 2-5
  Reporting Phase 2-10
  Accrual Versus Cash-Basis Accounting 2-22
  Computers and the Accounting Process 2-24

3 THE BALANCE SHEET AND NOTES TO THE FINANCIAL STATEMENTS 3-1
  Elements of the Balance Sheet 3-4
  Format of the Balance Sheet 3-16
  Balance Sheet Analysis 3-20
  Notes to the Financial Statements 3-27
  Limitations of the Balance Sheet 3-32

4 THE INCOME STATEMENT 4-1
  Income: What It Is and What It Isn't 4-3
  Why Is a Measure of Income Important? 4-5
  How Is Income Measured? 4-7
  Form of the Income Statement 4-13
  Components of the Income Statement 4-14
  Comprehensive Income and the Statement of Stockholders' Equity 4-30
  Forecasting Future Performance 4-34

5 STATEMENT OF CASH FLOWS AND ARTICULATION 5-1
  What Good Is a Cash Flow Statement? 5-3
  Structure of the Cash Flow Statement 5-6
  Reporting Cash Flow from Operations 5-10
  Preparing a Complete Statement of Cash Flows 5-17
  Using Cash Flow Data to Assess Financial Strength 5-23
  Articulation: How the Financial Statements Tie Together 5-26
  Forecasted Statement of Cash Flows 5-28
  Conclusion 5-32

6 EARNINGS MANAGEMENT 6-1
  Motivation for Earnings Management 6-5
  Earnings Management Techniques 6-10
  Pros and Cons of Managing Earnings 6-17
  Elements of Earnings Management Meltdowns 6-21
  Transparent Financial Reporting: The Best Practice 6-26

PART TWO: ROUTINE ACTIVITIES OF A BUSINESS

7 THE REVENUE/RECEIVABLES/CASH CYCLE 7-1
  The Operating Cycle of a Business 7-3
  Accounting for Sales Revenue 7-6
  Monitoring Accounts Receivable 7-15
  Cash Management and Control 7-18
  Presentation of Sales and Receivables in the Financial Statements 7-24
  Expanded Material
  Receivables as a Source of Cash 7-27
  Notes Receivable 7-33
  Impact of Uncollectible Accounts on the Statement of Cash Flows 7-38

8 REVENUE RECOGNITION 8-1
  Revenue Recognition 8-4
  SAB 101 8-6
  A Contract Approach to Revenue Recognition 8-11
  Revenue Recognition Prior to Delivery of Goods or Performance of Services 8-14
  Accounting for Long-Term Service Contracts: The Proportional Performance Method 8-27
  Revenue Recognition After Delivery of Goods or Performance of Services 8-29

Contents

9 INVENTORY AND COST OF GOODS SOLD 9-1
  What Is Inventory? 9-4
  Inventory Systems 9-7
  Whose Inventory Is It? 9-9
  What Is Inventory Cost? 9-11
  Inventory Valuation Methods 9-15
  More About LIFO 9-22
  Overall Comparison of FIFO, LIFO, and Average Cost 9-28
  Inventory Valuation at Other than Cost 9-30
  Gross Profit Method 9-37
  Effects of Errors in Recording Inventory 9-39
  Using Inventory Information for Financial Analysis 9-41
  Expanded Material
  Retail Inventory Method 9-44
  LIFO Pools, Dollar-Value LIFO, and Dollar-Value LIFO Retail 9-47
  Purchase Commitments 9-56
  Foreign Currency Inventory Transactions 9-57

10 INVESTMENTS IN NONCURRENT OPERATING ASSETS—ACQUISITION 10-1
  What Costs Are Included in Acquisition Cost? 10-4
  Acquisitions Other Than Simple Cash Transactions 10-8
  Capitalize or Expense? 10-22
  Accounting for the Acquisition of Intangible Assets 10-28
  Valuation of Assets at Fair Values 10-37
  Measuring Property, Plant, and Equipment Efficiency 10-38

11 INVESTMENTS IN NONCURRENT OPERATING ASSETS—UTILIZATION AND RETIREMENT 11-1
  Depreciation 11-4
  Depletion of Natural Resources 11-17
  Changes in Estimates of Cost Allocation Variables 11-18
  Impairment of Tangible Assets 11-20
  Amortization and Impairment of Intangibles 11-25
  Asset Retirements 11-30
  Expanded Material
  Depreciation for Partial Periods 11-37
  Income Tax Depreciation 11-39

PART THREE: ADDITIONAL ACTIVITIES OF A BUSINESS

12 DEBT FINANCING 12-1
  Classification and Measurement Issues Associated with Debt 12-4
  Accounting for Short-Term Debt Obligations 12-8
  Present Value of Long-Term Debt 12-13
  Financing with Bonds 12-14
  Fair Value Option 12-35
  Off-Balance-Sheet Financing 12-38
  Analyzing a Firm's Debt Position 12-43
  Disclosing Debt in the Financial Statements 12-45
  Expanded Material
  Accounting for Troubled Debt Restructuring 12-46

13 EQUITY FINANCING 13-1
  Nature and Classifications of Paid-In Capital 13-5
  Issuance of Capital Stock 13-10
  Stock Repurchases 13-14
  Stock Rights, Warrants, and Options 13-18
  Accounting for Share-Based Compensation 13-20
  Reporting Some Equity-Related Items as Liabilities 13-27
  Stock Conversions 13-33
  Factors Affecting Retained Earnings 13-34
  Accounting for Dividends 13-38
  Statement of Comprehensive Income and Other Equity Items 13-45
  Disclosures Related to the Equity Section 13-50

14 INVESTMENTS IN DEBT AND EQUITY SECURITIES 14-1
  Why Companies Invest in Other Companies 14-4
  Classification of Investment Securities 14-8
  Purchase of Securities 14-12
  Recognition of Revenue from Investment Securities 14-14
  Accounting for the Change in Value of Securities 14-24
  Sale of Securities 14-29
  Transferring Securities between Categories 14-33
  Investment Securities and the Statement of Cash Flows 14-36
  Classification and Disclosure 14-39
  Expanded Material
  Accounting for the Impairment of a Loan 14-43

15 LEASES 15-1
  Economic Advantages of Leasing 15-3
  Simple Example 15-4
  Nature of Leases 15-6
  Lease Classification Criteria 15-9
  Accounting for Leases—Lessee 15-13
  Accounting for Leases—Lessor 15-22
  Disclosure Requirements for Leases 15-34
  International Accounting of Leases 15-37
  Expanded Material
  Sale-Leaseback Transactions 15-38

Contents

16 INCOME TAXES 16-1
- Deferred Income Taxes: An Overview 16-3
- Annual Computation of Deferred Tax Liabilities and Assets 16-9
- Carryback and Carryforward of Operating Losses 16-22
- Scheduling for Enacted Future Tax Rates 16-25
- Financial Statement Presentation and Disclosure 16-26
- Deferred Taxes and the Statement of Cash Flows 16-30
- International Accounting for Deferred Taxes 16-31

17 EMPLOYEE COMPENSATION—PAYROLL, PENSIONS, AND OTHER COMPENSATION ISSUES 17-1
- Routine Employee Compensation Issues 17-3
- Nonroutine Employee Compensation Issues 17-8
- Accounting for Pensions 17-10
- Comprehensive Pension Illustration 17-21
- Disclosure of Pension Plans 17-37
- Postretirement Benefits Other than Pensions 17-41

PART FOUR: OTHER DIMENSIONS OF FINANCIAL REPORTING

18 EARNINGS PER SHARE (本章刪除)

19 DERIVATIVES, CONTINGENCIES, BUSINESS SEGMENTS, AND INTERIM REPORTS 19-1
- Simple Example of a Derivative 19-2
- Types of Risk 19-5
- Types of Derivatives 19-6
- Types of Hedging Activities 19-11
- Accounting for Derivatives and for Hedging Activities 19-12
- Accounting for Contingencies: Probable, Possible, and Remote 19-22
- Business Segments 19-29
- Interim Reports 19-33

20 ACCOUNTING CHANGES AND ERROR CORRECTIONS 20-1
- Accounting Changes 20-3
- Change in Accounting Estimate 20-5
- Change in Accounting Principle 20-8
- Pro Forma Disclosures after a Business Combination 20-14
- Error Corrections 20-15

21 STATEMENT OF CASH FLOWS REVISITED (本章刪除)

22 ACCOUNTING IN A GLOBAL MARKET (本章刪除)

23 ANALYSIS OF FINANCIAL STATEMENTS 23-1
- Framework for Financial Statement Analysis 23-2
- Impact of Alternative Accounting Methods 23-19
- Introduction to Equity Valuation 23-21

APPENDIX: INDEX OF REFERENCES TO APB AND FASB PRONOUNCEMENTS A-1

P1
Foundations of Financial Accounting

CHAPTER 1

Financial Reporting

Learning Objectives

1. Describe the purpose of financial reporting and identify the primary financial statements.

2. Explain the function of accounting standards and describe the role of the FASB in setting those standards in the United States.

3. Recognize the importance of the SEC, AICPA, AAA, and IRS to financial reporting.

4. Realize the growing importance and relevance of international accounting issues to the practice of accounting in the United States and understand the role of the IASB in international accounting standard setting.

5. Understand the significance of the FASB's conceptual framework in outlining the qualities of good accounting information, defining terms such as *asset* and *revenue*, and providing guidance about appropriate recognition, measurement, and reporting.

6. Identify career opportunities related to accounting and financial reporting and understand the importance of personal ethics in the practice of accounting.

It all started with a French accountant named René Ricol. In mid-2008, Mr. Ricol was commissioned by French President Nicolas Sarkozy to write a report on the impact of the worldwide financial crisis of 2007 and 2008.[1] This 148-page report covers a variety of topics including the origins of the crisis, the ongoing response by governments and business, and 30 detailed recommendations for additional actions. But on page 53, Mr. Ricol wrote something that was to have explosive consequences. He wrote: "At present, it is important to ensure that . . . a level playing field between European and U.S. [accounting] rules is achieved." By implication, according to Mr. Ricol, one reason that European banks were having such severe difficulties in the third quarter of 2008 was that U.S. accounting rules were giving an advantage to U.S. banks.

Mr. Sarkozy passed Mr. Ricol's report along to the assembled EU Finance Ministers, who happened to be meeting in Paris. These ministers were shocked—shocked to learn that U.S. accounting rules were creating an "unlevel playing field" to the advantage of U.S. banks. The Finance Ministers issued a communiqué on October 7, 2008, calling for: "[T]he necessity of avoiding any distortion of treatment between U.S. and European

---

[1] René Ricol, "Report to the President of the French Republic on the Financial Crisis," September 2008.

banks due to differences in accounting rules.... We also consider that the issue of asset reclassification must be resolved quickly.... We expect this issue to be solved by the end of the month, with the objective to implement as of the third quarter."[2]

So, to whom was the call to arms addressed? To the International Accounting Standards Board (IASB), based in London and designated by the European Union as the approved source of accounting standards for all EU nations. IASB standards, collectively known as International Financial Reporting Standards (IFRS), are also recognized as the source of generally accepted accounting principles in every sizable economy in the world... every sizable economy except one, the United States.

Attention turned to Sir David Tweedie, chairman of the IASB. Sir David was told that the IASB had three days to revise IFRS. Three *days*? The due process requirements of both the IASB and its U.S. counterpart, the Financial Accounting Standards Board (FASB), typically result in proposed accounting standards being circulated and discussed for *years*, not days. However, Sir David was told that without an immediate rule change, the EU would go around the IASB and unilaterally change the accounting rules for companies in its constituent countries. It is reported that Sir David considered resigning.[3] However, in order to live to fight another day, he succumbed to the EU pressure and rushed through the accounting change.

So, what was this accounting rule that was viewed as threatening the very survival of European banks? The accountants call it "fair value accounting," and in the business press it is often called "mark-to-market accounting." For companies, such as banks, that actively trade stocks and bonds, the mark-to-market rule says that the investments must be reported on the company's books at current market value, with any paper gains or losses (called "unrealized" gains or losses by the accountants) being reported in the company's income statement. Well, during the third quarter of 2008 (from July 2008 through September 2008), there had been HUGE paper losses for banks and other investors all over the world. These losses reduced the recorded capital of banks and threatened to put many banks in violation of their regulatory capital requirements. So, you can see why banks in particular were upset at "mark-to-market accounting." *Note:* No one seemed to complain much about mark-to-market accounting in the years when the market was up.

Back to Mr. Ricol. He claimed to have found a provision in the U.S. accounting rules that allowed U.S. banks to reclassify their investment securities into a category that accountants call "held to maturity." The important thing about held-to-maturity securities is that they are reported in the balance sheet at their original cost, not their current market value, with any changes in value being ignored. Thus, this appears to be a loophole that U.S. banks could use to sidestep the harsh impact of mark-to-market accounting. At least that is the way this U.S. rule was explained to the EU Finance Ministers. What the Finance Ministers were not told is that this reclassification is so rare that no one can think of an example of a U.S. company ever actually doing it. In addition, the U.S. rule requires the reclassification to "held-to-maturity" to be done at the prevailing market value on the date of the reclassification, so any paper gains or losses must be recorded in full on that day. This doesn't seem like much of a loophole. But remember, the EU Finance Ministers probably weren't given a full briefing on all the aspects of the U.S. rule; they were only told that this U.S. loophole allowed U.S. banks to avoid mark-to-market accounting, thus appearing to create an unlevel international playing field with European banks being the losers.

Now the story gets really interesting. In drafting the hasty revision to its rules, someone in the IASB (no one is saying who) made the IASB version of this reclassification rule applicable retroactively to July 1, 2008. Very clever. The IASB rule was approved on October 13, 2008, two weeks AFTER the end of the fiscal third quarter of the year.[4] By that time, European banks were able to see which of their investments had gone up and which had gone down during the third quarter. This new IASB rule allowed the European banks to roll back the clock to July 1, 2008, and with the benefit of hindsight, designate some investments to be accounted for using mark-to-market accounting (probably the ones that they now knew went up during the third quarter) and some investments to be reclassified as "held to maturity" at the value existing as of July 1 (probably the ones that they knew, with hindsight, went down during the third quarter).

So, this IASB rule revision, intended to "level" the international playing field, substantially tilted the playing field in favor of those European banks that chose to use it. Some European banks quickly backed away from this blatant manipulation of the accounting rules for their benefit. For example, in its third quarter 2008 financial report, BNP Paribas specifically stated that: "BNP Paribas did not use, in the third quarter 2008, the amendment to the *IAS 39* accounting standard authorising the transfer of certain assets... from the trading book to other portfolios."[5] On the other hand, Deutsche Bank gratefully used the retroactive provision to turn a loss into a profit. Without the retroactive reclassifications, Deutsche Bank would have reported a pretax loss of €732 million for the third quarter. With the reclassifications, Deutsche Bank was able report a pretax profit of €93 million, which it proudly hailed in its third quarter report.[6]

There are certainly historical examples of U.S. politicians putting pressure on the FASB to revise its rules for some perceived benefit or another. But in the United States, the FASB is somewhat shielded from these pressures by the Securities and Exchange Commission (SEC). Internationally, there is no global SEC, so the IASB was left on its own to experience the full force of the European Union's political pressure. Predictably, when faced with an EU ultimatum, the IASB buckled.

---

[2] Ecofin Council of 7 October 2008, "Immediate responses to financial turmoil."
[3] David Jetuah, "Tweedie nearly quit after fair value change," *Accountancy Age*, November 12, 2008.
[4] "Reclassification of Financial Assets—Amendments to *IAS 39 Financial Instruments: Recognition and Measurement and IFRS 7 Financial Instruments: Disclosures*," International Accounting Standards Board, London, October 2008.
[5] BNP Paribas Press Release, "Results as at 30 September 2008," November 5, 2008, Paris.
[6] Deutsche Bank, "Interim Report as of September 30, 2008," October 2008, Frankfurt am Main, pages 2 and 53.

Across the Atlantic, U.S. regulators and the U.S. business community could only stand back and watch this political power play with a mixture of amazement and disgust. As of October 2008, the SEC had an announced policy, a "time line," for shifting all U.S. accounting rule-making responsibility to the IASB by 2014. This policy stemmed from two incontrovertible facts: (1) global capital markets demand a uniform set of accounting rules, and (2) the world will never accept "Yankee" control of this one-world standard. So, the SEC had the choice of either watching the international harmonization parade go by or getting in line behind the IASB banner. However, the October 2008 IASB debacle caused both the SEC and the U.S. business community to reevaluate the benefits of ceding standard-setting power to the IASB, an organization that had now revealed itself as being subject to powers more interested in the well-being of European banks than in any abstract notion of global accounting harmony. It was time to rethink the "time line."

SEC Chairman Mary Shapiro was never as enthusiastic about international accounting convergence as her predecessor, Christopher Cox, was. She was fearful of "convergence" really being a "race to the bottom" in terms of a degradation in the quality of the U.S. financial reporting environment. During 2009, Chairman Shapiro said cautiously that the "time line" was on hold until the SEC determined exactly how it wanted to proceed.

The SEC's new international accounting convergence "work plan" was announced on February 24, 2010.[7] The SEC is still convinced that "a single set of high-quality globally accepted accounting standards would benefit U.S. investors." However, the SEC has expressed concern about both the quality of the international standards and the process by which those standards are set. Specifically, before ceding standard-making authority to the IASB (or any other international body, for that matter), the SEC wants to ensure that "accounting standards are set by an independent standard-setter and for the benefit of investors." The implication is that the SEC wants to be convinced that the IASB won't again cave in to EU pressure to twist an accounting rule to the benefit of European banks or some other powerful EU constituency. The SEC's "work plan" also states that the SEC will not switch over to IFRS until 2015, at the earliest.

The IASB has since attempted to create a barrier between itself and the political pressure aimed at it—a Monitoring Board that includes representation from a number of important international regulators, including SEC chair Shapiro. It isn't clear yet whether this Monitoring Board has or can serve as a shield between the IASB and international political pressure. Time will tell.

So, what has been the result of that report written by René Ricol? The primary result has been to bring home, dramatically, the remaining barriers to international convergence in financial reporting. The U.S. business community was forced to face the reality that it really doesn't want its reporting rules set by a London-based group that is essentially controlled by the European Union. In addition, all interested parties, both in the United States and overseas, have seen that the IASB differs from the FASB in one extremely important way—the pronouncements of the FASB have the force of law because the regulatory power of the SEC is behind them. But who will enforce the pronouncements of the IASB? Who will ensure that the provisions are applied in a consistent way in each country around the world? Will it ever really be possible to have one truly global set of accounting standards, uniformly interpreted, implemented, and audited? For now, it looks like the answer may be: No.

1. What is "mark-to-market accounting"?
2. When the IASB adopted its amended rule in October 2008, what was significant about the fact that the rule was written so that companies could apply the rule retroactively to July 1, 2008?
3. What impact did the October 2008 IASB debacle have in the United States?

Answers to these questions can be found on page 1-35.

In this text, you will learn about many of the key accounting issues integral to an understanding of the October 2008 IASB case described above: the accounting for investment securities in Chapter 14, fair value accounting in the Fair Value Module, and the ongoing effort by the IASB and the FASB to achieve convergence on a globally accepted set of high-quality accounting standards. In fact, this IASB-FASB convergence is such an important issue that it is discussed in every chapter in this book, starting with this one.

As the October 2008 IASB case illustrates, the intricacies of accounting often result in differences of opinion as to what accounting methods are appropriate and the level of

---

[7] SEC Press Release 2010-27, "SEC Approves Statement on Global Accounting Standards," U.S. Securities and Exchange Commission, February 24, 2010, Washington, D.C.

disclosure that should be required of companies. Arguments over appropriate accounting are facts of life because accounting involves judgment. Even in cases that don't involve financial statement scandal or political intrigue, the management of a company is likely to have some accounting disagreements with the independent auditor before the company's financial statements are released. If a company falters, outside analysts are sure to find accounting judgments with which, in retrospect, they disagree. If the FASB or IASB propose a new accounting rule, it is certain that some business executives will proclaim the rule to be utterly absurd. This is not because managers are sleazy, conniving, and self-serving (although such managers certainly exist); it is because the business world is a complex place filled with complex transactions, and reasonable people can disagree about how to account for those transactions. As the chapters in this book will explain in detail, accounting for the complex transactions that are commonplace today is much more than the simple "bean-counting" image portrayed of accounting in the popular press.

Your introductory accounting course gave you an overview of the primary financial statements and touched briefly on such topics as revenue recognition, depreciation, leases, pensions, deferred taxes, LIFO, and financial instruments. In intermediate accounting, all these topics are back, bigger and better than ever. Now, instead of getting an overview, you will actually get the nuts and bolts. Yes, some of these topics are complex—they are complex because the business world is a complex place. However, when you complete your course in intermediate accounting, you will be quite comfortable with a set of financial statements. In fact, you will probably find yourself skipping the statements themselves and turning directly to the really interesting reading—the notes.

Now is an exciting time to be studying accounting. Students have been learning double-entry bookkeeping for more than 500 years. Now it will be your privilege to witness the transformation of financial reporting via the twin forces of internationalization and information technology. Over the next five years, the increased integration of the worldwide market for capital will finally force diverse national accounting practices to converge to one global standard, with the United States being one of the last countries to accept that global standard. This text will help you understand the "how and why" of this process. In the longer term, the power of computers to create and analyze huge databases will change the very nature of accounting. Users will not learn about companies through a few pages of financial statements and notes but, ultimately, through online access to the raw financial data. It isn't clear what "accounting" will entail in the technological future, but it is certain that those professionals trained in the underlying concepts of accounting and in the importance of accounting judgment and accounting estimates will be best able to make the transition. This book is intended to prepare you for the future.

Accounting and Financial Reporting

LO1 学习目标1
描述财务报告的目的，了解主要的财务报表。

会计的全部目标就是为制定经济决策提供有用信息。

① Describe the purpose of financial reporting and identify the primary financial statements.

The overall objective of accounting is to provide information that can be used in making economic decisions.

> Accounting is a service activity. Its function is to provide quantitative information, primarily financial in nature, about economic entities that is intended to be useful in making economic decisions—in making reasoned choices among alternative courses of action.[8]

[8] *Statement of the Accounting Principles Board No. 4*, "Basic Concepts and Accounting Principles Underlying Financial Statements of Business Enterprises" (New York: American Institute of Certified Public Accountants, 1970), par. 40.

Several key features of this definition should be noted.

- Accounting provides a vital service in today's business environment. The study of accounting should not be viewed as a theoretical exercise—accounting is meant to be a practical tool.
- Accounting is concerned primarily with quantitative financial information that is used in conjunction with qualitative evaluations in making judgments.
- Accounting information is used in making decisions about how to allocate scarce resources. Economists and environmentalists remind us constantly that we live in a world with limited resources. The better the accounting system that measures and reports the costs of using these resources, the better decisions can be made for allocating them.
- Although accountants place much emphasis on reporting what has already occurred, this past information is intended to be useful in making economic decisions about the future.

> **Caution**
> Remember that accounting information is only one type of information used in decision making. In many cases, qualitative data are more useful than quantitative data.

Users of Accounting Information

Who uses accounting information and what information do they require to meet their decision-making needs? In general, all parties interested in the financial health of a company are called stakeholders.

stakeholders
利益相关者

Stakeholder users of accounting information are normally divided into two major classifications:

- Internal users, who make decisions directly affecting the internal operations of the enterprise
- External users, who make decisions concerning their relationship to the enterprise

Major internal and external stakeholder groups are listed in Exhibit 1-1.

Internal users need information to assist in planning and controlling company operations and managing company resources. The accounting system must provide timely information needed to control day-to-day operations and to make major planning decisions such as:

- Do we make this product or another one?
- Do we build a new production plant or expand existing facilities?

management accounting
管理会计

Management accounting (sometimes referred to as *managerial* or *cost accounting*) is concerned primarily with financial reporting for internal users. Internal users, especially management, have control over the accounting system and can specify precisely what information is needed and how the information is to be reported.

financial accounting
财务会计

Financial accounting focuses on the development and communication of financial information for external users. As a company grows and expands, it often finds its need for cash to be greater than that provided from profitable operations. In this situation, it will turn to people or organizations external to the company for funding. These external users need assurances that they will receive a return on their investment. Thus, they require information about the company's past performance because this information will allow them to forecast how the company can be expected to perform in the future.

Companies compete for external funding because external users have a variety of investment alternatives. The accounting information provided to external users aids in

Exhibit 1-1 | Major Internal and External Stakeholder Groups

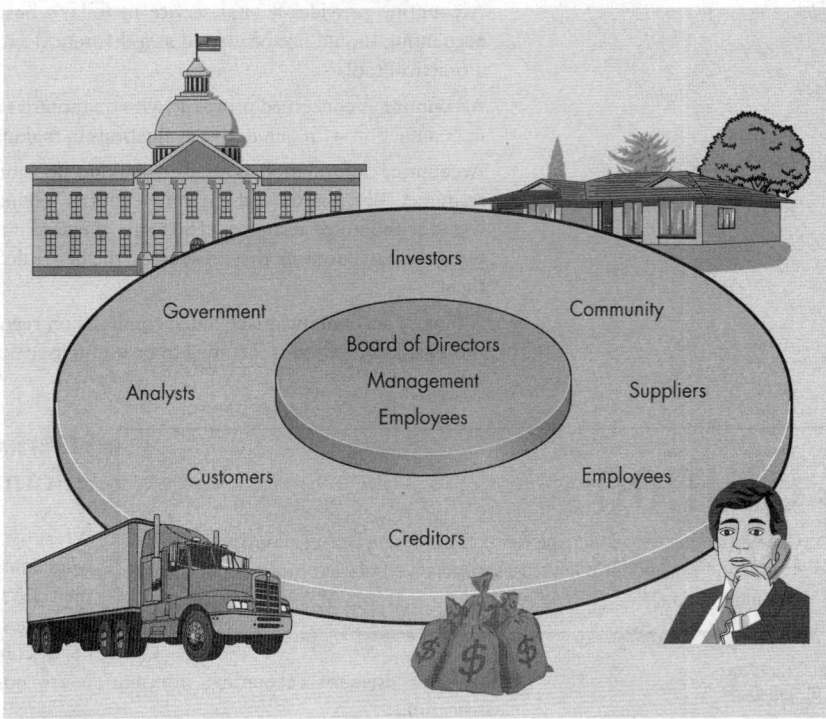

determining (1) whether a company's operations are profitable enough to justify additional funding and (2) how risky a company's operations are in order to determine what rate of return is necessary to compensate capital providers for the investment risk.

The types of decisions made by external users vary widely; therefore, their information needs are highly diverse. As a result, two groups of external users, creditors and investors, have been identified as the principal external users of financial information. Creditors need information about the profitability and stability of the company to decide whether to lend money to the company and, if so, what interest rate to charge. Investors (both existing stockholders and potential investors) need information concerning the safety and profitability of their investment.

creditors
债权人
investors
投资人

Incentives

As mentioned, companies often need external funding if they are to compete in the marketplace. Thus, the managers of these companies have an incentive to provide information that will attract external funding. They want to present information to external users that will make it appear as though their companies will be profitable in the future.

In their pursuit of external funding, management may not be as objective in evaluating and presenting accounting information as external users would like. As a result, care must be taken to ensure that accounting information is neutral. Standards have been established and safeguards have been implemented in an attempt to ensure that accounting information is neutral and objective.

Financial Reporting

Most accounting systems are designed to generate information for both internal and external reporting. The external information is much more highly summarized than the information reported internally. Understandably, a company does not want to disclose every detail of its internal financial dealings to outsiders. For this reason, external financial reporting is governed by an established body of standards or principles that are designed to carefully define what information a firm must disclose to outsiders. Financial accounting standards also establish a uniform method of presenting information so that financial reports for different companies can be more easily compared. The development of these standards is discussed in some detail later in this chapter.

This textbook focuses on financial accounting and external reporting. The **general-purpose financial statements** are the centerpiece of financial accounting. These financial statements include the balance sheet, income statement, and statement of cash flows.

The three major financial statements, along with the explanatory notes and the auditor's opinion, are briefly described here.

general purpose financial statements
通用财务报表

- The **balance sheet** reports, as of a certain point in time, the resources of a company (the assets), the company's obligations (the liabilities), and the net difference between its assets and liabilities, which represents the equity of the owners. The balance sheet addresses these fundamental questions: What does a company own? What does it owe?

balance sheet reports
资产负债表

- The **income statement** reports, for a certain interval, the net assets generated through business operations (revenues), the net assets consumed (expenses), and the difference, which is called *net income*. The income statement is the accountant's best effort at measuring the economic performance of a company for the given period.

income statement reports
利润表

- The **statement of cash flows** reports, for a certain interval, the amount of cash generated and consumed by a company through the following three types of activities: operating, investing, and financing. The statement of cash flows is the most objective of the financial statements because it is somewhat insulated from the accounting estimates and judgments needed to prepare a balance sheet and an income statement.

statement of cash flows reports
现金流量表

- Accounting estimates and judgments are outlined in the notes to the financial statements. In addition, the notes contain supplemental information as well as information about items not included in the financial statements. Using financial statements without reading the notes is like preparing for an intermediate accounting exam by just reading the table of contents of the textbook—you get the general picture, but you miss all of the important details. Each financial statement routinely carries the following warning printed at the bottom of the statement: "The notes to the financial statements are an integral part of this statement."

FYI

The cash flow statement is the most recent of the primary financial statements. It has been required only since 1988.

Stop & Think

In addition to the financial statements, the management of a company has a variety of other methods of communicating financial information to external users. Which ONE of the following is NOT one of those methods?
a) Press releases
b) Postings on the Internet
c) Interviews with financial reporters
d) Paid advertisements in the financial press
e) Preparation and dissemination of detailed operating budgets
f) Public meetings with analysts, institutional investors, and other interested parties

unqualified
无保留意见

unqualified, with explanatory language
无保留意见加解释说明段

qualified
保留意见

no opinion
拒绝表示意见

adverse
否定意见

Exhibit 1-2 | Relative Frequency of Audit Opinions

Types of Audit Opinions Relative Frequency For the Year 2006	Companies
UNQUALIFIED: Financial statements are in accordance with generally accepted accounting principles. They are consistent, and all material information has been disclosed.	2,369
UNQUALIFIED, WITH EXPLANATORY LANGUAGE: The opinion is unqualified, but the auditor has felt it necessary to emphasize some item with further language.	3,624
QUALIFIED: Either the audit firm was somehow constrained from performing all the desired tests, or some item is accounted for in a way with which the auditor disagrees.	5
NO OPINION: The auditor refuses to express an opinion, usually because there is great uncertainty about whether the audited firm will be able to remain in business.	0
ADVERSE: The financial statements are not in accordance with generally accepted accounting principles.	1
Total	5,999

Source: Standard and Poor's *COMPUSTAT*. The database includes firms traded on the New York, American, and NASDAQ exchanges.

- Auditors, working independently of a company's management and internal accountants, examine the financial statements and issue an auditor's opinion about the fairness of the statements and their adherence to proper accounting principles. The opinion is based on evidence gathered by the auditor from the detailed records and documents maintained by the company and from a review of the controls over the accounting system. Obviously, management is motivated to present the financial information in the most favorable manner possible. It is the responsibility of the auditors to review management's reports and to independently decide whether the reports are indeed representative of the actual conditions existing within the enterprise. The auditor's opinion adds credibility to the financial statements. The types of opinions issued by auditors, along with their relative frequencies, are outlined in Exhibit 1-2. As you can see, the audit opinion is almost always "unqualified."

The financial statements and accompanying notes (certified by the auditor's opinion) have historically been the primary mode of communicating financial information to external users.

Development of Accounting Standards

LO2 学习目标2
解释会计准则的功能，简述FASB在制定美国会计准则中所起的作用。

② Explain the function of accounting standards and describe the role of the FASB in setting those standards in the United States.

Consider this situation. A company decides to pay its managers partly in cash and partly in the form of options to buy the company's stock. The options would be very valuable if the company's stock price were to increase but would be worthless if the company's stock price were to decline. Because the company gives these potentially valuable options to employees, cash salaries don't need to be as high.

Should the value of the options be reported as salary expense or not? (You'll learn the answer to this surprisingly explosive question in Chapter 13.) One alternative is to let each company decide for itself. Users then must be careful about comparing the financial statements of two companies that have accounted for the same thing differently. Another alternative is to have one standard accounting treatment. Who sets the standard?

Accounting principles and procedures have evolved over hundreds of years in response to changes in business practices. The formal standard-setting process that exists today in the United States, however, has developed in just the past 75 years. The triggering event was the Stock Market Crash of 1929. In the aftermath of the crash, many market observers claimed that stock prices had been artificially inflated through questionable accounting practices. The Securities and Exchange Commission (SEC) was created to protect the interests of investors by ensuring full and fair disclosure. The SEC was also given specific legal authority to establish accounting standards for companies desiring to publicly issue shares in the United States. The emergence of the SEC forced the U.S. accounting profession to unite and to become more diligent in developing accounting principles. This led over time to the formation of a series of different private-sector organizations, each having the responsibility of issuing accounting standards. These organizations, their publications, and the time they were in existence are identified in Exhibit 1-3. The SEC has generally allowed these private-sector organizations to make the accounting standards in the United States. These standards are commonly referred to as generally accepted accounting principles (GAAP). Remember, however, that the SEC retains the legal authority to establish U.S. accounting standards if it so chooses.

Financial Accounting Standards Board

The Financial Accounting Standards Board (FASB) is currently recognized as the private-sector body responsible for the establishment of U.S. accounting standards. The FASB was organized in 1973, replacing the Accounting Principles Board (APB). The APB was replaced because it had lost credibility in the business community and was seen as being too heavily influenced by accountants. As a result, the seven full-time members of the FASB are drawn from a variety of backgrounds—auditing, corporate accounting, financial services, and academia.[9] The members are required to sever all connections with their firms

Exhibit 1-3 | U.S. Accounting Standard-Setting Bodies

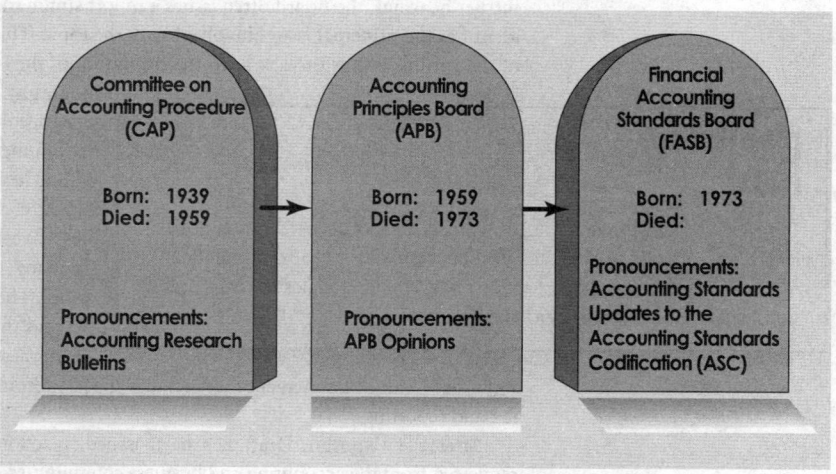

[9] When it was initially established, the FASB was structured to have seven board members. This number was reduced to five on July 1, 2008. In August 2010, it was announced that the FASB would return to seven board members in 2011.

or institutions prior to assuming membership on the Board. Members are appointed for five-year terms and are eligible for reappointment to one additional term. Headquartered in Norwalk, Connecticut, the Board has its own research staff and a 2011 operating budget of $35.6 million, much of which comes from fees levied under the Sarbanes-Oxley Act on companies publicly traded in the United States.

Appointment of new Board members is done by the Financial Accounting Foundation (FAF). The FAF is an independent, self-perpetuating body that, like the FASB, is made up of representatives from the accounting profession, the business world, government, and academia. However, the FAF has no standard-setting power, and its members are not full time. The FAF serves somewhat like a board of directors, overseeing the operations of the FASB. In addition to overseeing the FASB, the FAF is also responsible for selecting and supporting members of the Governmental Accounting Standards Board (GASB). The GASB was established in 1984 and sets financial accounting standards for state and local government entities.

Financial Accounting Foundation (FAF)
财务会计基金会

Governmental Accounting Standards Board (GASB)
政府会计准则委员会

The Standard-Setting Process

The major functions of the FASB are to study accounting issues and to establish accounting standards. These standards are published as Accounting Standards Updates. The FASB has also issued Statements of Financial Accounting Concepts that provide a framework within which specific accounting standards can be developed. The conceptual framework of the FASB is detailed later in the chapter.

Statements of Financial Accounting Concepts
财务会计概念公告

FASB准则制定程序的最大特点就是公开性。

The hallmark of the FASB's standard-setting process is openness. Because so many companies and individuals are impacted by the FASB's standards, the Board is meticulous about holding open meetings and inviting public comment. At any given time, the Board has a number of major projects under way. For example, as of September 10, 2012, the FASB was engaged in 21 agenda projects, 9 of which are joint projects with the IASB, which is described later in this chapter. These FASB projects address fundamental issues such as revenue recognition as well as technical issues relating to very complex business transactions such as insurance contracts.

Each major project undertaken by the Board involves a lengthy process. The FASB staff assembles background information and the Board holds public meetings before a decision is made to even add a project to the FASB's formal agenda. After more study and further hearings, the Board often issues a report summarizing its *Preliminary Views*, which identifies the principal issues involved with the topic. This document includes a discussion of the various points of view as to the resolution of the issues, as well as an extensive bibliography, but it does not include specific conclusions. Interested parties are invited to comment either in writing or orally at a public hearing.

After comments from interested parties have been evaluated, the Board meets as many times as necessary to resolve the issues. These meetings are open to the public, and the agenda is published in advance. From these meetings, the Board develops an Exposure Draft of a statement that includes specific recommendations for financial accounting and reporting.

> **FYI**
> The FASB is quite scrupulous about holding all of its deliberations in public. In fact, since four (of seven) votes are required to pass a FASB proposal, Board members are even careful not to discuss accounting issues at social occasions when three or more Board members are present.

After the Exposure Draft has been issued, reaction to the new document is again requested from the accounting and business communities. At the end of the exposure period, 60 days or longer if the topic is a major one, all comments are reviewed by the staff and

> **Caution**
>
> This description makes the standard-setting process seem orderly and serene. It is not. Fierce disagreements over accounting standards are common, and some people hate the FASB.

the Board. Further deliberation by the Board leads to either the issuance of an *Accounting Standards Update* (if at least four of the FASB members approve), a revised Exposure Draft, or in some cases, abandonment of the project. As you can see, the standard-setting process is a political one, full of consensus building, feedback, and compromise.

The final statement not only sets forth the actual standards but also establishes the effective date and method of transition. It also gives pertinent background information and the basis for the Board's conclusions, including reasons for rejecting significant alternative solutions. If any members dissent from the majority view, they may include the reasons for their dissent as part of the document. These dissents are interesting reading. For example, the dissent to the standard on the statement of cash flows (released in 1987) reveals that the Board members disagreed about a fundamental issue—whether payment of interest is an operating activity or a financing activity.[10]

Emerging Issues Task Force The methodical, sometimes slow, nature of the standard-setting process has been one of the principal points of criticism of the FASB. There seems to be no alternative to the lengthy process, however, given the philosophy that arriving at a consensus among members of the accounting profession and other interested parties is important to the Board's credibility.

In an effort to overcome this criticism and provide more timely guidance on issues, in 1984 the FASB established the Emerging Issues Task Force (EITF). The EITF assists the FASB in the early identification of emerging issues that affect financial reporting. Members of the EITF include the senior technical partners of the major national CPA firms plus representatives from major associations of preparers of financial statements. In addition, observers from the SEC, the AICPA, and the IASB (three organizations discussed later in this chapter) are invited to participate in the EITF discussions. The EITF meets periodically, typically at least once every quarter.

As an emerging issue is discussed, an attempt is made to arrive at a consensus treatment for the issue. If a consensus is reached by the EITF, that consensus must then be approved by a majority of the FASB members. That consensus opinion then defines the generally accepted accounting treatment unless and until the FASB decides to reconsider the issue. The EITF not only helps the FASB and its staff to better understand emerging issues but also in many cases determines that no immediate FASB action is necessary.

The consensus opinions of the EITF are published as Accounting Standards Updates. These updates are identified by a two-part number; the first part represents the year the issue was discussed, and the second part identifies the update number for that year. For example, among the consensuses reached in 2010 was Update No. 2010-17, "Milestone Method of Revenue Recognition," which deals with the timing of the reporting of revenue in long-term projects involving significant performance milestones such as the completion

---

[10] Three of the seven members of the FASB dissented to the issuance of the standard on the statement of cash flows. Prior to 1991, a majority of the seven-member board (four members) was the minimum requirement for approval of an Exposure Draft or a final statement of standards. This requirement was changed to a minimum approval of five members, or to what has been referred to as a "super-majority." A number of close, four to three, votes that resulted in standards not favored by many businesspeople led to strong pressure on the Financial Accounting Foundation to change the voting requirements. Although not favored by members of the FASB, the change was made in 1990. In April 2002, the voting requirement was changed back to four to three as an attempt to increase the efficiency and speed of the Board's deliberations.

of certain regulatory requirements in a pharmaceutical study. (*Note:* We will talk about revenue recognition at length in Chapter 8.) Although many of the issues are very specialized by topic and industry, the importance of the EITF to the standard-setting process cannot be overemphasized. Because discussions rarely last more than a day or two and a consensus is reached on a majority of the issues discussed, timely guidance is provided to the accounting profession without the lengthy due process of the FASB.

FASB Accounting Standards Codification™ As you saw in the discussion above, both the FASB standards and the EITF consensus opinions are published as Accounting Standards Updates. These Updates serve as formal notification that the official body of generally accepted accounting standards (GAAP) has been updated. This official source of U.S. GAAP is called the FASB Accounting Standards Codification (ASC) and is found on the FASB's Web site at **asc.fasb.org**.

Prior to the launching of the FASB ASC in July 2009, the FASB standards and the EITF consensus opinions were made available as numbered lists of items. So, if you wanted to know about the accounting for research and development costs, for example, you had to know that the accounting for normal R&D costs was contained in FASB *Statement of Financial Accounting Standards No. 2* (released in 1974), unless the R&D cost was for software development, in which case the accounting was described in *Statement No. 86* (released in 1985). In other words, for everyone except the experienced practitioners and the old accounting professors who had been around for a thousand years, finding a specific accounting rule on a specific topic involved a primitive hunt-and-peck strategy.

The FASB ASC employs a topical menu structure. Accounting topics are grouped under nine broad categories. Each category contains a collection of topics. For example, under the Presentation group of topics, you can find Topic 210 on the balance sheet, Topic 230 on the statement of cash flows, Topic 260 on earnings per share, and more. Under the Broad Transactions group of topics, you can find Topic 805 on business combinations, Topic 840 on leases, and more. A list of topic groupings and individual topics is given in Exhibit 1-4.[11]

Within each Topic, the accounting standard content is organized in additional menus leading eventually down to the paragraph level. A paragraph in the FASB ASC is identified with a four-part address: Topic-Subtopic-Section-Paragraph. For example, the paragraph that explains that cash paid for interest is to be classified in the statement of cash flows as an operating activity is FASB ASC 230-10-45-17.

- The first number, 230, designates the topic Statement of Cash Flows (which is in the Presentation group of topics).
- The second number, 10, indicates that this is an Overall issue, or subtopic. Other types of subtopics provide standards for particular types of transactions or industries. For example, under Topic 230, there are subtopics explaining statement of cash flow issues related to foreign currency exchange rates, cash flows in the film industry, and others.
- The third number, 45, indicates that this section addresses "Other Presentation Matters." The set of sections under each subtopic is standardized. For most subtopics you will see a section (10) on Objectives, another section (30) on how accounting items are to be initially measured, and so forth.
- Finally, the fourth number (17) indicates the exact paragraph where the text of the accounting standard is found. In this case, FASB ASC paragraph 230-10-45-17 reads

---

[11] For those who have a subscription to the "Professional View" of the FASB ASC, key word searches are also possible. The "Basic View" is free, and instructions for registering for the "Basic View" are given in this chapter. The "Professional View" costs about $800 per year. However, your college or university accounting department may have registered for free student access to the "Professional View." Ask your instructor.

as follows (in part): "All of the following are cash outflows for operating activities . . . (d) Cash payments to lenders and other creditors for interest."

In this textbook you will see many, many references to the FASB ASC. Any person who plans to work in a field where financial statements are prepared or used needs to become comfortable with the Codification. Each chapter in this book includes a short research

Exhibit 1-4 | Topics in the FASB Accounting Standards Codification as of September 2012

General Principles
- 105 Generally Accepted Accounting Principles

Presentation
- 205 Presentation of Financial Statements
- 210 Balance Sheet
- 215 Statement of Shareholder Equity
- 220 Comprehensive Income
- 225 Income Statement
- 230 Statement of Cash Flows
- 235 Notes to Financial Statements
- 250 Accounting Changes and Error Corrections
- 255 Changing Prices
- 260 Earnings Per Share
- 270 Interim Reporting
- 272 Limited Liability Entities
- 274 Personal Financial Statements
- 275 Risks and Uncertainties
- 280 Segment Reporting

Assets
- 305 Cash and Cash Equivalents
- 310 Receivables
- 320 Investments—Debt and Equity Securities
- 323 Investments—Equity Method and Joint Ventures
- 325 Investments—Other
- 330 Inventory
- 340 Other Assets and Deferred Costs
- 350 Intangibles—Goodwill and Other
- 360 Property, Plant, and Equipment

Liabilities
- 405 Liabilities
- 410 Asset Retirement and Environmental Obligations
- 420 Exit or Disposal Cost Obligations
- 430 Deferred Revenue
- 440 Commitments
- 450 Contingencies
- 460 Guarantees
- 470 Debt
- 480 Distinguishing Liabilities from Equity

Equity
- 505 Equity

Revenue
- 605 Revenue Recognition

Expenses
- 705 Cost of Sales and Services
- 710 Compensation—General
- 712 Compensation—Nonretirement Postemployment Benefits
- 715 Compensation—Retirement Benefits
- 718 Compensation—Stock Compensation
- 720 Other Expenses
- 730 Research and Development
- 740 Income Taxes

Broad Transactions
- 805 Business Combinations
- 808 Collaborative Arrangements
- 810 Consolidation
- 815 Derivatives and Hedging
- 820 Fair Value Measurement
- 825 Financial Instruments
- 830 Foreign Currency Matters
- 835 Interest
- 840 Leases
- 845 Nonmonetary Transactions
- 850 Related Party Disclosures
- 852 Reorganizations
- 855 Subsequent Events
- 860 Transfers and Servicing

Note: The specific Industry topics are omitted from this list of topics. Go to **asc.fasb.org** to see the entire list.

© Cengage Learning 2014

exercise to give you practice finding things in the ASC. And the end of each chapter includes a matrix that summarizes the FASB ASC material relating to the items covered in that chapter. This matrix also includes references to the old pre-Codification standard numbers, just in case you run across a long-time accountant who has refused to learn the new Codification references. Finally, these end-of-chapter matrices contain the corresponding references to the International Accounting Standards, which are discussed later in this chapter.

FASB Summary Remember this: The FASB has no enforcement power. Legal authority to set U.S. accounting standards rests with the SEC. FASB standards are "generally accepted," meaning that, overall, the FASB standards are viewed by the business community as being good accounting. However, the credibility of the FASB has fluctuated through the years as different issues have been resolved. For example, within the past 10 years the business community has been outraged by proposed standards for accounting for stock-based compensation and for goodwill. In both of those cases (which are discussed in Chapters 13 and 10, respectively), the FASB was forced to significantly revise its initial proposal. The FASB's job has been described as a "balancing act" between theoretical correctness and practical acceptability.

In addition to the FASB, several other bodies impact accounting standards and are important in other ways to the practice of accounting. Some of these bodies are discussed here.

Other Organizations Important to Financial Reporting

LO3 学习目标3
认识SEC、AICPA、AAA和IRS对财务报告的重要影响。

③ Recognize the importance of the SEC, AICPA, AAA, and IRS to financial reporting.

Securities and Exchange Commission

The SEC was created by an act of Congress in 1934. Its primary role is to regulate the issuance and trading of securities by corporations to the general public. Prior to offering securities for sale to the public, a company must file a registration statement with the Commission that contains financial and organizational disclosures. In addition, all publicly held companies are required to furnish annual financial statements (called a *10-K filing*), quarterly financial statements (*10-Q filing*), and other periodic information about significant events (*8-K filing*). The SEC also requires companies to have their external financial statements audited by independent accountants.

The Commission's intent is not to prevent the trading of speculative securities but to insist that investors have adequate information. As a result, the SEC is vitally interested in financial reporting and the development of accounting standards. The Commission carefully monitors the standard-setting process. The Commission also brings to the Board's attention emerging problems that need to be addressed and sends observers to meet with the EITF.

FYI
The first chairman of the SEC was Joseph P. Kennedy, father of the late President John F. Kennedy.

When the Commission was formed, Congress gave it power to establish accounting principles as follows:

> The Commission may prescribe, in regard to reports made pursuant to this title, the form or forms in which the required information shall be set forth, the items or details to be shown in

the balance sheet and the earning statement, and the methods to be followed in the preparation of reports in the appraisal or valuation of assets and liabilities....[12]

The Commission has generally refrained from fully using these powers, preferring to work through the private sector in the development of standards. Throughout its existence, however, the Commission has issued statements pertaining to accounting and auditing issues. These SEC statements are authoritative for companies that are publicly traded in the United States. This fact is made clear in FASB ASC paragraph 105-10-05-1, as follows.

Rules and interpretive releases of the Securities and Exchange Commission (SEC) under authority of federal securities laws are also sources of authoritative GAAP for SEC registrants. In addition to the SEC's rules and interpretive releases, the SEC staff issues Staff Accounting Bulletins that represent practices followed by the staff in administering SEC disclosure requirements, and it utilizes SEC Staff Announcements and Observer comments made at Emerging Issues Task Force meetings to publicly announce its views on certain accounting issues for SEC registrants.

The formal SEC rules are found in the Code of Federal Regulations (CFR). For example, on March 4, 2008, Chapter II of Title 17 of the CFR was amended by the SEC to allow non-U.S. companies to use International Accounting Standards, instead of U.S. GAAP, in their financial statement filings with the SEC. This is an extremely interesting development that will be discussed in more detail later in this chapter.

Although the SEC is generally supportive of the FASB, there have been disagreements between the two bodies. One of the most public of these disagreements occurred in the late 1970s and concerned the accounting for oil and gas exploratory costs. The FASB issued a standard in 1977, and the SEC publicly opposed the standard; the FASB finally succumbed to the pressure and reversed its position in 1979. In recent years, the SEC and FASB have increased their efforts at behind-the-scenes coordination and consultation. Still, the two bodies are not in complete harmony. For example, the SEC has been impatient with the FASB's slow progress on improving financial reporting. Often, the SEC establishes broad disclosure requirements in an area while the FASB deliberates about the specific accounting rules. In recent years, this was the pattern with stock-based compensation, environmental disclosures, and derivatives.

As mentioned above, the SEC requires all publicly traded companies in the United States to have their financial statements audited. The auditors of those financial statements must be registered and periodically inspected by the Public Company Accounting Oversight Board (PCAOB), which is a private-sector organization created by the Sarbanes-Oxley Act of 2002. The SEC has congressional authority to oversee the PCAOB's activities.

American Institute of Certified Public Accountants

The American Institute of Certified Public Accountants (AICPA) is the professional organization of practicing certified public accountants (CPAs) in the United States. The organization was founded in 1887, and it publishes a monthly journal, the *Journal of Accountancy*. (*Note:* Anyone interested in current developments in accounting should regularly read the *Journal of Accountancy*.) The AICPA has several important responsibilities, including certification and continuing education for CPAs, quality control, and standard setting.

---

[12] Securities Exchange Act of 1934, Section 13(b).

The AICPA is responsible for preparing and grading the Uniform CPA Examination. This computer-based examination is offered year round in authorized testing centers around the United States. In addition to passing the examination, an individual must meet the state education and experience requirements in order to obtain state certification as a CPA. Most states now require CPAs to meet continuing education requirements in order to retain their licenses to practice. The AICPA assists its members in meeting these requirements through an extensive Continuing Professional Education (CPE) program.

The AICPA is also concerned with maintaining the integrity of the profession through its Code of Professional Conduct and through a quality control program, which includes a process of peer review of CPA firms conducted by other CPAs. For CPA firms that audit publicly traded clients, these AICPA peer reviews are now somewhat overshadowed by the registration and inspection program of the PCAOB mentioned previously.

Prior to the formation of the FASB, accounting principles were established under the direction of the AICPA. Both the CAP and the APB were AICPA committees. Although the FASB replaced the APB as the official standard-setting body for the profession, the AICPA continues to influence the establishment of accounting standards. The AICPA helps the FASB identify emerging issues and communicates the concerns of CPAs on accounting issues to the FASB. In addition, the AICPA frequently establishes the specialized standards that relate to particular industries. For example, in *Statement of Position (SOP) 04-2*, the AICPA issued a set of rules for the accounting for a variety of real estate time-sharing transactions.

American Accounting Association

American Accounting Association (AAA)
美国会计学会

The American Accounting Association (AAA) is an organization for accounting professors, with 6,052 academic members as of August 2009. The AAA sponsors national and regional meetings where accounting professors discuss technical research and share innovative teaching techniques and materials. The AAA also organizes working committees of professors to study and comment on accounting standards issues. In addition, the AAA publishes a number of academic journals, including *The Accounting Review*, a quarterly research journal, and *Accounting Horizons*, which contains articles addressing many real-world accounting problems. In fact, *Accounting Horizons* is an excellent journal to read for more depth on intermediate accounting issues.

FYI
Ask your instructor if he or she is a member of the AAA.

One of the most significant actions of the AAA is to motivate and facilitate curriculum revision. As the accounting profession changes, it is critical that accounting educators continually revise their curricula to keep pace with these changes. The AAA provides forums for educators to share ideas about changes in curriculum and rewards innovative curriculum revision efforts. For example, in 1993, our university (Brigham Young University) was given the *Innovation in Accounting Education Award* for the integrative revision of our intermediate financial accounting, managerial accounting, tax, audit, and information systems courses. By the way, Brigham Young University received this accounting education innovation award again in 2007 (the only university to receive it twice), but we probably shouldn't tell you any more because you might think we are bragging.

Internal Revenue Service

Tax accounting and financial accounting are different, but the popular perception is that they are one and the same. Tax accounting and financial accounting were designed with different purposes in mind. In the **Thor Power Tool** case (1979), the Supreme Court stated:

> The primary goal of financial accounting is to provide useful information to management, shareholders, creditors, and others properly interested; the major responsibility of the accountant is to protect these parties from being misled. The primary goal of the income tax system, in contrast, is the equitable collection of revenue....

Although this text on intermediate financial accounting is not a study of income tax accounting, the U.S. tax rules as administered by the Internal Revenue Service (IRS) will still be discussed from time to time. In most areas, financial accounting and tax accounting are closely related. For example, your study of leases, depreciation, and inventory valuation in this text will aid your understanding of the corresponding tax rules.

What Is GAAP?

With all of these different bodies (FASB, EITF, AICPA, and SEC) being involved with accounting rules and accounting guidance, what is GAAP? Historically, the Auditing Standards Board of the AICPA has defined GAAP in the context of the phrase included in the standard auditor's opinion: "present fairly . . . in conformity with generally accepted accounting principles."[13] Both the SEC and the AICPA have recognized the FASB as the body entrusted with establishing GAAP in the United States. So, it is the FASB that determines what GAAP is. With the activation of the FASB Accounting Standards Codification in July 2009, the FASB clarified exactly which accounting rules and statements are "authoritative" GAAP and which are merely nonauthoritative suggestions. In FASB ASC paragraph 105-10-05-1, the FASB clearly states that the standards contained in the Codification itself are "the source of authoritative generally accepted accounting principles (GAAP) recognized by the FASB." In paragraph 3 of the same section, the FASB states: "Accounting and financial reporting practices not included in the Codification are nonauthoritative. . . . The appropriateness of other sources of accounting guidance depends on its relevance to particular circumstances, the specificity of the guidance, the general recognition of the issuer or author as an authority, and the extent of its use in practice." These sources of nonauthoritative guidance include widely recognized industry practices, the standards of the IASB (discussed later in this chapter), FASB Concepts Statements (also discussed later in this chapter), and even lowly accounting textbooks such as the one you are reading right now. The chapters in this textbook will, of course, focus on the authoritative standards in the FASB ASC.

For firms required to file financial statements with the SEC, the SEC rules and interpretive releases have the same authority as the FASB's Codification. These authoritative pronouncements are of particular importance to auditors because Rule 203 of the AICPA Code of Professional Conduct specifies that an auditor must not express an unqualified opinion when there is a material departure from these authoritative pronouncements.

In the description of the authoritative pronouncements, note that the Statements of Financial Accounting Concepts are relegated to a low-priority position, equal in authority with accounting textbooks(!). The FASB plans to address this issue in a broader project to improve the conceptual framework. As discussed later in this chapter, the conceptual framework embodied in the Statements of Financial Accounting Concepts forms an increasingly important foundation for all financial accounting standards.

---

[13] *Statement of Auditing Standards No. 69,* "The Meaning of Present Fairly in Conformity with Generally Accepted Accounting Principles in the Independent Auditor's Report" (New York: AICPA, December 1991).

FASB CODIFICATION

The Issue: You were at a party last night and, inevitably, the conversation turned to accounting and the FASB. You were embarrassed to learn that ALL of your friends have registered for access to the FASB Accounting Standards Codification (ASC). They were swapping amusing stories about various standards they had been looking at that day in the FASB ASC. You could feel your friends giving you the collective cold shoulder when it became obvious that you had never even seen the FASB ASC.

The Question: What are the steps I need to go through to register for access to the FASB ASC?

Searching the Codification: You start by going to **asc.fasb.org**. Follow the steps to register as a "New User." If you get stuck, take a look at the solution for this Codification item.

The Answer: The correct process is described on page 1-35.

International Accounting Issues

 Realize the growing importance and relevance of international accounting issues to the practice of accounting in the United States and understand the role of the IASB in international accounting standard setting.

LO4 学习目标4
认识国际会计问题对于美国会计实务的日益增强的重要性与相关性，理解国际会计准则理事会（IASB）在国际会计准则制定中的作用。

Divergent national accounting practices around the world can have an extremely significant impact on reported financial statements. With the increasing integration of the worldwide economy, these accounting differences have become impossible to ignore. For example, to raise debt or equity capital, many non-U.S. firms, such as **Sony**, **British Petroleum**, and **Nokia**, list their securities on U.S. exchanges and borrow from U.S. financial institutions. As of September 2012, over 420 non-U.S. share issues (from more than 45 countries) were trading on the New York Stock Exchange (NYSE). In addition, many U.S. companies have listed their shares on foreign exchanges; for example, **Boeing**'s shares trade on the Amsterdam, Brussels, London, Swiss, and Tokyo stock exchanges. U.S. companies also do substantial amounts of business in foreign currencies; **Disney** has significant amounts of business denominated in Japanese yen, European euros, British pounds, and Canadian dollars.

业务活动的国际化要求公司所编制的财务报表能够为世界各国的使用者所理解。各国会计准则的巨大差异增大了财务报表编制及使用者对报表理解的复杂性。

The international nature of business requires companies to be able to make their financial statements understandable to users all over the world. The significant differences in accounting standards that exist throughout the world complicate both the preparation of financial statements and the understanding of these financial statements by users.

International Differences in GAAP

As will be noted throughout this text, there are some differences between U.S. GAAP and GAAP of other countries. The good news is that the fundamental concepts underlying accounting practice are the same around the world. As a result, a solid understanding of U.S. GAAP will allow you to quickly grasp the variations that exist in different countries. Throughout this book, we will include specific coverage of the areas in which significant differences exist in accounting practices around the world. One other piece of good news is that the demands of international financial statement users are forcing accountants around the world to harmonize differing accounting standards. Accordingly, the differences that currently exist will gradually diminish over time.

International Accounting Standards Board

International Accounting Standards Board (IASB)
国际会计准则理事会

Just as the FASB establishes accounting standards for U.S. entities, other countries have their own standard-setting bodies. In an attempt to harmonize conflicting standards, the International Accounting Standards Board (IASB) was formed in 1973 to develop worldwide accounting standards. Like the FASB, the IASB develops proposals, circulates these among interested organizations, receives feedback, and then issues a final pronouncement. The 15 board members of the IASB come from many countries and represent a variety of professional backgrounds.[14]

As of September 2012, the 15 board members included individuals from the Netherlands, the United States, the United Kingdom, France, Sweden, China, Australia, South Africa, Brazil, Germany, Korea, India, and Japan. Most of the board members are CPAs with audit experience, but in May 2010 the IASB also included a financial analyst and several people with national regulatory experience.

The early standards of the IASB were primarily catalogs of the diverse accounting practices then used worldwide. Recent IASB projects have been more focused and innovative. For example, the substance of IASB decisions on improving earnings-per-share reporting was embraced by the FASB. In fact, the FASB and the IASB worked closely to develop compatible standards. In 2002, the IASB and the FASB entered into a joint agreement, called the Norwalk Agreement, in which they pledged to work together to develop a set of "fully compatible" accounting standards as soon as possible, and to continue to work together to make sure that those standards stay compatible. This agreement was confirmed and expanded in an FASB/IASB Memorandum of Understanding updated in 2008. This joint effort is proceeding along two fronts. First, the IASB and the FASB have identified several accounting standard issues on which they could achieve full compatibility without too much difficulty. These issues include the accounting for some inventory costs, accounting for the exchange of nonmonetary assets, and the reporting of accounting changes, all of which have been completed, and the computation of earnings per share, which is still in progress. Second, the IASB and FASB are working together on larger projects involving fundamental issues such as revenue recognition, the accounting for business combinations, and a joint conceptual framework.

The accounting standards produced by the IASB are referred to as *International Financial Reporting Standards (IFRS)* and *International Accounting Standards (IAS)*. The difference between these two sets of standards is merely one of timing; the IASB standards issued before 2001 are called *IAS* and those issued since 2001 are called *IFRS*. In practice, the entire body of IASB standards is referred to simply as *IFRS*. The international counterpart of the FASB's Emerging Issues Task Force (EITF) is called the International Financial Reporting Interpretations Committee (IFRIC), which was called the Standing Interpretations Committee (SIC) before 2002.

IFRSs are envisioned to be a set of standards that can be used by all companies regardless of where they are based. In fact, IFRS will supplement or even replace standards set by national standard setters such as the FASB. IASB standards have gained widespread acceptance throughout the world. And as mentioned earlier, in 2008 the SEC began allowing non-U.S. companies with shares trading on U.S. stock exchanges to issue their financial reports using IASB standards. Before this change, all non-U.S. companies wishing to have their shares traded in the United States were required to provide financial statements in

[14] The IASB will be expanded to 16 members by 2012.

FYI

In 2001, the IASB restructured itself as an independent body with closer links to national standard-setting bodies. At that time, the IASB adopted its current name and dropped its original name of the International Accounting Standards Committee (IASC).

Stop & Think

Consider these four organizations: FASB, AICPA, SEC, and IASB. Which ONE do you think will be making U.S. GAAP 10 years from now?
a) FASB
b) AICPA
c) SEC
d) IASB

accordance with U.S. GAAP. Historically, financial disclosure requirements in the United States have been the strictest in the world, and foreign companies have been reluctant to provide the U.S. GAAP disclosures. With the new SEC rule, the number of non-U.S. companies listed on U.S. stock exchanges may increase dramatically.

As mentioned in the opening scenario for this chapter, the SEC is considering whether to allow U.S. companies to use IASB standards, rather than FASB standards, in the financial reports that they provide to their U.S. shareholders. If this happens, the FASB may cease to exist. So pay attention because the next few years will be momentous ones in terms of the history of accounting standard setting. However, lest you despair over losing your good friend (the FASB) about whom you have just been reading, remember from the opening scenario of this chapter that the current SEC "work plan" does not envision a U.S. switch to IFRS until 2015 at the earliest. Remember, there are lots of issues of enforcement and independence to work out before the SEC turns the reins over to the IASB. In this textbook, you will learn both U.S. GAAP and, where there are substantive differences, IFRS.

In order to prepare you for a professional world in which both FASB and IASB standards will be used, both sets of standards will be covered in this textbook. The focus will be on FASB standards, but you will also receive comprehensive exposure to the IASB standards in each major topic area throughout the chapters of the text. In addition, Chapter 22 contains capstone coverage of International Accounting Standards.

A Conceptual Framework of Accounting

LO5 学习目标5

理解FASB概念框架在概括高质量会计信息的特征，定义资产、收入等概念，以及为合理确认、计量和报告提供指导方面所具有的重要意义。

conceptual framework
概念框架

⑤ Understand the significance of the FASB's conceptual framework in outlining the qualities of good accounting information, defining terms such as *asset* and *revenue*, and providing guidance about appropriate recognition, measurement, and reporting.

A strong theoretical foundation is essential if accounting practice is to keep pace with a changing business environment. Accountants are continually faced with new situations, technological advances, and business innovations that present new accounting and reporting problems. These problems must be dealt with in an organized and consistent manner. The conceptual framework plays a vital role in the development of new standards and in the revision of previously issued standards. Recognizing the importance of this role, the FASB stated that fundamental concepts "guide the Board in developing accounting and reporting standards by providing . . . a common foundation and basic reasoning on which to consider merits of alternatives."[15] In a very real sense, then, the FASB itself is a primary beneficiary of a conceptual framework.

---
[15] *Statement of Financial Accounting Concepts No. 6*, "Elements of Financial Statements" (Stamford, CT: Financial Accounting Standards Board, December 1985), p. i.

In addition, when accountants are confronted with new developments that are not covered by GAAP, a conceptual framework provides a reference for analyzing and resolving emerging issues. Thus, a conceptual framework not only helps in understanding existing practice but also provides a guide for future practice.

Nature and Components of the FASB's Conceptual Framework

Serious attempts to develop a theoretical foundation of accounting can be traced to the 1930s. Among the leaders in such attempts were accounting educators, both individually and collectively, as a part of the AAA. In 1936, the Executive Committee of the AAA began issuing a series of publications devoted to accounting theory, the last of which was published in 1965 and entitled "A Statement of Basic Accounting Theory." During the period from 1936 to 1973, the AAA and the AICPA issued several additional publications in their attempt to develop a conceptual foundation for the practice of accounting.[16]

> **Caution**
>
> Don't think that the conceptual framework is a useless exercise in accounting theory. Since its completion, the framework has significantly affected the nature of many accounting standards.

Although these publications made significant contributions to the development of accounting thought, no unified structure of accounting theory emerged from these efforts. When the FASB was established in 1973, it responded to the need for a general theoretical framework by undertaking a comprehensive project to develop a "conceptual framework for financial accounting and reporting." This project has been described as an attempt to establish a so-called constitution for accounting.

The conceptual framework project was one of the original FASB agenda items. Because of its significant potential impact on many aspects of financial reporting and, therefore, its controversial nature, progress was deliberately slow. The project had high priority and received a large share of FASB resources. In September 2010, after almost 40 years of discussions, the FASB issued the eighth of the Statements of Financial Accounting Concepts (usually referred to as *Concepts Statements*), which provide the basis for the conceptual framework.[17]

---

[16] Among the most prominent of these publications were the following:
- Maurice Moonitz, *Accounting Research Study No. 1*, "The Basic Postulates of Accounting" (New York: American Institute of Certified Public Accountants, 1961).
- William A. Paton and A. C. Littleton, "An Introduction to Corporate Accounting Standards, Monograph 3" (Evanston, IL: American Accounting Association, 1940).
- Thomas H. Sanders, Henry R. Hatfield, and W. Moore, "A Statement of Accounting Principles" (New York: American Institute of Accountants, Inc., 1938).
- Robert T. Sprouse and Maurice Moonitz, *Accounting Research Study No. 3*, "A Tentative Set of Broad Accounting Principles for Business Enterprises" (New York: American Institute of Certified Public Accountants, 1962).
- *Statement of the Accounting Principles Board No. 4*, "Basic Concepts and Accounting Principles Underlying Financial Statements of Business Enterprises" (New York: American Institute of Certified Public Accountants, October 1970).
- *Report of the Study Group on the Objectives of Financial Statements*, "Objectives of Financial Statements" (New York: American Institute of Certified Public Accountants, October 1973).

[17] The eight Concepts Statements issued by the FASB are
(1) Objectives of Financial Reporting by Business Enterprises (superseded by *Concepts Statement No. 8*)
(2) Qualitative Characteristics of Accounting Information (superseded by *Concepts Statement No. 8*)
(3) Elements of Financial Statements of Business Enterprises (superseded by *Concepts Statement No. 6*)
(4) Objectives of Financial Reporting by Nonbusiness Organizations
(5) Recognition and Measurement in Financial Statements of Business Enterprises
(6) Elements of Financial Statements (a replacement of No. 3, broadened to include not-for-profit as well as business enterprises)
(7) Using Cash Flow Information and Present Value in Accounting Measurements
(8) Chapter 1, *The Objective of General Purpose Financial Reporting*, and Chapter 3, *Qualitative Characteristics of Useful Financial Information* (a replacement of FASB *Concepts Statements No. 1* and *No. 2*)

Concepts Statement No. 8 is the first in an expected series of Concepts Statements that are the joint work of the FASB and the IASB.

The eight Concepts Statements address four major areas.

1. *Objectives:* What are the purposes of financial reporting?
2. *Qualitative characteristics:* What are the qualities of useful financial information?
3. *Elements:* What is an asset? a liability? a revenue? an expense?
4. *Recognition, measurement, and reporting:* How should the objectives, qualities, and elements definitions be implemented?

Objectives of Financial Reporting

Without identifying the goals for financial reporting (e.g., who needs what kind of information and for what reasons), accountants cannot determine the recognition criteria needed, which measurements are useful, or how best to report accounting information. The key financial reporting objectives outlined in the conceptual framework are as follows:

- Usefulness
- Understandability
- Target audience: investors and creditors
- Assessing future cash flows
- Evaluating economic resources
- Financial performance reflected by accrual accounting

Usefulness The overall objective of financial reporting is to provide information that is useful for decision making. The FASB states

> The objective of general purpose financial reporting is to provide financial information about the reporting entity that is useful to existing and potential investors, lenders, and other creditors in making decisions about providing resources to the entity.[18]

Understandability Financial reports cannot and should not be so simple as to be understood by everyone. Instead, the objective of understandability recognizes a fairly sophisticated user of financial reports, that is, one who has a reasonable understanding of accounting and business and who is willing to study and analyze the information presented.[19] In other words, the information should be comprehensible to someone like you.

Target Audience: Investors, Lenders, and Other Creditors Although there are many potential users of financial reports, the objectives are directed primarily toward investors and creditors. Other external users, such as the IRS or the SEC, can require selected information from individuals and companies. Investors and creditors, however, must rely to a significant extent on the information contained in the periodic financial reports supplied by management. In addition, information useful to investors and creditors in most cases will be useful to other external users (i.e., customers and employees).

Assessing Future Cash Flows Investors and creditors are interested primarily in a company's future cash flows. Creditors expect interest and loan principals to be paid in cash. Investors desire cash dividends and sufficient cash flow to allow the business to grow. Thus, financial reporting should provide information that is useful in assessing amounts, timing, and uncertainty (risk) of prospective cash flows.

概念框架中概括的财务报告主要目标如下:
- 有用性;
- 可理解性;
- 目标群体为投资者和债权人;
- 评估未来现金流量;
- 评估经济资源;
- 反映财务业绩。

---

[18] *Statement of Financial Accounting Concepts No. 8*, par. OB2.
[19] *Statement of Financial Accounting Concepts No. 8*, par. QC30 through QC32.

The estimated cost of environmental cleanup represents a trade-off of relevance and faithful representation.

Evaluating Economic Resources
Financial reporting should also provide information about a company's assets, liabilities, and owners' equity to help investors, creditors, and others evaluate the financial strengths and weaknesses of the enterprise and its liquidity and solvency. Such information will help users determine the financial condition of a company, which, in turn, should provide insight into the prospects of future cash flows.

Financial Performance Reflected by Accrual Accounting
Information about a company's financial performance (the change in its economic resources caused by its operations) is useful in assessing a company's ability to generate future cash flows. This financial performance is best reflected by accrual accounting.[20]

Qualitative Characteristics of Accounting Information

The overriding objective of financial reporting is to provide useful information. This is a very complex objective because of the many reporting alternatives. To assist in choosing among financial accounting and reporting alternatives, the conceptual framework identifies the qualitative characteristics of useful accounting information. These qualitative characteristics are separated into fundamental characteristics and enhancing characteristics. These characteristics are outlined in Exhibit 1-5.

Exhibit 1-5 | Qualitative Characteristics of Accounting Information

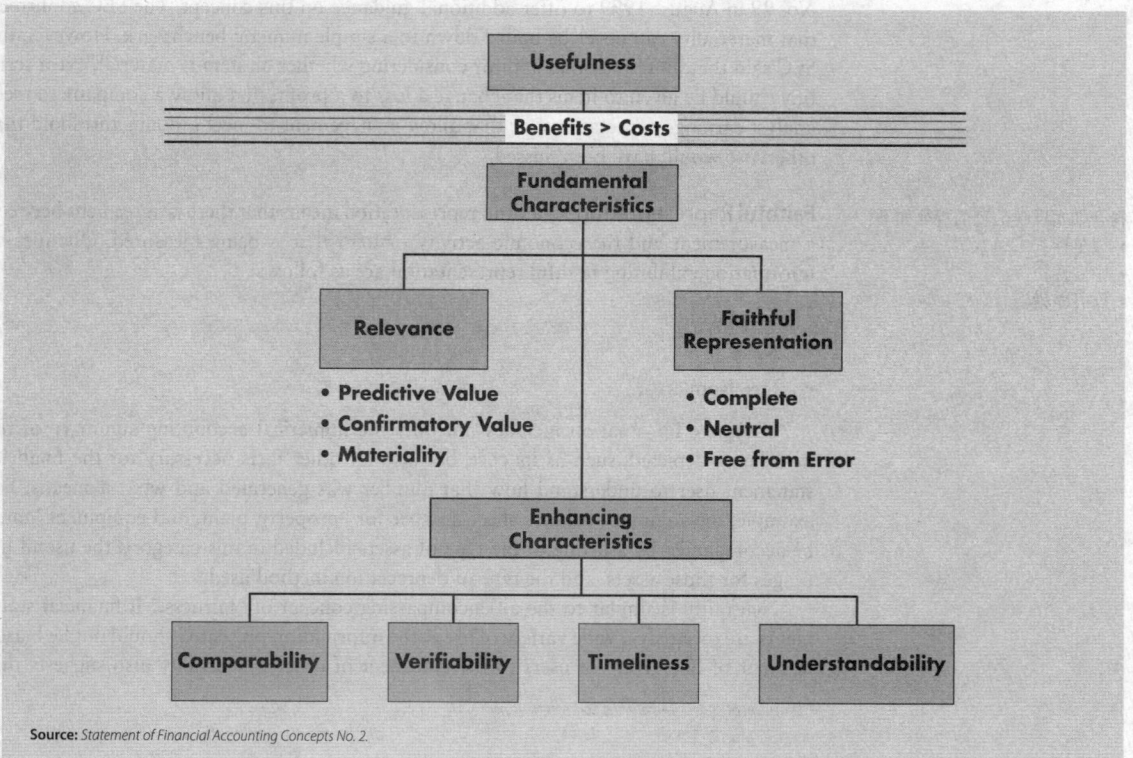

Source: *Statement of Financial Accounting Concepts No. 2.*

[20] *Statement of Financial Accounting Concepts No. 8*, par. OB17.

会计信息的基本特征有两个：相关性和如实反映。

Fundamental Characteristics The two fundamental characteristics of useful accounting information are relevance and faithful representation. These characteristics are viewed as being absolutely necessary; without both of them, accounting information is not useful.[21]

符合相关性信息的特征如下：
- 预测价值；
- 证实价值；
- 重要性。

Relevance The conceptual framework describes relevant information as information that can make a difference to a decision. Qualities of relevant information are as follows:

- Predictive value
- Confirmatory value
- Materiality

Relevant information normally provides both confirmatory value and predictive value at the same time. Feedback on past events helps confirm or correct earlier expectations. Such information can then be used to help predict future outcomes. For example, when a company presents comparative income statements, an investor has information to compare last year's operating results with this year's. This provides a general basis for evaluating prior expectations and for estimating what next year's results might be.

Materiality deals with this specific question: Is the item large enough to influence the decision of a user of the information? Quantitative guidance concerning materiality is lacking, so managers and accountants must exercise judgment in determining whether an item is material. All would agree that an item causing net income to change by 10% is material. How about 1%? Most accountants would say an item changing net income by 1% is immaterial unless the item results from questionable income manipulation or something else indicative of broader concern. Remember that there is no definitive numerical materiality threshold—the accountant must use her or his judgment. In recognition of the importance of the concept of materiality, the SEC released *Staff Accounting Bulletin (SAB) No. 99* in August 1999 to offer additional guidance on this concept. The SEC confirmed that materiality can never be boiled down to a simple numeric benchmark. However, the SEC said that, in terms of an auditor considering whether an item is material, extra scrutiny should be given to items that change a loss to a profit, that allow a company to meet analyst earnings expectations, or that allow management to meet a bonus threshold that otherwise would have been missed.

符合如实反映信息的特征如下：
- 完整性；
- 中立性；
- 没有差错。

Faithful Representation Faithful representation means that there is agreement between a measurement and the economic activity or item that is being measured. Qualities of information exhibiting faithful representation are as follows:

- Complete
- Neutral
- Free from error

Complete information includes not only the numerical accounting summary of the item being depicted, such as its cost, but also all other facts necessary for the financial statement user to understand how that number was generated and what it means. For example, the summary balance sheet number for "property, plant, and equipment" must be accompanied by a listing of the type of assets included in this category, the useful life ranges for those assets, and the type of depreciation method used.

Neutrality is similar to the all-encompassing concept of "fairness." If financial statements are to satisfy a wide variety of users, the information presented should not be biased in favor of one group of users to the detriment of others. Neutrality also suggests that

---

[21] *Statement of Financial Accounting Concepts No. 8, par. QC17.*

accounting standard setters should not be influenced by potential effects a new rule will have on a particular company or industry. In practice, neutrality is very difficult to achieve because firms that expect to be harmed by a new accounting rule often lobby vigorously against the proposed standard.

Accrual accounting information by its nature is based on judgments and includes estimates and approximations. Accordingly, the financial statement numbers cannot be perfectly "accurate." In fact, in a setting involving approximations and judgments, two different estimated numbers can reasonably be viewed as being equally "accurate." What can be expected of accounting numbers is that the process used to generate the final accounting numbers be applied in an error-free way.

Enhancing Characteristics The four enhancing characteristics of useful accounting information are comparability, verifiability, timeliness, and understandability. Once information exhibits both relevance and faithful representation, improvements in one or more of the four enhancing characteristics can make the accounting information even more useful.[22]

Comparability The essence of comparability is that information becomes much more useful when it can be related to a benchmark or standard. The comparison may be with data for other firms, or it may be with similar information for the same firm but for other periods of time. Comparability of accounting data for the same company over time is often called consistency. Comparability requires that similar events be accounted for in the same manner in the financial statements of different companies and for a particular company for different periods. It should be recognized, however, that uniformity is not always the answer to comparability. Different circumstances may require different accounting treatments.

Verifiability Verifiability implies consensus. Accountants seek to base the financial statements on measures that can be verified by other trained accountants using the same measurement methods.

Timeliness Timeliness is essential for information to "make a difference" because if the information becomes available after the decision is made, it isn't of much use. Financial reporting is increasingly criticized on the timeliness dimension because in the age of information technology, users are becoming accustomed to getting answers overnight, not at the end of a year or a quarter.

Understandability As stated earlier, business events can be complex, and the financial statements should not be simplified to the degree that this business complexity is concealed. However, the concept of understandability implies that this complexity should be explained clearly in order to be understood by users who are both familiar with business and willing to put in the time needed to analyze the financial reports.

Benefits Greater Than Cost Information is like other commodities in that it must be worth more than the cost of producing it. The difficulty in assessing cost effectiveness of financial reporting is that the costs and benefits, especially the benefits, are not always evident or easily measured. In addition, the costs are borne by an identifiable and vocal constituency, the companies required to prepare financial statements. The benefits are spread over the entire economy. Thus, the FASB more frequently hears complaints about the expected cost of a new standard than it hears praise about the expected benefits. When describing a new accounting standard, the FASB includes a section attempting to describe the expected costs and benefits of the standard.

[22] *Statement of Financial Accounting Concepts No. 8*, par. QC19.

What about Conservatism? No discussion of the qualities of accounting information is complete without a discussion of conservatism, which historically has been the guiding principle behind many accounting practices. The concept of conservatism can be summarized as follows: When in doubt, recognize all losses but don't recognize any gains. In formulating the conceptual framework, the FASB did not include conservatism in the list of qualitative characteristics. Financial statements that are deliberately biased to understate assets and profits lose the characteristics of relevance and faithful representation.

> **Caution**
> Although the conceptual framework excludes conservatism from its list of qualitative characteristics, most practicing accountants are still conservative in making their estimates and judgments.

Elements of Financial Statements

The FASB definitions of the 10 basic financial statement elements are listed in Exhibit 1-6. These elements compose the building blocks upon which financial statements are constructed. These definitions and the issues surrounding them are discussed in detail as the elements are introduced in later chapters.

Recognition, Measurement, and Reporting

To recognize or not to recognize... THAT is the question. One way to report financial information is to boil down all the estimates and judgments into one number and then use that one number to make a journal entry. This is called recognition. The key assumptions and estimates are then described in a note to the financial statements. Another approach is to skip the journal entry and just rely on the note to convey the information to users. This is called disclosure.

The recognition versus disclosure question has been at the heart of many accounting standard controversies and compromises in recent years. Two examples follow.

- The business community absolutely refused to accept the FASB's decision to require recognition of the value of employee stock options as compensation expense. The FASB initially compromised by requiring only disclosure of the information but finally insisted that, starting in 2006, businesses must recognize the expense rather than just disclose it.
- The FASB has used disclosure requirements to give firms some years of practice in reporting the fair value of financial instruments. Some standards now require recognition of those fair values, and the FASB provides extensive guidance on the use of and required disclosures regarding fair value measurements in the financial statements.

The conceptual framework provides guidance in determining what information should be formally incorporated into financial statements and when. These concepts are discussed here under the following three headings:

- Recognition criteria
- Measurement
- Reporting

Recognition Criteria For an item to be formally recognized, it must meet one of the definitions of the elements of financial statements.[23] For example, a receivable must meet the definition of an asset to be recorded and reported as such on a balance sheet. The same is true of liabilities, owners' equity, revenues, expenses, and other elements. An item must

---
[23] *Statement of Financial Accounting Concepts No. 5*, "Recognition and Measurement in Financial Statements of Business Enterprises" (Stamford, CT: Financial Accounting Standards Board, December 1984), par. 63.

Exhibit 1-6 | Elements of Financial Statements

Assets are probable future economic benefits obtained or controlled by a particular entity as a result of past transactions or events.

Liabilities are probable future sacrifices of economic benefits arising from present obligations of a particular entity to transfer assets or provide services to other entities in the future as a result of past transactions or events.

Equity, or Net Assets, is the residual interest in the assets of an entity that remains after deducting its liabilities.

Investments by Owners are increases in equity of a particular business enterprise resulting from transfers to it from other entities of something valuable to obtain or increase ownership interests (or equity) in it. Assets are most commonly received as investments by owners, but that which is received may also include services or satisfaction or conversion of liabilities of the enterprise.

Distributions to Owners are decreases in equity of a particular business enterprise resulting from transferring assets, rendering services, or incurring liabilities by the enterprise to owners. Distributions to owners decrease ownership interests (or equity) in an enterprise.

Comprehensive Income is the change in equity of a business enterprise during a period from transactions and other events and circumstances from nonowner sources. It includes all changes in equity during a period except those resulting from investments by owners and distributions to owners.

Revenues are inflows or other enhancements of assets of an entity or settlement of its liabilities (or a combination of both) from delivering or producing goods, rendering services, or other activities that constitute the entity's ongoing major or central operations.

Expenses are outflows or other using up of assets or incurrences of liabilities (or a combination of both) from delivering or producing goods, rendering services, or carrying out other activities that constitute the entity's ongoing major or central operations.

Gains are increases in equity (net assets) from peripheral or incidental transactions of an entity and from all other transactions and other events and circumstances affecting the entity except those that result from revenues or investments by owners.

Losses are decreases in equity (net assets) from peripheral or incidental transactions of an entity and from all other transactions and other events and circumstances affecting the entity except those that result from expenses or distributions to owners.

Material from FASB *Concepts Statement No. 6*, "Elements of Financial Statements," is copyrighted by the Financial Accounting Foundation (FAF), 401 Merritt 7, PO Box 5116, Norwalk, CT 06856-5116, USA, and is reproduced with permission. A complete copy of the document is available from the FAF.

also be reliably measurable in monetary terms to be recognized. For example, as mentioned earlier, many firms have obligations to clean up environmental damage. These obligations fit the definition of a liability, and information about them is relevant to users, yet they should not be recognized until they can be reliably quantified. Disclosure is preferable to recognition in situations in which relevant information cannot be reliably measured.

实务中常用的五种计量属性：
- 历史成本；
- 现行重置成本；
- 公允价值；
- 可变现净值；
- 现值（折现值）。

Measurement Closely related to recognition is measurement. Five different measurement attributes are currently used in practice.

1. *Historical cost* is the cash equivalent price exchanged for goods or services at the date of acquisition. (Examples of items measured at historical cost: land, buildings, equipment, and most inventories.)

2. *Current replacement cost* is the cash equivalent price that would be exchanged currently to purchase or replace equivalent goods or services. (Example: some inventories that have declined in value since acquisition.)

3. *Fair value* is the cash equivalent price that could be obtained by selling an asset in an orderly transaction. (Example: many financial instruments.)

4. Net realizable value is the amount of cash expected to be received from the conversion of assets in the normal course of business. (Example: accounts receivable.)
5. Present (or discounted) value is the amount of net future cash inflows or outflows discounted to their present value at an appropriate rate of interest. (Examples: long-term receivables, long-term payables, and long-term operating assets determined to have suffered an impairment in value.)

On the date an asset is acquired, all five of these measurement attributes have approximately the same value. The differences arise as the asset ages, business conditions change, and the original acquisition price becomes a less relevant measure of future economic benefit.

Current accounting practice in the United States is said to be based on historical costs, although, as illustrated, each of the five measurement attributes is used. Still, historical cost is the dominant measure and is used because of its high reliability. Many users believe that current replacement costs or fair values, though less reliable, are more relevant than historical costs for future-oriented decisions. Here we see the classic trade-off between relevance and reliability. In recent years, we have seen an increasing emphasis on relevance and thus a movement away from historical cost. Most financial instruments are now reported at fair value, and the present value of forecasted cash flows is becoming a more common measurement attribute. The importance of forecasted cash flow information is evidenced by the fact that a recent addition to the conceptual framework (*Concepts Statement No. 7* adopted in February 2000) outlines the appropriate approach to computing the present value of cash flows. In spite of this trend, the United States still lags behind other countries in the use of market values in financial statements. For example, many British companies report their land and buildings at estimated market values.

Most inventories are valued at historical cost—the cash equivalent price exchanged for the goods at the date of acquisition.

> **Caution**
>
> You will be doing lots of present value calculations during your course in intermediate accounting. Check the batteries in your calculator.

Reporting The conceptual framework indicates that a "full set of financial statements" is necessary to meet the objectives of financial reporting. Included in the recommended set of general-purpose financial statements are reports that show the following:

- Financial position at the end of the period
- Earnings (net income) for the period
- Cash flows during the period
- Investments by and distributions to owners during the period
- Comprehensive income (total nonowner changes in equity) for the period

The first three items have obvious reference to the three primary financial statements: balance sheet, income statement, and statement of cash flows. By the way, at the time the conceptual framework was formulated, there was no requirement to prepare a statement of cash flows. One of the early consequences of the completed conceptual framework was an increased emphasis on cash flow and the addition of the cash flow statement to the set of primary financial statements. The fourth reporting recommendation is typically satisfied with a statement of changes in owners' equity. Finally, a statement of comprehensive income is intended to summarize all increases and decreases in equity except for those

statement of changes in owners' equity
所有者权益变动表

综合收益与盈余的区别在于：它包括不在利润表中确认的未实现损益。这些未实现损益的例子包括因外币折算、可供出售债券价值变动和某些衍生合约价值变动所产生的未实现损益。

arising from owner investments and withdrawals. Comprehensive income differs from earnings in that it includes unrealized gains and losses not recognized in the income statement. Examples of these unrealized gains and losses include those arising from foreign currency translations, changes in the value of available-for-sale securities, and changes in the value of certain derivative contracts. Although the FASB discussed the concept of comprehensive income for 40 years, a forceful reporting requirement was not adopted until 2011. Beginning in 2011, companies are required to provide comprehensive income information at the bottom of the income statement or in a separate statement of comprehensive income that is shown immediately after the income statement.

For financial reporting to be most effective, all relevant information should be presented in an unbiased, understandable, and timely manner. This is sometimes referred to as the full disclosure principle. Because of the cost-benefit constraint discussed earlier, however, it would be impossible to report all relevant information. Further, too much information could adversely affect understandability and, therefore, decision usefulness. Those who provide financial information must use judgment in determining what information best satisfies the full disclosure principle within reasonable cost limitations.

Two final points to remember are that the financial statements represent just one part of financial reporting and that financial reporting is just one vehicle used by companies to communicate with external parties. Exhibit 1-7 illustrates the total information spectrum.

Exhibit 1-7 | Total Information Spectrum

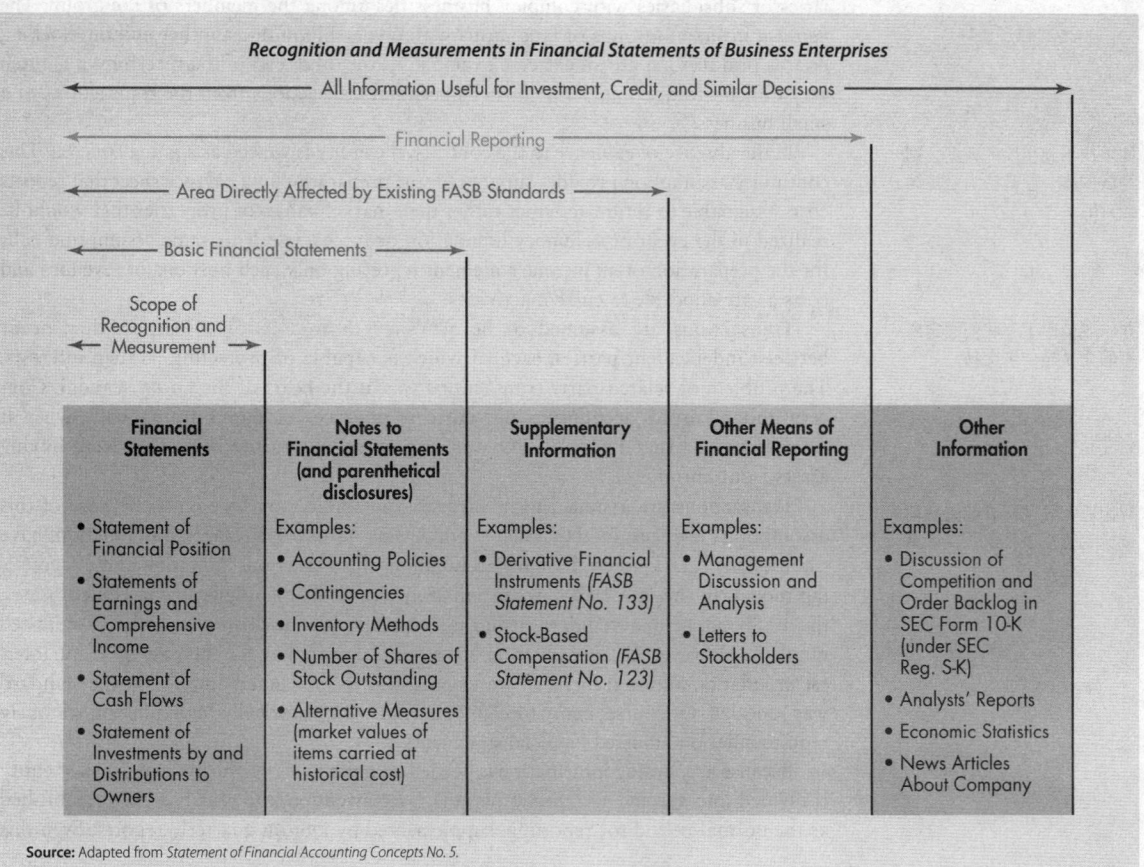

Source: Adapted from *Statement of Financial Accounting Concepts No. 5.*

In one way, this chart is somewhat misleading. Financial reporting is represented as four-fifths of the information spectrum, with other information comprising the other fifth. In reality, the proportions are probably reversed. In a world where online information is available 24 hours a day, the accounting profession faces the challenge of maintaining the relevance of financial reporting in the information spectrum.

Traditional Assumptions of the Accounting Model

The FASB conceptual framework is influenced by several underlying assumptions, although these assumptions are not addressed explicitly in the framework. These five basic assumptions are

- Economic entity
- Going concern
- Arm's-length transactions
- Stable monetary unit
- Accounting period

The business enterprise is viewed as a specific economic entity separate and distinct from its owners and any other business unit. Identifying the exact extent of the economic entity is difficult with large corporations that have networks of subsidiaries and subsidiaries of subsidiaries with complex business ties among the members of the group. The *keiretsu* in Japan (groups of large firms with ownership in one another and interlocking boards of directors) are an extreme example. At the other end of the spectrum, it is often very difficult to disentangle the owner's personal transactions from the transactions of a small business.

In the absence of evidence to the contrary, the entity is viewed as a going concern. This continuity assumption provides support for the preparation of a balance sheet that reports costs assignable to future activities rather than market values of properties that would be realized in the event of voluntary liquidation or forced sale. This same assumption calls for the preparation of an income statement reporting only such portions of revenues and costs as are allocable to current activities.

Transactions are assumed to be arm's-length transactions. That is, they occur between independent parties, each of which is capable of protecting its own interests. The problem of related-party transactions was at the heart of the Enron scandal. Concern about Enron's accounting and business practices escalated dramatically when it was discovered that Enron's CFO was also managing partnerships that were buying assets from Enron.

Transactions are assumed to be measured in stable monetary units. Because of this assumption, changes in the dollar's purchasing power resulting from inflation have traditionally been ignored. To many accountants, this is a serious limitation of the accounting model. In the late 1970s, when inflation was in double digits in the United States, the FASB adopted a standard requiring supplemental disclosure of inflation-adjusted numbers. However, because inflation has remained fairly low for the past 20 years, interest in inflation-adjusted financial statements died in the United States, and the standard was repealed. Of course, many foreign countries with historically high inflation routinely require inflation-adjusted financial statements.

Because accounting information is needed on a timely basis, the life of a business entity is divided into specific accounting periods. By convention, the year has been established as the normal period for reporting, supplemented by interim quarterly reports. Even this innocent traditional assumption has come under fire. Many users want "flash" reports and complain that a quarterly reporting period is too slow. On the other hand, U.S. business leaders often claim that the quarterly reporting cycle is too fast and forces managers to focus on short-term profits instead of on long-term growth. Many other countries require financial statements only semiannually.

Impact of the Conceptual Framework

The conceptual framework provides a basis for consistent judgments by standard setters, preparers, users, auditors, and others involved in financial reporting. A conceptual framework will not solve all accounting problems but if used on a consistent basis over time, it should help improve financial reporting.

The impact of the conceptual framework has been seen in many ways. For example, in *Concepts Statement No. 5*, the FASB outlines the need for a statement of comprehensive income that would contain all of the changes in the value of a company during a period whether those value changes were created by operations, by changes in market values, by changes in exchange rates, or by any other source. This statement of comprehensive income is now a required statement (see FASB ASC Section 220). In addition, the existence of this statement as a place to report changes in market values of assets has facilitated the adoption of standards that result in more relevant values in the balance sheet. Examples are the market values of investment securities and the market values of derivatives. Without the conceptual framework to guide the creation of these standards, their provisions would have been even more controversial than they were.

Related to the conceptual framework is the push toward more "principles-based" accounting standards. In theory, principles-based standards would not include any exceptions to general principles and would not include detailed implementation and interpretation guidance. Instead, a principles-based standard would have a strong conceptual foundation and be applicable to a variety of circumstances by a practicing accountant using his or her professional judgment. A number of accounting standards in the United States, including those dealing with the accounting for leases and derivatives, are full of exceptions, special cases, and tricky implementation rules requiring hundreds of pages of detailed interpretation. The cry for an emphasis on principles-based standards is a reaction to the huge costs of trying to understand and use these voluminous, detailed standards. The ideal of basing accounting standards on a strong conceptual foundation is what motivated the FASB's conceptual framework project in the first place and which continues to motivate the FASB and the IASB to work on a joint conceptual framework.

The framework discussed in this chapter will be a reference source throughout the text. In studying the remaining chapters, you will see many applications and a few exceptions to the theoretical framework established here. An understanding of the overall theoretical framework of accounting should make it easier for you to understand specific issues and problems encountered in practice.

Rules versus Principles

The most prominent difference between U.S. GAAP and IFRS is that U.S. GAAP contains many more detailed rules. In fact, a shorthand description is that U.S. GAAP is "rules oriented" and IFRS are "principles oriented." This is best summarized in a startling statistic—the entire body of U.S. accounting rules is estimated to occupy 25,000 pages. In contrast, the entire body of IFRS is estimated to occupy 2,500 pages. The theory with IFRS is that the application details in individual circumstances will be determined by the professional judgment of the accountant herself or himself.

For years, the FASB has been prodded to transition from a rules approach to a principles approach.[24] In July 2003, the SEC submitted a report to Congress recommending that the FASB move toward "objectives-oriented standards" which would have the following characteristics.

- Be based on an improved and consistently applied framework
- Clearly state the accounting objective of the standard
- Provide sufficient detail and structure so that the standard can be operationalized and applied on a consistent basis
- Minimize exceptions from the standard
- Avoid use of percentage tests ("bright-lines") that allow financial engineers to achieve technical compliance with the standard while evading the intent of the standard

As you can see, an improved conceptual framework is a key element of this transition from rules to principles. Since receipt of this SEC report, the FASB, in conjunction with the IASB, has been moving toward more principles-based standards. The question that continues to be asked in the U.S. business community is whether principles-based accounting standards will work in the U.S. legal environment. Accountants and auditors are concerned that they can never be sure their application of the accounting "principle," without the detailed guidance of rules, will bear up under the after-the-fact scrutiny of trial lawyers, juries, and judges. We'll just have to see what happens.

Careers in Financial Accounting and the Importance of Personal Ethics

LO6 学习目标6
了解与会计和财务报告有关的职业机会，理解个人职业道德在会计实务中的重要性。

6 Identify career opportunities related to accounting and financial reporting and understand the importance of personal ethics in the practice of accounting.

If you are like most students who take intermediate accounting, you aren't taking this class as a general social science elective. You intend to pursue a career in an accounting-related field. This introductory chapter closes with a brief discussion of some of the careers in accounting. One piece of advice: The best career move you can make right now (in addition to taking this class, of course) is to become familiar with your school's job placement office. Ask the people there where the jobs are and what kinds of candidates employers are hiring. Have them help you get started crafting a "killer" résumé. Find out about summer internships. The sooner you start gathering information and establishing a network of contacts, the better.

The three major career areas in financial accounting are:

1. Public accounting
2. Corporate accounting
3. User (analyst, banker, consultant)

[24] *Study Pursuant to Section 108(d) of the Sarbanes-Oxley Act of 2002 on the Adoption by the United States Financial Reporting System of a Principles-Based Accounting System*, Securities and Exchange Commission, July 2003.

Public Accounting

Public accountants do not work for a single business enterprise. Rather, they provide a variety of services for many different individual and business clients. In essence, a public accountant is a freelance accountant, an accountant for hire. Public accountants practice either individually or in firms.

A CPA is a certified public accountant. As mentioned earlier in connection with the discussion of the AICPA, in order to become a CPA, an individual must pass the CPA exam and satisfy education and work experience requirements that differ somewhat from state to state. One of the most significant (and controversial) developments in CPA licensing is the requirement adopted in many states that one must have 150 college credit hours (five years of full-time education) in order to become a CPA.

Traditionally, the most prominent role of CPAs has been as independent auditors of financial statements. Almost all large publicly held corporations are audited by a few large CPA firms. Listed in alphabetical order, the four largest firms are **Deloitte**, **Ernst & Young**, **KPMG**, and **PricewaterhouseCoopers**. Each of these firms is an international organization with many offices in the United States and abroad. Many small businesses are serviced by regional and local CPA firms, including a large number of sole practitioners. In these smaller firms, the role of auditing is often less important than the areas of tax reporting and planning and systems consulting. A CPA in a smaller firm is expected to be something of an accounting generalist as opposed to the more specialized positions of CPAs in large regional and national firms.

Corporate Accounting

Public accountants move from client to client as accountants for hire. Of course, businesses also employ their own staffs of in-house accountants. A large business enterprise employs financial accountants who are primarily concerned with external financial reporting; management accountants who are primarily concerned with internal financial reporting; tax accountants who prepare the necessary federal, state, and local tax returns and advise management in matters relating to taxation; and internal auditors who review the work performed by accountants and others within the enterprise and report their findings to management. In smaller organizations, there is less specialization and more combining of responsibility for the various accounting functions.

> **FYI**
> You might also consider a career as an accounting instructor. Ask your instructor what he or she thinks.

Not all CPAs are public accountants. Individuals who start their careers in public accounting and become CPAs often leave public accounting after a few years and join the in-house accounting staff of a business. Typically, the company they join is one of the clients they audited or consulted for as a public accountant. In fact, this is the most common career path for college graduates who start out working for one of the large accounting firms.

User (Analyst, Banker, Consultant)

Believe it or not, not everyone in the world wants to become an accountant. Many students take intermediate accounting in preparation for becoming a user of financial statements. Credit analysts in large banks are required to have a strong working knowledge of accounting to be able to evaluate the financial statements of firms seeking loans. Investment bankers and brokerage firms employ staffs of analysts to evaluate potential clients and to provide financial statement analysis services to customers. Consulting firms advise clients on how to improve operations. These days, most accounting-related consulting jobs require strong skills in information technology.

The Importance of Personal Ethics

Personal ethics is not a topic one typically expects to study in an intermediate financial accounting course. However, accounting-related scandals such as the one involving Enron have demonstrated that personal ethics and financial reporting are inextricably connected. The flexibility inherent in the assumptions underlying the preparation of financial statements means that an accountant can intentionally deceive financial statement users and yet still technically be in compliance with GAAP. Thus, our financial reporting system is of limited value if the accountants who operate the system do not have strong personal ethics.

Most of us believe that intentionally trying to deceive others is wrong. You will be reminded throughout this text that accounting choices often impact real economic decisions such as whether to grant a loan, make an investment, or fire an employee. Real economic decisions impact peoples' lives, and it is sobering to think that accountants have this power in their hands. Your personal ethical standards are of paramount importance.

Overview of Intermediate Accounting

This chapter has briefly described financial reporting and the accounting standard-setting process, introduced the organizations (and their acronyms) that all accountants should know, outlined the FASB conceptual framework (the "constitution" of accounting), discussed the major accounting-related careers, and reminded you of the importance of personal ethics. In the next four chapters, we will review everything you learned in introductory financial accounting, starting with the accountant's basic tools of analysis, the journal entry and the T-account. The text then covers the accounting standards for the different aspects of a business: operating, investing, and financing. The text concludes with individual chapters on a number of important topics such as deferred taxes, derivative financial instruments, and earnings per share.

As mentioned at the start of this chapter, now is an exciting time to be studying accounting because things are changing so fast. For example, one of the topics most discussed currently is the accounting for financial instruments. Thirty years ago when we took intermediate financial accounting, the accounting for financial instruments was a minor topic. The important point is that we really can't know what the important accounting issues will be 30 years from now. The best preparation for this unknown future is to learn the existing accounting rules, to understand how these rules arose, and to recognize the underlying concepts. That is the aim of this textbook.

SOLUTIONS TO OPENING SCENARIO QUESTIONS

1. Mark-to-market accounting is the practice of reporting investment securities in the balance sheet at their current market value. For securities that are in an active trading portfolio, the unrealized gains and losses (the "paper" gains and losses) are reported as part of net income.

2. The fact that the rule was retroactive allowed the European banks to roll back the clock to July 1, 2008, and, with the benefit of knowing which securities had increased and which had decreased in value, designate some investments to be accounted for using mark-to-market accounting (probably the ones that they now knew went up during the third quarter) and some investments to be reclassified as "held to maturity" at the value existing as of July 1 (probably the ones that they knew, with hindsight, went down during the third quarter).

3. The primary result of the October 2008 IASB debacle has been to highlight the remaining barriers to international convergence in financial reporting. The U.S. business community was forced to face the reality that it really doesn't want its reporting rules set by a London-based group that is essentially controlled by the European Union. In addition, all interested parties, both in the United States and overseas, have seen that the IASB differs from the FASB in one extremely important way—the pronouncements of the FASB have the force of law because the regulatory power of the SEC is behind them. Who will enforce the pronouncements of the IASB?

Stop & Think SOLUTIONS

1. (Page 1-7) The correct answer is E. Detailed operating budgets are an example of managerial accounting information. This budget information would typically not be revealed to external users.

2. (Page 1-20) The correct answer is a matter of personal opinion. As the business world becomes more global, the need for accounting rules that apply across borders increases. In 10 years, it is most likely that an international standard-setting body will be issuing accounting rules that apply to the global economy.

SOLUTION TO USING THE FASB'S CODIFICATION

1. Go to **asc.fasb.org**.
2. On the right side of the screen, click on the "Order Professional or Basic View" link. You can also see the "Academic Accounting Access" link. Your school's accounting department may have registered for academic access. If so, your instructor will have the information you need in order to log in.
3. The "Professional View," at the top of the page, costs over $800. Because this is your first experience with the FASB ASC, it is probably better to choose the "Basic View," at the bottom of the page, which is free. Click "Select."
4. Type in your e-mail address. Don't worry about security—they aren't going to ask for any personal data beyond your name and address. In addition, this is the FASB we are talking about. You can trust them. Click "Submit."
5. Enter your personal data. Then click to submit the data.
6. Accept the terms of the agreement.
7. Gleefully check out with your total bill being $0.00.
8. You are in. You should get an e-mail confirmation of your registration. However, even before you get the e-mail, you can go right to **asc.fasb.org** and log in as a Registered User by clicking in the bottom box on the right side of the ASC home page.
9. Enjoy! Each chapter in this textbook will contain an exercise that will require you to search the FASB ASC. *Hint:* Don't forget your FASB password. And it wouldn't hurt to tell your mom that you are officially registered with the FASB, with a password and everything. Nothing could make a mother prouder.

Review Chapter 1 Learning Objectives

① Describe the purpose of financial reporting and identify the primary financial statements.

The purpose of financial reporting is to aid interested parties in evaluating the company's past performance and in forecasting its future performance. The information about past events is intended to improve future operations and forecasts of future cash flows.

Internal users have the ability to receive custom-designed accounting reports. External users must rely on the general-purpose financial statements. The five major components of the financial statements follow:

- Balance sheet
- Income statement
- Statement of cash flows
- Explanatory notes
- Auditor's opinion

② Explain the function of accounting standards and describe the role of the FASB in setting those standards in the United States.

Accounting standards help accountants meet the information demands of users by providing guidelines and limits for financial reporting. Accounting standards also improve the comparability of financial reports among different companies. There are many different ways to account for the same underlying economic events, and users are never satisfied with the amount of financial information they receive—they always want to know more. By defining which methods to use and how much information to disclose, accounting standards save time and money for accountants. Users also benefit because they can learn one set of accounting rules to apply to all companies.

The Financial Accounting Standards Board (FASB) sets accounting standards in the United States. The FASB is a private-sector body and has no legal authority. Accordingly, the FASB must carefully balance theory and practice in order to maintain credibility in the business community. The issuance of a new accounting standard is preceded by a lengthy public discussion. The Emerging Issues Task Force (EITF) works under the direction of the FASB. The EITF formulates a timely expert consensus on how to handle new issues not yet covered in FASB pronouncements. The authoritative accounting standards are contained in the FASB Accounting Standards Codification.

③ Recognize the importance of the SEC, AICPA, AAA, and IRS to financial reporting.

- *Securities and Exchange Commission (SEC)*. The SEC has legal authority to establish U.S. accounting rules but generally allows the FASB to set the standards. To speed the improvement of disclosure, the SEC sometimes implements broad disclosure requirements in areas still being deliberated by the FASB.

- *American Institute of Certified Public Accountants (AICPA)*. The AICPA is a key professional organization of practicing accountants. The AICPA administers the CPA exam, polices the practices of its members, and establishes some accounting guidance, particularly related to specific industries.

- *American Accounting Association (AAA)*. The AAA is the professional organization of accounting professors. The AAA helps disseminate research results and facilitates improvements in accounting education.

- *Internal Revenue Service (IRS)*. Financial accounting is not the same as tax accounting. However, many specifics learned in intermediate accounting are similar to the corresponding tax rules.

④ Realize the growing importance and relevance of international accounting issues to the practice of accounting in the United States and understand the role of the IASB in international accounting standard setting.

Because business is increasingly conducted across national borders, companies must be able to use their financial statements to communicate with external users all over the world. As a result, divergent national accounting practices are converging to an overall global standard.

The International Accounting Standards Board (IASB) is an international body whose goal is to prepare a comprehensive set of financial accounting standards that can be used anywhere in the world. IASB standards have gained almost universal acceptance worldwide.

⑤ Understand the significance of the FASB's conceptual framework in outlining the qualities of good accounting information, defining terms such as *asset* and *revenue*, and providing guidance about appropriate recognition, measurement, and reporting.

The conceptual framework allows for the systematic adaptation of accounting standards to a changing business environment. The FASB uses the conceptual framework to aid in an organized and consistent development of new accounting standards. In addition, learning the FASB's conceptual framework allows one to understand and, perhaps, anticipate future standards.

The conceptual framework outlines the objectives of financial reporting and the qualities of good accounting information, precisely defines commonly used terms such as *asset* and *revenue*, and provides guidance about appropriate recognition, measurement, and reporting.

The key financial reporting objectives are as follows:

- Usefulness
- Understandability
- Target audience of investors, lenders, and other creditors
- Assessment of future cash flows and existing economic resources
- Financial performance reflected by accrual accounting

Qualities of useful accounting information are the following:

- Fundamental characteristics
  - Relevance—predictive value, confirmatory value, and materiality
  - Faithful representation—complete, neutral, and free from error
- Enhancing characteristics
  - Comparability
  - Verifiability
  - Timelinesss
  - Understandability

Recording an item in the accounting records through a journal entry is called *recognition*. To be recognized, an item must meet the definition of an element and be measurable, relevant, and reliable.

The following are the five measurement attributes used in practice:

- Historical cost
- Current replacement cost
- Fair value
- Net realizable value
- Present (or discounted) value

A full set of financial statements includes a balance sheet, income statement, statement of cash flows, statement of changes in owners' equity, and statement of comprehensive income.

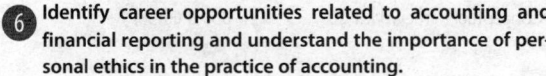
Identify career opportunities related to accounting and financial reporting and understand the importance of personal ethics in the practice of accounting.

Public accountants are freelance accountants who provide auditing, tax, and a variety of other customer services. In addition, since all companies have some financial reporting responsibilities, there are many financial accounting career opportunities in industry. Because accounting is the language of business, any business career requires a familiarity with financial accounting. Finally, our financial reporting system is of limited value if the accountants who operate the system do not have strong personal ethics.

FASB-IASB CODIFICATION SUMMARY

Topic	U.S. GAAP	IASB Standard
Accounting standard setter	Financial Accounting Standards Board (FASB)	International Accounting Standards Board (IASB)
Financial accounting standards	FASB Accounting Standards Codification (ASC)	• International Financial Reporting Standards (IFRS) • International Accounting Standards (IAS)
Group to address issues of interpretation or for which no formal standard currently exists	Emerging Issues Task Force (EITF)	• International Financial Reporting Interpretations Committee (IFRIC) • Standing Interpretations Committee (SIC) before 2002

KEY TERMS

Accounting 1-4
Accounting periods 1-30
Accounting Principles Board (APB) 1-9
Accounting Standards Updates 1-10
American Accounting Association (AAA) 1-16
American Institute of Certified Public Accountants (AICPA) 1-15
Arm's-length transactions 1-30
Certified public accountants (CPAs) 1-15
Comparability 1-25
Complete information 1-24
Comprehensive income 1-29
Conceptual framework 1-20
Confirmatory value 1-24
Conservatism 1-26
Consistency 1-25
Creditors 1-6
Current replacement cost 1-27
Disclosure 1-26
Economic entity 1-30
Emerging Issues Task Force (EITF) 1-11
Exposure Draft 1-10
Fair value 1-27
Faithful representation 1-24
Financial accounting 1-5
Financial Accounting Foundation (FAF) 1-10
Financial Accounting Standards Board (FASB) 1-9
Full disclosure principle 1-29
Generally accepted accounting principles (GAAP) 1-9
General-purpose financial statements 1-7
Going concern 1-30
Governmental Accounting Standards Board (GASB) 1-10
Historical cost 1-27
Internal Revenue Service (IRS) 1-17
International Accounting Standards Board (IASB) 1-19
Investors 1-6
Management accounting 1-5
Materiality 1-24
Net realizable value 1-28
Neutrality 1-24
Predictive value 1-24
Present (or discounted) value 1-28
Recognition 1-26
Relevance 1-24
Securities and Exchange Commission (SEC) 1-9
Stable monetary units 1-30
Stakeholders 1-5
Statement of changes in owners' equity 1-28
Statements of Financial Accounting Concepts 1-10
Timeliness 1-25
Understandability 1-25
Verifiability 1-25

Tutorial Activities

Tutorial Activities with author-written, content-specific feedback, available on *CengageNOW for Stice & Stice*.

QUESTIONS

1. *Accounting* has been defined as a service activity. Who is served by accounting, and how do they benefit?
2. How does the fact that there are limited resources in the world relate to accounting information?
3. Accounting is sometimes characterized as dealing only with the past. Give examples of how accounting information can be of value in dealing with the future.
4. Distinguish between management accounting and financial accounting.
5. What five items make up the general-purpose financial statements?
6. Contrast the roles of an accountant and an auditor.
7. Why are independent audits necessary?
8. What conditions led to the establishment of accounting standard-setting bodies in the United States?
9. Describe the structure of the FASB. Where does the FASB get its operating funds?
10. What are the differences in purpose and scope of the FASB Accounting Standards Codification and the FASB Statements of Financial Accounting Concepts?
11. What characteristics of the standard-setting process are designed to increase the acceptability of standards established by the FASB?
12. (a) What role does the EITF play in establishing accounting standards? (b) Why can it meet this role more efficiently than the FASB?
13. How does the SEC influence the setting of accounting standards?
14. What is the AICPA? The AAA?
15. Explain the relationship between financial accounting rules and tax accounting rules.

16. Why is standard setting such a difficult and complex task?
17. What constitutes authoritative GAAP in the United States?
18. Why are differing national accounting standards converging to a common global standard?
19. What is the IASB? What is the SEC position regarding IASB standards?
20. List and explain the main reasons why a conceptual framework of accounting is important.
21. Identify the major objectives of financial reporting as specified by the FASB.
22. One objective of financial reporting is understandability. Understandable to whom?
23. Why is it so difficult to measure the cost effectiveness of accounting information?
24. Distinguish between the qualities of relevance and faithful representation.
25. Does "free from error" imply absolute accuracy? Explain.
26. Define *comparability*.
27. Of what value is consistency in financial reporting?
28. What is the current numerical materiality standard in accounting?
29. What is conservatism in accounting? What is an example of conservatism in accounting practice?
30. Identify the criteria that an item must meet to qualify for recognition.
31. Identify and describe five different measurement attributes.
32. Briefly describe the five traditional assumptions that influence the conceptual framework.
33. What is the most common career path for a college graduate who starts out in public accounting?
34. What user careers require a knowledge of intermediate accounting issues?

EXERCISES

Exercise 1-1

Aspects of the FASB's Conceptual Framework
Determine whether the following statements are true or false. If a statement is false, explain why.

1. Comprehensive income includes changes in equity resulting from distributions to owners.
2. Confirmatory value and predictive value are both characteristics of relevant information.
3. The tendency to recognize favorable events early is an example of conservatism.
4. The conceptual framework focuses primarily on the needs of internal users of financial information.
5. The eight Statements of Financial Accounting Concepts are considered part of generally accepted accounting principles.
6. The overriding objective of financial reporting is to provide information for making economic decisions.
7. The term *recognition* is synonymous with the term *disclosure*.
8. Once an accounting method is adopted, it should never be changed.

Exercise 1-2

Conceptual Framework Terminology
Match the numbered statements below with the lettered terms. An answer (letter) may be used more than once, and some terms require more than one answer (letter).

1. Key ingredients in quality of relevance
2. Traditional assumptions that influence the FASB's conceptual framework
3. The idea that information should represent what it purports to represent
4. An important constraint relating to costs and benefits
5. An example of conservatism
6. The availability of information when it is needed
7. Recording an item in the accounting records
8. Determines the threshold for recognition

9. Implies consensus
10. Transactions between independent parties

(a) Cost effectiveness
(b) Faithful representation
(c) Recognition
(d) Verifiability
(e) Time periods
(f) Unrealized
(g) Completeness
(h) Timeliness
(i) Materiality
(j) Predictive value
(k) Economic entity
(l) Lower-of-cost-or-market rule
(m) Phrenology
(n) Arm's-length transactions

Exercise 1-3

Objectives of Financial Reporting

For each of the following independent situations, identify the relevant objective(s) of financial reporting that the company could be overlooking. Discuss each of these objectives.

1. The president of Daughters, Inc. believes that the financial statements should be prepared for use by management only, because they are the primary decision makers.
2. Sparkling Tile Co. believes that financial statements should reflect only the present financial standing and cash position of the firm and should not provide any future-oriented data.
3. The vice president of Greed Enterprises, Inc. believes that the financial statements are to present only current-year revenues and expenses, not to disclose assets, liabilities, and owners' equity.
4. Lohan Co. has a policy of providing disclosures of only its assets, liabilities, and owners' equity.
5. Bob Building, Inc. always discloses the assets, liabilities, and owners' equity of the firm along with the revenues and expenses. Bob's management believes that these items provide all of the information relevant to investing decisions.

Exercise 1-4

Applications of Accounting Characteristics and Concepts

For each situation listed, indicate by letter the appropriate qualitative characteristic(s) or accounting concept(s) applied. A letter may be used more than once, and more than one characteristic or concept may apply to a particular situation.

1. Goodwill is recorded in the accounts only when it arises from the purchase of another entity at a price higher than the fair value of the purchased entity's identifiable assets.
2. Land is valued at cost.
3. All payments out of petty cash are debited to Miscellaneous Expense.
4. Plant assets are classified separately as land or buildings, with an accumulated depreciation account for buildings.
5. Periodic payments of $2,300 per month for services of R. Robertson, who is the sole proprietor of the company, are reported as withdrawals.
6. Small tools used by a large manufacturing firm are recorded as expenses when purchased.
7. Investments in equity securities are initially recorded at cost.
8. A retail store estimates inventory rather than taking a complete physical count for purposes of preparing monthly financial statements.
9. A note describing the company's possible liability in a lawsuit is included with the financial statements even though no formal liability exists at the balance sheet date.
10. Depreciation on plant assets is consistently computed each year by the straight-line method.

(a) Understandability
(b) Verifiability
(c) Timeliness
(d) Faithful representation
(e) Neutrality
(f) Relevance
(g) Going concern
(h) Economic entity
(i) Historical cost
(j) Measurability
(k) Materiality
(l) Comparability

Exercise 1-5

Trade-Off between Qualitative Characteristics

In each of the following independent situations, an example is given requiring a trade-off between the qualitative characteristics discussed in the text. For each situation, identify the relevant characteristics and briefly discuss how satisfying one characteristic may involve not satisfying another.

1. The book value of an office building is approaching its originally estimated salvage value of $100,000. However, its fair value has been estimated at $10 million. The company's management would like to disclose to financial statement users the current value of the building on the balance sheet.
2. JCB Industries has used the FIFO inventory method for the past 20 years. However, all other major competitors use the LIFO method of accounting for inventories. JCB is contemplating a switch from FIFO to LIFO.
3. Hobson, Inc. is negotiating with a major bank for a significant loan. The bank has asked that a set of financial statements be provided as quickly after the year-end as possible. Because invoices from many of the company's suppliers are mailed several weeks after inventory is received, Hobson, Inc. is considering estimating the amounts associated with those liabilities to be able to prepare its financial statements more quickly.
4. Starship, Inc. produces and sells satellites to government and private industries. The company provides a warranty guaranteeing the performance of the satellites. A recent space launch placed one of its satellites in orbit, and several malfunctions have occurred. At year-end, Starship, Inc.'s auditors would like the company to disclose the potential liability in the notes to the financial statements. Officers of Starship, Inc. believe that the satellite can be repaired in orbit and that disclosure of a contingency such as this would unnecessarily bias the financial statements.

Exercise 1-6

Elements of Financial Reporting

For each of the following items, identify the financial statement element being discussed.

1. Changes in equity during a period except those resulting from investments by owners and distributions to owners
2. The net assets of an entity
3. The result of a transaction requiring the future transfer of assets to other entities
4. An increase in assets from the delivery of goods that constitutes the entity's ongoing central operations
5. An increase in an entity's net assets from incidental transactions
6. An increase in net assets through the issuance of stock
7. Decreases in net assets from peripheral transactions of an enterprise
8. The payment of a dividend
9. Outflows of assets from the delivery of goods or services
10. Items offering future value to an entity

Exercise 1-7

Assumptions of Financial Reporting

In each of the following independent situations, an example is given involving one of the five traditional assumptions of the accounting model. For each situation, identify the assumption involved (briefly explain your answer).

1. A subsidiary of Parent, Inc. was exhibiting poor earnings performance for the year. In an effort to increase the subsidiary's reported earnings, Parent, Inc. purchased products from the subsidiary at twice the normal markup.
2. When preparing the financial statements for MacNeil & Sons, the accountant included certain personal assets of MacNeil and his sons.
3. The operations of Uintah Savings & Loan are being evaluated by the federal government. During their investigations, government officials have determined that numerous loans made by top management were unwise and have seriously endangered the future existence of the savings and loan.
4. Pine Valley Ski Resort has experienced a drastic reduction in revenues because of light snowfall for the year. Rather than produce financial statements at the end of the fiscal year, as is traditionally done, management has elected to wait until next year and present results for a two-year period.

5. Colobri, Inc. has equipment that was purchased in 2001 at a cost of $150,000. Because of inflation, that same equipment, if purchased today, would cost $225,000. Management would like to report the asset on the balance sheet at its current value.

Exercise 1-8

Measurement Attributes and Going Concern Problems

One of the underlying assumptions of the accounting model is the going concern assumption. When this assumption is questionable, valuation methods used for assets and liabilities may differ from those used when the assumption is viable. For each of the following situations, identify the measurement attribute that would most likely be used if the company is not likely to remain a going concern.

1. Plant and equipment are carried at an amortized cost on a straight-line basis of $2,100,000.
2. Bonds with a maturity price of $1,500,000 and interest in arrears of $400,000 are reported as a noncurrent liability.
3. Accounts receivable are carried at $600,000, the gross amount charged for sales. No allowance for doubtful accounts is reported.
4. The reported LIFO cost of inventory is $250,000.
5. Investments in a subsidiary company are recorded at initial cost plus undistributed profits.

Exercise 1-9

Sample CPA Exam Questions

1. One of the elements on a financial statement is comprehensive income. Comprehensive income excludes changes in equity resulting from which of the following?
   (a) Loss from discontinued operations
   (b) Unrealized loss from foreign currency translation
   (c) Dividends paid to stockholders
   (d) Unrealized loss on investments in noncurrent marketable equity securities

2. According to the FASB conceptual framework, the objectives of financial reporting for business enterprises are based on
   (a) generally accepted accounting principles.
   (b) reporting on management's stewardship.
   (c) the need for conservatism.
   (d) the needs of users of the information.

3. Statements of Financial Accounting Concepts are intended to establish
   (a) generally accepted accounting principles in financial reporting by business enterprises.
   (b) the meaning of "Present fairly in accordance with generally accepted accounting principles."
   (c) the objectives and concepts for use in developing standards of financial accounting and reporting.
   (d) the hierarchy of sources of generally accepted accounting principles.

4. According to Statements of Financial Accounting Concepts, neutrality is an ingredient of faithful representation? Of relevance?
   (a) Yes   Yes
   (b) Yes   No
   (c) No   Yes
   (d) No   No

5. According to the FASB conceptual framework, which of the following statements conforms to the realization concept?
   (a) Equipment depreciation was assigned to a production department and then to product unit costs.
   (b) Depreciated equipment was sold in exchange for a note receivable.
   (c) Cash was collected on accounts receivable.
   (d) Product unit costs were assigned to cost of goods sold when the units were sold.

P1
Foundations of Financial Accounting

CHAPTER 2
A Review of the Accounting Cycle

Learning Objectives

1. Identify and explain the basic steps in the accounting process (accounting cycle).
2. Analyze transactions and make and post journal entries.
3. Make adjusting entries, produce financial statements, and close nominal accounts.
4. Distinguish between accrual and cash-basis accounting.
5. Discuss the importance and expanding role of computers to the accounting process.

Tom Clancy typed the first draft of his first novel, *The Hunt for Red October*, on an IBM Selectric typewriter while still holding down his full-time job as an insurance agent. The book was published in October 1984, and sales took off when it became known that the book was President Ronald Reagan's favorite. To date, Clancy has published a total of nine novels featuring the reluctant hero, Jack Ryan, two featuring Ryan's son, and one including both father and son. The stories have been so popular that Clancy has commanded a $25 million advance per book.

In *The Hunt for Red October*, Jack Ryan, who was trained as a historian, is a part-time analyst for the CIA. By the sixth novel in the series, *Debt of Honor*, a well-earned reputation for being a "good man in a storm" has landed Ryan, against his wishes, in the position of serving as the president's national security advisor. Jack Ryan's abilities are tested as an international crisis is touched off when a group of Japanese businessmen gain control of their government and determine that the only way to save the Japanese economy is through neutralization of U.S. power in the Pacific.

The first act of war against the United States is not an attack on a military target but on the bookkeeping system used by U.S. stock exchanges. A computer virus injected into the program used to record trades on all the major U.S. stock exchanges is activated at noon on Friday. The records of all trades made after that time are eliminated so that:

> No trading house, institution, or private investor could know what it had bought or sold, to or from

没有一家交易所、机构或私人投资者知道他们买或卖了什么、从哪里买的或者卖给了谁、买或卖了多少，因此没有人知道还剩余多少钱以进行其他交易，诸如周末去购买杂货。

whom, or for how much, and none could therefore know how much money was available for other trades, or for that matter, to purchase groceries over the weekend. (Tom Clancy, *Debt of Honor*, page 312)

The uncertainty created by the destruction of the stock exchanges' bookkeeping records threatens to throw the U.S. economy into a tailspin and distract U.S. policy makers from other moves being made by Japan in the Pacific. Jack Ryan saves the world as we know it and restores the U.S. economy to sound footing by . . . well, it wouldn't be fair to say—you'll have to read the book. Suffice it to say that a key part of the restoration plan is the repair of the stock exchanges' bookkeeping system.

This fictitious attack was an eerie precursor to the actual attack on the World Trade Center in New York City on September 11, 2001. In addition to the tragic loss of life, this attack also closed the New York Stock Exchange (NYSE) for four business days; it reopened the following Monday. The market fell by 7.1% when trading resumed. The impact on the U.S. economy could have been even greater if Wall Street firms had not had disaster recovery and data backup plans in place. In fact, within two months (November 9, 2001), the Dow Jones Industrial Average had recovered to its pre-attack level.

1. What would be the consequences to a customer if her bank could not tell her if her paycheck (which is direct deposited) had in fact been deposited? What would be the consequences to the bank?

2. Suppose the Internal Revenue Service and employers had no system established to track the amount of income tax withheld from employee salaries. How would taxpayers demonstrate to the U.S. government that they had paid taxes? How would the government verify tax payments?

Answers to these questions can be found on page 2-25.

These two examples, one fictitious and one tragically real, make a very good point: The business world in which we live and work would not be able to operate, for even one day, without a reliable method for recording the effects of transactions. A systematic method of recording transactions is necessary if companies such as IBM and **General Electric** (and even local music stores and Internet vendors) are to generate information with which to make sound business decisions.

This information is summarized in a variety of reports prepared from accounting records to assist users in making better economic decisions. Examples include the following:

general-purpose financial statements
通用财务报表

1. General-purpose financial statements prepared for external user groups, primarily current or potential investors and creditors, who are involved financially with an enterprise but who are not a part of its management team.

2. Reports received by user groups within organizations, especially those in managerial positions, to assist them in planning and controlling the day-to-day operations of their organizations.

tax returns
纳税申报单

3. Tax returns and similar reports prepared to comply with Internal Revenue Service (IRS) requirements.

4. Special reports required by various regulatory agencies such as the Securities and Exchange Commission (SEC).

accounting process
会计流程
accounting cycle
会计循环

Each of these reports is based on data that are the result of an accounting system and a set of procedures collectively referred to as the accounting process or the accounting cycle. While this process follows a fairly standard set of procedures that has existed for

2-2

accounting system
会计系统

centuries, the exact nature of the accounting system used to collect and report the data depends on the type of business, its size, the volume of transactions processed, the degree of automation employed, and other related factors. Every accounting system, however, should be designed to provide accurate information on a timely and efficient basis. At the same time, the system must provide controls that are effective in preventing mistakes and guarding against dishonesty.

Historically, accounting systems were maintained by hand and referred to as *manual systems*. Such systems continue to be used effectively in some situations. In today's business environment, however, most companies use computers to collect, process, and analyze financial information. Has the computer changed the accounting process? It allows businesses to collect and analyze much more information and do it quickly, but the computer has not changed the underlying accounting concepts involved—debits still equal credits; assets still equal liabilities plus owners' equity.

The purpose of this chapter is to review the basic steps of the accounting process, including a brief review of debits and credits and the mechanics of bookkeeping. Get ready for a discussion of double-entry accounting, a system described by the German poet Goethe as "an absolutely perfect one."[1]

Overview of the Accounting Process

 Identify and explain the basic steps in the accounting process (accounting cycle).

LO1 学习目标1
识别并解释会计流程（会计循环）中的基本步骤。

As you will recall from your introductory accounting class, the accounting process (or accounting cycle) consists of two interrelated parts, (1) the recording phase and (2) the reporting phase. The recording phase is concerned with collecting information about economic transactions and events and distilling that information into a form useful to the accounting process. For most businesses, the recording function is based on double-entry accounting procedures. In the reporting phase, the recorded information is organized and summarized using various formats for a variety of decision-making purposes. The two phases overlap because the recording of transactions is an ongoing activity that does not stop at the end of an accounting period but continues uninterrupted while events of the preceding period are being summarized and reported. The recording and reporting phases of the accounting process are reviewed and illustrated in this chapter. The form and content of the basic financial statements are discussed in depth and illustrated in Chapters 3, 4, and 5.

The accounting process, illustrated in Exhibit 2-1, generally includes the following steps in a well-defined sequence:

会计流程，即我们通常所指的会计循环，通常包括以下几个步骤：分析原始凭证、做相关交易的会计分录、登记相关账户、编制试算平衡表、编制调整分录、编制财务报表、结清虚账户以及编制结账后试算平衡表。

Recording Phase

1. **Business documents are analyzed.** Analysis of the documentation of business activities provides the basis for making an initial record of each transaction.

2. **Transactions are recorded.** Based on the supporting documents from step 1, transactions are recorded using journal entries.

3. **Transactions are posted.** Transactions, as classified and recorded, are posted to the appropriate accounts.

[1] Johann Wolfgang von Goethe, *Wilhelm Meister's Apprenticeship and Travels*, trans. Thomas Carlyle (Chapman and Hall, 1824).

Exhibit 2-1 | The Accounting Process

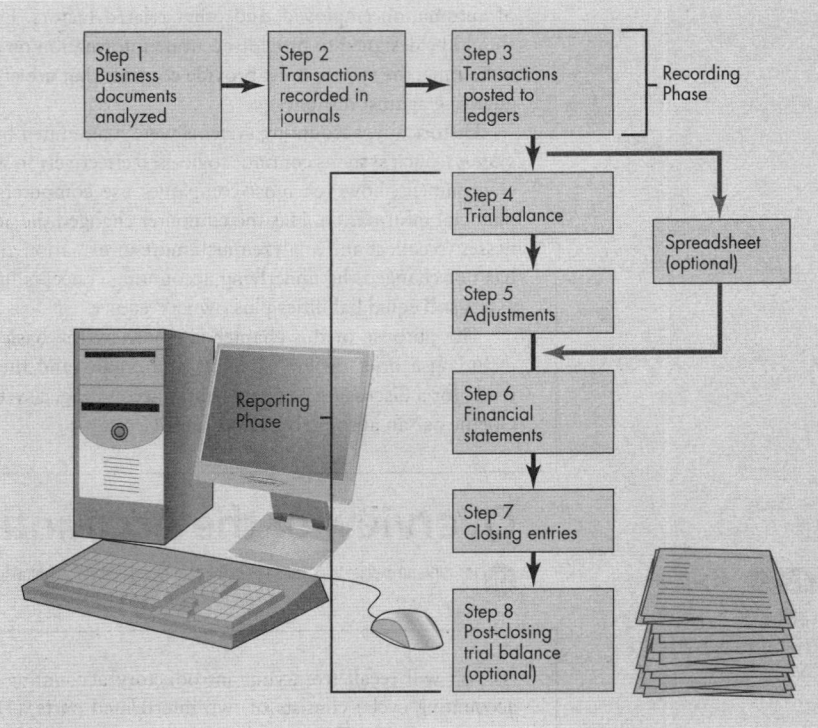

Reporting Phase

4. **A trial balance of the accounts in the general ledger is prepared.** The trial balance simply lists every account in the ledger along with its current debit or credit balance. This step in the reporting phase provides a general check on the accuracy of recording and posting.
5. **Adjusting entries are recorded.** Before financial statements can be prepared, all relevant information that has not been recorded must be determined and appropriate adjustments made. Adjusting entries must be recorded and posted so the accounts are current prior to the preparation of financial statements.
6. **Financial statements are prepared.** Statements summarizing operations and showing the financial position and cash flows are prepared from the information obtained from the adjusted accounts.
7. **Nominal accounts are closed.** Balances in the nominal (temporary) accounts are closed into the retained earnings account. This closing process results in beginning each accounting period with zero balances in all nominal accounts.
8. **A post-closing trial balance may be prepared** to determine the equality of the debits and credits after posting the adjusting and closing entries.

> **FYI**
>
> As noted in Exhibit 2-1, an optional spreadsheet can be used for the reporting process. This spreadsheet has columns for the trial balance, adjustments, an adjusted trial balance, and the financial statements. All accounts with their balances are listed on the spreadsheet in the appropriate columns. Computer spreadsheets are often used to facilitate this process.

Stop & Think

Which of the following would NOT be the role of a bookkeeper?
a) Analyzing and recording routine transactions
b) Posting journal entries
c) Interpreting accounting results
d) Preparing a post-closing trial balance

Before we are immersed in the details associated with the accounting process, it is important to remember that functions such as journalizing, posting, and closing are bookkeeping functions. You must be familiar with the mundane details of bookkeeping and know how to analyze transactions in terms of debits and credits, but you should not expect to spend your entire accounting career doing bookkeeping. As an accountant, you will spend a great deal of your time in designing information systems, analyzing complex transactions, and interpreting accounting results. A knowledge of the fundamentals of bookkeeping provides a foundation upon which these activities are based. These activities are vital to the management of an organization.

Recording Phase

LO2 学习目标2
分析交易，编制会计分录，并将每笔分录登入适当的分类账户。

② Analyze transactions and make and post journal entries.

Accurate financial statements can be prepared only if the results of business events and activities have been properly recorded. Certain events, termed transactions, involve the transfer or exchange of goods or services between two or more entities. Examples of business transactions include the purchase of merchandise or other assets from suppliers and the sale of goods or services to customers. In addition to transactions, other events and circumstances can affect the assets, liabilities, and owners' equity of the business. Some of those events and circumstances also must be recorded. Examples include the recognition of depreciation on plant assets or a decline in the market value of inventories and investments.

As indicated, the recording phase involves analyzing business documents, journalizing transactions, and posting to the ledger accounts. Before discussing these steps, the system of double-entry accounting will be reviewed because virtually all businesses use this procedure in recording their transactions.

Double-Entry Accounting

double-entry accounting
复式记账会计
debit
借
credit
贷

As explained in Chapter 1, financial accounting rests on a foundation of basic assumptions, concepts, and principles that govern the recording, classifying, summarizing, and reporting of accounting data. Double-entry accounting is an old and universally accepted system for recording accounting data. With double-entry accounting, each transaction is recorded in a way that maintains the equality of the basic accounting equation:

Assets = Liabilities + Owners' Equity

Caution

Remember that *debit* does not mean good (or bad) and *credit* does not mean bad (or good). *Debit* means left, and *credit* means right.

To review how double-entry accounting works, recall that a debit is an entry on the left side of an account and a credit is an

Exhibit 2-2 | Debit and Credit Relationships of Accounts

```
         Assets      =    Liabilities    +    Owners' Equity
        DR   CR           DR    CR             DR    CR
        (+)  (-)          (-)   (+)            (-)   (+)
                                               |           |
                                     Capital Stock    Retained Earnings
                                      DR   CR           DR    CR
                                      (-)  (+)          (-)   (+)
                                                    |              |
                                              Expenses         Revenues
                                              DR   CR          DR    CR
                                              (+)  (-)         (-)   (+)
                                                         |
                                                    Dividends
                                                    DR    CR
                                                    (+)   (-)
```
© Cengage Learning 2014

entry on the right side. The debit/credit relationships of accounts were explained in detail in your introductory accounting course. Exhibit 2-2 summarizes these relationships for a corporation. You will note that assets, expenses, and dividends are increased by debits and decreased by credits. Liabilities, capital stock, retained earnings, and revenues are increased by credits and decreased by debits. Note that while dividends reduce retained earnings, they are not classified as an expense and are not reported on the income statement.

Journal entries provide a systematic method for summarizing a business event's effect on the accounting equation. Every journal entry involves a three-step process:

journal entry
会计分录

1. Identify the accounts involved with an event or transaction.
2. Determine whether each account increased or decreased (this information, coupled with the answer to step 1, will tell you if the account was debited or credited).
3. Determine the amount by which each account was affected.

This three-step process, properly applied, will always result in a correct journal entry. Note that this process is used whether the accounting is being done manually or with a computer.

To illustrate double-entry accounting, consider the transactions and journal entries shown in Exhibit 2-3 and their impact on the accounting equation. In studying this illustration, you should note that for each transaction, total debits equal total credits. Therefore, the equality of the accounting equation is maintained.

Purchasing groceries at your local supermarket is a common example of a business transaction. Can you identify the accounts involved with this transaction?

应该掌握的复式记账会计的
重要特征。

Caution

Note in Exhibit 2-2 that dividends reduce retained earnings, but they are not classified as an expense and are not reported on the income statement.

To summarize, you should remember the following important features of double-entry accounting:

1. Assets are increased by debits and decreased by credits.
2. Liability and owners' equity accounts are increased by credits and decreased by debits.
3. Owners' equity for a corporation includes capital stock accounts and the retained earnings account.
4. Revenues, expenses, and dividends relate to owners' equity through the retained earnings account.

Exhibit 2-3 | Double-Entry Accounting: Illustrative Transactions and Journal Entries

	Three-Step Process				
Transaction	(1) Identify Accounts.	(2) Increase or Decrease?	(1) and (2) together indicate whether an account is debited or credited.	(3) By How Much?	Journal Entry
Investment by shareholder in a corporation, $10,000	Cash Capital Stock	Increase Increase	Asset ↑ = debit Owners' equity ↑ = credit	$10,000 $10,000	Cash 10,000 Capital Stock 10,000
Purchase of supplies on account, $5,000	Supplies Accounts Payable	Increase Increase	Asset ↑ = debit Liability ↑ = credit	$5,000 $5,000	Supplies 5,000 Accounts Payable 5,000
Payment of wages expense, $2,500	Cash Wages Expense	Decrease Increase	Asset ↓ = credit Expenses ↑ = debit	$2,500 $2,500	Wages Expense 2,500 Cash 2,500
Collection of accounts receivable, $1,000	Cash Accounts Receivable	Increase Decrease	Asset ↑ = debit Asset ↓ = credit	$1,000 $1,000	Cash 1,000 Accounts Receivable 1,000
Payment of account payable, $500	Cash Accounts Payable	Decrease Decrease	Asset ↓ = credit Liability ↓ = debit	$500 $500	Accounts Payable 500 Cash 500
Sale of merchandise on account, $20,000	Accounts Receivable Sales	Increase Increase	Asset ↑ = debit Revenues ↑ = credit	$20,000 $20,000	Accounts Receivable 20,000 Sales 20,000

Purchase of equipment: $15,000 down payment plus $40,000 long-term note	Cash
	Equipment
	Notes Payable
		Decrease
		Increase
		Increase
			Asset ↓ = credit
			Asset ↑ = debit
			Liability ↑ = credit
				$15,000
				$55,000
				$40,000
					Equipment 55,000
					    Cash 15,000
					    Notes Payable 40,000

Payment of cash dividend, $4,000	Cash Dividends	Decrease Increase	Asset ↓ = credit Dividends ↑ = debit	$4,000 $4,000	Dividends 4,000 Cash 4,000

© Cengage Learning 2014

5. Expenses and dividends are increased by debits and decreased by credits because they reduce owners' equity.
6. Revenues are increased by credits and decreased by debits.
7. The difference between total revenues and total expenses for a period is net income (loss), which increases (decreases) owners' equity through the retained earnings account.

With this brief overview of the accounting equation and journal entries, we are now ready to proceed through the steps in the accounting process.

Analyzing Business Documents

The recording phase begins with an analysis of the documentation showing what business activities have occurred. Normally, a business document, or source document, is the first record of each transaction. Such a document offers detailed information concerning the transaction. The business documents provide support for the data to be recorded in the journals. Copies of sales invoices, for example, are the evidence in support of sales transactions; canceled checks provide data concerning cash disbursements; and the corporation minutes book supports entries authorized by action of the board of directors. Documents underlying each recorded transaction provide a means of verifying the accounting records and thus form a vital part of the information and control systems.

business document, or source document
原始凭证

Journalizing Transactions

Once the information provided on business documents has been analyzed, transactions are recorded in chronological order in the appropriate journals. In some small businesses, all transactions are recorded in a single journal. Most business enterprises, however, maintain various special journals designed to meet their specific needs as well as a general journal. A special journal is used to record a particular type of frequently recurring transaction. Special journals are commonly used, for example, to record each of the following types of transactions: sales, purchases, cash disbursements, and cash receipts. A general journal is used to record all transactions for which a special journal is not maintained. As illustrated below, a general journal shows the transaction date and the accounts affected and allows for a brief description of each transaction. Special journals are illustrated and explained in the Web Material associated with this chapter (see www.cengagebrain.com).

journals
日记账
special journal
特种日记账
general journal
普通日记账

GENERAL JOURNAL Page 24

Date		Description	Post. Ref.	Debit	Credit
2015 July	1	Dividends	330	25,000	
		Dividends Payable	260		25,000
		Declared semiannual cash dividend on common stock.			
	10	Equipment	180	7,500	
		Notes Payable	220		7,500
		Issued note for new equipment.			
	31	Payroll Tax Expense	418	2,650	
		Payroll Taxes Payable	240		2,650
		Recorded payroll taxes for month.			

Posting to the Ledger Accounts

An account is used to summarize the effects of transactions on each element of the expanded accounting equation. For example, the cash account is used to provide detail for all transactions involving the inflow (debit) and outflow (credit) of cash. A ledger is a collection of accounts maintained by a business. The specific accounts required by a business unit vary depending on the nature of the business, its properties and activities, the information to be provided on the financial statements, and the controls to be employed in carrying out the accounting functions.

ledger
分类账

Information recorded in the journals is transferred to appropriate accounts in the ledger. This transfer is referred to as posting. Note that posting is a copying process; it involves no new analysis. Ledger accounts for Equipment and Notes Payable are presented by illustrating the posting of the July 10 transaction from the preceding general journal. The posting reference (J24) indicates that the transaction was transferred from page 24 of the general journal. Note that the account numbers for Equipment (180) and Notes Payable (220) are entered in the Posting Reference column of the journal.

posting
过账

GENERAL LEDGER

Account EQUIPMENT   Account No. 180

Date		Item	Post. Ref.	Debit	Credit	Balance
2015						
July	1	Balance				10,550
	10	Purchase Equipment	J24	7,500		18,050

Account NOTES PAYABLE   Account No. 220

Date		Item	Post. Ref.	Debit	Credit	Balance
2015						
July	1	Balance				5,750
	10	Purchase Equipment	J24		7,500	13,250

general ledger
总分类账
subsidiary ledgers
明细分类账
control account
统驭账户

It is often desirable to establish separate ledgers for detailed information in support of balance sheet or income statement items. The general ledger includes all accounts appearing on the financial statements, and separate subsidiary ledgers afford additional detail in support of certain general ledger accounts. For example, a single accounts receivable account is usually carried in the general ledger, and individual customer accounts are recorded in a subsidiary accounts receivable ledger. The general ledger account that summarizes the detailed information in a subsidiary ledger is known as a control account. Thus, Accounts Receivable is considered a control account. Subsidiary ledger accounts are illustrated in the Web Material associated with this chapter (see www.cengagebrain.com).

Stop & Think

The computer is very valuable in the posting process because it reduces the types of errors that can be made. Which of the following posting errors could a person make that a computer would not?
a) Posting to the wrong account
b) Posting the wrong amount
c) Posting a debit to a specific account instead of a credit
d) A well-functioning computer would not make any of these mistakes

Depending primarily on the number of transactions involved, amounts may be posted to ledger accounts on a daily, weekly, or monthly basis. If a computer system is being used, the posting process may be done automatically as transactions are recorded. At the end of an accounting period, when the posting process has been completed, the balances in the ledger accounts are used for preparing the trial balance.

Reporting Phase

 Make adjusting entries, produce financial statements, and close nominal accounts.

LO3 学习目标3
编制调整分录，编制财务报表并结清虚账户。

As noted earlier, the objective of the accounting process is to produce financial statements and other reports that will assist various users in making economic decisions. Once the recording phase is completed, the data must be summarized and organized into a useful format. The remaining steps of the accounting process are designed to accomplish this purpose. These steps will be illustrated using data from Rosi, Inc., a hypothetical merchandising company, for the year ended December 31, 2015.

Preparing a Trial Balance

After all transactions for the period have been posted to the ledger accounts, the balance for each account is determined. Every account will have either a debit, credit, or zero balance. A trial balance is a list of all accounts and their balances. The trial balance, therefore, indicates whether total debits equal total credits and thus provides a general check on the accuracy of recording and posting. When debits equal credits in a trial balance, however, it is no guarantee that the accounts are correct. For example, a journal entry involving a debit to Accounts Receivable could have been incorrectly posted as a debit to the notes receivable account. The trial balance would indeed balance, but the accounts would be in error. Thus, a balanced trial balance provides no guarantee of accuracy. However, a trial balance that does not balance indicates that we needn't go further into the reporting phase of the accounting process. An error exists somewhere and must be detected and corrected before proceeding. If we elect to proceed without correcting the error, we have one guarantee—the financial statements will contain errors. The trial balance for Rosi, Inc., is presented on the next page.

trial balance
试算平衡表

试算平衡表是编制财务报表的基础，不是管理层或者外部使用者的信息来源。

FYI

A fundamental difference between the trial balance and the financial statements is that no external users ever see the trial balance. Most managers have never seen a trial balance. It serves as the basis for the preparation of the financial statements but is not an information source to either management or external users.

Rosi, Inc.
Trial Balance
December 31, 2015

	Debit	Credit
Cash	$ 83,110	
Accounts Receivable	106,500	
Allowance for Bad Debts 坏账准备 (allowance for bad debts)		$ 1,610
Inventory	45,000	
Prepaid Insurance	8,000	
Interest Receivable	0	
Land	114,000	
Buildings	156,000	
Accumulated Depreciation—Buildings		39,000
Furniture and Equipment	19,000	
Accumulated Depreciation—Furniture and Equipment		3,800
Accounts Payable		37,910
Unearned Rent Revenue 预收租金收入 (unearned rent revenue)		0
Salaries and Wages Payable		0
Interest Payable		0
Income Taxes Payable		0
Dividends Payable 应付股利 (dividends payable)		3,400
Bonds Payable 应付债券 (bonds payable)		140,000
Common Stock, $0.10 par		150,000
Retained Earnings		103,900
Dividends	13,600	
Sales		479,500
Cost of Goods Sold	159,310	
Salaries and Wages Expense	172,450	
Heat, Light, and Power Expense	32,480	
Payroll Tax Expense 薪资税费 (payroll tax expense)	18,300	
Advertising Expense	18,600	
Bad Debt Expense	0	
Depreciation Expense—Buildings	0	
Depreciation Expense—Furniture and Equipment	0	
Insurance Expense	0	
Interest Revenue		1,100
Rent Revenue		2,550
Interest Expense	16,420	
Income Tax Expense 所得税费用 (income tax expense)	0	
Totals	$962,770	$962,770

adjusting entries
调整分录

Preparing Adjusting Entries

As discussed in the previous section, transactions generally are recorded in a journal in chronological order and then posted to the ledger accounts. The entries are based on the best information available at the time. Although the majority of accounts are up to date at the end of an accounting period and their balances can be included in the financial statements, some accounts require adjustment to reflect current circumstances. In general, these accounts are not updated throughout the period because it is impractical or inconvenient to make such entries on a daily or weekly basis. At the end of each accounting period, in order to report all asset, liability, and owners' equity amounts properly and to recognize all revenues and expenses for the period on an accrual basis, accountants are required to make any necessary adjustments prior to preparing the financial statements. The entries that reflect these adjustments are called adjusting entries.

One difficulty with adjusting entries is that the need for an adjustment is not signaled by a specific event such as the receipt of a bill or the receipt of cash from a customer. Rather, adjusting entries are recorded on the basis of an analysis of the circumstances at the close of each accounting period. This analysis involves just two steps:

> **FYI**
>
> **Disney**'s 1998 balance sheet included in its annual report did not balance. The preparers of that balance sheet transposed two numbers, and the result was a $9 (million) error. The balance sheet in the 1998 10-K that was filed with the SEC did not contain the transposition error.

1. Determine whether the amounts recorded for all assets and liabilities are correct. If not, debit or credit the appropriate asset or liability account. In short, fix the balance sheet.
2. Determine what revenue or expense adjustments are required as a result of the changes in recorded amounts of assets and liabilities indicated in step 1. Debit or credit the appropriate revenue or expense account. In short, fix the income statement.

It should be noted that these two steps are interrelated and may be reversed. That is, revenue and expense adjustments may be considered first to fix the income statement, indicating which asset and liability accounts need adjustment to fix the balance sheet. As you will see, each adjusting entry involves at least one income statement account and one balance sheet account. T-accounts are helpful in analyzing adjusting entries and will be used in the illustrations that follow.

The areas most commonly requiring analysis to see whether adjusting entries are needed include the following:

- *Transactions where cash will be exchanged in a future period*

1. Unrecorded assets
2. Unrecorded liabilities

- *Transactions where cash has been exchanged in a prior period*

3. Prepaid expenses
4. Unearned revenues

- *Transactions involving estimates*

For most transactions, the revenue or expense recognition and the flow of cash occur in the same accounting period. For those transactions, no adjustments are necessary as the entire transaction is accounted for in one accounting period. In some instances, the recognition of revenues and expenses and the flow of cash may occur in different accounting periods. In those instances, an adjusting entry is required to ensure that the proper amount of revenue and/or expense is recorded in each accounting period.

As we illustrate and discuss adjusting entries, remember that the basic purpose of adjustments is to make account balances current in order to report all asset, liability, and owners' equity amounts properly and to recognize all revenues and expenses for the period on an accrual basis. This is done so that the income statement and the balance sheet will reflect the proper operating results and financial position, respectively, at the end of the accounting period.

The adjusting entry part of the accounting process is illustrated using the adjusting data for Rosi, Inc., presented as follows.

Adjusting Data for Rosi, Inc.
December 31, 2015

Unrecorded Assets:
(a) Interest on notes receivable, $250.

Unrecorded Liabilities:
(b) Salaries and wages, $2,150.
(c) Interest on bonds payable, $5,000.
(d) Federal and state income taxes, $8,000.

Prepaid Expenses:
(e) Prepaid insurance remaining at year-end, $3,800.

Unearned Revenues:
(f) Unearned rent revenue remaining at year-end, $475.

Estimates:
(g) Depreciation Expense for buildings, 5% per year.
(h) Depreciation Expense for furniture and equipment, 10% per year.
(i) The Allowance for Bad Debts is to be increased by $1,100.

Transactions Where Cash Will Be Exchanged in a Future Period

In cases where work is performed in the current period but cash does not flow until a future period, an adjusting entry must be made to ensure that revenue is recognized (if you are the one who did the work) in the current period or that an expense is recognized (if the work was done on your behalf) in the current period. These adjusting entries are referred to as accrual entries, and there are generally two types: unrecorded (or accrued) assets and unrecorded (or accrued) liabilities.

unrecorded assets
未入账资产

Unrecorded Assets In accordance with the revenue recognition principle of accrual accounting, revenues should be recorded when earned, regardless of when the cash is received. If revenue is earned but not yet collected in cash, a receivable exists. To ensure that all receivables are properly reported on the balance sheet in the correct amounts, an analysis should be made at the end of each accounting period to see whether there are any revenues that have been earned but have not yet been collected or recorded. These unrecorded receivables are earned and represent amounts that are receivable in the future; therefore, they should be recognized as assets.

In recording unrecorded assets, an asset account is debited and a revenue account is credited. The illustrative entry recognizing the unrecorded receivable (and the accrued revenue) for Rosi, Inc., is as follows:

(a) Interest Receivable..	250	
Interest Revenue..		250

To record accrued interest on notes receivable.

After this adjusting entry has been journalized and posted, the receivable will appear as an asset on the balance sheet, and the interest revenue will be reported on the income statement. Through the adjusting entry, the asset (receivable) accounts are properly stated and revenues are appropriately reported.

Unrecorded Liabilities Just as assets are created from revenues being earned before they are collected or recorded, liabilities can be created by expenses being incurred prior to being paid or recorded. These expenses, along with their corresponding liabilities, should be recorded when incurred, no matter when they are paid. Thus, adjusting entries are required at the end of an accounting period to recognize any unrecorded liabilities in the proper period and to record the corresponding expenses. As the expense is recorded (increased by a debit), the corresponding liability is also recorded (increased by a credit), showing the entity's obligation to pay for the expense. If such adjustments are not made, the net income measurement for the period will not reflect all appropriate expenses and the corresponding liabilities will be understated on the balance sheet.

unrecorded liabilities
未入帐负债

The adjusting entries to record unrecorded liabilities (and accrued expenses) for Rosi, Inc., are as follows:

(b) Salaries and Wages Expense...	2,150	
Salaries and Wages Payable..		2,150

To record accrued salaries and wages.

(c) Interest Expense...	5,000	
Interest Payable...		5,000

To record accrued interest on bonds.

(d) Income Tax Expense..	8,000	
Income Taxes Payable..		8,000

To record income taxes.

Transactions Where Cash Has Been Exchanged in a Prior Period

For some transactions, cash has changed hands before the revenue is earned or the expense is incurred. If the revenue is not earned or the expense is not incurred prior to the end of the period, then an adjusting entry to reflect that fact is required.

prepaid expenses
预付费用

Prepaid Expenses Payments that a company makes in advance for items normally charged to expense are known as prepaid expenses. An example would be the payment of an insurance premium for three years. Theoretically, every resource acquisition is an asset, at least temporarily. Thus, the entry to record an advance payment should be a debit to an asset account (Prepaid Expenses) and a credit to Cash, showing the exchange of cash for another asset.

An expense is the using up of an asset. For example, when supplies are purchased, they are recorded as assets; when they are used, their cost is transferred to an expense account. The purpose of making adjusting entries for prepaid expenses is to show the complete or partial consumption of an asset. If the original entry is to an asset account, the adjusting entry reduces the asset to an amount that reflects its remaining future benefit and at the same time recognizes the actual expense incurred for the period.

> **Caution**
> Prepaid Expenses is a tricky name for an asset. Assets are reported in the balance sheet. Don't make the mistake of including Prepaid Expenses with the expenses on the income statement.

For the unrecorded assets and liabilities discussed earlier, there was no original entry; the adjusting entry was the first time these items were recorded in the accounting records. For prepaid expenses, this is not the case. Because cash has already been paid (in the case of prepaid expenses), an original entry has been made to record the cash transaction. Therefore, the amount of the adjusting entry is the difference between what the updated balance should be and the amount of the original entry already recorded.

The method of adjusting for prepaid expenses depends on how the expenditures were originally entered in the accounts. They could have been recorded originally as debits to (1) an asset account or (2) an expense account. Both methods, if consistently applied, result in the same end result. Thus, both methods are equally correct. An individual company would choose one method or the other and apply it each period.

Original Debit to an Asset Account. If an asset account was originally debited (Prepaid Insurance in this example), the adjusting entry requires that an expense account be debited for the amount applicable to the current period and the asset account be credited. The asset account remains with a debit balance that shows the amount applicable to future periods. An adjusting entry for Prepaid Insurance for Rosi, Inc., illustrates this situation as follows:

(e) Insurance Expense	4,200	
Prepaid Insurance		4,200
To record expired insurance ($8,000 − $3,800 = $4,200).		

Because the asset account Prepaid Insurance was originally debited, as shown in the trial balance, the amount of the prepayment ($8,000) must be reduced to reflect only the $3,800 that remains unexpired. The following T-accounts illustrate how this adjusting entry, when posted, would affect the accounts.

Prepaid Insurance				Insurance Expense	
Beg. Bal.	8,000			Beg. Bal.	0
		Adj. (e)	4,200	Adj. (e)	4,200
End. Bal.	3,800			End. Bal.	4,200

Original Debit to an Expense Account. If an expense account was originally debited (Insurance Expense in this example), the adjusting entry requires that an asset account be debited for the amount applicable to future periods and the expense account be credited.

The expense account then remains with a debit balance representing the amount applicable to the current period. For example, if Rosi, Inc., had originally debited Insurance Expense for $8,000, the adjusting entry would be as follows:

Prepaid Insurance	3,800	
Insurance Expense		3,800

To record prepaid insurance ($8,000 − $4,200 = $3,800).

The following T-accounts illustrate the effect that this adjusting entry would have on the relevant accounts.

Prepaid Insurance				Insurance Expense		
Beg. Bal.	0			Beg. Bal.	8,000	
Adj.	3,800					Adj. 3,800
End. Bal.	3,800			End. Bal.	4,200	

Note that regardless of which method is used, the ending balance in each account is the same. In this example, using either method results in an ending balance in Prepaid Insurance and Insurance Expense of $3,800 and $4,200, respectively.

> **Caution**
>
> The original debit to an asset account makes more sense conceptually. Remember, however, that the account balances reported in the financial statements are what matter; the working balances that exist in the accounting records on a day-to-day basis are not as important.

Unearned Revenues Amounts received before the actual earning of revenues are known as *unearned revenues*. They arise when customers pay in advance of the receipt of goods or services. Because the company has received cash but has not yet given the customer the purchased goods or services, the unearned revenues are in fact liabilities. That is, the company must provide something in return for the amounts received. For example, a building contractor may require a deposit before proceeding on construction of a house. Upon receipt of the deposit, the contractor has unearned revenue, a liability. The contractor must construct the house to earn the revenue. If the house is not built, the contractor will be obligated to repay the deposit.

unearned revenues
预收账款

The method of adjusting for unearned revenues depends on whether the receipts for undelivered goods or services were recorded originally as credits to (1) a revenue account or (2) a liability account.

Original Credit to a Revenue Account If a revenue account was originally credited (Rent Revenue in this example), this account is debited and a liability account is credited for the revenue applicable to a future period. The revenue account remains with a credit balance representing the earnings applicable to the current period. As indicated in the trial balance for Rosi, Inc., rent receipts are recorded originally in the rent revenue account. Unearned revenue at the end of 2015 is $475, and it is recorded as follows:

(f) Rent Revenue...	475	
Unearned Rent Revenue		475

To record unearned rent revenue.

The following T-accounts illustrate the effect that this adjusting entry would have on the related accounts.

Unearned Rent Revenue				Rent Revenue		
	Beg. Bal.	0			Beg. Bal.	2,550
	Adj. (f)	475	Adj. (f)	475		
	End. Bal.	475			End. Bal.	2,075

Original Credit to a Liability Account If a liability account was originally credited (Unearned Rent Revenue), this account is debited and a revenue account is credited for the amount applicable to the current period. The liability account remains with a credit balance that shows the amount applicable to future periods. For example, if Rosi, Inc., had originally credited Unearned Rent Revenue for $2,550, the adjusting entry (along with affected T-accounts) would be as follows:

Unearned Rent Revenue...	2,075	
Rent Revenue		2,075

To record rent revenue ($2,550 – $475).

Unearned Rent Revenue				Rent Revenue		
		Beg. Bal.	2,550		Beg. Bal.	0
Adj.	2,075				Adj.	2,075
		End. Bal.	475		End. Bal.	2,075

Again, note that using either method results in exactly the same balances for the income statement and balance sheet accounts.

Transactions Involving Estimates

In addition to timing differences associated with cash flows and the recognition of revenues and/or expenses, a third type of adjusting entry involves estimates. Accountants must constantly use judgment when applying the accrual accounting model. Questions such as "for how many periods will a machine generate revenues" or "how many of our credit customers will not pay" must be answered and reflected in the financial statements. The answers to these questions involve estimates. Two common types of these adjusting entries involve depreciation and bad debts.

asset depreciation
资产折旧

Asset Depreciation Charges to operations for the use of buildings, furniture, and equipment must be recorded at the end of the period. In recording asset depreciation, operations are charged with a portion of the asset's cost, and the carrying value of the asset is reduced by that amount. A reduction in an asset for depreciation is usually recorded by a credit to a contra account, Accumulated Depreciation. A *contra account* (or offset account) is set up to record subtractions from a related account.

contra account
抵销账户

Adjustments at the end of the year for depreciation for Rosi, Inc., are as follows:

(g) Depreciation Expense—Buildings...	7,800	
Accumulated Depreciation—Buildings.................................		7,800
To record depreciation on buildings at 5% per year.		
(h) Depreciation Expense—Furniture and Equipment..........................	1,900	
Accumulated Depreciation—Furniture and Equipment..................		1,900
To record depreciation on furniture and equipment at 10% per year.		

bad debts
坏账

Bad Debts Invariably, when a business allows customers to purchase goods and services on credit, some of the accounts receivable will not be collected, resulting in a charge to income for bad debt expense. Under the accrual concept, an adjustment should be made for the estimated expense in the current period rather than when specific accounts actually become uncollectible in later periods. This practice produces a better matching of revenues and expenses and therefore a better income measurement. Using this procedure, operations are charged with the estimated expense, and receivables are reduced by means of a contra account, Allowance for Bad Debts. To illustrate, the adjustment for Rosi, Inc., at the end of the year, assuming the allowance account is to be increased by $1,100, would be as follows:

(i) Bad Debt Expense... 1,100
    Allowance for Bad Debts... 1,100
To adjust for estimated bad debt expense.

在会计期末所做的调整分录是不涉及现金的。

We should emphasize two characteristics of adjusting entries. First, adjusting entries made at the end of an accounting period *do not involve cash*. Cash has either changed hands prior to the end of the period (as is the case with prepaid expenses or unearned revenues), or cash will change hands in a future period (as is the case with many unrecorded receivables and unrecorded liabilities). It is precisely because cash is not changing hands on the last day of the accounting period that most adjusting entries must be made.

每个调整分录涉及一个资产负债表账户和一个利润表账户。

Second, each adjusting entry involves a balance sheet account and an income statement account. In each case requiring adjustment, we are either generating an asset, using up an asset, recording an incurred but unrecorded expense, or recording revenue that has yet to be earned. Knowing that each adjusting entry has at least one balance sheet and one income statement account makes the adjustment process a little easier. Once you have determined that an adjusting entry involves a certain balance sheet account, you can then focus on identifying the corresponding income statement account that requires adjustment.

Preparing Financial Statements

Once all accounts have been brought up to date through the adjustment process, financial statements are prepared. Financial statements can be prepared directly from the data in the adjusted ledger accounts. The data must only be organized into appropriate sections and categories so as to present them as simply and clearly as possible. The following process describes how the financial statements are prepared from the information taken from the trial balance:

1. Identify all revenues and expenses—these account balances are used to prepare the income statement.
2. Compute net income—subtract expenses from revenues.
3. Compute the ending retained earnings balance—Retained Earnings from the previous period is the starting point. Net income (computed in step 2) is added to the beginning retained earnings balance and dividends for the period are subtracted.
4. Prepare a balance sheet using the balance sheet accounts from the trial balance and the modified retained earnings balance computed from step 3.

Once the financial statements are prepared, explanatory notes are written. These notes clarify the methods and assumptions used in preparing the statements. In addition, the auditor must review the financial statements to make sure they are accurate, reasonable, and in accordance with generally accepted accounting principles. Finally, the financial statements are distributed to external users who analyze them in order to learn more about the financial condition of the company.

How long does it take for large corporations to complete the accounting process to the point at which financial statements are available? For December 31 year-end firms, financial statement preparation is usually completed in February. The date of Disney's audit opinion (a rough measure of when financial statement preparation is essentially complete) for the fiscal year ended October 1, 2011, is November 23, 2011. For firms with publicly traded shares, the SEC requires the annual financial statements to be released within 60 days of fiscal year-end. The data used to prepare financial statements can be taken directly from the adjusted account balances in the ledger, or a spreadsheet may be used. Financial statements are prepared by determining which accounts go on which financial statement, appropriately listing those accounts, and summing to obtain totals.

Using a Spreadsheet

spreadsheet
电子工作表

An optional step in the accounting process is to use a spreadsheet (also called a work sheet) to facilitate the preparation of adjusting entries and financial statements. The availability of computer spreadsheets, such as Microsoft® Excel, makes the preparation of a spreadsheet quite easy. Remember, however, that preparing a spreadsheet is not a required step. As indicated, financial statements can be prepared directly from data in adjusted ledger account balances.

When a spreadsheet is constructed, trial balance data are listed in the first pair of columns. The adjusting entries are listed in the second pair of columns. Sometimes a third pair of columns is included to show the trial balance after adjustment. Account balances, as adjusted, are carried forward to the appropriate financial statement columns. A spreadsheet for a merchandising enterprise includes a pair of columns for the income statement accounts and a pair for the balance sheet accounts. There are no columns for the statement of cash flows because this statement requires additional analysis of changes in account balances for the period. A spreadsheet for Rosi, Inc., is shown on page 2-20. All adjustments illustrated previously are included.

Closing the Nominal Accounts

在结账的过程中，虚（暂计性）账户余额应转入实（永久性）账户，从而使得虚账户的余额为0。

Once adjusting entries have been formally recorded in the general journal and posted to the ledger accounts, the books are ready to be closed in preparation for a new accounting period. During this closing process, the nominal (temporary) account balances are transferred to a real (permanent) account, leaving the nominal accounts with a zero balance. Nominal accounts include all income statement accounts plus the dividends account for a corporation. The real account that receives the closing amounts from the nominal accounts is Retained Earnings. Because it is a real account, this and all other balance sheet accounts remain open and carry their balances forward to the new period.

The mechanics of closing the nominal accounts are straightforward. All revenue accounts with credit balances are closed by being debited; all expense accounts with debit balances are closed by being credited. This process reduces these temporary accounts to a zero balance. The difference between the closing debit amounts for revenues and the credit amounts for expenses is net income (or net loss) and is an increase (or decrease) to Retained Earnings. Dividends are also closed at the end of each period. The closing of Dividends serves to reduce Retained Earnings. Thus, the closing entries for revenues, expenses, and dividends can be made directly to Retained Earnings, as shown at the top of page 2-21.

FYI
No account on the trial balance shows up on both the income statement and the balance sheet.

Caution
Students often make the mistake of using the beginning retained earnings balance on the end-of-year balance sheet. As we shall see in the next section, the ending retained earnings balance is arrived at when the books are closed for the year.

Rosi, Inc.
Trial Balance
December 31, 2015

	Trial Balance		Adjustments				Income Statement		Balance Sheet	
	Debit	Credit		Debit		Credit	Debit	Credit	Debit	Credit
Cash	83,110								83,110	
Accounts Receivable	106,500								106,500	
Allowance for Bad Debts		1,610	(i)			1,100				2,710
Inventory	45,000								45,000	
Prepaid Insurance	8,000		(e)			4,200			3,800	
Interest Receivable	0		(a)	250					250	
Land	114,000								114,000	
Buildings	156,000								156,000	
Accumulated Depreciation—Buildings		39,000	(g)			7,800				46,800
Furniture and Equipment	19,000								19,000	
Accumulated Depreciation—Furniture and Equipment		3,800	(h)			1,900				5,700
Accounts Payable		37,910								37,910
Unearned Rent Revenue		0	(f)			475				475
Salaries and Wages Payable		0	(b)			2,150				2,150
Interest Payable		0	(c)			5,000				5,000
Income Taxes Payable		0	(d)			8,000				8,000
Dividends Payable		3,400								3,400
Bonds Payable		140,000								140,000
Common Stock, $0.10 par		150,000								150,000
Retained Earnings		103,900								103,900
Dividends	13,600								13,600	
Sales		479,500						479,500		
Cost of Goods Sold	159,310						159,310			
Salaries and Wages Expense	172,450		(b)	2,150			174,600			
Heat, Light, and Power Expense	32,480						32,480			
Payroll Tax Expense	18,300						18,300			
Advertising Expense	18,600						18,600			
Bad Debt Expense	0		(i)	1,100			1,100			
Depreciation Expense—Buildings	0		(g)	7,800			7,800			
Depreciation Expense—Furniture and Equipment	0		(h)	1,900			1,900			
Insurance Expense	0		(e)	4,200			4,200			
Interest Revenue		1,100			(a)	250		1,350		
Rent Revenue		2,550	(f)	475				2,075		
Interest Expense	16,420		(c)	5,000			21,420			
Income Tax Expense	0		(d)	8,000			8,000			
Totals	962,770	962,770		30,875		30,875	447,710	482,925	541,260	506,045
Net Income							35,215			35,215
							482,925	482,925	541,260	541,260

Revenues	xx	
Retained Earnings		xx
To close revenues to Retained Earnings.		
Retained Earnings	xx	
Expenses		xx
To close expenses to Retained Earnings.		
Retained Earnings	xx	
Dividends		xx
To close Dividends to Retained Earnings.		

The closing entries for Rosi, Inc., follow.

Closing Entries

2015				
Dec. 31	Sales		479,500	
	Interest Revenue		1,350	
	Rent Revenue		2,075	
	Retained Earnings			482,925
	To close revenue accounts to Retained Earnings.			
31	Retained Earnings		447,710	
	Cost of Goods Sold			159,310
	Salaries and Wages Expense			174,600
	Heat, Light, and Power Expense			32,480
	Payroll Tax Expense			18,300
	Advertising Expense			18,600
	Bad Debt Expense			1,100
	Depreciation Expense—Buildings			7,800
	Depreciation Expense—Furniture and Equipment			1,900
	Insurance Expense			4,200
	Interest Expense			21,420
	Income Tax Expense			8,000
	To close expense accounts to Retained Earnings.			
31	Retained Earnings		13,600	
	Dividends			13,600
	To close Dividends to Retained Earnings.			

The following T-accounts (revenues and expenses have each been combined into one account for illustrative purposes) illustrate the effect the closing process has on the nominal accounts and Retained Earnings.

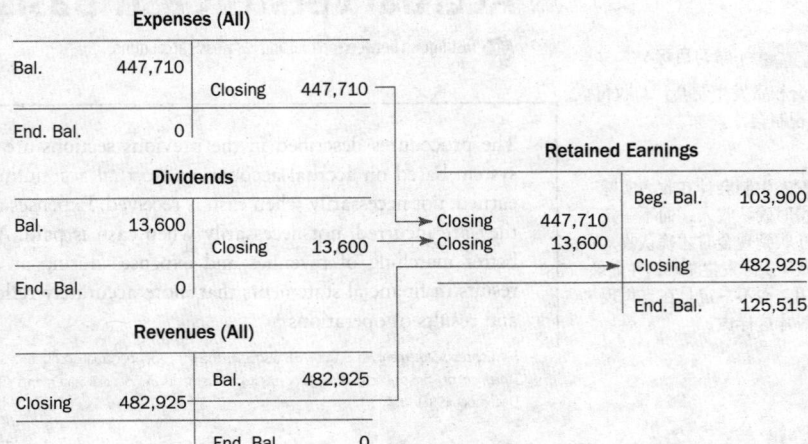

Preparing a Post-Closing Trial Balance

After the closing entries are posted, a post-closing trial balance can be prepared to verify the equality of the debits and credits for all real accounts. Recall that real accounts are only those accounts shown on the balance sheet. The post-closing trial balance represents the end of the accounting cycle. The post-closing trial balance for Rosi, Inc., follows:

Rosi, Inc.
Post-Closing Trial Balance
December 31, 2015

	Debit	Credit
Cash	$ 83,110	
Accounts Receivable	106,500	
Allowance for Bad Debts		$ 2,710
Inventory	45,000	
Prepaid Insurance	3,800	
Interest Receivable	250	
Land	114,000	
Buildings	156,000	
Accumulated Depreciation—Buildings		46,800
Furniture and Equipment	19,000	
Accumulated Depreciation—Furniture and Equipment		5,700
Accounts Payable		37,910
Unearned Rent Revenue		475
Salaries and Wages Payable		2,150
Interest Payable		5,000
Income Taxes Payable		8,000
Dividends Payable		3,400
Bonds Payable		140,000
Common Stock, $0.10 par		150,000
Retained Earnings		125,515
Totals	$527,660	$527,660

Accrual versus Cash-Basis Accounting

 Distinguish between accrual and cash-basis accounting.

The procedures described in the previous sections are those required in a double-entry system based on accrual accounting. Accrual accounting recognizes revenues as they are earned, not necessarily when cash is received. Expenses are recognized and recorded when they are incurred, not necessarily when cash is paid. Accrual accounting provides for a better matching of revenues and expenses during an accounting period and generally results in financial statements that more accurately reflect a company's financial position and results of operations.[2]

[2] In *Concepts Statement No. 6*, the FASB discusses the concept of accrual accounting and relates it to the objectives of financial reporting. *Statement of Financial Accounting Concepts No. 6*, "Elements of Financial Statements" (Stamford, CT: Financial Accounting Standards Board, December 1985).

收付实现制会计常见于那些不要求完整的复式记账记录的组织。

Some accounting systems are based on cash receipts and cash disbursements instead of accrual accounting. Cash-basis accounting procedures frequently are found in organizations not requiring a complete set of double-entry records. Such organizations might include small, unincorporated businesses and some nonprofit organizations. Professionals engaged in service businesses, such as CPAs, dentists, and engineers, also have traditionally used cash accounting systems. Even many of these organizations, however, periodically use professional accountants to prepare financial statements and other required reports on an accrual basis.

Discussion continues as to the appropriateness of using cash accounting systems, especially as a basis for determining tax liabilities. The FASB, in *Concepts Statement No. 1*, indicates that accrual accounting provides a better basis for financial reports than does information showing only cash receipts and disbursements.

The AICPA's position, however, is that the cash basis is appropriate for some small companies and especially for companies in the service industry. Accordingly, accountants will continue to be asked on occasion to convert cash-based records to generally accepted accrual-based financial statements. The procedures involved are illustrated in the Web Material associated with this chapter (see www.cengagebrain.com).

The AICPA calls cash-basis accounting an example of an "other comprehensive basis of accounting," or OCBOA. The most common alternatives to the accrual basis of accounting are the cash basis and the income tax basis.[3]

In July 2009, the IASB released a document detailing yet another accounting alternative to full GAAP. This alternative is called *IFRS for SMEs*, where "SME" stands for "small and medium-sized entities." The IASB intends this set of condensed standards to be appropriate for private companies around the world that have no need for all of the full-blown provisions of IFRS or U.S. GAAP. Because these standards fill just 230 pages, compared to 2,500 pages for IFRS and 25,000 pages for U.S. GAAP, implementation of *IFRS for SMEs* is certainly an attractive low-cost alternative for a small or medium-sized private company. The IASB has made this set of standards available for free to anyone who wants to use them. Go ahead and take a look at http://www.ifrs.org/Home.htm.

FASB CODIFICATION

The Issue: Because you are excited about your accounting class, you have spent a couple of days preparing a personal balance sheet. Of course, you have carefully used the principles of accrual accounting. Your brother, an extremely dense and unpleasant person, is now making fun of you. He claims that the FASB itself has stated that personal financial statements are to be prepared using the cash basis. You would love to put your brother in his place and show him that you are right and he is wrong ... again.

The Question: What is the proper basis for preparing a personal balance sheet?

Searching the Codification: The best place to start is with the FASB ASC topic group labeled "Presentation." In that menu you will find Topic 274, Personal Financial Statements. Look to see what basis should be used to recognize items that are reported in a personal balance sheet.

The Answer: The correct treatment is described on page 2-25.

---

[3] See Thomas A. Ratcliffe, "OCBOA: Financial Statements," *Journal of Accountancy*, October 2003, Vol. 196, Issue No. 4, p. 71. This article describes the AICPA's standards for auditing financial statements prepared under another comprehensive basis of accounting. These auditing standards are contained in the AICPA's Statement on Auditing Standards (SAS) No. 62, *Special Reports*.

Computers and the Accounting Process

LO5 学习目标5
讨论计算机在会计流程中的重要性及其日益扩大的用途。

⑤ Discuss the importance and expanding role of computers to the accounting process.

As an organization grows in size and complexity, its recording and summarizing processes become more involved, and it seeks to improve efficiency and reduce costs. Some enterprises could find that a system involving primarily manual operations is adequate in meeting their needs. Most find that information-processing needs can be handled effectively only through the use of computers.

The computer revolution has rapidly changed society and the way business is conducted and, therefore, the way accounting functions are performed. The 1990s are referred to as the *Decade of Networking*, indicating that the PCs on people's desks in the 1980s were increasingly being interconnected. The new millennium has seen increased use of the Internet, with business-to-business (B2B) and business-to-consumer (B2C) applications proliferating. The opportunities for information exchange have expanded exponentially. However, despite their tremendous capabilities, computers cannot replace skilled accountants. A computer, for example, does not know the difference between inventory and supplies until someone (the accountant) specifies the accounts involved in the transaction. Instead of reducing the responsibilities of accountants, the existence of computers places increased demands on them in directing the operations of the computer systems to ensure the use of appropriate procedures. For example, a poorly designed computer system may leave no document trail with which to verify accounting records. Although all arithmetical operations can be assumed to be done accurately by computers, the validity of the output data depends on the adequacy of the instructions given the computer. Unlike a human accountant, a computer cannot think for itself but must be given explicit instructions for performing each operation. Computers have certain advantages in that the accountant can be sure every direction will be carried out precisely. On the other hand, computers place a great responsibility on the information systems designer to anticipate any unusual situations that will require special consideration or judgment by an accountant.

在财务报告方面，计算机应用的最新发展是XBRL。XBRL的意思是可扩展商业报告语言，是将计算机制可读标签嵌入财务报告文件中的一种方法。XBRL的应用将大大简化财务报表数据分析的过程。

A recent development in the use of computers in financial reporting is the spread of XBRL. XBRL, which stands for eXtensible Business Reporting Language, is a method of embedding computer-readable tags in financial report documents. With these XBRL tabs, a company's financial statements can be downloaded directly into a spreadsheet where they can be compared to the financial statements of other companies that have also been downloaded. The use of XBRL greatly simplifies the process of analyzing financial statement data. The SEC initially required the use of XBRL for all financial statements filed by large public companies, and in June 2011 the requirement was extended to all companies publicly traded on U.S. stock exchanges. In the FASB's *Accounting Standards Codification*, XBRL elements are listed in many of the topic areas.

The question to be asked is this: If computers now take care of all of the routine accounting functions, why does an accounting student need to know anything about debits, credits, journals, posting, T-accounts, and trial balances? Good question. First, even though computers now do most of the routine work, the essence of double-entry accounting is unchanged from the days of quill pens and handwritten ledgers. Thus, the understanding of the process explained in this chapter is still relevant to a computer-based accounting system.

Second, with or without computers, the use of debits, credits, and T-accounts still provides an efficient and widespread shorthand method of analyzing transactions. At a minimum, all businesspeople should be familiar enough with the language of accounting to understand, for example, why a credit balance in the cash account or a debit balance in Retained Earnings is something unusual enough to merit investigation. Finally, an understanding of the accounting cycle—analyzing, recording, summarizing, and preparing—gives one insight into how information flows within an organization. Great advantages accrue to those who understand information flow.

SOLUTIONS TO OPENING SCENARIO QUESTIONS

1. If a customer could not tell if a deposit was made to her account, she would be unable to tell if the checks she had written would clear her account. If a bank cannot confirm for a customer that a deposit had been made, then the customer would search for a bank that could provide that basic service.

2. The burden of proof for tax payments would shift to the taxpayers. They would have to provide evidence that tax payments had been made. Currently, employers typically provide that evidence. The government would then need to have a system to match payments received from taxpayers with specific taxpayers. Fortunately for us, this system is already in place.

Stop & Think SOLUTIONS

1. (Page 2-5) The correct answer is C. Accountants and analysts interpret the accounting results for an accounting period.

2. (Page 2-9) The correct answer is D. If a computer is programmed properly, it will not post incorrect amounts, it will not post to incorrect accounts, and it will not mix its debits and credits.

SOLUTION TO USING THE FASB'S CODIFICATION

In Topic 274, you should find Section 274-10-25. There, in a very concise statement (in paragraph 1) that should silence your brother forever (at least on this issue), the FASB states:

"Assets and liabilities shall be recognized on the accrual basis of accounting."

So, once again your brother is wrong.

Review Chapter 2 Learning Objectives

1 Identify and explain the basic steps in the accounting process (accounting cycle).

The accounting process, often referred to as the *accounting cycle*, generally includes the following steps in a well-defined sequence: analyze business documents, journalize transactions, post to ledger accounts, prepare a trial balance, prepare adjusting entries, prepare financial statements (using a spreadsheet or working from the adjusted individual accounts), close the nominal accounts, and prepare a post-closing trial balance. This process of recording, classifying, summarizing, and reporting of accounting data is based on an old and universally accepted system called *double-entry accounting*.

2 Analyze transactions and make and post journal entries.

Transactions are events that transfer or exchange goods or services between or among two or more entities.

Business documents, such as invoices, provide evidence that transactions have occurred as well as the data required to record the transaction in the accounting records. The data are recorded with journal entries using a system of double-entry accounting. The journal entries are subsequently posted to ledger accounts.

③ Make adjusting entries, produce financial statements, and close nominal accounts.

Adjusting entries are made at the end of an accounting period prior to preparing the financial statements for that period. Adjusting entries are often required to update accounts so that the data are current and accurate. Generally, the required adjustments are the result of analysis rather than based on new transactions. Once adjusting entries are journalized and posted, the balance sheet, income statement, and statement of cash flows can be prepared and reported.

At the end of each accounting cycle, the balances in the nominal or temporary accounts must be transferred through the closing process to real or permanent accounts. The nominal accounts (all income statement accounts plus dividends) are left with a zero balance and are ready to receive transaction data for the new accounting period. The real (balance sheet) accounts remain open and carry their balances forward to the new period.

④ Distinguish between accrual and cash-basis accounting.

Accrual accounting recognizes revenues when they are earned, not necessarily when cash is received. Similarly, expenses are recognized and recorded under accrual accounting when they are incurred, not necessarily when cash is paid. Some organizations (and most individuals) use cash-basis accounting, which recognizes revenues when cash is received and expenses when cash is paid. The FASB has indicated that accrual accounting generally provides a better basis for financial reports, especially in reporting earnings, than does information showing only cash receipts and disbursements. However, both the FASB and SEC require a statement of cash flows to be presented along with an accrual-based income statement and a balance sheet as the primary financial statements of an enterprise.

⑤ Discuss the importance and expanding role of computers to the accounting process.

Computers play an increasing role in today's business environment as well as society in general. In the past, many companies used manual systems to record, classify, summarize, and report accounting data. Today, most companies use computers and electronic technology as an integral part of their accounting systems. In the future, technological advances will continue to significantly impact the accounting process of recording and reporting data for decision-making purposes.

KEY TERMS

Account 2-9	Closing entries 2-21	Journal entry 2-6	Source document 2-8
Accounting cycle 2-2	Contra account 2-17	Journals 2-8	Special journal 2-8
Accounting process 2-2	Control account 2-9	Ledger 2-9	Subsidiary ledgers 2-9
Accounting system 2-3	Credit 2-5	Nominal (temporary) account 2-19	Transactions 2-5
Accrual accounting 2-22	Debit 2-5	Post-closing trial balance 2-22	Trial balance 2-10
Adjusting entries 2-12	Double-entry accounting 2-5	Posting 2-9	Unearned revenues 2-16
Business document 2-8	General ledger 2-9	Prepaid expenses 2-14	Unrecorded liabilities 2-14
Cash-basis accounting 2-23	General journal 2-8	Real (permanent) account 2-19	Unrecorded receivables 2-13

Tutorial Activities

Tutorial Activities with author-written, content-specific feedback, available on *CengageNOW for Stice & Stice*.

QUESTIONS

1. What types of reports are generated from the accounting system?
2. What are the main similarities and differences between a manual and an automated accounting system?
3. Distinguish between the recording and reporting phases of the accounting process.
4. List and describe the steps in the accounting process. Why are these steps necessary? Are any steps optional?
5. Under double-entry accounting, what are the debit/credit relationships of accounts?
6. Distinguish between (a) real and nominal accounts, (b) general journal and special journals, and (c) general ledger and subsidiary ledgers.
7. Explain the nature and the purpose of (a) adjusting entries and (b) closing entries.
8. As Beechnut Mining Company's independent certified public accountant, you find that the company accountant posts adjusting and closing entries directly to the ledger without formal entries in the general journal. How would you evaluate this procedure in your report to management?
9. Give three common examples of contra accounts. Explain why contra accounts are used.
10. Payment of insurance in advance may be recorded in either (a) an expense account or (b) an asset account. Which method would you recommend? What periodic entries are required under each method?
11. Describe the nature and purpose of a work sheet.
12. What effect, if any, does the use of a work sheet have on the sequence of the reporting phase of the accounting process?
13. From the following list of accounts, determine which ones should be closed and whether each would normally be closed by a debit or by a credit entry.

Cash	Land
Rent Expense	Interest Revenue
Depreciation Expense	Advertising Expense
Sales	Notes Payable
Retained Earnings	Dividends
Capital Stock	Accounts Payable
Accounts Receivable	

14. Distinguish between accrual and cash-basis accounting.
15. Is greater accuracy achieved in financial statements prepared from double-entry accrual data as compared with cash data? Explain.
16. What are the major advantages of computers as compared with manual processing of accounting data?
17. One of your clients overheard a computer manufacturer sales representative saying that the computer will make the accountant obsolete. How would you respond to this comment?

PRACTICE EXERCISES

Practice 2-1

Journalizing
Make the journal entry to record each of the following transactions:
(a) The company purchased inventory for $5,000. The purchase was made on account.
(b) The company paid cash of $3,500 on its account with one of its suppliers from whom it regularly purchases inventory. The inventory purchase itself was recorded previously.

Practice 2-2

Journalizing
Make the journal entry (or entries) necessary to record the following transaction: Sold merchandise costing $8,000 for $14,000. Of the $14,000, $4,000 was received in cash and the remainder was on account. Assume a perpetual inventory system, meaning that the inventory reduction is recorded at the time of the sale.

Practice 2-3

Journalizing
Make the journal entry (or entries) necessary to record the following transaction: Purchased equipment with a fair market value of $100,000. Paid $10,000 cash as a down payment and signed two notes for the remaining cost—a 6% note for $20,000 that must be repaid (with interest) in six months and an 8% note for $70,000 that must be repaid (with interest) in two years.

Practice 2-4

Journalizing
Make the journal entry (or entries) necessary to record the following transaction: Sold land that had an original cost of $50,000. Received $40,000 cash. Also received a piece of equipment with a fair value of $75,000.

Practice 2-5

Journalizing
Make the journal entry (or entries) necessary to record the following transaction: Declared and paid a $12,000 cash dividend to shareholders.

Practice 2-6

Journalizing
Make the journal entry (or entries) necessary to record the following transaction: Gave land to an employee. The land originally cost $52,000, and it had that same value on the date it was given to the employee. This land was given in exchange for services rendered by the employee.

Practice 2-7

Posting
The beginning balance in the cash account was $10,000. During the month, the following four journal entries (involving cash) were recorded:

a.	Cash	2,775	
	Sales		2,775
b.	Accounts Payable	1,500	
	Cash		1,500
c.	Utilities Expense	6,200	
	Cash		6,200
d.	Cash	3,450	
	Gain		1,500
	Land		1,950

Create a Cash T-account and post the entries to this account. Compute an ending balance.

Practice 2-8

Posting
The beginning balance in the accounts payable account was $8,000. During the month, the following four journal entries (involving accounts payable) were recorded:

a.	Inventory	2,700	
	Accounts Payable		2,700
b.	Accounts Payable	6,500	
	Cash		6,500
c.	Accounts Payable	200	
	Inventory		200
d.	Inventory	3,000	
	Cash		450
	Accounts Payable		2,550

Create an Accounts Payable T-account and post the entries to this account. Compute an ending balance.

Practice 2-9

Trial Balance
Use the following account balance information to construct a trial balance:

Cost of Goods Sold	$9,000	Sales	$10,000
Accounts Payable	1,100	Dividends	700
Paid-In Capital	2,000	Retained Earnings (beginning)	1,000
Cash	400	Inventory	4,000

Practice 2-10

Trial Balance
Use the following account balance information to construct a trial balance:

Salary Expense	$24,000	Service Revenue	$32,000
Unearned Service Revenue	1,600	Rent Expense	5,300
Paid-In Capital	3,000	Retained Earnings (beginning)	1,200
Cash	3,500	Prepaid Rent Expense	5,000

Practice 2-11
Income Statement
Prepare two income statements, one using the information in Practice 2–9 and the other using the information in Practice 2–10.

Practice 2-12
Balance Sheet
Prepare two balance sheets, one using the information in Practice 2–9 and the other using the information in Practice 2–10.

Practice 2-13
Adjusting Entries
Make the adjusting journal entry necessary at the end of the period in the following situation: Equipment depreciation for the year was computed to be $5,500.

Practice 2-14
Adjusting Entries
Make the adjusting journal entry necessary at the end of the period in the following situation: Bad debts created by selling on credit during the year are estimated to be $1,200. So far, none of these accounts have been specifically identified and written off as uncollectible.

Practice 2-15
Adjusting Entries
Make the adjusting journal entry necessary at the end of the period in the following situation: On August 1, the company borrowed $10,000 under a one-year loan agreement. The annual interest rate is 12%. As of the end of the year, no entry has yet been made to record the accrued interest on the loan.

Practice 2-16
Adjusting Entries
Make the adjusting journal entry necessary at the end of the period in the following situation: On August 1, the company paid $3,600 in advance for 12 months of rent, with the rental period beginning on August 1. This $3,600 was recorded as Prepaid Rent. As of the end of the year, no entry has yet been made to adjust the amount initially recorded.

Practice 2-17
Adjusting Entries
Make the adjusting journal entry necessary at the end of the period in the following situation: On February 1, the company received $4,800 in advance for 12 months of service to be provided, with the service period beginning on February 1. This $4,800 was recorded as Unearned Service Revenue. The service is provided evenly throughout the year. As of the end of the year, no entry has yet been made to adjust the amount initially recorded.

Practice 2-18
Closing Entries
Make the closing entry (or entries) necessary to close the following accounts:

Cost of Goods Sold	$7,000	Sales	$11,000
Accounts Payable	900	Dividends	900
Paid-In Capital	1,500	Retained Earnings (beginning)	1,200
Cash	3,200	Inventory	3,500

Practice 2-19
Closing Entries
Make the closing entry (or entries) necessary to close the following accounts:

Salary Expense	$18,000	Service Revenue	$20,000
Unearned Service Revenue	4,700	Rent Expense	6,400
Paid-In Capital	2,000	Retained Earnings (beginning)	1,500
Cash	800	Prepaid Rent Expense	3,000

EXERCISES

Exercise 2-20

Recording Transactions in T-Accounts
Georgia Supply Corporation, a merchandising firm, prepared the following trial balance as of October 1:

	Debit	Credit
Cash	$150,000	
Accounts Receivable	21,540	
Inventory	32,680	
Land	15,400	
Building	14,000	
Accounts Payable		$ 9,190
Mortgage Payable		23,700
Common Stock		140,000
Retained Earnings		60,730
Totals	$233,620	$233,620

Georgia Supply engaged in the following transactions during October 2015. The company records inventory using the perpetual system.

Oct. 1   Sold merchandise on account to Tracker Corporation for $12,000; terms 2/10, n/30, FOB shipping point. Tracker paid $350 freight on the goods. The merchandise cost $6,850.
     5   Purchased inventory costing $10,250 on account; terms n/30.
     7   Received payment from Tracker for goods shipped October 1.
    15   The payroll paid for the first half of October was $22,000. (Ignore payroll taxes.)
    18   Purchased a machine for $8,600 cash.
    22   Declared a dividend of $0.45 per share on 45,000 shares of common stock outstanding.
    27   Purchased building and land for $125,000 in cash and a $225,000 mortgage payable, due in 30 years. The land was appraised at $150,000 and the building at $300,000.

1. Prepare T-accounts for all items in the October 1 trial balance and enter the initial balances.
2. Record the October transactions directly to the T-accounts.
3. Prepare a new trial balance as of the end of October.

Exercise 2-21

Adjusting Entries
In analyzing the accounts of Sydney Corporation, the adjusting data listed below are determined on December 31, the end of an annual fiscal period.

(a) The prepaid insurance account shows a debit of $6,000, representing the cost of a two-year earthquake insurance policy dated July 1.
(b) On August 1, Rent Revenue was credited for $9,450, representing revenue from subrental for a seven-month period beginning on that date.
(c) Purchase of advertising materials for $3,550 during the year was recorded in the advertising expense account. On December 31, advertising materials costing $500 are on hand.
(d) On November 1, $4,200 was paid for rent for a six-month period beginning on that date. The rent expense account was debited.
(e) Miscellaneous Office Expense was debited for office supplies of $950 purchased during the year. On December 31, office supplies of $125 are on hand.
(f) Interest of $534 has accrued on notes payable.

1. Give the adjusting entry for each item.
2. What sources would provide the information for each adjustment?

Exercise 2-22

Adjusting and Correcting Entries

Upon inspecting the books and records for Wernli Company for the year ended December 31, 2015, you find the following data:

(a) A receivable of $640 from Hatch Realty is determined to be uncollectible. The company maintains an allowance for bad debts for such losses.
(b) A creditor, E. F. Bowcutt Co., has just been awarded damages of $3,500 as a result of breach of contract by Wernli Company during the current year. Nothing appears on the books in connection with this matter.
(c) A fire destroyed part of a branch office. Furniture and fixtures that cost $12,300 and had a book value of $8,200 at the time of the fire were completely destroyed. The insurance company has agreed to pay $7,000 under the provisions of the fire insurance policy.
(d) Advances of $950 to salespersons have been previously recorded as sales salaries expense.
(e) Machinery at the end of the year shows a balance of $19,960. It is discovered that additions to this account during the year totaled $4,460, but of this amount, $760 should have been recorded as repairs. Depreciation is to be recorded at 10% on machinery owned throughout the year but at one-half this rate on machinery purchased or sold during the year.

Record the entries required to adjust and correct the accounts. (Ignore income tax consequences.)

Exercise 2-23

REVERSE SOLVABLE

Reconstructing Adjusting Entries

For each situation, reconstruct the adjusting entry that was made to arrive at the ending balance. Assume statements and adjusting entries are prepared only once each year.

1. Prepaid Insurance:
   Balance beginning of year $4,300
   Balance end of year   3,600

   During the year, an additional business insurance policy was purchased.
   A one-year premium of $1,200 was paid and charged to Prepaid Insurance.

2. Accumulated Depreciation:
   Balance beginning of year $103,400
   Balance end of year   106,100

   During the year, a depreciable asset that cost $10,700 and had a carrying value of $5,300 was sold for $6,000. The disposal of the asset was recorded correctly.

3. Unearned Rent:
   Balance beginning of year $ 8,000
   Balance end of year   12,000

   Warehouse quarterly rent received in advance is $14,000. During the year, equipment was rented to another company at an annual rent of $6,000. The quarterly rent payments were credited to Rent Revenue; the annual equipment rental was credited to Unearned Rent.

4. Salaries Payable:
   Balance beginning of year $36,540
   Balance end of year   29,480

   Salaries are paid biweekly. All salary payments during the year were debited to Salaries Expense.

Exercise 2-24

Adjusting and Closing Entries and Post-Closing Trial Balance

Accounts of Pioneer Heating Corporation at the end of the first year of operations showed the following balances. In addition, prepaid operating expenses are $4,000, and accrued sales commissions payable are $5,900. Investment revenue receivable is $1,000. Depreciation for the year on buildings is $4,500 and on machinery, $5,000. Federal and state income taxes for the year are estimated at $18,100.

	Debit	Credit
Cash	$ 39,000	
Inventory	50,000	
Investments	50,000	
Land	70,000	
Buildings	180,000	
Machinery	100,000	
Accounts Payable		$ 65,000
Common Stock		320,000
Additional Paid-In Capital		40,000
Sales		590,000
Cost of Goods Sold	230,000	
Sales Commissions	200,000	
General Operating Expenses	101,000	
Investment Revenue		5,000
Totals	$1,020,000	$1,020,000

1. Prepare the necessary entries to adjust and close the books.
2. Prepare a post-closing trial balance.

Exercise 2-25

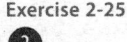

Adjusting and Closing Entries and Post-Closing Trial Balance
Below is the trial balance for Boudreaux Company as of December 31.

	Debit	Credit
Cash	$ 72,000	
Accounts Receivable	365,000	
Inventory	52,000	
Prepaid Expenses	36,000	
Land	70,000	
Plant and Equipment	1,254,000	
Other Assets	1,275,000	
Accounts Payable		$ 154,000
Wages, Interest, and Taxes Payable		218,000
Unearned Revenue		42,000
Long-Term Debt		1,190,000
Other Liabilities		297,000
Common Stock		195,000
Retained Earnings		915,000
Dividends	211,000	
Sales		2,762,000
Interest Revenue		29,000
Cost of Goods Sold	1,565,000	
Selling, General, and Administrative Expenses	615,000	
Interest Expense	82,000	
Income Tax Expense	205,000	
Totals	$5,802,000	$5,802,000

Consider the following additional information:
(a) Boudreaux uses a perpetual inventory system.
(b) The prepaid expenses were paid on September 1 and relate to a three-year insurance policy that went into effect on September 1.
(c) The unearned revenue relates to rental of an unused portion of the corporate offices. The $42,000 was received on April 1 and represents payment in advance for one year's rental.
(d) Plant and Equipment includes $15,000 for routine equipment repairs that were erroneously recorded as equipment purchases. The repairs were made on December 30.
(e) Other Assets includes $7,000 for miscellaneous office supplies, which were purchased in mid-October. An end-of-year count reveals that only $4,200 of the office supplies remain.
(f) Selling, General, and Administrative Expenses incorrectly includes $13,000 for office furniture purchases (Other Assets). The purchases were made on December 30.
(g) Inventory erroneously includes $7,500 of inventory that Boudreaux had purchased on account but that was returned to the supplier on December 28 because of unsatisfactory quality.

1. Record the entries necessary to adjust the books.
2. Record the entries necessary to close the books. Assume the adjustments in (1) do not affect Income Tax Expense.
3. Prepare a post-closing trial balance.

Exercise 2-26

REVERSE SOLVABLE

Analysis of Journal Entries

For each of the following journal entries, write a description of the underlying event.

1.	Cash...	300	
	Accounts Receivable...........................		300
2.	Accounts Payable................................	400	
	Inventory..		400
3.	Cash...	5,000	
	Loan Payable......................................		5,000
4.	Cash...	200	
	Accounts Receivable...........................	700	
	Sales...		900
	Cost of Goods Sold.............................	550	
	Inventory..		550
5.	Prepaid Insurance................................	200	
	Cash...		200
6.	Dividends..	250	
	Dividends Payable...............................		250
7.	Retained Earnings...............................	1,000	
	Dividends..		1,000
8.	Insurance Expense...............................	50	
	Prepaid Insurance................................		50
9.	Inventory..	600	
	Cash...		150
	Accounts Payable................................		450
10.	Allowance for Bad Debts.....................	46	
	Accounts Receivable...........................		46
11.	Interest Expense..................................	125	
	Interest Payable..................................		125
12.	Wages Payable....................................	130	
	Wages Expense...................................	75	
	Cash...		205
13.	Accounts Payable................................	500	
	Cash...		490
	Purchase Discounts.............................		10

Exercise 2-27

Adjusting Entries
The following accounts were taken from the trial balance of Cole Company as of December 31, 2015:

Sales	$70,000	Inventory	$23,000
Interest Revenue	3,000	Advertising Expense	1,500
Equipment	52,000	Selling Expense	7,500
Accumulated Depreciation—Equipment	9,600	Interest Expense	2,000

Given the information below, make the necessary adjusting entries.

(a) The equipment has an estimated useful life of 10 years and a salvage value of $4,000. Depreciation is calculated using the straight-line method.
(b) Of selling expense, $1,500 has been paid in advance.
(c) Interest of $800 has accrued on notes receivable.
(d) Of advertising expense, $440 was incorrectly debited to Selling Expense.

Exercise 2-28

Adjusting Entries
The following data were obtained from an analysis of the accounts of Noble Distributor Company as of March 31, 2015, in preparation of the annual report. Noble records current transactions in nominal accounts. What are the appropriate adjusting entries?

(a) Prepaid Insurance has a balance of $14,100. Noble has the following policies in force:

Policy	Date	Term	Cost	Coverage
A	1/1/2015	2 years	$ 3,600	Shop equipment
B	12/1/2014	6 months	1,800	Delivery equipment
C	7/1/2014	3 years	12,000	Buildings

(b) Unearned Subscription Revenue has a balance of $56,250. The following subscriptions were collected in the current year. There are no other unexpired subscriptions.

Effective Date	Amount	Term
July 1, 2014	$27,000	1 year
October 1, 2014	22,200	1 year
January 1, 2015	28,800	1 year
April 1, 2015	20,700	1 year

(c) Interest Payable has a balance of $825. Noble owes a 10%, 90-day note for $45,000 dated March 1, 2015.
(d) Supplies has a balance of $2,190. An inventory of supplies revealed a total of $1,410.
(e) Salaries Payable has a balance of $9,750. The payroll for the five-day workweek ended April 3 totaled $11,250.

Exercise 2-29

REVERSE SOLVABLE

Analyzing Adjusting Entries
Guidecom Consulting Company initially records prepaid items as assets and unearned items as liabilities. Selected account balances at the end of the current and prior year follow. Accrued expenses and revenues are adjusted only at year-end.

	Adjusted Balances, December 31, 2014	Adjusted Balances, December 31, 2015
Prepaid Rent	$ 5,100	$3,400
Salaries and Wages Payable	2,100	4,700
Unearned Consulting Fees	18,200	7,800
Interest Receivable	800	2,100

During 2015, Guidecom Consulting paid $14,000 for rent and $40,000 for wages. It received $112,000 for consulting fees and $3,200 as interest.

1. Provide the entries that were made at December 31, 2015, to adjust the accounts to the year-end balances shown on the previous page.
2. Determine the proper amount of Rent Expense, Salaries and Wages Expense, Consulting Fees Revenue, and Interest Revenue to be reported on the current-year income statement.

Exercise 2-30

Closing Entries

An accountant for Jolley, Inc., a merchandising enterprise, has just finished posting all year-end adjusting entries to the ledger accounts and now wishes to close the appropriate account balances in preparation for the new period.

1. For each of the accounts listed, indicate whether the year-end balance should be (a) carried forward to the new period, (b) closed by debiting the account, or (c) closed by crediting the account.

    (a) Cash $ 25,000
    (b) Sales   75,000
    (c) Dividends   3,500
    (d) Inventory   7,500
    (e) Selling Expenses   7,900
    (f) Capital Stock   100,000
    (g) Wages Expense   14,400
    (h) Dividends Payable   4,000
    (i) Cost of Goods Sold   26,500
    (j) Accounts Payable   12,000
    (k) Accounts Receivable   140,000
    (l) Prepaid Insurance   16,000
    (m) Interest Receivable   1,500
    (n) Sales Discounts   4,200
    (o) Interest Revenue   6,500
    (p) Supplies   8,000
    (q) Retained Earnings   6,500
    (r) Accumulated Depreciation   2,000
    (s) Depreciation Expense   1,800

2. Give the necessary closing entries.
3. What was Jolley's net income (loss) for the period?

Exercise 2-31

Closing Entries

Dylan's Taxidermy Corporation reports revenues and expenses of $142,300 and $91,500, respectively, for the period. Give the remaining entries to close the books assuming the ledger reports Additional Paid-In Capital of $400,000 and Retained Earnings of $125,000. Dividends during the year amounting to $29,200 were recorded in a dividends account.

Exercise 2-32

REVERSE SOLVABLE

Determining Income from Equity Account Analysis

An analysis of Goulding, Inc., disclosed changes in account balances for 2015 and the following supplementary data. From these data, calculate the net income or loss for 2015. (*Hint*: Net income can be thought of as the increase in net assets resulting from operations.)

Cash	$18,000 increase
Accounts Receivable	5,000 decrease
Inventory	14,000 increase
Equipment	58,000 increase
Accounts Payable	2,000 increase

Goulding sold 4,000 shares of its $5 par stock for $8 per share and received cash in full. Dividends of $20,000 were paid in cash during the year. Goulding borrowed $40,000 from the bank and made interest payments of $5,000. Goulding had no other loans payable. Interest of $2,000 was payable at December 31, 2015. There was no interest payable at December 31, 2014. Equipment of $15,000 was donated by stockholders during the year.

Exercise 2-33

Accrual Errors

Spilker Aviation, Inc., failed to make year-end adjustments to record accrued salaries and recognize interest receivable on investments over the last three years as follows:

	2013	2014	2015
Accrued salaries	$21,000	$17,500	$26,000
Interest receivable	8,500	11,400	12,100

What impact would the correction of these errors have on the net income for these three years? Ignore income taxes.

P1

Foundations of Financial Accounting

CHAPTER 3

The Balance Sheet and Notes to the Financial Statements

Learning Objectives

1. Describe the specific elements of the balance sheet (assets, liabilities, and owners' equity), and prepare a balance sheet with assets and liabilities properly classified into current and noncurrent categories.

2. Identify the different formats used to present balance sheet data.

3. Analyze a company's performance and financial position through the computation of financial ratios.

4. Recognize the importance of the notes to the financial statements, and outline the types of disclosures made in the notes.

5. Understand the major limitations of the balance sheet.

"Every man in uniform gets a bottle of Coca-Cola for 5 cents, wherever he is and whatever it costs." So said Robert Woodruff, Coca-Cola chairman, as U.S. soldiers entered the fighting in World War II. By 1941, Coca-Cola was such a part of U.S. life that Coke also became part of the war machine. In 1943, General Dwight Eisenhower requested the necessary equipment and bottles to refill 10 million Coca-Colas for soldiers in the European theater. Allied Headquarters in North Africa operated 64 bottling plants during the war.

From its beginnings in Atlanta, Georgia, in which 1886 sales averaged 9 drinks per day, to its current worldwide presence in which 2009 sales averaged 1.6 billion servings per day, Coca-Cola has grown to the point that it is now the most recognizable trademark on the planet—with sales in over 200 countries around the world.

Pharmacist Dr. John S. Pemberton mixed the first kettle of Coca-Cola in his backyard in 1886. Frank Robinson, Pemberton's bookkeeper and partner, named the drink and came up with the unique script that is Coke's signature. Bottled Coke (in contrast to Coca-Cola served at a soda fountain) was first offered in 1894, and five years later, Joseph Whitehead and Benjamin Thomas purchased the exclusive rights to bottle Coca-Cola for $1. Within 20 years, 1,000 bottlers around the world were bottling Coke. In 1915, the contoured bottle that symbolizes Coca-Cola was developed, and its shape was finally granted a patent in 1977.

With Coca-Cola's remarkable success, one must wonder what company executives were thinking in 1985 when they made a historic blunder. In April of that year, the company changed its secret formula, terminated the original Coke, and introduced "new" Coke. The public reaction was overwhelmingly negative, with consumers organizing and calling for the return of the original. After

Exhibit 3-1 | Coca-Cola's Balance Sheet

The Coca-Cola Company and Subsidiaries
Consolidated Balance Sheets
December 31, 2011 and 2010
(In millions except par value)

	2011	2010
ASSETS		
CURRENT ASSETS		
Cash and cash equivalents	$ 12,803	$ 8,517
Short-term investments	1,088	2,682
TOTAL CASH, CASH EQUIVALENTS, AND SHORT-TERM INVESTMENTS	13,891	11,199
Marketable securities	144	138
Trade accounts receivable, less allowances of $83 and $48, respectively	4,920	4,430
Inventories	3,092	2,650
Prepaid expenses and other assets	3,450	3,162
TOTAL CURRENT ASSETS	25,497	21,579
EQUITY METHOD INVESTMENTS	7,233	6,954
OTHER INVESTMENTS, PRINCIPALLY BOTTLING COMPANIES	1,141	631
OTHER ASSETS	3,495	2,121
PROPERTY, PLANT AND EQUIPMENT—net	14,939	14,727
TRADEMARKS WITH INDEFINITE LIVES	6,430	6,356
BOTTLERS' FRANCHISE RIGHTS WITH INDEFINITE LIVES	7,770	7,511
GOODWILL	12,219	11,665
OTHER INTANGIBLE ASSETS	1,250	1,377
TOTAL ASSETS	**$79,974**	**$72,921**
LIABILITIES AND EQUITY		
CURRENT LIABILITIES		
Accounts payable and accrued expenses	$ 9,009	$ 8,859
Loans and notes payable	12,871	8,100
Current maturities of long-term debt	2,041	1,276
Accrued income taxes	362	273
TOTAL CURRENT LIABILITIES	24,283	18,508
LONG-TERM DEBT	13,656	14,041
OTHER LIABILITIES	5,420	4,794
DEFERRED INCOME TAXES	4,694	4,261
THE COCA-COLA COMPANY SHAREOWNERS' EQUITY		
Common stock, $0.25 par value; Authorized—5,600 shares; Issued—3,520 and 3,520 shares, respectively	880	880
Capital surplus	11,212	10,057
Reinvested earnings	53,550	49,278
Accumulated other comprehensive income (loss)	(2,703)	(1,450)
Treasury stock, at cost—1,257 and 1,228 shares, respectively	(31,304)	(27,762)
EQUITY ATTRIBUTABLE TO SHAREOWNERS OF THE COCA-COLA COMPANY	31,635	31,003
EQUITY ATTRIBUTABLE TO NONCONTROLLING INTERESTS	286	314
TOTAL EQUITY	31,921	31,317
TOTAL LIABILITIES AND EQUITY	**$79,974**	**$72,921**

© Cengage Learning 2014

four months, the company reintroduced the original formula as Coca-Cola Classic.

Today, over 17,000 soft drink servings from The Coca-Cola Company are consumed around the world every second of every day.

Owning the most valuable brand name in the world (Interbrand, an international brand valuation company, estimated the value of the Coca-Cola brand name in 2011 at $71.861 billion), one might expect Coca-Cola's balance sheet to contain a significant amount assigned to this asset. One look at the company's balance sheet (see Exhibit 3-1), however, reveals that very little is recorded on Coke's balance sheet related to its intangible assets.

As illustrated with the brand name example, Coke's balance sheet is interesting as much for what it excludes as for what it includes. As an additional example, Coke owns between 20% and 30% of a number of bottling companies around the world. These bottlers all have the words "Coca-Cola" in their company names, but legally they are structured as companies separate from the Coca-Cola parent. In total, these Coca-Cola bottlers have $22.2 billion in liabilities; however, because The Coca-Cola Company does not own a controlling interest (more than 50%) in these bottlers, none of these liabilities are reported in Coke's balance sheet.

Coke's balance sheet appears relatively simple—deceptively simple. Although we are each comfortable with accounts such as Cash, Inventory, Accounts Payable, and Reinvested (or Retained) Earnings, a firm's balance sheet becomes much more complex as its business gets more complex. It is important that we understand what the balance sheet tells us, what it does not tell us, and the role that the financial statement notes play in assisting us in interpreting the financial statements.

1. As stated above, the Coca-Cola trademark has been estimated to be worth $71.861 billion. The value of this trademark is NOT reported in the Coca-Cola balance sheet in Exhibit 3-1, but trademarks valued at $6.430 billion are reported in 2011. What do you think is the difference between these trademarks and the original Coca-Cola trademark?

2. The liabilities of the Coca-Cola bottlers of which The Coca-Cola Company owns a significant percentage total $22.2 billion. As stated above, NONE of these liabilities is included in the balance sheet of The Coca-Cola Company. Look at Exhibit 3-1—what amount of total liabilities does The Coca-Cola Company report as of December 31, 2011?

3. Look at Exhibit 3-1. As of December 31, 2011, which amount is greater—total current assets or total current liabilities? If you were a banker making a short-term loan to a company, would you prefer that company to have more current assets or more current liabilities?

Answers to these questions can be found on page 3-34.

Coca-Cola's balance sheet, like the balance sheet of any company, lists the organization's accounting assets and liabilities. However, this does not mean that the balance sheet includes complete, up-to-date information about all of the organization's economic resources and obligations. As described in Chapter 1, the choice of how to include information in the financial statements is often a trade-off between relevance and reliability. The balance sheet has been criticized for being *too* reliable, with too many assets being recorded at historical cost instead of market value, and with many important economic assets (such as Microsoft's installed base of customers or Intel's market dominance) not being recorded at all. A characteristic of recent FASB statements is an effort to improve the relevance of the balance sheet.

Even with its limitations, the balance sheet is still *the* fundamental financial statement. In fact, the income statement and statement of cash flows can be thought of as simply providing supplemental information about certain balance sheet accounts: The income statement gives a detailed description of some of the yearly changes in retained earnings, and the statement of cash flows details the reasons for the change in the cash balance.

This chapter focuses on the strengths and limitations of the balance sheet and describes how companies report their assets, liabilities, and owners' equity. The chapter also introduces some financial ratios used to analyze the balance sheet and outlines the type of information contained in the notes to the financial statements.

Elements of the Balance Sheet

 Describe the specific elements of the balance sheet (assets, liabilities, and owners' equity), and prepare a balance sheet with assets and liabilities properly classified into current and noncurrent categories.

LO1 学习目标1
描述资产负债表的特定要素（资产、负债、所有者权益），编制一张资产负债表，将资产和负债合理地划分为流动性项目与非流动性项目。

Twenty years after his victory at the Battle of Hastings in 1066, William the Conqueror commissioned a royal survey of all the property in England. The survey was described as follows by one of the defeated Anglo-Saxons:

> He sent his men all over England into every shire and had them find out how many hundred hides there were in the shire, or what land and cattle the king himself had in the country, or what dues he ought to have in twelve months from the shire. Also, he had a record made of how much land his archbishops had, and his bishops and his abbots and his earls, and what or how much everybody had who was occupying land in England, in land or cattle, and how much money it was worth.

The survey thoroughly frightened the people of England, and it was called "Domesday [or Doomsday] Book" because it caused them to think of the final reckoning at the Last Judgment.[1]

Had the original Doomsday Book also included a listing of all the obligations, or liabilities, of the people of England, it would have comprised a balance sheet for England as of the year 1086. A balance sheet is a listing of an organization's assets and liabilities as of a certain point in time. The difference between assets and liabilities is called equity. Equity can be thought of as the amount of the assets that the owners of the organization can really call their own, the amount that would be left if all the liabilities were paid. The balance sheet is an expression of the basic accounting equation:[2]

$$\text{Assets} = \text{Liabilities} + \text{Owners' equity}$$

The three elements found on the balance sheet were precisely defined in Chapter 1. These definitions are repeated in Exhibit 3-2.

These definitions contain several key words and phrases that are briefly discussed here.

- *Probable*. Contrary to popular belief, accounting is not an exact science. Business is full of uncertainty, and this is acknowledged by the inclusion of the word *probable* in the definitions of assets and liabilities.
- *Future economic benefit*. Although the balance sheet summarizes the results of past transactions and events, its primary purpose is to help forecast the future. Hence, the only items included as assets and liabilities are those with implications for the future.
- *Obtained or controlled*. Accountants have a phrase, "substance over form," meaning that financial statements should reflect the underlying economic substance, not the superficial legal form. If a company economically controls the future economic benefits associated with an item, that item qualifies as an asset whether it is legally owned or not.
- *Obligation*. This term includes legal commitments as well as moral, social, and implied obligations. Again, the phrase "substance over form" applies.

[1] Elizabeth M. Hallam, *Domesday Book Through Nine Centuries* (Thomas and Hudson, 1986), pp. 16, 17.
[2] In abbreviated form, the basic accounting equation can be expressed as $A = L + E$. This can be rearranged algebraically to yield $E = A - L$. Notice the similarity with Einstein's famous equation: $E = mc^2$. Researchers thus far have had no luck in finding an underlying connection that would unify the fields of physics and accounting.

Exhibit 3-2 | Definitions of Asset, Liability, and Equity

Balance Sheet

Asset:
Probable future economic benefit obtained or controlled by a particular entity as a result of past transactions or events.

Liability:
Probable future sacrifice of economic benefit arising from a present obligation of a particular entity to transfer assets or provide services to other entities in the future as a result of past transactions or events.

Equity:
Residual interest in the assets of an entity that remains after deducting its liabilities. In a business enterprise, the equity is the ownership interest.

Source: Material from FASB Concepts Statement No. 6, Elements of Financial Statements, is copyrighted by the Financial Accounting Foundation (FAF), 401 Merritt 7, PO Box 5116, Norwalk, CT 06856-5116, USA, and is reproduced with permission. A complete copy of the document is available from the FAF.

- *Transfer assets or provide services.* Most liabilities involve an obligation to transfer assets in the future. However, an obligation to provide a service is also a liability. For example, having received your tuition check, your college or university now has a liability to you to provide a top-notch education.
- *Past transactions or events.* Assets and liabilities arise from transactions or events that have already happened. Consider a company that promises in April to pay a student $4,000 for a summer internship starting in June. If the company declares bankruptcy in May, does the student get to collect the $4,000? No, because the transaction, the actual summer internship work, has not yet occurred.[3]

Assets include financial items such as cash, receivables, and investments in financial instruments. Assets also include costs that are expected to provide future economic benefits. For example, expenditures made for inventories, equipment, and patents are expected to help generate revenues in future periods. Most assets are measured in terms of historical cost. As mentioned in Chapter 1 and outlined later in this chapter, however, some assets are measured in terms of replacement cost, market value, net realizable value, or discounted present value.

Liabilities include obligations with amounts denominated in precise monetary terms, such as accounts payable and long-term debt. The amounts of other liabilities must be estimated based on expectations about future events. These types of liabilities include warranties, pension obligations, and environmental liabilities.

Stop & Think

Alternatively, *asset* could be defined as everything legally owned by a company, and *liability* defined as all legal obligations. Which ONE of the following would NOT be a problem of these legalistic definitions?

a) Companies would be tempted to hire teams of lawyers to carefully craft contracts in order to obtain favorable accounting classification of assets and liabilities.
b) Companies could use legal technicalities in order to hide their economic liabilities in legally separate companies.
c) These law-based definitions of assets and liabilities would put too much power into the hands of the FASB.
d) The identification of accounting assets and liabilities would be greatly influenced by changing governmental standards of ownership.

---

[3] Whether the transaction has already occurred is sometimes difficult to determine. For example, if the student signs a summer internship contract guaranteeing payment of $4,000 whether or not any work is done, the contract signing itself might be viewed as creating an asset for the student and a liability for the company. This exact issue is important in determining the proper accounting treatment for long-term leases.

The total liability amount measures the amounts of the assets of the company that are claimed by various creditors. Owners' equity measures the amounts of the total assets of the company that remain and are thus claimed by the ownership group. Owners' equity equals the net assets of a company, or the difference between total assets and total liabilities. Owners' equity arises from investment by owners and is increased by net income and decreased by net losses and distributions to owners. Other items that can impact owners' equity are outlined later in the chapter.

Classified Balance Sheets

Although no standard categories must be used, the general framework for a balance sheet shown in Exhibit 3-3 is representative and will be used in this chapter. Balance sheet items are generally classified as current (or short-term) items and noncurrent (or long-term) items.

Exhibit 3-3 | Categories of a Classified Balance Sheet

investment securities
交易性金融资产

other current assets, such as prepaid expenses
其他流动资产，如预付费用

property, plant and equipment
不动产、厂房和设备

other noncurrent assets, such as deferred income tax assets
其他非流动资产，如递延所得税资产

long–term lease obligations
长期租赁义务

additional paid–in capital
资本溢价

ASSETS
Current assets:
    Cash
    Investment securities
    Accounts and notes receivable
    Inventories
    Other current assets, such as prepaid expenses
Noncurrent assets:
    Investments
    Property, plant, and equipment
    Intangible assets
    Other noncurrent assets, such as deferred income tax assets

LIABILITIES
Current liabilities:
    Accounts and notes payable
    Accrued expenses
    Current portion of long-term obligations
    Other current liabilities, such as unearned revenues
Noncurrent liabilities:
    Long-term debt, such as notes, bonds, and mortgages payable
    Long-term lease obligations
    Deferred income tax liabilities
    Other noncurrent liabilities, such as pension obligations

OWNERS' EQUITY
Contributed capital:
    Capital stock
    Additional paid-in capital
Retained earnings
Other equity, such as treasury stock (a subtraction)
Accumulated other comprehensive income

© Cengage Learning 2014

How long is *current*? For most companies, *current* means one year or less. Accordingly, assets expected to be used and liabilities expected to be paid or otherwise satisfied within a year are current items. When assets and liabilities are so classified, the difference between current assets and current liabilities may be determined. This difference is referred to as the company's working capital—the liquid buffer available in meeting financial demands and contingencies of the near future.

working capital
营运资本

The division of assets and liabilities into just two categories—current and noncurrent—is in some sense an arbitrary partition. Users of financial statements could desire a different partition. For example, some users exclude inventory when evaluating a company's working capital position. Users are certainly free to recast the balance sheet in whatever manner they wish. However, although there is some arbitrariness in the current/noncurrent classifications, its popularity among users as an indication of liquidity suggests that the classification does meet the test of decision usefulness.

Current Assets

The most common current assets are cash, receivables, and inventories. As depicted in Exhibit 3-4, the normal operating cycle involves the use of cash to purchase inventories, the sale of inventories resulting in receivables, and ultimately the cash collection of those receivables. In some industries, such as lumber and shipbuilding, this normal operating cycle is longer than one year. When the operating cycle is longer than a year, the length of the operating cycle should be used in defining current assets and liabilities. In practice, almost all companies use the one-year period.[4]

In addition to cash, receivables, and inventories, current assets typically include prepaid expenses and investments in certain securities. Prepaid items are a bit different from other current assets in that they are not expected to be converted into cash within a year. Instead, their expiration makes it possible to conserve cash that otherwise would have been required. Prepayments for periods extending beyond a year should be reported as noncurrent assets.

Debt and equity securities (often called bonds and stocks) that are purchased mainly with the intent of reselling the securities in the short term are called trading securities. Trading securities are classified as current assets. Other investments in debt and equity securities

Exhibit 3-4 | Operating Cycle

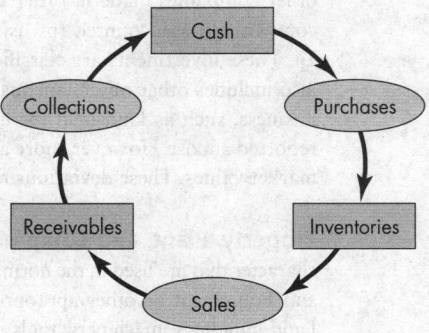

© Cengage Learning 2014

---

[4] In classifying items not related to the operating cycle, a one-year period is always used as the basis for current classification. For example, a note receivable due in 15 months that arose from the sale of land held as an investment would be classified as noncurrent even if the normal operating cycle exceeds 15 months.

are classified as current or noncurrent depending on whether management intends to convert them into cash within one year or one operating cycle, whichever is longer.[5]

The reported amounts for current assets are measured in a variety of ways. Cash and receivables are reported at their net realizable values. Thus, current receivable balances are reduced by allowances for estimated uncollectible accounts. Investments in debt and equity securities are reported, in most cases, at current market value. Inventories are reported at cost (FIFO, LIFO, etc.) or on the lower-of-cost-or-market basis. Prepaid expenses are reported at their historical costs.

Current assets are normally listed on the balance sheet before the noncurrent assets and in the order of their liquidity, with the most liquid terms (those closest to cash) first. This ordering is a tradition, not a requirement. Most utilities and insurance companies reverse the order and report their longer-lived assets first. In addition, as illustrated later, non-U.S. companies frequently start their balance sheets with their long-term assets.

Some exceptions to the normal classification of assets should be noted. If management intends to use an asset for a noncurrent purpose, that asset should be classified as noncurrent in spite of the usual classification. For example, cash that is restricted to a noncurrent use (e.g., for the acquisition of noncurrent assets or for the liquidation of noncurrent debts) should not be included in current assets. Similarly, land that is held for resale within the coming year should be classified as current. The overriding criterion is management intent.

> **Caution**
> As illustrated with current assets, a balance sheet is not restricted to reporting historical cost.

Noncurrent Assets

Assets not qualifying for presentation under the current heading are classified under a number of noncurrent headings. Noncurrent assets may be listed under separate headings, such as Investments; Property, Plant, and Equipment; Intangible Assets; and Other Noncurrent Assets.

Investments Investments held for such long-term purposes as regular income, appreciation, or ownership control are reported under the heading Investments. Debt and equity securities purchased as investments that management does not intend to sell in the coming year are classified as long-term investments. Acquisitions of the stock of other companies made in order to exert influence or control over the actions of those companies are accounted for using the equity method, which is explained in Chapter 14. These investments are classified as long-term investments. The Investments heading also includes other miscellaneous investments not used directly in the operations of the business, such as land held for investment purposes. Many long-term investments are reported at cost. However, more and more long-term assets are being reported at current market values. These deviations from cost will be discussed in later chapters.

Property, Plant, and Equipment Properties of a tangible and relatively permanent character that are used in the normal business operations are reported under Property, Plant, and Equipment or other appropriate headings such as Land, Buildings, and Equipment. Land, buildings, machinery, tools, furniture, fixtures, and vehicles are included in this section of the balance sheet. If an asset, such as land, is being held for speculation, it should be

---

[5] FASB ASC paragraphs 210-10-45-1(f) and 320-10-45-2.

> **FYI**
>
> When an investment in another company represents majority ownership of that company, no single investment amount is reported in the balance sheet. Instead, all of the individual assets and liabilities of the other company are included, or consolidated, in the balance sheet.

classified as an investment rather than under the heading Property, Plant, and Equipment. Tangible properties, except land, are normally reported at cost less accumulated depreciation. If the current value of a tangible property is less than its depreciated cost, the asset is said to be impaired. Guidelines for when and how to recognize asset impairments are given in Chapter 11.

无形资产包含了诸如商誉、专利、商标、特许权、版权、配方、租赁权和客户名单。

Intangible Assets The long-term rights and privileges of a nonphysical nature acquired for use in business operations are often reported under the heading Intangible Assets. Included in this class are items such as goodwill, patents, trademarks, franchises, copyrights, formulas, leaseholds, and customer lists. Intangible assets are an increasingly important part of most companies' economic value; accordingly, the FASB has placed more emphasis on the accounting for intangibles. Some intangible assets are depreciated, or amortized, in the same way as tangible assets. However, many intangible assets, including goodwill, are not amortized on a systematic basis. Instead, these intangible assets are regularly tested to determine whether their value has been impaired. The details of accounting for intangibles are in Chapters 10 and 11.

deferred income tax assets
递延所得税资产

Other Noncurrent Assets Those noncurrent assets not suitably reported under any of the previous classifications may be listed under the general heading "Other Noncurrent Assets" or may be listed separately under special descriptive headings. Such assets include, for example, long-term advances to officers, long-term receivables, deposits made with taxing authorities and utility companies, and deferred income tax assets. Deferred income tax assets arise when taxable income exceeds reported income for the period and the difference is expected to "reverse" in future periods. One common source of deferred income tax assets is large restructuring charges (including write-downs in asset values and recognition of relocation obligations) that are not yet deductible for income tax purposes; the deferred income tax asset reflects the expected future tax benefits that will arise when the elements of the restructuring charge become tax deductible in the future. The computation and reporting of deferred income tax assets is somewhat complex as well as interesting (as will be explained in Chapter 16).

Properties used in normal business operations, such as the printing press shown here, are classified as "property, plant, and equipment" on the balance sheet.

Current Liabilities

Current liabilities are those obligations that are reasonably expected to be paid using current assets or by creating other current liabilities. Generally, if a liability is reasonably expected to be paid within 12 months, it is classified as current. As with receivables, payables arising from the normal operating activities may be classified as current even if they are not to be paid within 12 months as long as they are to be paid within the operating cycle, which may exceed 12 months.

In addition to accounts payable and short-term borrowing, current liabilities also include amounts for accrued expenses. Common accruals include salaries and wages, interest, and taxes. The Current Liabilities section also includes amounts representing the portion of the long-term obligations due to be satisfied within one year.

The current liability classification generally does not include the following items that normally would be considered current.

- *Debts to be liquidated from a noncurrent sinking fund.* A sinking fund consists of cash and investment securities that have been accumulated for the stated purpose of repaying a specific loan. If the sinking fund is classified as a noncurrent asset, the associated loan is also classified as noncurrent.

- *Short-term obligations to be refinanced.* If a short-term loan is expected to be refinanced (either with a new long-term loan or with the issuance of equity) or paid back with the proceeds of a replacement loan, the existing short-term loan will not require the use of current assets even though it is scheduled to mature within a year. To reflect the economic substance of this situation, the existing loan is not classified as current as long as (1) the intent of the company is to refinance the loan on a long-term basis and (2) the company's intent is evidenced by an actual refinancing after the balance sheet date but before the financial statements are finalized or by the existence of an explicit refinancing agreement.[6]

> **FYI**
> The international standard for classification of short-term obligations to be refinanced is slightly different. According to *IAS 1*, for the obligation to be classified as long term the refinancing must take place by the balance sheet date, not the later date when the financial statements are finalized. The FASB is considering adopting this more stringent condition.

Callable Obligations Classification problems can arise when an obligation is callable by a creditor because it is difficult to determine exactly when the obligation will be paid. A callable obligation is one that is payable on demand and thus has no specified due date. If the terms of an agreement specify that an obligation is due on demand or will become due on demand within one year from the balance sheet date, the obligation should be classified as current.[7]

A loan can become callable because the debtor violates the provisions of the debt agreement. Loan agreement clauses that identify specific deficiencies (e.g., missing two consecutive interest payments) that can cause a loan to be immediately callable are referred to as objective acceleration clauses. If these specific deficiencies exist as of the balance sheet date, the associated liability should be classified as current unless the lender has agreed to waive the right to receive immediate payment or the deficiency has been fixed (e.g., an interest payment made) by the time the financial statements are issued.

In some cases, the debt agreement does not specifically identify the circumstances under which a loan will become callable, but it does indicate some general conditions that permit the lender to accelerate the due date. This type of provision is known as a subjective acceleration clause because the violation of the conditions cannot be objectively determined. Examples of the wording in such clauses are "if the debtor fails to maintain satisfactory operations . . ." or "if a material

> **FYI**
> Large banks have entire "compliance" departments that verify whether borrowers are following the terms of their loan agreements.

---

6 FASB ASC paragraph 470-10-45-14.
7 FASB ASC paragraph 470-10-45-10.

adverse change occurs...." If invoking of the clause is deemed probable, the liability should be classified as a current liability. If invoking of the clause is considered to be reasonably possible but not probable, only a note disclosure is necessary, and the liability continues to be classified as noncurrent.[8]

Noncurrent Liabilities

Obligations not reasonably expected to be paid or otherwise satisfied within 12 months (or within the operating cycle if it exceeds 12 months) are classified as *noncurrent liabilities*. Noncurrent liabilities are generally listed under separate headings, such as Long-Term Debt, Long-Term Lease Obligations, Deferred Income Tax Liability, and Other Noncurrent Liabilities.

Long-Term Debt Long-term notes, bonds, mortgages, and similar obligations not requiring the use of current funds for their retirement are generally reported on the balance sheet under the heading Long-Term Debt.

Long-term debt is reported at its discounted present value, which is initially measured by the proceeds from the debt issuance. When the amount borrowed is not the same as the amount ultimately required to be repaid, called the *maturity value*, a discount or premium is included as an adjustment to the maturity value to ensure that the debt is reported at its discounted present value. A discount should be subtracted from the amount reported for the debt, and a premium should be added to the amount reported for the debt.

When a note, a bond issue, or a mortgage formerly classified as a long-term obligation becomes payable within a year, it should be reclassified and presented as a current liability except when the obligation is to be refinanced, as discussed earlier, or is to be paid out of a fund classified as noncurrent.

长期债务以折现后的现值报告，这个价值最初以债务发行的收益计量。
当之前被归类为长期债务的票据、债券或抵押贷款将在一年内到期时，它们应当被重新归类为流动负债，除非该项债务将得到再融资，或者将由一笔非流动基金偿还。

Long-Term Lease Obligations Some leases of property, plant, and equipment are financially structured so that they are essentially debt-financed purchases. The FASB has established criteria to determine which leases are to be accounted for as purchases, or capital leases, rather than as ordinary operating leases. In accounting for capital leases, the present value of the future minimum lease payments is recorded as a long-term liability. That portion of the present value due within the next year is classified as a current liability. The long-term lease obligation reported by some firms is often more interesting for what it doesn't include than for what it does include. For example, as of May 31, 2011, the present value of future minimum lease payments for capital leases for FedEx was $146 million. At the same time, the present value of future minimum lease payments for operating leases (an amount *not* reported in the balance sheet) was approximately $10 billion. Be patient; in Chapter 15, you will learn more about leases than you ever wanted to know.

Deferred Income Tax Liability Almost all large companies include a deferred income tax liability in their balance sheets. This liability can be thought of as the income tax expected to be paid in future years on income that has already been reported in the income statement but which, because of the tax law, has not yet been taxed. The liability is valued using the enacted income tax rates expected to prevail in the future when the income is taxed. However, because the liability is not reported at its present (discounted) value, some analysts disregard it when evaluating a company's debt position. The accounting for deferred income taxes is very complex and controversial and has been the subject of considerable debate.

---

[8] FASB ASC paragraph 470-10-45-2.

Other Noncurrent Liabilities Those noncurrent liabilities not suitably reported under the separate headings outlined earlier may be listed under this general heading or may be listed separately under special descriptive headings. Examples of such long-term liabilities are pension plans and obligations resulting from advance collections on long-term contracts.

Contingent Liabilities Past activities or circumstances may give rise to possible future liabilities although obligations do not exist on the date of the balance sheet. These possible claims are known as contingent liabilities. They are potential obligations involving uncertainty as to possible losses. As future events occur or fail to occur, this uncertainty will be resolved. A good example of a contingent liability is the cosigner's obligation on a co-signed loan. The cosigner has no existing obligation but may have one in the future, depending on whether the borrower defaults on the loan.

Contingent liabilities are accounted for according to the judgment of management about the probability of the contingent obligation's becoming an actual obligation. If a future payment is considered probable, the liability should be recorded by a debit to a loss account and a credit to a liability account. If future payment is possible, the contingent nature of the loss is disclosed in a note to the financial statements. If future payment is remote, no accounting action is necessary.[9]

A contingent liability is distinguishable from an estimated liability. An estimated liability is a definite obligation with only the amount of the obligation in question and subject to estimation at the balance sheet date. Examples of estimated liabilities are pensions, warranties, and deferred taxes. Some liabilities combine the characteristics of contingent and estimated liabilities. A good example is a company's obligation for environmental cleanup costs. In many cases, a company is not certain if it is liable for environmental damage until the obligation is confirmed in the courts. However, even after the cleanup obligation is verified, estimating its amount is quite difficult; the cleanup typically extends over several years, the amount of the cost to be shared by other polluting companies is uncertain, and governmental environmental regulations can change at any time. If no reasonable estimate of an obligation can be made, it is not recognized as a liability in the balance sheet, but the nature of the obligation is disclosed in the financial statement notes. Chapter 19 contains more details on the accounting for contingent and estimated liabilities.

> 或有负债是潜在的义务，包含了不确定性，而这种不确定性会导致可能的损失。

> 或有负债不同于预计负债。预计负债是在资产负债表日能够确定的债务，只是金额不能确定并且需要估计。

Caution

This description makes it sound as if accounting for contingencies is cookbook simple, but the words "probable" and "possible" represent very complex concepts. For example, when exactly does a future event (such as a thunderstorm tomorrow) stop being possible and start being probable?

Stop & Think

The current/noncurrent classification scheme is only one way to split assets and liabilities into two groups. Below are three alternate two-way classification schemes. Which one would be most useful for: (1) A financial analyst trying to compare the company's core business with the core businesses of similar companies? (2) A U.S. congressperson concerned about the relocation of operations overseas? (3) An analyst trying to estimate the current market value of a company?

a) Located in the United States and located in a non-U.S. country
b) Used in the primary line of business and used in secondary lines of business
c) Measured at current fair value and measured on some other basis

---

9 FASB ASC paragraphs 450-20-25-2, 450-20-50-3, and 460-10-50-2.

Owners' Equity

The method of reporting the owners' equity varies with the form of the business unit. Business units are typically divided into three categories: proprietorships, partnerships, and corporations.[10] In the case of a proprietorship, the owner's equity in assets is reported by means of a single capital account. The balance in this account is the cumulative result of the owner's investments and withdrawals as well as past earnings and losses. In a partnership, capital accounts are established for each partner. Capital account balances summarize the investments and withdrawals and shares of past earnings and losses of each partner and thus measure the partners' individual equities in the partnership assets.

In a corporation, the difference between assets and liabilities is referred to as stockholders' (shareholders') equity or *owners' equity*. In presenting the owners' equity on the balance sheet, a distinction is made between the equity originating from the stockholders' investments, referred to as contributed capital or paid-in capital, and the equity originating from earnings, referred to as retained earnings.

Most financial statement analysis calculations use total stockholders' equity and do not distinguish between contributed capital and retained earnings. However, for some purposes the distinction can be very important. Historically, companies could legally pay cash dividends only in an amount not exceeding the retained earnings balance. This legal restriction has been relaxed in most states, but the retained earnings amount is still viewed as an informal limit to cash dividend payments.

Contributed Capital Contributed (or paid-in) capital is generally reported in two parts: (1) capital stock and (2) additional paid-in capital. The amount reported on the balance sheet as capital stock usually reflects the number of shares issued multiplied by the par value or stated value per share. Historically, par value was the market value of the shares at the time of their issue. In cases where shareholders invested less than the par value of the stock, courts sometimes held that the shareholders were contingently liable for the difference if corporate resources were insufficient to satisfy creditors. Today, most stocks are issued with low or no par values; par value no longer has much significance.

The two types of capital stock are preferred stock and common stock. In general, preferred stockholders are paid a fixed annual cash dividend and have a higher likelihood of recovering their investment if the company goes bankrupt.[11] Common stockholders are the real owners of the corporation; they vote for the board of directors and have legal ownership of the corporate assets after the claims of all creditors and preferred stockholders have been satisfied. For accounting purposes, when a corporation has issued more than one class of stock, the stock of each class is reported separately.

Additional paid-in capital represents investments by stockholders in excess of the par or stated value of the capital stock. Additional paid-in capital is also affected by a whole host of diverse transactions such as stock repurchases, stock dividends, share retirements, and stock conversions. In a sense, additional paid-in capital is the "dumping ground" of the Equity section.

---

10 In addition to these three general categories, there are many hybrids. Some of these are limited partnerships, S corporations, and limited liability companies (LLCs). In general, these organizations are taxed as partnerships but have some of the limited liability advantages of a corporation. All of the large accounting firms are organized as limited liability partnerships (LLP) to insulate uninvolved partners from client lawsuits directed at individual partners. According to IRS records, about 70% of U.S. businesses are organized as sole proprietorships.
11 In essence, preferred stock is an investment that has some of the characteristics of a loan: fixed periodic payment, no vote for the board of directors, and higher priority than common stock in case of bankruptcy liquidation. Increasingly, finance wizards are creating securities that combine characteristics of both debt and equity. The accounting question is where to put these creations. Distinguishing between debt and equity is addressed more fully in Chapter 13.

Retained Earnings The amount of undistributed earnings of past periods is reported as retained earnings. An excess of dividends and losses over earnings results in a negative retained earnings balance called a deficit. As detailed in Chapter 13, retained earnings can also be reduced as a result of stock retirements and the issuance of stock dividends. A sample of large positive and negative retained earnings balances for U.S. companies is given in Exhibit 3-5.

Portions of retained earnings are sometimes reported as restricted and unavailable as a basis for cash dividends. This ensures that a company does not distribute cash dividends to shareholders to the extent that the ability to repay creditors or make other planned expenditures comes into question. Retained earnings restrictions can be part of a loan agreement or can be voluntarily adopted by a company (called an *appropriation*). These restrictions are usually disclosed in a financial statement note.

Other Equity In addition to the two major categories of contributed capital and retained earnings, the Equity section can include a couple of other items: treasury stock and accumulated other comprehensive income. These are described in detail in later chapters, but they are briefly discussed here.

Treasury Stock When a company buys back its own shares, accountants call the repurchased shares treasury stock. Treasury shares can be retired, or they can be retained and reissued later. When the shares are retained, the amount paid to repurchase the treasury stock is usually shown as a subtraction from total stockholders' equity. In essence, a treasury stock purchase returns funds to shareholders.

Accumulated Other Comprehensive Income Beginning in 1998, the FASB required companies to summarize changes in owners' equity exclusive of net income and contributions by and distributions to owners. This summary, termed other comprehensive income, is typically provided by companies as part of their statement of stockholders' equity. The corresponding balance sheet item reflecting the cumulative total of these items over the years is titled Accumulated Other Comprehensive Income. The three most common components are certain unrealized gains and losses on investments, foreign currency adjustments, and certain unrealized gains and losses on derivative contracts.

Unrealized Gains and Losses on Available-for-Sale Securities Available-for-sale securities are those that were not purchased with the immediate intention to resell but also are not meant to be held permanently. These securities are reported in

> **FYI**
> For those interested in stock tips, buy the stocks of companies that announce treasury stock purchases. Those companies tend to outperform the market in the three to four years following the announcement.

Exhibit 3-5 | Large Positive and Negative Retained Earnings Balances for the Year 2011 (in millions)

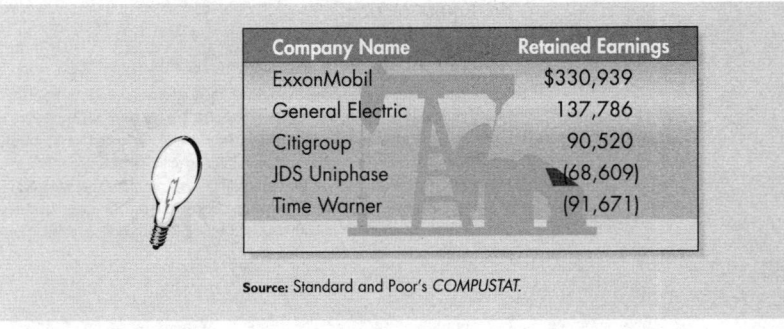

Company Name	Retained Earnings
ExxonMobil	$330,939
General Electric	137,786
Citigroup	90,520
JDS Uniphase	(68,609)
Time Warner	(91,671)

Source: Standard and Poor's *COMPUSTAT*.

the balance sheet at their current market values. The unrealized gains and losses from market value fluctuations are not included in the income statement but are instead shown as a separate equity item.[12]

Foreign Currency Translation Adjustments Almost every U.S. multinational corporation has a foreign currency translation adjustment in its Equity section. This adjustment arises from the change in the equity of foreign subsidiaries (as measured in terms of U.S. dollars) that occurs during the year as a result of changes in foreign currency exchange rates. These adjustments are discussed in Chapter 22.

Unrealized Gains and Losses on Derivatives A derivative is a financial instrument, such as an option or a future, that derives its value from the movement of a price, an exchange rate, or an interest rate associated with some other item. For example, an option to purchase a stock becomes more valuable as the price of the stock increases, and the right to purchase foreign currency at a fixed exchange rate becomes more valuable as that foreign currency becomes more expensive. As will be discussed in Chapter 19, companies often use derivatives in order to manage their exposure to risk stemming from changes in prices and rates. Some of the unrealized gains and losses from the fluctuations in the value of derivatives are reported as part of accumulated other comprehensive income.

Minority Interest When one company owns controlling interest (more than 50%) of the common stock of one or more other companies, the financial results of this group of companies are combined into a set of consolidated financial statements. The objective of consolidated financial statements is to reflect in one set of financial statements the results of all companies owned or controlled by the parent corporation. In the consolidated balance sheet, minority (or noncontrolling) interest is the amount of equity investment made by outside shareholders to consolidated subsidiaries that are not 100% owned by the parent. For example, if the parent owns 80% of the subsidiary, then the minority interest is the amount of financing provided by the outside shareholders who own the other 20% of the subsidiary. This minority interest is reported as part of owners' equity, but it is clearly listed separately from the parent's owners' equity.[13]

International Reserves The first thing one notices about the Equity portion of the balance sheets of many foreign companies, particularly those from countries influenced by the British accounting tradition, is the extended description of the company's "reserves." In familiar terms, reserves are merely different equity categories similar in nature, depending on the reserve, to additional paid-in capital or to restricted retained earnings. Reserve accounting is very important because in many foreign countries the legal ability to pay cash dividends is strictly tied to the balances in various reserve accounts. Common reserve category titles are revaluation reserve and capital redemption reserve. Reserves are discussed in more detail in Chapter 13, which is devoted to the Equity section.

Offsets on the Balance Sheet

As illustrated in the preceding discussion, a number of balance sheet items are reported at gross amounts not reflecting their actual values, thus requiring the recognition of offset balances in arriving at proper valuations. In the case of assets, for example, an allowance for bad debts is subtracted from the sum of the customer accounts in reporting the net amount

---

12 One never knows where controversy and compromise will rear their ugly heads. Accounting purists hoped to include these unrealized gains and losses in the income statement. Companies (particularly banks) fearful of the volatility that this would add to the income statement opposed the treatment. This equity item is the FASB's compromise.
13 FASB ASC paragraph 810-10-45-16.

FASB CODIFICATION

The Issue: You have just started working as a business manager for a local medical practice. As one of your first tasks, you have been asked to get the financial statements in shape to take to the bank to request a $500,000 loan for the practice. You have been examining the most recent balance sheet and noticed that there are no reported long-term liabilities. You are surprised to see this because you know that the practice has an existing five-year loan for $350,000. You asked one of the doctors about this and were told that the $350,000 loan was omitted because the doctors know that they have sufficient cash, in their personal savings, to pay the loan if needed. Thus, instead of going to the trouble of putting their personal cash in the business balance sheet, along with the $350,000 loan amount, they have just offset the two. Voilà.

The Question: Is there any accounting rule that specifically states that assets and liabilities shouldn't be offset in the way the doctors are doing? Are there any exceptions to the no-offset rule?

Searching the Codification: This issue relates to balance sheet presentation, so we should start with the Presentation group of topics in the FASB's Codification. One of the topics in that group is Topic 210—Balance Sheet. If we are lucky, "Offsetting" is one of the subtopics in the Balance Sheet topic.

The Answer: The correct treatment is described on page 3-35.

estimated as collectible; accumulated depreciation is subtracted from the related buildings and equipment balances in reporting the costs of the assets still assignable to future revenues. In the case of liabilities, a loan discount is subtracted from the maturity value of the loan in reporting the loan at its discounted present value. In the Stockholders' Equity section of the balance sheet, treasury stock is deducted in reporting total stockholders' equity.

The types of offsets described here, utilizing contra accounts, are required for proper reporting of particular balance sheet items. In addition, accounting rules require some assets and liabilities to be offset against one another, resulting in just one net amount being reported in the balance sheet. For example, a company's pension obligation is offset against the assets in the pension fund, and only the net number goes into the balance sheet. Deferred tax assets and liabilities are also offset against each other.

The cases just described are the exceptions. The general rule is that assets, liabilities, and equities should not be offset when compiling the balance sheet. Offsetting, or netting, can significantly reduce the information value of the balance sheet. If offsetting were taken to its extreme, the balance sheet would be just one line, total equity, embodying total liabilities offset against total assets.

Format of the Balance Sheet

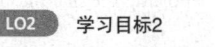
识别资产负债表的不同格式。

② Identify the different formats used to present balance sheet data.

When preparing a balance sheet, the order of asset and liability classifications may vary, but most businesses emphasize working capital position and liquidity, with assets and liabilities presented in the order of their liquidity. An exception to this order is generally found in the Property, Plant, and Equipment section where the more permanent assets with longer useful lives are listed first. The balance sheet of The Coca-Cola Company, reproduced in Exhibit 3-1, is an example of current assets and current liabilities being listed first.

As mentioned earlier, in some industries, such as the utility industry, the investment in plant assets is so significant that these assets are placed first on the balance sheet. Also, because long-term financing is so important in these industries, the equity capital and long-term debt obtained to finance plant assets are listed before current liabilities. To illustrate this type of presentation, the 2008 balance sheet for **Consolidated Edison** is given in Exhibit 3-6. Consolidated Edison, established in 1884, provides electric service to almost all of New York City.[14]

As seen in the Consolidated Edison illustration in Exhibit 3-6, balance sheets are generally presented in comparative form. With comparative reports for two or more dates, information is made available concerning the nature and trend of financial changes taking place within the periods between balance sheet dates. Currently, a minimum of two years of balance sheets and three years of income statements and cash flow statements are required by the SEC to be included in the annual report to shareholders.

Exhibit 3-6 | Consolidated Edison, Inc.

Consolidated Edison, Inc.
Consolidated Balance Sheet
December 31, 2008 and 2007

(Millions of Dollars)	At December 31, 2008	At December 31, 2007
Assets		
Utility Plant, at Original Cost (Note A)		
Electric	$17,483	$15,979
Gas	3,696	3,403
Steam	1,849	1,755
General	1,795	1,732
Total	24,823	22,869
Less: Accumulated depreciation	5,079	4,784
Net	19,744	18,085
Construction work in progress	1,109	1,028
Net Utility Plant	20,853	19,113
Non-Utility Plant (Note A)		
Non-utility property, less accumulated depreciation of $40 and $36 in 2008 and 2007, respectively	20	18
Non-utility property held for sale (Note V)	—	778
Construction work in progress	1	5
Net Plant	20,874	19,914
Current Assets		
Cash and temporary cash investments (Note A)	74	210
Accounts receivable—customers, less allowance for uncollectible accounts of $58 and $47 in 2008 and 2007, respectively	952	970
Accrued unbilled revenue (Note A)	131	149
Other receivables, less allowance for uncollectible accounts of $6 in 2008 and 2007	339	288
Fuel oil, at average cost	37	44
Gas in storage, at average cost	325	215
Materials and supplies, at average cost	154	146
Prepayments	697	119
Fair value of derivative assets	162	98

[14] In 2009, Consolidated Edison reordered its balance sheet and began using the more common sequencing with current assets first, then long-term assets, and so forth.

Exhibit 3-6 | Consolidated Edison, Inc. (Continued)

Consolidated Edison, Inc.
Consolidated Balance Sheet
December 31, 2008 and 2007

(Millions of Dollars)	At December 31, 2008	At December 31, 2007
Recoverable energy costs (Notes A and B)	$ 172	$ 213
Deferred derivative losses	260	45
Current assets held for sale (Note V)	—	40
Other current assets	16	13
Total Current Assets	**3,319**	**2,550**
Investments (Note A)	356	378
Deferred Charges, Regulatory Assets and Noncurrent Assets		
Goodwill (Note K)	411	408
Intangible assets, less accumulated amortization of $2 and $1 in 2008 and 2007, respectively	5	2
Regulatory assets (Note B)	8,105	4,511
Noncurrent assets held for sale (Note V)	—	88
Other deferred charges and noncurrent assets	428	411
Total Deferred Charges, Regulatory Assets and Noncurrent Assets	**8,949**	**5,420**
Total Assets	**$33,498**	**$28,262**

The accompanying notes are an integral part of these financial statements.

	2008	2007
Capitalization and Liabilities		
Capitalization		
Common shareholders' equity (See Statement of Common Shareholders' Equity)	$ 9,698	$ 9,076
Preferred stock of subsidiary (See Statement of Capitalization)	213	213
Long-term debt (See Statement of Capitalization)	9,232	7,611
Total Capitalization	**19,143**	**16,900**
Minority Interests	—	43
Noncurrent Liabilities		
Obligations under capital leases (Note J)	17	22
Provision for injuries and damages (Note G)	169	161
Pensions and retiree benefits	4,511	938
Superfund and other environmental costs (Note G)	250	327
Uncertain income taxes	118	155
Asset retirement obligations (Note R)	115	110
Fair value of derivative liabilities	120	15
Noncurrent liabilities held for sale (Note V)	—	61
Other noncurrent liabilities	79	95
Total Noncurrent Liabilities	**5,379**	**1,884**
Current Liabilities		
Long-term debt due within one year	482	809
Notes payable	363	840
Accounts payable	1,161	1,187
Customer deposits	265	249
Accrued taxes	57	26
Accrued interest	139	149
Accrued wages	88	82
Fair value of derivative liabilities	192	76
Deferred derivative gains (Note B)	23	10
Deferred income taxes—recoverable energy costs (Note L)	70	86
Current liabilities held for sale (Note V)	—	28
Other current liabilities	365	309
Total Current Liabilities	**3,205**	**3,851**
Deferred Credits and Regulatory Liabilities		
Deferred income taxes and investment tax credits (Notes A and L)	4,999	4,465
Regulatory liabilities (Note B)	737	1,097
Other deferred credits	35	22
Total Deferred Credits and Regulatory Liabilities	**5,771**	**5,584**
Total Capitalization and Liabilities	**$33,498**	**$28,262**

Consolidated Edison, Inc., 2008, 10K Report

Format of Foreign Balance Sheets

国外资产负债表通常将不动产、厂房及设备和无形资产列在前面。

Foreign balance sheets are frequently presented with property, plant, and equipment and intangibles listed first. In addition, foreign balance sheets frequently list the current assets and the current liabilities together and label the difference between the two as net current assets or working capital. This manner of reporting the current items reflects the business reality that a person starting a company needs to get long-term financing (long-term debt and equity) to finance the acquisition of long-term assets as well as to finance the portion of current assets that can't be acquired by incurring current liabilities. For example, if a company can acquire all of its inventory through credit purchases (accounts payable) and if the supplier will wait for payment until the inventory is sold and the cash collected, no long-term financing is needed to purchase the initial stock of inventory.

An example of a typical foreign balance sheet is provided in Exhibit 3-7, which contains the March 31, 2011, balance sheet of **British Telecommunications**. In addition to the format difference already mentioned, this balance sheet also reflects several other differences between a U.S. balance sheet and the balance sheet of a foreign company. The most obvious of these differences is in terminology. However, with some thought and a little accounting intuition, one can deduce that the item "ordinary shares" is what we would call "common stock," "share premium" is "additional paid-in capital," and so forth. Of course, there is more to accounting than formatting and terminology. Because British Telecommunications reports using International Financial Reporting Standards (IFRS), there are some slight differences in the company's reported numbers compared to what would be reported if British Telecommunications was a U.S. company reporting according to U.S. GAAP. Those U.S. GAAP–IFRS differences will be addressed throughout this textbook.

> **Stop & Think**
>
> From the information in Exhibit 3-7, compute total assets for British Telecommunications as of March 31, 2011.
> a) £18,559 million
> b) £23,540 million
> c) £24,540 million
> d) £21,052 million
> e) £32,630 million

Exhibit 3-7 | 2011 Balance Sheet of British Telecommunications

British Telecommunications Balance Sheet At 31 March 2011	
	2011 (In millions of British pounds)
Non-current assets	
Intangible assets	£ 3,389
Property, plant and equipment	14,623
Derivative financial instruments	625
Investments	61
Associates and joint ventures	164
Trade and other receivables	286
Deferred tax assets	461
	19,609
Current assets	
Inventories	121
Trade and other receivables	3,332
Derivative financial instruments	108
Investments	19
Cash and cash equivalents	351
	3,931

Exhibit 3-7 | 2011 Balance Sheet of British Telecommunications (Continued)

British Telecommunications
Balance Sheet
At 31 March 2011

	2011 (In millions of British pounds)
Current liabilities	
Loans and other borrowings	£ 485
Derivative financial instruments	62
Trade and other payables	6,114
Current tax liabilities	221
Provisions	149
	7,031
Total assets less current liabilities	**£16,509**
Non-current liabilities	
Loans and other borrowings	£ 9,371
Derivative financial instruments	507
Retirement benefit obligations	1,830
Other payables	831
Deferred tax liabilities	1,212
Provisions	807
	14,558
Equity	
Ordinary shares	408
Share premium	62
Capital redemption reserve	27
Other reserves	658
Retained earnings (loss)	770
Total parent shareholders' equity (deficit)	1,925
Non-controlling interests	26
Total equity (deficit)	**1,951**
	£16,509

British Telecommunications, 2011, 10K Report

Balance Sheet Analysis

LO3 学习目标3
计算财务比率，分析一家公司的业绩和财务状况。

③ Analyze a company's performance and financial position through the computation of financial ratios.

The purpose of classifying and ordering balance sheet items is to make the balance sheet easier to use. Look at Exhibit 3-8 and compare the two balance sheets for the fictitious Techtronics Corporation. The balance sheet on the left is just a list of assets, liabilities, and equities in alphabetical order, like a simple account listing. The balance sheet on the right uses the classification and ordering format described in the previous section. You decide which is easier to interpret.

The Techtronics numbers will be used to illustrate standard balance sheet analysis techniques. The simple techniques described in this overview will probably not help you to

Exhibit 3-8 | Techtronics' Balance Sheet, With and Without Classification

Techtronics Corporation
Balance Sheet
December 31, 2015

WITHOUT CLASSIFICATION		WITH CLASSIFICATION	
Assets		**Assets**	
Buildings and equipment (net of accumulated depreciation of $228,600)	$ 732,900	Current assets:	
Cash	52,650	Cash	$ 52,650
Intangible assets	165,000	Investment securities	67,350
Inventories	296,000	Receivables (less allowance for bad debts)	363,700
Investments	128,000	Inventories	296,000
Investment securities	67,350	Prepaid expenses	32,900
Land	76,300	Total current assets	$ 812,600
Other noncurrent assets	37,800	Noncurrent assets:	
Prepaid expenses	32,900	Investments	$ 128,000
Receivables (less allowance for bad debts)	363,700	Land	76,300
		Buildings and equipment (net of accumulated depreciation of $228,600)	732,900
		Intangible assets	165,000
		Other noncurrent assets	37,800
		Total noncurrent assets	$1,140,000
Total assets	$1,952,600	Total assets	$1,952,600
Liabilities		**Liabilities**	
Accounts payable	$ 312,700	Current liabilities:	
Accrued expenses	46,200	Notes payable	$ 50,000
Bonds payable	165,000	Accounts payable	312,700
Current portion of long-term debt	62,000	Accrued expenses	46,200
Deferred tax liability	126,700	Current portion of long-term debt	62,000
Long-term lease obligations	135,000	Other current liabilities	28,600
Notes payable — current	50,000	Total current liabilities	$ 499,500
Notes payable — noncurrent	100,000	Noncurrent liabilities:	
Other current liabilities	28,600	Notes payable	$ 100,000
Other noncurrent liabilities	72,500	Bonds payable	165,000
		Long-term lease obligations	135,000
		Deferred tax liability	126,700
		Other noncurrent liabilities	72,500
		Total noncurrent liabilities	$ 599,200
Total liabilities	$1,098,700	Total liabilities	$1,098,700
Stockholders' Equity		**Stockholders' Equity**	
Additional paid-in capital	$ 375,000	Contributed capital:	
Common stock	170,000	Common stock	$ 170,000
		Additional paid-in capital	375,000
			$ 545,000
Retained earnings	308,900	Retained earnings	308,900
Total stockholders' equity	$ 853,900	Total stockholders' equity	$ 853,900
Total liabilities and stockholders' equity	$1,952,600	Total liabilities and stockholders' equity	$1,952,600

© Cengage Learning 2014

pick "winning" stocks and become a millionaire, but they are a start. It is said that Warren Buffett (worth about $44 billion at last count) picks his investments only after "a careful balance sheet analysis."[15]

15 Robert Lenzner and David S. Fondiller, "The Not-So-Silent Partner," *Forbes*, January 22, 1996, p. 78.

Balance sheet information is analyzed in two major ways:
1. Relationships between balance sheet amounts
2. Relationships between balance sheet and income statement amounts

In general, relationships between financial statement amounts are called financial ratios.

Relationships Between Balance Sheet Amounts

Financial ratios comparing one balance sheet amount to another yield information about the operating and financial structure of a business. Three examples, which are discussed here, are liquidity, overall leverage, and asset mix.

Liquidity The relationship between current assets and current liabilities can be used to evaluate the liquidity of a company. Liquidity is the ability of a firm to satisfy its short-term obligations. Many companies with fantastic long-run potential have been killed by short-run liquidity problems.

A common indicator of the overall liquidity of a company is the current ratio. The current ratio is computed by dividing total current assets by total current liabilities. For Techtronics, the current ratio is computed as follows:

current ratio
流动比率

$$\text{Current ratio:} \quad \frac{\text{Current assets}}{\text{Current liabilities}} = \frac{\$812,600}{\$499,500} = 1.63$$

Historically, the rule of thumb has been that a current ratio below 2.0 suggests the possibility of liquidity problems. However, advances in information technology have enabled companies to be much more effective in minimizing the need to hold cash, inventories, and other current assets. As a result, current ratios for successful companies these days are frequently less than 1.0. Note that this is just a rule of thumb; proper evaluation of a company's liquidity involves comparing the current year's current ratio to current ratios in prior years and comparing the company's current ratio to those for other companies in the same industry.

Minimum current ratio requirements are frequently included in loan agreements. A typical agreement might state that if the current ratio falls below a certain level, the lender can declare the loan in default and require immediate repayment. This type of minimum current ratio restriction forces the borrower to maintain its liquidity and gives the lender an increased assurance that the loan will be repaid. When loan covenant restrictions are violated, the lender usually waives the right to immediate repayment, sometimes in exchange for a renegotiation of the loan at a higher interest rate. Exhibit 3-9 contains the 2011 current ratios for selected companies. Note that eBay and Microsoft have higher current ratios relative to the other companies. This is an indication of the need for liquidity in technology industries. As technology changes, companies in that industry need to be able to quickly adapt, and that ability requires liquidity. Note also the low current ratio of Disney, for example. At first glance you might think that 1.14 is dangerously low. Before jumping to that conclusion, think about what Disney's current assets are. Disney has cash and accounts receivable but very little inventory. It makes movies, and it runs theme parks, and these ventures require very little inventory. Therefore, the "secret" for Disney's low current ratio is its ability to collect its receivables quickly and reinvest the money into long-term productive assets.

Another ratio used to measure a firm's liquidity is the quick ratio, also known as the acid-test ratio. This ratio is computed as total *quick assets* divided by total current liabilities, where quick assets are defined as cash, investment securities, and net receivables. For Techtronics, the quick ratio is computed as follows:

quick ratio
速动比率

$$\text{Quick ratio:} \quad \frac{\text{Cash + Securities + Receivables}}{\text{Current liabilities}} = \frac{\$483,700}{\$499,500} = 0.97$$

Exhibit 3-9 | Selected 2011 Ratios

	Coca-Cola	Disney	McDonald's	Microsoft	eBay
Current ratio	1.05	1.14	1.25	2.60	1.88
Debt ratio	60.09%	45.30%	56.38%	47.49%	34.37%
Asset mix—PP&E*	18.68%	33.35%	69.22%	7.51%	7.27%
Asset turnover	0.58	0.57	0.82	0.64	0.43
Return on assets	10.72%	6.66%	16.68%	21.30%	11.82%
Return on equity	27.10%	12.86%	38.24%	40.55%	18.01%

* PP&E = property, plant, and equipment

The quick ratio indicates how well a firm can satisfy existing short-term obligations with assets that can be converted into cash without difficulty. For a bank considering a three-month loan or for a supplier considering selling to a company on short-term credit, the quick ratio yields information about the likelihood it will be repaid. Techtronics' quick ratio indicates it has $0.97 in quick assets for every $1.00 in current liabilities.

A lender wants to lend on a short-term basis to a company with high current and quick ratios, thus ensuring repayment. However, maintaining an excessively high current ratio is an inefficient use of company resources. Having excess investment securities will increase a company's current and quick ratios, giving comfort to lenders, but the resources used to buy those excess securities might be better utilized by buying trucks or buildings, paying off debts, or if nothing else, returning the cash to the owners for their personal use. A common characteristic of almost all financial ratios is that a ratio that deviates too much from the norm, either above or below, indicates a possible problem.[16]

> **Caution**
> A current ratio that is too high can also indicate trouble. Excess current assets, resulting in a high current ratio, can represent an inefficient use of resources. Cash management and just-in-time inventory systems are designed to keep current asset levels low.

Overall Leverage Comparing the amount of liabilities to the amount of assets held by a business indicates the extent to which borrowed funds have been used to leverage the owners' investments and increase the size of the firm. One frequently used measure of leverage is the debt ratio, computed as total liabilities divided by total assets. The debt ratio is frequently used as an indicator of the overall ability of a company to repay its debts. An intuitive interpretation of the debt ratio is that it represents the proportion of borrowed funds used to acquire the company's assets. For Techtronics, the debt ratio is computed as follows:

debt ratio
资产负债率

$$\text{Debt ratio:} \frac{\text{Total liabilities}}{\text{Total assets}} = \frac{\$1,098,700}{\$1,952,600} = 0.56$$

In other words, Techtronics borrowed 56% of the money it needed to buy its assets. The higher the debt ratio, the higher the likelihood that some of the debt might not be repaid. The general rule of thumb is that debt ratios should be below 50%. Again, this varies widely from one industry to the next. A bank, for example, could easily have a debt ratio in excess of 95%.

---

[16] Working capital management involves making sure a company does not have excess resources tied up in the form of cash, receivables, and inventory. An example is a just-in-time inventory system. An excess $1 million in working capital implicitly increases finance charges by $100,000 per year if the interest rate on borrowing is 10%.

See Exhibit 3-9; eBay has the lowest debt ratio, with each of the other companies having a debt ratio above 45%. As a general rule, companies in mature industries have a higher amount of debt than in newer industries because the proven track records of the companies make lenders willing to provide more debt financing.

Asset Mix A large fraction of a bank's assets is in financial investments, either loans receivable or securities. Property, plant, and equipment (PP&E) composes only a small fraction of a bank's assets. By comparison, the bulk of the assets of an electric utility is property, plant, and equipment. A company's asset mix, the proportion of total assets in each asset category, is determined to a large degree by the industry in which the company operates.

Asset mix is calculated by dividing each asset amount by the sum of total assets. For example, to determine what fraction of Techtronics' assets is buildings and equipment, perform the following calculation:

$$\frac{\text{Buildings and equipment}}{\text{Total assets}} = \frac{\$732,900}{\$1,952,600} = 0.38$$

Techtronics holds 38% of its assets in the form of buildings and equipment. To determine whether this proportion is appropriate requires looking at the comparable number for other firms in Techtronics' industry. We can tell, for example, that Techtronics is probably not an electric utility, since property, plant, and equipment is 62% ($20,874,000,000/$33,498,000,000) of the total assets of Consolidated Edison in 2008 (see Exhibit 3-6). Similar computations and comparisons can be done with any of the asset categories.

Not surprisingly, McDonald's has a large amount of its assets invested in property, plant, and equipment, as shown in Exhibit 3-9. It is also not surprising that Microsoft and eBay have very little invested in these long-term assets. What is somewhat surprising is Coca-Cola's low level of investment in PP&E. As mentioned at the beginning of the chapter, however, many of Coca-Cola's bottling facilities are owned by subsidiaries and are not reported on Coca-Cola's balance sheet.

Relationships Between Balance Sheet and Income Statement Amounts

Financial ratios comparing balance sheet and income statement amounts reveal information about a firm's overall profitability and about how efficiently the assets are being used. For this discussion, the following income statement data will be assumed for Techtronics: sales, $4,000,000; net income, $150,000.

Efficiency Techtronics' balance sheet reveals that it has $1,952,600 in assets. Are those assets being used efficiently? A financial ratio that gives an overall measure of company efficiency is called asset turnover and is computed as follows:

$$\text{Asset turnover:} \frac{\text{Sales}}{\text{Total assets}} = \frac{\$4,000,000}{\$1,952,600} = 2.05$$

Techtronics' asset turnover ratio of 2.05 means that for each dollar of assets, Techtronics is able to generate $2.05 in sales. The higher the asset turnover ratio, the more efficient the company is at using its assets to generate sales.

As indicated in Exhibit 3-9, McDonald's is the most efficient of the five companies in using assets to generate sales. Every dollar of McDonald's assets generates $0.82 in annual revenue.

Similar computations can be made for specific assets. The general principle is that in measuring whether a company has too much or too little of an asset, the amount of that asset is compared to an income statement item indicating the amount of business activity related to that asset. For example, evaluating the level of inventory involves comparing the inventory level to cost of goods sold for the year. Specific efficiency ratios for accounts receivable, inventory, and fixed assets will be described in the appropriate chapters later in the text.

Overall Profitability Techtronics' net income was $150,000. Is that a lot? It depends. If Techtronics is a small, garage computer-repair business, net income of $150,000 is a lot. If Techtronics is a multinational consumer electronics firm, net income of only $150,000 is terrible. To appropriately measure profitability, net income must be compared to some measure of the size of the investment. Two financial ratios used to assess a firm's overall profitability are return on assets and return on equity. Companies purchase assets with the intent of using them to generate profits. Return on assets is computed as follows:

衡量公司总体盈利能力的两个比率是资产收益率和权益收益率。

$$\text{Return on assets:} \frac{\text{Net income}}{\text{Total assets}} = \frac{\$150,000}{\$1,952,600} = 7.7\%$$

Techtronics' return on assets of 7.7% means that one dollar of assets generated 7.7 cents in net income. As with all ratios, this number must be evaluated in light of Techtronics' return on assets in previous years and the ratios for other firms in the same industry.

Note from Exhibit 3-9 that Microsoft stands out in terms of profitability, with Disney bringing up the rear. The 21.3% return on assets earned by Microsoft is unusually high.

One important factor not included when using return on assets to evaluate profitability is the effect of leverage. The stockholders of Techtronics did not have to invest the entire $1,952,600 needed to purchase the assets; they leveraged their investment through borrowing. Return on equity (ROE) measures the percentage return on the actual investment made by stockholders and is computed as follows:

$$\text{Return on equity:} \frac{\text{Net income}}{\text{Stockholders' equity}} = \frac{\$150,000}{\$853,900} = 17.6\%$$

Techtronics stockholders earned 17.6 cents for each dollar of equity investment. Computing return on equity is like taking a child's temperature: This one number is a summary indicator of the health of the entity. As a rule of thumb, companies with return on equity significantly below 15% are doing poorly. Companies with return on equity consistently above 15% are doing well.

> **Caution**
> A low ROE tells you only that a company is sick. Other financial ratios are the diagnostic tools used to pinpoint the exact nature of the illness.

Coca-Cola demonstrates how the effective use of debt can be of benefit to shareholders. Coca-Cola's shareholders earned a 27.1% return on their investment in 2011 (Exhibit 3-9). Contrast that with eBay's return of 18.01%. Also note that because eBay has a small debt ratio, there is a relatively small difference between the company's return on assets and its return on equity.

Proposed New Balance Sheet Format

The FASB and the International Accounting Standards Board (IASB) are currently engaged in a long-term project to restructure the way information is presented in the financial statements.[17] The focus of this effort is to clearly separate financial statement items that are related to a company's business activities from items that are related to other activities such as income taxes or financing. To give you an idea of what a restructured balance sheet might look like under this new proposal, the Techtronics balance sheet in Exhibit 3-8 has been reformatted and now appears in Exhibit 3-10.

17 "Preliminary Views on Financial Statement Presentation" (Norwalk, CT: Financial Accounting Standards Board, October 16, 2008), and "STAFF DRAFT of an Exposure Draft on Financial Statement Presentation" (Norwalk, CT: Financial Accounting Standards Board, July 1, 2010).

Exhibit 3-10

Techtronics Corporation
Balance Sheet (restructured according to FASB-IASB proposal)
December 31, 2015

BUSINESS
Operating
Current assets:
Receivables (less allowance for bad debts)	$ 363,700		
Inventories	296,000		
Prepaid expenses	32,900		
Total short-term assets		$ 692,600	
Land	$ 76,300		
Buildings and equipment (net of accumulated depreciation of $228,600)	732,900		
Intangible assets	165,000		
Other long-term assets	37,800		
Total long-term assets		1,012,000	
Accounts payable	$(312,700)		
Accrued expenses	(46,200)		
Other current liabilities	(28,600)		
Total short-term liabilities		(387,500)	
Other long-term liabilities		(72,500)	
Net operating assets		$1,244,600	
Investing			
Investment securities (short-term)	$ 67,350		
Investments (long-term)	128,000		
Total investing assets		195,350	
NET BUSINESS ASSETS			$1,439,950
FINANCING			
Financing assets			
Cash		$ 52,650	
Financing liabilities			
Notes payable	$ (50,000)		
Current portion of long-term debt	(62,000)		
Total short-term financing liabilities		(112,000)	
Notes payable	$(100,000)		
Bonds payable	(165,000)		
Long-term lease obligations	(135,000)		
Total long-term financing liabilities		(400,000)	
Total financing liabilities		$ (512,000)	
NET FINANCING LIABILITIES			(459,350)
INCOME TAXES			
Deferred tax liability			(126,700)
NET ASSETS			$ 853,900
EQUITY			
Common stock	$(170,000)		
Additional paid-in capital	(375,000)		
Retained earnings	(308,900)		
TOTAL EQUITY			$ (853,900)

Take a look at Exhibit 3-10 and note the following.

- The balance sheet contains four major sections: business, financing, income taxes, and equity. For a company that has decided to cease some of its operations, a fifth section would include the assets and liabilities related to "discontinued operations."
- Items related to activities associated with a company's financial operations (making investments and borrowing money) are reported separately from items related to the actual day-to-day function of the business. Responsibility for these items belongs to the treasury and financial people in the company, not to the people conducting the actual business operations.
- Items related to income taxes are also highlighted and reported separately. One way to think of this is that the people who run the business on a daily basis don't have anything to do with filing the income tax returns, planning income tax strategy, and so forth.
- This format makes it a little difficult to add up the traditional measures of total assets and total liabilities. The proposed restructuring would also require supplemental disclosure of these traditional numbers.

Under the current plan (as of June 2012), this proposed restructuring of the financial statements, which will also impact the income statement and the statement of cash flows, is expected to be discussed by the two accounting standards boards in 2012 and 2013 after other, more urgent issues (such as revenue recognition and the accounting for leases) are completed. Of course, lots could happen between now and then. But there is a strong sentiment for restructuring the financial statements to highlight a company's core business. So, take a good look at Exhibit 3-10: It could be your first look at the future.

Notes to the Financial Statements

 Recognize the importance of the notes to the financial statements, and outline the types of disclosures made in the notes.

LO4 学习目标4
认识财务报表附注的重要性，列出附注所披露的信息类型。

The basic financial statements do not provide all of the information desired by users. Among other things, creditors and investors need to know what methods of accounting were used by the company to arrive at the balances in the accounts. Sometimes the additional information desired is descriptive and is reported in narrative form. In other cases, additional numerical data are reported. To interpret the numbers contained in the financial statements and make useful comparisons with other companies, one must be able to read the notes and understand the assumptions applied.

The following types of notes are typically included by management as support to the basic financial statements.

- Summary of significant accounting policies.
- Additional information (both numerical and descriptive) to support summary totals found on the financial statements, usually the balance sheet. This is the most common type of note used.
- Information about items that are not reported on the basic statements because the items fail to meet the recognition criteria but are still considered to be significant to users in their decision making.
- Supplementary information required by the FASB or the SEC to fulfill the full disclosure principle.

These notes are considered to be an integral part of the financial statements and, unless specifically excluded, are covered by the auditor's opinion.

Summary of Significant Accounting Policies

GAAP requires that information about the accounting principles and policies followed in arriving at the amounts in the financial statements be disclosed to the users. The FASB Accounting Standards Codification contains the following statement:

> Information about the accounting policies adopted by an entity is essential for financial statement users. When financial statements that are issued . . . purport to present fairly financial position, cash flows, and results of operations in accordance with generally accepted accounting principles (GAAP), a description of all significant accounting policies of the entity shall be included as an integral part of the financial statements.[18]

Examples of the required disclosures of accounting policies include those relating to subsidiaries that have been included in the consolidated statements, depreciation methods (is straight-line used?), inventory valuation method (FIFO, LIFO, or something else?), implementation of any accounting changes, and special revenue recognition practices. This information is usually included as the initial note or as a separate summary preceding the notes to the financial statements. The summary of significant accounting policies for The Walt Disney Company is presented in Notes 2 and 3 to the company's 2011 financial statements. Much of the discussion is devoted to new accounting standards released by the FASB during the preceding year. Companies are required to outline the new standards that they are adopting for the first time. For example, in 2011 Disney reported that it had implemented a new FASB rule regarding the timing of the reporting of revenue from contracts that contain multiple elements. Companies are required to outline what impact, if any, the future adoption of new accounting standards will have on their financial statements.

Additional Information to Support Summary Totals

In order to prepare a balance sheet that is brief enough to be understandable but complete enough to meet the needs of users, notes are added that provide either quantitative or narrative information to support the postretirement amounts. For example, only summary totals for property, plant, and equipment and long-term debt are given in the balance sheet itself; the breakdown of these two items by category is usually given in the notes. Most large firms also have extended notes relating to leases, income taxes, and postemployment benefits. If a firm has entered into long-term leases, the length of the leases and the required future payments are outlined in a note. The income tax note identifies the major areas of difference between a company's financial accounting and tax accounting records. The tax note is also the place one has to look to find out what a company's actual income tax bill is. The postretirement benefit note describes a company's pension plan and plan for coverage of retiree medical benefits. Examination of this note reveals the

> **FYI**
>
> Financial statements in the United Kingdom are usually much more condensed than U.S. financial statements. For example, all current assets and current liabilities are often summed and reported as one net number. The details are given in the notes.

18 FASB ASC paragraph 235-10-50-1.

large amount of information that underlies the single summary numbers recognized in the balance sheet. Examples of these are Note 10 (income taxes) and Note 11 (pensions) to Disney's 2011 financial statements. Disney also includes notes detailing the summary totals for other assets (Note 14) and borrowings (Note 9).

Information About Items Not Included in Financial Statements

As discussed in Chapter 1, items included in the financial statements must meet certain recognition criteria. Even though an item might not meet the criteria for recognition in the statements, information concerning the item might be relevant to users. Loss contingencies are good examples of this type of item. As discussed earlier, if the probability of paying a contingent liability is estimated as "possible" or if the contingent liability is "probable but not reasonably estimable," the contingency should not be recognized but should be disclosed in the notes to the financial statements. The information provided should include as much data as possible to assist the user in evaluating the risk of the loss contingency. Along these lines, most large companies have an interesting note describing the lawsuits outstanding against them.

Conceptually, disclosure should not be an alternative to recognition. In other words, if an item meets the recognition criteria given in Chapter 1, it should be included in the financial statements themselves, not just disclosed in a note. However, recall that the FASB's standard-setting process has been described as a "balancing act" between conceptual purity and business practicality. One of the tools in this balancing act is disclosure. Two examples are the accounting for stock-based compensation and for derivative financial instruments.

- In 1993, the FASB tentatively decided to require firms to recognize as compensation expense the value of stock options given to employees. This decision caused an angry uproar in the business community. After deliberation, the FASB decided to use note disclosure as a compromise; recognition of the stock option values was not required; the values needed only be disclosed in a note. After this experience with disclosure, in 2004 the FASB again decided to require firms to recognize a stock option expense (starting in 2006).[19]

- With derivative financial instruments (e.g., options, futures, swaps, and other exotic financial contracts), the FASB responded to a public demand (backed by requests from the SEC) for more information about derivatives by requiring extensive disclosure.[20] This disclosure standard was a stopgap measure while the FASB studied the issue further with the view of establishing a recognition standard (which was accomplished in 1998).

Stop & Think

In analyzing a company, do users care whether they get the information from the financial statements themselves or from the notes? The answer to this question is "yes, in some circumstances." To understand this better, identify in which ONE of the following circumstances the financial analyst would be MOST LIKELY to prefer recognition over disclosure.

a) The analyst is performing a detailed financial statement analysis on a single company.
b) The analyst is performing a detailed financial statement comparison of two companies.
c) The analyst is performing a summary analysis of 50 different companies in 12 different industries.

---

19 FASB ASC Topic 218—Compensation-Stock Compensation, originally found in pre-Codification *Statement of Financial Accounting Standards No. 123* and *No. 123(R)*.
20 FASB ASC Section 815-10-50, originally found in pre-Codification *Statement of Financial Accounting Standards No. 119*.

One of the accounting controversies involved in the **Enron** scandal that exploded in 2001 and 2002 was the inadequacy of the disclosure in the notes to Enron's financial statements. For example, the existence of the controversial LJM2 investment partnerships, which were used to "hedge" (some would say "hide") $1 billion in Enron investment losses, was not disclosed anywhere in Enron's financial statements notes and was outlined in just three brief paragraphs in the company's proxy statement (which is sent to all shareholders in advance of the annual shareholder meeting).

Supplementary Information

The FASB and SEC require that supplementary information must be reported in separate schedules. For example, the FASB requires the disclosure of quarterly information for certain companies. While the information in these notes is important to the users, it may not be covered by the auditors' opinion. A note that is not covered by the opinion is marked "unaudited."

Another category of supplementary information is business segment information. For companies with geographically dispersed operations, this segment information outlines the results for the different geographic segments. For example, Coca-Cola reports that only 44.2% (2011) of its net operating revenues come from North America. For firms with diverse product lines (such as **PepsiCo**, with substantial operations in soft drinks and snack foods), segment information for the different product lines is presented.[21]

In addition to FASB requirements, the SEC also requires the disclosure of supplemental information about financial statement information for those publicly traded firms falling under the SEC's jurisdiction. For example, if the level of property, plant, and equipment is significant, the SEC requires a firm to provide details about changes in gross property, plant, and equipment and about changes in accumulated depreciation. The SEC also requires disclosure of the details of the changes in short-term borrowing and the average interest rate on short-term loans during the period.

Subsequent Events

Although a balance sheet is prepared as of a given date, it is usually between one and three months before the financial statements are issued and made available to external users. For example, the SEC requires large publicly traded companies to file their financial statements within 60 days of the fiscal year-end. During this time, the accounts are analyzed, adjusting entries are prepared, and for most companies, an independent audit is completed. During this "subsequent period," business doesn't shut down while the accountants huddle over the books. Business continues, and events could take place that have an impact upon the balance sheet and the other basic financial statements for the preceding year. Some of these events could even affect the amounts reported in the statements. These events are referred to in the accounting literature as subsequent events or post-balance sheet events. This subsequent period is illustrated in Exhibit 3-11.

Two different types of subsequent events require consideration by management and evaluation by the independent auditor.[22]

- Those that require retroactive recognition and thus affect the amounts to be reported in the financial statements for the preceding accounting period.
- Those that do not require recognition but should be disclosed in the notes to the financial statements.

21 FASB ASC Topic 280—Segment Reporting.
22 FASB ASC Topic 855—Subsequent Events.

Exhibit 3-11 | Subsequent Event Interval

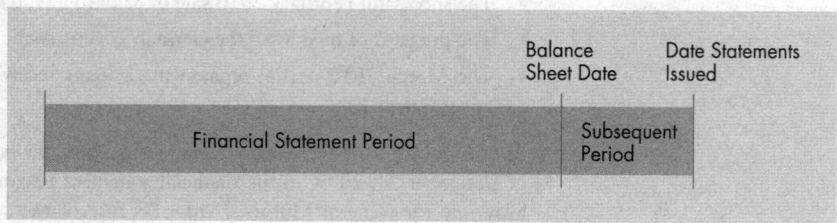

The first type of subsequent event usually provides additional information that affects the amounts included in the financial statements. The reported amounts in several accounts, such as Allowance for Bad Debts, Warranty Liability, and Income Taxes Payable, reflect estimates of the expected value. These estimates are based on information available as of a given date. If a subsequent event provides new information that shows that the conditions existing as of the balance sheet date were different from those assumed when making the estimate, a change in the amount to be reported in the financial statements is required.

To illustrate this type of event, assume that a month after the balance sheet date, the company learns that a major customer has filed for bankruptcy. This information was not known as of the balance sheet date, and only ordinary provisions were made in determining the Allowance for Bad Debts. In all likelihood, the customer was already in financial difficulty at the balance sheet date, but it was not general knowledge. The filing of bankruptcy reveals that the conditions at the balance sheet date were different than those assumed in preparing the statements, and a further adjustment to both the balance sheet and income statement is indicated.

The second type of subsequent event does not reveal a difference in the conditions as of the balance sheet date but involves an event that is considered so significant that its disclosure is highly relevant to readers of the financial statements. These events usually affect the subsequent year's financial statements and thus may affect decisions currently being made by users. Examples of such events include a catastrophe that destroys material portions of a company's assets, acquisition of a major subsidiary, sale of significant amounts of bonds or capital stock, and losses on receivables when the cause of the loss occurred subsequent to the balance sheet date. Information about this type of event is included in the notes to the financial statements and serves to notify the reader that the subsequent event could affect the predictive value of the statements.

The most common types of subsequent events reported by companies include events associated with debt refinancing, debt reduction, or incurring significant amounts of new debt; post-balance sheet developments associated with litigation; and changes in the status of a proposed merger or acquisition. Of course, many business events that occur during this subsequent period are related only to the subsequent year and therefore have no impact on the preceding year's financial statements.

As an example of the types of disclosure associated with subsequent events, the following items were discussed in Note 35 to the financial statements of **General Motors** dated December 31, 2009:

- A discussion of the financial statement impact of currency revaluations conducted by the Venezuelan government in early 2010
- The February 2010 sale of 1% of a joint venture (reducing GM's ownership to 49%) to a Hong Kong subsidiary of Shanghai Automotive Industry Corp (SAIC)—in essence, GM gave up joint control in exchange for some cash

- The February 2010 failure to complete a deal to sell HUMMER to a Chinese company
- The successful February 2010 sale of Saab to a Dutch company
- The progress of talks with the German government about the future of Opel
- The March 2010 partial repayment of loans received from the U.S. and Canadian governments

As you can see from these subsequent events notes, the period from the balance sheet date of December 31, 2009, to the financial statement issuance date on April 7, 2010, was a busy one for General Motors. (*Note:* Because of the company's ongoing restructuring, it was allowed to delay its financial statement issuance beyond the usual requirement of 60 days for companies publicly traded in the United States.)

International Accounting for Subsequent Events   The IASB has released a standard, IAS 10, dealing specifically with the accounting for subsequent events. This standard, which was originally issued in September 1974 and was revised in December 2003, is essentially the same as the accounting employed in the United States. Specifically, IAS 10 requires that companies adjust the reported amounts of assets and liabilities if events occurring after the balance sheet date provide additional information about conditions that existed at the balance sheet date. In addition, IAS 10 requires that disclosure be made of significant subsequent events even if those events do not impact the valuations reported in the balance sheet.

Limitations of the Balance Sheet

LO5 学习目标5
理解资产负债表的主要局限。

资产负债表一般无法反映公司的当前价值。

5 Understand the major limitations of the balance sheet.

Notwithstanding its usefulness, the balance sheet has some serious limitations. External users often need to know a company's worth. The balance sheet, however, does not generally reflect the current value of a business. A favorite ratio among followers of the stock market is the book-to-market ratio, computed as total book value of common equity divided by total market value of common equity. The book-to-market ratio reflects the difference between the balance sheet value of a company and the company's actual market value.[23] A company's book-to-market ratio is almost always less than 1.0 because many assets are reported at historical cost, which is usually less than market value, and other assets are not included in the balance sheet at all. In addition, many intangible economic assets, such as a reputation for superior products or customer service, are not recognized in the balance sheet. Accordingly, the balance sheet numbers often very poorly reflect what a company is worth.

The graph in Exhibit 3-12 shows the average book-to-market ratio, from 1924 through 2008, of the 30 companies making up the Dow Jones Industrial Average. Note the fairly steady decrease from an average book-to-market ratio of about 1.0 in 1980 to about 0.3 in 2008. This means that, in 2008, the accounting book value of the equity of the average company included in the Dow Jones Industrial Average was just 30% as large as the market value of the equity of that company. This low book-to-market ratio reflects the increas-

---

[23] Research into the behavior of stock prices has found that firms with high book-to-market ratios tend to outperform the market in future years. See Eugene F. Fama and Kenneth R. French, "The Cross-Section of Expected Stock Returns," *The Journal of Finance*, June 1992, p. 427. No one is sure why high book-to-market-ratio firms outperform the market. One suggestion is that the accounting numbers partially reflect fundamental underlying value, and a high book-to-market ratio indicates that the market is currently undervaluing a company.

Exhibit 3-12 | Average Book-to-Market Ratio of Companies Listed in the Dow Jones Industrial Average: 1924–2008

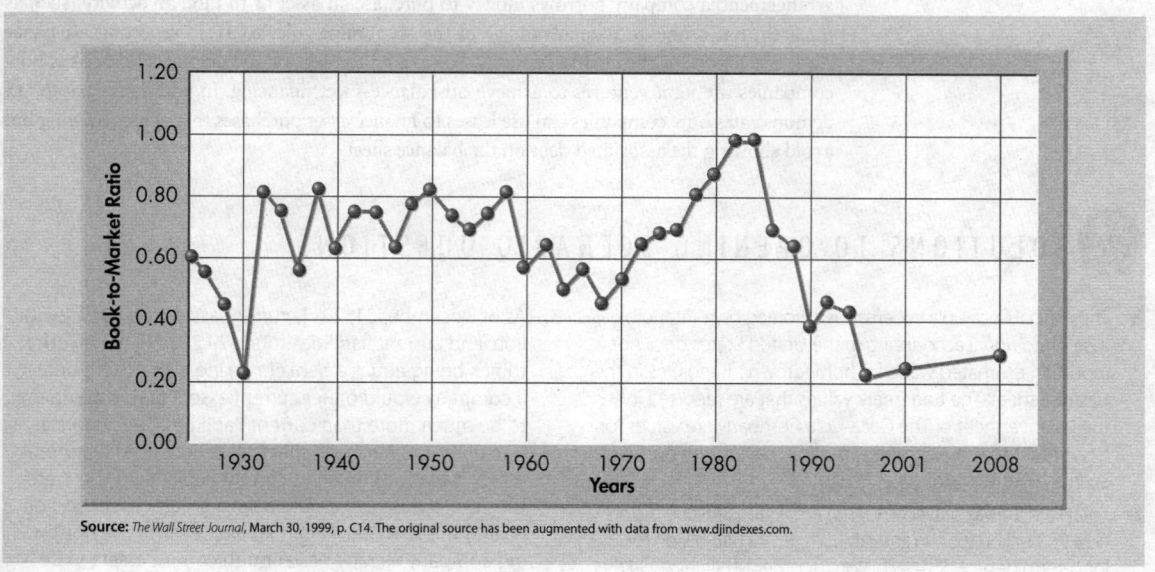

Source: *The Wall Street Journal*, March 30, 1999, p. C14. The original source has been augmented with data from www.djindexes.com.

ing importance of unreported, intangible assets as service and technology companies have become a more significant part of the U.S. economy.

A related problem with the balance sheet is the instability of the dollar, the standard accounting measuring unit in the United States. Because of general price changes in the economy, the dollar does not maintain a constant purchasing power, yet the historical costs of resources and equities shown on the balance sheet are not adjusted for changes in the purchasing power of the measuring unit. The result is a balance sheet that reflects assets, liabilities, and equities in terms of unequal purchasing power units. Some elements, for example, may be stated in terms of 1980 dollars and some in terms of current-year dollars. The variations in purchasing power of the amounts reported in the balance sheet make comparisons among companies, and even within a single company, less meaningful.

An additional limitation of the balance sheet, also related to the need for comparability, is that all companies do not classify and report all like items similarly. For example, titles and account classifications vary; some companies provide considerably more detail than others; and some companies with apparently similar transactions report them differently. Such differences make comparisons difficult and diminish the potential value of balance sheet analysis.

As mentioned, some entity resources and obligations are not reported on the balance sheet. For example, as mentioned at the beginning of the chapter in connection with Coca-Cola, the company's reputation and worldwide market presence are among its most valuable resources, yet those economic assets are not shown on the balance sheet because measuring them in monetary terms is quite difficult. The assumptions of the traditional accounting model identified in Chapter 1, specifically the requirements of arm's-length transactions or events measurable in monetary terms, add to the objectivity of balance sheet disclosures but at the same time cause some information to be omitted that is likely to be relevant to certain users' decisions.

One other limitation of the balance sheet is the increasing use of off-balance-sheet financing. In fact, a key aspect of the famous Enron accounting scandal was Enron's creative use of financing arrangements (with exotic names such as Rhythms and Raptor) to avoid reporting large amounts of debt in the company's balance sheet. In an off-balance-sheet financing arrangement, a company borrows money to purchase an asset or to fund an activity (such as research) but is able to take advantage of the accounting rules to avoid reporting a balance sheet obligation for the borrowed funds. For example, a section in Chapter 12 describes how companies use joint ventures to achieve off-balance-sheet financing. In addition, Chapter 15 demonstrates how companies can use leases to finance asset purchases through borrowing but avoid showing the associated debt on the balance sheet.

 SOLUTIONS TO OPENING SCENARIO QUESTIONS

1. The original Coca-Cola trademark is a "homegrown" intangible asset. Traditional accounting in the United States does not report an estimated value for homegrown intangibles in the balance sheet. The trademark values that are reported in the balance sheet of The Coca-Cola Company are values for trademarks that the company has purchased over the years, such as Minute Maid.

2. Total liabilities as of December 31, 2011, are $48.053 billion ($24.283 billion for current liabilities + $13.656 billion for long-term debt + $5.420 billion for other liabilities + $4.694 billion for deferred income taxes). Note that this amount of reported liabilities does *not* reflect the amount of unreported liabilities of the Coca-Cola bottlers of which The Coca-Cola Company owns a substantial percentage.

3. As of December 31, 2011, current assets total $25.497 billion, and current liabilities total $24.283 billion. All other things being equal, a banker making a short-term loan to a company would prefer current assets of that company to be much more than current liabilities. The historical rule of thumb has been that the desired level of current assets is twice as much as current liabilities. If this were the case, the banker would have a greater likelihood of having the short-term loan repaid because the borrowing company already has enough current assets to be able to repay all of its existing current liabilities. In the case of Coca-Cola, with a long history of generating cash from operations, a banker would take some comfort from its track record.

Stop & Think SOLUTIONS

1. (Page 3-5) The correct answer is C. Actually, defining assets and liabilities in terms of legal statutes would severely limit the FASB's influence. One of the key roles of the FASB is to apply the definitions in the conceptual framework to determine when assets and liabilities should be recognized. Legalistic definitions would take this exercise out of the FASB's hands and transfer it to the lawmakers responsible for contract law.

2. (Page 3-12)
   (1) A financial analyst trying to compare the company's core business with the core businesses of similar companies—Classification (b). This classification allows the analyst to compare the assets and liabilities associated with the primary lines of business of various companies.
   (2) A U.S. congressperson concerned about the relocation of operations overseas—Classification (a). This classification allows the congressperson to see how much of a company's assets and liabilities are located outside the United States. The congressperson would also be able to see the trend over time.
   (3) An analyst trying to estimate the current market value of a company—Classification (c). This classification allows the analyst to see what fraction of a company's assets is not reported at current fair value. This gives the analyst an idea of how much the company's market value might vary from its reported balance sheet value.

3. (Page 3-19) The correct answer is B. Total assets is the sum of current assets and long-term (fixed) assets. For British Telecommunications as of March 31, 2011, the amount of total assets is £23,540 million (£19,609 million + £3,931 million). Note that this is not the same total amount shown in the balance sheet—the balance sheet amount is total assets minus current liabilities.

4. (Page 3-29) The correct answer is C. When the analyst is doing a detailed analysis of one or two companies, then he or she can make any desired financial statement adjustments using note disclosure. Such adjustments might be necessary to make a company comparable to some benchmark or to make the financial statements of two different companies comparable. However, these detailed adjustments using note disclosure become expensive and time consuming when many companies are involved. In such a case, the analyst prefers to have all of the relevant data summarized and recognized in the financial statements themselves.

SOLUTION TO USING THE FASB'S CODIFICATION

In FASB ASC 210-20-05-1, we read the following: "This Subtopic provides criteria for offsetting amounts related to certain contracts and provides guidance on presentation. It is a general principle of accounting that the offsetting of assets and liabilities in the balance sheet is improper except if a right of setoff exists."

The "right of setoff" is defined as follows: "A right of setoff is a debtor's legal right, by contract or otherwise, to discharge all or a portion of the debt owed to another party by applying against the debt an amount that the other party owes to the debtor."

This "right of setoff" doesn't describe the situation with the doctors and their $350,000 bank loan. The "right of setoff" would exist if I owe you $1,000, and you owe me $1,000, and my contract with you allowed me to cancel my debt to you by "setting off" the amount you owe to me. I could then offset those amounts and eliminate both from my balance sheet.

To make a proper balance sheet for the medical practice, you need to include the existing $350,000 loan ... unless the doctors want to pull some of that cash out of their personal accounts and repay the loan.

Review Chapter 3 Learning Objectives

① Describe the specific elements of the balance sheet (assets, liabilities, and owners' equity), and prepare a balance sheet with assets and liabilities properly classified into current and noncurrent categories.

A balance sheet is a listing of a company's assets, liabilities, and equities as of a certain point in time.

- Assets are probable future economic benefits obtained or controlled as a result of past transactions or events.
- Liabilities are probable future sacrifices of economic benefits arising from present obligations to transfer assets or provide services in the future as a result of past transactions or events.
- Equity is the net assets of an entity, that is, the amount that remains after total liabilities have been deducted from total assets.

For balance sheet reporting, assets and liabilities are often separated into current and noncurrent categories. Current items are those expected to be used or paid within one year or within the normal operating cycle, whichever is longer.

When classifying assets and liabilities, the key considerations are how management intends to use an asset and when it expects to pay a liability.

Equity arises from owner investment, is increased by net income, and is decreased by losses and by distributions to owners. Equity is also impacted by stock repurchases, unrealized security gains and losses, and foreign exchange rate fluctuations.

② Identify the different formats used to present balance sheet data.

In most industries in the United States, assets and liabilities are listed in order of their liquidity with current items first. For some industries, particularly those with large investments in long-term assets, current items are not listed first. In addition, in other countries, the format of the balance sheet can vary widely.

③ Analyze a company's performance and financial position through the computation of financial ratios.

Balance sheet information is most often analyzed by looking at relationships between different balance sheet amounts and relationships between balance sheet and income statement amounts. Relationships between financial statement amounts are called *financial ratios*.

④ Recognize the importance of the notes to the financial statements, and outline the types of disclosures made in the notes.

The information in the financial statements is supported by explanatory notes. The notes include a description of the accounting policies, details of summary totals, disclosure of significant items that fail to meet the recognition criteria, and supplemental information required by FASB and SEC standards.

Note disclosure also sometimes relates to subsequent events. *Subsequent events* are significant events occurring between the balance sheet date and the date the financial statements are issued. Subsequent events come in two varieties: those requiring immediate retroactive recognition in the financial statements and those requiring only note disclosure.

 Understand the major limitations of the balance sheet.

The balance sheet often does not provide an accurate reflection of the value of a business. Reasons for this include the use of historical cost instead of current values, omission of some assets from the balance sheet, and failure to make adjustments for inflation. The balance sheet does not measure the market value of a company. The difference between balance sheet value and market value is captured in the book-to-market ratio (book value of equity divided by market value of equity), which is usually less than 1.0.

FASB-IASB CODIFICATION SUMMARY

Topic	FASB Accounting Standards Codification	Original FASB Standard	Corresponding IASB Standard	Differences Between U.S. GAAP and IFRS
Classified balance sheet	Section 210-10-05 par. 4 Section 210-10-45 par. 1 through 12	ARB 43 Ch., 3A par. 4-8	IAS 1 par. 60-61	No substantial differences in the descriptions and definitions of current assets and current liabilities
Classification of short-term obligations to be refinanced	Section 470-10-45 par. 14	SFAS No. 6 par. 10-11	IAS 1 par. 72	Under IFRS, for a short-term obligation to be classified as long term, the refinancing must take place by the balance sheet date
Subsequent events	Topic 855	SFAS No. 165	IAS 10	No substantial differences

KEY TERMS

Acid-test ratio 3-22
Additional paid-in capital 3-13
Asset mix 3-24
Assets 3-4
Asset turnover 3-24
Balance sheet 3-4
Book-to-market ratio 3-32
Callable obligation 3-10
Capital stock 3-13
Common stock 3-13
Contingent liabilities 3-12
Contributed capital 3-13
Corporations 3-13

Current assets 3-7
Current liabilities 3-9
Current ratio 3-22
Debt ratio 3-23
Deferred income tax assets 3-9
Deferred income tax liability 3-11
Deficit 3-14
Derivative 3-15
Equity 3-4
Estimated liability 3-12
Financial ratios 3-22
Leverage 3-23
Liabilities 3-4

Liquidity 3-22
Loan covenant 3-22
Minority (noncontrolling) interest 3-15
Objective acceleration clause 3-10
Other comprehensive income 3-14
Paid-in capital 3-13
Partnerships 3-13
Post-balance sheet events 3-30
Preferred stock 3-13
Proprietorships 3-13

Quick ratio 3-22
Retained earnings 3-13
Return on assets 3-25
Return on equity 3-25
Sinking fund 3-10
Stockholders' (shareholders') equity 3-13
Subjective acceleration clause 3-10
Subsequent events 3-30
Trading securities 3-7
Treasury stock 3-14
Working capital 3-7

Tutorial Activities

Tutorial Activities with author-written, content-specific feedback, available on *CengageNOW for Stice & Stice.*

QUESTIONS

1. What three elements are contained in a balance sheet?
2. What is the importance of the term *probable* in the definition of an asset?
3. "Liabilities are obligations denominated in precise monetary terms." Do you agree or disagree? Explain.
4. What does the difference between current assets and current liabilities measure?
5. What criteria are generally used (a) in classifying assets as current? (b) in classifying liabilities as current?
6. Indicate under what circumstances each of the following can be considered noncurrent: (a) cash and (b) receivables.
7. How can expected refinancing impact the classification of a liability?
8. (a) What is a subjective acceleration clause?
   (b) What is an objective acceleration clause?
   (c) How do these clauses in debt instruments affect the classification of a liability?
9. Distinguish between contingent liabilities and estimated liabilities.
10. How do the Equity sections of proprietorships, partnerships, and corporations differ from one another?
11. What are the three major categories in a corporation's Equity section?
12. Under what circumstances may offset balances be properly recognized on the balance sheet?
13. In what order are assets usually listed in the balance sheet?
14. What are financial ratios?
15. Explain how the asset turnover ratio provides a measure of a company's overall efficiency.
16. What one financial ratio summarizes everything about the performance of a company? How is it computed?
17. What are the major types of notes attached to the financial statements?
18. How has the FASB used note disclosure as a tool of compromise?
19. What are some examples of supplementary information included in the notes to financial statements?
20. Under what circumstances does a subsequent event lead to a journal entry for the previous reporting period?
21. "The balance sheet does not reflect the value of a business." Do you agree or disagree? Explain.

PRACTICE EXERCISES

Practice 3-1

Balance Sheet Relationships

The company has assembled the following partial balance sheet data.

Long-term assets.	$30,000
Long-term liabilities.	15,000
Paid-in capital.	4,000
Total assets	40,000
Current liabilities.	8,000

Use these data to compute the following quantities:

(a) Current assets
(b) Total liabilities
(c) Total equity
(d) Retained earnings

Practice 3-2

Working Capital

Using the following information, compute working capital:

Cost of Goods Sold	$ 9,000
Accounts Payable	2,400
Paid-In Capital	1,950
Cash	700
Sales	10,000
Accrued Wages Payable	150
Dividends	500
Retained Earnings (beginning)	1,000
Inventory	2,500

Practice 3-3

Current Assets

Using the following information, compute total current assets:

Goodwill	$ 9,000
Prepaid Expenses	1,100
Paid-In Capital	1,750
Cash	400
Property, Plant, and Equipment	10,000
Investment Securities (trading)	250
Accounts Receivable	700
Retained Earnings	1,000
Inventory	4,000

Practice 3-4

Current Liabilities

Using the following information, compute total current liabilities:

Accrued Income Taxes Payable	$ 9,000
Notes Payable (due in 14 months)	1,100
Paid-In Capital	1,750
Treasury Stock	400
Current Portion of Long-Term Debt	10,000
Unearned Revenue	250
Accounts Payable	700
Retained Earnings	1,000
Additional Paid-In Capital	4,000

Practice 3-5

Classification of Short-Term Loans to Be Refinanced

The company has the following three loans payable scheduled to be repaid in June of next year. As of December 31 of this year, identify which of the three should be classified as current and which should be classified as noncurrent.

(a) The company intends to repay Loan A when it comes due in June. In September, the company intends to get a new loan of equal amount from the same bank.

(b) The company intends to refinance Loan B when it comes due. The refinancing contract will be signed in May *after* the financial statements for this year have been released.

(c) The company intends to refinance Loan C when it comes due. The refinancing contract will be signed in January *before* the financial statements for this year have been released.

Practice 3-6

Callable Obligations

The company has the following three loans. As of December 31 of this year, identify which of the three should be classified as current and which should be classified as noncurrent.

(a) On July 15 of next year, Loan A will become payable on demand.

(b) Loan B is scheduled to be repaid in three years. In addition, the loan agreement specifies that if the company's current ratio falls below 1.5, the loan becomes payable on demand. On December 31, the current ratio is 1.8.

(c) Loan C is scheduled to be repaid in three years. In addition, the loan agreement specifies that if the company's "general financial condition deteriorates significantly," the loan becomes payable on demand. As of December 31, it is reasonably possible that this clause will be invoked.

Practice 3-7

Contingent Liabilities

The company has the following three potential obligations. Describe how each will be reported in the financial statements.

(a) The company has promised to make fixed pension payments to employees after they retire. The company is not certain how long the employees will work or how long they will live after they retire.

(b) The company has been sued by a group of shareholders who claim that they were deceived by the company's financial reporting practices. It is possible that the company will lose this lawsuit.

(c) The company is involved in litigation over who must clean up a toxic waste site near one of the company's factories. It is probable, but not certain, that the company will be required to pay for the cleanup.

Practice 3-8

Stockholders' Equity

Using the following information, compute: (a) total contributed capital, (b) ending retained earnings, and (c) total stockholders' equity:

Additional Paid-In Capital, Common.	$8,200
Accounts Payable	1,300
Total Expenses	5,650
Preferred Stock, at par	3,450
Common Stock, at par	300
Sales	9,700
Treasury Stock	375
Dividends	950
Retained Earnings (beginning)	6,500
Additional Paid-In Capital, Preferred	150

Practice 3-9

Stockholders' Equity

Using the following information, compute (a) total contributed capital, (b) total accumulated other comprehensive income, and (c) total stockholders' equity:

Additional Paid-In Capital, Common.	$9,000
Common Stock, at par	400
Cumulative Translation Adjustment (equity reduction), ending	2,000
Treasury Stock	700
Retained Earnings (post closing, or ending)	1,500
Cumulative Unrealized Gain on Available-for-Sale Securities, ending	1,100

Practice 3-10

Format of Foreign Balance Sheet
Following is a balance sheet presented in standard U.S. format. Rearrange this balance sheet to be in standard British format. Don't worry about differences in terminology; use the U.S. labels, but present the information in the British format.

Current Assets:		
Cash		$ 500
Inventory		2,000
Total current assets		$ 2,500
Noncurrent Assets:		
Property, plant, and equipment		$ 8,000
Long-term investments		1,700
Total noncurrent assets		$ 9,700
Total assets		$12,200
Current Liabilities:		
Accounts payable		$ 300
Short-term loans payable		1,100
Total current liabilities		$ 1,400
Noncurrent Liabilities:		
Long-term debt		$ 3,000
Stockholders' Equity:		
Common stock, at par		$ 50
Additional paid-in capital		2,000
Retained earnings		5,750
Total stockholders' equity		$ 7,800
Total liabilities and stockholders' equity		$12,200

Practice 3-11

Current Ratio
Use the following information to compute the current ratio:

Accounts Payable	$3,700
Paid-In Capital	3,650
Cash	750
Sales	9,500
Accrued Wages Payable	150
Inventory	6,300

Practice 3-12

Quick Ratio
Use the following information to compute the quick ratio:

Long-Term Loan Payable	$ 1,100
Accounts Receivable	1,750
Cash	400
Cost of Goods Sold	10,000
Accrued Wages Payable	315
Inventory	4,000

Practice 3-13

Debt Ratio
Use the information in Practice 3-4 to compute the debt ratio. Assume that the list includes all liability and equity items.

Practice 3-14
Debt Ratio
Use the information in Practice 3-8 to compute the debt ratio. Assume that the list includes all liability and equity items.

Practice 3-15
Asset Mix
Use the information in Practice 3-10 to compute the proportion of total assets in each of the following asset categories.

(a) Inventory
(b) Property, Plant, and Equipment

Practice 3-16
Asset Mix
Use the information in Practice 3-3 to compute the proportion of total assets in each of the following asset categories. Assume that the list contains all the asset items.

(a) Inventory
(b) Property, Plant, and Equipment

Practice 3-17
Measure of Efficiency
Refer to Practice 3-10. Sales for the year totaled $50,000. Compute asset turnover.

Practice 3-18
Return on Assets
Refer to Practice 3-10. Net income for the year totaled $3,600. Compute return on assets.

Practice 3-19
Return on Equity
Refer to Practice 3-10. Net income for the year totaled $2,000. Compute return on equity.

Practice 3-20
Accounting for Subsequent Events
On December 31, the warranty liability was estimated to be $100,000. On January 16 of the following year, results of a study done before December 31 were received. These study results indicate that products would require a much larger amount of warranty repairs than expected; total warranty repairs will be $175,000 instead of the estimated $100,000. The financial statements were issued on February 20. What amount should be reported as warranty liability in the December 31 balance sheet?

Practice 3-21
Accounting for Subsequent Events
On December 31, the warranty liability was estimated to be $100,000. On January 16 of the following year, it was learned that one week before, on January 9, poor-quality materials were introduced into the production process. This mistake is expected to create an additional $87,000 in warranty repairs. The financial statements were issued on February 20. What amount should be reported as warranty liability in the December 31 balance sheet?

Practice 3-22
Book-to-Market Ratio
Refer to Practice 3-10. As of the end of the year, the total market value of shares outstanding was $10,000. Compute the book-to-market ratio.

EXERCISES

Exercise 3-23
Balance Sheet Classification
A balance sheet contains the following classifications:

(a) Current assets
(b) Investments
(c) Property, plant, and equipment
(d) Intangible assets
(e) Other noncurrent assets
(f) Current liabilities
(g) Long-term debt
(h) Other noncurrent liabilities
(i) Capital stock
(j) Additional paid-in capital
(k) Retained earnings

Indicate by letter how each of the following accounts would be classified. Place a minus sign (–) for all accounts representing offset or contra balances.

1. Discount on Bonds Payable
2. Stock of Subsidiary Corporation
3. 12% Bonds Payable (due in six months)
4. U.S. Treasury Bills
5. Income Taxes Payable
6. Sales Taxes Payable
7. Estimated Claims under Warranties for Service and Replacements
8. Par Value of Stock Issued and Outstanding
9. Unearned Rent Revenue (six months in advance)
10. Long-Term Advances to Officers
11. Interest Receivable
12. Preferred Stock Retirement Fund
13. Trademarks
14. Allowance for Bad Debts
15. Dividends Payable
16. Accumulated Depreciation
17. Trading Securities
18. Prepaid Rent
19. Prepaid Insurance
20. Deferred Income Tax Asset

Exercise 3-24

Balance Sheet Classification
State how each of the following accounts should be classified on the balance sheet.

(a) Treasury Stock
(b) Retained Earnings
(c) Vacation Pay Payable
(d) Foreign Currency Translation Adjustment
(e) Allowance for Bad Debts
(f) Liability for Pension Payments
(g) Investment Securities (Trading)
(h) Paid-In Capital in Excess of Stated Value
(i) Leasehold Improvements
(j) Goodwill
(k) Receivables—U.S. Government Contracts
(l) Advances to Salespersons
(m) Premium on Bonds Payable
(n) Inventory
(o) Patents
(p) Unclaimed Payroll Checks
(q) Income Taxes Payable
(r) Subscription Revenue Received in Advance
(s) Interest Payable
(t) Deferred Income Tax Asset
(u) Tools
(v) Deferred Income Tax Liability

Exercise 3-25

Asset Definition
Using the definition of an asset from FASB *Concepts Statement No. 6*, indicate whether each of the following should be listed as an asset by Ingalls Company.

(a) Ingalls has legal title to a coal mine in a remote location. Historically, the mine has yielded more than $25 million in coal. Engineering estimates suggest that no additional coal is economically extractable from the mine.
(b) Ingalls employs a team of five geologists who are widely recognized as worldwide leaders in their field.
(c) Several years ago, Ingalls purchased a large meteor crater on the advice of a geologist who had developed a theory claiming that vast deposits of iron ore lay underneath the crater. The crater has no other economic use. No ore has been found, and the geologist's theory is not generally accepted.
(d) Ingalls claims ownership of a large piece of real estate in a foreign country. The real estate has a current market value of over $225 million. The country expropriated the land 35 years ago, and no representative of Ingalls has been allowed on the property since.
(e) Ingalls is currently negotiating the purchase of an oil field with proven oil reserves totaling 5 billion barrels.

Exercise 3-26

Liability Definition
Using the definition of a liability from FASB *Concepts Statement No. 6*, indicate whether each of the following should be listed as a liability by Pauli Company.

(a) Pauli was involved in a highly publicized lawsuit last year. Pauli lost and was ordered to pay damages of $125 million. The payment has been made.

(b) In exchange for television advertising services that Pauli received last month, Pauli is obligated to provide the television station with building maintenance service for the next four months.

(c) Pauli contractually guarantees to replace any of its stain-resistant carpets if they are stained and can't be cleaned.

(d) Pauli estimates that its total payroll for the coming year will exceed $35 million.

(e) In the past, Pauli has suffered frequent vandalism at its storage warehouses. Pauli estimates that losses due to vandalism during the coming year will total $3 million.

Exercise 3-27

Balance Sheet Preparation

From the following list of accounts, prepare a balance sheet showing all balance sheet items properly classified. (No monetary amounts are to be recognized.)

Accounts Payable	Interest Revenue
Accounts Receivable	Inventory
Accumulated Depreciation—Buildings	Investment in Subsidiary
Accumulated Depreciation—Equipment	Investment Securities (Trading)
Advertising Expense	Land
Allowance for Bad Debts	Loss on Purchase Commitments
Bad Debt Expense	Miscellaneous General Expense
Bonds Payable	Net Pension Asset
Buildings	Notes Payable (current)
Cash	Paid-In Capital from Sale of Treasury Stock
Common Stock	Paid-In Capital in Excess of Stated Value
Cost of Goods Sold	Patents
Deferred Income Tax Liability	Premium on Bonds Payable
Depreciation Expense—Buildings	Prepaid Insurance
Dividends	Property Tax Expense
Equipment	Purchase Discounts
Estimated Warranty Expense Payable (current)	Purchases
Gain on Sale of Investment Securities	Retained Earnings
Gain on Sale of Land	Salaries Payable
Goodwill	Sales
Income Tax Expense	Sales Salaries
Income Taxes Payable	Travel Expense
Interest Receivable	

Exercise 3-28

Computation of Working Capital

From the following data, compute the working capital for Hales Shipping Co. at December 31, 2015.

Cash in general checking account	$ 34,000	Used equipment to be sold	$ 9,000
Cash in fund to be used to retire bonds in 2019	59,000	Deferred tax asset—to be recovered in 2017	12,000
Cash held to pay sales taxes	18,000	Accounts payable	79,000
Notes receivable—due February 2017	113,000	Note payable—due July 2016	27,000
Accounts receivable	113,000	Note payable—due January 2017	18,000
Inventory	81,000	Bonds payable—maturity date 2019	219,000
Prepaid insurance—for 2016	15,000	Salaries payable	11,000
Vacant land held as investment	350,000	Sales taxes payable	23,000
		Goodwill	54,000

Exercise 3-29

Preparation of Corrected Balance Sheet

The following balance sheet was prepared for Jared Corporation as of December 31, 2015.

Jared Corporation
Balance Sheet
December 31, 2015

Assets		Liabilities and Owners' Equity	
Current assets:		Current liabilities:	
Cash	$ 12,500	Accounts payable	$ 3,400
Investment securities	8,000	Other current liabilities	2,000
Accounts receivable, net	21,350	Total current liabilities	$ 5,400
Inventory	31,000	Long-term liabilities	32,750
Other current assets	14,200	Total liabilities	$ 38,150
Total current assets	$ 87,050		
Noncurrent assets:		Owners' equity:	
Property, plant, and equipment, net	$ 64,800	Common stock	$ 50,000
Treasury stock	4,500	Retained earnings	81,800
Other noncurrent assets	13,600	Total owners' equity	$131,800
Total noncurrent assets	$ 82,900		
Total assets	$169,950	Total liabilities and owners' equity	$169,950

The following additional information relates to the December 31, 2015, balance sheet.

(a) Cash includes $4,000 that has been restricted to the purchase of manufacturing equipment (a noncurrent asset).

(b) Investment securities include $2,750 of stock that was purchased in order to give the company significant ownership and a seat on the board of directors of a major supplier.

(c) Other current assets include a $4,000 advance to the president of the company. No due date has been set.

(d) Long-term liabilities include bonds payable of $10,000. Of this amount, $2,500 represents bonds scheduled to be redeemed in 2016.

(e) Long-term liabilities also include a $7,000 bank loan. On May 15, the loan will become due on demand.

(f) On December 21, dividends in the amount of $15,000 were declared to be paid to shareholders of record on January 25. These dividends have not been reflected in the financial statements.

(g) Cash in the amount of $19,000 has been placed in a restricted fund for the redemption of preferred stock in 2016. Both the cash and the stock have been removed from the balance sheet.

(h) Property, plant, and equipment includes land costing $8,000 that is being held for investment purposes and that is scheduled to be sold in 2016.

Based on the information provided, prepare a corrected balance sheet.

Exercise 3-30

Balance Sheet Relationships

On the Clark and Company Inc. balance sheet, indicate the amount that should appear for each of the items (a) through (n) on the balance sheet.

REVERSE SOLVABLE

Clark and Company Inc.
Consolidated Balance Sheet
December 31, 2015

Assets

Current assets:			
Cash			$ 24,250
Investment securities			(a)
Accounts and notes receivable		$ (b)	
Allowance for doubtful accounts and notes receivable		7,851	121,664
Inventories			197,682
Other current assets			14,227
Total current assets			$ (c)
Noncurrent assets:			
Property, plant, and equipment		$694,604	
Accumulated depreciation		(d)	$398,832
Other noncurrent assets			13,217
Total noncurrent assets			412,049
Total assets			$792,514

Liabilities and Owners' Equity

Current liabilities:			
Accounts payable			$ (e)
Payable to banks			34,236
Income taxes payable			9,211
Current installments of long-term debt			6,341
Accrued expenses			7,100
Total current liabilities			$ (f)
Noncurrent liabilities:			
Long-term debt			$ (g)
Deferred income tax liability			41,218
Minority interest in subsidiaries			4,201
Total noncurrent liabilities			205,410
Total liabilities			$350,782
Contributed capital:			
Preferred stock, no par value (authorized 1,618 shares; issued 1,115 shares)			$ 12,392
Common stock, $1 par value per share (authorized 60,000 shares; issued 21,842 shares)		$ (h)	
Additional paid-in capital		(i)	(j)
Total contributed capital			$ (k)
Retained earnings			390,625
Total contributed capital and retained earnings			$ (l)
Less: Treasury stock, at cost (1,229 shares)			27,038
Total owners' equity			$ (m)
Total liabilities and owners' equity			$ (n)

Exercise 3-31

Balance Sheet Schedules

In its annual report to stockholders, Hakobe Inc. presents a condensed balance sheet with detailed data provided in supplementary schedules.

1. From the adjusted trial balance of Hakobe, prepare the following sections of the balance sheet, properly classifying all accounts as to balance sheet categories:

   (a) Current assets
   (b) Property, plant, and equipment
   (c) Intangible assets
   (d) Total assets
   (e) Current liabilities
   (f) Noncurrent liabilities
   (g) Owners' equity
   (h) Total liabilities and owners' equity

2. Compute the current ratio and debt ratio for Hakobe.

Hakobe Inc.
Adjusted Trial Balance
December 31, 2015

	Debit	Credit
Cash	$ 43,700	
Investment securities (trading)	15,000	
Notes receivable—trade debtors	22,000	
Accrued interest on notes receivable	2,100	
Accounts receivable	79,500	
Allowance for doubtful accounts		$ 4,600
Inventory	59,300	
Prepaid expenses	8,200	
Accounts payable		57,600
Notes payable—trade creditors		11,000
Accrued interest on notes payable		950
Land	103,000	
Buildings	192,000	
Accumulated depreciation—buildings		21,000
Equipment	37,000	
Accumulated depreciation—equipment		5,900
Patents	85,000	
Franchises	82,110	
Bonds payable, 8%—issue 1 (mature 12/31/17)		65,000
Bonds payable, 12%—issue 2 (mature 12/31/19)		125,000
Accrued interest on bonds payable		7,500
Premium on bonds payable—issue 1		2,500
Discount on bonds payable—issue 2	12,500	
Mortgage payable		72,000
Accrued interest on mortgage payable		4,320
Capital stock, par value $1; 10,000 shares authorized; 5,000 shares issued		5,000
Additional paid-in capital		123,700
Retained earnings		251,340
Treasury stock—at cost (500 shares)	16,000	
Totals	$757,410	$757,410

Exercise 3-32

Computation of Financial Ratios

The following data are from the financial statements of Riverton Company.

Current assets	$ 55,000	Total liabilities	$ 95,000
Total assets	125,000	Net income	18,000
Current liabilities	25,000	Sales	275,000

Compute Riverton's current ratio, debt ratio, asset turnover, return on assets, and return on equity.

Exercise 3-33

Computation of Financial Ratios

Schlofman Company has the following assets.

Cash	$ 20,000
Accounts receivable	60,000
Inventory	105,000
Property, plant, and equipment	220,000
Total assets	$405,000

Companies in Schlofman's industry typically have the following asset mix: cash, 7%; accounts receivable, 15%; inventory, 18%; property, plant, and equipment, 60%.

Compared to other companies in its industry, Schlofman has too much of one asset. Which one? Show your computations.

Exercise 3-34

Classification of Subsequent Events

The following events occurred after the end of the company's fiscal year but before the annual audit was completed. Classify each event as to its impact on the financial statements, that is: (1) reported by changing the amounts in the financial statements, (2) reported in notes to the financial statements, or (3) does not require reporting. Include support for your classification.

(a) A major customer went bankrupt due to a deteriorating financial condition.
(b) Company sustained extensive hurricane damage to one of its plants.
(c) Company lost a major lawsuit that had been pending for two years.
(d) Increasing U.S. trade deficit may have impact on company's overseas sales.
(e) Company sold a large block of preferred stock.
(f) Preparation of current year's income tax return disclosed that an additional $25,000 is due on last year's return.
(g) Company's controller resigned and was replaced by an audit manager from the company's audit firm.

Exercise 3-35

Reporting Financial Information

For each of the following items, indicate whether the item should be reflected in the 2015 financial statements for Tindall Company. If the item should be reflected, indicate whether it should be reported in the financial statements themselves or by note disclosure.

(a) As of December 31, 2015, the company holds $12.1 million of its own stock that it purchased in the open market and is holding for possible reissuance.
(b) As of December 31, 2015, the company was in violation of certain loan covenants. The violation does not cause the loans to be callable immediately but does increase the interest charge by 2.0%.
(c) The company's reported Provision for Income Taxes includes $4.2 million in current taxes and $7.8 million in deferred taxes.
(d) As of December 31, 2015, accounts receivable in the amount of $7.1 million are estimated to be uncollectible.

(e) The Environmental Protection Agency is investigating the company's procedures for disposing of toxic waste. Outside consultants have estimated that the company may be liable for fines of up to $10 million.
(f) During 2015, the company had a gain on the sale of manufacturing assets.
(g) During 2015, a long-term insurance agreement was signed. The company paid five years of insurance premiums in advance.
(h) The company uses straight-line depreciation for all tangible, long-term assets.
(i) During 2015, the company hired three prominent research chemists away from its chief competitor.
(j) Reported long-term debt is composed of senior subordinated bonds payable, convertible bonds payable, junior subordinated bonds payable, and capital lease obligations.
(k) Early in 2016, a significant drop in raw material prices caused the company's stock price to rise in anticipation of sharply increased profits for the year.

Exercise 3-36

Preparation of Notes to Financial Statements
The following information was used to prepare the financial statements for Delta Chemical Company. Prepare the necessary notes to accompany the statements.

Delta uses the LIFO inventory method on its financial statements. If the FIFO method were used, the ending inventory balance would be reduced by $50,000 and net income for the year would be reduced by $35,000 after taxes. Delta depreciates its equipment using the straight-line method. Revenue is generally recognized when inventory is shipped unless it is sold on a consignment basis. The current value of the equipment is $525,000, as contrasted to its depreciated cost of $375,000.

Delta has borrowed $350,000 on a 10-year note at 14% interest. The note is due on July 1, 2022. Delta's equipment has been pledged as collateral for the loan. The terms of the note prohibit additional long-term borrowing without the express permission of the holder of the note. Delta is planning to request such permission during the next fiscal year.

The board of directors of Delta is currently discussing a merger with another chemical company. No public announcement has yet been made, but it is anticipated that additional shares of stock will be issued as part of the merger. Delta's balance sheet will report receivables of $126,000. Included in this figure is a $25,000 advance to the president of Delta, $30,000 of notes receivable from customers, $10,000 in advances to sales representatives, and $70,000 of accounts receivable from customers. The reported balance reflects a deduction for anticipated collection losses.

Exercise 3-37

Book-to-Market Ratio
The following information relates to two companies, designated Company A and Company B. One of the companies is a traditional steel manufacturer. The other is a successful Internet retailer. Using the following information, identify which is which, and explain your answer.

	Reported Stockholders' Equity	Total Market Value of Equity
Company A	$15,000	$82,000
Company B	15,000	11,000

P1
Foundations of Financial Accounting

CHAPTER 4

The Income Statement

Learning Objectives

1. Define the concept of income.
2. Explain why an income measure is important.
3. Explain how income is measured, including the revenue recognition and expense-matching concepts.
4. Understand the format of an income statement.
5. Describe the specific components of an income statement.
6. Compute and present comprehensive income.
7. Construct simple forecasts of income for future periods.

Eliza Grace Symonds was an accomplished pianist, a feat additionally notable because she was deaf. Eliza met and married Melville Bell, who was the son of a famous elocutionist, Alexander Graham Bell. Melville's career followed that of his father. Eliza and Melville had three sons; the second son was named Alexander Graham Bell after his paternal grandfather. Young Alexander Graham Bell demonstrated an early interest in speech. In 1871, at the age of 24, Bell began teaching deaf children to speak at the Boston School for Deaf Mutes. Bell's approach was somewhat unorthodox because, at the time, it was common practice to teach deaf mutes only to sign or to simply institutionalize them. Mabel Hubbard, who would become Bell's wife, was one of his students.

Bell's interest in speech caused him to try to develop what he called the "harmonic telegraph." Samuel Morse completed his first telegraph line in 1843, allowing communication using Morse code between two points, and Bell was interested in transmitting speech in a similar way.

At an electrical machine shop, Bell met Thomas Watson. At the time, Watson was a repair mechanic and model maker who was regularly assigned to work with inventors. As Watson learned more of Bell's "harmonic telegraph," the two formed a partnership. In 1876, Bell, while working on their invention, spilled some battery acid and uttered those now-famous words, "Mr. Watson, come here. I want you!" On March 7, 1876, Bell was issued patent

> **FYI**
>
> Long after inventing the telephone, Bell continued his work with the deaf. In gratitude for his work, Helen Keller dedicated her autobiography to him.

number 174,465, covering "the method of, and apparatus for, transmitting vocal or other sounds telegraphically . . . by causing electrical undulations, similar in form to the vibrations of the air accompanying the said vocal or other sounds."

The **Bell Telephone Company** immediately presented immense competition to the **Western Union Telegraph Company**, which was developing its own telephone technology. Western Union hired Thomas Edison to develop a competing system, forcing the Bell Telephone Company to sue Western Union for patent infringement—and win. The Bell Telephone Company would be forced in subsequent years to defend its patent in more than 600 cases.

Alexander Graham Bell had little interest in the day-to-day operations of his company. Instead, he preferred studying science and nature. In 1888, he founded the National Geographic Society. Upon his death, on August 2, 1922, in a tribute to their inventor, all the phones in the nation were silent for one minute.

The Bell Telephone Company was to become the **American Telephone and Telegraph Company (AT&T)** in 1899. AT&T first transmitted the human voice across the Atlantic Ocean in 1915, and in 1927, AT&T introduced commercial transatlantic phone service at a cost of $75 for five minutes. Numerous AT&T inventions followed, including the transistor (1947), the first microwave relay system (1950), the laser (1958), and the first communications satellite (1962).

AT&T functioned as a regulated monopoly until January 1, 1984, when after an eight-year legal battle with the U.S. federal government, AT&T agreed to get out of the local telephone service business by divesting itself of its regional Bell operating companies. On that day, AT&T shrank from 1,009,000 employees to 373,000. In an interesting twist, one of the original seven regional Bell companies, **Southwestern Bell**, changed its name to **SBC Communications** and eventually bought three of the other regional companies and finally bought the original parent, AT&T, as well. The combination of these companies now uses the "AT&T" name. Exhibit 4-1 outlines the fate of the other regional Bells.

In recent years, all of this merger activity at AT&T has resulted in steady profits. For example, AT&T's 2011 financial statements reported the following income numbers (in millions):

	2011	2010	2009
Revenue	$126,723	$124,280	$122,513
Operating income	9,218	19,573	21,000
Income from continuing operations	4,184	19,400	12,427
Net income	3,944	19,864	12,138
Comprehensive income	4,412	19,898	15,234

In your parents' young adult years, they knew only one phone company—AT&T, or "Ma Bell," as it was sometimes called back then. These days, you have a confusing array of phone services, including AT&T, to choose from. And by the time your children enter college, AT&T might be just a historical curiosity.

Exhibit 4-1 | Fate of the Pieces from the 1984 AT&T Breakup

1984 Breakup	Where Are They in 2012?
	Companies comprising "AT&T" in 2012:
original AT&T	Purchased by SBC Communications in 2005
Ameritech	Purchased by SBC Communications in 1999
Bell South	Purchased by new AT&T in 2006
Pacific Telesis	Purchased by SBC Communications in 1997
Southwestern Bell	Renamed SBC Communications
	Companies included in Verizon in 2012:
Nynex	Purchased by Bell Atlantic in 1997
Bell Atlantic	Merged with GTE to form Verizon in 2000
	Company included in CenturyLink in 2012:
U S West	Purchased by Qwest in 2000, which was merged with CenturyLink in 2011

© Cengage Learning 2014

1. By what percentage did AT&T's revenue increase from 2009 to 2011?
2. By what percentage did AT&T's net income increase from 2009 to 2011?
3. AT&T's comprehensive income was down substantially in 2011. What factors can cause a decrease in comprehensive income?

Answers to these questions can be found on page 4-38.

In this chapter, we focus on one of the primary financial statements, the income statement. By analyzing the various components of the income statement, you will understand how the performance of a business is reported to financial statement users and how reported performance can change over time as a company changes the nature of its operations. In addition, we will discuss the format of the income statement, its more common components, and ways in which income statements from around the world differ as to the information they contain and the presentation of that information.

Income: What It Is and What It Isn't

LO1 学习目标1
理解利润的概念。

 Define the concept of income.

Individuals often confuse income with cash flows. Is income equal to the amount of cash generated from the successful operations of a business? No. For a variety of reasons, most of them related to accrual accounting, income and cash flows from operations are seldom the same number. Because both income and cash flows provide measures of a firm's performance, which provides the best measure? The FASB, in its conceptual framework, stated that "information about earnings and its components measured by accrual accounting generally provides a better indication of enterprise performance than information about current cash receipts and payments."[1] Information regarding cash flows is important. In fact, Chapter 5 focuses entirely on the statement of cash flows. Research supports the FASB's assertion, however, that the best indicator of a firm's performance is income.[2] So, an understanding of income, what it measures, and its components is essential in understanding and interpreting a firm's financial situation.

So, what is income? All of the varying ways to measure income share a common basic concept: Income is a return over and above the investment. One of the more widely accepted definitions of income states that it is the amount that an entity could return to its investors and still leave the entity as well-off at the end of the period as it was at the beginning.[3] What does it mean, however, to be "as well-off," and how can this be measured?

[1] *Statement of Financial Accounting Concepts No. 1*, "Objectives of Financial Reporting by Business Enterprises" (Stamford, CT: Financial Accounting Standards Board, 1984), par. 44.
[2] For example, see Gary C. Biddle, Robert M. Bowen, and James S. Wallace, "Does EVA® Beat Earnings? Evidence on Associations with Stock Returns and Firm Values," *Journal of Accounting and Economics*, December 1997, p. 301.
[3] Although many economists and accountants have adopted this view, a basic reference is J. R. Hicks' widely accepted book, *Value and Capital*, 2nd ed. (Oxford University Press, 1946).

Most measurements are based on some concept of capital or ownership maintenance. The FASB considered two concepts of capital maintenance in its conceptual framework: financial capital maintenance and physical capital maintenance.

Financial Capital Maintenance Concept of Income Determination

财务资本保全概念假设企业"在排除与所有者交易的影响后，只有期末净资产（资产−负债，或者所有者权益）的货币价值超过期初净资产的货币价值"时才有利润。

The financial capital maintenance concept assumes that a company has income "only if the dollar amount of an enterprise's net assets (assets − liabilities or, in other words, owners' equity) at the end of a period exceeds the dollar amount of net assets at the beginning of the period after excluding the effects of transactions with owners."[4] To illustrate, assume that Kreidler, Inc., had the following assets and liabilities at the beginning and at the end of a period.

	Beginning of Period	End of Period
Total assets	$510,000	$560,000
Total liabilities	430,000	390,000
Net assets (owners' equity)	$ 80,000	$170,000

If there were no investments by owners or distributions to owners during the period, income would be $90,000, the amount of the increase in net assets. Assume, however, that owners invested $40,000 in the business and received distributions (dividends) of $15,000. Income for the period would be $65,000, computed as follows:

Net assets, end of period	$170,000
Net assets, beginning of period	80,000
Change (increase) in net assets	$ 90,000
Deduct investment by owners	(40,000)
Add distributions (dividends) to owners	15,000
Income	$ 65,000

Physical Capital Maintenance Concept of Income Determination

实物资本保全是指在剔除与所有者交易的影响外，企业在一定时期最后阶段的实物生产能力应该超过这个时期开始阶段的实物生产能力。

Another way of defining capital maintenance is in terms of physical capital maintenance. Under this concept, income occurs "only if the physical productive capacity of the enterprise at the end of a period . . . exceeds the physical productive capacity at the beginning of the same period, also after excluding the effects of transactions with owners."[5] This concept requires that productive assets (inventories, buildings, and equipment) be valued at fair market values. Productive capital is maintained only if the current costs of these capital assets are maintained. Consider the beginning net asset value of $80,000 in the previous example. Now assume that, because of rising prices of buildings, inventory, equipment, and so forth, in order to maintain the same productive capacity the company would have had

---

[4] *Statement of Financial Accounting Concepts No. 5*, "Recognition and Measurement in Financial Statements of Business Enterprises" (Stamford, CT: Financial Accounting Standards Board, 1984), par. 47.
[5] Ibid.

> **Stop & Think**
>
> It would seem that the physical capital maintenance concept would provide the best theoretical measure of "well-offness." However, use of the physical capital maintenance concept of measuring income involves many practical difficulties. Identify ONE of those practical difficulties from the list below.
>
> a) Difficulty in estimating depreciation lives
> b) Difficulty in implementing internal control procedures
> c) Difficulty in providing cash flow information
> d) Difficulty in obtaining fair market values of assets and liabilities

to have $100,000 in net asset value by the end of the year. If the ending net asset value were $170,000, as before, and new investments and dividends were as shown, income would be $45,000 rather than $65,000. The $20,000 difference would be the amount necessary to "maintain physical productive capacity" and would not be part of income.

The FASB considered carefully these two ways of viewing income, and it adopted the financial capital maintenance concept as part of its conceptual framework. The acceptance of the financial capital maintenance concept rescued accountants from the difficult task of trying to measure productive capacity. Measuring income using the concept of financial capital maintenance, however, still leaves the question of how to value the net asset balance. Many suggest that net assets should be measured at their unexpired historical cost values as is often done. Others believe that replacement values or disposal values should be used. Some would include as assets intangible resources, such as human resources, goodwill, and geographic location, that have been attained over time without specifically identified payments. Others believe that only resources that have been acquired in arm's-length exchange activities should be included.

Likewise, controversy has developed over the recognition and measurement of liabilities. Should future claims against the entity for items such as pensions, warranties, and deferred income taxes be valued at their discounted values, valued at their future cash flow values, or eliminated completely from the financial statements until events clearly define the existence of a specific liability? The reported income under the financial maintenance concept varies widely depending on when and how the assets, liabilities, and changes in the valuation of assets and liabilities are measured. As it stands currently, a combination of historical costs, fair values, present values, and other valuation measures is used to measure a firm's "well-offness."

Why Is a Measure of Income Important?

② Explain why an income measure is important.

LO2 学习目标2
解释利润计量的重要性。

The recognition, measurement, and reporting (display) of business income and its components are considered by many to be the most important tasks of accountants. The users of financial statements who must make decisions regarding their relationship with the company are almost always concerned with a measure of its success in using the resources committed to its operation. Has the activity been profitable? What is the trend of profitability? Is it increasingly profitable, or is there a downward trend? What is the most probable result for future years? Will the company be profitable enough to pay interest on its debt and dividends to its stockholders and still grow at a desired rate? These and other questions all relate to the basic question: What is income?

利润的构成信息是非常重要的，并且能够被用于帮助预测未来的利润和现金流量。这不仅是因为这项信息对某一特定的使用者有用，还因为它对整体经济有价值。

Information about the components of income is important and can be used to help predict future income and cash flows. Not only can this information be helpful to a specific user, but it is also of value to the economy. As discussed in Chapter 1, many groups utilize accounting information, and accountants play a key role in providing information that will assist in allocating scarce resources to the most efficient and effective organizations or groups.

In the United States, the FASB has specified that financial accounting information is designed with investors and creditors in mind, while at the same time recognizing that many other groups will find the resulting information useful as well. Of course, accrual-based financial accounting information is not suited for every possible use. For example, governments, both federal and state, rely heavily on income taxes as a source of their revenues. The income figure used for assessing taxes is based on laws passed by Congress and regulations applied by the IRS and various courts. The income determined for financial reporting, however, is determined by adherence to accounting standards (GAAP) developed by the accounting profession. Thus, the amount of income reported to creditors and investors may not be the same as the income reported for tax purposes. Many items are the same for both types of reporting, but there are some significant differences. Most of these differences relate to the specific purposes Congress has for taxing income. Governments use an income figure as a base to assess taxes, but they must use one that relates closely with the ability of the taxpayer to pay the computed tax. For example, accrual accounting requires companies to defer recognition of revenues that are received before they are earned. Income tax regulations, however, often require these unearned revenues to be reported as income as soon as they are received in cash.

As mentioned in previous chapters, the increasing globalization of business is providing the impetus for a movement toward a unified body of International Accounting Standards. However, because financial accounting information plays different roles in different countries, it is probably not reasonable to assume that one set of standards can fit the business, legal, and cultural settings of every country in the world. For example, countries can be separated, broadly speaking, into two groups: code law countries and common law countries.[6] In code law countries, such as Germany and Japan, accounting standards have historically been set by legal processes. In such an environment, financial accounting numbers serve a variety of functions, including the determination of the amount of income tax and cash dividends to be paid. In common law countries, such as the United States and the United Kingdom, accounting standards are set in response to market forces. In a common law setting, financial accounting numbers are used more for informational purposes, not for deciding how the economic pie gets split among taxes, dividends, wages, and so forth. Given the significantly different roles played by financial accounting numbers in code law and common law countries, it may be unreasonable to expect one set of standards to work worldwide.

Accounting standards also play a different role in developing economies as compared to developed economies. In China, for example, the rudimentary state of the auditing and legal infrastructure makes the application of judgment-based accounting standards extremely problematic.[7] In a developing economy, it may be more important for financial reporting to satisfactorily fulfill its essential bookkeeping function rather than attempt to provide sophisticated investment information relevant for only a small set of companies trying to attract foreign investment. The fundamental question is this: How are accounting standards designed for use by international financial analysts going to help a domestic Chinese company with no plans to seek foreign investment and with a desire only to improve the monitoring of managers and the allocation of resources?

---

[6] Ray Ball, S. P. Kothari, and Ashok Robin, "The Effect of International Institutional Factors on Properties of Accounting Earnings," *Journal of Accounting and Economics*, February 2000, p. 1.

[7] Bing Xiang, "Institutional Factors Influencing China's Accounting Reforms and Standards," *Accounting Horizons*, June 1998, p. 105.

This text focuses on principles of accounting that are the supporting foundation for financial accounting and reporting as practiced in the United States. Income for tax purposes will be discussed, but only as it is used to determine the income tax expense and other tax-related amounts reported in the financial statements. Differences between U.S. and foreign accounting practices will be discussed where appropriate throughout the text.

How Is Income Measured?

LO3 学习目标3
解释利润是如何计量的，包括收入确认和费用配比的概念。

③ Explain how income is measured, including the revenue recognition and expense-matching concepts.

transaction approach
配比法

Comparing the net assets at two points in time, as was done previously in introducing the concept of financial capital maintenance, yields a single net income figure. However, this procedure discloses no detail concerning the components of income. To provide this detail, accountants have adopted a transaction approach to measuring income that stresses the direct computation of revenues and expenses. As long as the same measurement method is used, income will be the same under the transaction approach as with a single income computation.

The transaction approach, sometimes referred to as the *matching method*, focuses on business events that affect certain elements of financial statements, namely, revenues, expenses, gains, and losses. Income is measured as the difference between resource inflows (revenues and gains) and outflows (expenses and losses) over a period of time. Definitions for the four income elements are presented in Exhibit 4-2 as an aid to the following discussion.

As studying these definitions will indicate, by defining gains and losses in terms of changes in equity after providing for revenues, expenses, investments, and distributions to the owners, income determined by the transaction approach will be the same income as that determined under financial capital maintenance. However, by identifying intermediate income components, the transaction approach provides detail to assist in predicting future cash flows.

Exhibit 4-2 | Component Elements of Income

- Revenues are inflows or other enhancements of assets of an entity or settlements of its liabilities (or a combination of both) from delivering or producing goods, rendering services, or carrying out other activities that constitute the entity's ongoing major or central operations.

- Expenses are outflows or other "using up" of assets of an entity or incurrences of liabilities (or a combination of both) from delivering or producing goods, rendering services, or carrying out other activities that constitute the entity's ongoing major or central operations.

- Gains are increases in equity (net assets) from peripheral or incidental transactions of an entity and from all other transactions and other events and circumstances affecting the entity except those that result from revenues or investments by owners.

- Losses are decreases in equity (net assets) from peripheral or incidental transactions of an entity and from all other transactions and other events and circumstances affecting the entity except those that result from expenses or distributions to owners.

Material from FASB Concepts Statement No. 6, Elements of Financial Statements, is copyrighted by the Financial Accounting Foundation (FAF), 401 Merritt 7, PO Box 5116, Norwalk, CT 06856-5116, USA, and is reproduced with permission. A complete copy of the document is available from the FAF.

使用配比法确认和计量利润的关键是确定什么时候一项"资产的流入或增加"发生了，以及如何计量相应的"资产流出和其他耗用"。第一个是收入确认的问题，第二个是费用确认或费用配比的问题。

The key problem in recognizing and measuring income using the transaction approach is deciding when an "inflow or other enhancements of assets" has occurred and how to measure the "outflows or other 'using up' of assets." The first issue is identified as the revenue recognition problem, and the second issue is identified as the expense recognition, or expense-matching, problem.

Revenue and Gain Recognition

The transaction approach requires a clear definition of when income elements should be recognized, or recorded, in the financial statements. Under the GAAP of accrual accounting, revenue recognition does not necessarily occur when cash is received. The FASB's conceptual framework identifies two factors that should be considered in deciding when revenues and gains should be recognized: realization and the earnings process. Revenues and gains are generally recognized when:
1. they are realized or realizable, and
2. they have been earned through substantial completion of the activities involved in the earnings process.[8]

Stop & Think

Take a close look at Exhibit 4-2. Why is it important to disclose separately revenues and gains?

a) To distinguish between the profits generated by a company's core business and the profits generated by secondary, or peripheral, activities
b) To distinguish between profits generated through selling goods and profits generated through selling services
c) To distinguish between profits generated through business activities and profits generated through investments by owners
d) To distinguish between profits generated through the enhancement of assets and profits generated through the settlement of liabilities

Put in simple terms, revenues are recognized when the company generating the revenue has provided the bulk of the goods or services it promised (substantial completion) for the customer and when the customer has provided payment or at least a valid promise of payment (realizable) to the company. That is, the company has lived up to its end of an agreement, and the customer has the intention of paying.

In order for revenues and gains to be realized, inventory or other assets must be exchanged for cash or claims to cash, such as accounts receivable. Revenues are realizable when assets held or assets received in an exchange are readily convertible to known amounts of cash or claims to cash. The earnings process criterion relates primarily to revenue recognition. Most gains result from transactions and events, such as the sale of land or a patent, that involve no earnings process. Thus, being realized, or realizable, is of more importance in recognizing gains.

Application of these two criteria to certain industries and companies within these industries has resulted in recognition of revenue at different points in the revenue-producing cycle. This cycle can be a lengthy one. For a manufacturing company, it begins with the development of proposals for a certain product by an individual or by the research and development department and extends through planning, production, sale, collection, and finally expiration of the warranty period. Consider, for example, the revenue-producing cycle for **Ford Motor Company**. Engineers develop plans and create models and prototypes. Actual production of vehicles then occurs, followed by delivery to dealers for sale to customers. All

Construction contracts are an example of revenue that is recognized as services are performed.

---

[8] *Statement of Financial Accounting Concepts No. 5*, par. 83. The FASB and IASB are currently working on a refinement of the definition of "revenue recognition." This important topic is discussed at length in Chapter 8.

> **FYI**
>
> Most firms specify their revenue recognition policies in the notes to the financial statements. For example, the notes to **Disney**'s financial statements disclose the corporation's revenue recognition policies for movie tickets, video sales, movie licensing, TV advertising, Internet advertising, merchandise licensing, and theme park sales.

new vehicles are warranted against defect, in some cases for several years. All of these steps, which can take more than 10 years, are involved in generating sales revenue. If a failure occurs at any step, revenue may be seriously curtailed or even completely eliminated, yet there is only one aggregate revenue amount for the entire cycle, the selling price of the product.

For a service company, the revenue-producing cycle begins with an agreement to provide a service and extends through the planning and performance of the service to the collection of the cash and final proof through the passage of time that the service has been adequately performed. As an example, consider the revenue-producing cycle of **PricewaterhouseCoopers (PwC)**, one of the large accounting firms. For a typical audit, much of the planning and preparation occurs before the actual on-site visit. The on-site visit is then followed by an accumulation of data and the preparation of an audit report. And with increasing legal actions being taken against professionals, such as doctors and accountants, one could argue that the revenue-producing cycle does not end until the possibility of legal claims for services performed is remote, a period that extends until years after the actual service is provided.

Although some accountants have argued for recognizing revenue on a partial basis over these extended production or service periods, the prevailing practice has been to select one point in the cycle that best meets the revenue recognition criteria. Both of these criteria are generally met at the point of sale, which is generally when goods are delivered or services are rendered to customers and payment or a promise of payment is received. Thus, revenue for automobiles sold to dealers by Ford Motor Company will be recognized when the cars are shipped to the dealers. Similarly, PwC will record its revenue from audit and tax work when the services have been performed and billed. In both examples, the earnings process is deemed to be substantially complete, and the cash or receivable from the customer meets the realization criterion. Although the "point-of-sale" practice is the most common revenue recognition point, there are notable variations to this general rule.[9] The following discussion is merely an introduction to the subtleties associated with revenue recognition. A more complete treatment is given in Chapter 8.

Earlier Recognition

1. If a market exists for a product so that its sale at an established price is practically ensured without significant selling effort, revenues may be recognized at the point of completed

> **Stop & Think**
>
> Why do you think Kinross waits to recognize revenue from the sale of Kubaka gold until the gold is actually sold?
>
> a) Revenue from the sale of a product can never be recognized until after the product is actually sold.
> b) Uncertainty surrounds the ultimate shipment and sale of gold produced in the remote regions of eastern Russia.
> c) Revenue from the sale of a product can never be recognized until after the cash from the sale is actually collected.
> d) GAAP forbids the recognition of any revenue at the time of production.

如果一种产品因存在市场而不需要付出太大的销售努力即可确保在一个给定的价格售出，那么生产完成时就可以确认收入。

[9] Accounting Principles Board, *Statement No. 4*, "Basic Concepts in Accounting Principles Underlying Financial Statements of Business Enterprises," October 1970, par. 152. In 1999, the SEC released *SAB No. 101*, which gives specific guidance about when to recognize revenue. *SAB 101* is discussed in Chapter 8. In 2002, the FASB began a "Revenue Recognition" project in which the earnings and realization criteria would be replaced with an emphasis on the creation and extinguishment of performance obligations. As of June 2010, a final revised revenue recognition standard was expected to be released in 2011.

production. Examples of this situation may occur with certain precious metals and agricultural products that are sold in liquid and reliable markets at easily determinable prices.[10] In these situations, revenue is recognized when the mining or production of the goods is complete because the earnings process is considered to be substantially complete and the existence of a virtually guaranteed purchaser provides evidence of realizability. An example of this method of revenue recognition is provided by a Canadian mining company, **Kinross Gold Corporation**; the appropriate note from Kinross's financial statements is reproduced in Exhibit 4-3. According to the note, Kinross recognizes revenue prior to the point of sale with the expected sales price to be received being recorded in a current asset account, Bullion Settlements. Note that Kinross accounts for Kubaka bullion differently from its other ores; revenue recognition for Kubaka bullion occurs when it is sold. The Kubaka gold is produced in eastern Russia. For international purposes under *IAS 41*, gains and losses from increases and decreases in the fair value of biological assets (such as cows) and agricultural produce (such as harvested wheat) are recognized when they occur, without waiting until the items are subsequently sold. Similar treatment is allowed, but not required, under U.S. GAAP (see FASB ASC Section 905-330-35 Agriculture—Inventory—Subsequent Measurement).

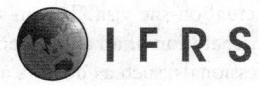

如果一项产品或服务已经提前签订了合同，则可能在进行生产或者提供服务时确认收入，特别是生产或者服务的周期超过了一个会计年度。由此产生了两种确认收入的会计方法，即完工百分比法和完工比例法。

2. If a product or service is contracted for in advance, revenue may be recognized as production takes place or as services are performed, especially if the production or performance period extends over more than one fiscal year. The percentage-of-completion and proportional performance methods of accounting have been developed to recognize revenue at several points in the production or service cycle rather than waiting until the final delivery or performance takes place. This exception to the general point-of-sale rule is necessary if the qualitative characteristics of relevance and representational faithfulness are to be met. Construction contracts for buildings, roads, and dams, and contracts for scientific research are examples of situations in which these methods of revenue recognition occur. In all cases when this revenue recognition variation is employed, a firm, enforceable contract must exist to meet the realizability criterion, and an objective measure of progress toward completion must be attainable to measure the degree of completeness. As an example of this type of revenue recognition, **The Boeing Company** indicates in its notes (see Exhibit 4-4) that a portion of its revenues are recognized prior to the point of sale.

Exhibit 4-3 | Kinross Gold Corporation Revenue Recognition Note Disclosure

Gold and silver poured, in transit and at refineries, are recorded at net realizable value and included in bullion settlements and other accounts receivable, with the exception of Kubaka bullion. The estimated net realizable value of Kubaka bullion is included in inventory until it is sold.

© Cengage Learning 2014

---

[10] Companies in these industries may recognize revenue prior to the point of sale, but a survey of revenue recognition policies for companies in these industries reveals that the vast majority recognize revenue at the point of sale. For example, Kinross Gold, which is used as an illustration, changed its accounting policy for revenue recognition effective January 1, 2001, so that revenue is now recognized upon shipment and passage of title to the customer. SEC rules adopted in 1999 frown on the recognition of revenue before delivery to a customer has taken place. See Chapter 8 for more details.

Exhibit 4-4 | The Boeing Company Note on Revenue Recognition

> Sales related to fixed-price contracts are recognized as deliveries are made except for certain fixed-price contracts that require substantial performance over an extended period before deliveries begin, for which sales are recorded based on attainment of performance milestones.

© Cengage Learning 2014

Later Recognition

3. If collectibility of assets received for products or services is considered doubtful, revenues and gains may be recognized as the cash is received. The installment sales and cost recovery methods of accounting have been developed to recognize revenue under these conditions. Sales of real estate, especially speculative recreational property, are often recorded using this variation of the general rule. In these cases, although the earnings process has been substantially completed, the questionable receivable fails to meet the realization criterion. For example, **Rent-A-Center** operates rent-to-own stores where consumers can obtain furniture, televisions, and other consumer goods on a rent-to-own basis. A big concern for Rent-A-Center is collecting the full amount of cash due under a rental contract. In fact, Rent-A-Center states that only 25% of its customers complete the full term of their agreement. With such a high likelihood of customers stopping payments on their rental agreements, Rent-A-Center recognizes revenue from a specific contract only gradually as the cash is actually collected. The general point-of-sale rule will be assumed for examples in this text unless specifically stated otherwise. Variations on this rule are discussed fully in Chapter 8.

Expense and Loss Recognition

In order to determine income, not only must criteria for revenue recognition be established, but also the principles for recognizing expenses and losses must be clearly defined. Some expenses are directly associated with revenues and can thus be recognized in the same period as the related revenues. Other expenditures are not recognized currently as expenses because they relate to future revenues and therefore are reported as assets. Still other expenses are not associated with specific revenues and are recognized in the time period when paid or incurred. Expense recognition, then, is divided into three cat- egories: (1) direct matching, (2) systematic and rational allocation, and (3) immediate recognition.

Direct Matching Relating expenses to specific revenues is often referred to as the matching process. For example, the cost of goods sold is clearly a direct expense that can be "matched" with the revenues produced by the sale of goods and reported in the same time period as the revenues are recognized. Similarly, shipping costs and sales commissions usually relate directly to revenues.[11]

Direct expenses include not only those that have already been incurred but also include anticipated expenses related to revenues of the current period. After delivery of goods to customers, there are still costs of collection, bad debt losses from uncollectible receivables, and possible warranty costs for product deficiencies. These expenses are directly related to revenues and should be estimated and matched against recognized revenues for the period.

Systematic and Rational Allocation The second general expense recognition category involves assets that benefit more than one accounting period. The cost of assets such as buildings, equipment, patents, and prepaid insurance are spread across the periods of expected benefit in some systematic and rational way. Generally, it is difficult, if not impossible, to relate these expenses directly to specific revenues or to specific periods, but it is clear that they are necessary if the revenue is to be earned. Examples of expenses that are included in this category are depreciation and amortization.

Immediate Recognition Many expenses are not related to specific revenues but are incurred to obtain goods and services that indirectly help to generate revenues. Because these goods and services are used almost immediately, their costs are recognized as expenses in the period of acquisition. Examples include most administrative costs, such as office salaries, utilities, and general advertising and selling expenses.

Immediate recognition is also appropriate when future benefits are highly uncertain. For example, expenditures for research and development may provide significant future benefits, but these benefits are usually so uncertain that the costs are written off in the period in which they are incurred.

Most losses also fit in the immediate recognition category. Because they arise from peripheral or incidental transactions, they do not relate directly to revenues. Examples include losses from disposition of used equipment, losses from natural catastrophes such as earthquakes or tornadoes, and losses from disposition of investments.

Gains and Losses from Changes in Market Values

An exception to the transaction approach in the recognition of gains and losses arises when gains or losses are recognized in the wake of changes in market values. For example, some investment securities, called trading securities (as explained fully in Chapter 14), are purchased by a company with the express intent of making money on short-term price fluctuations. Accordingly, even in the absence of a transaction to sell the trading securities, a gain (if the price of the securities has increased) or a loss (if the price of the securities has decreased) is recognized. Similarly, when a long-term asset such as a building has decreased substantially in value, a loss is recognized even though the building has not been sold and no transaction has occurred. (These impairment losses are explained in Chapter 11.)

The transaction approach is deeply ingrained in accounting practice. A primary attraction of the transaction approach is its reliability—increases and decreases in asset values can be verified by observing the transaction prices. However, as with the case of the trading securities mentioned in the preceding paragraph, many important economic factors

---

[11] *Statement of Financial Accounting Concepts No. 6*, "Elements of Financial Statements" (Stamford, CT: Financial Accounting Standards Board, December 1985), par. 144.

influence a company even in the absence of explicit transactions. Because of the information relevance of these changes in market values, more and more of these market value gains and losses are being recognized as part of income. As described more fully in Chapter 8, the FASB is currently working on a "revenue recognition" project that may go even further in stepping away from the transaction approach to instead embrace a focus on changes in values of assets and liabilities.

Form of the Income Statement

 Understand the format of an income statement.

All income statements prepared in accordance with GAAP report the same basic type of information and have certain common display features. Some sections of the income statement, especially irregular and extraordinary items, are specified by FASB pronouncements. Others have become standardized by wide usage.

Traditionally, the income from continuing operations category has been presented in multiple-step form. With the multiple-step form, the income statement is divided into separate sections (referred to as "intermediate components" in FASB *Concepts Statement No. 5*), and various subtotals are reported that reflect different levels of profitability. The income statement of IBM, shown in Exhibit 4-5, illustrates a multiple-step income statement. With the multiple-step form, the costs are partitioned so that intermediate components of income are presented. For example, IBM discloses gross profit, income before taxes, and net income in its income statements.

For discussion purposes, we will use the multiple-step income statement for Techtronics Corporation shown in Exhibit 4-6. This hypothetical income statement contains more categories and more detail than is usually found in actual published financial statements. It has become common practice to issue highly condensed statements, with details and supporting schedules provided in notes to the statements. The potential problem with this practice is that the condensed statements may not provide as much predictive and feedback value as statements that provide more detail about the components of income directly on the statement.

The Techtronics income statement differs from most published statements in other ways. For example, to simplify the illustration of the various income components, only one year is presented for Techtronics. To comply with SEC requirements, income statements of public companies are presented in comparative form for three years (see Exhibit 4-5). Comparative financial statements enable users to analyze performance over multiple periods and identify significant trends that might impact future performance. Also note that the Techtronics income statement is for a single business entity, but public companies often present consolidated financial statements that combine the financial results of a "parent company," such as IBM, with other companies that it owns, called *subsidiaries*.

All actual company statements illustrated in this chapter are consolidated statements.[12]

---

[12] Throughout this text, we will use many actual companies to illustrate financial reporting concepts and practices. You will observe many variations in statement titles, terminology, level of detail, and other aspects of reporting. As a result, you will develop an appreciation of the diversity in financial reporting and the ability to understand financial information presented in a wide variety of terms and formats.

Exhibit 4-5 | IBM's Income Statement

($ in millions except per share amounts) For the year ended December 31:	Notes	2011	2010	2009
Revenue				
Services		$ 60,721	$56,868	$55,128
Sales		44,063	40,736	38,300
Financing		2,132	2,267	2,331
Total revenue		106,916	99,870	95,758
Cost				
Services		40,740	38,383	37,146
Sales		14,973	14,374	13,606
Financing		1,065	1,100	1,220
Total cost		56,778	53,857	51,973
Gross profit		50,138	46,014	43,785
Expense and other income				
Selling, general and administrative		23,594	21,837	20,952
Research, development and engineering	O	6,258	6,026	5,820
Intellectual property and custom development income		(1,108)	(1,154)	(1,177)
Other (income) and expense		(20)	(787)	(351)
Interest expense	D&J	411	368	402
Total expense and other income		29,135	26,291	25,647
Income before income taxes		21,003	19,723	18,138
Provision for income taxes	N	5,148	4,890	4,713
Net income		$ 15,855	$14,833	$13,425
Earnings per share of common stock				
Assuming dilution	P	$ 13.06	$ 11.52	$ 10.01
Basic	P	$ 13.25	$ 11.69	$ 10.12
Weighted-average number of common shares outstanding				
Assuming dilution		1,213,767,985	1,287,355,388	1,341,352,754
Basic		1,196,951,006	1,268,789,202	1,327,157,410

Amounts may not add due to rounding.
The accompanying notes on pages 76 through 139 are an integral part of the financial statements.

© Cengage Learning 2014

Components of the Income Statement

  学习目标5

5 Describe the specific components of an income statement.

描述利润表的具体组成要素。

In the following sections, the content of the income statement will be discussed and illustrated using the statement for Techtronics Corporation. Variations in current reporting practices will be examined and illustrated with income statements of actual companies. Finally, the requirement to supplement reported net income with a measure of comprehensive income will be discussed.

Exhibit 4-6 | Techtronics Corporation Income Statement

Techtronics Corporation
Income Statement
For the Year Ended December 31, 2015

Revenue:			
Sales		$800,000	
Less: Sales returns and allowances	$ 12,000		
Sales discounts	8,000	20,000	$780,000
Cost of goods sold:			
Beginning inventory		$125,000	
Net purchases	$630,000		
Freight-in	32,000	662,000	
Cost of goods available for sale		$787,000	
Less ending inventory		296,000	491,000
Gross profit			$289,000
Operating expenses:			
Selling expenses:			
Sales salaries	$ 46,000		
Advertising expense	27,000		
Miscellaneous selling expenses	12,000	$ 85,000	
General and administrative expenses:			
Officers' and office salaries	$ 44,000		
Taxes and insurance	26,500		
Depreciation and amortization expense	30,000		
Bad debt expense	8,600		
Miscellaneous general expense	9,200	118,300	203,300
Operating income			$ 85,700
Other revenues and gains:			
Interest revenue		$ 12,750	
Gain on sale of investment		37,000	49,750
Other expenses and losses:			
Interest expense		$ (18,250)	
Loss on sale of equipment		(5,250)	(23,500)
Income from continuing operations before income taxes			$111,950
Income taxes on continuing operations			33,585
Income from continuing operations			$ 78,365
Discontinued operations:			
Loss from operations of discontinued business component			
(including loss on disposal of $16,000)		$ (51,000)	
Income tax benefit		15,300	(35,700)
Extraordinary gain (net of income taxes of $5,370)			12,530
Net income			$ 55,195
Change in translation adjustment		$ (2,450)	
Increase in unrealized gains on available-for-sale securities		1,180	(1,270)
Comprehensive income			$ 53,925
Earnings per common share:			
Income from continuing operations			$ 1.57
Discontinued operations			(0.71)
Extraordinary gain			0.25
Net income			$ 1.11

Income from Continuing Operations

The Techtronics Corporation income statement has two major categories of income: (1) income from continuing operations and (2) irregular or extraordinary items. Income from continuing operations includes all revenues and expenses and gains and losses arising from the ongoing operations of the firm. In the Techtronics example, income from continuing operations includes six separate sections as follows.

income from continuing operation
持续经营利润
irregular or extraordinary items
非常项目

1. Revenue
2. Cost of goods sold
3. Operating expenses
4. Other revenues and gains
5. Other expenses and losses
6. Income taxes on continuing operations

Also, a review of the Techtronics income statement discloses several subtotals in the income from continuing operations category. These subtotals are identified as follows.

1. Gross profit (Revenue − Cost of goods sold)
2. Operating income (Gross profit − Operating expenses)
3. Income from continuing operations before income taxes (Operating income + Other revenues and gains − Other expenses and losses)
4. Income from continuing operations (Income from continuing operations before income taxes − Income taxes on continuing operations)

Each of these major sections and related subtotals is discussed separately as a way to help you better understand current practices in reporting income from continuing operations. Then, we will examine the irregular and extraordinary components of income.

Revenue Revenue reports the total sales to customers for the period less any sales returns and allowances or discounts. This total should not include additions to billings for sales taxes and excise taxes that the business is required to collect on behalf of the government. These billing increases are properly recognized as current liabilities instead of as revenues because the sales tax and excise tax amounts must be forwarded to the appropriate government agency. Sales returns and allowances and sales discounts should be subtracted from gross sales in arriving at net sales revenue. When the sales price is increased to cover the cost of freight to the customer and the customer is billed accordingly, freight charges paid by the company should also be subtracted from sales in arriving at net sales. Freight charges not passed on to the buyer are recognized as selling expenses.

Cost of Goods Sold In any merchandising or manufacturing enterprise, the cost of goods relating to sales for the period must be determined. As illustrated in the Techtronics Corporation income statement, cost of goods available for sale is determined first. This is the sum of the beginning inventory, net purchases, and all other buying, freight, and storage costs relating to the acquisition of goods. (The net purchases balance is developed by subtracting purchase returns and allowances and purchase discounts from gross purchases, not shown.) Cost of goods sold is then calculated by subtracting the ending inventory from the cost of goods available for sale.

When the goods are manufactured by the seller, additional elements enter into the cost of goods sold. Besides material costs, a company incurs labor and overhead costs to convert the material from its raw material state to a finished good. A manufacturing company has three inventories rather than one: raw materials, goods in process, and finished goods. Techtronics Corporation is a merchandising company. The cost of goods sold for a manufacturing company is illustrated in Chapter 9.

Gross Profit For most merchandising and manufacturing companies, cost of goods sold is the most significant expense on the income statement. Because of its size, firms pay particular attention to changes in cost of goods sold relative to changes in sales. Gross profit is the difference between revenue from net sales and cost of goods sold; gross profit percentage, computed by dividing gross profit by revenue from net sales, provides a measure of profitability that allows comparisons for a firm from year to year. For **General Motors**, gross profit is the difference between the cost to manufacture a car and the price GM charges to dealers who buy cars. In a supermarket, gross profit is the difference between retail selling price and wholesale cost.

Gross profit is an important number. If a company is not generating enough from the sale of a product or service to cover the costs directly associated with that product or service, that company will not be able to stay in that line of business for long. For example, if IBM sells a mainframe computer for $126,000 and the materials, labor, and overhead costs associated with producing that computer are $139,000, the gross profit of negative $13,000 suggests that IBM is in serious difficulty. After all, with a negative gross profit, IBM would not be able to pay for advertising, executive salaries, interest expense, and so forth.

For example, using information from IBM's income statement in Exhibit 4-5, we can compute a gross profit percentage for each type of revenue.

IBM Corporation
Gross Profit Percentage

	2011	2010	2009
Services	32.9%	32.5%	32.6%
Sales	66.0%	64.7%	64.5%
Financing	50.0%	51.5%	47.7%
Total	46.9%	46.1%	45.7%

This analysis reveals that IBM's overall gross profit percentage has increased over the three-year period from 2009 to 2011. This increase can be attributed to increases in the gross profit percentage in each of the three reported categories.

Operating Expenses Operating expenses may be reported in two parts: (1) selling expenses and (2) general and administrative expenses. Selling expenses include items such as sales salaries and commissions and related payroll taxes, advertising and store displays, store supplies used, depreciation of store furniture and equipment, and delivery expenses. General and administrative expenses include officers' and office salaries and related payroll taxes, office supplies used, depreciation of office furniture and fixtures, telephone, postage, business licenses and fees, legal and accounting services, contributions, and similar items. For manufacturers, charges related jointly to production and administrative functions should be allocated in an equitable manner between manufacturing overhead and operating expenses.

Operating Income Operating income measures the performance of the fundamental business operations conducted by a company and is computed as gross profit minus operating expenses. A general rule of thumb is that all expenses are operating expenses except interest expense and income tax expense. Accordingly, another name for operating income is *earnings before interest and taxes (EBIT)*.

Operating income tells users how well a business is performing in the activities unique to that business, separate from the financing and income tax management policies that are handled at the corporate headquarters level. For example, operating income allows you to evaluate Wal-Mart's overall ability to choose store locations, establish pricing strategies, train and retain workers, and manage relations with its suppliers. Operating income does not tell you anything about the interest cost of Wal-Mart's loans or how successful Wal-Mart's tax planners have been at structuring and locating operations to minimize income taxes.

FASB CODIFICATION

The Issue: You have recently started working for an engineering company. The company is in the process of developing optical switches that will make computer memory storage and data transmission 200 times faster than current technology allows. The optical switches are still in the development stage, and the company has not yet shipped any products or recognized any revenue.

The CEO of the company is preparing to make a presentation to a group of venture capitalists. As part of the presentation, the CEO wants to provide the venture capitalists with a complete set of audited financial statements (balance sheet, income statement, and statement of cash flows). The CEO has heard that for a development stage company, the accounting rules are different. For example, items that would be recorded as expenses for a normal operating company can instead be viewed as investments in the future and recorded as assets by a development stage company. With this approach, the income statement of the engineering company won't look too bad even though the company has not yet had any revenue.

The CEO has asked you to confirm her general understanding of the accounting rules for development stage companies.

The Question: For development stage companies, can some expenses be reported not as expenses but instead as assets?

Searching the Codification: There are two different ways to get started on this one. First, you can go to the "Industry" set of topics and find Topic 915 (Development Stage Entities). Alternatively, you can go to the "Presentation" set of topics and find Topic 205 (Presentation of Financial Statements). Either way you start, you will end up at Subtopic 915-205 (Development Stage Entities—Presentation of Financial Statements). In the glossary for this subtopic, you can see that a "Development Stage Entity" is one for which either no operations have commenced or, if operations have commenced, no significant revenue has been generated. This certainly describes the optical switch company for which you work. Now it is time to find the answer to the question: *Hint:* You will find the most useful information in Section 45 (Other Presentation Matters).

The Answer: The accounting for expenses in development stage companies is discussed on page 4-39.

Other Revenues and Gains This section usually includes items identified with the peripheral activities of the company. Examples include revenue from financial activities, such as rents, interest, and dividends, and gains from the sale of assets such as equipment or investments. A gain reported on the income statement represents a net amount, that is, the difference between selling price and cost. This differs from revenues, which are reported in total and separately from related expenses.

Other Expenses and Losses This section is parallel to the previous one but results in deductions from, rather than increases to, operating income. Examples include interest expense and losses from the sale of assets. Losses, like gains, are reported at their net amounts.

A particularly controversial type of loss arises when companies propose a restructuring of their operations. A restructuring typically causes some assets to lose value because they no longer fit in a company's strategic plans. A restructuring also creates additional costs associated with the termination or relocation of employees. For example, in the notes to its financial statements, AT&T disclosed that its operating expenses for 2000 included a restructuring charge of $7.029 billion resulting from a combination of asset impairment charges (write-downs) and other one-time restructuring and exit costs to make the company more cost efficient in the future. The controversy over restructuring charges stems from the fact that companies exercise considerable discretion in determining the amount of a restructuring charge. The fear is that companies can use this discretion as a tool for manipulating the amount of reported net income. For example, companies that are already faced with the prospect of poor reported performance for a year may intentionally overstate the cost of a restructuring. The motivation for this so-called big-bath approach is that if a company is going to report poor results anyway, it makes sense to gather up all the bad news in the company and report it at the same time, thus diluting the effect of any single bad news item. Historically, if this approach was followed, reported performance in the years following the big-bath year would appear much improved, in large part because the restructuring charge resulted in many expenses of future years being estimated and reported as one lump sum in the big-bath year. In 2002, the FASB issued a clarifying standard to reduce the flexibility companies have to strategically estimate and recognize big-bath restructuring charges.[13]

The largest restructuring charge (to date) was recognized by **Time Warner** (then called AOL Time Warner) in 2002. The company recognized a total of $99.737 billion in restructuring charges, almost all of which related to write-downs of goodwill associated with the AOL and Time Warner merger in early 2001. This astronomical restructuring charge also contributed to Time Warner having the distinction of reporting the largest single-year net loss in history, $98.696 billion (on revenues of $40.961 billion!).

Income from Continuing Operations Before Income Taxes Subtracting other revenues and gains and other expenses and losses from operating income results in income from continuing operations before taxes.

Income Taxes on Continuing Operations Income tax expense is the sum of all the income tax consequences of all transactions undertaken by a company during a year. Some of those tax consequences may occur in the current year, and some may occur in future years. When transitory, irregular, or extraordinary items are reported, total taxes for the period must be allocated among the various components of income. One income tax amount is reported for all items included in the income from continuing operations

---

[13] FASB ASC Topic 420 (Exit or Disposal Cost Obligations).

> **Caution**
> Keep in mind that while a transaction may result in a gain or loss for one company, that same transaction may be treated differently for another. For example, if an office supplies store sells its delivery truck to a used car dealer, a gain or loss occurs for the office supplies store. However, when the used car dealer sells the delivery truck, the proceeds will be considered revenue. Why the different treatment? In the first instance, the sale of the truck is a peripheral activity. In the second case, the sale of the truck results from the dealer's ongoing operations.

category; it is presented as the last section in the category. In contrast, each item in the transitory, irregular, or extraordinary items category is reported net of its income tax effect, referred to as "net of income tax." This separation of income taxes into different sections of the income statement is referred to as intraperiod income tax allocation. The Web Material (**www.cengagebrain.com**) associated with Chapter 16 includes extensive coverage of intraperiod income tax allocation.

For example, in 2011 IBM generated enough taxable income to require it to pay $4.168 billion in income taxes in cash for the year. However, in 2011 IBM also entered into transactions creating tax liabilities that the company will pay in future years. Even though those taxes will not be paid until future years, they are recognized as an expense in the period in which they are incurred. So, as seen in Exhibit 4-5, IBM reports income tax expense of $5.418 billion for 2011, which represents the net tax effects, both now and in the future, of all transactions entered into during the year.

In the Techtronics illustration, an income tax rate of 30% was assumed. Thus, the amount of income tax related to continuing operations is $33,585 ($111,950 × 0.30). The same tax rate is applied to all income components in the Techtronics example. In practice, however, intraperiod income tax allocation may involve different rates for different components of income. This results from graduated tax rates and special, or alternative, rates for certain types of gains and losses.

Income from Continuing Operations A key purpose of financial accounting is to provide interested parties with information that can be used to predict how a company will perform in the future. Therefore, financial statement users desire an income amount that reflects the aspects of a company's performance that are expected to continue into the future. This is labeled Income from Continuing Operations. Income from continuing operations is computed by subtracting interest expense, income tax expense, and other gains and losses from operating income.

Transitory, Irregular, and Extraordinary Items

在持续经营利润之后分开报告的利润项目有时被称为线下项目。这些项目来自那些预期未来不会继续影响报告结果的交易和事项。独立于持续经营报告这些项目及相关的税务影响，可以为财务报表使用者披露更多的信息，以帮助他们估算报告提供公司预期在未来产生的利润和现金流量。

Components of income that are reported separately after income from continuing operations are sometimes called below-the-line items. These items arise from transactions and events that are not expected to continue to impact reported results in future years. Reporting these items and their related tax effects separately from continuing operations provides more informative disclosure to users of financial statements, helping them assess the income and cash flows the reporting company can be expected to generate in future years. Two types of transactions and events are reported in this manner: (1) discontinued operations and (2) extraordinary items. In addition to these two items, the effects of changes in accounting principles, changes in estimates, and changing prices also influence the income statement and related disclosures. Each of these items is discussed in turn.

Discontinued Operations A common irregular item involves the disposition of a separately identifiable component of a business either through sale or abandonment. The component of the company disposed of may be a major line of business, a major class of customer, a subsidiary company, or even just a single store with separately identifiable operations and cash flows. The size of the discontinued activity is not the factor that determines whether it is reported as a discontinued operation. Instead, to qualify as discontinued operations for reporting purposes, the operations and cash flows of the component must be clearly distinguishable from other operations and cash flows of the company, both physically and operationally, as well as for financial reporting purposes. For example, closing down one of five product lines in a plant in which the operations and cash flows from all of the product lines are intertwined would not be an example of a discontinued operation. Similarly, shifting production or marketing functions from one location to another would not be classified as a discontinued operation.

Management may decide to dispose of a component of a business for many reasons, such as the following:

- The component may be unprofitable.
- The component may not fit into the long-range plans for the company.
- Management may need funds to reduce long-term debt or to expand into other areas.
- Management may be fearful of a corporate takeover by new investors desiring to gain control of the company.

As companies constantly seek to fine-tune their strategic focus, they sometimes seek to sell peripheral operational components, especially unprofitable ones, and to consolidate the company around its principal business operations.

Regardless of the reason that a company sells a business component, the discontinuance of a substantial portion of company operations is a significant event. Therefore, information about discontinued operations should be presented explicitly to readers of financial statements.

Reporting Requirements for Discontinued Operations When a company discontinues operating a component of its business, future comparability requires that all elements that relate to the discontinued operation be identified and separated from continuing operations. Thus, in the Techtronics Corporation income statement illustrated in Exhibit 4-6, the first category after income from continuing operations is discontinued operations. The category is separated into two subdivisions: (1) the current-year income or loss from operating the discontinued component, in this case a $35,000 loss, plus any gain or loss on the disposal of the component, in this case a $16,000 loss; and (2) disclosure of the overall income tax impact of the income or loss associated with the component, in this case a tax benefit of $15,300. As previously indicated, all below-the-line items are reported net of their respective tax effects. If the item is a gain, it is reduced by the tax on the gain. If the item is a loss, it is deductible against other income, and thus its existence saves income taxes. The overall company loss can thus be reduced by the tax savings arising from being able to deduct the loss from otherwise taxable income.

Frequently, the disposal of a business component is initiated during the year but not completed by the end of the fiscal year. To be classified as a discontinued operation for reporting purposes, the ultimate disposal must be expected within one year of the period for which results are being reported. Accordingly, if a company made a decision in 2015 to dispose of a business component in April 2016, in the 2015 income statement the results of the operations of that business component should be reported as discontinued operations.

To illustrate the reporting for discontinued operations, consider the following example. Thom Beard Company has two divisions, A and B. The operations and cash flows of these two divisions are clearly distinguishable, so they both qualify as business components. On June 20, 2015, Thom Beard decides to dispose of the assets and liabilities of Division B; it is probable that the disposal will be completed early next year. The revenues and expenses of Thom Beard for 2015 and for the preceding two years are as follows:

	2015	2014	2013
Sales—A	$10,000	$9,200	$8,500
Total nontax expenses—A	8,800	8,100	7,500
Sales—B	7,000	8,100	9,000
Total nontax expenses—B	7,900	7,500	7,700

During the later part of 2015, Thom Beard disposed of a portion of Division B and recognized a pretax loss of $4,000 on the disposal. The income tax rate for Thom Beard Company is 40%. The 2015 comparative income statement would appear as follows:

	2015	2014	2013
Sales	$10,000	$9,200	$8,500
Expenses	8,800	8,100	7,500
Income before income taxes	$ 1,200	$1,100	$1,000
Income tax expense (40%)	480	440	400
Income from continuing operations	$ 720	$ 660	$ 600
Discontinued operations:			
Income (loss) from operations (including loss on disposal in 2015 of $4,000)	(4,900)	600	1,300
Income tax expense (benefit)—40%	(1,960)	240	520
Income (loss) on discontinued operations	$(2,940)	$ 360	$ 780
Net income	$(2,220)	$1,020	$1,380

Notice that this method of reporting allows users to distinguish between the part of Thom Beard's business that will continue to generate income in the future and the part that will not. This reporting format makes it much easier for financial statement users to attempt to forecast how Thom Beard will perform in subsequent years.

The reporting requirements for discontinued operations are contained in FASB ASC Subtopic 205-20.[14] On the balance sheet, assets and liabilities associated with discontinued components that have not yet been completely disposed of as of the balance sheet date are to be listed separately in the asset and liability sections of the balance sheet. Also, in addition to the summary income or loss number reported in the income statement, the total revenue associated with the discontinued operation should be disclosed in the financial statement notes. The objective of these disclosures is to report information that will assist external users in assessing future cash flows by clearly distinguishing normal recurring earnings patterns from those activities that are not expected to continue in the future yet are significant in assessing the total results of company operations for the current and prior years.

According to *International Financial Reporting Standard (IFRS) 5*, companies with discontinued operations must disclose the following: the amounts of revenue, expenses, and pretax profit or loss attributable to the discontinued operations and related income tax expense. In addition, separate disclosure of the assets, liabilities, and cash flows of the discontinued operations should be made. *IFRS 5* differs from U.S. GAAP in

---

[14] FASB ASC Subtopic 205-20 (Presentation of Financial Statements—Discontinued Operations).

that *IFRS 5* requires separate disclosure of the cash flows of the discontinued operations; this requirement does not exist in U.S. GAAP. In addition, *IFRS 5* requires that a discontinued operation be "a separate major line of business or geographical area of operations" (*IFRS 5* par. 32); under U.S. GAAP, the discontinued operation need not be a major line of business but must only have operations and cash flows that can be separately identified.

The reporting practices with respect to discontinued operations in the United Kingdom represent an interesting alternative to the U.S. approach. For example, in complying with *Financial Reporting Standard (FRS) 3* of the Accounting Standards Board in the United Kingdom, **British Telecommunications (BT)** provided the following information in its 2002 profit and loss account (income statement).

(In millions of £)	2002
Total turnover (sales)	
Ongoing activities	£21,815
Discontinued activities	2,827
Total operating profit	
Ongoing activities	(1,489)
Discontinued activities	(371)

British Telecommunications, 2002, 10K Report

This approach provides more information to financial statement users than does the U.S. approach because it allows for a comparison of the relative size and operating profitability of the continuing and discontinued operations.

非常项目是指在性质上不寻常、在概率上很少发生的事项和交易。

Extraordinary Items According to FASB ASC Subtopic 225-20, extraordinary items are events and transactions that are both unusual in nature and infrequent in occurrence. Thus, to qualify as extraordinary, an item must "possess a high degree of abnormality and be of a type clearly unrelated to, or only incidentally related to, the ordinary and typical activities of the entity ... [and] be of a type that would not reasonably be expected to recur in the foreseeable future. . . ."[15]

The intent of this standard is to restrict the items that can be classified as extraordinary. The presumption of the FASB is that an item should be considered ordinary and part of the company's continuing operations unless evidence clearly supports its classification as an extraordinary item. Examples of gains and losses that should *not* be reported as extraordinary items are as follows.

- The write-down or write-off of receivables, inventories, equipment leased to others, or intangible assets
- The gains or losses from exchanges or remeasurement of foreign currencies, including those relating to major devaluations and revaluations
- The gains or losses on disposal of a segment of a business
- Other gains or losses from sale or abandonment of property, plant, or equipment used in the business
- The effects of a strike
- The adjustment of accruals on long-term contracts

---

[15] FASB ASC paragraph 225-20-45-2.

For example, companies have reported as extraordinary items litigation settlements and write-offs of assets in foreign countries where expropriation risks were high.

Some items may not meet both criteria for extraordinary items but may meet one of them. Although these items do not qualify as extraordinary, they should be disclosed separately as part of income from continuing operations, either before or after operating income. Examples of these items include strike-related costs, obsolete inventory write-downs, and gains and losses from liquidation of investments. Most of us would consider the costs created by the September 11, 2001, World Trade Center attack to be the ultimate extraordinary item. However, these costs were *not* reported as extraordinary in 2001 income statements. The Emerging Issues Task Force determined that the economic effects of the World Trade Center attack were so pervasive as to make it impossible to separate the attack's direct costs from the economic costs (including lost revenue) due to the transformation of the economic landscape after the attack.

> **FYI**
>
> Before 2002, all gains and losses resulting from the early extinguishment of debt were reported as extraordinary. This classification was ended with the release of pre-Codification *SFAS No. 145* (now in FASB ASC paragraph 470-50-45-1); these gains and losses are now considered ordinary, subject to the normal criteria for extraordinary items.

In 2000 and 2001, **Verizon**'s financial statements exhibited examples of restructuring charges, extraordinary items, and catastrophic items that seemed extraordinary but were accounted for as part of ordinary operations. In 2001, Verizon reported a restructuring charge of $1.596 billion related to employee severance costs in the wake of the **Bell Atlantic–GTE** merger that created Verizon. In 2000, Verizon reported a $1.027 billion extraordinary loss (net of tax) stemming from the FCC-mandated sale of overlapping wireless services. See Exhibit 4-7 for Verizon's disclosure regarding costs created by the World Trade Center attack.

In an interesting departure from U.S. GAAP, the IASB does not allow for any income or expense items to be classified as "extraordinary," neither in the income statement itself nor in the notes to the financial statements. In the "Basis for Conclusions" for *IAS 1*, the IASB states that the normal risks of business involve unexpected and heretofore unexperienced events. In other words, the items classified as "extraordinary events" under U.S. GAAP are considered to be just another part of business by the IASB.

Exhibit 4-7 | Verizon Disclosure Regarding September 11, 2001, World Trade Center Attack

> **Note 2: Accounting for the Impact of the September 11, 2001, Terrorist Attacks**
>
> The terrorist attacks on September 11th resulted in considerable loss of life and property, as well as to exacerbate weakening economic conditions. Verizon was not spared any of these effects, given our significant operations in New York and Washington, D.C.
>
> The primary financial statement impact of the September 11th terrorist attacks pertains to Verizon's plant, equipment and administrative office space located either in, or adjacent to the World Trade Center complex, and the associated service restoration efforts. During the period following September 11th, we focused primarily on service restoration in the World Trade Center area and incurred costs, net of estimated insurance recoveries, totaling $285 million pretax ($172 million after-tax, or $.06 per diluted share) as a result of the terrorist attacks.
>
> Verizon's insurance policies are limited to losses of $1 billion for each occurrence and include a deductible of $1 million. As a result, we accrued an estimated insurance recovery of approximately $400 million in 2001, of which approximately $130 million has been received. The costs and estimated insurance recovery were recorded in accordance with Emerging Issues Task Force *Issue No. 01-10*, "Accounting for the Impact of the Terrorist Attacks of September 11, 2001."

Source: Verizon Wireless

Changes in Accounting Principles Although consistency in application of accounting principles increases the usefulness and comparability of the financial statements, the conditions of some occasions justify a change from one accounting principle to another. Occasionally a company will change an accounting principle (such as from LIFO to FIFO) because a change in economic conditions suggests that an accounting change will provide better information. More frequently, a change in accounting principle occurs because the FASB issues a new pronouncement requiring a change in principle; if GAAP is to be followed, the company has no choice but to change to conform with the new standard.

When there is a change in accounting principle or method, a company is required to determine how the income statement would have been different in past years if the new accounting method had been used all along. To improve comparability, income statements for all years presented (for example, for all three years if three years of comparative data are provided) must be restated using the new accounting method. The beginning balance of Retained Earnings for the oldest year presented reflects an adjustment for the cumulative income effect of the accounting change on the net incomes of all preceding years for which a detailed income statement is not presented.

As an illustration of the accounting for a change in accounting principle, consider the following example. Brandoni Company started business in 2013. In 2015, the company decided to change its method of computing cost of goods sold from FIFO to LIFO. To keep things simple, assume that Brandoni has only two expenses: cost of goods sold and income tax expense. The income tax rate for all items is 40%. The following sales and cost of goods sold information are for 2013–2015:

	2015	2014	2013
Sales	$8,000	$8,000	$8,000
Cost of goods sold—old method (FIFO)	5,600	6,100	7,500
Cost of goods sold—new method (LIFO)	4,500	4,500	4,500

The first impact of the change in inventory valuation method is to reduce cost of goods sold in 2015. The $4,500 cost of goods sold under the new method would be reported in the normal fashion in the income statement, and the $1,100 ($5,600 − $4,500) current-year impact of the accounting principle change would be disclosed in the notes to the financial statements. The 2015 comparative income statement would appear as follows:

	2015	2014	2013
Sales	$8,000	$8,000	$8,000
Cost of goods sold	4,500	4,500	4,500
Income before income taxes	$3,500	$3,500	$3,500
Income tax expense (40%)	1,400	1,400	1,400
Net income	$2,100	$2,100	$2,100

One drawback of this retroactive restatement approach is that the comparative income statements for 2013 and 2014 that are presented in the 2015 financial statements do NOT report the same 2013 and 2014 cost of goods sold and net income that were reported in the original 2013 and 2014 income statements. However, this drawback is more than compensated by the interyear comparability that is provided through retroactive restatement.

The approach described above for reporting the impact of a change in accounting principle is derived from FASB ASC Topic 250 (Accounting Changes and Error Corrections). This standard is modeled on *International Accounting Standard (IAS) 8*. Formerly, the FASB required companies to report the cumulative income effect (for all past years) of an accounting change as a single item in the current year's income statement. To increase international comparability of financial statements, the FASB decided in 2005 to change U.S. GAAP to conform with the international standard. The accounting for changes in accounting principles is discussed more fully in Chapter 20.

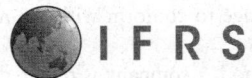

Changes in Estimates In reporting periodic revenues and in attempting to properly match those expenses incurred to generate current-period revenues, accountants must continually make judgments. The numbers reported in the financial statements reflect these judgments and are based on estimates of such factors as the number of years of useful life for depreciable assets, the amount of uncollectible accounts expected, and the amount of warranty liability to be recorded on the books. These and other estimates are made using the best available information at the statement date. However, conditions may subsequently change, and the estimates may need to be revised. Naturally, changing either revenue or expense amounts affects the income statement. The question is whether the previously reported income measures should be revised or whether the changes should impact only current and future periods.

在报告定期收入、试图恰当地匹配那些因产生收入而发生的费用时，会计人员必须持续做出判断。财务报表所报告的数据反映了这些判断，并且这些数据是基于对折旧资产使用年限、预期坏账金额及需记录的担保债务金额等因素的估计。这些及其他一些估计是根据财务报告日可获得的最佳信息做出的。然而，情况也许会改变，所以估计可能需要修订。

Changes in estimates should be reflected in the current period (the period in which the estimate is revised) and in future periods, if any, that are affected. No retroactive adjustments are to be made for a change in estimate. These changes are considered a normal part of the accounting process, not errors made in past periods.

To illustrate the computations for a change in estimate, assume that Springville Manufacturing Co., Inc., purchased a milling machine at a cost of $100,000. At the time of purchase, it was estimated that the machine would have a useful life of 10 years. Assuming no salvage value and that the straight-line method is used, the depreciation expense is $10,000 per year ($100,000/10). At the beginning of the fifth year, however, conditions indicated that the machine would be used for only three more years. Depreciation expense in the fifth, sixth, and seventh years should reflect the revised estimate, but depreciation expense recorded in the first four years would not be affected. Because the book value at the end of four years is $60,000 ($100,000 – $40,000 accumulated depreciation), annual depreciation charges for the remaining three years of estimated life would be $20,000 ($60,000/3). The following schedule summarizes the depreciation charges over the life of the asset:

Year	Depreciation
1	$ 10,000
2	10,000
3	10,000
4	10,000
5	20,000
6	20,000
7	20,000
Total (accumulated) depreciation	$100,000

Effects of Changing Prices The preceding presentation of revenue and expense recognition has not addressed the question of how, if at all, changing prices are to be recognized under the transaction approach. As indicated in Chapter 1, accountants have traditionally ignored this phenomenon, especially when gains would result from recognition. When an economy experiences high rates of inflation, users of financial statements become concerned that the statements do not reflect the impact of these changing prices. When the inflation rates are lower, this user concern decreases. When the price change rates are increasing, added pressure to adjust the financial statements is exerted by users of the income statement. Many foreign countries with high inflation rates require adjustments to remove the inflation effects. **McDonald's** addresses the effects of inflation in its 10-K filed with the SEC. This note disclosure (included in Exhibit 4-8) indicates that McDonald's is able to deal with inflation through a quick turnover of inventory and by increasing prices in those locations where costs change rapidly. Disclosure related to the impact of changing prices is encouraged, but not required, in FASB ASC Topic 255 (Changing Prices).

Net Income or Loss

Income or loss from continuing operations combined with the results of discontinued operations and extraordinary items provides users a summary measure of the firm's performance for a period: net income or net loss. This figure is the accountant's attempt to summarize in one number a company's overall economic performance for a given period. In the absence of any irregular items, net income is the same as income from continuing operations.

From the preceding discussion, you can see that when someone refers to a company's "income" or "profit," the person could be referring to any one of a host of numbers: gross profit, operating income, income from continuing operations, or net income. It is important to learn to be very specific when discussing a company's income. After all, comparing one company's net income to another company's operating income would be like comparing apples to oranges.

In order to compare this period's results with prior periods or with the performance of other firms, net income is divided by net sales to determine the return on sales. This measurement represents the net income percentage per dollar of sales. For example, **The Walt Disney Company** reported the following returns on sales.

	2011	2010	2009
Return on sales..	11.76%	10.41%	9.15%

Compare these results with a sample of returns on sales from various companies in different industries, shown in Exhibit 4-9.

When computing the return on sales, keep in mind that net income may include extraordinary or irregular items that can distort the results and hamper comparability. Adjustments may be needed in the analysis to account for such items.

Exhibit 4-8 | McDonald's—Note Disclosure

> The Company has demonstrated an ability to manage inflationary cost increases effectively. This is because of rapid inventory turnover, the ability to adjust menu prices, cost controls and substantial property holdings—many of which are at fixed costs and partly financed by debt made less expensive by inflation.

McDonald's, 2011, 10K Report

Exhibit 4-9 | Return on Sales

	2011	2010	2009
AT&T	3.1%	16.0%	9.9%
Microsoft	33.1%	30.0%	24.9%
IBM	14.8%	14.9%	14.0%
McDonald's	20.4%	20.5%	20.0%

© Cengage Learning 2014

Earnings per Share An individual shareholder is interested in how much of a company's net income is associated with his or her ownership interest. As a result, the income statement reports earnings per share (EPS), which is the amount of net income associated with each common share of stock. For example, in Exhibit 4-5 basic EPS for IBM in 2011 was $13.25. This means that an owner of 100 shares of IBM stock has claim on $1,325 ($13.25 EPS × 100 shares) of the $15.855 billion in IBM net income available to common shareholders for 2011.

To illustrate the importance of earnings per share, consider the following example. For the years 2013–2015, James Caird Company had net income, average shares outstanding, and earnings per share as follows:

	2015	2014	2013
Net income	$10,000	$6,000	$2,500
Average shares outstanding	10,000	5,000	1,000
Earnings per share (EPS)	$1.00	$1.20	$2.50

Note that if one looks only at the growth in net income, it appears that the shareholders of James Caird are doing very well, with net income growth rates of 140% in 2014 and 67% in 2015. However, a look at the data on shares outstanding reveals that this growth in net income has been driven by a substantial increase in the size of the company as evidenced by the large increases in shares outstanding. When viewed on a per-share basis, performance was actually steadily declining from 2013 to 2015; one of the original shareholders who earned $2.50 for each share owned in 2013 earned only $1.00 for each of those same shares in 2015.

Companies often disclose two earnings-per-share numbers. Basic EPS reports earnings based solely on shares actually outstanding during the year. Basic earnings per share is computed by dividing income available to common shareholders (net income less dividends paid to or promised to preferred shareholders) by the average number of common shares outstanding during the period.

Diluted earnings per share reflects the existence of stock options or other rights that can be converted into shares in the future. For example, in addition to having shares outstanding, a company could also have granted stock options that allow the option holders to buy shares of stock at some predetermined price. At present, the option holders don't own shares of stock, but they can acquire them from the company at any time. In other cases, a company might borrow money but also give the right to the lender to exchange the loan for shares of stock at some predetermined price. Diluted EPS is computed to give financial statement users an idea about the potential impact on EPS of the exercise of existing stock options or other rights to acquire shares.

IBM reports basic earnings per share and diluted earnings per share in 2011 of $13.25 and $13.06, respectively (see Exhibit 4-5). If all options and other convertible items that are likely to be converted were in fact converted into shares of IBM stock, the effect on IBM's earnings per share would be to reduce it by $0.19. A small difference of $0.19 (about 1% of basic EPS) indicates that IBM does not have many options and convertible securities outstanding.

Historically, the accounting rules in the United States governing the computation of EPS have been unnecessarily complex. In the mid-1990s, the FASB initiated a project, in conjunction with the IASB, to both improve U.S. accounting practice with respect to EPS and to increase international agreement on this important accounting issue. In 1997, the FASB and IASB issued almost identical standards prescribing the methods of computing the basic and diluted EPS numbers outlined earlier. This represented not only a big improvement in U.S. accounting practice but also was a milestone in that it was the first time that the FASB and the IASB worked jointly to issue an accounting standard.

When presenting EPS figures, separate earnings-per-share amounts are computed by dividing income from continuing operations and each irregular or extraordinary item by the weighted average number of shares of common stock outstanding for the reporting period.[16]

For example, the Techtronics Corporation income statement (Exhibit 4-6) shows earnings per common share of $1.57 for income from continuing operations, a $0.71 loss from discontinued operations, and $0.25 for extraordinary gain, for a total of $1.11 for net income. These figures were derived by dividing each identified component of net income by 50,000 shares of common stock outstanding during the period. When a company has only common stock outstanding, computing EPS is very straightforward. The computations become more complex, however, when a company has certain types of securities outstanding, such as convertible stock and stock options. These and other types of securities are discussed in Chapter 13, and more detail on the computation of earnings per share is given in Chapter 18.

Earnings per share is often used to calculate a firm's price-earnings (P/E) ratio. This ratio expresses the market value of common stock as a multiple of earnings and allows investors to evaluate the attractiveness of a firm's common stock. The price-earnings ratio is computed by dividing the market price per share of common stock by the annual basic EPS. Instead of using the average market value of shares for the period covered by earnings, the latest market value is normally used. *The Wall Street Journal* reports P/E ratios for most listed companies on a daily basis. Assuming that Techtronics Corporation's stock closed with a market value of $14.25 per share on December 31, 2015, its P/E ratio would be computed as follows:

$$\text{P/E ratio} = \frac{\text{Market value of per share}}{\text{Earnings per share}} = \frac{\$14.25}{\$1.11} = 12.8$$

To get an idea of how price-earnings ratios vary across time, consider the information contained in Exhibit 4-10. This exhibit summarizes data for thousands of companies over a 20-year period. The companies included in the analysis are the largest publicly traded companies in the United States, determined each year by ranking all publicly traded companies by market value and then computing the P/E ratios for the

---

[16] FASB ASC Topic 260 (Earnings per Share).

Exhibit 4-10 | P/E Ratios Over Time for Large, Publicly Traded U.S. Companies

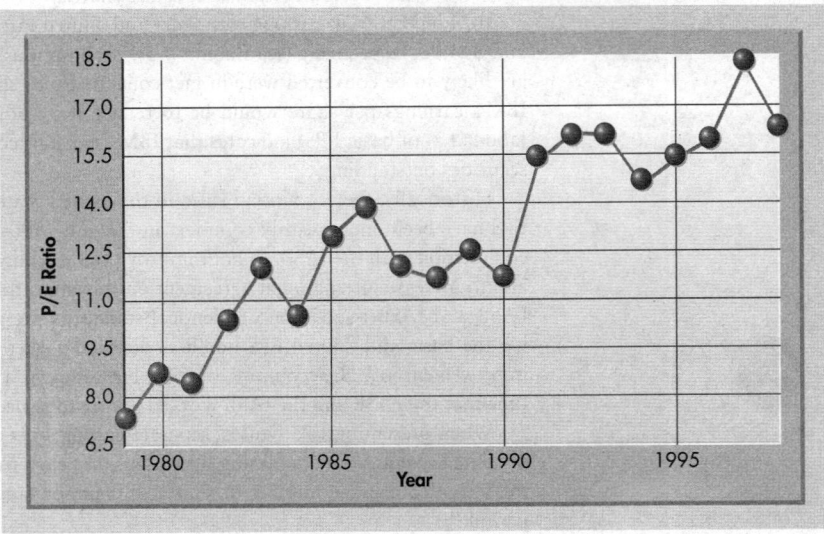

© Cengage Learning 2014

half with the largest market values. Note that over this 20-year period, P/E ratios tended to increase.

In general, the following types of firms have *higher* than average P/E ratios.

- Firms with strong future growth possibilities
- Firms with earnings for the year lower than average because of a nonrecurring event (e.g., a large write-off, a natural disaster)
- Firms with substantial unrecorded assets (e.g., appreciated land, unrecorded goodwill)

In general, the following types of firms have *lower* than average P/E ratios.

- Firms with earnings for the year higher than average because of a nonrecurring event (e.g., a one-time gain)
- Firms perceived as being very risky

Comprehensive Income and the Statement of Stockholders' Equity

LO6 学习目标6
计算综合收益并编制所有者权益表。

6 Compute and present comprehensive income.

The FASB requires companies to provide an additional measure of income: comprehensive income. This measure of a company's performance includes items in addition to those included in net income. Companies can either provide this additional information at the bottom of the income statement or include it in a separate statement of comprehensive income that is shown immediately after the income statement.

Comprehensive Income

Recall from the beginning of this chapter that a general definition of income is the increase in a company's wealth during a period. The wealth of a company is impacted in a variety of ways that have nothing to do with the business operations of the company. For example, changes in exchange rates can cause the U.S. dollar value of a company's foreign subsidiaries to increase or decrease. Comprehensive income is the number used to reflect an overall measure of the change in a company's wealth during the period. In addition to net income, comprehensive income includes items that, in general, arise from changes in market conditions unrelated to the business operations of a company. These items are excluded from net income because they are viewed as yielding little information about the economic performance of a company's business operations. However, they are reported as part of comprehensive income because they do impact the value of assets and liabilities reported in the balance sheet.

> **FYI**
>
> The FASB encourages companies to provide one continuous net income/comprehensive income statement. However, most companies report comprehensive income in a separate statement placed immediately after the income statement.

综合收益是对公司一定时期内财富变化总额的计量。除净利润外，综合收益还包括与公司经营无关的因市场状况变化而产生的项目。这些项目之所以被排除在净利润之外，是因为人们认为它们很少包含与公司经营的经济业绩相关的信息。然而，这些项目被当作综合收益报告是因为它们的确影响了资产负债表中资产和负债的价值。

The FASB discussed the concept of comprehensive income in its conceptual framework. However, it wasn't until 1998 that the concept was placed into practice with the issuance of pre-Codification *Statement No. 130*. This standard is now found in FASB ASC Topic 220 (Comprehensive Income). Exhibit 4-11 provides an example (IBM) of a statement of comprehensive income. Three of the more common adjustments made in arriving at comprehensive income are (1) foreign currency translation adjustments, (2) unrealized gains and losses on available-for-sale securities, and (3) deferred gains and losses on derivative financial instruments.

Foreign Currency Translation Adjustment During 2011, there was a decrease in the value of the currencies (relative to the U.S. dollar) in the countries where IBM has foreign subsidiaries. Thus, the U.S. dollar value of the net assets of those subsidiaries decreased $693 million during the year. This decrease was not the result of bad business performance by IBM; it was simply a function of the ebb and flow of the worldwide economy. This "loss" is not reported as part of net income but is included in the computation of comprehensive income.

Unrealized Gains and Losses on Available-for-Sale Securities To maintain a liquid reserve of assets that can be converted into cash if needed, most companies purchase an investment portfolio of stocks and bonds. For example, as of December 31, 2011, IBM owned $8.577 billion in securities that had been classified as "available for sale," meaning IBM does not intend to actively trade the securities in this portfolio but has them available to be sold if the need for cash arises. These securities are reported in the balance sheet at their fair value. As the fair value of these securities fluctuates, IBM experiences "unrealized" gains and losses. An unrealized gain or loss is the same as what is sometimes called a paper gain or loss, meaning that because the security has not yet been sold, the gain or loss is only on paper.

Because available-for-sale securities are not part of a company's operations, the associated unrealized gains and losses are excluded from the computation of net income and are instead reported as part of comprehensive income. During 2011, IBM recorded a $14 million loss on its available-for-sale portfolio; this amount was reported as a decrease in comprehensive income.

Exhibit 4-11 | IBM's Statement of Comprehensive Income for 2011

($ in millions) For the year ended December 31:	Notes	2011	2010	2009
Net income...		$15,855	$14,833	$13,425
Other comprehensive income/(loss), before tax:				
Foreign currency translation adjustments	L	(693)	712	1,675
Net changes related to available-for-sale securities	L			
Unrealized gains/(losses) arising during the period............		(14)	70	118
Reclassification of (gains)/losses to net income................		(231)	0	64
Subsequent changes in previously impaired securities arising during the period...................................		4	8	—
Total net changes related to available-for-sale securities		(241)	78	182
Unrealized gains/(losses) on cash flow hedges.................	L			
Unrealized gains/(losses) arising during the period............		(266)	371	(718)
Reclassification of (gains)/losses to net income................		511	203	(94)
Total unrealized gains/(losses) on cash flow hedges		245	573	(812)
Retirement-related benefit plans	L			
Prior service costs/(credits)		(28)	28	375
Net (losses)/gains arising during the period...................		(5,463)	(2,728)	1,433
Curtailments and settlements		11	10	(125)
Amortization of prior service (credits)/cost....................		(157)	(183)	(162)
Amortization of net gains/(losses)		1,847	1,249	1,105
Total retirement-related benefit plans		(3,790)	(1,624)	2,626
Other comprehensive income/(loss), before tax	L	(4,479)	(260)	3,671
Income tax (expense)/benefit related to items of other comprehensive income	L	1,339	348	(656)
Other comprehensive income/(loss).............................	L	(3,142)	87	3,015
Total comprehensive income.....................................		$12,713	$14,920	$16,440

Amounts may not add due to rounding.

The accompanying notes on pages 76 through 139 are an integral part of the financial statements.

IBM, 2011, 10K Report

Deferred Gains and Losses on Derivative Financial Instruments Companies frequently use derivative financial instruments to hedge their exposure to risk stemming from changes in prices and rates. As prices and rates change, the value of a derivative based on that price or rate also changes. As with available-for-sale securities, these value changes give rise to unrealized gains and losses. In some cases, these unrealized gains and losses on derivatives are included in net income and offset gains or losses on the items that were being hedged. In other cases, the reporting of the unrealized gains and losses on derivatives in net income is delayed until a subsequent year; in the meantime, the unrealized gains and losses are reported as part of comprehensive income. In 2011, IBM reported unrealized derivative losses of $266 million as part of comprehensive income. Additional discussion of derivatives is given in Chapter 19.

A few other comprehensive income items exist in addition to the three just described. For example, in 2011 IBM reported a decrease of $3.790 billion in comprehensive income stemming from changes in IBM's reported pension liability. The key point to remember is that these items represent changes in assets and liabilities reported in the balance sheet that are not deemed to reflect a company's own economic performance and are therefore excluded from the computation of net income. The net effect of each of these adjustments is to report a total comprehensive income of $12.713 billion in 2011, a net decrease of $3.142 billion from the reported amount of net income.

Proposed New Income Statement Format As mentioned in Chapter 3, the FASB and the IASB are currently engaged in a long-term project to restructure the way information is presented in the financial statements.[17] The focus of this effort is to clearly separate financial statement items that are related to a company's business activities from items that are related to other activities such as income taxes or financing. To give you an idea of what a restructured income statement might look like under this new proposal, the Techtronics income statement in Exhibit 4-6 (with some of the detail, including earnings per share data, omitted) has been reformatted and now appears in Exhibit 4-12.

Exhibit 4-12 | Techtronics Corporation Statement of Comprehensive Income

Techtronics Corporation
Statement of Comprehensive Income (restructured according to FASB-IASB proposal)
For the Year Ended December 31, 2015

BUSINESS	
Operating	
Sales	$ 780,000
Cost of goods sold	(491,000)
Gross profit	$ 289,000
Selling expenses	(85,000)
General and administrative expenses	(118,300)
Loss on sale of equipment	(5,250)
Gain (called "extraordinary" in Exhibit 4-6)	17,900
Operating income	**$ 98,350**
Investing	
Interest revenue	$ 12,750
Gain on sale of investment	37,000
Total investing income	**$ 49,750**
TOTAL BUSINESS INCOME	**$ 148,100**
FINANCING	
Interest expense	(18,250)
Income from continuing operations before income taxes	$ 129,850
INCOME TAX	
Total income tax expense ($33,585 + $5,370)	(38,955)
Income from continuing operations	$ 90,895
DISCONTINUED OPERATIONS	
Loss from operations of discontinued business component (including loss on disposal of $16,000)	$ (51,000)
Income tax benefit	15,300
NET LOSS ON DISCONTINUED OPERATIONS	**$ (35,700)**
NET INCOME	**$ 55,195**
OTHER COMPREHENSIVE INCOME (net of tax)	
Foreign currency translation adjustment	$ (2,450)
Unrealized gains on available-for-sale securities	1,180
TOTAL OTHER COMPREHENSIVE INCOME	**$ (1,270)**
TOTAL COMPREHENSIVE INCOME	**$ 53,925**

© Cengage Learning 2014

[17] Financial Accounting Standards Board, "Preliminary Views on Financial Statement Presentation" (Norwalk, CT: Financial Accounting Standards Board), October 16, 2008.

FASB和IASB提倡的新利润表格式——更名为综合收益表，分五部分分别列示公司主要业务、融资业务、所得税、非持续性项目和其他综合收益。这样的列示突出了综合收益的重要性。

Take a look at Exhibit 4-12 and note the following.

- When compared to the proposed change in the format of the balance sheet (see Chapter 3), this proposed new format for the income statement is really not that different from what we have been using for years.
- The income statement contains five major sections: business, financing, income taxes, discontinued operations, and other comprehensive income.
- This income statement does NOT include a separate line for extraordinary items. As mentioned earlier in this chapter, IFRS does NOT allow for the separate reporting of extraordinary items with the rationale that anything that happens to a business is part of the normal risk of running a business. The proposed new income statement format incorporates this provision of IFRS.
- Comprehensive income is an integral part of the proposed new statement, as evidenced by the statement title: "Statement of Comprehensive Income." The new income statement structure would put increased emphasis on comprehensive income.

As stated in Chapter 3, this proposed restructuring of the financial statements is expected to be discussed by the FASB and the IASB in 2012 and 2013 after other, more urgent issues (such as revenue recognition and the accounting for leases) are completed.

Forecasting Future Performance

7 Construct simple forecasts of income for future periods.

LO7 学习目标7
构建对未来期间利润的简单预测。

Financial statements report past results, but financial statement users are often interested in what will happen in the future. Therefore, an important skill for financial statement users to develop is using past financial statements to predict the future. This section presents a simple demonstration of how to use historical financial statement information to forecast a future income statement and balance sheet.

The key to a good financial statement forecast is identifying which underlying factors determine the level of a certain revenue or expense. For example, the level of cost of goods sold is closely tied to the level of sales, whereas the level of interest expense is only weakly tied to sales and is instead a direct function of the level of interest-bearing debt.

Most forecasting exercises start with a forecast of sales. The sales forecast indicates how fast the company is expected to grow and represents the general volume of activity expected in the company. This expected volume of activity influences the amount of assets that are needed to do business, which in turn determines the level of financing required. In short, for the resulting forecasted financial statements to be reliable, an accurate projection of sales is critical. The starting point for a sales forecast is last year's sales, with an addition for expected year-to-year growth based on the average sales growth experienced in previous years. This crude sales forecast should then be refined using as much company-specific information as is available. For example, in forecasting McDonald's sales, one should try to determine how many new outlets McDonald's expects to open during the coming year. The resulting sales forecast is the basis on which to forecast the remainder of the balance sheet, income statement, and statement of cash flows information.

Exhibit 4-13 contains financial statement information for the hypothetical Derrald Company. This information will be used as the basis for a simple forecasting exercise. The 2015 information for Derrald Company is historical information.

Exhibit 4-13 | Historical Financial Data for Derrald Company

Balance Sheet	2015
Cash	$ 10
Other current assets	250
Property, plant, and equipment, net	300
Total assets	$ 560
Accounts payable	$ 100
Bank loans payable	300
Total stockholders' equity	160
Total liabilities and stockholders' equity	$ 560
Income Statement	
Sales	$1,000
Cost of goods sold	700
Gross profit	$ 300
Depreciation expense	30
Other operating expenses	170
Operating profit	$ 100
Interest expense	30
Income before taxes	$ 70
Income taxes	30
Net income	$ 40

© Cengage Learning 2014

Forecast of Balance Sheet Accounts

Not all balance sheet accounts change according to the same process. Some items increase naturally as sales volume increases. Others increase only in response to specific long-term expansion plans, and other balance sheet items change only in response to specific financing choices made by management. How these different processes impact the forecast of a balance sheet is outlined next.

Natural Increase If Derrald Company plans to increase its sales volume by 40% in 2016, it seems logical to assume that Derrald will need about 40% more cash with which to handle this increased volume of business. In other words, the increased level of activity itself will create the need for more cash. The same is true of other current assets, such as accounts receivable and inventory, and of current operating liabilities, such as accounts payable and wages payable. In short, a planned 40% increase in the volume of Derrald's business means that, in the absence of plans to significantly change its methods of operation, Derrald will also experience a 40% increase in the levels of its current operating assets and liabilities. These forecasted natural increases are reflected in the forecasted balance sheet contained in Exhibit 4-14.

Long-Term Planning Long-term assets, such as property, plant, and equipment, do not increase naturally as sales volume increases. Instead, the addition of a new factory building, for example, occurs only as the result of a long-term planning process. Thus, a business anticipating an increase of sales in the coming year of only 10% may expand its productive capacity by 50% as part of its long-term strategic plan. Similarly, a business forecasting 25% sales growth may plan to use existing excess capacity to handle the entire sales increase without any increase in long-term assets. In short, forecasting future levels of long-term assets requires some knowledge of a company's strategic expansion plan. It is assumed that we know that Derrald Company plans to increase its property, plant, and equipment from $300 in 2015 to $500 in 2016. This forecasted increase is reflected in Exhibit 4-14.

Financing Choices The levels of long-term debt and of stockholders' equity are determined by management's decisions on how to best obtain financing. In fact, management often uses forecasted financial statements, prepared under a variety of different financing scenarios, to help determine financing choices. Because detailed treatment of the field of corporate finance is beyond the scope of this discussion, we will merely assume that Derrald is planning to finance its operations in 2016 by increasing its bank loans payable from $300 to $524 and by increasing stockholders' equity from $160 to $200. These forecasted increases are shown in Exhibit 4-14. Notice that the forecasted balance sheet for 2016 has total assets of $864 and total liabilities and stockholders' equity of $864. The numerical discipline imposed by the structure of the balance sheet ensures that the forecasted asset increases are consistent with Derrald Company's plans for additional financing.

Forecast of Income Statement Accounts

The amount of some expenses is directly tied to the amount of sales for the year. Derrald Company's sales are forecasted to increase by 40% in 2016, so it is reasonable to predict that cost of goods sold will increase by the same 40%. Another way to perform this calculation is to assume that the ratio of cost of goods sold to sales remains constant from year to year. Thus, because cost of goods sold was 70% of sales

Exhibit 4-14 | Forecasted Balance Sheet and Income Statement for Derrald Company

Balance Sheet	2015	2016 Forecasted	Basis for Forecast
Cash	$ 10	$ 14	40% natural increase
Other current assets	250	350	40% natural increase
Property, plant, and equipment, net	300	500	management decision
Total assets	$560	$864	
Accounts payable	$100	$140	40% natural increase
Bank loans payable	300	524	management decision
Total stockholders' equity	160	200	management decision
Total liabilities and stockholders' equity	$560	$864	

Income Statement	2015	2016 Forecasted	Basis for Forecast
Sales	$1,000	$1,400	40% increase
Cost of goods sold	700	980	70% of sales, same as last year
Gross profit	$ 300	$ 420	
Depreciation expense	30	50	10% of PPE, same as last year
Other operating expenses	170	238	17% of sales, same as last year
Operating profit	$ 100	$ 132	
Interest expense	30	52	10% of bank loans, same as last year
Income before taxes	$ 70	$ 80	
Income taxes	30	34	43% of pretax, same as last year
Net income	$ 40	$ 46	

© Cengage Learning 2014

in 2015 ($700/$1,000 = 70%), cost of goods sold should increase to $980 ($1,400 × 0.70) in 2016, as shown in Exhibit 4-14. Similarly, other operating expenses, such as wages and shipping costs, are also likely to maintain a constant relationship with the level of sales.

The amount of a company's depreciation expense is determined by how much property, plant, and equipment the company has. In 2015, Derrald Company had $30 of depreciation expense on $300 of property, plant, and equipment, that is, depreciation was 10% ($30/$300). If the same relationship holds in 2016, Derrald can expect to report depreciation expense of $50 ($500 × 0.10).

Interest expense depends on how much interest-bearing debt a company has. In 2015, Derrald Company reported interest expense of $30 with bank loans payable of $300. These numbers imply that the interest rate on Derrald's loans is 10% ($30/$300). Because the bank loans payable are expected to increase to $524 in 2016, Derrald can expect interest expense for the year of $52 ($524 × 0.10).

As shown in Exhibit 4-14, the assumptions made so far imply that Derrald's income before taxes in 2016 will total $80. Income tax expense is determined by how much pretax income a company has. The most reasonable assumption to make is that a company's tax rate, equal to income tax expense divided by pretax income, will stay constant from year to year. Derrald's tax rate in 2015 was 43% ($30/$70), which when applied to the forecasted pretax income of $80 for 2016, implies that income tax expense in 2016 will total $34 ($80 × 0.43).

The complete forecasted income statement for 2016 indicates that Derrald Company's income for the year will be $46. The quality of this forecast is only as good as the assumptions that underlie it. To determine how much impact the assumptions can have, it is often useful to conduct a sensitivity analysis. This involves repeating the forecasting exercise using a set of pessimistic and a set of optimistic assumptions. Thus, one can construct worst-case, standard-case, and best-case scenarios to use in making decisions with the forecasted numbers.

Financial statement forecasting is used to construct an estimate of how well a company will perform in the future. This forecasting exercise is useful for bankers worried about whether they can recover their money if they make a loan to a company and for investors who want to determine how much to invest in a company. Forecasted financial statements are also useful to company management for evaluating alternate strategies and determining whether the planned operating, investing, and financing activities appropriately mesh together. The Derrald Company example used in this chapter will also be used in Chapter 5 to illustrate how to forecast a company's statement of cash flows.

Concluding Comments

This chapter highlights the need for users of the income statement to use care with terminology. For example, income can mean gross profit, operating income, income from continuing operations, net income, or comprehensive income. One must be very careful with accounting terminology.

The income statement summarizes a firm's performance in its primary business activities (operating income) as well as peripheral activities (income from continuing operations). The income statement also includes two "below-the-line" items that are treated somewhat differently than other items included on the income statement. These are summarized in Exhibit 4-15.

Comprehensive income is a relatively new operational measure, and it will be interesting to see how the financial community uses this information in making investment decisions.

Exhibit 4-15 | Summary of Procedures for Reporting Irregular, Nonrecurring, or Unusual Items*

Where Reported	Category	Description	Examples
Part of income from continuing operations.	Changes in estimates.	Normal recurring changes in estimating future amounts. Included in normal accounts.	Changes in building and equipment lives, changes in estimated loss from uncollectible accounts receivable, changes in estimate of warranty liability.
	Unusual gains and losses, not considered extraordinary.	Unusual or infrequent, but not both. Related to normal operations. Material in amount. Shown in other revenues and gains or other expenses and losses.	Gains or losses from sale of assets, investments, or other operating assets. Write-off of inventories as obsolete.
On income statement, but after income from continuing operations.	Discontinued operations.	Disposal of completely separate business component. Include gain or loss from sale or abandonment.	Sale by conglomerate company of separate line of business, such as milling company selling restaurant segment.
	Extraordinary items.	Both unusual and infrequent. Not related to normal business operations. Material in amount.	Material gains and losses from some casualties or legal claims if meet criteria.

* This chart describes the usual case. Exceptions to the descriptions occasionally do occur.

© Cengage Learning 2014

SOLUTIONS TO OPENING SCENARIO QUESTIONS

1. 3.4% = ($126,723 − $122,513)/$122,513.
2. −66.3% = ($4,184 − $12,427)/$12,427.
3. As explained in this chapter, the factors that impact comprehensive income are (1) net income and (2) unrealized gains and losses from market movements in investment values or foreign currency exchange rates. The substantial drop in comprehensive income for AT&T in 2011 was the result of several large one-time operating expenses such as impairment of intangible assets and actuarial losses from AT&T's pension plans. These topics are discussed in later chapters.

Stop & Think SOLUTIONS

1. (Page 4-5) The correct answer is D. Measuring physical well-offness would require firms to obtain fair market value measures of each of their assets and liabilities each period. The difficulties of obtaining these measures along with the associated costs would, in most cases, cause the costs of the information to exceed its benefits.
2. (Page 4-8) The correct answer is A. Revenues and expenses are associated with what a business does. That is, they relate to a company's central activities. An investor or creditor would want to evaluate a business's performance in its central activities. Additional information relating to gains and losses associated with the peripheral activities of a business would be useful but should not be combined with revenues and expenses for reporting purposes.
3. (Page 4-9) The correct answer is B. Recall that revenue recognition at the time of production is acceptable when sale at an established price is practically assured. For the gold produced by Kinross in eastern Russia, enough uncertainty surrounds the shipment and sale of the gold that revenue is not recognized until the actual sale occurs.

SOLUTION TO USING THE FASB'S CODIFICATION

FASB ASC paragraph 915-205-45-1 says the following: "Financial statements issued by a development stage entity shall present financial position, results of operations, and cash flows in conformity with the generally accepted accounting principles (GAAP) that apply to established operating entities." In short, a development stage company must use the same accounting standards used by regular companies. So, the answer to your CEO's question is "No. A development stage company must report expenses using the same standards used by regular companies."

FASB ASC Subtopic 915-205 comes from pre-Codification *SFAS No. 7*, which was adopted by the FASB in 1975. Before *SFAS No. 7*, special accounting practices used in development stage companies included: "(a) deferral of all types of costs without regard to their recoverability, (b) nonassignment of dollar amounts to shares of stock issued for consideration other than cash, and (c) offset of revenue against deferred costs." (*SFAS No. 7*, par. 2)

Review Chapter 4 Learning Objectives

① Define the concept of income.

Income is a return over and above the investment of the owners. It measures the amount that an entity could return to its investors and still leave the entity as well off at the end of the period as at the beginning. Two concepts can be used to measure "well-offness:" financial capital maintenance (the dollar amount of net assets) and physical capital maintenance (physical productive capacity). The FASB has chosen to use the financial capital maintenance concept in measuring income.

② Explain why an income measure is important.

Many consider the recognition, measurement, and reporting of income to be among the most important tasks performed by accountants. Many individuals use this measure for business and economic decisions that result in the allocation of resources, which in turn contributes to the standard of living in society.

③ Explain how income is measured, including the revenue recognition and expense-matching concepts.

Income is measured as the difference between resource inflows (revenues and gains) and outflows (expenses and losses) over a period of time. Revenues are recognized when (1) they are realized or realizable and (2) they have been earned through substantial completion of the activities involved in the earning process. Usually, this is at the point of sale of goods or services. Expenses are matched against revenues directly, in a systematic and rational manner, or are immediately recognized as a period expense.

④ Understand the format of an income statement.

The general format of a multiple-step income statement is to subtract cost of goods sold and operating expenses from operating revenues to derive operating income. Gains and losses are then included to arrive at income from continuing operations. Regardless of the format, irregular and extraordinary items are disclosed separately to determine net income.

⑤ Describe the specific components of an income statement.

Most companies will report on some or all of the following specific components of an income statement:

- Revenue
- Cost of goods sold
- Gross profit
- Operating expenses
- Operating income
- Other revenues and gains
- Other expenses and losses
- Income from continuing operations before income taxes
- Income taxes on continuing operations
- Income from continuing operations
- Discontinued operations
- Extraordinary items

6 Compute and present comprehensive income.

In its conceptual framework, the FASB suggests reporting comprehensive income reflecting all changes in equity during a period except those resulting from investments by owners and distributions to owners. Comprehensive income is the number used to reflect an overall measure of the change in a company's wealth during the period. In addition to net income, comprehensive income includes items that, in general, arise from changes in market conditions unrelated to the business operations of a company. The FASB encourages companies to provide one continuous net income/comprehensive income statement. However, most companies report comprehensive income in a separate statement placed immediately after the income statement.

7 Construct simple forecasts of income for future periods.

An important use of an income statement is to forecast income in future periods. Good forecasting requires an understanding of what underlying factors determine the level of a revenue or an expense. Most financial statement forecasting exercises start with a forecast of sales, which establishes the expected scale of operations in future periods. Some balance sheet items increase naturally as the level of sales increases; examples of such accounts are cash, accounts receivable, inventory, and accounts payable. Other balance sheet items, such as property, plant, and equipment, change in response to a company's long-term strategic plans. Finally, the amounts of the balance sheet items associated with financing, such as long-term debt and paid-in capital, are determined by the financing decisions made by a company's management.

Some income statement items, such as cost of goods sold, maintain a constant relationship with sales. Depreciation expense is more likely to be related to the amount of a company's property, plant, and equipment. Interest expense is tied to the balance in interest-bearing debt. Finally, income tax expense is typically a relatively constant percentage of income before taxes.

FASB-IASB CODIFICATION SUMMARY

Topic	FASB Accounting Standards Codification	Original FASB Standard	Corresponding IASB Standard	Differences Between U.S. GAAP and IFRS
Discontinued operations	Subtopic 205-20	SFAS No. 144	IFRS 5	Under IFRS, a discontinued operation must be a major line of business or geographic segment. Also, under IFRS, separate disclosure must be made of the cash flows of the discontinued operations.
Extraordinary items	Subtopic 225-20	APB Opinion No. 30	IAS 1 par. 87	Under IFRS, no income or expense items are allowed to be classified as "extraordinary."
Change in accounting principle	Section 250-10-45 par. 1-16 Section 250-10-50 par. 1-3	SFAS No. 154 par. 4-18 APB No. 28 par. 28	IAS 8 par. 14-31	No substantial differences.

KEY TERMS

- Comparative financial statements 4-13
- Comprehensive income 4-31
- Consolidated financial statements 4-13
- Discontinued operations 4-21
- Earnings per share (EPS) 4-28
- Expense recognition 4-11
- Expenses 4-7
- Extraordinary items 4-23
- Financial capital maintenance 4-4
- Gains 4-7
- Gross profit 4-17
- Gross profit percentage 4-17
- Income 4-3
- Income from continuing operations 4-16
- Intraperiod income tax allocation 4-20
- Losses 4-7
- Matching 4-11
- Multiple-step form 4-13
- Operating income 4-18
- Physical capital maintenance 4-4
- Price-earnings ratio (P/E ratio) 4-29
- Restructuring charge 4-19
- Return on sales 4-27
- Revenue recognition 4-8
- Revenues 4-7
- Transaction approach 4-7

Tutorial Activities

Tutorial Activities with author-written, content-specific feedback, available on *CengageNOW for Stice & Stice.*

QUESTIONS

1. FASB *Concepts Statement No. 1* states, "The primary focus of financial reporting is information about an enterprise's performance provided by measures of earnings and its components." Why is it unwise for users of financial statements to focus too much attention on the income statement?

2. After the necessary definitions and assumptions that support the determination of income have been made, what are the two methods of income measurement that may be used to determine income? How do they differ?

3. What different measurement methods may be applied to net assets in arriving at income under the capital maintenance approach?

4. Income as determined by income tax regulations is not necessarily the same as income reported to external users. Why might there be differences?

5. What is the difference between a code law country and a common law country?

6. How are revenues and expenses different from gains and losses?

7. What two factors must be considered in deciding the point at which revenues and gains should be recognized? At what point in the revenue cycle are these conditions usually met?

8. Name three exceptions to the general rule that assumes revenue is recognized at the point of sale. What is the justification for these exceptions?

9. What guidelines are used to match costs with revenues in determining income?

10. What are some possible disadvantages of a multiple-step income statement?

11. Identify the major sections (components of income) that are included in a multiple-step income statement.

12. What are restructuring charges, and why do they generate controversy?

13. What is the meaning of "intraperiod" income tax allocation?

14. Pop-Up Company has decided to sell its lid manufacturing division even though the division is expected to show a small profit this year. The division's assets will be sold to another company at a loss of $10,000. What information (if any) should Pop-Up disclose in its financial reports with respect to this division?

15. Which of the following would not normally qualify as an extraordinary item?
    (a) The write-down or write-off of receivables
    (b) Major devaluation of foreign currency

(c) Loss on sale of plant and equipment
(d) Gain from early extinguishment of debt
(e) Loss due to extensive flood damage to an asphalt company in Las Vegas, Nevada
(f) Loss due to extensive earthquake damage to a furniture company in Los Angeles, California
(g) Farming loss due to heavy spring rains in the Northwest

16. Explain briefly the difference in accounting treatment of (a) a change in accounting principle and (b) a change in accounting estimate.

17. Under IASB standards, how is a change in accounting principle reported?
18. What is the general practice in reporting earnings per share?
19. Define *comprehensive income*. How does it differ from net income?
20. What is the starting point for the preparation of forecasted financial statements?
21. Describe the process one should use in forecasting depreciation expense.

PRACTICE EXERCISES

Practice 4-1

Identifying Income Statement Items
Using the data below, compute net income.

Accounts payable	$ 120
Capital stock	400
Cash	100
Cost of goods sold	250
Dividends	160
Equipment	1,640
Inventory	550
Loans payable	860
Prepaid rent	50
Rent expense	200
Retained earnings (beginning)	700
Sales revenue	1,200
Utilities expense	330

Practice 4-2

Financial Capital Maintenance
The company had the following total asset and total liability balances at the beginning and the end of the year:

	Beginning	Ending
Total assets	$400,000	$625,000
Total liabilities	230,000	280,000

During the year, the company received $100,000 in new investment funds contributed by the owners. Using the financial capital maintenance concept, determine the company's income for the year.

Practice 4-3
Physical Capital Maintenance
Refer to Practice 4-2. Assets with the same productive capacity as the assets comprising the $400,000 beginning asset balance had a current cost of $465,000 at the end of the year. Using the physical capital maintenance concept, determine the company's income for the year.

Practice 4-4
Computation of Income Using Matching
The company sells custom-designed engineering equipment. During the most recent year, the company received the following customer orders:

For Machine A, selling price = $125,000, production cost = $67,000
For Machine B, selling price = $235,000, production cost = $140,000
For Machine C, selling price = $72,000, production cost = $41,000
For Machine D, selling price = $370,000, production cost = $150,000

Machines A and C were completed and shipped during the year; the total revenue from the sale of these machines will be reported in the income statement for the year. Machines B and D have not yet been completed; the total production cost incurred so far for these two machines is $240,000. The revenue from the sale of these two machines will *not* be reported in the income statement for the year. Using the transaction approach (the matching method), compute the company's income for the year.

Practice 4-5
Revenue Recognition
The following information describes the company's sales for the year:

(a) A sale for $100,000 was made on March 23. As of the end of the year, all work associated with the sale has been completed. Unfortunately, the customer is a significant credit risk, and the collection of the cash for the sale is very uncertain. No cash has been collected as of the end of the year.

(b) A sale for $130,000 was made on July 12. The $130,000 cash for the sale was collected in full on July 12. The work associated with the sale has not yet begun but is expected to be completed early next year.

(c) A sale for $170,000 was made on November 17. No cash has been collected as of the end of the year, but all of the cash is expected to be collected early next year. As of the end of the year, all of the work associated with the sale has been completed.

How much revenue should be recognized for the year?

Practice 4-6
Expense Recognition
The following information describes the company's costs incurred during the year:

	Amount of Cost	Expense Recognition Method	Length of Allocation Period	Matched Revenue Recognized?
(a)	$30,000	Direct matching	Not applicable	Yes
(b)	70,000	Immediate recognition	Not applicable	Not applicable
(c)	15,000	Rational allocation	Three years	Not applicable
(d)	27,000	Immediate recognition	Not applicable	Not applicable
(e)	45,000	Rational allocation	Five years	Not applicable
(f)	50,000	Direct matching	Not applicable	No

How much expense should be recognized for the year?

Practice 4-7
Multiple-Step Income Statement
Using the following information, prepare a multiple-step income statement.

Cost of goods sold	$ 6,000	Extraordinary gain (net of income taxes)	$ 250
Interest expense	1,100	Dividends	700
Selling and administrative expense	750	Retained earnings (beginning)	1,000
Cash	400	Income tax expense (on	
Sales	10,000	continuing operations)	1,200

Practice 4-8

Multiple-Step Income Statement

Using the following information, prepare a multiple-step income statement.

Cost of goods sold	$ 8,000	Accrued wages payable	$ 320
Interest expense	900	Dividends	500
Selling and administrative expense	1,000	Retained earnings (beginning)	700
Cash	600	Income tax expense	1,000
Sales	13,000		

Practice 4-9

Computation of Gross Profit Percentage

Refer to the **IBM** information in Exhibit 4-5. Compute the overall gross profit percentage for 2009, 2010, and 2011.

Practice 4-10

Income from Continuing Operations

Refer to the **IBM** information in Exhibit 4-5. Compute income from continuing operations as a percentage of total revenue for 2009, 2010, and 2011.

Practice 4-11

Computation of Income from Continuing Operations

Use the following information to compute *income from continuing operations*. Assume that the income tax rate on all items is 40%.

Cost of goods sold	$ 5,000	Extraordinary loss	$ (350)
Interest expense	900	Sales	12,000
Income (loss) from discontinued operations	(1,500)	Dividends	750
		Loss on sale of discontinued operations	(300)
Selling and administrative expense	1,450		

Practice 4-12

Computation of Income from Discontinued Operations

Fleming Company has two divisions, E and N. Both qualify as business components. In 2015, the firm decides to dispose of the assets and liabilities of Division N; it is probable that the disposal will be completed early next year. The revenues and expenses of Fleming for 2014 and 2015 are as follows:

	2015	2014
Sales—E	$5,000	$4,600
Total nontax expenses—E	4,400	4,100
Sales—N	3,500	5,100
Total nontax expenses—N	3,900	4,500

During the later part of 2015, Fleming disposed of a portion of Division N and recognized a pretax loss of $2,000 on the disposal. The income tax rate for Fleming Company is 30%. Prepare the 2015 comparative income statement.

Practice 4-13

Computation of Income from Discontinued Operations

Refer to the data in Practice 4-12. Repeat the exercise, assuming that Division E is being discontinued. Also assume that instead of a $2,000 pretax loss on the disposal, there was a $1,500 pretax gain.

Practice 4-14

Gains and Losses on Extraordinary Items

Use the following information to compute *income from continuing operations* and *net income*. Assume that the income tax rate on all items is 40%.

Cost of goods sold	$14,000	Loss from an unusual and infrequent event	$ (800)
Interest expense	2,400	Sales	25,000
Loss from an unusual but frequent event	(3,000)	Gain from a normal but infrequent event	1,350
Selling and administrative expense	2,250	Dividends	1,000

C4 | The Income Statement
EOC 4-45

Practice 4-15

Cumulative Effect of a Change in Accounting Principle
The company started business in 2013. In 2015, the company decided to change its method of computing oil and gas exploration expense. The company has only two expenses: oil and gas exploration expense and income tax expense. The following sales and oil and gas exploration expense information are for 2013–2015:

	2015	2014	2013
Sales	$5,000	$3,000	$2,000
Oil and gas exploration expense—old method	1,000	600	400
Oil and gas exploration expense—new method	700	1,200	1,500

Prepare the 2015 comparative income statement. The income tax rate for all items is 30%.

Practice 4-16

Accounting for Changes in Estimates
A building was purchased for $100,000 on January 1, 2010. It was estimated to have no salvage value and to have an estimated useful life of 20 years. On January 1, 2015, the estimated useful life was changed from 20 years to 30 years. Compute depreciation expense for 2015. Use straight-line depreciation.

Practice 4-17

Return on Sales
Use the following information to compute return on sales.

Earnings per share	$ 1.67	Market price per share	$ 20
Cost of goods sold	10,000	Net income	200
Cash	550	Total stockholders' equity	6,700
Sales	13,000		

Practice 4-18

Earnings per Share
For the years 2013–2015, Robbins Soccer Company had net income and average shares outstanding as follows:

	2015	2014	2013
Net income	$12,250	$9,000	$5,500
Average shares outstanding	3,500	3,000	2,000

What was the percentage of change in earnings per share (EPS) in 2014? In 2015?

Practice 4-19

Price-Earnings (P/E) Ratio
Refer to Practice 4-17. Use that information to compute the price-earnings ratio.

Practice 4-20

Comprehensive Income
Use the following information to compute *net income* and *comprehensive income*. For simplicity, ignore income taxes.

Income from continuing operations	$ 9,000	Extraordinary loss	$(1,200)
Unrealized loss on available-for-sale securities	(1,700)	Foreign currency translation adjustment (equity increase)	1,500
Dividends	850		

Practice 4-21

Forecasted Balance Sheet
The following balance sheet asset information is for 2015:

Cash	$ 100	Land	$2,500
Accounts receivable	500	Plant and equipment (net)	5,000
Inventory	1,000		

Sales are expected to increase by 25% in 2016. No new land will be needed to support this increased level of sales. This sales increase will require significantly expanded production capacity; net plant and equipment will increase by 40%. Prepare a forecast of the Assets section of the 2016 balance sheet.

Practice 4-22

Forecasted Income Statement
The following balance sheet information represents actual data for 2015 and forecasted data for 2016:

	Actual 2015	Forecasted 2016
Current assets	$2,000	$2,600
Property, plant, and equipment (net)	5,000	6,000
Accounts payable	500	650
Long-term debt	4,000	5,000
Total stockholders' equity	2,500	2,950

The actual income statement for 2015 is as follows:

Sales	$10,000
Cost of goods sold	6,000
Depreciation expense	1,000
Interest expense	400
Income before income taxes	$ 2,600
Income tax expense	910
Net income	$ 1,690

Sales are expected to increase by 30% in 2016. Prepare a forecasted income statement for 2016.

EXERCISES

Exercise 4-23

Calculation of Net Income
Changes in the balance sheet account balances for the Bubble Bobble Co. during 2015 follow. Dividends declared during 2015 were $15,000. Calculate the net income for the year assuming that no transactions other than the dividends affected retained earnings.

	Increase (Decrease)
Cash	$ 38,500
Accounts Receivable	57,000
Inventory	(32,500)
Buildings and Equipment (net)	160,000
Patents	(4,000)
Accounts Payable	(45,000)
Bonds Payable	135,000
Capital Stock	25,000
Additional Paid-In Capital	35,000

Exercise 4-24

Revenue Recognition

For each of the following transactions, events, or circumstances, indicate whether the recognition criteria for revenues and gains are met and provide support for your answer.

(a) An order of $25,000 for merchandise is received from a customer.

(b) The value of timberlands increases by $40,000 for the year due to normal growth.

(c) Accounting services are rendered to a client on account.

(d) A 1991 investment was made in land at a cost of $80,000. The land currently has a fair market value of $107,000.

(e) Cash of $5,600 is collected from the sale of a gift certificate that is redeemable in the next accounting period.

(f) Cash of $7,500 is collected from subscribers for subscription fees to a monthly magazine. The subscription period is two years.

(g) You owe a creditor $1,500, payable in 30 days. The creditor has cash flow difficulties and has agreed to allow you to retire the debt in full with an immediate payment of $1,200.

Exercise 4-25

Revenue Recognition

Indicate which of the following transactions or events gives rise to the recognition of revenue in 2015 under the accrual basis of accounting. If revenue is not recognized, what account, if any, is credited?

(a) On December 15, 2015, Howe Company received $20,000 as rent revenue for the six-month period beginning January 1, 2016.

(b) Monroe Tractor Co., on July 1, 2015, sold one of its tractors and received $10,000 in cash and a note for $50,000 at 12% interest, payable in one year. The fair market value of the tractor is $60,000.

(c) Oswald, Inc., issued additional shares of common stock on December 10, 2015, for $30,000 above par value.

(d) Balance Company received a purchase order in 2015 from an established customer for $10,200 of merchandise. The merchandise was shipped on December 20, 2015. The company's credit policy allows the customer to return the merchandise within 30 days and a 3% discount if paid within 20 days from shipment.

(e) Gloria, Inc., sold merchandise costing $2,000 for $2,500 in August 2015. The terms of the sale are 15% down on a 12-month conditional sales contract, with title to the goods being retained by the seller until the contract price is paid in full.

(f) On November 1, 2015, Jones & Whitlock entered into an agreement to audit the 2015 financial statements of Lehi Mills for a fee of $35,000. The audit work began on December 15, 2015, and will be completed around February 15, 2016.

Exercise 4-26

Expense Recognition

For each of the following items, indicate whether the expense should be recognized using (1) direct matching, (2) systematic and rational allocation, or (3) immediate recognition. Provide support for your answer.

(a) Johnson & Smith, Inc., conducts cancer research. The company's hope is to develop a cure for the deadly disease. To date, its efforts have proven unsuccessful. It is testing a new drug, Ebzinene, which has cost $400,000 to develop.

(b) **Sears** offers warranties on many of the products it sells. Although the warranty periods range from days to years, Sears can reasonably estimate warranty costs.

(c) Stocks Co. recently signed a two-year lease agreement on a warehouse. The entire cost of $15,000 was paid in advance.

(d) John Clark assembles chairs for the Stone Furniture Company. The company pays Clark on an hourly basis.

(e) Hardy Co. recently purchased a fleet of new delivery trucks. The trucks are each expected to last for 100,000 miles.

(f) Taylor Manufacturing Inc. regularly advertises in national trade journals. The objective is to acquire name recognition, not to promote a specific product.

Exercise 4-27

Change in Estimate
Borgquist Corporation purchased a patent on January 2, 2012, for $400,000. Its original life was estimated to be 10 years. However, in December of 2015, Borgquist's controller received information proving conclusively that the product protected by the Borgquist patent would be obsolete within three years. Accordingly, the company decided to write off the unamortized portion of the patent cost over four years beginning in 2015. How would the change in estimate be reflected in the accounts for 2015 and subsequent years?

Exercise 4-28

Classification of Income Statement Items
Where in a multiple-step income statement would each of the following items be reported?

(a) Purchase discounts
(b) Gain on early retirement of debt
(c) Interest revenue
(d) Loss on sale of equipment
(e) Casualty loss from hurricane
(f) Sales commissions
(g) Loss on disposal of business component
(h) Income tax expense
(i) Gain on sale of land
(j) Sales discounts
(k) Loss from long-term investments written off as worthless
(l) Direct labor cost
(m) Vacation pay of office employees
(n) Ending inventory

Exercise 4-29

Analysis and Preparation of Income Statement
The selling expenses of Caribou Inc. for 2015 are 13% of sales. General expenses, excluding doubtful accounts, are 25% of cost of goods sold but only 15% of sales. Doubtful accounts are 2% of sales. The beginning inventory was $136,000, and it decreased 30% during the year. Income from operations for the year before income taxes of 30% is $160,000. Extraordinary gain, net of tax of 30%, is $21,000. Prepare an income statement, including earnings-per-share data, giving supporting computations. Caribou Inc. has 130,000 shares of common stock outstanding.

Exercise 4-30

Intraperiod Income Tax Allocation
Nephi Corporation reported the following income items before tax for the year 2015:

Income from continuing operations before income taxes	$260,000
Loss from operations of a discontinued business component	70,000
Gain from disposal of a business component	40,000
Extraordinary gain	110,000

The income tax rate is 35% on all items. Prepare the portion of the income statement beginning with Income from continuing operations before income taxes for the year ended December 31, 2015, after applying proper intraperiod income tax allocation procedures.

Exercise 4-31

Discontinued Operations
On May 31, 2015, top management of Stafford Manufacturing Co. decided to dispose of an unprofitable business component. An operating loss of $210,000 associated with the component was incurred during the year. The plant facilities associated with the business segment were sold on November 30, and a $23,000 gain was realized on the sale of the plant assets.

(a) Assuming a 30% tax rate, prepare the discontinued operations section of Stafford Manufacturing Co.'s income statement for the year ending December 31, 2015.

(b) What additional information about the discontinued segment would be provided by Stafford Manufacturing if it were reporting using the accounting standards of the United Kingdom?

Exercise 4-32

Discontinued Operations

Jason Bond Company operates two restaurants, one in Valencia and one in Saugus. The operations and cash flows of each of the two restaurants are clearly distinguishable. During 2015, Jason Bond decided to close the restaurant in Saugus and sell the property; it is probable that the disposal will be completed early next year. The revenues and expenses of Jason Bond for 2015 and for the preceding two years are as follows:

	2015	2014	2013
Sales—Valencia	$60,000	$48,000	$40,000
Cost of goods sold—Valencia	26,000	22,000	18,000
Other expenses—Valencia	14,000	13,000	12,000
Sales—Saugus	23,000	30,000	52,000
Cost of goods sold—Saugus	14,000	19,000	20,000
Other expenses—Saugus	17,000	16,000	15,000

The other expenses do not include income tax expense. During the later part of 2015, Jason Bond sold much of the kitchen equipment of the Saugus restaurant and recognized a pretax gain of $15,000 on the disposal. The income tax rate for Jason Bond is 35%.

Prepare the three-year comparative income statement for 2013–2015.

Exercise 4-33

Change in Accounting Principle

In 2015, Compliance Industries changed its method of inventory valuation. The summary effect of those changes is as follows:

	Old Method	New Method
Cost of goods sold—2015	$25,000	$19,000
Cost of goods sold—2014	29,000	21,000
Cost of goods sold—2013	31,000	24,000
Cost of goods sold—2012 and before	51,000	38,000

Net income was $128,000, $119,000, and $98,000 for 2015, 2014, and 2013, respectively. The income tax rate is 30%.

1. Compute the reported net income for each year if three years of financial statements are issued at the end of 2015.
2. Compute the amount of adjustment that would be made to Retained Earnings as of January 1, 2013.

Exercise 4-34

Reporting Items on Financial Statements

Under what classification would you report each of the following items on the financial statements?

(a) Revenue from sale of obsolete inventory

(b) Loss on sale of the fertilizer production division of a lawn supplies manufacturer

(c) Loss stemming from expropriation of assets by a foreign government

(d) Gain resulting from changing asset balances to adjust for the effect of excessive depreciation charged in error in prior years

(e) Loss resulting from excessive accrual in prior years of estimated revenues from long-term contracts

(f) Costs incurred to purchase a valuable patent

(g) Net income from the discontinued dune buggy operations of a custom car designer

(h) Costs of rearranging plant machinery into a more efficient order

(i) Error made in capitalizing advertising expense during the prior year

(j) Gain on sale of land to the government
(k) Loss from destruction of crops by a hailstorm
(l) Additional depreciation resulting from a change in the estimated useful life of an asset
(m) Gain on sale of long-term investments
(n) Loss from spring flooding
(o) Sale of obsolete inventory at less than book value
(p) Additional federal income tax assessment for prior years
(q) Loss resulting from the sale of a portion of a business component
(r) Costs associated with moving a U.S. business to Japan
(s) Loss resulting from a patent that was recently determined to be worthless

Exercise 4-35

Multiple-Step Income Statement

From the following list of accounts, prepare a multiple-step income statement in good form showing all appropriate items properly classified, including disclosure of earnings-per-share data. (No monetary amounts are to be reported.)

Accounts Payable
Accumulated Depreciation—Office Building
Accumulated Depreciation—Office Furniture and Fixtures
Advertising Expense
Allowance for Bad Debts
Bad Debt Expense
Cash
Common Stock, $1 par (10,000 shares outstanding)
Depreciation Expense—Office Building
Depreciation Expense—Office Furniture and Fixtures
Dividend Revenue
Dividends Payable
Dividends Receivable
Extraordinary Gain (net of income taxes)
Federal Unemployment Tax Payable
Freight-In
Goodwill
Income Tax Expense
Income Taxes Payable
Insurance Expense
Interest Expense—Bonds
Interest Expense—Other
Interest Payable
Interest Receivable
Interest Revenue
Inventory—Beginning
Inventory—Ending
Loss from Discontinued Operations (net of income taxes)
Miscellaneous General Expense
Miscellaneous Selling Expense
Office Salaries Expense
Office Supplies
Office Supplies Expense
Officers' Salaries Expense
Property Taxes Expense
Purchase Discounts
Purchase Returns and Allowances
Purchases
Retained Earnings
Royalties Received in Advance
Royalty Revenue
Salaries and Wages Payable
Sales
Sales Discounts
Sales Returns and Allowances
Sales Salaries and Commissions
Sales Taxes Payable

Exercise 4-36

Multiple-Step Income Statement and Statement of Retained Earnings

Jacksonville Window Co. reports the following for 2015:

Retained earnings, January 1	$335,200	Cost of goods sold	$772,000
Selling expenses	$290,200	Dividends declared this year	$40,000
Sales revenue	$1,420,000	Tax rate for all items	40%
Interest expense	$14,100	Average shares of common stock	
General and administrative expenses	$224,800	outstanding during the year	30,000

Prepare a multiple-step income statement (including earnings-per-share data) and a statement of retained earnings for Jacksonville.

Exercise 4-37

REVERSE SOLVABLE

Correction of Retained Earnings Statement

J. Mair has been employed as a bookkeeper at Problems Inc. for a number of years. With the assistance of a clerk, Mair handles all accounting duties, including the preparation of financial statements. The following is a statement of earned surplus prepared by Mair for 2015:

Problems Inc.
Statement of Earned Surplus for 2015

Balance at beginning of year		$ 76,843
Additions:		
Change in estimate of 2015 amortization expense	$ 3,100	
Gain on sale of land	17,420	
Interest revenue	3,900	
Profit and loss for 2015	12,760	
Total additions		37,180
Total		$114,023
Deductions:		
Increased depreciation due to change in estimated life	$ 6,400	
Dividends declared and paid	12,000	
Loss on sale of equipment	2,490	
Loss from major casualty (extraordinary)	25,310	
Total deductions		46,200
Balance at end of year		$ 67,823

1. Prepare a schedule showing the correct net income for 2015. (Ignore income taxes.)
2. Prepare a retained earnings statement for 2015.
3. Explain why you have changed the retained earnings statement.

Exercise 4-38

Statement of Comprehensive Income

Svedin Incorporated provides the following information relating to 2015:

Net income	$17,650
Unrealized losses on available-for-sale securities	1,285
Foreign currency translation adjustment	287
Deferred loss on derivatives	315

The foreign currency adjustment resulted from a weakening in the currencies of Svedin's foreign subsidiaries relative to the U.S. dollar. The deferred loss on derivatives required the recognition of a liability with a resulting decrease in equity. (*Note*: These items represent the results of events occurring during 2015, not the cumulative result of events in prior years.)

1. Determine the effect that each of these items would have when computing comprehensive income for 2015. Explain your rationale.
2. Prepare a statement of comprehensive income for Svedin Incorporated for 2015.

Exercise 4-39

Forecasted Income Statement

Romney and Associates wishes to forecast its net income for the year 2016. Romney has assembled balance sheet and income statement data for 2015 and has also done a forecast of the balance sheet for 2016. In addition, Romney has estimated that its sales in 2016 will rise to $3,600. This information is summarized in the following table.

Balance Sheet	2015	2016 Forecasted
Cash	$ 40	$ 48
Other current assets	450	540
Property, plant, and equipment (net)	500	700
Total assets	$ 990	$1,288
Accounts payable	$ 190	$ 228
Bank loans payable	500	400
Total stockholders' equity	300	660
Total liabilities and stockholders' equity	$ 990	$1,288

Income Statement	2015	2016 Forecasted
Sales	$3,000	$3,600
Cost of goods sold	1,200	
Gross profit	$1,800	
Depreciation expense	100	
Other operating expenses	1,440	
Operating profit	$ 260	
Interest expense	50	
Income before taxes	$ 210	
Income taxes	84	
Net income	$ 126	

Prepare a forecasted income statement for 2016. Clearly state what assumptions you make.

Exercise 4-40

Forecasted Balance Sheet and Income Statement

Ryan Company wishes to prepare a forecasted income statement and a forecasted balance sheet for 2016. Ryan's balance sheet and income statement for 2015 follow.

Balance Sheet	2015
Cash	$ 10
Other current assets	250
Property, plant, and equipment, net	800
Total assets	$1,060
Accounts payable	$ 100
Bank loans payable	700
Total stockholders' equity	260
Total liabilities and stockholders' equity	$1,060

Income Statement	2015
Sales	$1,000
Cost of goods sold	750
Gross profit	$ 250
Depreciation expense	40
Other operating expenses	80
Operating profit	$ 130
Interest expense	70
Income before taxes	$ 60
Income taxes	20
Net income	$ 40

In addition, Ryan has assembled the following forecasted information regarding 2016:

(a) Sales are expected to increase to $1,500.

(b) Ryan expects to become more efficient at utilizing its property, plant, and equipment in 2016. Therefore, Ryan expects that the sales increase will not require any increase in property, plant, and equipment. Accordingly, the year 2016 property, plant, and equipment balance is expected to be $800.

(c) Ryan's bank has approved a new long-term loan of $200. This loan will be in addition to the existing loan payable.

Prepare a forecasted balance sheet and a forecasted income statement for 2016. Clearly state what assumptions you make.

P1
Foundations of Financial Accounting

CHAPTER 5

Statement of Cash Flows and Articulation

Learning Objectives

1. Describe the circumstances in which the cash flow statement is a particularly important companion of the income statement.

2. Outline the structure of and information reported in the three main categories of the cash flow statement: operating, investing, and financing.

3. Compute cash flow from operations using either the direct or the indirect method.

4. Prepare a complete statement of cash flows and provide the required supplemental disclosures.

5. Assess a firm's financial strength by analyzing the relationships among cash flows from operating, investing, and financing activities and by computing financial ratios based on cash flow data.

6. Demonstrate how the three primary financial statements tie together, or articulate, in a unified framework.

7. Use knowledge of how the three primary financial statements tie together to prepare a forecasted statement of cash flows.

Karl Eller started out in the billboard business. After his company was acquired by Gannett, he sat on the firm's board and was one of a group of directors who opposed Gannett's risky plan to start up the first U.S. national daily newspaper, *USA Today*. He left Gannett and went to Columbia Pictures, where he was one of the driving forces behind the purchase of Columbia by Coca-Cola. (Columbia Pictures was subsequently purchased again, this time by Sony in one of the most overpriced Hollywood deals of all time—but that is another story.) In 1983, Mr. Eller went into the convenience store business and took on the challenge of transforming Circle K from a regional 1,200-store convenience store chain centered in Arizona into the second-largest chain in the United States (behind 7-Eleven). At its peak, Circle K operated 4,685 stores in 32 states.

Circle K's rapid expansion was financed through long-term borrowing. Its long-term debt increased from $41 million in 1983, when Mr. Eller took over, to $1.2 billion in 1990. The interest on this large debt, along with increased price competition from convenience stores operated by oil companies, combined to squeeze Circle K's profits.[1] Net income dropped from a record high of $60 million in 1988 to $15 million in 1989. For the year ended April 30, 1990, Circle K reported a loss of $773 million. In May 1990, Circle K filed for Chapter 11 bankruptcy protection.

As illustrated in Exhibit 5-1, at the same time it was reporting the disastrous $773 million loss, Circle K was reporting a record high positive cash flow from operations of more than $100 million. How could Circle K report positive cash flow at the same time it was reporting a record-breaking net loss? There are many causes for a difference between accrual net income and cash flow; these causes are discussed in this chapter. In Circle K's case, there were three primary contributing factors:

- Much of the reported loss was due to a $639 million restructuring charge. For example, goodwill previously recorded as a $300 million asset was written off. This drastically reduced net income but did not affect cash flow.

- Circle K added $75 million to its estimated liability for environmental cleanup charges resulting from leaky underground gasoline storage tanks. Again, this charge reduced income but did not involve an immediate cash outflow.

- Financial distress forced Circle K to make its operations more efficient. One result was that Circle K reduced its inventory by $65 million in 1990. This action increased cash flow because $65 million in cash was liberated that otherwise would have been tied up in the form of gasoline, beer, and Twinkies®.

In 1991, Circle K again showed positive cash flow from operations while reporting a large net loss. In an interesting twist, this positive cash flow was partially a result of the bankruptcy filing. When a company files for Chapter 11 bankruptcy, the courts allow the company to cease making interest payments on its old debts. During the fiscal year ended April 30, 1990, the year before the bankruptcy filing, Circle K paid more than $100 million in interest. In 1991, after the filing, Circle K paid only $6 million in interest. In addition, the bankruptcy filing strengthened the willingness of suppliers to sell to Circle K on credit because bankruptcy

Exhibit 5-1 | Circle K Income vs. Cash Flow

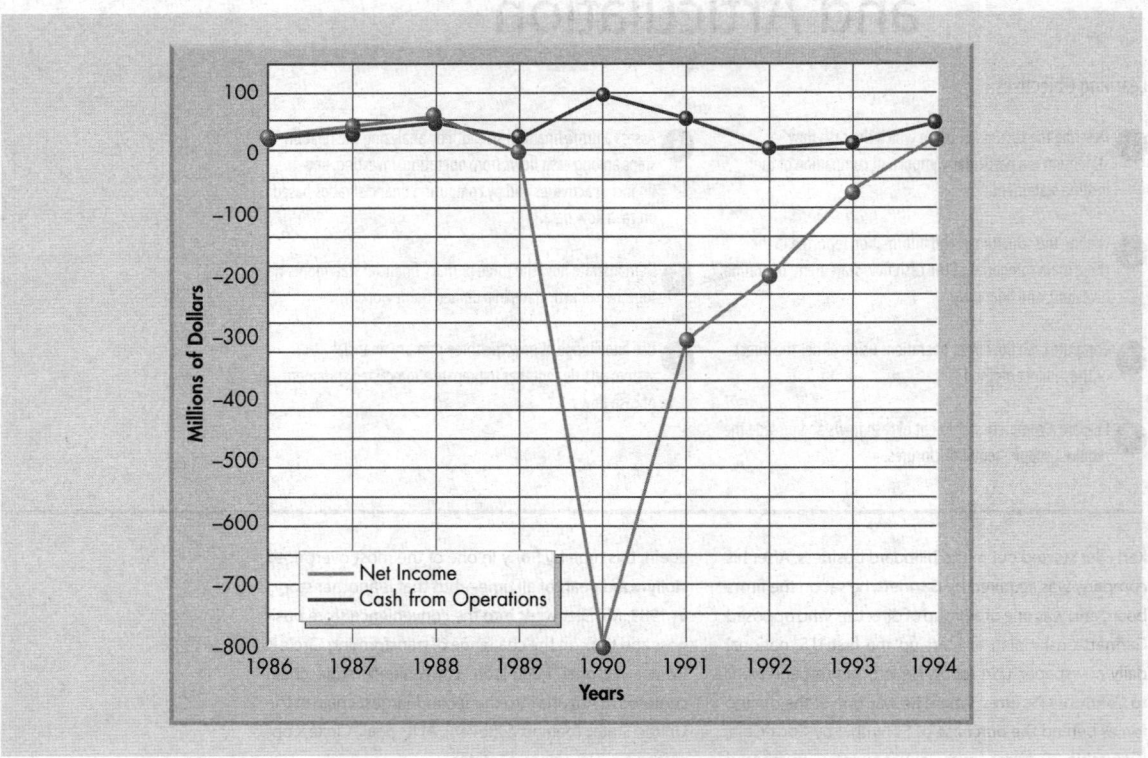

[1] Roy J. Harris Jr., "Karl Eller of Circle K, Always Pushing Luck, Now Lives to Regret It," *The Wall Street Journal*, March 28, 1990, p. A1.

laws place postbankruptcy lenders near the top of the creditor priority list. As a result, Circle K's accounts payable increased $80 million in 1991. This accounts payable increase freed up cash that otherwise would have been used to pay current bills.

Because of this positive cash flow from operations, Circle K was able to stay in business while its management devised a reorganization plan. As part of its bankruptcy restructuring, Circle K replaced Karl Eller as chief executive officer (CEO) in 1990. Following a lengthy debate among the creditors, Circle K's bankruptcy reorganization plan was formally approved by a federal bankruptcy court judge, and in 1993 Circle K was purchased for $400 million by a diverse group of private investors from Barcelona, Kuwait, and Pittsburgh. Subsequently, Circle K was taken over by Tosco, the largest independent refiner and marketer of petroleum products in the United States.[2] In September 2001, Tosco itself was acquired by Phillips Petroleum, temporarily combining the Circle K brand under the same umbrella as 76 and Phillips 66. In 2003, Circle K was acquired by a Canadian company, Alimentation Couche-Tard.

And what about Mr. Eller, who started this whole thing? Well, you can't keep a good entrepreneur down. Karl Eller returned to his roots and became CEO of Eller Media, the largest billboard company in the United States.[3] On April 10, 1997, Eller Media was acquired by Clear Channel Communications, which has billboards across the United States and in the United Kingdom and operates radio and TV stations in the United States, Mexico, Australia, and New Zealand. Mr. Eller served on the board of directors of Clear Channel until his retirement in 2001 at age 73. Mr. Eller, a longtime sports fan, served on the National Collegiate Athletic Association (NCAA) Leadership Advisory Board of Directors along with other luminaries such as Peyton Manning. He was given the NCAA's Flying Wedge Award to recognize his service to the NCAA. How is that for landing on your feet?

1. How was Circle K able to report a record amount of positive operating cash flow at the same time it was reporting an income statement loss of $773 million?
2. How did filing for Chapter 11 bankruptcy help Circle K's cash flow situation?
3. In what kind of business did Karl Eller both start and end his business career?

Answers to these questions can be found on page 5-32.

The Circle K case illustrates that cash flow data sometimes reveal aspects of operations not captured by earnings. In addition, recall that assessing the amounts, timing, and uncertainty of future cash flows is one of the primary objectives of financial reporting.[4] The statement that provides information needed to meet this objective is a statement of cash flows. This chapter provides an overview of reporting cash flows and outlines the techniques for preparing and analyzing a cash flow statement.

What Good Is a Cash Flow Statement?

LO1 学习目标1
阐述现金流量表是利润表的重要补充形式。

① Describe the circumstances in which the cash flow statement is a particularly important companion of the income statement.

The key question is whether a cash flow statement tells us anything we don't already know from the balance sheet and income statement. This is a legitimate question because the conceptual framework says that the primary focus of financial reporting is earnings, and

---

[2] Jonathan Auerbach and Louise Lee, "Circle K Pact Gives Tosco Fuel Injection," *The Wall Street Journal*, February 20, 1996, p. A4. (Interestingly, Tosco's corporate headquarters were in Stamford, Connecticut, the same city where the FASB was formerly located—small world.)
[3] William P. Barrett, "The Phoenix of Phoenix," *Forbes*, January 1, 1996, p. 44.
[4] *Statement of Financial Accounting Concepts No. 8*, "Conceptual Framework for Financial Reporting: Chapter 1, *The Objective of General Purpose Financial Reporting*, and Chapter 3, *Qualitative Characteristics of Useful Financial Information*" (Norwalk, CT: Financial Accounting Standards Board, September 2010), par. OB3.

earnings information is a better indicator of a firm's ability to generate cash in the future than is current cash flow information.

To answer the question: Yes, we need the cash flow statement. Some of the important reasons discussed in this chapter follow.

- Sometimes earnings fail.
- Everything is on one page.
- It is used as a forecasting tool.

Sometimes Earnings Fail

In some situations, net income does not give us an accurate picture of the economic performance of a company for a certain period. Three such scenarios are illustrated here by reference to actual company examples: (1) the Circle K scenario, (2) the **Home Depot** scenario, and (3) the **KnowledgeWare** scenario.

The Big Loss Scenario When a company reports large noncash expenses, such as write-offs, depreciation, and provisions for future obligations, earnings may give a gloomier picture of current operations than is warranted. As discussed in the opening scenario of the chapter, Circle K reported record losses in the same years it was reporting record positive cash flow from operations. In such cases, cash flow from operations is a better indicator of whether the company can continue to honor its commitments to creditors, customers, employees, and investors in the near term. Don't misunderstand this to mean that a reported loss is nothing to worry about as long as cash flow is positive; the positive cash flow indicates that business can continue for the time being, but the reported loss may hint at looming problems in the future.

> **Caution**
> Note that the heading to this section says that "sometimes" earnings fail. In most cases, net income is the single best measure of a firm's economic performance.

The Rapid Growth Scenario Rapidly growing firms use large amounts of cash to expand inventory. In addition, cash collections on the growing accounts receivable often lag behind the need to pay creditors. In these cases, reported earnings may be positive, but operations are actually consuming rather than generating cash. This can make it difficult to service debt and satisfy investors' demands for cash dividends. For example, in the mid-1980s, The Home Depot was faced with a crisis as exponential sales growth necessitated operating cash infusions every year in spite of the fact that earnings were positive.[5] The lesson is this: For high-growth companies, positive income is no guarantee that sufficient cash flow is there to service current needs.

The Reality Check Scenario Accounting assumptions are the heart of accrual accounting. For companies entering phases in which it is critical that reported earnings look good, those assumptions can be stretched—sometimes to the breaking point. Such phases include just before making a large loan application, just before the initial public offering of stock (when founding entrepreneurs cash in all those years of struggle and sweat), and just before being bought out by another company. In these cases, cash flow from operations, which is not impacted by accrual assumptions, provides an excellent reality check

---

[5] The cash flow problems of Home Depot in 1985 are the subject of a very popular Harvard Business School case written by Professor Krishna Palepu.

for reported earnings. For example, in 1994, KnowledgeWare, an Atlanta-based software company, was acquired by Sterling Software. Negotiations over the purchase price were thrown into chaos when it was disclosed that KnowledgeWare had been overly optimistic with its revenue recognition assumptions. At the time, one accounting professor commented: "Cash from operations is the critical number investors should be looking at when evaluating one of these companies."[6]

Everything Is on One Page

As discussed in more detail later, the cash flow statement includes information on operating, investing, and financing activities. In essence, everything you ever wanted to know about a company's performance for the year is summarized in this one statement. How successful were operations for the year? Look at the Operating Activities section. What new investments were made in property, plant, and equipment? Look in the Investing Activities section. Where did the money come from this year to finance all this stuff? See the Financing Activities section. If you were stuck on a desert island and could receive only a single financial statement each year (by bottle floated in on the waves), you would probably choose the cash flow statement.

It Is Used as a Forecasting Tool

When forecasting the future, a cash flow statement is an excellent tool to analyze whether the operating, investing, and financing plans are consistent and workable. To do this, one constructs a pro forma, or projected, cash flow statement. A pro forma cash flow statement

FASB CODIFICATION

The Issue: You have interrupted a successful acting career and are now following your dream of studying accounting. However, you still have a fondness for the film industry. You recently overheard an extremely disturbing conversation between two accounting professors. One of the professors said to the other: "Yes, exploitation is one of the primary operating cash outflows in the film business."

You are shocked to hear such an unfair characterization of the business where you got your start. You are planning to confront this professor and denounce him for voicing such an odious stereotype. However, before you visit the offending professor in his office, you want to do some research in the accounting standards to find out a bit more about accounting in the film industry, particularly as it relates to operating cash outflows.

The Question: What has "exploitation" got to do with operating cash outflows in the film business?

Searching the Codification: This is a great opportunity to use the Industry topics in the FASB Codification. Under the Industry topics, you should see the collection of Entertainment topics in the group 92X. One of those entertainment industries is Topic 926—Films. A look at the menu under this topic should allow you to find some information on the statement of cash flows in the film industry.

The Answer: The correct treatment is described on page 5-32.

[6] Timothy L. O'Brien, "KnowledgeWare Accounting Practices Are Questioned," *The Wall Street Journal*, September 7, 1994, p. B2.

is a prediction of what the actual cash flow statement will look like in future years if the operating, investing, and financing plans are implemented. For example, most lenders would be reluctant to loan money to a company to finance new investing activities when the pro forma cash flow statement indicates that there will be no positive operating cash flow to repay the loan. Construction of a pro forma cash flow statement is illustrated later in this chapter.

Structure of the Cash Flow Statement

2 Outline the structure of and information reported in the three main categories of the cash flow statement: operating, investing, and financing.

A statement of cash flows explains the change during the period in cash and cash equivalents. A cash equivalent is a short-term, highly liquid investment that can be converted easily into cash. To qualify as a cash equivalent, an item must be:[7]

1. Readily convertible to cash.
2. So near to its maturity that there is insignificant risk of changes in value due to changes in interest rates.

Generally, only investments with original maturities of three months or less qualify as cash equivalents. Original maturity in this case is determined from the date an investment is acquired by the reporting entity, which often does not coincide with the date the security is issued. For example, both a three-month U.S. Treasury bill and a three-year Treasury note purchased three months prior to maturity qualify as cash equivalents. However, if the Treasury note were purchased three years ago, it would not qualify as a cash equivalent during the last three months prior to its maturity.[8] In addition to U.S. Treasury obligations, cash equivalents can include items such as money market funds and commercial paper. Investments in marketable equity securities (common and preferred stock) normally would not be classified as cash equivalents because such securities have no maturity date.

Not all investments qualifying as cash equivalents need be reported as such. Management establishes a policy concerning which short-term, highly liquid investments are to be treated as cash equivalents. Once a policy is established, management should disclose which items are being treated as cash equivalents in presenting its cash flow statement. Any change in the established policy should be disclosed.

Three Categories of Cash Flows

In the statement of cash flows, cash receipts and payments are classified according to three main categories:

- Operating activities
- Investing activities
- Financing activities

Exhibit 5-2 summarizes the major types of cash receipts and cash payments included in each category and includes the income statement and balance sheet accounts that are typically related to each category in the statement of cash flows.

[7] FASB ASC Section 230-10-20 (Glossary)—Cash equivalents.
[8] Ibid.

Exhibit 5-2 | Major Cash Receipts and Payments by Category

Operating Activities

Cash receipts from:
- Sale of goods or services
- Sale of trading securities*
- Interest revenue
- Dividend revenue

Cash payments for:
- Inventory purchases
- Wages and salaries
- Taxes
- Interest expense
- Other expenses (e.g., utilities, rent)
- Purchase of trading securities*

Related items: income statement; current operating assets; current operating liabilities; some long-term operating assets and liabilities

*Cash flows associated with trading securities are usually, but not always, classified as operating activities.

Investing Activities

Cash receipts from:
- Sale of plant assets
- Sale of a business segment
- Sale of nontrading securities
- Collection of principal on loans

Cash payments for:
- Purchase of plant assets
- Purchase of nontrading securities
- Making loans to other entities

Related items: property, plant, and equipment; long-term investments; other long-term assets

Financing Activities

Cash receipts from:
- Issuance of stock
- Borrowing (e.g., bonds, notes, mortgages)

Cash payments for:
- Cash dividends
- Repayment of loans
- Repurchase of stock (treasury stock)

Related items: short-term and long-term debt; common stock; treasury stock; dividends

© Cengage Learning 2014

Operating Activities Operating activities include those transactions and events associated with the revenues and expenses that enter into the determination of net income. Cash receipts from selling goods or from providing services are the major cash inflows for most businesses. Other cash receipts come from interest, dividends, and similar items. Major cash outflows include payments to purchase inventory and to pay wages, taxes, interest, utilities, rent, and similar expenses. The net amount of cash provided or used by operating activities is the key figure in a statement of cash flows. In the same way that net income is used to summarize everything in an income statement, net cash from operations is the "bottom line" of the cash flow statement.

> **Caution**
>
> Whether an activity is an operating activity depends upon the nature of the business. The purchase of machinery is an investing activity for a manufacturing business, but it is an operating activity for a machinery sales business.

Although cash inflows from interest or dividends logically might be classified as investing or financing activities, the FASB decided to classify them as operating activities. The guiding principle is that the Operating Activities section contains the cash flow effects of revenues and expenses included in the income statement.

主要的投资活动是买卖土地、建筑物、机器设备和其他不以交易为目的持有的资产。此外，投资活动还包括购买或出售以非交易目的持有的金融工具，以及贷款的发放和收回。

Investing Activities The primary investing activities are the purchase and sale of land, buildings, equipment, and other assets not generally held for resale. In addition, investing activities include the purchase and sale of financial instruments not intended for trading purposes, as well as the making and collecting of loans. These activities occur regularly and result in cash receipts and payments, but they are not classified as operating activities because they relate only indirectly to the central, ongoing operation of a business.

Financing Activities Financing activities include transactions and events whereby cash is obtained from or repaid to owners (equity financing) and creditors (debt financing). For example, the cash proceeds from issuing stock or bonds would be classified under financing activities. Similarly, payments to reacquire stock (treasury stock) or to retire bonds and the payment of dividends are considered financing activities.

> **Stop & Think**
>
> There is conceptual difficulty in categorizing some cash flow items into just one of the three cash flow activities specified by the FASB. Two items that the FASB insists be classified as operating activities can be classified in other ways, or even in their own categories, according to the IASB. Look at the list below and identify these two problematic items.
>
> a) Payment of wages and payment for inventory purchases
> b) Payment of rent and payment of insurance
> c) Payment of interest and payment of income taxes
> d) Payment of utilities and payment for repairs

The nature of financing activities is the same no matter what industry a company is in, but operating and investing activities differ considerably across industries. For example, the operating and investing activities of a supermarket chain are quite different from those of a sand and gravel company. However, for both companies, the process of borrowing money, selling stock, paying cash dividends, and repaying loans is almost the same.

Cash Flow Pattern The normal pattern of positive inflows or negative outflows of cash reported in the cash flow statement is as follows:

- Cash from operating activities, +
- Cash from investing activities, –
- Cash from financing activities, + or –

Most companies (73% in the United States in 2006) generate positive cash flow from operations. In fact, several periods of negative cash from operations is a sure indicator of financial trouble. In normal times, most companies use cash to expand or enhance long-term assets, so cash from investing activities is usually negative (83% of the time in the United States in 2006). A company with positive cash flows from investing activities is selling off its long-term assets faster than it is replacing them.

融资活动没有一般模式，在一个正常经营的公司中，其数量可能为正也可能为负，取决于公司所处的成长阶段。

No general statements can be made about cash flows from financing activities; in healthy companies the number can be either positive or negative. As an example, positive cash flows from financing activities can be a sign of a young company that is expanding so fast that operations cannot provide enough cash to finance the expansion. Hence, additional cash must come from financing. Negative cash flows from financing activities might be exhibited by a mature company that has reached a stable state and has surplus cash from operations that can be used to repay loans or to pay higher cash dividends. Accordingly, a company's cash flow pattern is a general reflection of where the company is in its life cycle. As shown in Exhibit 5-3, a young or rapidly growing

> **FYI**
>
> A contender for the world record "cash cow" year is **ExxonMobil** in 2008. In that year, ExxonMobil's operating cash flow of $59.7 billion was enough to pay for its investing activities ($15.5 billion), repay debt ($0.5 billion), pay cash dividends ($8.1 billion), and repurchase stock ($35.7 billion).

Exhibit 5-3 | Cash Flow Patterns Over the Life of a Company

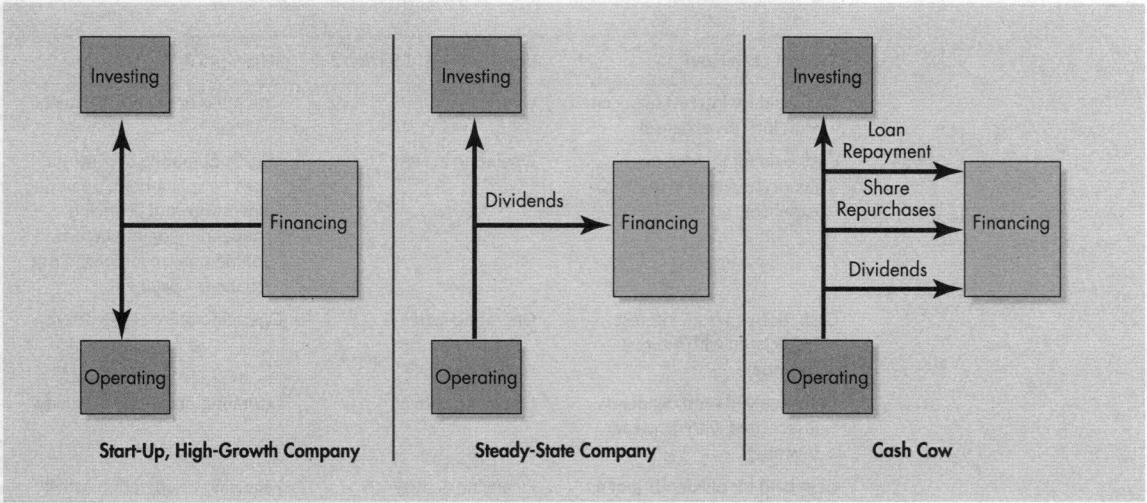

company requires cash inflows from financing activities in order to pay for its capital expansion (investing activities) and to subsidize negative operating cash flow resulting from a buildup in inventories and receivables. In a company that has stopped growing and is focused on maintaining its position, cash from operations is sufficient to finance the replenishment of long-term assets and to pay dividends to the investors. Finally, a mature, successful company (sometimes called a *cash cow*) generates so much cash from operations that it can pay for capital expansion and have cash left over to repay loans, pay cash dividends, and even repurchase shares of stock.

Further discussion of the interpretation of the cash flow pattern is in a later section of this chapter.

Noncash Investing and Financing Activities

一些投资和融资活动可能影响某个实体一个期间内的财务状况，但不影响现金流。

Some investing and financing activities affect an entity's financial position but not the entity's cash flow during the period. For example, equipment may be purchased with a note payable, or land may be acquired by issuing stock. Such noncash investing and financing activities should be disclosed separately, either in the notes to the financial statements or in an accompanying schedule, but not in the cash flow statement itself.[9] For example, when **Chevron Corporation** acquired a 50% interest in a joint venture with Kazakhstan to develop the Tengiz oil field, the $709 million deferred portion of the acquisition price was disclosed in the notes to Chevron's financial statements as a noncash transaction.

Cash Flow Categories under *IAS 7*

A cash flow statement has been required under IFRS since 1992. The provisions of *IAS 7, Statement of Cash Flows*, are more flexible than the U.S. rules contained in FASB *ASC Section 230* (originally *SFAS No. 95*). Total cash flow, operating plus investing plus financing, is the same under both sets of rules, but a few common types of cash flows can be

[9] FASB ASC paragraph 230-10-50-3.

classified in different categories depending on whether U.S. GAAP or IFRS is used to make the categorization. A summary of those differences is given below.

Type of Cash Flow	U.S. GAAP—ASC Section 230	IFRS—IAS 7
Cash paid for interest (associated with interest expense)	Operating activity	Operating or financing activity
Cash paid for income taxes (associated with income tax expense)	Operating activity	Usually operating activity, but can be split among operating, investing, and financing depending on the nature of the transaction giving rise to the tax payment
Cash received from interest (associated with interest revenue)	Operating activity	Operating or investing activity
Cash received from dividends (associated with dividend revenue)	Operating activity	Operating or investing activity
Cash paid for dividends (not an income statement item)	Financing activity	Financing or operating activity

The key number in a cash flow statement is total operating cash flow. As you can see from the table above, total operating cash flow for a company using IFRS could be greater than, less than, or the same as what the same company would report under U.S. GAAP, depending on the classification choices made under IFRS.

The particulars for computing operating cash flow, as illustrated in the next section, are slightly different under IFRS if some of the items above are classified differently from what is required under U.S. GAAP. Those slight differences are demonstrated in Chapter 21 when we revisit the statement of cash flows.

Reporting Cash Flow from Operations

3 Compute cash flow from operations using either the direct or the indirect method.

Exhibit 5-4 illustrates the general format, with details omitted, for a statement of cash flows using data from Intel's statement of cash flows. The statement should report the net cash provided by or used in operating, investing, and financing activities and the net effect of total cash flow on cash and cash equivalents during the period. The information is to be presented in a manner that reconciles beginning and ending cash and cash equivalent amounts.[10]

The preparation of the Investing and Financing Activities sections of the statement of cash flows is straightforward. The Operating Activities section, however, is more complex. Operating cash flow is actually a simple concept: It is merely the difference between cash received and cash disbursed for operating activities. The computation of operating cash

---

[10] Additional disclosures are required in reconciling the change in cash and cash equivalents for a company that has subsidiaries located in foreign countries. Because of changes in exchange rates, the U.S. dollar equivalent of foreign cash balances can change during the year even if the foreign subsidiary enters into no transactions. If the amount is material, the effect of this change is shown as a separate line in the cash flow statement of U.S. multinationals.

Exhibit 5-4 | General Format for a Statement of Cash Flows— Intel Corporation 2011 (Amounts in millions)

Cash provided by (or used for):	
Operating activities	$ 20,963
Investing activities	(10,301)
Financing activities	(11,100)
Effect of exchange rate fluctuations on cash and cash equivalents	5
Net increase (decrease) in cash and cash equivalents	$ (433)
Cash and cash equivalents at beginning of year	5,498
Cash and cash equivalents at end of year	$ 5,065

© Cengage Learning 2014

Exhibit 5-5 | Relationship Between Net Income and Operating Cash Flow

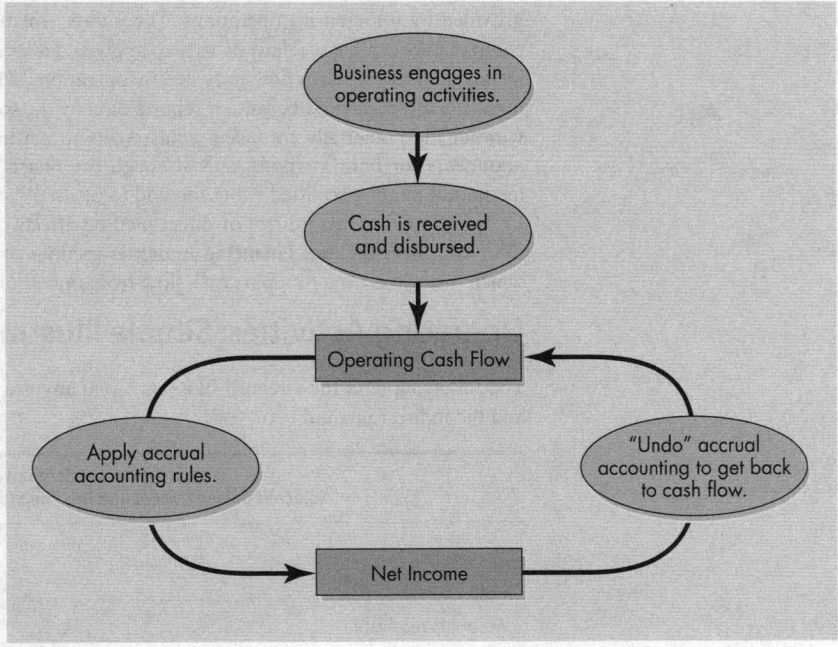

© Cengage Learning 2014

直接法和间接法都可以用于计算与报告经营活动的净现金流量。在财务报表中，更为广泛的是间接法，美国大型公司中约95%使用间接法。

flow is difficult because accounting systems are designed to adjust cash flow numbers to arrive at accrual net income. Computing operating cash flow requires undoing all the accrual accounting adjustments. This is illustrated in Exhibit 5-5.

Two methods may be used in calculating and reporting the amount of net cash flow from operating activities: the indirect method and the direct method. The most popular method used in reported financial statements is the indirect method; it is used by approximately 95% of large U.S. corporations.

> **Caution**
> The choice of the direct or indirect method is not a way to manipulate the amount of reported cash flow from operations. Both methods yield the same number.

The direct method is essentially a reexamination of each income statement item with the objective of reporting how much cash was received or disbursed in association with the item. For example, for the item Sales in the income statement, there is a corresponding item in the cash flow statement called *cash collected from customers*. For cost of goods sold, the corresponding item is *cash paid for inventory*. To prepare the Operating Activities section using the direct method, one must adjust each income statement item for the effects of accruals.

The indirect method begins with net income as reported on the income statement and adjusts this accrual amount for any items that do not affect cash flow. The adjustments are of three basic types.

- Revenues and expenses that do not involve cash inflow or outflow
- Gains and losses associated with investing or financing activities
- Adjustments for changes in current operating assets and liabilities that indicate non-cash sources of revenues and expenses

Both methods produce identical results—that is, the same amount of net cash flow provided by (or used in) operations. The indirect method is favored and used by most companies because it is relatively easy to apply and it reconciles the difference between net income and the net cash flow provided by operations. Many users of financial statements favor the direct method because it reports directly the sources of cash inflow and outflow without the potentially confusing adjustments to net income. The FASB considered the arguments for both methods, and although the Board favored the clarity of the direct method, it finally permitted either method to be used.[11]

The choice of the indirect or direct method affects only the Operating Activities section. The Investing and Financing Activities sections are exactly the same regardless of which method is used to report cash flow from operations.

Operating Activities: Simple Illustration

The following data for Orchard Blossom Company are used to illustrate both the direct and the indirect methods:

Orchard Blossom Company Selected Balance Sheet and Income Statement Data		
	End of Year	Beginning of Year
Balance sheet:		
Cash	$ 25	$ 15
Accounts receivable	60	40
Inventory	75	100
Wages payable	10	7
Income statement:		
Sales	$150	
Cost of goods sold	(80)	
Wages expense	(25)	
Depreciation expense	(30)	
Net income	$ 15	

Direct Method The best way to do the direct method is to systematically go down the list of income statement items and calculate how much cash is associated with each item.

[11] FASB ASC paragraphs 230-10-45-25 and 28.

直接法的最好方式是系统地记下利润表所列项目，计算出与每个项目相关联的现金。

Sales and Cash Collected from Customers

The beginning accounts receivable balance, along with sales for the year, constitutes potential collections from customers. The ending accounts receivable balance represents accounts not collected. Thus, cash collected from customers is computed as follows:

	Beginning accounts receivable	$ 40
+	Sales	150
=	Cash available for collection	$190
−	Ending accounts receivable	60
=	Cash collected from customers	$130

Note that a faster way to do this is to adjust the $150 sales amount by the $20 change in accounts receivable. The question is whether to add or subtract the $20. An increase in accounts receivable means less cash, so subtract the $20 increase ($150 − $20 = $130).

Cost of Goods Sold and Cash Paid for Inventory

The ending inventory balance, along with cost of goods sold for the year, represents the total amount of inventory the company must have purchased some time in the past. The beginning inventory balance represents inventory purchased in prior years. Thus, inventory purchased this year is computed as follows:

	Ending inventory	$ 75
+	Cost of goods sold	80
=	Required inventory	$155
−	Beginning inventory	100
=	Inventory purchased this year	$ 55

Alternatively, adjust the $80 cost of goods sold amount by the $25 change in inventory. Should you add or subtract the $25? First, remember that in the absence of any inventory changes, the $80 in cost of goods sold would have represented an $80 OUTFLOW to replenish the inventory that was sold. A decrease in inventory during the year means that you purchased less than you sold, so less cash was paid to replenish the inventory. Accordingly, add the decrease in inventory (−$80 + $25 = −$55) to arrive at the net $55 outflow for inventory purchased during the year.

> **Caution**
> Students who try to prepare cash flow statements solely by memorization of rules (e.g., add all decreases) usually end up getting only 50% of their computations correct. The best approach is to stop and use your business intuition.

Note that in this simple illustration, all inventory is paid for in cash. A subsequent illustration in this chapter will show how to make adjustments for accounts payable.

Wages Expense and Cash Paid for Wages

The beginning wages payable balance, along with wages expense for the year, constitutes the total obligation to employees. The ending wages payable balance represents the amount of that obligation not yet paid. Thus, cash paid to employees for wages is computed as follows:

	Beginning wages payable	$ 7
+	Wages expense	25
=	Total obligation to employees	$32
−	Ending wages payable	10
=	Cash paid for wages	$22

This can also be computed by adding the $3 increase in wages payable to the $25 cash outflow represented by wages expense (−$25 + $3 = −$22). You ADD the $3 increase because the increase represents wages that were not paid in cash during the year.

Depreciation Expense Here's a trick question: How much cash is paid for depreciation? None, because depreciation is a noncash expense.

The Operating Activities section of Orchard Blossom's cash flow statement, using the direct method, appears as follows:

Orchard Blossom Company
Statement of Cash Flows
Operating Activities: Direct Method

Cash collected from customers	$130
Cash paid for inventory	(55)
Cash paid for wages	(22)
Cash paid for depreciation	0
Net cash from operating activities	$ 53

Of course, in a proper cash flow statement, there would be no line for cash paid for depreciation. It is included here only to remind you that no cash is paid for depreciation.

Indirect Method With the indirect method, we start with net income, which incorporates the net effect of all the income statement items, and then report the adjustments necessary to convert all income statement items into cash flow numbers. Only the adjustments themselves are reported. As with the direct method, the best way to perform the indirect method is to go right down the income statement, item by item.

Sales What adjustment is necessary to convert this item to a cash flow number? The $20 increase in accounts receivable means that cash collected is $20 less than the $150 sales number indicates. So, the necessary adjustment to convert net income into cash flow is to subtract the $20 increase in accounts receivable.

Cost of Goods Sold The $25 decrease in inventory means that, although cost of goods sold of $80 is included in the income statement, less cash was used to purchase inventory than is suggested by the cost of goods sold number. Therefore, add the $25 inventory decrease to convert net income into cash flow.

Wages Expense The income statement includes a $25 subtraction for wages expense. However, the $3 increase in wages payable indicates that not all of that $25 wages expense was paid in cash. Accordingly, the $3 increase in wages payable is added to net income.

Depreciation Expense The $30 depreciation expense is a noncash expense. Because it was subtracted in computing net income, it must be added back to net income in computing cash flow. Add the $30 depreciation expense to net income.

The Operating Activities section of Orchard Blossom's cash flow statement, using the indirect method, follows.

Orchard Blossom Company
Statement of Cash Flows
Operating Activities: Indirect Method

Net income	$ 15
Plus: Depreciation	30
Less: Increase in accounts receivable	(20)
Plus: Decrease in inventory	25
Plus: Increase in wages payable	3
Net cash from operating activities	$ 53

Note that net cash from operating activities, commonly referred to as *cash flow from operations*, is the same, $53, whether the direct or the indirect method is used. Also note that depreciation is the first item listed after net income. This is the traditional presentation. This ordering is unfortunate because it reinforces two wrong ideas.

- Depreciation is a source of cash. *Wrong*.
- Cash flow is equal to net income plus depreciation. *Wrong*.

Depreciation is not a source of cash.[12] Depreciation is added back to net income to offset the effect of subtracting depreciation expense in the original computation of net income. The net effect is to eliminate depreciation in the computation of cash flow.

The definition "cash flow equals net income plus depreciation" is widely used. A quick look at Orchard Blossom's indirect method Operating Activities section shows, however, that the "net income plus depreciation" definition ignores all of the changes in current assets and current liabilities. Sometimes the changes in current items cancel (as they almost do in Orchard Blossom's case), so "net income plus depreciation" can be a good estimate of true cash from operations. However, many times, particularly with rapidly expanding firms, the current item changes do not cancel out. In those situations, true cash from operations is much lower than the "net income plus depreciation" definition would indicate. The "net income plus depreciation" definition is used widely in finance, and many finance professors believe it with all their hearts. Don't let them deceive you.

> **FYI**
>
> One advantage of the indirect method is that it highlights how cash flow can be improved in the short run by adjusting operating procedures. In the Orchard Blossom example, both cutting back on inventory levels and slowing payments of wages increased the amount of cash generated by operations.

Comparison of Direct and Indirect Methods The computations of Orchard Blossom's net income and operating cash flow are compared as follows:

Income Statement		Adjustments		Cash Flows from Operations	
Sales	$150	− 20	(increase in accounts receivable)	$130	Cash collected from customers
Cost of goods sold	(80)	+ 25	(decrease in inventory)	(55)	Cash paid for inventory
Wages expense	(25)	+ 3	(increase in wages payable)	(22)	Cash paid for wages
Depreciation expense	(30)	+ 30	(not a cash flow item)	0	
Net income	$ 15	+ 38	net adjustment	$ 53	Cash flows from operations

With the direct method of reporting cash from operations, each of the individual cash flow items is reported. The Operating Activities section of a statement of cash flows prepared using the direct method is, in effect, a cash-basis income statement and involves reporting the shaded information from the following work sheet.

---

[12] Depreciation is not a source of cash in a financial accounting context. However, when income taxes are considered, the depreciation tax deduction lowers the income tax liability. Thus, when analyzing the cash flow of a business or a project, the depreciation tax deduction is a source of cash to the extent that it lowers the amount of income taxes paid. This issue is covered in most textbook discussions of capital budgeting.

Income Statement		Adjustments		Cash Flows from Operations	
Sales	$150	−20	(increase in accounts receivable)	$130	Cash collected from customers
Cost of goods sold	(80)	+25	(decrease in inventory)	(55)	Cash paid for inventory
Wages expense	(25)	+3	(increase in wages payable)	(22)	Cash paid for wages
Depreciation expense	(30)	+30	(not a cash flow item)	0	
Net income	$ 15	+38	net adjustment	$ 53	Cash flows from operations

With the indirect method, only net income and the adjustments are reported. Therefore, the Operating Activities section of the statement of cash flows for Orchard Blossom includes the shaded information in the following table.

Income Statement		Adjustments		Cash Flows from Operations	
Sales	$150	−20	(increase in accounts receivable)	$130	Cash collected from customers
Cost of goods sold	(80)	+25	(decrease in inventory)	(55)	Cash paid for inventory
Wages expense	(25)	+3	(increase in wages payable)	(22)	Cash paid for wages
Depreciation expense	(30)	+30	(not a cash flow item)	0	
Net income	$ 15	+38	net adjustment	$ 53	Cash flows from operations

Both methods of reporting operating cash flow have advantages. The primary advantage of the direct method is that it is very straightforward and intuitive. The primary advantage of the indirect method is that it highlights the factors that cause net income and cash from operations to differ. As mentioned earlier, almost all large U.S. companies use the indirect method. Some actual examples of the large differences that can exist between income and cash from operations are given in Exhibit 5-6.

Exhibit 5-6 | Large Differences Between Income and Cash from Operations for the Year 2011 (in millions of U.S. dollars)

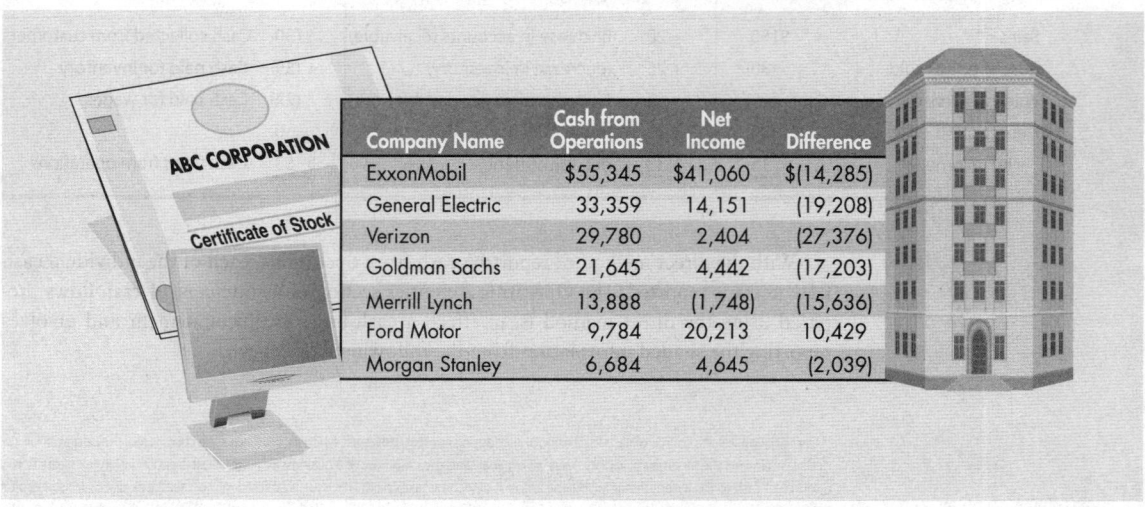

Company Name	Cash from Operations	Net Income	Difference
ExxonMobil	$55,345	$41,060	$(14,285)
General Electric	33,359	14,151	(19,208)
Verizon	29,780	2,404	(27,376)
Goldman Sachs	21,645	4,442	(17,203)
Merrill Lynch	13,888	(1,748)	(15,636)
Ford Motor	9,784	20,213	10,429
Morgan Stanley	6,684	4,645	(2,039)

Preparing a Complete Statement of Cash Flows

LO4 学习目标4
编制一张完整的现金流量表，同时提供所要求的补充披露信息。

4 Prepare a complete statement of cash flows and provide the required supplemental disclosures.

In this section, we will expand the Orchard Blossom Company example into a comprehensive problem in order to illustrate the preparation of a complete statement of cash flows. For this example, we will need complete balance sheet data as of the beginning and end of the year, as well as income statement data for the year. These data are as follows:

Orchard Blossom Company
Complete Balance Sheet and Income Statement Data

	End of Year	Beginning of Year
Balance Sheet:		
Cash	$ 25	$ 15
Accounts receivable	60	40
Inventory	75	100
Land	120	105
Buildings	200	160
Accumulated depreciation	(66)	(50)
Total assets	$414	$370
Accounts payable	$ 50	$ 37
Wages payable	10	7
Long-term debt	169	190
Paid-in capital	100	60
Retained earnings	85	76
Total liabilities and equity	$414	$370
Income Statement:		
Sales	$150	
Gain on sale of building	10	
Cost of goods sold	(80)	
Wages expense	(25)	
Depreciation expense	(30)	
Interest expense	(10)	
Net income	$ 15	

Before proceeding with this example, please note three changes from the original Orchard Blossom data used in the preceding section. These changes are made to enrich the example so that it will illustrate all of the major items you need to learn at this point with respect to preparing a complete statement of cash flows.

- Accounts payable have been added to the balance sheet. This will change the operating cash flow calculation done previously. We will assume that all of these accounts payable relate to inventory purchases.

- Interest expense has been added to the income statement. This will change the operating cash flow calculation done previously.
- A gain on sale of building has been added to the income statement. From supplemental information (not found in the balance sheet or income statement), we learn that buildings with an original cost of $36 and a book value of $22 were sold for a total of $32, resulting in the reported gain of $10 ($32 sales price − $22 book value). The sale of a building is an investing activity, yet the gain is shown as part of net income, which we use as our basis for computing operating cash flow. We will have to be careful how we handle this gain.

The following six-step process outlines a systematic method that can be used in analyzing the income statement and comparative balance sheets in preparing a statement of cash flows:

1. Compute how much the cash balance changed during the year. The statement of cash flows is not complete until the sum of cash from operating, investing, and financing activities exactly matches the total change in the cash balance during the year.
2. Convert the income statement from an accrual-basis to a cash-basis summary of operations. This is done in three steps.
   (a) Eliminate expenses that do not involve the outflow of cash, such as depreciation expense.
   (b) Eliminate gains and losses associated with investing or financing activities to avoid counting these items twice.
   (c) Adjust for changes in the balances of current operating assets and operating liabilities because these changes indicate cases in which the operating cash flow associated with an item does not match the revenue or expense reported for that item.

   The final result of these adjustments is that net income is converted into cash flow from operating activities.

3. Analyze the long-term assets to identify the cash flow effects of investing activities. Changes in property, plant, and equipment may indicate that cash has either been spent or received.
4. Analyze the long-term debt and stockholders' equity accounts to determine the cash flow effects of any financing transactions. These transactions include borrowing or repaying debt, issuing or buying back stock, and paying dividends. Also, examine changes in short-term loan accounts; borrowing and repaying under short-term arrangements are also classified as financing activities.
5. Make sure that the total net cash flow from operating, investing, and financing activities is equal to the net increase or decrease in cash as computed in step 1. Then, prepare a formal statement of cash flows by classifying all cash inflows and outflows according to operating, investing, and financing activities. The net cash flows from each of the three main activities should be highlighted.
6. Prepare supplemental disclosure, including the disclosure of any significant investing or financing transactions that did not involve cash. This disclosure is done outside the cash flow statement itself. The types of transactions disclosed in this way include the purchase of land by issuing stock and the retirement of bonds by issuing stock. In addition, supplemental disclosure of cash paid for interest expense and taxes is required.

We will illustrate this six-step process using the expanded information from the Orchard Blossom example. Because we will prepare the statement of cash flows without reference to the detailed cash flow transaction data, we are going to have to make some informed inferences about cash flows by examining the balance sheet and income statement accounts.

Step 1. Compute How Much the Cash Balance Changed During the Year

Orchard Blossom began the year with a cash balance of $15 and ended with a cash balance of $25. Thus, our target in preparing the statement of cash flows is to explain why the cash account increased by $10 during the year.

Step 2. Convert the Income Statement from an Accrual-Basis to a Cash-Basis Summary of Operations

Recall that converting accrual net income into cash from operations involves eliminating noncash expenses, removing the effects of gains and losses, and adjusting for the impact of changes in current operating asset and liability balances. These adjustments are shown in the work sheet, Exhibit 5-7, and are explained below. Many of the adjustment are the same as those illustrated in the simple Orchard Blossom example in the previous section.

Depreciation Expense (Adjustment A1) The first adjustment involves adding the amount of depreciation expense. As explained previously, because depreciation expense does not involve an outflow of cash, and because depreciation was initially subtracted to arrive at net income, this adjustment effectively eliminates depreciation from the computation of cash from operations. It can be seen in the far right column of the work sheet in Exhibit 5-7 that adjustment A1 results in a $0 (–$30 + $30) cash flow effect from depreciation.

Gain on Sale of Building (Adjustment B1) Adjustment must also be made for any gains or losses included in the computation of net income. Orchard Blossom sold buildings during the year and recorded a gain of $10 on the sale. The $32 cash flow effect of the building sale (mentioned above) will be shown in the Investing Activities section of the cash flow statement. To avoid counting any part of the $32 sales amount twice, the gain should be excluded from the Operating Activities section. However, the gain has already been added in the computation of net income. In order to exclude the gain from the Operating Activities section, it must be subtracted from net income. If there had been a loss on the building sale, that loss would be added back to net income in the Operating Activities section so that it would not impact cash flows from operations. The full $32 cash flow impact of the sale of this building (to be analyzed later) is reported in the Investing Activities section.

Exhibit 5-7 | Adjustments to Convert Orchard Blossom's Accrual Net Income to Cash from Operations

	Income Statement		Adjustments		Cash Flows from Operations
Sales	$150	C1	$(20)	Increase in accounts receivable	$130
Gain on sale of building	10	B1	(10)	Investing activity item	0
Cost of goods sold	(80)	C2	25	Decrease in inventory	(42)
		C3	13	Increase in accounts payable	
Wages expense	(25)	C4	3	Increase in wages payable	(22)
Depreciation expense	(30)	A1	30	Not a cash flow item	0
Interest expense	(10)			No interest payable balance	(10)
Net income	$ 15		$ 41		$ 56

© Cengage Learning 2014

A company's statement of cash flows must reflect the amount of cash paid for inventory during the year. For example, in the computation of cash from operations, Reebok must reduce the cost of goods sold number to reflect that part of the inventory sold in the current period was actually purchased in the prior period.

Changes in Current Assets and Liabilities The remaining adjustments (C1–C4 in Exhibit 5-7) are needed because the computation of accrual net income involves reporting revenues and expenses when economic events occur, not necessarily when cash is received or paid. The timing differences between the receipt or payment of cash and the earning of revenue or the incurring of an expense are reflected in the shifting balances in the current operating assets and liabilities. This is illustrated through a discussion of each of Orchard Blossom's current operating asset and liability accounts.

Accounts receivable (adjustment C1) Recall from our analysis earlier in the chapter that the amount of cash Orchard Blossom collected from customers during the year differed from sales for the period. The $20 increase in accounts receivable is subtracted, as shown in Exhibit 5-7.

Inventory (adjustment C2) The statement of cash flows should reflect the amount of cash paid for inventory during the year, which is not necessarily the same as the cost of inventory sold. Orchard Blossom's inventory decreased by $25 during the year, indicating that the amount of inventory purchased during the year was less than the amount of inventory sold. Accordingly, in the computation of cash from operations we must reduce the cost of goods sold number to reflect the fact that part of the inventory sold this period was actually purchased last period. To reduce cost of goods sold (which is subtracted in the computation of net income), the adjustment involves adding $25, as shown in Exhibit 5-7. This addition of $25 represents an increase in cash flow because less cash was used to replenish inventory during the year.

Accounts payable (adjustment C3) The balance in Orchard Blossom's accounts payable account increased by $13 during the year. This increase occurred because Orchard Blossom paid for less than it bought from its suppliers during the year. The adjustment necessary to reflect this reduction in cash outflow is to add $13 in computing cash from operations, shown as adjustment C3 in Exhibit 5-7. As seen in the exhibit, total cash paid to purchase inventory during the year was $42.

Wages expenses (adjustment C4) The balance in Orchard Blossom's wages payable account increased by $3 during the year. This increase occurred because Orchard Blossom did not pay all wages due to its employees during the year. The adjustment necessary to reflect this reduction in cash outflow for wages is to add $3 in computing cash from operations, shown as adjustment C4 in Exhibit 5-7. Again, when the wages payable account increases, the company has more cash because cash was conserved and not used to pay its operating obligations.

Interest expense Because an interest payable account does not exist, we can safely assume that all interest expense was paid for in cash. Therefore, there is no need for an adjustment. If there were an interest payable account, the reasoning used when analyzing the accounts payable and wages payable accounts would apply.

Note that the total cash inflow from operating activities is $56, which is $3 more than the $53 we computed in the earlier example. The $3 difference arises because in this expanded example we included $10 in interest expense (which reduces operating cash flow by $10) and also included a $13 increase in the accounts payable balance (which increases operating cash flow by $13). The net effect is to increase operating cash flow by $3 relative to the previous simple example.

Step 3. Analyze the Long-Term Assets to Identify the Cash Flow Effects of Investing Activities
Orchard Blossom reports two long-term asset accounts.

- Land
- Buildings

We will analyze each of these in turn to determine how much cash flow was associated with each during the year.

Land The land account increased by $15 ($120 – $105) during the year. This could be a combination of purchases and sales of land. Because there is no indication of land sales during the year, we conclude that the $15 represents the price of new land purchased during the year.

Buildings The balance in Orchard Blossom's buildings account increased by $40 ($200 – $160) during the year. In the absence of any other information, this increase would suggest that Orchard Blossom purchased buildings with a cost of $40. However, in this case, additional information mentioned above is available indicating that buildings were sold for $32 during the year. This $32 cash proceeds from the sale is a cash inflow from investing activities. This building sale complicates our calculations so that we aren't yet sure how much was paid to purchase new buildings during the year.

A useful way to summarize all of the purchase and sale information for buildings is to reconstruct the T-accounts for both the buildings account and the associated accumulated depreciation account. Those T-accounts appear as follows:

Buildings				Accumulated Depreciation			
Beg. Bal.	160					Beg. Bal.	50
		Historical cost		Accum. dep.			
Purchases	[76]	of items sold	36	on items sold	[14]	Dep. exp.	30
End. Bal.	200					End. Bal.	66

The amounts in boxes (amount of purchases and amount of accumulated depreciation associated with the items sold) can be inferred given the other information. With this information, we can compute whether the sale of buildings resulted in a gain or in a loss as follows:

Cash proceeds (given earlier)	$32
Book value of items sold ($36 – $14)	22
Gain on sale of buildings	$10

The existence of a $10 gain is confirmed in the Orchard Blossom income statement. Note that with the income statement information and the amounts inferred using the T-accounts above, we could have traced backward and computed the cash proceeds from the sale of the buildings and equipment. The T-accounts are very useful devices for structuring the information that we have so that we can infer the missing values needed to complete the statement of cash flows.

Step 4. Analyze the Long-Term Debt and Stockholders' Equity Accounts to Determine the Cash Flow Effects of Any Financing Transactions
Long-term debt accounts increase when a company borrows more money—an inflow of cash—and decrease when the company pays back the debt—an outflow of cash. In the case of Orchard Blossom, we observe that the company's balance in Long-Term Debt decreased by $21 ($190 – $169) during the year. Accordingly, we can infer that Orchard Blossom

repaid $21 in loans during the year. This $21 loan repayment represents cash used by financing activities. The same analysis would apply to short-term debt. The $40 ($200 − $160) increase in Orchard Blossom's paid-in capital account during the year represents a cash inflow from the issuance of new shares of stock. This cash inflow is reported as part of cash from financing activities.

The retained earnings account increases from the recognition of net income (an operating activity), decreases as a result of net losses (also an operating activity), and decreases through the payment of dividends (a financing activity). In the absence of detailed information, it is possible to infer the amount of dividends declared by identifying the unexplained change in the retained earnings account balance. An efficient way to do this is to recreate the retained earnings T-account as follows:

Retained Earnings

		Beg. Bal.	76
Dividends	6	Net income	15
		End. Bal.	85

So, the amount of dividends paid during the year was $6. Of course, it is usually the case that the amount of dividends paid is disclosed somewhere in the financial statements. However, you never know the level of detailed information to which you will have access. And, after all, it is a relatively simple (and fun!) analytical exercise.

Step 5. Prepare a Formal Statement of Cash Flows Based on our analyses of the income statement and balance sheet accounts, we have identified all inflows and outflows of cash for Orchard Blossom for the year, and we have categorized those cash flows based on the type of activity. The resulting statement of cash flows (prepared using the indirect method, which is by far the more common method of presentation) is shown in Exhibit 5-8. Note that the statement indicates that the total change in cash for the year is an increase of $10, which matches the $10 increase (from $15 to $25) shown on the balance sheet.

Step 6. Prepare Supplemental Disclosure Two categories of supplemental disclosure are associated with the statement of cash flows. These are as follows:

- Cash paid for interest and income taxes
- Noncash investing and financing activities

Cash Paid for Interest and Income Taxes FASB *ASC Topic 230* requires separate disclosure of the cash paid for interest and for income taxes during the year. When the direct method is used, the amounts of cash paid for interest and for income taxes are part of the Operating Activities section, so no additional disclosure is needed. When the indirect method is used, these amounts must be shown separately, either at the bottom of the cash flow statement, or in an accompanying note. In the case of Orchard Blossom (which has no income taxes), the supplemental information might be presented as follows:

Supplemental Disclosure:
Cash paid for interest $10

Noncash Investing and Financing Activities When a company has significant noncash transactions, such as purchasing property, plant, and equipment by issuing debt or in exchange for shares of stock, these transactions must be disclosed in the notes to the

Exhibit 5-8 | Complete Statement of Cash Flows for Orchard Blossom Company

Orchard Blossom Company
Statement of Cash Flows
For the Year Ended December 31

Cash flows from operating activities:		
Net income..		$ 15
Adjustments:		
Add: Depreciation expense.................................	$ 30	
Subtract: Gain on sale of building.......................	(10)	
Subtract: Increase in accounts receivable............	(20)	
Add: Decrease in inventory.................................	25	
Add: Increase in accounts payable......................	13	
Add: Increase in wages payable..........................	3	41
Net cash provided by operating activities........		$ 56
Cash flows from investing activities:		
Sold buildings..	$ 32	
Purchased land..	(15)	
Purchased buildings...	(76)	
Net cash used by investing activities...............		(59)
Cash flows from financing activities:		
Issued stock to shareholders..............................	$ 40	
Repaid long-term debt.......................................	(21)	
Paid dividends...	(6)	
Net cash provided by financing activities.........		13
Net increase in cash...		$ 10
Beginning cash balance...		15
Ending cash balance..		$ 25

© Cengage Learning 2014

financial statements. Orchard Blossom did not have any of these noncash transactions, so no additional disclosure is necessary in this case.

This Orchard Blossom example includes all the common items that are encountered in preparing a statement of cash flows. In Chapter 21, we will revisit the statement of cash flows and learn how to handle some more complex items.

Using Cash Flow Data to Assess Financial Strength

LO5 学习目标5

分析经营活动、投资活动和融资活动之间现金流的关系，并计算基于现金流数据的财务比率，评估一家公司的财务实力。

5 Assess a firm's financial strength by analyzing the relationships among cash flows from operating, investing, and financing activities and by computing financial ratios based on cash flow data.

Various analytical techniques are used to assess a company's financial strength. Key variables are profitability, efficiency, leverage, and liquidity. By tradition, analysts have concentrated on the relationships captured in the income statement and the balance sheet. More and more emphasis is now placed, however, on cash flows and the relationships of data reported on the cash flow statement in conjunction with the income statement and the balance sheet.

Cash Flow Patterns

It is possible to gain useful insights about a company by analyzing the relationships among the three cash flow categories. Exhibit 5-9 shows the eight different possible patterns. Patterns 1 and 8 are unusual. Pattern 1 might exist when a firm is experiencing positive cash flows from all three activities and is seeking to significantly increase its cash position for some strategic reason. Pattern 8 shows negative cash flows from all activities and could exist, even in the short term, only if a company had existing cash reserves to draw upon. Patterns 2 through 4 show positive operating cash flows that are sufficient by themselves (pattern 2) or are supplemented by investing (pattern 3) or financing (pattern 4) activities to settle debt, pay owners, or expand the business. Patterns 5 through 7 are not healthy over the long term, because operating cash shortfalls have to be covered by selling long-term assets and/or by securing external financing.

These cash flow patterns stress the importance of operating cash flows. A positive operating cash flow allows a company to pay its bills, its creditors, and its shareholders and to grow and expand. A negative operating cash flow means a company has to look at other sources of cash, which eventually dry up if operations are not successful.

Exhibit 5-9 | Analysis of Cash Flow Statement: Patterns

	CF from Operating	CF from Investing	CF from Financing	General Explanation
#1	+	+	+	Company is using cash generated from operations and from sale of assets and from financing to build up pile of cash—very liquid company—possibly looking for acquisition.
#2	+	−	−	Company is using cash flow generated from operations to buy fixed assets and to pay down debt or pay owners.
#3	+	+	−	Company is using cash from operations and from sale of fixed assets to pay down debt or pay owners.
#4	+	−	+	Company is using cash from operations and from borrowing (or from owner investment) to expand.
#5	−	+	+	Company's operating cash flow problems are covered by sale of fixed assets and by borrowing or by shareholder contributions.
#6	−	−	+	Company is growing rapidly but has shortfalls in cash flow from operations and from purchase of fixed assets financed by long-term debt or new investment.
#7	−	+	−	Company is financing operating cash flow shortages and payments to creditors and/or stockholders via sale of fixed assets.
#8	−	−	−	Company is using cash reserves to finance operation shortfall and pay long-term creditors and/or investors.

Source: Michael T. Dugan, Benton E. Gup, and William D. Samson, "Teaching the Statement of Cash Flows," *Journal of Accounting Education*, Vol. 9, 1991, p. 36 with permission from Elsevier.

Cash Flow Ratios

The data from a cash flow statement also can be used to compute selected ratios that help determine a company's financial strength. If such ratios are compared for the same company over a period of time or with other companies in the same industry, they can be helpful in evaluating relative performance. To illustrate the computation of selected cash flow ratios, selected data from Circle K's 1989 and 1988 financial statements (before Circle K's disastrous year in 1990) will be used (Exhibit 5-10).

> **FYI**
>
> Most courses in financial statement analysis still make only passing mention of cash flow ratios. Familiarity with the ratios discussed in this section is a quick and easy way to set oneself apart from the crowd.

最重要的现金流关系可能是营运现金和报告净利润之间的关系。

Cash Flow to Net Income Perhaps the most important cash flow relationship is the relationship between cash from operations and reported net income. The cash-flow-to-net-income ratio reflects the extent to which accrual accounting assumptions and adjustments have been included in computing net income. The formula is cash from operations divided by net income. For Circle K, computation of the cash-flow-to-net-income ratios is as follows:

	1989	1988
Cash from operations	$57,767	$84,333
Net income	÷15,414	÷60,411
Cash-flow-to-net-income ratio	3.75	1.40

In general, the cash-flow-to-net-income ratio has a value more than 1.0 because of the existence of significant noncash expenses (such as depreciation) that reduce reported net income but have no impact on cash flow. For a given company, the cash-flow-to-net-income ratio should remain fairly stable from year to year. A significant increase in the ratio, such as that reported by Circle K in 1989, indicates that accounting assumptions were instrumental in reducing reported net income. This ratio reveals that, from the standpoint of management concerned about being able to pay the bills and creditors concerned about timely repayment of loans, Circle K's performance in 1989 was actually somewhat better than indicated by just looking at net income. From the numbers reported earlier in the chapter, it is apparent that the same was true in 1990 when the reported net loss was $773 million but the cash generated by operations was $108 million.

cash flow adequacy ratio
现金流充足率

Cash Flow Adequacy As defined earlier, a *cash cow* is a business that is generating enough cash from operations to completely pay for all new plant and equipment purchases with cash left over to repay loans or to distribute to investors. The cash flow adequacy ratio,

Exhibit 5-10 | Selected Cash Flow Data for Circle K for 1988 and 1989

(In thousands of dollars)	1989	1988
Net income	$ 15,414	$ 60,411
Cash from operations	57,767	84,333
Cash paid for capital expenditures	193,338	233,087
Cash paid for acquisitions	68,139	147,500
Cash paid for interest	89,928	49,267
Cash paid for income taxes	11,233	28,439

© Cengage Learning 2014

computed as cash from operations divided by expenditures for fixed asset additions and acquisitions of new businesses, indicates whether a business is a cash cow. Computation of the cash flow adequacy ratio for Circle K is as follows:

	1989	1988
Cash from operations	$ 57,767	$ 84,333
Cash paid for capital expenditures	$193,338	$233,087
Cash paid for acquisitions	68,139	147,500
Cash required for investing activities	$261,477	$380,587
Cash flow adequacy ratio	0.22	0.22

> **FYI**
> Cash paid for dividends is sometimes added to the denominator of the cash flow adequacy ratio. With this formulation, the ratio indicates whether operating cash flow is sufficient to pay for both capital additions and regular dividends to stockholders.

The calculations indicate that in both 1988 and 1989, Circle K's cash from operations fell well short of being able to pay for its expansion. This means that Circle K was forced to seek substantial amounts of external financing, either new debt or additional funds from investors, during both years.

Cash Times Interest Earned Because interest payments must be made with cash, an informative indicator of a company's interest-paying ability compares cash generated by operations to cash paid for interest. This cash times interest earned ratio is computed for Circle K as follows:

cash times interest earned
现金利息保障倍数

	1989	1988
Cash from operations	$ 57,767	$ 84,333
Cash paid for interest	89,928	49,267
Cash paid for income taxes	11,233	28,439
Cash before interest and taxes	$158,928	$162,039
Cash paid for interest	÷ 89,928	÷ 49,267
Cash times interest earned ratio	1.77	3.29

Pretax cash flow is used because interest is paid before any taxes are deducted. From this calculation, we can see that Circle K's creditors experienced a significant drop in security in 1989 because Circle K's operations generated only 1.77 times the amount of cash that was needed in order to make its required interest payments. Ultimately, the inability to continue making its interest payments forced Circle K into bankruptcy.[13]

Articulation: How the Financial Statements Tie Together

LO6 学习目标6
论证三张主要财务报表如何联系在一起并形成一个统一的框架。

Demonstrate how the three primary financial statements tie together, or articulate, in a unified framework.

In an accounting context, articulation means that the three primary financial statements are not isolated lists of numbers but are an integrated set of reports on a company's financial

---

[13] For additional cash flow ratios, see Don E. Giacomino and David E. Mielke, "Cash Flows: Another Approach to Ratio Analysis," *Journal of Accountancy*, March 1993, p. 57.

health. The statement of cash flows contains the detailed explanation for why the balance sheet cash amount changed from beginning of year to end of year. The income statement, combined with the amount of dividends declared during the year, explains the change in retained earnings shown in the balance sheet. Cash from operations in the statement of cash flows is transformed into net income through the accounting adjustments applied to the raw cash flow data. These relationships are illustrated in Exhibit 5-11 using the financial statement numbers from the Orchard Blossom Company example in the preceding section.

资产负债表可被视为所有财务报表的根本，现金流量表仅仅给出资产负债表中现金余额的详细信息，而利润表也仅仅给出留存收益余额变化的一些详情。

The balance sheet can be viewed as the mother of all financial statements, with the statement of cash flows merely giving some details about changes in the cash balance in the balance sheet and the income statement merely giving some details about changes in the retained earnings balance. Of course, before we get too carried away in our admiration of the balance sheet, we should remind ourselves that these "mere changes" in the cash balance and the retained earnings balance capture much of what business is all about.

Now let's take a detailed look at Exhibit 5-11. Note that the $10 increase in cash during the year, from a beginning balance of $15 to an ending balance of $25, is explained by the sum of the cash flows from operating, investing, and financing activities reported in the statement of cash flows. The $9 increase in the retained earnings balance during the year, from a beginning balance of $76 to an ending balance of $85, is explained by the $15 net income, reported in the income statement, less the $6 paid in dividends. The link between the statement of cash flows (or, more precisely, the Operating section of the statement of cash flows) and the income statement is the accrual adjustments made during the year. One of the beauties of the indirect method of reporting cash flow from operating activities is that these accrual adjustments are summarized in one place. Look back at Exhibit 5-8

Exhibit 5-11 | Articulation of the Financial Statements

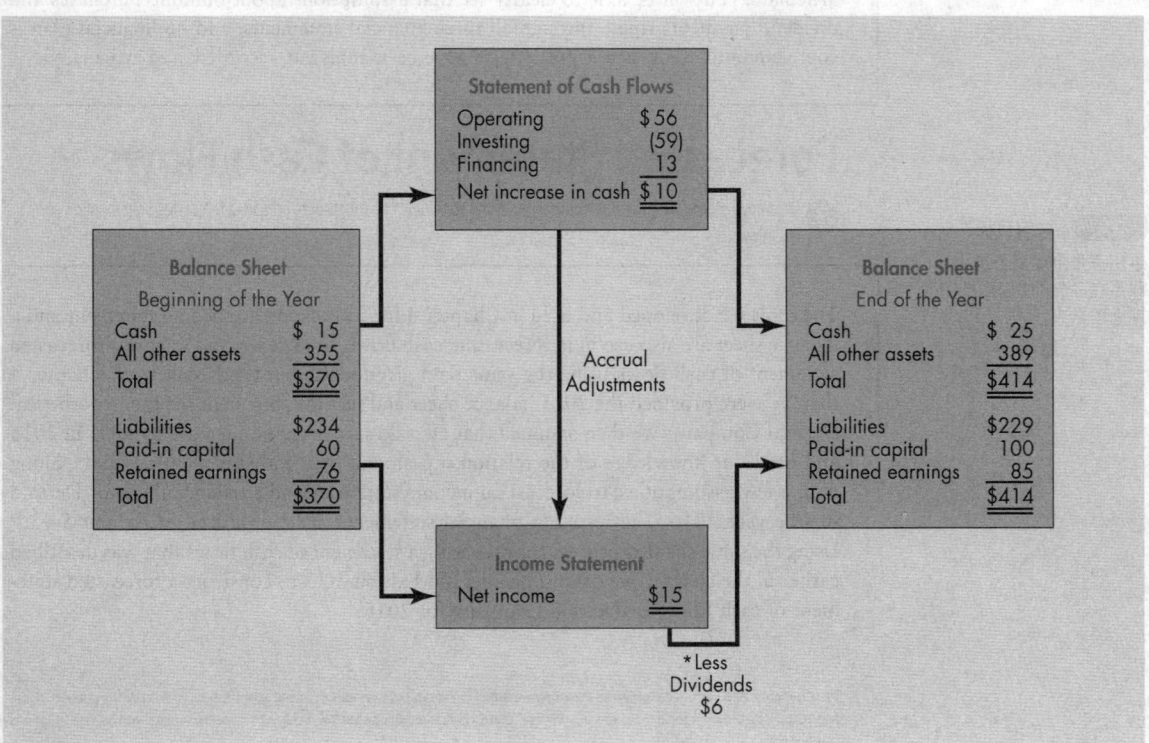

and see that the body of the Operating Activities section is a listing of the net effects of the operating accrual adjustments made during the year.

The articulation diagram in Exhibit 5-11 gives just a glimpse of the interrelationships among the financial statements. As you saw when we prepared the Investing Activities section of the Orchard Blossom Company statement of cash flows, the beginning and ending balances in the buildings and accumulated depreciation accounts, along with reported Depreciation Expense from the income statement, combine to indicate the amount of cash flow from investing activities as reported in the statement of cash flows. Similarly, the changes in long-term debt and paid-in capital are explained in the Financing Activities section of the statement of cash flows. Look again at Exhibit 5-11 and imagine a complex web connecting the beginning and ending balance sheets with the income statement and the statement of cash flows; this web represents the complete articulation of the financial statements.

The articulation of the three primary financial statements is perhaps the most beautiful, and useful, aspect of the financial accounting model. The constraints of this articulation framework require that all of the recorded transactions and the accrual assumptions for a company for a year must fit together and add up. In Chapter 6, we will discuss some of the practices of earnings management that are attempted by desperate managers seeking to make their company look better on paper. Earnings management can deceive financial statement users for a limited time, but the inexorable requirements of financial statement articulation mean that ultimately any deception practiced in the income statement will show up as increasingly unlikely amounts in the balance sheet and increasingly disturbing differences between net income and operating cash flow.

Similarly, the articulation of the financial statements is an important disciplinary tool in making financial forecasts. In the concluding section of this chapter, you will learn how to prepare a forecasted statement of cash flows. Because the financial statements must articulate, you will be able to clearly see that assumptions about building purchases and dividend payments ripple through all three financial statements, and no financial plan is complete until all of these ripple effects have been analyzed, recorded, and articulated.

Forecasted Statement of Cash Flows

LO7 学习目标7
运用三张主要财务报表如何联系在一起的知识编制预测现金流量表。

 Use knowledge of how the three primary financial statements tie together to prepare a forecasted statement of cash flows.

The tools we developed and used in Chapter 4 for forecasting an income statement and a balance sheet are also useful in forecasting cash flows. In fact, we can prepare a forecasted statement of cash flows using the same data given in Chapter 4. Recall from Chapter 4 that we were provided the 2015 balance sheet and income statement for the hypothetical Derrald Company. We then assumed that Derrald's sales would increase by 40% in 2016 and used our knowledge of the relationship among financial statement amounts, along with a few assumptions, to forecast an income statement and a balance sheet for Derrald for the year 2016. The resulting financial statements are reproduced in Exhibit 5-12.[14] Using the same six-step process for preparing a statement of cash flows that was described earlier in the chapter, we can use the data in Exhibit 5-12 to construct a forecasted statement of cash flows for Derrald Company for 2016.

---

[14] In Chapter 4, Accounts Receivable and Inventory were grouped under one heading, Other Current Assets, to simplify the analysis. These two accounts are shown separately here. In addition, Total Stockholders' Equity has been split into its paid-in capital and retained earnings components.

Exhibit 5-12 | Forecasted Balance Sheet and Income Statement for Derrald Company

Balance Sheet	2015	2016 Forecasted	Basis for Forecast
Cash	$ 10	$ 14	40% natural increase
Accounts receivable	100	140	40% natural increase
Inventory	150	210	40% natural increase
Property, plant, and equipment, net	300	500	management decision
Total assets	$560	$864	
Accounts payable	$100	$140	40% natural increase
Bank loans payable	300	524	management decision
Paid-in capital	50	50	management decision
Retained earnings	110	150	plus net income less dividends
Total liabilities and stockholders' equity	$560	$864	

Income Statement	2015	2016 Forecasted	Basis for Forecast
Sales	$1,000	$1,400	40% increase
Cost of goods sold	700	980	70% of sales, same as last year
Gross profit	$ 300	$ 420	
Depreciation expense	30	50	10% of PP&E, same as last year
Other operating expenses	170	238	17% of sales, same as last year
Operating profit	$ 100	$ 132	
Interest expense	30	52	10% of bank loan, same as last year
Income before taxes	$ 70	$ 80	
Income taxes	30	34	43% of pretax, same as last year
Net income	$ 40	$ 46	

© Cengage Learning 2014

Step 1. Compute the Change in Cash Cash is forecasted to increase by $4 ($14 − $10) from 2015 to 2016. Hence, we know that the sum of cash from operating, investing, and financing activities in the forecasted statement of cash flows must be $4.

Step 2. Convert the Income Statement from an Accrual Basis to a Cash Basis
Beginning with the forecasted income statement, the following adjustments are necessary:

	Income Statement	Adjustments		Cash Flows from Operations
Sales	$ 1,400	A.	−40	$ 1,360
Cost of goods sold	(980)	B.	−60	(1,000)
		C.	+40	
Depreciation expense	(50)	D.	+50	0
Other operating expenses	(238)	E.	0	(238)
Interest expense	(52)	F.	0	(52)
Income taxes	(34)	G.	0	(34)
Net income	$ 46			$ 36

Adjustment A Accounts Receivable is forecasted to increase by $40 ($140 − $100) during 2016, indicating that more sales will be made during the year than will be collected in cash. To compute cash collected from customers, sales must be reduced by the amount of the $40 forecasted increase in Accounts Receivable.

Adjustment B Inventory is forecasted to increase by $60 ($210 − $150), indicating that more inventory will be purchased than will be sold. This $60 Inventory increase represents an additional cash outflow.

Adjustment C Accounts Payable is forecasted to increase by $40 ($140 − $100), signifying that not all inventory that will be purchased on account during 2016 will be paid for during 2016. Thus, the Accounts Payable increase represents a cash savings.

Adjustment D Forecasted depreciation expense of $50 does not involve cash and must be added back in computing cash from operating activities.

Adjustments E Through G For this example, we are assuming that the accounts payable account relates strictly to the purchase of inventory and that all other expenses involving the outflow of cash are paid for immediately. As a result, there are no payable accounts relating to other operating expenses, interest, or taxes. If payable accounts relating to these expenses were to exist, the analysis would be similar to that conducted for Accounts Payable: Increases would be added (indicating a cash savings by allowing the payable to increase) and decreases would be subtracted (indicating an additional outflow of cash to reduce the payable balance).

The resulting Operating section of the forecasted statement of cash flows indicates that Derrald Company will generate $36 from operations in 2016.

Step 3. Analyze the Long-Term Asset Accounts The only long-term asset account is Property, Plant, and Equipment (PP&E). PP&E is forecasted to increase from $300 to $500 in 2016. Note that the PP&E amount is reported "net," meaning that accumulated depreciation is subtracted from the reported PP&E amount rather than being shown as a separate amount. As a result, the "net" PP&E amount can be affected by any of three events: purchase of new PP&E (an addition), sale of old PP&E (a subtraction), and depreciation of existing PP&E (a subtraction). Using the forecasted information, and assuming that no old PP&E will be sold during 2016, we can conclude the following.

	Beginning PP&E...	$300
	PP&E to be sold during the year	0
−	PP&E depreciation	(50)
=	Ending PP&E without purchase of new PP&E	$250

The fact that the projected ending PP&E balance is $500 implies that Derrald Company expects to purchase $250 ($500 − $250) in new PP&E during 2016. This $250 forecasted purchase represents cash to be used for investing activities.

Step 4. Analyze the Long-Term Debt and Stockholders' Equity Accounts The bank loans payable account is projected to increase from $300 to $524. This difference of $224 represents a cash inflow from financing. Because Paid-In Capital is projected to remain at $50, Derrald Company is not expecting to raise any new cash by issuing shares of stock during 2016.

The $40 ($150 − $110) projected increase in Retained Earnings must be analyzed in light of expected net income for 2016. Because Derrald Company is expected to have net income of $46 in 2016, it must also be expecting to pay dividends of $6 to result in the net increase in Retained Earnings of $40. The $6 forecasted dividend payment is reported as a cash outflow from financing activities.

Step 5. Prepare the Statement of Cash Flows All information necessary to prepare the forecasted statement of cash flows is now assembled. The forecasted statement is shown in Exhibit 5-13, with forecasted operating cash flows being reported using the indirect method. Note that the sum of the forecasted operating, investing, and financing cash flows ($36 − $250 + $218) is equal to the total forecasted change in cash of $4.

Step 6. Disclose Any Significant Noncash Activities Derrald Company does not anticipate any significant noncash activities during 2016, so the forecasted cash flow statement completely summarizes the important events that are expected to occur.

From the forecasted cash flow statement, we can see that Derrald's expected operating cash flow will not be nearly enough to pay for the additional PP&E it expects to acquire during 2016. As a result, Derrald plans to make up the shortfall with a significant $224 increase in its bank loan payable account. When used internally, the projected statement of cash flows allows Derrald Company to plan ahead; Derrald can start investigating the likelihood of obtaining such a large new loan. Alternatively, Derrald could consider scaling back the expansion plans if obtaining the required financing doesn't appear feasible. An external user, such as a bank, can use the forecasted cash flow statement to see whether it seems likely that Derrald can continue to meet its existing obligations. An investor can use the projected cash flow statement to evaluate the likelihood that Derrald will be able to continue making dividend payments. In summary, construction of a full set of projected financial statements—a balance sheet, an income statement, and a statement of cash flows—allows the financial statement user to see whether a company's strategic plans concerning operating, investing, and financing activities are consistent with one another.

Exhibit 5-13 | Forecasted Statement of Cash Flows for Derrald Company for 2016

Derrald Company Forecasted Statement of Cash Flows For the Year Ended December 31, 2016		
Cash flows from operating activities:		
Net income		$ 46
Adjustments:		
Add depreciation	$ 50	
Subtract increase in accounts receivable	(40)	
Subtract increase in inventory	(60)	
Add increase in accounts payable	40	
		(10)
Net cash provided by operating activities.............................		$ 36
Cash flows from investing activities:		
Purchase of property, plant, and equipment	$(250)	
Net cash used in investing activities		(250)
Cash flows from financing activities:		
Borrowing (bank loan payable)	$ 224	
Payment of dividends	(6)	
Net cash provided by financing activities		218
Net increase in cash		$ 4
Beginning cash balance		10
Ending cash balance		$ 14

© Cengage Learning 2014

Conclusion

This chapter has been an overview of the statement of cash flows. Along with the balance sheet and the income statement, the statement of cash flows is one of the three primary financial statements. However, because it is relatively new (required only since 1988), it sometimes does not receive the emphasis that it deserves. Cash flow variables and ratios are only now starting to make it into the mainstream of financial statement analysis. You are now a cash flow statement expert; be patient with those who have not yet caught the vision.

All basic aspects of cash flow reporting and disclosure have been covered in this chapter. Additional complexities are introduced in later chapters as appropriate. An expanded discussion, incorporating these complexities, is provided in Chapter 21. You might start thinking now about how that will be affected by revenue recognition assumptions, FIFO and LIFO, capitalize or expense decisions, operating leases, bonds issued at a discount, stock splits, and dividends. Chapter 21 also includes material on international differences in the statement of cash flows.

SOLUTIONS TO OPENING SCENARIO QUESTIONS

1. Some of the expenses included in Circle K's $773 million loss were noncash expenses. Two examples are the $300 million write-off of goodwill and the $75 million expense recorded for estimated future environmental cleanup costs. In addition, Circle K reduced its inventory level by $65 million, which doesn't affect the computation of net income but does free up $65 million in cash.

2. Under Chapter 11 bankruptcy protection, Circle K was able to reduce the cash it paid for interest in 1991 by $100 million. In addition, collection protection given to new creditors allowed Circle K to increase its accounts payable by $80 million, freeing up a substantial amount of cash.

3. Karl Eller started and ended his business career in the billboard business.

Stop & Think SOLUTION

1. (Page 5-8) The correct answer is C. Conceptually, payment of interest can be thought of as a financing activity. And because income taxes relate to all activities (for example, income tax must be paid on a gain from the sale of land, which is an investing activity), one could argue that categorization of the payment of income taxes depends on the underlying activity that gave rise to these income taxes. The IASB provides flexibility in the classification of the payment of interest and income taxes. In addition, as explained in this chapter, although the FASB requires these items to be classified as operating activities, it also requires that these two specific items be separately disclosed so that financial statement users can reclassify them, if desired, to meet their own needs.

SOLUTION TO USING THE FASB'S CODIFICATION

The glossary in FASB ASC Subtopic 926-230-20 includes the following definition of "exploitation costs" in the film industry: "All direct costs (including marketing, advertising, publicity, promotion, and other distribution expenses) incurred in connection with the distribution of a film."

So, exploitation is indeed a primary operating cash outflow in the film industry. However, the word "exploitation" as used in the accounting standards does not have the same meaning as it does in everyday speech. By the way, it does seem extremely insensitive of the accountants to use the term "exploitation" when talking about marketing, advertising, publicity, and promotion.

Review Chapter 5 Learning Objectives

① Describe the circumstances in which the cash flow statement is a particularly important companion of the income statement.

A cash flow statement is an important companion to the income statement. When noncash expenses are high, earnings give an overly pessimistic view of a company's performance; cash flow from operations could give a better picture. In addition, the operations of rapidly growing companies can consume cash even when reported net income is positive. Finally, the cash flow statement provides a reality check in situations in which companies have an incentive to bias the accrual accounting assumptions.

The cash flow statement offers a one-page summary of the results of a company's operating, investing, and financing activities for the period. A pro forma, or projected, cash flow statement is an excellent tool to analyze whether a company's operating, investing, and financing plans are consistent and workable.

② Outline the structure of and information reported in the three main categories of the cash flow statement: operating, investing, and financing.

The three sections of a cash flow statement are operating, investing, and financing. Significant noncash investing and financing transactions must also be disclosed.

- *Operating.* For purposes of preparing a cash flow statement, operating activities are those activities that enter into the calculation of net income. Net cash provided by operating activities is the "bottom line" of the cash flow statement.
- *Investing.* The primary investing activities are the purchase and sale of land, buildings, equipment, and nontrading financial instruments.
- *Financing.* Financing activities involve the receipt of cash from and the repayment of cash to owners and creditors. An exception is that the payment of interest is considered an operating activity.
- *Noncash investing and financing transactions.* These include the purchase of long-term assets in exchange for the issuance of debt or stock.

③ Compute cash flow from operations using either the direct or the indirect method.

There are two ways to present cash flow from operations: the direct method and the indirect method. The direct method is more intuitive; the indirect method emphasizes a reconciliation between net income and cash flow. Almost all companies use the indirect method.

The direct method is a recap of the income statement with the objective of reporting how much cash was received or disbursed in association with each income statement item.

The indirect method starts with net income and then reports adjustments for operating items not involving cash flow. The three types of adjustments are

- Revenues and expenses that do not involve cash inflows or outflows
- Gains and losses associated with investing or financing activities
- Adjustments for changes in current operating assets and liabilities that indicate noncash sources of revenues and expenses

Net cash from operations is the same whether it is computed using the direct method or the indirect method.

④ Prepare a complete statement of cash flows and provide the required supplemental disclosures.

Basic information to prepare the three sections of the cash flow statement comes from the following portions of the balance sheet and the income statement:

- Operating—income statement and current assets and liabilities
- Investing—long-term assets
- Financing—long-term liabilities and owners' equity

A complete cash flow statement is not prepared until each income statement item has been considered, all changes in balance sheet items have been explained, and the net change in cash has been exactly reconciled.

Six steps to preparing a cash flow statement are as follows:

1. Determine the change in cash (including cash equivalents). This is the target number.
2. Operating activities—analyze each income statement item and the changes in all current operating assets and operating liabilities.
3. Investing activities—analyze the changes in all noncurrent assets, such as land, buildings, and so forth.
4. Financing activities—analyze the changes in all noncurrent liabilities, all owners' equity accounts, and all nonoperating current liabilities.

5. Prepare a formal statement of cash flows, reconciling the beginning and ending cash balances. If the sum of operating, investing, and financing activities does not equal the total balance sheet change in cash, something in the cash flow statement is wrong. Fix it.

6. Prepare supplemental disclosure, including the disclosure of any significant investing or financing transactions that did not involve cash.

5 **Assess a firm's financial strength by analyzing the relationships among cash flows from operating, investing, and financing activities and by computing financial ratios based on cash flow data.**

Patterns of positive and negative cash flow in the three categories of operating, investing, and financing yield insights into the health and current strategy of a business. Most companies have positive cash from operations and negative cash from investing activities.

Data from the cash flow statement can be used in conjunction with balance sheet and income statement data to compute financial ratios.

6 **Demonstrate how the three primary financial statements tie together, or articulate, in a unified framework.**

Complete understanding of financial statements requires familiarity with how the three primary financial statements are linked together. This linkage is called financial statement articulation. The essence of financial statement articulation is summarized in these three relationships.

(a) Balance sheet and income statement—The income statement for the year details the change in the retained earnings balance (less dividends) for the year.

(b) Balance sheet and statement of cash flows—The statement of cash flows details the change in the cash balance for the year.

(c) Income statement and statement of cash flows—The important accrual adjustments made during the year explain the difference between the income statement and the Operating section of the statement of cash flows.

7 **Use knowledge of how the three primary financial statements tie together to prepare a forecasted statement of cash flows.**

A projected cash flow statement can be constructed using information from a projected balance sheet and income statement. The cash flow projection allows a company to plan ahead as far as timing of new loans, stock issuances, long-term asset acquisitions, and so forth. Projected cash flow statements also allow potential lenders to evaluate the likelihood that the loan will be repaid and allow potential investors to evaluate the likelihood of receiving cash dividends in the future.

FASB-IASB CODIFICATION SUMMARY

Topic	FASB Accounting Standards Codification	Original FASB Standard	Corresponding IASB Standard	Differences between U.S. GAAP and IFRS
Definition of cash equivalents	Section 230-10-20 (Glossary)—Cash equivalents	SFAS No. 95 par. 8	IAS 7 par. 7	No substantial differences
Noncash investing and financing activities	Section 230-10-50 par. 3	SFAS No. 95 par. 32	IAS 7 par. 43	No substantial differences
Direct and indirect methods	Section 230-10-45 par. 25,28	SFAS No. 95 par. 27-28	IAS 7 par. 18-19	No substantial differences
Classification of interest paid	Section 230-10-45 par. 17(d)	SFAS No. 95 par. 23(d)	IAS 7 par. 33	U.S. GAAP—operating IFRS—operating or financing
Classification of income taxes paid	Section 230-10-45 par. 17(c)	SFAS No. 95 par. 23(c)	IAS 7 par. 35	U.S. GAAP—operating IFRS—operating, investing, or financing
Classification of interest received	Section 230-10-45 par. 16(b)	SFAS No. 95 par. 22(b)	IAS 7 par. 33	U.S. GAAP—operating IFRS—operating or investing
Classification of dividends received	Section 230-10-45 par. 16(b)	SFAS No. 95 par. 22(b)	IAS 7 par. 33	U.S. GAAP—operating IFRS—operating or investing
Classification of dividends paid	Section 230-10-45 par. 15(a)	SFAS No. 95 par. 20(a)	IAS 7 par. 34	U.S. GAAP—financing IFRS—operating or financing

KEY TERMS

Articulation 5-26
Cash equivalent 5-6
Cash flow adequacy ratio 5-25
Cash-flow-to-net-income ratio 5-25
Cash times interest earned ratio 5-26
Direct method 5-12
Financing activities 5-8
Indirect method 5-12
Investing activities 5-8
Noncash investing and financing activities 5-9
Operating activities 5-7
Pro forma cash flow statement 5-5
Statement of cash flows 5-6

Tutorial Activities

Tutorial Activities with author-written, content-specific feedback, available on *CengageNOW for Stice & Stice*.

QUESTIONS

1. Under what circumstances does cash flow from operations offer a clearer picture of a company's performance than does net income?
2. What criteria must be met for an item to be considered a cash equivalent in preparing a statement of cash flows?
3. What are the three categories in a statement of cash flows? What types of items are included in each?
4. What is the normal pattern of cash flow (positive or negative) for operating, investing, and financing activities?
5. Either the direct method or the indirect method may be used to report cash flows from operating activities. What is the difference in approach for the two methods?
6. Why do many users prefer the direct method? Why do the majority of preparers prefer the indirect method?
7. How is depreciation expense handled when the direct method is used? The indirect method?
8. What is wrong with the statement, "Cash flow is equal to net income plus depreciation"?
9. Why does the FASB treat interest payments as an operating activity rather than as a financing activity?
10. When preparing a cash flow statement, what is the "target number"?
11. When using the direct method, what items must be considered in the calculation of cash paid for inventory purchases?
12. How is a loss on the sale of a long-term asset treated when using the direct method? The indirect method?
13. Is the purchase of securities an operating activity or an investing activity? Explain.
14. What supplemental disclosures are required by the FASB if a company elects to use the direct method in preparing its statement of cash flows? What disclosures are required if the indirect method is used?
15. How are significant noncash investing and financing transactions reported in connection with a statement of cash flows?
16. How is interest paid classified in a statement of cash flows under the provisions of FASB *ASC Topic 230*?
17. On average, which number is larger, net income or cash from operations? Explain.
18. What does it mean when the value of a company's cash flow adequacy ratio is less than 1.0?
19. The income statement provides detail as to transactions that occurred during the period relating to what balance sheet account? The statement of cash flows provides detail as to the transactions that occurred during the period relating to what balance sheet account?
20. A forecasted statement of cash flows allows management to plan ahead. What information is contained in the statement that can be used for planning purposes?
21. How can external users use a forecasted statement of cash flows?

PRACTICE EXERCISES

Practice 5-1

Classifying Cash Flows
The company provided the following information.

(a) Cash sales for the year were $50,000; sales on account totaled $60,000.
(b) Cost of goods sold was $55,000.
(c) All inventory is purchased on account.
(d) Depreciation on building was $31,000 for the year.
(e) Depreciation on equipment was $2,000.
(f) Cash collections of accounts receivable were $38,000.
(g) Cash payments on accounts payable for inventory equaled $39,000.
(h) Rent expense paid in cash was $11,000.
(i) 20,000 shares of common stock were issued for $240,000 in cash.
(j) Land valued at $106,000 was acquired in exchange for signing a mortgage note payable.
(k) Equipment was purchased for cash at a cost of $84,000.
(l) Dividends of $46,000 were declared but not yet paid.
(m) $15,000 of dividends that had been declared the previous year were paid in cash.
(n) Interest totaling $16,000 was paid in cash during the year.
(o) A machine used on the assembly line was sold for $12,000 in cash. The machine had a book value of $7,000.
(p) On January 1, the company entered into an operating lease to secure the use of a building having a cash price of $200,000. The first lease payment of $19,000 in cash was made on January 1.

1. Compute cash from operating activities.
2. Compute cash from investing activities.
3. Compute cash from financing activities.

Practice 5-2

Cash and Cash Equivalents
A company reports the following information as of the end of the year. Using the information, determine the total amount of cash and cash equivalents.

(a) Investment securities of $10,000. These securities are common stock investments in 30 companies that compose the Dow Jones Industrial average. As a result, the stocks are very actively traded in the market.
(b) Investment securities of $5,700. These securities are U.S. government bonds. The bonds are 30-year bonds; they were purchased on December 31 at which time they had two months to go until they mature.
(c) Cash of $3,400 in the form of coin, currency, savings accounts, and checking accounts.
(d) Investment securities of $6,600. These securities are commercial paper (short-term IOUs from other companies). The term of the paper is nine months; they were purchased on December 31 at which time they had four months to go until they mature.

Practice 5-3

Three Categories of Cash Flows
Using the following information, compute cash flow from operating activities, cash flow from investing activities, and cash flow from financing activities.

	Cash Inflow (Outflow)
(a) Cash received from sale of a building	$ 4,200
(b) Cash paid for interest	(600)
(c) Cash paid to repurchase shares of stock (treasury stock)	(1,100)
(d) Cash collected from customers	13,400
(e) Cash paid for dividends	(930)
(f) Cash paid for income taxes	(1,850)

Practice 5-4

Cash Flow Patterns

Identify which of the following cash flow patterns most likely belongs to: (1) a start-up, high-growth company; (2) a steady-state company; and (3) a cash cow.

	Operating Cash Flow	Investing Cash Flow	Financing Cash Flow
Company A	$(10,000)	$(27,000)	$ 40,000
Company B	40,000	(27,000)	(10,000)
Company C	30,000	(27,000)	(1,500)

Practice 5-5

Noncash Investing and Financing Activities

Combining the following information, compute the total amount of (1) cash flow from investing activities and (2) cash flow from financing activities.

(a) Purchased a building for $120,000. Paid $40,000 and signed a mortgage with the seller for the remaining $80,000.

(b) Executed a debt-equity swap: replaced a $67,000 loan by giving the lender shares of common stock worth $67,000 on the date the swap was executed.

(c) Purchased land for $100,000. Signed a note for $35,000 and gave shares of common stock worth $65,000.

(d) Borrowed $56,000 under a long-term loan agreement. Used the cash from the loan proceeds as follows: $15,000 for purchase of additional inventory, $30,000 to pay cash dividends, and $11,000 to increase the cash balance.

Practice 5-6

General Format for a Statement of Cash Flows

Organize the following summary information into the proper format for a statement of cash flows.

Cash balance, beginning of year	$ 2,800	Cash balance, end of year	$ 4,600
Cash flow from financing activities	5,000	Cash flow from investing activities	(9,400)
Total stockholders' equity, end of year	24,300		
Cash flow from operating activities	6,200	Total stockholders' equity, beginning of year	21,500

Practice 5-7

Cash Collected from Customers

Using the following information, compute cash collected from customers.

Sales	$10,000
Cost of goods sold	5,300
Operating expenses	3,800

	End of Year	Beginning of Year
Prepaid operating expenses	$1,000	$ 700
Accounts payable	1,350	1,200
Inventory	2,500	2,100
Accounts receivable	1,400	1,375

Practice 5-8

Cash Paid for Inventory Purchases
Refer to the information in Practice 5-7. Compute cash paid for inventory purchases. (*Note:* All Accounts Payable relate to inventory purchases.)

Practice 5-9

Cash Paid for Operating Expenses
Refer to the information in Practice 5-7. Compute cash paid for operating expenses.

Practice 5-10

Direct Method
Using the following income statement and cash flow adjustment information, prepare the Operating Cash Flow section of the statement of cash flows using the *direct* method.

Sales	$7,800
Cost of goods sold	3,100
Interest expense	450
Depreciation expense	600
Net income	$3,650

Adjustments:

(a) Interest payable *increased* by $80.

(b) Accounts receivable *decreased* by $320.

(c) Inventory *decreased* by $180.

(d) Accounts payable *decreased* by $210. (*Note:* All accounts payable relate to inventory purchases.)

Practice 5-11

Indirect Method
Refer to Practice 5-10. Prepare the Operating Cash Flow section of the statement of cash flows using the *indirect* method.

Practice 5-12

Complete Statement of Cash Flows from Detailed Data
Using the following information, prepare a complete statement of cash flows.

(a) Cash balance, beginning	$ 1,500
(b) Cash paid to purchase inventory	7,800
(c) Cash received from sale of a building	5,600
(d) Cash paid for interest	450
(e) Cash paid to repay a loan	1,000
(f) Cash collected from customers	10,000
(g) Cash balance, ending	?
(h) Cash received from issuance of new shares of common stock	1,200
(i) Cash paid for dividends	780
(j) Cash paid for income taxes	1,320
(k) Cash paid to purchase machinery	1,950

Practice 5-13

Operating Cash Flow: Gains and Losses
Using the following information, compute cash flow from operating activities. (*Note:* With the limited information given, only the indirect method can be used.)

Increase in accounts receivable		$ 300
Decrease in income taxes payable		170
Depreciation		1,000
Net income		250
Gain on sale of equipment		440
Loss on sale of building		210

Practice 5-14

Operating Cash Flow: Restructuring Charges

Using the following information, compute cash flow from operating activities. (*Note:* With the limited information given, only the indirect method can be used.)

Decrease in inventory	$ 300
Increase in wages payable	170
Restructuring charge	2,300
Depreciation	1,000
Net income	500

The restructuring charge consists of two elements: (1) $1,500 for the write-down in value of certain assets and (2) $800 for recognition of an obligation to relocate employees; none of the relocation has yet taken place.

Practice 5-15

Operating Cash Flow: Deferred Income Taxes

Using the following information, compute cash paid for income taxes.

Reported income tax expense $32,000

	End of Year	Beginning of Year
Income taxes payable	$ 2,950	$ 2,560
Deferred income tax liability	32,100	28,600

Practice 5-16

Operating Cash Flow: Deferred, or Unearned, Sales Revenue

Using the following information, compute cash collected from customers.

Sales $10,000

	End of Year	Beginning of Year
Accounts receivable	$1,250	$1,430
Deferred sales revenue	1,000	750

Practice 5-17

Operating Cash Flow: Prepaid Operating Expenses

Using the following information, compute cash paid for operating expenses.

Operating expenses:	
Depreciation	$10,000
Insurance	7,500
Wages	14,600
Total operating expenses	$32,100

	End of Year	Beginning of Year
Prepaid insurance	$1,500	$1,430
Wages payable	600	750

Practice 5-18

Computing Cash Paid to Purchase Property, Plant, and Equipment
Using the following information, compute cash paid to purchase property, plant, and equipment.

Depreciation expense... $13,000

	End of Year	Beginning of Year
Property, plant, and equipment............................	$134,000	$124,000
Accumulated depreciation...................................	32,000	41,000

During the year, property, plant, and equipment with an original cost of $28,000 was sold for a gain of $6,500.

Practice 5-19

Computing Cash Received from the Sale of Property, Plant, and Equipment
Refer to Practice 5-18. Compute the amount of cash received from the sale of the property, plant, and equipment.

Practice 5-20

Computing Cash Paid for Dividends
Using the following information, compute cash paid for dividends.

Net income $10,000

	End of Year	Beginning of Year
Retained earnings...	$112,000	$106,000
Paid-in capital...	50,000	44,000
Cash	1,300	1,000
Dividends payable	200	450

Practice 5-21

Computing Cash Flow Ratios
Using the following information, compute the following ratios: (1) cash-flow-to-net-income, (2) cash flow adequacy, and (3) cash times interest earned.

Net income	$18,000
Cash flow from operating activities	21,000
Cash paid for capital expenditures	23,500
Cash paid for acquisitions	11,000
Cash paid for interest	3,800
Cash paid for income taxes	6,700

Practice 5-22

Articulation
Use the following information to answer the questions below:

Dividends declared and paid...	$ 8,000
Cash from investing activities	(25,000)
Cash from financing activities	(8,000)

	End of Year	Beginning of Year
Cash	$ 21,000	$ 12,000
Other assets..	210,000	227,000
Liabilities..	106,500	117,000
Common stock	21,000	21,000
Retained earnings...	105,000	?

Compute the (a) cash from operating activities and (b) net income.

C5 | Statement of Cash Flows and Articulation

Practice 5-23

Preparing a Forecasted Statement of Cash Flows
The following balance sheet and income statement information includes actual data for 2015 and forecasted data for 2016:

	Actual 2015	Forecasted 2016
Cash	$ 100	$ 130
Accounts receivable	600	780
Inventory	1,300	1,690
Property, plant, and equipment (net)	5,000	6,300
Accounts payable	500	650
Long-term debt	4,000	5,000
Paid-in capital	1,000	1,400
Retained earnings	1,500	1,850
Sales	$10,000	$13,000
Cost of goods sold	6,000	7,800
Depreciation expense	1,000	1,200
Interest expense	400	500
Income before income taxes	$ 2,600	$ 3,500
Income tax expense	910	1,225
Net income	$ 1,690	$ 2,275

Prepare a forecasted statement of cash flows for 2016. Use the indirect method of reporting cash flow from operating activities.

EXERCISES

Exercise 5-24

Classification of Cash Flows
Indicate whether each of the following items would be classified as (1) an operating activity, an investing activity, or a financing activity or (2) as a noncash transaction or noncash item.

(a) Cash collected from customers.
(b) Cash paid to suppliers for inventory.
(c) Cash received for interest on a nontrade note receivable.
(d) Cash received from issuance of stock.
(e) Cash paid for dividends.
(f) Cash received from bank on a loan.
(g) Cash paid for interest on a loan.
(h) Cash paid to retire bonds.
(i) Cash paid to purchase stock of another company as a long-term investment.
(j) Cash received from the sale of a business segment.
(k) Cash paid for property taxes.
(l) Cash received for dividend revenue.
(m) Cash paid for wages.
(n) Cash paid for insurance.
(o) Preferred stock retired by issuing common stock.
(p) Depreciation expense for the year.
(q) Cash paid to purchase machinery.
(r) Cash received from the sale of land.

Exercise 5-25

Cash Flow Analysis
State how each of the following items would be reflected on a statement of cash flows.

(a) Securities classified as available for sale were purchased for $4,200.

(b) Buildings were acquired for $210,000, the company paying $60,000 cash and signing an 11% mortgage note, payable in five years, for the balance.

(c) Cash of $54,200 was paid to purchase a business whose assets consisted of inventory, $16,700; furniture and fixtures, $8,400; land and buildings, $20,100; and goodwill, $9,000.

(d) A cash dividend of $2,600 was declared in the current period, payable at the beginning of the next period.

(e) Accounts Payable shows a decrease for the period of $1,250.

Exercise 5-26

Cash Receipts and Cash Payments
The accountant for Alpine Hobby Stores prepared the following selected information for the year ended December 31, 2015:

	Dec. 31, 2015	Dec. 31, 2014
(a) Equipment	$55,000	$62,000
(b) Accumulated Depreciation	13,900	12,800
(c) Long-Term Debt	20,000	25,000
(d) Common Stock	16,000	12,000

Equipment with a book value of $18,000 was sold for $16,000 cash. The original cost of the equipment was $21,000.

Determine the cash inflows and outflows during 2015 associated with each of the accounts listed. Indicate how the cash flows for each item would be presented on the statement of cash flows.

Exercise 5-27

Preparing the Operating Activities Section of the Statement of Cash Flows
Anakin, Inc., provides the following account balances for 2015 and 2014:

	Dec. 31, 2015	Dec. 31, 2014
Accounts Receivable	$ 18,700	$15,500
Inventory	25,440	27,200
Accounts Payable	21,650	22,400
Salaries Payable	1,500	1,350
Sales	278,700	
Cost of Goods Sold	197,000	
Depreciation Expense	16,700	
Salaries Expense	35,200	
Other Expenses	24,300	

Using the format presented in the chapter, prepare the Operating Activities section of the statement of cash flows and present that information using (a) the direct method and (b) the indirect method.

Exercise 5-28

Preparing the Operating Activities Section of a Statement of Cash Flows

Norrington Trading Co. provides the following income statement for 2015:

Sales	$675,400
Cost of goods sold	243,500
Gross margin	$431,900
Depreciation expense	51,000
Salaries expense	124,600
Interest expense	11,300
Other expenses	98,700
Income taxes expense	44,000
Net income	$102,300

In addition, the following balance sheet information is available:

	Dec. 31, 2015	Dec. 31, 2014
Accounts receivable	$52,000	$47,000
Inventory	78,100	72,300
Prepaid other expenses	5,600	6,700
Accounts payable	53,600	52,300
Interest payable	800	1,200
Income taxes payable	5,200	3,400

Using the format presented in the chapter, prepare the Operating Activities section of the statement of cash flows and present that information using (a) the direct method and (b) the indirect method.

Exercise 5-29

Format of Statement of Cash Flows with Indirect Method

From the following information for Carter Corporation, prepare a statement of cash flows for the year ended December 31, 2015, using the indirect method.

Amortization of patent	$ 4,000	Retirement of long-term debt	$40,000
Depreciation expense	7,000	Sale of land (includes $6,000 gain)	35,000
Issuance of common stock	25,000	Decrease in accounts receivable	2,100
Issuance of new bonds payable	30,000	Increase in inventory	1,200
Net income	55,000	Increase in accounts payable	1,500
Payment of dividends	22,500	Increase in cash	56,700
Purchase of equipment	33,200	Cash balance, January 1, 2015	82,800

Exercise 5-30

Cash Flow from Operations—Indirect Method

The following information was taken from the books of Tapwater Company. Compute the amount of net cash provided by (used in) operating activities during 2015 using the indirect method.

	Dec. 31, 2015	Dec. 31, 2014
Accounts receivable	$18,900	$16,750
Accounts payable	11,500	14,000
Accumulated depreciation (no plant assets retired during year)	29,000	22,000
Inventories	24,500	20,000
Other current liabilities	5,000	3,000
Prepaid insurance	1,200	2,000
Net income	35,500	—

Exercise 5-31

Cash Flow from Operations—Direct Method

A summary of revenues and expenses for Norwalk Company for 2015 follows:

Sales	$ 7,200,000
Cost of goods manufactured and sold	3,500,000
Gross profit	$ 3,700,000
Selling, general, and administrative expenses	2,300,000
Income before income taxes	$ 1,400,000
Income taxes	500,000
Net income	$ 900,000

Net changes in working capital accounts for 2015 were as follows:

	Debit	Credit
Cash	$104,000	
Trade Accounts Receivable	420,000	
Inventories		$110,000
Prepaid Expenses (selling and general)	15,000	
Accrued Expenses (75% of increase related to manufacturing activities and 25% to general operating activities)		48,000
Income Taxes Payable		54,000
Trade Accounts Payable		170,000

Depreciation on plant and equipment for the year totaled $700,000; 60% was related to manufacturing activities and 40% to general and administrative activities.

Prepare a schedule of net cash provided by (used in) operating activities for the year using the direct method.

Exercise 5-32

Cash Flow from Operations—Indirect Method

The following information was taken from the comparative financial statements of Tulip Corporation:

Net income for year	$ 75,000
Sales revenue	450,000
Cost of goods sold (except depreciation)	275,000
Depreciation expense for year	50,000
Amortization of intangible assets for year	20,000
Interest expense on short-term debt for year	5,200
Dividends declared and paid during year	35,000

Selected account balances:

	Beginning of Year	End of Year
Accounts Receivable	$22,000	$15,000
Inventory	35,000	40,000
Accounts Payable	47,500	52,000
Interest Payable	1,200	400

Using the indirect method, compute the net amount of cash provided by (used in) operating activities for the year.

Exercise 5-33

Cash Flow from Operations—Direct Method
Based on the information given in Exercise 5-32 and using the direct method, compute the net amount of cash provided by (used in) operating activities for the year.

Exercise 5-34

Cash Computations
A comparative balance sheet, income statement, and additional information for Shillig Doors Inc. follow.

Shillig Doors Inc.
Condensed Comparative Income Statement
For the Years Ended December 31, 2015 and 2014

	2015	2014
Net sales	$3,946,000	$3,112,000
Cost of goods sold	2,385,000	2,364,000
Gross profit	$1,561,000	$ 748,000
Expenses	792,000	506,000
Net income	$ 769,000	$ 242,000

Shillig Doors Inc.
Comparative Balance Sheet
December 31, 2015 and 2014

	2015	2014
Assets		
Current assets:		
Cash	$ 131,000	$ 102,000
Available-for-sale securities	400,000	—
Accounts receivable	409,000	372,000
Inventory	289,000	304,000
Prepaid expenses	36,000	24,000
Total current assets	$1,265,000	$ 802,000
Property, plant, and equipment	$ 656,000	$ 541,000
Accumulated depreciation	(81,000)	(42,000)
	$ 575,000	$ 499,000
Total assets	$1,840,000	$1,301,000
Liabilities and Stockholders' Equity		
Current liabilities:		
Accounts payable	$ 191,000	$ 174,000
Accrued expenses	124,000	110,000
Dividends payable	165,000	100,000
Total current liabilities	$ 480,000	$ 384,000
Notes payable—due 2017	210,000	106,000
Total liabilities	$ 690,000	$ 490,000
Stockholders' equity:		
Common stock	$ 625,000	$ 600,000
Retained earnings	525,000	211,000
Total stockholders' equity	$1,150,000	$ 811,000
Total liabilities and stockholders' equity	$1,840,000	$1,301,000

Additional information for Shillig:

(a) All accounts receivable and accounts payable relate to trade merchandise.
(b) The proceeds from the notes payable were used to finance plant expansion.
(c) Capital stock was sold to provide additional working capital.

Compute the following for 2015:

    Cash collected from accounts receivable, assuming all sales are on account.
    Cash payments made on accounts payable to suppliers, assuming that all purchases of inventory are on account.
    Cash payments for dividends.
    Cash receipts that were not provided by operations.
    Cash payments for assets that were not reflected in operations.

Exercise 5-35

Statement of Cash Flows—Indirect Method
Following is information for Goulding Manufacturing Company:

(a) Long-term debt of $500,000 was retired at face value.
(b) New machinery was purchased for $62,000.
(c) Common stock with a par value of $100,000 was issued for $160,000.
(d) Dividends of $22,000 declared in 2014 were paid in January 2015, and dividends of $30,000 were declared in December 2015, to be paid in 2016.
(e) Net income was $450,700. Included in the computation were depreciation expense of $70,000 and intangible assets amortization of $10,000.

	Dec. 31, 2015	Dec. 31, 2014
Current assets:		
Cash and cash equivalents	$189,200	$130,000
Accounts receivable	175,000	156,000
Inventory	178,000	160,000
Current liabilities:		
Accounts payable	64,000	87,400
Dividends payable	30,000	22,000
Interest payable	12,900	7,000
Wages payable	24,000	17,000

Prepare a statement of cash flows for the year ended December 31, 2015, using the indirect method.

Exercise 5-36

Articulation
The following information is available for Kelsey Inc. (*Note:* All inventory is purchased on account, and Accounts Payable relates only to the purchase of inventory.)

	Dec. 31, 2015	Dec. 31, 2014
Accounts receivable	$?	$75,000
Inventory	72,000	83,000
Accounts payable	56,000	44,000
Sales	540,000	
Cost of goods sold	?	
Cash collected from customers	551,000	
Cash paid for inventory	?	
Inventory purchased on account	279,000	

Compute the following for 2015:

1. The ending balance in accounts receivable
2. The amount of cash paid for inventory
3. The amount of cost of goods sold

Exercise 5-37

Articulation

The following information is available for Santiago Inc.:

	Dec. 31, 2015	Dec. 31, 2014
Cash	$ 141,000	$ 97,000
Retained earnings	665,000	543,000
Cash from operating activities	?	
Cash from investing activities	(483,000)	
Cash from financing activities	(287,000)	
Dividends declared and paid	47,000	
Net income	?	

REVERSE SOLVABLE

Compute the following for 2015:

1. Net income
2. Cash from operating activities

Exercise 5-38

Cash Flow Ratios

Following are data from the financial statements for Houma Company.

Houma Company
Selected Financial Statement Data
For the Years Ended December 31, 2015 and 2014

	2015	2014
Net income	$34,000	$ 65,200
Cash from operating activities	28,900	158,130
Cash paid for purchase of fixed assets	42,000	156,000
Cash paid for interest	26,000	24,000
Cash paid for income taxes	15,000	25,670

Compute the following for both 2014 and 2015:

1. Cash-flow-to-net-income ratio
2. Cash flow adequacy ratio
3. Cash times interest earned ratio

Exercise 5-39

Forecasted Income Statement and Statement of Cash Flows

(*Note:* This exercise uses the same information used in Exercise 4-39.) Romney and Associates wishes to forecast its net income for the year 2016. In addition, for planning purposes Romney intends to construct a forecasted statement of cash flows for 2016. Romney has assembled balance sheet and income statement data for 2015 and has forecast a balance sheet for 2016. In addition, Romney has estimated that its sales in 2016 will rise to $3,600 and does not anticipate paying any dividends in the coming year. This information is summarized here.

Balance Sheet	2015	2016 Forecasted
Cash	$ 40	$ 48
Other current assets	450	540
Property, plant, and equipment (net)	500	700
Total assets	$990	$1,288
Accounts payable	$190	$ 228
Bank loans payable	500	400
Total stockholders' equity	300	660
Total liabilities and stockholders' equity	$990	$1,288

Income Statement	2015	2016 Forecasted
Sales	$3,000	$3,600
Cost of goods sold	1,200	
Gross profit	$1,800	
Depreciation expense	100	
Other operating expenses	1,440	
Operating profit	$ 260	
Interest expense	50	
Income before taxes	$ 210	
Income taxes	84	
Net income	$ 126	

1. Prepare a forecasted income statement for 2016. Clearly state what assumptions you make.
2. Prepare a forecasted statement of cash flows for 2016. Use the indirect method of reporting cash from operating activities. (*Hint:* In computing cash paid to purchase new property, plant, and equipment, don't forget to consider the effect of depreciation expense in 2016.)

Exercise 5-40

Forecasted Balance Sheet, Income Statement, and Statement of Cash Flows
(*Note*: This exercise uses the same information used in Exercise 4-40.) Ryan Company wishes to prepare a forecasted income statement, balance sheet, and statement of cash flows for 2016. Ryan's balance sheet and income statement for 2015 follow:

Balance Sheet	2015
Cash	$ 10
Other current assets	250
Property, plant, and equipment, net	800
Total assets	$1,060
Accounts payable	$ 100
Bank loans payable	700
Total stockholders' equity	260
Total liabilities and stockholders' equity	$1,060

Income Statement	2015
Sales	$1,000
Cost of goods sold	750
Gross profit	$ 250
Depreciation expense	40
Other operating expenses	80
Operating profit	$ 130
Interest expense	70
Income before taxes	$ 60
Income taxes	20
Net income	$ 40

In addition, Ryan has assembled the following forecasted information regarding 2016.

(a) Sales are expected to increase to $1,500.
(b) Ryan expects to become more efficient at utilizing its property, plant, and equipment in 2016. Therefore, Ryan expects that the sales increase will not require any overall increase in property, plant, and equipment. Accordingly, the year 2016 property, plant, and equipment balance is expected to be $800.
(c) Ryan's bank has approved a new long-term loan of $200. This loan will be in addition to the existing loan payable.
(d) Ryan Company does not anticipate paying any dividends in the coming year.

1. Prepare a forecasted balance sheet for 2016. Clearly state what assumptions you make.
2. Prepare a forecasted income statement for 2016. Clearly state what assumptions you make.
3. Prepare a forecasted statement of cash flows for 2016. Use the indirect method of reporting cash from operating activities. (*Hint:* In computing cash paid to purchase new property, plant, and equipment, don't forget to consider the effect of depreciation expense in 2016.)

P1

Foundations of Financial Accounting

CHAPTER 6

Earnings Management

Learning Objectives

1. Identify the factors that motivate earnings management.
2. List the common techniques used to manage earnings.
3. Critically discuss whether a company should manage its earnings.
4. Describe the common elements of an earnings management meltdown.
5. Explain how good accounting standards and ethical behavior by accountants lower the cost of obtaining capital.

Chester Carlson was a patent attorney. He was frustrated at the time and expense involved in producing copies of patent documents. Copies of text documents could be produced by retyping them with carbon paper inserted between multiple sheets of blank typing paper. Drawings were reproduced by sending them out to be professionally photographed. Carlson pondered how he might make single copies of any sort of document right in the office with just the push of a button. Carlson had a technical background, having graduated from Cal Tech and worked at Bell Labs for a time. Accordingly, he was aware of the fairly recent discovery of the photoconductivity of some materials. These materials, when exposed to light, were transformed from electrical insulators to electrical conductors. Carlson combined the phenomena of photoconductivity and static electricity to devise a process for making copies; he applied for his first patent in 1937.

Patent application notwithstanding, Chester Carlson didn't have the necessary engineering skills to bring his copying process to life. Accordingly, he hired a young engineer, and the two of them worked on the process in a back room behind a beauty parlor in Astoria, Long Island. They made their first successful copy on October 22, 1938; the text of the copy was "10-22-38 Astoria." Carlson called the process "electrophotography." This was later changed to *xerography*, from the Greek words for dry (xeros) and writing (graphein). The five steps in xerography are outlined in Exhibit 6-1; as you can tell from the description and from your experience with copy machines today, the general xerography process is the same today as it was back in 1938.

Chester Carlson approached 20 companies with his new process, but none were interested. For several years, IBM considered buying the patent from Carlson but ultimately decided against it. Finally, in

1944 Carlson was able to convince Batelle Memorial Institute of Columbus, Ohio, to commercially develop his xerography process. Batelle was to get 60% of the proceeds, leaving Carlson with 40%. The progress of Batelle scientists was slow initially because of their continuing work on war-related research. By 1946, after the conclusion of World War II, the Batelle researchers had refined xerography to the point at which it was commercially viable. On January 2, 1947, Batelle licensed the process to Haloid Company, a producer of photographic paper based in Rochester, New York, for $50,000 plus royalties on sales. When this deal was signed, Chester Carlson quit his job as a patent attorney and prepared to sit back and let the sales royalties roll in. He soon realized that there was still much work to be done before Haloid could mass-produce xerography machines; Carlson was back at his job within a month. Ultimately, Chester Carlson wound up with $2 million and 150,000 shares of Haloid stock.

Haloid produced its first xerography machine, the Xerox Model A, in 1949. This initial model required the user to perform 14 steps and took 45 seconds to make a single copy. Between 1949 and 1961, Haloid invested more than $90 million in improving its xerography machines. In 1959, Haloid released the Xerox 914. Following the practice of renting rather than selling its machines (a practice made popular by IBM), Haloid was able to place 20,000 Xerox 914 machines by 1962. Each machine produced yearly rental revenue averaging $4,000, and it had cost Haloid just $2,500 to manufacture each machine. Haloid became the original high-tech, high-flying glamour stock; the company had a price-earnings ratio of over 100 in 1961. In that same year, Haloid changed its name to Xerox.

Through the 1960s and 1970s, Xerox continued to be a very profitable company known for its innovative products. In 1970, the company opened its Palo Alto Research Center (PARC) near Stanford University. During the 1970s, many of the products developed at PARC were truly 20 years ahead of their time. For example, by 1974 PARC researchers had developed a personal computer, the Alto, that employed a Windowslike screen, allowed the user to execute commands by pointing and clicking with a mouse, and was networked with other machines through Ethernet. In 1977, PARC researchers were able to add the computer industry's first laser printer to this networked configuration. Unfortunately for Xerox, the traditional East Coast executives of the company didn't share the enthusiasm for personal computers expressed by the West Coast PARC researchers. The Alto (and its successor, the Star) were never fully embraced by either customers (because of their relatively high price) or the Xerox sales force. Xerox stopped producing personal computers in the early 1980s.

In the 1980s, Xerox faced stiff competition from Japanese copy machine makers such as Canon and Ricoh. Xerox was able to maintain its profitability through aggressive cost cutting and improvement in quality. Then in the 1990s, Xerox faced another threat as companies focused more on "digital documents," calling into question the need for large-scale paper copy machines. Xerox fought back again with its digital and color copiers and its slogan, "The Document Company." Through mid-1999, the Xerox business strategy seemed to be working. In July 1999, the company's shares were trading for $50 each, and financial analysts were expecting the

>
>
> Xerox has been so successful in the copy machine business that the company has had difficulty preserving the trademark status of the word *xerox*. Like the words *aspirin*, *escalator*, and *zipper*, which were once the trade names of specific products, the word *xerox* runs the risk of passing into generic usage and losing its legal protection. For example, on its Web site, Xerox advises that the word "xerox" never be used as a verb.

Exhibit 6-1 | The Five Key Steps in Xerography

1. A plate (or drum) made of a photoconductive material is charged with positive static electricity. The original material used by Chester Carlson was sulfur; commonly used photoconductive materials now are selenium, germanium, and silicon.

2. The plate is exposed to light reflected from the page to be copied. Where the light falls on the photoconductive material, the material becomes an electrical conductor and the positive charge is dissipated. In the shadows (corresponding to the image to be copied), the positive static charge remains.

3. The plate is dusted with a negatively charged powder, the toner. The toner particles stick to the positively charged areas of the plate, duplicating the image to be copied.

4. A piece of paper that has been supercharged with positive static electricity is placed over the plate. The negatively charged toner is attracted away from the plate by the supercharged paper.

5. The paper is heated, melting the toner and fusing the image onto the paper.

© Cengage Learning 2014

next year (fiscal 2000) to be a record-breaking one, with earnings forecasted to top $3.00 per share (compared to the $2.67 per share expected to be reported in fiscal 1999).

Unknown to analysts and investors in July 1999, the favorable revenue and earnings numbers reported by Xerox from 1997 through 1999 were more the result of accounting manipulations

> **FYI**
>
> On March 17, 1988, **Apple Computer** brought suit against **Microsoft**, claiming that Windows 2.03 illegally copied the "look and feel" of the Apple Macintosh graphical user interface. Reportedly, Bill Gates' response was that both he and Apple cofounder Steve Jobs had taken the idea from PARC.

than effective business practices. As revealed through a subsequent SEC investigation, Xerox had accelerated the recognition of revenue and boosted reported earnings through the use of both non-GAAP accounting practices and changes in GAAP accounting practices that were not disclosed to financial statement users. Descriptions of some of these practices follow:

Lease discount rates in Brazil. Xerox sometimes accounts for the lease of a copy machine as a sale, with financing provided by Xerox. This is entirely acceptable and is discussed in Chapter 15 in the section on sales-type leases. A sales-type lease involves both initial sales revenue and interest revenue over the life of the lease. An accounting assumption about the appropriate interest rate associated with the financing aspect of the lease determines the mix between initial sales revenue and subsequent interest revenue. For example, assume that a copy machine is leased for 10 years with annual lease payments of $1,000. Over the life of the lease, total revenue of $10,000 (10 years × $1,000) will be recognized. If it is

> **FYI**
>
> The corporate headquarters of Xerox is located in Norwalk, Connecticut. This is also the home of the FASB!

assumed that the appropriate interest rate is 6%, immediate sales revenue is $7,360 (the present value of $1,000 per year for 10 years at a 6% discount rate), and interest revenue over the life of the lease is $2,640 ($10,000 − $7,360). In contrast, if the appropriate interest rate is assumed to be 25%, immediate sales revenue is $3,571, and subsequent interest revenue is $6,429. The key difference between sales revenue and interest revenue is that the sales revenue is reported immediately whereas the interest revenue is spread over the life of the lease. To increase reported revenue in its Brazilian subsidiary, Xerox's accounting staff assumed interest rates as low as 6% when accounting for its leases. This assumption was made even though Xerox's own borrowing rate in Brazil was in excess of 25%. Xerox did not disclose details about this key accounting assumption to financial statement users.

Income tax refund receivable in the United Kingdom. In 1995, Xerox won a tax dispute in the United Kingdom. As a result, the company was entitled to a refund of $237 million in overpaid taxes. Xerox recorded this victory by debiting tax refund receivable. However, instead of crediting income for the entire $237 million immediately, as required by GAAP, Xerox deferred much of the income to be recognized in future periods. As explained later in the chapter, this is known as creating a "cookie jar reserve." Basically, through this accounting procedure Xerox was free to recognize the $237 million in income in whatever quarter it needed in order to meet performance targets or analyst expectations.

Bad debts and sales returns at Xerox Mexico. In the mid-1990s, the managers of Xerox Mexico relaxed credit standards for customers in order to increase sales to meet revenue targets set by corporate headquarters. This practice did increase immediate sales, but it also increased the estimated amount of bad debts by $127 million. To avoid recognizing this $127 million in bad debts, the managers of Xerox Mexico renegotiated the credit terms, lengthening payment periods for delinquent accounts to maintain the appearance that the accounts were actually collectible. In addition, Xerox Mexico received $27 million in sales returns from 1996 through 2000. To avoid recording this return of merchandise (and associated reduction in net sales), secret warehouses were rented to store the returned merchandise. Again, these activities were done in order to allow the managers of Xerox Mexico to meet the aggressive targets imposed by Xerox company headquarters.

In total, Xerox accelerated the reporting of more than $6 billion in revenue in the period 1997–2000 and increased reported earnings by $1.4 billion during the same period. At the peak of the earnings manipulation in 1998, more than 30% of Xerox's reported earnings stemmed from undisclosed changes in accounting practices. An SEC investigation uncovering Xerox's accounting abuses resulted in a $10 million fine for the company; at the time, this was the largest fine ever imposed for misleading financial reporting.

Until 2001, Xerox's auditor was KPMG. KPMG required Xerox to make many adjustments to its financial statements over the 1997–2000 period. For example, when Xerox proposed the creation of an off-balance-sheet entity dubbed "Project Mozart," KPMG stood firm against the plan because it appeared to be a blatant attempt to transfer reported losses from the Xerox income statement to the Project Mozart income statement. In addition, in early 2000, KPMG refused to sign off on the 1999 audit until Xerox had completed an internal investigation of its accounting practices and had made a number of restatements. As a result of this firm stance by KPMG, the Xerox financial statements for the year ended December 31, 1999, were not released until June 7, 2000. However, many businesspeople and regulators argue that KPMG was not tough enough. In response to the KPMG claim that the vast majority of the $6 billion overstatement in revenue by Xerox stemmed from honest differences in accounting judgment and estimates, Lynn E. Turner, at the time an accounting professor at Colorado State University and former chief accountant of the SEC, said, "As I tell my students, they will flunk if they can't get the answers on their homework any closer than to the nearest billion dollars." In April 2005, KPMG agreed to pay $22 million to settle a civil suit filed by the SEC stemming from the Xerox audit.

Sources: James Bandler and Mark Maremont, "KPMG's Auditing with Xerox Tests Toughness of SEC," *The Wall Street Journal*, May 6, 2002, p. A1.

Richard Hamner, "There Isn't Any Profit Squeeze at Xerox," *Fortune*, July 1962, pp. 151–155 and 208–216.

Jeremy Kahn, "The Paper Jam from Hell," *Fortune*, November 13, 2000.

"Publishing: Revolution Ahead?" *Time*, November 1, 1948, pp. 82–83.

"Printing With Powders," *Fortune*, June 1949, pp. 113–122.

Securities and Exchange Commission, Plaintiff, v. Xerox Corporation, Defendant, Civil Action No. 02-272789 (DLC), April 11, 2002.

Lynn E. Turner, "Just a Few Rotten Apples? Better Audit Those Books," *The Washington Post*, July 14, 2002, p. B1.

1. What business events of the 1980s and 1990s put pressure on Xerox's reported profits?
2. What was done by the managers of Xerox Mexico to avoid reducing reported net sales for $27 million in returned merchandise?
3. What happened to KPMG as a result of its work auditing the financial statements of Xerox?

Answers to these questions can be found on page 6-29.

The final outcomes of this exercise in earnings and revenue management at Xerox were all negative. By August 2002, after all of the public revelations and accounting restatements had been assimilated by the market, Xerox's total market value had fallen to $5 billion. Xerox also bore a tarnished reputation that will take years to restore; by April 2010, the company's market value had only risen back to $15 billion, a far cry from its $46 billion peak in 1999. The CEO and CFO who presided over Xerox during the accounting manipulations were let go, and a group of six former Xerox executives agreed to personally pay more than $20 million to settle SEC charges. KPMG lost the Xerox audit engagement, with the $60 million in fees earned by the successor auditor in 2001 alone. The biggest loser, however, was the U.S. economy. The crisis in investor confidence sparked by the relentless barrage of accounting scandals in 2001 and 2002 helped lower stock values in the United States by more than 20%, eliminating in excess of $2 trillion in wealth for U.S. investors.

This chapter explores the topic of earnings management. Because accounting numbers are so important in so many decisions, there is a predictable tendency of managers to try to manipulate the reported numbers to be as favorable as possible. And because financial accounting involves so many judgments and estimates, such manipulation is possible. In this chapter, we will discuss the common techniques used to manage earnings, as well as the difficult issue of whether it is in the best interest of a company to try to manage its reported earnings. We will also walk through the typical sequence of events associated with an earnings management catastrophe. The Xerox case that started the chapter is an accurate model of the mess that can result from managers trying to manipulate reported accounting numbers to try to compensate for lackluster operating performance. The chapter ends with a discussion of the great value that can be added to an economy by good accounting standards and ethical accountants.

Motivation for Earnings Management

LO1 Identify the factors that motivate earnings management.

学习目标1
识别引起盈余管理动机的因素。

Numbers are very important in framing peoples' opinions. Rarely do we question how the numbers are computed. For example, the too-close-to-call U.S. presidential election of 2000 resulted in very close scrutiny of the voting process in Florida. This close scrutiny made all of us aware that rather than just take vote totals as a given, we should instead exercise more care and healthy skepticism about vote tabulation in future elections. As another example, U.S. federal government budget decisions are not made based on some theoretical "real economic" budget surplus or deficit but are based on the reported surplus or deficit. Pressure to raise or lower taxes, to increase or cut spending, to elect different representatives, and so forth, are based on that one reported number, and hardly anyone delves into how the number is computed. In the government budgetary arena, the following statement, though perhaps a bit overstated, still contains a grain of truth:

> Perception dictates policy,
>
> accounting determines perception,
>
> therefore, accounting rules the world.

Reported numbers have a similar power to frame opinions in the corporate arena. Because reported net income is the number that receives the most attention, it is also the number that corporate managers might be most tempted to manipulate. This section describes four reasons for managing reported earnings. These aren't necessarily good reasons, as illustrated in the Xerox opening scenario and as discussed more fully later in the chapter. However, they do reflect the forces that are often spoken of as pushing managers to manipulate reported earnings. These four reasons are as follows:

盈余管理的动机主要有：
- 满足内部目标；
- 满足外部预期；
- 平滑利润；
- 为IPO或贷款申请进行粉饰。

1. Meet internal targets
2. Meet external expectations
3. Provide income smoothing
4. Provide window dressing for an IPO or a loan

Each of these earnings management motivations will be discussed in turn in this section.

Meet Internal Targets

As discussed in the Xerox scenario at the beginning of the chapter, managers in Xerox Mexico felt pressured by corporate earnings and revenue targets and resorted to relaxing credit standards, biasing estimates of bad debts, and finally fraudulently concealing sales returns. One of the most notorious examples of accounting manipulation to meet internal goals is the MiniScribe case from 1989. To meet the nearly impossible earnings targets set by the flamboyant and volatile CEO, employees of MiniScribe, a seller of disk drives, reportedly resorted to shipping disk drive boxes filled with bricks to meet sales targets at the end of a quarter.

Internal earnings targets represent an important tool in motivating managers to increase sales efforts, control costs, and use resources more efficiently. As with any performance measurement tool, however, it is a fact of life that the person being evaluated will have a tendency to forget the economic factors underlying the measurement and instead focus on the measured number itself. If you doubt this tendency, consider whether during this intermediate accounting course you have maintained your focus solely on learning financial accounting or whether you have occasionally concentrated primarily on scoring points to get a good grade.

学术研究证实，当存在以利润为基础的内部红利时，将出现盈余管理倾向。例如，如果盈余很接近红利门槛，管理层就更可能操纵利润使其向上；如果盈余大大超过最高红利水平，则管理层更可能操纵利润使其向下。

Academic research has also confirmed that the existence of earnings-based internal bonuses contributes to the incidence of earnings management. For example, research has demonstrated that managers subject to an earnings-based bonus plan are more likely to manage earnings upward if they are close to the bonus threshold and are also more likely to manage earnings downward if reported earnings are substantially in excess of the maximum bonus level.[1] This latter tendency basically means that managers have a tendency to defer some earnings "for a rainy day," which could occur the next period when operating results are not as favorable. This tendency has been found using company-level information as well as using earnings reported by managers of divisions of companies.[2] Because the existence of an earnings-based bonus plan increases the incentive of managers to manipulate the reported numbers, auditors consider such plans a risk factor as they plan the nature and extent of their audit work.

Meet External Expectations

A wide variety of external stakeholders has an interest in a company's financial performance. For example, employees and customers want a company to do well so that it can survive for the long run and make good on its long-term pension and warranty obligations. Suppliers want assurance that they will receive payment and, more important, that the purchasing company will be a reliable purchaser for many years into the future. For these stakeholders, signs of financial weakness, such as reporting negative earnings, are very bad news indeed. Accordingly, we shouldn't be surprised that in some companies when the initial computations reveal that a company will report a net loss, the company's accountants are asked to go back to the accrual judgments and estimates to see whether just a few more dollars of earnings can be squeezed to obtain positive earnings. If this scenario is true, we should expect that there should be a lower-than-expected number of companies with earnings just a little bit negative and a higher-than-expected number of companies with earnings just a little bit positive. This result should occur because any company that has a small negative earnings number has a strong incentive to try to use accounting assumptions to nudge the earnings into positive territory. This intuition is verified by the earnings distribution information reproduced in Exhibit 6-2. As seen in

> **FYI**
>
> As China prepared to apply for World Trade Organization (WTO) membership, the official Chinese government target was 8% economic growth in 1998. Government officials biased the reported numbers upward, concealing the fact that actual growth was just 4%. See Nicholas R. Lardy, "Integrating China into the Global Economy," Brookings Institution Press, 2002.

1 P. Healy, "The Effect of Bonus Schemes on Accounting Decisions," *Journal of Accounting and Economics*, 1985, p. 85.
2 F. Guidry, A. Leone, and S. Rock, "Earnings-Based Bonus Plans and Earnings Management by Business-Unit Managers," *Journal of Accounting and Economics*, 1999, p. 113.

在正常情况下，净利润在0上下的公司的数值分布应该呈钟形曲线；然而，在0以下，你可以看到数值分布形成一个凹槽，这说明利润恰好在0下一点的公司严重低于预期；恰好在0以上的数值分布出现一个突起，这说明利润恰好在0上一点的公司严重高于预期。

the diagram, annual net income for an average company is equal to about 7% of the company's market value. And except around zero, the numerical distribution of companies that have net income above and below that average amount follows the familiar bell-shaped curve. However, just below zero you can see a trough in the distribution, indicating that the number of companies with earnings just below zero is significantly lower than expected. In addition, there is a lump on the distribution just above zero, indicating that the number of companies with earnings just above zero is significantly greater than expected. This simple picture provides strong evidence that companies manage earnings to avoid reporting losses and disappointing external stakeholders.

Financial analysts are a very important set of external financial statement users. In addition to making buy and sell recommendations about shares of a company's stock, financial analysts also generate forecasts of company earnings. Extensive research has

> **FYI**
>
> According to *CFO.com*, chief financial officer (CFO) turnover among the Fortune 500 increased by 21% from 2003 to 2004. Failing to meet analysts' earnings expectations and the pressure to comply with Sarbanes-Oxley were cited as the most frequent causes for the turnover of CFOs. See Lisa Yoon, "CFO Resignations Soared in 2004," *CFO.com*, April 5, 2005.

Exhibit 6-2 | Standardized Distribution of Annual Net Income

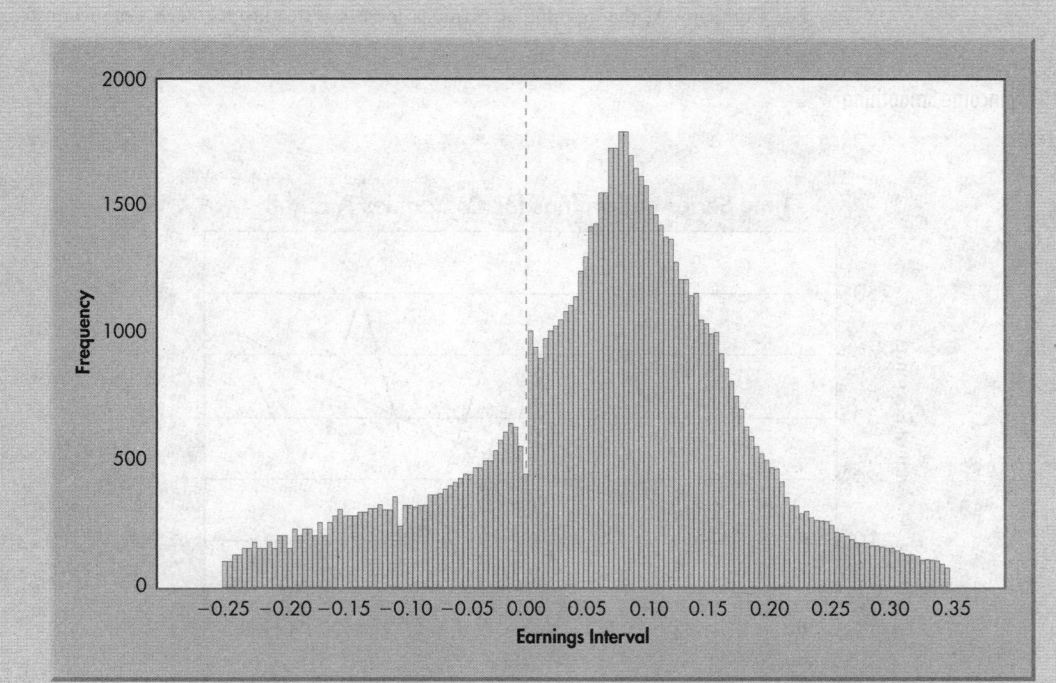

Observations are computed as net income divided by beginning-of-year market value. For example, 0.05 represents net income that is 5% of market value. "Frequency" is the number of observations in a given earnings interval.

Source: D. Burgstahler and I. Dichev, "Earnings Management to Avoid Earnings Decreases and Losses," *Journal of Accounting and Economics*, 1997, p. 99. The diagram is from Figure 3 on page 109.

shown that announcing net income less than the income forecast by analysts results in a drop in stock price. As a result, companies have an incentive to manage earnings to make sure that the announced number is at least equal to the earnings expected by analysts.

The uncanny ability of many companies to consistently meet analysts' earnings expectations would not be possible unless those companies were practicing at least some earnings management. For example, until the unexpected earnings decline associated with the September 11, 2001, World Trade Center attack, **General Electric** had met or exceeded analysts' earnings expectations for 29 consecutive quarters. Microsoft met or exceeded analysts' expectations for 52 quarters in a row, a streak that ended in the first quarter of 2000. Streaks like this defy the laws of probability. If analysts make an unbiased forecast of earnings and if companies don't make any efforts to manage earnings to reach the forecasted level, reported earnings should exceed the forecast half the time and fall short of the forecast half the time. In this setting, a string of 52 quarters in a row of meeting or beating analysts' forecast has a 1-in-4.5 quadrillion chance of occurring randomly. Research has demonstrated that managers not only manage earnings to make sure they meet analysts' forecasts but also provide overly pessimistic "guidance" to analysts to ensure that the forecasts made are not too high to reach.[3]

Provide Income Smoothing

Examine the time series of earnings for Company A and Company B shown in Exhibit 6-3. For Company A, the amount of earnings increases steadily for each year from Year 1

Exhibit 6-3 | Income Smoothing

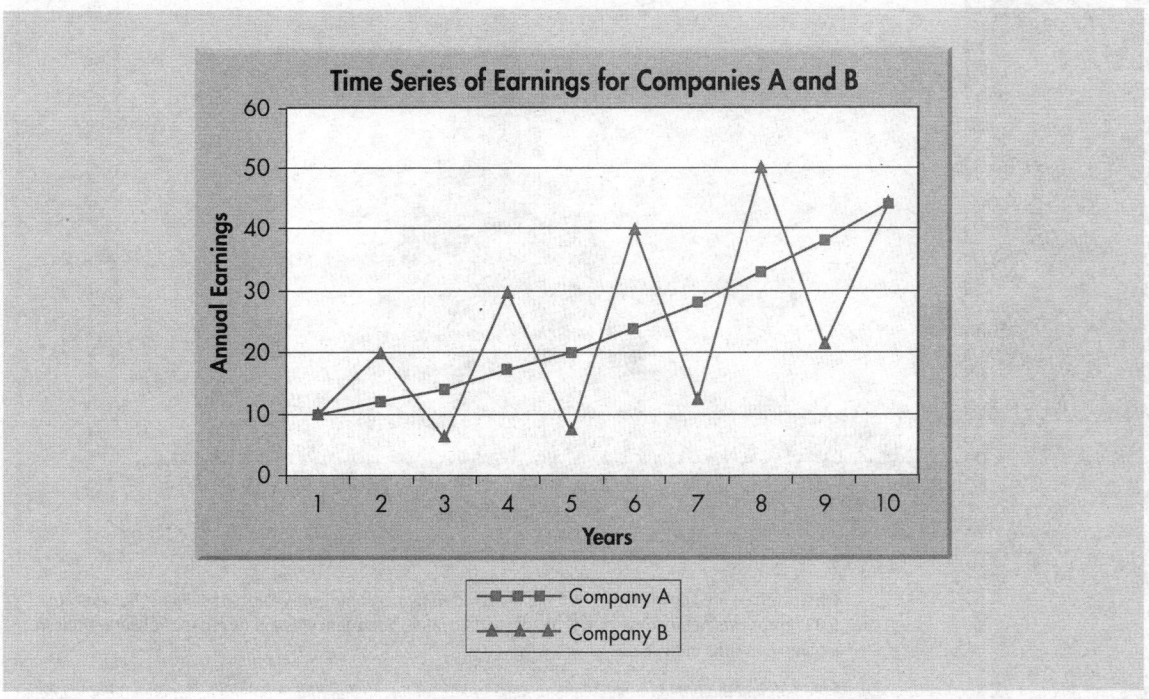

© Cengage Learning 2014

3 D. Matsumoto, "Management's Incentives to Avoid Negative Earnings Surprises," *The Accounting Review*, July 2002, p. 483.

through Year 10. For Company B, the earnings series is like a roller coaster ride. Companies A and B have the same earnings in Year 1, the same earnings in Year 10, and the same total earnings over the 10-year period included in the graph. At the end of Year 10, if you were asked which company you would prefer to loan money to or to invest in, you would almost certainly choose Company A. The earnings stream of Company A gives you a sense of stability, reliability, and reduced risk.

Now imagine yourself as the chief executive officer of Company B. You know that through aggressive accounting assumptions, you can strategically defer or accelerate the recognition of some revenues and expenses and smooth your reported earnings stream to be exactly like that shown for Company A. Would you be tempted to do so? Of course you would. The practice of carefully timing the recognition of revenues and expenses to even out the amount of reported earnings from one year to the next is called income smoothing. By making a company appear to be less volatile, income smoothing can make it easier for a company to obtain a loan on favorable terms and easier to attract investors.[4]

利润平滑能够使公司更容易以有利的条件获得贷款和吸引投资者。

The champion of all income-smoothing companies is General Electric. In fact, GE's ability to report steadily increasing earnings is legendary. As of the end of 2001, General Electric had reported 105 consecutive quarters of earnings growth (a streak that ended in 2002). GE's business structure is particularly well suited to earnings management because of the company's large number of diverse operating units (financial services, heavy manufacturing, home appliances, and so forth). A large one-time loss reported by one business unit can frequently be matched with an offsetting gain reported by another unit. By carefully timing the recognition of these gains and losses, GE can avoid reporting earnings that bounce up and down from quarter to quarter. For example, in its press release announcing results for the fourth quarter of 2001, GE reported that its **GE Capital Services** subsidiary reported a $642 million after-tax gain from the restructuring of its investment in a global satellite partnership. During the same quarter, GE Capital Services reported a $656 million after-tax loss associated with its exit from certain unprofitable insurance and financing product lines. The timing of one of these transactions could have been delayed so that it would have occurred in the first quarter of 2002, but by making sure that they were both recognized in the same quarter, General Electric was able to show a more smooth earnings stream. In 1994, an article in *The Wall Street Journal* accused General Electric of income smoothing.[5] Shortly after the article came out, one of GE's financial executives was speaking to a group of accounting professors, one of whom was brazen enough to ask if it were true that GE practiced income smoothing. The GE executive quietly smiled and responded, "Well, the timing of the recognition of some of our gains and losses has been rather fortuitous"—the implication of the response being that, of course, GE did all that it could, within the accounting rules, to smooth reported earnings.

Provide Window Dressing for an IPO or a Loan

As mentioned in Chapter 5, for companies entering phases in which it is critical that reported earnings look good, accounting assumptions can be stretched—sometimes to the breaking point. Such phases include just before making a large loan application or just before the IPO of stock. Many studies have demonstrated the tendency of managers in U.S. companies to boost their reported earnings using accounting assumptions in the

---

4 See R. Dye, "Earnings Management in an Overlapping Generations Model," *Journal of Accounting Research*, 1988, p. 195; and B. Trueman and S. Titman, "An Explanation for Accounting Income Smoothing," *Journal of Accounting Research* (supplement), 1988, p. 127. For a more general discussion of earnings management, see K. Schipper, "Commentary on Earnings Management," *Accounting Horizons*, December 1989, p. 91.

5 Randall Smith, Steven Lipin, and Amal Kumar Naj, "Managing Profits: How General Electric Damps Fluctuations in its Annual Earnings," *The Wall Street Journal*, November 3, 1994, p. A1.

period before an IPO.[6] A study of IPOs in China found that even socialist managers in Chinese state-owned enterprises manipulate reported earnings in advance of shares of the company being sold to the public.[7] If both capitalist managers in the United States and socialist managers in China are engaged in the same pattern of window dressing before an IPO, the phenomenon is truly a universal one.

An interesting case of reverse window dressing was discovered through an examination of companies applying to the U.S. International Trade Commission (ITC) for relief from the importation of competing foreign products. Important pieces of evidence that U.S. companies can submit when petitioning for import barriers are financial statements showing a reduction in profitability corresponding to an increase in the import of competing foreign products. In this setting, a company would have an incentive to make pessimistic accounting assumptions and report the lowest earnings possible, within the accounting rules. Research has shown that this tendency does in fact exist.[8]

This section has outlined a number of settings in which managers have strong economic incentives to manipulate reported earnings. Whether a manager should attempt to manage earnings is the topic of a later section in this chapter.

Earnings Management Techniques

LO2 学习目标2
列出盈余管理的常用技术手段。

② List the common techniques used to manage earnings.

With all of the incentives to manage earnings mentioned in the previous section, it isn't surprising that managers occasionally do use the flexibility inherent in accrual accounting to actually manage earnings. The more accounting training one has, the easier it is to see ways in which accounting judgments and estimates can be used to "enhance" the reported numbers. In fact, there have been nationwide seminars on exactly how to effectively manage earnings. One popular seminar sponsored by the National Center for Continuing Education in 2001 was "How to Manage Earnings in Conformance with GAAP." The target audience for the two-day seminar was described as CFOs, CPAs, controllers, auditors, bankers, analysts, and securities attorneys.

> **FYI**
>
> In the wake of the accounting scandals that occurred in 2001 and 2002, the National Center for Continuing Education decided to change the title of the earnings management seminar to "How to Detect Manipulative Accounting Practices." However, the course outline was exactly the same as the original "How to Manage Earnings" seminar.

Using the concepts of accrual accounting and the accounting standards that have been promulgated, accountants add information value by using estimates and assumptions to convert the raw cash flow data into accrual data. However, the same flexibility that allows accountants to use professional judgment to produce financial statements that accurately portray a company's financial condition also allows desperate managers to manipulate the reported numbers. The following sections describe the common techniques used in managing earnings.

---

6 As one example, see S. Teoh, T. Wong, and G. Rao, "Are Accruals during Initial Public Offerings Opportunistic?" *Review of Accounting Studies*, May 1998, p. 175.
7 J. Aharony, J. Lee, and T. Wong, "Financial Packaging of IPO Firms in China," *Journal of Accounting Research*, 2000, p. 103.
8 J. Jones, "Earnings Management during Import Relief Investigations," *Journal of Accounting Research*, 1991, p. 193.

Earnings Management Continuum

Not all earnings management schemes are created equal. The continuum in Exhibit 6-4 illustrates that earnings management can range from savvy timing of transactions to outright fraud. This section provides examples of each activity on the earnings management continuum. Keep in mind that in most companies, earnings management, if it is practiced at all, does not extend beyond the savvy transaction timing found at the left end of the continuum in Exhibit 6-4. However, because of the importance and economic significance of the catastrophic reporting failures that are sometimes associated with companies that engage in more elaborate earnings management, the entire continuum is discussed here.

Strategic Matching As mentioned in the earlier discussion of income smoothing, General Electric is the acknowledged master at timing its transactions so that large one-time gains and losses occur in the same quarter, resulting in a smooth upward trend in reported earnings. Through awareness of the benefits of consistently meeting earnings targets or of reporting a stable income stream, a company can make extra efforts to ensure that certain key transactions are completed quickly or delayed so that they are recognized in the most advantageous quarter.

Change in Methods or Estimates with Full Disclosure Companies frequently change accounting estimates respecting bad debts, return on pension funds, depreciation lives, and so forth. For example, in 1998 Delta Air Lines increased the depreciation life for some of its aircraft from 20 to 25 years, reducing depreciation expense and increasing pretax income by $92 million. Although such changes are a routine part of adjusting accounting estimates to reflect the most current information available, they can be used to manage the amount of reported earnings. Because the impact of such changes is fully disclosed, any earnings management motivation could be detected by financial statement users willing to do a little detective work.

Change in Methods or Estimates with Little or No Disclosure In contrast to the accounting changes referred to in the preceding paragraph, other accounting changes are sometimes made without full disclosure. For example, the Xerox opening scenario reported that the company changed the estimated interest rate used in recording sales-type leases without describing the change in the notes to the financial statements. One might debate whether the new estimated interest rate was more appropriate, but what is certain is that failing to disclose the impact of the change misled financial statement users. These users evaluated the reported earnings of Xerox under the incorrect assumption that the results were compiled using a consistent set of accounting methods and estimates and could therefore be meaningfully compared to prior-year results. As indicated by the label in Exhibit 6-4, this constitutes deceptive accounting.

Exhibit 6-4 | The Earnings Management Continuum

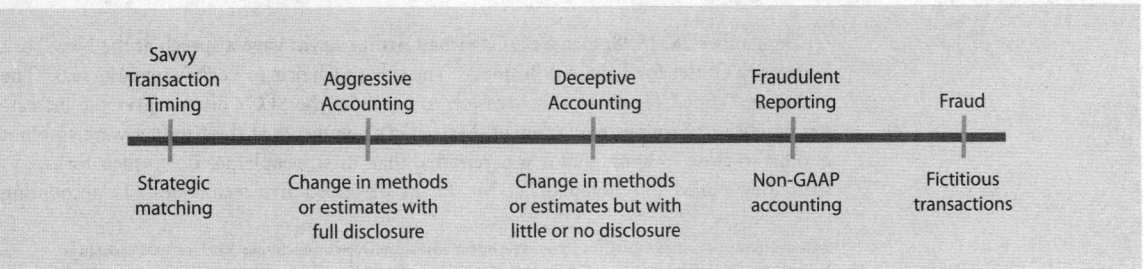

Non-GAAP Accounting Toward the right end of the earnings management continuum lies the earnings management tool that can be politely called "non-GAAP accounting." A more descriptive label in many cases is "fraudulent reporting," although non-GAAP accounting can also be the result of inadvertent errors. For example, part of the accounting deception practiced by Enron was the inappropriate use of special-purpose entities (SPEs). SPEs are small companies affiliated with, and often indirectly controlled by, a larger company. It is clear that some (although certainly not all) of Enron's SPEs were established for the express purpose of hiding information from financial statement users. In so doing, Enron violated the spirit of the accounting standards. In some cases, Enron also violated the letter of the standards by using SPE accounting when it was not allowed under GAAP. As another example, it was revealed in 2002 that WorldCom had capitalized (i.e., recognized as an asset) $3.8 billion in expenditures for local phone access charges that should have been reported as operating expenses. By the way, when the smoke finally cleared on the WorldCom scandal, the estimate of the total amount of accounting fraud climbed to $11 billion.

Fictitious Transactions The opening scenario for this chapter mentioned that managers at Xerox Mexico rented secret warehouses in which to store returned merchandise to avoid recording the returns. This is an example of outright fraud, which is the deceptive concealment of transactions (like the sales returns) or the creation of fictitious transactions. A classic example of the latter is the famous ZZZZ Best case. The founder of ZZZZ Best, a carpet cleaning and fire damage restoration business, started inventing sales contracts to meet increasing operating performance expectations by banks and investors. For example, ZZZZ Best claimed to have a contract for a $2.3 million restoration job on an eight-story building in Arroyo Grande, California, a town that had no buildings over three stories.

The five items displayed in Exhibit 6-4 also mirror the progression in earnings management strategies followed by individual companies. These activities start small and legitimately and really reflect nothing more than the strategic timing of transactions to smooth reported results. In the face of operating results that fall short of targets, a company might make some cosmetic changes in accounting estimates to meet earnings expectations but would fully disclose these changes to avoid deceiving serious financial statement users. If operating results are far short of expectations, an increasingly desperate management might cross the line into deceptive accounting by making accounting changes that are not disclosed or by violating GAAP completely. Finally, when the gap between expected results and actual results is so great that it cannot be closed by any accounting assumption, a manager who is still fixated on making the target number must resort to out-and-out fraud by inventing transactions and customers. The key things to remember are that the forces encouraging managers and accountants to manage earnings are real and that if one is not aware of those forces, it is easy to gradually slip from the left side of the earnings management continuum to the right side.

Chairman Levitt's Top Five Accounting Hocus-Pocus Items

On September 28, 1998, then-SEC Chairman Arthur Levitt gave a speech at the New York University Center for Law and Business.[9] The title of Chairman Levitt's remarks was "The Numbers Game." He chose this occasion to proclaim the SEC's dismay over the increasing practice of earnings management. Mr. Levitt's comments at the banquet were so blunt and hit so close to home that it was reported that "first, people put down their forks, . . . then they pulled out notepads."[10] Mr. Levitt described five techniques of "accounting

---

[9] A text of this entire landmark speech can be found at **http://www.sec.gov/news/speech/speecharchive/1998/spch220.txt**.
[10] Carol Loomis, "Lies, Damned Lies, and Managed Earnings," *Fortune*, August 2, 1999, p. 74.

FYI

Traditionally, companies have sometimes timed a big bath to coincide with a change in management. In this way, the "bath" year can be blamed on past management.

hocus-pocus" that summarized the most blatant abuses of the flexibility inherent in accrual accounting. A description of these five techniques follows. The discussion includes both a description of the abuses that prompted Chairman Levitt's comments as well as a description of how accounting standards and practices have been changed to address these abuses.

big-bath charges
巨额冲销，俗称"洗大澡"

Big-Bath Charges Examine the time series of earnings for Company C and Company D shown in Exhibit 6-5. For Company C, the amount of earnings increases steadily until Year 5 when the trend turns around and earnings decrease steadily thereafter. For Company D, earnings drop dramatically in Year 5 but then are steady at $15 each year thereafter. Companies C and D have the same total earnings over the 10-year period included in the graph. At the end of Year 10, if you were asked which company you would prefer to loan money to or to invest in, you would almost certainly choose Company D. Any problems that Company D may have had appear to have been put behind it in Year 5, and the recent earnings picture exudes stability. In contrast, Company C's problems seem to be continuing without end. The big drop in earnings in Year 5 for Company D is an example of a "big bath." The concept behind a big bath is that if a company expects to have a series of hits to earnings in future years, it is better to try to recognize all of the bad news in one year, leaving future years unencumbered by continuing losses. One way

Exhibit 6-5 | A Big Bath

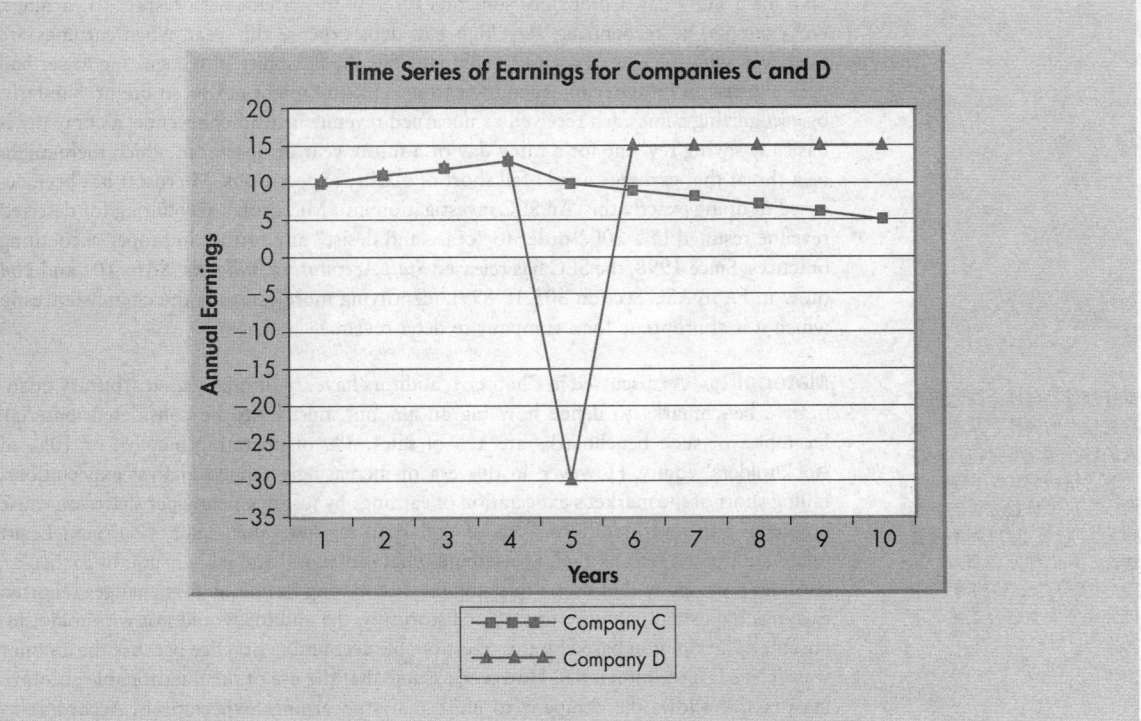

© Cengage Learning 2014

to execute a big bath is through a large restructuring charge, as discussed in Chapter 4. As part of a restructuring charge, assets are written off and the expenses associated with future restructuring obligations are recognized immediately. Since Mr. Levitt's speech in 1998, the FASB has substantially limited the flexibility a company has to recognize a big-bath restructuring charge by adopting stricter rules on the accounting for impairment losses (FASB ASC Section 360-10-35) and on the timing of the recognition of restructuring obligations (FASB ASC Topic 420).

Creative Acquisition Accounting A key accounting task after one company has acquired another is the allocation of the total purchase price to the individual assets of the acquired company. This process is described in Chapter 10. A practice common at the time Mr. Levitt gave his speech was that of allocating a large amount of a purchase price to the value of ongoing research and development projects. As described in Chapter 10, at the time of Mr. Levitt's speech, the cost assigned to "purchased in-process R&D" was expensed immediately in accordance with the mandated U.S. GAAP treatment of all R&D expenditures. The net result of this treatment is similar to a big bath in that a large R&D expense is recorded in the acquisition year, and expenses in subsequent years are lower than they would have been if the purchase price had been allocated to a depreciable asset. Since 1998, new acquisition accounting rules have been adopted (FASB ASC Topic 805, Business Combinations); these standards give more extensive guidelines on how the purchase price in a business acquisition should be allocated. In the immediate aftermath of Mr. Levitt's speech, the SEC staff informed companies that they would be very skeptical in their review of the accounting for any business acquisition in which a large portion of the purchase price was allocated to in-process R&D.

Cookie Jar Reserves We are all familiar with the advice that in good times we should save for a rainy day. Companies sometimes follow this advice with respect to earnings. For example, by recognizing very high bad debt expense this year, when earnings are high even with the extra expense, a company has the flexibility of recognizing lower bad debt expense in future years when the earnings picture might not be so bright. Similarly, by recognizing some cash received as unearned revenue instead of revenue, a company is basically saving revenue for a rainy day or a future year or quarter in which there might be a threat that earnings would fall short of market expectations. Microsoft has been accused of doing exactly this. An SEC investigation into Microsoft's accounting for deferred revenue resulted in a 2002 order to "cease and desist" any further improper accounting practices. Since 1998, the SEC has released *Staff Accounting Bulletins (SAB) 101* and *104* (now in FASB ASC Section 605-10-S99), identifying more carefully the circumstances in which it is appropriate for a company to defer revenue.

Materiality As discussed in Chapter 1, auditors have traditionally used arbitrary quantitative benchmarks to define how big an amount must be to be considered material. Examples of such benchmarks are 1% of sales, 5% of operating income, or 10% of stockholders' equity. However, in this era of increasingly refined analyst expectations, falling short of the market's expectation of earnings by just one penny per share can cause a company to lose literally billions of dollars in market value. Thus, Chairman Levitt urged auditors to rethink their ideas about what is material and what is not. In particular, consider a company that uses a questionable accounting technique that changes reported earnings by a small amount, just 1%. Historically, the auditor would not withhold a favorable audit opinion based on this questionable accounting practice because the amount was deemed to be immaterial. However, assume that the use of the questionable accounting practice allows the company to meet analysts' earnings expectations. According to

审计师对重要性金额的确定存在较大的弹性，从销售收入的1%、营业利润的5%到所有者权益的10%不等；然而，在这个日益完善的分析师预期年代，可以毫不夸张地说，利润即使偏离市场预期达1美分/股，也将导致特定公司损失上百万美元的市场价值。

Chairman Levitt, the impact of that technique should be considered material. Thus, the auditor should not sign off on the audit opinion until the company had changed the practice or convinced the auditor that it was in accordance with GAAP. In 1999, the SEC released *SAB 99* (now in FASB ASC Section 250-10-S99) that outlines this more comprehensive definition of materiality.

Revenue Recognition More common than Microsoft's efforts to defer revenue are the efforts of companies to accelerate the reporting of revenue. In particular, start-up companies, eager to show operating results to lenders and potential investors, would like to report revenue when contracts are signed or partially completed rather than waiting until the promised product or service has been fully delivered. For example, the opening scenario for Chapter 8 describes the rise and fall of MicroStrategy, a software firm. When the operating performance of the company fell short of analysts' expectations in the third quarter of 1999, the company recognized $17.5 million in revenue from a $27.5 million multiyear licensing agreement that was signed very near the end of the quarter. Given that the company had not really provided any of the promised service in the short time that had elapsed since the signing of the contract, it would have been more appropriate not to report any revenue at all. However, to do so would have resulted in MicroStrategy's reporting a loss for the quarter on revenues that were 20% lower than revenues reported the quarter before. As mentioned earlier, in response to the abuses mentioned by Mr. Levitt, the SEC released *SAB 101*, which reduces the flexibility companies have in the timing of revenue recognition. The revenue recognition guidance contained in *SAB 101* is described in detail in Chapter 8. As also described in Chapter 8, the FASB and IASB are in the midst of a joint project involving a comprehensive revisiting of the rules regarding when revenue should be reported.

As mentioned earlier, action has been taken to reduce the incidence of each of these five hocus-pocus items. However, this list is still a useful starting point to see how companies attempt to manage earnings. As new accounting standards and SEC regulations reduce or eliminate one particular type of earnings management, rest assured that resourceful managers and accountants will invent new ones, but these new techniques will be variations on the general theme shared by all of Chairman Levitt's hocus-pocus items. The exercise of judgment inherent in the accrual process gives desperate managers the ability to accelerate or defer the reporting of profit to best suit their purposes.

Pro Forma Earnings

An interesting twist in the practice of earnings management is the reporting of pro forma earnings. A pro forma earnings number is the regular GAAP earnings number with some revenues, expenses, gains, or losses excluded. The exclusions are made because, companies claim, the GAAP results do not fairly reflect the company's performance.

The concern with pro forma earnings is that companies can abuse the practice and report pro forma earnings merely in an effort to make their results seem better than they actually were. In fact, pro forma earnings have been labeled as "EBS," or "everything but the bad stuff."[11] There are many examples of questionable pro forma earnings reporting. For example, on August 8, 2001, Waste Management announced its earnings for the second quarter of 2001. Reported GAAP earnings were $191 million, somewhat short of analysts' expectations. However, pro forma earnings were $212 million for the quarter, beating analysts' expectations. The difference between GAAP earnings and pro forma

---

11 Lynn Turner, SEC Chief Accountant, Remarks to the 39th Annual Corporate Counsel Institute, Northwestern University School of Law, Evanston, Illinois, October 12, 2000.

earnings resulted because, on a pro forma basis, Waste Management decided to exclude $1 million in truck-painting costs and $30 million in consulting costs from the operating expenses. Waste Management's claim was that the trucks were painted early, making the paint job economically equivalent to a capital expenditure (an asset) rather than an expense. The consulting costs were part of a strategic improvement initiative; again, Waste Management claimed that these costs were more appropriately reported as an asset rather than as an expense as required under GAAP.[12]

The key question with respect to pro forma earnings is whether the number helps financial statement users better understand a company or whether it is a blatant attempt to cover up poor performance. Research on this issue has revealed that both answers are correct. For many companies, the pro forma earnings number is in fact a better reflection of the underlying economic performance than is GAAP net income. Thus, a manager can use the flexibility of pro forma earnings reports to reveal additional, useful information. On the other hand, there is also evidence that some managers use a pro forma earnings release in an attempt to hide poor operating performance. A study of 1,149 pro forma earnings announcements made from January 1998 through December 2000 found that while only 38.7% of the announcing companies had GAAP earnings that met or exceeded analysts' expectations, the pro forma earnings numbers reported by these same companies met or exceeded analysts' expectations 80.1% of the time.[13]

One way to view the flexible reporting options a manager has in choosing what to report as "pro forma earnings" is that these options are just an exaggerated version of the options the same manager has in reporting GAAP earnings. If the manager is trustworthy, the GAAP earnings are reliable, and the manager can reveal even better information about the underlying economics of the business through appropriate adjustments in computing pro forma earnings. This advantage of pro forma earnings is offset (some would say swamped) by the opportunity that reporting pro forma earnings gives a desperate manager seeking to gloss over operating problems by reporting deceptively positive pro forma results. This potential for misleading reporting of pro forma earnings prompted the Financial Executives International (FEI) and the National Investor Relations Institute in April 2001 to recommend that firms give a reconciliation to GAAP net income whenever reporting pro forma numbers. This reconciliation highlights the adjustments made by management in reporting pro forma earnings. In 2003, the SEC formalized this requirement of providing a reconciliation between GAAP and pro forma earnings in its Regulation G. An example of one such reconciliation is reproduced in Exhibit 6-6. This illustration is for Intuit Inc., maker of the popular software products QuickBooks, Quicken, and TurboTax. Note that the largest adjustment (for share-based compensation expense, which will be explained in Chapter 13) is a noncash item that Intuit believes does not relate to the company's core operating performance.

This section has discussed the earnings management continuum, which illustrates how a company can imperceptibly slide from intelligent transaction timing to unquestionably fraudulent deception in its attempts to report the most attractive earnings possible. The

> **FYI**
>
> The first SEC cease and desist order with respect to pro forma earnings was issued to **Trump Hotels & Casino Resorts**. For the third quarter of 1999, Trump had a GAAP loss of $67 million. However, by excluding a one-time charge of $81 million, Trump was able to report pro forma earnings of $14 million, exceeding the prevailing analyst forecast of $12 million. What Trump deceptively failed to mention is that the $14 million in pro forma earnings included a $17 million one-time gain. See Securities and Exchange Commission, *Accounting and Auditing Enforcement Release No. 1499*, Administrative Proceeding File No. 3-10680, January 16, 2002.

---

12 Aaron Elstein, "Unusual Expenses Raise Concerns," *The Wall Street Journal*, August 23, 2001, p. C1.
13 N. Bhattacharya, E. Black, T. Christensen, and C. Larson, "Assessing the Relative Informativeness and Permanence of Pro Forma Earnings and GAAP Operating Earnings," *Journal of Accounting and Economics*, 2002.

Exhibit 6-6 | Reconciliation of Pro Forma Earnings to GAAP Earnings

Intuit Inc.
GAAP to Pro Forma Operating Income Reconciliation

(in millions)	Three Months Ended January 31, 2010	Three Months Ended January 31, 2009
GAAP operating income	$139	$111
Amortization of purchased intangible assets	16	14
Acquisition-related charges	11	13
Professional fees for business combinations	3	—
Share-based compensation expense	37	34
Non-GAAP operating income	$206	$172

Share-based compensation expenses. These consist of non-cash expenses for stock options, restricted stock units and purchases of common stock under our Employee Stock Purchase Plan. When considering the impact of equity awards, we place greater emphasis on overall shareholder dilution rather than the accounting charges associated with those awards.

Amortization of purchased intangible assets and acquisition-related charges. When we acquire an entity, we are required by GAAP to record the fair values of the intangible assets of the entity and amortize them over their useful lives. Amortization of purchased intangible assets in cost of revenue includes amortization of software and other technology assets of acquired entities. Acquisition-related charges in operating expenses include amortization of other purchased intangible assets such as customer lists, covenants not to compete and trade names.

Professional fees for business combinations. We exclude from our non-GAAP financial measures the professional fees we incur to complete business combinations. These include investment banking, legal and accounting fees.

Gains and losses on marketable equity securities and other investments. We exclude from our non-GAAP financial measures gains and losses that we record when we sell or impair marketable equity securities and other investments.

© Cengage Learning 2014

five accounting hocus-pocus techniques are examples of the accounting tactics companies use to manage earnings. Finally, pro forma earnings announcements can be either an effort by management to add information value to the reported GAAP numbers or a last-ditch attempt to meet earnings targets that were not attainable using generally accepted accounting principles. Keep in mind that accounting standards and SEC enforcement activities will undoubtedly change in the future to eliminate some earnings management techniques that are common now. However, desperate managers will continue to work with creative accountants to develop new ways for companies to manage their reported results.

Pros and Cons of Managing Earnings

 Critically discuss whether a company should manage its earnings.

The preceding two sections have discussed why and how a company manages earnings. This section explores the difficult issue of whether a company *should* manage earnings. The perfect-world response that a company should never manage earnings under any circumstances is both naïve in today's financial reporting environment and is also not necessarily correct. On the other hand, there can be great risk in starting down the slippery slope of managing reported results.

Financial Reporting as a Part of Public Relations

On the Web sites of most publicly traded companies, the financial statements can be found under the heading "Investor Relations." In essence, financial reporting is just a subcategory of public relations. A financial statement is one of a large number of vehicles that managers of a company use to communicate information about the company to the public. And as with other forms of corporate communications, a company must balance its desire to frame information in the best light possible with the need to maintain credibility with company stakeholders.

In the context of financial statements being one way for a company to communicate with the public, consider your answers to the following questions:

QUESTION Does a manager have an ethical and fiduciary responsibility to carefully manage the resources of a publicly traded company in order to maximize the value to the shareholders?

Answer. *Yes. In fact, this is the very definition of the responsibility of a corporate manager.*

QUESTION Does the public perception of a company impact the company's success in terms of finding customers, securing relationships with suppliers, attracting employees, and obtaining cooperation from elected officials and regulators?

Answer. *Certainly. It is impossible to rally people to put their time and money behind a company unless they are convinced that the company can be successful.*

QUESTION Does the amount of reported earnings impact the public's perception of a company?

Answer. *Absolutely. Accounting net income is not the only piece of information relevant to assessing a company's viability, but it certainly is one influential data point.*

QUESTION Does a manager have a responsibility to manage reported earnings, within the constraints of generally accepted accounting principles?

Answer. *It is difficult to answer no to this question. In light of the answers to the preceding questions, it would be an irresponsible manager indeed who did not do all possible, within the constraints of GAAP, to burnish the company's public image.*

> **FYI**
> Of course, a manager who spends too much time managing earnings, at the expense of pushing forward the strategic efforts of the company, is wasting corporate resources. One CEO estimated that 35% of his/her time was spent considering preliminary financial reports and providing earnings guidance to analysts and company stakeholders.

Is Earnings Management Ethical?

Refer back to Exhibit 6-4. Everyone agrees that the creation of fictitious transactions, at the far right side of the earnings management continuum, is unethical. But there the universal agreement ends with respect to what is and is not ethical. For example, managers and their auditors frequently disagree about what constitutes fraudulent, non-GAAP reporting. In the WorldCom example mentioned earlier, the company's CFO vigorously defended the capitalization rather than the expensing of the disputed $3.8 billion in local phone access charges. The CFO reiterated this defense, based on his understanding of the appropriate accounting standards, in a multiday series of meetings with the external auditor and the audit committee.[14] In the view of the CFO, this "fraudulent reporting" was both ethical and in conformity with GAAP. As one moves even further to the left on the earnings management continuum, disagreement about whether a certain act is or is not ethical increases. For example, when a company makes an accounting change, how can a bright line be drawn between sufficient and deceptive disclosure? Who is to judge whether the strategic timing of gains and losses by General Electric is unethical or just prudent business practice?

Exhibit 6-7 contains a figure titled "The GAAP Oval." This oval represents the flexibility a manager has, within GAAP, to report one earnings number from among many possibilities based on different methods and assumptions. Clearly, reporting a number corresponding with points D or E, which are both outside the GAAP oval, is unethical. The difficult ethical question is whether the manager has a responsibility to try to report an earnings number exactly in the middle of the possible range, point B in Exhibit 6-7. Or does the manager have a responsibility to report the most conservative, worst-case number, point A in the exhibit? Is it wrong for the manager to try to use accounting flexibility to report an earnings number corresponding with point C, which is the highest possible earnings number that is still in conformity with GAAP? What cost is there, in terms of credibility, for a manager who makes a conservative set of accounting assumptions one year, perhaps when overall operating performance is good, and an aggressive set of assumptions the next year, perhaps to try to hide lackluster operating performance? Finally, note that the boundary of the oval is fuzzy, so it sometimes is not clear whether a certain set of computations is or is not in conformity with GAAP.

一名管理人员是否确实进行了盈余管理及其是否超过界限违反了GAAP，部分归因于被查获的畏惧（成本）和公司道德文化的作用。

Of course, whether a manager actually does manage earnings and whether he or she crosses the line and violates GAAP to do so is partially a function of the fear (and costs) of getting caught and of the general ethical culture of the company. It is also a function of the manager's personal ethics and ability to recognize that fraudulent and deceptive financial reporting is part of a continuum that starts with innocent window dressing but can end with full-scale fraud. There is no neon sign giving a final warning saying, "Beware: Don't cross this line!" Thus, each individual must be constantly aware of where he or she is with respect to the earnings management continuum in Exhibit 6-4

Exhibit 6-7 | The GAAP Oval

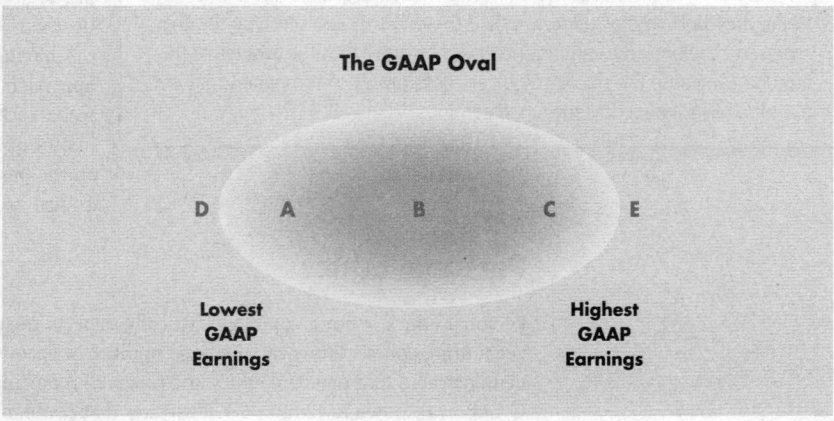

© Cengage Learning 2014

---

14 Jared Sandberg, Deborah Solomon, and Rebecca Blumenstein, "Inside WorldCom's Unearthing of a Vast Accounting Scandal," *The Wall Street Journal*, June 27, 2002, p. A1. WorldCom's CFO, Scott Sullivan, later pleaded guilty to charges of conspiracy, securities fraud, and filing false statements. Mr. Sullivan was released from prison in 2009 after serving four years.

ARTHUR ANDERSEN: A TALE OF TWO CHOICES

As with any company that has a long history, Arthur Andersen has a number of internal legends that helped define its character over the years. One of these legends, included in the official history covering the firm's first 50 years, is as follows:

> About 1915, Mr. [Arthur] Andersen [the founder of the firm] was confronted with a difficult situation with respect to the financial statements of a midwestern interurban railway company. The company had distorted its earnings by deferring relatively large charges that properly should have been absorbed in current operating expenses. Mr. Andersen was insistent that the financial statements to which he attached his report should disclose the facts. The president of the company . . . came to Chicago and demanded that Mr. Andersen issue a report approving the company's procedure in deferring these operating charges. Mr. Andersen informed the president that there was not enough money in the city of Chicago to induce him to change his report. We lost the client, of course, at a time when the small firm was not having easy sailing, and the loss of a client was almost a life and death matter. The soundness of Mr. Andersen's judgment in this case was clearly indicated when, a few months later, the company was forced to file a petition in bankruptcy.

Contrast this account with the behavior of Arthur Andersen personnel associated with the Enron scandal. In connection with the Enron engagement, Andersen helped Enron structure SPEs that were used to improve the reported accounting numbers of the Enron parent company. Andersen partners also failed to warn Enron's board of directors of their concerns about Enron's accounting. And finally, Andersen professionals shredded documents in a desperate attempt to cover up the firm's involvement in Enron's accounting deception. These questionable actions, taken without careful consideration of their long-term consequences, ultimately brought down the firm started by Mr. Andersen back in 1913.

Question:
In what specific ways can a reputation for unbending integrity help an audit firm? A manufacturing firm? A service firm?

Source: Arthur Andersen & Co., "The First Fifty Years: 1913–1963," Chicago, 1963, pp. 19–20.

FYI

Nonaccountants are under the impression that there is no GAAP oval. Instead, they believe that there is only a GAAP point, a single quantity that represents the one, true earnings number. Managers must be aware that this attitude can cause the public to be very unforgiving of companies that are found to have "innocently" managed earnings.

---

and the GAAP oval in Exhibit 6-7. Boards of directors and financial statement preparers should also be aware that, as a group, managers are notoriously overoptimistic about the future business prospects of their companies. A company policy of having a consistently conservative approach to accounting is a good counterbalance to managers who might try to justify optimistic accounting assumptions on the basis of a business turnaround that is "just around the corner."

Personal Ethics

Personal ethics is not a topic one typically expects to study in an intermediate financial accounting course. However, the large number of accounting scandals in 2001 and 2002 demonstrated that personal ethics and financial reporting are inextricably connected. The GAAP oval shown in Exhibit 6-7 illustrates that companies can report a range of earnings numbers for a year and still be in strict conformity with GAAP. In other words, earnings management can and does occur without any violation of the accounting rules. If one takes a strictly legalistic view of the world, then it is clear that managers should manage earnings, when they have concluded that the potential costs in terms of lost credibility are outweighed by the financial reporting benefits, because earnings can be managed without violating any rules.

A contrasting view is that the practice of financial accounting is not a matter of simply applying a list of rules to a set of objective facts. Management intent often enters into the decision of how to report a particular item. For example, land is reported as a long-term asset in the balance sheet unless management intends to sell the land within one year of the balance sheet date. In the context of earnings management, an important consideration is whether savvy transaction timing or changes in accounting methods or estimates are done to better communicate the economic performance of the business to financial statement users or whether the earnings management techniques are used with the intent to deceive. And if earnings management is done to deceive, whom is management trying to deceive? If management is trying to deceive potential investors, lenders, regulatory authorities, employees, or other company stakeholders, then managing earnings poses a real risk of lost credibility in the future. One final important item should be considered—most people believe that intentionally trying to deceive others is wrong, regardless of the economic consequences.

> **FYI**
>
> In an effort to increase the personal cost to company executives of allowing a company to report earnings that violate GAAP, the SEC in 2002 began requiring CEOs and CFOs to submit sworn statements asserting that they had personally confirmed that their company's financial statements contained no materially misleading items.

Elements of Earnings Management Meltdowns

4 Describe the common elements of an earnings management meltdown.

Since the start of the new millennium, astounding numbers of catastrophic accounting failures have occurred. The list includes, but is not limited to, Xerox, Enron, WorldCom, Lehman Brothers, Freddie Mac, and undoubtedly many more by the time you read this chapter. Of course, the details of each failure are different, but they all stem from unsuccessful attempts to manage earnings, and they all have common elements. These common elements are outlined in the timeline in Exhibit 6-8 and are discussed in this section.

Downturn in Business

Excessive earnings management almost always begins with a downturn in business. When operating results are consistently good, the need for earnings management is not

Exhibit 6-8 | Seven Elements of an Earnings Management Meltdown

1	2	3	4	5	6	7
Downturn in business	Pressure to meet expectations	Attempted accounting solution	Auditor's calculated risk	Insufficient user skepticism	Regulatory investigation	Massive loss of reputation

© Cengage Learning 2014

as great. For example, the first step along the path to accounting scandal for Xerox was a slowdown in sales associated with the increased use of digital documents in the United States and general business woes in the company's Mexican and Brazilian subsidiaries. WorldCom was caught in the massive collapse of the telecommunications companies. From 1997 through 2002, telecom companies spent $4 trillion (with a t!) laying fiber optic cable in the expectation of doubling or tripling of data traffic every quarter. When this volume of traffic didn't materialize, the aggregate market values of telecom companies dropped by $2.5 trillion.[15] In this industry setting, WorldCom was bound to feel some earnings pressure. For Enron, the company's rapid revenue growth partially masked a substantial decline in operating profitability. Exhibit 6-9 displays the return on assets (operating income/assets) of Enron's largest segment from 1996 through 2000. Note that the Enron accounting scandal did not break until late in 2001. You should note that return on assets was not only declining but it was also at a very low absolute level of less than 2%. This dwindling profitability increased the pressure on Enron's management to manage earnings.

FYI

In 1993, the CFO for **Daimler-Benz** was concerned that the company was using loopholes in the German accounting standards to manage earnings and hide the company's poor operating performance, allowing management to delay making the tough decisions needed to fix the company. See Case 22-8 (and the associated solution) to find out what happened.

Pressure to Meet Expectations

As mentioned earlier, a powerful factor motivating managers to manage earnings is the desire to continue to meet expectations, both internal and external. According to the SEC, without the accounting manipulations outlined at the beginning of the chapter, Xerox would have failed to meet analysts'

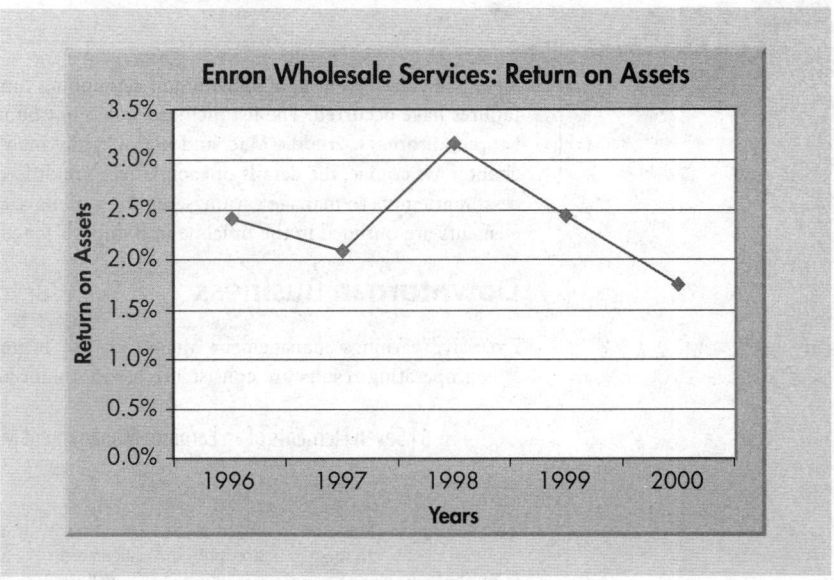

Exhibit 6-9 | Enron's Declining Operating Profitability

15 Geoffrey Colvin, "When Scandal Isn't Sexy," *Fortune*, June 10, 2002.

earnings expectations in 11 of the 12 quarters in 1997, 1998, and 1999. As it was, Xerox met or exceeded expectations in each of the 12 quarters. As described in Chapter 8, when MicroStrategy fell short of market expectations in March 2000, the company's stock price started into a tailspin that reduced the value of the company by 99.9% within 16 months.

Attempted Accounting Solution

One response to a downturn in business and a looming failure to meet market expectations is to go back to the drawing board and try to improve the business. For example, as described in the opening scenario for Chapter 23, Home Depot was in exactly this situation at the beginning of 1986. The company's earnings had dropped and a disappointed market had reduced the value of Home Depot's stock by 23%. Home Depot's response in 1986 was to more efficiently manage inventory, cut overhead, and aggressively collect its outstanding accounts receivable. This approach propelled Home Depot to years of double-digit sales and earnings growth. Alternatively, when the accountants, instead of the operations or marketing people, are asked to return a company to profitability through earnings management, the solution is a temporary one at best. At worst, the counterproductive mentality associated with papering over a company's problems through earnings management can ultimately lead to even larger business problems.

Auditor's Calculated Risk

财务报表的决策有用性观点认为，审计师的预计风险代表了公司管理层和公司审计师磋商达成的结果。

A useful view of the financial statements is that they represent a negotiated settlement between the management of the company and the company's auditor. As described throughout this chapter, management has many incentives to use the financial statements to paint the best picture possible. On the other hand, the audit firm wishes to preserve its reputation and to avoid investor lawsuits, so the audit firm has an incentive to push back against any accounting treatment that appears overly optimistic. As management and the auditor discuss the appropriate accounting treatment of items when a difference of opinion exists, they eventually reach agreement on a set of financial statements that both management and the auditor can sign and release to the public.

FYI

Companies that pay more nonaudit fees (such as for tax work) to auditors more frequently meet or just beat analysts' expectations through the use of accounting accruals. This is evidence that companies with more extensive economic ties with their auditor tend to manage earnings more. See R. Frankel, M. Johnson, and K. Nelson, "The Relation between Auditors' Fees for Nonaudit Services and Earnings Management," *The Accounting Review*, Vol. 77, Supplement 2002.

As you can imagine, an auditor is frequently required to decide whether to accept a debatable accounting treatment, engage in further discussions to try to convince management to abandon the treatment, or as a final resort, withdraw from the audit. In making this decision, the auditor must balance the multiyear future revenues from continuing as a company's auditor with the potential costs of being swept up in an accounting scandal, losing valuable reputation, and perhaps losing a large lawsuit. Thus, the decision to sign the audit opinion is always a calculated risk.

One lesson we can learn from the Enron case is that all auditors, not just Arthur Andersen, had been underweighting the potential cost of signing an audit opinion on financial statements that contain questionable accounting. In the case of Enron and Arthur Andersen, this calculated risk by Andersen's Enron audit team resulted in the rapid demise of a venerable firm with the loss of the jobs of tens of thousands of Andersen employees along with billions of dollars in partners' equity. Probably more than any new regulation from the SEC or new law from Congress, this huge economic loss resulting from Andersen's calculated risk with respect to the Enron audit has caused other audit firms to be more careful and less willing to compromise on accounting treatments as the negotiated settlement over the financial statements is reached.

Insufficient User Skepticism

With the benefit of hindsight, it is often very easy to look back and see advance warning signs of an impending accounting scandal. For example, as we look now at Enron's declining return on asset numbers in Exhibit 6-9, we wonder why more people weren't skeptical about the company's fundamental operating performance before accounting scandal engulfed the company. In fact, in October 2001, just before the Enron earnings restatement that led to the company's bankruptcy less than two months later, 11 of the 13 financial analysts following Enron recommended the company's stock as a "buy" or "strong buy." Again, with the benefit of hindsight, it seems that even though Enron's published financial statements were misleadingly positive, there were still indications in those financial statements that should have led a skeptical analyst and investment community to question the company's fundamental business model.

> **FYI**
>
> An analysis of 26,000 analysts' recommendations as of April 2, 2001, revealed that only 0.3% of the recommendations were a "strong sale." By comparison, 67.7% of the recommendations were "buy" or "strong buy." See Lynn E. Turner, "The State of Financial Reporting Today: An Unfinished Chapter III," SEC Chief Accountant, Remarks at Glasser LegalWorks Third Annual SEC Disclosure & Accounting Conference, San Francisco, California, June 21, 2001.

The question of why financial statement users have historically not exhibited enough healthy skepticism is an interesting one without a definitive answer. One contributing factor is similar to the calculated risk idea mentioned earlier with respect to auditors. Financial statement users have usually accepted companies' financial statements at face value with the realization that there was some risk of deceptive reporting but without being sufficiently aware of the massive losses that might stem from that deception. Just as auditors are now weighing their risks in a new light after the large losses stemming from the Enron, WorldCom, and other accounting scandals, financial statement users are now exercising a greater degree of skepticism about reported financial results.

Another reason that analysts and the investment community have not exhibited enough financial statement skepticism is that these parties often stand to benefit economically as companies obtain loans, issue stock, set up complicated financing vehicles, and engage in merger and acquisition activity. Wall Street investment firms such as GE Capital, **J.P. Morgan Capital, Merrill Lynch,** and **Morgan Stanley** all benefited as investors in the SPEs that Enron used to keep some information off its balance sheet.

An extreme example of financial analysts intentionally overlooking poor performance comes in the case of the $100 million fine levied by the state of New York against Merrill Lynch. Investigation revealed that at the same time that the Merrill Lynch analysts were publicly recommending stocks as a "buy," they were internally circulating highly negative comments about those same stocks. For example, one stock, **InfoSpace**, was listed on Merrill Lynch's "Favored 15" buy list for four months in 2000 even though the firm's analysts were saying internally that InfoSpace was a "powder keg" and a "piece of junk" and that the analysts had received many "bad smell comments" about the company.[16] The motivation behind this public recommendation of stocks that the analysts privately were very

---

16 Affidavit in Support of an Inquiry by Eliot Spitzer, Attorney General of the State of New York, Pursuant to Article 23-A of the General Business Law of the State of New York with regard to the acts and practices of Merrill Lynch & Co., Inc., and others, April 2002.

skeptical about was as follows: "The research analysts were acting as quasi-investment bankers for the companies at issue, often initiating, continuing, and/or manipulating research coverage for the purpose of attracting and keeping investment banking clients."

Regulatory Investigation

Just as New York investigated the Merrill Lynch analyst team as described earlier, investigations are often conducted when companies are suspected of passing outside the boundary of the GAAP oval in Exhibit 6-7 into the area of fraudulent financial reporting. As described at the beginning of the chapter, the SEC launched an investigation of Xerox and uncovered evidence of systematic financial misrepresentation, resulting in a $10 million fine and a $22 million civil judgment being levied against Xerox. The SEC frequently investigates questionable accounting and requires the offending company to sign an order agreeing to "cease and desist" its misleading accounting practices.

In addition to regulatory investigations, fraudulent financial reporting can also lead to criminal charges. In the Enron case, for example, Arthur Andersen was convicted of obstruction of justice for its destruction of audit work papers.[17] Some Enron executives pleaded guilty to criminal charges, and one of the former CEOs of the company is currently sitting in a federal prison. As mentioned earlier, the CFO of WorldCom pleaded guilty to charges of fraud, and the CEO of WorldCom was found guilty of fraud in a highly publicized trial.

Massive Loss of Reputation

The final step in an earnings management meltdown is the huge loss of credibility experienced by the company that has been found to have manipulated its reported earnings. This loss of credibility harms all of the company's relationships and drastically impairs its economic value. As mentioned earlier, the SEC imposed $32 million in penalties on Xerox for its improper reporting practices. However, the amount of these penalties pales in comparison to the $764 million in market value that Xerox shareholders lost on April 3, 2001, the day after the company announced that it was delaying the release of its 2000 financial statements pending an additional review by the company's auditor. Overall, from the peak of the earnings manipulation in 1999 to the final resolution of the accounting scandal in June 2002, Xerox shareholders lost approximately $40 billion in market value.

From 1997 through 2010, five major periods of decline in worldwide stock prices occurred. The first, in 1997, was touched off by a concern about the reliability of banking and financial information in a number of Asian countries. The second, in 2000, was primarily a return to reality after initial euphoria about the business possibilities associated with the Internet. The third decline occurred in 2001 in the wake of the political and economic uncertainty created by the September 11, 2001, attack on the World Trade Center. The fourth broad-based decline in stock values occurred in 2002 and was largely fueled by widespread uncertainty about the credibility of the financial reports of U.S. corporations. The fifth large decline occurred in 2008. Of course, this decline was a natural result of the real estate greed that had inflated U.S. real estate prices. However, the decline was made worse because of investor uncertainty about what was really inside the mortgage-backed securities that had flooded the market. This credibility crisis has graphically illustrated the real economic value of high-quality and transparent (i.e., easy to understand) financial reporting.

---

17 In a strange twist to the Enron and Arthur Andersen story, the U.S. Supreme Court later overturned the Arthur Andersen conviction because of erroneous instructions given by the judge to the jury. Unfortunately for Arthur Andersen, the firm's operations had long since ceased because of the loss of its reputation stemming from the conviction.

Exhibit 6-10 | Seven Elements of an Earnings Management Meltdown

1	2	3	4	5	6	7
Downturn in business	Pressure to meet expectations	Attempted accounting solution	Auditor's calculated risk	Insufficient user skepticism	Regulatory investigation	Massive loss of reputation

Through stage 5, the public is unaware of an earnings management meltdown.

© Cengage Learning 2014

We close this section with one final thought about earnings management meltdowns. Refer to Exhibit 6-10, which repeats the seven elements of an earnings management meltdown. If we had been discussing this topic in 1999, the Xerox meltdown would have been at stage 5, meaning that the earnings management manipulations were in full swing, the auditor had made a calculated risk and signed off on past financial statements, and the investment community was bullish on Xerox's stock and pleasantly unaware of the catastrophe that was waiting to happen. Similarly, as you are reading this chapter, it is certain that some major corporations are at stage 5 of an earnings management meltdown about which the public is as yet completely oblivious. Accordingly, an attitude of healthy skepticism about financial reports is always appropriate, whether you are an accountant, an auditor, a financial analyst, a regulator, a private investor, or just a conscientious citizen.

Transparent Financial Reporting: The Best Practice

LO5 学习目标5
解释好的会计准则和会计人员职业道德行为如何降低融资成本。

 Explain how good accounting standards and ethical behavior by accountants lower the cost of obtaining capital.

An important fact often forgotten by financial statement preparers and users is that the entire purpose of accounting, both financial and managerial, is to lower the cost of doing business. A good managerial accounting system allows managers more efficient access to the information needed to make good business decisions. Good financial accounting reduces the information uncertainty surrounding a company so that external parties, such as lenders and investors, do not bear as much risk when they provide financing to the company. This section explains how transparent financial reporting, even in a setting in which there are great incentives for managers to manipulate earnings in the short run, represents the best business practice for the long run.

What Is the Cost of Capital?

The cost of capital is the cost a company bears to obtain external financing. The cost of debt financing is simply the after-tax interest cost associated with borrowing the money. The cost of equity financing is the expected return (both as dividends and an increase in the market value of the investment) necessary to induce investors to provide equity capital. A company often computes its weighted-average cost of capital, which is the average of the cost of debt and equity financing weighted by the proportion of each type of financing.

A company's cost of capital is critical because it determines which long-term projects are profitable to undertake. In a capital budgeting setting, the cost of capital can be thought

FYI

Financial statements that have no credibility can actually be worse than no financial statements at all. When managers are willing to try to deceive lenders and investors through misleading financial reporting, those same lenders and investors naturally wonder what other types of deception the managers are attempting. This is called the "cockroach theory:" If you discover one deceptive practice, there are likely to be more.

决定公司资本成本的一个重要因素是与公司相关的风险。

of as the *discount rate* or *hurdle rate* used in evaluating long-term projects. The higher the cost to obtain funds, the fewer long-term projects are profitable for the company to undertake. A project that makes economic sense to a company with a low cost of capital could very well be unprofitable to a company with a higher cost of capital.

A key factor in determining a company's cost of capital is the risk associated with the company. For a very risky company, lenders and investors are going to require a higher return to induce them to provide capital to the company. Thus, the more risk associated with a company, the higher its cost of capital. One risk factor is the information risk associated with uncertainty about the company's future prospects. A company produces financial statements to better inform lenders and investors about its past performance; they can then use this information to make better forecasts of the company's future performance. Consequently, good financial statements reduce the uncertainty of lenders and investors so that they will provide financing at a lower cost. However, when the financial statements lose their credibility, they do nothing to reduce the information risk surrounding a company, and the company's cost of capital is higher.

The Role of Accounting Standards

Chapter 1 introduced you to the organizations important in setting accounting standards: the FASB, the AICPA, the SEC, and the IASB. In the context of our discussion here, it is useful to view each of these organizations as helping to lower the cost of capital. The FASB and the AICPA help lower the U.S. cost of capital by promulgating uniform recognition and disclosure standards for use by companies in the United States. In spite of the accounting scandals that have been discussed in this chapter, the financial reporting system in the United States is still viewed as being the best in the world. Put another way, the extensive and high-quality accounting standards used in the United States result in financial statements that reduce information risk more than do the statements prepared under the standards used anywhere else in the world.

According to the SEC, its "primary mission . . . is to protect investors and maintain the integrity of the securities markets." In terms of financial reporting, this protection of investors means that the SEC monitors the accounting standard-setting process of the FASB, requires publicly traded companies to make quarterly financial statements available to investors on a timely basis, and as in the case of Xerox, investigates (and punishes) cases of deceptive financial reporting. All of these actions increase the reliance that capital providers can place on the financial statements of companies trading on U.S. securities markets. Thus, the SEC's actions contribute toward reducing information risk and lowering the cost of capital.

The IASB is playing an increasingly important role in enhancing the credibility of international financial reporting. In the international arena, transparent and reliable financial reports are extremely important to providers of capital because the company requiring the investment capital may be in a different business environment and a different culture than those providing the capital. Therefore, the important efforts of the IASB also serve to lower the cost of capital by lowering information risk.

However, not everyone agrees that the mandated adoption of IFRS by U.S. companies will lower the cost of capital for those companies. U.S. GAAP is famous for containing

detailed accounting rules. In contrast, IFRS is known for being based on general principles, with the detailed application being left up to the professional judgment of the accountant. By some counts, U.S. GAAP contains about 25,000 pages and IFRS contains just 2,500 pages; those extra 22,500 pages allow for a lot of detailed U.S. GAAP accounting guidance that doesn't exist under IFRS. The question being considered in the U.S. business community is whether principles-based accounting standards will work in the U.S. legal environment. Accountants and auditors are concerned that they can never be sure their application of the accounting "principle," without the detailed guidance of rules, will bear up under the after-the-fact scrutiny of trial lawyers, juries, and judges. And financial statement users are concerned that this increased reliance on accounting judgment will make the reported numbers under IFRS more vulnerable to management manipulation, increasing information risk and thus increasing the cost of capital. These are issues that will be played out over the next few years as the SEC guides the U.S. transition to IFRS.

The Necessity of Ethical Behavior

A nagging question concerns why accounting scandals continue to occur in the United States even when we have high-quality accounting standards supplemented by an active regulatory system. The answer to this question has been mentioned over and over in this chapter: Managers have strong economic incentives to report favorable financial results, and these incentives can lead to deceptive or fraudulent reporting. But managers also have strong incentives to maintain a reputation for credibility for both their company and for themselves personally. This existence of conflicting forces is not unique to the area of financial reporting. We are all faced with situations in which we have incentives to deceive or commit fraud. For example, the income tax collection system in the United States works reasonably well only because the vast majority of taxpayers honestly report their taxable income, even though they could benefit economically by understating their income. Without this voluntary compliance, the Internal Revenue Service would find it prohibitively costly to audit and investigate every Form 1040 to enforce tax compliance.

As all college students know, good grades make it easier to secure a spot on the interview schedules of campus recruiters. Thus, there are some incentives to cheat when writing papers or taking exams. As a result, the internal control systems surrounding the security of exams on some campuses are truly impressive. Other universities have found that an honor code, or a code of conduct, is a less costly way to reduce the incidence of cheating. For example, at Rice University in Houston, Texas, incoming students commit to abide by the university's Honor System. Under this system, class instructors are specifically prohibited from monitoring students during an examination. In place of this external monitoring, each student is required to write the following statement on his or her exam: "On my honor, I have neither given nor received any aid on this examination."

Accountants have their own honor system; it is called the *AICPA Code of Professional Conduct*. An important concept from this code of conduct is contained in the following paragraph:

> In discharging their professional responsibilities, members may encounter conflicting pressures. . . . In resolving those conflicts, members should act with integrity, guided by the precept that when members fulfill their responsibility to the public, clients' and employers' interests are best served.[18]

In essence, this paragraph says that ethical behavior is also the best long-run business practice. To illustrate that this is so, consider again the Xerox scenario that started this chapter. The deceptive accounting practices undertaken at Xerox to hide poor operating

---

18 *AICPA Code of Professional Conduct*, Section 53–Article II: The Public Interest, par. 02 (New York: AICPA, 19).

performance merely delayed the inevitable. When these problems were eventually revealed, the economic loss suffered by all Xerox stakeholders—investors, lenders, customers, employees—was greatly magnified because of the accounting deception. The company lost economic value not just because of reduced opinions about its operating performance but also because the company had lost its credibility. Xerox researchers and marketers may soon design and promote products that will reverse the company's operating woes, but the impairment of the company's credibility will not be reversed for many, many years.

In a perfectly rational world, efforts to manipulate public perception through earnings management would be fruitless because appropriately skeptical users of the financial data would be aware of the potential for earnings management and would perfectly adjust the reported numbers using alternative sources of information to remove any bias. However, the world is not perfectly rational. Rarely do financial statement users have the time or resources to unravel the potential manipulations in every set of numbers that they see. Instead, financial statement users rely on the soundness of the accounting standards, the integrity of the managers who prepared the numbers, and the skills and thoroughness of the auditors. One of the disappointing lessons stemming from the accounting scandals of 2001 and 2002 is that financial statement users probably placed too much unquestioning reliance on the reported financial statement numbers of some companies. Because of the large amounts of money lost by investors and creditors, they will be more skeptical in the future. Hopefully, one of the positive lessons drawn from these same scandals will be that society at large will see the massive impact that credible (or questionable) financial reporting can have on the economy. Hopefully, both users and preparers of financial statements will insist on transparency in reporting in order to reduce information risk and lower the cost of capital. And hopefully individual managers, accountants, and financial statement users will be reminded again that ethical behavior really is the best long-run business practice.

SOLUTIONS TO OPENING SCENARIO QUESTIONS

1. In the 1980s, Xerox faced stiff competition from Japanese copy machine makers. In the 1990s, Xerox faced another threat as companies focused more on "digital documents," calling into question the need for large-scale paper copy machines.

2. To avoid recording $27 million in sales returns, the Xerox Mexico managers rented secret warehouses to store the returned merchandise.

3. In April 2005, KPMG agreed to pay $22 million to settle a civil suit filed by the SEC stemming from the Xerox audit. In addition, KPMG lost the Xerox audit account, resulting in lost audit fees of tens of millions of dollars per year.

Review Chapter 6 Learning Objectives

 Identify the factors that motivate earnings management.

Four factors that motivate managers to manage reported earnings follow:

- Meet internal targets
- Meet external expectations
- Provide income smoothing
- Provide window dressing for an IPO or a loan

 List the common techniques used to manage earnings.

The earnings management continuum contains the following five items:

- Strategic matching of one-time gains and losses
- Change in methods or estimates with full disclosure
- Change in methods or estimates with little or no disclosure

- Non-GAAP accounting
- Fictitious transactions

The five techniques of accounting hocus-pocus identified by then-Chairman Arthur Levitt of the SEC in 1998 are as follows:

- Big-bath charges
- Creative acquisition accounting
- Cookie jar reserves
- Materiality
- Revenue recognition

A pro forma earnings number is the regular GAAP earnings number with some revenues, expenses, gains, or losses excluded. Managers can use the flexibility of pro forma disclosures to reveal better information about a company's underlying economic performance. However, pro forma disclosures can also be used in an attempt to hide poor performance.

3 Critically discuss whether a company should manage its earnings.

Financial reporting is a normal part of a company's overall public relations effort. As such, a responsible manager should consider what impact the financial statements will have on the company's ability to satisfy the needs of its stakeholders. There is no "true" earnings number, and a manager is not necessarily expected to report earnings that are somewhere in the middle of the possible range of numbers. Computing earnings using non-GAAP methods is clearly unethical, but the boundary between GAAP and non-GAAP treatment is not always a bright line. If the intent in using earnings management techniques is to deceive, then most people would consider the earnings management wrong, independent of whether it was in strict conformity with GAAP.

4 Describe the common elements of an earnings management meltdown.

The seven stages in an earnings management meltdown are as follows:

- Downturn in business
- Pressure to meet expectations
- Attempted accounting solution
- Auditor's calculated risk
- Insufficient user skepticism
- Regulatory investigation
- Massive loss of reputation

At any given time, at least a few large corporations are somewhere in the middle of an earnings management meltdown that has not yet been publicly revealed.

5 Explain how good accounting standards and ethical behavior by accountants lower the cost of obtaining capital.

By reducing information risk, good financial reporting can lower a company's cost of capital. High-quality accounting standards and vigorous regulatory enforcement activity alone cannot ensure the credibility of financial reports. Without ethical behavior by individual managers and accountants, the regulatory cost to ensure credible financial statements would be prohibitively high. Because of the high value of a company's reputation, ethical financial reporting is also a good long-run business practice.

FASB-IASB CODIFICATION SUMMARY

Topic	U.S. GAAP	IASB Standard
General characterization of the standards	Rules oriented. U.S. GAAP contains about 25,000 pages with lots of detailed guidance.	Principles oriented. IFRS contains just 2,500 pages with many detailed accounting decisions left up to the professional judgment of the accountant.

KEY TERMS

Big bath 6-13
Cost of capital 6-26
Cost of debt financing 6-26
Cost of equity financing 6-26
Earnings management continuum 6-11
GAAP oval 6-19
Income smoothing 6-9
Internal earnings target 6-6
Pro forma earnings number 6-15
Weighted-average cost of capital 6-26
Window dressing 6-10

Tutorial Activities

Tutorial Activities with author-written, content-specific feedback, available on *CengageNOW for Stice & Stice*.

QUESTIONS

1. What are the four factors that might motivate a manager to attempt to manage earnings?
2. (a) What is the purpose of internal earnings targets?
   (b) What is the risk associated with internal earnings targets?
3. What has academic research shown with respect to earnings-based bonus thresholds?
4. How do auditors react to the existence of an earnings-based bonus plan in the company being audited?
5. Explain the significance of the figure in Exhibit 6-2.
6. Explain the significance of a company meeting or beating analysts' earnings forecasts for many quarters in a row.
7. What does the term *income smoothing* mean?
8. **General Electric** has long been known as a company that smoothes its reported earnings. What is it about General Electric that makes it possible for the company to smooth earnings?
9. Research has discovered a phenomenon common to both capitalist managers in the West and socialist managers in China. What is this phenomenon?
10. Describe one setting in which a manager might have an incentive to manipulate the accrual assumptions so that lower earnings are reported.
11. The flexibility that is a key part of the estimates and judgments inherent in accrual accounting allows desperate managers to manipulate the reported numbers. Why not do away with this flexibility and just require companies to report raw cash flow data without any assumptions about bad debt percentage, depreciation life, estimated future warranty repairs, and so forth?
12. What are the five labels in the earnings management continuum (see Exhibit 6-4), and what general types of actions are associated with each label?
13. Is there anything wrong with using a different accounting estimate this year compared to last year so long as both estimates fall within a generally accepted range for your industry?
14. What are two potential causes of non-GAAP accounting?
15. Company A has created fictitious transactions to report more favorable earnings. Is it likely that this is the only action Company A has taken to manage earnings? Explain.
16. In 1998, then-SEC Chairman Arthur Levitt gave a speech in which he identified five techniques of accounting hocus-pocus. List those five techniques.
17. What is the benefit of "taking a big bath"?
18. What accounting actions have been taken since Chairman Levitt's speech in 1998 to limit the use of big-bath charges to manage earnings?
19. What type of company would be most likely to establish a cookie jar reserve?
20. In what way is the concept of materiality contained in *SAB 99* different from the traditional concept of materiality?
21. What major accounting action has been taken since Chairman Levitt's speech in 1998 to limit the abuse of revenue recognition to manage earnings?
22. What is a pro forma earnings number?
23. What is a benefit of a company's reporting a pro forma earnings number? What is a danger with pro forma earnings numbers?
24. With respect to pro forma earnings numbers, what recommendation made by the FEI and the National Investor Relations Institute did the SEC endorse?

25. In what sense is financial reporting part of a company's general public relations effort?
26. Refer to the GAAP oval in Exhibit 6-7.
    (a) In what important way is point E different from point C?
    (b) In what important way is point A different from point C?
27. What factors influence whether a manager actually violates GAAP in an effort to manage earnings?
28. What is one way to distinguish between earnings management that is ethically right and earnings management that is ethically wrong?
29. What are the seven elements of an earnings management meltdown?
30. A manager being pressured to meet expectations in the face of a downturn in operating performance can be tempted to turn to an accounting solution and use accrual estimates and judgments to manage reported earnings. How else might the manager respond to this pressure?
31. What costs and risks is an auditor balancing when signing an audit opinion?
32. What economic incentives do financial analysts sometimes have for overlooking a company's glaring deficiencies and continuing to recommend it to investors as a "buy"?
33. When the SEC launches an investigation against a company and finds evidence of misleading financial reporting, historically what type of punishments has the SEC used?
34. The text of the chapter includes discussion of seven stages in an earnings management meltdown. At what stage does the earnings management meltdown become public knowledge?
35. What does the *cost of capital* mean?
36. How does financial reporting impact a company's cost of capital?
37. How do accounting standards impact the cost of capital?
38. According to the AICPA Code of Professional Conduct, what precept should guide members of the AICPA as they encounter conflicting pressures among their clients, investors, the business community, the government, and so forth?
39. What is the best long-run business practice?

P2

Routine Activities of a Business

CHAPTER 7

The Revenue/Receivables/Cash Cycle

Learning Objectives

1. Explain the normal operating cycle of a business.

2. Prepare journal entries to record sales revenue, including the accounting for bad debts and warranties for service or replacement.

3. Analyze accounts receivable to measure how efficiently a firm is using this operating asset.

4. Discuss the composition, management, and control of cash, including the use of a bank reconciliation.

5. Recognize appropriate disclosures for presenting sales and receivables in the financial statements.

EM EXPANDED MATERIAL

6. Explain how receivables may be used as a source of cash through secured borrowing or sale.

7. Describe proper accounting and valuation of notes receivable.

8. Understand the impact of uncollectible accounts on the statement of cash flows.

A. P. Giannini was born in 1870 in San Jose, California. When Giannini was seven, his father was killed. His mother remarried, and the family moved to San Francisco where Giannini's stepfather started a fruit wholesaling business. Giannini worked full-time in the business and by age 19 was made a junior partner in what was by then the most successful fruit wholesaling firm on the West Coast. He invested his profits in San Francisco real estate and by age 31 was financially secure enough to retire.

Giannini's retirement was an active one. He continued to manage his real estate portfolio, and he was a member of the board of directors of Columbus Savings & Loan Association, which was San Francisco's first Italian-owned bank. In spite of its immigrant roots, Columbus Savings followed the practice of the other area banks, lending only a portion of the deposits it took in to a few large local businesses and sending the rest to the money center banks in New York and Chicago. Giannini was disturbed to see that the farmers, merchants, and workers he was accustomed to dealing with were not able to get loans. When he was unable to get Columbus to change the policy, he quit the board and vowed to start his own bank. On October 17, 1904, A. P. Giannini, a man with no prior experience as a banker, embarked on a second career by opening the Bank of Italy in a converted saloon in San Francisco.

By April 1906, Giannini's bank was still an obscure little bank in the Italian section of town. On the morning of April 18, 1906, San Francisco was rocked by the worst earthquake in its history. About one-third of the town was destroyed, and 500 people were killed. In the quake's aftermath, many local business and civic leaders advocated a slow rebuilding, with a moratorium on all building loans for six months. Giannini disagreed strongly: "Gentlemen, you are making a vital mistake. The time for doing business is right now. Tomorrow morning I am putting a desk on Washington Street wharf with a Bank of Italy sign over it. Any man who wants to rebuild San Francisco can come there and get as much cash as he needs to do it."

Giannini's little bank would eventually grow to become one of the largest banks in the world—**Bank of America**. As of December 31, 2011, Bank of America reported total assets exceeding $2.1 trillion, making it the largest commercial bank in the United States in terms of assets (although only the eleventh largest worldwide). Bank of America's largest asset is its loan portfolio, which totals $892 billion; Bank of America's loan portfolio alone is almost three times as large as **ExxonMobil**'s entire asset base (at $331 billion). As you can imagine, with a loan portfolio of this size, Bank of America is continually dealing with customers who don't pay. In 2011, Bank of America recognized an expense of $13.4 billion for loans that it does not expect its customers to repay.

1. What do you think is a bank's largest revenue category? Its largest expense category?

2. Loans made by banks can be lumped into two general categories: consumer loans and commercial, or business, loans. Bank of America had total loans outstanding of $892 billion as of the end of 2011. Do you think most of these loans were to individuals (consumer loans) or to businesses (commercial loans)?

3. Bank of America reports a "net charge-off ratio" for each major loan category. This ratio is computed as the amount of loans in a category that were written off during the year, divided by the average daily loan balance in that category during the year. The four largest categories of consumer loans for Bank of America in 2011 were residential mortgages, home equity loans, direct/indirect consumer loans, and domestic credit cards. Which one of these four loan categories do you think had the lowest net charge-off ratio? The highest net charge-off ratio?

Answers to these questions can be found on page 7-41.

Our discussion of the income statement in Chapter 4 focused our attention on the importance of net income in the decisions made by investors and creditors. In this and the subsequent chapter, we focus on the event that begins the income-producing process—the sale. Because the financial statements are interrelated, a study of the sale contained in the income statement is also a study of the resulting accounts receivable and/or cash contained in the balance sheet.

Exhibit 7-1 illustrates the time line associated with the revenue/receivables/cash cycle. The chapter will begin with a discussion of the events relating to this time line. We will first discuss the journal entries that result from the sale of goods or services. With this background, we then introduce additional complexities associated with sales—sales discounts, sales returns and allowances, bad debts, and warranties—and their effect on the

Exhibit 7-1 | Revenue/Receivables/Cash Time Line

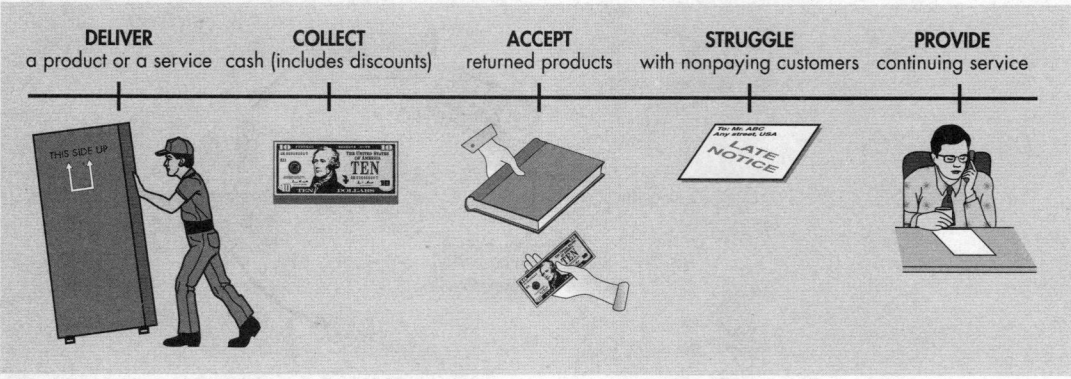

financial statements. As illustrated by the large amount of bad debt expense recognized by Bank of America in 2011, proper recognition of revenues and the valuation of receivables can have a very significant impact on the financial statements.

Once we discuss the events relating to the revenue/receivables/cash cycle, we also present and discuss methods for monitoring accounts receivable, cash management and control, and the presentation of sales, receivables, and cash on the financial statements. In the Expanded Material section of this chapter, we discuss how receivables can be used as a source of cash. The chapter concludes with a discussion of the impact of bad debt expense on computing cash flows from operations. Chapter 8 contains a further discussion of the important issues surrounding revenue recognition.

The Operating Cycle of a Business

LO1 学习目标1
说明一家公司的正常经营周期。

➊ Explain the normal operating cycle of a business.

The normal operating cycle of a business involves purchasing inventory (using either cash or credit), which is then sold, often on account. Once the receivable is collected, the cycle begins again. This cycle, illustrated in Exhibit 7-2, continually repeats itself and is the lifeblood of any business enterprise. An understanding of this operating cycle (which involves the recognition of revenue, the recording of a receivable, and the subsequent collection of cash) is critical if you are to understand how businesses operate and the role of accounting information in that business. Thus, we begin our detailed discussion of accounting with a look at the revenue/receivables/cash cycle.

The recognition of revenue is generally related to the recognition of accounts receivable. Because revenues are generally recorded when the earning process is complete and a valid promise of payment (or payment itself) is received, it follows that a receivable arising from the sale of goods is generally recognized when title

FYI

When a company accepts another company's credit card (such as Visa, MasterCard, and American Express) as payment, the credit card company charges a service fee. This fee is recognized as an expense by the seller.

Exhibit 7-2 | The Operating Cycle

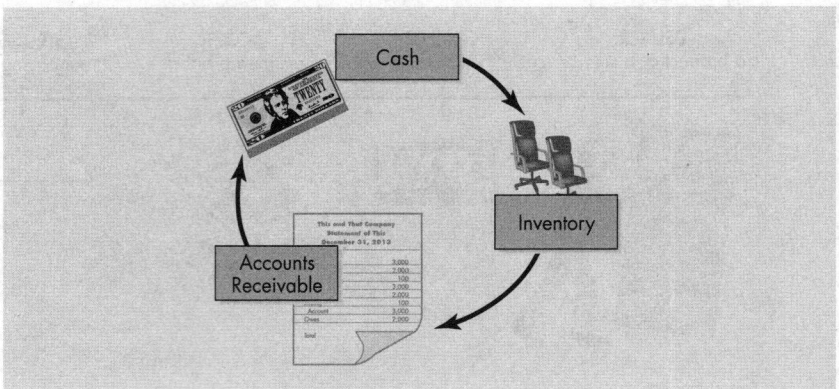

to the goods passes to a bona fide buyer. The point at which title passes may vary with the terms of the sale; therefore, it is normal practice to recognize the receivable when goods are shipped to the customer. It is at this point in time that the revenue recognition criteria are normally satisfied. Revenue should not be recognized for goods shipped on approval when the shipper retains title until there is a formal acceptance, or for goods shipped on consignment when the shipper retains title until the goods are sold by the consignee. Receivables for services to customers are properly recognized when the services are performed. It is worth again mentioning that the complexities of revenue recognition (and there are many) are discussed in Chapter 8.

The entry for recognizing revenue and a receivable from the sale of goods or services is as follows:

Accounts Receivable..	xx
Sales..	xx

When the amount is collected, Accounts Receivable is credited, and Cash is debited as follows:

Cash..	xx
Accounts Receivable	xx

For department stores and major oil and gas companies that have their own credit cards, a significant portion of revenues arises from sales using these credit cards. For example, Target has both a Target credit card and a Target Visa card (although as of June 2012, all new cards issued are Target cards). By maintaining its own credit card, Target makes money both from its store operations as well as financial income from its credit card receivables portfolio.

Before we move on and introduce some additional aspects of sales, let's take a moment and discuss the different types of receivables that are typical. In its broadest sense, the term *receivables* is applicable to all claims against others for money, goods, or services. For accounting purposes, however, the term is generally employed in a narrower sense to designate claims expected to be settled by the receipt of cash.

Stop & Think

Consider the question of why a company would sell on account in the first place. In other words, why not just have a policy of "all sales are for cash"? Which ONE of the following is the most reasonable explanation for why companies sell on account?

a) Allowing customers to buy on credit attracts more customers.
b) The creation of accounts receivable allows a company to more precisely manage its asset mix.
c) An excess of cash sales can overwhelm a company's cash management system.
d) State incorporation laws require businesses with more than $100,000 in total assets to allow customers to buy on credit.

trade receivables
销售应收款
nontrade receivables
其他应收款

In classifying receivables, an important distinction is made between trade and nontrade receivables. Trade receivables, generally the most significant category of receivables, result from the normal operating activities of a business, that is, credit sales of goods or services to customers. Trade receivables may be evidenced by a formal written promise to pay and classified as notes receivable. In most cases, however, trade receivables are unsecured "open accounts," often referred to simply as *accounts receivable*.

Accounts receivable represent an extension of short-term credit to customers. Payments are generally due within 30 to 90 days. The credit arrangements are typically informal agreements between seller and buyer supported by such business documents as invoices, sales orders, and delivery contracts. Normally, trade receivables do not involve interest, although an interest or service charge may be added if payments are not made within a specified period. Trade receivables are the most common type of receivable and are generally the most significant in total dollar amount.

Nontrade receivables include all other types of receivables. They arise from a variety of transactions, such as (1) the sale of securities or property other than inventory, (2) deposits to guarantee contract performance or expense payment, (3) claims for rebates and tax refunds, and (4) dividends and interest receivable. Nontrade receivables should be summarized in appropriately titled accounts and reported separately in the financial statements. Another way of classifying receivables relates to the current or short-term versus noncurrent or long-term nature of receivables. As indicated in Chapter 3, the *current assets* classification, as broadly conceived, includes all receivables identified as collectible within one year or the normal operating cycle, whichever is longer. Thus, for classification purposes, all trade receivables are considered current receivables; each nontrade item requires separate analysis to determine whether it is reasonable to assume that it will be collected within one year. Noncurrent receivables are reported under the Investments or Other Noncurrent Assets caption or as a separate item with an appropriate description.

In summary, receivables are classified in various ways, for example, as accounts or notes receivable, as trade or nontrade receivables, and as current or noncurrent receivables. These categories are not mutually exclusive. For example, accounts receivable are trade receivables and are current; notes receivable may be trade receivables and therefore current in some circumstances, but they may be nontrade receivables, either current or noncurrent, in other situations. The classifications used most often in practice and throughout this book will be simply *accounts receivable*, *notes receivable*, and *other receivables*.

Companies must pay a fee for accepting another company's credit card. What do you think this fee is for?

Accounting for Sales Revenue

LO2 学习目标2
编制反映销售收入的分录，包括坏账和保修与更换保证的核算。

2 Prepare journal entries to record sales revenue, including the accounting for bad debts and warranties for service or replacement.

The amount of sales or revenues is always the largest item on the income statement (if it's not, the company has bigger problems to worry about than how to account for transactions), and accounts receivable is typically one of the largest current assets on a company's balance sheet. The large magnitude of these two account balances should not, however, cause us to overlook some additional aspects of sales transactions. Although these items are significantly smaller when compared to sales and receivables, knowledge of them is critical in properly accounting for the transactions of a company. The items we will examine in this section include the following:

- *Discounts*—Discounts are offered at the time of the sale or at the time of payment.
- *Sales Returns and Allowances*—Returns and allowances occur subsequent to the sale and can occur before or after payment has been made.
- *Accounting for Bad Debts*—Once a credit sale is made, the issue of collection remains. Bad debts must be estimated in any period in which credit sales are made or accounts receivable are outstanding.
- *Warranties for Service or Replacement*—Long after a sale occurs and collection is made, a warranty period associated with that sale may still be in place.

Discounts

trade discount
商业折扣

Many companies bill their customers at a gross sales price less an amount designated as a trade discount. The discount may vary by customer, depending on the volume of business or size of order from the customer. In effect, the trade discount reduces the *list* sales price to the *net* sales price actually charged the customer. This net price is the amount at which the receivable and corresponding revenue should be recorded; the list price is merely the starting point in the price negotiation between buyer and seller.

cash (sales) discount
现金折扣

Another type of discount is a cash (sales) discount offered to customers by some companies to encourage prompt payment of bills. Cash discounts may be taken by the customer only if payment is made within a specified period of time, generally 30 days or less. Receivables are generally recorded at their gross amounts, without regard to any cash discount offered. If payment is received within the discount period, Sales Discounts (a contra account to Sales) is debited for the difference between the recorded amount of the receivable and the total cash collected. This method (called the *gross method*), which is simple and widely used, is illustrated as follows with credit terms of 2/10, n/30 (2% discount if paid within 10 days, net amount due in 30 days).

Cash (Sales) Discounts—Gross Method

Sales of $1,000; terms 2/10, n/30:

Accounts Receivable	1,000	
Sales		1,000

Partial payment of $300, received within discount period:

Cash	294	
Sales Discounts	6	
Accounts Receivable		300

Payment of the remaining $700, received after discount period:

Cash	700	
Accounts Receivable		700

The net method of accounting for sales discounts records the sale and the receivable net of the discount. Using the preceding example, the receivable and the sale would be recorded at $980 ($1,000 × 0.98). If payment is not made within the discount period, the additional amount paid by the customer through failure to take the sales discount would be recorded in a revenue account. Illustrations of the journal entries using the net method follow.

Cash (Sales) Discounts—Net Method

Sales of $1,000; terms 2/10, n/30:

Accounts Receivable	980	
Sales		980

Partial payment of $294, received within discount period:

Cash	294	
Accounts Receivable		294

Payment of the remaining $700, received after discount period:

Cash	700	
Sales Discounts Not Taken		14
Accounts Receivable ($700 × 0.98)		686

Sales Returns and Allowances

In the normal course of business, some goods will be returned by customers and some allowance will have to be made for factors such as goods damaged during shipment, spoiled or otherwise defective goods, or shipment of an incorrect quantity or type of goods. When an allowance is necessary, net sales and accounts receivable are reduced. To illustrate, assume that red sweaters costing $600 are sold to a customer for $1,000. The customer calls and states that green sweaters were ordered and should have been shipped. Rather than return the sweaters, the customer agrees to keep the

FYI

Contra accounts are used because they often yield valuable information. For example, suppose Firm A and Firm B both have net sales of $10,000. Firm A has gross sales of $1,000,000 and sales returns of $990,000. Firm B has gross sales of $10,000 and no sales returns. Might this information affect decisions made about these two firms?

sweaters in return for a reduction in the price—an allowance—of $200. The entry to record this sales allowance is as follows:

Sales Returns and Allowances..	200	
Accounts Receivable		200

Although the debit could be made directly to Sales, reducing the Sales amount, the use of a separate contra account preserves the information about the original amount of Sales. Knowledge of the amount of Sales Returns and Allowances relative to total Sales may be useful to management.

Suppose that instead of an allowance, the customer elects to return the sweaters. The return is recorded as follows:

Sales Returns and Allowances..	1,000	
Accounts Receivable		1,000
Inventory	600	
Cost of Goods Sold		600

As will be discussed in Chapter 9, management must ensure that inventory is not recorded in the books at more than its current value. This lower-of-cost-or-market test is especially important for damaged inventory, as is often the case with returned inventory.

The Valuation of Accounts Receivable—Accounting for Bad Debts

present value
现值

Theoretically, all receivables should be valued at an amount representing the present value of the expected future cash receipts. Because accounts receivable are short term, usually being collected within 30 to 90 days, the amount of interest is small relative to the amount of the receivable. Consequently, the accounting profession has chosen to ignore the interest element for these trade receivables.[1]

net realizable value
可变现净值

Instead of valuing accounts receivable at a discounted present value, they are reported at their net realizable value, that is, their expected cash value. This means that accounts receivable should be recorded net of estimated uncollectible items. The objective is to report the receivables at the amount actually expected to be collected in cash.

Uncollectible Accounts Receivable Invariably, some receivables will prove uncollectible. The simplest method for recognizing the loss from these uncollectible accounts is to debit an expense account, such as Doubtful Accounts Expense, Bad Debt Expense, or Uncollectible Accounts Expense, and credit Accounts Receivable at the time it is determined that an account cannot be collected. This approach is called the direct write-off method and is often used by small businesses because of its simplicity. Although the recognition of uncollectibles in the period of their discovery is simple and convenient, this method does not provide for the matching of expenses with current revenues and does not report receivables at their net realizable value. Therefore, use of the direct write-off method is not allowed under generally accepted accounting principles. The following sections describe the procedures used in estimating uncollectibles with the allowance method, which is required by GAAP.[2]

direct write-off method
直接转销法

The direct write-off method of accounting for bad debts is the method required by the IRS in most cases when computing taxable income.

[1] FASB ASC paragraph 835-30-15-3(a).
[2] FASB ASC paragraphs 310-10-35-7 through 9.

establishing an allowance for bad debts
坏账准备的备抵法

Establishing an Allowance for Bad Debts When using the allowance method, the amount of receivables estimated to be uncollectible is recorded by a debit to Bad Debt Expense and a credit to Allowance for Bad Debts. The terminology for these account titles may vary somewhat. For example, other possibilities for Allowance for Bad Debts include Allowance for Uncollectible Accounts and Allowance for Doubtful Accounts. The expense account title usually is consistent with that of the allowance account.

The allowance for bad debts account is a contra asset account that is offset against Accounts Receivable, resulting in the Accounts Receivable balance being reported at its net realizable value. The credit side of the allowance account represents estimated future uncollectible accounts. The debit side of the account reflects verified uncollectible accounts. If a large credit balance builds up in the account over time, this indicates that estimated bad debts are running higher than actual bad debts and that the estimation technique being used may need to be revised.

A typical entry to recognize bad debt expense, normally made as an end-of-the-period adjustment, is as follows:

Bad Debt Expense...	xx	
Allowance for Bad Debts		xx
To record estimated uncollectible accounts receivable for the period.		

The expense would be reported as a selling or general and administrative expense, and the allowance account would be shown as a deduction from Accounts Receivable, thereby reporting the net realizable amount of the receivables.

Writing off an Uncollectible Account Under the Allowance Method When positive evidence is available concerning the partial or complete worthlessness of an account, the account is written off by a debit to the allowance account, which was previously established, and a credit to Accounts Receivable. Positive evidence of a reduction in value is found in the bankruptcy, death, or disappearance of a debtor, failure to enforce collection legally, or barring of collection by the statute of limitations. Write-offs should be supported by evidence of the uncollectibility of the accounts from appropriate parties, such as courts, lawyers, or credit agencies. The entry to write off an uncollectible receivable is as follows:

Allowance for Bad Debts..	xx	
Accounts Receivable		xx
To record the write-off of an uncollectible account.		

Note that no entry is made to Bad Debt Expense at this time. That entry was made when the allowance was established. The expense was thus estimated and recorded in the period when the sale was made, not necessarily in the period when a particular account was verified as being uncollectible.

Occasionally, an account that has been written off as uncollectible is unexpectedly collected. Entries are required to reverse the write-off entry and to record the collection. Assuming an account of $1,500 was written off as uncollectible but was subsequently collected, the following entries would be made at the time of collection.

Accounts Receivable..	1,500	
Allowance for Bad Debts		1,500
To reverse the entry made to write off the account.		
Cash	1,500	
Accounts Receivable		1,500
To record collection of the account.		

Exhibit 7-3 | Bank of America's Note Disclosure Relating to Recoveries

(Dollars in millions)	2011	2010	2009
Allowance for loan and lease losses, January 1	$ 41,885	$ 47,988	$ 23,071
Loans and leases charged off	(24,742)	(37,390)	(35,483)
Recoveries of loans and leases previously charged off	3,909	3,056	1,795
Net charge-offs	(20,833)	(34,334)	(33,638)
Provision for loan and lease losses	13,629	28,195	48,366
Other	(898)	36	(549)
Allowance for loan and lease losses, December 31	**$ 33,783**	**$ 41,885**	**$ 37,200**

Bank of America, 2011, 10K Report

For many companies, the issue of collection of accounts previously written off is not significant. For companies in some industries, however, it is a multimillion-dollar issue. For example, in 2011, Bank of America recovered $3.9 billion of loans that had been previously written, or charged, off. Exhibit 7-3 provides the note from Bank of America's 2011 10-K filing, which illustrates that over the preceding three years, Bank of America recovered $8.8 billion in accounts previously charged off.

To summarize using a T-account, the allowance account typically increases (with a credit) as estimates of bad debts are made and recognized as an expense, and decreases (with a debit) as actual bad debts are identified and written off. In addition, the allowance account will increase if accounts that had previously been written off are subsequently recovered; the reason for this increase is that, if the original bad debt estimate was correct, the recovery of one would-be bad debt means that there must still be another bad debt out there somewhere.

Allowance for Bad Debts	
Actual bad debts written off	Estimated bad debt expense
	Recovery of previously written off bad debts

estimating uncollectibles based on percentage of sales
基于销售百分比法估计坏账损失

For a firm in a steady state, that is, one that has been in business for a number of years and has a stable level of accounts receivable, bad debt expense estimated on current year's credit sales will be approximately the same as actual write-offs.

Estimating Uncollectibles Based on Percentage of Sales The estimate for uncollectible accounts may be based on sales for the period or the amount of receivables outstanding at the end of the period. When a sales basis is used, the amount of uncollectible accounts in past years relative to total sales provides a percentage of estimated uncollectibles. This percentage may be modified by expectations based on current experience. Because doubtful accounts occur only with credit sales, it is logical to develop a percentage of doubtful accounts based on credit sales of past periods. This percentage is then applied to credit sales of the current period. However, because extra work may be required in maintaining separate records of cash and credit sales or in analyzing sales data, the percentage is frequently developed in terms of total sales. Unless there is considerable periodic fluctuation in the proportion of cash and credit sales, the percentage-of-total-sales method will normally give satisfactory results.

To illustrate, if 2% of sales is considered doubtful in terms of collection and sales for the period are $100,000, the charge for Bad Debt Expense would be 2% of the current period's sales, or $2,000. Note that any existing balance in the allowance account resulting from past period charges to Bad Debt Expense is ignored. The entry for this period is simply as follows:

Bad Debt Expense..	2,000	
Allowance for Bad Debts		2,000
To record estimated bad debt expense for the period		
($100,000 × 0.02 = $2,000).		

The percentage-of-sales method for estimating bad debts is widely used in practice because it is simple to apply. Companies often use this method to estimate bad debts periodically during the year and then adjust the allowance account at year-end in relationship to the Accounts Receivable balance, as explained in the next section.

estimating uncollectibles based on accounts receivable balance
基于应收账款余额估计坏账损失

Estimating Uncollectibles Based on Accounts Receivable Balance Instead of using a percentage of sales to estimate bad debts, companies may base their estimates on a percentage of total accounts receivable outstanding. This method emphasizes the relationship between the Accounts Receivable and the Allowance for Bad Debts balances. For example, if total Accounts Receivable are $50,000 and it is estimated that 3% of those accounts will be uncollectible, the allowance account should have a balance of $1,500 ($50,000 × 0.03). If the allowance account already has a $600 credit balance from prior periods, the current-period adjusting entry is as follows:

Bad Debt Expense..	900	
Allowance for Bad Debts		900
To record estimated bad debt expense for the period		
($1,500 required balance − $600 current balance = $900 adjustment).		

After posting this entry, the balance in the allowance account would be $1,500, or 3% of total Accounts Receivable. Note that this method adjusts the existing balance to the desired balance based on a percentage of total receivables outstanding. If, in the example, the allowance account had a $200 debit balance caused by writing off more bad debts than had been estimated previously, the adjusting entry would be for $1,700 in order to bring the allowance account to the desired credit balance of $1,500, or 3% of total receivables.

The most commonly used method for establishing an allowance based on outstanding receivables involves aging receivables. Individual accounts are analyzed to determine those not yet due and those past due. Past-due accounts are classified in terms of the length of the period past due. An analysis sheet used in aging accounts receivable is shown on the following page.

Overdue balances can be evaluated individually to estimate the collectibility of each item as a basis for developing an overall estimate. An alternative procedure is to develop a series of estimated loss percentages and apply these to the different receivables classifications. ICO Products' calculation of the allowance on the latter basis is illustrated on the next page.

ICO Products, Inc.
Analysis of Receivables
December 31, 2015

Customer	Amount	Not Yet Due	Not More Than 30 Days Past Due	31–60 Days Past Due	61–90 Days Past Due	91–180 Days Past Due	181–365 Days Past Due	More Than One Year Past Due
A. B. Andrews	$ 450			$ 450				
B. T. Brooks	300				$100	$200		
B. Bryant	200		$ 200					
L. B. Devine	2,100	$ 2,100						
K. Martinez	200						$200	
~~								
M. A. Young	1,400	1,000		100	300			
Total	$47,550	$40,000	$3,000	$1,200	$650	$500	$800	$1,400

ICO Products, Inc.
Estimated Amount of Uncollectible Accounts
December 31, 2015

Classification	Balances	Uncollectible Accounts Experience Percentage	Accounts Estimated Amount of Uncollectible
Not yet due	$40,000	2%	$ 800
Not more than 30 days past due	3,000	5	150
31–60 days past due	1,200	10	120
61–90 days past due	650	20	130
91–180 days past due	500	30	150
181–365 days past due	800	50	400
More than one year past due	1,400	80	1,120
	$47,550		$2,870

Just as with the previous method based on a percentage of total receivables outstanding, Bad Debt Expense is debited and Allowance for Bad Debts is credited for an amount bringing the allowance account to the required balance. Assuming uncollectibles estimated at $2,870 as shown in the ICO Products calculation and a credit balance of $620 in the allowance account before adjustment, the following entry is made:

Bad Debt Expense...	2,250	
Allowance for Bad Debts		2,250

To record bad debt expense for the period

($2,870 required balance − $620 current balance = $2,250 adjustment).

The aging method provides the most satisfactory approach to the valuation of receivables at their net realizable amounts. Furthermore, data developed through aging receivables may be quite useful to management for purposes of credit analysis and control.

> **Caution**
>
> The most common error when computing bad debt expense is to confuse the two methods—percentage of sales and percentage of receivables. Remember that when you are using the percentage-of-sales method, bad debt expense is computed and the balance in the allowance account is then determined. When you are using the percentage-of-receivables method, the balance in the allowance account is computed, and then the amount of bad debt expense for the period is determined.

> **FYI**
>
> In FASB ASC paragraph 954-605-45-4, the FASB requires that healthcare entities, such as hospitals, report the bad debt "expense" amount not as an operating expense but instead as a contra revenue line item shown right below "revenue." The resulting difference is then called "net revenue." The FASB and the IASB are currently considering requiring this same bad debt contra revenue approach for all companies, not just hospitals. For now, however, all companies outside of health care report bad debt expense as an operating expense.

> **FYI**
>
> Many companies that sell items such as electronics or appliances make large amounts of profits by selling *maintenance agreements*. Because of the high profit margins associated with these agreements, salespersons are often given big incentives to sell them. Some consumer magazines have warned readers that these maintenance agreements are not cost effective and should not be purchased.

Corrections to Allowance for Bad Debts

As previously indicated, the Allowance for Bad Debts balance is established and maintained by means of adjusting entries at the close of each accounting period. If the allowance provisions are too large, the allowance account balance will be unnecessarily inflated and earnings and accounts receivable will be understated; if the allowance provisions are too small, the allowance account balance will be inadequate, and both accounts receivable and earnings will be overstated.

Care must be taken to see that the allowance balance follows the credit experience of the particular business. The process of aging receivables at different intervals may be employed as a means of checking the allowance balance to be certain that it is being maintained satisfactorily. Such periodic reviews may indicate a need for a correction in the allowance as well as a change in the rate or in the method employed.

When the uncollectible accounts experience approximates the estimated losses, the allowance procedure may be considered satisfactory, and no adjustment is required. When it appears that there has been a failure to estimate uncollectible accounts accurately, resulting in an allowance balance that is clearly inadequate or excessive, an adjustment is in order. The effect of this change in accounting estimate would be reported in the current and future periods as an ordinary item on the income statement, usually as an addition to or subtraction from Bad Debt Expense.

The actual write-off of receivables as uncollectible by debits to the allowance account and credits to the receivables account may temporarily result in a debit balance in the allowance account. A debit balance arising in this manner does not mean necessarily that the allowance is inadequate; debits to the allowance account simply predate the end-of-period adjustment for uncollectible accounts. Once an adjustment is made, the allowance account will have a credit balance. Think about what it would mean if, after adjustment, the allowance account still had a debit balance—when combined with the balance in Accounts Receivable, it would mean that you expect to receive more than you are owed, which is a very low probability event.

Warranties for Service or Replacement

As you have just read, bad debts must be estimated so that proper expenses can be matched with revenues in the period in which the revenues were earned. The same is true in the case of warranties. Many

保修项目。很多公司为那些对产品不满意或退回瑕疵产品的顾客提供免费服务。如果这些服务协议或保证包含较少的花费，那么这些消耗应当在发生时被确认为当期损益；如果这些服务协议包含较大数额的未来花费且经验表明公司存在确定的未来，那么就应当估计这些费用并抵减当期收入。

companies agree to provide free service on units failing to perform satisfactorily or to replace defective goods. When these agreements, or warranties, involve only minor costs, such costs may be recognized in the periods incurred. When these agreements involve significant future costs and when experience indicates that a definite future obligation exists, estimates of such costs should be made and matched against current revenues.[3]

Such estimates are usually recorded by a debit to an expense account and a credit to a liability account. Subsequent costs of fulfilling warranties are debited to the liability account and credited to an appropriate account, for example, Cash or Inventory. As was the case with the allowance for bad debts account, the debit side of the estimated liability under warranties account tracks actual warranty costs while the credit side of the account represents estimated costs.

To illustrate accounting for warranties, consider the following example. MJW Video & Sound sells compact stereo systems with a two-year warranty. Past experience indicates that 10% of all systems sold will need repairs in the first year and 20% will need repairs in the second year. The average repair cost is $50 per system. The number of systems sold in 2014 and 2015 was 5,000 and 6,000, respectively. Actual repair costs were $12,500 in 2014 and $55,000 in 2015; it is assumed that all repair costs involved cash expenditures.

2014	Warranty Expense	75,000	
	Estimated Liability under Warranties		75,000
	To record estimated warranty expense based on systems sold		
	(5,000 × 0.30 × $50 = $75,000).		
	Estimated Liability under Warranties	12,500	
	Cash		12,500
	To record cost of actual repairs in 2014.		
2015	Warranty Expense	90,000	
	Estimated Liability under Warranties		90,000
	To record estimated warranty expense based on systems sold		
	(6,000 × 0.30 × $50 = $90,000).		
	Estimated Liability under Warranties	55,000	
	Cash		55,000
	To record cost of actual repairs in 2015.		

Periodically, the warranty liability account should be analyzed to see whether the actual repairs approximate the estimate. Adjustment to the percentages used in estimating future warranty obligations will be required if experience differs materially from the estimates. These adjustments are changes in estimates and are reported prospectively, that is, in current and future periods. If sales and repairs in the preceding example are assumed to occur evenly through two years, analysis of the liability account at the end of 2015 shows that the ending balance of $97,500 ($75,000 + $90,000 − $12,500 − $55,000) is reasonably close to the predicted amount of $100,000 based upon the 10% and 20% estimates. (*Note:* Assuming that sales occur evenly throughout the year is mathematically the same as assuming that all of the sales occur halfway through the year.)

[3] FASB ASC paragraphs 460-10-25-5 through 7. This guidance relates to warranties that are not separately sold but instead are included in the overall price of the product. For separately priced warranties, the revenue for the sale should be divided between the product and the warranty service. Revenue associated with providing the warranty service is recognized in a straight-line fashion over the term on the separately priced warranty. See FASB ASC paragraphs 605-20-25-1 through 6.

FASB CODIFICATION

The Issue: Your company sells lawn care equipment—lawn mowers, aerators, trimmers, and so forth. Your salespersons are trained to aggressively sell extended warranty agreements to all customers. These extended warranty agreements are a HUGE profit center for your business. To give the salespersons an incentive to sell these agreements, your company pays the salespersons a 30% commission on every extended warranty they sell.

The Question: What is the proper accounting treatment for these commissions—should they be recognized as an expense in the period they are paid, or should they be deferred and amortized as an expense over the warranty agreement period?

Searching the Codification: On this one, we are going to cheat just a little bit. We note in the chapter that regular warranties are discussed in FASB ASC paragraphs 460-10-25-5 through 7. Let's go there and see if we can pick up any clues about the accounting for commissions on separately priced warranties.

The Answer: The correct treatment is described on page 7-42.

Computation:

2014 sales still under warranty for six months:

$50 × [5,000 units × (6/12 × 0.20)] .... $ 25,000

2015 sales still under warranty for 18 months:

$50 × [[6,000 units × (6/12 × 0.10)] + [6,000 units × (12/12 × 0.20)]] 75,000

Total $100,000

On occasion, an estimate may differ significantly from actual experience. Misleading financial statements may result if an adjustment is not made. In those instances, an adjustment is made to the liability account in the current period. Continuing the previous example, assume that warranty costs incurred in 2015 were only $35,000. Then the ending balance of $117,500 would be much higher than the $100,000 estimate. If the $17,500 difference was considered to be material, an adjustment to warranty expense would be made in 2015 as follows:

Estimated Liability under Warranties 17,500
    Warranty Expense 17,500
    To record adjustment of estimate for warranty repairs.

Monitoring Accounts Receivable

 Analyze accounts receivable to measure how efficiently a firm is using this operating asset.

Managers as well as external users of financial information need to measure how efficiently a firm is utilizing its operating assets, particularly significant working capital elements such as receivables, inventories, and accounts payable. The most common relationship used to monitor receivables is the average collection period.

Average Collection Period

Average receivables are sometimes expressed in terms of the average collection period, which reflects the average number of days that elapse between the time that a sale is made and the time that cash is collected. Average receivables outstanding divided by average daily sales gives the average collection period. This measure is computed for the WS Corporation as illustrated here.

	2015	2014
Average receivables	$397,500	$354,250
Net sales	$1,425,000	$1,650,000
Average daily sales (net sales/365)	$3,904	$4,521
Average collection period (average receivables/average daily sales)	102 days	78 days

这种衡量方法也可通过以应收账款周转率划分一年天数来获得。用当年平均应收账款除以净销售额，并且据此决定应收账款周转率。为了更准确地计量平均应收账款，通常会用到年初余额和年末余额，但是利用季末余额或月末余额是个更好的方法。

This same measurement can be obtained by dividing the number of days in the year by the receivables turnover. Accounts receivable turnover is determined by dividing net sales by the average trade accounts receivable outstanding during the year. In developing an average receivables amount, the average of the beginning-of-year and end-of-year balances is normally used; however, a better measure of the average balance can be obtained using quarterly or monthly balances.

Accounts receivable turnover rates for WS Corporation for 2015 and 2014 are computed as follows:

	2015	2014
Net sales	$1,425,000	$1,650,000
Net receivables:		
Beginning of year	$375,000	$333,500
End of year	$420,000	$375,000
Average receivables [(beginning balance + ending balance)/2]	$397,500	$354,250
Receivables turnover for year	3.6 times	4.7 times

The value computed for receivables turnover represents the average number of revenue/receivables/cash cycles completed by the firm during the year.

In some cases, instead of computing the average collection period for the entire year, it may be more useful to report the average collection period for the receivables existing at the end of the period. This information would be significant in evaluating current position and, particularly, the receivable position as of a given date. This information for WS Corporation is computed as follows:

	2015	2014
Receivables at end of year	$420,000	$375,000
Average daily sales	$3,904	$4,521
Average collection period (end of year)	108 days	83 days

What constitutes a reasonable average collection period varies with individual businesses. For example, if merchandise is sold on terms of net 45 days, a 40-day average collection period would be reasonable, but if terms are net 30 days, a receivable balance equal to 40 days' sales would indicate slow collections. The average collection period for a number of companies is given in Exhibit 7-4. Notice the difference between the 60-day average collection period of **Caterpillar**, a company that makes its money selling and financing heavy equipment, and the six-day average collection period of **Home Depot**, which emphasizes the sales of inventory and devotes relatively little effort to credit issues. Also, note the relatively short six-day average collection period for **Sears**. Before Sears sold its in-house credit card business to **Citicorp** in 2003, Sears routinely had an average collection period in excess of 200 days, driven by the long time period that Sears credit card customers took to pay for their credit purchases.

Sales activity just before the close of a period should be considered when interpreting accounts receivable measurements. If sales are unusually light or heavy just before the end of the fiscal period, this affects total receivables as well as the related measurements. When such unevenness prevails, it may be better to analyze accounts receivable according to their due dates, as was illustrated earlier in the chapter.

The problem of minimizing accounts receivable without losing desirable business is important. Receivables often do not earn interest revenue, and the cost of carrying them must be covered by the profit margin. The longer the accounts are carried without interest being earned, the smaller will be the percentage return realized on invested capital.

To attract business, credit frequently is granted for relatively long periods. The cost of granting long-term credit should be considered. Assume that a business has average daily sales of $5,000 and average accounts receivable of $250,000, which represents 50 days' sales. If collections and the credit period can be improved so that accounts receivable represent only 30 days' sales, accounts receivable will be reduced to $150,000. Assuming a total cost of 10% to carry and service the accounts, the $100,000 decrease would yield annual savings of $10,000.

Exhibit 7-4 | Average Collection Period (in days) for 2011

Company	Average Collection Period
Caterpillar	59.7
ExxonMobil	27.7
Home Depot	6.0
McDonald's (franchise fees)	52.7
Microsoft	73.1
Sears	6.1

© Cengage Learning 2014

Cash Management and Control

4 Discuss the composition, management, and control of cash, including the use of a bank reconciliation.

LO4 学习目标4
讨论现金的构成、管理与控制，包括银行存款余额调节表的作用。

To this point, our focus has been primarily on revenues and receivables. However, revenues and receivables have value because they will eventually be converted to cash. Cash is important because it provides the basis for measurement and accounting for all other items. Another reason that cash is so important is that individuals, businesses, and even governments must maintain an adequate liquidity position; that is, they must have a sufficient amount of cash on hand to pay obligations as they come due if they are to remain viable operating entities. In the early stages of its conceptual framework project, the FASB identified the need to report information on cash and liquidity as one of the key objectives of financial reporting. This emphasis eventually led to the requirement of providing a statement of cash flows as one of the primary financial statements.

In striking contrast to the importance of cash as a key element in the liquidity position of an entity is its unproductive nature. Because cash is the measure of value, it cannot expand or grow unless it is converted into other properties. Cash kept under a mattress, for example, will not grow or appreciate, whereas land may increase in value if held. Excessive balances of cash on hand are often referred to as *idle cash*. Efficient cash management requires available cash to be continuously working in one of several ways as part of the operating cycle or as a short- or long-term investment. The management of cash is therefore a critical business function.

Because cash is the most liquid of all assets, it is also the one that needs to be safeguarded the most. Thus, we will spend some time discussing cash and its equivalents as well the most common safeguard—a bank reconciliation—often employed to ensure the proper accounting for cash.

Composition of Cash

Cash is the most liquid of current assets. To be reported as "cash," an item must be readily available and not restricted for use in the payment of current obligations. A general guideline is whether an item is acceptable for deposit at face value by a bank or other financial institution.

Items that are classified as cash include coin and currency on hand and unrestricted funds available on deposit in a bank, which are often called demand deposits, because they can be withdrawn upon demand. Demand deposits include amounts in checking, savings, and money market deposit accounts. Petty cash funds or change funds and negotiable instruments, such as personal checks and cashiers' checks, are also items commonly reported as cash. The total of these items plus undeposited coin and currency is sometimes called *cash on hand*. In addition, many companies report investments in very short-term, interest-earning securities (such as three-month U.S. Treasury securities) as cash equivalents in the balance sheet. Deposits that are not immediately available for withdrawal or have other restrictions are sometimes referred to as time deposits. These deposits are sometimes separately classified as *temporary investments*. Examples of time deposits include certificates of deposit (CDs) and money market savings certificates. CDs, for example, generally may be withdrawn without penalty only at specified maturity dates.

demand deposits
活期存款

cash equivalents
现金等价物

time deposits
定期存款

Deposits in foreign banks that are subject to immediate and unrestricted withdrawal generally qualify as cash and are reported at their U.S. dollar equivalents as of the date of the balance sheet. However, cash in foreign banks that is restricted as to use or withdrawal should be designated as receivables of a current or noncurrent nature and reported subject to appropriate allowances for estimated uncollectibles.

Some items do not meet the "acceptance at face value on deposit" test and should not be reported as cash. Examples include postage stamps (which are office supplies) and postdated checks, IOUs, and not-sufficient-funds (NSF) checks (all of which are, in effect, receivables).

Cash balances specifically designated by management for special purposes should be reported separately. An example would be cash set aside specifically for the purpose of retiring a bond issue in the future; this cash is called a *sinking fund*. Restricted cash should be reported as a current item only if it is to be applied to some current purpose or obligation. Classification of the cash balance as current or noncurrent should parallel the classification applied to the liability.

A credit balance in the cash account resulting from the issuance of checks in excess of the amount on deposit is known as a cash overdraft and should be reported as a current liability.

cash overdraft
现金透支

In summary, cash is a current asset comprising coin, currency, and other items that (1) serve as a medium of exchange and (2) provide the basis for measurement in accounting. Most negotiable instruments (e.g., checks, bank drafts, and money orders) qualify as cash because they can be converted to currency on demand or are acceptable for deposit at face value by a bank. For many companies, the bulk of "cash" is held in the form of short-term, interest-earning securities. Components of cash restricted as to use or withdrawal should be disclosed or reported separately and classified as an investment, a receivable, or other asset. Exhibit 7-5 summarizes the classification of various items that have been discussed. The objective of disclosure is to provide the user of financial statements with information to assist in evaluating the entity's ability to meet obligations (i.e., its liquidity and solvency) and in assessing the effectiveness of cash management.

Exhibit 7-5 | Classification of Cash and Noncash Items

Item	Classification
Undeposited coin and currency	Cash
Unrestricted funds on deposit at bank (demand deposits)	Cash
Petty cash and change funds	Cash
Negotiable instruments, such as checks, bank drafts, and money orders	Cash
Company checks written but not yet mailed or delivered	Cash
Restricted deposits, such as CDs and money market savings certificates (time deposits)	Investment
Deposits in foreign banks:	
Unrestricted	Cash
Restricted	Receivables
Postage stamps	Office supplies
IOUs, postdated checks, and not-sufficient-funds (NSF) checks	Receivables
Cash restricted for special purposes	Restricted cash*
Cash overdraft	Current liability

*Separately reported as current or noncurrent asset depending on the purpose for which it is restricted.

© Cengage Learning 2014

Compensating Balances

In connection with financing arrangements, it is common practice for a company to agree to maintain a minimum or average balance on deposit with a bank or other lending institution. These compensating balances are defined by the SEC as "that portion of any demand deposit (or any time deposit or certificate of deposit) maintained by a corporation . . . which constitutes support for existing borrowing arrangements of the corporation . . . with a lending institution. Such arrangements would include both outstanding borrowings and the assurance of future credit availability."[4]

Compensating balances provide a source of funds to the lender as partial compensation for credit extended. In effect, such arrangements raise the interest rate of the borrower because a portion of the amount on deposit with the lending institution cannot be used. These balances present an accounting problem from the standpoint of disclosure. Readers of financial statements are likely to assume the entire cash balance is available to meet current obligations when, in fact, part of the balance is restricted.

The solution to this problem is to disclose the amount of compensating balances. The SEC recommends that any "legally restricted" deposits held as compensating balances be segregated and reported separately. If the balances are the result of short-term financing arrangements, they should be shown separately among the "cash items" in the Current Assets section; if the compensating balances are in connection with long-term agreements, they should be classified as noncurrent, either as investments or "other assets." In many instances, deposits are not legally restricted, but compensating balance agreements still exist as business commitments in connection with lines of credit. In these situations, the amounts and nature of the arrangements should be disclosed in the notes to the financial statements, as illustrated in Exhibit 7-6 for **Chiquita Brands International** (the banana company) in 2011.

> **FYI**
> The effective interest rate on a loan can be thought of as interest ÷ "take home" amount of loan. Because a compensating balance requirement reduces the amount of the loan that can be "taken home" while still requiring that interest be paid on the entire loan, it would increase the effective interest rate.

compensating balances
补偿性余额

补偿性余额是给予提供信用贷款债权人的部分资金补偿。

Management and Control of Cash

As noted earlier, a business enterprise must maintain sufficient cash for current operations and for paying obligations as they come due. Any excess cash should be invested temporarily to earn an additional return for the shareholders. Effective cash management also requires controls to protect cash from loss by theft or fraud. Because cash is the most liquid asset, it is particularly susceptible to misappropriation unless properly safeguarded.

Exhibit 7-6 | Chiquita Brands International—Disclosure of Compensating Balance

> Cash and equivalents include cash and highly liquid investments with a maturity of three months or less at the time of purchase. At December 31, 2011, the company had €5 million ($6 million) of cash equivalents in a compensating balance arrangement relating to an uncommitted credit line for bank guarantees used primarily for import licenses and duties in European Union countries.
>
> Chiquita Brands, 2011, 10K Report

[4] FASB SEC paragraph 210-10-S99-1.

The system for controlling cash must be adapted to a particular business. It is not feasible to describe all features and techniques employed in businesses of various kinds and sizes. In general, however, systems of cash control deny access to the accounting records to those who handle cash. This reduces the possibility of improper entries to conceal the misuse of cash receipts and cash payments. The probability of misappropriation of cash is greatly reduced if two or more employees must conspire in an embezzlement. Furthermore, systems normally provide for separation of the receiving and paying functions. The basic characteristics of a system of cash control are as follows:

1. Specifically assigned responsibility for handling cash receipts
2. Separation of handling and recording cash receipts
3. Daily deposit of all cash received
4. Voucher system to control cash payments
5. Internal audits at irregular intervals
6. Double record of cash—bank and books, with reconciliations performed by someone outside the accounting function

These controls are more likely to be found in large companies with many employees. Small companies with few employees generally have difficulty in totally segregating accounting and cash-handling duties. Even small companies, however, should incorporate as many control features as possible.

To the extent that a company can incorporate effective internal controls, it can reduce significantly the chances of theft, loss, or inadvertent errors in accounting for and controlling cash. Even the most elaborate control system, however, cannot totally eliminate the possibilities of misappropriations or errors. The use of periodic bank reconciliations can help identify any cash shortages or errors that may have been made in accounting for cash. Another common cash control, a petty cash fund, is discussed in the Web Material associated with this chapter. The text support Web site is **www.cengagebrain.com**.

Bank Reconciliations

银行对账表也称银行存款余额调节表。

When daily receipts are deposited and payments are made by check, the bank's statement of its transactions with the depositor can be compared with the record of cash as reported on the depositor's books. A comparison of the bank balance with the balance reported on the books is usually made monthly by means of a summary known as a bank reconciliation. A bank reconciliation is prepared to disclose any errors or irregularities in either the records of the bank or those of the business unit. It is developed in a form that points out the reasons for discrepancies in the two balances. It should be prepared by an individual who neither handles nor records cash because if a person who was embezzling from the cash account also was in charge of the reconciliation, it would be too easy to cover his or her tracks.

When the bank statement and the depositor's records are compared, certain items may appear on one but not the other, resulting in a difference in the two balances. Most of these differences result from temporary timing lags and are thus normal. Four common types of differences arise in the following situations:

1. A deposit made near the end of the month and recorded on the depositor's books is not received by the bank in time to be reflected on the bank statement. This amount, referred to as a deposit in transit, has to be added to the bank statement balance to make it agree with the balance on the depositor's books.
2. Checks written near the end of the month have reduced the depositor's cash balance but have not cleared the bank as of the bank statement date. These outstanding checks must be subtracted from the bank statement balance to make it agree with the depositor's records.
3. The bank sometimes charges a monthly fee for servicing an account. The bank automatically reduces the depositor's account balance for this bank service charge and notes the amount on the bank statement. The depositor must deduct this amount from the recorded cash balance to make it agree with the bank statement balance. The return of a customer's check for which insufficient funds are available, known as a not-sufficient-funds (NSF) check, is handled in a similar manner.
4. An amount owed to the depositor is paid directly to the bank by a third party and is added to the depositor's account. Upon receipt of the bank statement (assuming prior notification has not been received from the bank), this amount must be added to the cash balance on the depositor's books. Examples include a direct payroll deposit by an individual's employer and interest added by the bank on a savings account. Similarly, the depositor may have items deducted from the account by a third party (such as transfers to savings plans). These items must be deducted from the depositor's cash balance.

deposit in transit
未达账项

> **Caution**
> In preparing a bank reconciliation, it is essential to know how the bank handled a transaction (e.g., the entry made, if any, on an NSF check) so that a proper reconciliation can be made from the company's books' perspective.

> **Caution**
> Adjustments to the book balance should reflect new information learned upon receiving the bank statement. Adjustments to the bank balance should reflect checks written and deposits made that the bank doesn't know about yet.

If, after considering these items, the bank statement and the book balances cannot be reconciled, a detailed analysis of both the bank's records and the depositor's books may be necessary to determine whether errors or irregularities exist on the records of either party.

Preparing a Bank Reconciliation An illustration of a common form of bank reconciliation follows. This form is prepared in two sections, the bank statement balance being adjusted to the corrected cash balance in the first section, and the book balance being adjusted to the same corrected cash balance in the second section. Any items not yet recognized by the bank (e.g., deposits in transit or outstanding checks) as well as any errors made by the bank are recorded in the first section. The second section contains any items the depositor has not yet recognized (e.g., direct deposits, NSF checks, or bank service charges) and any corrections for errors made on the depositor's books.

The reconciliation of bank and book balances to a corrected balance has two important advantages: It develops a corrected cash figure, and it shows separately all items requiring adjustment on the depositor's books.

An alternative form of reconciliation would be to reconcile the bank statement balance to the book balance. This form would not develop a corrected cash figure, however, and would make it more difficult to determine the adjustments needed on the depositor's books.

Svendsen, Inc.
Bank Reconciliation
November 30, 2015

Balance per bank statement, November 30, 2015		$2,979.72
Add: Deposits in transit	$658.50	
Charge for interest made to depositor's account by bank in error	12.50	671.00
		$3,650.72
Deduct outstanding checks:		
No. 1125	$ 58.16	
No. 1138	100.00	
No. 1152	98.60	
No. 1154	255.00	
No. 1155	192.07	703.83
Corrected bank balance		$2,946.89
Balance per books, November 30, 2015		$2,952.49
Add: Interest earned during November	$ 98.50	
Check No. 1116 to Ace Advertising for $46 recorded by depositor as $64 in error	18.00	116.50
		$3,068.99
Deduct: Bank service charges	$ 3.16	
Customer's check deposited November 25 and returned marked NSF	118.94	122.10
Corrected book balance		$2,946.89

After preparing the reconciliation, the depositor should record any items appearing on the bank statement and requiring recognition on the company's books as well as any corrections for errors discovered on its own books. The bank should be notified immediately of any bank errors. The following entries would be required on the books of Svendsen, Inc., as a result of the November 30 reconciliation:

Cash	98.50	
Interest Revenue		98.50
To record interest earned during November.		
Cash	18.00	
Advertising Expense		18.00
To record correction for check in payment of advertising recorded as $64 instead of the actual amount, $46.		
Accounts Receivable	118.94	
Miscellaneous General Expense	3.16	
Cash		122.10
To record customer's uncollectible check and bank charges for November.		

Stop & Think

Suppose that after employing the procedures outlined here, a company's bank and book balances are not the same. Further suppose that the corrected bank balance is *greater than* the corrected book balance. Which ONE of the following errors could cause this type of difference?

a) A deposit in transit made the last day of the month was omitted from the bank reconciliation. The deposit was recorded in the company's books.
b) The company mistakenly recorded a check it made out to one of its suppliers as being for $50 instead of $500. The bank cleared the check at the correct amount of $500.
c) The company mistakenly recorded a deposit made in the middle of the month as $500 instead of $50. The bank recorded the deposit at the correct amount of $50.
d) A check written three months ago, which has still not cleared the bank, was omitted from the outstanding checks list in the bank reconciliation.

After these entries are posted, the cash account will show a balance of $2,946.89. If financial statements were prepared at November 30, this is the amount that would be reported as cash on the balance sheet. It should be noted that the bank reconciliation is not presented to external users. It is used as a control procedure and as an accounting tool to determine the adjustments required to bring the cash account and related account balances up to date.

Presentation of Sales and Receivables in the Financial Statements

LO5 学习目标5
确认财务报表对销售收入和应收账款的恰当披露。

5 Recognize appropriate disclosures for presenting sales and receivables in the financial statements.

Companies often provide a breakdown of the sources of their revenues in the body of the income statement. For example, Note 1 of **The Walt Disney Company**'s financial statements indicates four sources of revenues: media networks, parks & resorts, studio entertainment, and consumer products. As another example, **McDonald's** provides information in the notes to its financial statements partitioning revenues, operating income, and identifiable assets by geographical area (see Exhibit 7-7). This information is useful to users of the financial statements as they determine future sources of a firm's revenue. This information also allows users to determine how efficiently assets are being used to generate revenues and profits. In the case of McDonald's, we can compute the percentage of revenues generated from each geographical area and conclude that the percentage of revenues generated in Europe has decreased slightly over time (from 40.8% in 2009 to 40.3% in 2011). In computing the amount of revenue dollars generated in the United States per dollar of assets, we note that the amount has increased slightly over time (from 0.762 in 2009 to 0.785 in 2011). That amount has also increased for McDonald's European operations (from 0.807 in 2009 to 0.906 in 2011). With this analysis, we can see that the European operations are generating more revenue dollars per dollar of assets than are their American counterparts.

Receivables qualifying as current items may be grouped for presentation on the balance sheet in the following classes: (1) notes receivable—trade debtors, (2) accounts receivable—trade debtors, and (3) other receivables. Alternatively, trade notes and

Exhibit 7-7 | McDonald's Notes to Consolidated Financial Statements

Segment and geographic information			
In millions	2011	2010	2009
U.S.	$ 8,528.2	$ 8,111.6	$ 7,943.8
Europe	10,886.4	9,569.2	9,273.8
APMEA	6,019.5	5,065.5	4,337.0
Other Countries & Corporate	1,571.9	1,328.3	1,190.1
Total revenues	$ 27,006.0	$ 24,074.6	$ 22,744.7
U.S.	$ 3,666.2	$ 3,446.5	$ 3,231.7
Europe	3,226.7	2,796.8	2,588.1
APMEA	1,525.8	1,199.9	989.5
Other Countries & Corporate	111.0	29.9	31.7
Total operating income	$ 8,529.7	$ 7,473.1	$ 6,841.0
U.S.	$10,865.5	$10,467.7	$10,429.3
Europe	12,015.1	11,360.7	11,494.4
APMEA	5,824.2	5,374.0	4,409.0
Other Countries & Corporate	4,285.1	4,772.8	3,892.2
Total assets	$ 32,989.9	$ 31,975.2	$ 30,224.9

McDonald's, 2011, 10K Report

在资产负债表中，长期应收款和其他应收款被划分为"其他流动资产"。企业应披露其应收账款是否有使用限制，比如该款项是否已被用来支付某项负债或者为某项贷款提供抵押担保。

accounts receivable can be reported as a single amount. The detail reported for other receivables depends on the relative significance of the various items included. Valuation accounts are deducted from the individual receivable balances or combined balances to which they relate. Any long-term trade and nontrade receivables would be reported as "other noncurrent assets" on the balance sheet. A company should also disclose whether restrictions have been placed on any receivables, such as when receivables have been set aside to satisfy a specific obligation or have been pledged as collateral on a loan. Finally, a company should disclose any significant concentrations of credit risk relating to its receivables. For example, if a significant percentage of a company's sales (and corresponding receivables) are with one debtor, that would represent a concentration of credit risk and should be disclosed.

As is explained in the Expanded Material later in the chapter, when receivables have been sold or used as collateral for loans, the details associated with the sale or borrowing transaction should be disclosed. Disclosure would include factors such as the terms of the agreement, the value of the receivables involved, and the recourse available to the lender.

Accounts and notes receivable as presented by Caterpillar, Inc., in its 2011 10-K filing are shown in Exhibit 7-8. In Exhibit 7-8, Caterpillar's note disclosure relating to its finance receivables is presented. Information relating to maturity dates of receivables, residual values of leased equipment, and credit loss estimates are presented. Notice that Caterpillar's estimate for credit losses in 2011 is substantially less than the actual write-offs during the same year.[5]

---

[5] In FASB ASC paragraph 310-10-50-7A, the FASB requires companies to disclose a receivables aging analysis, similar to what was illustrated earlier in this chapter.

Exhibit 7-8 | Reporting Receivables—Caterpillar Note Disclosure

TABLE III—Finance Receivables Information (Millions of dollars)
Contractual maturities of outstanding finance receivables

Amounts Due In	December 31, 2011			
	Retail Installment Contracts	Retail Finance Leases	Retail Notes	Total
2012	$1,771	$3,052	$2,993	$ 7,816
2013	1,199	2,002	1,941	5,142
2014	772	1,070	1,261	3,103
2015	371	458	996	1,825
2016	111	211	766	1,088
Thereafter	19	125	880	1,024
	$4,243	$6,918	$8,837	$19,998
Residual value	—	854	—	854
Less: Unearned income	(59)	(738)	(75)	(872)
Total	$4,184	$7,034	$8,762	$19,930

Impaired loans and leases:

	2011	2010	2009
Average recorded investment	$ 665	$ 604	$ 425
At December 31:			
Recorded investment	$ 527	$ 641	$ 513
Impaired loans/finance leases for which there is a related allowance for credit losses	249	358	448
Related allowance for credit losses on impaired loans/finance leases	56	79	117
Impaired loans/finance leases for which there is no related allowance for credit losses	278	283	65

Allowance for credit loss activity:

	2011	2010	2009
Balance at beginning of year	$ 362	$ 376	$ 391
Provision for credit losses	168	205	225
Receivables written off	(210)	(288)	(281)
Recoveries on receivables previously written off	52	51	28
Other—net	(6)	18	13
Balance at end of year	$ 366	$ 362	$ 376

In estimating the allowance for credit losses, we review accounts that are past due, non-performing, or in bankruptcy.

Caterpillar, Inc., 2011, 10K Report

EXPANDED MATERIAL

In the first part of this chapter, we focused on the central activity of a business—selling a product or service and collecting the resulting receivable. We also discussed other events or activities related to this revenue/receivables/cash cycle. In this section of the chapter, we address the issue of using accounts receivable as a source of cash. Often, for a variety of reasons, a company will have an immediate need for cash. A number of methods are available to a company to convert its receivables into cash without waiting for payment from the customer. The most common of those methods are discussed here. We also discuss notes receivable and how they are valued and used as a source of cash. The Expanded Material also includes a brief discussion of the impact of uncollectible accounts on the statement of cash flows.

Receivables as a Source of Cash

LO6 学习目标6
解释如何通过担保借款或者销售将应收账款转化为现金资源。

6 Explain how receivables may be used as a source of cash through secured borrowing or sale.

As stated previously, receivables are a part of the normal revenue/receivables/cash operating cycle of a business. Frequently, this cycle takes several months to complete. Sometimes companies need immediate cash and cannot wait for completion of the normal cycle. At other times, companies are not in financial stress but want to accelerate the receivables collection process, shift the risk of credit and the effort of collection to someone else, or merely use receivables from customers as a source of financing.

Receivables may be converted to cash in one of two ways: as a sale (either with or without recourse) or as a secured borrowing. The FASB specifies in Topic 860 the conditions that must be met if a transfer of receivables is to be accounted for as a sale.[6] Those conditions are as follows:

1. The transferred assets have been isolated from the transferor. That is, the transferor and its creditors cannot access the assets.
2. The transferee has the right to pledge or exchange the transferred assets.
3. The transferor does not maintain effective control over the assets through either (a) an agreement to repurchase them before their maturity or (b) the ability to cause the transferee to return specific assets.

These three conditions are designed to carefully define cases in which the transfer of a financial asset is being made with no substantial strings attached. If there are no strings attached, meaning that the transferor does not have the right to get the assets back and the transferee has the right to use the assets in any way desired, then the transfer is accounted for as a sale. If these three conditions are not met, then the transfer of receivables is accounted for as a secured borrowing. In the sections that follow, we discuss both the sale of receivables and their use as collateral in a borrowing arrangement.

Sale of Receivables without Recourse

Certain banks, dealers, and finance companies purchase receivables from companies. In many cases, these purchases are done without recourse, meaning that the purchaser

---
[6] FASB ASC paragraph 860-10-40-5.

Exhibit 7-9 | Flow of Activities Involved in Factoring

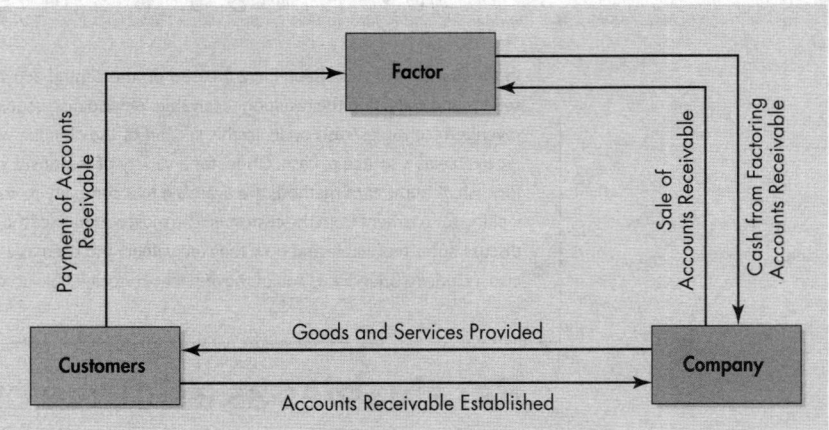

assumes the risks associated with the collectibility of the receivables. If the terms of the sale are with recourse, then if the receivables are not collected, the purchaser has the right to collect from the company that originally sold the receivable. A sale of accounts receivable without recourse is commonly referred to as accounts receivable factoring, and the buyer is referred to as a *factor*.[7] Customers are usually notified that their bills are payable to the factor, and this party assumes the burden of billing and collecting accounts. The flow of activities involved in factoring is presented in Exhibit 7-9.

In many cases, factoring involves more than the purchase and collection of accounts receivable. Factoring frequently involves a continuing agreement whereby a financing institution assumes the credit function as well as the collection function. Under such an arrangement, the factor grants or denies credit, handles the accounts receivable records, bills customers, and makes collections. The business unit is relieved of all these activities, and the sale of goods provides immediate cash for business use. Because the factor absorbs the losses from bad accounts and frequently assumes credit and collection responsibilities, the charges associated with factoring generally exceed the interest charges on a loan with receivables used as collateral. Often, the factor will charge a fee of 10% to 30% of the net amount of receivables purchased, except for credit card factoring where the rate is 3% to 5%. The factor may withhold a portion of the purchase price for possible future charges for customer returns and allowances or other special adjustments. Final settlement is made after receivables have been collected.

When receivables are sold outright, without recourse, Cash is debited, receivables and related allowance balances are closed, and a loss account is debited for factoring charges. When part of the purchase price is withheld by the factor, a receivable from the factor is established pending final settlement. Upon receipt of the total purchase price from the bank or finance company, the factor receivable account is eliminated. To illustrate, assume that $10,000 of receivables are factored, that is, sold without recourse, to a

应收账款在很多情形下是不附追索权的，意味着购买者承担了应收账款不能回收的风险。若附追索权，则在应收账款无法回收时，受让方有权向最初的转让方偿还。出售不附追索权的应收账款被称为应收账款售让。

> **FYI**
> Student loans are often factored to specialized loan servicing companies.

---
[7] Recourse is defined by the FASB as "the right of a transferee of receivables to receive payment from the transferor of those receivables for any of the following: (a) failure of the debtors to pay when due, (b) the effects of prepayments, or (c) adjustments resulting from defects in the eligibility of the transferred receivables." FASB ASC Section 860-10-20-Glossary.

finance company for $8,500. An allowance for bad debts equal to $300 was previously established for these accounts. This amount will need to be written off along with the accounts receivable being sold. The finance company withheld 5% of the purchase price as protection against sales returns and allowances. The entry to record the sale of the accounts is as follows:

Cash	8,075	
Receivable from Factor	425	
Allowance for Bad Debts...	300	
Loss from Factoring Receivables	1,200	
Accounts Receivable		10,000

To record the factoring of receivables. Computations:

Cash = $8,500 − $425 = $8,075; Factor receivable =

$8,500 × 0.05 = $425; Factoring loss =

($10,000 − $300) − $8,500 = $1,200.

The loss from factoring is determined by comparing the book value of the receivables ($10,000 − $300) to the proceeds to be received ($8,500). Assuming there were no returns or allowances, the final settlement would be recorded as follows:

Cash	425	
Receivable from Factor...		425

To record the final settlement associated with previously factored receivables.

Sale of Receivables with Recourse

Cash can be obtained by selling receivables with recourse. This is different from factoring, which generally is on a nonrecourse basis. Selling receivables with recourse means that a purchaser (bank or finance company) advances cash in return for receivables but retains the right to collect from the seller if debtors (seller's customers) fail to make payments when due.

The FASB requires the seller to estimate the value of the recourse obligation and recognize that liability. That is, the seller must estimate the amount that will be paid to the purchaser as a result of default on the receivables that were sold. Continuing the previous example, assume that the receivables were sold with recourse and the recourse obligation has an estimated fair value of $500. In this instance, the loss to be recognized on the transaction is $1,700 and is computed as follows:

> **FYI**
>
> The estimation of the recourse obligation essentially involves a reexamination of the receivables being sold to determine whether the allowance for bad debts associated with those receivables is sufficient.

Cash received	$ 8,500
Estimated value of recourse obligation...................................	(500)
Net proceeds...	$ 8,000
Book value of the receivables...	$ 9,700
Net proceeds to be received...	(8,000)
Loss on sale of receivables..	$ 1,700

The entry to record the sale of receivables with recourse would be as follows:

Cash	8,075	
Receivable from Factor	425	
Allowance for Bad Debts	300	
Loss on Sale of Receivables	1,700	
Accounts Receivable		10,000
Recourse Obligation		500

> **Stop & Think**
>
> Why would a company ever factor receivables with recourse when it could factor those same receivables without recourse?
>
> a) Factoring receivables without recourse is illegal in many states.
> b) FASB ASC Topic 860 does not apply when receivables are factored with recourse.
> c) The fee paid to the factor is lower when factoring receivables with recourse.
> d) The recourse obligation is always exactly equal to the allowance for bad debts.

If in the future the estimate of the recourse obligation turns out to have been incorrect, then the company will recognize income if the actual amount paid relating to the recourse obligation is less than $500 and will recognize an additional loss if the amount turns out to be greater than $500.

As mentioned earlier, the recourse provisions of a receivable transfer may leave the transferor with such a large degree of control over or large amount of risk from the transferred receivables that the receivables should remain on the books of the transferor. Specifically, if the three conditions mentioned earlier are not met, then the transfer of receivables is accounted for as a secured borrowing, as illustrated in the next section.

Secured Borrowing

Loans are frequently obtained from banks or other lending institutions by assigning or pledging receivables as security. The loan is evidenced by a written note that provides for either a general assignment of receivables or an assignment of specific receivables. With an assignment of receivables, no special accounting problems are involved. The books simply report the loan (a debit to Cash and a credit to Notes Payable) and subsequent settlement of the obligation (a debit to Notes Payable and a credit to Cash). However, disclosure should be made on the balance sheet, by a parenthetical comment or a note, of the amount and nature of receivables pledged to secure the obligation to the lender.

> **FYI**
>
> Packaging and transfer of receivables is sometimes called *securitization*. In this context, when you see the term *securitization*, think of it as the process of turning receivables into cash immediately.

The procedures involved are illustrated in the following example. It is assumed that the assignor (the borrower) collects the receivables, which is often the case.

On July 1, 2015, Provo Mercantile Co. assigns receivables totaling $300,000 to Salem Bank as collateral on a $200,000, 12% note. Provo Mercantile does not notify its account debtors and will continue to collect the assigned receivables. Salem assesses a 1% finance charge on assigned receivables in addition to the interest on the note. Provo is to make monthly payments to Salem with cash collected on assigned receivables. The entries shown below would be made.

If in the following example Salem Bank assumes responsibility for collecting the assigned receivables, the account debtors would have to be notified to make their payments to the bank. Salem would then use a liability account (e.g., Payable to Provo Mercantile) to account for cash collections during the period. Because the receivables are still owned by Provo Mercantile, the bank would not record them as assets. Upon full payment of the note plus interest, the bank would remit to Provo Mercantile any cash collections in excess of the note, along with any uncollected accounts.

Illustrative Entries for Assignment of Specific Receivables

Provo Mercantile Co.			Salem Bank		

Issuance of note and assignment of specific receivables on July 1, 2015:

Cash	197,000		Notes Receivable	200,000	
Finance Charge	3,000*		Finance Revenue		3,000*
Notes Payable		200,000	Cash		197,000

*(0.01 × $300,000)

Collections of assigned accounts during July, $180,000 less cash discounts of $1,000; sales returns in July, $2,000:

Cash	179,000		(No Entry)		
Sales Discounts	1,000				
Sales Returns and Allowances	2,000				
Accounts Receivable		182,000			

Paid Salem Bank amounts owed for July collections plus accrued interest on note to August 1:

Interest Expense	2,000*		Cash	181,000	
Notes Payable	179,000		Interest Revenue		2,000
Cash		181,000	Notes Receivable		179,000

* ($200,000 × 0.12 × 1/12)

Collections of remaining assigned accounts during August less $800 written off as uncollectible:

Cash	117,200		(No Entry)		
Allowance for Bad Debts	800				
Accounts Receivable		118,000*			

* ($300,000 − $182,000)

Paid Salem Bank remaining balance owed plus accrued interest on note to September 1:

Interest Expense	210*		Cash	21,210	
Notes Payable	21,000†		Interest Revenue		210*
Cash		21,210	Notes Receivable		21,000†

* ($21,000 × 0.12 × 1/12)
† ($200,000 − $179,000)

In summary, receivables provide an important source of cash for many companies. The transfer of receivables to third parties in return for cash generally takes the form of secured borrowing (borrowing with the receivables pledged as collateral) or factoring (a sale without recourse). The financing arrangements are often complex and may involve a transfer of receivables on a recourse basis. Each transaction must be analyzed carefully to see if in form and substance it is a borrowing transaction or a sales transaction and treated accordingly.

Derecognition of Receivables: *IAS 39*

IAS 39用两步法进行应收账款的终止确认：（1）与应收账款所有权相关的主要风险和报酬是否转移；（2）控制权是否已发生转移。

IASB standards address the transfer of receivables in *IAS 39*. *IAS 39* covers a lot of ground such as the accounting for investment securities, the accounting for derivatives, and the accounting for the transfer of financial assets such as receivables. As seen above in the discussion of FASB ASC Topic 860, the key accounting issue with the transfer of receivables is whether the transfer should be recorded as a sale, with the receivable then removed from the books of the transferor, or whether the transfer should be accounted for as a secured loan with the receivable remaining on the books of the transferor. Frequently the term "derecognition" is used to signify the removal of the receivable from the books of the transferor.

Recall that the purpose of the three conditions in FASB ASC Section 860-10-40 is to identify receivable transfers in which economic ownership of the receivable has been transferred. *IAS 39* contains the same concept but applied slightly differently. *IAS 39* contains a two-step test for derecognition.

1. Determine whether the receivable transfer involves a transfer of "substantially all the risks and rewards of ownership of the [receivable]." If so, the transfer should be accounted for as a sale of the receivable, as illustrated previously. If not, go on to step 2.
2. If the receivable transfer does not involve the transfer of substantially all the risks and rewards of ownership, determine whether control of the receivable has been transferred. If so, account for the receivable transfer as a sale. If not, the transfer is accounted for as a secured loan, as illustrated previously.[8]

The *IAS 39* two-step test emphasizes the question of whether the risks and rewards of ownership have been transferred. With respect to receivables, the risks and rewards of ownership are the receipt, or nonreceipt, of cash depending on whether the customer who owes the receivable amount ultimately pays. For example, a transferor of a receivable who receives a nonrefundable fixed cash payment in exchange for the receivable has transferred the risks and rewards of ownership because the transferor gets to keep the nonrefundable fixed cash payment whether the customer pays the receivable amount or not. In contrast, if the transferor receives an upfront cash payment but then agrees to give back some of the cash, or to receive extra cash, depending on how much the customer ultimately pays, then the risks and rewards of ownership have not been transferred.

Compare the three criteria in *SFAS No. 140* with the two-step test contained in *IAS 39*. As is typically the case, the U.S. standard is more detailed and the international standard is more conceptual. In the large majority of cases, the two standards will result in the same accounting treatment for a receivable transfer.

---

[8] *International Accounting Standard 39,* "Financial Instruments: Recognition and Measurement" (London: International Accounting Standards Board, August 18, 2005), par. 20.

Notes Receivable

LO7 学习目标7
描述应收票据的正确核算和估值。

7 Describe proper accounting and valuation of notes receivable.

A promissory note is an unconditional written promise to pay a certain sum of money at a specified time. The note is signed by the maker and is payable to the order of a specified payee or bearer. Notes usually involve interest, stated at an annual rate and charged on the face amount of the note. Most notes are negotiable notes that are legally transferable by endorsement and delivery.

For reporting purposes, trade notes receivable should include only negotiable short-term instruments acquired from trade debtors and not yet due. Trade notes generally arise from sales involving relatively high dollar amounts when the buyer wants to extend payment beyond the usual trade credit period of 30 to 90 days. Also, sellers sometimes request notes from customers whose accounts receivable are past due. Most companies, however, have relatively few trade notes receivable.

Nontrade notes receivable should be separately designated on the balance sheet under an appropriate title. For example, notes arising from loans to customers, officers, employees, and affiliated companies should be reported separately from trade notes.

Valuation of Notes Receivable

Notes receivable are initially recorded at their present value, which may be defined as the sum of future receipts discounted to the present date at an appropriate rate of interest.[9] In a lending transaction, the present value is the amount of cash received by the borrower. When a note is exchanged for property, goods, or services, the present value equals the current cash selling price of the items exchanged. The difference between the present value and the amount to be collected at the due date or maturity date is a charge for interest.

带息票据是承诺支付票据面值加上一定利息的书面保证。

All notes arising in arm's-length transactions between unrelated parties involve an element of interest. However, a distinction as to form is made between interest-bearing and non-interest-bearing notes. An interest-bearing note is written as a promise to pay principal (or face amount) plus interest at a specified rate. In the absence of special valuation problems discussed in the next section, the face amount of an interest-bearing note is the present value upon issuance of the note.

Another name for Discount on Notes Receivable is Unearned Interest Revenue.

A non-interest-bearing note does not specify an interest rate, but the face amount includes the interest charge. Thus, the present value is the difference between the face amount and the interest included in that amount, sometimes called the implicit (or effective) interest.

无息票据的票面上没有标示利率，但面值包含了利息费用。因此，现值就是面值与在票据期内发生的利息的差额，这个利息通常称作内含利息。

In recording receipt of a note, Notes Receivable is debited for the face amount of the note. When the face amount differs from the present value, as is the case with non-interest-bearing

---

[9] See the text module, Time Value of Money Review, for a discussion of present value concepts and applications.

notes, the difference is recorded as a premium or discount and amortized over the life of the note. In the example to follow, a note receivable is established with credits to sales and discount on notes receivable accounts. The amount of discount is the implicit interest on the note and will be recognized as interest revenue as the note matures.

To illustrate, assume that High Value Corporation sells goods on January 1, 2015, with a price of $1,000. The buyer gives High Value a promissory note due December 31, 2016. The maturity value of the note includes interest at 10%. Thus, High Value will receive $1,210 ($1,000 × 1.21) when the note is paid.[10] The entries below show the accounting procedures for an interest-bearing note and one written in a non-interest-bearing form.

At December 31, 2015, the unamortized discount of $110 on the non-interest-bearing note would be deducted from Notes Receivable on the balance sheet. If the non-interest-bearing note were recorded at face value with no recognition of the interest included therein, the sales price and profit to the seller would be overstated. In subsequent periods, interest revenue would be understated. Failure to record the discount would also result in an overstatement of assets.

Illustrative Entries for Notes

Interest-Bearing Note
Face Amount = Present Value = $1,000
Stated Interest Rate = 10%

Non-Interest-Bearing Note
Face Amount = Maturity = $1,210
No Stated Interest Rate

To record note received in exchange for goods selling for $1,000:

2015
Jan. 1	Notes Receivable	1,000		Notes Receivable	1,210	
	Sales		1,000	Sales		1,000
				Discount on Notes Receivable		210

To recognize interest earned for one year, $1,000 × 0.10:

Dec. 31	Interest Receivable	100		Discount on Notes Receivable	100	
	Interest Revenue		100	Interest Revenue		100

To record settlement of note at maturity and recognize interest earned for one year, ($1,000 + $100) × 0.10:

2016
Dec. 31	Cash	1,210		Cash	1,210	
	Notes Receivable		1,000	Discount on Notes Receivable	110	
	Interest Receivable		100	Notes Receivable		1,210
	Interest Revenue		110	Interest Revenue		110

Although the proper valuation of receivables calls for the amortization procedure just described, exceptions may be appropriate in some situations due to special limitations or practical considerations. Among the exceptions are the following:

> "... receivables and payables arising from transactions with customers or suppliers in the normal course of business which are due in customary trade terms not exceeding approximately one year."[11]

---

[10] The future value of $1 to be received two years from now, if the interest rate is 10% compounded annually, is $1.21.
[11] FASB ASC paragraph 835-30-15-3(a).

Accordingly, short-term notes and accounts receivable arising from trade sales may be properly recorded at the amounts collectible in the customary sales terms without separately recording the implicit interest embedded in those amounts.

Notes, like accounts receivable, are not always collectible. If notes receivable comprise a significant portion of regular trade receivables, a provision should be made for uncollectible amounts and an allowance account established using procedures similar to those for accounts receivable already discussed.

Special Valuation Problems

Special valuation issues arise with respect to nontrade long-term notes, such as secured and unsecured notes, debentures (bonds), equipment obligations, and mortgage notes. Examples are provided for notes exchanged for cash and for property, goods, or services.

Notes Exchanged for Cash When a note is exchanged for cash and no other rights or privileges are involved, the present value of the note is presumed to be the amount of the cash proceeds. The note should be recorded at its face amount, and any difference between the face amount and the cash proceeds should be recorded as a premium or discount on the note. The premium or discount should be amortized over the life of the note as illustrated previously for High Value Corporation. The total interest is measured by the difference in actual cash received by the borrower and the total amount to be received in the future by the lender. Any unamortized premium or discount on notes is reported on the balance sheet as a direct addition to or deduction from the face amount of the receivables, thus showing their net present value.

Notes Exchanged for Property, Goods, or Services When a note is exchanged for property, goods, or services in an arm's-length transaction, the present value of the note is usually evidenced by the terms of the note or supporting documents. There is a general presumption that the interest specified by the parties to a transaction represents fair and adequate compensation for the use of borrowed funds.[12] Valuation problems arise, however, when one of the following conditions exists:

1. No interest rate is stated.
2. The stated rate does not seem reasonable, given the nature of the transaction and surrounding circumstances.
3. The stated face amount of the note is significantly different from the current cash equivalent sales price of similar property, goods, or services, or from the current market value of similar notes at the date of the transaction.

Under any of the preceding conditions, the note should be recorded at (1) the fair value of the property, goods, or services exchanged or (2) the fair value of the note, whichever is more clearly determinable. The difference between the face amount of the note and the recorded value is recognized as a discount or premium and is amortized over the life of the note.

> **Caution**
> Make sure you are comfortable with the time value of money concepts discussed in the text module before proceeding with this example.

To illustrate, assume that on July 1, 2015, Timberline Corporation sells a tract of land purchased three years ago at a cost of $250,000. The buyer gives Timberline a one-year note with a face amount of $310,000, bearing interest at a stated rate of 8%. An appraisal of the land prior to the

---
[12] FASB ASC paragraph 835-30-25-2.

sale indicated a market value of $300,000, which in this example is considered to be the appropriate basis for recording the sale as follows:

2015
July 1 Notes Receivable 310,000
          Discount on Notes Receivable 10,000
          Land 250,000
          Gain on Sale of Land 50,000

When the note is paid at maturity, Timberline will receive the face value ($310,000) plus stated interest of $24,800 ($310,000 × 0.08), or a total of $334,800. The interest to be recognized, however, is $34,800—the difference between the maturity value of the note and the market value of the land at the date of the exchange. Thus, the effective rate of interest on the note is 11.6% ($34,800/$300,000).

Assuming straight-line amortization of the discount and that Timberline's year-end is December 31, the following entries would be made to recognize interest revenue and to record payment of the note at maturity:

2015
Dec. 31 Interest Receivable 12,400*
           Discount on Notes Receivable 5,000
              Interest Revenue 17,400
           *$310,000 × 0.08 × 6/12 = $12,400

2016
June 30 Cash 334,800
           Discount on Notes Receivable 5,000
              Notes Receivable 310,000
              Interest Receivable 12,400
              Interest Revenue 17,400

The unamortized discount balance of $5,000 would be subtracted from Notes Receivable on the December 31, 2015, balance sheet.

Imputing an Interest Rate If there is no current market price for either the property, goods, or services or the note, then the present value of the note must be determined by selecting an appropriate interest rate and using that rate to discount future receipts to the present. The imputed interest rate is determined at the date of the exchange and is not altered thereafter.

The selection of an appropriate rate is influenced by many factors, including the credit standing of the issuer of the note and prevailing interest rates for debt instruments of similar quality and length of time to maturity. The objective is as follows:

> In any event, the rate used for valuation purposes should be the rate at which the debtor can obtain financing of a similar nature from other sources at the date of the transaction.[13]

To illustrate the process of imputing interest rates, assume that Horrocks & Associates surveyed 800,000 acres of mountain property for Mountain Meadow Ranch. On December 31, 2015, Horrocks accepted a $45,000 note as payment for services. The note is non-interest-bearing and comes due in three yearly installments of $15,000 each, beginning December 31, 2016. Assume there is no market for the note and no basis for estimating objectively the fair value of the services rendered. After considering the current prime interest rate, the credit standing of the ranch, the

内含报酬率。如果资产、商品或服务与票据均没有当前市价，那么就要选择一个合适的利率将未来价值折现到当前价值作为票据的现值。

[13] FASB ASC 835-30-25-12.

SELLING A NOTE RECEIVABLE: WHAT'S IT WORTH?

As discussed earlier in the chapter, accounts and notes receivable can be used as an immediate source of cash by selling them to a factor. When a note receivable is sold, the value of the receivable depends on several factors including the interest rate on the note, the interest rate charged by the factor, and the time period involved.

Suppose for a moment that you are a bank official. What factors will affect the amount you are willing to pay to a company that wants to discount (sell) a note? First and foremost will be the creditworthiness of the maker; a second factor will be the length of time you must wait to get the money; and a third factor will be how much money you are going to receive when the note matures. Each of these factors will be reflected in your computation of the present value of that note. The steps to determine the amount to be received by the bank (the proceeds) are as follows:

1. Determine the maturity value of the note.

   Maturity value = Face amount + Interest
   Interest = Face amount × Interest rate × Interest period
   Interest period = Date of note to date of maturity

   The maturity value is the amount you will receive when the note matures.

2. Determine the amount of discount.

   Discount = Maturity value × Discount rate × Discount period
   Discount period = Date of discount to date of maturity

Once the maturity value is determined, the second factor comes into play: how long you have to wait to get the money. This time period is termed the *discount period*. Finally, the creditworthiness of the maker enters into the equation. The riskier the maker, the higher the discount rate will be. Also affecting the discount rate are general economic variables.

3. Determine the proceeds.
   Proceeds = Maturity value − Discount

Once the proceeds are determined, the transaction can be recorded, recognizing the applicable liability and net interest revenue or expense (if a borrowing transaction) or the gain or loss (if a sales transaction).

Consider the following example. Meeker Corporation received a three-month, $5,000, 10% note from a customer on September 1 to settle a past-due accounts receivable. One month later, the note is discounted at a bank at a discount rate of 15%. The amount received from the bank would be computed as follows:

Maturity value of the note = $5,000 + ($5,000 × 0.10 × 3/12)
= $5,125
Amount of discount = $5,125 × 0.15 × 2/12
= $128.13
Proceeds = $5,125 − $128.13 = $4,996.87

In this instance, Meeker would recognize a loss of $3.13 ($5,000 − $4,996.87) as a result of discounting the note.

---

collateral available, the terms for repayment, and the prevailing rates of interest for the issuer's other debt, a 10% imputed interest rate is considered appropriate. The note should be recorded at its present value and a discount recognized. The computation is based on the present value calculations as follows:

Face amount of note	$45,000
Less present value of note:	
PV_n: PMT = $15,000; N = 3; I = 10%...	37,303*
Discount on note..	$ 7,697

*Rounded to nearest dollar.

The entry to record the receipt of the note would be:

2015
Dec. 31 Notes Receivable... 45,000
             Discount on Notes Receivable................................. 7,697
             Service Revenue 37,303
   To record a non-interest-bearing note receivable at its present value based on an imputed interest rate of 10% per year.

A schedule showing the amortization of the discount on the note follows. This type of computation is commonly referred to as the *effective interest amortization method*.

	(1) Face Amount Before Current Installment	(2) Unamortized Discount	(3) Net Amount (1) – (2)	(4) Discount Amortization 10% × (3)	(5) Payment Received
Dec. 31, 2016	$45,000	$7,697	$37,303	$3,730	$15,000
Dec. 31, 2017	30,000	3,967*	26,033	2,603	15,000
Dec. 31, 2018	15,000	1,364†	13,636	1,364	15,000
				$7,697	$45,000

*$7,697 − $3,730 = $3,967
†$3,967 − $2,603 = $1,364

At the end of each year, an entry similar to the following would be made:

2016
Dec. 31　Cash 15,000
　　　　　Discount on Notes Receivable 3,730
　　　　　　Interest Revenue.. 3,730
　　　　　　Notes Receivable.. 15,000

To record the first year's installment on notes receivable and recognize interest earned during the period.

By using these procedures, at the end of the three years the discount will be completely amortized to interest revenue, the face amount of the note receivable will have been collected, and the appropriate amount of service revenue will have been recognized in the year it was earned. At the end of each year, the balance sheet will reflect the net present value of the receivable by subtracting the unamortized discount balance from the outstanding balance in Notes Receivable.

It is necessary to impute an interest rate only when the present value of the receivable cannot be determined through evaluation of existing market values of the elements of the transaction. The valuation and income measurement objectives remain the same regardless of the specific circumstances: to report notes receivable at their net present values and to record appropriate amounts of interest revenue during the collection period of the receivables.

Impact of Uncollectible Accounts on the Statement of Cash Flows

LO8 学习目标8
理解坏账对现金流量表的影响。

8 Understand the impact of uncollectible accounts on the statement of cash flows.

As noted in Chapter 5, the amount of reported sales or net income on an accrual basis must be adjusted for the change in the accounts receivable balances to derive the corresponding amount of cash flow from operations. The establishment of a provision for bad debts with a corresponding allowance for bad debts and the subsequent writing off of uncollectible accounts will impact the adjustments made, depending on whether the analysis considers gross or net accounts receivable balances.

To this point, we have assumed that any decrease in accounts receivable represents a payment received on account. Actually, two possibilities are associated with a decrease in receivables: Customers pay, or customers never pay, and the account is written off. Thus, a decrease in receivables may reflect a receipt of cash, or it may reflect the writing off of an account.

To illustrate the adjustments required for accounts receivable when preparing a statement of cash flows, consider the following information:

	Beginning Balances	Ending Balances
Accounts receivable	$20,000	$ 25,000
Allowance for bad debts	4,000	4,800
Net accounts receivable	$16,000	$ 20,200
Sales for the year		$1,000,000
Net income for the year		100,000
Bad debt expense for the year		2,000
Write-off of uncollectible amounts for the year		1,200
Cash expenses for the year		898,000

In order to focus on the impact of uncollectible accounts, the illustration assumes that all operating expenses other than bad debt expense were paid in cash. Also, it is assumed that—with the exception of accounts receivable—there were no changes in the amounts of current assets and current liabilities.

In T-account form, the receivables account and the associated allowance account appear as follows:

Accounts Receivable			Allowance for Bad Debts		
Beg. Bal.	20,000			Beg. Bal.	4,000
	1,000,000		1,200		2,000
		993,800		End. Bal.	4,800
		1,200			
End. Bal.	25,000				

The accounts receivable account increased from $20,000 to $25,000. Given sales of $1,000,000, credits to Accounts Receivable must have totaled $995,000, but this $995,000 does not relate entirely to cash collections. A portion of the decline, $1,200, relates to the fact that some cash will never be collected and is no longer an asset; it must be written off. Therefore, cash collections total $993,800.

How is this information reflected in the statement of cash flows? Using the format discussed in Chapter 5, we will begin with the income statement and make adjustments as follows:

Income Statement		Adjustments		Cash Flows from Operations
Sales	$1,000,000	$(5,000)	$995,000	Cash collected from customers
Bad debt expense	(2,000)	800	(1,200)	
Cash expenses	(898,000)	0	(898,000)	Cash paid for expenses
Net income	$ 100,000	$(4,200)	$ 95,800	Cash from operations

The first adjustment of ($5,000) reflects the increase in the accounts receivable account resulting from sales (the debit side of the receivables account) exceeding credits to the accounts receivable account (cash collections and actual bad debts). The second adjustment converts the accrual basis measure, the bad debt expense (the credit side of the allowance account), to its cash flow counterpart, actual bad debts (the debit side of the allowance account). These two adjustments, considered together, tell us that $993,800 ($995,000 − $1,200) was collected from customers during the period.

Using the preceding information, the net cash flow provided by operations during the period is as follows:

Direct Method	
Cash collected from customers	$ 993,800
Cash expenses	(898,000)
Net cash flow provided by operations	$ 95,800

Indirect Method	
Net income	$ 100,000
Less: Increase in accounts receivable	(5,000)
Add: Increase in allowance for bad debts	800
Net cash flows provided by operations	$ 95,800

Often, accounts receivable will be presented net of the bad debt expense. Take a look at the following T-account in which "netting" occurs.

Accounts Receivable (net)

Beg. Bal.	16,000		
Sales	1,000,000		
		Collections	993,800
		Bad debt expense	2,000
End. Bal.	20,200		

What happened to the $1,200 related to the amounts written off as uncollectible? Because that amount appeared as a credit in the receivables account and a debit in the allowance account, it will net out to $0 when the two accounts are combined.

The statement of cash flows, when net accounts receivable are presented, can be prepared from the following information.

Income Statement		Adjustments		Cash Flows from Operations
Sales	$1,000,000	$(4,200)	$995,800	Cash collected from customers
Bad debt expense	(2,000)	0	(2,000)	
Cash expenses	(898,000)	0	(898,000)	Cash paid for expenses
Net income	$ 100,000	$(4,200)	$ 95,800	Cash from operations

Sales is simply adjusted for the change in the net receivables account. Why is there no adjustment to Bad Debt Expense in this case? Because when the two accounts are netted together, all adjustments are netted together as well and result in the $4,200 adjustment.

Using net receivables, the net cash flows provided by operations during the period is presented as follows:

Direct Method	
Cash collected from customers	$993,800
Cash expenses	(898,000)
Net cash flow provided by operations	$ 95,800
Indirect Method	
Net income	$100,000
Less: Increase in accounts receivable	(4,200)
Net cash flows provided by operations	$ 95,800

In the vast majority of cases, net receivables are presented and the indirect method is used. In these instances, the only adjustment required relates to the change in the net accounts receivable balance.

SOLUTIONS TO OPENING SCENARIO QUESTIONS

1. The largest revenue amount for a bank is interest revenue on its loans. In 2011, Bank of America reported interest revenue on its loans of $45.0 billion. In addition, Bank of America reported interest revenue from investments of an additional $9.5 billion. The largest expense amount for a bank is usually its interest expense. In 2011, Bank of America reported interest expense of $21.6 billion of which $3.0 billion was interest paid to depositors.

2. As of December 31, 2011, Bank of America had consumer loans outstanding of $609 billion and commercial loans outstanding of $317 billion. By far the largest loan category was residential mortgages/home equity loans at $387 billion. (*Note:* Because of various classifications on Bank of America's balance sheet, these numbers do NOT add up to the total reported loans receivable amount of $892 billion.)

3. The net charge-off ratio for the residential mortgage loans was just 1.45%. For home equity loans the net charge-off ratio was slightly higher at 3.42%. The net charge-off ratio for direct/indirect consumer loans was 1.64%, and the net charge-off ratio for domestic credit card loans was 6.90%.

Stop & Think SOLUTIONS

1. (Page 7-5) The correct answer is A. The use of credit allows businesses to attract customers. A policy of "cash only" may cause customers to shop elsewhere, especially if all of a company's competitors are offering credit terms.

2. (Page 7-24) The correct answer is D. If an outstanding check is omitted from the outstanding check list in the reconciliation, the corrected bank balance will be greater than the corrected book balance. When a bank reconciliation does not reconcile, it is good practice to look at the reconciliation for the preceding month to see whether all outstanding checks listed in that month have subsequently cleared the bank. The other potential errors listed (a, b, and c) would all cause the corrected bank balance to be less than the corrected book balance.

3. (Page 7-30) The correct answer is C. The factor would charge a fee based on the risk he or she is assuming. Factoring without recourse involves the factor assuming all the risk associated with collections. To assume that risk, the factor will charge a higher fee. If the risk of collection remains with the company (with recourse), then the factor would be willing to charge a lower fee.

SOLUTION TO USING THE FASB'S CODIFICATION

By going to the paragraphs on regular warranties, you should run across FASB ASC paragraph 460-10-25-8 which leads to Section 605-20-25. Paragraph 4 of that Section says the following: "Costs that are directly related to the acquisition of a contract and that would have not been incurred but for the acquisition of that contract (incremental direct acquisition costs) shall be deferred and charged to expense in proportion to the revenue recognized."

So, those salespersons' commissions should be deferred (recorded as a prepaid expense) and amortized to expense over the life of the associated extended warranty agreement. This matches the commission expense recognition with the timing of the recognition of the revenue from the extended warranty.

Review Chapter 7 Learning Objectives

① Explain the normal operating cycle of a business.

The operating cycle is the lifeblood of almost every business. The critical event for a business is the sale of goods or services. This sale often results in the recording of an account receivable. The account receivable is then collected, the resulting cash is reinvested in the business, and the cycle begins again.

② Prepare journal entries to record sales revenue, including the accounting for bad debts and warranties for service or replacement.

A sale is recorded with a credit to Sales Revenue and a debit to either Accounts Receivable or Cash. The matching principle requires that expenses associated with the sale be recorded in the period of the sale. As a result, items such as bad debts and warranties must be estimated and recorded.

Bad debts are estimated using one of two methods: percentage of sales or percentage of receivables. Each of these methods involves estimating the likelihood that some receivables will not be collected. The journal entry involves a debit to Bad Debt Expense and a credit to Allowance for Bad Debts. The allowance account is a contra asset account that, when offset against the accounts receivable account, values the asset at its net realizable value.

Warranties are quantified by estimating, based on past experience, the probable amount of future warranty costs and are recorded with a debit to Warranty Expense and a credit to a liability account. When the warranty claim is presented, the liability account is reduced and a credit is made to cash, parts, labor, and so forth.

③ Analyze accounts receivable to measure how efficiently a firm is using this operating asset.

The effective management of accounts receivable is critical to the cash flows of any business. The most common tool used to monitor receivables is the average collection period, which reflects the average number of days that lapse between the time a sale is made and cash is collected. First, the accounts receivable turnover ratio is computed by dividing sales by average accounts receivable. The resulting number is divided into 365 (the number of days in a year) to compute the average collection period.

④ Discuss the composition, management, and control of cash, including the use of a bank reconciliation.

Cash management and control are critical to the success of every business. Because cash is the most liquid of assets, safeguards must be in place to ensure that cash is properly handled and accounted for. A common control involves the use of a bank reconciliation. A bank reconciliation requires the accountant to reconcile the bank's balance for cash with the company's balance. Any discrepancies are identified and appropriate corrections are made.

⑤ Recognize appropriate disclosures for presenting sales and receivables in the financial statements.

Disclosure of sales and receivables in the financial statements vary from company to company. In the body of the financial statements, sales are generally reported net of discounts and allowances. Receivables are often reported net of their allowance account with supplemental information provided in the notes to the financial statements.

EXPANDED MATERIAL

6 **Explain how receivables may be used as a source of cash through secured borrowing or sale.**

In most cases, a receivable is converted into cash when a customer, in the normal cycle of business, pays the company. However, companies can accelerate the cash collection process by using accounts receivable to assist in obtaining a loan. The method employed and the cost to the firm depend on the degree of risk to which the company wishes to expose itself. In the case of secured borrowing, the company is simply pledging the receivable as collateral on a loan. Receivables can also be sold to a third party, usually a bank or other financial institution. When a receivable is sold with recourse, the selling company must quantify the expected payout that will be made as a result of the recourse provision.

7 **Describe proper accounting and valuation of notes receivable.**

Notes receivable represent a formal borrowing arrangement between two parties. A note receivable typically specifies an interest rate and a payment date. Notes receivable are valued using techniques that compute the present value of the principal and interest to be received. Problems can arise in the valuation of notes receivable when the note is exchanged for goods or services and the fair market value of those goods and services is difficult to determine. In some instances, an effective interest rate for the note must be imputed.

8 **Understand the impact of uncollectible accounts on the statement of cash flows.**

The accounts Allowance for Bad Debts and Bad Debt Expense must be interpreted with care when determining the amount of cash flows related to receivables for a certain period. Different adjustments are made to the statement of cash flows, depending on whether the direct or indirect method is being used. The objective of these adjustments is to correctly identify cash collections from customers for the period.

FASB-IASB CODIFICATION SUMMARY

Topic	FASB Accounting Standards Codification	Original FASB Standard	Corresponding IASB Standard	Differences between U.S. GAAP and IFRS
Bad debts	Section 310-10-35 par. 7-9	SFAS No. 5 par. 22	No explicit standard	No apparent differences
Warranties	Section 460-10-25 par. 5-7	SFAS No. 5 par. 24	IAS 37 par. 14, 39	No substantial differences
Compensating balances	Section 210-10-S99 par. 1	SEC Regulation S-X, Rule 5-02, Caption 1	IAS 7 par. 48	No substantial differences
Imputation of interest on receivables	Section 835-30-25 par. 2, 12	APB No. 21 par. 9, 13	No explicit standard	No apparent differences
Derecognition of receivables	Section 860-10-40 par. 5	SFAS No. 140 par. 9	IAS 39 par. 20	U.S. GAAP includes a list of three criteria that must be satisfied for derecognition. IFRS has a conceptual two-step test based on risks and rewards and control. In practice, the derecognition result is almost always the same.

KEY TERMS

Accounts receivable 7-3
Accounts receivable turnover 7-16
Aging receivables 7-11
Allowance method 7-8
Average collection period 7-16
Bank reconciliation 7-21
Bank service charge 7-22
Cash 7-18
Cash (sales) discount 7-6

Cash equivalents 7-18
Cash overdraft 7-19
Compensating balances 7-20
Demand deposits 7-18
Deposit in transit 7-22
Direct write-off method 7-8
Net realizable value 7-8
Nontrade receivables 7-5
Notes receivable 7-5
Not-sufficient-funds (NSF) check 7-22

Outstanding checks 7-22
Present value 7-8
Revenue 7-3
Time deposits 7-18
Trade discount 7-6
Trade receivables 7-5
Warranties 7-13

EXPANDED MATERIAL

Accounts receivable factoring 7-28

Assignment of receivables 7-30
Implicit (effective) interest 7-33
Imputed interest rate 7-36
Interest-bearing note 7-33
Negotiable notes 7-33
Non-interest-bearing note 7-33
Principal (face amount) 7-33
Promissory note 7-33
Selling receivables with recourse 7-29

Tutorial Activities

Tutorial Activities with author-written, content-specific feedback, available on *CengageNOW for Stice & Stice*.

QUESTIONS

1. Explain how each of the following factors affects the classification of a receivable: (a) the form of a receivable, (b) the source of a receivable, and (c) the expected time to maturity or collection.
2. (a) Describe the methods for establishing and maintaining an allowance for bad debts account.
   (b) How would the percentages used in estimating uncollectible accounts be determined under each of the methods?
3. In accounting for uncollectible accounts receivable, why does GAAP require the allowance method rather than the direct write-off method?
4. An analysis of the accounts receivable balance of $8,702 on the records of Jorgenson, Inc., on December 31 reveals the following:

Accounts from sales of last three months (appear to be fully collectible)	$7,460
Accounts from sales prior to October 1 (of doubtful value).....................	1,312
Accounts known to be worthless..........	320
Dishonored notes charged back to customers' accounts....................	800
Credit balances in customers' accounts ...	1,190

   (a) What adjustments are required?
   (b) How should the various balances be shown on the balance sheet?
5. Why should a company normally account for product warranties on an accrual basis?
6. (a) How is accounts receivable turnover computed?
   (b) How is average collection period computed?
   (c) What do these two measurements show?
7. Why is cash on hand necessary yet potentially unproductive?
8. The following items were included as cash on the balance sheet for Lawson Co. How should each of the items have been reported?
   (a) Demand deposits with bank
   (b) Restricted cash deposits in foreign banks
   (c) Bank account used for payment of salaries and wages
   (d) Cash in a special cash account to be used currently for the construction of a new building
   (e) Customers' checks returned by the bank marked "Not Sufficient Funds"
   (f) Customers' postdated checks
   (g) IOUs from employees

(h) Postage stamps received in the mail for merchandise
(i) Postal money orders received from customers not yet deposited
(j) Notes receivable in the hands of the bank for collection
(k) Special bank account in which sales tax collections are deposited
(l) Customers' checks not yet deposited

9. Melvin Company shows in its accounts a cash balance of $66,500 with Bank A and an overdraft of $1,500 with Bank B on December 31. Bank B regards the overdraft as, in effect, a loan to Melvin Company and charges interest on the overdraft balance. How would you report the balances with Banks A and B? Would your answer be any different if the overdraft arose as a result of certain checks that had been deposited and proved to be uncollectible and if the overdraft was cleared promptly by Melvin Company at the beginning of January?

10. Mills Manufacturing is required to maintain a compensating balance of $15,000 with its bank to maintain a line of open credit. The compensating balance is legally restricted as to its use. How should the compensating balance be reported on the balance sheet and why?

11. (a) Give at least four common sources of differences between depositor and bank balances.

(b) Which of the differences in (a) require an adjusting entry on the books of the depositor?

EXPANDED MATERIAL

12. How are attitudes regarding the financing of accounts receivable changing? Why do you think this is so?

13. (a) Distinguish between the practices of (1) selling receivables and (2) using receivables as collateral for borrowing.
   (b) Describe the accounting procedures to be followed in each case.

14. Under U.S. GAAP, what three conditions must be met to record the transfer of receivables with recourse as a sale?

15. Describe the two-step test required under the provisions of *IAS 39* to determine whether a receivable should be derecognized.

16. (a) When should a note receivable be recorded at an amount different from its face amount?
   (b) Describe the procedures employed in accounting for the difference between a note's face amount and its recorded value.

17. Explain what special accounting procedures are required when receivables are assigned as collateral for a secured loan.

18. What is meant by *imputing a rate of interest*? How is such a rate determined?

PRACTICE EXERCISES

Practice 7-1

Journal Entries for Sales

The company recorded the following summary journal entries during July.

a. Cash	30,000	
Sales		30,000
b. Cash	8,000	
Accounts Receivable	40,000	
Sales		48,000
c. Inventory	25,000	
Accounts Payable		25,000
d. Cash	33,000	
Accounts Receivable		33,000
e. Accounts Payable	19,000	
Cash		19,000

1. Write a brief description of each of the five transactions represented by the journal entries in (a) through (e).
2. At the beginning of July, the Accounts Receivable balance was $5,000. What is the Accounts Receivable balance at the end of July?

Practice 7-2

Simple Credit Sale Journal Entries
Credit sales for the year were $100,000. Collections on account were $88,000. Make the necessary summary journal entries to record this information.

Practice 7-3

Sales Discounts: Gross Method
On January 16, two credit sales were made, one for $300 and one for $400. Terms for both sales were 3/15, n/30. Cash for the $300 sale was collected on January 25; cash for the $400 sale was collected on February 14. Make all journal entries necessary to record both the sales and the cash collections. Use the gross method of accounting for sales discounts.

Practice 7-4

Sales Discounts: Net Method
Refer to Practice 7-3. Make all journal entries necessary to record both the sales and the cash collections. Use the net method of accounting for sales discounts.

Practice 7-5

Sales Returns and Allowances
On July 15, goods costing $7,000 were sold for $10,000 on account. The customer returned the goods before paying for them. Make the journal entry or entries necessary on the books of the seller to record the return of the goods. Assume that the goods are not damaged and can be resold at their normal selling price. Also assume that the selling company uses a perpetual inventory system.

Practice 7-6

Basic Bad Debt Journal Entries
Bad debt expense for the year was estimated to be $12,000. Total accounts written off as uncollectible during the year were $8,100. Make the necessary summary journal entries to record this information.

Practice 7-7

Recovery of an Account Previously Written Off
Because of the extreme deterioration in the financial condition of a customer, the customer's account in the amount of $7,500 was written off as uncollectible on July 23. By November 1, the customer's financial condition had improved such that the customer was able to pay the account in full. Make the journal entries necessary to write the account off on July 23 and then to record the collection of the account on November 1.

Practice 7-8

Bad Debts: Percentage-of-Sales Method
Bad debt expense is estimated using the percentage-of-sales method. Total sales for the year were $500,000. The ending balance in Accounts Receivable was $100,000. Historically, bad debts have been 3% of total sales. The economic circumstances of credit customers this year are about the same as they have been in past years. Total accounts written off as uncollectible during the year were $13,700. Make the necessary summary journal entries to record this bad debt-related information.

Practice 7-9

Bad Debts: Percentage-of-Accounts-Receivable Method
Bad debt expense is estimated using the percentage-of-accounts-receivable method. Total sales for the year were $600,000. The ending balance in Accounts Receivable was $200,000. An examination of the outstanding accounts at the end of the year indicates that approximately 14% of these accounts will ultimately prove to be uncollectible. Before any adjustment, the balance in Allowance for Bad Debts is $900 (credit). Total accounts written off as uncollectible during the year were $16,600. Make the necessary summary journal entries to record this bad debt-related information.

Practice 7-10

Aging Accounts Receivable
The following aging of accounts receivable is as of the end of the year:

	Overall	Less Than 30 Days	31–60 Days	61–90 Days	Over 90 Days
Ken Nelson	$ 10,000	$ 8,000		$1,000	$1,000
Elaine Anderson	40,000	31,000	$ 4,000		5,000
Bryan Crist	12,000	3,000	4,000	2,000	3,000
Renee Warner	60,000	50,000	10,000		
Nelson Hsia	16,000	10,000	6,000		
Stella Valerio	25,000	20,000		5,000	
Total	$163,000	$122,000	$24,000	$8,000	$9,000

Historical experience indicates the following:

Age of Account	Percentage Ultimately Uncollectible
Less than 30 days	2%
31 to 60 days	10
61 to 90 days	30
Over 90 days	75

Compute the appropriate amount of Allowance for Bad Debts as of the end of the year.

Practice 7-11

Estimation and Recognition of Warranty Expense
Historically, warranty expenditures have been equal to 4% of sales. Total sales for the year were $650,000. Actual warranty repairs made during the year totaled $29,000. Make the necessary summary journal entries to record this warranty-related information.

Practice 7-12

Comparison of Actual and Expected Warranty Expense
The company offers a one-year warranty to its customers. Warranty expenditures are estimated to be 4% of sales. Sales occur evenly throughout the year. The following information relates to the company's first two years of business:

Sales—Year 1	$100,000
Actual warranty repairs—Year 1	3,000
Sales—Year 2	$150,000
Actual warranty repairs—Year 2	6,500

(1) Compute the balance in the warranty liability account at the end of Year 2. (2) Evaluate whether that balance is too high or too low given the company's experience.

Practice 7-13

Average Collection Period
Sales for the year were $400,000. The Accounts Receivable balance was $50,000 at the beginning of the year and $65,000 at the end of the year. Compute the average collection period using (1) the average accounts receivable balance and (2) the ending accounts receivable balance.

Practice 7-14

Computation of Cash Balance
Using the following information, compute the cash balance.

Restricted deposits in foreign bank accounts	$ 5,200
Cash overdraft	(1,000)
Postdated customer checks	750
Savings account balance	10,000
Coin and currency	2,300

Practice 7-15

Bank Reconciliation
The company received a bank statement at the end of the month. The statement contained the following:

Ending balance	$9,500
Bank service charge for the month	65
Interest earned and added by the bank to the account balance	45

In comparing the bank statement to its own cash records, the company found the following:

Deposits made but not yet recorded by the bank	$2,700
Checks written and mailed but not yet recorded by the bank	3,900

Before making any adjustment suggested by the bank statement, the cash balance according to the books is $8,320. What is the correct cash balance as of the end of the month? Verify this amount by reconciling the bank statement with the cash balance on the books.

E X P A N D E D   M A T E R I A L

Practice 7-16
Sale of Receivables without Recourse
Cammo Company sold receivables (without recourse) for $53,000. Cammo received $50,000 cash immediately from the factor (the company to whom the receivables were sold). The remaining $3,000 will be received once the factor verifies that none of the receivables is in dispute. The receivables had a face amount of $60,000; Cammo had previously established an Allowance for Bad Debts of $2,500 in connection with these receivables. Make the journal entry necessary on Cammo's books to record the sale of these receivables.

Practice 7-17
Sale of Receivables with Recourse
Refer to Practice 7-16. Assume that the sale of the receivables was done *with* recourse. The estimated value of the recourse obligation is $1,300. Make the journal entry necessary on Cammo's books to record the sale of these receivables with recourse.

Practice 7-18
Accounting for a Secured Borrowing
Refer to Practice 7-16. Assume that Cammo received the entire $53,000 in cash immediately. Also assume that the transfer of receivables did *not* satisfy the three conditions contained in FASB ASC paragraph 860-10-40-5. Make the journal entry necessary on Cammo's books to record the transfer of these receivables.

Practice 7-19
Journal Entries for Interest-Bearing Note
As payment for services rendered, the company received an 18-month note on January 1. The face amount of the note is $3,000, and the stated rate of interest is 9%, compounded annually. The 9% rate is equal to the market rate. The full amount of the note, including accrued interest, will be received at the end of the 18-month period. Make *all* journal entries necessary on the books of the recipient of the note during the 18-month life of this note. Don't forget any necessary year-end adjusting entry.

Practice 7-20
Journal Entries for Non-Interest-Bearing Note
As payment for services rendered, the company received a 24-month note on January 1. The face amount of the note is $1,000; the note is non-interest-bearing. The cash price of the services rendered is $857. The market rate of interest is 8%, compounded annually. The $1,000 face amount of the note will be received at the end of the 24-month period. Make *all* journal entries necessary on the books of the recipient of the note during the 24-month life of this note. Don't forget any necessary year-end adjusting entry. The cash will be received on December 31 of the second year.

Practice 7-21
Note Exchanged for Goods or Services
In exchange for land, the company received a 12-month note on January 1. The face amount of the note is $2,000, and the stated rate of interest is 12%, compounded annually. The 12% rate is equal to the market rate. The original cost of the land was $2,450. The full amount of the note, including accrued interest, will be received at the end of the 12-month period, on December 31. Make *all* journal entries necessary on the books of the recipient of the note during the 12-month life of this note.

Practice 7-22
Effective Interest Amortization Method
As payment for services rendered, the company received a 36-month note on January 1. The face amount of the note is $1,000; the note is non-interest-bearing. There is no reasonable basis for determining the cash price of the services rendered. The market rate of interest is 10%, compounded annually. The $1,000 face amount of the note will be received at the end of the 36-month period. Make *all* journal entries necessary

on the books of the recipient of the note during the 36-month life of this note. Don't forget any necessary year-end adjusting entries.

Practice 7-23

Bad Debts and the Direct Method

	Ending Balances	Beginning Balances
Accounts receivable..	$ 9,500	$13,000
Allowance for bad debts	3,100	3,000
Sales for the year..	75,000	
Net income for the year..	20,000	
Bad debt expense for the year	2,000	
Write-off of uncollectible amounts for the year.......................	1,900	
Cash expenses for the year...	53,000	

Prepare the Operating Activities section of the statement of cash flows using the direct method.

Practice 7-24

Bad Debts and the Indirect Method
Refer to Practice 7-23. Prepare the Operating Activities section of the statement of cash flows using the indirect method.

EXERCISES

Exercise 7-25

Classifying Receivables
Classify each of the following items as: (A) Accounts Receivable, (B) Notes Receivable, (C) Trade Receivables, (D) Nontrade Receivables, or (E) Other (indicate nature of item). Because the classifications are not mutually exclusive, more than one classification may be appropriate. Also indicate whether the item would normally be reported as a current or noncurrent asset assuming a six-month operating cycle.

1. **MasterCard** or **VISA** credit card sale of merchandise to customer
2. Overpayment to supplier for inventory purchased on account
3. Insurance claim on automobile accident
4. Charge sale to regular customer
5. Advance to sales manager
6. Interest due on five-year note from company president, interest payable annually
7. Acceptance of three-year note on sale of land held as investment
8. Acceptance of six-month note for past-due account arising from the sale of inventory
9. Claim for a tax refund from last year
10. Prepaid insurance—four months remaining in the policy period
11. Overpayment by customer of an account receivable

Exercise 7-26

Computing the Accounts Receivable Balance
The following information from Tiny Company's first year of operations is to be used in testing the accuracy of Accounts Receivable. The December 31, 2015, balance is $28,300.

(a) Collections from customers, $48,000
(b) Merchandise purchased, $74,000
(c) Ending merchandise inventory, $31,500

(d) Goods sell at 60% above cost
(e) All sales on account

Compute the balance that Accounts Receivable should show and determine the amount of any shortage or overage.

Exercise 7-27

Sales Discounts

On November 1, Rosario Company sold goods on account for $7,000. The terms of the sale were 3/10, n/40, allowing sales discounts to be taken against partial payments. Payment in satisfaction of $3,000 of this amount was received on November 9. Payment in satisfaction of the remaining $4,000 was received on December 9.

1. How much cash did Rosario Company collect from this $7,000 account?
2. Using the gross method, what journal entries would Rosario make on November 9 and December 9?
3. Using the net method, what journal entries would Rosario make on November 9 and December 9?

Exercise 7-28

Sales Returns

On July 23, Louie Company sold goods costing $3,000 on account for $4,500. The terms of the sale were n/30. Payment in satisfaction of $3,000 of this amount was received on August 17. Also on August 17, the customer returned goods costing $1,000 (with a sales price of $1,500). The customer reported that the goods did not meet the required specifications.

1. Make the journal entry necessary on July 23 to record the sale. Louie uses a perpetual inventory system.
2. Make the journal entry necessary on August 17 to record the cash collection.
3. Make the journal entry necessary on August 17 to record the return of the goods.
4. What question exists with respect to the valuation of the returned inventory?

Exercise 7-29

Estimating Bad Debts

Accounts Receivable of the Chalet Housing Co. on December 31, 2015, had a balance of $550,000. Allowance for Bad Debts had a $4,500 debit balance. Sales in 2015 were $3,450,000 less sales discounts of $51,000. Give the adjusting entry for estimated Bad Debt Expense under each of the following independent assumptions.

1. Of 2015 net sales, 1.5% will probably never be collected.
2. Of outstanding accounts receivable, 8% are doubtful.
3. An aging schedule shows that $41,000 of the outstanding accounts receivable are doubtful.

Exercise 7-30

Journal Entries for Receivable Write-Offs

McGraw Medical Center has received a bankruptcy notice for Phillip Hollister. Hollister owes the medical center $1,350. The bankruptcy notice indicates that the medical center can't expect to receive payment of any of the $1,350.

1. Make the journal entry necessitated by receipt of the bankruptcy notice.
2. Six months after the medical center received the bankruptcy notice, Hollister appeared requesting medical treatment. He agreed to pay his old bill in its entirety. Make the journal entry or entries necessary to record receipt of the $1,350 payment from Hollister.

Exercise 7-31

Aging Accounts Receivable

Blanchard Company's accounts receivable subsidiary ledger reveals the following information:

Customer	Account Balance Dec. 31, 2015	Invoice Amounts and Dates	
Allison, Inc.	$ 8,795	$3,500	12/6/2015
		5,295	11/29/2015
Banks Bros.	5,230	3,000	9/27/2015
		2,230	8/20/2015
Barker & Co.	7,650	5,000	12/8/2015
		2,650	10/25/2015
Marrin Co.	11,285	5,785	11/17/2015
		5,500	10/9/2015
Ring, Inc.	7,900	4,800	12/12/2015
		3,100	12/2/2015
West Corp.	4,350	4,350	9/12/2015

Blanchard Company's receivable collection experience indicates that, on average, losses have occurred as follows:

Age of Accounts	Uncollectible Percentage
0–30 days	0.7%
31–60 days	1.4
61–90 days	3.5
91–120 days	10.2
Over 120 days	60.0

The Allowance for Bad Debts credit balance on December 31, 2015, was $2,245 before adjustment.

1. Prepare an accounts receivable aging schedule.
2. Using the aging schedule from (1), compute the Allowance for Bad Debts balance as of December 31, 2015.
3. Prepare the end-of-year adjusting entry.
4. (a) Where accounts receivable are few in number, such as in this exercise, what are some possible weaknesses in estimating bad debts by the aging method?
   (b) Would the other methods of estimating bad debts be subject to these same weaknesses? Explain.

Exercise 7-32

Analysis of Allowance for Bad Debts

The Intercontinental Publishing Company follows the procedure of debiting Bad Debt Expense for 2% of all new sales. Sales for four consecutive years and year-end allowance account balances were as follows:

Year	Sales	Allowance for Bad Debts End-of-Year Credit Balance
2012	$1,500,000	$22,300
2013	1,425,000	30,800
2014	1,800,000	41,400
2015	1,970,000	61,500

1. Compute the amount of accounts written off for the years 2013, 2014, and 2015.
2. The external auditors are concerned with the growing amount in the allowance account. What action do you recommend the auditors take?

Exercise 7-33

Warranty Liability

In 2014, Carver Electronics Co. began selling a new computer that carried a two-year warranty against defects. Based on the manufacturer's recommendations, Carver projects estimated warranty costs (as a percentage of dollar sales) as follows:

First year of warranty	4%
Second year of warranty	7%

Sales and actual warranty repairs for 2014 and 2015 are as follows.

	2015	2014
Sales	$850,000	$700,000
Actual warranty repairs	30,750	18,500

1. Give the necessary journal entries to record the liability at the end of 2014 and 2015, assuming that there were no collections of previously reserved balances.
2. Analyze the warranty liability account as of the year ended December 31, 2015, to see if the actual repairs approximate the estimate. Should Carver revise the manufacturer's warranty estimate? (Assume sales and repairs occur evenly throughout the year.)

Exercise 7-34

Extended Service Contract

Hitech Appliance Company's accountant has been reviewing the firm's past television sales. For the past two years, Hitech has been offering an extended service contract on all televisions sold. With the purchase of a television, the customer has the right to purchase a three-year service contract for an extra $75. Information concerning past television and warranty contract sales follows.

Plasma-All Model II Television	2015	2014
Television sales in units	700	590
Sales price per unit	$900	$800
Number of service contracts sold	420	380
Expenses relating to television warranties	$8,250	$4,240

Hitech's accountant has estimated from past records that the pattern of repairs has been 32% in the first year after sale, 40% in the second year, and 28% in the third year. Give the necessary journal entries related to the service contracts for 2014 and 2015. In addition, indicate how much profit on service contracts would be recognized in 2015. Assume sales of the contracts are made evenly during the year and that the company recognizes revenue based on estimated annual exposure as a percentage of total exposure.

Exercise 7-35

Analyzing Accounts Receivable

Trend Industries Company reported the following amounts on its 2014 and 2015 financial statements:

	2015	2014
Accounts receivable	$ 235,000	$ 210,000
Allowance for bad debts	12,000	8,000
Net sales	2,145,000	1,890,000
Cost of sales	1,067,000	856,000

1. Compute the accounts receivable turnover for 2015.
2. What is the average collection period during 2015? (Use 365 days.)

Exercise 7-36

Reporting Cash on the Balance Sheet

1. Indicate how each of the items below should be reported using the following classifications: (a) cash, (b) restricted cash, (c) temporary investment, (d) receivable, (e) liability, or (f) office supplies.

(1)	Checking account at First Security	$ (20)
(2)	Checking account at Second Security	350
(3)	U.S. t-bills	650
(4)	Payroll bank account	100
(5)	Sales tax bank account	150
(6)	Foreign bank account—restricted (in equivalent U.S. dollars)	750
(7)	Postage stamps	22
(8)	Employee's postdated check	30
(9)	IOU from president's brother	75
(10)	Credit memo from a vendor for a purchase return	87
(11)	Traveler's check	50
(12)	NSF check	18
(13)	Petty cash fund ($16 in currency and expense receipts for $84)	100
(14)	Money order	36

2. What amount would be reported as unrestricted cash on the balance sheet?

Exercise 7-37

Restricted Cash

Baltic Group, Inc., operates Baltic Group resorts in the United States, Mexico, the Caribbean, Asia, the South Pacific, and the Indian Ocean Basin. Baltic Group routinely receives payment in advance from vacationers. In some countries, Baltic Group is required by law to deposit cash received as payment for future vacations in special accounts. Cash in these accounts is restricted as to its use.

Assume that on December 31, Baltic Group received cash totaling $7,450,000 as payment in advance for vacations at one of its resorts. The resort is in a country that requires that the cash be deposited in a special account.

1. Prepare the journal entry necessary to record receipt of the $7,450,000.
2. Explain how the $7,450,000 would be disclosed in the December 31 balance sheet.

Exercise 7-38

Composition of Cash

Ortiz Company had the following cash balances at December 31, 2015:

Undeposited coin and currency	$ 29,500
Unrestricted demand deposits	1,375,000
Company checks written (and deducted from the demand deposits amount) but not scheduled to be mailed until January 2	265,000
Time deposits restricted for use (expected use in 2016)	2,500,000

In exchange for a guaranteed line of credit, Ortiz has agreed to maintain a minimum balance of $225,000 in its unrestricted demand deposits account. How much should Ortiz report as Cash in its December 31, 2015, balance sheet?

Exercise 7-39

Correct Cash Balance

Sterling Company's bank statement for the month of March included the following information:

Ending balance, March 31	$28,046
Bank service charge for March	130
Interest paid by bank to Sterling for March	107

In comparing the bank statement to its own cash records, Sterling found the following:

Deposits made but not yet recorded by the bank $3,689

Checks written and mailed but not yet recorded by the bank 6,530

In addition, Sterling discovered that it had erroneously recorded a check for $46 that should have been recorded for $64. What is Sterling's correct Cash balance at March 31?

Exercise 7-40

Correct Cash Balance

Lewiston Corporation's bank statement for the month of April included the following information:

Bank service charge for April $110

Check deposited by Lewiston during April was not collectible
and has been marked "NSF" by the bank and returned 350

In comparing the bank statement to its own cash records, Lewiston found:

Deposits made but not yet recorded by the bank $1,674

Checks written and mailed but not yet recorded by the bank 677

All the deposits in transit and outstanding checks have been properly recorded in Lewiston's books. Lewiston also found a check for $275, payable to Lewiston Corporation, that had not yet been deposited and had not been recorded in Lewiston's books. Lewiston's books show a bank account balance of $7,842 (before any adjustments or corrections). What is Lewiston Corporation's correct Cash balance at April 30?

Exercise 7-41

Bank Reconciliation and Adjusting Entries

The accounting department supplied the following data in reconciling the September 30 bank statement for Clegg Auto.

Ending cash balance per bank $18,972.67

Ending cash balance per books 16,697.76

Deposits in transit... 3,251.42

Bank service charge... 20.00

Outstanding checks.. 4,163.51

Note collected by bank including $50 interest (Clegg not yet notified) 2,150.00

Error by bank—check drawn by Gregg Corp. was charged to Clegg's account............ 713.18

A sale and deposit of $1,628.00 were entered in the sales journal and cash receipts journal as $1,682.00.

1. Prepare the September 30 bank reconciliation.
2. Give the journal entries required on the books to adjust the cash account.

Exercise 7-42

REVERSE SOLVABLE

Bank Reconciliation—Analysis of Outstanding Checks

The following information was included in the bank reconciliation for Bryant, Inc., for June. What was the total of outstanding checks at the beginning of June? Assume all other reconciling items are listed.

Checks and charges recorded by bank in June, including a June service charge of $35 ...... $16,320

Service charge made by bank in May and recorded on the books in June 30

Total of credits to Cash in all journals during June... 21,705

Customer's NSF check returned as a bank charge in June (no entry made on books) 200

Customer's NSF check returned in May and redeposited in June
   (no entry made on books in either May or June)... 275

Outstanding checks at June 30.. 11,470

Deposits in transit at June 30... 500

EXPANDED MATERIAL

Exercise 7-43

Accounting for the Sale of Accounts Receivable

On July 15, Mann Company sold $600,000 in accounts receivable for cash of $500,000. The factor withheld 10% of the cash proceeds to allow for possible customer returns or account adjustments. An Allowance for Bad Debts of $80,000 had previously been established by Mann in relation to these accounts.

1. Make the journal entry necessary on Mann's books to record the sale of the accounts.
2. Make the journal entry necessary on Mann's books to record final settlement of the factoring arrangement. No customer returns or account adjustments occurred in relation to the accounts.

Exercise 7-44

Accounting for a Non-Interest-Bearing Note

Zobell Corporation sells equipment with a book value of $8,000, receiving a non-interest-bearing note due in three years with a face amount of $10,000. There is no established market value for the equipment. The interest rate on similar obligations is estimated at 12%. Compute the gain or loss on the sale and the discount on notes receivable, and make the necessary entry to record the sale. Also, make the entries to record the amortization of the discount at the end of the first, second, and third year using effective-interest amortization. (Round to the nearest dollar.)

Exercise 7-45

Accounting for an Interest-Bearing Note

Abacus, Inc., purchased inventory costing $95,000. Terms of the purchase were 3/10, n/30. Abacus uses a perpetual inventory system. In order to take advantage of the cash discount, Abacus borrowed $75,000 from Commercial First Bank, signing a two-month, 8% note. The bank requires monthly interest payments. Make the entries to record the following:

1. Initial purchase of inventory on account
2. Payment to the supplier within the discount period
3. Loan from the bank
4. First month's payment to the bank
5. Second and final payment to the bank

Exercise 7-46

Receivables and the Statement of Cash Flows

The following selected information is provided for Lynez Company. All sales are credit sales and all receivables are trade receivables.

Accounts receivable, January 1 net balance	$125,000
Accounts receivable, December 31 net balance	165,000
Sales for the year	800,000
Uncollectible accounts written off during the year	14,000
Bad debt expense for the year	24,000
Cash expenses for the year	681,000
Net income for the year	95,000

Using the format illustrated in the chapter and the preceding information, answer the following questions:

1. Using the *direct* method, what is the net cash flow from operations that Lynez Company would report in its statement of cash flows?
2. Assuming the use of the *indirect* method, what adjustments to net income would be required in reporting net cash flow from operations?

P2
Routine Activities of a Business

CHAPTER 8

Revenue Recognition

Learning Objectives

1. Identify the primary criteria for revenue recognition.
2. Discuss the revenue recognition issues, and abuses, underlying the examples used in *SAB 101*.
3. Describe the contract approach to revenue recognition that is currently being considered by the FASB and IASB.
4. Record journal entries for long-term construction-type contracts using percentage-of-completion and completed-contract methods.
5. Record journal entries for long-term service contracts using the proportional performance method.
6. Explain when revenue is recognized after delivery of goods or services through installment sales, cost recovery, and cash methods.

The rise and fall of MicroStrategy encapsulates the boom and bust, sprinkled with accounting scandal, associated with the high-tech economy from 1998 through 2002. At its peak, MicroStrategy was worth $31.1 billion and was trading at a price-to-sales ratio of 152 and a price-to-earnings ratio of 2,220. But in a sell-off precipitated by a revenue-related accounting restatement, the shares reached a low of $0.45 on July 26, 2002, down from their peak of $333.00 on March 10, 2000 (a 99.9% drop). In the wake of this price collapse, MicroStrategy's CEO was fined by the SEC, and the company's auditor was sued by outraged investors. An outline of MicroStrategy's rise and fall follows.

Many people have described MicroStrategy's CEO Michael Saylor as the smartest person they know.[1] He grew up outside Dayton, Ohio, the son of an Air Force sergeant, and entered MIT on an ROTC scholarship, intending to become an Air Force pilot. While at MIT, Saylor developed skills in computer simulation, and he wrote his undergraduate thesis using a computer

---

[1] Mark Leibovich, "MicroStrategy's CEO Sped to the Brink," *The Washington Post*, January 6, 2002, p. A01. This article was the first in a four-part series by Mr. Leibovich that ran January 6–9, 2002, in *The Washington Post*. All four articles serve as source material for this brief history of MicroStrategy.

simulation to model the reactions of different types of government systems to catastrophes such as wars or epidemics. Since a heart murmur had cut short his chances of becoming a pilot, Saylor became a computer modeler for DuPont.

In 1989, Saylor started his own computer modeling business, called MicroStrategy, in partnership with his MIT roommate, Sanju Bansal. The foundation of MicroStrategy's product line has been its corporate data mining program. The program combs through terabytes of data in an unwieldy corporate database, looking for interesting relationships. For example, MicroStrategy customers McDonald's and Wal-Mart could use the program to detect customer buying trends on, say, Monday afternoons in the summer in California compared to Texas to help in targeting local marketing efforts. This data mining program was very successful, and MicroStrategy doubled its revenues each year from 1994 through 1998, growing from 1994 revenues of $4.98 million to 1998 revenues of $106.43 million. The company went public on June 11, 1998, with the shares opening at $12 per share and ending the first day of trading at $21 per share.

In early 1999, MicroStrategy was a solid software company with an impressive record of revenue and profit growth. However, the company's price-to-sales ratio was just 12, compared to ratios routinely more than 100 for dot.com companies. This was because MicroStrategy was not benefiting from any of the "Internet halo" that seemed to surround all companies that were in any way affiliated with the Web in those days. And Michael Saylor had a vision of making his company much more than a software company. This vision is captured in the company motto: "Information like water." Saylor wanted to place the power of the data mining software that MicroStrategy provided to corporations into the hands of individuals. Accordingly, in July 1999 MicroStrategy launched Strategy.com, which promised to make personalized information available to individuals by email, through the Web, and by wireless phone. Subscribers could receive tailored messages about finance, news, weather, sports, and traffic, and that was just the beginning. By the end of 1999, Strategy.com had not yet generated a single dollar of revenue for MicroStrategy, but the initiative had brought the aura of the Internet to the valuation of MicroStrategy's stock, causing the price-to-sales ratio to increase from 12 to 150. In January 2000, while all 1,600 MicroStrategy employees were on a company cruise in the Cayman Islands, the company's stock increased in value by 19% on one day, and Michael Saylor's holdings alone increased in value by $1 billion. "We should go on cruises more often," joked Saylor.

A price-to-sales ratio of 150 means that investors expect substantial sales growth (and ultimately substantial profit and cash flow growth) in the future. It also means that any stumbling on the part of the company can result in a catastrophic drop in stock price. For example, if a company has a market value of $30 billion with a price-to-sales ratio of 150, like MicroStrategy in early 2000, then negative news about the future that causes the price-to-sales ratio to drop to a lower but still respectable level of, say, 6 (which was the price-to-sales ratio for Coca-Cola in early 2000) would cause the company's stock price to drop 96% to $1.2 billion. This type of precarious valuation puts huge pressure on managers to continue to report revenue growth that meets or exceeds the market's expectation. In the face of this pressure, MicroStrategy, like many firms before and many since, broke the accounting rules governing when sales can be reported.

On March 12, 2000, MicroStrategy's chief financial officer (CFO) received a call from the partner in charge of the company's audit. The audit firm, PricewaterhouseCoopers (PwC), had been reviewing MicroStrategy's revenue recognition practices and believed that a restatement was necessary. This investigation had been initiated in part in response to a March 6, 2000, *Forbes* article by reporter David Raymond questioning MicroStrategy's reporting of sales.[2] MicroStrategy's board of directors was reluctant to restate revenue because preliminary revenue numbers for 1999 had already been announced, helping to drive the company's stock price to its all-time high. However, with the board finally convinced of the necessity, a press release was drafted explaining that MicroStrategy was lowering its 1999 revenues from the previously announced $205 million to between $150 and $155 million. The news announcement was issued at 8:06 a.m. on Monday, March 20, 2000. MicroStrategy's stock opened the day trading at $226.75 per share; by the end of the day, the shares had dropped 62% to $86.75 per share.

Subsequent SEC investigation confirmed that MicroStrategy had overstated its revenue, and the inquiry uncovered a number of questionable practices.[3] Two samples are given below.

- Contract signing. *The final report on MicroStrategy from the SEC included the following: "To maintain maximum flexibility to achieve the desired quarterly financial results, MicroStrategy held, until after the close of the quarter, contracts that had been signed by customers but had not yet been signed by MicroStrategy. Only after MicroStrategy determined the desired financial results were the unsigned contracts apportioned, between the just-ended quarter and the then-current quarter, signed and given an 'effective date.' In some instances, the contracts were signed without affixing a date, allowing the company further flexibility to assign a date at a later time."*

- The NCR deal. *On October 4, 1999, MicroStrategy announced that it had sold software and services to NCR for $27.5 million under a multiyear licensing agreement. Although the deal was announced four days after the end of the third quarter and although the licensing agreement extended for several years, MicroStrategy recognized over half the amount as revenue immediately (and perhaps retroactively) and added $17.5 million to third quarter revenue. Without this $17.5 million in revenue, MicroStrategy's*

---

[2] David S. Raymond, "MicroStrategy's Curious Success," *Forbes*, March 6, 2000.
[3] Securities and Exchange Commission, *Accounting and Auditing Enforcement Release No. 1350*, Administrative Proceeding File No. 3-10388: In the Matter of MicroStrategy, Inc., December 14, 2000.

reported revenue for the third quarter would have been down 20% from the quarter before. The reported profit for the quarter would have instead been a loss. And perhaps worst of all, MicroStrategy would have fallen well short of analysts' expectations, sending the stock price spiraling downward. As it was, MicroStrategy's stock price soared 72% during the month of October 1999.

The aftermath of the MicroStrategy meltdown was bad for all of the principal characters involved. Michael Saylor was judged by the SEC to have committed fraud. He paid a fine of $350,000 and was required to forfeit an additional $8.3 million in gains from stock sales. As of March 10, 2010, his stake in MicroStrategy was worth just $238 million, down from $14 billion at his company's pinnacle. In May 2001, PricewaterhouseCoopers agreed to pay $55 million to settle a class-action lawsuit brought by MicroStrategy shareholders who accused the audit firm of negligence in allowing MicroStrategy's financial reporting to go uncorrected for so long. And in August 2003, the SEC announced that it had settled a suit with the PwC partner in charge of the MicroStrategy audit, with the partner agreeing to be barred from auditing public clients. MicroStrategy itself is slowly recovering from the bursting of its revenue bubble. The company reported losses in three of the four years from 2000 through 2003, but the company has reported positive net income in each year from 2004 through 2011. And as of October 2012, the company's price-to-sales ratio was 2.29, up from its low point of just 0.25 in the wake of the revenue recognition scandal, but still a far cry from its pre-scandal peak of 152.

1. Why do you think the price-to-sales ratio (as opposed to the price-earnings ratio) is often used in valuing the stocks of start-up technology companies, especially those related to the Internet?

2. On Monday, March 20, 2000, MicroStrategy issued a press release stating that revenues for the year 1999 were about $155 million, not $205 million as previously announced. This represented a drop of 24% in reported revenue. Why did a drop of just 24% in reported revenue result in a stock price drop of 62%? In other words, why wasn't the drop in stock price also 24%?

3. In early March 2000, MicroStrategy's board of directors received word that the company's auditor was requesting a revenue restatement. The board was reluctant to go forward with the restatement because of fears (justified, as it turns out) that the restatement would hurt the company's stock price. List and explain two or three arguments that you, as a member of the board, could have made in support of the restatement.

Answers to these questions can be found on pages 8-34–8-35.

In the MicroStrategy case, both the boom and the bust are tied to the accounting rules for revenue recognition. With high-growth companies boasting price-to-sales ratios of 150 or higher, a delay in reporting revenue from a $10 million contract can easily lead to losses in market value in excess of $1 billion. Because so much rides on how much revenue a company reports, many companies have succumbed to the temptation to either manage reported revenue or to commit outright fraud in boosting reported revenue. Because of the large number of revenue recognition abuses in the 1990s, many involving technology companies such as MicroStrategy, the SEC released *Staff Accounting Bulletin (SAB) No. 101*, "Revenue Recognition in Financial Statements," in December 1999. *SAB 101* was one of the most influential, and controversial, accounting pronouncements in the last 20 years. Following the release of *SAB 101*, the FASB, in cooperation with the IASB, has undertaken a comprehensive examination of the accounting standards related to revenue recognition. As investors struggle to guide their investment capital to its most valuable use in the uncertain, high-tech business playing field, reliable financial reporting with respect to revenue recognition is critical.

This chapter will proceed as follows. The first section includes a review of the general principles associated with revenue recognition. The next section uses selected components of *SAB 101* to provide illustrations of the difficult revenue recognition issues that can arise through a combination of complex business transactions and aggressive, or desperate, managers who are trying to meet revenue targets. The following section outlines the revised revenue recognition provisions developed in recent years by the FASB and IASB. The concluding sections cover specific revenue recognition practices and illustrate the percentage-of-completion, proportional performance, and installment sales methods of accounting.

Revenue Recognition

LO1 Identify the primary criteria for revenue recognition.

学习目标1
识别收入确认的主要原则。

Recognition refers to the time when transactions are recorded on the books. The FASB's two criteria for recognizing revenues and gains, articulated in FASB *Concepts Statement No. 5*, were identified in Chapter 4 and are repeated here for emphasis. Revenues and gains are generally recognized when:

1. They are realized or realizable.
2. They have been earned through substantial completion of the activities involved in the earnings process.

Both of these criteria generally are met at the point of sale, which most often occurs when goods are delivered or when services are rendered to customers. Usually, assets and revenues are recognized concurrently. Thus, a sale of inventory results in an increase in Cash or Accounts Receivable and an increase in Sales Revenue. However, assets are sometimes received before these revenue recognition criteria are met. For example, if a client pays for consulting services in advance, an asset, Cash, is recorded on the books even though revenue has not been earned. In these cases, a liability, Unearned Revenue, is recorded. When the revenue recognition criteria are fully met, revenue is recognized and the liability account is reduced.

销售收入确认的条件：
（1）顾客已付款或承诺付款；
（2）公司已提供产品或服务。
如果顾客提供有效的付款承诺并且根据合同保证随后销售的条件存在，则可以在销售之前确认收入；如果顾客在收到产品或服务后不提供有效的付款承诺或有重要的合同未完成事项，则应该在销售之后确认收入。

In general, revenue is not recognized prior to the point of sale because either (1) a valid promise of payment has not been received from the customer or (2) the company has not provided the product or service. An exception occurs when the customer provides a valid promise of payment and conditions exist that contractually guarantee the sale. The most common example of this exception occurs in the case of long-term contracts where the two parties involved are legally obligated to fulfill the terms of the contract. In this case, revenue (or at least a portion of the total contract price) may be recognized prior to the point of final sale.

Another exception to the general rule occurs when either of the two revenue recognition criteria is not satisfied at the point of sale. In some cases, a product or service may be provided to the customer without receiving a valid promise of payment. In these instances, revenue is not recognized until payment or the valid promise is received. Now you are saying to yourself, "Why would anyone provide a product or service to a customer without receiving a valid promise of payment?" A common example is a family doctor

FYI

"Realized" or "realizable" can be interpreted as having received cash or other assets or a valid promise of cash or other assets to be received at some future time.

> **FYI**
>
> The notes to **Walt Disney**'s financial statements provide an example of how one firm might have several different revenue recognition policies, depending on what is being sold.

who frequently provides treatment first and then tries to collect payment later.[4] Also, if a customer provides payment yet substantial services must still be provided by the company, then the recognition of revenue must be postponed until those services are provided. In any case, if both of the two revenue recognition criteria are met prior to the point of sale, revenue may be recognized. If either of the two criteria is not met at the point of sale, then the recognition of revenue must wait.

Although the point-of-sale rule has dominated the practice of revenue recognition, there have been notable variations to this rule. In fact, cases in which revenue should be recognized after the point of sale have proved to be very controversial. As illustrated in the MicroStrategy scenario at the beginning of the chapter, pressure to meet market and analyst revenue expectations has made companies, especially startup companies, reluctant to defer the recognition of revenue past the point of sale.

In addition, the timing of revenue recognition has become more complicated as business arrangements have become more complex. Companies frequently enter into multi-faceted transactions that specify one overall transaction price but require delivery of several different elements of value to the customer. For example, a technology services company may sign a contract, with one single overall price, with a customer to provide hardware, software, installation, service, and off-site data backup for two years. Accounting for these transactions involving "multiple deliverables" is a focus of much study and debate by both the FASB and the IASB. Multiple-deliverable arrangements will be discussed in detail later in the chapter.

Because every income statement begins with total revenue, the measurement of revenue is fundamental to the practice of accrual accounting. As you can imagine, the topic of revenue recognition has been studied very thoroughly through the years. However, from about 1995 through 2005, rapid innovations in business practices, especially involving transactions associated with technology, outstripped the FASB's ability keep up in the area of revenue recognition. In other words, the FASB's thorough and open standard-setting process was just not fast enough to address the revenue recognition abuses and deceptions that were being created seemingly on a daily basis. But the SEC, tasked with making sure investors have full and fair information on which to make informed investment decisions, was alarmed at the increasingly cavalier revenue recognition practices in the late 1990s, especially by high-tech companies. As a result, in 1999, the SEC became impatient with the FASB's slow process and made a preemptive strike, issuing a nuts-and-bolts revenue recognition document, *SAB 101*, based on the real-world cases they were seeing every day.

From this discussion, you should get the sense that the FASB had temporarily lost the lead in establishing the concepts and standards that define appropriate revenue recognition. This was a troubling development because other bodies such as the SEC tend to approach accounting standards from a practical, problem-solving viewpoint as compared to the conceptual approach preferred by the FASB. The problem-solving viewpoint is great for quick action, but it results in a set of standards that has no unifying conceptual underpinning. The FASB's approach, although sometimes excruciatingly slow, gives more predictability and logical structure to accounting standards. The FASB is currently (October 2012) engaged in a revenue recognition project in conjunction with the IASB. The FASB has decided to emphasize the measurement of a seller's satisfaction of performance obligations created through contracts with its customers. This new revenue recognition approach proposed by the FASB will be described later in the chapter.

---

[4] Anyone who has visited a doctor recently can attest to the fact that most medical personnel now do all they can to secure payment or a valid promise (generally through insurance) prior to providing the service. They have learned the hard way.

SAB 101

LO2 学习目标2
基于SAB 101中使用的例子运用收入确认概念。

2 Discuss the revenue recognition issues, and abuses, underlying the examples used in *SAB 101*.

SAB 101 is a very interesting document. It is in a question-and-answer format. Most of the questions follow the pattern: "May a company recognize revenue in the following situation?" The answers given in *SAB 101* are invariably "No." *SAB 101* arose in response to specific abuses seen by the SEC staff. As illustrated with the MicroStrategy scenario at the beginning of the chapter, these abuses were often driven by the desire of high-flying companies to maintain their aura of invincibility by continuing to report astronomical revenue growth each quarter.

Because *SAB 101* was released to curtail specific abuses, it should not be seen as a comprehensive treatise on the entire area of revenue recognition. Remember that the vast majority of companies apply the revenue recognition criteria in a very straightforward way with no questions from their auditor, the SEC, or investors. But it is precisely in the financial reporting of high-growth, start-up companies doing innovative transactions where reliable and transparent accounting practices add greatest value. Thus, the revenue recognition issues covered in *SAB 101* may not be comprehensive, but they are extremely important.

The release by the SEC of *SAB 101* caused quite a stir in the accounting community. *SAB 101* deals with a fundamental accounting topic (revenue recognition), is blunt in its provisions, and was released without the years of discussion and lobbying typically involved in the release of an FASB statement. As a result, *SAB 101* was like a bomb going off. In the aftermath of this bomb, the FASB has undertaken a comprehensive review of the topic of revenue recognition, as mentioned above. The discussion below presents a sample of the practical revenue recognition problems and abuses that caused the SEC to release *SAB 101*. Through new revenue recognition guidance, the FASB subsequently has addressed many of the points of concern raised in *SAB 101*. However, it is informative, and historically interesting, to see the kind of revenue recognition mess that existed near the turn of the millennium.

> **FYI**
>
> When the SEC releases accounting guidance, it is in response to an immediate need to safeguard investors from what the SEC views as faulty, and perhaps deceptive, financial reporting practices. In these cases, the SEC sometimes grows impatient with the long deliberative process that the FASB follows before releasing a standard.

SAB 101, Question 1

The best evidence of a sale is that the seller and buyer have concluded a routine, arm's-length agreement that is conducted entirely according to the normal business practices of both the seller and the buyer. Question number 1 in *SAB 101* highlights areas in which a seller might bend the revenue recognition rules to strategically time the reporting of a sale. Without a reliable internal control system, it is easier for the management of a seller to manipulate the timing of the reporting of a sale.

> Company A requires each sale to be supported by a written sales agreement signed by an authorized representative of both Company A and of the customer. May Company A recognize revenue in the current quarter if the product is delivered before the end of the quarter but the sales agreement is not signed by the customer until a few days after the end of the quarter?[5]

---

[5] Each of the *SAB 101* questions covered in this section has been simplified and adapted from its original wording. The original wording is available at **http://www.sec.gov**. Because this section does not cover all of the *SAB 101* questions, in most cases the question numbering here differs from the original numbering.

If a company does not have a reliable, systematic, predictable procedure in place for processing customer contracts, then it becomes much easier for company executives to succumb to temptation at the end of a quarter and strategically accelerate the booking of revenue. Thus, even though *SAB 101* Question 1 seems narrowly focused, it should instead be seen as encouraging companies to implement good internal controls surrounding revenue recognition. Companies with such controls are much less likely to be called into question about their revenue recognition practices. This emphasis on internal control is a precursor to the expanded emphasis embodied in the Sarbanes-Oxley Act of 2002. Section 404 of Sarbanes-Oxley instructs the SEC to require all publicly traded companies to provide a report on the condition of the company's internal control over the financial reporting process. These financial reporting controls include company procedures to ensure that all transactions are recorded so that the public financial statements are not rendered irrelevant by secret side agreements. Proper internal controls also include procedures to ensure that no transaction takes place unless it is approved by the proper authority. In addition, a good internal control system establishes procedures to safeguard the value of the company's assets.

As explained in the opening scenario of the chapter, MicroStrategy executives deliberately delayed signing customer contracts near the end of a quarter until it was determined how many of the contracts were needed to meet revenue targets for the quarter.

> The Coca-Cola Company was found by the SEC to have engaged in "channel stuffing" in its Japan subsidiary. On April 18, 2005, the SEC made the following statement: "The Commission found that, at or near the end of each reporting period between 1997 and 1999, Coca-Cola implemented an undisclosed 'channel stuffing' practice in Japan known as 'gallon pushing' for the purpose of pulling sales forward into a current period. To accomplish gallon pushing's purpose, Japanese bottlers were offered extended credit terms to induce them to purchase quantities of beverage concentrate the bottlers otherwise would not have purchased until a following period. . . . This practice contributed approximately $0.01 to $0.02 to Coca-Cola's quarterly earnings per share and was the difference in 8 out of the 12 quarters from 1997 through 1999 between Coca-Cola meeting and missing analysts' consensus or modified consensus earnings estimates."

SAB 101, Question 2

> Company H requires customers to pay an up-front, nonrefundable fee in addition to monthly payments for its services. When should Company H recognize the revenue from this up-front, nonrefundable fee?

The situation described in Question 2 relates to the recognition of revenue when service periods cover extended periods and when there are several different activities that the seller must perform in providing the service. The concern in cases such as this is that sellers will wish to front-load the recognition of revenue; in the extreme, the seller would like to recognize all of the revenue immediately. The guidance given in *SAB 101* is that, in general, revenue should be recognized on a straight-line basis over the life of the contract and that recognition of an extra chunk of revenue for completion of a specific service act under the contract can be justified only if that service can be sold as a separate product.

In the situation described in Question 2, immediate recognition of the nonrefundable up-front fee as revenue cannot be justified because no customer would pay separately to simply be "signed up" for a service. Instead, the sign-up and payment of the up-front fee are integral parts of the entire service arrangement, and the entire package should be accounted for as a unit. An example given in *SAB 101* is the nonrefundable initiation fee paid when a customer buys a lifetime membership to a health club. The initiation fee and the subsequent monthly payments should be accounted for as a unit because no customer would pay a separate fee merely to sign up for the club without the expectation of using the club in the future. This general approach has been approved and included in the FASB Codification in FASB ASC Subtopic 605-25 (Revenue Recognition—Multiple-Element Arrangements). The terminology used in Subtopic 605-25 is that in a business arrangement with several components, revenue is recognized separately for each "unit of accounting" where a "unit of accounting" is defined as a component that has "value to the customer on a standalone basis."

> **ITT Educational Services** offers technology-oriented degree programs to more than 30,000 students in the United States. *SAB 101* impacted the company's revenue recognition policy as follows: "Effective January 1, 2000, we implemented *SAB 101* and changed the method by which we recognize the laboratory and application fees charged to a student as revenue. We began recognizing those fees as revenue on a straight-line basis over the average student's program length of 24 months. Previously, we recognized the quarterly laboratory fee as revenue at the beginning of each academic quarter and the application fee as revenue when we received the fee."

More About Subtopic 605-25 The focus of Subtopic 605-25 is on the "unit of accounting." An element of a multiple-element arrangement is considered to be a unit of accounting if that element has standalone value. An element has standalone value if it is sold separately (by anyone, not necessarily the seller) or if the customer can resell it.

To illustrate the accounting for a multiple-element arrangement under Subtopic 605-25, assume that on April 2 Lily Kay Company sold elements A and B to a customer for a single price of $1,000; Lily Kay collected the $1,000 selling price in cash on April 2. Also assume that both element A and element B are sold separately (not necessarily by Lily Kay), so each has standalone value to the customer. Lily Kay has three different methods to use in determining the separate selling prices of the two elements. The three different methods are as follows and are to be used in the following order.

1. Vender-specific objective evidence (VSOE). VSOE consists of the individual prices that Lily Kay itself uses in selling elements A and B. If these prices exist, then, of course, they are the best measure of the separate selling prices, for Lily Kay, of the two elements. It is possible that VSOE exists for one, or both, or neither of the two elements.
2. Third-party evidence (TPE). If Lily Kay itself does not sell one or both of the two elements separately, then the next best source of evidence for a separate selling price is the price at which the elements are sold separately by other companies.
3. Best estimate using other data. It is possible that neither Lily Kay nor a third-party competitor sells either element A or element B separately. This does not mean that the elements have no standalone value; if the customer can resell the elements separately, then they have standalone value. However, this does mean that Lily Kay must develop

an estimate of what the separate selling price would be. Possible inputs into this estimation process are the cost of the element (plus a standard profit margin) and observable selling prices of similar items.

In this case, Lily Kay sometimes sells element A separately for $700 (VSOE). Also, even though neither Lily Kay nor its competitors sell element B separately, an estimate using costs and normal profit margins indicates that the separate selling price of element B would be approximately $400. Lily Kay would make the following journal entries on April 2 (to record the receipt of cash), on June 6 (to record the delivery of element A), and on July 15 (to record the delivery of element B).

April 2

Cash	1,000	
Unearned Revenue—Element A		636*
Unearned Revenue—Element B		364**

*Element A: [$700/($700 + $400)] × $1,000 = $636
**Element B: [$400/($700 + $400)] × $1,000 = $364

June 6

Unearned Revenue—Element A	636	
Revenue—Element A		636

July 15

Unearned Revenue—Element B	364	
Revenue—Element B		364

Note the impact of the accounting for the revenue associated with this multiple-element transaction. If Lily Kay's fiscal second quarter ends on June 30, then only the $636 in revenue from the delivery of element A will be included in the second quarter results, even though all of the $1,000 in cash was collected during the quarter. The amount of revenue recognized during the second quarter is determined by the relative amount of value received by the customer during that quarter.

SAB 101, Question 3: Income Statement Presentation of Revenue: Gross or Net

Question 3 related to *SAB 101* does not deal with when revenue should be recognized but instead with how the revenue should be reported in the income statement.

> Company A operates an Internet site through which customers can order the products of traditional Company T. Company T ships the products directly to the customers, and Company A never takes title to the product. The typical sales price is $175, of which Company A receives $25. Should Company A report revenue of $175 with cost of goods sold of $150, or should Company A merely report $25 in commission revenue?

The issue dealt with in Question 3 is labeled "gross versus net" revenue reporting. In gross reporting, Company A reports the total sales price as revenue, and the difference between the $25 proceeds to Company A and the $175 sales price is reported as cost of goods sold. Before *SAB 101*, this was the preferred accounting treatment by Internet brokers. The alternative is the net method in which Company A merely reports the $25 it receives as commission revenue. The reason that Internet companies preferred the gross presentation is illustrated by referring back to the MicroStrategy story. Recall that with MicroStrategy there was frequent reference to the company's price-to-sales ratio. Because most companies report losses in their early years, earnings-based valuation methods don't work. An alternative approach is to value the company based on its reported sales under the assumption that as the company becomes established, those sales will eventually generate positive earnings and cash flows. But a revenue-based valuation model also gives companies an incentive to maximize their reported revenue, even if there is no impact on bottom-line earnings. Thus, the gross method is preferred over the net method by companies wishing to boost reported revenue.

SAB 101 made clear that the gross method (reporting $175 in revenue and $150 in cost of goods sold in the Question 3 example) is inappropriate when a company merely serves as an agent or broker and never takes legal and economic ownership of the goods being sold. This same issue was subsequently addressed in more detail in FASB ASC Section 605-45-45 (Revenue Recognition—Principal Agent Considerations—Other Presentation Matters), where characteristics of a transaction in which a company should report revenue on a net basis are given as follows.

- The company does not maintain an inventory of the product being sold but simply forwards orders to a supplier.
- The company is not primarily responsible for satisfying customer requirements, requests, complaints, and so forth; those requirements are satisfied by the supplier of the goods.
- The company earns a fixed amount, or a fixed percentage, and doesn't bear the risk of fluctuations in the margin between the selling price and the cost of goods sold.
- The company does not bear the credit risk associated with collecting from the customer; that risk is borne by the supplier.

> Enron shot to Number 5 in the *Fortune* 500 list for 2002 by virtue of its reported revenue of $139 billion. Using a gap in the accounting rules with respect to revenue reporting for energy trading companies, Enron reported its energy trades using gross reporting instead of net reporting. To illustrate, assume that Enron brokered a deal between a natural gas supplier and a local utility. Enron guaranteed a selling price of $1,000,000 to the natural gas supplier and guaranteed a purchase price of $1,050,000 to the local utility. When the natural gas supplier then provided the natural gas to the utility, Enron would keep the $50,000 excess. Because of the lack of a definite standard for revenue reporting for energy trading, Enron was able to report revenue of $1,050,000 (with cost of goods sold of $1,000,000) rather than the more appropriate reporting of simply $50,000 in commission revenue.

This section has included a review of some of the topics addressed in *SAB 101*. Remember, *SAB 101* was never intended to be a comprehensive treatise on revenue recognition. Instead, *SAB 101* was the SEC's attempt to curtail specific accounting abuses seen in the revenue recognition practices of companies such as MicroStrategy. *SAB 101*, issued in 1999, has proved to be very influential. The big splash made by *SAB 101* prompted the FASB, followed by the IASB, to reexamine the fundamental topic of revenue recognition. The next section introduces the results of that FASB/IASB revenue recognition effort.

A Contract Approach to Revenue Recognition

 Describe the contract approach to revenue recognition that is currently being considered by the FASB and IASB.

LO3 学习目标3
描述FASB和IASB正在考量的合同法下的收入确认。

Both the FASB and IASB have conceptual frameworks that have long directed their standard setting. Key elements in these frameworks are the definitions of assets and liabilities. Both standard setters focus on correct reporting of assets and liabilities in any new standard that they contemplate. This asset-and-liability focus is at the heart of the joint FASB/IASB project on revenue recognition.[6] The insight used in the FASB/IASB project is that when a seller enters into a contract with a buyer, the seller accepts certain performance obligations (liabilities) in exchange for the promise of receiving assets from the buyer.

With this contractual performance obligation focus, the FASB and the IASB have agreed that revenue arises when a seller satisfies a performance obligation to a buyer. Although this contract approach will not change the end result of accounting for revenue in many common situations, the new approach does represent a substantial conceptual shift from the historic focus on reflecting the results of a company's earnings processes. The intent is to make the model robust enough to be used in a wide variety of settings for which there now exists a patchwork of situation-specific and industry-specific revenue recognition practices.

For a particular contract between a buyer and a seller, the three basic steps in recognizing revenue under the contract approach are as follows:

1. Identify the performance obligations accepted by the seller. Delivery of a good or service represents a distinct performance obligation if the seller, or another company in the same line of business as the seller, sells that good or service separately. If no one sells the good or service separately, its delivery can still represent a distinct performance obligation if the good or service has a distinct function and a distinct profit margin so that it could be sold separately, if desired.

2. Allocate transaction prices based on relative separate selling prices of any distinct elements of a multiple-element arrangement. Recall that under Subtopic 605-25, data about separate selling prices are to be considered in a specific sequence: first, vender-specific objective evidence, then third-party evidence, and finally, other evidence. In their contract approach proposal, the FASB and IASB are suggesting that the same types of evidence be used. However, the emphasis in the proposal is on generating the best possible measure of the separate selling price, without specifying any particular priority among the data items used.

3. Recognize revenue as the performance obligations are satisfied. Under the contract approach proposed by the FASB and the IASB, a performance obligation is satisfied when the buyer obtains control of the good or service from the seller. This control means that the buyer can use the good or service in any way desired and can prevent others from using the good or service.

---

[6] See Proposed Accounting Standards Update (Revised)—*Revenue Recognition (Topic 605): Revenue from Contracts with Customers*, November 14, 2011, FASB Web site at **http://www.fasb.org**.

You should recognize this approach as being virtually the same as the approach explained earlier in the chapter in the discussion of multiple-element arrangements under Subtopic 605-25. This is no coincidence because the material in this subtopic was developed and adopted at the same time the FASB and IASB were deliberating their new overall revenue recognition approach. And the general idea that no revenue should be recognized until something of value has been delivered to the customer goes back to *SAB 101* and even back to the traditional revenue recognition criteria.

A difference associated with the contract approach is the increased use of selling price estimates in accounting for multiple-element arrangements. Historically, the use of selling price estimates to account for these arrangements was almost forbidden. For example, under the provisions of pre-Codification *EITF 00-21*, if no observable price (either vendor specific or third party) were available for an undelivered element in a multiple-element arrangement, then NO revenue could be recognized, even for the delivered items with observable prices, until that undelivered item was delivered. And a price estimate could not be used in place of a verifiable, observable price. This draconian treatment has since been superseded (as discussed earlier in the treatment of Subtopic 605-25), and it will be put even further in the past as the contract approach embraces a more reasonable use of estimates in the area of revenue recognition.

To illustrate the contract approach to revenue recognition, consider the example of Wilks Company selling a plasma TV and two-year warranty to a customer for a joint price of $2,000. For simplicity, assume that Wilks collects all of the cash up front on the contract-signing date, and also assume that the probability of product return is 0%. Wilks Company has generated the following information regarding sales of this type.

- Cost of plasma TV, $1,500
- Sales price of plasma TV if sold separately, unknown. Neither Wilks nor any of its competitors sell the plasma TV without the two-year warranty. However, the TV has a distinct function and a distinct profit margin and could be sold separately, if desired. Wilks does sell other consumer electronic products separately. The profit margins for these products range between 16% and 22% of cost.
- Sales price of two-year warranty if sold separately, unknown. The two-year warranty on the plasma TV is not sold separately, but Wilks does sell warranties of various lengths for a variety of other consumer electronics products. A two-year warranty for a refrigerator/freezer with the same wholesale cost sells for $300. Wilks estimates that the two-year cost of repairs for the plasma TV would be about 5% higher than for a refrigerator/freezer.

When the customer signs the contract to buy the plasma TV and two-year warranty from Wilks Company, Wilks has created two performance obligations that should be recognized as liabilities: the obligation to deliver the plasma TV and the obligation to provide two years of warranty service. The difficulty is in measuring the liabilities for the TV delivery and warranty service. Neither element has an observable price, but both elements do have standalone value to the customer. In order to allocate the total contract price of $2,000, Wilks must estimate standalone selling prices for each of the two elements. With the data given above, those estimates can be generated as follows:

TV screen delivery obligation

Low estimate: $1,500 cost + ($1,500 × 0.16) = $1,740

High estimate: $1,500 cost + ($1,500 × 0.22) = $1,830

Average: ($1,740 + $1,830)/2 = $1,785

Warranty service obligation

$300 + (\$300 \times 0.5) = \$315$

Of course, if separate, observable selling prices were available, either from Wilks or from one of its competitors, it may be preferable to use those prices rather than these estimates.

The transaction price allocation, using the estimated separate selling prices of the TV screen and the warranty, is as follows:

TV delivery obligation $1,700 = \$2,000 \times [\$1,785/(\$1,785 + \$315)]$

Warranty service obligation $300 = \$2,000 \times [\$315/(\$1,785 + \$315)]$

These two quantities, $1,700 and $300, are estimates of the two performance obligations Wilks Company accepted when signing the contract. These two obligations are balanced by the asset, $2,000 in cash, that Wilks received. The journal entry to record this asset and these two liabilities created at the contract signing is as follows:

Cash	2,000	
Contract Liability—TV		1,700
Contract Liability—Warranty		300

When the plasma TV is delivered to the customer, that performance obligation has been satisfied and the associated liability has decreased to zero. Revenue is recognized when a liability created as part of a contractual arrangement with a customer has decreased. The journal entry (assuming a perpetual inventory system) is as follows:

Contract Liability—TV	1,700	
Sales Revenue		1,700
Cost of Goods Sold	1,500	
Inventory		1,500

Additional revenue will be recognized as the performance obligation associated with the warranty services is reduced. This reduction may be in a straight-line fashion, or the obligation may be reduced more, say, in the first year than in the second year; if this is true, more warranty revenue will be recognized in the first year than in the second year.

The contract approach has the benefits of being easy to understand, relatively easy to use, and generally consistent with past practice. In fact, in this simple example the contract approach may seem so much like existing practice that it doesn't seem worth the bother. However, the shift from an earnings process focus to a focus on the creation and satisfaction of performance obligation liabilities makes this revenue recognition approach both consistent with the conceptual frameworks of the FASB and IASB and flexible enough to be applied in a wide variety of settings.

On November 14, 2011, the FASB and the IASB jointly released a revised Exposure Draft proposing a formal revenue recognition standard based on the contract approach. At this point, it is highly likely that some variation of the contract approach will be adopted by both the FASB and the IASB sometime in 2013 as the foundation for revenue recognition standards. As stated above, from a practical standpoint the contract approach is generally consistent with existing standards.

FASB CODIFICATION

The Issue: Your sister is an economics major. She is always using sophisticated phrases such as "utility maximization," "downward-sloping demand curve," and "Pareto optimal." You wish you knew what she was talking about.

Last night she was saying something about "principal-agent models." A light went off in your head—you know that in your accounting studies you have seen something about principals and agents. You also remember that it had something to do with revenue recognition.

The Question: In the context of revenue recognition, what is a principal and what is an agent?

Searching the Codification: In the FASB Codification, all of the material about revenue recognition is in Topic 605. Good luck!

The Answer: The accounting use of the terms "principal" and "agent" is given on page 8-35.

Revenue Recognition Prior to Delivery of Goods or Performance of Services

 Record journal entries for long-term construction-type contracts using percentage-of-completion and completed-contract methods.

LO4 学习目标4
使用完工百分比和完成合同法核算长期建造合同。

At this point, it is important to remember that the contract approach to revenue recognition discussed in the previous section is still being considered and refined by the FASB and the IASB. Revenue recognition under current U.S. GAAP is still based on the historical focus on the earnings process. The next three sections explain how this general approach to revenue recognition works in three different settings.

Under some circumstances, revenue can be meaningfully reported prior to the delivery of the finished product or completion of a service contract. For example, under *IAS 41*, biological assets, such as cattle, fruit trees, and lumber forests, are recorded in the balance sheet at their fair value (less estimating selling costs) as of the balance sheet date. Increases in this fair value are recognized as gains, and decreases are recognized as losses. Accordingly, under International Accounting Standards, a lumber company would report the timber in its forests at fair value (less selling cost) in each balance sheet during, say, the 30-year period the timber is growing. The yearly increases or decreases in fair value would be reported in the income statement as gains or losses before the timber is ever sold or delivered to a customer. This approach is allowed in some circumstances under U.S. GAAP but is not required.[7]

Under U.S. GAAP, the most common occurrence of revenue recognition before final delivery is when the construction period of the asset being sold or the period of service performance is relatively long, that is, more than one year. In these cases, if a company waits until the production or service period is complete to recognize revenue, the income

---

[7] See FASB ASC Section 905-330-35 (Agriculture—Inventory—Subsequent Measurement).

statement may not report meaningfully the periodic achievement of the company. Under this approach, referred to as the completed-contract method, all income from the contract is related to the year of completion, even though only a small part of the earnings may be attributable to effort in that period. Previous periods receive no credit for their efforts; in fact, they may be penalized through the absorption of selling, general, and administrative and other overhead costs relating to the contract but not considered part of the inventory cost.

Percentage-of-completion accounting, an alternative to the completed-contract method, was developed to relate recognition of revenue on long term construction-type contracts to the activities of a firm in fulfilling these contracts. Similarly, the proportional performance method has been developed to reflect revenue earned on service contracts under which many acts of service are to be performed before the contract is completed.

Examples of such service contracts include contracts covering maintenance on electronic office equipment, correspondence schools, trustee services, health clubs, professional services such as those offered by attorneys and accountants, and servicing of mortgage loans by mortgage bankers. Percentage-of-completion accounting and proportional performance accounting are similar in their application. However, some special problems arise in accounting for service contracts. The discussion and examples in the following sections relate first to long-term construction-type contracts and then to the special problems encountered with service contracts.

General Concepts of Percentage-of-Completion Accounting

Under the percentage-of-completion method, a company recognizes revenues and costs on a contract as it progresses toward completion rather than deferring recognition of these items until the contract is completed. The amount of revenue to be recognized each period is based on some measure of progress toward completion. This requires an estimate of costs yet to be incurred. Changes in estimates of future costs arise normally, and the necessary adjustments are made in the year the estimates are revised. Thus, the revenues and costs to be recognized in a given year are affected by the revenues and costs already recognized. As work progresses on the contract, the actual costs incurred are charged to inventory. The amount of profit earned each period also is charged to this asset account. Thus, the inventory account is valued at its net realizable value: the sales (or contract) price less the cost to complete the contract and less the unearned profit on the unfinished contract. (See Chapter 9 for a review of the concepts and computations associated with net realizable value.) If a company projects a loss on the contract prior to completion, the full amount of the loss should be recognized immediately. This loss recognition results in a write-down of the asset to its estimated net realizable value. If only a percentage of the loss were recognized, the asset value would exceed the net realizable value. This would violate the lower-of-cost-or-market rule discussed more fully in Chapter 9.

> **Stop & Think**
>
> Which ONE of the following is NOT a good way to measure a contract's percentage of completion?
> a) The cost expended on contract work so far, relative to the estimate of the total cost to be expended on the contract.
> b) The percentage of revenue that will result in the company meeting its revenue and profit goals for the period.
> c) An engineer's estimate of the percentage of the work that has been completed.
> d) The amount of output produced under the contract (such as the number of feet of roadway completed on a highway construction job), relative to the estimated total amount of output to be produced under the contract.

Necessary Conditions to Use Percentage-of-Completion Accounting

Most long-term construction-type contracts should be reported using the percentage-of-completion method. The guidelines presently in force, however, are not specific as to when a company must use the percentage-of-completion method and when it must use the alternative completed-contract method. The accounting standards that still govern this area were issued by the Committee on Accounting Procedure in 1955.[8] In 1981, the AICPA identified several elements that should be present if percentage-of-completion accounting is to be used.[9]

使用完工百分比法时需要确定的几个要素。

1. Dependable estimates can be made of contract revenues, contract costs, and the extent of progress toward completion.
2. The contract clearly specifies the enforceable rights regarding goods or services to be provided and received by the parties, the consideration to be exchanged, and the manner and terms of settlement.
3. The buyer can be expected to satisfy obligations under the contract.
4. The contractor can be expected to perform the contractual obligation.

The completed-contract method should be used only when an entity has primarily short-term contracts, when the conditions for using percentage-of-completion accounting are not met, or when there are inherent uncertainties in the contract, beyond the normal business risks. By the way, under *IAS 11*, the completed-contract method is not allowed under International Financial Reporting Standards.

For many years, income tax regulations permitted contractors wide latitude in selecting either the percentage-of-completion or completed-contract method. Beginning with the Tax Reform Act of 1986, the tax laws have limited the use of the completed-contract method and have required increased use of the percentage-of-completion method. This results in accelerated revenues from taxes without increasing the tax rates, and it also results in similar revenue recognition treatment for both taxes and financial reporting.

Measuring the Percentage of Completion

Various methods are currently used in practice to measure the earnings process. They can be conveniently grouped into two categories: input and output measures.

---

[8] Pre-Codification *Committee on Accounting Procedure, Accounting Research Bulletin No. 45*, "Long-Term Construction-Type Contracts" (New York: American Institute of Certified Public Accountants, 1955). These provisions are now contained in FASB ASC Subtopic 605-35 (Revenue Recognition—Construction-Type and Production-Type Contracts).

[9] FASB ASC paragraph 605-35-25-57. These provisions were originally found in *AICPA Statement of Position 81–1*, "Accounting for Performance of Construction-Type and Certain Production-Type Contracts" (New York: American Institute of Certified Public Accountants, 1981), par. 23.

Input Measures Input measures are made in relation to the costs or efforts devoted to a contract. They are based on an established or assumed relationship between a unit of input and productivity. They include the widely used cost-to-cost method and several variations of efforts-expended methods.

Cost-to-Cost Method Perhaps the most popular of the input measures is the cost-to-cost method. Under this method, the degree of completion is determined by comparing costs already incurred with the most recent estimates of total expected costs to complete the project. The percentage that costs incurred bear to total expected costs is applied to the contract price to determine the revenue to be recognized to date as well as to the expected net income on the project in arriving at earnings to date. Some of the costs incurred, particularly in the early stages of the contract, should be disregarded in applying this method because they do not relate directly to effort expended on the contract. These include such items as subcontract costs for work that has yet to be performed and standard fabricated materials that have not yet been installed. One of the most difficult problems in using this method is estimating the costs yet to be incurred. Engineers are often consulted to help provide estimates as to a project's percentage of completion. However difficult the estimation process may be, it is required in reporting income, regardless of how the percentage of completion is computed.

To illustrate, assume that in January 2014 Strong Construction Company was awarded a contract with a total price of $3,000,000. Strong expected to earn $400,000 profit on the contract, or in other words, total costs on the contract were estimated to be $2,600,000. The construction was completed over a three-year period, and the cost data and cost percentages shown below were compiled during that time.

Note that the cost percentage is computed by dividing cumulative actual costs incurred by total cost, an amount that is estimated for the first two years.

Year	(1) Actual Cost Incurred	(2) Estimated Cost to Complete	(3) Total Cost (1) + (2)	(4) Cost Percentage (1)/(3)
2014	$1,040,000	$1,560,000	$2,600,000*	40
2015	910,000			
Total	$1,950,000	650,000	2,600,000*	75
2016	650,000			
Total	$2,600,000	0	2,600,000†	100

* Estimated total contract cost.
† Actual total contract cost.

Efforts-Expended Methods The efforts-expended methods are based on some measure of work performed. They include labor hours, labor dollars, machine hours, or material quantities. In each case, the degree of completion is measured in a way similar to that used in the cost-to-cost approach: the ratio of the efforts expended to date to the estimated total efforts to be expended on the entire contract. For example, if the measure of work performed is labor hours, the ratio of hours worked to date to the total estimated hours would produce the percentage for use in measuring income earned.

Output Measures Output measures are made in terms of results achieved. Included in this category are methods based on units produced, contract milestones reached, and values added. For example, if the contract calls for units of output, such as miles of roadway, a measure of completion would be a ratio of the miles completed to the total miles in the contract. Architects and engineers are sometimes asked to evaluate jobs and estimate what percentage of a job is complete. These estimates are, in reality, output measures and usually are based on the physical progress made on a contract. In its current deliberations on revenue recognition (discussed in the preceding section), the FASB has indicated that "output methods often result in the most faithful depiction of the transfer of goods or services."[10]

Accounting for Long-Term Construction-Type Contracts

For both the percentage-of-completion and the completed-contract methods, all direct and allocable indirect costs of the contracts are charged to an inventory account. The difference in recording between the two methods relates to the timing of revenue and expense recognition; that is, when the estimated earned income is recognized with its related effect on the income statement and the balance sheet. During the construction period, the annual reported income under these two accounting methods will differ. However, after the contract is completed, the combined income for the total construction period will be the same under each method of accounting. The balance sheet at the end of the construction and collection periods also will be identical.

Usually, contracts require progress billings by the contractor and payments by the customer on these billings. The billings and payments are accounted for and reported in the same manner under both methods. The amount of these billings usually is specified by the contract terms and may be related to the costs actually incurred. Generally, these contracts require inspection before final settlement is made. The billings are debited to Accounts Receivable and credited to a deferred account, Progress Billings on Construction Contracts, that serves as an offset to the inventory account, Construction in Progress. The billing of the contract thus transfers the asset value from inventory to receivables, but because of the long-term nature of the contract, the construction costs continue to be reflected in the accounts.

To illustrate accounting for a long-term construction contract, we will continue the Strong Construction Company example mentioned earlier. Recall that construction was completed over a three-year period and the contract price was $3,000,000. The direct and allocable indirect costs, billings, and collections[11] for 2014, 2015, and 2016 are as follows:

Year	Direct and Allocable Indirect Costs	Billings	Collections
2014	$1,040,000	$1,000,000	$ 800,000
2015	910,000	900,000	850,000
2016	650,000	1,100,000	1,350,000

---

[10] FASB *Proposed Accounting Standards Update, Revenue Recognition (Topic 605): Revenue from Contracts with Customers*, June 24, 2010, par. 33. In its revised 2011 Exposure Draft, the FASB softened its endorsement of output methods in response to some concerns expressed through public comment letters. However, the Board still affirmed that, conceptually, a reliable output measure is often the best measure of performance with long-term contracts.

[11] As a protection for the customer, long-term contracts frequently provide for an amount to be retained from the progress payments. This retention is usually a percentage of the progress billings, for example, 10% to 20%, and is paid upon final acceptance of the construction. Thus, the amount collected is often less than the amount billed in the initial years of the contract.

The following entries for the three years would be made on the contractor's books under either the percentage-of-completion or the completed-contract method.

	2014		2015		2016	
Construction in Progress.......	1,040,000		910,000		650,000	
Materials, Cash, etc.		1,040,000		910,000		650,000
To record costs incurred.						
Accounts Receivable	1,000,000		900,000		1,100,000	
Progress Billings on						
Construction Contracts ...		1,000,000		900,000		1,100,000
To record billings.						
Cash	800,000		850,000		1,350,000	
Accounts Receivable		800,000		850,000		1,350,000
To record cash collections.						

No other entries would be required in 2014 and 2015 under the completed-contract method. In both years, the balance of Construction in Progress exceeds the amount in Progress Billings on Construction Contracts; thus, the latter account would be offset against the inventory account in the balance sheet.

Before proceeding further, let's examine the relationship between the accounts Construction in Progress and Progress Billings on Construction Contracts. Amounts recorded in Construction in Progress represent the costs that have been incurred to date relating to a specific contract. If the customer has not been billed, then the entire cost represents a probable future benefit to the company and should be disclosed on the balance sheet as an asset. If, however, the customer has been billed for a portion of these costs, then the company has in effect traded one asset for another. In place of inventory, the company now has a receivable (or cash if the receivable has been collected).

Thus, if the balance in Construction in Progress exceeds the balance in Progress Billings on Construction Contracts, the excess represents the amount of the construction costs for which the customer has not been billed.[12] The amount for which the customer has been billed is included in either Accounts Receivable or Cash. If Progress Billings on Construction Contracts is greater than Construction in Progress, the difference represents a liability because the customer has been billed (and a receivable has been recorded) for more than the costs actually incurred.

FYI

The reason these entries are the same under either revenue recognition method is because they are a function of the terms of the contract that specifies when payment will be made.

Stop & Think

Progress Billings on Construction Contracts is offset against the construction in progress account. What does the resulting net figure represent?

a) The estimated fair market value of the portion of the construction that has been completed.
b) The amount of cash that has been collected under the contract.
c) The value of the completed construction for which the customer has not yet been billed.
d) The estimated amount of uncollectible accounts associated with the construction project.

---

[12] As we will soon learn, under the percentage-of-completion method, Construction in Progress includes both costs and the portion of expected gross profit earned to date.

Because the operating cycle of a company that emphasizes long-term contracts is usually more than one year, all of the preceding balance sheet accounts would be classified as current. The balance sheet at the end of 2015 under the completed-contract method would disclose the following balances related to the construction contract:

Current assets:

Accounts receivable..			$250,000
Construction in progress...	$1,950,000		
Less: Progress billings on construction contracts.....................	1,900,000		50,000

If the billings exceeded the construction costs, the excess would be reported in the Current Liability section of the balance sheet.

Under the completed-contract method, the following entries would be made to recognize revenue and costs and to close out the inventory and billings accounts at the completion of the contract, that is, in 2016.

Progress Billings on Construction Contracts............................	3,000,000	
Revenue from Long-Term Construction Contracts.....................		3,000,000
Cost of Long-Term Construction Contracts...............................	2,600,000	
Construction in Progress...		2,600,000

The first entry represents the billings on the contract that, at the end of the contract, equal the total revenue from the contract. The second journal entry transfers the inventoried cost from the contract to the appropriate expense account on the income statement. The income statement for 2016 would report the gross revenues and the matched costs, thus recognizing the entire $400,000 profit in one year.

Using Percentage-of-Completion Accounting: Cost-to-Cost Method

If the company used the percentage-of-completion method of accounting, the $400,000 profit would be spread over all three years of construction according to the estimated percentage of completion for each year. The information provided previously details Strong's estimated cost to complete the contract at the end of 2014 and 2015 as well as the total actual costs at the end of 2016. Recall that the percentage of completion for each year, determined on a cost-to-cost basis, is as follows:

	2014	2015	2016
Percentage of completion to date.................................	40%	75%	100%

These percentages may be used to determine directly the gross profit that should be recognized on the income statement; that is, the income statement for 2014 would report only the gross profit from construction contracts in the amount of $160,000 (estimated gross profit—2014, $400,000 × 0.40 = $160,000). Preferably, the percentages should be used to determine both revenues and costs. The income statement will then disclose revenues, costs, and the resulting gross profit, a method more consistent with normal income statement reporting.[13] The procedures are as follows:

1. Cumulative revenue to date should be computed by multiplying total estimated contract revenue by the percentage of completion. Revenue for the current period is the difference between the cumulative revenue at the end of the current period and the cumulative revenue recognized in prior periods.

2. Cumulative costs to date should be computed in a manner similar to revenue and should be equal to the total estimated contract cost multiplied by the percentage of completion on the contract. Cost for the current period is the difference between the cumulative costs at the end of the current period and the cumulative costs reported in prior periods.

3. Cumulative gross profit is the excess of cumulative revenue over cumulative costs, and the current period gross profit is the difference between current revenue and current costs.

Since spacecraft like the *Endeavour* space shuttle may take many years to build, aerospace companies must account for this construction using the percentage-of-completion method.

If the cost-to-cost method is used to estimate earned revenue, the proportional cost for each period will typically equal the actual cost incurred.

To illustrate, for 2014, 40% of the fixed contract price of $3,000,000 would be recognized as revenue ($1,200,000) and 40% of the expected total cost of $2,600,000 would be reported as cost ($1,040,000). The following revenue recognition entries would be made for each of the three years of the contract. These entries are in addition to the transaction entries illustrated previously.

	2014	2015	2016
Cost of Long-Term Construction Contracts*	1,040,000	910,000	650,000
Construction in Progress	160,000	140,000	100,000
Revenue from Long-Term Construction Contracts		1,200,000	1,050,000†	750,000‡

* Actual costs.
† ($3,000,000 × 0.75) − $1,200,000 = $1,050,000.
‡ $3,000,000 − $1,200,000 − $1,050,000 = $750,000.

The gross profit recognized each year is added to the construction in progress account, thereby valuing the inventory on the books at its net realizable value. Note that the procedures used in recognizing revenue under the percentage-of-completion method do not affect the progress billings made or the amount of cash collected. These amounts are determined by contract and not by the accounting method used.

Because the construction in progress account contains costs incurred plus recognized profit (the two together equaling total revenues recognized to date), at the completion of the contract the balance in this account will exactly equal the amount in Progress Billings

[13] *Construction Contractor Guide Committee of the Accounting Standards Division, AICPA*, "AICPA Audit and Accounting Guide for Construction Contractors" (New York: American Institute of Certified Public Accountants, 1999).

on Construction Contracts, because the progress billings account reflects the contract price (or total revenues). The following closing entry would complete the accounting process:

Progress Billings on Construction Contracts	3,000,000	
Construction in Progress		3,000,000

Using Percentage-of-Completion Accounting: Other Methods

If the cost-to-cost method is not used to measure progress on the contract, the proportional costs recognized under this method may not be equal to the actual costs incurred. For example, assume in 2014 that an engineering estimate measure was used, and 42% of the contract was assumed to be completed. The gross profit recognized would therefore be computed and reported as follows:

Recognized revenue (42% of $3,000,000)	$1,260,000
Cost (42% of $2,600,000)	1,092,000
Gross profit (42% of $400,000)	$ 168,000

Because some accountants believe that the amount of cost recognized should be equal to the costs actually incurred, there is an alternative to the preceding approach.[14] Under this actual cost approach, revenue is defined as the actual costs incurred on the contract plus the gross profit earned for the period on the contract. Using the data from the previous example, the revenue and costs to be reported on the 2014 income statement would be as follows:

Actual cost incurred to date	$1,040,000
Recognized gross profit (42% of $400,000)	168,000
Recognized revenue	$1,208,000

This contrasts with the $1,260,000 revenue using the proportional cost approach. Both approaches report gross profit as $168,000.

The actual cost approach and the proportional cost approach are equally acceptable. However, because the actual cost approach results in a varying gross profit percentage from period to period whenever the measurement of completion differs from that which would occur if the cost-to-cost method were used, the authors feel that the proportional cost approach is preferable. Unless a different method is explicitly stated, text examples and end-of-chapter material will assume the *proportional cost approach*.

Revision of Estimates

In the previous example, it was assumed that the estimated cost did not vary from the beginning of the contract. This rarely would be the case. As estimates change, catch-up adjustments are made in the year of the change. To illustrate the impact of changing estimates, assume that at the end of 2015, it was estimated that the remaining cost to complete the construction was $720,000 rather than $650,000. This would increase the total estimated cost to $2,670,000, reduce the expected profit to $330,000, and change the percentage of completion at the end of 2015 to 73% ($1,950,000/$2,670,000).

The following analysis shows how this change would affect the revenue and costs to be reported each year, assuming that the actual costs incurred in 2016 were $700,000.

[14] FASB ASC paragraphs 605-35-25-83 and 84.

	2014	2015	2016
Contract price	$3,000,000	$3,000,000	$3,000,000
Actual cost incurred to date	$1,040,000	$1,950,000	$2,650,000
Estimated cost to complete	1,560,000	720,000	0
Total estimated cost	$2,600,000	$2,670,000	$2,650,000
Total expected gross profit	$ 400,000	$ 330,000	$ 350,000
Percentage of completion to date	40%	73%	100%

	To Date	Recognized—Prior Years	Recognized—Current Year
2014:			
Recognized revenue ($3,000,000 × 0.40)	$1,200,000	0	$1,200,000
Cost (actual cost)	1,040,000	0	1,040,000
Gross profit	$ 160,000		$ 160,000
2015:			
Recognized revenue ($3,000,000 × 0.73)	$2,190,000	$1,200,000	$ 990,000
Cost (actual cost)	1,950,000	1,040,000	910,000
Gross profit	$ 240,000	$ 160,000	$ 80,000
2016:			
Recognized revenue	$3,000,000	$2,190,000	$ 810,000
Cost (actual cost)	2,650,000	1,950,000	700,000
Gross profit	$ 350,000	$ 240,000	$ 110,000

The entries to record revenue and cost for the three years, given the assumed estimate revision, would be as follows:

	2014	2015	2016
Cost of Long-Term Construction Contracts	1,040,000	910,000	700,000
Construction in Progress	160,000	80,000	110,000
Revenue from Long-Term Construction Contracts	1,200,000	990,000	810,000

> **Stop & Think**
>
> What circumstances would give rise to a loss being reported this year on a contract that is profitable overall?
> a) Underestimates of the percentage completed in this period
> b) Overestimates of the percentage completed in this period
> c) Underestimates of the percentage completed in prior periods
> d) Overestimates of the percentage completed in prior periods

In some cases, an increase in total estimated cost can result in recognition of a loss in the year of the increase. Revising the preceding example, assume that at the end of 2015 the estimated cost to complete construction was $836,000, and this was the actual cost incurred in 2016. The following analysis shows how this change in estimated cost would reduce the percentage of completion at the end of 2015 to 70%, and the cumulative profit at the end of 2015 to $150,000. Because

$160,000 was already recognized as gross profit in 2014, a loss of $10,000 would be recognized in 2015.

	2014	2015	2016
Contract price	$3,000,000	$3,000,000	$3,000,000
Actual cost incurred to date	$1,040,000	$1,950,000	$2,786,000
Estimated cost to complete	1,560,000	836,000	0
Total estimated cost	$2,600,000	$2,786,000	$2,786,000
Total expected gross profit	$ 400,000	$ 214,000	$ 214,000
Percentage of completion to date	40%	70%	100%

	To Date	Recognized—Prior Years	Recognized—Current Year
2014:			
Recognized revenue ($3,000,000 × 0.40)	$1,200,000	0	$1,200,000
Cost (actual cost)	1,040,000	0	1,040,000
Gross profit	$ 160,000		$ 160,000
2015:			
Recognized revenue ($3,000,000 × 0.70)	$2,100,000	$1,200,000	$ 900,000
Cost (actual cost)	1,950,000	1,040,000	910,000
Gross profit	$ 150,000	$ 160,000	$ (10,000)
2016:			
Recognized revenue	$3,000,000	$2,100,000	$ 900,000
Cost (actual cost)	2,786,000	1,950,000	836,000
Gross profit	$ 214,000	$ 150,000	$ 64,000

The entries to record revenue and cost for the three years, given the assumed loss estimate in 2015, would be as follows:

	2014	2015	2016
Cost of Long-Term Construction Contracts	1,040,000	910,000	836,000
Construction in Progress	160,000	10,000	64,000
Revenue from Long-Term Construction Contracts	1,200,000	900,000	900,000

Reporting Anticipated Contract Losses

In the example above, an increase in estimated total cost resulted in recognition of a loss in the year the estimate was revised, but overall, the contract resulted in a profit. In some cases, an increase in estimated total cost is so great that a loss on the entire contract is anticipated; that is, total estimated costs are expected to exceed the total revenue from the contract. When a loss on the total contract is anticipated, GAAP requires reporting the loss in its entirety in the period when the loss is first anticipated. This is true under either the completed-contract or the percentage-of-completion method.

> **Caution**
> Do not confuse a loss on an entire contract with a loss for a period on a profitable contract. The accounting for these two possibilities is entirely different.

For example, assume that in the earlier construction example, the estimated cost to complete the contract at the end of 2015 was $1,300,000. Because $1,950,000 of costs had already been incurred, the total estimated cost of the contract would be $3,250,000 ($1,950,000 + $1,300,000), or $250,000 more than the contract price. Assume also that actual costs equaled expected costs in 2016.

	2014	2015	2016
Contract price	$3,000,000	$3,000,000	$3,000,000
Actual cost incurred to date	$1,040,000	$1,950,000	$3,250,000
Estimated cost to complete	1,560,000	1,300,000	0
Total estimated cost	$2,600,000	$3,250,000	$3,250,000
Total expected gross profit (loss)	$ 400,000	$ (250,000)	$ (250,000)
Percentage of completion to date	40%	60%	100%

Using this example, accounting for a contract loss is illustrated first for the completed-contract method and then for the percentage-of-completion method.

Anticipated Contract Loss: Completed-Contract Method If the completed-contract method is used, the recognition of an anticipated contract loss is simple. The amount of the loss is debited to a loss account, and the inventory account, Construction in Progress, is credited by that amount to reduce the inventory to its expected net realizable value. To record the anticipated loss of $250,000 on the construction contract, the following entry would be made at the end of 2015:

Anticipated Loss on Long-Term Construction Contracts	250,000	
Construction in Progress		250,000

> 在完工百分比法下确认预计合同损失的金额较在完成合同法下更为复杂。为了正确地反映在首个会计期间的预计合同总损失，从累计已确认收入中扣除的累计成本并不是实际发生的成本之和，而是累计已确认收入加上预计损失。

> **FYI**
> Because the construction in progress inventory account is used to accumulate actual construction costs under the completed-contract method, this journal entry will ensure that at the end of the contract, the inventory account is not reported at an amount higher than the contract price.

Anticipated Contract Loss: Percentage-of-Completion Method Recognition of an anticipated contract loss under the percentage-of-completion method is more complex. To properly reflect the entire loss in the year it is first anticipated, the cumulative cost to deduct from cumulative recognized revenue cannot be the actual cost incurred but must be the cumulative recognized revenue plus the entire anticipated loss. Thus, continuing the construction contract example, the cumulative recognized revenue at the end of 2015 would be $1,800,000 (60% × $3,000,000), and the cumulative cost at the same date would be $2,050,000 ($1,800,000 + $250,000). Because the example assumes that $160,000 profit was recognized on this contract in 2014, the total loss to be recognized in 2015 is $410,000 ($160,000 + $250,000). The analysis that follows reflects the amounts to be reported for each of the three years of the contract life under the anticipated loss assumption.

	To Date	Recognized—Prior Years	Recognized—Current Year
2014:			
Recognized revenue ($3,000,000 × 0.40)	$1,200,000	0	$1,200,000
Cost (actual cost)	1,040,000	0	1,040,000
Gross profit	$ 160,000		$ 160,000
2015:			
Recognized revenue ($3,000,000 × 0.60)	$1,800,000	$1,200,000	$ 600,000
Cost (recognized revenue plus entire anticipated loss)	2,050,000	1,040,000	1,010,000
Gross profit (loss)	$ (250,000)	$ 160,000	$ (410,000)
2016:			
Recognized revenue	$3,000,000	$1,800,000	$1,200,000
Cost	3,250,000	2,050,000	1,200,000
Gross profit	$ (250,000)	$ (250,000)	$ 0

The entry to record the revenue, costs, and adjustments to Construction in Progress for the loss in 2015 would be as follows:

Cost of Long-Term Construction Contracts	1,010,000	
Revenue from Long-Term Construction Contracts		600,000
Construction in Progress		410,000

Note that the construction in progress account under both methods would have a balance of $1,700,000 at the end of 2015, computed as shown below.

Completed-Contract Method
Construction in Progress

2014 cost	1,040,000	2015 loss	250,000
2015 cost	910,000		
Balance	1,700,000		

Percentage-of-Completion Method
Construction in Progress

2014 cost	1,040,000	2015 loss	410,000
2014 gross profit	160,000		
2015 cost	910,000		
Balance	1,700,000		

Accounting for Long-Term Service Contracts: The Proportional Performance Method

5 Record journal entries for long-term service contracts using the proportional performance method.

LO5 学习目标5

使用完工百分比法核算长期劳务合同。

Thus far, the discussion in this chapter has focused on long-term construction-type contracts. As indicated earlier, another type of contract that frequently extends over a long period of time is a service contract. When the service to be performed is completed as a single act or over a relatively short period of time, no revenue recognition problems arise. The revenue recognition criteria previously defined apply, and all direct and indirect costs related to the service are charged to expense in the period the revenue is recognized. However, when several acts over a period of time are involved, the same revenue recognition problems illustrated for long-term construction-type contracts arise.

As explained in the earlier discussion of *SAB 101*, partial recognition of revenue under a multiple-element service contract is appropriate only if each element of the contract constitutes a service that can be sold separately. This approach is confirmed in FASB ASC Subtopic 605-25 (Revenue Recognition—Multiple-Element Arrangements). If a contract involves a specified number of identical or similar acts, for example, the playing of a sports contest under a season ticket arrangement, then each sports contest represents a separate product and proportional performance accounting is appropriate. In such a case, revenue should be recognized by relating the number of acts performed to the total number of acts to be performed over the contract life. If a contract involves a specified number of defined but not identical acts, revenue should be recognized using the relationship of the sales value of the individual acts to the total sales value of the service contract. If no pattern of performance can be determined, or if a service contract involves an unspecified number of similar or identical acts with a fixed period for performance, for example, a maintenance contract for electronic office equipment, the straight-line method, that is, recognizing revenue equally over the periods of performance, should be used. In Exhibit 8-1, **Microsoft**'s revenue recognition note provides an example of how a company recognizes revenue for services when a lengthy time period is involved. Of course, proportional revenue recognition is applicable only if cash collection is reasonably assured and if losses from nonpayment can be objectively determined.

Exhibit 8-1 | Microsoft's Revenue Recognition Note—Partial

Revenue from multi-year licensing arrangements are accounted for as subscriptions, with billings recorded as unearned revenue and recognized as revenue ratably over the billing coverage period. Certain multi-year licensing arrangements include rights to receive future versions of software product.

Source: Microsoft

与长期使用费有关的收入按照订购进行账务处理，买方应付的合同成本按照使用时间长短确认为未实现收入。使用费合同应包括允许用户使用新软件产品的权利。

The cost recognition problems of service contracts are somewhat different from those of long-term construction-type contracts. Most service contracts involve three different types of costs: (1) initial direct costs related to obtaining and performing initial services on the contract, such as commissions, legal fees, credit investigations, and paper processing; (2) direct costs related to performing the various acts of service; and (3) indirect costs related to maintaining the organization to service the contract, for example, general and administrative expenses. Initial direct costs generally are charged, that is, matched, against revenue using the same measure used for revenue recognition. Direct costs usually are charged to expense as incurred because they relate directly to the acts for which revenue is recognized. Similarly, all indirect costs should be charged to expense as incurred. As is true for long-term construction-type contracts, any indicated loss on completion of the service contract is to be charged to the period in which the loss is first indicated. If collection of a service contract is highly uncertain, revenue recognition should not be related to performance but to the collection of the receivable using one of the methods described in the latter part of this chapter.

To illustrate accounting for a service contract using the proportional performance method, assume a correspondence school enters into 100 contracts with students for an extended writing course. The fee for each contract is $500, payable in advance. This fee includes many different services such as providing the text material, evaluating written assignments and examinations, and awarding of a certificate. Total incremental direct costs incurred to get these 100 students to decide to sign up for the extended writing course are $5,000.[15] Direct costs for the lessons actually completed during the first period are $12,000. The separate sales value of the lessons completed during the first period is $24,000; if sold separately, the total sales value of all the lessons would be $60,000. The following entries would be made to record these transactions:

Cash	50,000	
Deferred Course Revenue (liability account)		50,000
Deferred Initial Costs (asset account)	5,000	
Cash		5,000
Contract Costs (expense account)	12,000	
Cash		12,000
Deferred Course Revenue	20,000*	
Recognized Course Revenue		20,000
Contract Costs	2,000†	
Deferred Initial Costs		2,000

* Relative sales value percentage: $24,000/$60,000 = 40%; $50,000 × 0.40 = $20,000
† $5,000 × 0.40 = $2,000

The gross profit reported on these contracts for the period would be $6,000 ($20,000 − $12,000 − $2,000). The deferred initial cost and deferred course revenues would normally be reported as current balance sheet deferrals, because the operating cycle of a correspondence school would be equal to the average time to complete a contract or one year, whichever is longer.

---

[15] These "incremental direct acquisition costs" should be recorded as assets and then subsequently expensed in proportion to the amount of revenue that is recognized. See FASB ASC paragraph 605-20-25-4.

Revenue Recognition after Delivery of Goods or Performance of Services

LO6 学习目标6

解释通过分期收款法、成本补偿法及现金法，在交付产品或者提供服务后何时才确认收入。

6 Explain when revenue is recognized after delivery of goods or services through installment sales, cost recovery, and cash methods.

One of the FASB's two revenue recognition criteria, listed at the beginning of this chapter, states that revenue should not be recognized until the earnings process is substantially completed. Normally, the earnings process is substantially completed by the delivery of goods or performance of services. Collection of receivables is usually routine, and any future warranty costs can be reasonably estimated. In some cases, however, the circumstances surrounding a revenue transaction are such that considerable uncertainty exists as to whether payments will indeed be received. This can occur if the sales transaction is unusual in nature or involves a customer in such a way that default carries little cost or penalty. Under these circumstances, the uncertainty of cash collection suggests that revenue recognition should await the actual receipt of cash.

根据收到现金方式的不同，确认收入至少有三种方法：分期收款法、成本补偿法和现金法。

There are at least three different approaches to revenue recognition that depend on the receipt of cash: installment sales, cost recovery, and cash. These methods differ as to the treatment of costs incurred and the timing of revenue recognition. They are summarized and contrasted with the full accrual method in the table below.

These methods are really not alternatives to each other; however, the guidelines for applying them are not well defined. As the uncertainty of the environment increases, GAAP would require moving from the full accrual method to installment sales, cost recovery, and, finally, a strict cash approach. The cash method is the most conservative approach, because it would not permit the deferral of any costs but would charge them to expense as those costs are paid. In the following pages, each of these revenue recognition methods will be discussed and illustrated.

Method	Timing of Revenue and/or Income Recognition	Treatment of Product Costs or Direct Costs under Service Contracts
Full accrual	At point of sale.	Charge against revenue at time of sale or rendering of service.
Installment sales	At collection of cash. Usually a portion of the cash payment is recognized as income.	Defer to be matched against a part of each cash collection. Usually done by deferring the estimated profit.
Cost recovery	At collection of cash, but only after all costs are recovered.	Defer to be matched against total cash collected.
Cash	At collection of cash.	Charge to expense as incurred.

Installment Sales Method

Traditionally, the most commonly applied method for dealing with the uncertainty of cash collections has been the installment sales method. Under this method, profit is recognized as cash is collected rather than at the time of sale.[16] The installment sales method is used most commonly in cases of real estate sales where contracts may involve little or no down

---

[16] FASB ASC paragraphs 605-10-25-3 through 5 and 360-20-55-7 through 10.

> **Caution**
>
> Do not confuse installment sales with the installment sales method of accounting. Remember that most installment sales are accounted for using accrual accounting. Only those sales with a high degree of uncertainty as to collection are accounted for using the installment sales method.

payment, payments are spread over 10 to 30 or 40 years, and a high probability of default in the early years exists because of a small investment by the buyer in the contract and because the market prices of the property often are unstable. Application of the accrual method to these contracts frequently overstates income in the early years due to the failure to realistically provide for future costs related to the contract, including losses from contract defaults. The FASB considered these types of sales and concluded that accrual accounting applied in these circumstances often results in "front-end loading," that is, a recognition of all revenue at the time of the sales contract with improper matching of related costs. Thus, the Board has established criteria that must be met before real estate and retail land sales can be recorded using the full accrual method of revenue recognition. If the criteria are not fully met, then the use of the installment sales method, or in some cases the cost recovery or deposit methods, is recommended to reflect the conditions of the sale more accurately.[17] **General Growth Properties, Inc.**, a real estate development firm, provides disclosure, shown in Exhibit 8-2, relating to its revenue recognition policy. Note that General Growth Properties uses one of four revenue recognition policies (full accrual, installment, cost recovery, or percentage of completion) for its transactions, depending on whether or not the transaction meets established revenue recognition criteria.

Accounting for installment sales using the deferred gross profit approach requires determining a gross profit rate for the sales of each year and establishing an accounts receivable and a deferred gross profit account identified by the year of the sale. As collections are made of a given year's receivables, a portion of the deferred profit equal to the gross profit rate times the collections made is recognized as income. To keep things relatively simple, the following examples of transactions and journal entries will illustrate the installment sales method assuming the sale of merchandise.

分期收款法的账务处理：根据递延的毛利确认收入，要求确定当年的毛利率并在发生销售业务的当期设立应收账款账户和递延毛利账户。

> **FYI**
>
> The installment sales method is frequently used for income tax purposes. The primary rationale for allowing its use in that setting is that when the cash is collected over an extended period, at the time the sale is made the taxpayer does not have the wherewithal to pay all of the income tax due on the total profit.

Exhibit 8-2 | General Growth Properties' Revenue Recognition Note

> Revenues from land sales are recognized using the full accrual method provided that various criteria relating to the terms of the transactions and our subsequent involvement with the land sold are met. Revenues relating to transactions that do not meet the established criteria are deferred and recognized when the criteria are met or using the installment or cost recovery methods, as appropriate in the circumstances. For land sale transactions in which we are required to perform additional services and incur significant costs after title has passed, revenues and cost of sales are recognized on a percentage of completion basis.

© Cengage Learning 2014

[17] FASB ASC Subtopic 360-20 (Property, Plant, and Equipment—Real Estate Sales).

Installment Sales of Merchandise Assume that the Riding Corporation sells merchandise on the installment basis and that the uncertainties of cash collection make the use of the installment sales method necessary. The following data relate to three years of operations. To simplify the presentation, interest charges are excluded from the example.

	2014	2015	2016
Installment sales	$150,000	$200,000	$300,000
Cost of installment sales	100,000	140,000	204,000
Gross profit	$ 50,000	$ 60,000	$ 96,000
Gross profit percentage	33.333%	30%	32%
Cash collections:			
2014 sales	$ 30,000	$ 75,000	$ 30,000
2015 sales		70,000	80,000
2016 sales			100,000

The entries to record the transactions for 2014 would be as follows:

During the year:

Installment Accounts Receivable—2014	150,000	
Installment Sales		150,000
Cost of Installment Sales	100,000	
Inventory		100,000
Cash	30,000	
Installment Accounts Receivable—2014		30,000

End of year:

Installment Sales	150,000	
Cost of Installment Sales		100,000
Deferred Gross Profit—2014		50,000
Deferred Gross Profit—2014	10,000*	
Realized Gross Profit on Installment Sales		10,000

* $30,000 × 33.33%

The sales and costs related to sales are recorded in a manner identical to the accounting for sales discussed in Chapter 7. At the end of the year, however, the sales and cost of sales accounts are closed to a deferred gross profit account rather than to Retained Earnings. The realized gross profit is then recognized by applying the gross profit percentage to cash collections. All other general and administrative expenses are normally written off in the period incurred.

For 2014, the income statement would begin with sales from which is subtracted deferred gross profit and to which is added realized gross profit for the year to arrive at a net figure. Cost of sales would then be subtracted along with other operating expenses (assumed to be $5,000 in this example) as illustrated:

Sales	$ 150,000
Less: Deferred gross profit	(50,000)
Add: Realized gross profit	10,000
	$ 110,000
Less: Cost of installment sales	(100,000)
Other operating expenses	(5,000)
Operating income	$ 5,000

Entries for the next two years are summarized in the schedule below.

	2015		2016	
During the year:				
Installment Accounts Receivable—2015	200,000			
Installment Accounts Receivable—2016			300,000	
Installment Sales.....................................		200,000		300,000
Cost of Installment Sales.............................	140,000		204,000	
Inventory		140,000		204,000
Cash	145,000		210,000	
Installment Accounts Receivable—2014		75,000		30,000
Installment Accounts Receivable—2015		70,000		80,000
Installment Accounts Receivable—2016				100,000
End of year:				
Installment Sales	200,000		300,000	
Cost of Installment Sales		140,000		204,000
Deferred Gross Profit—2015.........................		60,000		
Deferred Gross Profit—2016.........................				96,000
Deferred Gross Profit—2014	25,000*		10,000†	
Deferred Gross Profit—2015	21,000‡		24,000§	
Deferred Gross Profit—2016			32,000#	
Realized Gross Profit on Installment Sales...........		46,000		66,000

*$75,000 × 0.33333 = $25,000
† $30,000 × 0.33333 = $10,000
‡ $70,000 × 0.30 = $21,000
§ $80,000 × 0.30 = $24,000
# $100,000 × 0.32 = $32,000

If a company is heavily involved in installment sales, the operating cycle of the business is normally the period of the average installment contract. Thus, the currently accepted definition of current assets and current liabilities requires that the receivables and their related deferred gross profit accounts be reported in the Current Assets section of classified balance sheets. The deferred gross profit accounts should be reported as an offset to the related accounts receivable. Thus, at the end of 2014, the Current Assets section would include the following account balances:

> **Caution**
>
> Note that a separate deferred gross profit account is kept for each year and that accounts receivable collections must be accounted for by year. This is to ensure that the appropriate gross profit percentage is applied to the cash collected.

Installment accounts receivable..	$120,000	
Less: Deferred gross profit	40,000	$80,000

Complexities of Installment Sales of Merchandise In the previous example, no provision was made for interest. In reality, installment sales contracts always include interest, either expressed or implied. The interest portion of the contract payments is recognized as income in the period in which cash is received, and the balance of the payment is treated as a collection on the installment sale. Thus, if in the example discussed previously, the $75,000 collection of 2014 sales in 2015 included interest of $40,000, only $35,000 would be used to compute the realized gross profit from 2014 sales. The resulting journal entries made in 2015 relating to the $75,000 collection of 2014 sales would be as follows:

Cash	75,000	
Interest Revenue		40,000
Installment Accounts Receivable—2014		35,000
Deferred Gross Profit—2014	11,666*	
Realized Gross Profit on Installment Sales		11,666

* $35,000 × 0.33333 = $11,666

Stop & Think

What does the $80,000 net amount represent?

a) The cost of the inventory associated with the $120,000 installment accounts receivable
b) The amount of cash expected to be ultimately collected from the $120,000 installment accounts receivable
c) The net present value of the installment accounts receivable amount of $120,000
d) The current portion of the installment accounts receivable amount of $120,000

Additional complexities can arise in installment sales accounting in providing for uncollectible accounts. Because of the right to repossess merchandise in the event of nonpayment, the provision for uncollectible accounts can be less than might be expected. Only the amount of the receivable in excess of the current value of the repossessed merchandise is a potential loss. Accounting for repossessions is discussed in Chapter 9. Theoretically, a proper matching of estimated losses against revenues would require allocating the expected losses over the years of collection. Practically, however, the provision is made and charged against income in the period of the sale. Thus, the accounting entries for handling estimated uncollectible accounts are the same as illustrated in Chapter 7. However, normally the impact of accounting for bad debts with respect to installment sales is not great because revenue and receivables are not recognized until the probability of cash collection is quite high.

Cost Recovery Method

在成本补偿法下，只有在业务发生的成本收到现金补偿时才确认收入。收到的现金，不管是利息还是本金，必须首先补偿所消耗的成本费用。

Under the cost recovery method, no income is recognized on a sale until the cost of the item sold is recovered through cash receipts.[18] All cash receipts, both interest and principal portions, are applied first to the cost of those items sold. Then all subsequent receipts are reported as revenue. Because all costs have been recovered, the recognized revenue after cost recovery represents income. This method is used only when the circumstances surrounding a sale are so uncertain that earlier recognition is impossible.

Using the information from the Riding Corporation example, assume that collections are so uncertain that the use of the cost recovery method is deemed appropriate. While the entries to record the installment sale, the receipt of cash, and the deferral of the gross profit are identical for both the installment sales and cost recovery methods, the entry for recognizing gross profit differs.

In 2014 no gross profit would be recognized, because the amount of cash collected ($30,000) is less than the cost of the inventory sold ($100,000). The cash collections in 2015 relating to 2014 sales result in total cash receipts exceeding the cost of sales

---

[18] FASB ASC paragraphs 360-20-55-13 through 15.

($30,000 + $75,000 > $100,000). Thus, in 2015 gross profit of $5,000 would be recognized on 2014 sales. The journal entry to recognize this gross profit in 2015 follows:

Deferred Gross Profit—2014	5,000	
Realized Gross Profit on Installment Sales		5,000

Because the cash collected in 2015 for 2015 sales ($70,000) is less than the cost of inventory sold ($140,000), no gross profit would be recognized in 2015 on 2015 sales. In 2016 the $30,000 collected in cash from the 2014 sales would all be recognized as gross profit. The cash collected relating to 2015 sales, $80,000, when added to the cash received in 2015, $70,000, exceeds the cost of the 2015 sales of $140,000. Thus, $10,000 of gross profit that was deferred in 2015 will be recognized in 2016. The journal entry to recognize gross profit in 2016 would be:

Deferred Gross Profit—2014	30,000	
Deferred Gross Profit—2015	10,000	
Realized Gross Profit on Installment Sales		40,000

Comparing the amount of gross profit that is recognized using the various revenue recognition methods for the period 2014–2016 indicates how the income statement can be materially impacted by the method used.

	Gross Profit Recognized		
Revenue Recognition Method	2014	2015	2016
Full accrual	$50,000	$60,000	$96,000
Installment sales	10,000	46,000	66,000
Cost recovery	0	5,000	40,000

Cash Method

If the probability of recovering product or service costs is remote, the cash method of accounting could be used. Seldom would this method be applicable for sales of merchandise or real estate because the right of repossession would leave considerable value to the seller. However, the cash method might be appropriate for service contracts with high initial costs and considerable uncertainty as to the ultimate collection of the contract price. Under this method, all costs are charged to expense as incurred, and revenue is recognized as collections are made. This extreme method of revenue and expense recognition would be appropriate only when the potential losses on a contract cannot be estimated with any degree of certainty.

SOLUTIONS TO OPENING SCENARIO QUESTIONS

1. First, start-up companies, particularly Internet start-ups, often have not yet reported any earnings. Thus, the price-earnings ratio is virtually worthless in estimating appropriate stock values. Second, the Internet has been, and still is, characterized by huge upside potential but great uncertainty about which Internet-related business models will ultimately succeed. In this uncertain setting, the best measure of a company's future Internet-related profitability is the size of its Internet presence now. This is measured by volume of business, or sales.

2. Here are two contributing factors.
   a. Change in expected growth trend: MicroStrategy's stock price was based on investors' forecasts of future sales and profits. Investors had extrapolated past growth trends into the future. So, the restatement of revenue not only lowered the level of revenue, but also drastically lowered the expected future growth trend.

b. Cockroach theory: When you see one cockroach in your kitchen, what do you know? You know that there are others. The announcement of the revenue restatement called into question everything that MicroStrategy was doing. All of the company's past statements were now being reevaluated in light of this newly discovered lack of credibility.

3. Here are three possibilities.

   a. This is the ethical thing to do. All public figures should feel a fiduciary responsibility to see that those who don't have access to information are not deceived. The big guys (the banks, the institutional investors, and so forth) can take care of themselves. The small guys, who have to rely on the integrity of the big guys, are the ones who should be watched after.

   b. From a crisis management standpoint, we have seen over and over (Watergate, Enron, and any other scandal that you can think of) that the fallout from a mistake is worse if a company has tried to cover up the mistake. Just take your medicine, tell all of the bad news up front, take your lumps, and move on.

   c. Companies with more transparent reporting and with a reputation for integrity will, in the long run, have a lower cost of capital. These companies are trusted, so there is less information risk.

Stop & Think SOLUTIONS

1. (Page 8-16) The correct answer is B. The other three methods are all acceptable ways to measure a contract's percentage of completion. Because this percentage can greatly influence a company's reported profits, the percentage must be arrived at objectively to avoid management pressure to bias the estimated percentage completed in order to meet profit targets.

2. (Page 8-19) The correct answer is C. When the progress billings on construction contracts account is netted against the construction in progress account, the resulting net figure represents the amount of the construction (which includes costs as well as a portion of expected profits) for which the customer has not yet been billed.

3. (Page 8-23) The correct answer is D. If estimates in prior periods were overstated by a significant amount, too much revenue (and profit) could end up being reported in the early periods. This error would require a loss to be recorded for this period so that the revenue (and profit) recognized to date would be correct.

4. (Page 8-33) The correct answer is A. The $80,000 amount represents the cost of the inventory associated with the $120,000 in sales that is reflected in the accounts receivable balance. Because collection of the receivable balance is uncertain, it is recorded at a lesser amount. This $80,000 number assumes that if worse came to worst and customers didn't pay, the seller could at least get the inventory back.

SOLUTION TO USING THE FASB'S CODIFICATION

You are in luck—Subtopic 605-45 addresses "Principal Agent Considerations." You may recall that this subtopic came up in the text discussion of whether an Internet grocer should report revenue "gross" or "net." FASB ASC paragraph 605-45-45-1 says the following: "It is a matter of judgment whether an entity should report revenue based on either of the following: (a) The gross amount billed to a customer because it has earned revenue (as a principal) from the sale of the goods or services. (b) The net amount retained (that is, the amount billed to the customer less the amount paid to a supplier) because it has earned a commission or fee as an agent."

So, a "principal" is the primary owner of a business, the risk taker and the person ultimately responsible for the actions of the business. An "agent" merely works for a principal, doing certain tasks as directed by the principal. In some sense, the "principal" is the entrepreneur, and the "agent" is the employee.

Review Chapter 8 Learning Objectives

1. Identify the primary criteria for revenue recognition.

Revenue has historically been recognized and recorded when two criteria have been met. The first criterion is realizability, which means that the seller has received payment or a valid promise of payment from the purchaser. The second criterion is met when the earnings process is substantially complete. Substantial completion means that the seller has provided the product or service (or a large portion of the product or service) to the purchaser. More recently, the key principle in revenue recognition has become that revenue is recognized when performance obligations to customers are satisfied.

2. Discuss the revenue recognition issues, and abuses, underlying the examples used in *SAB 101*.

SAB 101 was released in 1999 by the SEC staff to curtail specific abuses in revenue recognition practices. *SAB 101* requires companies to implement better internal control processes so that the records about the timing of sales transactions are reliable. In addition, up-front fees should be recognized as revenue over the life of a service agreement, generally on a straight-line basis. Finally, revenue for most Internet broker arrangements should be reported net instead of gross. *SAB 101* proved to be a stimulus to the FASB and the IASB to reconsider the area of revenue recognition.

3. Describe the contract approach to revenue recognition that is currently being considered by the FASB and IASB.

With respect to revenue recognition, the FASB and IASB are considering a contract approach that is more consistent with the underlying conceptual framework of accounting standards than is the patchwork of approaches, focused on the earnings process, that have arisen over time. The contract approach uses the relative amounts of the estimated separate selling prices of the various elements in the arrangement to measure the performance obligations created when a contractual arrangement with a customer is entered into. Revenue is recognized when those performance obligations are eventually satisfied. A performance obligation is satisfied when control of the contractual good or service passes from the buyer to the seller.

4. Record journal entries for long-term construction-type contracts using percentage-of-completion and completed-contract methods.

In some instances, revenue may be recognized prior to the actual delivery of goods or services. The most common example of this is a long-term contract. In this case, revenue may be recognized prior to delivery if four criteria are met: (1) estimates can be made of the amount of work remaining, (2) a contract exists outlining each party's responsibilities, (3) the buyer can be expected to fulfill the contract, and (4) the seller can be expected to fulfill the contract. If these conditions are met, revenue may be recognized prior to the point of sale and the revenue recognition method is termed *percentage of completion*. With this method, revenue is recognized based on an estimate of the degree to which the contract is complete. Using the cost-to-cost method for estimating the degree of completion results in matching actual contract costs with estimated revenues. With long-term contracts, journal entries are required to record costs incurred, billings made to customers, and collections from customers. These entries are the same for both the percentage-of-completion method and the completed-contract method. An additional journal entry is made each period under the percentage-of-completion method to record the recognition of revenue and related expenses for the period. The amount of revenue recognized is a function of the percentage of the work completed to date. With the completed-contract method, revenue is recognized only when the contract has been completed.

5. Record journal entries for long-term service contracts using the proportional performance method.

With long-term service contracts, revenue can be recognized prior to completion based on the degree to which the contract is completed. Estimates of completion are made based on the percentage of identical acts completed or the relative sales value of the acts completed. The amount of revenue to be recognized is computed by multiplying this ratio by the contract price.

6. Explain when revenue is recognized after delivery of goods or services through installment sales, cost recovery, and cash methods.

In some cases, it is not appropriate to recognize revenue at the point of sale when a valid promise of payment has not been received. In these instances, the recognition of revenue is deferred until cash is actually received. Several methods exist for recognizing revenue. The installment sales method recognizes profit based on a gross profit percentage. Of every dollar collected, a portion is recorded as profit based on the gross profit percentage. With the cost recovery method, cash collections are first considered to be a recovery of the costs associated with the sale. Once costs are recovered, each subsequent dollar received is recorded as profit. When the cash method is employed, profit is determined by comparing the cash received from customers with the cash expended during the period relating to inventory or services.

FASB-IASB CODIFICATION SUMMARY

Topic	FASB Accounting Standards Codification	Original FASB Standard	Corresponding IASB Standard	Differences between U.S. GAAP and IFRS
Revenue recognition	Topic 605	Contained in a large number of different standards	IAS 18, IAS 11	U.S. GAAP and IFRS are generally consistent, but many detailed differences exist. The FASB and IASB are currently working on a joint revenue recognition project.
Completed-contract method	Subtopic 605-35	ARB 45 and SOP 81-1	IAS 11	Under IFRS, the completed contract method is not allowed.
Pre-sale revenue recognition for biological assets	Section 905-330-35	SOP 85-3	IAS 41	Under IFRS, changes in the fair value of biological assets are recognized as gains and losses. Under U.S. GAAP, a similar procedure is acceptable under some circumstances, but not required.
Multiple-element arrangements	Subtopic 605-25	EITF 08-1	IAS 18	IFRS does not contain any specific provisions related to multiple-element arrangements.

KEY TERMS

Cash method 8-34
Completed-contract method 8-15
Cost recovery method 8-33
Cost-to-cost method 8-17
Efforts-expended methods 8-17
Input measures 8-17
Installment sales method 8-29
Output measures 8-17
Percentage-of-completion accounting 8-15
Proportional performance method 8-15
Recognition 8-4

Tutorial Activities

Tutorial Activities with author-written, content-specific feedback, available on *CengageNOW for Stice & Stice*.

QUESTIONS

1. What are the two traditional general revenue recognition criteria?
2. Why did the SEC issue *Staff Accounting Bulletin (SAB) 101*?
3. Why does Question 1 in *SAB 101* emphasize the proper signing of a sales agreement?
4. In general, why are up-front, nonrefundable fees not recognized as revenue immediately?
5. Under FASB ASC Subtopic 605-25, when is an element of a multiple-element arrangement considered to be a unit of accounting?
6. Under FASB ASC Subtopic 605-25, what are the three different methods for determining the separate selling price of a single element in a multiple-element transaction?
7. What are the three basic steps in applying the contract method for revenue recognition?
8. Why would a company prefer gross revenue reporting over net revenue reporting?
9. Under what conditions is percentage-of-completion accounting recommended for construction contractors?
10. Distinguish between the cost-to-cost method and efforts-expended methods of measuring the percentage of completion.
11. Output measures of percentage of completion are sometimes preferred to input measures. What are some examples of commonly used output measures?
12. What is the relationship between the construction in progress account and the progress billings on construction contracts account? How should these accounts be reported on the balance sheet?
13. When a measure of percentage of completion other than cost-to-cost is used, the amount of cost charged against revenue using the percentage of completion usually will be different from the costs incurred. What accounting alternative exists to make it so that the costs charged against revenue are equal to the costs incurred?
14. The construction in progress account is used to accumulate all costs of construction. What additional item is included in this account when percentage-of-completion accounting is followed?
15. The gross profit percentage reported on long-term construction contracts often varies from year to year. What is the major reason for this variation?
16. How are anticipated contract losses treated under the completed-contract and percentage-of-completion methods?
17. What input and output measures usually are applicable to the proportional performance method for long-term service contracts?
18. The proportional performance method spreads the profit over the periods in which services are being performed. What arguments could be made against this method of revenue recognition for newly formed service-oriented companies?
19. Distinguish among the three different approaches to revenue recognition that await the receipt of cash. How does the treatment of costs incurred vary depending on the approach used?
20. Under what general conditions is the installment sales method of accounting preferred to the full accrual method?
21. The normal accounting entries for installment sales require keeping a separate record by year of receivables, collections on receivables, and the deferred gross profit percentages. Why are these separate records necessary?
22. Installment sales contracts generally include interest. Contrast the method of recognizing interest revenue from the method used to recognize the gross profit on the sale.
23. Under what conditions would the cash method of recognizing revenue be acceptable for reporting purposes?

PRACTICE EXERCISES

Practice 8-1

Basic Journal Entries for Revenue Recognition
The company collected $1,000 cash in advance from a customer for services to be rendered. Subsequently, the company rendered the services. Make the journal entries necessary to record (1) the receipt of the cash and (2) the subsequent completion of the services.

Practice 8-2

Revenue in a Multiple-Element Arrangement under Subtopic 605-25
On June 4, Seller Company signed a sales agreement with Buyer Company to deliver and install a piece of factory equipment. The total contract price is $300,000. Customers usually buy an equipment/installation package, but Seller Company does sell equipment without installation and also installs equipment sold by other companies. The selling price of the equipment without installation is $290,000. The separate price

for installation of this piece of equipment is $20,000. How much revenue should be recognized by Seller Company when the equipment is delivered but before it is installed?

Practice 8-3

Reporting Revenue Gross and Net

Shop-at-Home Company operates a Web grocer. Customers submit their orders online to Shop-at-Home Company; Shop-at-Home then forwards the orders to a national grocery chain. The grocery chain arranges for assembly and shipment of the order. Shop-at-Home Company receives 3% of the retail value of all orders it takes. During January, Shop-at-Home Company received orders for groceries with a retail selling price of $400,000. These groceries cost the grocery store chain $280,000. The grocery store chain collected cash of $400,000 from the customers and paid the appropriate commission in cash to Shop-at-Home Company. Based on this information, make all journal entries necessary in January (1) on the books of Shop-at-Home Company and (2) on the books of the grocery store chain. Assume that the grocery store chain uses a perpetual inventory system.

Practice 8-4

Cost-to-Cost Method

The company signed an $880,000 contract to build an environmentally friendly access trail to South Willow Lake. The project was expected to take approximately three years. The following information was collected for each year of the project—Year 1, Year 2, and Year 3:

	Cost Expended During the Year	Expected Additional Cost to Completion	Support Timbers Laid during the Year	Additional Support Timbers to Be Laid	Trail Feet Constructed during the Year	Additional Trail Feet to Be Constructed
Year 1	$100,000	$450,000	150	850	3,000	15,200
Year 2	150,000	280,000	300	520	7,500	8,200
Year 3	250,000	0	500	0	8,000	0

The company uses the percentage-of-completion method of computing revenue from long-term construction contracts. Assume that the company employs the cost-to-cost method of estimating the percentage of completion. Compute the amount of revenue to be recognized in (1) Year 1, (2) Year 2, and (3) Year 3. (*Note:* Round percentage to three decimal places for percentage completed.)

Practice 8-5

Efforts-Expended Method

Refer to Practice 8-4. Assume that the company employs the efforts-expended method of estimating the percentage of completion. In particular, the company measures its progress by the number of support timbers laid in the trail. Compute the amount of revenue to be recognized in (1) Year 1, (2) Year 2, and (3) Year 3. (*Note:* Round percentage to three decimal places for percentage completed.)

Practice 8-6

Percentage of Completion Based on Output Measures

Refer to Practice 8-4. Assume that the company employs an output measure to estimate the percentage of completion. In particular, the company measures its progress by the number of trail feet that have been completed. Compute the amount of revenue to be recognized in (1) Year 1, (2) Year 2, and (3) Year 3. (*Note:* Round percentage to three decimal places for percentage completed.)

Practice 8-7

Basic Construction Journal Entries

Refer to Practice 8-4. In addition to the percentage-of-completion information, the following information is available regarding billing and cash collection for the project:

	Year 1	Year 2	Year 3
Progress billings	$200,000	$200,000	$480,000
Cash collections	180,000	170,000	530,000

Make the journal entries necessary to record the construction cost, the progress billings, and the cash collections in (1) Year 1, (2) Year 2, and (3) Year 3.

Practice 8-8

Completed-Contract Journal Entries
Refer to Practice 8-4 and Practice 8-7. Assume that the company uses the completed-contract method. Make the journal entries necessary in Year 3 to recognize revenue and costs for the completed project.

Practice 8-9

Percentage-of-Completion Journal Entries
Refer to Practice 8-4 and Practice 8-7. Assume that the company uses the percentage-of-completion method and uses a cost-to-cost approach in estimating the percentage of completion. Make the journal entries to record revenue and cost for the construction project in (1) Year 1, (2) Year 2, and (3) Year 3.

Practice 8-10

Construction Contracts: Balance Sheet Reporting
Refer to Practice 8-4, Practice 8-7, and Practice 8-9. Indicate how, and in what amount, the following accounts will be reported in the company's balance sheet for Year 1, Year 2, and Year 3: (1) Accounts Receivable, (2) Progress Billings, and (3) Construction in Progress. Assume that as of the end of Year 3, the progress billings and construction in progress accounts have not yet been closed.

Practice 8-11

Multiple Years of Revenues and Costs: Cost-to-Cost Method
The company signed a $1,800,000 contract to build an environmentally friendly access trail to Timpanogas Caves. The project was expected to take approximately three years. The following information was collected for each year of the project, Year 1, Year 2, and Year 3:

	Cost Expended during the Year	Expected Additional Cost to Completion	Trail Feet Constructed during the Year	Additional Trail Feet to Be Constructed
Year 1	$280,000	$760,000	9,800	20,300
Year 2	390,000	380,000	10,200	10,000
Year 3	370,000	0	10,000	0

The company uses the percentage-of-completion method of computing revenue from long-term construction contracts. Assume that the company employs the cost-to-cost method of estimating the percentage of completion. Make the journal entries to record revenue and cost for the construction project—(1) Year 1, (2) Year 2, and (3) Year 3. (*Note:* Round percentage to four decimal places for percentage completed.)

Practice 8-12

Multiple Years of Revenues and Costs: Output Measure
Refer to Practice 8-11. Assume that the company uses the percentage of trail feet constructed in estimating the percentage of completion. Make the journal entries to record revenue and cost for the construction project in (1) Year 1, (2) Year 2, and (3) Year 3. (*Note:* Round percentage to four decimal places for percentage completed.)

Practice 8-13

Multiple Years of Revenues and Costs: Anticipated Loss
The company signed a $1,450,000 contract to build an environmentally friendly access trail to Stansbury Peak. The project was expected to take approximately three years. The following information was collected for each year of the project—Year 1, Year 2, and Year 3:

	Cost Expended during the Year	Expected Additional Cost to Completion
Year 1	$200,000	$1,150,000
Year 2	350,000	1,020,000
Year 3	915,000	0

The company uses the percentage-of-completion method of computing revenue from long-term construction contracts, and the company employs the cost-to-cost method to estimate the percentage of completion. Make the journal entries to record revenue and cost for the construction project in (1) Year 1, (2) Year 2, and (3) Year 3. (*Note:* Round percentage to four decimal places for percentage completed.)

Practice 8-14

Journal Entries for the Proportional Performance Method

The Washington Blue Sox is a minor league baseball team. The team has 55 home games during a season and sells season tickets for $600 each. For the most recent season, the Blue Sox sold 1,900 season tickets. The total initial direct costs (in cash) related to the season tickets (including product giveaways for signing up early, costs of processing the transactions, and so forth) were $180,000. Direct costs (in cash) are $3 per customer per game. The team's fiscal year ends on June 30. As of that date, 21 of the home games have been played. Make the journal entries necessary to record (1) the receipt of cash for the 1,900 season tickets sold, (2) the payment (in cash) for the initial direct costs, and (3) the recognition of all season ticket revenues and expenses for the fiscal year.

Practice 8-15

Installment Sales: Basic Journal Entries

The company had sales during the year of $350,000. The gross profit percentage during the year was 20%. Cash collected during the year related to these sales was 40% of the sales. Give all journal entries necessary during the year, assuming use of the installment sales method.

Practice 8-16

Installment Sales: Financial Statement Reporting

Refer to Practice 8-15. Indicate how the installment sales receivable would be reported in the balance sheet at the end of the year.

Practice 8-17

Installment Sales: Interest on Receivables

Transistor Electronics makes all of its sales on credit and accounts for them using the installment sales method. For simplicity, assume that all sales occur on the first day of the year and that all cash collections are made on the last day of the year. Transistor Electronics charges 21% interest on the unpaid installment balances. Data for Year 1 and Year 2 are as follows:

	Year 1	Year 2
Sales	$200,000	$220,000
Cost of goods sold	110,000	130,000
Cash collections (principal and interest):		
From Year 1 sales	90,000	100,000
From Year 2 sales	0	100,000

Prepare *all* necessary journal entries for (1) Year 1 and (2) Year 2.

Practice 8-18

Cost Recovery Method: Basic Journal Entries

The company had installment sales in Year 1 of $350,000, in Year 2 of $270,000, and in Year 3 of $210,000. The gross profit percentage of each year, in order, was 20%, 25%, and 30%. Past history has shown that 40% of total sales are collected in the year of the sale, 50% in the year after the sale, and no collections are made in the second year after the sale or thereafter. Because of uncertainty about cash collection, the company uses the cost recovery method. Make all necessary journal entries for (1) Year 1, (2) Year 2, and (3) Year 3.

EXERCISES

Exercise 8-19

Completed-Contract Method

On June 1, 2015, bids were submitted for a construction project to build a new municipal building and fire station. The lowest bid was $5,000,000, submitted by the Shannon Construction Company. Shannon was awarded the contract. Shannon uses the completed-contract method to report gross profit. The following data are given to summarize the activities on this contract for 2015 and 2016. Give the entries to record these transactions using the completed-contract method.

Year	Cost Incurred	Estimated Cost to Complete	Billings on Contract	Collections of Billings
2015	$1,930,000	$2,420,000	$2,100,000	$1,800,000
2016	2,290,000	0	2,900,000	3,200,000

Exercise 8-20

Percentage-of-Completion Analysis

Espiritu Construction Co. has used the cost-to-cost percentage-of-completion method of recognizing revenue. Tony Espiritu assumed leadership of the business after the recent death of his father, Howard. In reviewing the records, Tony finds the following information regarding a recently completed building project for which the total contract was $2,000,000.

	2014	2015	2016
Gross profit (loss)	$ 75,000	$140,000	$ (20,000)
Cost incurred	360,000	?	820,000

Espiritu wants to know how effectively the company operated during the last three years on this project and, because the information is not complete, has asked for answers to the following questions.

1. How much cost was incurred in 2015?
2. What percentage of the project was completed by the end of 2015?
3. What was the total estimated gross profit on the project by the end of 2015?
4. What was the estimated cost to complete the project at the end of 2015?

Exercise 8-21

Percentage-of-Completion Accounting

Perfectionist Construction Company was the low bidder on an office building construction contract. The contract bid was $9,000,000, with an estimated cost to complete the project of $7,000,000. The contract period was 30 months starting May 1, 2014. The company uses the cost-to-cost method of estimating earnings. Because of changes requested by the customer, the contract price was adjusted downward to $8,600,000 on May 1, 2015.

A record of construction activities for the years 2014–2017 is as follows:

Year	Actual Cost— Current Year	Progress Billings	Cash Receipts
2014	$1,900,000	$2,500,000	$1,900,000
2015	3,600,000	3,400,000	3,100,000
2016	1,670,000	2,700,000	2,500,000
2017			1,100,000

The estimated cost to complete the contract as of the end of each accounting period is:

2014	$5,150,000
2015	1,600,000
2016	0

Calculate the gross profit for the years 2014–2016 under the percentage-of-completion method of revenue recognition. (*Note:* Round percentage to two decimal places for percentage completed.)

Exercise 8-22

Percentage-of-Completion Analysis

Smokey International Inc. recently acquired the Kurtz Builders Company. Kurtz has incomplete accounting records. On one particular project, only the information below is available.

REVERSE SOLVABLE

	2014	2015	2016
Costs incurred during year	$200,000	$250,000	?
Estimated cost to complete	450,000	190,000	$ 0
Recognized revenue	220,000	?	?
Gross profit on contract	?	10,000	(10,000)
Contract price	850,000		

Because the information is incomplete, you are asked the following questions assuming the percentage-of-completion method is used, an output measure is used to estimate the percentage completed, and revenue is recorded using the actual cost approach.

1. How much gross profit should be reported in 2014?
2. How much revenue should be reported in 2015?
3. How much revenue should be reported in 2016?
4. How much cost was incurred in 2016?
5. What are the total costs on the contract?
6. What would be the gross profit for 2015 if the cost-to-cost percentage-of-completion method were used rather than the output measure? (*Hint:* Ignore the revenue amount shown for 2014 and gross profit amount reported for 2015.) (*Note:* Round percentage to two decimal places.)

Exercise 8-23

Reporting Construction Contracts

Kylie Builders Inc. is building a new home for Cassie Proffit at a contracted price of $200,000. The estimated cost at the time the contract is signed (January 2, 2015) is $115,000. At December 31, 2015, the total cost incurred is $60,000 with estimated costs to complete of $59,000. Kylie has billed $80,000 on the job and has received a $55,000 payment. This is the only contract in process at year-end. Prepare the sections of the balance sheet and the income statement of Kylie Builders Inc. affected by these events assuming use of (1) the percentage-of-completion method and (2) the completed-contract method. (*Note:* Round percentage to two decimal places for percentage completed.)

Exercise 8-24

Percentage of Completion Using Architect's Estimates

Southern California Builders Inc. entered into a contract to construct an office building and plaza at a contract price of $30,000,000. Income is to be reported using the percentage-of-completion method as determined by estimates made by the architect. The data below summarize the activities on the construction for the years 2014–2016. For the years 2014–2016, what entries are required to record this information, assuming the architect's estimate of the percentage completed is used to determine revenue (proportional cost approach)?

Year	Actual Cost Incurred	Estimated Cost to Complete	Percentage Completed— Architect's Estimate	Project Billings	Collections on Billings
2014	$7,600,000	$18,400,000	30%	$ 9,500,000	$ 9,000,000
2015	9,700,000	8,900,000	80	11,500,000	10,300,000
2016	8,800,000	0	100	9,000,000	10,700,000

Exercise 8-25

Completed-Contract Method

On January 1, 2014, the Kobe Construction Company entered into a three-year contract to build a dam. The original contract price was $21,000,000 and the estimated cost was $19,400,000. The following cost data relate to the construction period.

Year	Cost Incurred	Estimated Cost to Complete	Billings	Cash Collected
2014	$7,200,000	$12,500,000	$7,200,000	$6,500,000
2015	6,700,000	7,800,000	6,500,000	6,400,000
2016	7,900,000	0	7,300,000	8,100,000

Prepare the required journal entries for the three years of the contract, assuming Kobe uses the completed-contract method.

Exercise 8-26

Percentage-of-Completion Method with Change Orders

The Build-It Construction Company enters into a contract on January 1, 2015, to construct a 20-story office building for $42,000,000. During the construction period, many change orders are made to the original contract. The following schedule summarizes the changes made in 2015.

	Cost Incurred—2015	Estimated Cost to Complete	Contract Price
Basic contract	$8,000,000	$28,000,000	$42,000,000
Change Order 1	50,000	50,000	125,000
Change Order 2	0	50,000	0
Change Order 3	300,000	300,000	Still to be negotiated; at least cost.
Change Order 4	125,000	0	100,000

Compute the revenues, costs, and gross profit to be recognized in 2015, assuming use of the cost-to-cost method to determine the percentage completed. (*Note:* Round percentage to two decimal places.)

Exercise 8-27

Service Industry Accounting

The Spectrum Fitness Club charges a nonrefundable annual membership fee of $1,200 for its services. For this fee, each member receives a fitness evaluation (value $200), a monthly magazine (annual value $25), and two hours' use of the equipment each week (annual value $1,100). Each of the three elements of the annual membership can be purchased separately. The initial direct costs to obtain the membership are $180. The direct cost of the fitness evaluation is $100, and the monthly direct costs to provide the other services are estimated to be $25 per person. Give the journal entries to record the transactions in 2015 relative to a membership sold on May 1, 2015.

Exercise 8-28

Installment Sales Accounting

Jordan Corporation had sales in 2014 of $150,000, in 2015 of $180,000, and in 2016 of $225,000. The gross profit percentage of each year, in order, was 25%, 30%, and 35%. Past history has shown that 20% of total sales are collected in the first year, 40% in the second year, and 20% in the third year. Assuming these collections are made as projected, give the journal entries for 2014, 2015, and 2016, assuming the installment sales method. Ignore provisions for bad debts and interest.

Exercise 8-29

Installment Sales Analysis
Complete the following table.

	2014	2015	2016
Installment sales	$50,000	$80,000	$ (7)
Cost of installment sales	(1)	(5)	91,800
Gross profit	(2)	(6)	28,200
Gross profit percentage	(3)	25%	(8)
Cash collections:			
2014 sales	(4)	25,000	10,000
2015 sales		20,000	50,000
2016 sales			45,000
Realized gross profit on installment sales	1,100	10,500	(9)

Exercise 8-30

Cost Recovery Method
K. B. Sayer Furnishings Inc. had the following sales and gross profit percentages for the years 2014–2017.

	Sales	Gross Profit Percentage
2014	$60,000	55%
2015	65,000	51
2016	72,000	56
2017	76,000	57

Historically, 60% of sales are collected in the year of the sale, 25% in the following year, and 10% in the third year. Assuming collections are as projected, give the journal entries for the years 2014–2017, assuming the cost recovery method. (Ignore provision for bad debts.) Prepare a table comparing the gross profit recognized for 2014–2017 using the full accrual method and the cost recovery method.

Exercise 8-31

Cost Recovery Analysis
Hatch Enterprises uses the cost recovery method for all installment sales. Complete the following table.

	2014	2015	2016
Installment sales	$92,000	$103,000	$ (1)
Cost of installment sales	(2)	62,830	74,750
Gross profit percentage	36%	(3)	35%
Cash collections:			
2014 sales	27,200	48,300	12,200
2015 sales		36,600	(4)
2016 sales			43,450
Realized gross profit on installment sales	(5)	(6)	19,250

P2

Routine Activities of a Business

CHAPTER 9

Inventory and Cost of Goods Sold

Learning Objectives

1. Define inventory for a merchandising business, and identify the different types of inventory for a manufacturing business.

2. Explain the advantages and disadvantages of both periodic and perpetual inventory systems.

3. Determine when ownership of goods in transit changes hands and what circumstances require shipped inventory to be kept on the books.

4. Compute total inventory acquisition cost.

5. Use the four basic inventory valuation methods: specific identification, average cost, FIFO, and LIFO.

6. Explain how LIFO inventory layers are created, and describe the significance of the LIFO reserve.

7. Choose an inventory valuation method based on the trade-offs among income tax effects, bookkeeping costs, and the impact on the financial statements.

8. Apply the lower-of-cost-or-market (LCM) rule to reflect declines in the market value of inventory.

9. Use the gross profit method to estimate ending inventory.

10. Determine the financial statement impact of inventory recording errors.

11. Analyze inventory using financial ratios, and properly compare ratios of different firms after adjusting for differences in inventory valuation methods.

EM EXPANDED MATERIAL

12. Compute estimates of FIFO, LIFO, average cost, and lower-of-cost-or-market inventory using the retail inventory method.

13. Use LIFO pools, dollar-value LIFO, and dollar-value LIFO retail to compute ending inventory.

14. Account for the impact of changing prices on purchase commitments.

15. Record inventory purchase transactions denominated in foreign currencies.

Let's go back to 1974. America was captivated by the Watergate investigation culminating in the resignation of President Nixon in August. In the spring, Hank Aaron hit his 715th career home run and broke Babe Ruth's long-standing record. Rock 'n' roll had fallen into the doldrums with best-selling songs for the year including forgettable numbers such as "Billy, Don't Be a Hero" by Bo Donaldson and the Heywoods and "Seasons in the Sun" by Terry Jacks. To add insult to injury, the first "disco" hit—"Rock the Boat" by The Hues Corporation—came out in 1974. At the movies, Americans were lining up to see disaster pictures such as *Earthquake* and *The Towering Inferno*.

From an accounting standpoint, 1974 was an interesting year because it was the first year since World War II in which consumer price inflation in the United States exceeded 10%. High inflation wreaks havoc on the reliability of historical cost financial statements. In fact, the high inflation experienced throughout the latter half of the 1970s caused the FASB to experiment with inflation-adjusted financial statements.

High inflation also magnifies the difference between the FIFO (first-in, first-out) and LIFO (last-in, first-out) inventory methods. In times of rising prices, FIFO results in low cost of goods sold because the old, lower-cost inventory is assumed to be sold. Similarly, LIFO results in high cost of goods sold because the new, higher-cost inventory is assumed to be sold. This is illustrated in Exhibit 9-1. As an example of the FIFO/LIFO difference caused by the high inflation in 1974, the 1974 cost of goods sold of **DuPont** was $600 million higher using LIFO than it would have been if DuPont had used FIFO.

By the way, 1974 happened to be the year that DuPont switched from FIFO to LIFO. DuPont was not alone—over 700 U.S. companies adopted LIFO in 1974. Why did these companies voluntarily adopt LIFO and subject themselves to higher cost of goods sold and lower reported profits? The one-word answer is taxes. The IRS requires firms using LIFO for income tax purposes to also use LIFO for financial reporting. So, if a company wants to get a reduction in taxes through higher LIFO cost of goods sold, the company must also accept a lower reported net income.[1] In DuPont's case, the adoption of LIFO in 1974 saved over $250 million in taxes but lowered its reported net income by over $300 million.

A question that has intrigued accounting researchers is whether investors viewed the 1974 LIFO adoptions as good news or bad news—good news because of the LIFO tax savings or bad news because of the reduction in reported net income. The answer to this question provides insight into whether investors are sophisticated in their knowledge of accounting. A sophisticated investor would view a LIFO adoption in a time of high inflation as good news, realizing that the adopting firm was focusing on real cash savings (lower taxes) and not worried about just looking good in the reported financial statements. An unsophisticated investor is fixated on reported earnings and would view LIFO adoption as bad news because it lowers net income.

In 1982, Professor William E. Ricks published a study suggesting that the LIFO adoptions were viewed as bad news, implying that investors back in 1974 were unsophisticated in their understanding of LIFO and FIFO.[2] He found that the market value of firms adopting LIFO dropped an average of 2% in the week surrounding the public announcement of 1974 earnings. Many studies have reexamined this result, and the overall conclusion is that it isn't clear exactly what caused this market value drop. After a careful analysis of competing

Exhibit 9-1 | LIFO and FIFO in Times of Inflation

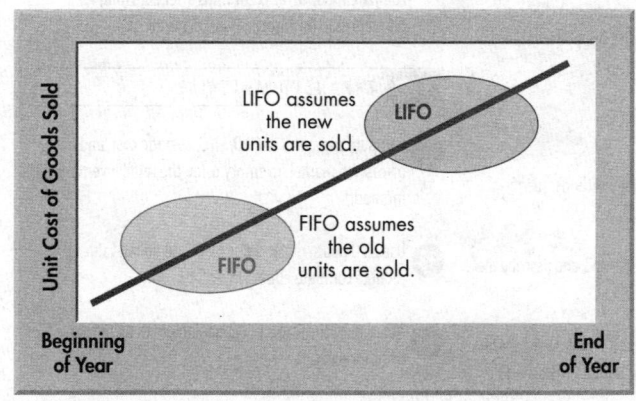

© Cengage Learning 2014

---

[1] This "LIFO conformity rule" is an exception—in most cases, the choice of a tax accounting method does not necessarily dictate the same choice for financial reporting.
[2] William E. Ricks, "The Market's Response to the 1974 LIFO Adoptions," *Journal of Accounting Research*, Autumn 1982, p. 367.

explanations, Professor John R. M. Hand concluded: "[Negative] stock returns at 1974 LIFO adoption dates appear to reflect both sophisticated and unsophisticated responses to information on LIFO adopters. It is hard to disentangle the two responses...."[3]

Your job is to study this chapter and make sure that your understanding of inventory accounting puts you in the set of sophisticated users of financial statements.

1. What causes a big difference between LIFO and FIFO?
2. What prompted so many U.S. companies to switch from FIFO to LIFO in 1974?
3. On what does an unsophisticated investor focus?

Answers to these questions can be found on page 9-59.

The time line in Exhibit 9-2 illustrates the business issues involved with inventory. The accounting questions associated with the items in the time line are as follows:

- When is inventory considered to have been purchased—when it is ordered, when it is shipped, when it is received, or when it is paid for?
- Similarly, when is the inventory considered to have been sold?
- Many costs are associated with the "value-added" process—which of these costs are considered to be part of the cost of inventory and which are simply business expenses for that period?
- How should total inventory cost be divided between the inventory that was sold (cost of goods sold) and the inventory that remains (ending inventory)?

Determining what items should be included in inventory involves more than recognizing inventory when you see it. Some inventory that should be included in a company's balance sheet cannot be found in the company's warehouses but instead is in transit in trucks, trains, or ships or is temporarily in the custody of some other company. A proper physical determination of how much inventory a company owns as of a certain date is one of the most daunting tasks of an independent external auditor.

Exhibit 9-2 | Time Line of Business Issues Involved with Inventory

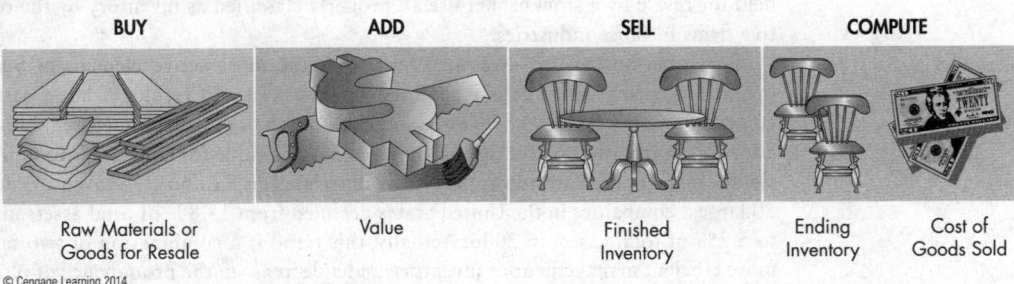

© Cengage Learning 2014

---

[3] John R. M. Hand, "1974 LIFO Excess Stock Return and Analyst Forecast Error Anomalies Revisited," *Journal of Accounting Research*, Spring 1995, p. 175.

Attaching the proper costs to inventory is one of the primary functions of a cost accounting system. Advances made since 1980 in the practice of cost accounting have turned the sleepy topic of overhead allocation into a key element of product pricing and marketing focus. The important area of cost accounting is briefly covered in this chapter, but detailed treatment is left to a cost accounting course. The majority of the chapter is devoted to the topic of inventory valuation. Almost all companies in the United States use one or more of three basic inventory valuation methods: FIFO (first-in, first-out), LIFO (last-in, first-out), and average cost. The objective of inventory valuation is to divide the total cost of goods available for sale during the period into two categories: the cost associated with goods that were sold (cost of goods sold) and the cost associated with goods that still remain (ending inventory). Coverage of the LIFO inventory valuation method takes up a large proportion of the chapter because the apparently simple assumption of last-in, first-out introduces all kinds of interesting twists into inventory accounting.

The chapter continues with a discussion of the accounting treatment required when the market value of inventory declines. We then discuss a common technique used to estimate inventory—the gross profit method. In addition to providing a means of determining the amount of inventory lost in a fire or flood, the gross profit method is also used with periodic inventory systems to provide ending inventory estimates for preparing monthly or quarterly financial statements when a full physical inventory count is not feasible. Inventory estimates are also compared to perpetual inventory records to provide an early warning of unusual inventory shrinkage. Finally, external auditors and the IRS use inventory estimates to test the reasonableness of reported trends in cost of goods sold. In the Expanded Material, a more elaborate method of inventory estimation is introduced, and accounting for purchase commitments and for foreign currency inventory purchases is discussed.

What Is Inventory?

 Define inventory for a merchandising business, and identify the different types of inventory for a manufacturing business.

LO1 学习目标1
定义商贸企业的存货，并区分制造企业存货的不同种类。

The term inventory designates goods held for sale in the normal course of business and, in the case of a manufacturer, goods in production or to be placed in production. The nature of goods classified as inventory varies widely with the nature of business activities and in some cases includes assets not normally thought of as inventory. For example, land and buildings held for resale by a real estate firm, partially completed buildings to be sold in the future by a construction firm, and investment securities held for resale by a stockbroker are all properly classified as inventory by the respective firms in those industries.

For some businesses, inventory represents the most active element in business operations, being continuously acquired or produced and resold. A large part of a company's resources can be invested in goods purchased or manufactured. However, advances in information technology have made it possible for companies to more efficiently manage their inventory levels. As illustrated in Exhibit 9-3, inventory for the 50 largest companies in the United States declined from 15.8% of total assets in 1979 to 5.2% of total assets in 2006. Actually, this trend is a combination of two factors: more efficient management of inventory and a decrease in the prominence of old-style smokestack industries that carried large inventories. Companies in the growth industries of service, technology, and information often have little or no inventory.

Exhibit 9-3 | How Much Inventory Do Companies Have?

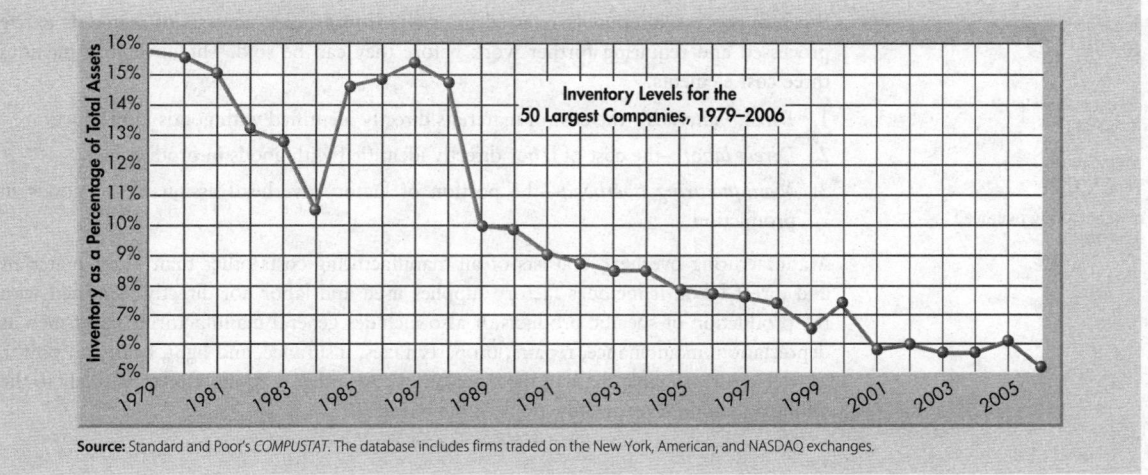

Source: Standard and Poor's *COMPUSTAT*. The database includes firms traded on the New York, American, and NASDAQ exchanges.

The term *inventory* (or *merchandise inventory*) is generally applied to goods held by a merchandising firm, either wholesale or retail, when such goods have been acquired in a condition for resale. The terms *raw materials*, *work in process*, and *finished goods* refer to the inventories of a manufacturing enterprise.

Raw Materials

Raw materials are goods acquired for use in the production process. Some raw materials are obtained directly from natural sources. More often, however, raw materials are purchased from other companies and represent the finished products of the suppliers. For example, high-quality acid-free paper (like that used for this book) is the finished product of a paper mill but represents raw material to a textbook publishing company.

Although the term *raw materials* can be used broadly to cover all materials used in manufacturing, this designation is usually restricted to materials that will be physically incorporated in the products being manufactured. Because these materials are used directly in the production of goods, they are frequently referred to as direct materials. The term indirect materials is then used to refer to auxiliary materials, that is, materials that are necessary in the production process but are not directly incorporated in the products. Oils and fuels for factory equipment, cleaning supplies, and similar items fall into this grouping because these items are not incorporated in a product but simply facilitate production.

Although indirect materials may be summarized separately, they should be reported as a part of a company's inventories since they ultimately will be consumed in the production process. Supplies purchased for use in the delivery, sales, and general administrative functions of the enterprise should not be reported as part of the inventories, but as selling and administrative supplies. Remember, *inventory* is the label given to assets to be sold in the normal course of business or to assets to be incorporated, directly or indirectly, into goods that are manufactured and then sold.

Work in Process

Work in process, alternately referred to as *goods in process*, consists of materials partly processed and requiring further work before they can be sold. This inventory includes three cost elements.

1. *Direct materials*—the cost of materials directly identified with goods in production
2. *Direct labor*—the cost of labor directly identified with goods in production
3. *Manufacturing overhead*—the portion of factory overhead assignable to goods in production

Manufacturing overhead consists of all manufacturing costs other than direct materials and direct labor. It includes factory supplies used and labor not directly identified with the production of specific products. It also includes general manufacturing costs such as depreciation, maintenance, repairs, property taxes, insurance, and light, heat, and power, as well as a reasonable share of the managerial costs other than those relating solely to the selling and administrative functions of the business.

Finished Goods

Finished goods are the manufactured products awaiting sale. As products are completed, the costs accumulated in the production process are transferred from Work in Process to the finished goods inventory account. The diagram in Exhibit 9-4 illustrates the basic flow of product costs through the inventory accounts of a manufacturer.

Note the vertical dotted line in Exhibit 9-4 separating Work in Process from Finished Goods. This line represents the factory wall. Historically, the rule of thumb was that costs incurred inside the factory wall were allocated to inventory, and costs incurred outside the factory wall (e.g., in the finished goods warehouse) were expensed as incurred. This simple rule doesn't always work because the IRS adopted inventory cost capitalization rules in 1986 that require some outside-the-factory costs to be capitalized as part of inventory cost. Although IRS rules do not govern financial accounting treatment, in this case

Exhibit 9-4 | Inventory Cost Flow

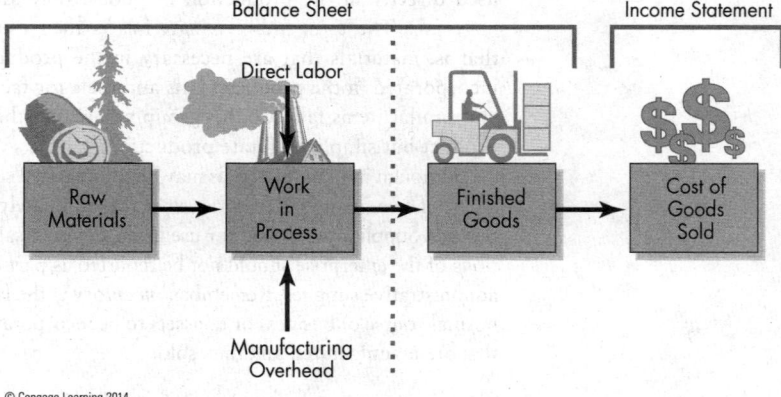

some companies use the IRS rules for financial reporting to reduce the cost of maintaining separate records.[4]

Inventory Systems

LO2 Explain the advantages and disadvantages of both periodic and perpetual inventory systems.

学习目标2
解释定期盘存制和永续盘存制的优缺点。

Consider the last time you made a purchase. Did the business where you made the purchase keep a record of what item it sold you, or did it just record the selling price? With a traditional cash register system, the seller records only the sales price; the seller has no record of how many units of a particular inventory item have been sold. Accountants call this type of system a periodic inventory system because the only way to verify what inventory has been sold and what remains is to do a periodic physical count.

The alternative to a periodic system is a perpetual inventory system in which both the selling price and the type of item sold are recorded for each sale. A bar code scanning system is an example of a perpetual inventory system. With a perpetual system, the seller knows the number of each item sold and the number that should still be in inventory. With a perpetual system, periodic physical inventory counts are useful in revealing the amount of inventory "shrinkage"—inventory lost, stolen, or spoiled.

To illustrate the differences between periodic and perpetual inventory systems, assume the following transactions occurred during the period for CyBorg Incorporated.

Beginning inventory...................................	50 units @ $10	$ 500
Purchases during the period.........................	300 units @ $10	3,000
Sales during the period.................................	275 units @ $15	4,125
Ending inventory (physical count)..................	70 units @ $10	700

The journal entries to record these purchases and sales for both periodic and perpetual inventory systems are as follows:

Periodic Inventory System			Perpetual Inventory System		
Purchases during the period			*Purchases during the period*		
Purchases.................	3,000		Inventory.....................	3,000	
Accounts Payable.........		3,000	Accounts Payable........		3,000
Sales during the period			*Sales during the period*		
Accounts Receivable.......	4,125		Accounts Receivable.......	4,125	
Sales........................		4,125	Sales............................		4,125
			Cost of Goods Sold........	2,750	
			Inventory.................		2,750

定期盘存制和永续盘存制有两点不同：第一，在永续盘存制下多出一个分录，该分录是根据销售库存记录销售成本的；而在定期盘存制下，销售成本的数据并不可知。第二，在定期盘存制下，购买存货时记入采购账户的借方而非存货账户的借方。采购账户是为了计算存货成本而设置的临时性账户，在期末时会分配到存货和销售成本中；对定期盘存制来说，存货账户的数值在期间内不会发生变化，只有在期末实地盘存结束后才会根据盘存结果予以变更。

There are two differences between these two sets of journal entries. First, with a perpetual system an additional entry is made upon the sale of inventory to record the cost of goods sold. With a periodic system, cost of goods sold data are not known (or at least are not recorded) at the time of the sale. The second difference is that

[4] In 1986, the Emerging Issues Task Force (EITF) discussed whether the capitalization of an inventory cost for tax purposes requires that the same cost be included in inventory for financial reporting purposes. The EITF reached a consensus that the tax treatment should be considered but should not dictate the financial accounting treatment. See FASB ASC paragraphs 330-10-55-3 and 4.

with the periodic system the debit for the inventory purchase is to Purchases instead of to Inventory. The purchases account is a temporary holding tank for inventory costs that are allocated between Inventory and Cost of Goods Sold at the end of the period. Under a periodic system, to debit Inventory directly for the amount of purchases during the period would yield misleading information about the level of inventory because the inventory account is not reduced for the cost of goods sold during the period. With a periodic system, the inventory account remains untouched until a physical inventory count is done at the end of the period.

When a perpetual inventory system is employed, the company knows how much inventory should be on hand at any point in time. Comparing the inventory records to the result of a physical count allows the company to track discrepancies in inventory totals. Thus, even when a perpetual system is employed, physical counts of units on hand should be made at least once a year to confirm the balances on the books. The frequency of physical inventories varies depending on the nature of the goods, their rate of turnover, and the degree of internal control.[5] A plan for continuous counting of inventory items on a rotation basis is frequently employed.

Variations may be found between the recorded amounts and the amounts actually on hand as a result of recording errors, shrinkage, breakage, theft, and other causes. The inventory accounts should be adjusted to agree with the physical count when a discrepancy exists. To illustrate, cost of goods sold in the CyBorg example is computed as follows:

	Periodic System	Perpetual System
Beginning inventory	$ 500	$ 500
+ Purchases	3,000	3,000
= Cost of goods available for sale	$3,500	$3,500
− Ending inventory	700 (count)	750 (records)
= Preliminary cost of goods sold	$2,800	$2,750 (records)
+ Cost of missing inventory	Unknown	50 ($750 − $700)
= Reported cost of goods sold	$2,800	$2,800

With the perpetual system, the accounting records contain amounts for ending inventory and cost of goods sold before the physical count is ever done. The physical count serves to verify the accounting records. And in this case, it appears that CyBorg has lost $50 in inventory: the difference between the $750 inventory recorded in the books and the $700 physically counted. The entry to adjust the perpetual system inventory account for this shrinkage would be as follows:

Cost of Goods Sold 50
   Inventory 50

As indicated, this type of inventory adjustment for shrinkage and breakage would typically be included as part of cost of goods sold on the income statement.

With the periodic system, ending inventory is known only from the physical count. In addition, cost of goods sold can be computed only after the physical count is done. No shrinkage calculation is possible with a periodic system because the accounting records contain no

---

[5] While paying for gas and soft drinks at a mini-convenience store, one of the authors noticed the cashier marking the soft drink purchases on an inventory sheet. Aha, thought the author, this place uses a perpetual inventory system. When asked how often a physical count was done to verify the inventory records, the cashier replied, "At the end of every shift." Obviously, the store manager was using the combination of a perpetual inventory system and frequent physical counts to minimize shoplifting by customers and pilferage by employees.

> **Stop & Think**
>
> If perpetual inventory systems have so many clear advantages, why aren't they used by all companies?
> a) A perpetual inventory system can increase the level of a company's bad debts.
> b) Perpetual inventory systems are illegal in most countries outside the United States.
> c) A perpetual inventory system is more costly to operate than a periodic system.
> d) A perpetual inventory system is only appropriate for businesses with low-value identical items with a high turnover.

indication of how much inventory should be found in the physical count. In fact, with a periodic system, the label "cost of goods sold" might be better replaced by "cost of goods sold, stolen, lost, and spoiled"—all that is known is that the goods are gone. For external reporting purposes, both the periodic and perpetual systems yield the same reported cost of goods sold. However, for internal purposes, the perpetual system divides that number into cost of goods sold and cost of inventory shrinkage.

Practically all large trading and manufacturing enterprises and many small organizations have adopted perpetual inventory systems. With the costs of computers and point-of-sale systems so low, perpetual inventory systems are now more economical and, in today's fast-moving world, almost a necessity. These systems offer a continuous check and control over inventories. Purchasing and production planning are facilitated, adequate on-hand inventories are ensured, and losses incurred through damage and theft are fully disclosed.

Whose Inventory Is It?

LO3 学习目标3
确认存货在交易中的所有权问题，以及在何种情况下需要把运输过程中的存货记录在账上。

③ Determine when ownership of goods in transit changes hands and what circumstances require shipped inventory to be kept on the books.

As a general rule, goods should be included in the inventory of the business holding legal title. The *passing of title* is a legal term designating the point at which ownership changes. When the rule of passing title is not observed, statements should include appropriate disclosure of the special practice followed and the factors supporting such practice. Application of the legal test under a number of special circumstances is described in the following paragraphs.

Goods in Transit

因为所有权从起运点开始转移，年末即使买方没有收到商品，在途物资也应该包含在买方的存货内。

When goods are in transit from the seller to the buyer, who owns them? The answer depends on the terms of the sale. When terms of sale are FOB (free on board) shipping point, title passes to the buyer with the loading of goods at the point of shipment. Because title passes at the shipping point, goods in transit at year-end should be included in the inventory of the buyer even though the buyer hasn't received them yet.

When terms of a sale are FOB destination, legal title does not pass until the goods are received by the buyer. Even though it can be difficult to determine whether goods have reached their destination by the end of the period, when the terms are FOB destination the seller should not recognize a sale, and a corresponding inventory decrease, until the goods are received by the buyer.

To summarize, when goods are shipped FOB shipping point, they belong to the buyer while they are in transit and should normally be included in the buyer's inventory while in transit. When goods are shipped FOB destination, they belong to the seller while in transit and are normally included in the seller's inventory. The impact of shipping terms on the ownership of goods in transit is summarized in Exhibit 9-5.

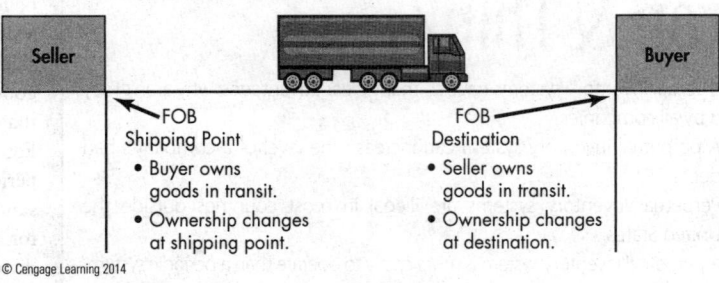

Exhibit 9-5 | Ownership Transfer for Goods in Transit

In some cases, title to goods may pass before shipment takes place. For example, if goods are produced on special customer order, they may be recorded as a sale as soon as they are completed and segregated from the regular inventory. If the sale is recognized upon segregation by the seller, the goods should be excluded from the seller's inventory. The buyer could recognize the goods as part of inventory as soon as they are separated.

Keep in mind that the shipping terms related to inventory are only an issue at the end of an accounting period. For most shipments, the goods will be shipped by the seller and received by the buyer in the same accounting period, thereby presenting no accounting problems.

Goods on Consignment

Goods are frequently transferred to a dealer or customer on a consignment basis. The shipper retains title and includes the goods in inventory until their sale or use by the dealer or customer. For example, NN, Inc., a company that makes precision steel balls and rollers for use in manufacturing antifriction bearings, provides goods on consignment to some of its major customers. Through this arrangement, the customers are able to maintain low inventory levels. NN, Inc., benefits from this consignment arrangement because this added service improves customer satisfaction and, hopefully, increases sales. Consigned goods are properly reported by the shipper at the sum of their costs and the handling and shipping costs incurred in their transfer to the dealer or customer. The goods may be separately designated on the shipper's balance sheet as merchandise on consignment. Alternatively, the amount of inventory on consignment may be disclosed in the financial statement notes. For example, in the notes to its December 31, 2011, financial statements, NN, Inc., disclosed that $4.2 million of its $46.0 million in inventory was inventory on consignment. The dealer or customer does not own the consigned goods; hence, neither consigned goods nor obligations for such goods are reported on the dealer's or customer's financial statements. Recall that revenue recognition accounting for consignments was discussed in Chapter 8.

Other merchandise owned by a business but in the possession of others, such as goods in the hands of salespersons and agents, goods held by customers on approval, and goods held by others for storage, processing, or shipment, also should be shown as a part of the ending inventory of the business that owns the goods.

> **FYI**
>
> Twenty years ago, when auditors got together, they exchanged "war stories" about difficult inventory audits. These days you are more likely to hear auditors complaining about lawsuits and nasty computer systems.

Auditing consigned inventory presents the auditor with a special set of problems. Inventory that is on the premises may not belong to the company because the company is holding it on consignment, yet inventory that is located with a vendor on consignment, hundreds of miles away, still belongs to the company. Imagine an auditor walking out into a warehouse and seeing row upon row of inventory. "That's not ours; we are just holding it on consignment," quips the warehouse manager. Then the warehouse manager leads the auditor to the shipping platform. "See that truck just leaving the gate? That truck and hundreds more just like it contain inventory that is still ours but has been shipped on consignment. Audit that!"

Conditional Sales, Installment Sales, and Repurchase Agreements

附条件买卖和分期付款销售合同可能会一直保留卖方所有权直至销售款全部收齐。

Conditional sales and installment sales contracts may provide for a retention of title by the seller until the sales price is fully recovered. Under these circumstances, the seller, who retains title, may continue to show the goods on its records, reduced by the buyer's equity in such goods as established by collections; the buyer, in turn, can report an equity in the goods accruing through payments made. However, in the usual case when the possibilities of returns and defaults are very low, the seller, anticipating completion of the contract and the ultimate passing of title, recognizes the transaction as a regular sale and removes the goods from reported inventory at the time of the sale; the buyer, intending to comply with the contract and acquire title, recognizes the transaction as a regular purchase. Revenue recognition accounting for installment sales also was discussed in Chapter 8.

FYI
In some countries, it is common for the seller to retain legal title of goods until the buyer pays for them. The SEC has stated (in *SAB 104*) that in cases like this, it is appropriate to assume that accounting ownership changes hands at delivery if the seller's title is limited to the right to ensure recovery of the goods if payment is not made. See FASB ASC paragraph 605-10-S99-1 (Question 3).

As a creative way to obtain cash on a short-term basis, firms sometimes sell inventory to another company but at the same time agree to repurchase the inventory at some future date. The repurchase price typically includes the original selling price of the inventory plus finance and holding charges. In essence, the "selling" company has used inventory to secure a short-term loan but agrees to buy back the inventory later. For those familiar with such things, this is similar to how a pawnshop works. The FASB has decided that these arrangements should be accounted for according to their economic substance—no sale is recorded, the inventory is not removed from the selling company's balance sheet, and the seller must record a liability for the proceeds received in the "sale."[6]

What Is Inventory Cost?

LO4 学习目标4
计算存货的总获取成本。

4 Compute total inventory acquisition cost.

After the goods to be included as inventory have been identified, the accountant must assign a dollar value to the physical units. Both U.S. and international accounting standards agree that historical cost should normally be used in valuing inventory. Attention is directed in this section to identifying the elements that comprise inventory cost.

---

[6] FASB ASC paragraph 470-40-25-1. The FASB calls this type of transaction a "product financing arrangement."

Items Included in Inventory Cost

Inventory cost consists of all expenditures, both direct and indirect, relating to inventory acquisition, preparation, and placement for sale. In the case of raw materials or goods acquired for resale, cost includes the purchase price, freight, receiving, storage, and all other costs incurred to the time goods are ready for sale. Certain expenditures can be traced to specific acquisitions or can be allocated to inventory items in some equitable manner. Other expenditures may be relatively small and difficult to allocate. Such items are normally excluded in the calculation of inventory cost and are recognized as expenses in the current period. These items are called period costs.

The charges to be included in the cost of manufactured products have already been mentioned. These costs are called product or inventoriable costs. Proper accounting for materials, labor, and manufacturing overhead items and their identification with goods in process and finished goods inventories are achieved through a cost accounting system. Certain costs relating to the acquisition or the manufacture of goods may be considered abnormal and may be excluded in arriving at inventory cost. For example, costs arising from idle capacity, excessive spoilage, and reprocessing are usually considered abnormal and are expensed in the current period.[7] Only those portions of general and administrative costs that are clearly related to procurement or production should be included in inventory cost.

Inventory costing is important for financial reporting purposes, but it is absolutely critical for making production, pricing, and strategy decisions. For example, if competitive pressures dictate that a business can sell a product for no more than $10 per unit, it is essential to that business to know whether it costs $8 or $11 to produce the unit. As mentioned earlier in the chapter, recent advances in techniques for allocating manufacturing overhead have greatly improved cost accounting systems.

Traditionally, manufacturing overhead costs have been allocated to products based on the amount of direct labor required in production. This allocation scheme often fails because direct labor can be a small part of the cost of a product that actually causes a large amount of manufacturing overhead through requiring frequent machine maintenance, lots of invoice paperwork, heavy administrative supervision, and so forth. Activity-based cost (ABC) systems strive to allocate overhead based on clearly identified cost drivers—characteristics of the production process (e.g., number of required machine reconfigurations or average frequency of production glitches requiring management intervention) that are known to create overhead costs. The real benefit of a good inventory costing system is seen in better information for internal decision making. As such, this important topic is covered fully in managerial accounting courses.

A schedule of cost of goods manufactured is often prepared by manufacturing companies to illustrate how various costs affect inventories and, ultimately, cost of goods sold. An illustration of this schedule is presented in Exhibit 9-6.[8]

In practice, companies take different positions in classifying certain costs. For example, costs of the purchasing department, costs of accounting for manufacturing activities,

> **Caution**
> One last warning—don't let the short coverage of overhead allocation here deceive you. This is a vital topic that has spawned arguments, textbooks, and lots of consulting revenue for the experts.

---

[7] FASB ASC paragraph 330-10-30-7.
[8] To make this schedule more intuitive for the financial accounting audience using this text, the actual manufacturing overhead costs are shown. In a proper schedule of cost of goods manufactured, this total would be adjusted for the amount of over- or underapplied overhead such that the amount of applied (instead of actual) manufacturing overhead would be included in the computation of total manufacturing costs.

Exhibit 9-6 | Schedule of Cost of Goods Manufactured

Bartlett Corporation
Schedule of Cost of Goods Manufactured
For the Year Ended December 31, 2015

Direct materials:		
Raw materials inventory, January 1, 2015	$ 21,350	
Purchases	107,500	
Cost of raw materials available for use	$128,850	
Less: Raw materials inventory, December 31, 2015	22,350	
Raw materials used in production		$106,500
Direct labor		96,850
Manufacturing overhead:		
Indirect labor	$ 40,000	
Factory supervision	29,000	
Depreciation—factory buildings and equipment	20,000	
Light, heat, and power	18,000	
Factory supplies	15,000	
Miscellaneous manufacturing overhead	12,055	134,055
Total manufacturing costs		$337,405
Add: Work in process inventory, January 1, 2015		29,400
		$366,805
Less: Work in process inventory, December 31, 2015		26,500
Cost of goods manufactured		$340,305

© Cengage Learning 2014

and costs of pensions for production personnel may be treated as inventoriable costs by some companies and period costs by others.

Discounts as Reductions in Cost

Discounts associated with the purchase of inventory should be treated as a reduction in the cost assigned to the inventory. Trade discounts refer to the difference between a catalog price and the price actually charged to a buyer. *Cost* is defined as the list price less the trade discount. No record needs to be made of a trade discount, and the purchases should be recorded at the net price.

Cash discounts are discounts granted for payment of invoices within a limited time period. Cash discounts are usually stated as a certain percentage to be allowed if the invoice is paid within a certain number of days, with the full amount due within another time period. For example, 2/10, n/30 (two ten, net thirty) means that 2% is allowed as a cash discount if the invoice is paid within 10 days after the invoice date but the full or "net" amount is due within 30 days.

Theoretically, inventory should be recorded at the discounted amount (i.e., the gross invoice price less the allowable discount). This net method reflects the fact that discounts not taken are in effect a finance charge incurred for failure to pay within the discount period. Discounts not taken are recorded in the discounts lost account and reported as a separate item on the income statement. Discounts lost usually represent a relatively high rate of interest. To illustrate, assume a purchase of $10,000 provides for payment on a 2/10, n/30 basis. This purchase and the payment options are illustrated in Exhibit 9-7.

Exhibit 9-7 | Impact of Cash Discounts

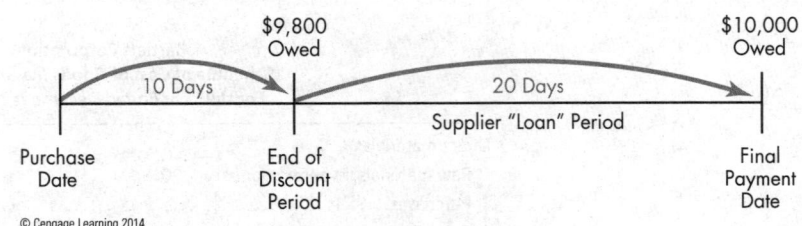

If the buyer pays for the purchase by the 10th day, only $9,800 must be paid. Twenty days later the full $10,000 is due. Thus, an additional $200 must be paid in exchange for delaying payment for an extra 20 days. In essence, this is a 20-day "loan" from the supplier to the purchaser. The effective interest rate on this 20-day "loan" is 2.04% ($200/$9,800). Because there are about eighteen 20-day periods in a year, the annual interest cost on this "loan" exceeds 36%, suggesting that missing a cash discount is a very costly mistake. Failure on the part of management to take a cash discount usually represents carelessness in considering payment alternatives. If cash discounts are accounted for using the net method, the $200 cost of a missed discount is not included as part of the inventory cost but is expensed immediately as a finance charge.

Under the gross method, cash discounts are booked only when they are taken. While the net method tracks discounts not taken, the gross method provides no such information, and inventory records are maintained at the gross unit price. When a periodic system is used, cash discounts taken are reflected through a contra purchases account, Purchase Discounts. With a perpetual inventory system, discounts are credited directly to Inventory.

The net method of accounting for purchases is strongly preferred; however, many companies still follow the historical practice of recognizing cash discounts only as payments are made. The entries required for both the gross and net methods are illustrated in the following table. A perpetual inventory method is assumed.

在总值法下，现金折扣只在取得时被记录。净值法记录没有取得的折扣，而总值法没有提供这些信息，存货以总单位价值计量。当存货计价采用定期盘存制时，现金折扣通过备抵购买账户反映；当存货计价采用永续盘存制时，现金折扣被直接记入存货贷方。

Transaction	Purchases Reported Net		Purchases Reported Gross	
Purchase of merchandise priced at $10,000 along with a cash discount of 2%.	Inventory............ 9,800 Accounts Payable ..	9,800	Inventory............ 10,000 Accounts Payable ..	10,000
(a) Assuming payment of the invoice within discount period.	Accounts Payable..... 9,800 Cash	9,800	Accounts Payable..... 10,000 Inventory .... Cash	200 9,800
(b) Assuming payment of the invoice after discount period.	Accounts Payable..... 9,800 Discounts Lost........ 200 Cash	10,000	Accounts Payable..... 10,000 Cash	10,000
(c) Required adjustment at the end of the period assuming that the invoice has not been paid and the discount period has lapsed.	Discounts Lost .... 200 Accounts Payable ..	200	No entry required	

The difference in the two methods is that the net method shows the cost of missed discounts as a separate finance charge (Discounts Lost), whereas the gross method lumps this finance charge into the inventory cost. This result is the same if a periodic inventory system is used. The difference in journal entries with a periodic system is that Purchases, instead of Inventory, is debited to record the original purchase. In addition, Purchase Discounts, instead of Inventory, is credited under the gross method when payment is within the discount period.

Purchase Returns and Allowances

Adjustments to invoice cost are also made when merchandise either is damaged or is of a lesser quality than ordered. Sometimes the merchandise is physically returned to the supplier. In other instances, a credit is allowed to the buyer by the supplier to compensate for the damage or the inferior quality of the merchandise. A purchase allowance of $400 given for defective merchandise would be recorded as follows:

Periodic Inventory System		Perpetual Inventory System	
Accounts Payable 400		Accounts Payable 400	
Purchase Returns and Allowances	400	Inventory	400

Purchase Returns and Allowances is a contra purchases account.

The computation of total inventory acquisition cost is summarized as follows:

Invoice cost plus freight, storage, and preparation cost
− Cash discounts (only cash discounts taken if using the gross method)
− Purchase returns and allowances
= Inventory cost

Inventory Valuation Methods

 Use the four basic inventory valuation methods: specific identification, average cost, FIFO, and LIFO.

At the end of an accounting period, total inventory cost must be allocated between inventory still remaining (to be reported on the balance sheet as an asset) and inventory sold during the period (to be reported on the income statement as the expense "cost of goods sold"). Numerous methods have evolved to make this allocation between cost of goods sold and inventory. The most common methods are as follows:

- Specific identification
- Average cost
- First-in, first-out (FIFO)
- Last-in, first-out (LIFO)

Each of these methods has certain characteristics that make it preferable under certain conditions. All four methods have in common the fact that inventory cost is allocated between the income statement and the balance sheet. Only the specific identification method determines the cost allocation according to the physical inventory flow. Unless individual inventory items, such as automobiles, are clearly definable, inventory items are exchangeable. Thus, the emphasis in inventory valuation usually is on the accounting cost allocation, not the physical flow.

FIFO is by far the most common inventory valuation method in the United States. Exhibit 9-8 reports the frequency of use of inventory valuation methods by U.S. companies in both

LO5 学习目标5
使用四种基本的存货计价方法：个别计价法、平均成本法、先进先出法和后进先出法。

Exhibit 9-8 | Frequency of Inventory Valuation Method Use

Frequency of Use of Inventory Valuation Methods
U.S. Companies
1979 and 2006

Inventory Method	1979 All Companies	2006 All Companies	2006 Large Companies
FIFO	75.6%	67.8%	62.2%
LIFO	25.8	13.1	26.8
Average cost	20.8	31.7	45.6
Specific identification	3.7	4.7	3.8

Source: Standard and Poor's *COMPUSTAT*. The database includes firms traded on the New York, American, and NASDAQ exchanges.

1979 and 2006. The percentages sum to more than 100%, indicating that many companies use more than one inventory method, applying different methods to different classes of inventory. Recall from the opening scenario of the chapter that LIFO generates income tax savings in times of inflation. The reduction in the rate of inflation in the United States from 1979 to 2006 is probably the cause of the overall decline in usage of LIFO. Finally, notice the difference in usage of LIFO between large and small firms. This is probably the consequence of the potentially sizable bookkeeping costs of maintaining a LIFO system.

There have been few guidelines developed by the profession to assist companies in choosing among these alternative inventory valuation methods. Some argue that cost flow should mirror the physical flow of goods. Others think that inventory valuation should concentrate on matching current costs with current revenues. Still others think that the emphasis should be on the proper valuation of inventory on the balance sheet. The following discussion of the allocation methods demonstrates how each method relates to these different viewpoints.

The four methods will be illustrated using the following simple example for Dalton Company. Dalton has no beginning inventory for 2015.

	Number of Units	Unit Cost	Total Cost
Purchases:			
January 1	200	$10	$ 2,000
March 23	300	12	3,600
July 15	500	11	5,500
November 6	100	13	1,300
Total purchases	1,100		$12,400

Sales: 700 units at $15 per unit. For simplicity, assume that all sales occurred on December 31.

Specific Identification

Costs may be allocated between goods sold during the period and goods on hand at the end of the period according to the actual cost of specific units. This specific identification method requires a way to identify the historical cost of each individual unit of inventory. With specific identification, the flow of recorded costs matches the physical flow of goods.

From a theoretical standpoint, the specific identification method is very attractive, especially when each inventory item is unique and has a high cost. However, when inventory is composed of a great many items or identical items acquired at different times and at different prices, specific identification is likely to be slow, burdensome, and costly. Even a computer tracking system won't answer all these practical concerns. Consider the task of implementing a specific identification inventory system in a do-it-yourself hardware store with the requirement to specifically track all costs associated with each screwdriver, each bolt, each piece of lumber, and each can of paint.

Apart from practical concerns, when units are identical and interchangeable, the specific identification method opens the door to possible profit manipulation through the selection of particular units for delivery. Consider the Dalton Company example. If Dalton Company wants to minimize its cost of goods sold for 2015 (and thus maximize reported net income), it can strategically choose to ship the 700 units with the lowest cost. Cost of goods sold would be computed as follows:

Dalton Company
Specific Identification Method
Shipment of the Lowest Cost Units
Cost of Goods Sold Computation

	Number of Units	Unit Cost	Total Cost
Batch purchased on:			
January 1	200	$10	$2,000
July 15	500	11	5,500
Total cost of goods sold	700		$7,500

个别计价法是四种方法中最不常用的。

The specific identification method is the least common of the four methods discussed in this chapter. Exhibit 9-8 indicates that in 2006 it was used by only 4.7% of U.S. companies. Amazon.com is one company that has used the specific identification method. The company has an extremely sophisticated inventory tracking system, and this same system makes it easy to implement the specific identification method. Exhibit 9-9 provides the company's note disclosure relating to its inventory valuation method.

However, as of January 1, 2002, Amazon.com changed its inventory valuation method from specific identification to FIFO, reflecting the continuing shift away from the specific identification method for financial reporting purposes. Note that this does not mean that Amazon.com changed the way it actually tracks its goods; the switch from the specific identification method merely represents a change in assumption for financial reporting purposes.

Average Cost Method

The average cost method assigns the same average cost to each unit. This method is based on the assumption that goods sold should be charged at an average cost, with

Exhibit 9-9 | Amazon.com—Inventory Valuation Method (before 2002)

Inventories, consisting of products available for sale, are recorded using the specific-identification method and valued at the lower of cost or market value.

Source: Amazon.com

the average being weighted by the number of units acquired at each price. Using the cost data for Dalton Company, the weighted-average cost of each unit would be computed as follows:

Total purchases: 1,100 units at a total cost of $12,400

Weighted-average cost: $12,400/1,100 units = $11.27 per unit (rounded)

Using the average cost method, cost of goods sold is simply the number of units sold multiplied by the average cost per unit: $7,890 (700 units × $11.27 per unit, rounded).

The average cost method can be supported as realistic and as paralleling the physical flow of goods, particularly where there is an intermingling of identical inventory units. Unlike the other inventory methods, the average cost approach provides the same cost for similar items of equal utility. The method does not permit profit manipulation. A limitation of the average cost method is that inventory values may lag significantly behind current prices in periods of rapidly rising or falling prices.

> **FYI**
>
> When Western accounting practices were first introduced into the former Soviet Union, Soviet accountants complained that LIFO and FIFO didn't make any sense. They were attracted by the logic of the average cost method.

First-In, First-Out Method

The first-in, first-out (FIFO) method is based on the assumption that the units sold are the oldest units on hand. For Dalton Company, FIFO cost of goods sold is computed as follows:

Dalton Company
FIFO Method
Cost of Goods Sold Computation

	Number of Units	Unit Cost	Total Cost
Batch purchased on:			
January 1	200	$10	$2,000
March 23	300	12	3,600
July 15	200	11	2,200
Total cost of goods sold	700		$7,800

Note that only 200 units from the July 15 batch are assumed to be sold; the remaining 300 units from that batch are assumed to be in ending inventory.

FIFO can be supported as a logical and realistic approach to the flow of costs when it is impractical or impossible to achieve specific cost identification. FIFO assumes a cost flow closely paralleling the usual physical flow of goods sold. Expense is charged with costs considered applicable to the goods actually sold. FIFO affords little opportunity for profit manipulation because the assignment of costs is determined by the order in which costs are incurred. In addition, with FIFO the units remaining in ending inventory are the most recently purchased units, so their reported cost would most closely match end-of-period replacement cost.

Last-In, First-Out Method

The last-in, first-out (LIFO) method is based on the assumption that the newest units are sold. For Dalton Company, LIFO cost of goods sold is computed as follows:

Dalton Company
LIFO Method
Cost of Goods Sold Computation

	Number of Units	Unit Cost	Total Cost
Batch purchased on:			
November 6	100	$13	$1,300
July 15	500	11	5,500
March 23	100	12	1,200
Total cost of goods sold	700		$8,000

Note that only 100 units from the March 23 batch are assumed to be sold; the remaining 200 units from that batch are assumed to be in ending inventory.

> **Caution**
> There is no required connection between the actual physical flow of goods and the inventory valuation method used.

LIFO is frequently criticized from a theoretical standpoint. It does not match the usual flow of goods in a business (although it does unfortunately match the flow of food in and out of a college student's refrigerator—with nasty implications for "ending inventory"). As seen in the following sections, LIFO results in old values on the balance sheet and can yield very strange cost of goods sold numbers when inventory levels decline. However, LIFO is the best method at matching current inventory costs with current revenues. The difficulties and quirks of maintaining a LIFO inventory system are detailed later in the chapter.

Comparison of Methods: Cost of Goods Sold and Ending Inventory

Recall that the purpose of an inventory valuation method is to allocate total inventory cost between cost of goods sold and inventory. For Dalton Company, total inventory cost for 2015 is $12,400. The allocation of this cost between cost of goods sold and ending inventory is shown in Exhibit 9-10 for each of the four inventory valuation methods. Note that the average cost method differs from the other three methods in that no assumption is made about the sale of specific units. Instead, all sales are assumed to be of the hypothetical "average" unit at the average cost per unit.

Use of FIFO in a period of rising prices matches oldest low-cost inventory with rising sales prices, thus expanding the gross profit margin. In a period of declining prices, oldest high-cost inventory is matched with declining sales prices, thus narrowing the gross profit margin. Using average cost, the gross profit margin tends to follow a similar pattern in response to changing prices. On the other hand, use of LIFO in a period of rising prices relates current high costs of acquiring goods with rising sales prices. Thus, LIFO tends to have a stabilizing effect on gross profit margins.

In using FIFO, inventories are reported on the balance sheet at or near current costs. With LIFO, inventories are reported at the cost of the earliest purchases. If LIFO has been used for a long time, the disparity between current value of inventory and reported LIFO cost can grow quite large. Use of the average method generally provides inventory values similar to FIFO values, because average costs are heavily influenced by current costs. Specific identification can produce any variety of results depending on which particular units are chosen for shipment.

When the prices paid for merchandise do not fluctuate significantly, alternative inventory methods may provide only minor differences in the financial statements. However, in periods of steadily rising or falling prices, the alternative methods may produce material differences.

在先进先出法下，存货以近期的成本在资产负债表中予以报告；在后进先出法下，存货则以最初的采购价格进行报告。

Exhibit 9-10 | Comparison of Inventory Valuation Methods

Dalton Company
Comparison of Four Inventory Valuation Methods
Cost of Goods Sold and Ending Inventory

	Unit Cost	Specific Identification	Average Cost*	FIFO	LIFO
Purchased on:					
January 1	$10	200	200	200	200
March 23	12	300	300	300	200 / 100
July 15	11	500	500	200 / 300	500
November 6	13	100	100	100	100

Units sold ▓   Units remaining ☐

Cost of goods sold (700 units):

Specific Identification	Average Cost	FIFO	LIFO
200 × $10 = $ 2,000	700 × $11.27 = $ 7,890 †	200 × $10 = $ 2,000	100 × $13 = $ 1,300
500 × $11 = 5,500		300 × $12 = 3,600	500 × $11 = 5,500
		200 × $11 = 2,200	100 × $12 = 1,200
$ 7,500	$ 7,890	$ 7,800	$ 8,000

Ending inventory (400 units):

Specific Identification	Average Cost	FIFO	LIFO
300 × $12 = $ 3,600	400 × $11.27 = $ 4,510 †	300 × $11 = $ 3,300	200 × $10 = $ 2,000
100 × $13 = 1,300		100 × $13 = 1,300	200 × $12 = 2,400
$ 4,900	$ 4,510	$ 4,600	$ 4,400

Total inventory cost:

$12,400	$12,400	$12,400	$12,400

*With the average cost method, no assumption is made about the sale of specific units. The average cost per unit is computed as follows: $12,400/1,100 units = $11.27 per unit, rounded.
†Rounded to the nearest $10.

© Cengage Learning 2014

Complications with a Perpetual Inventory System

In the Dalton Company example, the simplifying assumption was made that all 700 units were sold on December 31. In essence, this is the assumption made when a periodic inventory system is used. Computation of average cost and LIFO under a perpetual system is complicated because the average cost of units available for sale changes every time a purchase is made, and the identification of the "last-in" units also changes with every purchase. The complications of a perpetual system are illustrated in Exhibit 9-11, in which Dalton Company's cost of goods sold and ending inventory for 2015 are computed assuming that 300 units were sold on June 30 and 400 units were sold on December 31.

Examine Exhibit 9-11 and consider the following observations:

- Even in this more complicated example, the net result of each of the inventory valuation methods is to allocate the total inventory cost of $12,400 between cost of goods sold and ending inventory.

Exhibit 9-11 | Inventory Valuation Methods and a Perpetual Inventory System

Dalton Company
Complications of a Perpetual Inventory System

	Unit Cost	Average Cost*	FIFO	LIFO
300 units sold on June 30:				
Purchased on:				
January 1	$10	200	200	200
March 23	12	300	100 / 200	300
		Units sold	Units remaining	

Cost of goods sold (300 units):

	Average	FIFO	LIFO
	300 × $11.20 = $3,360	200 × $10 = $2,000	300 × $12 = $3,600
		100 × $12 = 1,200	
	$3,360	$3,200	$3,600

Inventory on June 30 (200 units):

	200 × $11.20 = $2,240	200 × $12 = $2,400	200 × $10 = $2,000

	Unit Cost	Average Cost†	FIFO	LIFO
400 units sold on December 31:				
Purchased on:				
Inventory on June 30	—	200 × $11.20	200 × $12	200 × $10
July 15	$11	500	200 / 300	200 / 300
November 6	13	100	100	100
		Units sold	Units remaining	

Cost of goods sold (400 units):

	Average	FIFO	LIFO
	400 × $11.30 = $4,520	200 × $12 = $2,400	100 × $13 = $1,300
		200 × $11 = 2,200	300 × $11 = 3,300
	$4,520	$4,600	$4,600

Ending inventory (400 units):

	Average	FIFO	LIFO
	400 × $11.30 = $4,520	300 × $11 = $3,300	200 × $10 = $2,000
		100 × $13 = 1,300	200 × $11 = 2,200
	$4,520	$4,600	$4,200

Total inventory cost:

	Average	FIFO	LIFO
Sold on June 30	$ 3,360	$ 3,200	$ 3,600
Sold on December 31	4,520	4,600	4,600
Total cost of goods sold	$ 7,880	$ 7,800	$ 8,200
Inventory on December 31	4,520	4,600	4,200
Total inventory cost	$12,400	$12,400	$12,400

*With the average cost method, no assumption is made about the sale of specific units. The average cost per unit is computed as follows:
[(200 × $10) + (300 × $12)]/500 units = $11.20 per unit
†[(200 × $11.20) + (500 × $11) + (100 × $13)]/800 units = $11.30 per unit

© Cengage Learning 2014

- For FIFO, cost of goods sold and ending inventory are the same whether a periodic system (all sales assumed to occur at year-end) or a perpetual system (sales occur throughout the year) is used. Compare Exhibits 9-10 and 9-11. This is because no matter when in the year the sales are assumed to occur, the oldest units (first in) are always the same ones.
- Because the newest units (last in) as of June 30 are not the same as the newest units on December 31, applying LIFO on a perpetual basis gives a different cost of goods sold and ending inventory than if a periodic system is used.
- Similarly, the average cost of units in inventory on June 30 ($11.20) is not the same as the average cost of all units purchased for the year ($11.27). Thus, applying average cost on a perpetual and a periodic basis yields different results.

Because of the unnecessary complications of perpetual LIFO and perpetual average cost, many businesses that use average cost or LIFO for financial reporting use a simple FIFO assumption in the maintenance of their day-to-day perpetual inventory records. These perpetual FIFO records are then converted to periodic average cost or LIFO for the financial reports.

More About LIFO

LO6 学习目标6
解释在后进先出法计量下账务中新增的存货是怎样计量的，并叙述后进先出储备的重要性。

6 Explain how LIFO inventory layers are created, and describe the significance of the LIFO reserve.

In the simple Dalton Company example of the previous section, the LIFO calculations did not seem any more difficult than the calculations using the other three methods. In a more involved example, the complexities of LIFO become apparent. In this section, a multiyear example is used to illustrate LIFO layers and LIFO liquidation. The advantages of using LIFO pools and dollar-value LIFO to reduce the recordkeeping burden associated with LIFO are illustrated later in the chapter.

LIFO Layers

The following data are for Ryanes Company for the first three years of its existence:

	2012	2013	2014
Purchases	120 units @ $ 5	150 units @ $10	160 units @ $15
Sales	100 units @ $10	120 units @ $15	120 units @ $20

At the end of 2012, 20 units with a total cost of $100 (20 units × $5 per unit) remain in ending inventory. Are these units sold in 2013? If a FIFO assumption is made, the answer is yes. Under FIFO, the 120 units sold in 2013 are the oldest available units: the 20 units left over from 2012 plus 100 units purchased in 2013. However, if a LIFO assumption is made, the 20 units left over at the end of 2012 are not sold in 2013. Instead, the newest units are sold, and those are 120 of the units purchased in 2013. Using LIFO, cost of goods sold and ending inventory for each of the three years are as follows:

Caution

Pay close attention to this part of the chapter. You may think you understand LIFO, but until you work through the wrinkles and quirks presented here, you don't.

	2012	2013	2014
LIFO cost of goods sold	100 × $5 = $500	120 × $10 = $1,200	120 × $15 = $1,800
Ending inventory:			
Year units purchased			
2012	20 × $5 = $100	20 × $ 5 = $ 100	20 × $ 5 = $ 100
2013		30 × $10 = 300	30 × $10 = 300
2014			40 × $15 = 600
Ending inventory	20 units $100	50 units $ 400	90 units $1,000

Notice that each year in which the number of units purchased exceeds the number of units sold, a new LIFO layer is created in ending inventory. As long as inventory continues to grow, a new LIFO layer is created each year and the old LIFO layers remain untouched.

The creation of LIFO layers illustrates one of the drawbacks of LIFO in that after a few years, the LIFO assumption results in ending inventory containing old inventory at old prices. In the Ryanes example, 2014 ending inventory is assumed to contain inventory purchased back in 2012. And, because inventory costs have increased during the period, the $1,000 amount reported for 2014 ending inventory does not represent the current value of the 90 units of inventory. For example, if FIFO were used, the 90 units in 2014 ending inventory would be valued using the 2014 purchase price of $15 per unit, giving them a value of $1,350 (90 units × $15 per unit). The difference between the LIFO ending inventory amount and the amount obtained using another inventory valuation method (like FIFO or average cost) is called the *LIFO reserve*. In this example, the LIFO reserve is $350 ($1,350 FIFO ending inventory − $1,000 LIFO ending inventory).

Exhibit 9-12 contains the note disclosure of DuPont's LIFO reserve from the

Stop & Think

Refer to the original Ryanes Company data and compute the FIFO cost of goods sold for 2012, 2013, and 2014.
a) 2012 = $500; 2013 = $1,200; 2014 = $1,550
b) 2012 = $100; 2013 = $400; 2014 = $1,550
c) 2012 = $500; 2013 = $1,100; 2014 = $1,550
d) 2012 = $100; 2013 = $1,100; 2014 = $1,550

Exhibit 9-12 | DuPont's LIFO Reserve Note

9. Inventories December 31	2011	2010
Finished products	$4,541	$3,733
Semifinished products	2,293	2,022
Raw materials, stores and supplies	1,262	855
Total	$8,096	$6,610
Adjustment of inventories to a LIFO basis	(901)	(643)
	$7,195	$5,967

Inventory values, before LIFO adjustment, are generally determined by the average cost method, which approximates current cost. Excluding seeds, certain food-ingredients, enzymes, stores and supplies, inventories valued under the LIFO method comprised 78% of consolidated inventories before LIFO adjustment as of December 31, 2011 and 2010.

DuPont, 2011, 10K Report

company's 2011 annual report. Note that DuPont uses the average cost method for maintaining its accounting records during the year and then adjusts its inventory to the LIFO method for financial reporting purposes.

Many companies that use LIFO report the amount of their LIFO reserve, either as a parenthetical note in the balance sheet or in the notes to the financial statements. The size of the LIFO reserve for several large U.S. companies is given in Exhibit 9-13. These LIFO reserve disclosures can aid financial statement users in comparing companies that use different inventory valuation methods. The disclosures can be used to recalculate LIFO ending inventory and cost of goods sold on a FIFO or average cost basis. To illustrate, the following data can be used to calculate FIFO cost of goods sold for Ryanes for 2014.

	2013	2014
LIFO ending inventory	$ 400	$1,000
LIFO reserve	100	350
LIFO cost of goods sold	1,200	1,800

The FIFO calculation can be done as follows:

LIFO			FIFO	
$ 400	Beginning inventory		$ 500	($400 + $100 LIFO reserve)
2,400	+ Purchases		2,400	(160 units × $15; same for LIFO and FIFO)
$2,800	= Cost of goods available		$2,900	
1,000	− Ending inventory		1,350	($1,000 + $350 LIFO reserve)
$1,800	= Cost of goods sold		$1,550	

Exhibit 9-13 | Size of LIFO Reserve for Selected U.S. Companies—2011

U.S. Companies with Large LIFO Reserves for the Year 2011 (in millions of U.S. dollars)

Company Name	Reported LIFO Inventory	LIFO Reserve
Caterpillar	$14,544	$2,422
Ford Motor	5,901	928
Deere & Co.	4,371	1,486

© Cengage Learning 2014

In this simple example, purchases can be computed from the original data. Alternatively, purchases can be inferred from the beginning inventory, ending inventory, and cost of goods sold amounts. The important insight is that purchases are the same whether LIFO or FIFO is used.

LIFO Liquidation

Continuing the Ryanes Company example, assume purchases and sales for 2015 are as follows:

Purchases .... 60 units @ $20
Sales .... 150 units @ $25

Because the number of units purchased does not exceed the number sold, no new LIFO layer is added in 2015. In fact, because 2015 purchases are so low, inventory in the old LIFO layers must be sold. This is called *LIFO liquidation*. Computation of 2015 LIFO cost of goods sold is as follows:

Year	Units Purchased	
2015	60 units @ $20	$1,200
2014	40 units @ $15	600
2013	30 units @ $10	300
2012	20 units @ $ 5	100
Total	150 units	$2,200

LIFO liquidation causes old LIFO layer costs to flow through cost of goods sold, sometimes with bizarre results. In this example, if Ryanes had not reduced inventory during 2015, LIFO cost of goods sold would have been $3,000 (150 units × $20 per unit). Thus, the impact of reducing inventory levels and dragging old LIFO layers into cost of goods sold is to reduce reported cost of goods sold by $800 ($3,000 − $2,200). This LIFO liquidation effect would be disclosed in the notes to the financial statements.

Drastic inventory reductions can be caused by work stoppages, a slowdown in business, or financing problems. When a company has used LIFO during a period of rising prices (as illustrated in the Ryanes example), the odd result of an unfortunate inventory reduction is that LIFO liquidation causes cost of goods sold to go down and net income to go up. The potential for this LIFO liquidation effect is one reason given under IFRS for banning the use of LIFO.

Interim LIFO Liquidation Frequently, a company experiences a decline in inventory at an interim reporting date but fully expects to replenish the inventory by the end of the fiscal year. This would be common, for example, in any business with seasonal fluctuations in inventory levels. For companies using LIFO, temporary interim inventory reductions

Retail stores must account for interim inventory reductions due to the seasonal fluctuation of inventory levels.

interim LIFO liquidation
临时后进先出法清算

are not viewed as the liquidation of LIFO layers. To maintain the recorded historical cost of the LIFO layers, a temporary provision account is established and then reversed when the inventory is replenished.[9]

To illustrate the appropriate journal entry, assume that the LIFO liquidation for Ryanes for 2015 had actually occurred at the end of the first quarter of 2015 and that the inventory was expected to be replenished by year-end. The $800 LIFO liquidation effect would be recorded as follows:

Cost of Goods Sold	800
Provision for Temporary Decline in LIFO Inventory	800

The provision account represents a liability to replace the inventory at a cost exceeding its recorded LIFO amount. This provision account is recorded only for interim reports; a LIFO liquidation is recorded at the end of the fiscal year whether a year-end inventory decline is temporary or not.

LIFO and Income Taxes

The LIFO inventory method was developed in the United States during the late 1930s as a method of reducing income taxes during periods of rising prices. However, when Congress authorized the use of LIFO for income tax purposes, a unique provision was attached to the law. This provision has become known as the LIFO conformity rule and specifies that only those taxpayers who use LIFO for financial reporting purposes may use it for tax purposes. LIFO is the only accounting method that must be reported the same way for tax and book purposes. In the early years, the LIFO conformity rule was strictly applied, and companies were not permitted to report inventory values using any other method, either in the body of the financial statements or in the attached notes. In 1981, the IRS regulations were relaxed by permitting companies to provide supplemental non-LIFO disclosures (such as the LIFO reserve disclosures discussed previously) as long as the information is not presented on the face of the income statement.[10]

Prior to the relaxation of the LIFO conformity rule, the income tax regulations governed the detailed application of LIFO for financial reporting purposes as well. And in fact, the IRS rules are still very important in determining how companies apply LIFO for financial reporting. However, both the SEC and the AICPA have issued guidelines outlining how proper application of LIFO for financial reporting might differ from the IRS regulations concerning LIFO.[11] The FASB has never addressed the issue of LIFO, deciding that the AICPA and SEC guidelines on the topic are sufficient.

> **Caution**
>
> LIFO is the exception! In every other case, companies are not required to use the same accounting methods in the financial statements as they use for income tax purposes. Therefore, a financial accounting decision usually has no impact on income taxes payable—LIFO is the exception.

To illustrate how LIFO reduces taxes in times of inflation, refer back to the data for Ryanes Company. For simplicity, assume that cost of goods sold is the only expense and that the tax rate is 40%. Calculation of income taxes using both LIFO and FIFO is given in Exhibit 9-14.

[9] FASB ASC paragraph 270-10-45-6b.
[10] The IRS LIFO conformity relaxation went so far as to state that, as far as the IRS is concerned, companies that use LIFO for tax purposes can prepare financial statements for external users using FIFO for inventory valuation on the balance sheet provided that LIFO cost of goods sold is reported on the income statement. However, this mismatch between the balance sheet and the income statement would be a violation of U.S. GAAP.
[11] See *Issues Paper*, "Identification and Discussion of Certain Financial Accounting and Reporting Issues Concerning LIFO Inventories" (New York: American Institute of Certified Public Accountants, 1984); and *Staff Accounting Bulletin (SAB) 58* (Topic 5.L.) (Washington, D.C: Securities and Exchange Commission, March 1985). See FASB ASC paragraph 330-10-S99-1.

Exhibit 9-14 | Ryanes Example: Comparison of Income Taxes Using LIFO and FIFO

LIFO:

	2012		2013		2014		2015	
Sales	100 @ $10	$1,000	120 @ $15	$1,800	120 @ $20	$2,400	150 @ $25	$3,750
Cost of goods sold	100 @ $5	500	120 @ $10	1,200	120 @ $15	1,800	60 @ $20	
							40 @ $15	
							30 @ $10	
							20 @ $5	2,200
Gross profit		$ 500		$ 600		$ 600		$1,550
Income taxes (40%)		$ 200		$ 240		$ 240		$ 620

FIFO:

	2012		2013		2014		2015	
Sales	100 @ $10	$1,000	120 @ $15	$1,800	120 @ $20	$2,400	150 @ $25	$3,750
Cost of goods sold	100 @ $5	500	20 @ $5		50 @ $10		90 @ $15	
			100 @ $10	1,100	70 @ $15	1,550	60 @ $20	2,550
Gross profit		$ 500		$ 700		$ 850		$1,200
Income taxes (40%)		$ 200		$ 280		$ 340		$ 480

© Cengage Learning 2014

From 2012 through 2014, with prices and inventory levels rising, the use of LIFO saves a total of $140 in income taxes [($280 − $240) + ($340 − $240)]. Because sales, collections, purchases, and payments are all the same whether LIFO or FIFO is used, the only cash flow difference between using LIFO and using FIFO is in cash paid for income taxes. Therefore, by the end of 2014, Ryanes will have additional cash of $140 (from tax savings) if LIFO is used.

Note also that this cumulative tax savings is exactly equal to the LIFO reserve at the end of 2014 (computed to be $350 in the previous section) multiplied by the tax rate ($350 × 0.40 = $140). Recall that the LIFO reserve represents the difference between the value of FIFO ending inventory and the value of LIFO ending inventory. Another way to think of the LIFO reserve is that it represents an inventory holding gain—an increase in the value of inventory because of price increases. In essence, when FIFO is used, this inventory holding gain becomes taxable income as it occurs, whereas with LIFO the inventory holding gain is not taxed until the inventory is liquidated, which happens in 2015 in this example.

The inventory liquidation in 2015 also illustrates that the use of LIFO for tax purposes results in tax deferral, not tax reduction. But because many companies have a low probability of liquidating their inventories in the foreseeable future, use of LIFO can defer payment of taxes on inventory holding gains for a long time.

LIFO Pools and Dollar-Value LIFO

As a means of simplifying the valuation process and extending its applicability to more items, the IRS developed the technique of establishing LIFO inventory pools of substantially identical goods. The purpose of forming LIFO pools is to simplify the LIFO calculations associated with large numbers of products. The simplification results in an estimate of what cost of goods sold would be if LIFO were applied strictly and laboriously.

Even the grouping of substantially identical items into quantity pools does not produce all the benefits desired from the use of LIFO. To further simplify the recordkeeping associated with LIFO and to eliminate the issues associated with new products replacing old products, the dollar-value LIFO inventory method was developed. Under this method, LIFO layers are determined based on total dollar changes rather than quantity changes. LIFO pools and dollar-value LIFO are discussed in detail in the Expanded Material section of this chapter.

Overall Comparison of FIFO, LIFO, and Average Cost

LO7 学习目标7
依据经营中不同方法对所得税、库存成本及财务状况的影响选择存货计价方法。

⑦ Choose an inventory valuation method based on the trade-offs among income tax effects, bookkeeping costs, and the impact on the financial statements.

The chart in Exhibit 9-15 gives a summary comparison of the advantages and disadvantages of FIFO and LIFO. Average cost can be viewed as being somewhere between these two.

So, which inventory valuation method should a company pick? Circumstances differ from firm to firm, and the decision would be based on an analysis of the following four factors:

- Income tax effects
- Bookkeeping costs
- Impact on financial statements
- Industry comparison

Exhibit 9-15 | Summary Comparison of FIFO and LIFO

	FIFO	LIFO
Income Statement	**Advantage:** • Usually corresponds with the physical flow of goods. **Disadvantages:** • Can cause older costs to be matched with current revenues. • Inventory holding gains and losses are included as part of gross profit.	**Advantages:** • Matches current costs with current revenues. • Excludes inventory holding gains and losses from gross profit. **Disadvantages:** • Usually does not correspond with the physical flow of goods. • Potential LIFO liquidation means old costs in LIFO layers can be drawn into cost of goods sold.
Balance Sheet	**Advantage:** • Ending inventory balance agrees closely with current replacement cost.	**Disadvantage:** • Ending inventory balance is composed of old costs in LIFO layers and can be substantially lower than current replacement cost. This is partially offset by supplemental disclosure.
Income Taxes	**Disadvantage:** • Yields higher taxable income in times of inflation if inventory levels are stable or increasing.	**Advantage:** • Yields lower taxable income in times of inflation if inventory levels are stable or increasing. **Disadvantage:** • LIFO liquidation can result in greatly increased tax payments when inventory levels decline.

© Cengage Learning 2014

Income Tax Effects

If a company has large inventory levels, is experiencing significant inventory cost increases, and does not anticipate reducing inventory levels in the future, LIFO gives substantial cash flow benefits in terms of tax deferral. This is the primary reason for LIFO adoption by most firms. For the many firms with small inventory levels or with flat or decreasing inventory costs, LIFO gives little, if any, tax benefit. Such firms are unlikely to use LIFO.

Bookkeeping Costs

As seen in this chapter, the bookkeeping associated with LIFO is a bit more complicated than with FIFO or average cost. In dollars and cents, a LIFO system costs more to operate. For this reason, LIFO is less common among small firms where any LIFO tax benefits can be swamped by increased bookkeeping costs. However, with improved information technology and with the simplifications of LIFO pools and dollar-value LIFO (discussed in the Expanded Material associated with this chapter), the incremental LIFO bookkeeping costs can be minimized.

Impact on Financial Statements

While LIFO gives tax benefits, it also gives reduced reported income and reduced reported inventory. These negative financial statement effects can harm a company by scaring off stockholders, potential investors, and banks. One way around this is to provide supplemental disclosure to allow users to see what the financial statements would look like if FIFO or average cost were used.

Stop & Think

Why wouldn't it be possible to use LIFO for the income statement and FIFO for the balance sheet?
a) The amount of income taxes paid would double.
b) The ending inventory amount and the amount of cost of goods sold would always be equal.
c) Gross profit would always be negative.
d) Without a special adjustment, the balance sheet wouldn't balance.

Industry Comparison

Although financial statement users should be sophisticated in their understanding of inventory accounting, they often are not. They ignore supplemental LIFO disclosures and just compare the unadjusted numbers. If other companies in an industry use FIFO, the reported performance of a LIFO company can look poor by comparison.

International Accounting and Inventory Valuation

The International Accounting Standards Board (IASB) has waffled in its opinion about LIFO. In its initial standard on inventory (*IAS 2*), the IASB identified LIFO, along with FIFO, average cost, and something called the base stock method (an extreme form of LIFO), as allowable inventory valuation methods. In 1989, the IASB proposed eliminating the base stock method, and in 1991, it tentatively decided to eliminate both the base stock method and LIFO. In 1992, the IASB decided to officially endorse FIFO and average cost, to kill the base stock method, and to let LIFO live on as a second-class "allowed alternative treatment." Finally, in December 2003 the IASB adopted a revised version of *IAS 2* and did away with LIFO once and for all.

Inventory Accounting Changes

When a company changes its method of valuing inventory, the change is accounted for as a change in accounting principle. If the change is to average cost or FIFO, both the beginning and ending inventories can usually be computed on the new basis. Thus, the effect of changing inventory methods can be determined and reported in the financial statements, as explained in Chapter 20. If the change is to LIFO from another method, however, a company's records are generally not complete enough to reconstruct the prior years' inventory layers. Therefore, the base-year layer for the new LIFO inventory is the opening inventory for the year in which LIFO is adopted (also the ending inventory for the year before LIFO is adopted). There is no adjustment to the financial statements to reflect the change to LIFO. However, the impact of the change on income for the current year must be disclosed in a note to the statements. In addition, the note should explain why there is no effect on the financial statements. Required disclosures for a change to LIFO are illustrated in Exhibit 9-16 in a description from the 2001 10-K filing of **Duane Reade**, the largest drugstore chain in New York City. Note the company's forthright description of the income tax benefits of using LIFO when inventory costs are rising.

When inventories are a material item, a change in the inventory method by a company may impair comparability of that company's financial statements with prior years' statements and with the financial statements of other entities. Such changes require careful consideration and should be made only when management can clearly demonstrate the preferability of the alternative method.[12]

Inventory Valuation at Other than Cost

8 Apply the lower-of-cost-or-market (LCM) rule to reflect declines in the market value of inventory.

The basic procedures for allocating total cost of goods available for sale between ending inventory and cost of goods sold were explained in the previous sections. In some cases, these cost allocation procedures result in inventory cost that exceeds the current market value of the inventory. The following section discusses how to determine when inventory

Exhibit 9-16 | Duane Reade: Disclosure of Change to LIFO Method

Accounting Change

During the first quarter of 2002, we plan to adopt a change in accounting method to convert from our current retail dollar based first-in, first-out ("FIFO") method of inventory valuation to an item specific cost based last-in, first-out ("LIFO") method of inventory valuation. This change is expected to result in a separate one-time non-cash after tax charge of approximately $9.0 million to be recorded in the first quarter. In addition, expected 2002 inflation in inventory acquisition costs will likely result in increased charges to cost of goods to be sold during 2002. We estimate that a 1.0% inflation in the annual inventory acquisition costs in 2002 would approximate a $1.2 million reduction in fiscal 2002 net earnings. Adoption of the specific cost LIFO method will result in the recognition of the latest item costs in our reported gross margins, and will make our results more comparable to other major retailers in our industry. In an inflationary period, the LIFO method also has the added favorable impact of increasing cash flow through reduced income taxes.

Duane Reade, 2001, 10K Report

[12] FASB ASC paragraph 250-10-45-12.

should be "written down" to reflect a decline in its market value. The section concludes with a discussion of inventory valuation when inventory is acquired in a nonmarket transaction (e.g., the return of defective merchandise) and a value must be assigned.

Lower of Cost or Market

One of the traditional concepts of accounting is conservatism, sometimes summarized as "when in doubt, recognize all unrealized losses, but don't recognize any unrealized gains." When applied to asset valuation, conservatism results in the rule of lower of cost or market (LCM), meaning that assets are recorded at the lower of their cost or their market value.[13] LCM has the effect of recognizing unrealized decreases in the value of assets but not unrealized increases.[14]

In applying the lower-of-cost-or-market rule, the cost of the ending inventory, as determined under an appropriate cost allocation method, is compared with market value at the end of the period. If market is less than cost, an adjusting entry is made to record the loss and restate ending inventory at the lower value.[15]

What Is "Market"? The term market in "lower of cost or market" is interpreted as meaning replacement cost, with potential adjustments for a ceiling and a floor value. Replacement cost, sometimes referred to as entry cost, includes the purchase price of the product or raw materials plus all other costs incurred in the acquisition or manufacture of goods. Replacement cost is frequently a good measure of the amount of future economic benefit embodied in inventory because declines in acquisition costs (entry cost) usually indicate a decline in selling prices (exit value). However, selling prices do not always respond immediately and in proportion to changes in replacement costs. Accordingly, the following ceiling and floor constraints are placed on the use of replacement cost as the measure of the market value of inventory:[16]

- Ceiling. The market value of inventory is not greater than the net realizable value of the inventory. Net realizable value (NRV) is equal to the estimated selling price of the inventory minus any normal selling costs. The reasoning behind this ceiling is that the market value of inventory could never reasonably be considered to be more than the net amount that can be received upon sale of the inventory.

- Floor. The market value of the inventory is not less than net realizable value minus a normal profit margin. If inventory is recorded below this floor amount, then the inventory can be sold in the future netting a return that is more than the normal profit margin.

In summary, market value of inventory is never less than the floor value, is never more than the ceiling value, and is equal to replacement cost when replacement cost is between the floor and the ceiling. These relationships are summarized in Exhibit 9-17.

市场价值在成本与市价孰低法中被解释为重置成本，重置成本包括产品或者原材料的购买价格，减去所有其他收购成本和制造成本。
重置成本作为衡量存货市场价值的一种方法，受到上下限的约束。一是存货的市值不能大于存货的可变现净值，二是存货的市值不能小于可变现净值减去正常毛利。

> **FYI**
> A good way to apply the ceiling and floor rules is to remember that the market value will always be the middle value of these three—replacement cost and ceiling and floor amounts.

---

[13] Historically, investment securities, inventory, and property, plant, and equipment were recorded at the lower of cost or market. With the adoption of FASB pre-Codification *Statement No. 115* in 1993, most investment securities are now recorded at their current market value whether that amount is lower or higher than cost. See FASB ASC Topic 320 (Investments—Debt and Equity Securities).

[14] For a time, the FASB required firms to make supplemental disclosure of the replacement cost of inventory. This requirement (FASB pre-Codification *Statement No. 33*) was a response to the high inflation of the late 1970s that frequently caused reported historical inventory cost to be much lower than current replacement cost. When inflation abated, interest in this supplemental disclosure waned and *Statement No. 33* was repealed.

[15] No adjustment to LIFO cost is permitted for tax purposes. Application of LCM to LIFO inventories for financial reporting purposes does not violate the "LIFO conformity" rule if IRS approval is obtained.

[16] FASB ASC Master Glossary: "Market."

Exhibit 9-17 | Market Value Equals Replacement Cost, Constrained by the Ceiling and the Floor

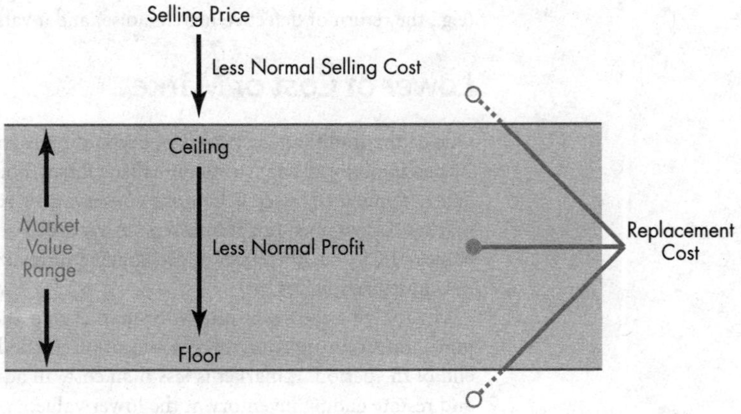

Applying the Lower-of-Cost-or-Market Method Application of the LCM rule to determine the appropriate inventory valuation may be summarized in the following steps:

1. Define pertinent values: historical cost, floor (NRV—normal profit), replacement cost, ceiling (NRV).
2. Determine "market" (replacement cost as constrained by ceiling and floor limits).
3. Compare cost with market (as defined in step 2 above), and select the lower amount.

To illustrate these steps, assume that Fezzig Company sells six products identified with the letters A through F. For each product, the selling price per unit is $1.00, selling expenses are $0.20 per unit, and the normal profit is 25% of sales, or $0.25 per unit. The historical cost and the current replacement cost are different for each product. The lower-of-cost-or-market valuation for each product is shown below with the appropriate "market" value highlighted.

Item	Historical Cost	Floor	Replacement Cost	Ceiling	Market	Lower of Cost or Market
A....	$0.65	$0.55	$0.70	$0.80	$0.70	$0.65
B....	0.65	0.55	0.60	0.80	0.60	0.60
C....	0.65	0.55	0.50	0.80	0.55	0.55
D....	0.50	0.55	0.45	0.80	0.55	0.50
E....	0.75	0.55	0.85	0.80	0.80	0.75
F....	0.90	0.55	1.00	0.80	0.80	0.80

A: Market is equal to replacement cost; historical cost is less than market.
B: Market is equal to replacement cost; market is less than historical cost.
C: Market is equal to the floor; market is less than historical cost.
D: Market is equal to the floor; replacement and historical costs are less than market.
E: Market is equal to the ceiling; historical cost is less than market.
F: Market is equal to the ceiling; market is less than historical and replacement costs.

For products A and B, the replacement cost is between the floor and the ceiling, so the market value is the replacement cost. For products C and D, replacement cost is below the floor, so the market value is the floor value. For products E and F, replacement cost is greater than the ceiling, so the market value is the ceiling value.

> **Caution**
>
> Don't get carried away—remember that an actual adjusting entry is made only if market value is less than historical cost. For products A, D, and E, no LCM adjustment is needed.

To see the wisdom in using the floor and ceiling values in calculating market value, consider products C and F. Without the floor, the market value for product C would be $0.50 and the inventory would be written down from the cost of $0.65 to the market value of $0.50. But this $0.50 value is too low because it would result in extra profits being recorded next period when the inventory is sold. For example, selling price of $1.00 minus selling costs of $0.20 minus recorded inventory amount of $0.50 leaves a reported profit of $0.30 per unit, whereas the normal profit is just $0.25 per unit. Without the floor, product C would be written down too much this period, resulting in unusually high profits next period.

For product F, without the ceiling value the market value would be the $1.00 replacement cost. Because this exceeds the cost of $0.90, the inventory would continue to be recorded at cost. However, the ceiling amount suggests that the maximum that can be expected to be realized upon sale of units of product F is the net realizable value of $0.80. In this case, the ceiling amount ensures that the inventory cost is written down so that reported inventory does not exceed the amount expected to be realized upon sale of the inventory.

The LCM method may be applied to each inventory item, to the major classes or categories of inventory items, or to the inventory as a whole. Application of LCM to the individual inventory items will result in the lower inventory value because increases in the market value of some inventory items are not allowed to offset decreases in the value of other items.[17]

To illustrate the difference in valuation applications, assume that Fezzig Company's inventory includes 1,000 units each of products A through F. The table below illustrates how the LCM valuation of Fezzig's inventory would differ, depending on whether the LCM rule is applied individually to each product or to the inventory as a whole.

If the individual product method is used, the LCM rule is applied separately to products A through F, resulting in a total LCM inventory valuation of $3,850. If the LCM rule is applied to the inventory as a whole, the aggregate market value of $4,000 is compared to the aggregate cost of $4,100, and the inventory is recorded at $4,000.

Product	Number of Units	Total Cost	Total Market	Total LCM
A.	1,000	$ 650	$ 700	$ 650
B.	1,000	650	600	600
C.	1,000	650	550	550
D.	1,000	500	550	500
E.	1,000	750	800	750
F.	1,000	900	800	800
	6,000	$4,100	$4,000	$3,850

[17] The IRS requires application of the LCM rule to individual products. To reduce the burden of keeping two sets of inventory records, companies frequently use this same method for financial reporting purposes. Many disputes have arisen between taxpayers and the IRS through the years as to what constitutes a recognizable decline in inventory value. An important tax case in this area was settled by the U.S. Supreme Court in 1979. The taxpayer, **Thor Power Tool Co.**, had followed the practice of writing down the value of spare parts inventories that were being held to cover future warranty requirements. Although the sales prices did not decline, the probability of the parts being sold, and thus their net realizable value, decreased as time passed. The write-down to reflect the current decline in value is consistent with the accounting principle of recognizing declines in value as they occur. The Supreme Court, however, ruled that for tax purposes the reduction must await the actual decline in the sales price for the parts in question.

The journal entry to record the write-down of the inventory on an individual item basis is usually made as follows:

Loss from Decline in Value of Inventory	250	
Inventory		250

($4,100 − $3,850)

The loss on the decline in market value may be shown as a separate item on the income statement, or included as part of cost of goods sold. Separate reporting of the loss has the advantage of providing readers with increased information to forecast operations and cash flows. As an example, Cisco Systems recognized an inventory write-down of $2.77 billion in 2001 "due to a sudden and significant decrease in demand for the Company's products."[18]

Once an individual item is reduced to a lower market price, the new market price is considered to be the item's cost for future inventory valuations; cost reductions once made are not restored. Thus, inventory records must be adjusted to reflect the new values.

Rather than reducing the inventory directly, the inventory account can be maintained at cost, and an allowance for inventory decline can be used to record the decline in value. This method would generally be used when inventory is valued on a category or entire inventory basis. The entry to record the write-down on an entire inventory basis and using an allowance account would be as follows:

Loss from Decline in Value of Inventory	100	
Allowance for Decline in Value of Inventory		100

($4,100 − $4,000)

The allowance account would be reported as an offset to the inventory account on the balance sheet. The question then arises of what to do with this allowance in subsequent years. Assume that in the subsequent year, Fezzig Company sells its entire existing inventory of products A through F. The allowance is no longer needed because the inventory to which the allowance applied has been sold. The adjusting entry necessary in the subsequent year is as follows:

Allowance for Decline in Value of Inventory	100	
Cost of Goods Sold		100

The credit is entered appropriately to Cost of Goods Sold, rather than to a gain, for the following reasons:

- The recorded cost of the old inventory sold during the year, $4,100, is an overstatement of the carrying amount of the inventory. The net carrying amount is only $4,000 ($4,100 cost − $100 allowance), and Cost of Goods Sold has been overstated by the amount of the allowance.

- Recording a gain gives the misleading impression that recoveries of inventory market values are recognized as gains. On the contrary, once a particular inventory item or group of items is written down, no subsequent market value increases for those items are recognized.

The inventory at the end of the subsequent year is then evaluated to determine whether the establishment of a new Allowance for Decline in Value of Inventory is needed.[19]

Caution

No gains are recorded on inventory market value recoveries.

---

[18] According to FASB ASC paragraph 420-10-S99-3, inventory write-downs such as that made by Cisco should be classified as an increase in cost of goods sold.

[19] The two adjusting entries eliminating the allowance from the previous year and creating a new allowance can be combined into one entry that merely changes the net balance in the allowance account. However, making the two entries separately greatly clarifies the reasoning underlying the entries.

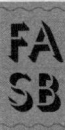

FASB CODIFICATION

The Issue: You come from the small town of Grantsville. Historically, many people in your community have been farmers. You are combining your love of accounting with your love of the farm and are doing some bookkeeping for a hometown farmer. The farmer has been asked by the local bank to prepare a balance sheet and income statement in connection with the farmer's application for a loan to finance an expansion of cultivated land for next year's planting season. The balance sheet will be dated September 30. The farmer has harvested all of her crop but has not yet sold it. The farmer is uncertain about how to report this harvested crop inventory in the balance sheet.

The Question: At what amount should harvested crop inventory be reported in the balance sheet?

Searching the Codification: If you look under the "Inventory" topic (Topic 330) in the "Assets" collection of topics in the Codification, you will see that there is an entire special topic (905) addressing agricultural accounting issues. You are interested in the "subsequent measurement" of harvested crops.

The Answer: The accounting treatment for harvested crop inventory is discussed on page 9-60.

Assigned Inventory Value: The Case of Returned Inventory

In some cases, the ceiling and floor values discussed provide guidance in assigning an appropriate inventory value when inventory cost is difficult to determine. As an illustration, consider the following data on defective inventory returned to Inigo Company by angry customers.

- Number of defective units returned: 1,000
- Selling price of normal units: $5
- Cost of normal units: $3
- Normal gross profit percentage: ($5 − $3)/$5 = 40%
- Scrap selling price of units returned as defective: $2
- For simplicity, assume that there are no extra expenses associated with the scrap sale of units that have been returned as defective.

In this case, it is clearly wrong to record the defective inventory units at their historical cost of $3 per unit because they can be sold for only $2 per unit. No replacement cost number can be used to determine the appropriate lower-of-cost-or-market write-down because no supplier will quote a price on entire batches of defective units. Thus, the appropriate inventory valuation is somewhere between the ceiling and the floor:

Ceiling: $2 selling price − $0 selling costs = $2 net realizable value
Floor: $2 net realizable value − $0.80 normal gross profit ($2 × 40%) = $1.20

If the inventory is written down to the ceiling value of $2, the loss on the write-down is $1,000 [($3 − $2) × 1,000 units]. If the inventory is written down to the floor value, the write-down loss is $1,800 [($3 − $1.20) × 1,000 units]. The write-down loss, and profit on subsequent scrap sale of defective units, is summarized as follows:

	Write-Down to Ceiling	Write-Down to Floor
Loss on write-down	$(1,000)	$(1,800)
Scrap sales of defective units	$2,000	$2,000
Cost of goods sold	2,000	1,200
Gross profit on scrap sales	0	800
Total loss on defective units	$(1,000)	$(1,000)

In the absence of a reliable replacement cost number, should the returned inventory be recorded at the ceiling value, the floor value, or somewhere in between? Or does it make any difference? You might contend that it makes no difference because the total loss on defective units is $1,000 in all cases. However, if you are the manager in charge of scrap sales and your annual bonus is based on the profit generated by your department, which inventory valuation number would you prefer? You would prefer the floor value because this lowers your cost of goods sold and allows your department to show a profit. The general point of the illustration is this: When there is some leeway in the assigning of inventory values, the assigned value can be very important in determining how profits and losses associated with the inventory are allocated among different reporting units within the business.

In summary, the absence of a reliable measure of entry values (historical cost or replacement cost) means that an inventory value must be assigned based on exit values (net realizable value and normal selling profit). The decision of what inventory value to choose within the floor-to-ceiling interval can be an interesting exercise in intracompany bargaining as managers try to set the inventory values to maximize the reported profits in their departments and push losses off to other departments. This is the same issue that arises in the context of transfer pricing (assigning inventory values to goods "sold" from one division of a company to another) and is discussed at length in courses on cost accounting.[20]

> **FYI**
> These same issues arise when assigning values to used items given in trade for new items. For example, how does a car dealer value the used car inventory accepted in trade for new cars?

Accounting for Declines in Inventory Values: *IAS 2*

The inventory write-down rule under *IAS 2* can best be labeled "lower of cost or net realizable value." This net realizable value is the same as described earlier: estimated selling price of the inventory minus any normal selling costs. Under *IAS 2*, if the selling price of inventory has declined enough (or if the normal selling costs have increased enough) that the cost of the inventory cannot be recovered, then the inventory is written down to the net realizable value. This approach is much easier to apply than the U.S. GAAP "lower-of-cost-or-market" rule—there is no ceiling, no floor, and no replacement cost. Instead, the *IAS 2* rule involves a simple comparison between cost and net realizable value. The write-down journal entry is the same as illustrated earlier.

---

[20] As illustrated, assigned inventory values can determine where within a company profits and losses are reported. Imagine how important this issue is in the context of tax reporting for multinational companies. Assigned inventory values determine whether a taxable profit is reported (and taxed) in a foreign subsidiary or in the U.S. parent company.

One additional difference in the provisions of *IAS 2* is that if the depressed selling price of written-down inventory subsequently recovers, the inventory write-down loss is reversed. This reversal would probably be reported as a decrease in cost of goods sold resulting in an increase in gross profit.

Gross Profit Method

LO9 学习目标9
使用毛利法估计期末存货价值。

9 Use the gross profit method to estimate ending inventory.

Inventory estimation techniques are used to generate inventory values when a physical inventory count is not practical and to provide an independent check of the validity of the inventory figures generated by the accounting system. The simplest inventory estimation technique is the gross profit method. The gross profit method is based on the observation that the relationship between sales and cost of goods sold is usually fairly stable. The gross profit percentage [(Sales − Cost of goods sold)/Sales] is applied to sales to estimate cost of goods sold. This cost of goods sold estimate is subtracted from the cost of goods available for sale to arrive at an estimated inventory balance.

gross profit percentage
毛利率

毛利法的应用基础是销售收入和销售成本的关系比较稳定。

To be useful, the gross profit percentage used must be a reliable measure of current experience. In developing a reliable rate, reference is made to past rates, and these are adjusted for changes in current circumstances. For example, the historical gross profit percentage would be adjusted if the pricing strategy has changed (e.g., because of increased competition), if the sales mix has changed, or if a different inventory valuation method has been adopted (e.g., a switch from FIFO to LIFO).

To illustrate the application of the gross profit method, consider the following information for Rugen Company.

Beginning inventory, January 1	$25,000
Sales, January 1–January 31	50,000
Purchases, January 1–January 31	40,000
Historical gross profit percentages:	
Last year	40%
Two years ago	37%
Three years ago	42%

Rugen wishes to prepare financial statements as of January 31 and wants to use an estimate of ending inventory rather than performing a physical inventory count. Last year's gross profit percentage of 40% is considered to be a good estimate of the current gross profit percentage.

The inventory estimate is a two-step process: An assumed gross profit percentage is used to determine estimated gross profit, which then allows computation of estimated cost of goods sold. That number is then used to estimate ending inventory.

Sales (actual)	$50,000	100%
Cost of goods sold (estimate)	30,000	60%
Gross profit (estimate)	$20,000	40%
Beginning inventory (actual)		$25,000
+ Purchases (actual)		40,000
= Cost of goods available for sale (actual)		$65,000
− Ending inventory (estimate)		35,000
= Cost of goods sold (estimate)		$30,000

This ending inventory estimate can now be used in the January 31 financial statements or can be compared to perpetual inventory records if they exist, or can be used as the basis of an insurance reimbursement if the inventory on January 31 is destroyed in an accident. This two-step process is illustrated in Exhibit 9-18.

Assume that Rugen does a physical inventory count indicating that January 31 inventory is $32,000, compared to the $35,000 estimate computed earlier. Is this a reasonable difference, or is there reason for further investigation? One way to make this determination is to see what range of ending inventory estimates is possible given the differences observed in historical gross profit percentages. These calculations are as follows.

	Gross Profit Percentage		
	40%	37%	42%
Sales (actual)	$50,000	$50,000	$50,000
Cost of goods sold (estimate)	30,000	31,500	29,000
Gross profit (estimate)	$20,000	$18,500	$21,000
Beginning inventory (actual)	$25,000	$25,000	$25,000
+ Purchases (actual)	40,000	40,000	40,000
= Cost of goods available for sale (actual)	$65,000	$65,000	$65,000
− Ending inventory (estimate)	35,000	33,500	36,000
+ Cost of goods sold (estimate)	$30,000	$31,500	$29,000

The range of estimates for January 31 inventory is from $33,500 to $36,000. The $32,000 value derived from the physical count is outside this range. Possible explanations are:

- This year's gross profit percentage is outside the historically observed range, suggesting that there has been a significant change in pricing strategy or product mix.
- Inventory shrinkage has occurred.
- Sales have been underreported. The IRS sometimes uses the gross profit method to detect underreporting of sales to avoid income taxes.

Exhibit 9-18 | The Gross Profit Method

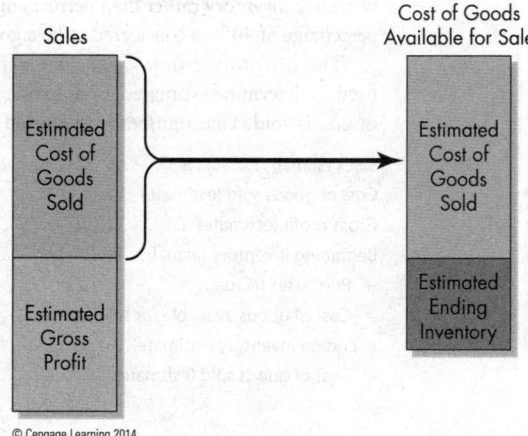

Stop & Think

Assume that the actual amount of inventory is much lower than the estimated amount. Which ONE of the following is NOT a possible explanation?

a) The estimation process is flawed.
b) The actual amount of purchases was greater than the reported amount of purchases.
c) The missing inventory was lost or stolen.
d) The missing inventory was sold, but the sales were not reported.

Sometimes the hardest part of applying the gross profit method is deciphering language about the relationship between sales and cost of goods sold. In the example just completed, the sales/cost of goods sold relationship was summarized by saying that the gross profit percentage is 40%. The same relationship could be described in at least two other ways:

1. Sales are made at a markup of 40% of the selling price.
2. Sales are made at a markup of 66⅔% of cost. (Gross profit/Cost = 66⅔%)

Be careful.

Like the gross profit method, the retail inventory method can be used to generate a reliable estimate of inventory position whenever desired. This method, like the gross profit method, permits the estimation of an inventory amount without the time and expense of taking a physical inventory or maintaining detailed perpetual inventory records. The retail inventory method is more flexible than the gross profit method in that it allows estimates to be based on FIFO, LIFO, or average cost assumptions, and it even permits estimation of lower-of-cost-or-market values. The retail inventory method is covered in detail in the Expanded Material associated with this chapter.

Effects of Errors in Recording Inventory

LO10 学习目标10
确认存货记录错误对财务报告的影响。

10 Determine the financial statement impact of inventory recording errors.

Failure to correctly report inventory results in misstatements on both the balance sheet and the income statement. The effect on the income statement is sometimes difficult to evaluate because of the different amounts that can be affected by an error. Analysis of the impact is aided by recalling the simple computation:

Beginning inventory
+ Purchases
= Goods available for sale
− Ending inventory
= Cost of goods sold

For example, an overstatement of the beginning inventory will result in an overstatement of goods available for sale and cost of goods sold. Because the cost of goods sold is deducted from sales to determine the gross profit, the overstated cost of goods sold results in an understated gross profit and finally an understated net income.

Sometimes an error may affect two of the amounts in such a way that they offset each other. For example, if a purchase in transit is neither recorded as a purchase nor included in the ending inventory, the

FYI

Because inventory errors reverse themselves in the following year, persons using inventory fraud to overstate income must create larger and larger amounts of fictitious inventory in succeeding years to maintain the bogus income growth. This escalation is often what causes the fraud to be detected.

有时一个错误可能影响计算过程中的两个环节，但这两个环节互相抵消了。例如，如果一笔购入存货还在运输过程中，其既不能作为购买行为记录也不能包括在期末存货中，所以购入存货的低估会导致可供销售商品的低估；但是，当可供销售商品减去低估的期末存货时，两者的低估相互抵消了，从而产生了一个正确的销售成本、毛利及净利润，但资产负债表中的存货及应付账款仍被低估。

understatement of purchases results in an understatement of goods available for sale; however, the understatement of ending inventory subtracted from goods available for sale offsets the error and creates a correct cost of goods sold, gross profit, and net income. Inventory and accounts payable, however, will be understated on the balance sheet.[21]

Because the ending inventory of one period becomes the beginning inventory of the next period, undetected inventory errors affect two accounting periods. If left undetected, the errors will offset each other under a FIFO or average method. Errors in LIFO layers, however, may perpetuate themselves until the layers are eliminated.

It is unwise to try to memorize the impact a particular type of inventory error has on the financial statements. It is preferable to analyze each situation. Analysis of the following three typical inventory errors provides further practice.

1. Overstatement of ending inventory through an improper physical count
2. Understatement of ending inventory through an improper physical count
3. Understatement of ending inventory through delay in recording a purchase until the following year.

Stop & Think

Why might a manager risk his or her reputation by fraudulently overstating inventory in light of the fact that the resulting income increase is completely counterbalanced in the following year?

a) The manager is confident that operating profits next year will be strong enough to cover the impact of the counterbalancing inventory error.
b) The manager knows that not all inventory errors are counterbalancing.
c) The manager knows that inventory errors do not have any impact on reported operating profit.

The impact of the three errors on the income statement and the balance sheet in the year of the error and the following year is summarized in Exhibit 9-19.

Error 1, overstatement of ending inventory, sometimes results when a company fraudulently manipulates its inventory count. As seen in Exhibit 9-19, this ending inventory overstatement reduces cost of goods sold and increases net income in the year of the error. A counterbalancing reduction in net income occurs in the following year because beginning inventory is overstated.

Error 2, understatement of ending inventory, is the opposite of Error 1 and results in a reduction in net income in the error year. As with Error 1, a counterbalancing error occurs in the following year.

Error 3, delay recording purchase or understatement of ending inventory and purchases, commonly occurs when a company fails to consider end-of-period goods in transit as part of purchases and inventory. As seen in Exhibit 9-19, this error has no impact on net income but does cause inventory and payables to be understated in the year of the error.

The correcting entry for each of these errors depends on when the error is discovered. If it is discovered in the current year, adjustments can be made to current accounts and the reported net income and balance sheet amounts will be correct. If the error is not discovered until the subsequent period, the correcting entry qualifies as a prior-period adjustment if the net income of the prior period was misstated. The error to a prior year's income is corrected through Retained Earnings. To illustrate these entries, assume that an incorrect physical count has resulted in an overstatement of ending

---

[21] This analysis is strictly true only if the FIFO inventory valuation method is used. With both LIFO and average cost, end-of-period purchases impact the calculation of cost of goods sold.

Exhibit 9-19 | Analysis of Inventory Errors

	#1 Overstatement of Ending Inventory		#2 Understatement of Ending Inventory		#3 Delay Recording Purchase	
	Error Year	Next Year	Error Year	Next Year	Error Year	Next Year
Beginning inventory	OK	over*	OK	under	OK	under
+ Purchases	OK	OK	OK	OK	under	over
= Goods available for sale	OK	over	OK	under	under	OK
− Ending inventory	over	OK	under	OK	under	OK
= Cost of goods sold	under	over	over	under	OK	OK
Income Statement:						
Cost of goods sold	under	over	over	under	OK	OK
Net income	over	under	under	over	OK	OK
Balance Sheet:						
Inventory	over	OK	under	OK	under	OK
Payables	OK	OK	OK	OK	under	OK
Retained earnings	over	OK	under	OK	OK	OK

*(Over) indicates overstatement, (under) indicates understatement, and (OK) indicates no effect.

© Cengage Learning 2014

inventory by $1,000 (Error 1). The correcting entry required, depending on when the error is discovered, would be as follows:

Error discovered in current year:

| Cost of Goods Sold | 1,000 | |
| Inventory | | 1,000 |

Error discovered in subsequent year:

| Retained Earnings | 1,000 | |
| Inventory | | 1,000 |

Using Inventory Information for Financial Analysis

LO11 Analyze inventory using financial ratios, and properly compare ratios of different firms after adjusting for differences in inventory valuation methods.

学习目标11
运用财务比率分析存货，并且针对不同企业间不同存货计价方法调整后的比值进行财务比率对比分析。

inventory turnover
存货周转

The inventory balances contained in the financial statements are often used to measure how efficiently the company is utilizing its inventory. The amount of inventory carried frequently relates closely to sales volume. The inventory position and the appropriateness of its size may be evaluated by computing the *inventory turnover*. The inventory turnover is measured by dividing cost of goods sold by average inventory [(beginning balance + ending balance) ÷ 2].

Consider the financial information relating to inventories for **Deere & Co.** provided below.

Deere & Co.
Major Classes of Inventories
(Dollars in millions)

	2011	2010
Raw materials and supplies	$ 1,626	$ 1,201
Work-in-process	647	483
Finished machines and parts	3,584	2,777
Total FIFO value	$ 5,857	$ 4,461
Adjustment to LIFO value	1,486	1,398
Inventories	$ 4,371	$ 3,063
Cost of sales	$21,919	$17,399

The inventory turnover rate for Deere & Co. would be computed as follows:

$$\frac{\text{Cost of goods sold}}{\text{Average inventory*}} = \frac{\$21,919}{\$3,717} = 5.90 \text{ times}$$

Calculation:

* 2011: ($4,371 + $3,063)/2 = $3,717

Inventory turnover of 5.90 times means that if Deere & Co. were to completely use up all of its inventory, and then instantaneously replace it, this process would be repeated 5.90 times during the year. The higher the inventory turnover number, the faster a company is using its inventory.

Using total inventory, this example has been simplified. If separate turnovers were computed for raw materials, work in process, and finished goods, the appropriate numerators for each computation would be raw materials used in production, cost of goods manufactured, and cost of goods sold, respectively. Note that total sales is never appropriate to use in inventory turnover calculations because sales numbers are stated in terms of selling prices, whereas inventory is stated in terms of acquisition or production cost. For example, in a retail setting, sales is a retail number and inventory is a wholesale number. Mixing them in the same calculation seriously impairs the interpretation of the inventory turnover ratio.[22]

Deere & Co. uses LIFO. From the disclosure about Deere's LIFO reserve, FIFO values for inventory and cost of goods sold can be calculated. If Deere & Co. had used FIFO instead of LIFO, inventory turnover for 2011 would have been 4.23 (instead of 5.90 under LIFO), computed as follows:

$$\frac{\text{FIFO cost of goods sold*}}{\text{FIFO average inventory}^\dagger} = \frac{\$21,831}{\$5,159} = 4.23 \text{ times}$$

Calculations:

*$21,919 + ($1,398 − $1,486) = $21,831
†($5,857 + $4,461)/2 = $5,159

This calculation illustrates that the ratios of two companies that are essentially the same will differ if one uses LIFO and the other uses FIFO. In any serious comparative ratio analysis, one must first make the necessary adjustments for differences in accounting methods to ensure that the accounting numbers are comparable.

[22] In spite of the incomparability of sales and inventory, in practice many inventory turnover calculations are done using sales. Obviously, not everyone in the financial community has studied this textbook... yet.

> **Caution**
>
> Anyone can compute and compare a bunch of financial ratios. What sets you apart from someone without an accounting background is that you can clean up the accounting numbers, making adjustments for accounting method differences, before you compute the ratios.

Average inventories are sometimes expressed as number of days' sales in inventories. Information is thus provided concerning the average time it takes to turn over the inventory. The number of days' sales in inventory is calculated by dividing average inventory by average daily cost of goods sold. The number of days' sales in inventory also can be obtained by dividing the number of days in the year by the inventory turnover rate. The latter procedure for Deere & Co. is illustrated below, using the originally reported LIFO numbers:

Inventory turnover for the year	5.90 times
Number of days' sales in inventory (365/inventory turnover) or [average inventory/(cost of goods sold/365)]	61.9 days

Number of days' sales in inventory of 61.9 days means that, on average, Deere & Co. has enough inventory to continue operations for 61.9 days using just its existing inventory.

With an increased inventory turnover, the investment necessary for a given volume of business is smaller, and consequently, the return on invested capital is higher. This assumes a company can acquire goods in smaller quantities (with more frequent orders) without paying a higher price. If merchandise must be bought in very large quantities to get favorable prices, then the savings on quantity purchases must be weighed against the savings of carrying lower inventory. Inventory investments and turnover rates vary among industries, and each business must be judged in terms of its financial structure and operations. Management must establish an inventory policy that avoids the extremes of a dangerously low stock, which may impair sales, and an overstocking of goods, which involves a heavy capital investment along with risks of spoilage, obsolescence, and price declines.

Exhibit 9-20 contains a listing of the number of days' sales in inventory of several large companies for 2011. As you can see, the numbers vary widely both across and within industries.

Exhibit 9-20 | Number of Days' Sales in Inventory for Selected Companies, 2011

Company	Number of Days' Sales in Inventory
IBM	16.22
Dell	10.23
General Motors	33.38
Ford Motor Company	19.03
Nike, Inc.	76.45
K Swiss	163.40
Wal-Mart Stores, Inc.	42.01
Target	59.16

© Cengage Learning 2014

Required Disclosures Related to Inventories

The balance sheet typically contains a single amount for a firm's inventory. For a manufacturing firm, the breakdown of inventory into raw materials, work in process, and finished goods is detailed in the financial statement notes. Merchandising firms also sometimes provide note disclosure of the quantities of major classes of inventory. The basis of valuation (such as cost or lower of cost or market), together with the inventory valuation method (LIFO, FIFO, average, or other method), must be disclosed either in a parenthetical note in the balance sheet or in the accompanying notes. A special note is included when a firm changes its valuation method. This note describes the change, the reason for the change, and the quantitative effect of the change on the financial statements.

The amount of write-downs of inventory to lower of cost or market is also disclosed in the notes. As mentioned earlier, the amount of the write-down should be included in cost of goods sold. If significant inventory price declines take place between the balance sheet date and the date the financial statements are issued, no adjustment of the financial statements is needed, but the declines should be disclosed as a subsequent event.

When inventories have been pledged as security on loans from banks, finance companies, or factors, the amounts pledged should be disclosed either parenthetically in the Inventory section of the balance sheet or in the notes.

EXPANDED MATERIAL

Retail Inventory Method

LO12 学习目标12

使用零售盘存法计算先进先出法、后进先出法、平均成本法及成本与市价孰低法下的存货估值。

零售盘存法可以广泛地应用于零售企业，以克服其库存多变的特点。这种方法就像毛利法一样允许存货估值，可以节省实地盘存或维持详细的永续盘存记录所耗费的时间和费用。

12 Compute estimates of FIFO, LIFO, average cost, and lower-of-cost-or-market inventory using the retail inventory method.

The retail inventory method is widely employed by retail firms to arrive at reliable estimates of inventory position whenever desired. This method, like the gross profit method, permits the estimation of an inventory amount without the time and expense of taking a physical inventory or maintaining detailed perpetual inventory records. The retail inventory method is more flexible than the gross profit method in that it allows estimates to be based on FIFO, LIFO, or average cost assumptions, and it even permits estimation of LCM values. The retail inventory method also offers the advantage that when a physical inventory is actually taken for financial statement purposes, the inventory can be taken at retail and then converted to cost without reference to individual costs and invoices, thus saving time and expense.[23]

When the retail inventory method is used, records of goods purchased are maintained at two amounts—cost and retail. Computers have made it feasible to maintain cost records for the thousands of items normally included in a retail inventory. A cost percentage is computed by dividing the goods available for sale at cost by the goods

---

[23] The retail inventory method is acceptable for income tax purposes, provided the taxpayer maintains adequate and satisfactory records supporting inventory calculations and applies the method consistently on successive tax returns.

available for sale at retail. This cost percentage can then be applied to the ending inventory at retail, an amount that can be readily calculated by subtracting sales for the period from the total goods available for sale at retail. This process is illustrated in Exhibit 9-21.

The computation of retail inventory at the end of January is illustrated with the example for Wesley Company. The simple process illustrated in this example is based on an average cost assumption because beginning inventory and purchases are lumped together to compute one cost percentage.

	Cost	Retail
Inventory, January 1	$30,000	$50,000
Purchases in January	30,000	40,000
Goods available for sale	$60,000	$90,000
Cost percentage ($60,000 ÷ $90,000) = 66.7%		
Deduct sales for January		65,000
Inventory, January 31, at retail		$25,000
Inventory, January 31, at estimated cost ($25,000 × 66.7%)	$16,675	

Exhibit 9-21 | Retail Inventory Method

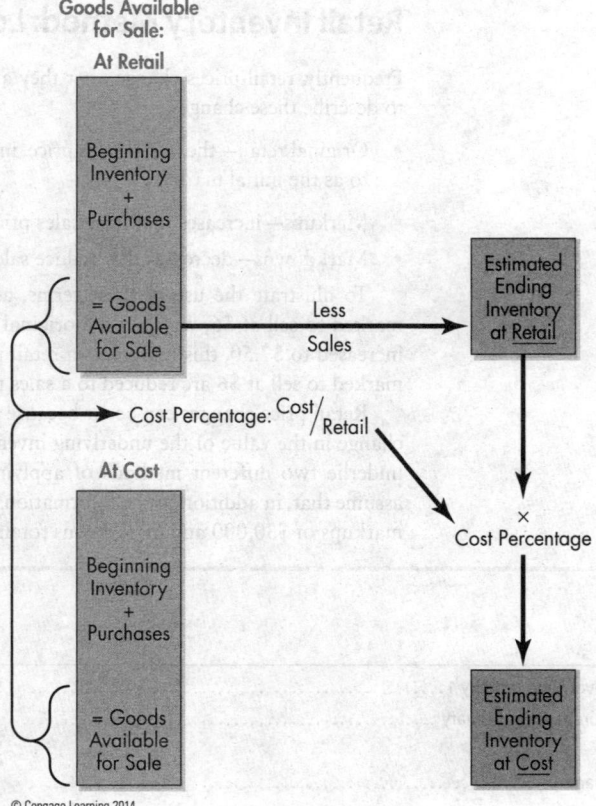

© Cengage Learning 2014

FIFO and LIFO assumptions can be incorporated by computing different cost percentages for beginning inventory and purchases, as shown in the table below.

	Cost	Retail
Inventory, January 1	$30,000	$50,000
Purchases in January	30,000	40,000
Goods available for sale	$60,000	$90,000
Cost percentage:		
Beginning inventory ($30,000 ÷ $50,000) = 60.0%		
Purchases ($30,000 ÷ $40,000) = 75.0%		
Deduct sales for January		65,000
Inventory, January 31, at retail		$25,000
Inventory, January 31, at estimated cost:		
FIFO ($25,000 × 75.0%)	$18,750	
LIFO ($25,000 × 60.0%)	$15,000	

With a FIFO assumption, the retail inventory is converted to cost using the cost percentage applicable to the most recently acquired goods (purchases). With a LIFO assumption, the retail-to-cost conversion for ending inventory is done using the old cost percentage (beginning inventory).

Retail Inventory Method: Lower of Cost or Market

Frequently, retail prices change after they are originally set. The following terms are used to describe these changes.

- **Original retail**—the initial sales price, including the original increase over cost referred to as the *initial markup*.
- **Markups**—increases that raise sales prices above original retail.
- **Markdowns**—decreases that reduce sales prices below original retail.

To illustrate the use of these terms, assume that merchandise costing $4 a unit is marked to sell at $6, which is the original retail price. If the retail price is subsequently increased to $7.50, this represents a retail price markup of $1.50. If the goods originally marked to sell at $6 are reduced to a sales price of $5, this represents a markdown of $1.

Retail price changes can occur because of a change in pricing strategy or because of a change in the value of the underlying inventory. These two causes of retail price changes underlie two different methods of applying the retail inventory method. To illustrate, assume that, in addition to the information given earlier, Wesley Company had retail price markups of $30,000 and markdowns totaling $20,000 during the month of January.

	Average Cost		Lower of Cost or Market	
	Cost	Retail	Cost	Retail
Inventory, January 1	$30,000	$ 50,000	$30,000	$ 50,000
Purchases in January	30,000	40,000	30,000	40,000
	$60,000	$ 90,000	$60,000	$ 90,000
Markups		30,000		30,000
Markdowns		(20,000)		
		$100,000		$120,000

	Average Cost		Lower of Cost or Market	
	Cost	Retail	Cost	Retail
Cost percentage:				
Average cost: ($60,000 ÷ $100,000) = 60.0%				
Lower of cost or market: ($60,000 ÷ $120,000) = 50.0%				
Markdowns		—		(20,000)
Goods available for sale		$100,000		$100,000
Deduct sales for January		65,000		65,000
Inventory, January 31, at retail		$ 35,000		$ 35,000
Inventory, January 31, at estimated cost:				
Average cost: ($35,000 × 60.0%)	$21,000			
Lower of cost or market: ($35,000 × 50.0%)			$17,500	

> **Caution**
> The only difference between the average cost and the lower-of-cost-or-market estimates is in the treatment of markdowns.

Operationally, the simple difference between the two estimates is in when the markdowns are subtracted—before computation of the cost percentage or after. And this simple computational difference reflects the two different assumptions about the cause of markups and markdowns. Subtracting the markdowns before calculation of the cost percentage is equivalent to assuming that the markdowns result from a change in pricing strategy. Under this assumption, all markups and markdowns should be reflected in the computation of the cost percentage. The resulting calculation gives an estimate of the average cost of ending inventory. Subtracting the markdowns after calculation of the cost percentage reflects the assumption that the markdowns are the result of a decline in the value of the inventory. As a result, markdowns do not affect the normal cost percentage but are instead reflected as a direct decline in the recorded value of inventory. This assumption yields an estimate of inventory at lower of cost or market.

The illustrations in this section demonstrate the flexibility of the retail inventory method. The retail inventory method can be used to estimate ending inventory using FIFO, LIFO, average cost, and lower of cost or market.

LIFO Pools, Dollar-Value LIFO, and Dollar-Value LIFO Retail

LO13 Use LIFO pools, dollar-value LIFO, and dollar-value LIFO retail to compute ending inventory.

学习目标13
使用后进先出法、美元币值下的后进先出法和美元币值下的后进先出零售法计算期末存货价值。

With large and diversified inventories, application of LIFO procedures to specific goods can be extremely burdensome. In addition, if LIFO layers are defined in terms of specific products, frequent LIFO liquidations can occur as demand for individual products declines. Two approaches have been developed to simplify the application of LIFO: LIFO pools and dollar-value LIFO. Also, the retail inventory method can be combined with the dollar-value LIFO inventory method to use retail costs to estimate LIFO ending inventory values.

LIFO Pools

As a means of simplifying the valuation process and extending its applicability to more items, the IRS developed the technique of establishing LIFO inventory pools of substantially identical goods. At the end of a period, the quantity of items in the pool is determined, and costs are assigned to those items. Units equal to the beginning quantity in the pool are assigned the beginning unit costs. If the number of units in ending inventory exceeds the number of beginning units, the additional units are regarded as an incremental layer within the pool.

To illustrate the formation of LIFO pools, the following data will be used for Elohar Company, a seller of fine neckties:

Beginning inventory:

	Wide ties	1,000 units @ $10 =	$10,000
	Narrow ties	1,500 units @ $ 8 =	12,000
		2,500 units	$22,000

Purchases:

January 16	Wide	800 units @ $13 =	$10,400
	Narrow	1,000 units @ $11 =	11,000
December 19	Wide	1,500 units @ $15 =	22,500
	Narrow	2,000 units @ $16 =	32,000
		5,300 units	$75,900

Sales:

December 31	Wide	1,700 units
	Narrow	3,200 units

Ending inventory:

	Wide	1,600 units
	Narrow	1,300 units

If the two types of neckties are accounted for separately, computations of LIFO ending inventory and cost of goods sold are as follows:

LIFO ending inventory:

Wide Ties	Narrow Ties
1,000 units @ $10 = $10,000	1,300 units @ $8 = $10,400
600 units @ $13 = 7,800	
1,600 units $17,800	

LIFO cost of goods sold:

	Wide Ties	Narrow Ties
Beginning inventory...	$10,000	$12,000
+ Purchases...	10,400	11,000
	22,500	32,000
= Cost of goods available.....................................	$42,900	$55,000
− Ending inventory	17,800	10,400
= Cost of goods sold	$25,100	$44,600

Total cost of goods sold: $25,100 + $44,600 = $69,700

Rather than account for the wide ties and narrow ties separately, they can be combined into one LIFO pool. This will simplify the accounting (as illustrated on the following page) and also makes conceptual sense because the two types of ties form a natural business group. Similarly, a large appliance wholesaler might form a pool of all major kitchen appliances such as refrigerators, freezers, and ovens.

The data requirements for computing LIFO cost of goods sold with the two types of ties forming one LIFO pool are few. The three items below are all that are needed:

- Total beginning inventory: 2,500 units with a total cost of $22,000
- Number of units in the new LIFO layer: 400 units (2,900 ending − 2,500 beginning)
- Average cost per unit of ties purchased during the year: $14.32 ($75,900/5,300 units)

LIFO ending inventory using a LIFO pool is computed as follows:

Beginning inventory..	2,500 units	= $22,000
New LIFO layer	400 units @ $14.32 =	5,728
		$27,728

LIFO cost of goods sold is then:

	LIFO Pool
Beginning inventory...	$22,000
+ Purchases	75,900
= Cost of goods available	$97,900
− Ending inventory	27,728
= Cost of goods sold...	$70,172

Remember that the purpose of forming LIFO pools is to simplify the LIFO calculations associated with large numbers of products. The simplification results in an estimate of what cost of goods sold would be if LIFO were applied strictly and laboriously. In this example, the LIFO pool cost of goods sold estimate ($70,172) differs from the total of the individual LIFO calculations ($69,700) because of the simplifying assumption of using the average cost of purchases to value the new LIFO layer.[24]

LIFO pooling was originally developed as part of the IRS regulations but was quickly adopted as acceptable for financial reporting as well. Although it is not necessary for companies to use the same pools for tax and financial reporting purposes, most companies do, even when the IRS regulations require more pools than might be necessary for accounting purposes.[25]

Because companies can choose to have many LIFO pools or, in the extreme, just one pool, what factors determine the choice of the optimal number of pools? Focusing on the income tax effect, the conventional wisdom is that the fewer pools, the better, with one pool being the best of all. This is because lumping all inventories together into one LIFO pool allows decreases in the inventory of one product to be offset by increases in another product, making it less likely that a LIFO liquidation will result in a sudden increase in income taxes. This conventional wisdom emphasizes avoidance of LIFO liquidations but ignores the primary purpose of LIFO, which is the deferral of income taxes in normal times. Choosing the number of pools that gives maximum tax deferral in normal times (i.e., in times of steady or rising inventory levels) requires careful analysis and depends partly on whether different categories of inventory have different rates of price change.[26]

---

[24] The unit cost assigned to the items in the new layer may be based on any one of the following measurements:
• The weighted-average cost of acquisitions within the period
• Actual costs of earliest acquisitions within the period (LIFO)
• Actual costs of the latest acquisitions within the period (FIFO)

[25] James M. Reeve and Keith G. Stanga, "The LIFO Pooling Decision: Some Empirical Results from Accounting Practice," *Accounting Horizons*, June 1987, p. 27.

[26] William R. Cron and Randall B. Hayes, "The Dollar-Value LIFO Pooling Decision: The Conventional Wisdom Is Too General," *Accounting Horizons*, December 1989, p. 57.

Dollar-Value LIFO

Even the grouping of substantially identical items into quantity pools does not produce all the benefits desired from the use of LIFO. For example, technological advances and marketing developments are constantly causing specific products to be phased out and replaced by something new that fills the market niche of the old product. The music store business has seen its inventory change from vinyl albums to eight-track tapes to cassettes to CDs to digital files in the past 50 years. The accounting question is whether old LIFO layers should be liquidated whenever a new product replaces an old one. To address this question, and also to further simplify the recordkeeping associated with LIFO, the dollar-value LIFO inventory method was developed. Under this method, LIFO layers are determined based on total dollar changes rather than quantity changes. The dollar-value method has become the most widely used adaptation of the LIFO concept. In a survey of LIFO users, Professors Reeve and Stanga found that 95% of the 206 companies responding to their survey used some version of the dollar-value method.[27]

With dollar-value LIFO, the unit of measurement is the dollar. All goods in the inventory pool to which dollar-value LIFO is to be applied are viewed as though they are identical items. To determine if the dollar quantity of inventory has increased during the year, it is necessary to value the ending inventory in a pool at base-year prices (i.e., those in effect when LIFO was first adopted by the company) and compare the total with that at the beginning of the year, also valued at base-year prices. If the end-of-year inventory at base-year prices exceeds the beginning-of-year inventory at base-year prices, a new LIFO layer is created. If there has been a decrease, the most recent LIFO layer (or layers) is reduced.

Dollar-value LIFO calculations are illustrated using the same Elohar Company example from the previous section.

First, the replacement cost of ending inventory is computed using prices prevailing at the end of the period. In this example, the end-of-period prices come from the December 19 purchase. For Elohar Company, the replacement cost of ending inventory is:

Ending inventory at ending prices:

Wide ties	1,600 units @ $15 = $24,000
Narrow ties	1,300 units @ $16 = 20,800
	$44,800

Since beginning inventory was only $22,000, it appears that there was an increase in inventory during the period, suggesting that a new LIFO layer should be added. However, the increase in inventory may be a result of price increases rather than an actual increase in the quantity of inventory. To make this determination, computation is made of what the value of beginning inventory would be at ending prices:

Beginning inventory at ending prices:

Wide ties	1,000 units @ $15 = $15,000
Narrow ties	1,500 units @ $16 = 24,000
	$39,000

After adjusting for price increases during the year, we can see that the dollar value of inventory increased by $5,800:

Ending inventory at ending prices	$44,800
− Beginning inventory at ending prices	39,000
Dollar value of new LIFO layer, at ending prices	$ 5,800

---

[27] James M. Reeve and Keith G. Stanga, "The LIFO Pooling Decision: Some Empirical Results from Accounting Practice," *Accounting Horizons*, June 1987, p. 2.

Finally, dollar-value LIFO ending inventory is computed as follows:

Beginning inventory, at base-year prices	$22,000
New LIFO layer, at ending prices	5,800
LIFO ending inventory	$27,800

This LIFO ending inventory is then used in the computation of LIFO cost of goods sold. To summarize, the dollar-value LIFO computations are:

1. Compute ending inventory at ending prices.
2. Compute beginning inventory at ending prices.
3. Compute the difference. An increase represents a new LIFO layer.
4. LIFO ending inventory is beginning inventory at base-year prices plus the new LIFO layer.

In the example, the new LIFO layer was valued at ending prices. This is acceptable but is somewhat inconsistent with the LIFO assumption. In fact, this approach essentially results in the new layer being valued using a FIFO assumption. Alternatively, the new LIFO layer can be valued using average prices for the period, or by using the prices of the first purchases of the period. The only computational difference is that "ending prices" are replaced by "first purchase prices" or "average prices" in steps 1 and 2 above. The computations using first purchase prices to value the new LIFO layer are given below. The first purchase made during the period was on January 16.

Ending inventory at first purchase prices:

Wide ties	1,600 units @ $13 =	$20,800
Narrow ties	1,300 units @ $11 =	14,300
		$35,100

Beginning inventory at first purchase prices:

Wide ties	1,000 units @ $13 =	$13,000
Narrow ties	1,500 units @ $11 =	16,500
		$29,500

Ending inventory at first purchase prices	$35,100
− Beginning inventory at first purchase prices	29,500
Dollar value of new LIFO layer, at first purchase prices	$ 5,600
Beginning inventory, at base-year prices	$22,000
New LIFO layer, at first purchase prices	5,600
LIFO ending inventory	$27,600

Use of an Index

美元币值下的后进先出法只需每种存货的基年价格和期末价格的记录，这种方法也称双重乘数法。

The dollar-value LIFO illustration just completed required a record of base-year prices and end-of-year prices for each individual inventory item. This technique is called the double extension method. Imagine how messy the computations would be with several thousand products. Recall that the purpose of LIFO pools and dollar-value LIFO is to reduce the bookkeeping costs associated with LIFO. Dollar-value LIFO is greatly simplified if a price index is used in place of the double extension method.

A price index is simply an overall measure of how much prices have increased during the year. A common example is the Consumer Price Index (CPI). The CPI measures how much consumer prices increase in the United States during a given period. If the CPI goes up from 100 to 103 during a year, we say that prices for the year increased by 3%, or in other words, inflation for the year was 3%.

A price index in the Elohar Company example can be computed by comparing beginning inventory at beginning prices to beginning inventory at ending prices:

Beginning inventory at ending prices:
Wide ties	1,000 units @ $15 = $15,000
Narrow ties	1,500 units @ $16 = 24,000
	$39,000

Beginning inventory at beginning prices:
Wide ties	1,000 units @ $10 = $10,000
Narrow ties	1,500 units @ $8 = 12,000
	$22,000

End-of-year price index: $39,000/$22,000 = 1.77, or 177

With the beginning-of-year index being 100, an end-of-year-index of 177 means that prices increased an average of 77% during the year. This index would be used in the following work sheet to compute ending inventory for Elohar Company using dollar-value LIFO:

Inventory at End-of-Year Prices		Year-End Price Index		Inventory at Base-Year Prices	Layers in Base-Year Prices		Incremental Layer Index		Dollar-Value LIFO Cost
$44,800	÷	1.77	=	$25,311	$22,000	×	1.00	=	$22,000
					3,311	×	1.77	=	5,860
					$25,311				$27,860

This ending inventory of $27,860 differs from the $27,800 computed earlier (with the new layer valued at ending prices) only because the index is rounded at 1.77 (instead of carrying it out to 1.7727272727 . . .).

Note that the index calculations in the work sheet result in the new layer being valued at ending prices. In order to value the new layer at first purchase prices, an additional index must be computed:

Beginning inventory at first purchase prices:
Wide ties	1,000 units @ $13 = $13,000
Narrow ties	1,500 units @ $11 = 16,500
	$29,500

First purchase price index: $29,500/$22,000 = 1.34

The first purchase price index would be used to value the new LIFO layer as follows:

Inventory at End-of-Year Prices		Year-End Price Index		Inventory at Base-Year Prices	Layers in Base-Year Prices		Incremental Layer Index		Dollar-Value LIFO Cost
$44,800	÷	1.77	=	$25,311	$22,000	×	1.00	=	$22,000
					3,311	×	1.34	=	4,437
					$25,311				$26,437

To recap, the new LIFO layer can be valued using a year-end price index, a first purchase price index, or an average price index.

Dollar-Value LIFO: Multiyear Example

One more illustration of dollar-value LIFO is given on the following pages. This example illustrates how dollar-value LIFO works when LIFO layers are liquidated.

Assume the index numbers and inventories at end-of-year prices for Hsu Wholesale Co. are as follows:

Date	Year-End Price Index*	Inventory at End-of-Year Prices
December 31, 2011	1.00	$38,000
December 31, 2012	1.20	54,000
December 31, 2013	1.32	66,000
December 31, 2014	1.40	56,000
December 31, 2015	1.25	55,000

* Many published indexes appear as percentages without decimals, e.g., 100, 120, 132, 140, 125.

The work sheet in Exhibit 9-22 shows the calculation of LIFO ending inventory for Hsu for each year. The following items should be observed in the example:

- *December 31, 2012*—With an ending inventory of $45,000 in terms of base prices, the inventory has increased in 2012 by $7,000; however, the $7,000 increase is stated in terms of base-year prices and needs to be restated in terms of 2012 year-end prices, which are 120% of the base level.
- *December 31, 2013*—With an ending inventory of $50,000 in terms of base prices, the inventory has increased in 2013 by another $5,000; however, the $5,000 increase is stated in terms of base-year prices and needs to be restated in terms of 2013 year-end costs, which are 132% of the base level.

Exhibit 9-22 | Dollar-Value LIFO: Multiyear Example

Date	Inventory at End-of-Year Prices		Year-End Price Index		Inventory at Base-Year Prices	Layers in Base-Year Prices		Incremental Layer Index		Dollar-Value LIFO Cost
December 31, 2011	$38,000	÷	1.00	=	$38,000	$38,000	×	1.00	=	$38,000
December 31, 2012	$54,000	÷	1.20	=	$45,000	$38,000	×	1.00	=	$38,000
						7,000	×	1.20	=	8,400
						$45,000				$46,400
December 31, 2013	$66,000	÷	1.32	=	$50,000	$38,000	×	1.00	=	$38,000
						7,000	×	1.20	=	8,400
						5,000	×	1.32	=	6,600
						$50,000				$53,000
December 31, 2014	$56,000	÷	1.40	=	$40,000	$38,000	×	1.00	=	$38,000
						2,000	×	1.20	=	2,400
						$40,000				$40,400
December 31, 2015	$55,000	÷	1.25	=	$44,000	$38,000	×	1.00	=	$38,000
						2,000	×	1.20	=	2,400
						4,000	×	1.25	=	5,000
						$44,000				$45,400

- *December 31, 2014*—When the ending inventory of $40,000 (expressed in base-year dollars) is compared to the beginning inventory of $50,000 (also expressed in base-year dollars), it is apparent that the inventory has been decreased by $10,000 in base-year terms. Under LIFO procedures, the decrease is assumed to take place in the most recently added layers, reducing or eliminating them. As a result, the 2013 layer, priced at $5,000 in base-year terms, is completely eliminated, and $5,000 of the $7,000 layer from 2012 is eliminated. This leaves only $2,000 of the 2012 layer, plus the base-year amount. The remaining $2,000 of the 2012 layer is multiplied by 1.20 to restate it to 2012 dollars and is added to the base-year amount to arrive at the ending inventory amount of $40,400.
- *December 31, 2015*—The ending inventory of $44,000 in terms of the base prices indicates an inventory increase for 2015 of $4,000. This increase requires restatement in terms of 2015 year-end prices, which are 125% of the base level.

In some cases, the index for the first year of the LIFO layers is not 1.00. This is especially true when an externally generated index is used. When this occurs, it is simpler to convert all inventories to a base of 1.00 rather than to use the index for the initial year of the LIFO layers. The computations are done in the same manner as in the previous example except the inventory is stated in terms of the base year of the index, not the first year of the inventory layers. To illustrate, assume the same facts as stated earlier except that the base year of the external index is 2007; in 2011, the index is 1.20; and in 2012, it is 1.44. The schedule showing the LIFO inventory computations would be modified as follows for the first two years. Note that the inventory cost is the same under either situation.

Date	Inventory at End-of-Year Prices		Year-End Price Index		Inventory at Base = 1.00 (2007 Prices)	Layers in Base = 1.00 (2007 Prices)		Incremental Layer Index		Dollar-Value LIFO Cost
December 31, 2011	$38,000	÷	1.20	=	$31,667	$31,667	×	1.20	=	$38,000
December 31, 2012	$54,000	÷	1.44	=	$37,500	$31,667	×	1.20	=	$38,000
						5,833	×	1.44	=	8,400
						$37,500				$46,400

Dollar-Value LIFO Retail Method

The dollar-value LIFO procedures described in the preceding section can be combined with the retail inventory method described earlier in developing LIFO inventory values. With the dollar-value LIFO retail method, LIFO layers are stated in terms of retail values. After the LIFO retail layers have been identified and priced using a price index, a further adjustment is needed to state the inventory at cost. This is done by multiplying the retail inventory of each layer by the appropriate cost percentage.

One thing to keep in mind when computing cost percentages for the dollar-value LIFO retail method is that beginning inventory values are ignored. When LIFO is used, a new inventory layer is converted from retail to cost using the cost percentage applicable to current year purchases.

The following LIFO retail layer data for Miracle Max Department Store as of December 31, 2014, are used to illustrate the computations associated with the dollar-value LIFO retail method.

Layer Year	Year-End Price Index	Incremental Cost Percentage	Inventory at End-of-Year Retail Prices
2011	1.00	0.60	$60,000
2012	1.05	0.62	69,300
2013	1.10	0.64	77,000
2014	1.12	0.65	71,120

Assume that the 2015 year-end price index is 1.08. The incremental cost percentage and 2015 ending inventory at end-of-year retail prices are computed as follows.

	Cost	Retail
Beginning inventory, December 31, 2014	—	$ 71,120
Purchases	$59,780	$ 98,000
Incremental cost percentage: ($59,780 ÷ $98,000) = 61%		
Goods available for sale		$169,120
Deduct: Sales		90,820
Ending inventory at retail (year-end prices)		$ 78,300

From these data, a work sheet similar to that illustrated earlier for dollar-value LIFO can be constructed to determine the LIFO retail inventory layers. One additional column is necessary to record the incremental cost percentage that will convert the retail inventory to cost. It is important to note that the incremental cost percentage is used only if an incremental layer is added to the inventory in the current period. In the example, no layer was added in 2014, so the cost percentage applicable to purchases made in 2014 is not used. As seen with the dollar-value LIFO method, when an inventory layer is eliminated, it is not reintroduced in subsequent

Date	End-of-Year Retail Prices		Year-End Price Index		Base-Year Retail Prices	Layers		Incremental Layer Index		Incremental Cost Percentage		Dollar-Value LIFO Retail Cost
December 31, 2011	$60,000	÷	1.00	=	$60,000	$60,000	×	1.00	×	0.60	=	$36,000
December 31, 2012	$69,300	÷	1.05	=	$66,000	$60,000	×	1.00	×	0.60	=	$36,000
						6,000	×	1.05	×	0.62	=	3,906
						$66,000						$39,906
December 31, 2013	$77,000	÷	1.10	=	$70,000	$60,000	×	1.00	×	0.60	=	$36,000
						6,000	×	1.05	×	0.62	=	3,906
						4,000	×	1.10	×	0.64	=	2,816
						$70,000						$42,722
December 31, 2014	$71,120	÷	1.12	=	$63,500	$60,000	×	1.00	×	0.60	=	$36,000
						3,500	×	1.05	×	0.62	=	2,279*
						$63,500						$38,279
December 31, 2015	$78,300	÷	1.08	=	$72,500	$60,000	×	1.00	×	0.60	=	$36,000
						3,500	×	1.05	×	0.62	=	2,279*
						9,000	×	1.08	×	0.61	=	5,929*
						$72,500						$44,208

*Rounded to nearest dollar

years when layers are added. This is illustrated in the example when, in 2014, the $4,000 layer formed in 2013 is eliminated. In 2015, the 2013 $4,000 layer is not resurrected. Instead, the new layer consists of 2015 percentages.

Purchase Commitments

LO14 Account for the impact of changing prices on purchase commitments.

Extreme fluctuations in the price of inventory purchases can expose a company to excessive risk. Of the different ways to manage this risk, the simplest is a purchase commitment that locks in the inventory purchase price in advance. For example, rather than being exposed to the ups and downs of oil prices, an airline can contract in advance to purchase its next month's fuel at a set price.

The first accounting issue raised by purchase commitments is whether the company committing to the future purchase should record an asset (for the inventory to be received) and a liability (for the payment obligation) at the commitment date. This type of contract is an exchange of promises about future actions and is known as an *executory contract*. Another example of an executory contract is an employment agreement in which a firm and an employee agree to employment terms for a future period. Accounting rules require some executory contracts to be recognized in the financial statements.[28]

With purchase commitments, no journal entry is required to record the commitment prior to delivery of the goods. However, in an adaptation of the LCM rule, when price declines take place subsequent to such a commitment and the commitment is outstanding at the end of an accounting period, the loss is recorded just as losses on goods on hand are recognized.[29] A decline is recorded by a debit to a special loss account and a credit to either a contra asset account or an accrued liability account, such as Estimated Loss on Purchase Commitments. Acquisition of the goods in a subsequent period is recorded by a credit to Accounts Payable, a debit canceling the credit balance in the contra asset or accrued liability account, and a debit to Purchases for the difference.

> **FYI**
>
> As you will see in Chapter 19, a purchase commitment is very similar to one type of derivative called a *forward contract*.

To manage their risk, airlines often contract in advance to purchase fuel at a set price.

---

[28] A lease is a good example of an executory contract. A lease is an exchange of promises about the future—the lessor promises to provide the use of an asset (like a building) and the lessee promises to pay for the use of the asset. As discussed in Chapter 15, some leases are recognized in the financial statements (capital leases) and some are not (operating leases).

[29] FASB ASC paragraph 330-10-35-17.

To illustrate the accounting for purchase commitments, we'll use the following example. Rollins Oat Company entered into a purchase commitment on November 1, 2014, for 100,000 bushels of wheat at $3.40 per bushel to be delivered in March 2015. At the end of 2014, the market price for wheat had dropped to $3.20 per bushel. The entries to record this decline in value and the subsequent delivery of the wheat would be as follows:

2014				
Dec.	31	Loss on Purchase Commitments	20,000	
		Estimated Loss on Purchase Commitments		20,000
		(100,000 bushels × $0.20 per bushel)		
2015				
Mar.	31	Estimated Loss on Purchase Commitments	20,000	
		Purchases...	320,000	
		Accounts Payable		340,000

The loss is thus assigned to the period in which the inventory price decline took place. Current loss recognition would not be appropriate when commitments can be canceled, when commitments provide for price adjustment, or when declines do not suggest reductions in sale prices. If, prior to delivery, the market price increases, the estimated loss on purchase commitments account would be reduced and a gain would be recorded. The amount of gain to be recognized is limited to the amount of loss previously recorded.

Foreign Currency Inventory Transactions

15 Record inventory purchase transactions denominated in foreign currencies.

The discussion of inventories thus far has centered around the purchase and valuation of inventories in a domestic environment, that is, within the United States. As noted in Chapter 1, business has become increasingly global. Exports and imports of materials and finished goods are a significant part of many companies' purchases and sales. Depending on how a purchase transaction is structured, additional gains or losses may occur in foreign inventory transactions because of fluctuations in the currency exchange rates between two countries.

Not all international transactions involve foreign currency risk. Only transactions denominated in currencies other than the U.S. dollar are foreign currency transactions for U.S. companies. For example, if a U.S. company buys inventory from a German firm, the transaction is a normal purchase (for the U.S. company) if the inventory price is set in U.S. dollars. But if the price is set in euros, the U.S. company is exposed to foreign currency exchange risk during the period the account payable is outstanding.

To illustrate the complexities associated with foreign currency transactions, assume that on November 1, 2014, Washington Company purchased inventory from Swiss Company and that the invoice was denominated in Swiss francs with a purchase price of 50,000 francs. At the time of the purchase, the exchange rate was 5 francs per U.S. dollar. This rate is called

LO15 学习目标15
记录以外币计量的存货购买交易。

foreign currency transactions
外币交易

Caution
If the transaction contract is written in terms of U.S. dollars, there is no foreign currency risk whether the other company is based in Azerbaijan or Zimbabwe.

spot rate
即期汇率

the spot rate, the rate at which the two currencies can be exchanged right now. Washington Company would make the following journal entry to record the purchase:

2014
Nov. 1   Inventory 10,000
            Accounts Payable (fc) 10,000
            (50,000 francs/5 = $10,000)

The (fc) designation is used for convenience to indicate those items that are denominated in a foreign currency. It is important to recognize, however, that the amounts in Washington's journal entry represent U.S. dollars.

The impact of a foreign currency inventory purchase is recognized when the liability is paid. If the terms call for payment of the liability on February 1, 2015, Washington Company will have to credit cash on that date, but for how much? Recall that the invoice requires payment in francs, not in dollars. Washington Company will have to purchase 50,000 francs from a foreign currency broker. How much will the company be required to pay the broker? The answer depends on the spot rate on that date. If the spot rate is 4.7 francs per U.S. dollar on February 1, 2015, then Washington Company will have to pay $10,638 (50,000/4.7) to purchase 50,000 francs. The journal entry to record the payment to Swiss Company is as follows:

2015
Feb. 1   Accounts Payable (fc)... 10,000
            Exchange Loss... 638
            Cash.. 10,638

Washington Company incurs a loss in this situation because it had a liability denominated in a currency (francs) that increased in value—the number of francs required to purchase one U.S. dollar declined. On November 1, 2014, Washington Company would have had to pay only $10,000 to purchase 50,000 francs. However, to purchase the same number of francs on February 1, 2015, requires $10,638. The exchange loss would be included as an expense in the income statement in the period incurred.

This situation could just as easily have resulted in an exchange gain for Washington Company. If the franc had weakened relative to the dollar, then fewer dollars would have been required to purchase 50,000 francs. Suppose the exchange rate for Swiss francs had been 5.1 per U.S. dollar on February 1, 2015. Washington Company would have recorded the following journal entry and recognized an exchange gain:

2015
Feb. 1   Accounts Payable (fc)... 10,000
            Exchange Gain 196
            Cash (50,000 francs/5.1).. 9,804

If a balance sheet date occurs while a foreign currency asset or liability is outstanding, the asset or liability is valued at the spot rate on the balance sheet date.[30] Continuing the initial example, suppose that Washington Company's fiscal year ends on December 31 and the exchange rate on December 31, 2014, is 4.8 francs per U.S. dollar. On that date, Washington Company would make the following adjusting entry to record the change in the amount of cash required to pay the liability:

2014
Dec. 31 Exchange Loss... 417
            Accounts Payable (fc) 417
            [(50,000 francs/4.8) − $10,000 = $417]

[30] FASB ASC paragraph 830-20-35-2.

This journal entry adjusts the liability to its value of $10,417, given the balance sheet date spot rate, and allocates the exchange rate loss to the period in which the change in exchange rates occurred. When the liability is subsequently paid on February 1, 2015, and the spot rate is 4.7 francs per dollar, the journal entry would be as follows:

2015
Feb. 1 Accounts Payable (fc)... 10,417
        Exchange Loss.. 221
            Cash (50,000 francs/4.7)....................................... 10,638

Note that the exchange losses of $417 and $221 recorded on December 31 and February 1, respectively, total $638, which is the same amount that is obtained if no adjusting entry is made. The adjusting entry simply allocates the exchange loss to the appropriate accounting periods.

An obvious question at this point is, why didn't Washington Company avoid the exchange loss and pay the liability early? If Washington knew that the franc was going to become more expensive, it probably would have. However, predicting the direction and amount of change in the exchange rate for a particular currency is as difficult as predicting whether the price of a specific stock on the New York Stock Exchange is going to rise or fall, and by how much.

Foreign currency exchange risk is another form of price risk. And, just like domestic price risk, foreign currency exchange risk can be hedged. *Hedging* involves contracting with a foreign currency broker to deliver or receive a specified foreign currency at a specified future date and at a specified exchange rate. A fully hedged transaction results in no exchange gain or loss to the company. The cost of hedging is the fee charged by the broker. For that fee, the broker assumes all of the risks associated with exchange rate changes. Accounting for foreign currency hedging is discussed in Chapter 19. For coverage of how multinational companies combine the financial statements of subsidiaries located in different countries, see Chapter 22.

 SOLUTIONS TO OPENING SCENARIO QUESTIONS

1. High inflation causes a big difference between the ending inventory and cost of goods sold numbers produced by LIFO and FIFO. Drastic deflation would do the same, in the opposite direction.
2. The high inflation of 1974 made it so that LIFO cost of goods sold was much greater than FIFO cost of goods sold. By adopting LIFO, companies could report higher cost of goods sold, leading to lower payment of income taxes.
3. An unsophisticated investor focuses on reported earnings without paying attention to the accounting methods and assumptions used in computing those reported earnings.

Stop & Think SOLUTIONS

1. (Page 9-9) The correct answer is C. Choosing between two acceptable accounting procedures is an exercise in cost-benefit analysis. Perpetual inventory systems provide better information, but they also usually cost more to operate. For some businesses, the costs exceed the benefits, so those businesses use a periodic system. Businesses most likely to use a periodic system are those with lots of low-value identical items with a high turnover. In addition, very small businesses, because they don't make much profit, are less likely to be able to afford a computerized inventory system.

2. (Page 9-23) The correct answer is C, computed as follows:

	2012	2013	2014
FIFO cost of goods sold:	100 × $5 = $500	20 × $ 5 = $ 100 100 × $10 = 1,000 $1,100	50 × $10 = $ 500 70 × $15 = 1,050 $1,550
Ending inventory:	20 × $5 = $100	50 × $10 = $ 500	90 × $15 = $1,350

3. (Page 9-29) The correct answer is D. Use of LIFO for the income statement and FIFO for the balance sheet would result in a cost allocation discrepancy. In essence, the FIFO inventory valuation on the balance sheet includes inventory-holding gains, but the LIFO gross profit on the income statement excludes those holding gains. Unless this discrepancy is handled appropriately, the balance sheet will not balance. A possible way to handle this discrepancy is to create a special equity item, perhaps a new type of accumulated other comprehensive income. This equity item would normally have a credit balance (unrecognized inventory holding gain), reflecting the fact that FIFO ending inventory is typically greater than LIFO ending inventory.

4. (Page 9-39) The correct answer is B. An understatement of the amount of purchases would cause the actual amount of inventory to be greater than the estimated amount. If the actual amount of inventory is much lower than the estimated amount, there are three possible explanations: (1) the estimation process is flawed; (2) inventory was lost or stolen; or (3) the missing inventory was sold but the sales were not reported. A clever fraud artist can cover his or her tracks by making sure that the reported gross profit percentage is close to industry norms and by avoiding any large swings in the level of unreported sales from one year to the next. Like anything else, successful fraud requires consistent, patient effort over the course of many years.

5. (Page 9-40) The correct answer is A. All managers are confident that any current difficulties are only temporary. They think that if they can just get past their immediate problems, business will turn around in the future. Thus, managers don't worry about the counterbalancing impact of inventory errors because they know (or think they know) that business will be better next year. In addition, when a manager is facing termination for missing this year's profit target, concerns about the counterbalancing effort of any inventory error next year are of no significance.

SOLUTION TO USING THE FASB'S CODIFICATION

In FASB ASC Subtopic 905-330 (Agriculture—Inventory), you can see Section 35 (Subsequent Measurement). Inventories of harvested crops are to be accounted for in the same way as animals held for sale. There are two acceptable treatments. First, the harvested crops (or animals) can be accounted for at lower of cost or market, just like any other inventory item. Second, the harvested crop inventory can be recorded at "sales price less estimated costs of disposal." This is a description of net realizable value.

Note that not all crops are eligible for this net realizable value reporting. The criteria listed in FASB ASC paragraph 905-330-35-3 indicate that this treatment is appropriate only for crops that are ready to ship to reliable markets.

Review Chapter 9 Learning Objectives

1 Define inventory for a merchandising business, and identify the different types of inventory for a manufacturing business.

For a merchandising firm, inventory is the label given to assets sold in the normal course of business. The types of items included in the inventory of a merchandising company are determined by the nature of the business, not the nature of the items. For example, a truck is a fixed asset for an overnight mail delivery company but is inventory for a truck dealership. For a manufacturing firm, there are three types of inventory.

- *Raw materials* are goods obtained for use in the manufacturing process. Direct materials are incorporated directly into the manufactured product (e.g., steel in

an automobile, wood in furniture) and indirect materials are used to facilitate production (e.g., lubricant for factory equipment, factory cleaning supplies).
- *Work in process* consists of materials only partly processed that require further work before they can be sold. The three categories of costs that go into work in process are direct materials, direct labor, and manufacturing overhead.
- *Finished goods* are the manufactured products awaiting sale. Upon sale, the cost of finished goods becomes cost of goods sold. A rough rule of thumb is that costs incurred inside the factory are assigned to the cost of inventory, and costs incurred outside the factory are classified as selling, general, or administrative expenses.

② Explain the advantages and disadvantages of both periodic and perpetual inventory systems.

The following chart summarizes the differences between periodic and perpetual inventory systems:

Periodic	Perpetual
Inventory	
Known only after an end-of-period physical count.	Known on a day-to-day basis.
Cost of Goods Sold	
Known only after an end-of-period physical count.	Known on a day-to-day basis.
Inventory Shrinkage	
Can't be calculated.	Can be calculated by comparing inventory records with physical count.
Journal Entries	
No entry made to record cost of goods sold until the end of the period.	Cost of goods sold entry made in association with each sale.
Inventory purchases debited to a temporary purchases account.	Inventory purchases debited directly to the inventory account.
Quality of Information vs. Cost to Operate	
Lower quality of information but less costly to operate.	Higher quality of information but more costly to operate.

③ Determine when ownership of goods in transit changes hands and what circumstances require shipped inventory to be kept on the books.

With a few exceptions, goods should be included in the reported inventory of the business that owns them, regardless of the physical location of the inventory.
- *Goods in transit.* Goods shipped FOB shipping point belong to the buyer while in transit. Goods shipped FOB destination belong to the seller while in transit.
- *Goods on consignment.* Goods on consignment should be included in the consignor's inventory. The consignee does not include the goods in inventory even though the consignee has physical possession of the goods.
- *Installment sales and conditional sales.* Even though the seller may retain legal title to the inventory until the end of the installment period, the seller should remove the goods from inventory at the time of sale if successful completion of the contract is anticipated.
- *Repurchase agreements.* When the seller promises to buy back goods at a specified price at a future date, the goods should not be removed from the seller's reported inventory. In addition, a liability is recorded for the "sales" proceeds.

④ Compute total inventory acquisition cost.

For purchased goods, the recorded inventory amount includes all costs related to purchase, receipt, and preparation of the goods. For manufactured inventory, cost includes direct materials, direct labor, and manufacturing overhead.

The cost of purchased inventory is summarized as follows:

Invoice cost plus freight, storage, and preparation cost
− Cash discounts
− Purchase returns and allowances
= Inventory cost

The two ways to account for cash discounts are the net method and the gross method. With the net method, the cost of missed discounts is reported as a separate financing expense. With the gross method, missed cash discounts are included as part of the cost of inventory.

The most difficult part of computing the cost of manufactured inventory is allocating manufacturing overhead. Traditionally, overhead allocation has been proportioned on the amount of direct labor associated with a product. An activity-based cost (ABC) system allocates overhead based on clearly identified cost drivers—characteristics of the production process known to create overhead costs.

⑤ Use the four basic inventory valuation methods: specific identification, average cost, FIFO, and LIFO.

Inventory valuation methods allocate total inventory cost between inventory remaining and inventory sold. The four most common methods are specific identification, average cost, first-in, first-out (FIFO), and last-in, first-out (LIFO).
- *Specific identification.* The actual physical units sold are specifically identified and their aggregate cost is reported as cost of goods sold.
- *Average cost.* The same average cost is assigned to each unit. Cost of goods sold is computed by multiplying units sold by the average cost per unit.

- *FIFO.* The units sold are assumed to be the oldest units on hand.
- *LIFO.* The units sold are assumed to be the newest units on hand.

With a perpetual inventory system, computation of average cost and LIFO is more complicated because the average cost of goods available and the identification of the newest units change with each purchase and sale. In practice, perpetual records are usually maintained on a FIFO basis and then converted to average cost or LIFO for the financial reports.

6 Explain how LIFO inventory layers are created, and describe the significance of the LIFO reserve.

A LIFO inventory layer is created in each year in which purchases exceed sales. The difference between LIFO inventory value and FIFO or average cost is called the *LIFO reserve.*

The LIFO assumption means that all sales are made from current purchases as long as purchases are greater than or equal to sales. Thus, inventory acquired in previous years remains on the books in LIFO layers.

When inventory levels decline, inventory in LIFO layers is sold, starting with the most recently created layer. In times of rising prices, these old LIFO layer costs are lower than current replacement cost. Consequently, LIFO liquidation often results in lower cost of goods sold and higher net income.

Companies using LIFO are allowed to disclose the difference between the inventory cost in old LIFO layers and the current replacement cost (approximated by FIFO or average cost inventory). These LIFO reserve disclosures can be used to compute what cost of goods sold and ending inventory would have been if the company had used FIFO (or average cost) instead of LIFO.

The primary motivation for a company to adopt LIFO is to defer payment of income taxes on inventory holding gains.

7 Choose an inventory valuation method based on the trade-offs among income tax effects, bookkeeping costs, and the impact on the financial statements.

FIFO
- *Advantages:* corresponds with physical flow of goods; ending inventory balance is close to current replacement cost
- *Disadvantages:* matches older costs with current revenues; inventory holding gains and losses are part of gross profit; no income tax deferral

LIFO
- *Advantages:* matches current costs with current revenues; excludes inventory holding gains from gross profit; income tax deferral
- *Disadvantages:* does not correspond with the physical flow of goods; potential LIFO liquidation can draw old costs into cost of goods sold; ending inventory balance can be much lower than current replacement cost

The cash flow benefits of LIFO income tax deferral must be weighed against increased bookkeeping costs and poorer reported financial statement performance. For firms with small inventory levels or low inventory cost increases, the tax deferral benefits of LIFO are probably insignificant. Currently, the LIFO method is not acceptable under IASB standards.

8 Apply the lower-of-cost-or-market (LCM) rule to reflect declines in the market value of inventory.

The lower-of-cost-or-market (LCM) rule results in recognition of decreases in the market value of inventory. Applying the LCM rule requires careful specification of the "market" value. To use the LCM rule, the cost of the ending inventory is compared with its market value. If market is less than cost, ending inventory is written down to the market value.

The market value of inventory is equal to its replacement cost, subject to floor and ceiling constraints. The ceiling constraint is that the market value of inventory is not greater than net realizable value. The floor constraint is that the market value of the inventory is not less than net realizable value minus a normal profit margin. In summary, market value of inventory is never less than the floor value, is never more than the ceiling value, and is equal to replacement cost when replacement cost is between the floor and the ceiling.

The comparable inventory write-down rule under *IAS 2* can be labeled "lower of cost or net realizable value." Under *IAS 2,* inventory write-downs can be subsequently reversed if the inventory selling price recovers.

9 Use the gross profit method to estimate ending inventory.

The gross profit method is a simple technique for estimating ending inventory. Inventory estimates are used to confirm the accounting records and to substitute for inventory counts when a physical count is not practical. The gross profit method is as follows:

- Estimate a gross profit percentage [(Sales − Cost of goods sold)/Sales] based on historical values adjusted for significant changes in pricing policy and sales mix.
- Apply the gross profit percentage to sales to estimate cost of goods sold.
- Subtract the cost of goods sold estimate from the cost of goods available for sale to arrive at an estimated ending inventory balance.

10 **Determine the financial statement impact of inventory recording errors.**

Undetected inventory recording errors impact financial statements in both the year of the error and the subsequent year. Depending on the nature of the error, income can be understated or overstated.

Analysis of inventory errors is aided by recalling the simple computation:

> Beginning inventory
> + Purchases
> = Goods available for sale
> − Ending inventory
> = Cost of goods sold

Because the ending inventory of one period becomes the beginning inventory of the next period, undetected inventory errors affect two accounting periods. A common error is the overstatement of ending inventory. This error has the effect of reducing cost of goods sold and increasing net income in the year of the error. A counterbalancing reduction in net income occurs in the following year.

11 **Analyze inventory using financial ratios, and properly compare ratios of different firms after adjusting for differences in inventory valuation methods.**

Inventory ratios provide information on whether the level of inventory is appropriate for the volume of sales.

Inventory turnover is computed as cost of goods sold divided by average inventory, in which average inventory is usually the simple average of beginning and ending inventory. This ratio is the number of times a business completely uses and replaces its inventory during the year.

Number of days' sales in inventory is 365 divided by inventory turnover. This ratio is the number of days a firm can continue in business without buying/manufacturing additional inventory.

These ratios can differ significantly, depending on whether a company uses FIFO, LIFO, or average cost. Use the LIFO reserve disclosures to convert a company's LIFO numbers before comparing them to another company's FIFO or average cost numbers.

EXPANDED MATERIAL

12 **Compute estimates of FIFO, LIFO, average cost, and lower-of-cost-or-market inventory using the retail inventory method.**

When the retail inventory method is used, records of goods purchased are maintained at both cost and retail amounts. A cost percentage is computed by dividing the goods available for sale at cost by the goods available for sale at retail. This cost percentage is then applied to the ending inventory at retail to get an estimate of the cost of ending inventory.

Variations on the computation of the cost percentage yield inventory estimates for a variety of valuation assumptions, such as:

- *FIFO*. The cost percentage is based on current purchases.
- *LIFO*. The cost percentage is based on beginning inventory, adjusted for the addition of any new LIFO layers.
- *Average cost*. The cost percentage is computed using both beginning inventory and current purchases and includes the effects of both markups and markdowns.
- *Lower of cost or market*. The cost percentage is computed using both beginning inventory and current purchases and includes the effects of markups but not of markdowns.

13 **Use LIFO pools, dollar-value LIFO, and dollar-value LIFO retail to compute ending inventory.**

Use of LIFO pools simplifies LIFO by eliminating the need to keep detailed LIFO layer information on many different products. When the quantity of items in a LIFO pool increases during a year, a new LIFO layer is added. Decreases in the quantity of some items can be offset by increases in other items, reducing the frequency of LIFO liquidations. Choosing the correct number of LIFO pools to maximize the tax deferral benefits of LIFO involves analysis of the probability of LIFO liquidation and the comparative rate of price increases for different categories of inventory.

Dollar-value LIFO further simplifies LIFO bookkeeping. With dollar-value LIFO, the dollar value of inventory (instead of the physical quantity) is the basic unit of measurement.

Dollar-value LIFO is applied as follows:

- Compute the value of ending inventory using ending prices.
- Convert this value to base-year prices by dividing by the end-of-period price index.
- Compare this number to the beginning inventory (in base-year prices) to determine whether a new LIFO layer has been added.
- All LIFO layers are then converted from base-year prices using the appropriate price index from the year in which the layer was created. New layers can be valued using an end-of-period price index (a FIFO assumption), an average price index (an average cost assumption), or a first purchase price index (a LIFO assumption).

Almost all retail companies that use LIFO employ the dollar-value LIFO retail method. The dollar-value LIFO retail method is used as follows:

- A cost percentage for the current year is computed using cost and retail information for current purchases.
- A price index is used to determine whether a new LIFO layer has been created.
- The retail values of all LIFO layers are converted to cost using the appropriate cost percentages.

⑭ Account for the impact of changing prices on purchase commitments.

With a purchase commitment, a company locks in the cost of inventory before the inventory is actually purchased. The LCM rule is applied if prices decline between the commitment date and the purchase date. No journal entry is made to record the commitment. However, when price declines take place after a purchase commitment has been made, a loss is recorded in the period of the price decline.

⑮ Record inventory purchase transactions denominated in foreign currencies.

Transactions denominated in currencies other than the U.S. dollar are foreign currency transactions for U.S. companies. Foreign currency transactions expose companies to exchange rate risk during the time between the purchase and the payment of the foreign currency obligation. Gains or losses resulting from exchange rate changes are recognized in the period in which the exchange rate changes occur.

FASB-IASB CODIFICATION SUMMARY

Topic	FASB Accounting Standards Codification	Original FASB Standard	Corresponding IASB Standard	Differences between U.S. GAAP and IFRS
LIFO	Section 330-10-30 par. 9-11	ARB 43, Chapter 4	IAS 2 par. 23-27	LIFO is not allowable under IFRS.
Lower of cost or market	Section 330-10-35 par. 1-12	ARB 43, Chapter 4	IAS 2 par. 28-33	Under IFRS, inventory is recorded at lower of cost or net realizable value, and inventory write-down losses can be reversed if the selling price subsequently recovers.
Foreign currency transactions	Section 830-20-35 par. 2	SFAS No. 52 par. 16b	IAS 21 par. 23a, 28	No substantial differences

KEY TERMS

Activity-based cost (ABC) system 9-12
Average cost method 9-17
Cash discount 9-13
Ceiling 9-31
Consigned goods 9-10
Cost driver 9-12
Direct materials 9-5
Dollar-value LIFO 9-28
Entry cost 9-31
Exit value 9-31
Finished goods 9-6

First-in, first-out (FIFO) method 9-18
Floor 9-31
FOB (free on board) destination 9-9
FOB (free on board) shipping point 9-9
Gross method 9-14
Gross profit method 9-37
Gross profit percentage 9-37
Indirect materials 9-5
Inventory 9-4
Inventory turnover 9-41

Last-in, first-out (LIFO) method 9-18
LIFO conformity rule 9-26
LIFO inventory pools 9-27
LIFO layer 9-23
LIFO liquidation 9-25
LIFO reserve 9-23
Lower of cost or market (LCM) 9-31
Manufacturing overhead 9-6
Market (in "lower of cost or market") 9-31
Net method 9-13

Number of days' sales in inventory 9-43
Period costs 9-12
Periodic inventory system 9-7
Perpetual inventory system 9-7
Product (inventoriable) cost 9-12
Raw materials 9-5
Replacement cost 9-31
Shrinkage 9-8
Specific identification method 9-16
Trade discount 9-13
Work in process 9-6

EXPANDED MATERIAL
Cost percentage 9-44
Dollar-value LIFO retail method 9-54
Double extension 9-51
Foreign currency transaction 9-57
Initial markup 9-46
Markdowns 9-46
Markups 9-46
Original retail 9-46
Price index 9-51
Purchase commitment 9-56
Retail inventory method 9-44
Spot rate 9-58

Tutorial Activities

Tutorial Activities with author-written, content-specific feedback, available on *CengageNOW* for Stice & Stice.

QUESTIONS

1. What four questions are associated with the accounting for inventory?
2. **General Motors'** finished goods inventory is composed primarily of automobiles. Are automobiles always classified as "inventory" on the balance sheets of all companies? Explain.
3. What is the difference between direct materials and indirect materials?
4. (a) What are the three cost elements entering into work in process and finished goods?
   (b) What items enter into manufacturing overhead?
5. What is the general rule for distinguishing between inventory-related costs that should be included in the cost of inventory and those that should be expensed as incurred?
6. A campus bookstore has a computerized inventory system. Is it more likely that the system is a periodic system or a perpetual system? Explain.
7. Would you expect to find a perpetual or a periodic inventory system used in each of the following situations?
   (a) Diamond ring department of a jewelry store
   (b) Computer department of a college bookstore
   (c) Candy department of a college bookstore
   (d) Automobile dealership—new car department
   (e) Automobile dealership—parts department
   (f) Wholesale dealer of small tools
   (g) A plumbing supply house—plastic fittings department
8. How is inventory shrinkage computed under a perpetual inventory system?
9. Under what conditions are goods in transit legally reported as inventory by the (a) seller? (b) buyer?
10. How should (a) consigned goods and (b) installment sales be treated in computing year-end inventory costs?
11. What is the appropriate way to account for inventory sold under a repurchase agreement?
12. What is an activity-based cost (ABC) system?
13. (a) What are the two methods of accounting for cash discounts? (b) Which method is generally preferred? Why?
14. What objections can be raised to the use of the specific identification method?
15. What advantages are there to using the average cost method of inventory valuation?
16. Which better matches the normal physical flow of goods—FIFO or LIFO? Which better matches current costs and current revenues?
17. Why are LIFO and average cost more complicated with a perpetual inventory system than with a periodic system?
18. (a) Under what conditions is a LIFO layer created? (b) What is meant by "LIFO reserve"?
19. (a) What is the LIFO conformity rule? (b) How has the rule changed since it was first adopted?
20. Assume there is no change in the physical quantity of inventory for the current accounting period. During a period of rising prices, which inventory valuation method (LIFO or FIFO) will result in the greater dollar value of ending inventory? The lower payment of income taxes?
21. What kinds of companies would be *least* likely to use LIFO? Explain.
22. What is the current status of LIFO under IASB standards?
23. The use of lower of cost or market is an unnecessary continuation of the tradition of conservative accounting. Comment on this view.
24. Why are ceiling and floor limitations on replacement cost considered necessary?
25. What differences result from applying lower of cost or market to individual inventory items instead of to the inventory as a whole?
26. Why would a manager care about the value assigned to inventory transferred in from another department?

27. How do the provisions of *IAS 2* differ from the LCM rule contained in U.S. GAAP?
28. What information is needed to develop a reliable gross profit percentage for use with the gross profit method?
29. State the effect of each of the following errors made by Clawson Inc. on the income statement and the balance sheet (1) of the current period and (2) of the succeeding period:
    (a) The ending inventory is overstated as a result of a miscount of goods on hand.
    (b) The company fails to record a purchase of merchandise on account, and the merchandise purchased is not recognized in recording the ending inventory.
    (c) The ending inventory is understated as a result of a miscount of goods on hand.
30. Company A has an inventory turnover ratio of 8.0 times. Company B has an inventory turnover ratio of 10.0 times. Both companies are in the same industry. Which company manages its inventory more efficiently? Explain.

EXPANDED MATERIAL

31. What advantages does the retail inventory method have over the gross profit method?
32. How can FIFO and LIFO assumptions be incorporated into the retail inventory method?
33. (a) How are markdowns treated when estimating average cost using the retail inventory method? (b) How are markdowns treated when estimating lower of cost or market using the retail inventory method?
34. What factors should a company consider in identifying the appropriate number of dollar-value LIFO pools?
35. What are the major advantages of dollar-value LIFO?
36. Indexes are used for two different purposes in computing the cost of LIFO layers with dollar-value LIFO. Clearly distinguish between these uses and describe how the indexes are applied.
37. Identify three different indexes that can be used in valuing a new LIFO layer with dollar-value LIFO. Which index is most consistent with the LIFO assumption?
38. When applying the dollar-value LIFO retail method: (a) How do beginning inventory values impact the computation of the cost percentage? (b) How are markdowns treated?
39. What journal entry is made when a purchase commitment is originally entered into? Explain.
40. Are all transactions with foreign companies classified as foreign currency transactions? If not, what determines if a transaction is a foreign currency transaction?
41. Why is an adjustment made on the balance sheet date to reflect exchange rate changes?

PRACTICE EXERCISES

Practice 9-1

Perpetual and Periodic Journal Entries

The company uses a *perpetual* inventory system and made the following summary journal entries for the month.

Inventory	3,000	
Accounts Payable		3,000
Accounts Receivable	10,000	
Sales		10,000
Cost of Goods Sold	4,500	
Inventory		4,500
Cash	9,000	
Accounts Receivable		9,000

1. If the inventory balance at the beginning of the month was $10,000, what is the inventory balance at the end of the month?
2. If the accounts receivable balance at the beginning of the month was $3,500, what is the accounts receivable balance at the end of the month?
3. What is the amount of *gross profit* for the month?

Practice 9-2

Perpetual and Periodic Journal Entries

During the month, the company purchased inventory on account for $3,000. Sales (all on account) during the period totaled $10,000. The items sold had a cost of $4,500. Cash collections on account during the period totaled $9,000. Make the journal entries necessary to record these transactions using (1) a periodic inventory system and (2) a perpetual inventory system.

Practice 9-3

Perpetual and Periodic Computations

Beginning inventory for the period was $220,000. Purchases for the period totaled $720,000 and sales were $1,250,000. A physical count of ending inventory revealed inventory of $145,000. (1) Compute cost of goods sold assuming that a periodic system is used and (2) make the journal entry to record inventory shrinkage assuming that a perpetual system is used and cost of goods sold according to the system was $710,000.

Practice 9-4

Goods in Transit and on Consignment

The company counted its ending inventory on December 31. *None of the following items were included when the total amount of the company's ending inventory was computed:*

- $15,000 in goods located in the company's warehouse that are on consignment from another company.
- $20,000 in goods that were *sold* by the company and shipped on December 30 and were in transit on December 31; the goods were received by the customer on January 2. Terms were FOB destination.
- $30,000 in goods that were *purchased* by the company and shipped on December 30 and were in transit on December 31; the goods were received by the company on January 2. Terms were FOB shipping point.
- $40,000 in goods that were *sold* by the company and shipped on December 30 and were in transit on December 31; the goods were received by the customer on January 2. Terms were FOB shipping point.

The company's reported inventory (before any corrections) was $200,000. What is the correct amount of the company's inventory on December 31?

Practice 9-5

Schedule of Cost of Goods Manufactured

The company reported the following information for the year:

Ending work-in-process inventory	$100,000
Depreciation on factory building	32,000
Salespersons' salaries	27,000
Beginning raw materials inventory	40,000
Direct labor	198,000
Factory supervisor's salary	56,000
Depreciation on company headquarters building	21,000
Beginning work-in-process inventory	76,000
Ending raw materials inventory	34,000
Indirect labor	36,000
Advertising costs	50,000
Purchases of raw materials	230,000

Prepare a schedule of cost of goods manufactured for the year.

Practice 9-6

Accounting for Purchase Discounts

On May 23, the company purchased $450,000 in inventory on account. The purchase terms are 2/10, n/30. Make the journal entries to record the purchase of and subsequent payment for these goods assuming: (1) the company uses the net method and paid for the goods on June 1; (2) the company uses the net method and paid for the goods on June 15; (3) the company uses the gross method and paid for the goods on June 1; and (4) the company uses the gross method and paid for the goods on June 15. Assume a perpetual inventory system.

Practice 9-7

Inventory Valuation: FIFO, LIFO, and Average

The company reported the following inventory data for the year:

	Units	Cost per Unit
Beginning inventory	300	$17.50
Purchases:		
March 23	900	18.00
September 16	1,200	18.25
Units remaining at year-end	400	

Compute (1) cost of goods sold and (2) ending inventory assuming (a) FIFO inventory valuation, (b) LIFO inventory valuation, and (c) average cost inventory valuation. The company uses a periodic inventory system.

Practice 9-8

Inventory Valuation: Complications with a Perpetual System

Refer to Practice 9-7. Assume that the sales occurred as follows:

	Units Sold
January 16	100
July 15	600
November 1	1,300
Total	2,000

Compute (1) cost of goods sold and (2) ending inventory assuming (a) FIFO inventory valuation, (b) LIFO inventory valuation, and (c) average cost inventory valuation. The company uses a *perpetual* inventory system.

Practice 9-9

LIFO Layers

The company started business at the beginning of Year 1. Inventory purchases and sales during the first four years of the company's business are as follows:

	Units Purchased	Cost per Unit	Units Sold
Year 1	50	$2.50	40
Year 2	80	3.00	65
Year 3	90	3.40	90
Year 4	130	4.00	100

Compute the company's ending inventory as of the end of Year 4. The company uses LIFO inventory valuation.

Practice 9-10

LIFO Reserve and LIFO Liquidation

Refer to Practice 9-9. Compute the following:

1. LIFO reserve at the end of Year 4.
2. Cost of goods sold for Year 4.
3. Cost of goods sold for Year 4 assuming that units purchased had been 75 instead of 130.

Practice 9-11

LIFO and Income Taxes

Refer to Practice 9-9. Assume that the company has no expenses except for cost of goods sold, the selling price per unit is $6 in each year, and that the income tax rate is 40%. Compute the total amount of income taxes owed for Year 1 through Year 4 assuming that (1) the company uses LIFO inventory valuation and (2) the company uses FIFO inventory valuation.

Practice 9-12

Lower of Cost or Market

The following information pertains to the company's ending inventory:

	Original Cost	Selling Price	Selling Cost	Replacement Cost	Normal Profit
Item A	$ 575	$ 700	$ 50	$ 600	$100
Item B	700	820	80	550	150
Item C	1,180	1,250	100	1,100	300

Apply lower-of-cost-or-market accounting to each inventory item individually. What *total* amount should be reported as inventory in the balance sheet?

Practice 9-13

Lower of Cost or Market: Individual vs. Aggregate

Refer to Practice 9-12. Apply lower-of-cost-or-market accounting to the inventory as a whole. What *total* amount should be reported as inventory in the balance sheet?

Practice 9-14

Lower-of-Cost-or-Market Journal Entries

The company started business at the beginning of Year 1. The company applies the LCM rule to its inventory as a whole. Inventory cost and market values as of the end of Year 1 and Year 2 were as follows:

	Cost	Market Value
Year 1	$1,000	$ 800
Year 2	1,700	1,650

The market value numbers already include consideration of the replacement cost, the ceiling, and the floor. Make the journal entry necessary to record the LCM adjustment at the end of (1) Year 1 and (2) Year 2. The company uses an allowance account for any LCM adjustments.

Practice 9-15

Returned Inventory

The company sells large industrial equipment. A piece of equipment with an original cost of $250,000 and an original selling price of $390,000 was recently returned. It is expected that the equipment will be able to be resold for just $225,000. The company normally earns a gross profit of 35.9% of the selling price. How much loss is recorded when the inventory is returned and how much gross profit will be reported when the equipment is resold assuming that the returned inventory is recorded at (1) its original cost, (2) its net realizable value, and (3) its net realizable value minus a normal gross profit?

Practice 9-16

Gross Profit Method

On July 23, the company's inventory was destroyed in a hurricane-related flood. For insurance purposes, the company must reliably estimate the amount of inventory on hand on July 23. The company uses a periodic inventory system. The following data have been assembled:

Inventory, January 1	$1,000,000
Purchases, January 1–July 23	3,700,000
Sales, January 1–July 23	5,000,000
Historical gross profit percentages:	
Last year	60%
Two years ago	55%

Estimate the company's inventory as of July 23 using (1) last year's gross profit percentage and (2) the gross profit percentage from two years ago.

Practice 9-17

Inventory Errors

At the beginning of Year 1, the company's inventory level was stated correctly. At the end of Year 1, inventory was overstated by $2,000. At the end of Year 2, inventory was understated by $450. At the end of Year 3, inventory was correctly stated. Reported net income was $3,000 in Year 1, $3,000 in Year 2, and $3,000 in Year 3. Compute the correct amount of net income in (1) Year 1, (2) Year 2, and (3) Year 3. Ignore income taxes.

Practice 9-18

Computing Inventory Ratios

The company reported the following information for the year:

Beginning accounts receivable	$2,000	Ending accounts receivable	$2,400
Sales	8,000	Cost of goods sold	4,200
Ending inventory	3,000	Beginning inventory	2,600

Compute (1) inventory turnover and (2) number of days' sales in inventory.

EXPANDED MATERIAL

Practice 9-19

Retail Inventory Method

The company reported the following information for the month:

	Cost	Retail
Inventory, January 1	$20,000	$30,000
Purchases in January	20,000	35,000

Sales for the month totaled $47,000. Compute the estimated cost of inventory on hand at the end of the month using the average cost assumption.

Practice 9-20

Markups and Markdowns

The company reported the following information relating to inventory for the month of April:

	Cost	Retail
Inventory, January 1	$25,000	$ 50,000
Purchases in January	40,000	70,000
Markups		30,000
Markdowns		(25,000)

Sales for the month totaled $80,000. Compute the estimated cost of inventory on hand at the end of the month using the average cost assumption.

Practice 9-21

LIFO Pools

The company has one LIFO pool. Information relating to the products in this pool is as follows:

Beginning inventory, January 1	25 units @ $20 each
Purchase, February 12	30 units @ $22 each
Purchase, February 28	45 units @ $26 each
Purchase, March 15	60 units @ $28 each
Sales for the first quarter	120 units

Compute the ending LIFO inventory value for the first quarter assuming new layers are valued based on a LIFO cost assumption.

Practice 9-22
Dollar-Value LIFO

The company manufactures a single product and has decided to adopt the dollar-value LIFO inventory method. The inventory value on that date using the newly adopted dollar-value LIFO method was $100,000. Inventory at year-end prices was $120,000, and the year-end price index was 1.05. Compute the inventory value at year-end assuming incremental layers are valued at year-end prices.

Practice 9-23
Dollar-Value LIFO Retail

The company compiled the following information concerning inventory for the current year:

Date	Year-End Price Index at Retail	Incremental Layer Index	Incremental Cost Percentage	Inventory at Retail
Jan. 1	1.00	1.00	65%	$ 80,000
Dec. 31	1.10	1.05	70%	110,000

Compute the inventory cost at year-end using the dollar-value LIFO retail method.

Practice 9-24
Purchase Commitments

On November 17 of Year 1, the company entered into a commitment to purchase 250,000 ounces of gold on February 14 of Year 2 at a price of $1,910.20 per ounce. On December 31 of Year 1, the market price of gold is $1,875.10 per ounce. On February 14, the price of gold is $1,892.00 per ounce. Make the journal entries necessary to record (1) the November 17 purchase commitment, (2) any necessary adjustment at December 31, and (3) the actual purchase (for cash) on February 14. The company uses a perpetual inventory system.

Practice 9-25
Foreign Currency Inventory Purchases

On November 6 of Year 1, the company purchased inventory (on account) from a supplier located in Indonesia. The purchase price is 100,000,000 Indonesian rupiah. On November 6, the exchange rate was 8,700 rupiah for 1 U.S. dollar. On December 31, the exchange rate was 10,000 rupiah for 1 U.S. dollar. The company paid the account on March 23 of Year 2. On that date, the exchange rate was 9,100 rupiah for 1 U.S. dollar. Make the journal entries necessary on (1) November 6, (2) December 31, and (3) March 23. The company uses a perpetual inventory system.

EXERCISES

Exercise 9-26
Identification of Inventory Costs and Categories

The records of Burtone Company contain the following cost categories. Burtone manufactures exercise equipment and iron weights.

(a) Cost of materials used to repair factory equipment
(b) Depreciation on the fleet of salespersons' cars
(c) Cost to purchase iron
(d) Salaries of the factory supervisors
(e) Cost of heat, electricity, and insurance for the company office building
(f) Wages of the workers who shape the iron weights
(g) Property taxes on the factory building
(h) Cost of oil for the factory equipment
(i) Salary of the company president
(j) Pension benefits of workers who repair factory equipment

For each category, indicate whether the cost is an inventory cost (I) or if it should be expensed as incurred (E). For each inventory cost, indicate whether the cost is part of direct materials (DM), direct labor (DL), or manufacturing overhead (MOH).

Exercise 9-27

Perpetual and Periodic Inventory Systems
The following inventory information is for Stevenson Company.

Beginning inventory	200 units @ $8
Purchases	350 units @ $8
Ending inventory	100 units

Sales for the year totaled $5,900. All sales and purchases are on account.

1. Make the journal entries necessary to record purchases and sales during the year assuming a periodic inventory system.
2. Assume that a periodic inventory system is used. Compute cost of goods sold.
3. Assume that a perpetual inventory system is used. The perpetual records indicate that the sales of $5,900 represent 400 units with a total cost of $3,200. Make the journal entries necessary to record purchases, sales, and inventory shrinkage for the year.

Exercise 9-28

Computing Cash Expenditure for Inventory
Using the following data, compute the total cash expended for inventory in 2015.

Accounts payable:	
January 1, 2015	$ 350,000
December 31, 2015	525,000
Cost of goods sold—2015	1,080,000
Inventory balance:	
January 1, 2015	$ 600,000
December 31, 2015	540,000

Exercise 9-29

Passage of Title
The management of Kauer Company has engaged you to assist in the preparation of year-end (December 31) financial statements. You are told that on November 30, the correct inventory level was 150,000 units. During the month of December, sales totaled 50,000 units including 25,000 units shipped on consignment to Towsey Company. A letter received from Towsey indicates that as of December 31, it had sold 20,000 units and was still trying to sell the remainder. A review of the December purchase orders to various suppliers shows the following:

Purchase Order Date	Invoice Date	Number of Units	Date Shipped	Date Received	Terms
Dec. 2, 2014	Jan. 3, 2015	10,000	Jan. 2, 2015	Jan. 3, 2015	FOB shipping point
Dec. 11, 2014	Jan. 3, 2015	8,000	Dec. 22, 2014	Dec. 24, 2014	FOB destination
Dec. 13, 2014	Jan. 2, 2015	13,000	Dec. 28, 2014	Jan. 2, 2015	FOB shipping point
Dec. 23, 2014	Dec. 26, 2014	12,000	Jan. 2, 2015	Jan. 3, 2015	FOB shipping point
Dec. 28, 2014	Jan. 10, 2015	10,000	Dec. 31, 2014	Jan. 5, 2015	FOB destination
Dec. 31, 2014	Jan. 10, 2015	15,000	Jan. 3, 2015	Jan. 6, 2015	FOB destination

Kauer Company uses the "passing of legal title" for inventory recognition. Compute the number of units that should be included in the year-end inventory.

Exercise 9-30

Passage of Title

The Anson Manufacturing Company reviewed its year-end inventory and found the following items. Indicate which items should be included in the inventory balance at December 31, 2015. Give your reasons for the treatment you suggest.

(a) A packing case containing a product costing $1,210 was standing in the shipping room when the physical inventory was taken. It was not included in the inventory because it was marked "Hold for shipping instructions." The customer's order was dated December 21, but the case was shipped and the customer billed on January 8, 2016.

(b) Merchandise costing $545 was received on December 28, 2015, and the invoice was recorded. The invoice was in the hands of the purchasing agent; it was marked "On consignment."

(c) Merchandise received on January 4, 2016, costing $905 was entered in the purchase register on January 5. The invoice showed shipment was made FOB shipping point on December 31, 2015. Because it was not on hand during the inventory count, it was not included.

(d) A special machine, fabricated to order for a particular customer, was finished and in the shipping room on December 30. The customer was billed on that date and the machine was excluded from inventory although it was shipped January 2, 2016. The customer had requested, in writing, that the special machine be held for shipment until January 2016.

(e) Merchandise costing $1,960 was received on January 3, 2016, and the related purchase invoice was recorded January 5. The invoice showed the shipment was made on December 29, 2015, FOB destination.

(f) Merchandise costing $2,400 was sold on an installment basis on December 15. The customer took possession of the goods on that date. The merchandise was included in inventory because, technically, Anson still holds legal title in order to enforce payment. Historical experience suggests that full payment on installment sales is received approximately 99% of the time.

(g) Goods costing $1,730 were sold and delivered on December 20. The goods were included in inventory because the sale was accompanied by a repurchase agreement requiring Anson to buy back the inventory in February 2016.

Exercise 9-31

Cost of Goods Manufactured Schedule

The following quarterly cost data have been accumulated for Oakeson Mfg. Inc.:

Raw materials—beginning inventory (Jan. 1, 2015)	90 units @ $7.00
Purchases	75 units @ $8.00
	120 units @ $8.50

Transferred 195 units of raw materials to work in process:

Work in process—beginning inventory (Jan. 1, 2015)	53 units @ $14.00
Direct labor	$3,100
Manufacturing overhead	$2,950
Work in process—ending inventory (Mar. 31, 2015)	47 units @ $14.25

Prepare a cost of goods manufactured schedule for Oakeson Mfg. Inc. for the quarter ended March 31, 2015. Assume the use of FIFO for raw materials inventory.

Exercise 9-32

Cash Discounts

Olavssen Hardware regularly buys merchandise from Dawson Suppliers. Olavssen uses the net method to record purchases and discounts. On August 15, Olavssen Hardware purchased material from Dawson Suppliers. The invoice received from Dawson showed an invoiced price of $15,536 and payment terms of 2/10, n/30. Payment was sent to Dawson Suppliers on August 28. Prepare entries to record the purchase and subsequent payment assuming a periodic inventory system. (*Note:* Round to nearest dollar.)

Exercise 9-33

Net and Gross Methods—Entries
On December 3, Ainge Printing purchased inventory listed at $7,400 from Craig Paper Supply. Terms of the purchase were 3/10, n/20. Ainge Printing also purchased inventory from Tippetts Ink Wholesale on December 10 for a list price of $10,300. Terms of the purchase were 3/10, n/30. On December 16, Ainge paid both suppliers for these purchases. Ainge does not use a perpetual inventory system.

1. Give the entries to record the purchases and invoice payments assuming that (a) the net method is used and (b) the gross method is used.
2. Assume that Ainge has not paid either of the invoices at December 31. Give the year-end adjusting entry if the net method is used.

Exercise 9-34
Recording Purchase Returns
On July 23, Stevensonville Company purchased goods on account for $6,000. Stevensonville later returned defective goods costing $450.

Record the purchase and the return of the defective goods assuming (1) a periodic inventory system and (2) a perpetual inventory system.

Exercise 9-35

Inventory Computation Using Different Cost Flows
The Webster Store shows the following information relating to one of its products.

Inventory, January 1	300 units @ $17.50
Sales, January 8	200 units
Purchases, January 10	900 units @ $18.00
Sales, January 18	800 units
Purchases, January 20	1,200 units @ $19.50
Sales, January 25	1,000 units

What are the values of ending inventory under a periodic inventory system assuming a (1) FIFO, (2) LIFO, and (3) average cost flow? (*Note:* Round unit costs to three decimal places.)

Exercise 9-36

Inventory Computation Using Different Cost Flows
Brooklyn Corporation had the following transactions relating to product X during September.

Date		Units	Unit Cost
September 1	Balance on hand	600 units	$1.50
6	Purchase	200 units	2.00
12	Sale	400 units	
13	Sale	100 units	
18	Purchase	250 units	3.00
20	Purchase	150 units	3.50
25	Sale	300 units	

Determine the ending inventory value under each of the following costing methods:

1. FIFO (perpetual)
2. FIFO (periodic)
3. LIFO (perpetual)
4. LIFO (periodic)

Exercise 9-37

Comparison of Inventory Methods

Dutch Truck Sales sells semitrailers. The current inventory includes the following five semitrailers (identical except for paint color) along with purchase dates and costs:

Semitrailer	Purchase Date	Cost
1	April 3, 2015	$73,000
2	April 10, 2015	70,000
3	April 10, 2015	71,000
4	May 4, 2015	77,000
5	May 12, 2015	78,500

On May 20, 2015, a trucking firm purchased semitrailer 3 from Dutch for $86,000.

1. Compute the gross margin on this sale assuming Dutch uses the:
   (a) FIFO inventory method
   (b) LIFO inventory method
   (c) Specific identification method
2. Which inventory method do you think Dutch should use? Why?

Exercise 9-38

LIFO Inventory Computation

White Farm Supply's records for the first three months of its existence show purchases of commodity Y2 as follows:

	Number of Units	Cost
August	5,500	$28,050
September	8,000	41,600
October	5,100	27,030

The inventory of commodity Y2 at the end of October using FIFO is valued at $36,390.

1. Assuming that none of commodity Y2 was sold during August and September, what value would be shown at the end of October if LIFO cost was assumed?
2. If White Farm uses LIFO, what disclosure could it make in its October 31 quarterly report concerning the FIFO value of inventory?

Exercise 9-39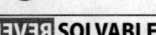

Inventory Computation from Incomplete Records

A flood recently destroyed many of the financial records of Yak Manufacturing Company. Management has hired you to recreate as much financial information as possible for the month of July. You are able to find out that the company uses an average cost inventory valuation system. You also learn that Yak makes a physical count at the end of each month in order to determine monthly ending inventory values. By examining various documents, you are able to gather the following information:

Ending inventory at July 31	58,500 units
Total cost of units available for sale in July	$145,210
Cost of goods sold during July	$117,130
Cost of beginning inventory, July 1	$0.40 per unit
Gross profit on sales for July	$93,590

July purchases:

Date	Units	Unit Cost
July 5	55,000	$0.51
11	53,000	0.50
15	45,000	0.55
16	47,000	0.53

You are asked to provide the following information.

1. Number of units on hand, July 1
2. Units sold during July
3. Unit cost of inventory at July 31
4. Value of inventory at July 31

Exercise 9-40

Computation of Beginning Inventory from Ending Inventory
The Atlas Company sells product T. During a move to a new location, the inventory records for product T were misplaced. The bookkeeper has been able to gather some information from the sales records and gives you the data shown below.

July sales:
82,100 units at $9.00

July purchases:

Date	Quantity	Unit Cost
July 5	17,000	$4.50
9	17,800	5.25
12	18,100	5.00
25	19,000	5.50

On July 31, 24,000 units were on hand with a total value of $129,500. Atlas has always used a periodic FIFO inventory costing system. Gross profit on sales for July was $358,100. Reconstruct the beginning inventory (quantity and dollar value) for the month of July.

Exercise 9-41

Impact on Profit of Failure to Replace LIFO Layers
Harrison Lumber Company uses a periodic LIFO method for inventory costing. The following information relates to the plywood inventory carried by Harrison Lumber.

Plywood inventory:

Date	Quantity	LIFO Costing Layers
May 1	600 sheets	300 sheets at $ 8.00
		225 sheets at $11.00
		75 sheets at $13.00

Plywood purchases:

May 8		115 sheets at $14.00
17		95 sheets at $15.00
29		200 sheets at $14.50

All sales of plywood during May were at $20 per sheet. On May 31, there were 360 sheets of plywood in the storeroom.

1. Compute the gross profit on sales for May, as a dollar value and as a percentage of sales.
2. Assume that because of a lumber strike, Harrison Lumber is not able to purchase the May 29 order of lumber until June 10. Assuming sales remained the same, recompute the gross profit on sales for May, as a dollar value and as a percentage of sales.
3. Compare the results of (1) and (2) and explain the difference.

Exercise 9-42

Computation of Beginning Inventory

A note to the financial statements of Highland Inc. at December 31, 2015, reads as follows:

> Because of the manufacturer's production problems for our Humdinger Limited line, our inventories were unavoidably reduced. Under the LIFO inventory accounting method currently being used for tax and financial accounting purposes, the net effect of all the inventory changes was to increase pretax income by $1,000,000 over what it would have been had the inventory of Humdinger Limited been maintained at the normal physical levels on hand at the start of the year.

The unit purchase price of the merchandise was $25 per unit during the year. Highland Inc. uses the periodic inventory system. Additional data concerning Highland's inventory were as follows:

Date	Physical Count of Inventory	LIFO Cost of Inventory
January 1, 2015	500,000 units	$?
December 31, 2015	400,000 units	$3,600,000

1. What was the unit average cost for the 100,000 units sold from the beginning inventory?
2. What was the reported value for the January 1, 2015, inventory?

Exercise 9-43

Income Differences—FIFO vs. LIFO

First-in, first-out has been used for inventory valuation by the Bartlett Co. since it was organized in 2012. Using the data that follow, redetermine the net incomes for each year on the assumption of inventory valuation on the last-in, first-out basis:

	2012	2013	2014	2015
Reported net income—FIFO basis.	$22,300	$42,400	$61,350	$58,200
Reported ending inventories—FIFO basis	44,300	89,900	112,000	125,000
Ending inventories—LIFO basis	35,100	65,300	80,000	113,000

Exercise 9-44

Gross Margin Differences—FIFO vs. LIFO

Assume the Bullock Corporation had the following purchases and sales of its single product during its first three years of operation.

	Purchases		Sales	
Year	Units	Unit Cost	Units	Unit Price
1	10,000	$10	8,000	$14
2	9,000	12	9,000	17
3	8,000	15	10,000	18
	27,000		27,000	

Cost of goods sold is Bullock's only expense. The income tax rate is 40%.

1. Determine the net income (after tax) for each of the three years assuming FIFO historical cost flow.
2. Determine the net income (after tax) for each of the three years assuming LIFO historical cost flow.
3. Compare the total net income over the life of the business. How do the different cost flow assumptions affect net income and cash flows over the life of the business? From a cash flow perspective, which cost flow assumption is better? Explain.

Exercise 9-45

Lower-of-Cost-or-Market Valuation
Determine the proper carrying value of the following inventory items.

Item	Cost	Replacement Cost	Sales Price	Selling Expenses	Normal Profit
Product 431	$2.50	$2.60	$3.20	$0.45	$0.20
Product 432	1.12	1.00	1.28	0.32	0.07
Product 433	0.54	0.50	0.68	0.13	0.10
Product 434	0.75	0.85	1.07	0.23	0.04
Product 435	1.69	1.60	1.86	0.18	0.04
Product 436	2.03	1.95	2.26	0.26	0.30

Exercise 9-46

Lower-of-Cost-or-Market Valuation
The following inventory data are available for Nordic Ski Shop at December 31.

	Cost	Market
Skis	$55,000	$62,000
Boots	42,500	38,000
Ski equipment	18,000	16,500
Ski apparel	10,000	12,000

1. Determine the value of ending inventory using the lower-of-cost-or-market method applied to (a) individual items and (b) total inventory.
2. Prepare any journal entries required to adjust the ending inventory if lower of cost or market is applied to (a) individual items and (b) total inventory.

Exercise 9-47

Lower-of-Cost-or-Market Valuation
Newcomer, Inc., values inventories using the lower-of-cost-or-market method applied to total inventory. Inventory values at the end of the company's first and second years of operation follow.

	Cost	Market
Year 1	$58,000	$53,000
Year 2	75,000	73,800

1. Prepare the journal entries necessary to reflect the proper inventory valuation at the end of each year. (Assume Newcomer uses an inventory allowance account.)
2. For Year 1, assume sales were $510,000 and purchases were $440,000. What amount would be reported as cost of goods sold on the income statement for Year 1 if: (a) the inventory decline is reported separately and (b) the inventory decline is not reported separately?

Exercise 9-48

Comparison of Inventory Valuation Methods

The Crevier Corporation began business on January 1, 2015. The following table shows information about inventories, as of December 31, for three consecutive years under different valuation methods. Assume that purchases are $60,000 each year. Using this information and assuming that the same method is used each year, you are to answer each of the questions that follow.

	LIFO	FIFO	Market	Lower of Cost or Market*
2015	$12,300	$15,100	$14,800	$14,500
2016	10,400	11,600	8,800	11,500
2017	11,600	13,400	13,000	12,900

* FIFO cost, item-by-item valuation.

1. Which inventory basis would result in the highest net income for 2015?
2. Which inventory basis would result in the highest net income for 2016?
3. Which inventory basis would result in the lowest net income for the three years combined?
4. For the year 2016, how much higher or lower would net income be on the FIFO cost basis than on the lower-of-cost-or-market basis?

Exercise 9-49

Valuation of Return

Napali Inc. sells new equipment with a $5,300 list price. A dissatisfied customer returned one piece of equipment. Napali determines that the returned equipment can be resold if it is reconditioned. The expected sales price of the reconditioned equipment is $4,500; the reconditioning expenses are estimated to be $600; and normal profit is 35% of the sales price.

1. Prepare the journal entry to record the sale of the reconditioned equipment for cash assuming that the floor value is used to record the returned equipment.
2. Prepare the journal entry to record the sale of the reconditioned equipment for cash assuming that the original list price is used to record the returned equipment.
3. Evaluate the entries.

Exercise 9-50

Inventory Loss—Gross Profit Method

On August 15, 2015, a hurricane damaged a warehouse of Rheinhart Merchandise Company. The entire inventory and many accounting records stored in the warehouse were completely destroyed. Although the inventory was not insured, a portion could be sold for scrap. Through the use of the remaining records, the following data are assembled:

Inventory, January 1	$ 375,000
Purchases, January 1–August 15	1,385,000
Cash sales, January 1–August 15	225,000
Collection of accounts receivable, January 1–August 15	2,115,000
Accounts receivable, January 1	175,000
Accounts receivable, August 15	265,000
Salvage value of inventory	5,000
Gross profit percentage on sales	32%

Compute the inventory loss as a result of the hurricane.

Exercise 9-51

Inventory Loss—Gross Profit Method

On June 30, 2015, a flash flood damaged the warehouse and factory of Magna Corporation, completely destroying the work-in-process inventory. There was no damage to either the raw materials or finished goods inventories. A physical inventory taken after the flood revealed the following valuations:

Finished goods.	$123,000
Work in process	0
Raw materials	46,100

The inventory on January 1, 2015, consisted of the following:

Finished goods.	$109,000
Work in process	103,000
Raw materials	49,300
	$261,300

A review of the books and records disclosed that the gross profit margin historically approximated 42% of sales. The sales for the first six months of 2015 were $584,000. Raw materials purchases were $88,000. Direct labor costs for this period were $130,000, and manufacturing overhead has historically been applied at 70% of direct labor.

Compute the value of the work-in-process inventory lost on June 30, 2015.

Exercise 9-52

Correction of Inventory Errors

Annual income for the Stoker Co. for the period 2011–2015 appears below. However, a review of the records for the company reveals inventory misstatements as listed. Calculate corrected net income for each year.

	2011	2012	2013	2014	2015
Reported net income (loss)	$18,000	$13,000	$2,000	$ (5,800)	$16,000
Inventory overstatement, end of year		5,500			3,600
Inventory understatement, end of year	4,500			10,500	

Exercise 9-53

Effect on Net Income of Inventory Errors

The Martin Company reported income before taxes of $370,000 for 2014 and $526,000 for 2015. A later audit produced the following information:

(a) The ending inventory for 2014 included 2,000 units erroneously priced at $5.90 per unit. The correct cost was $9.50 per unit.

(b) Merchandise costing $17,500 was shipped to the Martin Company, FOB shipping point, on December 26, 2014. The purchase was recorded in 2014, but the merchandise was excluded from the ending inventory because it was not received until January 4, 2015.

(c) On December 28, 2014, merchandise costing $2,900 was sold to Deluxe Paint Shop. Deluxe had asked Martin in writing to keep the merchandise for it until January 2, when it would come and pick it up. Because the merchandise was still in the store at year-end, the merchandise was included in the inventory count. The sale was correctly recorded in December 2014.

(d) Craft Company sold merchandise costing $1,500 to Martin Company. The purchase was made on December 29, 2014, and the merchandise was shipped on December 30. Terms were FOB shipping point. Because the Martin Company bookkeeper was on vacation, neither the purchase nor the receipt of goods was recorded on the books until January 2015.

Assume that all amounts are material and a physical count of inventory was taken every December 31.

1. Compute the corrected income before taxes for each year.
2. By what amount did the total income before taxes change for the two years combined?
3. Assume all errors were found in February 2015, just after the books were closed for 2014. What journal entry would be made? Martin uses a periodic inventory system.

Exercise 9-54

Correction of LIFO Inventory

The Manwaring Products Company's inventory record appears below.

	Purchases		Sales
	Quantity	Unit Cost	Quantity
2013	8,200	$4.30	5,800
2014	8,900	4.80	9,200
2015	6,800	5.10	6,300

The company uses a LIFO cost flow assumption. It reported ending inventories as follows for its first three years of operations:

2013	$10,320
2014	9,630
2015	12,120

Determine if the Manwaring Products Company has reported its inventory correctly. Assuming that 2015 accounts are not yet closed, make any necessary correcting entries.

Exercise 9-55

Inventory Turnover

The Rigby Supplement Company showed the following data in its financial statements.

	2015	2014
Cost of goods sold	$1,400,000	$1,125,000
Beginning inventory	275,000	175,000
Ending inventory	405,000	275,000

1. Compute the number of days' sales in average inventory for both 2014 and 2015. What can you infer from these numbers?
2. How would you interpret the answer to (1) if this company were in the business of selling fresh fruits and vegetables? What if the company sold real estate?

E X P A N D E D   M A T E R I A L

Exercise 9-56

Retail Inventory Method

The Evening Out Clothing Store values its inventory using the retail inventory method. The following data are available for the month of November 2015:

	Cost	Retail
Inventory, November 1	$ 53,800	$ 80,000
Purchases	154,304	220,000
Sales		244,000

Compute the estimated inventory at November 30, 2015, assuming:
1. FIFO
2. LIFO
3. Average cost

Exercise 9-57

Retail Inventory Method

The Help-U-Succeed Bookstore recently received a shipment of accounting textbooks from the publisher. Following the receipt of the shipment, the FASB issued a major new accounting standard that related directly to the contents of one chapter of the text. Portions of this chapter became "obsolete" immediately as a result of the FASB's action. In order to sell the books, the bookstore marked down the selling price and offered a separate supplement covering the new standard, which was provided at no cost by the publisher. Information relating to the cost and selling price of the text for the month of September is given below.

	Cost	Retail
Beginning inventory	$ 2,400	$ 3,000
Purchases	27,000	36,000
Freight-in	1,800	
Markdowns		2,600
Sales		31,200

Based on the data given, compute the estimated inventory at the end of the month using the retail inventory method and assuming:

1. LCM valuation
2. Average cost valuation

Exercise 9-58

Retail Inventory Method

Carmel Department Store uses the retail inventory method. On December 31, 2015, the following information relating to the inventory was gathered:

	Cost	Retail
Inventory, January 1, 2015	$ 26,550	$ 45,000
Sales		430,000
Purchases	309,000	435,000
Purchase discounts	4,200	
Freight-in	5,250	
Markups		30,000
Markdowns		40,000
Sales discounts		5,000

Compute the ending inventory value at December 31, 2015, using the:

1. Average cost method
2. Lower-of-cost-or-market method

Exercise 9-59

Computing Inventory Using LIFO Pools

Miller Mfg. has one LIFO pool. Information relating to the products in this pool is as follows:

Beginning inventory, January 1	60 units @ $10 each
Purchase, February 12	45 units @ $12 each
Purchase, February 28	75 units @ $18 each
Purchase, March 15	65 units @ $12.50 each
Sales for the first quarter	135 units

Compute the ending LIFO inventory value for the first quarter assuming new layers are valued based on:

1. A FIFO assumption
2. A LIFO assumption
3. An average cost assumption

Exercise 9-60

Dollar-Value LIFO Inventory Method

The Wernli Manufacturing Company manufactures a single product. The managers, Brandon and Chris Wernli, decided on December 31, 2012, to adopt the dollar-value LIFO inventory method. The inventory value on that date using the newly adopted dollar-value LIFO method was $700,000. Additional information follows:

Date	Inventory at Year-End Prices	Year-End Price Index
Dec. 31, 2013	$803,000	1.10
Dec. 31, 2014	806,400	1.12
Dec. 31, 2015	894,000	1.20

Compute the inventory value at December 31 of each year using the dollar-value method, assuming incremental layers are valued at year-end prices.

Exercise 9-61

Dollar-Value LIFO Inventory Method

Jennifer Inc. adopted dollar-value LIFO on December 31, 2012. Data for 2012–2015 follow:

Inventory and index on the adoption date, December 31, 2012:

Dollar-value LIFO inventory	$250,000
Price index at year-end (the base year)	1.00

Inventory information in succeeding years:

Date	Inventory at Year-End Prices	Year-End Price Index	Average Price Index
Dec. 31, 2013	$314,720	1.12	1.04
Dec. 31, 2014	361,800	1.20	1.14
Dec. 31, 2015	353,822	1.27	1.20

1. Compute the inventory value at December 31 of each year under the dollar-value method, assuming new layers are valued using the average price index.
2. Compute the inventory value at December 31, 2015, assuming that dollar-value procedures were adopted at December 31, 2013, rather than in 2012. The beginning layer is the December 31, 2013, balance.

Exercise 9-62

Dollar-Value LIFO Retail Method

On February 15, 2016, Rooker, Madras & Associates compiled the following information concerning inventory for five years. It used the dollar-value LIFO retail inventory method.

Date	Year-End Price Index at Retail	Incremental Layer Index	Incremental Cost Percentage	Inventory
Dec. 31, 2011	1.00	1.00	71%	$155,000
Dec. 31, 2012	1.04	1.02	72	188,600
Dec. 31, 2013	1.14	1.09	64	192,500
Dec. 31, 2014	1.12	1.11	63	194,200
Dec. 31, 2015	1.16	1.12	67	195,800

Compute the inventory cost at the end of each year under the dollar-value LIFO retail method. (*Note:* Round all dollar amounts to the nearest dollar.)

Exercise 9-63

Loss on Purchase Commitments

On October 1, 2015, Sloan Oil Inc. entered into a six-month, $650,000 purchase commitment for a supply of oil. On December 31, 2015, the market value of oil had fallen to $552,500. Make the journal entries necessary on December 31, 2015, and on March 31, 2016, assuming that the market value of the inventory on March 31 is $430,000.

Exercise 9-64

Foreign Currency Purchase

Wittenbecher's, a German company that supplies your firm with a necessary raw material, recently shipped 15,000 units of the material to your production facility.

1. Prepare the necessary journal entries to record the purchase of the goods and the subsequent payment 30 days later if the selling price on the invoice is $3 per unit.
2. Prepare the necessary journal entries to record the purchase of the goods and the subsequent payment 30 days later if the selling price on the invoice is 6 euros per unit. On the date of purchase, 1 euro is worth $0.50, and the rate on the date of payment is $0.60.

Exercise 9-65

Foreign Currency Purchase

Kyoto Manufacturing produces automobile mufflers, which are then sent to the United States where they are installed in domestically built cars. Truck Inc., a U.S. auto company, received a shipment of mufflers on December 15, 2014. The mufflers were subsequently paid for on January 30, 2015. The invoice was denominated in Korean won and totaled 4,500,000 won. The number of Korean won required to purchase 1 U.S. dollar fluctuated as follows:

	Exchange Rates
December 15, 2014	1,000
December 31, 2014	900
January 30, 2015	880

Provide the necessary journal entries for Truck Inc. to record the above transactions assuming Truck Inc.'s fiscal year-end is December 31.

Routine
Activities
of a Business

CHAPTER 10

Investments in Noncurrent Operating Assets—Acquisition

Learning Objectives

1. Identify those costs to be included in the acquisition cost of different types of noncurrent operating assets.

2. Properly account for noncurrent operating asset acquisitions using various special arrangements, including deferred payment, self-construction, and acquisition of an entire company.

3. Separate costs into those that should be expensed immediately and those that should be capitalized, and understand the accounting standards for research and development and oil and gas exploration costs.

4. Recognize intangible assets acquired separately, as part of a basket purchase, and as part of a business acquisition.

5. Discuss the pros and cons of recording noncurrent operating assets at their fair values.

6. Use the fixed asset turnover ratio as a general measure of how efficiently a company is using its property, plant, and equipment.

Jerry Jones didn't win many friends in Texas when one of his first acts after buying the Dallas Cowboys in 1989 was to fire Tom Landry, who had been the head coach of the Cowboys ever since the team entered the NFL. Jones became even less popular when the Cowboys lost 15 of 16 games in their first year under new head coach Jimmy Johnson.[1] In those days, the Cowboys stunk as a football team but looked like a pretty shrewd business investment. When Jones, an Arkansas oil man, purchased the Cowboys for $150 million, he acquired a diverse array of assets. These assets included miscellaneous football equipment, stadium leases, radio and TV broadcast rights, cable TV rights, luxury stadium suites, player contracts, a lease on the Cowboys' luxurious Valley Ranch training facility, and the Cowboys' NFL franchise rights.

Allocating the purchase price among these assets and defining their useful lives were difficult and

[1] William P. Barrett, "Maybe They Should Let Jerry Play," *Forbes*, February 19, 1990, p. 140.

Exhibit 10-1 | Time Line of the Dallas Cowboys' Franchise Value, 1991–2012

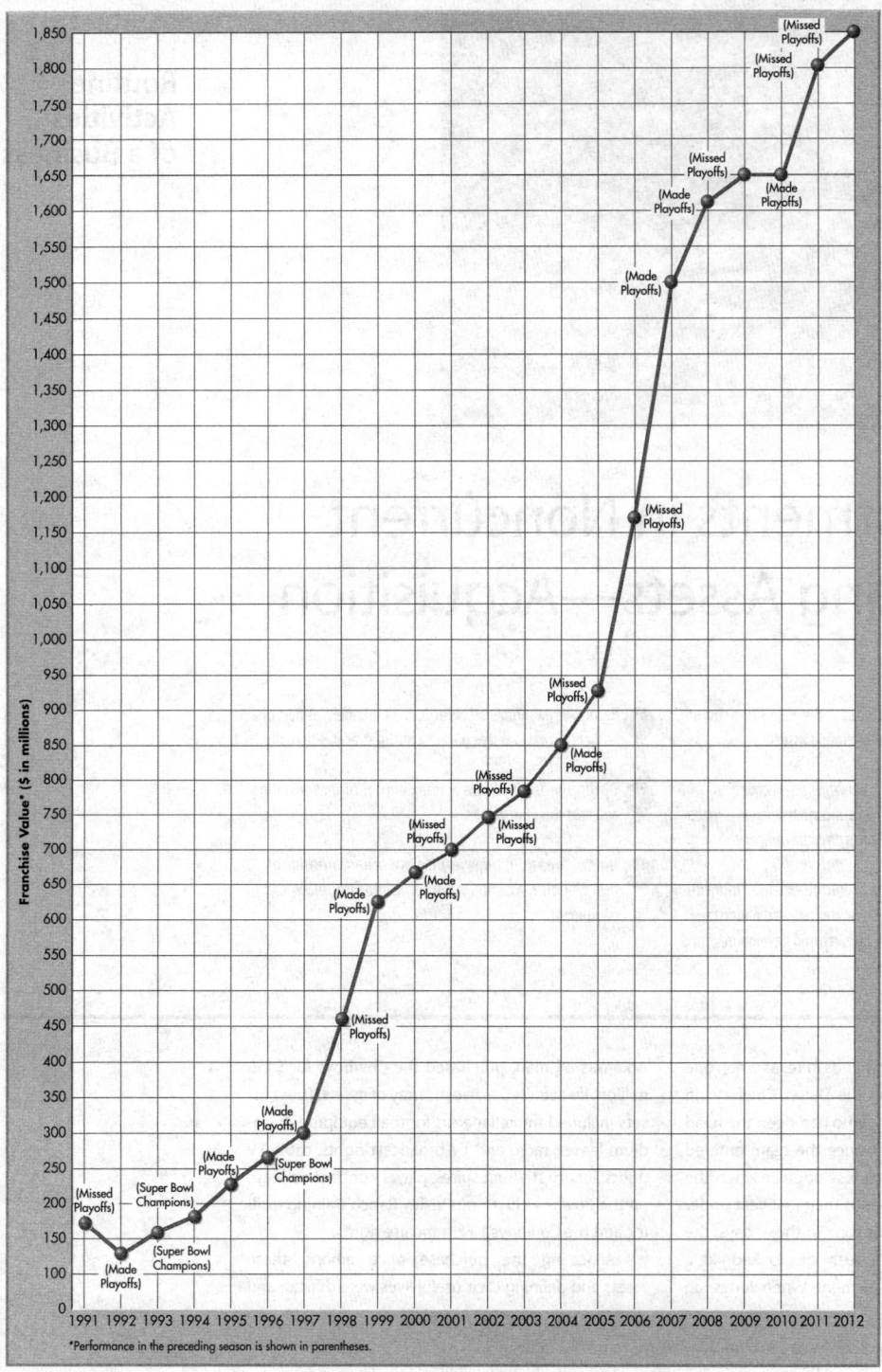

*Performance in the preceding season is shown in parentheses.

© Cengage Learning 2014

strategic tasks. When H. R. "Bum" Bright, Jones' predecessor, bought the Dallas Cowboys for $85 million in 1984, he was able to allocate half the purchase price to players' contracts. These were amortizable assets that, for tax purposes, were written off over four years.[2] Jones received a similar tax break when he acquired the Cowboys.

But entrepreneurs like Jerry Jones don't get rich by relying solely on depreciation tax breaks. Jones quickly set about putting the Cowboys' finances back in the black—in 1988, the Cowboys had lost $9.5 million. Jones encouraged the team's treasurer to look for ways to cut expenses—renegotiate insurance policy premiums, seek competitive bids for printing tickets and providing training room supplies, and remove the floodlights from the parking lot of the training center. Jones also moved to increase revenues by signing leases for 99 unleased luxury boxes (generating an extra $8.5 million per year in revenue) and then building an additional 68 luxury boxes. By 1992, the Cowboys were again profitable with net income of $20.6 million.[3]

The on-field performance of the Cowboys matched their financial success. In 1990, the Cowboys improved their record to 7 and 9, and in 1991 they made the playoffs, advancing to the second round. The Cowboys' return to glory was capped in January 1993 when they returned to the Super Bowl for the first time since 1978 and routed the Buffalo Bills, 52–17. In January 1996, the Cowboys became the first NFL franchise to win three Super Bowls in a four-year time period. The subsequent so-so on-field performance of the team (it has not been back to the Super Bowl since 1996 and made the playoffs just seven times from 1996 through 2012, winning a total of just two playoff games in that span) has not seemed to hurt its financial performance. (See Exhibit 10-1.) In a 2011 estimate by *Forbes*, the Cowboys were rated the most valuable sports franchise in North America (tied with baseball's New York Yankees) with an estimated value of $1.85 billion; the most valuable sports team in the world, at $1.9 billion, is the English soccer team Manchester United.[4]

1. From an accounting standpoint, what difficult asset valuation exercise is necessary when buying an entire business such as the Dallas Cowboys?

2. Why do buyers of a sports franchise wish to allocate as much of the purchase price as possible to the asset "players' contracts"?

Answers to these questions can be found on page 10-41.

Many billions of dollars are invested each year in new property, plant, and equipment and increasingly in intangible assets as well. A time line of the business and accounting issues associated with property, plant, and equipment is shown in Exhibit 10-2.

One of the keys to successful business is correctly choosing which long-term assets to buy. Capital budgeting and discounted cash flow analysis are essential elements in making the best choices. In addition to the difficult financial decisions surrounding long-term assets, many accounting questions are introduced when long-term items are acquired. These accounting issues include the following:

- Which costs should be capitalized as assets, and which ones should be expensed?
- What costs should be included in the acquisition cost of a long-term asset?
- How should intangible assets be recorded?
- At what amounts should long-term assets be recorded when the financing of the purchase is more complex than a simple cash payment?
- How should expenditures made subsequent to acquisition be recorded?
- What recognition should be given to changes in the market value of long-term assets?

This chapter discusses these general issues and describes many of the historic controversies that have led to changes in the accounting standards over the years. The chapter also discusses

---

[2] Hal Lancaster, "Football Team's Sale Is Strictly Business," *The Wall Street Journal*, April 18, 1989, p. B1.
[3] David Whitford, "America's Owner," *Inc.*, December 1993, p. 102.
[4] Go to **http://www.forbes.com** and look under "Lists" for the current valuation of professional sports franchises.

Exhibit 10-2 | Time Line of Business and Accounting Issues Involved with Long-Term Operating Assets

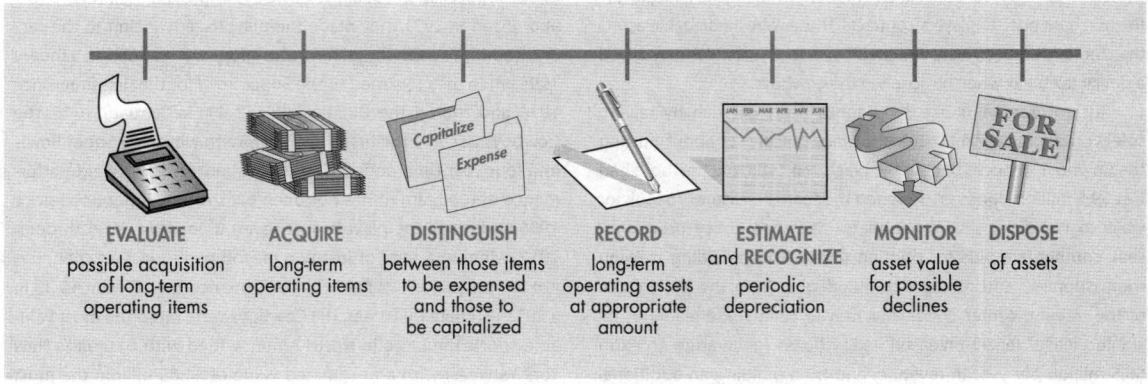

© Cengage Learning 2014

the controversial decision by the FASB to require all research and development costs to be expensed immediately (a decision that may soon be revised in order to harmonize with the international standard), the embarrassing flip-flop the FASB was forced to make on oil and gas accounting, the historical roots of the capitalization of interest, and the question of historical cost versus current cost. Chapter 11 will address the important issues of recognizing depreciation on long-term operating assets, recording impairment losses when asset values have significantly declined, and recording the disposal of long-term operating assets.

What Costs Are Included in Acquisition Cost?

LO1 学习目标1
确认各种类型非流动性经营资产的购买成本。

1 Identify those costs to be included in the acquisition cost of different types of noncurrent operating assets.

Noncurrent operating assets are recorded initially at cost—the original bargained or cash sales price. In theory, the maximum price a company should be willing to pay for an operating asset is the present value of the net benefit the company expects to obtain from the use and final disposition of the asset. In a competitive economy, the market value or cost of an asset at acquisition is assumed to reflect the present value of its future benefits.

The cost of property includes not only the original purchase price or equivalent value but also any other expenditures required in obtaining and preparing the asset for its intended use. Any taxes, freight, installation, and other expenditures related to the acquisition should be included in the asset's cost. Postacquisition costs—costs incurred after the asset is placed into service—are usually expensed rather than added to the acquisition cost. Exceptions to this general rule apply to some major replacements or improvements and will be discussed later in the chapter.

Although most noncurrent operating asset categories have similar acquisition costs, over time accounting practice has identified some specific costs that are included for different asset categories. Exhibits 10-3 and 10-4 summarize the types of costs normally included as acquisition costs for each major noncurrent asset category.

> **Caution**
> Classification of an asset as a noncurrent operating asset depends on how management intends to use the asset. For example, land held for long-term investment purposes is not an operating asset; land held for resale within a year is a current asset.

Exhibit 10-3 | Acquisition Costs of Tangible Noncurrent Operating Assets

Land	Realty used for business purposes.	COST: Purchase price, commissions, legal fees, escrow fees, surveying fees, clearing and grading costs, street and water line assessments.
Land improvements	Items such as landscaping, paving, and fencing that improve the usefulness of property.	COST: Cost of improvements, including expenditures for materials, labor, and overhead.
Buildings	Structures used to house business operations.	COST: Purchase price, commissions, reconditioning costs.
Equipment	Assets used in the production of goods or in providing services. Examples include automobiles, trucks, machinery, patterns and dies, and furniture and fixtures.	COST: Purchase price, taxes, freight, insurance, installation, and any expenditures incurred in preparing the asset for its intended use (e.g., reconditioning and testing costs).

© Cengage Learning 2014

Exhibit 10-4 | Acquisition Costs of Goodwill and Other Intangible Assets

Patent	An exclusive right granted by a national government that enables an inventor to control the manufacture, sale, or use of an invention. In the United States, legal life is 20 years from patent application date.	COST: Purchase price, filing and registry fees, cost of subsequent litigation to protect right. Does not include internal research and development costs.
Trademark	An exclusive right granted by a national government that permits the use of distinctive symbols, labels, and designs (e.g., McDonald's Golden Arches, Nike's Swoosh®, Apple Computer's name and logo). Legal life is virtually unlimited.	COST: Same as patent.
Copyright	An exclusive right granted by a national government that permits an author to sell, license, or control his or her work. In the United States, copyrights expire 70 years after the death of the author.	COST: Same as patent.
Franchise agreement	An exclusive right or privilege received by a business or individual to perform certain functions or sell certain products or services.	COST: Expenditures made to purchase the franchise. Legal fees and other costs incurred in obtaining the franchise.
Acquired customer list	A list or database containing customer information such as name, address, past purchases, and so forth. Companies that originally develop such a list often sell or lease it to other companies unless prohibited by customer confidentiality agreements.	COST: Purchase price when acquired from another company. Costs to internally develop a customer list are expensed as incurred.
Goodwill	Miscellaneous intangible resources, factors, and conditions that allow a company to earn above normal income with its identifiable net assets. Goodwill is recorded only when a business entity is acquired by a purchase.	COST: Portion of purchase price that exceeds the sum of the current market value for all identifiable net assets, both tangible and intangible.

Some of these illustrations are taken from FASB ASC Topic 805 (Business Combinations).

© Cengage Learning 2014

Tangible Assets

土地是不计提折旧的资产，归属于它的成本应该是与土地无限寿命直接相关的支出。

Land Because land is a nondepreciable asset, costs assigned to it should be those costs that directly relate to land's unlimited life. Together with clearing and grading costs, costs of removing unwanted structures from newly acquired land are considered part of the cost to prepare the land for its intended use and are added to its purchase price. Government assessments for water lines, sewers, roads, and other such items are considered part of the land's

Five Largest Land Accounts[5] 2006 (in millions)	
Wal-Mart	$18,612
Home Depot	8,355
MGM Mirage	7,905
Peabody Energy	7,127
Lowe's	5,496

Five Largest Building Accounts 2006 (in millions)	
Wal-Mart	$64,052
AES (electricity generation and distribution)	23,977
McDonald's	21,682
Verizon	19,207
Target	16,110

Five Largest Equipment Accounts 2006 (in millions)	
Verizon	$176,369
Qwest Communication	40,249
Dow Chemical	33,457
Intel	29,482
IBM	27,585

Five Largest Total Intangible Asset Accounts 2006 (in millions)	
AT&T	$127,397
Time Warner	92,806
Procter & Gamble	89,027
General Electric	83,928
Bank of America	78,129

cost because maintenance of these items is the responsibility of the government; thus, to the landowner, they have unlimited life. These types of improvements are distinguished from similar costs for landscaping, parking lots, and interior sidewalks that are installed by the owner and must be replaced over time. The improvements that owners are responsible for are generally classified as land improvements and depreciated.

Buildings The cost of purchased buildings includes any reconditioning costs necessary before occupancy. Because self-constructed buildings have many unique costs, a separate discussion of self-constructed assets is included later in this chapter.

Equipment Equipment costs include freight and insurance charges while the equipment is in transit and any expenditures for testing and installation. Costs for reconditioning purchased used equipment are also part of the asset cost.

Intangible Assets

Intangible assets are defined as those assets (not including financial assets) that lack physical substance. Many intangible assets arise from contractual or governmental rights. A well-known example of this type of intangible asset is the right to operate a taxicab in a metropolitan area, such as New York City. Although this right is evidenced by a physical object, the taxicab medallion, it is the legal right itself that is valuable. Other intangible assets are not created by a specific contract or legal right. The existence of these intangibles is evidenced by the fact that they are bought, sold, or licensed, either separately or in conjunction with a broader assortment of assets. A good example of this type of intangible is a customer list. Magazine subscription companies, Web travel services, and real estate listing services all generate substantial revenues by selling or "leasing" their customer lists. In addition, a purchaser must pay a premium when buying an existing business location because of the value of the customer list (and customer relationships) that is tied to the business; the value of this premium should be reported as a separate intangible asset.

The most important distinction in intangible assets for accounting purposes is between those intangible assets that are internally generated and those that are externally purchased. This distinction is important because the transfer of externally purchased intangible assets in an arm's-length market transaction provides reliable evidence that the intangibles have probable future economic benefit. Such reliable evidence does not exist for most internally generated intangibles. Accordingly, most costs associated with generating and maintaining internally generated intangibles are expensed as incurred.[6] Only the actual legal and filing costs are included as part of the intangible asset cost for these internally developed items. Any costs to defend the rights in court are added to the intangible asset cost if the action is successful. If it is not successful, all asset costs related to the rights are written off as expenses.

Most externally obtained intangible assets arise in transactions involving other assets. For example, the purchase of the tangible assets of a factory building and its associated machinery also might involve the acquisition of the intangible assets of the operating permit for the factory, the water rights tied to the property, and the customer relationships developed by the prior factory owner. Accounting for this kind of "basket purchase" of assets will be discussed later in the chapter. A short description of some of the common types of intangible assets follows.

Trademark A trademark is a distinctive name, symbol, or slogan that distinguishes a product or service from similar products or services. Well-known examples include

---
[5] Standard & Poor's *COMPUSTAT*.
[6] FASB ASC paragraph 350-20-25-3.

> **FYI**
>
> The original Coca-Cola bottling franchise sold for $1.

Coke®, Windows®, Yahoo!®, and the Nike Swoosh®. As shown in Exhibit 10-10 later in the chapter, the value of the Coca-Cola trademark was estimated in 2011 to be almost $72 billion. Because the Coca-Cola trademark is an internally generated intangible asset, it is not reported in **The Coca-Cola Company**'s balance sheet. However, the company has purchased other trademarks (such as Minute Maid®), with a total cost of $6.4 billion; these are reported in The Coca-Cola Company's balance sheet, as shown in Chapter 3.

Franchises Franchise operations have become so common in everyday life that we often don't realize we are dealing with them. In fact, these days it is difficult to find a nonfranchise business in a typical shopping mall. When a business obtains a franchise, the recorded cost of the franchise includes any sum paid specifically for the franchise right as well as legal fees and other costs incurred in obtaining it. Although the value of a franchise at the time of its acquisition may be substantially in excess of its cost, the amount recorded should be limited to actual outlays. For example, approximately 81% of **McDonald's** locations are operated under franchise agreements. A McDonald's franchisee must contribute an initial cash amount of around $500,000, which is used to buy some of the equipment and signs and to pay the initial franchise fee. The value of a McDonald's franchise alone is much more than $500,000, but the franchisee would only record a franchise asset in his or her financial statements equal to the cost (not value) of the franchise. However, if a franchise right is included when one company purchases another company, presumably the entire value is included in the purchase price, and the fair value attributable to the franchise right is recorded as an intangible asset in the acquirer's books.

Order Backlog To some companies, especially capital equipment manufacturers, the order backlog is a key economic asset. The *order backlog* is the amount of orders the company has received for equipment that has not yet been produced or delivered. Note that these orders do not constitute sales because they do not satisfy the revenue recognition requirement that the product be completed and shipped. However, this order backlog does represent future valuable economic activity, and the contractual right to these backlogged orders constitutes an important intangible asset. In its 2011 10-K filing, **Boeing** reported the following about its order backlog:

Contractual Backlog (unaudited, in millions) Years ended December 31,	2011	2010	2009
Contractual backlog:			
Commercial Airplanes	$293,303	$255,591	$250,476
Boeing Defense, Space & Security:			
Boeing Military Aircraft	$ 24,085	$ 25,094	$ 26,354
Network & Space Systems	9,056	9,586	7,746
Global Services & Support	13,213	13,684	11,924
Total Boeing Defense, Space & Security	$ 46,354	$ 48,364	$ 46,024
Total contractual backlog	$339,657	$303,955	$296,500

As with other intangible assets, this internally generated order backlog would not be recognized as an intangible asset on Boeing's balance sheet. However, if another company were to buy Boeing, part of the purchase price would be identified with the economic value of the order backlog, and a corresponding intangible asset would be recognized in the books of the acquiring company.

Goodwill Goodwill represents the business contacts, reputation, functioning systems, staff camaraderie, and industry experience that make a business much more than just a collection of assets. As mentioned earlier, if these factors are the result of a contractual right or are associated with intangibles that can be bought and sold separately, the value of the factor should be reported as a separate intangible asset. In essence, goodwill is a residual number, the value of all of the synergies of a functioning business that cannot be specifically identified with any other intangible factor. Goodwill is recognized only when it is purchased as part of the acquisition of another company. In other words, a company's own goodwill, its homegrown goodwill, is not recognized. Goodwill will be defined and discussed more in depth later in the chapter.

> **FYI**
> The most important recent development in accounting for intangibles is the FASB's emphasis on companies reporting separate amounts for all of the individual intangible assets that can be identified. Previously, these assets were typically tossed in with goodwill.

Acquisitions Other Than Simple Cash Transactions

LO2 学习目标2
正确做出各种特别方式（包括延期支付、自建和企业合并）下非流动性经营资产取得的会计处理。

② Properly account for noncurrent operating asset acquisitions using various special arrangements, including deferred payment, self-construction, and acquisition of an entire company.

When an asset is purchased for cash, the acquisition is simply recorded at the amount of cash paid, including all outlays relating to its purchase and preparation for intended use. Assets can be acquired under a number of other arrangements, however, some of which present special problems relating to the cost to be recorded. The acquisition of assets is discussed under the following headings:

1. Basket purchase
2. Deferred payment
3. Leasing
4. Exchange of nonmonetary assets
5. Acquisition by issuing securities
6. Self-construction
7. Acquisition by donation or discovery
8. Acquisition of an asset with significant restoration costs at retirement
9. Acquisition of an entire company

Basket Purchase

basket purchase
一篮子购买

In some purchases, a number of assets may be acquired in a basket purchase for one lump sum. For example, the opening scenario of this chapter described how Jerry Jones acquired football equipment, cable TV rights, player contracts, and the Cowboys' NFL franchise rights when he purchased the Dallas Cowboys. To account for the assets on an individual basis, the total purchase price must be allocated among the individual assets. When part of a purchase price can be clearly identified with specific assets, such a cost assignment should be made and the balance of the purchase price allocated among the remaining assets. When no part of the purchase price can be related to specific assets, the entire amount must be allocated among the different assets acquired. Appraisal values or similar evidence provided by a competent independent authority should be sought to support the allocation.

To illustrate the allocation of a joint asset cost, assume that land, buildings, and equipment are acquired for $160,000. Assume further that a professional appraiser valued each of the assets at the acquisition date. The cost allocation is made as follows:

Assigned to	Appraised Values	Cost Allocation According to Relative Appraised Values	Cost Assigned to Individual Assets
Land	$ 56,000	56,000/200,000 × $160,000	$ 44,800
Buildings	120,000	120,000/200,000 × $160,000	96,000
Equipment	24,000	24,000/200,000 × $160,000	19,200
	$200,000		$160,000

The entry to record this acquisition, assuming a cash purchase, is as follows:

```
Land .............................................................. 44,800
Buildings ......................................................... 96,000
Equipment ........................................................ 19,200
    Cash ......................................................................... 160,000
```

This cost allocation of a basket purchase price is not merely a theoretical exercise. Some assets in the group may be depreciable, others nondepreciable. Depreciable assets may have different useful lives. Periodic depreciation expense can be significantly impacted by the proportion of the purchase price that is allocated to assets with relatively long useful lives.

Deferred Payment

The acquisition of real estate or other property frequently involves deferred payment of all or part of the purchase price. The buyer signs a note or a mortgage that specifies the terms of settlement of the obligation. The debt contract may call for one payment at a given future date or a series of payments at specified intervals. Interest charged on the unpaid balance of the contract should be recognized as an expense.

To illustrate the accounting for a deferred payment purchase contract, assume that land is acquired on January 2, 2015, for $100,000; $35,000 is paid at the time of purchase, and the balance is to be paid in semiannual installments of $5,000 plus interest on the unpaid principal at an annual rate of 10%. Entries for the purchase and for the first payment on the contract follow.

> **Caution**
>
> In this example, each semiannual payment declines since the interest is calculated on a declining balance in Notes Payable. For example, on January 1, 2016, the total payment would be just $8,000 ($5,000 + $3,000 interest). Alternatively, a contract can provide for a constant payment, or annuity. With an annuity, the amount applied to the note principal increases (and the Interest Expense decreases) each period as the liability decreases.

Transaction	Entry		
January 2, 2015	Land..........................	100,000	
Purchased land for $100,000, paying $35,000 down, the balance to be paid in semiannual payments of $5,000 plus interest at 10%.	Cash.......................		35,000
	Notes Payable		65,000
June 30, 2015	Interest Expense..............	3,250	
Made first payment. Amount of payment: $5,000 + $3,250 (5% of $65,000) = $8,250	Notes Payable................	5,000	
	Cash.......................		8,250

在这个例子中，合同明确规定了购买价格和未支付余额的给定利率；有时，合同只简单提供了支付金额和方式，而没有涉及利息或提供一个在市场中不合理的给定利率。在这种情形下，以票据、销售价格、资产成本、商品和服务交换票据的成本应该按资产、商品、服务的公允价值或票据的当期市场价值（可明确认定）记录。

In the preceding example, the contract specified both a purchase price and interest at a stated rate on the unpaid balance. Sometimes, however, a contract may simply provide for a payment or series of payments without reference to interest or may provide for a stated interest rate that is unreasonable in relation to the market. In these circumstances, the note, sales price, and cost of the property, goods, or services exchanged for the note should be recorded at the fair value of the property, goods, or services or at the current market value of the note, whichever value is more clearly determinable.[7] The following example illustrates the accounting by the purchaser in this circumstance.

Assume that certain equipment, which has a cash price of $50,000, is acquired under a deferred payment contract. The contract specifies a down payment of $15,000 plus seven annual payments of $7,189 each, or a total price, including interest, of $65,323. Although not stated, the effective interest rate implicit in this contract is 10%, the rate that discounts the annual payments of $7,189 to a present value of $35,000, the cash price less the down payment.[8] If the fair value of the asset varies from the contract price because of delayed payments, the difference should be recorded as a discount (contra liability) and amortized over the life of the contract using the implicit or effective interest rate. Using the earlier example, the entries to record the purchase, the amortization of the discount for the first two years, and the first two payments would be as follows:

Transaction	Entry		
January 2, 2015	Equipment.....................	50,000	
Purchased equipment with a cash price of $50,000 for $15,000 down plus seven annual payments of $7,189 each, or a total contract price of $65,323.	Discount on Notes Payable	15,323	
	Notes Payable		50,323
	Cash.........................		15,000
December 31, 2015	Notes Payable.................	7,189	
Made first payment of $7,189. Amortization of debt discount: $50,323 − $15,323 = $35,000 10% × $35,000 = $3,500	Cash.........................		7,189
	Interest Expense................	3,500	
	Discount on Notes Payable...		3,500

[7] FASB ASC paragraph 835-30-25-10.
[8] As illustrated in the Time Value of Money Review Module, the effective or implicit interest rate may be computed as follows:
    Business calculator keystrokes:
    First toggle to make sure that the payments are assumed to occur at the end (END) of the period.
    The difference between the cash price and the down payment is $35,000.
    $PV = (\$35,000); N = 7; PMT = \$7,189 \rightarrow I = 10.00\%$.
Additional examples of computing an implicit rate of interest are presented in the Module.

Transaction	Entry		
December 31, 2016	Notes Payable.................	7,189	
Made second payment of $7,189. Amortization of debt discount: 10% × $31,311* = $3,131	Cash........................		7,189
	Interest Expense...............	3,131	
	Discount on Notes Payable...		3,131

$*\$50{,}323 - \$7{,}189 = \$43{,}134$ Notes payable
$\$15{,}323 - \$3{,}500 = \underline{11{,}823}$ Discount on notes payable
$\underline{\$31{,}311}$ Present value of notes payable at end of first year

> **Caution**
> The account Discount on Notes Payable is a contra liability account and is reported as an offset to Notes Payable. It represents that portion of the remaining payments on the note that will be for interest.

When there is no established cash price for the property, goods, or services and there is no stated rate of interest on the contract, or the stated rate is unreasonable under the circumstances, an imputed interest rate must be used. The imputed interest rate is an estimate of what interest rate the borrowing company would have to pay on a loan given its creditworthiness and current market interest rates.

Leasing

A lease is a contract whereby one party (the lessee) is granted a right to use property owned by another party (the lessor) for a specified period of time for a specified periodic cost. Most leases are similar in nature to rentals. These leases are called operating leases. However, other leases, referred to as capital leases, are economically equivalent to a sale of the leased asset with the lessor allowing the lessee to pay for the asset over time with a series of "lease" payments. In these circumstances, the lease payments are exactly equivalent to mortgage payments.

operating leases
经营性租赁

> **FYI**
> In this text, the word *amortization* is used to refer to the periodic expensing of the cost of intangible assets and leasehold improvements; depreciation is used for tangible assets.

capital leases
融资性租赁

In such cases, the leased property should be recorded as an asset on the books of the company using the asset (the lessee), not on the books of the company that legally owns the asset (the lessor). The capital lease asset is recorded at the present value of the future lease payments. Because lease accounting is a complex area, an entire chapter (Chapter 15) is devoted to accounting for leases.

Even when a lease is not considered to be the same as a purchase and the periodic payments are recorded as rental expense, certain lease prepayments or improvements to the property by the lessee may be treated as capital expenditures. Because leasehold improvements such as partitions in a building, additions, and attached equipment revert to the owner at the expiration of the lease, they are properly capitalized on the books of the lessee and amortized over the remaining life of the lease. Some lease costs are really expenses of the period and should not be capitalized. These include improvements that are made in lieu of rent; for example, a lessee builds partitions in a leased warehouse for storage of its product, and the lessor allows the lessee to offset the cost against rental expense for the period. These costs should be expensed by the lessee.

Exchange of Nonmonetary Assets

In some cases, an enterprise acquires a new asset by exchanging or trading existing nonmonetary assets.[9] Generally, the new asset should be valued at its fair value or at the fair value of the asset given up, whichever is more clearly determinable.[10] If the nonmonetary asset is used equipment, the fair value of the new asset is generally more clearly determinable and therefore used to record the exchange. If one of the parties in the exchange could have chosen to receive cash instead of the nonmonetary asset, that amount of cash is a good reflection of the fair value of the assets exchanged.

It should be observed that determining the fair value of a new asset can sometimes be difficult. The quoted or list price for an asset is not always a good indicator of the market value and is often higher than the actual cash price for the asset. An inflated list price permits the seller to increase the indicated trade-in allowance for a used asset. The price for which the asset could be sold in a cash transaction is the fair value that should be used to record the acquisition.

To illustrate, assume the sticker on the window of a new car sitting in a dealer's showroom lists a total selling price of $33,500. The sticker includes a base price plus an itemized listing of all the options that have been added. If you, as a buyer, approached the dealer with your old clunker as a trade-in, you might be surprised to be offered $3,000 for a car you know is worth no more than $1,000. If you offered to pay cash for the new car with no trade-in, however, you could probably buy it for approximately $31,500 or the list price reduced by the inflated amount of allowance offered for the trade-in. The fair value of the new asset is thus not the list price of $33,500 but the true cash price of $31,500.

If the nonmonetary asset given up to acquire the new asset is also property or equipment, a sale of property occurs simultaneously with the acquisition. When an exchange of a nonmonetary asset takes place, the use of fair value results in a gain or loss on the disposal of the nonmonetary asset. Under some limited circumstances, a gain may be deferred and recognized (through lower depreciation expense) over the life of the newly acquired asset.[11] Because of the need to first discuss depreciation methods before explaining the accounting for the sale of assets, the full discussion of acquisition and disposal by exchange is covered in Chapter 11.

Acquisition by Issuing Securities

A company may acquire certain property by issuing its own bonds or stocks. When a fair value for the securities can be determined, that value is assigned to the asset; in the absence of a fair value for the securities, the fair value of the asset acquired would be used. To illustrate, assume that a company issues 1,000 shares of $1 par common stock in acquiring land; the stock has a current market price of $45 per share. An entry should be made as follows:

Land	45,000	
Common Stock		1,000
Paid-In Capital in Excess of Par		44,000

When securities do not have an established market value, appraisal of the acquired assets by an independent authority may be required to arrive at an objective determination of their fair value.

As discussed in Chapter 5, purchasing noncurrent assets in exchange for long-term debt and/or stock is an example of a significant noncash transaction. This kind of noncash

---

[9] Monetary assets are those assets whose amounts are fixed in terms of currency, by contract, or otherwise. Examples include cash and accounts receivable. Nonmonetary assets include all other assets, such as inventories, land, buildings, and equipment.
[10] FASB ASC paragraph 845-10-30-1.
[11] FASB ASC paragraph 845-10-30-3.

transaction is not included in the body of the statement of cash flows as an investing or a financing activity. Instead, the transaction, if material, is disclosed separately.

Self-Construction

Sometimes buildings or equipment are constructed by a company for its own use. This may be done to save on construction costs, to utilize idle facilities, or to achieve a higher quality of construction.

Self-Constructed Assets Like purchased assets, these are recorded at cost, including all expenditures incurred to build the asset and make it ready for its intended use. Some considerations in determining the cost of self-constructed assets are discussed in the following sections.

Overhead Chargeable to Self-Construction All costs that can be related to construction should be charged to the assets under construction. There is no question about the inclusion of charges for material and labor directly attributable to the new construction. However, there is a difference of opinion regarding the amount of overhead properly assignable to the construction activity. Some accountants take the position that assets under construction should be charged with no more than the incremental overhead, the increase in a company's total overhead resulting from the special construction activity. Others maintain that overhead should be assigned to construction just as it is assigned to normal operations. This would call for the inclusion of not only the increase in overhead resulting from construction activities but also a pro rata share of the company's fixed overhead. Common practice is to allocate both variable overhead and a pro rata share of fixed overhead to self-construction projects. An illustration of the capitalization of overhead costs is given in the December 31, 2011, 10-K filing of **Gyrodyne Company of America**. The company began in 1946 as a producer of helicopters and has since transitioned to managing real estate operations. Gyrodyne reports, "In addition to land, land development, and construction costs, real estate held for development includes legal, engineering and other related soft development costs, interest, real estate taxes, and related development and construction overhead costs which are capitalized during the development and construction period."

Savings or Loss on Self-Construction When the cost of self-construction of an asset is less than the cost to acquire it through purchase or construction by outsiders, the difference for accounting purposes is not a profit but a savings. The construction is properly reported at its actual cost. The savings will emerge as an increase in net income over the life of the asset as lower depreciation is charged against periodic revenue. Assume, on the other hand, the cost of self-construction is greater than bids originally received for the construction. There is generally no assurance that the asset under alternative arrangements might have been equal in quality to that which was self-constructed. In recording this transaction, just as in recording others, accounts should reflect those courses of action taken, not the alternatives that might have been selected. However, if there is evidence indicating cost has been materially excessive because of construction inefficiencies or failures, the asset should be evaluated for possible recording of an impairment loss. Recognition of impairment losses is discussed in Chapter 11.

Interest During Period of Construction When a construction company bids on a job, the bid includes a charge for interest that will be incurred on funds borrowed to finance the construction. The interest cost is viewed as being an integral part of the cost of construction, just like materials, labor, and equipment rental costs. In a similar way, when a company constructs an asset for its own use, long-standing accounting practice is for the company to capitalize the interest costs incurred to finance the construction.

Capitalization of interest first began with public utilities. Public utilities self-construct a large portion of their assets, so the capitalized interest amount can be very material. More importantly, public utility rates are frequently set by government bodies and are tied to the utility's rate base, which is the utility's book value of assets. The higher the rate base, the higher the utility rates. Accordingly, public utilities have a great incentive to include all possible costs, including capitalized interest, in the reported cost of their self-constructed assets.

Although capitalization of interest began with public utilities, it is now generally accepted accounting practice for all firms that construct assets for their own use. Remember that interest capitalization is not merely a ploy used by utilities to get higher rates; interest is a legitimate cost of construction, and the proper matching of revenues and expenses suggests that interest be deferred and charged over the life of the constructed asset. If buildings or equipment were acquired by purchase rather than by self-construction, a charge for interest during the construction period would be implicit in the purchase price.

Capitalization of interest is required for assets, such as buildings and equipment, that are being self-constructed for an enterprise's own use and assets that are intended to be leased or sold to others that can be identified as discrete projects. These are projects that can be clearly identified as to the assets involved. Interest should not be capitalized for inventories manufactured or produced on a repetitive basis, for assets that are currently being used, or for assets that are idle and are not undergoing activities to prepare them for use. Thus, land that is being held for future development does not qualify for interest capitalization.[12]

Once it is determined that the construction project qualifies for interest capitalization, the amount of interest to be capitalized must be determined. The following basic guidelines govern the computation of capitalized interest:

1. Interest charges begin when the first expenditures are made on the project and continue as long as work continues and until the asset is completed and actually ready for use.
2. The amount of interest to be capitalized is computed using the accumulated expenditures for the project, weighted based on when the expenditures were made during the year. *Expenditures* mean cash disbursements, not accruals.
3. The interest rates to be used in calculating the amount of interest to capitalize are, in the following order:
   (a) Interest rate incurred for any debt specifically incurred for funds used on the project.
   (b) Weighted-average interest rate from all other enterprise borrowings regardless of the use of funds.
4. If the construction period covers more than one fiscal period, accumulated expenditures include prior years' capitalized interest.

The maximum interest that can be capitalized is the total interest accrued for the year.

The following illustration demonstrates the application of these guidelines. Cutler Industries, Inc., has decided to construct a new computerized assembly plant. It is estimated that the construction period will be about 18 months and that the cost of construction will be approximately $6.4 million (excluding capitalized interest). A 12% construction loan for $2 million is obtained on January 1, 2015, at the beginning of construction.

---

[12] FASB ASC paragraph 835-20-15-6.

In addition to the construction loan, Cutler has the following outstanding debt during the construction period:

Five-year notes payable, 11% interest	$3,000,000
Mortgage on other plant, 9% interest	4,800,000

The weighted-average interest rate on this general nonconstruction debt is computed as follows:

Nonconstruction Debt	Principal	Rate	Interest Cost
Notes payable	$3,000,000	11%	$330,000
Mortgage	4,800,000	9	432,000
	$7,800,000	9.8*	$762,000

*Weighted-average rate = $762,000 ÷ $7,800,000 = 9.8% (rounded)

The following expenditures were incurred on the project during 2015.

January 1, 2015	$1,200,000
October 1, 2015	1,800,000

Computation of the amount of interest to be capitalized for 2015 is as follows:

Expenditure Date	Amount	Interest Capitalization Rate	Fraction of the Year Outstanding	Capitalized Interest
January 1, 2015	$1,200,000	12%	12/12	$144,000
October 1, 2015	800,000	12	3/12	24,000
	1,000,000	9.8	3/12	24,500
Total capitalized interest for 2015				$192,500

注意：资本化利息金额只以未偿还时间内的支出为基础计算。1月1日的支出导致整年借款成本的提高，而10月1日的支出只是最后三个月的未偿付成本。如果支出用来偿还负债而非用于在建工程，这种方法可得出免于被资本化的利息总额估计数。

Notice first that capitalized interest is computed only for the amount of time the expenditures were outstanding. The January 1 expenditures caused increased borrowing costs for the entire year, but the October 1 expenditures were outstanding for only the final three months of the year. This approach results in an approximation of the amount of interest that could have been avoided if the expenditures had been used to repay debt instead of being used for the construction project.

This approach also assumes that the most avoidable interest is the interest on the borrowing specifically for the construction project. Accordingly, the interest rate of 12% on the specific construction borrowing is used. However, the amount of that loan is only $2,000,000; expenditures above this $2,000,000 amount could have been used to repay general company debt. Therefore, the October 1 expenditure of $1,800,000 has been split into two pieces—the first $800,000 could have been used to repay the balance of the construction loan ($800,000 = $2,000,000 − $1,200,000), so the amount of avoidable interest is computed using the 12% rate. The remaining $1,000,000 could

> **Stop & Think**
>
> Which ONE of the following describes the financial statement impact of a company neglecting to capitalize interest that should be capitalized?
>
> a) Net income overstated and total assets overstated
> b) Net income understated and total assets overstated
> c) Net income overstated and total assets understated
> d) Net income understated and total assets understated

have been used to repay general company debt, so the weighted-average rate of 9.8% on general borrowing is used.

Finally, recall that the amount of interest capitalized cannot exceed total interest incurred for the year. Total interest incurred during 2015 was as follows:

Debt	Amount	Interest Rate	Annual Interest
Construction loan	$2,000,000	12%	$ 240,000
Notes payable	3,000,000	11%	330,000
Mortgage payable	4,800,000	9%	432,000
Total interest incurred			$1,002,000

Because total interest incurred exceeds the computed amount of interest to be capitalized, the entire indicated amount of $192,500 is capitalized. The journal entry to record total interest incurred by Cutler Industries during 2015 (assuming that all interest was paid in cash) is as follows:

Construction in Progress	192,500	
Interest Expense ($1,002,000 − $192,500)	809,500	
Cash		1,002,000

Assume that additional construction expenditures of $3,200,000 were made on February 1, 2016, and the project was completed on May 31, 2016.

The amount of interest to be capitalized for the year 2016 follows.

Expenditure Date	Amount	Interest Capitalization Rate	Fraction Outstanding of the Year	Capitalized Interest
Accumulated in 2015	$2,000,000	12%	5/12	$100,000
	1,192,500	9.8	5/12	48,694
February 1, 2016	3,200,000	9.8	4/12	104,533
Total capitalized interest for 2016				$253,227

> **FYI**
>
> This is an unusual project indeed! It finished ahead of schedule (in only 17 months), and the actual total cost of construction (excluding capitalized interest) is only $6.2 million, $200,000 less than forecasted.

Avoidable interest in 2016 includes interest on all the loans that could have been repaid with the construction expenditures made in 2015. These expenditures total $3,192,500 ($1,200,000 + $1,800,000 + $192,500) and include interest capitalized in 2015. Interest is capitalized only until May 31 (five months) when construction is completed and the building is ready for use. Because $253,227 is less than the actual annual interest of $1,002,000, the entire indicated amount of $253,227 is capitalized in 2016.

Total recorded cost of the building on May 31, 2016, when it is put into service, is $6,645,727, computed as follows:

Expenditures incurred in 2015	$3,000,000
Interest capitalized in 2015	192,500
Expenditures incurred in 2016	3,200,000
Interest capitalized in 2016	253,227
Total building cost, May 31, 2016	$6,645,727

FASB ASC Subtopic 835-20 (Interest—Capitalization of Interest) requires disclosure of the total interest expense for the year and the amount capitalized. This disclosure can be made either in the body of the income statement or in a note to the statements.

To illustrate these two methods, assume that Cutler Industries reported the 2015 interest information on the income statement and the 2016 interest information in a note.

Cutler Industries, Inc.
Income Statement
For the Year Ended December 31, 2015

Operating income..		$XXX,XXX
Other expenses and losses:		
Total interest incurred...............................	$1,002,000	
Less: Capitalized interest	192,500	809,500
Income before income taxes		$XXX,XXX
Income taxes...		XXX,XXX
Net income		$XXX,XXX

Cutler Industries, Inc.
Financial Statement Notes
For the Year Ended December 31, 2016

Note X—Interest expense. Interest of $253,227 was capitalized in 2016 as part of the cost of construction for the computerized assembly plant in accordance with the requirements of FASB ASC Subtopic 835-20.

The amount of capitalized interest reported for 2011 by several large U.S. companies and its percentage of total interest reported by those companies are displayed in Exhibit 10-5. As you can see, **General Electric** capitalized only an insignificant amount of its $14,595 million in interest during 2011. On the other hand, **ExxonMobil** capitalized more interest than it expensed in 2011.

Exhibit 10-5 | Capitalized Interest for Several Large U.S. Companies in 2011 (in millions of U.S. dollars)

Company	Capitalized Interest	Interest Expense	Capitalized as a Percentage of Total Interest
General Electric	$ 25	$14,570	0.2%
AT&T	162	3,535	4.4
ExxonMobil	593	247	70.6
McDonald's	14.0	492.8	2.8
The Walt Disney Company	91	343	21.0

Complexities arise in computing the amount of interest to capitalize when a company secures new loans in the middle of the year. These complexities and an alternate approach to computing capitalized interest are explained in the Web Material associated with this chapter (www.cengagebrain.com).

Not everyone agrees that interest on funds used to finance the self-construction of assets should be capitalized. In fact, the original FASB vote was only four to three in favor of pre-Codification *SFAS No. 34*, which mandated the capitalization of interest in the United States back in 1979. The changing stance of the IASB and its predecessor, the IASC, perfectly illustrates the split view on interest capitalization. In the original international standard on interest capitalization *(IAS 23)*, companies were allowed to either capitalize (or *capitalise*, to use the international spelling) interest or not, but the company should be consistent in its practice. In a 1989 exposure draft, the IASC then proposed establishing a benchmark treatment requiring interest capitalization. But the revised version of *IAS 23* issued in 1993 said that all interest should be expensed, regardless of how the funds are used, with interest capitalization as an allowable alternative. Finally, in 2007 the IASB revised *IAS 23* again to require, starting on January 1, 2009, that all companies capitalize "borrowing costs" incurred in the construction of a long-term asset. An important difference between this revised version of *IAS 23* and the U.S. standard is that the international standard requires that companies capitalize the *net* amount of interest incurred rather than the *gross* amount. This means that under *IAS 23* a company capitalizes the amount of interest, computed as shown above under the explanation of the U.S. standard, *less* the amount of investment income generated by borrowed construction funds that are temporarily invested before they are needed to pay for construction expenditures. Accordingly, the amount of interest capitalized under the international standard is generally less than the amount that would be capitalized under the U.S. standard.

Acquisition by Donation or Discovery

When property is received through donation, there is no cost that can be used as a basis for its valuation. Even though certain expenditures may have to be made incidental to the gift, these expenditures are generally considerably less than the value of the property. Here cost obviously fails to provide a satisfactory basis for asset valuation.

Property acquired through donation should be appraised and recorded at its fair value. A donation is recognized as a revenue or gain in the period in which it is received.[13] To illustrate, Netty's Ice Cream Parlor is given a donation of land and a building by an eccentric ice cream lover. The entry on Netty's books, using the appraised values of the land and the building, is as follows:

Land..	400,000	
Buildings...	1,500,000	
Revenue or Gain..		1,900,000

Depreciation of an asset acquired by gift should be recorded in the usual manner, the value assigned to the asset providing the basis for the depreciation charge.

If a gift is contingent upon some act to be performed by the recipient, no asset should be reported until the conditions of the gift have been met. At that time, both the increase in assets and the revenue or gain should be recognized in the accounts and in the financial statements.[14]

---

[13] FASB ASC paragraph 958-310-25-1.
[14] FASB ASC paragraph 958-605-25-11.

Publicly traded oil and gas firms are required to disclose the quantity of their proved oil and gas reserves, as well as a forecast of the discounted value of future net cash flows expected to be generated by the reserves.

Occasionally, valuable resources are discovered on land already owned. The discovery greatly increases the value of the property. However, because the cost of the land is not affected by the discovery, it is common practice in the United States to ignore this increase in value. Similarly, the increase in value for assets that change over time, such as growing timber or aging wine, is ignored in common practice in the United States. Failure to recognize these discovery or accretion values ignores the economic reality of the situation and tends to materially understate the assets of the entity. Nevertheless, asset write-ups are generally not allowable under U.S. accounting standards, although they are routine in some other countries. More information on asset write-ups is given later in the chapter.

One exception to the practice of ignoring the value of assets discovered is the supplemental disclosure required regarding oil and gas reserves. Publicly traded oil and gas firms are required to disclose the amount of their proved oil and gas reserves, along with summary data on why the amount of proved reserves changed during the period. In addition, the oil and gas firms are required to disclose a forecast of the discounted value of future net cash flows expected to be generated by the reserves.[15] The oil and gas firms are skeptical about the usefulness of this disclosure as illustrated by this quote from Chevron's 2011 annual report:

FYI

Valuation issues in transactions that are not arm's length can be very difficult. FASB ASC paragraph 845-10-S99-1 requires that when a corporation receives nonmonetary assets as an investment by a shareholder, the assets are recorded by the company at the shareholder's historical cost.

> The information provided does not represent management's estimate of the company's expected future cash flows or value of proved oil and gas reserves. Estimates of proved-reserve quantities are imprecise and change over time as new information becomes available. Moreover, probable and possible reserves, which may become proved in the future, are excluded from the calculations. . . . The calculations . . . should not be relied upon as an indication of the company's future cash flows or value of its oil and gas reserves.[16]

The international standard for recognizing increases in the value of property from growth or discovery is substantially different from U.S. practice. Under *IAS 41*, biological assets, such as cattle, fruit trees, and lumber forests, are recorded in the balance sheet at their fair value (less estimating selling costs) as of the balance sheet date. Increases in this fair value are recognized as gains, and decreases are recognized as losses. Accordingly, under international accounting standards, a lumber company would report

[15] FASB ASC paragraph 932-235-50-2.
[16] Chevron, 2011, 10K Report.

> **FYI**
>
> In 2004, **Royal Dutch/Shell Group** was fined a total of $150 million by U.S. and British authorities for deceptive reporting of its proved oil and gas reserves. The company was forced to reduce its reported oil reserves by 4.47 billion barrels, a reduction of 23%. This reserve restatement knocked about 10% off the market value of the company.

the timber in its forests at fair value (less selling cost) in each balance sheet during, say, the 30-year period the timber is growing. The yearly increases or decreases in fair value would be reported in the income statement as gains or losses. In summary, International Financial Reporting Standards allow, and sometimes require, the recognition of changes in long-term asset values in many more cases than do U.S. standards.

Acquisition of an Asset with Significant Restoration Costs at Retirement

取得长期经营资产的行为在法律上使得企业负有在资产使用结束后支付修复费用的义务。该义务的正确会计处理要求在义务发生时以估计的公允价值记录，其公允价值应加入所获得的长期经营资产的成本中。

Sometimes, the act of acquiring a long-term operating asset legally obligates a company to incur restoration costs in the future when the asset is retired. For example, when an oil exploration firm erects an oil platform to support drilling operations, it becomes legally obligated to dismantle and remove the platform when the drilling is done.[17] Proper accounting for this obligation requires that it be recognized, at its estimated fair value, at the time that it is incurred and that the fair value of the obligation be added to the cost of acquiring the long-term operating asset.

To illustrate the initial recognition of an asset retirement obligation, assume that Bryan Beach Company purchases and erects an oil platform at a total cost of $750,000. The oil platform will be in use for 10 years, at which time Bryan Beach is legally obligated to ensure that the platform is dismantled and removed from the site. Bryan Beach can estimate the fair value of this asset retirement obligation by referring to market prices for the settlement of these obligations or by using present value techniques. If, for example, there are firms that will contract in advance to dismantle and remove an oil platform 10 years from now, Bryan Beach can use the price of those contracts to estimate the fair value of its asset retirement obligation. In this case, assume that no such

> **FYI**
>
> Adding the fair value of asset retirement obligations to the cost of the associated long-term operating asset applies only to normal restoration costs that are unavoidable in the routine use of the asset. Unforeseen restoration costs, such as from a catastrophic toxic waste spill, are accounted for differently. The present value of these catastrophic cleanup costs is expensed in the period in which the unforeseen cost is incurred and the related liability is recognized.

market exists. However, Bryan Beach estimates that it will have to pay $100,000 to have the platform dismantled and removed from the site in 10 years. If the appropriate interest rate to use in computing the present value is 8%,[18] the present value of the $100,000 obligation is computed as follows:

$$FV = \$100{,}000;\ I = 8\%;\ N = 10\ \text{years} \rightarrow \$46{,}319$$

---

[17] This oil platform illustration and the nuclear plant illustration used later are adapted from FASB ASC Section 410-20-55 (Asset Retirement and Environmental Obligations—Asset Retirement Obligations—Implementation Guidance and Illustration).

[18] In FASB ASC paragraphs 410-20-55-13 through 17, the FASB states that the appropriate interest rate to use is the credit-adjusted risk-free rate, meaning the rate on U.S. Treasury securities (typically 5% or less), plus premiums to reflect both the credit standing of the company doing the calculation as well as a "market-risk premium" that a third party would demand for accepting the uncertainties associated with taking on the asset retirement obligation. See the Time Value of Money Review Module of this text for more discussion on present-value calculations.

The journal entries to record the purchase of the oil platform and the recognition of the asset retirement obligation are as follows:

Oil Platform	750,000	
Cash		750,000
Oil Platform	46,319	
Asset Retirement Obligation		46,319

In this oil platform example, the entire asset retirement obligation was created by the initial acquisition and deployment of the long-term operating asset. In other situations, additional asset retirement obligation is created over time. For example, assume that Homer Company constructs and commences operation of a nuclear power plant. Total construction cost is $400,000. The cost of cleaning up the routine contamination caused by the initial stockpile of nuclear material is estimated to be $500,000; this cost will be incurred in 30 years when the plant is decommissioned. Additional contamination will occur each year that the plant is in operation. In its first year of operation, that additional contamination adds $40,000 to the estimated cleanup cost, which will occur after 29 years (because one year has elapsed). The journal entries to record the purchase of the nuclear plant and the recognition of the initial asset retirement obligation (assuming that the appropriate interest rate is 9%) and the additional obligation created after one year are as follows:

Initial Acquisition

Nuclear Plant	400,000	
Cash		400,000
Nuclear Plant	37,686	
Asset Retirement Obligation		37,686

$FV = \$500{,}000; I = 9\%; N = 30 \text{ years} \rightarrow \$37{,}686$

After One Year

Nuclear Plant	3,286	
Asset Retirement Obligation		3,286

$FV = \$40{,}000; I = 9\%; N = 29 \text{ years} \rightarrow \$3{,}286$

The asset retirement cost added to the basis of the nuclear plant would be depreciated over the useful life of the plant. In addition, the amount of the asset retirement obligation would increase each year through the passage of time (because the time until the payment of the restoration costs would be shorter). Accounting for depreciation and the systematic increase in the recorded amount of the asset retirement obligation will be discussed in Chapter 11.

Acquisition of an Entire Company

Instead of buying selected assets from another firm, as in a basket purchase, sometimes a company will buy the entire firm. This is called a *business combination*. The procedures for accounting for a business combination are similar to those used for a basket purchase. The primary difference is that in a business combination the sum of the fair values of the identifiable assets is usually less than the total amount paid to buy the company. As discussed earlier, this excess is called *goodwill* and reflects the value of the synergy of having all of the productive assets together as a functioning unit. The accounting for business combinations and goodwill is discussed in detail later in the chapter when the acquisition of intangible assets is covered.

Capitalize or Expense?

③ Separate costs into those that should be expensed immediately and those that should be capitalized, and understand the accounting standards for research and development and oil and gas exploration costs.

The decision as to whether a given expenditure is an asset or an expense is one of the many areas in which an accountant must exercise judgment. Conceptually, the issue is straightforward: If an expenditure is expected to benefit future periods, it is an asset; otherwise, it is an expense.

In practice, the capitalize-or-expense question is much more difficult. To illustrate, look at the continuum in Exhibit 10-6.

Few people would disagree with the claim that the cost of office supplies used is an expense. Once the supplies are used, they offer no more future benefit. Similarly, the cost of a building clearly should be capitalized because the building will provide economic benefit in future periods. The endpoints of the continuum are easy, but it is the vast middle ground where accountants must exercise their judgment.

The difficulty with making capitalize-or-expense decisions is that many expenditures have some probability of generating future economic benefit, but uncertainty surrounds that benefit. Research and development expenditures are a good example. Companies spend money on research and development because they expect to reap future benefits. However, there is no guarantee that the benefits will materialize. The following sections examine several categories of expenditures to give you practice in analyzing the issues relevant to a capitalize-or-expense decision.

Before examining the conceptual issues, here is one practical note. Many companies establish a lower limit on amounts that will be considered for capitalization to avoid wasting time agonizing about the proper

FYI

This seemingly simple capitalize-or-expense issue blew up in the face of **WorldCom** in 2002 when it was revealed that the company had capitalized $3.8 billion in expenditures that it should have expensed. Uproar over this accounting abuse harmed the company's public image and hastened its bankruptcy, the largest in U.S. history to that time.

Exhibit 10-6 | Expense/Asset Continuum

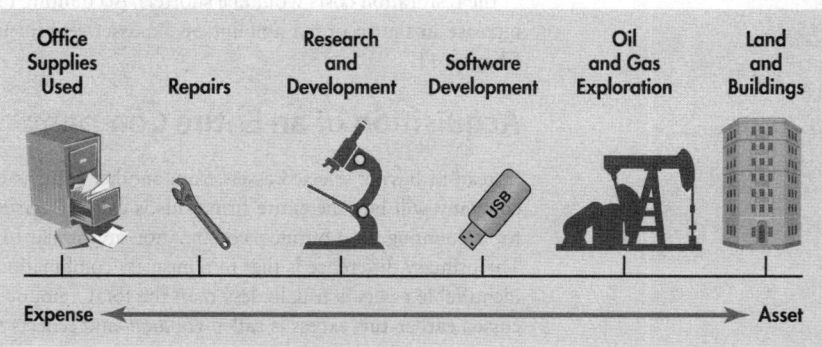

© Cengage Learning 2014

accounting for trivial amounts. Thus, any expenditure under the established limit is always expensed currently even though future benefits are expected from that expenditure. This practice is justified on the grounds of expediency and materiality. Of course, the amount of the limit varies with the size of the company. In the published financial statements of large corporations, for example, amounts are rounded to the nearest million. Detailed accounting for amounts smaller than this will have no impact on the reported numbers. This treatment is acceptable as long as it is consistently applied and no material misstatements arise due to unusual expenditure patterns or other causes.

Postacquisition Expenditures

Over the useful lives of plant assets, regular as well as special expenditures are incurred. Certain expenditures are required to maintain and repair assets; others are incurred to increase their capacity or efficiency or to extend their useful lives. Each expenditure requires careful analysis to determine whether it should be expensed or capitalized.

The words *maintenance, repairs, renewals, replacements, additions, betterments, improvements,* and *rearrangements* are often used in describing expenditures made in the course of asset use. A more systematic way to view these postacquisition expenditures is how they relate to the components of a recorded piece of property, plant, or equipment.[19] A component is a portion of a property, plant, or equipment item that is separately identifiable and for which a separate useful life can be estimated. An example of a component is the heating and cooling system of a building. The acquisition cost of this system can be separately identified, and typically the heating and cooling system has a different life than the building itself. In accounting for postacquisition expenditures, the important consideration is whether the expenditure results in the replacement of an existing component, the addition of a component, or is merely intended to maintain an existing component in working order. Exhibit 10-7 summarizes the accounting for these postacquisition expenditures.

Exhibit 10-7 | Summary of Expenditures Subsequent to Acquisition

Type of Expenditure	Definition	Accounting Treatment
Maintenance and repairs	Normal cost of keeping property in operating condition.	Expense as incurred because the cost is intended to keep an existing component in working order.
Renewals and replacements:		
1. No extension of useful life or increase in future cash flows.	Unplanned replacement. Expenditure needed to fulfill original plans.	Expense as incurred; no new component acquired.
2. Extends useful life or increases future cash flows.	Improvement resulting from replacement with better component.	Replacement of a component. Capitalize the cost of the new component. The remaining book value of the replaced component is added to depreciation expense for the period.
Additions and betterments	Expenditures that add to asset usefulness by either extending life or increasing future cash flows.	Account for as a separate component of the asset with a separate estimated useful life.

© Cengage Learning 2014

[19] AcSEC Exposure Draft, Proposed Statement of Position, "Accounting for Certain Costs and Activities Related to Property, Plant, and Equipment" (New York: American Institute of Certified Public Accountants, June 29, 2001). On April 14, 2004, the FASB met to consider the AcSEC's final proposed Statement of Position (SOP). The Board objected to the release of the SOP, so it was withheld. Among other things, the Board members thought that intercompany differences in defining "components" would result in a lack of comparability of financial statements. The FASB may undertake a review of the accounting for property, plant, and equipment in conjunction with its general effort to increase international convergence. Ultimately, the concept of a "component" of a certain item of property, plant, or equipment may not be retained by the FASB. However, the "component" approach is part of International Financial Reporting Standards; see *IAS 16*, par. 43.

Maintenance and Repairs Expenditures to maintain plant assets in good operating condition are referred to as maintenance. Among these are expenditures for painting, lubricating, and adjusting equipment. Maintenance expenditures are ordinary, recurring, and do not improve the asset or add to its life; therefore, they are recorded as expenses when they are incurred.

Expenditures to restore assets to good operating condition upon their breakdown or to restore and replace broken parts are referred to as repairs. These are ordinary and recurring expenditures that benefit only current operations; thus, they also are charged to expense immediately.

Renewals and Replacements Expenditures for overhauling plant assets are frequently referred to as renewals. These amounts should be expensed as incurred. Substitutions of parts or entire units are referred to as replacements. If a part is removed and replaced with a different part, the cost and accumulated depreciation related to the replaced part should be removed from the accounts, and the remaining book value of the replaced part is added to depreciation expense for the period. If the replacement component has a useful life different from the remaining useful life of the large plant asset of which it is a component, its cost should be accounted for as a separate depreciable asset. To illustrate replacements, assume that Mendon Fireworks Company replaces the roof of its manufacturing plant for $40,000. Assume that the original cost of the building was $1,600,000 and it is three-fourths depreciated. If the original roof cost $20,000, this roof was recorded as part of the building cost, and the new roof is recorded as a separate component. The following entry could be made to remove the undepreciated book value of the old roof and record the expenditure for the new one.

Roof	40,000	
Accumulated Depreciation—Buildings (old roof)	15,000	
Depreciation Expense	5,000	
Buildings (old roof)		20,000
Cash		40,000

Additions and Betterments Enlargements and extensions of existing facilities are referred to as additions. Changes in assets designed to provide increased or improved services are referred to as betterments. If the addition or betterment does not involve a replacement of component parts of an existing asset, the expenditure should be capitalized by adding it to the cost of the asset, or if the new component has a useful life different from the larger asset of which it is a component, establishing a separate asset account for the component. If a replacement is involved, it is accounted for as discussed in the Mendon roof example.

Research and Development Expenditures

Historically, expenditures for research and development (R&D) purposes were reported sometimes as assets and sometimes as expenses. The FASB inherited this problem from the Accounting Principles Board and made this area the subject of its first definitive standard.[20] The Board defined research activities as those undertaken to discover new knowledge that will be useful in developing new products, services, or processes or that will result in significant improvements of existing products or processes. Development activities involve the application of research findings to develop a plan or design for new or improved products and processes. Development activities include the formulation, design, and testing of products; construction of prototypes; and operation of pilot plants.

[20] *Pre-Codification Statement of Financial Accounting Standards No. 2*, "Accounting for Research and Development Costs" (Stamford, CT: Financial Accounting Standards Board, 1974).

Because of the uncertainty surrounding the future economic benefit of R&D activities, the FASB concluded that research and development expenditures should be expensed in the period incurred. Among the arguments for expensing R&D costs is the frequent inability to find a definite causal relationship between the expenditures and future revenues. Sometimes very large expenditures do not generate any future revenue, but relatively small expenditures lead to significant discoveries that generate large revenues. The Board found it difficult to establish criteria that would distinguish between those R&D expenditures that would most likely benefit future periods and those that would not.[21]

Research and development costs include those costs of materials, equipment, facilities, personnel, purchased intangibles, contract services, and a reasonable allocation of indirect costs that are related specifically to research and development activities and that have no alternative future uses. Such activities include the following:

- Research aimed at discovery of new knowledge
- Search for applications of research findings
- Search for possible product or process alternatives
- Design, construction, and testing of preproduction prototypes
- Design, construction, and operation of a pilot plant

Expenditures for certain items having alternative future uses, either in additional research projects or for productive purposes, can be recorded as assets and allocated against future projects or periods as research and development expenses. This exception permits the deferral of costs incurred for materials, equipment, facilities, and purchased intangibles, but only if an alternative use can be identified.

Computer Software Development Expenditures

The FASB's requirement that all R&D costs be expensed seemed particularly ill-suited for the many software developers that sprang up in the early 1980s. The only economic assets owned by these firms were the software they developed, and strict application of pre-Codification *Statement No. 2* dictated that all development costs be expensed. The FASB, with strong support from the SEC, reexamined the R&D issue in the context of software developers and in 1985 issued pre-Codification *Statement No. 86*, "Accounting for the Costs of Computer Software to Be Sold, Leased, or Otherwise Marketed."

The Board's conclusions concerning computer software development costs are summarized in Exhibit 10-8.

Exhibit 10-8 | Development of Successful Software

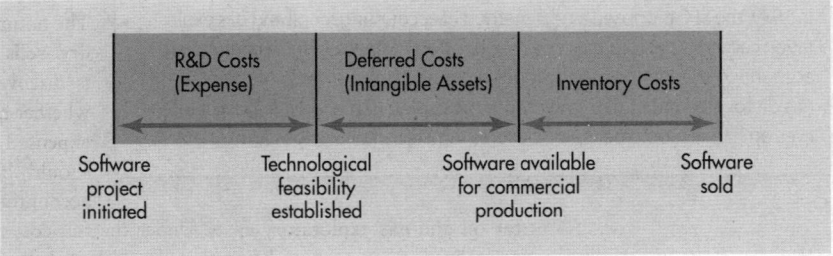

© Cengage Learning 2014

[21] FASB ASC paragraphs 730-10-05-1 through 3.

As demonstrated by Exhibit 10-8, all costs incurred up to the point where technological feasibility is established are to be expensed as research and development. These include costs incurred for planning, designing, and testing activities. In essence, the uncertainty surrounding the future benefits of these costs is so great that they should be expensed. After technological feasibility has been established, uncertainty about future benefits is decreased to the extent that costs incurred after this point can be capitalized. Capitalizable software development costs include the costs of coding and testing done after the establishment of technological feasibility and the cost to produce masters. Additional costs to actually produce software from the masters and package the software for distribution are inventoriable costs and will be expensed as part of cost of goods sold.

Considerable judgment is required to determine when technological feasibility has been established. At a minimum, technological feasibility is attained when an enterprise has produced either of the following:[22]

- A detailed program design of the software, or
- A working model of the software

International Accounting for Research and Development: *IAS 38* The IASB has established an R&D accounting rule that many think is superior to the FASB rule. *IAS 38* requires research costs to be expensed and development costs to be capitalized. *Research costs*, as defined in this standard, are those R&D costs incurred before technical and commercial feasibility has been established, and development costs are those incurred after technical and commercial feasibility. As you can see, the FASB rule for the accounting for software development costs is quite similar to the IASB standard for all research and development costs.

The Future of R&D Accounting in the United States On April 22, 2004, the FASB and the IASB held a joint meeting to discuss the convergence of their respective sets of accounting standards. One area identified as a candidate for convergence in the short term is the accounting for research and development. To date, the staffs of the FASB and the IASB are still studying this issue. Preliminary indications are that the general approach to R&D accounting in *IAS 38* will be adopted by the FASB, with the IASB borrowing some of the criteria included in pre-Codification FASB *Statement No. 86* (on computer software R&D) in order to make *IAS 38* easier to implement. However, remember that, until the FASB and the IASB come to an agreement on a joint R&D accounting standard, U.S. GAAP requires that all R&D costs be expensed except for postfeasibility computer software development costs.

FYI

In 1979, the SEC proposed a new method of accounting for oil and gas exploration called *reserve recognition accounting (RRA)*. RRA was a form of discovery accounting that would have recognized as an asset the value of the oil and gas discovered rather than the cost of the exploration efforts. A form of RRA lives on in the supplemental disclosures required of oil and gas firms.

Oil and Gas Exploration Costs

The nature of oil exploration is that several dry wells are drilled for each "gusher" that is discovered. The accounting question is whether the cost of the dry holes should be expensed as incurred or whether the costs should be capitalized. Two methods of accounting have been developed to account for oil and gas exploratory costs. Under the full cost method, all exploratory costs are capitalized, the reasoning being that the cost of drilling dry wells is part of the cost of

---

[22] FASB ASC paragraph 985-20-25-2.

locating productive wells. Under the successful efforts method, exploratory costs for dry holes are expensed, and only exploratory costs for successful wells are capitalized. Most large, successful oil companies use the successful efforts method. Exhibit 10-9 contains a description of the successful efforts method given by ExxonMobil in the notes to its 2011 financial statements.

For smaller companies, the full cost method has been more popular. The claim is that the full cost method encourages small companies to continue exploration by not imposing the severe penalty of recognizing all costs of unsuccessful projects as immediate expenses. Exhibit 10-9 also contains an excerpt from the 2011 financial statements of **Glen Rose Petroleum Corporation**, a small company based in Texas, which drills for oil and gas and accounts for its oil and gas operations using the full cost method.

The issue of how to account for exploratory costs in the oil and gas industry has attracted the attention of the FASB, the SEC, and even the U.S. Congress. When an apparent oil shortage developed in the 1970s, strong pressure was placed on oil companies to expand their exploration to discover new sources of oil and gas. One provision of the Energy Policy and Conservation Act of 1975 was that the SEC establish accounting rules for U.S. firms engaged in the production of oil and gas. The SEC allowed the FASB to take the lead. In 1977, the FASB decided that the successful efforts method (i.e., expense the cost of dry holes) was the appropriate accounting treatment and issued pre-Codification FASB *Statement No. 19*, "Financial Accounting and Reporting by Oil and Gas Producing Companies."

The uproar over *SFAS No. 19* was immediate and loud. Small, independent oil exploration firms argued that using the successful efforts method would require them to expense costs that they had been capitalizing, resulting in lower profits, depressed stock prices, and more difficulty in getting loans. The Department of Energy held hearings, and the Justice Department's antitrust division expressed concern. A bill was introduced in the Senate that would have made it *illegal* for the FASB to eliminate the full cost method. The SEC ran for cover and declared that in spite of the FASB standard, financial statements prepared using the full cost method would be acceptable to the SEC. In February 1979, the FASB

Exhibit 10-9 | ExxonMobil and Glen Rose Petroleum—Exploration Costs

ExxonMobil
The Corporation uses the "successful efforts" method to account for its exploration and production activities. Under this method, costs are accumulated on a field-by-field basis with certain exploratory expenditures and exploratory dry holes being expensed as incurred. Costs of productive wells and development dry holes are capitalized and amortized on the unit-of-production method. The Corporation uses this accounting policy instead of the "full cost" method because it provides a more timely accounting of the success or failure of the Corporation's exploration and production activities. If the full cost method were used, all costs would be capitalized and depreciated on a country-by-country basis. The capitalized costs would be subject to an impairment test by country. The full cost method would tend to delay the expense recognition of unsuccessful projects.

Glen Rose Petroleum
We employ the full cost method of accounting for our oil and gas production assets, which are located in the southwestern United States. Under the full cost method, all costs associated with the acquisition, exploration and development of oil and gas properties are capitalized and accumulated in cost centers on a country-by-country basis. The sum of net capitalized costs and estimated future development and dismantlement costs for each cost center is depleted on the equivalent unit-of-production basis using proved oil and gas reserves as determined by independent petroleum engineers.

© Cengage Learning 2014

succumbed to the pressure and issued pre-Codification *SFAS No. 25*, reinstating the full cost method.

The oil and gas controversy is a perfect illustration of the difficulties surrounding the capitalize-or-expense decision. Conceptual arguments can usually be made on both sides of the issue. Some expenditures, such as R&D and oil and gas exploration costs, are covered by specific authoritative pronouncements. Other expenditures, such as repairs or renewals, require accounting judgment. Material in the cases at the end of the chapter allows you to test your judgment on such issues as the accounting for advertising and asbestos removal.

Accounting for the Acquisition of Intangible Assets

LO4 学习目标4
单独取得、一揽子交易取得和商业并购取得的无形资产的确认。

④ Recognize intangible assets acquired separately, as part of a basket purchase, and as part of a business acquisition.

One of the most striking trends in business in the past 20 years is the increasing importance of intangible assets. This trend has proved to be a difficult challenge for financial reporting. The classic financial reporting model is based on manufacturing and retail companies with a focus on inventory, accounts receivable, buildings, equipment, and so forth. In a world driven by information technology, global brand names, and human capital, this accounting model often excludes the most important economic assets of a business. For example, in 2006, it was estimated that an average of 213 gigabytes of digital information was generated for each man, woman, and child in North America.[23] In 2001, Federal Reserve economist Leonard Nakamura estimated that U.S. companies invest approximately $1 trillion per year in intangible assets and that the value of the existing stock of intangibles is $5 trillion.[24] Finally, in 2001, Professor Erik Brynjolfsson of MIT's Sloan School estimated that U.S. companies had invested $1.3 trillion over the preceding 10 years in their "organization capital," or their processes and ways of doing things effectively and efficiently; this is comparable to the amount those same companies had invested in new equipment and factories over the same period.[25]

In August 1996, the FASB began a project on the accounting for intangibles. The FASB noted, "Intangible assets make up an increasing proportion of the assets of many (if not most) entities, but despite their importance, those assets often are not recognized as such."[26] The result of the FASB's project was a requirement that companies make greater efforts to identify and separately recognize more intangible assets. Theoretically, this requirement has existed since 1970; pre-Codification *APB Opinion No. 17* (paragraphs 24 through 26) stipulated that the cost of identifiable intangible assets should be separately recognized in the financial statements. However, in practice most companies had reported intangibles as an ill-defined conglomeration, with little detail about separate intangibles. The revised standards are contained in FASB ASC 350 (Intangibles—Goodwill and Other).

These revised standards also substantially change the practice of amortizing the cost of intangible assets. Under these standards, many intangible assets are assumed to have

---

[23] Michelle Kessler, "Days of Officially Drowning in Data Almost upon Us," *USA Today*, March 7, 2007.
[24] Leonard I. Nakamura, "What Is the U.S. Gross Investment in Intangibles? (At Least) One Trillion Dollars a Year!" Federal Reserve Bank of Philadelphia, Working Paper No. 01-15, October 2001.
[25] Mark Kindley, "Hidden Assets," *CIO Insight*, October 1, 2001.
[26] FASB, August 1996.

indefinite useful lives and thus are not systematically amortized. The amortization (and nonamortization) of intangible assets is discussed in Chapter 11. The different types of intangible assets and the process through which they are recognized are discussed below.

Internally Generated Intangibles

One thing the new FASB standards do *not* attempt is to require companies to identify and value internally generated, or homegrown, intangibles. In most cases, these are the most valuable intangible assets that a company has. As an illustration, consider Exhibit 10-10, which lists the 10 most valuable brands in the world in 2011. Each of these brands represents a valuable economic asset that was internally generated. For example, the $71.86 billion Coca-Cola brand name has been created over the years by The Coca-Cola Company through successful business operations and relentless marketing. Because the valuation of this asset is not deemed sufficiently reliable to meet the standard for financial statement recognition, it is not included in The Coca-Cola Company's balance sheet. However, as explained later, if another company were to buy The Coca-Cola Company, an important part of recording the transaction would be allocating the total purchase price to the various economic assets acquired, including previously unrecorded intangible assets. In the future, financial reporting will move toward providing more information about internally generated intangibles. Whether this will involve actual valuation and recognition of these intangibles in the financial statements or simply more extensive note disclosure remains to be seen.

Intangibles Acquired in a Basket Purchase

A common method of acquiring intangible assets is in conjunction with a collection of associated assets. For example, a company might pay $700,000 to purchase a patent along with a functioning factory and special equipment used in producing the patented product. Helpful information is lost if the entire $700,000 purchase price is merely recorded as a generic "asset." Accordingly, as demonstrated earlier in the chapter with a basket purchase involving only tangible assets, the total purchase price of $700,000 is allocated among

Exhibit 10-10 | Ten Most Valuable Brands in the World for 2011

Brand	Brand Value (in billions)
1 Coca-Cola	$71.86
2 IBM	69.91
3 Microsoft	59.09
4 Google	55.32
5 General Electric	42.81
6 McDonald's	35.59
7 Intel	35.22
8 Apple	33.49
9 Disney	29.02
10 Hewlett-Packard (HP)	28.48

Source: Interbrand at http://www.interbrand.com.

all of the assets, tangible and intangible, according to the relative fair values of the assets. If the fair values of the patent, factory, and equipment are estimated to be $200,000, $450,000, and $100,000, respectively, the $700,000 cost would be allocated as follows:

	Estimated Fair Values	Cost Allocation According to Relative Estimated Values	Cost Assigned to Individual Assets
Patent.........................	$200,000	200,000/750,000 × $700,000	$186,667
Factory	450,000	450,000/750,000 × $700,000	420,000
Equipment	100,000	100,000/750,000 × $700,000	93,333
	$750,000		$700,000

Five General Categories of Intangible Assets To aid companies in identifying different types of intangible assets that should be recognized separately, in FASB ASC Section 805-20-55, the FASB includes a description of five general categories of intangible assets. Those five general categories are:

1. *Marketing-related* intangible assets such as trademarks, brand names, and Internet domain names.
2. *Customer-related* intangible assets such as customer lists, order backlogs, and customer relationships.
3. *Artistic-related* intangible assets such as items protected by copyright.
4. *Contract-based* intangible assets such as licenses, franchises, and broadcast rights.
5. *Technology-based* intangible assets including both patented and unpatented technologies as well as trade secrets.

> **Caution**
> Of course, an intangible can be acquired by itself. If a company buys a single intangible asset, the purchase price allocation is simple: The entire purchase price is recorded as the cost of the single intangible asset.

These five categories do not comprise a comprehensive catalogue of all possible intangible assets. In addition, the identification of intangibles should not be viewed as merely matching up an acquired basket of assets with items from the FASB's list. As with all other assets, intangible assets must meet specific criteria to be recognized. The conceptual background for those criteria is laid out in *Concepts Statement No. 5* (paragraph 63), which indicates that to be recognized as an asset, an item must have probable future economic benefit, must be relevant to decision makers, and must be reliably measurable. In addition, intangible assets must be identifiable in order to be separately recognized in the financial statements. The criterion of identifiability is presumed to be satisfied with intangibles that are based on contracts or that are separately traded.

Contract-Based Intangibles Most of the intangible assets briefly described at the beginning of this chapter arise from contracts or other legal rights. Examples are trademarks, patents, copyrights, and franchise agreements. An intangible asset that is based on contractual or legal rights should be recognized as a separate asset, even if the right is inseparably connected with another asset. For example, the legal right to operate a specific nuclear power plant would often be sold with the nuclear power plant itself. Although these assets are not practically separable, the right to operate the factory is established by a specific legal permit and should be valued and reported separately in the books of the company that acquires the plant.

Separately Tradable Intangibles Some intangible assets arise as companies establish and maintain relationships of trust with their customers. These relationships are not imposed by legal right or contract but are voluntary and are based on past positive experiences. Companies are increasingly recognizing the value in these relationships and are even learning how to sell or rent these relationships. One example is the sale (exclusive use) or rental (nonexclusive use) of a customer database to another company. The fact that there is a market for these databases is taken as evidence that intangibles of this sort are reliably measurable assets that should be recognized as a separate asset when acquired by a company. Another example is the relationship a bank has with its depositors. Although these relationships themselves are not typically traded in separate transactions, they are inherent in the trading of portfolios of customer deposits. When a bank acquires a set of depositor liabilities from another bank, included in that transaction is the transfer of the depositor relationships to the acquiring bank. In such a transaction, a fair value should be estimated for the depositor relationships and a separate intangible asset recognized.

一些无形资产随着公司的建立而产生，并维持着与客户形成的信任关系。这些关系并不是产生于法律权利或合同的，而是一种自发的、形成于过去的积极正面的经历。例如，向其他公司出售（排他性使用）或者租赁（非排他性使用）客户数据库，以及银行与存款客户的关系。

> **FYI**
>
> One of the dangers in these tradable intangibles is that the very relationship of trust that created the valuable intangible in the first place may be impaired when it is sold. For example, subscribers to a magazine may cancel their subscription when they learn that the magazine publisher has sold their subscriber database to a telemarketing firm or a political fund-raising organization.

Estimating the Fair Value of an Intangible The most difficult part of recording an amount for an intangible asset is not in identifying the asset but in estimating its fair value. The objective in estimating the fair value is to duplicate the price at which the intangible asset would change hands in an arm's-length market transaction. If there is a market for similar intangible assets, the best estimate of fair value is made with reference to these observable market prices. In the absence of such a market, present value techniques should be used to estimate the fair value. As described in *Concepts Statement No. 7*, the present value of future cash flows can be used to estimate fair value in one of two ways. In the traditional approach, which is often used in situations where the amount and timing of the future cash flows are determined by contract, the present value is computed using a risk-adjusted interest rate that incorporates expectations about the uncertainty of receipt of the future contractual cash flows. In the expected cash flow approach, a range of possible outcomes is identified, the present value of the cash flows in each possible outcome is computed (using the risk-free interest rate), and a weighted-average present value is computed by summing the present value of the cash flows in each outcome, multiplied by the estimated probability of that outcome. To illustrate the traditional and the expected cash flow approaches, consider the following two examples.

> **FYI**
>
> In forming a corporation, certain organization costs are incurred, including legal fees, promotional costs, stock certificate costs, underwriting costs, and state incorporation fees. It can be argued that the benefits to be derived from these expenditures extend beyond the first fiscal period. However, the AICPA, with the approval of the FASB, has decided that organization costs (and the costs associated with other types of start-up activities) should be expensed as they are incurred. See FASB ASC paragraph 720-15-25-1.

Traditional Approach Intangible Asset A is the right to receive royalty payments in the future. The future royalty cash flows are $1,000 at the end of each year for the next five years. The risk-free interest rate is 5%; the receipt of these royalty cash flows is not certain, so a risk-adjusted interest rate of 12% is used in computing their present value. The fair value of Intangible Asset A is estimated as follows:

<blockquote>
Business calculator keystrokes
$N = 5$ years
$I = 12\%$
$PMT = \$1,000$
$FV = \$0$ (there is no additional payment at the end of five years)
$PV = \$3,605$
</blockquote>

FYI

In the traditional approach to computing present values, all of the "art" goes into determining the appropriate risk-adjusted interest rate.

If Intangible Asset A is acquired as part of a basket purchase with other assets, this $3,605 amount would be used as the estimated fair value of the intangible asset in the allocation of the total purchase price.

Expected Cash Flow Approach Intangible Asset B is a secret formula to produce a fast-food cheeseburger that contains 25 essential vitamins and minerals, reduces cholesterol levels, and replenishes the ozone layer. Future cash flows from the secret formula are uncertain; the following estimates have been generated, with the associated probabilities:

Outcome 1   10% probability of cash flows of $5,000 at the end of each year for 10 years
Outcome 2   30% probability of cash flows of $1,000 at the end of each year for four years
Outcome 3   60% probability of cash flows of $100 at the end of each year for three years

In the expected cash flow approach, the uncertainty of the future cash flows is not reflected in a risk-adjusted interest rate but is incorporated through the assessment of the various possible outcomes and the probabilities of each. Thus, the risk-free interest rate (5% in this case) is used in computing the present value of the cash flows in each outcome:[27]

	Present Value	Probability	Probability Weighted Present Value
Outcome 1	$38,609	0.10	$3,861
Outcome 2	3,546	0.30	1,064
Outcome 3	272	0.60	163
Total estimated fair value			$5,088

To summarize, the fair value of an intangible can be determined by referring to market prices, by computing present value using the traditional approach, or by computing present value using the expected cash flow approach. Again, these present value computation procedures are reviewed in the Time Value of Money Module of this text.

Acquired In-Process Research and Development One valuable intangible sometimes involved when one company purchases a collection of assets from another is existing research and development projects, often called *acquired in-process R&D*. For

---

[27] In applying the expected cash flow approach, we really should take the analysis one step further and convert the expected cash flows into "certainty equivalents." The basic idea is that there is a lower amount of cash that you would accept for sure in exchange for a higher, uncertain amount. We will leave this more complete "certainty equivalent" analysis to a more detailed course in valuation.

example, on October 1, 2001, **Bristol-Myers Squibb**, a large pharmaceuticals company, acquired the pharmaceuticals division of **DuPont** for $7.8 billion. Of this amount, $2.009 billion was associated with five ongoing research projects, as described in the following financial statement note:

> The [$2.009 billion] charge was associated with five research projects in the Cardiovascular, Central Nervous System, Oncology, and Anti-Infective therapeutic areas ranging from the preclinical to the phase II development stage. The amount was determined by identifying research projects for which technological feasibility has not been established and for which there is no alternative future use. The projected FDA approval dates are years 2005 through 2008, at which time the Company expects these projects to begin to generate cash flows. The cost to complete these research projects is estimated at $1.2 billion.[28]

Acquired in-process R&D creates a somewhat embarrassing situation for financial accountants in the United States. As mentioned earlier in the chapter, under U.S. GAAP normal R&D costs are expensed as incurred. The rationale behind this treatment is that there is too much uncertainty over the future economic value of research and development. However, as demonstrated in the Bristol-Myers Squibb case, the value of ongoing R&D can be verified in a market transaction. On this issue, the FASB has provided inconsistent answers. In summary, in-process R&D is to be recognized as an intangible asset if it is acquired as part of a business combination but is to be expensed if acquired as part of a basket purchase outside of a business combination.[29]

This patchwork approach is a perfect illustration of two general forces operating in the development of U.S. GAAP: (1) the steady influence of the desire for the FASB and the IASB to converge on a common set of high-quality International Accounting Standards and (2) the great caution of accountants in general and the FASB in particular when considering any change to long-standing practice. The FASB has stated that it intends to revisit this inconsistency in the future.

To summarize this section on the acquisition of intangibles as part of a basket purchase, the key point is that it is important to itemize and recognize intangible assets separately as much as possible. The total purchase price is allocated to the intangible assets according to their relative fair values. As discussed in Chapter 11, some of these intangibles will be amortized and some will not.

Intangibles Acquired in the Acquisition of a Business

In the previous section, we discussed the acquisition of intangible assets as part of a basket purchase. In this section we cover the acquisition of an entire company. When one company acquires another, the acquiring company pays for an assorted collection of tangible assets, liabilities, identifiable intangible assets, and usually an additional intangible asset, goodwill, that is essentially the synergistic value of the acquired business that can't be associated with any specific tangible or intangible asset.

One objective of the FASB standards on accounting for a business acquisition (also called a business combination) is to curtail the use of the goodwill asset account as a "kitchen sink" containing a hodgepodge of costs that would more appropriately be allocated to individual intangible assets. Goodwill is best thought of as a residual amount, the amount of the purchase price of a business that is left over after all other tangible and intangible assets have been identified. As such, goodwill is that intangible something that makes the whole company worth more than its individual parts. In general, goodwill represents all of the special advantages, not otherwise separately identifiable, enjoyed by an enterprise,

[28] Bristol-Myers Squibb, 2001, 10K Report.
[29] See FASB ASC paragraphs 350-30-35-17A, 805-20-35-5, and 730-10-25-1 and 2.

such as a high credit standing, reputation for superior products and services, experience with development and distribution processes, favorable government relations, and so forth. These factors allow a business to earn above normal income with the identifiable assets, tangible and intangible, employed in the business.

The accounting for the acquisition of an entire company is very similar to the accounting for a basket purchase; the total purchase price is allocated to all of the acquired items in accordance with their estimated fair values. A key difference in the accounting for acquisition of a basket of assets and acquisition of an entire business is as follows:

- The acquisition cost is not allocated in proportion to the fair values of the identifiable assets. Instead, each identifiable asset is recorded at an amount equal to its estimated fair value; any residual is reported as goodwill.

In determining fair values of assets and liabilities for the purpose of allocating the overall acquisition price, current market values should be sought rather than the values reported in the accounts of the acquired company. Receivables should be stated at amounts expected to be realized. Inventories and securities should be restated in terms of current market values. Land, buildings, and equipment may require special appraisals in arriving at their fair values. Intangible assets, such as patents and franchises, should be included at their estimated fair values whether or not they were recorded as assets on the books of the acquired company. Care should be taken to determine that liabilities are fully recognized.

To the extent possible, the amount paid for any existing company should be related to identifiable assets. If an excess does exist, it is recognized as an asset and called *goodwill* or "cost in excess of fair value of net assets acquired."

To illustrate the recording of the purchase of an ongoing business, assume that Airnational Corporation purchases the net assets of Speedy Freight Airlines for $1,500,000 in cash. A schedule of net assets for Speedy Freight, as recorded on Speedy Freight's books at the time of acquisition, follows.

企业合并的会计处理与一篮子购买交易的会计处理非常相似；总购买价格依据估计的公允价值分配到这些项目上。企业合并和一篮子交易会计处理的一个主要区别是：企业合并的购买成本并不是按比例分配到可辨认资产的公允价值中，而是每项可辨认资产均以估计公允价值记录，超过部分记为商誉。

Assets		
Cash	$ 37,500	
Receivables	246,000	
Inventory	392,000	
Land, buildings, and equipment (net)	361,200	
		$1,036,700
Liabilities		
Current liabilities	$ 86,000	
Long-term debt	183,500	269,500
Book value of net assets		$ 767,200

Analysis of the $732,800 difference between the purchase price of $1,500,000 and the net asset book value of $767,200 ($1,036,700 − $269,500) reveals the following differences between the recorded costs and market values of the assets:

	Cost	Market
Inventory	$392,000	$ 427,000
Land, buildings, and equipment	361,200	389,500
Patents	0	50,000
Purchased in-process R&D	0	400,000
Totals	$753,200	$1,266,500

The identifiable portion of the $732,800 difference amounts to $513,300 ($1,266,500 − $753,200) and is allocated to the respective items. The remaining difference of $219,500 ($732,800 − $513,300) is recorded as goodwill.

The entry to record the purchase is shown below. The estimated fair value associated with purchased in-process research and development projects is recognized as a separate intangible asset, consistent with the treatment of other research and development expenditures.

Cash	37,500	
Receivables	246,000	
Inventory	427,000	
Land, Buildings, and Equipment	389,500	
Patents	50,000	
In-Process R&D Asset	400,000	
Goodwill	219,500	
Current Liabilities		86,000
Long-Term Debt		183,500
Cash		1,500,000

After it is recognized, goodwill is left on the books at its originally recorded amount unless there is evidence that its value has been impaired. As mentioned earlier, this treatment is viewed by some as a compromise by the FASB. Whether goodwill should be amortized is an interesting theoretical discussion, but the existing standard says that goodwill is not to be amortized. Goodwill impairment is discussed in Chapter 11.

Notice that the patent asset was not recorded on the books of Speedy Freight before the acquisition. This could be because the patent cost had been fully amortized or because the patent had been developed through in-house research and development and all of those costs had been immediately expensed. However, when Speedy Freight is acquired, the patent is recognized as an identifiable economic asset.

The Speedy Freight example was simplified because Airnational purchased 100% of Speedy Freight. The accounting is changed a little if Airnational were to purchase, say, only 80% of Speedy Freight. All of the acquired assets, including goodwill, are still recognized at 100% of their fair values, but an additional item, called *noncontrolling interest*, is recognized to represent the outside ownership of the nonpurchased 20% of Speedy Freight. Noncontrolling interest is reported in the Equity section of the acquiring company's balance sheet; this topic is covered in Chapter 13.

Because goodwill is recorded on the books only when another company is acquired, one must be careful in interpreting a company's reported goodwill balance. The reported goodwill balance does not reflect the company's own goodwill but the goodwill of other companies it has acquired. So, **Microsoft**'s goodwill is not recognized on Microsoft's balance sheet, nor is **PepsiCo**'s goodwill shown on the balance sheet of PepsiCo. There is substantial goodwill on Pepsi's balance sheet, but that has arisen from the acquisitions of other companies, such as **Frito-Lay**. Thus, companies with sizable economic goodwill may have no recorded goodwill at all, and the goodwill that a company does report was developed by someone else. Current accounting principles may result in misleading users of financial statements as far as goodwill is concerned. On the other hand, to allow companies to place a value on their own goodwill and record this amount on the balance sheet would introduce a significant amount of added subjectivity to the financial statements.

Bargain Purchase Occasionally, the amount paid for another company is less than the fair value of the net identifiable items of the acquired company. This condition can arise when the existing management of a company is using the assets in a suboptimal fashion. When this bargain purchase exists, the acquiring company should first review all of the fair value estimates to make sure that they are reliable. If after doing this there is still an excess of identifiable net fair value over the purchase price, any remaining excess is recognized as a gain.

To illustrate, assume that the Speedy Freight acquisition described earlier was for $1,000,000 instead of $1,500,000. The acquisition is recorded as follows:

Cash	37,500	
Receivables	246,000	
Inventory	427,000	
Land, Buildings, and Equipment	389,500	
Patents	50,000	
In-Process R&D Asset	400,000	
Gain		280,500
Current Liabilities		86,000
Long-Term Debt		183,500
Cash		1,000,000

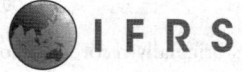

International Accounting for Intangibles: *IAS 38* and *IFRS 3*   The IASB's standard for the accounting for intangible assets is *IAS 38*. This IASB standard is very much compatible with U.S. GAAP. The International Accounting Standard for business combinations, *IFRS 3*, is also quite similar to the U.S. standard. This similarity in the accounting for intangibles is not accidental; the FASB and IASB worked jointly on their business combinations standards in order to eliminate almost all differences in accounting for the related intangible assets. In addition, the FASB worked with several non-U.S. standard setters in developing its standards on goodwill and intangibles. The most significant differences between U.S. GAAP and IASB standards in the accounting for intangible assets are in the testing of these assets for impairment. This topic is covered in Chapter 11.

FASB CODIFICATION

The Issue: You are the accountant for a company in the carpet cleaning business. Because of your company's innovative cleaning system (no harsh detergents, no damaging brushes, and extremely small carbon footprint), you have been very successful and have begun to drive your competitors out of business. In fact, just today your company's CEO has decided to start buying a number of your competitors. As you walked out the door at the end of the day, she said: "You had better learn how to account for a bargain purchase."

The Question: What is a bargain purchase, and why is a bargain purchase likely to arise in this situation?

Searching the Codification: Bargain purchases are covered in this chapter, but you would like to show your boss that you can find accounting standards for yourself in the authoritative literature. The best place to start is in Topic 805 (Business Combinations), which is in the "Broad Transactions" collection of topics.

The Answer: The authoritative accounting standards relative to bargain purchases are described on page 10-41.

Valuation of Assets at Fair Values

LO5 学习目标5
讨论以公允价值记录非流动性经营资产的优缺点。

⑤ Discuss the pros and cons of recording noncurrent operating assets at their fair values.

Throughout this chapter, the valuation of assets has been based on historical costs. As discussed in Chapter 1, asset measurement is frequently a trade-off between relevance and reliability. Historical cost is a reliable number, but the fair value of noncurrent assets can be more relevant.

The reduction in the recorded amount of noncurrent operating assets that have declined in value has long been part of generally accepted accounting principles. Writing down assets to recognize market value declines is a reflection of the conservative bias that is a fundamental part of accounting practice. The rules governing these impairment write-downs are discussed in Chapter 11. On the other hand, asset write-ups have not been generally accepted in recent times. Before the formation of the SEC in 1934, it was common for U.S. companies to report the upward revaluation of property and equipment. However, by 1940 the SEC had effectively eliminated this practice, not by explicitly banning it but through informal administrative pressure. Much of the suspicion about asset revaluations stemmed from a Federal Trade Commission investigation, completed in 1935, that uncovered a number of cases in the public utility industry in which a utility had improperly revalued assets upward to boost its rate base. In the late 1980s, the absence of advance warning of the $500 billion collapse of the savings and loan (S&L) industry was blamed in part on the failure of S&Ls to report current market values of their loan portfolios. Reexamination of the accounting for financial institutions led to pre-Codification FASB *Statement No. 115*, which required most investment securities to be reported at their current market values; this provision continues in FASB ASC Topic 320. It is likely that the continuing call by financial statement users for current value information will result in a reconsideration of the appropriateness of historical cost accounting for noncurrent operating assets. In fact, between 1980 and 1986 the FASB required large companies to report the current value of noncurrent operating assets in a note to the statements.

In *IAS 16*, the IASB permits the inclusion of upward revaluations of noncurrent operating assets in the financial statements as an allowable alternative to reporting the historical cost of those assets. Because fair values are often based on subjective appraisals rather than objective historical cost, accountants and auditors have traditionally been concerned that companies might use upward asset revaluations to artificially boost reported balance sheet and income statement values. This concern is reflected in the careful rules laid out in *IAS 16*, some of which are summarized here.

- If a company revalues its noncurrent operating assets to fair value, it must do so on a regular basis (not as a one-time event) and must revalue entire classes of assets rather than just picking and choosing certain assets in an effort to report the fair values of only those assets that have increased in value.
- Downward revaluations are recorded as a loss.
- Upward revaluations are recorded as a debit to the asset and a credit to a special "revaluation" equity account. This practice means that upward revaluations cannot be used to boost reported income. In addition, when an asset that has been revalued upward is subsequently sold, any associated balance in the special revaluation equity

Stop & Think

Which ONE of the following statements is true regarding the fair value of noncurrent operating assets?

a) International standards prohibit companies from recognizing the fair value of noncurrent operating assets.
b) The fair value of noncurrent operating assets can be estimated by professional appraisers, just as the pension liability is currently estimated by actuaries.
c) The fair value of noncurrent operating assets is not relevant information to most financial statement users.

account is credited directly to retained earnings and is not reported as an income statement gain. The implication of this accounting treatment is that the choice to recognize the increase in the value of a noncurrent operating asset through an asset revaluation means that the increase will never be reported in the income statement as a gain, even when the asset is sold.

One example of a company that revalues its assets on an annual basis is **Bank of China (Hong Kong) Limited** (BOC). The company indicates in the notes to its financial statements that valuations are done at least annually by external independent appraisers. As of December 31, 2011, the reported net amount of land and buildings ("premises") for BOC was HK$37.0 billion. This number is a mix of historical cost numbers and amounts obtained from professional revaluations. Without the revaluations, the net amount of land and buildings would have been HK$6.7 billion. Further explanation of the accounting for upward asset revaluations is given in Chapter 11.

IASB standards also allow investment property to be reported at fair value in the balance sheet. According to the provisions of *IAS 40*, investment property is land or a building that is held in order to earn rentals or for price appreciation, or both. This investment property can be accounted for using the traditional cost method. Alternatively, under *IAS 40*, a company can elect to use a fair value approach in which the investment property is reported in the balance sheet at its fair value, and any resulting gains or losses are reported in the income statement. This option is very important to real estate companies which are in business to make money through price appreciation; requiring these companies to report investment property at cost in the balance sheet conceals key operating information.

Measuring Property, Plant, and Equipment Efficiency

LO6 学习目标6
运用固定资产周转率衡量一家公司使用不动产、厂房和设备的效率。

6 Use the fixed asset turnover ratio as a general measure of how efficiently a company is using its property, plant, and equipment.

fixed asset trunover ratio
固定资产周转率

The result of proper capital budgeting analysis should be a level of property, plant, and equipment that is appropriate to the amount of sales a company is doing. As with any other asset, excess funds tied up in the form of property, plant, and equipment reduce a company's efficiency, increase financing costs, and lower return on equity.

In this section, we discuss the fixed asset turnover ratio, which uses financial statement data to roughly indicate how efficiently a company is utilizing its property, plant, and equipment to generate sales. We also illustrate that careful interpretation of the fixed asset turnover ratio is necessary because the recorded book value of long-term operating assets can differ significantly from the actual value of those assets.

Evaluating the Level of Property, Plant, and Equipment

Fixed asset turnover ratio is computed as sales divided by average property, plant, and equipment (fixed assets) and is interpreted as the number of dollars in sales generated by each dollar of fixed assets. This ratio is also called *PP&E turnover*. The computation of the fixed asset turnover ratio for General Electric is given below. (All financial statement numbers are in millions.)

The fixed asset turnover ratios suggest that General Electric was slightly more efficient at using its fixed assets to generate sales in 2011 than it was in 2010. In 2011, each dollar of fixed assets generated $2.23 in sales, up from $2.21 in 2010.

	2011	2010
Sales	$147,300	$149,593
Property, plant, and equipment:		
Beginning of year	$ 66,212	$ 69,212
End of year	$ 65,739	$ 66,212
Average fixed assets [(beginning balance + ending balance) ÷ 2]	$ 65,976	$ 67,712
Fixed asset turnover ratio	2.23	2.21

Dangers in Using the Fixed Asset Turnover Ratio

运用固定资产周转率可能得出错误的结论，不同行业的固定资产周转率无法进行有意义的对比，而且所报告的不动产、厂房、设备的价值与这些正被公司使用的资产的实际公允价值可能不同。

As with all ratios, the fixed asset turnover ratio must be used carefully to ensure that erroneous conclusions are not made. For example, fixed asset turnover ratio values for two companies in different industries cannot be meaningfully compared. This point can be illustrated using the fact that General Electric is composed of two primary parts: General Electric, the manufacturing company, and **GE Capital Services**, the financial services firm. The fixed asset turnover ratio computed earlier was for both parts. Because GE Capital Services does not use property, plant, and equipment for manufacturing but leases assets to other companies to earn financial revenue, one would expect GE Capital Services' fixed asset turnover ratio to be quite unlike that for a manufacturing firm. In fact, as shown next, the fixed asset turnover ratio for the manufacturing segments of General Electric was 7.99 times in 2011, more than triple the ratio value for the entire company.

Fixed Asset Turnover Ratio General Electric—Manufacturing Segments Only		
	2011	2010
Sales	$106,737	$104,528
Property, plant, and equipment:		
Beginning of year	$ 12,444	$ 12,495
End of year	$ 14,283	$ 12,444
Average fixed assets [(beginning balance + ending balance) ÷ 2]	$ 13,364	$ 12,470
Fixed asset turnover ratio	7.99	8.38

Another difficulty in comparing values for the fixed asset turnover ratio among different companies is that the reported amount for property, plant, and equipment can be a poor indicator of the actual fair value of the fixed assets being used by a company. As discussed earlier, the accounting rules in the United States require fixed assets to be written down when their value is impaired but do not allow the writing up of fixed asset amounts to reflect increases in fair value. This creates

> **Stop & Think**
>
> Why did Safeway's accumulated depreciation decrease so dramatically from 1985 to 1986?
>
> a) The accumulated depreciation balance fluctuates depending on the current values of property, plant, and equipment.
> b) The accumulated depreciation balance represented a large cash amount that was used to finance the leveraged buyout.
> c) When company ownership changes, as in a leveraged buyout, the existing assets are recorded as if they had just been purchased at their fair values (as in a business combination).
> d) According to the U.S. tax code, accumulated depreciation is a deferred tax item that must be reduced when a company experiences a leveraged buyout.

a comparability problem when one company has relatively new fixed assets, which are recorded at close to market value, and another company has older fixed assets, which are recorded at depreciated historical cost values that may significantly understate the real value of the assets.

A graphic illustration of this comparability problem is provided by **Safeway**, the supermarket chain. Safeway was taken private in a leveraged buyout near the end of 1986. When the leveraged buyout occurred, Safeway became a new company, for accounting purposes at least, and Safeway's assets were restated to their current market values as of the leveraged buyout date. This provides a rare opportunity to see how significantly the fixed asset turnover ratio is impacted by whether a company has its fixed assets recorded at market values or at depreciated historical cost. Listed below are the cost, accumulated depreciation, and fixed asset turnover ratios for Safeway for 1985, just before the leveraged buyout, and 1986, just after the leveraged buyout.

Safeway had almost the same fixed assets in place at the end of 1986 as it had at the end of 1985; the difference in the reported numbers is due almost entirely to the revaluation that took place as part of the leveraged buyout. Notice that the book value of Safeway's fixed assets increased by more than $1 billion from 1985 to 1986. This increase reflects the impact of reporting the fixed assets at market value rather than at depreciated historical cost. Also, note the significant decline in the computed fixed asset turnover ratio: from 7.45 in 1985 to 5.44 in 1986. Actually, Safeway's use of its fixed assets was almost exactly the same in 1986 as it had been in 1985; the difference in the ratio is caused by the use of the artificially low depreciated cost numbers in 1985 to compute the ratio. In summary, the fixed asset turnover ratio can be significantly impacted by the difference between the market value of fixed assets and their reported depreciated cost. For some companies, this difference can be very large indeed.

	1986	1985
Cost	$3,854	$4,641
Less: Accumulated depreciation	120	2,004
Book value	$3,734	$2,637
Fixed asset turnover ratio	5.44	7.45

Another complication with analysis using the fixed asset turnover ratio is caused by leasing. As will be discussed in Chapter 15, many companies lease the bulk of their fixed assets, and, as a result, many of these assets are not included in their balance sheets. This biases the fixed asset turnover ratio for these companies upward because the sales generated by the leased assets are included in the numerator of the ratio but the leased assets generating the sales are not included in the denominator.

SOLUTIONS TO OPENING SCENARIO QUESTIONS

1. When Jerry Jones purchased the Dallas Cowboys for $150 million, his accountants were then faced with the problem of allocating this $150 million purchase price among the many and varied assets of the Cowboys such as miscellaneous football equipment, stadium leases, radio and TV broadcast rights, cable TV rights, luxury stadium suites, player contracts, a lease on the Cowboys' luxurious Valley Ranch training facility, and the Cowboys' NFL franchise rights.

2. The desire to allocate as much of the purchase price as possible to the asset "players' contracts" is motivated by tax considerations. The asset players' contracts can be written off over four years for tax purposes, thus accelerating the tax break associated with depreciation of some or all of the original purchase price.

Stop & Think SOLUTIONS

1. (Page 10-15) The answer is D. Capitalized interest is not extra interest. If a company were to forget to capitalize interest that should be capitalized, interest expense would be overstated and long-term assets would be understated. Total cash flow would be unaffected, but cash from operations would be understated and cash from investing activities would be overstated.

2. (Page 10-38) The answer is B. It is unlikely that within the next 10 years U.S. companies will be required to recognize the current value of property, plant, and equipment, although such revaluation is allowable under International Accounting Standards. The historical cost tradition is strong in the United States, and the FASB is having enough trouble getting the business community to accept the recognition of the fair value of financial instruments and derivatives. But fair value recognition of property, plant, and equipment is only a matter of time—the information is very relevant and can be estimated by professional appraisers, just as the pension liability is currently estimated by actuaries.

3. (Page 10-40) The answer is C. One event that reduces accumulated depreciation is the disposal of old assets. This is not what happened to Safeway between 1985 and 1986. Instead, when Safeway's assets were revalued in late 1986, the accumulated depreciation account was set to zero. It was as if Safeway had disposed of all of its old assets and then repurchased them at their current market values.

SOLUTION TO USING THE FASB'S CODIFICATION

Under Topic 805 (Business Combinations), you should have seen Subtopic 805-30 (Goodwill or Gain from Bargain Purchase, Including Consideration Transferred). Section 805-30-25 includes material on "Gain from Bargain Purchase." With respect to the circumstances under which a bargain purchase might occur, the following is contained in FASB ASC paragraph 805-30-25-3: "A bargain purchase might happen, for example, in a business combination that is a forced sale in which the seller is acting under compulsion." In this particular case, your CEO expects to be able to buy her struggling competitors for a low price.

As explained in the textbook, if the purchase price is less than the fair value of the net assets of the acquired company, the difference is recognized as a "gain in earnings on the acquisition date" (FASB ASC paragraph 805-30-25-2). In past years, this gain has sometimes been called "negative goodwill," representing the negative value associated with the acquired company created by poor management, poor reputation, and poor operating circumstances.

Review Chapter 10 Learning Objectives

(1) Identify those costs to be included in the acquisition cost of different types of noncurrent operating assets.

The cost of tangible noncurrent operating assets includes not only the original purchase price or equivalent value but also any other expenditures required in obtaining and preparing the asset for its intended use. For example, land cost includes surveying fees and the cost of removing old buildings. Equipment cost includes the costs of testing and installation.

Intangible noncurrent operating assets are also generally recorded at cost. The cost is the purchase price if copyrights, patents, or trademarks are purchased from another company. For internally generated intangibles, the cost often includes only the actual legal and filing costs, as well as any cost to successfully defend the rights in court.

(2) Properly account for noncurrent operating asset acquisitions using various special arrangements, including deferred payment, self-construction, and acquisition of an entire company.

- *Basket purchase.* Acquisition cost is allocated to the various assets based on the relative fair values of the assets.
- *Deferred payment.* The acquisition is recorded at the discounted present value of the payments.
- *Leasing.* Property leased under a capital lease is recognized as an asset; property leased under an operating lease is not included in the balance sheet.
- *Exchange of nonmonetary assets.* The transaction is recorded at the fair value of the asset received or the asset given, whichever is more clearly determinable.
- *Acquisition by issuing securities.* The transaction is recorded at the fair value of the asset acquired or the securities issued, whichever is more clearly determinable.
- *Self-construction.* The cost of self-constructed assets includes an allocation of overhead and the cost of interest incurred to finance the construction. The amount of capitalized interest is an estimate of interest that could have been avoided if the construction expenditures had been used to repay loans instead.
- *Acquisition by donation or discovery.* Assets received as donations are recorded as revenue in an amount equal to the fair value of the assets. Discovered assets are not recognized.
- *Acquisition and an associated asset retirement obligation.* The estimated fair value of the asset retirement obligation is recognized as a liability and added to the cost of the asset acquired.
- *Acquisition of an entire company.* In a business combination accounted for as a purchase, acquired assets are recorded at their fair values, and any excess is recognized as goodwill.

(3) Separate costs into those that should be expensed immediately and those that should be capitalized, and understand the accounting standards for research and development and oil and gas exploration costs.

- *Postacquisition costs.* Repair and maintenance costs are expensed. Expenditures for new components, either as replacements or as additional components, are capitalized.
- *Research and development costs.* In the United States, all general research and development expenditures are expensed as incurred. The FASB may reconsider this rule some time soon.
- *Software development costs.* In the United States, software development expenditures incurred before technological feasibility has been established are expensed; expenditures after technological feasibility has been established are capitalized.
- *Oil and gas exploration costs.* With the successful efforts method, costs of drilling dry wells are expensed immediately; with the full cost method, these costs are capitalized.

(4) Recognize intangible assets acquired separately, as part of a basket purchase, and as part of a business acquisition.

In a basket purchase including intangibles, the total purchase price is allocated in proportion to the estimated fair values of all of the acquired assets, including the intangibles. Recorded intangibles can be either contract based, separately tradable, or relevant items that have probable future economic benefit and are reliably measurable. Fair values of intangibles are estimated by reference to market prices, by the traditional present value approach (using a risk-adjusted interest rate), or by the expected cash flow approach. Amounts allocated to acquired in-process research and development should be expensed immediately.

In a business acquisition, only those intangibles that are contract based or separately tradable are recognized; other intangible items are included in the recorded amount of goodwill. In the case of a bargain purchase, the fair value estimates should be carefully reviewed. If the purchase price is still less than the fair value of the net assets acquired, a gain is recognized for the difference.

(5) Discuss the pros and cons of recording noncurrent operating assets at their fair values.

Recording noncurrent operating assets at their fair values represents a trade-off between relevance and reliability.

In the United States, reliability concerns have resulted in the prohibition of asset write-ups. Under *IAS 16*, upward asset revaluations are an allowable alternative to reporting the historical cost of those assets.

6 **Use the fixed asset turnover ratio as a general measure of how efficiently a company is using its property, plant, and equipment.**

The fixed asset turnover ratio is computed as sales divided by average property, plant, and equipment (fixed assets) and is interpreted as the number of dollars in sales generated by each dollar of fixed assets. Meaningful comparison of fixed asset turnover ratios can only be done between firms in similar industries. Another difficulty in comparing values for the fixed asset turnover ratio among different companies is that the reported amount for property, plant, and equipment can be a poor indicator of the actual fair value of the fixed assets being used by a company. This is true when fixed assets have increased in value, relative to their depreciated cost, and when a significant number of assets have been leased and are not reported in the balance sheet.

FASB-IASB CODIFICATION SUMMARY

Topic	FASB Accounting Standards Codification	Original FASB Standard	Corresponding IASB Standard	Differences between U.S. GAAP and IFRS
Interest capitalization	Subtopic 835-20	SFAS No. 34	IAS 23	Under IFRS, net "borrowing costs" are capitalized. The net amount is the gross interest paid less interest received on investment of idle funds.
Asset retirement obligation	Subtopic 410-20	SFAS No. 143	IAS 16 and IAS 37	No substantial differences
Business combinations	Topic 805	SFAS No. 141R	IFRS 3	No substantial differences
Intangible assets	Topic 350	SFAS No. 142	IAS 38	No substantial differences
Research and development	Topic 730	SFAS No. 2 SFAS No. 86	IAS 38	Under IFRS, development costs, which are costs incurred after technological feasibility, are capitalized. This matches U.S. GAAP for software development costs, but not for ordinary R&D.

KEY TERMS

Additions 10-24
Asset retirement obligation 10-20
Bargain purchase 10-36
Basket purchase 10-8
Betterments 10-24
Capital leases 10-11
Capitalized interest 10-14
Component 10-23
Development 10-24
Discovery 10-19
Donation 10-18
Fixed asset turnover ratio 10-38
Full cost method 10-26
Goodwill 10-33
Intangible assets 10-6
Maintenance 10-24
Noncurrent operating assets 10-4
Operating leases 10-11
Renewals 10-24
Repairs 10-24
Replacements 10-24
Research 10-24
Research and development (R&D) 10-24
Software development costs 10-25
Successful efforts method 10-27
Technological feasibility 10-26
Trademark 10-6

Tutorial Activities

Tutorial Activities with author-written, content-specific feedback, available on *CengageNOW for Stice & Stice.*

QUESTIONS

1. On the balance sheets of many companies, the largest classification of assets in amount is noncurrent operating assets. Name the items, other than the amount paid to the former owner or contractor, that may be properly included as part of the acquisition cost of the following property items: (a) land, (b) buildings, and (c) equipment.
2. What acquisition costs are included in (a) copyrights, (b) franchises, and (c) trademarks?
3. What procedure should be followed to allocate the cost of a basket purchase of assets among specific accounts?
4. What special accounting problems are introduced when a company purchases equipment on a deferred payment contract rather than with cash?
5. (a) Why is the "list price" of an asset often not representative of its fair market value? (b) Under these conditions, how should a fair value be determined?
6. Gaylen Corp. decides to construct a building for itself and plans to use existing plant facilities to assist with such construction. (a) What costs will enter into the cost of construction? (b) What two positions can the company take with respect to general overhead allocation during the period of construction? Evaluate each position and indicate your preference.
7. What characteristics must a construction project have before interest can be capitalized as part of the project cost?
8. What amount of interest is capitalized under *IAS 23*?
9. Parkhurst Corporation acquires land and buildings valued at $250,000 as a gift from a local philanthropist. The president of the company maintains that because there was no cost for the acquisition, neither the cost of the facilities nor depreciation needs to be recognized for financial statement purposes. Evaluate the president's position assuming (a) the donation is unconditional and (b) the donation is contingent upon the employment by the company of a certain number of employees for a 10-year period.
10. What type of asset value increases are recognized under *IAS 41*?
11. What is an asset retirement obligation? What is the proper accounting for an asset retirement obligation?
12. Why do some companies expense asset expenditures that are less than an established monetary amount?
13. Indicate the effects of the following errors on the balance sheet and the income statement in the current year and succeeding years.
    (a) The cost of a depreciable asset is incorrectly recorded as an expense.
    (b) An expense expenditure is incorrectly recorded as an addition to the cost of a depreciable asset.
14. Which of the following items would be recorded as expenses, and which would be recorded as assets?
    (a) Cost of installing machinery
    (b) Cost of unsuccessful litigation to protect patent
    (c) Extensive repairs as a result of a fire
    (d) Cost of grading land
    (e) Insurance on machinery in transit
    (f) Interest incurred during construction period
    (g) Cost of replacing a major machinery component
    (h) New safety guards on machinery
    (i) Commission on purchase of real estate
    (j) Special tax assessment for street improvements
    (k) Cost of repainting offices
15. What happens to the remaining net book value of a component that is replaced?
16. (a) What type of activities are considered to be research and development activities?
    (b) Under what conditions, if any, are research and development costs capitalized?
17. Distinguish between the full cost and successful efforts methods of recording exploratory costs for oil and gas properties.
18. In general, how is the cost of internally generated intangibles accounted for?
19. What are the five general categories of intangible assets?
20. What two approaches are used in estimating fair values using present value computations? Briefly explain the difference between the two approaches.
21. (a) Under what conditions may goodwill be reported as an asset? (b) Roper Company engages in a widespread advertising campaign on behalf of new products, charging above normal expenditures to goodwill. Do you approve of this practice? Why or why not?
22. How is acquired in-process research and development accounted for under U.S. GAAP?
23. What argument is given for reporting noncurrent operating assets at their historical costs instead of at current values?
24. Under the provisions of *IAS 16*, what is the credit entry when noncurrent operating assets are written up to reflect an increase in market value?
25. Describe the fair value option that is available under *IAS 40* to companies that own investment property.
26. How is the fixed asset turnover ratio calculated, and what does the resulting ratio measure?
27. Briefly describe the dangers to financial statement users inherent in the use of the fixed asset turnover ratio.

PRACTICE EXERCISES

Practice 10-1

Categories of Tangible Noncurrent Operating Assets

The following costs were incurred in the most recent year:

(a) Paid $20,000 to purchase a piece of equipment. In addition, paid $1,000 to have the equipment shipped to and installed in its final location. Spent $1,750 to have the equipment tested before beginning its production use. Paid $2,000 for lubrication and normal maintenance during the first year of operation of the equipment.

(b) Paid $100,000 to buy a piece of land. Also paid $10,000 to construct a parking lot and sidewalks.

(c) Paid $50,000 to buy another piece of land. Then paid $10,000 to have an old building demolished and have the land cleared. Paid $125,000 to have a building constructed.

Compute the total cost that should be reported in each of the following categories:

1. Land
2. Buildings
3. Equipment
4. Land Improvements

Practice 10-2

Categories of Intangible Noncurrent Operating Assets

For each of the brief descriptions given below, identify the label typically associated with the intangible asset being described.

1. An exclusive right or privilege received by a business or individual to perform certain functions or sell certain products or services
2. Miscellaneous intangible resources, factors, and conditions that allow a company to earn above normal income with its identifiable net assets
3. An exclusive right granted by a national government that enables an inventor to control the manufacture, sale, or use of an invention
4. An exclusive right granted by a national government that permits an author to sell, license, or control her or his work
5. An exclusive right granted by a national government that permits the use of distinctive symbols, labels, and designs

Practice 10-3

Basket Purchase

The company paid $750,000 to buy a collection of assets. The assets had the following appraised values:

Equipment	$250,000
Building	425,000
Land	125,000

Compute the cost to be allocated to each asset.

Practice 10-4

Deferred Payment

The company purchased a piece of equipment. Terms of the purchase were as follows: $10,000 in cash immediately, followed by note payments of $20,000 at the end of each year for the next eight years. The market rate of interest is 9%. Make the journal entries necessary to record (1) the initial purchase and (2) the first cash payment of $20,000 at the end of the first year.

Practice 10-5

Exchange of Nonmonetary Assets

The company exchanged a piece of land for a new piece of equipment. The equipment has a list price of $100,000, and the land has a historical cost of $35,000. The land has a current market value of $93,000. Make the journal entry necessary to record the exchange.

Practice 10-6

Cost of a Self-Constructed Asset
The company constructed its own building. The cost of materials was $400,000. Labor cost incurred on the construction project was $600,000. Total overhead cost for the company for the year was $8,000,000; total labor cost (including the cost of construction) was $4,000,000. Interest incurred to finance the construction cost was $140,000. Compute the total cost of the building.

Practice 10-7

Capitalized Interest: Single-Year Computation
The company had the following loans outstanding for the entire year:

	Amount	Interest Rate
Specific construction loan.	$ 100,000	10%
General loan	2,000,000	12

The company began the self-construction of a building on January 1. The following expenditures were made during the year:

January 1	$100,000
May 1	200,000
November 1	300,000
Total	$600,000

Construction was completed on December 31. Compute (1) the amount of interest capitalized during the year and (2) the recorded cost of the building at the end of the year.

Practice 10-8

Capitalized Interest: Journal Entry
Refer to Practice 10-7. Make the journal entry necessary to record *total* interest paid for the year. Assume that all of the interest was paid in cash on December 31.

Practice 10-9

Capitalized Interest: Multiple-Year Computation
Refer to Practice 10-7. Assume that construction was *not* completed on December 31 of Year 1. Also assume that the same loans were outstanding for all of Year 2. The following expenditure was made during Year 2:

July 1	$500,000

Final construction was completed on December 31 of Year 2. Compute (1) the amount of interest capitalized during Year 2 and (2) the recorded cost of the building at the end of Year 2.

Practice 10-10

Acquisition by Donation
The company has received a donation of land from a rich local philanthropist. The land originally cost the philanthropist $48,000. On the date of the donation, it had a market value of $111,000. Make the journal entry necessary on the books of the company to record the receipt of the land.

Practice 10-11

Accounting for an Asset Retirement Obligation
The company purchased a mining site that will have to be restored to certain specifications when the mining production ceases. The cost of the mining site is $800,000, and the restoration cost is expected to be $200,000. It is estimated that the mine will continue in operation for 15 years. The appropriate interest rate is 7%. Make the appropriate journal entries to record the purchase of the mining site and the recognition of the obligation to restore the mining site.

Practice 10-12

Renewals and Replacements
The company recently replaced the heating/cooling system for its building. The old system cost $160,000, and was 80% depreciated. The new system cost $210,000, which was paid in cash. The new system will

extend the economic useful life of the building by five years. Make the journal entry necessary to record the removal of the old system and the installation of the new system, assuming that the separate cost of the old system is identifiable and has been accounted as part of the building cost.

Practice 10-13

Research and Development
During the year, the company made the following research and development expenditures:

Date	Amount	Comment
July 23	$100,000	Before technological feasibility established.
December 31	120,000	After technological feasibility established.

Compute the total research and development (R&D) expense for the year assuming (1) the expenditures were for normal R&D, (2) the expenditures were for software R&D, *and* (3) the expenditures were for normal R&D and the company does its accounting according to International Financial Reporting Standards.

Practice 10-14

Oil and Gas Exploration Costs
The company started business on January 1 and during the year had oil and gas exploration costs of $500,000. Of these costs, $100,000 was associated with successful wells and $400,000 with so-called dry holes. For simplicity, assume that all of the costs were incurred on December 31. Compute the total oil and gas exploration expense to be reported for the year, assuming that (1) the company uses the successful efforts method and (2) the company uses the full cost method.

Practice 10-15

Accounting for the Acquisition of an Entire Company
Stafford Company purchased Deaver Manufacturing for $1,400,000 cash on January 1. The book value and fair value of the assets of Deaver as of the date of the acquisition follow:

	Book Value	Fair Value
Cash	$ 20,000	$ 20,000
Accounts receivable	190,000	190,000
Inventory	260,000	320,000
Patent	0	80,000
Property, plant, and equipment	600,000	750,000
Totals	$1,070,000	$1,360,000

In addition, Deaver had liabilities totaling $500,000 at the time of the acquisition. Deaver has no other separately identifiable intangible assets. Make the journal entry necessary on the books of Stafford Company to record the acquisition.

Practice 10-16

Accounting for a Bargain Purchase
Refer to Practice 10-15. Assume that the cash acquisition price is $720,000 instead of $1,400,000. Make the journal entry necessary on the books of Stafford Company to record the acquisition.

Practice 10-17

Intangibles and a Basket Purchase
The company paid $500,000 to purchase the following: a building with an appraised value of $200,000, an operating permit valued at $100,000, and ongoing research and development projects valued at $150,000. In addition, it is estimated that the fair value of the order backlog associated with the products manufactured in the building is $100,000: this order backlog is included as part of the purchase. Make the journal entry necessary to record this cash purchase.

Practice 10-18

Intangibles and a Business Acquisition

Buyer Company purchased Target Company for $800,000 cash. Target Company had total liabilities of $300,000. Buyer Company's assessment of the fair values it obtained when it purchased Target Company is as follows:

Cash	$100,000
Inventory	50,000
In-process R&D	500,000

Make the journal entry necessary to record this business acquisition.

Practice 10-19

Fixed Asset Turnover Ratio

Company A had sales for the year totaling $480,000. The net property, plant, and equipment balance at the beginning of the year was $160,000; the ending balance was $200,000. Compute the fixed asset turnover ratio.

Practice 10-20

Danger in Using Fixed Asset Turnover Ratio

Refer to Practice 10-19. Company A's competitor, Company B, had sales for the year totaling $360,000. The net property, plant, and equipment balance at the beginning of the year was $200,000; the ending balance was $220,000. Company B is a very young company; all of its fixed assets have been purchased in the past two years. In contrast, Company A's assets are 10 years old, on average. It is estimated that Company A's fixed assets had a market value of $290,000 at the beginning of the year and $310,000 at the end of the year. Which company is more efficient at using its fixed assets to generate sales, Company A or Company B? Explain.

EXERCISES

Exercise 10-21

Cost of Specific Plant Items

The following expenditures were incurred by Peterson Enterprises Co. in 2015:

Purchase of land	$270,000	Special assessment tax for street project	$ 2,400
Land survey	4,800	Dividends	4,000
Fees for search of title for land	500	Damages awarded for injuries sustained in construction (no insurance was carried)	8,750
Building permit	4,000		
Temporary quarters for construction crews	11,200	Costs of construction	2,640,000
Payment to tenants of old building for vacating premises	4,450	Cost of paving parking lot adjoining building	55,000
Razing old building	41,000		
Excavating basement	13,000	Cost of shrubs, trees, and other landscaping	36,000

What is the cost of the land, land improvements, and building?

Exercise 10-22

Determining Cost of Patent

Dean Lang Enterprises Inc. developed a new machine that reduces the time required to insert the fortunes into its fortune cookies. Because the process is considered very valuable to the fortune cookie industry, Dean Lang patented the machine. The following expenses were incurred in developing and patenting the machine:

Research and development laboratory expenses	$34,000
Metal used in the construction of the machine	6,000
Blueprints used to design the machine	2,600
Legal expenses to obtain patent	13,400
Wages paid for the employees' work on the research, development, and building of the machine (60% of the time was spent in actually building the machine)	42,000
Expense of drawing required by the patent office to be submitted with the patent application	2,500
Fee paid to government patent office to process application	3,200

One year later, Dean Lang Enterprises Inc. paid $19,300 in legal fees to successfully defend the patent against an infringement suit by Chinese Cookie Co.

Give the entries on Dean Lang's books indicated by the preceding events. Ignore any amortization of the patent or depreciation of the machine.

Exercise 10-23

Basket Purchase

Allred Shipping Co. acquired land, buildings, and equipment at a lump-sum price of $920,000. An appraisal of the assets at the time of acquisition disclosed the following values.

Land	$250,000
Buildings	600,000
Equipment	200,000

What cost should be assigned to each asset?

Exercise 10-24

Basket Purchase

Ratcliff Corporation purchased land, a building, a patent, and a franchise for the lump sum of $1,450,000. A real estate appraiser estimated the building to have a resale value of $600,000 (two-thirds of the total worth of land and building). The franchise had no established resale value. The patent was valued by management at $325,000. Give the journal entry to record the acquisition of the assets.

Exercise 10-25

Equipment Purchase on Deferred Payment Contract

Custom Industries purchased new specialized manufacturing equipment on July 1, 2015. The equipment cash price was $96,000. Custom signed a deferred payment contract that provided for a down payment of $10,000 and a 10-year note for $112,420. The note is to be paid in 10 equal annual payments of $11,242. The payments include 5.193% interest and are made to be on June 30 of each year, beginning June 30, 2016. Prepare the journal entries for 2015, 2016, and 2017 related to the equipment purchase and the contract. Custom's fiscal year ends on June 30.

Exercise 10-26

Purchase on Deferred Payment Contract

HiTech Industries purchased new electronic equipment for its telecommunication system. The contractual arrangement specified 10 payments of $8,600 each to be made over a 10-year period. If HiTech had borrowed money to buy the equipment, it would have paid interest at 9%. HiTech's accountant recorded the purchase as follows:

Equipment	86,000	
Notes Payable		86,000

Prepare the correcting acquisition entry, considering the implicit interest in the purchase.

Exercise 10-27

Basket Purchase in Exchange for Stock

On May 31, 2015, Julienne Corp. exchanged 20,000 shares of its $1 par common stock for the following assets:

(a) A trademark valued at $183,000.

(b) A building, including land, valued at $732,000 (20% of the value is for the land).

(c) A franchise right. No estimate of the value is available at time of exchange.

Julienne Corp. stock is selling at $50 per share on the date of the exchange. Give the entries to record the exchange on Julienne's books.

Exercise 10-28

Purchase of Building with Bonds and Stock

Sayer Co. entered into a contract with Bradford Construction Co. for construction of an office building at a cost of $680,000. Upon completion of construction, Bradford agreed to accept in full payment of the contract price Sayer Co.'s 10% bonds with a face value of $350,000 and common stock with a par value of $90,000 and no established fair market value. Sayer Co.'s bonds are selling in the market at this time at 106. How would you recommend the building acquisition be recorded?

Exercise 10-29
Acquisition of Land and Building for Stock and Cash
Valdilla's Music Store acquired land and an old building in exchange for 50,000 shares of its common stock, par $0.50, and cash of $80,000. The auditor ascertains that the company's stock was selling for $15 per share when the purchase was made. The following additional costs were incurred to complete the transaction:

Legal cost to complete transaction	$10,000
Property tax for previous year	30,000
Cost of building demolition	21,000
Salvage value of demolished building	(6,000)

What entry should be made to record the acquisition of the property?

Exercise 10-30
Cost of Self-Constructed Asset
Brodhead Manufacturing Company has constructed its own special equipment to produce a newly developed product. A bid to construct the equipment by an outside company was received for $1,200,000. The actual costs incurred by Brodhead to construct the equipment were as follows:

Direct material	$320,000
Direct labor	200,000

It is estimated that incremental overhead costs for construction amount to 140% of direct labor costs. In addition, fixed costs (exclusive of interest) of $700,000 were incurred during the construction period and allocated to production on the basis of total prime costs (direct labor plus direct material). The prime costs incurred to build the new equipment amounted to 35% of the total prime costs incurred for the period. The company follows the policy of capitalizing all possible costs on self-construction projects.

To assist in financing the construction of the equipment, a $500,000, 10% loan was acquired at the beginning of the six-month construction period. The company carries no other debt except for trade accounts payable. For simplicity, assume that all construction expenditures took place exactly midway through the project: That is, all expenditures took place with three months remaining in the construction period. Compute the cost to be assigned to the new equipment.

Exercise 10-31
Capitalization of Interest
Carver Department Stores, Inc., constructs its own stores. In the past, no cost has been added to the asset value for interest on funds borrowed for construction. Management has decided to correct its policy and desires to include interest as part of the cost of a new store just being completed. Based on the following information, how much interest would be added to the cost of the store (1) in 2015 and (2) in 2016?

Total construction expenditures:

January 2, 2015	$ 500,000
May 1, 2015	450,000
November 1, 2015	700,000
March 1, 2016	950,000
September 1, 2016	800,000
November 30, 2016	600,000
	$4,000,000

Outstanding company debt:

Mortgage related directly to new store; interest rate, 10%; term, five years from beginning of construction	$1,500,000
General bond liability:	
Bonds issued just prior to construction of store; interest rate, 8% for 10 years	$ 500,000
Bonds issued prior to construction; interest rate, 12%, mature in five years	$ 800,000
Estimated cost of equity capital	14%

Exercise 10-32

Interest Capitalization Decision

For each of the situations described here, indicate when interest should be capitalized (C) and when it should not be capitalized (NC).

(a) Queen Company is constructing a piece of equipment for its own use. Total construction costs are expected to be $4 million, and the construction period will be one month.

(b) Ferney Company is constructing a piece of equipment for sale. Total construction costs are expected to exceed $10 million, and the construction period will be about 15 months. This is a special order. Ferney has never produced a piece of equipment like this before.

(c) Patterson Company is constructing a piece of equipment for its own use. Total construction costs are expected to be $15 million, and the construction period will be about two years. The forecasted total construction cost is only a very rough estimate because Patterson has no system in place to accumulate separately the costs associated with this project.

(d) Savis Company is constructing a piece of equipment for its own use. Total construction costs are expected to be $350, and the construction period will be nine months.

(e) Platt Company is constructing a piece of equipment for sale. Total construction costs are expected to exceed $10 million, and the construction period will be about 15 months. This particular piece of equipment is Platt's best seller.

(f) Stowell Company is in the process of renovating its corporate office building. The project will cost $7.5 million and will take about 15 months. The building will remain in use throughout the project.

(g) Jackson Company owns a piece of undeveloped land. The land originally cost $21 million. Jackson plans to hold onto the land for three to four years and then develop it into a vacation resort.

Exercise 10-33

Asset Retirement Obligation

Simpson Company purchased a nerve gas detoxification facility. The facility cost $900,000. The cost of cleaning up the routine contamination caused by the initial location of nerve gas on the property is estimated to be $1,300,000; this cost will be incurred in 20 years when all of the existing stockpile of nerve gas is detoxified and the facility is decommissioned. Additional contamination will occur each year that the facility is in operation. In its first year of operation, that additional contamination adds $100,000 to the estimated cleanup cost, which will occur after 19 years (because one year has elapsed). Make the journal entries necessary to record the purchase of the detoxification facility and the recognition of the initial asset retirement obligation (assuming that the appropriate interest rate is 7%). Also make the journal entry to recognize the additional obligation created after one year.

Exercise 10-34

Postacquisition Expenditures

GoodeHill Company replaced some parts of its factory building during 2015:

(a) The outside corrugated covering on the factory walls was removed and replaced. The job was done by an expert crew from Hollister Construction Company and will extend the life of the building by six years. The cost of the new wall was $84,000. The cost of the old wall is estimated to be $60,000. The building is 20% depreciated.

(b) Dust filters in the interior of the factory were replaced at a cost of $20,000. The new filters are expected to reduce employee health hazards and thus reduce wage and fringe benefit costs. The original filters cost $11,000. The old filters are one-fourth depreciated.

Prepare journal entries for the preceding information.

Exercise 10-35

Research and Development Costs

In 2015, the Slidell Corporation incurred research and development costs as follows:

Materials and equipment	$160,000
Personnel	105,000
Indirect costs	60,000
	$325,000

These costs relate to a product that will be marketed in 2016. It is estimated that these costs will be recouped by December 31, 2019.

1. What is the amount of research and development costs that should be expensed in 2015?
2. Assume that of these costs, equipment of $80,000 can be used on other research projects. Estimated useful life of the equipment is five years with no salvage value, and it was acquired at the beginning of 2015. What is the amount of research and development costs that should be expensed in 2015 under these conditions? Assume that depreciation on all equipment is computed on a straight-line basis.

Exercise 10-36

What Are the R&D Costs?

Pringle Company has a substantial research department. Following are listed, in chronological order, some of the major activities associated with one of Pringle's research projects.

Project Started

(a) Purchased special equipment to be used solely for this project.
(b) Purchased general equipment that will be usable in Pringle's normal operations.
(c) Allocated overhead to the project.

Technological Feasibility Established

(d) Purchased more special equipment to be used solely for this project.
(e) Performed tests on an early model of the product.
(f) Allocated overhead to the project.

Product Becomes Ready for Production

(g) Incurred direct production costs.
(h) Allocated overhead to the products.

1. For each activity (a) through (h), indicate whether the cost should be capitalized (C), expensed (E), or included in cost of inventory (I).
2. Repeat (1), assuming that Pringle is a computer software development company.

Exercise 10-37

Full Cost and Successful Efforts

Exploratory Company is an oil and gas exploration firm. During 2015, Exploratory engaged in 86 different exploratory projects, only 20 of which were successful. The total cost of this exploration effort was $24 million, $5.6 million of which was associated with the successful projects. As of the end of 2015, production had not yet begun at the successful sites.

1. Using the successful efforts method of accounting for oil and gas exploration costs, how much exploration expense would be shown in Exploratory's income statement for 2015? How much of the exploration cost will be capitalized and shown as an asset on the company's balance sheet as of December 31, 2015?
2. Repeat (1) using the full cost method.

Exercise 10-38

Classifying Expenditures as Assets or Expenses

One of the most difficult problems facing an accountant is the determination of which expenditures should be capitalized and which should be immediately expensed. What position would you take in each of the following instances?

(a) Painting partitions in a large room recently divided into four sections.
(b) Labor cost of tearing down a wall to permit extension of assembly line.
(c) Replacement of motor on a machine. Life used to depreciate the machine is eight years. The machine is four years old. Replacement of the motor was anticipated when the machine was purchased.
(d) Cost of grading land prior to construction.
(e) Assessment for street paving.
(f) Cost of tearing down a previously occupied old building in preparation for new construction; old building is fully depreciated.

Exercise 10-39

Purchase of a Company

Conglomerate Company purchased Individual Company for $860,000 cash. A schedule of the fair values of Individual's assets and liabilities as of the purchase date follows.

Individual Company
Schedule of Asset and Liability Fair Values

Assets		
Cash	$ 12,000	
Receivables	96,000	
Inventory	145,000	
Land, buildings, and equipment	519,000	$772,000
Liabilities		
Current liabilities	$ 75,000	
Long-term debt	116,000	191,000
Net asset fair value		$581,000

1. Make the journal entry necessary for Conglomerate Company to record the purchase.
2. Assume that the purchase price is $460,000 cash. Make the journal entry necessary to record the purchase.

Exercise 10-40

Purchase of a Company

Landers Inc. is considering purchasing J&B Properties, which has the following assets and liabilities.

	Cost	Fair Value
Accounts receivable	$ 210,000	$ 200,000
Inventory	250,000	260,000
Prepaid insurance	12,000	12,000
Buildings and equipment (net)	88,000	168,000
Accounts payable	(130,000)	(130,000)
Net assets	$ 430,000	$ 510,000

1. Make the journal entry necessary for Landers Inc. to record the purchase if the purchase price is $650,000 cash.
2. Assume that the purchase price is $320,000 cash. Make the journal entry necessary to record the purchase.

Exercise 10-41

Basket Purchase of Intangible Assets

Taraz Company paid $500,000 to purchase the following portfolio of intangibles with estimated fair values as indicated:

	Estimated Fair Value
Internet domain name	$150,000
Order backlog	100,000
In-process research and development	200,000
Operating permit	80,000

In addition, Taraz spent $300,000 to run an advertising campaign to boost its image in the local community. Make the journal entries necessary to record the purchase of the intangibles and the payment for the advertising.

Exercise 10-42

Purchase of Intangible Assets in a Business Acquisition

Omniportal Company purchased Network Enterprises. The following fair values were associated with the items acquired in this business acquisition:

	Cost	Fair Value
Accounts receivable	$ 180,000	$ 180,000
Inventory	120,000	75,000
Government contacts	0	92,000
Equipment (net)	68,000	84,000
Short-term loan payable	(160,000)	(160,000)
Net assets	$ 208,000	$ 271,000

The fair value associated with Network Enterprises' government contacts is not based on any legal or contractual relationship. In addition, for obvious reasons, there is no open market trading for intangibles of this sort.

1. Make the journal entry necessary for Omniportal Company to record the purchase if the purchase price is $790,000 cash.
2. Assume that the purchase price is $28,000 cash. Make the journal entry necessary to record the purchase.

Exercise 10-43

Fixed Asset Turnover

Dandy Hardware Stores reported the following asset values in 2014 and 2015:

	2015	2014
Cash	$ 40,000	$ 25,000
Accounts receivable	380,000	330,000
Inventory	590,000	410,000
Land	150,000	125,000
Buildings	500,000	450,000
Equipment	260,000	250,000

In addition, Dandy Hardware had sales of $3,500,000 in 2015. Cost of goods sold for the year was $2,200,000. Compute Dandy Hardware's fixed asset turnover ratio for 2015.

P2
Routine Activities of a Business

CHAPTER 11

Investments in Noncurrent Operating Assets— Utilization and Retirement

Learning Objectives

1. Use straight-line, accelerated, use-factor, and group depreciation methods to compute annual depreciation expense.

2. Apply the productive-output method to the depletion of natural resources.

3. Incorporate changes in estimates and methods into the computation of depreciation for current and future periods.

4. Identify whether an asset is impaired, and measure the amount of impairment loss using both U.S. GAAP and IASB standards.

5. Discuss the issues impacting proper recognition of amortization or impairment for intangible assets.

6. Account for the sale of depreciable assets in exchange for cash and in exchange for other depreciable assets.

EM EXPANDED MATERIAL

7. Compute depreciation for partial periods, using both straight-line and accelerated methods.

8. Understand the depreciation methods underlying the MACRS income tax depreciation system.

Garbage—that's how H. Wayne Huizenga made his first splash on the national scene. In the early 1960s, he started with one garbage truck in southern Florida. Huizenga went on to buy up hundreds of local garbage companies across the country, combining them into Waste Management Inc. (which later merged with USA Waste Services but kept the Waste Management name), the largest trash hauler in the world.

After his retirement from the trash business in 1984, Huizenga's eye fell on a small, 20-store, video chain in Dallas called Blockbuster Video.[1] By the end of 1987, Huizenga had acquired

[1] Eric Calonius, "Meet the King of Video," *Fortune*, June 4, 1990, p. 208.

control of Blockbuster and had increased the number of stores to 130. Through a combination of aggressive expansion and the acquisition of existing video chains, Blockbuster soon became the nation's largest video chain. By the end of 2007, there were 7,830 Blockbuster Video stores, primarily located in the United States, Great Britain, and Canada.

On May 8, 1989, a Bear Stearns investment report was released that was critical of some of Blockbuster's accounting practices, particularly its depreciation policies. The report suggested that the 40-year life Blockbuster used for amortizing goodwill was much too long; to quote from the report: "Have you ever seen a 40-year-old videotape store?" Five years was suggested as a more reasonable amortization period. The report also criticized Blockbuster for increasing the depreciation period for videotapes from 9 months to 36 months.[2] Revising both these items to use the shorter amortization periods would have cut Blockbuster's 1988 net income almost in half—from $0.57 per share to $0.32 per share.

Release of the Bear Stearns report caused Blockbuster's stock price to drop from $33.50 to $26.25 in two days, a 22% drop. (See Exhibit 11-1.) This represented a total decline in market value of approximately $200 million. Wayne Huizenga was livid. In a meeting with stock analysts, he showed a letter from the SEC ordering Blockbuster to use the longer videotape amortization period. He criticized the Bear Stearns researchers for not understanding his business and said that their report wasn't "worth the powder to blow it to hell."[3] Huizenga was vindicated when within two weeks of the release of the report, Blockbuster's stock had regained most of the 22% loss.

In 1994, Wayne Huizenga left Blockbuster after presiding over its acquisition by Viacom in a deal valued at over $8 billion. This completed an incredible run by Huizenga: He had entered, dominated, and successfully exited two very different industries, garbage and video rentals. So, what was next? Selected as America's number 1 entrepreneur by Success magazine in 1995, it was certain that Wayne Huizenga would not just sit around and count his money (about $1.4 billion). At one time he owned three professional sports teams in southern Florida: the Miami Dolphins (football), the Florida Marlins (baseball), and the Florida Panthers (hockey). His new company, AutoNation, is busy doing for auto dealerships what Huizenga already did for garbage hauling and video stores: taking fragmented businesses across the country and consolidating them into a nationwide network. At age 66, after creating three Fortune 1000 companies from scratch, Mr. Huizenga announced that he was stepping down from the board of AutoNation in April 2004. Currently, AutoNation is the largest automotive retailer in the United States with 258 new vehicle franchises as of December 31, 2011.

Exhibit 11-1 | Blockbuster Video Daily Stock Prices in May 1989

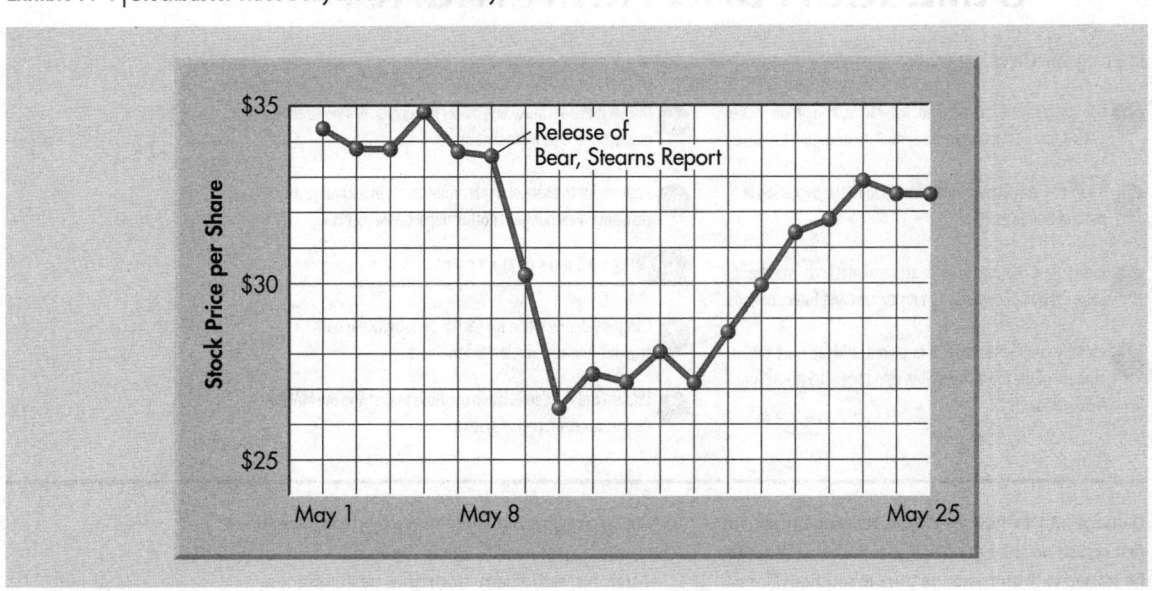

© Cengage Learning 2014

[2] Dana Weschsler, "Earnings Helper," Forbes, June 12, 1989, p. 15. As explained later in the chapter, GAAP has been changed, and goodwill is no longer amortized but is instead tested for impairment on a regular basis.
[3] Duncan Maxwell Anderson and Michael Warshaw, "The #1 Entrepreneur in America," Success, March 1995, p. 32.

1. Why would the Bear Stearns report cause Blockbuster's stock price to decline by 22%?
2. Look carefully at Exhibit 11-1 to see the behavior of Blockbuster's stock price around the release of the Bear Stearns report. When did "the market" better understand Blockbuster's accounting for depreciation—on May 7, just before the release of the Bear Stearns report, or on May 10, two days after the release of the report? Explain your answer.

Answers to these questions can be found on page 11-41.

A fundamental task of accrual accounting is appropriately allocating the cost of long-lived assets to expense. If you are a Venetian shipmaster setting the price that you will charge for the use of your ship on a spice-trading voyage to the Orient, you must somehow allocate the cost of the ship over the expected number of voyages the ship can complete. If you are a Silicon Valley research firm, proper measurement of annual income requires you to allocate the cost of your research patents over their expected economic life. Computing asset depreciation is an exercise in accounting judgment, and as illustrated in the Blockbuster/Bear Stearns example, reasonable people can disagree, with huge implications for reported profits.

Three different terms are used to describe the process of allocating the cost of long-lived assets to periodic expense. The allocation of tangible property costs is referred to as depreciation. For minerals and other natural resources, the cost allocation process is called depletion. For intangible assets, such as patents and copyrights, the process is referred to as amortization. Sometimes amortization is used generically to encompass all three terms.

This chapter discusses what happens to a long-lived asset after acquisition. The first decision facing management relates to estimating and recognizing the expense associated with a long-lived asset's use. We will cover the common depreciation methods and the depletion of natural resources. We will also address the issues associated with the proper treatment of changes in depreciation estimates. The chapter also describes when an impairment loss should be recognized and the proper accounting for the retirement of depreciable assets. The chapter includes discussion of three types of intangibles: those that are amortized, those that are not amortized but are tested for impairment, and goodwill, which is not amortized and is tested for impairment using a special test. The time line in Exhibit 11-2 illustrates the issues to be discussed. The Expanded Material at the end of the chapter offers more detail on depreciating assets acquired and retired in midyear and on the modified accelerated cost recovery system (MACRS), a depreciation system used for income tax purposes.

Exhibit 11-2 | Time Line of Business Issues Involved with Long-Term Operating Assets

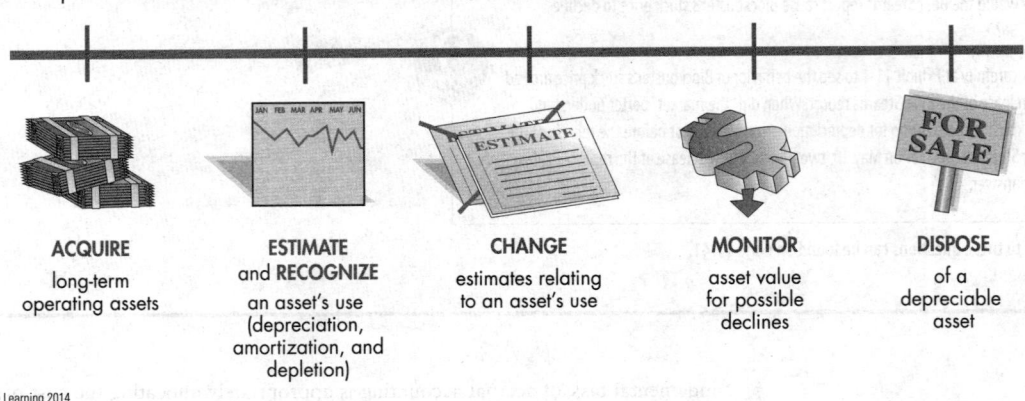

© Cengage Learning 2014

Depreciation

LO1 学习目标1
使用直线折旧法、加速折旧法、工作量折旧法和分类折旧法计算年度折旧费用。

① Use straight-line, accelerated, use-factor, and group depreciation methods to compute annual depreciation expense.

Depreciation is *not* a process through which a company accumulates a cash fund to replace its long-lived assets. Depreciation is also *not* a way to compute the current value of long-lived assets. Instead, depreciation is the systematic allocation of the cost of an asset over the different periods benefited by the use of the asset. Accumulated depreciation is not an asset replacement fund but is the sum of all the asset cost that has been expensed in prior periods. Similarly, the book value of an asset (historical cost less accumulated depreciation) is the asset cost remaining to be allocated to future periods but is not an estimate of the asset's current value.

Depreciation expense is the recognition of the using up of the service potential of an asset. The nature of depreciation expense is conceptually no different from the expenses that recognize the expiration of insurance premiums or prepaid rent; the practical difference is that noncurrent assets are depreciated over several years, whereas prepaid rent is usually expensed over a period of months.

FYI

Depreciation expense was not widely reported in income statements until the early 1900s. The passage of the Sixteenth Amendment in 1913, allowing the taxation of income, spurred companies to demand some depreciation deduction for the use of long-term assets.

影响折旧费的四项因素为：
- 资产成本；
- 剩余价值；
- 可使用期限；
- 使用模式。

Factors Affecting the Periodic Depreciation Charge

Four factors are taken into consideration in determining the appropriate amount of annual depreciation expense:

- Asset cost
- Residual or salvage value
- Useful life
- Pattern of use

Asset Cost The cost of an asset includes all the expenditures relating to its acquisition and preparation for use as described in Chapter 10. The cost of property less the expected residual value, if any, is the depreciable cost or depreciation base, that is, the portion of asset cost to be expensed in future periods.

资产的剩余价值（残值）是当资产报废时所能卖出的估计金额。剩余价值依赖于公司的弃置政策及市场条件等。

Residual or Salvage Value The residual (salvage) value of property is an estimate of the amount for which the asset can be sold when it is retired. The residual value depends on the retirement policy of the company as well as market conditions and other factors. If, for example, the company normally uses equipment until it is physically exhausted and no longer serviceable, the residual value, represented by the scrap or junk value that can be salvaged, may be quite small. If, however, the company normally replaces its equipment after a short period of use, the residual value, represented by the selling price or trade-in value, may be relatively high.

> **Caution**
> Ignoring small residual values bothers some students who want to compute depreciation correctly to the penny. Remember that depreciation is an *estimate*—forget the pennies.

From a theoretical point of view, any estimated residual value should be subtracted from cost in arriving at the portion of asset cost to be charged to depreciation. In practice, however, residual values are frequently ignored in determining periodic depreciation charges. This practice is acceptable when residual values are relatively small or are not subject to reasonable estimation.

资产可使用年限受物理或功能性因素的影响。其中，影响资产使用期限的物理因素包括磨损、退化和腐蚀及损毁；功能性因素主要是过时。

Useful Life Noncurrent operating assets other than land have a limited useful life as a result of certain physical and functional factors. The physical factors that limit the service life of an asset are (1) wear and tear, (2) deterioration and decay, and (3) damage or destruction. Everyone is familiar with the processes of wear and tear that render an automobile, a building, or furniture no longer usable. A tangible asset, whether used or not, also is subject to deterioration and decay through aging. Finally, fire, flood, earthquake, or accident may reduce or terminate the useful life of an asset.

The primary functional factor limiting the useful lives of assets is obsolescence. An asset may lose its usefulness when as a result of altered business requirements or technological progress, it no longer can produce sufficient revenue to justify its continued use. Although the asset is still physically usable, its inability to produce sufficient revenue has cut short its economic life. Look around: How many old personal computers are stored in corners, still perfectly operational, but unable to run the software that is currently being used?

Both physical and functional factors must be considered in estimating the useful life of a depreciable asset. This recognition requires estimating what events will take place in the future and requires careful judgment on the part of the accountant. Physical factors are more readily apparent than functional factors in predicting asset life. When functional factors are expected to hasten the retirement of an asset, these also must be considered.

In practice, many companies as a matter of policy dispose of certain classes of assets after a predetermined period without regard to the serviceability of individual

Computers have short useful lives due to the quick progress of technology.

assets within a class. Company automobiles, for example, may be replaced routinely every two or three years.

The useful life of a depreciable plant asset may be expressed in terms of either an estimated time factor or an estimated use factor. The time factor may be a period of months or years; the use factor may be a number of hours of service or a number of units of output. The cost of the asset is allocated in accordance with the lapse of time or extent of use. The rate of cost allocation may be modified by other factors, but basically depreciation must be recognized on a time or use basis.

Pattern of Use To match asset cost against revenues, periodic depreciation charges should reflect as closely as possible the pattern of use. If the asset produces a varying revenue pattern, the depreciation charges should vary in a corresponding manner. When depreciation is measured in terms of a time factor, the pattern of use must be estimated. Because of the difficulty in identifying a pattern of use, several somewhat arbitrary methods have come into common practice. Each method represents a different pattern and is designed to make the time basis approximate the use basis. The time factor is employed in two general classes of methods: straight-line depreciation and accelerated depreciation. When depreciation is measured in terms of a use factor, the units of use must be estimated. The depreciation charge varies periodically in accordance with the services provided by the asset. As illustrated later, the use factor is employed in service-hours depreciation and in productive-output depreciation.

Recording Periodic Depreciation

The general form of the journal entry used to recognize depreciation is as follows:

Depreciation Expense xx
    Accumulated Depreciation xx

In manufacturing operations, depreciation is sometimes charged to a production overhead account and then allocated to the cost of inventory. This merely extends the period of deferral; instead of going straight to an expense account, depreciation goes to inventory and then to expense (Cost of Sales).

The allowance account that is credited in recording periodic depreciation is commonly titled *Accumulated Depreciation*. The accumulation of expired cost in a separate account rather than crediting the asset account directly permits identification of the original cost of the asset and the accumulated depreciation. Companies are required to disclose both cost and accumulated depreciation for plant assets on the balance sheet or in the notes to the financial statements. This enables the user to estimate the relative age of plant assets and provides some basis for predicting future cash outflows for the replacement of plant assets.

Methods of Depreciation

There are a number of different methods for computing depreciation expense. The depreciation method used in any specific instance is a matter of judgment and, conceptually, should be selected to most closely approximate the actual pattern of use expected from the asset. In practice, most firms select one depreciation method, such as straight-line, and use it for substantially all their depreciable assets. The following methods are described in this section:

Time-Factor Methods
- Straight-line depreciation
- Accelerated methods
  - Sum-of-the-years'-digits depreciation
  - Declining-balance depreciation

Use-Factor Methods
- Service-hours depreciation
- Productive-output depreciation

Group and Composite Methods

The examples that follow assume the acquisition of a polyurethane plastic-molding machine at the beginning of 2015 by Schuss Boom Ski Manufacturing, Inc., at a cost of $100,000 with an estimated residual value of $5,000. The following symbols are used in the formulas for the development of depreciation rates and charges:

C = Asset cost
R = Estimated residual value
n = Estimated life in years, hours of service, or units of output
r = Depreciation rate per period, per hour of service, or per unit of output
D = Periodic depreciation charge

Time-Factor Methods The most common methods of cost allocation are related to the passage of time. A productive asset is used up over time, and possible obsolescence due to technological changes is also a function of time. Of the time-factor depreciation methods, straight-line depreciation is by far the most popular.

The use of accelerated depreciation methods is based largely on the assumption that there will be rapid reductions in a depreciable asset's efficiency, output, or other benefits in the early years of that asset's life. As assets age, they often require increased charges for maintenance and repairs. Charges for depreciation decline, then, as the economic advantages afforded through ownership of the asset decline. The most commonly used accelerated method is the declining-balance method; the sum-of-the-years'-digits method is also sometimes used.

Straight-Line Depreciation Straight-line depreciation relates depreciation to the passage of time and recognizes equal depreciation in each year of the life of the asset. The simple assumption behind the straight-line method is that the asset is equally useful during each time period, and depreciation is not affected by asset productivity or efficiency variations. In applying the straight-line method, an estimate is made of the useful life of the asset, and the depreciable asset cost (the difference between the asset cost and residual value) is divided by the useful life of the asset in arriving at the periodic depreciation amount.

Using data for the machine acquired by Schuss Boom Ski Manufacturing and assuming a five-year life, annual depreciation is computed as follows:

$$D = \frac{C-R}{N}, \text{ or } \frac{\$100{,}000 - \$5{,}000}{5 \text{ years}} = \$19{,}000 \text{ per year}$$

A table summarizing annual depreciation for the entire life of the asset, using the straight-line method, follows.

End of Year	Computation		Depreciation Amount	Accumulated Depreciation	Asset Book Value
					$100,000
2015	$95,000/5	=	$19,000	$19,000	81,000
2016	95,000/5	=	19,000	38,000	62,000
2017	95,000/5	=	19,000	57,000	43,000
2018	95,000/5	=	19,000	76,000	24,000
2019	95,000/5	=	19,000	95,000	5,000
			$95,000		

It was indicated earlier that residual value is frequently ignored when it is a relatively minor amount. If this were done in the preceding example, depreciation would be $20,000 per year instead of $19,000.

When assets are acquired or disposed of in the middle of a year, depreciation for the partial year should be recognized. The examples in this chapter assume that partial-year depreciation is recognized for the number of months an asset was held during the year. A variety of other approaches to computing partial-year depreciation are covered in the Expanded Material at the end of the chapter.

Sum-of-the-Years'-Digits Depreciation The sum-of-the-years'-digits depreciation method yields decreasing depreciation in each successive year. The computations are done by applying a series of fractions, each of a smaller value, to depreciable asset cost. The numerator of the fraction is the number of years remaining in the asset life as of the beginning of the year. The denominator of the fraction is the sum of all the digits from one to the original useful life. There is no great conceptual insight behind this method; it is merely a clever arithmetic scheme that gives decreasing depreciation each year and results in the entire depreciable cost being allocated over the asset's useful life.

In the Schuss Boom example, the useful life is five years, so the denominator of the fraction is 15 (1 + 2 + 3 + 4 + 5). Annual depreciation is computed as follows:

年限总和折旧法下连续年份的折旧是递减的。

End of Year	Computation		Depreciation Amount	Accumulated Depreciation	Asset Book Value
					$100,000
2015	$95,000 × 5/15	=	$31,667	$31,667	68,333
2016	95,000 × 4/15	=	25,333	57,000	43,000
2017	95,000 × 3/15	=	19,000	76,000	24,000
2018	95,000 × 2/15	=	12,667	88,667	11,333
2019	95,000 × 1/15	=	6,333	95,000	5,000
			$95,000		

FYI

The famous mathematician Carl Friedrich Gauss deduced this formula in 1878 during a test in school when he was 10 years old.

Note that under this method, annual depreciation expense declines by 1/15 of the depreciation asset base each year, or by $6,333 (by $6,334 in 2016 and 2019 due to effects of rounding).

When an asset has a long useful life, such as 20 years, computing the sum of the years' digits can be cumbersome. The following formula is a shortcut to computing the sum of the years' digits:

$$\frac{[n(n+1)]}{2} = (1 + 2 + 3 + \cdots + n)$$

With a useful life of 20 years, the sum-of-the-years'-digits denominator determined by the formula is $[20(20 + 1)]/2 = 210$. The fraction applied to depreciable cost in the first year would be 20/210, in the second year, 19/210, and so forth.

Declining-Balance Depreciation The declining-balance depreciation methods provide decreasing charges by applying a constant percentage rate to a declining asset book value. The most popular rate is two times the straight-line rate, and this method is often called double-declining-balance depreciation. The percentage to be used is double the straight-line rate, calculated for various useful lives as follows:

Estimated Useful Life in Years	Straight-Line Rate	2 Times Straight-Line Rate
3	33 1/3%	66 2/3%
5	20	40
7	14 2/7	28 4/7
8	12 1/2	25
10	10	20
20	5	10

Residual value is not used in the computations under this method; however, it is generally recognized that depreciation should not continue once the book value is equal to the residual value. Depreciation using the double-declining-balance method for the Schuss Boom asset described earlier is summarized in the following table:

End of Year	Computation	Depreciation Amount	Accumulated Depreciation	Asset Book Value
				$100,000
2015	$100,000 × 40% =	$40,000	$40,000	60,000
2016	60,000 × 40% =	24,000	64,000	36,000
2017	36,000 × 40% =	14,400	78,400	21,600
2018	21,600 × 40% =	8,640	87,040	12,960
2019	12,960 × 40% =	5,184	92,224	7,776
		$92,224		

It should be noted that the rate of 40% is applied to the decreasing book value of the asset each year. This results in a declining amount of depreciation expense. In applying this rate, the book value after five years exceeds the residual value by $2,776 ($7,776 − $5,000). This condition arises whenever residual values are relatively low in amount. Companies usually switch to the straight-line method when the remaining annual depreciation

> **Caution**
>
> With both the straight-line and sum-of-the-years'-digits methods, the residual value is subtracted from the asset cost before calculating depreciation. Residual value is not subtracted when using the double-declining-balance method.

> **Stop & Think**
>
> Imagine that at the beginning of 2015, Schuss Boom had five different machines: one brand new, and the others one year, two years, three years, and four years old. Which depreciation method—straight-line, sum-of-the-years'-digits, or double-declining-balance—would give the highest total depreciation expense in 2015?
>
> a) Straight-line gives the highest total depreciation expense in 2015.
> b) Sum-of-the-years'-digits gives the highest total depreciation expense in 2015.
> c) Double-declining-balance gives the highest total depreciation expense in 2015.
> d) All three depreciation methods give the same total depreciation expense in 2015.

computed using straight line exceeds the depreciation computed by continuing to apply the declining-balance rate. In the Schuss Boom example, the depreciation expense for the year 2019 would be $7,960 if a switch was made from the double-declining-balance to the straight-line method. This would reduce the book value of the asset to its $5,000 residual value. In this example, the switch would be made in the last year of the asset's life, and the final year's depreciation expense is simply the amount necessary to reduce the asset's book value to its residual value. However, if the asset in the example had a lower residual value, the switch could have been made in the fourth year. For example, assume the asset is expected to have no residual value. The book value under the double-declining-balance method at the end of the third year as shown previously is $21,600; thus, the straight-line depreciation for the fourth and fifth years would be $10,800 ($21,600/2); because the straight-line depreciation of $10,800 exceeds the double-declining depreciation of $8,640, the straight-line amount would be used.

Evaluation of Time-Factor Methods Exhibit 11-3 illustrates the pattern of depreciation expense for the time-factor methods discussed in the preceding sections. Note that when the straight-line method is used, depreciation is a constant or fixed charge each period. When the life of an asset is affected primarily by the lapse of time rather than by the degree of use, recognition of depreciation as a constant charge is generally appropriate. However, when the straight-line method is used, net income measurements become particularly sensitive to changes in the volume of business activity. With above normal activity, there is no increase in the depreciation charge; with below normal activity, there is no decrease in the depreciation charge.

As mentioned, straight-line depreciation is the most widely used procedure for financial reporting purposes. It is readily understood and frequently parallels asset use. It has the advantage of simplicity and under normal conditions offers a satisfactory means of cost allocation. Normal asset conditions exist when (1) assets have been accumulated over a period of years so that the total of depreciation plus maintenance is comparatively even from period to period and (2) service potentials of assets are being steadily reduced by functional as well as physical factors. The absence of either of these conditions may suggest the use of some depreciation method other than straight line.

Accelerated methods can be supported as reasonable approaches to cost allocation when the annual benefits provided by an asset decline as it grows older. These methods, too, are suggested when an asset requires increasing maintenance and repairs over its

直接折旧法的适用条件为：（1）不同时期内资产折旧费和保养费的总和在各期是可比的；（2）出于功能性因素和物理因素，资产的潜在服务能力稳定减弱。如果这两个条件中任何一个不满足，建议使用直接折旧法以外的折旧方法。

Exhibit 11-3 | Time-Factor Methods: Depreciation Patterns Compared

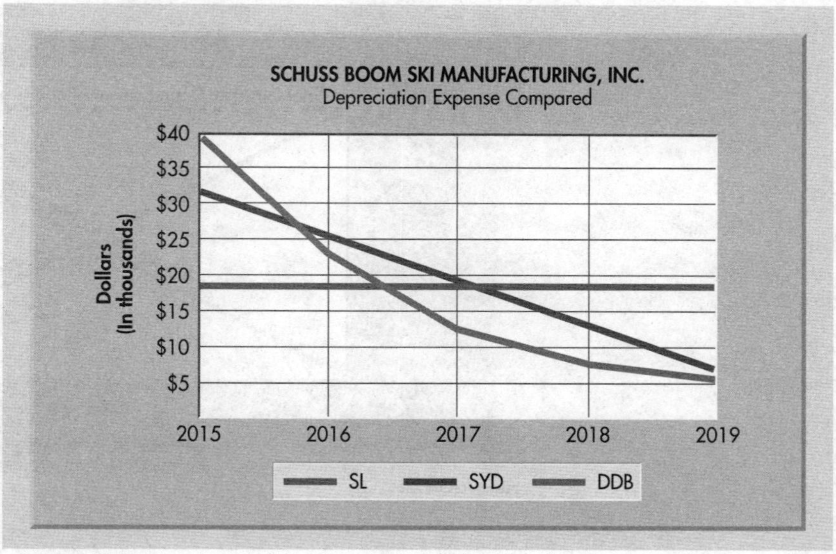

SCHUSS BOOM SKI MANUFACTURING, INC.
Depreciation Expense Compared

[Chart showing depreciation expense in dollars (in thousands) from 2015 to 2019 comparing SL, SYD, and DDB methods]

© Cengage Learning 2014

useful life.[4] When straight-line depreciation is employed, the combined charges for depreciation, maintenance, and repairs will increase over the life of the asset; when an accelerated method is used, the combined charges will tend to be equalized. Exhibit 11-4 illustrates this relationship.

Other factors suggesting the use of an accelerated method include (1) the anticipation of a significant contribution in early periods with the extent of the contribution to be realized in later periods being less definite and (2) the possibility that inadequacy or obsolescence may result in premature retirement of the asset.

use-factor methods
工作量折旧法

Use-Factor Methods Use-factor depreciation methods view asset exhaustion as related primarily to asset use or output and provide periodic charges varying with the degree of such service. Service life for certain assets can best be expressed in terms of hours of service but for others in terms of units of production.

service-hours depreciation
服务期折旧法

Service-Hours Depreciation Service-hours depreciation is based on the theory that the purchase of an asset represents the purchase of a number of hours of direct service. This method requires an estimate of the life of the asset in terms of service hours. Depreciable cost is divided by total service hours in arriving at the depreciation rate to be assigned for each hour of asset use. The use of the asset during the period is measured, and the number of service hours is multiplied by the depreciation rate in arriving at the periodic depreciation charge. Depreciation charges against revenue fluctuate periodically according to how much the asset is used.

---

[4] The following is found in FASB ASC paragraph 360-10-35-7: "The declining-balance method is an example of one of the methods that meet the requirements of being systematic and rational. If the expected productivity or revenue-earning power of the asset is relatively greater during the earlier years of its life, or maintenance charges tend to increase during later years, the declining-balance method may provide the most satisfactory allocation of cost. That conclusion also applies to other methods, including the sum-of-the-years'-digits method, that produce substantially similar results."

Exhibit 11-4 | Accelerated Depreciation and Repairs and Maintenance Expense

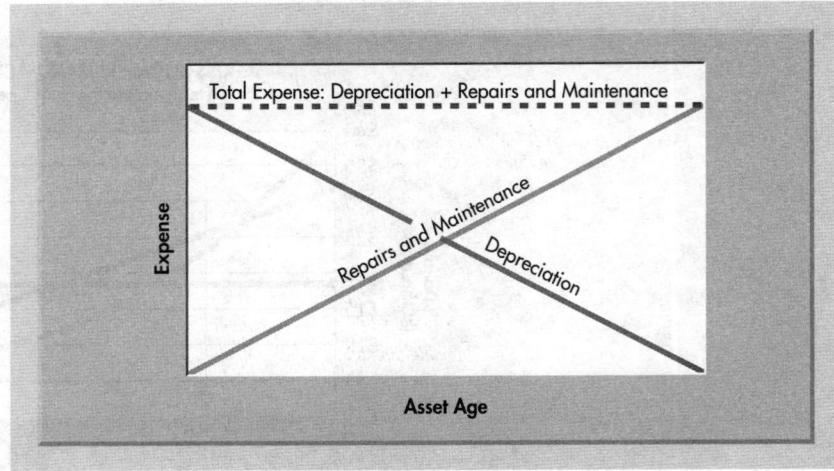

© Cengage Learning 2014

Using the Schuss Boom asset data previously given and an estimated service life of 20,000 hours, the rate to be applied for each service hour is determined as follows:

$$r \text{ (per hour)} = \frac{C - R}{n}, \text{ or } \frac{\$100{,}000 - \$5{,}000}{20{,}000 \text{ hours}} = \$4.75 \text{ per hour}$$

Computation of annual depreciation is summarized in the following table:

End of Year	Service Hours	Computation	Depreciation Amount	Accumulated Depreciation	Asset Book Value
					$100,000
2015	3,000	3,000 × $4.75 =	$14,250	$14,250	85,750
2016	5,000	5,000 × 4.75 =	23,750	38,000	62,000
2017	5,000	5,000 × 4.75 =	23,750	61,750	38,250
2018	4,000	4,000 × 4.75 =	19,000	80,750	19,250
2019	3,000	3,000 × 4.75 =	14,250	95,000	5,000
	20,000		$95,000		

In this illustration, the original estimate of service hours is correct, and the asset is retired after 20,000 hours are reached in the fifth year. Such precise estimation would seldom be found in practice. Procedures for handling changes in estimates are discussed later in the chapter.

Recall that straight-line depreciation resulted in annual depreciation of $19,000

> **FYI**
>
> The productive-output method approximates the technique used to depreciate the cost of producing a motion picture. This technique is discussed in Discussion Case 11-75.

regardless of fluctuations in how much the asset was used. When asset life is affected directly by the degree of use and when there are significant fluctuations in such use, the service-hours method, which recognizes hours used instead of hours available for use, normally provides the more appropriate charge to operations.

Productive-Output Depreciation Productive-output depreciation is based on the theory that an asset is acquired for the service it can provide in the form of production output. This method requires an estimate of the total unit output of the asset. Depreciable cost divided by the total estimated output gives the equal charge to be assigned for each unit of output. The measured production for a period multiplied by the charge per unit gives the charge to be made against revenue. Depreciation charges fluctuate periodically according to the contribution the asset makes in unit output.

Using the Schuss Boom asset data and an estimated productive life of 25,000 units, the rate to be applied for each unit produced is determined as follows:

$$r \text{ (per unit)} = \frac{C-R}{n}, \text{ or } \frac{\$100,000 - \$5,000}{25,000 \text{ units}} = \$3.80 \text{ per unit}$$

A table for the productive-output method would be similar to that prepared for the service-hours method.

当对资产使用的定量衡量可以比较合理地估计出来时，工作量折旧法是一种满意度较高的资产成本分配方法。

Evaluation of Use-Factor Methods When quantitative measures of asset use can be reasonably estimated, the use-factor methods provide highly satisfactory approaches to asset cost allocation. Depreciation as a fluctuating charge tends to follow the revenue curve: High depreciation charges are assigned to periods of high activity; low charges are assigned to periods of low activity. When the useful life of an asset is affected primarily by the degree of its use, recognition of depreciation as a variable charge is particularly appropriate.

However, certain limitations in applying the use-factor methods need to be noted. Asset performance in terms of service hours or productive output is often difficult to estimate. Measurement solely in terms of these factors could fail to recognize special conditions, such as increasing maintenance and repair costs, as well as possible inadequacy and obsolescence. Furthermore, when service life expires even in the absence of use, a use-factor method may conceal actual fluctuations in earnings; by relating periodic depreciation charges to the volume of operations, periodic operating results may be smoothed out, thus creating a false appearance of stability.

Group and Composite Methods It was assumed in preceding discussions that depreciation expense is associated with individual assets and is applied to each separate unit. This practice is called unit depreciation. From a practical standpoint, it often makes sense to compute depreciation for an entire group of assets as if the group were one asset. Group cost allocation procedures are referred to as group depreciation when the assets in the group are similar (e.g., all of a company's delivery vans) and composite depreciation when the assets in the group are related but dissimilar (e.g., all of a company's desks, chairs, and computers). In the following discussion, the term *group depreciation* will be used generically to refer to both methods.

The group depreciation procedure treats a collection of assets as a single group. Depreciation is accumulated in a single account, and the depreciation rate is based on the average life of assets in the group. Group depreciation is generally computed as an adaptation of the straight-line method, and the illustrations in this chapter assume this approach. A group rate is established by initially analyzing the various assets or classes of assets in use and computing the depreciation as an average of the straight-line annual depreciation as follows:

Asset	Cost	Residual Value	Depreciable Cost	Estimated Life in Years	Annual Depreciation Expense (Straight-Line)
A.	$ 2,000	$ 120	$ 1,880	4	$ 470
B.	6,000	300	5,700	6	950
C.	12,000	1,200	10,800	10	1,080
	$20,000	$1,620	$18,380		$2,500

Group depreciation rate to be applied to cost: $2,500/$20,000 = 12.5%
Average life of assets: $18,380/$2,500 = 7.352 years

The rate of 12.5% applied to the cost of the existing assets, $20,000, results in annual depreciation of $2,500. Annual depreciation of $2,500 will accumulate to a total of $18,380 in 7.352 years; hence, 7.352 years is the average life of the assets.

After the group rate of 12.5% has been set, it is used to compute annual depreciation for all assets subsequently included in the group. For example, if Asset D is acquired for $5,000, the total cost of the assets in the group becomes $25,000 ($2,000 + $6,000 + $12,000 + $5,000), and annual depreciation expense is $3,125 ($25,000 × 0.125). The group rate is ordinarily left the same in subsequent years in the absence of significant changes in the lives of assets included in the group. It is assumed that the assets are replaced with similar assets when retired. The group rate should be reviewed periodically to confirm that it is still appropriate for the assets in the group.

Because the accumulated depreciation account under the group procedure applies to the entire group of assets, it is not related to any specific asset. Thus, no book value can be calculated for any specific asset, and there are no fully depreciated assets. No gains or losses are recognized at the time individual assets are retired. For example, if asset B is sold for $3,500 after two years of use, the entry to record the sale using the group depreciation method would be as follows:

Cash	3,500	
Accumulated Depreciation	2,500	
Equipment		6,000

Because no gain or loss is recognized, the debit to Accumulated Depreciation is the difference between the cost of the asset and the cash received. Gains and losses due solely to normal variations in asset lives are not recognized.

In instances when assets in a group are continued in use after their cost has been assigned to operations, no further depreciation charges are recognized. On the other hand, when all the assets in a group are retired before their costs have been assigned to operations, a special charge related to such retirement would be recognized, either as a loss or as an addition to depreciation expense.

FASB CODIFICATION

The Issue: You are interviewing for a job with a mid-size accounting firm. Just before lunch you had a fairly unpleasant interview with a person who has been with the firm for six years. He decided to test your knowledge of depreciation methods, so he asked you to list all of the depreciation methods you know. When you mentioned "group depreciation," he stopped you and challenged you to name one industry that uses group depreciation. He said that in his long experience in the "real world," he has never seen a company using group depreciation. You can hear this person down the hall boasting to his colleagues about how he "stumped" the job applicant with a simple question about depreciation.

You feel that your credibility is at stake. You have just 30 minutes until your afternoon set of interviews begins.

The Question: According to the authoritative accounting literature, what industry uses group depreciation?

Searching the Codification: You have found that with respect to questions about accounting standards and practices, your best online friend is the FASB's Codification. You know that depreciation expense relates to property, plant, and equipment, which is discussed in Topic 360 of the Codification. You also know that depreciation expense is an issue of "subsequent measurement," which is found in Section 35 of whatever subtopic it is under. So, start with Topic 360 and start looking for some descriptions of depreciation standards in specific industries.

The Answer: The use of group depreciation in a specific industry is described on page 11-42.

Depreciation and *IAS 16*

Some items of property, plant, and equipment are composed of identifiable subitems. A perfect example is a building which has a roof, a heating/cooling system, windows, a general supporting structure, and so forth. Those subitems almost certainly do not depreciate over the same life. However, standard U.S. practice has been to treat the building as one composite asset depreciated as a group. An alternate approach is to depreciate each subitem, or component, separately. This component approach was mentioned briefly in Chapter 10. Mandatory use of the component approach was proposed by the AICPA in 2001 but rejected by the FASB in 2004; under current U.S. GAAP, companies are allowed, but not required, to use the component approach.

In contrast, the component approach is required under IASB standards. The following requirement is contained in *IAS 16*:

> Each part of an item of property, plant and equipment with a cost that is significant in relation to the total cost of the item shall be depreciated separately.[5]

Conceptually, the component approach presents no great difficulty because it merely requires that the standard depreciation calculations be applied separately to each significant

---

[5] *International Accounting Standard 16*, "Property, Plant and Equipment" (London: International Accounting Standards Board, December 9, 2004), par. 43.

component of a larger asset, such as a building. In practice, there is a slight increase in bookkeeping effort to keep track of the separate components.

Depreciation and Accretion of an Asset Retirement Obligation

As discussed in Chapter 10, the act of acquiring a long-term operating asset sometimes legally obligates a company to incur restoration costs in the future when the asset is retired. The fair value of this obligation is estimated when the asset is acquired; the fair value of the obligation is recognized as a liability and is added to the cost of the acquired asset. To continue the example introduced in Chapter 10, assume that Bryan Beach Company purchases and erects an oil platform at a total cost of $750,000. The oil platform will be in use for 10 years, at which time Bryan Beach is legally obligated to ensure that the platform is dismantled and removed from the site. Bryan Beach estimates that it will have to pay $100,000 to have the platform dismantled and removed from the site in 10 years. If the appropriate interest rate to use in computing the present value of the restoration obligation is 8%, the present value of the $100,000 obligation is computed as follows:

$$FV = \$100{,}000;\ I = 8\%;\ N = 10 \text{ years} \rightarrow \$46{,}319$$

The journal entries to record the purchase of the oil platform and the recognition of the asset retirement obligation are as follows:

Oil Platform	750,000	
Cash		750,000
Oil Platform	46,319	
Asset Retirement Obligation		46,319

The cost of the oil platform asset, including the estimated retirement obligation, is depreciated just like any other long-term asset. If straight-line depreciation is used and a zero residual value is assumed, the depreciation entry each year is as follows:

Depreciation Expense [($750,000 + $46,319)/10]	79,632	
Accumulated Depreciation—Oil Platform		79,632

In addition to this entry, each year an entry must be made to recognize the increase in the present value of the asset retirement obligation as the time until the obligation must be satisfied grows closer. This increase is similar to interest expense, but the FASB ruled that it should not be classified as interest expense.[6] Instead, the expense is called *accretion expense* and is recognized through the following journal entry:

Accretion Expense ($46,319 × 0.08)	3,706	
Asset Retirement Obligation		3,706

---

[6] FASB ASC paragraph 410-20-35-5.

Depletion of Natural Resources

LO2 学习目标2
运用工作量折旧法对自然资源进行折旧

② Apply the productive-output method to the depletion of natural resources.

Natural resources, also called *wasting assets*, are consumed as the physical units representing these resources are removed and sold. The withdrawal of oil or gas, the cutting of timber, and the mining of coal, sulfur, iron, copper, or silver ore are examples of processes leading to the exhaustion of natural resources. Depletion expense is a charge for the "using up" of the resources.

The computation of depletion expense is an adaptation of the productive-output method of depreciation. Perhaps the most difficult problem in computing depletion expense is estimating the amount of resources available for economical removal from the land. Generally, a geologist, mining engineer, or other expert is called upon to make the estimate, and it is subject to continual revision as the resource is extracted or removed.

Developmental costs, such as costs of drilling, sinking mine shafts, and constructing roads, should be capitalized and added to the original cost of the property in arriving at the total cost subject to depletion. These costs are often incurred before normal activities begin.

To illustrate the computation of depletion expense, assume the following facts: Land containing mineral deposits is purchased at a cost of $5,500,000. After all of the mineral deposits have been extracted, it is expected that the land will have a residual value of $250,000. The natural resource supply is estimated at 1,000,000 tons. The unit-depletion charge and the total depletion charge for the first year, assuming the withdrawal of 80,000 tons, are calculated as follows:

$$\text{Depletion charge per ton: } (\$5,500,000 - \$250,000) \div 1,000,000 = \$5.25$$

$$\text{Depletion charge for the first year: } 80,000 \text{ tons} \times \$5.25 = \$420,000$$

The following entries should be made to record these events:

Mineral Deposits	5,500,000	
Cash		5,500,000
Depletion Expense	420,000	
Accumulated Depletion (or Mineral Deposits)		420,000

如果80 000吨矿产在当年就被卖掉，420 000美元就会被全部当作销货成本的一部分；如果只有60 000吨被卖掉，那么将有105 000美元作为期末存货被记录在资产负债表中。

If the 80,000 tons are sold in the current year, the entire $420,000 would be included as part of the cost of goods sold. If only 60,000 tons are sold, $105,000 is reported as part of ending inventory on the balance sheet.

When buildings and improvements are constructed in connection with the removal of natural resources and their usefulness is limited to the duration of the project, it is reasonable to recognize depreciation on such properties on an output basis consistent with the charges to be recognized for the natural resources themselves. For example, assume that buildings are constructed at a cost of $250,000; the useful lives of the buildings are expected to terminate upon exhaustion of the natural resource consisting of 1,000,000 units. Under these circumstances, a depreciation charge of $0.25 ($250,000/1,000,000) should accompany the depletion charge recognized for each unit. When improvements provide benefits expected to terminate prior to the exhaustion of the natural resource, the cost of such improvements should be allocated on the basis of the units to be removed during the life of the improvements or on a time basis, whichever is considered more appropriate.

Changes in Estimates of Cost Allocation Variables

3 Incorporate changes in estimates and methods into the computation of depreciation for current and future periods.

The allocation of asset costs benefiting more than one period cannot be precisely determined at acquisition because so many of the variables must be estimated. Only one factor in determining the periodic charge for depreciation, amortization, or depletion is based on historical information: asset cost. Other factors—residual value, useful life or output, and the pattern of use or benefit—must be estimated. The question frequently facing accountants is how adjustments to these estimates, which arise as time passes, should be reflected in the accounts. A change in estimate is reported in the current and future periods rather than as an adjustment of prior periods. This type of adjustment is made for residual value and useful-life changes. A change in depreciation method (e.g., from double-declining-balance to straight-line) based on a revised expected pattern of use is also reported in the current and future periods rather than as an adjustment of prior periods.[7]

Change in Estimated Life

To illustrate the procedure for a change in estimated life affecting allocation of asset cost, assume that a company purchased $50,000 of equipment and estimated a 10-year life. Using the straight-line method with no residual value, the annual depreciation would be $5,000. After four years, accumulated depreciation would amount to $20,000, and the remaining undepreciated book value would be $30,000. Early in the fifth year, a reevaluation of the life indicates only four more years of service can be expected from the asset. An adjustment must therefore be made for the fifth and subsequent years to reflect the change. A new annual depreciation charge is calculated by dividing the remaining book value by the remaining life of four years. This would result in an annual charge of $7,500 for the fifth through eighth years ($30,000/4 = $7,500).

Year	Computation		Depreciation Amount	Accumulated Depreciation
1	$50,000/10	=	$ 5,000	$ 5,000
2	$50,000/10	=	5,000	10,000
3	$50,000/10	=	5,000	15,000
4	$50,000/10	=	5,000	20,000
5	($50,000 − $20,000)/4	=	7,500	27,500
6	($50,000 − $20,000)/4	=	7,500	35,000
7	($50,000 − $20,000)/4	=	7,500	42,500
8	($50,000 − $20,000)/4	=	7,500	50,000
			$50,000	

[7] FASB ASC paragraph 250-10-45-19.

Note that no attempt is made to go back and "fix" the first four years. The $5,000 depreciation charge recognized in those years was computed using the best information available. When revised information becomes available in the fifth year, the impact is reflected in the current and future periods.

注意：并没有对前4年的折旧数据进行追溯和修正，每年确认的5 000美元折旧额是利用所能获得的最恰当信息计算所得，在第5年可以获得更精准的信息时，产生的影响将在第5年及以后几年里予以反映。

Change in Estimated Units of Production

Another change in estimate occurs in accounting for natural resources when the estimate of the recoverable units changes as a result of further discoveries, improved extraction processes, or changes in sales prices that indicate changes in the number of units that can be extracted profitably. A revised depletion rate is established by dividing the remaining resource cost balance by the estimated remaining recoverable units.

To illustrate, assume the facts used in the earlier depletion example. Land is purchased at a cost of $5,500,000 with estimated net residual value of $250,000. The original estimated supply of natural resources in the land is 1,000,000 tons. As indicated previously, the depletion rate under these conditions would be $5.25 per ton, and the depletion charge for the first year when 80,000 tons were mined would be $420,000. Assume that in the second year of operation, 100,000 tons of ore are withdrawn, but before the books are closed at the end of the second year, appraisal of the expected recoverable tons indicates a remaining tonnage of 950,000. The new depletion rate and the depletion charge for the second year would be computed as follows:

Cost assignable to recoverable tons as of the beginning of the second year:

Original costs applicable to depletable resources	$5,250,000
Deduct: Depletion charge for the first year	420,000
Balance of cost subject to depletion	$4,830,000

Estimated recoverable tons as of the beginning of the second year:

Number of tons withdrawn in the second year	100,000
Estimated recoverable tons as of the end of the second year	950,000
Total recoverable tons as of the beginning of the second year	1,050,000

Depletion charge per ton for the second year: $4,830,000/1,050,000 = $4.60

Depletion charge for the second year: 100,000 × $4.60 = $460,000

Sometimes an increase in estimated recoverable units arises from additional expenditures for capital developments. When this occurs, the additional costs should be added to the remaining recoverable cost and divided by the number of tons remaining to be extracted. To illustrate this situation, assume in the preceding example that $525,000 of additional costs had been incurred at the beginning of the second year. The preceding computation of depletion rate and depletion expense would be changed as follows:

Cost assignable to recoverable tons as of the beginning of the second year:

Original costs applicable to depletable resources	$5,250,000
Add: Additional costs incurred in the second year	525,000
	$5,775,000
Deduct: Depletion charge for the first year	420,000
Balance of cost subject to depletion	$5,355,000
Estimated recoverable tons as of the beginning of the second year (as stated previously)	1,050,000

Depletion charge per ton for the second year: $5,355,000/1,050,000 = $5.10

Depletion charge for the second year: 100,000 × $5.10 = $510,000

Accounting is made up of many estimates. The procedures outlined in this section are designed to prevent the continual restating of reported income from prior years. Adjustments to prior-period income figures are made only if actual errors have occurred, not when reasonable estimates have been made that later prove inaccurate.

Change in Depreciation Method

Another change in estimate occurs when the actual pattern of consumption of an asset doesn't match the pattern of consumption implicit in the depreciation method used. For example, an asset for which straight-line depreciation has been used might be observed to be wearing out in an accelerated fashion. Accordingly, a change in depreciation method is indicated.

To illustrate, assume that an asset is purchased for $120,000 with a 12-year expected useful life and zero expected salvage value. Straight-line depreciation is used with the asset resulting in annual depreciation expense of $10,000 [($120,000 − $0)/12 years]. After two years of use, the asset has a remaining book value of $100,000 ($120,000 − $10,000 depreciation for Year 1 − $10,000 depreciation for Year 2) and a remaining useful life of 10 years. Observation of the pattern of consumption of this asset for these two years indicates that the double-declining-balance method of depreciation would yield a better estimate of periodic depreciation. This change in estimate related to the pattern of asset consumption is reflected in the year in which the change is implemented (Year 3 in this example) and the subsequent years. Depreciation expense for Year 3 is computed as follows:

- Straight-line rate = 100%/Remaining life = 100%/10 years = 10%
- Double the straight-line rate = 10% × 2 = 20%
- Remaining book value = $100,000 (computation shown above)
- Year 3 depreciation expense = $100,000 × 0.20 = $20,000

When a change in estimate impacting the computation of depreciation expense is made, the current-year impact of the change on net income must be disclosed in the notes to the financial statements. When the change is implemented through a change in depreciation method, the note disclosure must also include an explanation of the change. Further discussion of accounting changes is contained in Chapter 20.

Impairment of Tangible Assets

 Identify whether an asset is impaired, and measure the amount of the impairment loss using both U.S. GAAP and IASB standards.

Events sometimes occur after the purchase of an asset and before the end of its estimated life that impair its value and require an immediate write-down of the asset rather than making a normal allocation of cost over a period of time. Until 1995, the authoritative accounting literature did not include a clear statement of accounting standards governing the recognition of asset impairment.

As an example, in 1994, Eli Lilly, a large pharmaceutical company, paid $4.1 billion to acquire PCS Health Systems, a company that helps insurance companies and HMOs manage their prescription drug benefit plans. By the second quarter of 1997, it had become apparent that the PCS acquisition was not turning out as planned. The movement toward managed health care had not been as fast as Lilly had expected, and the ominous possibility of increased government regulation of prescription drug benefit plans had tempered enthusiasm about PCS's prospects. In reviewing the acquisition, Eli Lilly decided that it should recognize a

FYI

In a final act of surrender, Eli Lilly sold its PCS division to **Rite Aid** on January 22, 1999, for just $1.6 billion.

loss and reduce the recorded value of PCS's assets by $2.4 billion.

As illustrated by the Eli Lilly/PCS Health Systems case, whether to recognize the impairment of operating assets is not a simple decision. In addition, once the decision to recognize the impairment has been made, one is still faced with the question of the amount of the write-down. This section discusses the concepts and procedures associated with the recognition of an asset impairment.

Accounting for Asset Impairment

资产减值计算涉及四个问题:
- 资产什么时候应该进行减值测试?
- 资产什么时候减值?
- 如何计量减值?
- 应当披露哪些减值信息?

Guidance on the accounting for asset impairment addresses the following four questions:[8]

1. When should an asset be reviewed for possible impairment?
2. When is an asset impaired?
3. How should an impairment loss be measured?
4. What information should be disclosed about an impairment?

1. When Should an Asset Be Reviewed for Possible Impairment? Conducting an impairment review of every asset at the end of every year would be unlikely to provide sufficiently improved financial information to justify the cost of the reviews. Instead, companies are required to conduct impairment tests whenever there has been a material change in the way an asset is used or in the business environment. In addition, if management obtains information suggesting that the market value of an asset has declined, an impairment review should be conducted.

2. When Is an Asset Impaired? According to the FASB, an entity should recognize an impairment loss only when the undiscounted sum of estimated future cash flows from an asset is less than the book value of the asset. As illustrated in the following example, this is rather a strange impairment threshold; a more intuitive test would be to compare the book value to the fair value of the asset. Because the undiscounted cash flows do not incorporate the time value of money, the sum of undiscounted future cash flows will always be greater than the fair value of the asset.

3. How Should an Impairment Loss Be Measured? The impairment loss is the difference between the book value of the asset and the fair value. The fair value can be approximated using the present value of estimated future cash flows from the asset.

4. What Information Should Be Disclosed about an Impairment? Disclosure should include a description of the impaired asset, reasons for the impairment, a description of the measurement assumptions, and the business segment or segments affected. An impairment loss should be included as part of income from continuing operations, and note disclosure of the amount should be made if the impairment loss is not shown as a separate income statement item.

Caution

The existence of an impairment loss is determined using undiscounted future cash flows. The amount of the impairment loss is measured using fair value, or *discounted*, future cash flows.

[8] FASB ASC Subtopic 360-10 (Property, Plant, and Equipment—Overall), various subsections on "Impairment."

Application of the impairment rules is illustrated with the following example. Guangzhou Company purchased a building five years ago for $600,000. The building has been depreciated using the straight-line method with a 20-year useful life and no residual value. Several other buildings in the immediate area have recently been abandoned, and Guangzhou has decided that the building should be evaluated for possible impairment. Guangzhou estimates that the building has a remaining useful life of 15 years, that net cash inflow from the building will be $25,000 per year, and that the fair value of the building is $230,000.

Annual depreciation for the building has been $30,000 ($600,000/20 years). The current book value of the building is computed as follows:

Original cost	$600,000
Accumulated depreciation ($30,000 × 5 years)	150,000
Book value	$450,000

The book value of $450,000 is compared to the $375,000 ($25,000 × 15 years) undiscounted sum of future cash flows to determine whether the building is impaired. The sum of future cash flows is less, so an impairment loss should be recognized. The loss is equal to the $220,000 ($450,000 − $230,000) difference between the book value of the building and its fair value. The impairment loss would be recorded as follows:

Accumulated Depreciation—Building	150,000	
Loss on Impairment of Building	220,000	
Building ($600,000 − $230,000)		370,000

The new recorded value of $230,000 ($600,000 − $370,000) is considered to be the cost of the asset. After an impairment loss is recognized, no restoration of the loss is allowed even if the fair value of the asset recovers.

The odd nature of the undiscounted cash flow threshold can be seen if the facts in the Guangzhou example are changed slightly. Assume that net cash inflow from the building will be $35,000 per year and that the fair value of the building is $330,000. With these numbers, no impairment loss is recognized, even though the fair value of $330,000 is less than the book value of $450,000 because the undiscounted sum of future cash flows of $525,000 ($35,000 × 15 years) exceeds the book value.

In many cases, it is more appropriate to estimate a range of possible future cash flows rather than to make a specific point estimate. In the preceding example, assume that instead of estimating future cash flows of $25,000 per year, it is estimated that the following two cash flow scenarios are possible, with the indicated probabilities:

	Future Cash Inflows	Probability
Scenario 1	$20,000 per year for 15 years	85%
Scenario 2	50,000 per year for 15 years	15%

> **Stop & Think**
>
> Which ONE of the following statements best describes the effect of the undiscounted cash flow threshold used in the impairment test?
>
> a) Use of the undiscounted cash flow threshold means that an asset must suffer a significant drop in fair value before an impairment loss is recognized.
> b) Use of the undiscounted cash flow threshold means that any drop in fair value, no matter how small, will result in the recognition of an impairment loss.
> c) Use of the undiscounted cash flow threshold means that impairment losses will occasionally be recognized even when assets have increased in value.
> d) Use of the undiscounted cash flow threshold means that it is unlikely that any company will ever recognize an impairment loss.

In applying the impairment test, the weighted-average undiscounted cash flows are computed as follows:

	Undiscounted Future Cash Inflows	Probability	Probability-Weighted Future Cash Flows
Scenario 1	$20,000 × 15 years = $300,000	85%	$255,000
Scenario 2	50,000 × 15 years = 750,000	15%	112,500
Total			$367,500

The $367,500 probability-weighted sum of undiscounted future cash flows is compared to the $450,000 book value of the building, indicating that the asset is impaired ($367,500 < $450,000). Assume that in this case there is no observable market value of the building and that the market value must be estimated using present value techniques. If the risk-free interest rate is 6.0%, the expected present value is computed as follows:

	Future Cash Inflows	Present Value (6.0% discount rate)	Probability	Probability-Weighted Present Value
Scenario 1	$20,000 × 15 years	$194,245	85%	$165,108
Scenario 2	50,000 × 15 years	485,612	15%	72,842
Estimated fair value				$237,950

The impairment loss would be recorded as follows:

Accumulated Depreciation—Building	150,000	
Loss on Impairment of Building ($450,000 − $237,950)	212,050	
Building ($600,000 − $237,950)		362,050

International Accounting for Asset Impairment: *IAS 36*

The IASB's standard for impairment is *IAS 36*, "Impairment of Assets." This international standard is, from a conceptual standpoint, superior to the impairment standard embodied in U.S. GAAP. The IASB standard requires that a company recognize an impairment loss whenever the "recoverable amount" of an asset is less than its book value. *Recoverable amount* is defined as the higher of the selling price of the asset or the discounted future cash flows associated with the asset's use. Both of these measures are based on the discounted value of the future cash flows from the asset, which means that the IASB has completely rejected the conceptually unappealing undiscounted cash flow threshold adopted by the FASB.

IAS 36 also differs from U.S. GAAP in that the international standard allows for the reversal of an impairment loss if events in subsequent years suggest the asset is no longer impaired. Therefore, if an asset has increased in value and is no longer deemed to be impaired, the portion of the impairment loss that has been recovered should be reversed and recognized as a gain. Under the FASB standard, no subsequent recovery of an impairment loss is allowed.

IASB准则要求，一旦公司资产的"可收回金额"小于其账面价值就要确认减值。可回收金额被定义为资产销售价格和与资产使用有关的未来现金流折现值中的较高者。

Accounting for Upward Asset Revaluations: *IAS 16*

As mentioned in Chapter 10, an allowable alternative under *IAS 16* is to recognize increases in the value of long-term operating assets. Because the accounting procedures associated with asset revaluation are similar to those used to recognize an asset impairment, they are illustrated in this section.

Recognizing an Upward Asset Revaluation
Earlier, we used an example of a building purchased by Guangzhou Company to illustrate the accounting for an asset impairment. Recall that after five years, the book value of that building was as follows:

Original cost	$600,000
Accumulated depreciation ($30,000 × 5 years)	150,000
Book value	$450,000

Now assume that Guangzhou Company uses International Accounting Standards, the building's fair value is $540,000, and Guangzhou employs the allowable alternative under international standards, electing to recognize this increase in asset value. The journal entry to recognize the asset revaluation is as follows:

Accumulated Depreciation—Building	150,000	
Revaluation Equity Reserve		90,000
Building ($600,000 − $540,000)		60,000

After the entry is posted, the balance in the accumulated depreciation account is $0, and the balance in the building account is $540,000 ($600,000 − $60,000), resulting in a net recorded amount of $540,000. As discussed in Chapter 13, the revaluation equity reserve is a separate category of equity and reflects the increase in the reported value of the total assets of the company stemming from increases in the market value of long-term operating assets. After the revaluation, annual depreciation expense is computed based on the revalued amount; the revalued amount is depreciated over the remaining estimated life of the asset.

> **Caution**
> Remember that the upward revaluation of long-term operating assets is an allowable alternative under International Accounting Standards but is *not* allowable under U.S. GAAP.

Recording the Disposal of a Revalued Asset
An interesting twist in the provisions of *IAS 16* makes it somewhat costly for a company to revalue its assets upward. To illustrate, assume that, immediately after revaluing its building to $540,000, Guangzhou Company sells the building for $540,000 in cash. This disposal would be recorded as follows:

Cash	540,000	
Building		540,000
Revaluation Equity Reserve	90,000	
Retained Earnings		90,000

Note that because Guangzhou chose to revalue the asset, the $90,000 "gain" from the increase in the value of the asset is never reported as a gain in Guangzhou's income statement. The "gain" is initially reflected as an increase in the equity reserve; on disposal, the "gain" is transferred directly to Retained Earnings, bypassing the income statement completely. Thus, although *IAS 16* gives companies the benefit of recognizing increases in the value of long-term operating assets, the provisions of *IAS 16* also impose a cost in the sense that these increases are then never reflected as increases in earnings in the income statement.

Amortization and Impairment of Intangibles

LO5 学习目标5
讨论影响无形资产正确摊销和减值的事项。

5 Discuss the issues impacting proper recognition of amortization or impairment for intangible assets.

For accounting purposes, recorded intangible assets come in three varieties:

- *Intangible assets that are amortized.* The impairment test for these intangibles is the same as the two-step test described earlier in the chapter for tangible long-term operating assets.
- *Intangible assets that are not amortized.* The impairment test for these intangibles involves a simple one-step comparison of the book value to the fair value.
- *Goodwill, which according to FASB ASC Topic 350 (Intangibles—Goodwill and Other) is not amortized.* The goodwill impairment test is a process that first involves estimating the fair value of the entire reporting unit to which the goodwill is allocated.

In accounting for an intangible asset after its acquisition, a determination first must be made as to whether the intangible asset has a finite life. If no economic, legal, or contractual factors cause the intangible to have a finite life, then its life is said to be indefinite, and the asset is not to be amortized until its life is determined to be finite. An indefinite life is one that extends beyond the foreseeable horizon.[9] An example of an intangible asset that has an indefinite life is a broadcast license that includes an extension option that can be renewed indefinitely. If an intangible asset is determined to have a finite life, the asset is to be amortized over its estimated life; the useful life estimate should be reviewed periodically.[10]

Amortization and Impairment of Intangible Assets Subject to Amortization

The very nature of intangible assets makes estimating their useful lives a difficult problem. The useful life of an intangible asset may be affected by a variety of economic, legal, regulatory, and contractual factors. These factors, including options for renewal or extension, should be evaluated in determining the appropriate period over which the cost of the intangible asset should be allocated. A patent, for example, has a legal life of 20 years from the date of application in the United States; but if the competitive advantages afforded by the patent are expected to terminate after five years, the patent cost should be amortized over the shorter period.

---

[9] FASB ASC paragraph 350-30-35-4.
[10] Before the adoption of pre-Codification *SFAS No. 142* in 2001 (which is the basis for FASB ASC Topic 350), intangible assets were amortizable over a maximum period of 40 years. The FASB considered imposing a maximum amortization period of 20 years on intangibles. However, the final standard does not include any arbitrary cap on the useful life of amortizable intangible assets.

Intangible assets are to be amortized by the straight-line method unless there is strong justification for using another method. Amortization, like depreciation, may be charged as an operating expense of the period or allocated to production overhead if the asset is related directly to the manufacture of goods. Because companies must disclose both the original cost and the accumulated amortization for amortizable intangibles, the credit entry should be made to a separate accumulated amortization account.

To illustrate the accounting for amortizable intangibles, consider the following example. Ethereal Company markets products to real-estate agents and to new homeowners. Ethereal purchased a customer list for $30,000 on January 1, 2015. Because of turnover among real-estate agents and because new homeowners gradually become established homeowners, the list is expected to have economic value for only four years. As with all amortizable intangibles, the presumption is that the residual value of the customer list is zero; in this case, there is no evidence to rebut this presumption. Similarly, there is no evidence to justify the use of any amortization method other than straight line. On December 31, 2015, the following journal entry is made to recognize amortization expense:

Amortization Expense ($30,000/4 years)	7,500	
Accumulated Amortization—Customer List		7,500

During 2016, before amortization expense for the year is recognized, the customer list intangible asset is tested for impairment. The impairment test is the same as that explained previously for tangible long-term operating assets. The impairment test for the real-estate customer list was prompted by a substantial downturn in the real-estate market in the area. At the time of the impairment test, the book value of the intangible asset is $22,500 ($30,000 − $7,500). It is estimated that the customer list will generate future cash flows of $5,000 per year for the next three years and that the fair value of the customer list on December 31, 2016, is $12,000. The customer list intangible asset is impaired because the $15,000 ($5,000 × 3 years) sum of the future undiscounted cash flows is less than the book value of $22,500. The amount of the impairment loss is the $10,500 ($22,500 − $12,000) difference between the book value and the fair value and is recorded as follows:

Impairment Loss ($22,500 − $12,000)	10,500	
Accumulated Amortization—Customer List	7,500	
Customer List ($30,000 − $12,000)		18,000

The $12,000 fair value is the new basis for the intangible asset; no entry is made to recognize any subsequent recovery in the value of the intangible. Amortization in subsequent years will be based on the new book value of $12,000 and the estimated remaining useful life of three years. In the notes to the financial statements for 2016, Ethereal Company would be required to disclose the amount of amortization expense it expects to recognize for all of its intangibles in each year for the next five years.

Impairment of Intangible Assets Not Subject to Amortization

Some intangibles are identified as having indefinite lives and are not amortized. The FASB described the following examples of intangibles with indefinite lives:

- *Broadcast license.* Broadcast licenses often have a renewal period of 10 years. Renewal is virtually automatic if the license holder maintains an acceptable level of service to

the public. Accordingly, there is no foreseeable end to the useful life of the broadcast license; it has an indefinite life.
- *Trademark.* A trademark right is granted for a limited time, but trademarks can be renewed almost routinely. If economic factors suggest that the trademark will continue to have value in the foreseeable future, then its useful life is indefinite.[11]

Intangibles with indefinite lives are not amortized. However, an intangible with an indefinite life is evaluated at least annually to determine (1) whether the end of the useful life is now foreseeable and amortization should begin and/or (2) whether the intangible is impaired. The impairment test is a very simple one: The fair value of the intangible is compared to its book value, and if the fair value is less than the book value, an impairment loss is recognized for the difference.

To illustrate, assume that Impalpable Company has a broadcast license that has no foreseeable end to its useful life. The broadcast license is recorded at its original acquisition cost of $60,000. In the past, it was estimated that the broadcast license would generate cash flows of $7,000 per year. Recent changes in the broadcast environment have reduced the cash flows expected to be generated by the license. The data gathered by Impalpable Company suggest that, although the useful life of the license is still indefinite, the possible future cash flows will be reduced to either $2,000 per year (with 70% probability) or to $4,000 per year (with 30% probability). The risk-free interest rate to be used in the probability-weighted present value calculation is 5%. The estimate of the fair value of the intangible is computed as follows:

> **Stop & Think**
>
> Why wouldn't the regular two-step impairment test (using the undiscounted sum of future cash flows) work for intangible assets that are not amortized?
> a) The undiscounted sum of future cash flows is zero.
> b) The undiscounted sum of future cash flows is always equal to the book value of the intangible asset, by definition.
> c) The undiscounted sum of future cash flows is infinite.
> d) The undiscounted sum of future cash flows is always less than the fair value of the asset.

	Future Cash Inflows	Present Value* of Indefinite Annual Cash Flows	Probability	Probability-Weighted Present Value
Scenario 1.....................	$2,000 per year	$40,000	70%	$28,000
Scenario 2.....................	$4,000 per year	80,000	30%	24,000
Total estimated fair value				$52,000

*The present value of a stream of indefinite, or infinite, annual cash flows is simply (Annual cash flow/Discount rate).

Because the estimated fair value of the broadcast license is less than its book value ($52,000 < $60,000), the intangible asset is impaired. The impairment loss is recognized with the following journal entry:

Impairment Loss ($60,000 − $52,000)... 8,000
    Broadcast License... 8,000

---

[11] FASB ASC paragraphs 350-30-55-11 through 13 and 20 through 22.

As with the recognition of other impairment losses, the $52,000 fair value is the new basis for the intangible asset; no entry is made to recognize any subsequent recovery in the value of the intangible.[12]

Impairment of Goodwill

When goodwill is recognized in conjunction with the acquisition of a business, that goodwill is assigned to an existing "reporting unit" of that business. For example, if Disney were to acquire another TV network in addition to its existing ABC network, any goodwill associated with the acquisition would be assigned to Disney's Media Networks segment. If necessary, goodwill created in an acquisition can be split up and assigned to several different existing operating segments.

As discussed in Chapter 10, for accounting purposes goodwill is computed as the residual amount left over after the purchase price of a business has been allocated to all of the identifiable tangible and intangible assets. This residual nature of goodwill is the key to testing whether goodwill is impaired after its acquisition. Clearly, by definition goodwill cannot be valued by itself but is instead the remaining value not explained by the fair values of all the identifiable assets. The procedures in testing goodwill for impairment stem from this idea and are outlined as follows:

Procedures in Testing Goodwill for Impairment

1. Conduct a *qualitative* assessment of reporting units that include recorded goodwill. Determine whether it is more likely than not (a probability of greater than 50%) that the fair value of the reporting unit is less than its net book value (recorded assets less recorded liabilities). *Note:* This is an OPTIONAL step; a company can choose to skip directly to Procedure 2 below.[13]

2. Compute the fair value of each reporting unit to which goodwill has been assigned. This can be done by using the present value of expected future cash flows or earnings or revenue multiples.

3. If the fair value of the reporting unit exceeds the net book value of the assets (including goodwill) and liabilities of the reporting unit, the goodwill is assumed to not be impaired and no impairment loss is recognized.

4. If the fair value of the reporting unit is less than the net book value of the assets and liabilities of the reporting unit, then a new fair value of goodwill is computed. The value of goodwill cannot be measured directly. Instead, goodwill value is always a residual amount; it is the amount of fair value of a reporting unit that is left over after the values of all identifiable assets and liabilities of the reporting unit have been considered. Accordingly, the fair values of all assets and liabilities of the reporting unit are estimated, these amounts are compared to the overall fair value of the reporting unit, and the implied amount of goodwill is computed.

5. If the implied amount of goodwill computed in (4) is less than the amount initially recorded, a goodwill impairment loss is recognized for the difference.

To illustrate the goodwill impairment test, assume that Buyer Company acquired Target Company on January 1, 2015. As part of the acquisition, $1,000 in goodwill was

---

[12] In January 2012, the FASB proposed an optional qualitative impairment assessment that a company can perform before diving into the detailed calculation of the fair value of its indefinite-lived intangibles. This qualitative assessment option is intended to reduce the cost of performing the impairment analysis of intangibles. An Accounting Standards Update on this subject is expected to be released in the latter half of 2012. As discussed in the next section, such an option is already included in the impairment testing of goodwill.

[13] FASB ASC paragraphs 350-20-35-3A through 3G.

recognized; this goodwill was assigned to Buyer's Manufacturing reporting unit. For 2015, earnings from the Manufacturing reporting unit were $350. Separately traded companies with operations similar to the Manufacturing reporting unit have market values approximately equal to six times earnings (i.e., their price-earnings ratios are 6.0). As of December 31, 2015, book and fair values of assets and liabilities of the Manufacturing reporting unit are as follows:

	Book Values	Fair Values
Identifiable assets	$3,500	$4,000
Goodwill	1,000	?
Liabilities	2,000	2,000

Procedure 1 A qualitative assessment indicates that both the general economic and the specific industry conditions affecting the Manufacturing reporting unit suggest that there is more than a 50% probability that the fair value of the reporting unit is less than its net book value. Thus, there is a strong possibility that the Manufacturing reporting unit goodwill has been impaired; accordingly, the additional, quantitative goodwill impairment test procedures must be now be completed. Other qualitative factors that can indicate a possible goodwill impairment are negative operating cash flows or earnings or a shake-up in top management.

Procedure 2 Using the earnings multiple, the fair value of the Manufacturing reporting unit is estimated to be $2,100 ($350 × 6). This fair value estimation could also be done using cash flow estimates and present value techniques.

Procedure 3 The net book value of the assets and liabilities of the Manufacturing reporting unit is computed as follows:

$$\text{Assets } (\$3,500 + \$1,000) - \text{Liabilities } (\$2,000) = \$2,500$$

Because the estimated fair value of the reporting unit ($2,100) is less than the net book value of the reporting unit ($2,500), further computations are needed to determine the amount of a goodwill impairment loss, if any.

Procedure 4 Using the $2,100 estimated fair value of the Manufacturing reporting unit, along with the estimated fair values of the identifiable assets and liabilities, the implied fair value of goodwill is computed as follows:

Estimated fair value of Manufacturing reporting unit	$2,100
Fair value of identifiable assets – fair value of liabilities ($4,000 – $2,000)	2,000
Implied fair value of goodwill	$ 100

Procedure 5 The implied fair value of goodwill is less than the recorded amount of goodwill ($100 < $1,000). Accordingly,

---

Stop & Think

It has been suggested that the goodwill impairment test is a costly one to apply in practice. Which one of the five procedures of the goodwill impairment test do you think is the most costly to perform?

a) Conduct a qualitative assessment of reporting units to which goodwill has been assigned.
b) Compute the fair value of each reporting unit to which goodwill has been assigned.
c) Compare the fair value of the reporting unit to the net book value of the assets (including goodwill) and liabilities of the reporting unit.
d) Estimate the fair value of all assets and liabilities of the reporting unit and use these amounts to compute the implied amount of goodwill.
e) Compare the newly computed estimate of goodwill to the recorded amount of goodwill.

> **FYI**
>
> During 2002, **Time Warner** (formerly known as AOL Time Warner) recognized goodwill impairment losses totaling $98.884 billion. The goodwill initially arose as part of the ill-fated acquisition of Time Warner by AOL.

the goodwill is impaired. The journal entry necessary to recognize the goodwill impairment loss is as follows:

Goodwill Impairment Loss	900	
Goodwill ($1,000 − $100)		900

The total amount of goodwill impairment losses should be reported as a separate line item in the income statement.

International Accounting for Intangible Impairment: *IAS 36*

As explained in the preceding section, U.S. GAAP contains three different impairment tests for intangible assets—one for intangibles with finite lives, a different one for intangible assets with indefinite lives, and a third test for goodwill. Well, the good news with respect to International Financial Reporting Standards is that there is basically just one impairment test for intangibles, explained in *IAS 36*, and this is the same impairment test used with tangible assets: the recorded amount of the intangible asset is compared to its "recoverable amount." As explained earlier, the recoverable amount is the higher of the fair value of the intangible (less the cost to sell the intangible) and the value of the intangible in use.[14] If the recoverable amount is less than the recorded amount, the intangible is impaired, and an impairment loss is recognized. When testing goodwill for impairment, the test is applied to the business unit to which the goodwill has been assigned. Goodwill is impaired if the recoverable amount of the entire business unit is less than the recorded amount of the net assets of the unit (including goodwill); this test is similar to the goodwill impairment test under U.S. GAAP.

Asset Retirements

 Account for the sale of depreciable assets in exchange for cash and in exchange for other depreciable assets.

LO6 学习目标6
对出售折旧资产换取现金和其他折旧资产的会计处理。

Assets may be retired by sale, exchange, or abandonment. Generally, when an asset is disposed of, any unrecorded depreciation or amortization for the period is recorded at the date of disposition. A book value as of the date of disposition can then be computed as the difference between the cost of the asset and its accumulated depreciation. If the disposition price exceeds the book value, a gain is recognized. If the disposition price is less than the book value, a loss is recorded. As part of the disposition entry, the balances in the asset and accumulated depreciation accounts for the asset are canceled. The following sections illustrate the asset retirement process under varying conditions.

---

[14] The difference between "fair value" and "value in use" is that "fair value" is a market-based quantity reflecting what market participants outside a company would pay to buy the intangible. In contrast, "value in use" is a company-specific quantity based on the present value of the discounted cash flows expected to be generated by the intangible given how the company plans to use that intangible internally. "Value in use" is usually greater than "fair value" because if the internal value of an asset is less than its value in the external market, the company would likely have already sold the asset.

Asset Retirement by Sale

If the proceeds from the sale of an asset are in the form of cash or a receivable, the recording of the transaction follows the order outlined in the previous paragraph. For example, assume that on July 1, 2015, Landon Supply Co. sells for $43,600 machinery that is recorded on the books at cost of $83,600 with accumulated depreciation as of January 1, 2015, of $50,600. The company depreciates its machinery using a straight-line, 10% rate. Before recording the asset sale, a half-year of depreciation is recognized representing use of the asset for the first six months of the year.

The following entries would be made to record this transaction:

Depreciation Expense—Machinery	4,180	
Accumulated Depreciation—Machinery		4,180
To record depreciation for six months in 2015 ($83,600 × 0.10 × 6/12).		
Cash	43,600	
Accumulated Depreciation—Machinery	54,780	
Machinery		83,600
Gain on Sale of Machinery		14,780*
To record sale of machinery at a gain.		

*Sales price	$43,600
Book value ($83,600 − $54,780)	28,820
Gain on sale	$14,780

Asset Classification as Held for Sale

Often, a plan is made to dispose of an asset before the actual sale takes place. Special accounting is required if the following conditions are satisfied:

- Management commits to a plan to sell a long-term operating asset.
- The asset is available for immediate sale.
- An active effort to locate a buyer is underway.
- It is probable that the sale will be completed within one year.

If these criteria are satisfied, two uncommon accounting actions are required. During the interval between being classified as held for sale and actually being sold

1. No depreciation is to be recognized, and
2. The asset is to be reported at the lower of its book value or its fair value (less the estimated cost to sell).[15]

To illustrate the accounting for a long-term asset that is classified as held for sale, assume that as of July 1, 2015, Haan Company has a building with a cost of $100,000 and accumulated depreciation of $35,000. Haan commits to a plan to sell the building by March 1, 2016. On July 1, 2015, the building has an estimated fair value of $40,000, and it is estimated that selling costs associated with the disposal of the building will be $3,000. On July 1, 2015, Haan must make the following journal entry:

[15] FASB ASC paragraph 360-10-35-43.

Building—Held for Sale..	37,000	
Loss on Held-for-Sale Classification	28,000	
Accumulated Depreciation—Building...	35,000	
Building		100,000

After this journal entry is made, the building is recorded at its net realizable value of $37,000 ($40,000 selling price − $3,000 selling costs). If the net realizable value had been greater than the book value of $65,000 ($100,000 − $35,000), no journal entry would have been made. This measurement approach is exactly the same as that used to record inventory at the lower of cost or market, as illustrated in Chapter 9.

> **Caution**
> Recognition of this loss did *not* involve use of the two-step impairment test explained earlier. Instead, the net selling price of the asset held for sale is compared directly to the book value; no comparison is made to the sum of future undiscounted cash flows.

On December 31, 2015, no adjusting entry is made for depreciation of the building. As mentioned, no depreciation expense is recognized on a long-term asset classified as held for sale. The rationale behind this approach is that because the asset is now designated for disposal, the key accounting point is no longer long-term cost allocation using depreciation but is instead proper current valuation of the asset. Accordingly, in the Haan Company example, the $37,000 carrying value of the building on December 31, 2015, would be compared to a revised estimate of the selling price (less selling cost) on that date. If this revised estimate is even lower than $37,000, an additional loss would be recognized. If the estimated net selling price had increased since the initial loss was recognized, a gain would be recognized to the extent of the $28,000 loss initially recognized. For example, if the estimated selling price as of December 31, 2015, was $58,000 (with $3,000 estimated selling costs), the following journal entry would be necessary:

利得只能在之前确认的损失范围内转回。例如，2015年12月31日的净售价估计为80 000美元，那么只有28 000美元被确认为收入，而非总收入43000美元（80 000−37 000）。

Building Held for Sale..	18,000	
Gain on Recovery of Value—Held for Sale......................................		18,000

Computation of gain: ($58,000 − $3,000) − $37,000 = $18,000

> **Caution**
> This partial recovery of the loss recognized on the held-for-sale classification is not the usual practice with impairment losses. For regular long-term assets (not being held for sale), no recovery of impairment losses is allowed.

A gain is recognized only to the extent that it offsets a previously recognized loss. For example, if the net selling price of the building on December 31, 2015, was estimated to be $80,000, a gain of only $28,000 would be recognized instead of the entire indicated gain of $43,000 ($80,000 − $37,000).

当一项经营资产与另一项非货币性资产交易时，换入资产要以其市场公允价值或换出资产的公允价值中更容易确定的一项入账。然而，如果交易没有真正的商业价值，则有时换入资产必须以账面价值（而非公允价值）入账。

Asset Retirement by Exchange for Other Nonmonetary Assets

As indicated in Chapter 10, when operating assets are acquired in exchange for other nonmonetary assets, the new asset acquired is generally recorded at its fair value or the fair value of the nonmonetary asset given in exchange, whichever is more clearly determinable. However, if the exchange has no real commercial substance, the asset received is sometimes recorded at the BOOK value (not fair value) of the asset given.

The entries required to record the exchange of most nonmonetary assets are identical to those illustrated in the previous section except that a nonmonetary asset is received in exchange rather than cash or receivables. Gains and losses arising from these exchanges are recognized when the exchange takes place.

To illustrate, assume in the earlier example that the retirement of the described asset was done by exchanging it for delivery equipment that had a market value of $43,600. The entries would be the same as illustrated except that instead of a debit to Cash, Delivery Equipment would be debited for $43,600. The gain would still be computed by comparing the book value of the machine and the market value of the asset acquired in the exchange. (*Note:* In the examples in this section, the entry to record depreciation expense for the first six months of the year will not be shown.)

Delivery Equipment	43,600	
Accumulated Depreciation—Machinery	54,780	
Machinery		83,600
Gain on Exchange of Machinery		14,780

If the machinery's market value were more clearly determinable than the value of the delivery equipment, the value of the machinery would be used to compute the gain or loss and to determine the value for the delivery equipment. Assume that the delivery equipment is used and has no readily available market price, but the machinery had a market value of $25,000. Under these circumstances, a loss of $3,820 ($28,820 – $25,000) would be indicated, and the entry to record the exchange would be as follows:

Delivery Equipment	25,000	
Accumulated Depreciation—Machinery	54,780	
Loss on Exchange of Machinery	3,820	
Machinery		83,600

Often, the exchange of nonmonetary assets includes a transfer of cash because the nonmonetary assets in most exchange transactions do not have identical market values. The cash part of the transaction adjusts the market values of the assets received to those of the assets given up. Thus, if in the previous example the machinery (with a market value of $25,000) were given in exchange for the delivery equipment and $3,000 cash, the entry would be as follows:

Cash	3,000	
Delivery Equipment ($25,000 – $3,000 cash received)	22,000	
Accumulated Depreciation—Machinery	54,780	
Loss on Exchange of Machinery	3,820	
Machinery		83,600

Remember that for most exchanges of nonmonetary assets, the asset received is recorded on the books at its fair value on the date of exchange. An exception to this general rule is explained in the next section.

Nonmonetary Exchange without Commercial Substance

Not all exchanges of nonmonetary assets involve substantive business transactions. For example, the Tri-City Cadillac dealership has a blue DeVille in its inventory but really wishes that it had a red one in stock. Another dealership in a nearby town has a red DeVille and is willing to exchange its car for Tri-City's blue one. This exchange of nonmonetary assets is not intended to be an earnings transaction for either party. Using the FASB's terminology, this exchange has no "commercial substance" because it does nothing to affect the risk, timing, or amount of Tri-City's cash flows.[16] Another example of such an exchange without commercial substance would occur if two manufacturing companies exchanged similar equipment that both companies used in similar ways in their production processes.

To illustrate the application of the notion of "commercial substance" to the accounting for nonmonetary exchanges, three examples follow. In the first example, no cash is involved in the exchange. In the second example, the exchange includes a "small" transfer of cash. In the third example, cash makes up a "large" part of the value of the transaction.

Example 1—No Cash Involved Republic Manufacturing Company owns a molding machine which it has decided to exchange for a similar machine owned by Logan Square Company. The following cost and market data relate to the two machines:

	Republic	Logan
Costs of machines to be exchanged	$46,000	$54,000
Accumulated depreciation on machines to be exchanged	32,000	37,700
Book values of machines to be exchanged	14,000	16,300
Fair values of machines to be exchanged	16,000	16,000

This exchange does not have commercial substance because the machines are essentially the same, will be used in the same way, and have the same fair values. In short, this exchange will not affect the risk, timing, or amount of either company's cash flows. In such a case, both companies will record the asset received at the book value of the asset or assets given up. The entry on Republic's books to record the exchange is as follows:

Machinery (new)	14,000	
Accumulated Depreciation—Machinery (old)	32,000	
Machinery (old)		46,000

The entry on Logan's books to record the exchange is as follows:

Machinery	16,000	
Accumulated Depreciation—Machinery (old)	37,700	
Loss on Exchange of Machinery	300	
Machinery (old)		54,000

> **Caution**
> Indicated losses are *always* recognized. Indicated gains are sometimes recognized and sometimes not.

Note that in Republic's entry, no gain is recognized even though there is an indicated gain because the fair value of the asset received is $2,000 more than the book value of the asset given. The exchange does not have commercial

---

[16] FASB ASC Section 845-10-30 (Nonmonetary Transactions—Overall—Initial Measurement).

substance, so no gain is recognized and the new asset is slotted into Republic's accounting records at the same book value as the old asset.

For Logan's entry, the fair value of the asset exchanged is less than its book value, so there is an indicated loss. The loss is recognized, and the newly acquired molding machine is recorded on Logan's books at its fair value. This is a good example of conservatism in accounting: Losses are recognized as soon as they are objectively determinable; gains are not recognized until realized. Another way to view the recognition of this loss is that the exchange prompted a reevaluation of the recorded amount of the machine, suggesting that Logan should recognize a loss similar to an impairment loss.

Example 2—Transfer of a "Small" Amount of Cash in the Exchange Assume the same facts as in Example 1, except that it is agreed that Republic's machine has a fair value of $16,000 and Logan's machine is worth $17,000. To make the exchange equal, Republic agrees to pay Logan $1,000 cash. The entry on Republic's books for Example 2 is as follows:

Machinery (new)	15,000	
Accumulated Depreciation—Machinery (old)	32,000	
Machinery (old)		46,000
Cash		1,000

As was true for Example 1, Republic does not recognize any of the indicated gain. The fair value of the assets surrendered ($16,000 + $1,000) exceeds their book values ($14,000 + $1,000), indicating a $2,000 gain. The exchange does not have commercial substance because the machines are essentially the same except for a minor difference ($1,000) in fair value. Technically, the immediate payment of the $1,000 in cash impacts the risk, timing, and amount of both companies' cash flows, but the impact is not significant. The indicated gain, therefore, is not recognized. The new machine is recorded at $15,000, equal to the book value of the assets given in the exchange.

In Example 2, the book value of Logan's machine is less than the fair value, indicating a $700 gain ($17,000 − $16,300). Because Logan received cash as part of the transaction, a portion of the $700 indicated gain should be recognized as having been earned.[17]

The amount to be recognized is computed using the following formula:

$$\text{Recognized gain} = \frac{\text{Cash received}}{\text{Cash received} + \text{Fair value of acquired asset}} \times \text{Total indicated gain}$$

Using the figures from Example 2, Logan would recognize $41 of the indicated gain, computed as follows:

$$\frac{\$1,000}{\$1,000 + \$16,000} \times \$700 = \$41$$

The recorded value of the molding machine on Logan's books is $15,341, the book value of the packaging machine exchanged less the cash received plus the gain recognized

---

[17] FASB ASC paragraph 845-10-30-6.

($16,300 − $1,000 + $41). Another way of computing the recorded value is by deducting the deferred gain from the fair value of the asset received ($16,000 − $659, or $15,341).

The entry on Logan's books to record the exchange is as follows:

Cash	1,000	
Machinery (new)	15,341	
Accumulated Depreciation—Machinery (old)	37,700	
Machinery (old)		54,000
Gain on Exchange of Machinery		41

The effect of this treatment is to defer a portion of the indicated gain and reduce the recorded book value of the new machinery. In essence, the deferred gain will be recognized over time through lower depreciation charges.

Example 3—Transfer of a "Large" Amount of Cash in the Exchange

Assume the same facts as in Example 2 except that it is agreed that Republic's machine has a fair value of $12,750 and that Republic must pay $4,250 cash to make the exchange equal; remember that in Example 2 the fair value of Logan's machine was $17,000. In this case, the cash comprises a "large" part of the fair value of the exchange. When cash comprises a large part of the transaction, the exchange has commercial substance, all gains and losses are recognized, and assets received are recorded at their fair values. The entry on Republic's books for Example 3 is as follows:

Machinery (new)	17,000	
Accumulated Depreciation—Machinery (old)	32,000	
Loss on Exchange of Machinery	1,250	
Machinery (old)		46,000
Cash		4,250

The entry on Logan's books for the exchange is as follows:

Cash	4,250	
Machinery (new)	12,750	
Accumulated Depreciation—Machinery (old)	37,700	
Machinery (old)		54,000
Gain on Exchange of Machinery		700

The question that remains is how much cash constitutes an amount large enough to have a significant impact on the risk, amount, or timing of the cash flows of the companies involved in the exchange. In Example 3, the $4,250 in cash comprises 25% ($4,250/$17,000) of the transaction. A 25% threshold is used by the FASB to distinguish a small amount of cash from a large amount of cash. So, if the amount of cash is 25% or more of the fair value of the transaction, then the transaction is accounted for as a monetary transaction.[18]

---

[18] FASB ASC paragraph 845-10-25-6.

EXPANDED MATERIAL

The kind of depreciation that businesspeople are most interested in is income tax depreciation. By lowering taxable income, tax depreciation reduces the payments for income taxes. The Expanded Material for this chapter shows how the MACRS income tax depreciation system is derived from the financial reporting depreciation methods illustrated earlier. An important part of MACRS is the depreciation computation for assets acquired or disposed of in the middle of the year. Accordingly, computation of depreciation for partial periods is also explained in more detail.

Depreciation for Partial Periods

LO7 学习目标7
使用直线法和加速折旧法计算部分周期的折旧。

7 Compute depreciation for partial periods, using both straight-line and accelerated methods.

Most of the illustrations in this chapter have assumed that assets were purchased on the first day of a company's fiscal period. In reality, of course, asset transactions occur throughout the year. When a time-factor method is used, depreciation on assets acquired or disposed of during the year may be based on the number of days the asset was held during the period. When the level of acquisitions and retirements is significant, however, companies often adopt a less burdensome policy for recognizing depreciation for partial periods. Some alternatives found in practice include the following:

1. Depreciation is recognized to the nearest whole month. Assets acquired on or before the 15th of the month are considered owned for the entire month; assets acquired after the 15th are not considered owned for any part of the month; assets sold after the 15th are considered owned for the entire month.

   折旧被确认到最接近的某个整月。某月15日当日或之前购得的资产被认为属于本月；15日之后购得的资产不计入当月；15日之后变卖的资产仍确认当月的折旧。

2. Depreciation is recognized to the nearest whole year. Assets acquired during the first six months are considered held for the entire year; assets acquired during the last six months are not considered in the depreciation computation. Conversely, no depreciation is recorded on assets sold during the first six months, and a full year's depreciation is recorded on assets sold during the last six months.

> **Caution**
> Remember that depreciation is an estimate, and computing depreciation for the exact number of days or months gives only an illusion of precision.

3. One-half year's depreciation is recognized on all assets purchased or sold during the year. A full year's depreciation is taken on all other assets. This approach is required for income tax purposes and is illustrated in the next section.

4. No depreciation is recognized on acquisitions during the year, but depreciation for a full year is recognized on retirements.

5. Depreciation is recognized for a full year on acquisitions during the year, but no depreciation is recognized on retirements.

Alternatives 2 through 5 are attractive because of their simplicity. Alternative 1 makes the most intuitive sense, and its use is assumed in the examples and problems in the text unless otherwise noted.

If a company uses the sum-of-the-years'-digits method of depreciation and recognizes a partial year's depreciation on assets in the year purchased, the depreciation expense for the second year must be determined by the following allocation procedure. To illustrate, the example used earlier in the chapter of the asset acquired by Schuss Boom Ski Manufacturing will be used. To repeat, the asset cost $100,000 and has an estimated residual value of $5,000 and an estimated useful life of five years. Assume that the asset was purchased three-fourths of the way through the fiscal year. The computation of depreciation expense for the first two years, using sum-of-the-years'-digits depreciation, is as follows:

First year:
Depreciation for full year ($95,000 × 5/15).................................... $31,667
One-fourth year's depreciation ($31,667/4)..................................... $ 7,917

Second year:
Depreciation for balance of first year ($31,667 − $7,917)....................... $23,750
Depreciation for second full year ($95,000 × 4/15)............................ $25,333
One-fourth year's depreciation ($25,333/4)..................................... 6,333
Total depreciation—second year $30,083

From this point, each year's depreciation will be $6,333 less than the previous year's depreciation. This difference equals 1/15 of the original depreciable asset base of $95,000. A summary of the depreciation charges for the five-year period is as follows:

	Depreciation	Asset Book Value (Cost Less Accumulated Depreciation)
Year 1	$ 7,917	$92,083
Year 2	30,083	62,000
Year 3	23,750	38,250
Year 4	17,417	20,833
Year 5	11,083	9,750
Year 6	4,750	5,000
Total	$95,000	

Year 5 depreciation is $6,334 less than the previous year due to effects of rounding.

Alternatively, depreciation for Years 2 through 6 can be computed using the standard sum-of-the-years'-digits computation with the numerator being the number of years remaining in the asset's useful life as of the beginning of the year. For Year 2, the number of years remaining in the asset's useful life at the beginning of the year is 4.75. The depreciation for Year 2 is $95,000 × 4.75/15 = $30,083.

If a company uses a declining-balance method of depreciation, the computation of depreciation when partial years are involved is relatively straightforward. After Year 1's depreciation is computed, the remaining years are calculated in the same manner as illustrated earlier in the chapter; a constant percentage is multiplied by a declining book value. Again assuming a purchase three-fourths of the way through the fiscal year and the use of alternative 1, the double-declining-balance depreciation expense for the Schuss Boom asset would be as shown on page 11-39, assuming a switch to straight-line depreciation in Year 5.

Year	Computation		Depreciation Amount	Asset Book Value
1	$100,000 × 0.40 × 1/4	=	$10,000	$90,000
2	$90,000 × 0.40	=	36,000	54,000
3	$54,000 × 0.40	=	21,600	32,400
4	$32,400 × 0.40	=	12,960	19,440
5	($19,440 − $5,000)/1.75	=	8,251*	11,189
6	$11,189 − $5,000	=	6,189	5,000
			$95,000	

*Rounded.

Income Tax Depreciation

LO8 Understand the depreciation methods underlying the MACRS income tax depreciation system.

学习目标8
理解修正的加速成本回收制中所得税折旧系统的基本折旧方法。

The Economic Recovery Tax Act (ERTA) of 1981 introduced an adaptation of the declining-balance depreciation method to be used for income tax purposes. It is referred to as the accelerated cost recovery system (ACRS). Subsequent revisions to the income tax laws have altered the original provisions. Because the Tax Reform Act of 1986 made several significant changes to ACRS, the new system is now referred to as the modified accelerated cost recovery system (MACRS).

The term *cost recovery* was used in the tax regulations to emphasize that ACRS is not a standard depreciation method because the system is not based strictly on asset life or pattern of use. ACRS has largely replaced traditional depreciation accounting for income tax purposes. Its original purpose was to both simplify the computation of tax depreciation and provide for a more rapid write-off of asset cost to reduce income taxes and thus stimulate investment in noncurrent operating assets. Simplification was to be achieved by using one of three cost recovery periods for all assets rather than a specific useful life for each class of asset as previously prescribed by the income tax regulations. In addition, salvage values were to be ignored. A more rapid write-off was achieved by allowing companies to write off most machinery and equipment over three to five years, and all real estate over 15 years, even though previously prescribed income tax class lives were for much longer periods.

> **FYI**
> Firms can choose MACRS for tax purposes and another method for financial reporting. Unlike LIFO elections, there is no necessary connection between income tax depreciation and depreciation for financial reporting.

The subsequent modifications to ACRS by Congress have tended to dampen both of its original objectives, primarily because tightening tax depreciation rules is a way to increase tax revenues without increasing income tax rates.[19] The original three recovery periods have been replaced with six recovery periods for personal property, such as

美国国会对加速折旧法的一系列修正是为了控制最初的目标，这主要是因为严格控制税费折旧规则可以在不增加所得税税率的基础上增加税收收入。

[19] For example, the Revenue Reconciliation Act of 1993 increased the recovery period for nonresidential real property from 31.5 years to 39 years. *RIA United States Tax Reporter, Tax Bulletin*, No. 33, August 12, 1993.

Exhibit 11-5 | MACRS Cost Recovery Periods and Depreciation Methods

IRS–Defined Class Lives	MACRS Cost Recovery Period	Depreciation Method	Examples of Assets
Personal Property:			
4 years or less	3.0 years	200% declining balance	Race horses
4 to < 10 years	5.0	200 declining balance	Cars, trucks, office machinery
10 to < 16 years	7.0	200 declining balance	Office furniture, most factory machinery
16 to < 20 years	10.0	200 declining balance	Ships
20 to < 25 years	15.0	150 declining balance	Service station
More than 25 years	25.0	150 declining balance	Water treatment facilities
Real Property—Buildings:			
Residential rental	27.5	Straight line	
Nonresidential	39.0	Straight line	

© Cengage Learning 2014

equipment, automobiles, and furniture, and two periods for real property or land and buildings.[20] At the same time, the recovery periods for most assets have been extended so that less rapid write-off of asset cost is permitted.

Exhibit 11-5 illustrates the cost recovery periods and depreciation methods under MACRS. For personal property, the appropriate cost recovery period is determined by reference to the IRS class lives defined in the tax regulations. The real property recovery periods relate to the type of real property involved rather than class lives. ACRS initially provided for 150% declining-balance depreciation. The 1986 Reform Act increased the number of asset recovery periods and extended the recovery periods for most assets. The effects of these changes were partially offset by changing the method of depreciation for most personal property to the 200% (or double-) declining-balance method.

The MACRS method for personal property also incorporates a half-year convention, meaning that one-half of a year's depreciation is recognized on all assets purchased or sold during the year. To illustrate, assume that office equipment is purchased for $100,000 on October 1, 2015. The office equipment has a $5,000 estimated residual value. The equipment is five-year property according to the IRS classification. Using the half-year convention, the double-declining-balance method, and ignoring the residual value, the MACRS depreciation for the equipment would be computed as follows:

---

[20] *Personal property* is a general term that encompasses all property other than real property (land and buildings).

Year	Computation		MACRS Depreciation Amount	Asset Book Value
1	$100,000 × 0.40 × 1/2	=	$ 20,000	$80,000
2	80,000 × 0.40	=	32,000	48,000
3	48,000 × 0.40	=	19,200	28,800
4	28,800 × 0.40	=	11,520	17,280
5	17,280/1.5	=	11,520	5,760
6	Remaining book value	=	5,760	0
			$100,000	

> **FYI**
>
> Of course, regular taxpayers aren't prepared to do these calculations. The IRS has summarized the MACRS method in a series of tables listing the percentage of the original asset cost that should be depreciated each year.

Even though the asset was purchased three-fourths of the way through the year, for tax purposes $20,000 is reported as the cost recovery in the first year rather than $10,000 determined by computing depreciation to the nearest month. Note that a switch to the straight-line method was made in Year 5. If the double-declining-balance method had been applied to this year, only $6,912 ($17,280 × 0.40) would have been reported rather than $11,520 using straight-line for the remaining one and one-half years.

 SOLUTIONS TO OPENING SCENARIO QUESTIONS

1. The stock price decline was likely caused by a number of factors. First, if investors were convinced that they had previously been valuing Blockbuster's stock based on artificially inflated earnings, the stock price would drop upon realization of that fact. In addition, if this announcement caused investors to doubt the integrity of Blockbuster's management, the stock price would drop in anticipation of the uncovering of even more bad news.

2. Interpretation of daily stock price movements is a very uncertain business in spite of the impression you might get from Wall Street analysts every evening on the news. With that said, here is one explanation for the pattern in Blockbuster's stock price movement around the release of the Bear Stearns report. First, investors understood the valuation implications of Blockbuster's depreciation practices before the release of the report on May 8. In response to the report, investors panicked and drove the price down. Over the course of the next two weeks, investors reevaluated their valuation of Blockbuster and decided that they had been correct in the first place. The fact that the stock price ended up a little below where it had stood before the report indicates, perhaps, a little lingering uncertainty about Blockbuster.

Stop & Think SOLUTIONS

1. (Page 11-10) The correct answer is D. Total depreciation expense for the five assets is computed below. (*Note*: With double-declining-balance, the depreciation for the four-year-old asset is the amount that reduces the book value to the residual value of $5,000.) For each depreciation method, total annual depreciation expense for the five assets is the same—$95,000. For a company with a stable base of assets, all depreciation methods yield the same total depreciation expense. If a company is growing, and thus has more new assets than old assets, the accelerated methods yield higher total depreciation expense than does straight-line.

Age of Asset	Straight-Line	Sum-of-the-Years'-Digits	Double-Declining-Balance
Brand new	$19,000	$31,667	$40,000
One year old	19,000	25,333	24,000
Two years old	19,000	19,000	14,400
Three years old	19,000	12,667	8,640
Four years old	19,000	6,333	7,960
Total depreciation	$95,000	$95,000	$95,000

2. (Page 11-22) The correct answer is A. The undiscounted sum of future cash flows is always greater than an asset's fair value because the undiscounted amount does not reflect the time value of money. Accordingly, in order for the undiscounted sum of future cash flows to be less than an asset's book value, the fair value of the asset must be substantially less than the book value.

3. (Page 11-27) The correct answer is C. For an intangible asset with an indefinite life, there is no foreseeable end to the future cash flows to be generated by the asset. Accordingly, the undiscounted sum of future cash flows will always be infinite, and using the two-step impairment test, no impairment loss would ever be recognized. This is an unreasonable outcome, so a separate impairment test, using the discounted present value of the future cash flows, is used.

4. (Page 11-29) The correct answer is D. Procedure 4 is the most costly to perform. Optional Procedure 1 involves a low-cost qualitative assessment. In many cases, Procedure 2 can be done using simple earnings or revenue multiples to estimate the fair value of the reporting unit. Procedure 3 is a simple calculation using the estimated fair value and the reported amounts of assets and liabilities for the reporting unit. Once Procedure 4 is completed, Procedure 5 simply involves the comparison of two numbers. However, Procedure 4 requires the estimation of the fair value of *all* the assets and liabilities of the reporting unit.

SOLUTION TO USING THE FASB'S CODIFICATION

Under Topic 360 (Property, Plant, and Equipment), you see a number of industries listed—agriculture, airlines, contractors, and so forth. Let's start with agriculture. In Section 35 (Subsequent Measurement) under Subtopic 905-360, you see subsections on topics such as breeding animals, production animals, and trees and vines. This doesn't look like the right place.

The next industry listed is airlines covered in Subtopic 908-360. In Section 35 on subsequent measurement, you see a subsection on "Depreciation Methods." There you find the following: "A depreciation method may be applied to a single asset (unit depreciation) or to a group or pool of assets that are similar in nature (group depreciation). An air carrier can use unit or group depreciation methods on different groups of assets.... Under the group method, the airline depreciates the aggregate cost of a group of equipment that is fairly homogeneous, despite differences in the service lives of individual items. Group depreciation usually is applied to groups of assets that are significant in number but have relatively small unit values, such as rotable parts and assemblies."

So, here is one example, the airline industry, where group depreciation is so routine that it is mentioned in the authoritative accounting standards.

Review Chapter 11 Learning Objectives

① Use straight-line, accelerated, use-factor, and group depreciation methods to compute annual depreciation expense.

The four factors that are considered in computing annual depreciation are asset cost, residual (or salvage) value, useful life, and pattern of use. The most common methods for computing annual depreciation are as follows:

Time-Factor Methods

- *Straight-line depreciation.* The difference between asset cost and residual value is divided by the useful life of the asset.
- *Accelerated methods*
  - *Sum-of-the-years'-digits depreciation.* The depreciable asset cost is multiplied by a fraction; the numerator is the number of years remaining in the asset life as of the beginning of the year, and the denominator is the sum of all the digits from 1 to the original useful life.
  - *Declining-balance depreciation.* The asset book value is multiplied by a constant percentage rate derived from the useful life. The most commonly used percentage is double the straight-line rate.

Use-Factor Methods

- *Service-hours depreciation.* Depreciable cost is divided by total expected lifetime service hours to compute a per-hour depreciation rate. The number of service hours in a period multiplied by the rate yields the periodic depreciation charge.
- *Productive-output depreciation.* This is similar to service-hours depreciation except the rate is based on expected number of output units during the life of the asset.

Group and Composite Methods

A collection of assets is depreciated as one group. A group rate, derived from an initial analysis of the type of assets in the group, is multiplied by the total cost of group assets to compute periodic depreciation expense. Gains and losses resulting from normal variations in asset lives are not recognized.

② Apply the productive-output method to the depletion of natural resources.

The depletion rate is based on total development cost of the natural resource divided by the estimated amount of resource units to be removed. Periodic depletion expense is the depletion rate multiplied by the number of units removed during the period. Structures and improvements related specifically to removal of the natural resource should be depreciated based on the fraction of natural resources extracted during the period.

③ Incorporate changes in estimates and methods into the computation of depreciation for current and future periods.

A change in estimate impacts the current and future periods and is not used to adjust amounts reported in prior periods. The undepreciated book value is allocated over the remaining life based on the revised estimates. Changes in depreciation method are accounted for as changes in estimates and are reflected in the current and future periods.

④ Identify whether an asset is impaired, and measure the amount of the impairment loss using both U.S. GAAP and IASB standards.

Under U.S. GAAP, assets are reviewed for possible impairment whenever there is a significant change in operations or in the way an asset is used. An asset is impaired when the undiscounted sum of future cash flows from the asset is less than the reported book value. An impaired asset is written down to its fair value. IASB standards differ from U.S. GAAP in that the discounted sum of future cash flows—rather than the undiscounted sum—is used to determine whether an impairment loss exists. International standards also allow for the upward revaluation of long-term operating assets that have increased in value.

⑤ Discuss the issues impacting proper recognition of amortization or impairment for intangible assets.

An intangible asset with a finite life is amortized over its estimated useful life, usually with zero residual value and using the straight-line method. These intangibles are tested for impairment using the standard two-step impairment test. An intangible asset with an indefinite life is not amortized. Instead, these intangibles are tested for impairment simply by comparing their carrying value to their estimated fair value. Goodwill is not amortized. Goodwill is tested for impairment each year using a process that starts with either a qualitative assessment or an estimate of the fair value of the entire reporting unit to which the goodwill was assigned when it was acquired.

⑥ Account for the sale of depreciable assets in exchange for cash and in exchange for other depreciable assets.

Indicated losses are always recognized. In cash transactions and in other exchanges involving commercial substance, indicated gains are recognized and all assets exchanged are recorded on the books of the company receiving them at their fair values. Some nonmonetary exchanges do not have commercial substance, meaning that they do not impact the risk, timing, or amount of the cash flows of the parties in the exchange. In this case, the assets received are recorded at the book value of the assets given up in the exchange.

EXPANDED MATERIAL

7 Compute depreciation for partial periods, using both straight-line and accelerated methods.

Depreciation is not always computed for the exact number of days or months an asset is owned. One common simplifying assumption is the half-year convention: One-half of a year's depreciation is recognized on all assets purchased or sold during the year.

8 Understand the depreciation methods underlying the MACRS income tax depreciation system.

MACRS is based on the 200% declining-balance depreciation method with no residual value and a half-year convention. To streamline the system, the IRS has established eight classes of assets with set depreciation lives.

FASB-IASB CODIFICATION SUMMARY

Topic	FASB Accounting Standards Codification	Original FASB Standard	Corresponding IASB Standard	Differences between U.S. GAAP and IFRS
Impairment of tangible assets	Subtopic 360-10 various subsections on "Impairment"	SFAS No. 144	IAS 36	Under U.S. GAAP, the impairment test is a two-step test. Under IFRS, the impairment test involves just one step, a comparison of the book value to the "recoverable amount" of the asset.
Impairment of intangible assets	Topic 350	SFAS No. 142	IAS 36	U.S. GAAP includes three different impairment tests for intangibles. Under IFRS, there is just one test, which is the same as is used for tangible assets.
Upward revaluation	Not part of U.S. GAAP	Not part of U.S. GAAP	IAS 16	Upward revaluations of property, plant, and equipment are generally not allowable under U.S. GAAP.
Asset retirement obligations	Subtopic 410-20	SFAS No. 143	IAS 16 and IAS 37	No substantial differences
Assets classified as held for sale	Section 360-10-45	SFAS No. 144	IFRS 5	No substantial differences

KEY TERMS

Accelerated depreciation 11-7
Amortization 11-3
Book value 11-4
Composite depreciation 11-13
Declining-balance depreciation 11-9
Depletion 11-3
Depreciation 11-3

Double-declining-balance depreciation 11-9
Gain 11-30
Group depreciation 11-13
Impairment 11-20
Indicated gain 11-34
Indicated loss 11-35
Loss 11-30
Natural resources 11-17

Productive-output depreciation 11-13
Residual (salvage) value 11-5
Service-hours depreciation 11-11
Straight-line depreciation 11-7
Sum-of-the-years'-digits depreciation 11-8
Time-factor depreciation 11-7
Unit depreciation 11-13

Use-factor depreciation 11-11
Useful life 11-5

EXPANDED MATERIAL

Accelerated cost recovery system (ACRS) 11-39
Half-year convention 11-40
Modified accelerated cost recovery system (MACRS) 11-39

Tutorial Activities

Tutorial Activities with author-written, content-specific feedback, available on *CengageNOW for Stice & Stice*.

QUESTIONS

1. Distinguish among depreciation, depletion, and amortization expenses.
2. What factors must be considered in determining the periodic depreciation charges that should be made for a company's depreciable assets?
3. What role does residual, or salvage, value play in the various methods of time-factor depreciation?
4. Distinguish between the functional and physical factors affecting the useful life of a tangible noncurrent operating asset.
5. Distinguish between time-factor and use-factor methods of depreciation.
6. Briefly describe group depreciation, and describe how asset retirements are recorded under this method.
7. Describe the component approach to computing depreciation.
8. How does the recognition of an asset retirement obligation impact periodic depreciation expense? Interest expense?
9. Describe the proper accounting treatment for a change in estimated useful life.
10. What procedures must be followed when the estimate of recoverable natural resources is changed due to subsequent development work?
11. Under U.S. GAAP, what test is used to determine whether a long-term tangible asset is impaired? How is an impairment loss measured?
12. How does the International Accounting Standard for asset impairment differ from the standard used in the United States?
13. If a non-U.S. company chooses to revalue a long-term operating asset upward in accordance with *IAS 16*, how is the unrealized "gain" on the revaluation recognized in the financial statements?
14. Briefly describe the three types of intangible assets in terms of amortization and impairment.
15. Briefly describe the five procedures followed in testing goodwill for impairment.
16. Under *IAS 36*, there is basically one impairment test for intangible assets. Briefly describe the structure of that test.
17. What two unusual accounting actions are taken when a long-term operating asset is classified as held for sale?
18. Under what circumstances is a gain recognized when a productive asset is exchanged for a similar productive asset? A loss?

EXPANDED MATERIAL

19. Why isn't depreciation expense always computed for the exact number of days an asset is owned?
20. What were the original reasons for the development of the ACRS income tax depreciation method?

PRACTICE EXERCISES

Practice 11-1

Recording Depreciation Expense
Depreciation expense for the year was $1,000. Make the necessary journal entry.

Practice 11-2

Depreciation Expense, Accumulated Depreciation, and Book Value
A machine was acquired for $7,000 on May 1 of Year 1. Depreciation expense on the machine for Year 1 was $1,000. Depreciation expense on the machine for Year 2 was $1,500. (1) Make the journal entry necessary on December 31 of Year 2 to record depreciation expense on the machine for the year. (2) Compute the accumulated depreciation on the machine as of December 31 of Year 2. (3) Compute the book value of the machine as of December 31 of Year 2.

Practice 11-3

Computing Straight-Line Depreciation
The company acquired a machine on January 1 at an original cost of $115,000. The machine's estimated residual value is $20,000, and its estimated life is five years. (1) Compute the annual straight-line depreciation amount, (2) make the journal entry necessary to record depreciation expense for the first year, and (3) compute the machine's book value at the end of the first year.

Practice 11-4

Computing Sum-of-the-Years'-Digits Depreciation
The company acquired a machine on January 1 at an original cost of $115,000. The machine's estimated residual value is $20,000, and its estimated life is five years. Assume that the company uses sum-of-the-years'-digits depreciation. Compute (1) depreciation expense for each year of the machine's five-year life and (2) book value at the end of each year of the machine's five-year life.

Practice 11-5

Computing Double-Declining-Balance Depreciation
The company acquired a machine on January 1 at an original cost of $100,000. The machine's estimated residual value is $10,000, and its estimated life is four years. The company uses double-declining-balance depreciation and switches to straight-line in the final year of the machine's life. Compute (1) depreciation expense for each year of the machine's four-year life and (2) book value at the end of each year of the machine's four-year life.

Practice 11-6

Computing Service-Hours Depreciation
The company acquired a machine on January 1 at an original cost of $75,000. The machine's estimated residual value is $15,000, and its estimated life is 20,000 service hours. The actual usage of the machine was as follows: Year 1, 9,000 hours; Year 2, 5,000 hours; Year 3, 4,000 hours; Year 4, 2,000 hours. Compute (1) depreciation expense for each year of the machine's life and (2) book value at the end of each year of the machine's life.

Practice 11-7

Computing Productive-Output Depreciation
The company acquired a machine on January 1 at an original cost of $70,000. The machine's estimated residual value is $5,000, and its estimated lifetime output is 13,000 units. The actual output of the machine was as follows: Year 1, 3,000 units; Year 2, 5,000 units; Year 3, 2,000 units; Year 4, 3,000 units. Compute (1) depreciation expense for each year of the machine's life and (2) book value at the end of each year of the machine's life.

Practice 11-8
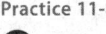
Computing Group Depreciation
The company has decided to use group depreciation based on the straight-line depreciation method. The initial pool of assets on which the group depreciation rate is based is as follows:

	Acquisition Cost	Salvage Value	Useful Life
Asset 1	$64,000	$ 4,000	6 years
Asset 2	90,000	10,000	10
Asset 3	42,000	6,000	9
Asset 4	30,000	0	5

Compute the group depreciation rate.

Practice 11-9

Group Depreciation: Recording Asset Sales
Refer to Practice 11-8. (1) Make the journal entry to record the sale of Asset 3 after two years for $22,000 cash. (2) Compute depreciation expense in the third year if Asset 5 is purchased at the beginning of the year for $50,000. This purchase is made at the same time that Asset 3 is sold.

Practice 11-10
Asset Retirement Obligation
On January 1, Lewis Company purchased land it will use as a landfill for the next 12 years. The cost of the land was $525,000. At the end of 12 years, Lewis Company will be required to spend $250,000 to landscape and reforest the landfill site. The appropriate discount rate is 9%. Because the useful life of the land is limited in this case, the cost of the land is depreciated. Lewis uses the straight-line method. Compute the amount of depreciation expense and accretion expense in Year 1.

Practice 11-11
Computing Depletion Expense
On January 1, the company purchased a mine for $100,000. At that time, it was estimated that the mine contained 5,000 tons of ore. It is also estimated that the mine will have a residual value of $20,000 when all of the ore is extracted. During the year, the company extracted 900 tons of ore from the mine. (1) Compute depletion expense for the year and (2) make the journal entry necessary to record the depletion expense.

Practice 11-12
Change in Estimated Life
The company purchased a machine for $40,000. The machine had an estimated residual value of $4,000 and an estimated useful life of nine years. After three full years of experience with the machine, it was determined that its total useful life would be only seven years instead of nine. In addition, a revised estimate of $8,000 was made for the residual value, instead of the original $4,000. Compute depreciation expense for the fourth year. The company uses straight-line depreciation.

Practice 11-13
Change in Estimated Units of Production
On January 1 of Year 1, the company purchased a mine for $150,000. At that time, it was estimated that the mine contained 2,000 tons of ore. During Year 1, the company extracted 900 tons of ore from the mine. On January 1 of Year 2, the company spent $60,000 on mine improvements. During Year 2, the company extracted 600 tons of ore. On December 31 of Year 2, it was estimated that the mine contained 700 tons of ore. Compute depletion expense for (1) Year 1 and (2) Year 2.

Practice 11-14
Change in Depreciation Method
On January 1, the company purchased a machine for $80,000. The machine had an estimated useful life of eight years and an estimated salvage value of $8,000. After three full years of using the machine, the company changed its depreciation method from straight-line to double-declining-balance. Compute depreciation expense for the fourth year.

Practice 11-15
Determining Whether a Tangible Asset Is Impaired
The cost and the accumulated depreciation for a piece of equipment are $1,500,000 and $600,000, respectively. Management is concerned that the equipment has become impaired. Management hired several independent appraisers who agreed that the current value of the equipment is $500,000. Management also estimates that the equipment will generate cash inflows of $65,000 per year for the next 14 years. Is the equipment impaired? Explain.

Practice 11-16
Recording a Tangible Asset Impairment
A building has a cost of $750,000 and accumulated depreciation of $125,000. The fair value of the building is estimated to be $300,000. The building is expected to generate net cash inflows of $20,000 per year for the next 30 years. (1) Determine whether the building is impaired and (2) if it is impaired, make the journal entry necessary to record the impairment loss.

Practice 11-17
Recording Upward Asset Revaluations
A building has a cost of $500,000 and accumulated depreciation of $40,000. The current value of the building is estimated to be $730,000. The company that owns the building is based in Genovia and uses International Financial Reporting Standards. The company has chosen to recognize increases in the value of long-term operating assets. Make the necessary journal entry.

Practice 11-18

Recording Amortization Expense

On January 1, the company purchased the rights to a valuable Internet domain name for $250,000. Given current market conditions, the company estimates that these rights have an economic life of four years at which time they will have no residual value. Make the journal entry necessary to recognize amortization expense for the year.

Practice 11-19

Goodwill Impairment

Buyer Company acquired Target Company on January 1. As part of the acquisition, $1,000 in goodwill was recognized; this goodwill was assigned to Buyer's Manufacturing reporting unit. A qualitative assessment of general economic and industry conditions indicates that it is more likely than not that the fair value of the Manufacturing reporting unit is less than its net book value. On December 31, it was estimated that the future cash flows expected to be generated by the Manufacturing reporting unit are $350 at the end of each year for the next 10 years. The appropriate interest rate is 10%. The fair values and book values of the assets and liabilities of the Manufacturing reporting unit are as follows:

	Book Values	Fair Values
Identifiable assets	$3,500	$4,000
Goodwill	1,000	?
Liabilities	2,000	2,000

Make the journal entry necessary to recognize any goodwill impairment loss.

Practice 11-20

Exchange of Assets

A building has a cost of $700,000 and accumulated depreciation of $340,000. The building is exchanged for land. Make the necessary journal entry if (1) the land has a market value of $400,000 and (2) the land has a market value of $200,000.

Practice 11-21

Classifying an Asset as Held for Sale

On October 1, 2015, the company has a building with a cost of $375,000 and accumulated depreciation of $225,000. The company commits to a plan to sell the building by February 1, 2016. On October 1, 2015, the building has an estimated selling price of $145,000, and it is estimated that selling costs associated with the disposal of the building will be $9,000. On December 31, 2015, the estimated selling price of the building has increased to $170,000, with estimated selling costs remaining at $9,000. Make the journal entries necessary to record (1) the initial classification of the building as held for sale on October 1, 2015, and (2) any adjustment necessary on December 31, 2015. Remember that no depreciation expense is recognized once an asset is classified as held for sale.

Practice 11-22

Exchange of Assets

The company exchanged an asset for a similar asset. The exchange was with another company in the same line of business. The old asset had a cost of $1,000 and accumulated depreciation of $850. The old asset had a market value of $400 on the date of the exchange. Make the journal entry necessary to record the exchange assuming that (1) the company received the new machine and no cash, (2) the company received the new machine and a "large" amount of cash of $300, and (3) the company received the new machine and a "small" amount of cash of $80. [*Hint:* In all three cases, the total market value of assets received (cash plus new asset) is the same as the market value of the asset given up ($400).]

EXPANDED MATERIAL

Practice 11-23

Depreciation for Partial Periods

The company purchased a machine on April 1 for $100,000. The machine has an estimated useful life of five years and an estimated salvage value of $15,000. The company computes partial-year depreciation to the nearest whole month. Compute the amount of depreciation expense for this year *and* next year using (1) sum-of-the-years'-digits depreciation and (2) double-declining-balance depreciation.

Practice 11-24

Income Tax Depreciation
The company purchased a ship for $850,000. The ship has an estimated residual value of $100,000. Compute the amount of MACRS depreciation deduction for the first two years of the life of the ship.

EXERCISES

Exercise 11-25

Computation of Asset Cost and Depreciation Expense
A machine is purchased at the beginning of 2015 for $42,000. Its estimated life is eight years. Freight costs on the machine are $3,000. Installation costs are $1,600. The machine is estimated to have a residual value of $600 and a useful life of 32,000 hours. It was used 3,000 hours in 2015.

1. What is the cost of the machine for accounting purposes?
2. Compute the depreciation charge for 2015 using (a) the straight-line method and (b) the service-hours method.

Exercise 11-26

Service-Hours Depreciation
Jen and Barry's Ice Milk Company used cash to purchase a new ice milk mixer on January 1, 2015. The new mixer is estimated to have a 20,000-hour service life. Jen and Barry's depreciates equipment on the service-hours method. The total price paid for the machine was $57,000. This price included $2,000 freight in, $1,800 installation costs, and $3,000 for a two-year maintenance contract.

During 2015, Jen and Barry's used the machine for 2,500 hours; in 2016, 3,000 hours. Prepare all related journal entries for the purchase of equipment, annual depreciation, and maintenance expense for 2015 and 2016.

Exercise 11-27

REVERSE SOLVABLE

Inferring Useful Lives
The information that follows is from the balance sheet of Hampton Company for December 31, 2015, and December 31, 2014.

	Dec. 31, 2015	Dec. 31, 2014
Equipment—cost	$ 680,000	$ 680,000
Accumulated depreciation—equipment	(250,000)	(160,000)
Buildings—cost	2,450,000	2,450,000
Accumulated depreciation—buildings	(340,000)	(230,000)

Hampton did not acquire or dispose of any buildings or equipment during 2015. Hampton uses the straight-line method of depreciation. If residual values are assumed to be 10% of asset cost, what is the average useful life of Hampton's (1) equipment and (2) buildings?

Exercise 11-28

Computation of Depreciation Expense
Limestone Construction purchased a concrete mixer on July 15, 2015. Company officials revealed the following information regarding this asset and its acquisition:

Purchase price	$210,000
Residual value	$20,000
Estimated useful life	9 years
Estimated service hours	50,000
Estimated production in units	375,000 yards

The concrete mixer was operated by construction crews in 2015 for a total of 6,500 hours, and it produced 49,500 yards of concrete.

It is company policy to take a half-year's depreciation on all assets for which it used the straight-line or double-declining-balance depreciation method in the year of purchase.

Calculate the resulting depreciation expense for 2015 under each of the following methods, and specify which method allows the greatest depreciation expense.

1. Double-declining-balance
2. Productive-output
3. Service-hours
4. Straight-line

Exercise 11-29

Productive-Output Depreciation and Asset Retirement

Equipment was purchased at the beginning of 2013 for $100,000 with an estimated product life of 300,000 units. The estimated salvage value was $4,000. During 2013, 2014, and 2015, the equipment produced 80,000 units, 120,000 units, and 40,000 units, respectively. The machine was damaged at the beginning of 2016, and the equipment was scrapped with no salvage value.

1. Determine depreciation using the productive-output method for 2013, 2014, and 2015.
2. Give the entry to write off the equipment at the beginning of 2016.

Exercise 11-30

Group Depreciation

Allwood, Inc., a small furniture manufacturer, purchased the following assets at the end of 2014:

Description	Cost	Salvage	Life
Delivery truck	$37,000	$8,000	7 years
Circular saws	725	180	5 years
Workbench	460	—	10 years
Forklift	11,000	950	6 years

Compute the following amounts for 2015 using group depreciation on a straight-line basis:

1. Depreciation expense
2. Group depreciation rate
3. Average life of the assets

Exercise 11-31

Group Depreciation Entries

Lundquist, Inc., uses the group depreciation method for its furniture account. The depreciation rate used for furniture is 21%. The balance in the furniture account on December 31, 2014, was $125,000, and the balance in Accumulated Depreciation—Furniture was $61,000. The following purchases and dispositions of furniture occurred in the years 2015–2017 (assume that all purchases and disposals occurred at the beginning of each year):

		Assets Sold	
Year	Assets Purchased—Cost (Cash)	Cost	Selling Price (Cash)
2015	$35,000	$27,000	$8,000
2016	27,600	15,000	6,000
2017	24,500	32,000	8,000

1. Prepare the summary journal entries Lundquist should make each year (2015–2017) for the purchase, disposition, and depreciation of the furniture.
2. Prepare a summary of the furniture and accumulated depreciation accounts for the years 2015–2017.

Exercise 11-32

Depreciation of Special Components

Jackson Manufacturing acquired a new milling machine on April 1, 2010. The machine has a special component that requires replacement before the end of the useful life. The asset was originally recorded in two accounts, one representing the main unit and the other for the special component. Depreciation is recorded by the straight-line method to the nearest month, residual values being disregarded. On April 1, 2016, the special component is scrapped and is replaced with a similar component. This component is expected to have a residual value of approximately 25% of cost at the end of the useful life of the main unit, and because of its materiality, the residual value will be considered in calculating depreciation. Specific asset information is as follows:

Main milling machine:
   Purchase price in 2010 .... $74,800
   Residual value $6,200
   Estimated useful life .... 10 years

First special component:
   Purchase price $12,000
   Residual value $500
   Estimated useful life .... 6 years

Second special component:
   Purchase price $16,500

What are the depreciation charges to be recognized for the years (1) 2010, (2) 2016, and (3) 2017?

Exercise 11-33

Asset Retirement Obligation

On January 1, 2015, Major Company purchased a uranium mine for $800,000. On that date, Major estimated that the mine contained 1,000 tons of ore. At the end of the productive years of the mine, Major Company will be required to spend $4,200,000 to clean up the mine site. The appropriate discount rate is 8%, and it is estimated that it will take approximately 14 years to mine all of the ore. Major uses the productive-output method of depreciation. During 2015, Major extracted 100 tons of ore from the mine.

1. Compute the amount of depreciation (or depletion) expense for 2015.
2. Compute the amount of accretion expense for 2015.

Exercise 11-34

Depletion Expense

On January 2, 2014, Adelaide Rose purchased land with valuable natural ore deposits for $13 million. The estimated residual value of the land was $4 million. At the time of purchase, a geological survey estimated 3 million tons of removable ore were under the ground. Early in 2014, roads were constructed on the land to aid in the extraction and transportation of the mined ore at a cost of $975,000. In 2014, 75,000 tons were mined. In 2015, Adelaide fired her mining engineer and hired a new expert. A new survey made at the end of 2015 estimated 4.5 million tons of ore were available for mining. In 2015, 265,000 tons were mined. Assuming that all the ore mined was sold, how much was the depletion expense for 2014 and 2015?

Exercise 11-35

Change in Estimated Useful Life

Goff Corporation purchased a machine on January 1, 2010, for $500,000. At the date of acquisition, the machine had an estimated useful life of 20 years with no salvage value. The machine is being depreciated on a straight-line basis. On January 1, 2015, as a result of Goff's experience with the machine, it was decided that the machine had an estimated useful life of 15 years from the date of acquisition. What is the amount of depreciation expense on this machine in 2015 using a new annual depreciation charge for the remaining 10 years?

Exercise 11-36

Change in Estimated Useful Life
Finn Corporation purchased a machine on July 1, 2012, for $225,000. The machine was estimated to have a useful life of 12 years with an estimated salvage value of $15,000. During 2015, it became apparent that the machine would become uneconomical after December 31, 2019, and that the machine would have no scrap value. Finn uses the straight-line method of depreciation for all machinery. What should be the charge for depreciation in 2015 using the new estimates for useful life and salvage value?

Exercise 11-37

Change in Depreciation Method
Franklin Company purchased a machine on January 1, 2012, paying $150,000. The machine was estimated to have a useful life of eight years and an estimated salvage value of $30,000. In early 2014, the company elected to change its depreciation method from straight-line to sum-of-the-years'-digits for future periods. What should be the charge for depreciation for 2014?

Exercise 11-38

Recording an Impairment Loss
Della Bee Company purchased a manufacturing plant building 10 years ago for $1,300,000. The building has been depreciated using the straight-line method with a 30-year useful life and 10% residual value. Della Bee's manufacturing operations have experienced significant losses for the past two years, so Della Bee has decided that the manufacturing building should be evaluated for possible impairment. Della Bee estimates that the building has a remaining useful life of 15 years, that net cash inflow from the building will be $50,000 per year, and that the fair value of the building is $380,000.

1. Determine whether an impairment loss should be recognized.
2. If an impairment loss should be recognized, make the appropriate journal entry.
3. How would your answer to (1) change if the fair value of the building was $560,000?

Exercise 11-39

Impairment and Revaluation under International Accounting Standards
Use the information given in Exercise 11-38 and assume that Della Bee Company is located in Hong Kong and uses International Financial Reporting Standards. Della Bee also has chosen to recognize increases in the value of long-term operating assets in accordance with the allowable alternative under *IAS 16*.

1. Determine whether an impairment loss should be recognized.
2. If an impairment loss should be recognized, make the appropriate journal entry.
3. What journal entry would Della Bee make if the fair value of the building was $1,250,000?

Exercise 11-40

Accounting for Patents
The Rockington Co. applied for and received numerous patents at a total cost of $31,195 at the beginning of 2010. It is assumed the patents will have economic value for their remaining legal life of 16 years. At the beginning of 2012, the company paid $9,350 in successfully prosecuting an attempted infringement of these patent rights. At the beginning of 2015, $32,400 was paid to acquire patents that could make its own patents worthless; the patents acquired have a remaining life of 15 years but will not be used.

1. Give the entries to record the expenditures relative to patents.
2. Give the entries to record patent amortization for the years 2010, 2012, and 2015.

Exercise 11-41

Impairment of Intangibles
An intangible asset cost $300,000 on January 1, 2015. On January 1, 2016, the asset was evaluated to determine whether it was impaired. As of January 1, 2016, the asset was expected to generate future cash flows of $25,000 per year (at the end of the year). The appropriate discount rate is 5%.

1. Give the entries to record amortization in 2015 and any impairment loss in 2016 assuming that as of January 1, 2015, the asset was assumed to have a total useful life of 10 years and that as of January 1, 2016, there were nine years remaining.

2. Give the entries to record amortization in 2015 and any impairment loss in 2016 assuming that as of January 1, 2015, the asset was assumed to have an indefinite useful life and that as of January 1, 2016, the remaining life was still indefinite.

Exercise 11-42

Impairment of Goodwill

Largest Company acquired Large Company on January 1. As part of the acquisition, $10,000 in goodwill was recognized; this goodwill was assigned to Largest's Production reporting unit. The fact that both operating cash flow and net income were significantly negative in the past year indicates that it is more likely than not that the fair value of the Production reporting unit is less than its net book value. During the year, the Production reporting unit reported revenues of $13,000. Publicly traded companies with operations similar to those of the Production unit had price-to-revenue ratios averaging 1.60. The fair values and book values of the assets and liabilities of the Production reporting unit are as follows:

	Book Values	Fair Values
Identifiable assets	$21,300	$20,500
Goodwill	10,000	?
Liabilities	7,600	7,600

Make the journal entry necessary to recognize any goodwill impairment loss.

Exercise 11-43

Recording the Sale of Equipment with Note

On December 31, 2015, Debenham Corporation sold an old machine for $15,000, having an original cost of $84,000 and a book value of $9,000. The terms of the sale were as follows: $3,000 down payment, $6,000 payable on December 31 of the next two years. The sales agreement made no mention of interest; however, 10% would be a fair rate for this type of transaction. Give the journal entries on Debenham's books to record the sale of the machine and receipt of the two subsequent payments. (*Note:* Round to the nearest dollar.)

Exercise 11-44

Long-Term Operating Asset Held for Sale

On April 1, 2015, Brandoni Company has a piece of machinery with a cost of $100,000 and accumulated depreciation of $75,000. On April 1, Brandoni decided to sell the machine within one year. As of April 1, 2015, the machine had an estimated selling price of $10,000 and a remaining useful life of two years. It is estimated that selling costs associated with the disposal of the machine will be $1,000. On December 31, 2015, the estimated selling price of the machine had increased to $15,000, with estimated selling costs increasing to $1,600.

1. Make the entry to record the initial classification of the machine as held for sale on April 1, 2015.
2. Make the entry to record depreciation expense on the machine for the period April 1 through December 31, 2015.
3. Make the entry, if any, needed on December 31, 2015, to reflect the change in the expected selling price.

Exercise 11-45

Exchange of Machinery

Assume that Coaltown Corporation has a machine that cost $52,000, has a book value of $35,000, and has a fair value of $40,000. The machine is used in Coaltown's manufacturing process. For each of the following situations, indicate the value at which the company should record the new asset and why it should be recorded at that value.

(a) Coaltown exchanged the machine for a truck with a list price of $43,000.
(b) Coaltown exchanged the machine with another manufacturing company for a similar machine with a list price of $41,000.
(c) Coaltown exchanged the machine for a newer model machine from another manufacturing company. The new machine had a list price of $62,000, and Coaltown paid a "large" amount of cash of $15,000.

(d) Coaltown exchanged the machine plus a "small" amount of cash of $3,000 for a similar machine from Newton Inc., a manufacturing company. The newly acquired machine is carried on Newton's books at its cost of $55,000 with accumulated depreciation of $42,000; its fair value is $43,000. In addition to determining the value, give the journal entries for both companies to record the exchange.

Exercise 11-46
Exchange of Truck
On January 2, 2015, Joshon Hardware Company traded an old delivery truck to a dealer for a newer model. Data relative to the old and new trucks follow:

Old truck:

Original cost	$22,750
Accumulated depreciation as of January 2, 2015	19,000

New truck:

List price	$24,000
Cash price without trade-in	23,100
Cash paid with trade-in	20,900

1. Give the journal entries on Joshon's books to record the purchase of the new truck.
2. Give the journal entries on Joshon's books if the cash paid was $18,000 and that amount is considered "large."

E X P A N D E D   M A T E R I A L

Exercise 11-47
Computation of Depreciation Expense
Feng Company purchased a machine for $180,000 on September 1, 2015. It is estimated that the machine will have a 10-year life and a salvage value of $18,000. Its working hours and production in units are estimated at 36,000 and 750,000, respectively. It is the company's policy to depreciate assets for the number of months they are held during a year. During 2015, the machine was operated 1,500 hours and produced 21,000 units. Which of the following methods will give the greatest depreciation expense for 2015: (1) double-declining-balance (2) sum-of-the-years'-digits, (3) productive-output, or (4) service-hours? (Show computations for all four methods.)

Exercise 11-48
Computation of Book and Tax Depreciation
Rocky Point Foundry purchased factory equipment on March 15, 2014. The equipment will be depreciated for financial purposes over its estimated useful life, counting the year of acquisition as a half-year. The company accountant revealed the following information regarding this machine:

Purchase price	$110,000
Residual value	$17,000
Estimated useful life	12 years

1. What amount should Rocky Point Foundry record for depreciation expense for 2015 using the (a) double-declining-balance method and (b) sum-of-the-years'-digits method?
2. Assuming the equipment is classified as eight-year property under the modified accelerated cost recovery system (MACRS), what amount should Rocky Point Foundry deduct for depreciation on its tax return in 2015?

Exercise 11-49
MACRS Computation
Olympus Equipment Company purchased a new piece of factory equipment on May 1, 2015, for $29,200. For income tax purposes, the equipment is classified as a seven-year asset. Because this is similar to the economic life expected for the asset, Olympus decides to use the tax depreciation for financial reporting purposes. The equipment is not expected to have any residual value at the end of the seven years. Prepare a depreciation schedule for the life of the asset using the MACRS method of cost recovery.

P3
Additional Activities of a Business

CHAPTER 12
Debt Financing

Learning Objectives

1. Understand the various classification and measurement issues associated with debt.

2. Account for short-term debt obligations, including those expected to be refinanced, and describe the purpose of lines of credit.

3. Apply present value concepts to the accounting for long-term debts such as mortgages.

4. Understand the various types of bonds; compute the price of a bond issue; and account for the issuance, interest, and redemption of bonds.

5. Discuss the use of the fair value option for financial assets and liabilities.

6. Explain various types of off-balance-sheet financing, and understand the reasons for this type of financing.

7. Analyze a firm's debt position using ratios.

8. Review the notes to financial statements, and understand the disclosure associated with debt financing.

EM EXPANDED MATERIAL

9. Understand the conditions under which troubled debt restructuring occurs, and be able to account for troubled debt restructuring.

Analysis of the data gathered in the U.S. census of 1880 took almost 10 years. For the census of 1890, the U.S. government commissioned Herman Hollerith to provide data tabulation machines to speed up the process. This system of mechanized data handling saved the Census Bureau $5 million and slashed the data analysis time by two years. In 1924, Hollerith's company adopted the name International Business Machines Corporation (IBM). IBM became the largest office machine producer in the United States with sales of more than $180 million in 1949.

In 1950, there was great resistance to the idea of electronic computers at IBM. IBM's engineers were specialists in electromechanical devices and were uncomfortable working with vacuum tubes, diodes, and magnetic recording tapes. In addition, there were many questions about the customer demand for electronic computers. One IBM executive forecast that the size of the total worldwide market for computers was no more than five. However, following significant internal debate, IBM pressed forward with the production of its first electronic computer, the 701. Through the 1960s and 70s, with its aggressive leasing program, emphasis on sales and service, and continued investment in research and development, IBM established a dominant (some claimed a monopolistic) position in the mainframe computer market.

When the IBM personal computer was released in 1981, it quickly became the industry standard for PCs. By 1986, IBM held 40% of the PC market. Amid this success, IBM made what, in retrospect, was a crucial error—it chose to focus on producing and selling hardware and to leave software development, by and large, to others. In fact, IBM did not develop the operating system for its first PC, instead electing to use a system called DOS, licensed from a 32-person company named Microsoft. In the early 1990s, as profits of software developers such as Microsoft exploded, the profits of IBM slumped badly. In 1990, IBM reported an operating profit of $11 billion. Operating profit in 1991 fell to $942 million, and operations showed a loss of $45 million in 1992, which was IBM's first operating loss ever. As of December 31, 1992, the total market value of IBM stock was $29 billion, down from $106 billion in 1987 when IBM was the most valuable company in the world.

Interestingly, in the midst of these problems—decreasing market share, lower profit margins, and record losses—IBM found high demand for its record-setting bond issue. In 1993, IBM issued $1.25 billion of seven-year notes and $550 million of 20-year debentures.

At the time, this was the largest U.S. bond issue in history. The stated interest rates were 6.375% for the notes and 7.50% for the bonds. On their issue date, these two bond issues provided investors with a yield just 0.7% above that provided by U.S. Treasury instruments with comparable maturity periods. Because of IBM's financial woes and increased risk at the time, many thought that the difference would be much higher. Nonetheless, investors' concerns about IBM's future did increase the perceived risk associated with loaning money to the company. In January 1993, Standard & Poor's downgraded IBM's credit rating from the highest rating, AAA, to AA−. In March 1993, Moody's Investor's Service also lowered IBM's rating from A−1 to AA−2.[1] Prior to these downgrades, IBM was able to finance debt in the market at approximately 0.5% above the U.S. Treasury yield.[2]

In a bid to turn IBM around, the board of directors looked outside the company for a new CEO in 1993. They picked Louis V. Gerstner, Jr., who had been the CEO at RJR Nabisco for four years. In his 1997 address to IBM's shareholders, Mr. Gerstner looked back on the task that had faced him when he took the reins in 1993. When he came aboard, he reported, IBM's board was considering dismantling the company, thinking that a collection of smaller, more nimble businesses would hopefully be worth more to IBM's shareholders than the lumbering, inefficient parent company. Mr. Gerstner changed the direction of the company, deciding to keep the company together and to rely on IBM's unique market position in terms of product breadth and strong customer ties.

Under Mr. Gerstner's leadership, IBM recovered. Mr. Gerstner led the company, as the chairman of the board of directors, through 2002. Exhibit 12-1 shows the relationship between IBM's total

Exhibit 12-1 | IBM's Total Debt, Total Assets, and Total Market Value of Equity

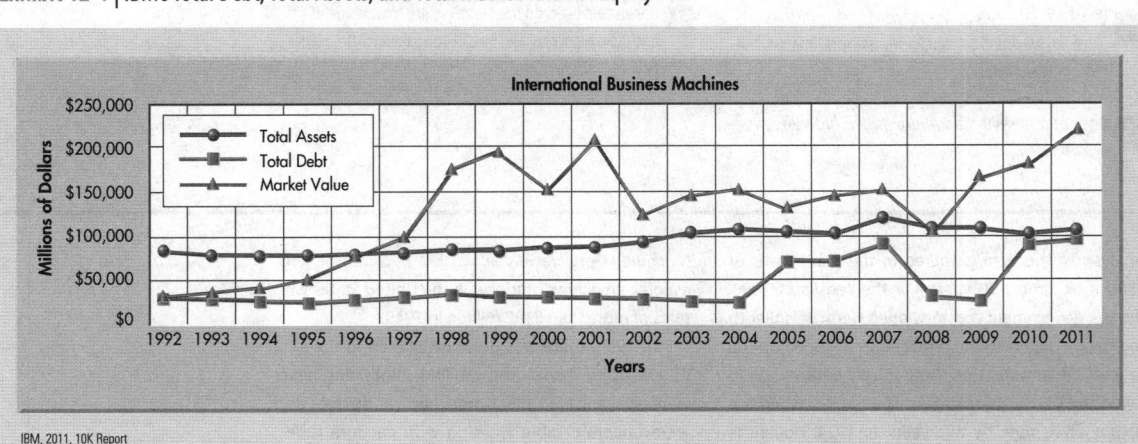

IBM, 2011, 10K Report

[1] These bond rating scales have since been modified.
[2] Thomas T. Vogel, Jr., and Leslie Scism, "Investors Snap Up $1.8 Billion of IBM Securities as Corporations Scramble to Best Higher Interest Rates," *The Wall Street Journal*, June 9, 1993, p. C16.

short- and long-term debt, its total assets, and its market value from 1992 through 2011. Note that IBM's total short- and long-term debt and total market value were almost equal in 1992. Although the company's assets and debt have remained relatively constant over the 16-year period, the firm's market value increased significantly, peaking at $208 billion on December 31, 2001, before easing in the wake of the burst of the dot.com bubble.

An examination of IBM's 2011 liabilities reveals the following (in millions):

Current liabilities:

Taxes	$ 3,313
Short-term debt	8,463
Accounts payable	8,517
Compensation and benefits	5,099
Deferred income	12,197
Other accrued expenses and liabilities	4,535

Long-term:

Long-term debt	$22,857
Retirement and nonpension postretirement benefit obligations	18,374
Deferred income	12,197
Other liabilities	4,535

IBM's largest liability is its long-term debt. A review of this debt reveals debentures, some of which will mature as far out as 2096. In addition, the long-term debt includes notes and foreign currency debt denominated in euros, Japanese yen, and Swiss francs.

In this chapter, we will discuss many of these liabilities. A discussion of the liabilities relating to compensation (compensation and benefits and retirement and nonpension postretirement benefits) will be saved for Chapter 17.

---

1. What was the interest rate impact of the downgrading of IBM's debt by the bond rating agencies?
2. Why is the market interest rate on corporate bonds ALWAYS higher than the market interest rate associated with comparable U.S. Treasury bonds?
3. In 2011, IBM's long-term debt and its long-term retirement obligation were the two largest liabilities on the balance sheet. However, the financial characteristics of these two obligations are dramatically different. On what important dimension do these two long-term obligations differ?

Answers to these questions can be found on page 12-51.

In addition to the routine notes and debentures issued by IBM, a long list of more creative types of debt-financing instruments has been created by the U.S. financial industry. For years, we've had convertible bonds, junk bonds, zero-interest bonds, and commodity-backed bonds, to name a few. The objective of each of these debt instruments is to assist a company in raising needed funds for its business. In this chapter, we will discuss various methods available to companies for borrowing money. We begin with a quick review of liabilities: What they are and how they are measured. Then we will discuss short-term obligations and lines of credit. We then review the concept of present value and examine a mortgage to illustrate how present values apply to the accounting for long-term debt obligations. We then focus on the accounting for various types of bonds, including the option to report these bonds in the balance sheet at their fair value. Following our discussion of bonds, we will introduce some common methods that companies use to avoid disclosing debt on the financial statements. These methods are collectively referred to as *off-balance-sheet financing*. Once you have been exposed to various types of debt financing available to a company, we will talk about how one can analyze a firm's debt position as well as common note disclosures associated with debt.

Exhibit 12-2 | Time Line of Business Issues Associated with Long-Term Debt

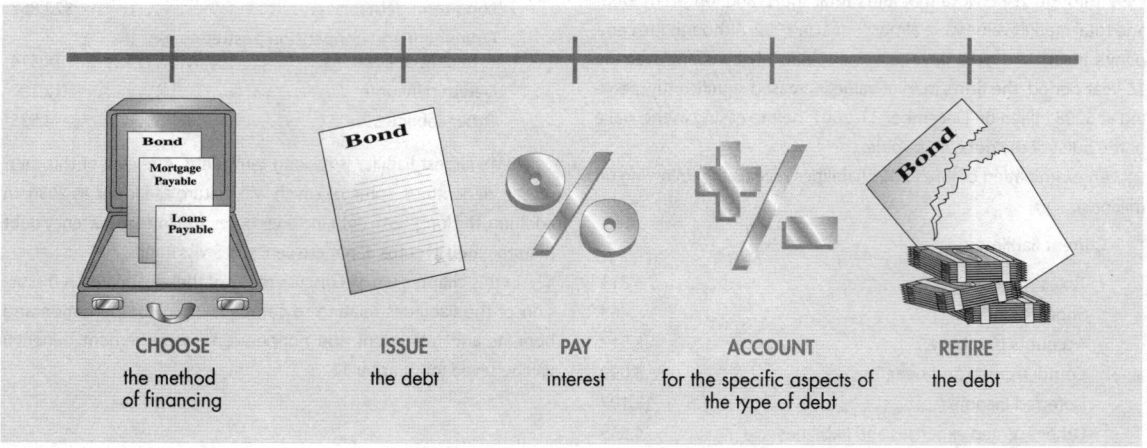

In the Expanded Material section of the chapter, we discuss troubled debt restructuring. The topic of troubled debt restructuring covers those instances when a company is in poor financial condition and is in danger of defaulting on its debt payments. The negotiations between the bond issuer and the holders of the bonds (or troubled debt) often require journal entries to account for the concessions made on the part of the bondholders.

A time line illustrating the business issues associated with long-term financing is given in Exhibit 12-2. The first action is to choose the appropriate form of financing. For example, a company must decide whether to negotiate a private loan with a bank or to seek public financing through the issuance of bonds. After the debt is issued, it is usually serviced through periodic interest payments, although some forms of long-term debt defer payment of all interest until the end of the loan period. An important part of issuing and monitoring long-term debt is the accounting for the specific features of the debt. As discussed in this chapter, bonds require specialized accounting procedures to ensure that the proper amount of interest expense is reported in the income statement and that the long-term debt obligation is reported at the appropriate amount in the balance sheet. Finally, the long-term debt is repaid, either as originally scheduled or, sometimes, in advance.

Classification and Measurement Issues Associated with Debt

LO1 学习目标1
理解各种与债务相关的分类与计量事项。

① Understand the various classification and measurement issues associated with debt.

Before we get into the specifics of debt, let's first take a moment and review just what liabilities are and how they are classified and measured.

Definition of Liabilities

The FASB has defined liabilities as "probable future sacrifices of economic benefits arising from present obligations of a particular entity to transfer assets or provide services to

A liability, such as a bank loan, has the following characteristics: (1) is a result of past transactions or events, (2) involves a probable future transfer of assets or services, and (3) is the obligation of a particular entity.

负债是由过去的交易或事项形成的，因此负债必须在发生时才能予以确认。如果双方的合同义务是以承诺换取承诺的形式存在的，且合同双方义务变更将在未来发生，就不形成负债，这种合同通常被称作待执行合同。

FYI

The FASB is considering a change in the conceptual framework definition of a liability. The change intends to extend the definition of a liability beyond obligations to transfer assets or services to also include obligations to deliver a certain dollar value of equity shares.

other entities in the future as a result of past transactions or events."[3] This definition contains significant components that need to be explained before individual liability accounts are discussed.

A liability is a result of *past transactions or events*. Thus, a liability is not recognized until incurred. This part of the definition excludes contractual obligations from an exchange of promises if performance by both parties is still in the future. Such contracts are referred to as *executory contracts*. Determining when an executory contract qualifies as a liability is not always easy. For example, the signing of a labor contract that obligates both the employer and the employee does not give rise to a liability in current accounting practice nor does the placing of an order for the purchase of merchandise. However, under some conditions, the signing of a lease is recognized as an event that requires the current recognition of a liability even though a lease is essentially an executory contract.

A liability must involve a *probable future transfer of assets or services*. Although liabilities result from past transactions or events, an obligation may be contingent upon the occurrence of another event sometime in the future. When occurrence of the future event seems probable, the obligation is defined as a *liability*. Although the majority of liabilities are satisfied by payment of cash, some obligations are satisfied by transferring other types of assets or by providing services. For example, revenue received in advance requires recognition of an obligation to provide goods or services in the future. Usually, the time of payment is specified by a debt instrument, for example, a note requiring payment of interest and principal on a given date or series of dates. Some obligations, however, require the transfer of assets or services over a period of time, but the exact dates cannot be determined when the liability is incurred, for example, obligations to provide parts or service under a warranty agreement.

A liability is the *obligation of a particular entity*, that is, the entity that has the responsibility to transfer assets or provide services. As long as the payment or transfer is probable, it is not necessary that the entity to whom the obligation is owed be identified. Thus, a warranty to make any repairs necessary to an item sold by an entity is an obligation of that entity even though it is not certain which customers will receive benefits. Generally, the obligation rests on a foundation of legal rights and duties. However, obligations created, inferred, or construed from the facts of a particular situation may also be recognized as liabilities. For example, if a company regularly pays vacation pay or year-end bonuses, accrual of these items as a liability is warranted even though no legal agreement exists to make these payments.

Although the FASB's definition is helpful, the question of when a liability exists is not always easy to answer. Examples of areas in which there are continuing controversies

---

[3] *Statement of Financial Accounting Concepts No. 6*, "Elements of Financial Statements" (Stamford, CT: Financial Accounting Standards Board, December 1985), par. 35. As discussed in this chapter and in Chapter 13 on equity financing, the FASB is currently considering a revision of this liability definition.

include the problems associated with off-balance-sheet financing, deferred income taxes, leases, pensions, and even some equity securities, such as redeemable preferred stock. Once an item is accepted as having met the definition of a liability, there is still the need to appropriately classify, measure, and report the liability.

Classification of Liabilities

For reporting purposes, liabilities are usually classified as current or noncurrent. The distinction between current and noncurrent liabilities was introduced and explained in Chapter 3, where it was pointed out that the computation of working capital is considered by many to be a useful measure of the liquidity of an enterprise.

As noted in Chapter 3, the same rules generally apply for the classification of liabilities as for assets. If a liability arises in the course of an entity's normal operating cycle, it is considered current if current assets will be used to satisfy the obligation within one year or one operating cycle, whichever period is longer. On the other hand, bank borrowings, notes, mortgages, and similar obligations are related to the general financial condition of the entity, rather than directly to the operating cycle, and are classified as current only if they are to be paid with current assets within one year.

> **FYI**
>
> The classification of a liability as current or noncurrent can impact significantly a company's ability to raise additional funds. Most lending institutions and investors look carefully at the current ratio—current assets divided by current liabilities—as a measure of liquidity.

当非流动负债将在一年内到期时，这项负债应按流动负债在资产负债表中明确列示，以反映当前资产的预期流出。

When debt that has been classified as noncurrent will mature within the next year, the liability should be reported as a current liability in order to reflect the expected drain on current assets. However, if the liability is to be paid by transfer of noncurrent assets that have been accumulated for the purpose of liquidating the liability, the obligation continues to be classified as noncurrent.

The distinction between current and noncurrent liabilities is important because of the impact on a company's current ratio. This fundamental measurement of a company's liquidity is computed by dividing total current assets by total current liabilities.

The current ratio is a measure of an entity's ability to meet current obligations. Care must be taken to determine that proper items have been included in the current asset and current liability categories. Historically, the rule of thumb has been that a current ratio below 2.0 suggests the possibility of liquidity problems. However, advances in information technology have enabled companies to be much more effective in minimizing the need to hold cash, inventories, and other current assets. As a result, current ratios for successful companies these days are frequently less than 1.0. Current ratios for selected U.S. companies are given in Exhibit 12-3. Note that most of the companies have current ratios substantially below the 2.0 historical benchmark, and the current ratio of **Delta Air Lines** is only 0.61.

A reasonable margin of current assets over current liabilities suggests that a company will be able to meet maturing obligations even in the event of unfavorable business

> **Stop & Think**
>
> Look at Exhibit 12-3. The 2011 current ratio of **Wal-Mart** is only 0.88. How will Wal-Mart most likely meet its current obligations as they come due?
> a) By the issuance of new shares of common stock
> b) By liquidating long-term assets such as land or buildings
> c) Wal-Mart will probably not be able to meet its current obligations as they come due.
> d) Through the generation of operating cash flow in the normal course of business

Exhibit 12-3 | Current Ratios for Selected U.S. Companies for Fiscal 2011

	Current Ratio
Coca-Cola	1.05
Delta Air Lines	0.61
Dow Chemical	1.72
IBM	1.21
McDonald's	1.25
Microsoft	2.60
Wal-Mart	0.88

© Cengage Learning 2014

conditions or losses on such assets as securities, receivables, and inventories. A current ratio of 1.4 means, for example, that a company could liquidate its total current liabilities 1.4 times using only its current assets.

Measurement of Liabilities

The distinction between current and noncurrent liabilities is also an important consideration in the measurement of liabilities. Obviously, before liabilities can be reported on the financial statements, they must be stated in monetary terms. The fair value measurement used for liabilities is typically the present value of the future cash outflows to settle the obligation. Generally, this is the amount of cash required to pay someone else to accept responsibility for the obligation today.

If a claim isn't to be paid until sometime in the future, as is the case with noncurrent liabilities, either the claim should provide for interest to be paid on the debt or the obligation should be reported at the discounted value of its maturity amount. Current obligations that arise in the course of normal business operations are generally due within a short period, for example, 30 to 60 days, and normally are not discounted.[4] Thus, trade accounts payable are not reported at their present value even though they carry no interest provision. However, this is an exception to the general rule; most nonoperating business transactions, such as the borrowing of money, purchasing of assets over time, and long-term leases, do involve the computation of present values. The obligation in these instances is the present value of the future resource outflows. The use of present value concepts with long-term debt obligations is illustrated in detail later in the chapter.

For measurement purposes, liabilities can be divided into three categories:

1. Liabilities that are definite in amount
2. Estimated liabilities
3. Contingent liabilities

[4] FASB ASC paragraph 835-30-15-3a.

The measurement of liabilities always involves some uncertainty because a liability, by definition, involves a future outflow of resources. However, for the first category, both the existence of the liability and the amount to be paid are determinable because of a contract, trade agreement, or general business practice. An example of a liability that is definite in amount is the principal payment on a note.

The second category includes items that are definitely liabilities; that is, they involve a definite future resource outflow, but the actual amount of the obligation cannot be established currently. In this situation, the amount of the liability is estimated so that the obligation is reflected in the current period, even though at an approximated value. A warranty obligation that is recorded on an accrual basis is an example of an estimated liability.

Generally, liabilities from both of the first two categories are reported on the balance sheet, either as current or noncurrent liabilities, whichever is appropriate. However, items that resemble liabilities but are contingent upon the occurrence of some future event are not recorded until it is probable that the event will occur. Even though the amount of the potential obligation may be known, the actual existence of a liability is questionable because it is contingent upon a future event for which there is considerable uncertainty. An example of a contingent liability is a pending lawsuit. Only if the lawsuit is lost or is settled out of court will a sacrifice of economic benefits be necessary. Although not recorded in the accounts, some contingent liabilities should be disclosed in the notes to the financial statements as discussed and illustrated in Chapter 19.

一些因或有事项而产生的负债只有在未来事项很可能发生的情形下才被记录。由于决定或有事项发生与否的未来事项具有很大的不确定性，即使潜在义务的金额已经知晓，负债的产生仍受质疑。

> **Caution**
>
> A contingent liability results only when there is a significant degree of uncertainty as to the outcome of the event associated with the potential liability. Recall from its definition that a liability involves a "probable future sacrifice...." If the contingent event is probable, it meets the definition of a liability and should be recorded as such.

Accounting for Short-Term Debt Obligations

LO2 学习目标2
解释包括预期再融资在内的短期负债，以及信用额度的目的。

② Account for short-term debt obligations, including those expected to be refinanced, and describe the purpose of lines of credit.

As noted in the previous section, liabilities that have been classified as current are typically not discounted, that is, they are not reported at their present value. Instead, they are reported on the balance sheet at their face value. Representative of this type of debt are accounts payable, notes payable, and miscellaneous operating payables including salaries, payroll taxes, property and sales taxes, and income taxes. Short-term obligations that are expected to be refinanced require special consideration. Problems that can arise in determining the balances to be reported for these various types of debt are described in the following sections.

Short-Term Operating Liabilities

Businesses with good internal processes purchase most goods and services on credit. The term account payable usually refers to the amount due for the purchase of materials by a manufacturing company or merchandise by a wholesaler or retailer. Other obligations, such as salaries and wages, rent, interest, and utilities, are reported as separate liabilities in accounts descriptive of the nature of the obligation. Accounts payable are not recorded when purchase orders are placed but instead when legal title to the goods passes to the buyer. The rules for the customary recognition of legal passage of title were presented in Chapter 9. If goods are in transit at year-end, the purchase should be recorded if the shipment terms indicate that title has passed. This means that care must be exercised to review the purchase of goods and services near the end of an accounting period to ensure a proper cutoff and reporting of liabilities and inventory. It is customary to report accounts payable at the expected amount of the payment. Because the payment period is normally short, no recognition of interest is required.

Short-Term Debt

Companies often borrow money on a short-term basis for operating purposes other than for the purchase of materials or merchandise involving accounts payable. Collectively, these obligations may be referred to as *short-term debt*. In most cases, such debt is evidenced by a promissory note, a formal written promise to pay a sum of money in the future, and is usually reflected on the debtor's books as Notes payable.

Notes issued to trade creditors for the purchase of goods or services are called trade notes payable. Nontrade notes payable are notes issued to banks or to officers and stockholders for loans to the company and those issued to others for the purchase of noncurrent operating assets. It is normally desirable to classify current notes payable on the balance sheet as trade or nontrade because such information would reveal to statement users the sources of indebtedness and the extent to which the company has relied on each source in financing its activities.

The problems encountered in the valuation of notes payable are the same as those discussed in Chapter 7 with respect to notes receivable. Thus, a short-term note payable is recorded and reported at its present value, which is normally the face value of the note. This presumes that the note bears a reasonable stated rate of interest. However, if a note has no stated rate of interest, or if the stated rate is unreasonable, then the face value of the note would need to be discounted to its present value to reflect the effective rate of interest implicit in the note. This is accomplished by debiting Discount on Notes Payable when the note is issued and by writing off the discount to Interest Expense over the life of the note in the same manner as was illustrated for the discount on notes receivable in Chapter 7.

Discount on Notes Payable is a contra account to Notes Payable and would be reported on the balance sheet as follows; the $90,000 net amount represents the present value of the note.

Current liabilities:		
Notes payable...	$100,000	
Less: Discount on notes payable	10,000	$90,000

Short-Term Obligations Expected to Be Refinanced

Misclassification of debt can create serious problems for users of financial statements. Because the "current" classification is reserved for those obligations that will be satisfied with current assets within a year, a short-term obligation that is expected to be refinanced on a long-term basis should not be reported as a current liability. This applies to the currently maturing portion of a long-term debt and to all other short-term obligations except those arising in the normal course of operations that are due in customary terms. Similarly, it should not be assumed that a short-term obligation will be refinanced and therefore classified as a noncurrent liability unless the refinancing arrangements are secure. Thus, to avoid potential manipulation, the refinancing expectation must be realistic, not just a mere possibility.

An example will illustrate this last point and show the importance of proper classification. Assume that a company borrows a substantial amount of money that it expects to pay back at the end of five years. The president of the company signs a six-month note, which the loan officer at the bank verbally agrees will be renewed "automatically" until the actual maturity date in five years. The only current obligation expected is payment of the accrued interest each renewal period. Under these circumstances, the company reports the obligation as noncurrent, except for the accrued interest obligation. Assume further that the loan officer leaves the bank and that the new bank official will not allow the short-term note to be refinanced. The financial picture of the company is now dramatically changed. What was considered a long-term obligation because of refinancing expectations is suddenly a current liability requiring settlement with liquid assets in the near future.

The authoritative guideline for classifying short-term obligations expected to be refinanced is contained in FASB ASC Topic 470 (Debt). According to the FASB, both of the following conditions must be met before a short-term obligation may be properly excluded from the current liability classification:[5]

根据FASB的准则，我们应将短期义务排除在短期负债之外，列入长期负债必须满足以下情形：
- 管理层必须明确是基于长期基础上的融资义务；
- 管理当局必须有能力进行再融资。

1. Management must *intend to refinance* the obligation on a long-term basis.
2. Management *must demonstrate an ability to refinance* the obligation.

Concerning the second point, an ability to refinance may be demonstrated by either of the following:

(a) Actually refinancing the obligation during the period between the balance sheet date and the date the statements are issued.

(b) Reaching a firm agreement that clearly provides for refinancing on a long-term basis.

The terms of the refinancing agreement should be noncancellable as to all parties and extend beyond the current year. In addition, the company should not be in violation of the agreement at the balance sheet date or the date of issuance, and the lender or investor should be financially capable of meeting the refinancing requirements.

If an actual refinancing does occur before the balance sheet is issued, the portion of the short-term obligation that is to be excluded from current liabilities cannot exceed the proceeds from the new debt or equity securities issued to retire the old debt. For example, if a $400,000 long-term note is issued to partially refinance $750,000 of short-term obligations, only $400,000 of the short-term debt can be excluded from current liabilities.

如果在财务报表报出日之前，实际再融资发生时的资金已提前支付，那么这笔款项应包含在资产负债表中的流动负债项目。

An additional question relates to the timing of the refinancing. If the obligation is paid prior to the actual refinancing and before the issuance of the financial statements, the obligation should be included in current liabilities on the balance sheet.[6] To illustrate, assume that the liabilities of CareFree Inc. at December 31, 2014, include a note payable for $200,000, due January 15, 2015. The management of CareFree intends to refinance the note by issuing 10-year bonds. The bonds are actually issued before the issuance of the December 31, 2014, balance sheet on February 15, 2015. If the bonds are issued prior to payment of the note, the note should be classified as noncurrent on the December 31, 2014, balance sheet. If payment of the note precedes the issuance of the bonds, however, the note should be included in current liabilities as of December 31, 2014.

The international standard for classification of short-term obligations to be refinanced is slightly different. According to *IAS 1*, for the obligation to be classified as long term, the refinancing must take place by the balance sheet date, not the later date when the financial statements are finalized. In other words, under the international standard post-balance-sheet-date events are NOT considered when determining whether a refinanceable obligation is reported as current or noncurrent. The FASB is considering adopting this more stringent condition.

[5] FASB ASC paragraph 470-10-45-14.
[6] FASB ASC paragraph 470-10-45-15.

Normally, classified balance sheets are presented showing a total for Current Liabilities. If a short-term obligation is excluded from that category due to refinancing expectations, disclosure should be made in the notes to the financial statements. The note should include a general description of the refinancing agreement.

Lines of Credit

Some companies have temporary borrowing needs necessitated by the seasonal nature of their business. **Toys "R" Us** is an example of this type of business. Even nonseasonal companies have predictable short-term funding needs that they prefer to arrange for in advance. A way to handle these temporary funding needs is to arrange lines of credit with banks. The lines of credit can be used for automatic borrowing as cash is needed, and then the loans can be repaid when cash is plentiful. For example, in 2011, Toys "R" Us had a $1.85 billion line of credit to finance seasonal inventory buildup and store construction costs. IBM also has lines of credit established with numerous banks that allow it to quickly borrow money. A *line of credit* is a negotiated arrangement with a lender in which the terms are agreed to prior to the need for borrowing. When a company finds itself in need of money, an established line of credit allows the company access to funds immediately without having to go through the credit approval process. IBM disclosed the following in the notes to its 2010 financial statements:

LINES OF CREDIT

The company maintains a five-year, $10 billion Credit Agreement (the "Credit Agreement"), which expires on June 28, 2012. The total expense recorded by the company related to this facility was $6.2 million in 2010, $6.3 million in 2009 and $6.2 million in 2008. The Credit Agreement permits the company and its Subsidiary Borrowers to borrow up to $10 billion on a revolving basis. Borrowings of the Subsidiary Borrowers will be unconditionally backed by the company. The company may also, upon the agreement of either existing lenders, or of the additional banks not currently party to the Credit Agreement, increase the commitments under the Credit Agreement up to an additional $2.0 billion. Subject to certain terms of the Credit Agreement, the company and Subsidiary Borrowers may borrow, prepay and reborrow amounts under the Credit Agreement at any time during the Credit Agreement. Interest rates on borrowings under the Credit Agreement will be based on prevailing market interest rates, as further described in the Credit Agreement. The Credit Agreement contains customary representations and warranties, covenants, events of default, and indemnification provisions. The company believes that circumstances that might give rise to breach of these covenants or an event of default, as specified in the Credit Agreement, are remote. The company's other lines of credit, most of which are uncommitted, totaled approximately $14,679 million and $9,790 million at December 31, 2010 and 2009, respectively. Interest rates and other terms of borrowing under these lines of credit vary from country to country, depending on local market conditions.

($ in millions) At December 31:	2010	2009
Unused lines:		
From the committed global credit facility	$ 9,926	$ 9,910
From other committed and uncommitted lines	11,462	7,405
Total unused lines of credit	$21,388	$17,314

IBM, 2010, 10K Report

虽然信用额度本身不是一项负债，但是信用额度一旦用于借款就形成了形式上的负债，我们应根据还款协议中偿付时间的长短将其划分为流动负债或长期负债。

The line of credit itself is *not* a liability. However, once the line of credit is used to borrow money, the company has a formal liability that will be reported as either a current or

Exhibit 12-4 | Unused Lines of Credit—2011

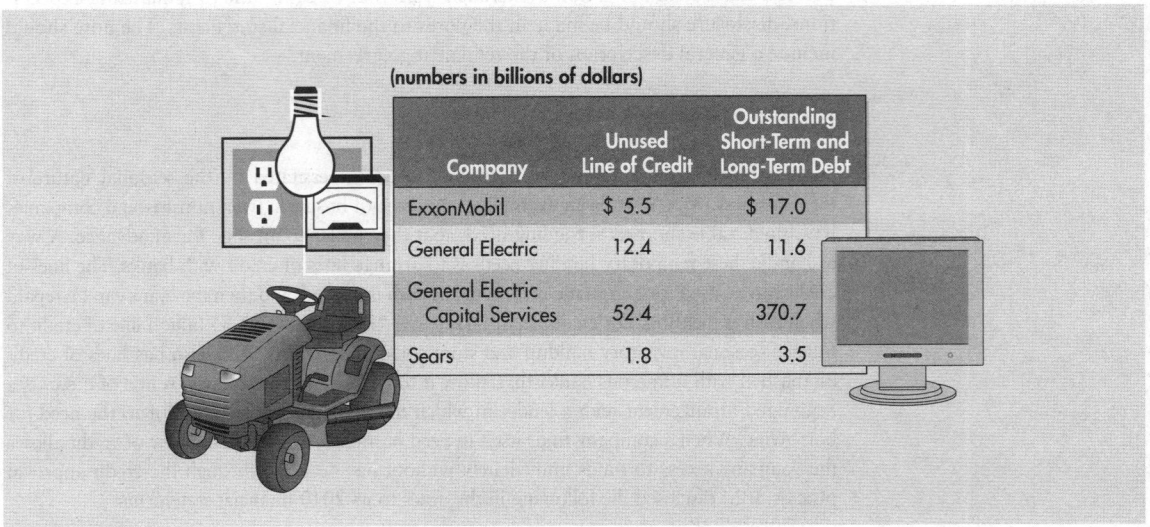

(numbers in billions of dollars)

Company	Unused Line of Credit	Outstanding Short-Term and Long-Term Debt
ExxonMobil	$ 5.5	$ 17.0
General Electric	12.4	11.6
General Electric Capital Services	52.4	370.7
Sears	1.8	3.5

© Cengage Learning 2014

long-term liability, depending on the repayment terms of the agreement. A sample of U.S. companies with large unused lines of credit is given in Exhibit 12-4. Note especially that the lines of credit are quite large relative to the amount of outstanding debt; in the case of Sears, use of the full amount of credit would increase its amount of outstanding debt by 50%. Details regarding the terms of the line of credit, for example, the used and unused portions and the applicable interest rates, are disclosed in the financial statement notes.

Maintaining a line of credit is not costless. Banks typically charge a small amount, a fraction of 1% per year, in exchange for the commitment to provide a company with guaranteed credit. For example, on December 31, 2011, McDonald's had a $1.5 billion line of credit (expiring in 2016) that had a fee of 0.065% per year. Of course, if McDonald's uses the line of credit, interest on the borrowed amount would have to be paid in addition to this fee. The fee is the cost that McDonald's pays in order to have guaranteed access to credit. The cost of maintaining this $1.5 billion credit line for one year is $975,000 ($1.5 billion × 0.00065).

Seasonal businesses often use lines of credit to handle temporary borrowing needs.

Present Value of Long-Term Debt

 Apply present value concepts to the accounting for long-term debts such as mortgages.

The reporting of long-term debt obligations is more complex than for short-term obligations because the sum of the future cash payments to be made on a long-term debt is not a good measure of the actual economic obligation. For example, repaying a 30-year, $200,000 mortgage with a 7% interest rate will require monthly payments totaling $479,018 over the 30-year life of the mortgage. However, the entire obligation could be settled with one payment of $200,000 today. In reporting long-term debt obligations, the emphasis is on reporting what the real economic value of the obligation is today, not what the total debt payments will be in the future.

To illustrate the application of present value concepts to the accounting for long-term debt, a simple mortgage example will be used. A mortgage is a loan backed by an asset that serves as collateral for the loan. If the borrower cannot repay the loan, the lender has the legal right to claim the mortgaged asset and sell it in order to recover the loan amount. Mortgages are generally payable in equal installments; a portion of each payment represents interest on the unpaid mortgage balance, and the remainder of the payment is designated as repayment of part of the principal of the loan. As an example, assume that on January 1, 2015, Crystal Michae purchases a house for $250,000 and makes a down payment of $50,000. The remaining $200,000 of the purchase price is financed through a mortgage on the house. The mortgage is payable over 30 years at a rate of $2,057 monthly. The interest rate is 12% compounded monthly, and the first payment is due on February 1, 2015. An interest rate of 12% compounded monthly is the same as 1% per month (12%/12 months). (See the Time Value of Money Review module for a review of present value concepts.)

As the mortgage payments are made, each monthly payment of $2,057 must be divided between principal and interest. The interest is based on 1% of the mortgage balance at the beginning of the month. On February 1, the interest is $2,000 ($200,000 × 0.01), and the principal portion of the payment is $57 (or $2,057 − $2,000). In March, the interest is $1,999, 1% of $199,943 ($200,000 − $57), and this pattern continues monthly. The division of these payments into interest and principal components for the first five monthly payments is shown in Exhibit 12-5. This process is called loan (or mortgage) amortization.

If Crystal were to maintain a set of personal financial records, she would make the following journal entry on February 1:

Interest Expense...	2,000
Mortgage Payable..	57
Cash..	2,057

As with other forms of long-term financing, a mortgage obligation is reported in a company's balance sheet at its present value, which approximates the cash amount that would fully satisfy the obligation today. So, for example, if Crystal were to prepare a quarterly balance sheet as of April 1, 2015 (after the third payment was made), she would show a mortgage liability of $199,827 (see Exhibit 12-5). Because most mortgages are payable in monthly installments, the principal payments for the next 12 months following the balance sheet date must be shown in the Current Liability section as the current portion of a long-term debt. The remaining portion is classified as a long-term liability.

Exhibit 12-5 | Loan (Mortgage) Amortization Schedule

Date	(1) Payment Amount	(2) Interest Expense (4) × 0.01	(3) Amount Applied to Reduce Principal (1) − (2)	(4) Balance
January 1, 2015	—	—	—	$200,000
February 1, 2015	$2,057	$2,000	$57	199,943
March 1, 2015	2,057	1,999	58	199,885
April 1, 2015	2,057	1,999	58	199,827
May 1, 2015	2,057	1,998	59	199,768
June 1, 2015	2,057	1,998	59	199,709

© Cengage Learning 2014

A secured loan is similar to a mortgage in that it is a loan backed by certain assets as collateral. If the borrower cannot repay the loan, the lender can claim the securing assets. Secured loans are more common among firms experiencing financial difficulties. The fact that the loan is secured reduces the risk to the lender and therefore reduces the interest cost for the borrower. For example, in its 2011 annual report, Delta Air Lines disclosed the following regarding its secured loans:

> In 2011, we entered into senior secured first-lien credit facilities to borrow up to $2.6 billion. The Senior Secured Credit Facilities consist of a $1.4 billion first-lien term loan facility and a $1.2 billion first-lien revolving credit facility, up to $500 million of which may be used for the issuance of letters of credit. Our obligations under the Senior Secured Credit Facilities are guaranteed by substantially all of our domestic subsidiaries. The Senior Secured Credit Facilities and the related guarantees are secured by liens on certain of our and the Guarantors' assets, including accounts receivable, inventory, flight equipment, ground property and equipment, certain non-Pacific international routes, domestic slots, real estate and certain investments.

Financing with Bonds

LO4 学习目标4
理解各类债券，计算债券的发行价格并解释债券的发行、利息及债券回购。

④ Understand the various types of bonds; compute the price of a bond issue; and account for the issuance, interest, and redemption of bonds.

The long-term financing of a corporation is accomplished either through the issuance of long-term debt instruments, usually bonds or notes, or through the sale of additional stock. The issuance of bonds or notes instead of stock may be preferred by management and stockholders for the following reasons:

1. Present owners remain in control of the corporation.
2. Interest is a deductible expense in arriving at taxable income; dividends are not.
3. Current market rates of interest may be favorable relative to stock market prices.
4. The charge against earnings for interest may be less than the amount of dividends that might be expected by shareholders.

There are, however, certain limitations and disadvantages of financing with long-term debt securities. Debt financing is possible only when a company is in satisfactory financial condition and can offer adequate security to creditors. Furthermore, interest obligations must be paid regardless of the company's earnings and financial position. If a company has operating losses and is unable to raise sufficient cash to meet periodic interest payments, secured debt holders may take legal action to assume control of company assets.

A complicating factor is that the distinction between debt and equity securities may become fuzzy. Usually, a debt instrument has a fixed interest rate and a definite maturity date when the principal must be repaid. Also, holders of debt instruments generally have no voting privileges. A traditional equity security, on the other hand, has no fixed repayment obligation or maturity date, and dividends on stock become obligations only after being formally declared by the board of directors of a corporation. In addition, common stockholders generally have voting and other ownership privileges. The problem is that certain convertible debt securities have many equity characteristics, and some preferred stocks have many of the characteristics of debt. This makes it important to recognize the distinction between debt and equity and to provide the accounting treatment that is most appropriate under the specific circumstances.

> **FYI**
>
> Often, companies in poor financial condition can still obtain financing. However, the terms of the debt are typically very restrictive and the interest rate is very high. Bonds issued by high-risk companies are often classified as *junk bonds*. Junk bonds are discussed later in this chapter.

Accounting for Bonds

Conceptually, bonds and long-term notes are similar types of debt instruments. There are some technical differences, however. For example, the trust indenture (i.e., the bond contract), associated with bonds generally provides more extensive detail than the contract terms of a note, often including restrictions on the payment of dividends or incurrence of additional debt. The length of time to maturity is also generally longer for bonds than for notes. Some bonds do not mature for 20 years or longer, while most notes mature in one to five years. Other characteristics of bonds and notes are similar. Therefore, although the discussion that follows deals specifically with bonds, the accounting principles and reporting practices related to bonds can also be applied to long-term notes.

There are three main considerations in accounting for bonds:

1. Recording the issuance or purchase
2. Recognizing the applicable interest during the life of the bonds
3. Accounting for the retirement of bonds either at maturity or prior to the maturity date

Before these considerations are discussed, the nature of bonds and the determination of bond market prices will be reviewed.

Nature of Bonds

The power of a corporation to create bond indebtedness is found in the corporation laws of a state and may be specifically granted by charter. In some cases, formal authorization by a majority of stockholders is required before a board of directors can approve a bond issue.

Borrowing by means of bonds involves the issuance of certificates of indebtedness. Bond certificates, commonly referred to simply as *bonds*, are frequently issued in denominations of $1,000, referred to as the face value, par value, or maturity value of the bond, although in some cases bonds are issued in varying denominations.

The group contract between the corporation and the bondholders is known as the bond indenture. The indenture details the rights and obligations of the contracting parties, indicates the property pledged as well as the protection offered on the loan, and names the bank or trust company that is to represent the bondholders.

Bonds may be sold by the company directly to investors, or they may be underwritten by investment bankers or a syndicate. The underwriters may agree to purchase the entire bond issue or that part of the issue not sold by the company, or they may agree simply to manage the sale of the security on a commission basis, often referred to as a "*best efforts*" *basis.*

Most companies attempt to sell their bonds to underwriters to avoid incurring a loss after the bonds are placed on the market. An interesting example of this occurred when IBM went to the bond market for the first time and issued a record $1 billion worth of bonds and long-term notes. After the issue was released by IBM to the underwriters, interest rates soared as the Federal Reserve Bank sharply increased its discount rate. The market price of the IBM securities fell, and the brokerage houses and investment bankers participating in the underwriting incurred a loss in excess of $50 million on the sale of the securities to investors.

Issuers of Bonds Bonds and similar debt instruments are issued by private corporations; the U.S. government; state, county, and local governments; school districts; and government-sponsored organizations, such as the Federal Home Loan Bank and the Federal National Mortgage Association. As of December 2009, the Securities Industry and Financial Markets Association estimated that the amount of outstanding bonds for corporations was $6.9 trillion.

The U.S. government's debt includes not only U.S. Treasury bonds but also U.S. Treasury bills, which are notes with less than one year to maturity date, and U.S. Treasury notes, which mature in one to seven years. Outstanding U.S. government debt securities as of December 2009 totaled $9.2 trillion.

Debt securities issued by state, county, and local governments and their agencies are collectively referred to as municipal debt. A unique feature of municipal debt is that the interest received by investors from such securities is exempt from federal income tax. Because of this tax advantage, "municipals" generally carry lower interest rates than debt securities of other issuers, enabling these governmental units to borrow at favorable interest rates. The tax exemption is in reality a subsidy granted by the federal government to encourage capital investment in state and local governments. Municipal bonds outstanding as of December 2009 were $2.8 trillion.

Types of Bonds Bonds may be categorized in many different ways, depending on the characteristics of a particular bond issue. The major distinguishing features of bonds are identified and discussed in the following sections.

Term versus Serial Bonds
一次还本付息债券与分期还本付息债券

Term versus Serial Bonds Bonds that mature on a single date are called term bonds. When bonds mature in installments, they are referred to as serial bonds. Serial bonds are much less common than term bonds.

Secured versus Unsecured Bonds
担保债券与无担保债券

Secured versus Unsecured Bonds Bonds issued by private corporations may be either secured or unsecured. Secured bonds offer protection to investors by providing some form of security, such as a mortgage on real estate or a pledge of other collateral. A first-mortgage bond represents a first claim against the property of a corporation in the event of the company's inability to meet bond interest and principal payments. A second-mortgage bond is a secondary claim ranking only after the claim of the first-mortgage bond or senior issue has been completely satisfied. A collateral trust bond is usually secured by stocks and bonds of other corporations owned by the issuing company. Such securities are generally transferred to a trustee, who holds them as collateral on behalf of the bondholders and, if necessary, will sell them to satisfy the bondholders' claim.

Unsecured bonds are not protected by the pledge of any specific assets and are frequently termed debenture bonds, or debentures. Holders of debenture bonds simply rank as general creditors along with other unsecured parties. The risk involved in these securities varies with the financial strength of the debtor. Debentures issued by a strong company may involve little risk; debentures issued by a weak company whose properties are already heavily mortgaged may involve considerable risk. Quality ratings for bonds are published by both Moody's and Standard & Poor's investor service companies. For example, Moody's bond ratings range from (Aaa), for prime or high-quality bonds to (C), for very high-risk bonds. Standard & Poor's range is from AAA, AA, A, BBB, and so forth, to D.

Registered versus Bearer (Coupon) Bonds 记名债券与不记名债券   Registered bonds call for the registry of the owner's name on the corporation books. Transfer of bond ownership is similar to that for stock. When a bond is sold, the corporate transfer agent cancels the bond certificate surrendered by the seller and issues a new certificate to the buyer. Interest checks are mailed periodically to the bondholders of record. Bearer bonds, or coupon bonds, are not recorded in the name of the owner; title to these bonds passes with delivery. Each bond is accompanied by coupons for individual interest payments covering the life of the issue. Coupons are clipped by the owner of the bond and presented to a bank for deposit or collection. The issue of bearer bonds eliminates the need for recording bond ownership changes and preparing and mailing periodic interest checks. Coupon bonds fail to offer the bondholder the protection found in registered bonds in the event the bonds are lost or stolen. In some cases, bonds provide interest coupons but require registry as to principal. Here, ownership safeguards are provided while the time-consuming routines involved in making interest payments are avoided. Bonds of recent issue are registered rather than coupon bonds.

Zero-Interest Bonds and Bonds with Variable Interest Rates   In recent years, some companies have issued long-term debt securities that do not bear interest. Instead, these securities sell at a significant discount that provides an investor with a total interest payoff at maturity. These bonds are known as zero-interest bonds or deep-discount bonds. Another type of zero-interest bond delays interest payments for a period of time.

Because of potentially wide fluctuations in interest rates, some bonds and long-term notes are issued with variable (or floating) interest rates. Over the life of these obligations, the interest rate changes as prevailing market interest rates increase or decrease. A variable interest rate security benefits the investor when interest rates are rising and the issuer when interest rates are falling.

Junk Bonds   High-risk, high-yield bonds issued by companies that are heavily in debt or otherwise in weak financial condition are often referred to as junk bonds. These bonds are rated Ba2 or lower by Moody's and BB or lower by Standard & Poor's. Junk bonds typically yield higher interest rates, some yielding in excess of 20%.

Junk bonds are issued in at least three types of circumstances. First, they are issued by companies that once had high credit ratings but have fallen on hard times. As an example,

Standard & Poor's issued a rating of B for debt issued by **Little Traverse Bay Band of Odawa Indians**, owners of a hotel and casino resort in Michigan, and provided the following information:

> Standard & Poor's Ratings Services assigned its 'B' rating to Harbor Springs, Mich.-based Little Traverse Bay Band of Odawa Indians' $195 million senior notes due 2013. At the same time, Standard & Poor's assigned its 'B' issuer credit rating to the Tribe. The outlook is negative.
>
> The ratings on the Tribe reflect very high leverage during the construction period of the Tribe's expansion project, a narrow gaming operation, a competitive marketplace that is facing additional intermediate-term gaming supply, and challenges managing a larger gaming facility. These are only partially tempered by the escrowing of the first four interest payments on the notes, totaling $33 million, and stable cash flow from the existing gaming facility.
>
> Source: Standard & Poor's.

Second, junk bonds are issued by emerging growth companies, such as **Amazon.com**'s issue of junk bonds priced at $275 million in 1998, that lack adequate cash flow, credit history, or diversification to permit them to issue higher grade (i.e., lower risk) bonds (Amazon's fortunes have since changed with the company reporting its first positive cash flow from operations in 2002 and its first positive net income in 2003). The third circumstance is that junk bonds are issued by companies undergoing restructuring, often in conjunction with a leveraged buyout (LBO).

Convertible and Commodity-Backed Bonds Bonds may provide for their conversion into some other security at the option of the bondholder. Such bonds are known as convertible bonds. The conversion feature generally permits the owner of bonds to exchange them for common stock. The bondholder is thus able to convert the claim into an ownership interest if corporate operations prove successful and conversion becomes attractive; in the meantime, the special rights of a creditor are maintained. Bonds may also be redeemable in terms of commodities, such as oil or precious metals. These types of bonds are referred to as commodity-backed bonds.

Callable Bonds Bond indentures frequently give the issuing company the right to call and retire the bonds prior to their maturity. Such bonds are termed callable bonds. When a corporation wishes to reduce its outstanding indebtedness, bondholders are notified of the portion of the issue to be surrendered, and they are paid in accordance with call provisions. Interest does not accrue after the call date.

Mortgage-Backed Securities One of the culprits of the 2008 worldwide financial crises was mortgage-backed securities. In many cases, these securities are just a special form of secured bonds. The underlying collateral for these bonds is the collection of mortgages owned by the issuing entity (either a private company or, more often, a U.S. government sponsored entity such as the Federal National Mortgage Association, or Fannie Mae). Problems with this type of secured bond arise when the people who own the mortgaged homes can no longer make their payments. These defaults cause the portfolio of mortgage loans to have decreased value as collateral for the mortgage-backed bonds.

FASB CODIFICATION

The Issue: You are in charge of preparing the financial statements for the start-up company for which you work. The CEO has just come to your office to criticize your liability classification of the subordinated debentures that the company has issued. These debentures are "subordinated" to the company's other loans, meaning that those other loans must be repaid first before the subordinated debentures are repaid. As a result, from an economic standpoint, the holders of the subordinated debentures are close to being common stockholders. Your CEO thinks that these debentures should be reported in the equity section of your company's balance sheet. She points out, correctly, that banks often classify subordinated debentures as "equity" in the definition of debt covenant calculations for borrowers. Your accounting instinct tells you that subordinated debentures must be classified as liabilities, but you don't have any authoritative support for your position.

The Question: Where can one find the authoritative statement requiring subordinated debt to be classified as a liability in the balance sheet?

Searching the Codification: Of course, we are going to start by looking in FASB ASC Topic 470 (Debt). Here is a hint—the classification of subordinated debt was addressed by the SEC in a Staff Accounting Bulletin.

The Answer: The authoritative guidance for the balance sheet classification of subordinated debt is given on page 12-52.

Market Price of Bonds

The market price of bonds varies with the safety of the investment and the current market interest rate for similar instruments. When the financial condition and earnings of a corporation are such that payment of interest and principal on bond indebtedness is virtually ensured, the interest rate a company must offer to sell a bond issue is relatively low. As the risk factor increases, a higher interest return is necessary to attract investors. The amount of interest paid on bonds is a specified percentage of the face value. This percentage is termed the stated rate, or contract rate. This rate, however, may not be the same as the prevailing or market rate for bonds of similar quality and length of time to maturity at the time the issue is sold. Furthermore, the market rate fluctuates constantly. These factors often result in a difference between bond face values and the prices at which the bonds actually sell in the market.

The purchase of bonds at face value implies agreement between the bond's stated rate of interest and the prevailing market rate of interest. If the stated rate exceeds the market rate, the bonds will sell at a premium; if the stated rate is less than the market rate, the bonds will sell at a discount. The bond premium or the bond discount is the amount needed to adjust the stated rate of interest to the actual market rate of interest or yield for that particular bond. Thus, the stated rate adjusted for the premium or the discount gives the actual rate of return on the bonds, known as the market, yield, or effective interest rate. A declining market rate of interest subsequent

> **Caution**
>
> When the stated interest rate on a company's bonds is less than the market rate for similar bonds, investors will pay less than the face value of the bond because they are going to receive a lower interest payment. The amount paid below the face value is termed a *discount*. The reverse is true for a premium.

to issuance of the bonds results in an increase in the market value of the bonds; a rising market rate of interest results in a decrease in their market value.

Bond prices are quoted in the market as a percentage of face value. For example, a bond quotation of 96.5 means the market price is 96.5% of face value; thus, the bond is trading at a discount. A bond quotation of 104 means the market price is 104% of face value; thus, the bond is trading at a premium. U.S. government note and bond quotations are made in 32s rather than 100s. This means that a government bond selling at 98.16 (sometimes written 98:16) is selling at 98 16/32, or in terms of decimal equivalents, 98.5%.

The market price of a bond at any date can be determined by discounting the maturity value of the bond and each remaining interest payment at the market rate of interest for similar debt on that date. The present value calculations explained in the Time Value of Money Review module can be used for computing bond market prices.

To illustrate the computation of a bond market price, assume 10-year, 8% bonds of $100,000 are to be sold on the bond issue date. Further assume that the effective interest rate for bonds of similar quality and maturity is 10%, compounded semiannually.

The computation of the market price of the bonds may be divided into two parts:

Part 1 Present value of principal (maturity value):

Maturity value of bonds after 10 years, or 20 semiannual periods......	$100,000
Effective interest rate = 10% per year, or 5% per semiannual period;	
$FV = \$100{,}000; N = 20; I = 5\%$...................................	$37,689

Part 2 Present value of 20 interest payments:

Semiannual payment, 4% of $100,000	$ 4,000
Effective interest rate, 10% per year, or 5% per semiannual period;	
$PMT = \$4{,}000; N = 20; I = 5\%$.....................................	49,849
Total present value (market price) of bond	$87,538

The market price for the bonds would be $87,538, the sum of the present values of the two parts. Because the effective interest rate is higher than the stated interest rate, the bonds would sell at a $12,462 discount at the issuance date. It should be noted that if the effective rate on these bonds were 8% instead of 10%, the sum of the present values of the two parts would be $100,000, meaning that the bonds would sell at their face value, or at par. If the effective interest rate were less than 8%, the market price of the bonds would be more than $100,000, and the bonds would sell at a premium.

The bonds of public corporations are traded on various bond exchanges, which are similar to stock exchanges. Exhibit 12-6 presents a selection of bond listings as of July 23, 2012.

Exhibit 12-6 | Bond Listing

	Price	Coupon %	Maturity Date	Yield to Maturity %	Current Yield%	Rating
Hewlett-Packard.......................	114.43	5.400	1-Mar-2017	2.711	4.719	A
Hewlett-Packard.......................	113.91	5.500	1-Mar-2018	3.218	4.828	A
PepsiCo Inc.............................	102.57	3.600	13-Aug-2042	3.461	3.510	AA
Atlantic Richfield	130.09	8.250	1-Feb-2022	4.661	6.432	A

Source: finance.yahoo.com/bonds, July 23, 2012. Data provided by ValuBond.

Stop & Think

In computing the market price for bonds, what is the only thing for which the stated rate of interest is used?

a) Computing the amount of the periodic interest payments
b) Computing the amount of the maturity value
c) Computing the present value of the periodic interest payments
d) Computing the present value of the maturity value

Notice that **Hewlett-Packard** has more than one bond issue listed; the first listing is for bonds that mature in 2017, and the second listing is for bonds that mature in 2018. The current yield for the first Hewlett-Packard bond listing is 4.719, which means that if the bonds were purchased at their closing price of 114.43, the interest payments would give the investor a 4.719% annual return. These Hewlett-Packard bonds were trading at a premium, which means that the coupon rate on these bonds of 5.400% is higher than was the market rate required on bonds of similar riskiness. The yield-to-maturity percentage is the overall rate of return that would be earned by an investor (through receipt of periodic interest payments as well as the maturity amount) who purchases the bonds today and holds them until their maturity. The yield-to-maturity percentage can be thought of as the rate of return necessary to induce an investor to buy the bonds, given the riskiness of the bond issuer.

Issuance of Bonds

Bonds may be sold directly to investors by the issuer, or they may be sold in the open market through securities exchanges or through investment bankers. Regardless of how they are placed, when bonds are issued (sold), the issuer must record the receipt of cash and recognize the long-term liability. The purchaser must record the payment of cash and the bond investment.

FYI

Where capital markets are less well developed, banks are the major source of debt financing of companies. As economies develop, such as in China, the relative amount of bond financing increases.

An issuer normally records the bond obligation at its face value—the amount that the company must pay at maturity. Hence, when bonds are issued at an amount other than face value, a bond discount or premium account is established for the difference between the cash received and the bond face value. The premium is added to or the discount is subtracted from the bond face value to report the bonds at their present value. Although an investor could also record the investment in bonds at their face value by using a premium or discount account, traditionally investors record their bond investments at cost, that is, the face value net of any premium or discount.

发行公司一般以债券面值（债券到期日公司必须支付的本金）确定应付债券的金额。因此，当债券按折价或溢价而非按面值发行时，应以债券溢价或折价科目反映实际收到的现金与债券面值的差额。在溢价时，以债券面值加上增值部分作为债券的当前价值入账；在折价时，则扣除减值部分。

Bonds issued or acquired in exchange for noncash assets or services are recorded at the fair value of the bonds unless the value of the exchanged assets or services is more clearly determinable. A difference between the face value of the bonds and the cash value of the bonds or the value of the property acquired is recognized as bond discount or bond premium. When bonds and other securities are acquired for a lump sum, an apportionment of such cost among the securities is required.

As indicated earlier, bonds may be issued at par, at a discount, or at a premium. They may be issued on an interest payment date or between interest dates, which calls for the recognition of accrued interest. Each of these situations will be illustrated using the following data: $100,000, 8%, 10-year bonds are issued; semiannual interest of $4,000 ($100,000 × 0.08 × 6/12) is payable on January 1 and July 1.

Bonds Issued at Par on Interest Date When bonds are issued at par, or face value, on an interest date, there is no premium or discount to be recognized nor any accrued interest at the date of issuance. The appropriate entries for the first year on the issuer's books and on the investor's books, assuming the data in the preceding paragraph and issuance on January 1 at par value, are as follows:

		Issuer's Books			**Investor's Books**	
Jan. 1	Cash....................	100,000		Bond Investment	100,000	
	Bonds Payable		100,000	Cash		100,000
July 1	Interest Expense	4,000		Cash	4,000	
	Cash		4,000	Interest Revenue		4,000
Dec. 31	Interest Expense	4,000		Interest Receivable...........	4,000	
	Interest Payable		4,000	Interest Revenue		4,000

Bonds Issued at Discount on Interest Date Now assume that the bonds were issued on January 1 but that the effective rate of interest was 10%, requiring recognition of a discount of $12,462 ($100,000 − $87,538; see computations on page 12-20). The appropriate entries on January 1 follow. The interest entries on July 1 and December 31 are illustrated in a later section of this chapter that discusses the amortization of discounts and premiums.

		Issuer's Books			**Investor's Books**	
Jan. 1	Cash....................	87,538		Bond Investment	87,538	
	Discount on Bonds Payable	12,462		Cash		87,538
	Bonds Payable		100,000			

Bonds Issued at Premium on Interest Date Again using the preceding data, assume that the bonds were sold at an effective interest rate of 7%. Using present value techniques, it can be computed that the bond will sell for a premium of $7,106. In this case, the entries on January 1 are as follows:

		Issuer's Books			**Investor's Books**	
Jan. 1	Cash....................	107,106		Bond Investment	107,106	
	Premium on Bonds Payable...		7,106	Cash		107,106
	Bonds Payable		100,000			

当债券在两个付息日之间发行时，则要调整上期付款日到交易日期间的应计利息。

Bonds Issued at Par between Interest Dates When bonds are issued between interest dates, an adjustment is made for the interest accrued between the last interest payment date and the date of the transaction. A buyer of the bonds pays the amount of accrued interest along with the purchase price and then receives the accrued interest plus interest earned subsequent to the purchase date when the next interest payment is made. This practice avoids the problem an issuer of bonds would have in trying to split interest payments for a given period between two or more owners of the securities. To illustrate, if the bonds in the previous example were issued at par on March 1, the appropriate entries are as follows:[7]

---

[7] As an alternative, the accrued interest could be initially credited to Interest Expense by the issuer and debited to Interest Revenue by the investor. When the first interest payment is made, the debit to Interest Expense for the issuer, when combined with the initial entry, would result in the proper amount of interest expense being recognized. A similar procedure can be applied by the investor in determining interest revenue.

	Issuer's Books		**Investor's Books**	
Mar. 1	Cash................................ 101,333		Bond Investment................. 100,000	
	Bonds Payable..............	100,000	Interest Receivable.............. 1,333	
	Interest Payable..............	1,333*	Cash.............................	101,333
	*($100,000 × 0.08 × 2/12)			
July 1	Interest Expense................ 2,667†		Cash............................. 4,000	
	Interest Payable................. 1,333		Interest Receivable............	1,333
	Cash...........................	4,000	Interest Revenue..............	2,667
	†($100,000 × 0.08 × 4/12)			

Bond Issuance Costs The issuance of bonds normally involves costs to the issuer for legal services, printing and engraving, taxes, and underwriting. Traditionally, these costs have been offset against any premium or added to any discount arising on the issuance and thus netted against the face value of the bonds. In *Statement of Financial Accounting Concepts No. 3* paragraph 161, since superseded, the FASB stated that "deferred charges" such as bond issuance costs fail to meet the definition of assets. In its recent consideration of the accounting for the issuance of debt and equity financing, the FASB has made a preliminary determination that all issuance costs, for both debt and equity financing, should be expensed as incurred. However, this decision has not yet been formalized into an official standard. Accordingly, until such time as the FASB releases a formal standard, these bond issuance costs will still be reported as assets by some companies.[8]

Accounting for Bond Interest

With coupon bonds, cash is paid by the issuing company in exchange for interest coupons on the interest dates. Payments on coupons may be made by the company directly to bondholders, or payments may be cleared through a bank or other disbursing agent. Subsidiary records with bondholders are not maintained because coupons are redeemable by bearers. In the case of registered bonds, interest checks are mailed either by the company or its agent. When bonds are registered, the bonds account requires subsidiary ledger support. The subsidiary ledger shows holdings by individuals and changes in such holdings. Checks are sent to bondholders of record as of the interest payment dates.

当债券以溢价或折价发行时，市场会将票面利率调整为市场利率或实际利率。由于初始溢价或折价的存在，发行方在债券发行期间每期所支付的利息不能代表该期间包含的所有利息，因此有必要对现金支付利息进行调整以反映债券的实际收益率，这种调整被称为债券溢价或折价调整，这种周期性的调整使得债券账面价值与票面价值逐步靠拢。

When bonds are issued at a premium or discount, the market acts to adjust the stated interest rate to a market or effective interest rate. Because of the initial premium or discount, the periodic interest payments made over the bond's life by the issuer do not represent the total interest expense for the periods involved. An adjustment to the interest expense associated with the cash payment is necessary to reflect the effective interest being incurred on the bonds. This adjustment is referred to as bond premium or discount amortization. This periodic adjustment results in a gradual adjustment of the bond's carrying value toward the bond's face value.

A premium on issued bonds recognizes that the stated interest rate is higher than the market interest rate. Amortization of the premium reduces the interest expense below the amount of cash paid. A discount on issued bonds recognizes that the stated interest rate is lower than the market interest rate. Amortization of the discount increases the amount

---

[8] FASB ASC paragraph 835-30-45-3. In some cases, these bond issuance costs, or "deferred charges," can be thought of as "points," or interest paid in advance, that are then capitalized and expensed over the life of the bond. The FASB also states that debt issuance costs for financial liabilities that are reported at fair value should be expensed as incurred. This "fair value option" is discussed in more detail later in the chapter.

of interest expense above the amount of cash paid. In summary, the amortization of a discount or premium on bonds accomplishes two things: The bond's carrying value is gradually adjusted to be equal to the maturity value, and the periodic interest expense is adjusted to reflect the fact that the effective interest rate on the bonds is either higher (with a discount) or lower (with a premium) than the actual amount of cash paid each period.

Two main methods are used to amortize the premium or discount: (1) the straight-line method and (2) the effective-interest method. The straight-line method is explained first because the computations are simpler. This method is acceptable, however, only when its application results in periodic interest expense that does not differ materially from the amounts that would be reported using the effective-interest method.[9]

Straight-Line Method The straight-line method provides for the recognition of an equal amount of premium or discount amortization each period. The amount of monthly amortization is determined by dividing the premium or discount at purchase or issuance date by the number of months remaining to the bond maturity date. For example, if a 10-year, 10% bond issue with a maturity value of $200,000 was sold on the issuance date at 103, the $6,000 premium would be amortized evenly over the 120 months until maturity, or at a rate of $50 per month ($6,000/120). If the bonds were sold three months after the issuance date, the $6,000 premium would be amortized evenly over 117 months, or at a rate of $51.28 per month ($6,000/117). The amortization period is always the time from original sale to maturity. The premium amortization would reduce both interest expense on the issuer's books and interest revenue on the investor's books. A discount amortization would have the opposite results: Both accounts would be increased.

To illustrate the accounting for bond interest using straight-line amortization, consider again the earlier example of the $100,000, 8%, 10-year bonds issued on January 1. When sold at a $12,462 discount, the appropriate entries to record interest on July 1 and December 31 would be as follows:

	Issuer's Books			Investor's Books	
July 1	Interest Expense................	4,623		Cash...........................	4,000	
	Discount on Bonds Payable...		623*	Bond Investment...............	623	
	Cash........................		4,000†	Interest Revenue.............		4,623

*$12,462/120 × 6 months = $623 (rounded) discount amortization for six-month period
†$100,000 × 0.08 × 6/12 = $4,000 cash

Dec. 31	Interest Expense................	4,623		Interest Receivable.............	4,000	
	Discount on Bonds Payable...		623	Bond Investment...............	623	
	Interest Payable..............		4,000	Interest Revenue.............		4,623

As explained in Chapter 14, this amortization of bond premiums and discounts on the books of the investor is most important when the bond investment is classified as held to maturity. For trading and available-for-sale securities, the bond investment is revalued at the end of each period and reported at its fair value.

Note that the discount amortization has the effect of increasing the effective interest rate over the life of the bond from the 8% stated rate to the 10% market rate of interest that the bonds were sold to yield. Over the life of the bond, the $12,462 discount will be charged to interest expense for the issuer and recognized as interest revenue by the investor.

[9] FASB ASC paragraphs 835-30-35-2 through 4.

To illustrate the entries that would be required to amortize a bond premium, consider again the situation in which the 8% bonds were sold to yield 7%, or $107,106. The $7,106 premium would be amortized on a straight-line basis as follows:

	Issuer's Books			Investor's Books	
July 1	Interest Expense	3,645	Cash	4,000	
	Premium on Bonds Payable	355*	Bond Investment		355
	Cash	4,000	Interest Revenue		3,645
Dec. 31	Interest Expense	3,645	Interest Receivable	4,000	
	Premium on Bonds Payable	355	Bond Investment		355
	Interest Payable	4,000	Interest Revenue		3,645

*$7,106/120 × 6 months = $355 (rounded) premium amortization for six-month period

The amortization of the premium has the effect of reducing the amount of interest expense or interest revenue over the life of the bond to the actual yield or market rate of the bonds, 7%.

实际利率法是根据不变利率、基于不断变化的摊余成本计算每期的溢价与折价摊销。

Effective-Interest Method The effective-interest method of amortization uses a uniform interest rate based on a changing loan balance and provides for an increasing premium or discount amortization each period. The mortgage (or loan) amortization schedule in Exhibit 12-5 on page 12-14 employs the effective-interest method. In order to use this method, the effective-interest rate for the bonds must be known. This is the rate of interest at bond issuance that discounts the maturity value of the bonds and the periodic interest payments to the market price of the bonds. This rate is used to determine the amount of revenue or expense to be recorded on the books.

To illustrate the amortization of a bond discount using the effective-interest method, consider once again the $100,000, 8%, 10-year bonds sold for $87,538, based on an effective interest rate of 10%. The discount amortization for the first six months using the effective-interest method is computed as follows:

Bond balance (carrying value) at beginning of first period	$87,538
Effective rate per semiannual period	5%
Stated rate per semiannual period	4%
Interest amount based on carrying value and effective rate ($87,538 × 0.05)	$ 4,377
Interest payment based on face value and stated rate ($100,000 × 0.04)	4,000
Discount amortization—difference in interest based on effective rate and stated rate	$ 377

Caution

Students often interchange the stated and market interest rates when computing interest expense for the period. Remember that the stated rate is used only once—to determine the amount of cash paid or received as interest. The market, or effective, rate is used to calculate the amount of interest expense or interest revenue.

This difference between the amount paid (received) and the compound interest expense (revenue) is the discount amortization for the first period using the effective-interest method. For the second semiannual period, the bond carrying value increases by the amount of discount amortized. The amortization for the second semiannual period would be computed as follows:

Bond balance (carrying value) at beginning of second period ($87,538 + $377)	$87,915
Interest amount based on carrying value and effective rate ($87,915 × 0.05)	$ 4,396
Interest payment based on face value and stated rate ($100,000 × 0.04)	4,000
Discount amortization—difference in interest based on effective rate and stated rate	$ 396

Stop & Think

When preparing a bond amortization schedule like the one that follows, there are certain numbers within that schedule that you know without having to do any elaborate computations. Which ONE of the following numbers can be determined using a very simple computation?

a) The periodic interest expense
b) The periodic interest payment
c) The periodic premium (or discount) amortization
d) The carrying value of the bond

The amount of interest to be recognized each period is computed at a uniform rate on an increasing balance. This results in an increasing discount amortization over the life of the bonds, which is graphically demonstrated and compared with straight-line amortization in Exhibit 12-7.

The entries for amortizing the discount would be the same as those shown for straight-line amortization; only the amounts would be different.

Premium amortization would be computed in a similar way except that the interest payment based on the stated interest rate would be higher than the interest amount based on the effective rate. For example, assume that the $100,000, 8%, 10-year bonds were sold on the issuance date for $107,106, thus providing an effective interest rate of 7%. The premium amortization for the first and second six-month periods would be computed as follows (amounts are rounded to the nearest dollar):

Bond balance (carrying value) at beginning of first period	$107,106
Effective rate per semiannual period	3.5%
Stated rate per semiannual period	4.0%
Interest payment based on face value and stated rate ($100,000 × 0.04)	$ 4,000
Interest amount based on carrying value and effective rate ($107,106 × 0.035)	3,749
Premium amortization—difference in interest based on stated rate and effective rate	$ 251
Bond balance (carrying value) at beginning of second period ($107,106 − $251)	$106,855
Interest payment based on face value and stated rate ($100,000 × 0.04)	$ 4,000
Interest amount based on carrying value and effective rate ($106,855 × 0.035)	3,740
Premium amortization—difference in interest based on stated rate and effective rate	$ 260

Exhibit 12-7 | Comparison of Straight-Line and Effective-Interest Amortization Methods

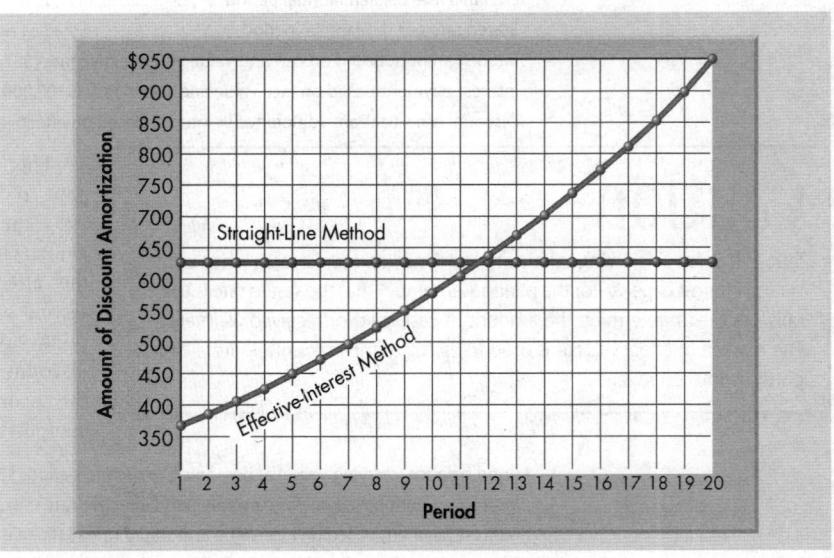

© Cengage Learning 2014

As illustrated, as the investment or liability balance is reduced by the premium amortization, the interest, based on the effective rate, also decreases. The difference between the interest payment and the effective interest amount increases in a manner similar to discount amortization. Bond amortization tables may be prepared to determine the periodic adjustments to the bond carrying value, that is, the present value of the bond. A partial bond amortization table follows.

Because the effective-interest method adjusts the stated interest rate to an effective interest rate, it is theoretically more accurate as an amortization method than is the straight-line method. Note that the total amortization over the life of the bond is the same under either method; only the interim amounts differ. The effective-interest method is the recommended amortization method. However, as stated previously, the straight-line method may be used by a company if the interim results of using it do not differ materially from the amortization using the effective-interest method.

Amortization of Bond Premium—Effective-Interest Method $100,000, 10-Year Bonds, Interest at 8% Payable Semiannually, Sold at $107, 106 to Yield 7%

Interest Payment	A Interest Paid (0.04 × $100,000)	B Interest Expense (0.035 × Bond Carrying Value)	C Premium Amortization (A − B)	D Unamortized Premium (D − C)	E Bond Carrying Value ($100,000 + D)
				$7,106	$107,106
1	$4,000	$3,749 (0.035 × $107,106)	$251	6,855	106,855
2	4,000	3,740 (0.035 × $106,855)	260	6,595	106,595
3	4,000	3,731 (0.035 × $106,595)	269	6,326	106,326
4	4,000	3,721 (0.035 × $106,326)	279	6,047	106,047
5	4,000	3,712 (0.035 × $106,047)	288	5,759	105,759

Cash Flow Effects of Amortizing Bond Premiums and Discounts

The amortization of a bond discount or premium does not involve the receipt or payment of cash and, like other noncash items, must be considered in preparing a statement of cash flows. Recall that when the indirect method is used to report cash flows from operating activities, net income is adjusted for noncash items. When a bond discount is amortized, interest expense reported on the income statement is higher than interest paid, and net income, on a cash basis, is understated. The appropriate adjustment is to add the amount of discount amortization back to net income. The reverse is true in the case of a bond premium. That is, the amount of bond premium amortization is subtracted from net income to arrive at cash flow from operations.

Using the direct method requires conversion of individual accrual-basis revenue and expense items to a cash basis. Thus, to convert interest expense to cash paid for interest, the expense reported on the income statement is decreased by the amount of discount amortization for the period or increased by the amount of premium amortization.

The following example illustrates the adjustments necessary when preparing a statement of cash flows. Consider the information used in the previous examples related to a bond discount: The company issues $100,000, 8%, 10-year bonds when the effective rate of interest is 10%. The bonds are issued at a price of $87,538. The calculations for the discount amortization during the first year are on page 12-25. The amount of discount amortized during the first year is $773 ($377 + $396). The amount of interest expense disclosed on the income statement for the year is $8,773 ($4,377 + $4,396), and the amount of cash paid to bondholders is $8,000 (if, for simplicity, we assume that the second payment of $4,000 is made on December 31). To keep the example simple, assume that the company reported net income of $90,000 for the year and that sales for the year (all cash) were $98,773, meaning that the $8,773 in interest expense was the only expense. An analysis of the cash flow impact of the discount amortization is included in the following matrix:

Income Statement		Adjustments		Cash Flows from Operations
Sales	$98,773	None	$98,773	Cash collected from customers
Interest expense	(8,773)	+ $773 (bond discount amortization; not a cash item)	(8,000)	Cash paid for interest
Net income	$90,000	+ $773 net adjustment	$90,773	Cash flow from operations

Reporting using the indirect method, the amount of discount amortized ($773) is added back to net income. Reporting using the direct method, the amount of the discount is subtracted from reported interest expense to convert that amount to a cash basis as follows: $8,773 interest expense − $773 discount amortization = $8,000 cash paid for interest. In this case, in which only one bond issue is involved, cash paid for interest could instead be computed by multiplying the stated interest rate by the face value of the bonds ($100,000 × 0.08).

Retirement of Bonds at Maturity

In most cases, bonds include a specified termination or maturity date. At that time, the issuer must pay the current investors the maturity, or face, value of the bonds. When bond discount or premium and issuance costs have been properly amortized over the life of the bonds, bond retirement at maturity simply calls for elimination of the liability or the investment by a cash transaction, illustrated as follows assuming a $100,000 bond:

Issuer's Books		Investor's Books	
Bonds Payable	100,000	Cash	100,000
Cash	100,000	Bond Investment	100,000

任何在到期时显示未支付的债券应从发行方账户的应付债券余额中剔除，作为应付到期债券单独记录。这些债券被划分为流动负债，除非它们是用来支付债券偿还基金的。到期未支付债券不须支付累计利息。如果债券偿还基金用于清偿债券，那么清偿后剩余的现金可返还至现金账户。

There is no recognition of any gain or loss on retirement because the carrying value is equal to the maturity value, which is also equal to the market value of the bonds at that point in time.

Any bonds not presented for payment at their maturity date should be removed from the Bonds Payable balance on the issuer's books and reported separately as Matured Bonds Payable; these are reported as a current liability except when they are to be paid out of a bond retirement fund. Interest does not accrue on matured bonds not presented for payment. If a bond retirement fund is used to pay off a bond issue, any cash remaining in the fund may be returned to the cash account.

FYI

In 1975, high interest rates had caused a decline in the market value of bonds issued during the 1960s. Many companies were retiring these bonds early in order to be able to report accounting gains on the retirement. In order to stop companies from including these gains as part of ordinary income from continuing operations, the FASB decreed that they be classified as extraordinary. In 2002, the FASB rescinded this special accounting for gains and losses on early extinguishment of debt.

Caution

Note that a gain or loss is determined by comparing the carrying value of the bond to its fair value. If a company can retire a bond for less than its carrying value, a gain results. If the company must pay more than the carrying value, the result is a loss.

Extinguishment of Debt Prior to Maturity

When debt is retired, or "extinguished," prior to the maturity date, a gain or loss must be recognized for the difference between the carrying value of the debt security and the amount paid to satisfy the obligation.

The problems that arise in retiring bonds or other forms of long-term debt prior to maturity are described in the following sections. Bonds may be retired prior to maturity in one of the following ways:

1. Bonds may be *redeemed* by the issuer by purchasing the bonds on the open market or by exercising the call provision that is frequently included in bond indentures.
2. Bonds may be *converted*, that is, exchanged for other securities.
3. Bonds may be *refinanced* (sometimes called *refunded*) by using the proceeds from the sale of a new bond issue to retire outstanding bonds.

redemption by purchase of bonds in the market
公开市场购买方式的债券赎回

Redemption by Purchase of Bonds in the Market Corporations frequently purchase their own bonds in the market when prices or other factors make such actions desirable. When bonds are purchased, amortization of bond premium or discount and issue costs should be brought up to date. Purchase by the issuer calls for the cancellation of the bond's face value together with any related premium, discount, or issue costs as of the purchase date.

To illustrate a bond redemption prior to maturity, assume that $100,000, 8% bonds of Triad Inc. are not held until maturity but are redeemed by the issuer on February 1, 2015, at 97. The carrying value of the bonds on both the issuer's and investor's books is $97,700 as of February 1. Interest payment dates on the bonds are January 31 and July 31. Entries on both the issuer's and investor's books at the time of redemption are as follows:

	Issuer's Books			Investor's Books	
Feb. 1	Bonds Payable.................	100,000	Cash............................	97,000	
	Discount on Bonds Payable...		2,300	Loss on Sale of Bonds	700
	Cash		97,000	Bond Investment—Triad Inc...		97,700
	Gain on Bond Redemption....		700*		
Computation:					
*Carrying value of bonds, February 1, 2015		$97,700			
Purchase (redemption) price..............		97,000			
Gain on bond redemption		$ 700			

If the redemption had occurred between interest payment dates, adjusting entries would have to be made to recognize the accrued interest and to amortize the bond discount or premium.

redemption by exercise of call provision
通过可赎回条款的债券赎回

Redemption by Exercise of Call Provision A call provision gives the issuer the option of retiring bonds prior to maturity. Frequently, the call must be made on an interest payment date, and no further interest accrues on the bonds not presented at this time. When only a part of an issue is to be redeemed, the bonds called may be determined by lot.

The inclusion of call provisions in a bond agreement is a feature favoring the issuer. The company is in a position to terminate the bond agreement and eliminate future interest charges whenever its financial position makes such action feasible. Furthermore, the company is protected in the event of a fall in the market interest rate by being able to retire the old issue from proceeds of a new issue paying a lower rate of interest. A bond contract normally requires payment of a premium if bonds are called. A bondholder is thus offered special compensation if the investment is terminated early.

> **FYI**
>
> Until the issuance of pre-Codification FASB *Statement No. 125* in 1996, early extinguishment of debt could also be accomplished through *in-substance defeasance*. This process involved transferring assets into an irrevocable trust, using those assets to satisfy the cash flow requirements of a certain debt obligation, and removing both the assets and the associated debt from the balance sheet. The requirement now is that the assets and debt in an in-substance defeasance arrangement still be reported in the balance sheet.

When bonds are called, the difference between the amount paid and the bond carrying value is reported as a gain or a loss on both the issuer's and investor's books. Any interest paid at the time of the call is recorded as a debit to Interest Expense on the issuer's books and a credit to Interest Revenue on the investor's books. The entries to be made are the same as illustrated previously for the purchase (redemption) of bonds by the issuer.

Convertible Bonds Convertible debt securities raise specific questions as to the nature of the securities, that is, whether they should be considered debt or equity securities, the valuation of the conversion feature, and the treatment of any gain or loss on conversion.

Convertible debt securities usually have the following features:[10]

1. An interest rate lower than the issuer could establish for nonconvertible debt
2. An initial conversion price higher than the market value of the common stock at time of issuance
3. A call option retained by the issuer

The popularity of these securities may be attributed to the advantages to both an issuer and a holder. An issuer is able to obtain financing at a lower interest rate because of the value of the conversion feature to the holder. Because of the call provision, an issuer is in a position to exert influence on the holders to exchange the debt for equity securities if stock values increase; the issuer has had the use of relatively low interest rate financing if stock values do not increase. On the other hand, the holder has a debt instrument that, barring default, ensures the return of investment plus a fixed return and, at the same time, offers an option to transfer his or her interest to equity capital should such transfer become attractive.

Accounting for Convertible Debt Issuance When the Conversion Feature Is Nondetachable Differences of opinion exist as to whether convertible debt securities should be treated by an issuer solely as debt or whether part of the proceeds received from

[10] FASB ASC paragraph 470-20-25-11.

the issuance of debt should be recognized as equity capital. One view holds that the debt and the conversion privilege are inseparably connected, and therefore, the debt and equity portions of a security should not be separately valued. A holder cannot sell part of the instrument and retain the other. An alternate view holds that there are two distinct elements in these securities and that each should be recognized in the accounts: The portion of the issuance price attributable to the conversion privilege should be recorded as a credit to Paid-In Capital; the balance of the issuance price should be assigned to the debt. This would decrease the premium otherwise recognized in the debt or perhaps result in a discount.

These views are compared in the example that follows. Assume that 500 ten-year bonds, face value $1,000, are sold at 105, or a total issue price of $525,000 (500 × $1,000 × 1.05). The bonds contain a conversion privilege that provides for exchange of a $1,000 bond for 20 shares of stock, par value $1. The interest rate on the bonds is 8%. It is estimated that without the conversion privilege, the bonds would sell at 96. Assume that a separate value of the conversion feature cannot be determined. The journal entries to record the issuance on the issuer's books under the two approaches are as follows:

Debt and Equity Not Separated		Debt and Equity Separated	
Cash 525,000		Cash 525,000	
Bonds Payable	500,000	Discount on Bonds Payable 20,000*	
Premium on Bonds Payable	25,000	Bonds Payable	500,000
		Paid-In Capital Arising from	
		Bond Conversion Feature	45,000†
Computations:			
*Par value of bonds (500 × $1,000)...............	$500,000	†Total cash received on sale of bonds	$525,000
Selling price of bonds without conversion feature ($500,000 × 0.96)	480,000	Selling price without conversion feature	480,000
Discount on bonds without conversion feature ..	$ 20,000	Amount applicable to conversion feature (equity portion)	$ 45,000

The periodic charge for interest will differ, depending on which method is employed. To illustrate the computation of interest charges, assume that the straight-line method is used to amortize bond premium or discount. Under the first approach, the annual interest charge would be $37,500 ($40,000 paid less $2,500 premium amortization). Under the second approach, the annual interest charge would be $42,000 ($40,000 paid plus $2,000 discount amortization).

The provisions of FASB ASC Section 470-20-25 (Debt—Debt with Conversion and Other Options—Recognition) state that when convertible debt is sold at a price or with a value at issuance not significantly in excess of the face value, "no portion of the proceeds from the issuance . . . should be accounted for as attributable to the conversion feature."[11] On the other hand, there would seem to be strong theoretical support for separating the debt and equity portions of the proceeds from the issuance of convertible debt on the issuer's books. Despite these theoretical arguments, current practice follows the provisions in Topic 470, and no separation is usually made between debt and equity when the conversion feature of the debt is not detachable, or separately tradable, from the debt instrument itself. This is true even when separate values are determinable.[12]

---

[11] FASB ASC paragraphs 470-20-25-10 and 12.
[12] Separation is required when the initial conversion price is *lower* than the market value of the common stock at the time of issuance. These convertible bonds are said to be "in the money" at the date of issuance, and the accounting standards refer to this as a "beneficial conversion feature." According to FASB ASC paragraph 470-20-25-5, the magnitude of the excess of the market value over the conversion price at issuance is to be recognized as additional paid-in capital.

Accounting for Convertible Debt Issuance When the Conversion Feature Is Detachable Sometimes, bonds are issued in conjunction with stock warrants. The warrants allow the holder to buy shares of stock at a set price. The bonds and the warrants are issued as elements of a single security; in essence, the combination of the bonds and the stock warrants is economically equivalent to a convertible debt security. The practical difference is that investors can trade the stock warrants separately from the bonds themselves. In this case, the issuer of the bonds and the stock warrants is required to allocate the joint issuance price between the two instruments; the bonds are accounted for as debt, and the stock warrants are accounted for as part of paid-in capital as illustrated in the "Debt and Equity Separated" journal entry shown previously. The FASB has expressed a preliminary preference for ultimately requiring the proceeds of *all* convertible debt issues to be separated into their debt and equity components. If the value of the convertibility feature cannot be separately determined, as in the preceding example, the "with-and-without" method of allocating the bond proceeds between the debt and the equity components can be used. This is the method illustrated earlier in the "Debt and Equity Separated" example. An alternative method of separating the proceeds, the "relative-fair-value" method, is recommended by the FASB when reliable fair values of both the bond and the conversion feature can be determined.[13] This relative-fair-value method is illustrated in the section on accounting for stock warrants in Chapter 13. The Board has not yet produced a formal standard on this issue.

Accounting for Convertible Debt Issuance According to *IAS 32* *IAS 32*, "Financial Instruments: Disclosure and Presentation," does not differentiate between convertible debt with nondetachable and detachable conversion features. Instead, *IAS 32* states that for all convertible debt issues, the issuance proceeds should be allocated between the debt and equity. Accordingly, the international standard mandates that in all cases, the "Debt and Equity Separated" journal entry illustrated previously should be used.

Accounting for Conversion When conversion takes place, a special valuation question must be answered: Should the issuer of the convertible bonds use the fair value of the securities to compute a gain or loss on the date of the conversion? This question has two answers, and the correct answer depends on the nature of the conversion feature as of the issuance date of the convertible bonds. If, as of the issuance date, the probability of eventual conversion of the convertible bonds was deemed to be "at least reasonably possible," then the conversion is really just a routine transition in the life of the convertible bonds, and no gain or loss is recognized upon conversion.[14] For example, consider a convertible bond for which, as of the issuance date, the fair value of the common stock into which the bond can be converted is close to the fair value of the convertible bond itself. In such a case, it is "at least reasonably possible" that at some time during the life of the convertible bond, the fair value of the common stock will increase and create conditions favorable to the conversion of the bonds by the bondholder. Upon conversion of these bonds, no gain or loss would be recognized on the books of the bond issuer. Instead, the carrying value of the bonds is simply transferred from the bond-related accounts to the common stock accounts.

To illustrate bond issuer accounting for a conversion when no gain or loss is recognized, assume HiTec Co. offers bondholders 40 shares of HiTec Co. common stock, $1 par, in exchange for each $1,000, 8% bond held. An investor exchanges bonds

---

[13] FASB ASC paragraph 470-20-30-1.
[14] FASB ASC paragraphs 470-20-40-4 and 5.

with a face value of $10,000 (carrying value as of the conversion date, $9,850) for 400 shares of common stock having a market price at the time of the exchange of $26 per share. To keep things simple, assume that the exchange is completed at an interest payment date *after* interest has been paid and properly recorded, including bond discount amortization. Also assume that, as of the issuance date, the fair value of 40 shares of HiTec Co. common stock was close to the issuance price of the convertible bonds. In this case, no gain or loss is recognized on the conversion date. The bond's carrying value is transferred to the common stock accounts on the theory that the company, upon issuing the bonds, is aware of the fact that bond proceeds are at least reasonably likely to ultimately represent the consideration identified with stock. Thus, when bondholders exercise their conversion privileges, the value identified with the obligation is transferred to the common stock that replaces it. The conversion is recorded as follows:

Bonds Payable	10,000	
Common Stock, $1 par		400
Paid-In Capital in Excess of Par		9,450
Discount on Bonds Payable		150

The accounting for the conversion is different if, as of the issuance date, there is not a reasonable possibility that the convertible bonds will eventually be converted. This occurs if, for example, the fair value of the common stock into which the bond can be converted is substantially lower than the fair value of the convertible bond itself on the issuance date. In this case, the most likely future for the convertible bonds is that they will never be converted into common stock. Thus, it is a significant event if and when they are converted. Refer again to the HiTec example, but now assume that, as of the issuance date, the fair value of 40 shares of HiTec Co. common stock was substantially below the issuance price of the convertible bonds. The subsequent "unexpected" conversion is recorded as shown below.

Bonds Payable	10,000	
Loss on Conversion of Bonds	550*	
Common Stock, $1 par		400
Paid-In Capital in Excess of Par		10,000
Discount on Bonds Payable		150
Computation:		
*Market value of stock issued (400 shares at $26)		$10,400
Face value of bonds payable	$10,000	
Less unamortized discount	150	9,850
Loss to company on conversion of bonds		$ 550

In summary, if subsequent conversion is at least reasonably possible as of the issuance date, then no gain or loss is recognized upon that subsequent conversion. If subsequent conversion was unexpected as of the issuance date, the fair value of the shares issued on conversion is used to compute a gain or loss on the conversion date.

From the standpoint of the bondholder, or investor, the exchange of the bonds for common stock of HiTec Co. represents a nonmonetary exchange of one asset for another. Nonmonetary exchanges were discussed in Chapter 10. The general rule is that an asset received in a nonmonetary exchange is to be recorded on the books at its fair value on the exchange date, and any gain or loss arising from a difference between this fair value and the carrying value of the exchanged asset is to be recognized. An exception to this rule occurs when the exchange lacks "commercial substance" meaning that the cash flows expected to come from the newly received asset have the same risk, timing, and amount as the cash flows that had been expected from the exchanged asset.[15] In the case of a bond conversion into common stock, cash flows from a bond investment have substantially different risk, timing, and amount compared to cash flows from a common stock investment, so the exchange does have commercial substance.

Refer again to the HiTec example. Assume that the bond investment carrying value is the same on the books of the investor as it is on the books of the issuer. The exchange is recorded on the books of the investor as follows:

Investment in HiTec Co. Common Stock...	10,400	
Bond Investment—HiTec Co..		9,850
Gain on Conversion of HiTec Co. Bonds..		550

Bond Refinancing Cash for the retirement of a bond issue is frequently raised through the sale of a new issue and is referred to as bond refinancing, or refunding. Bond refinancing may take place when an issue matures, or bonds may be refinanced prior to their maturity when the interest rate has dropped and the interest savings on a new issue will more than offset the cost of retiring the old issue. To illustrate, assume that a corporation has outstanding $1,000,000 of 12% bonds callable at 102 and with a remaining 10-year term, and similar 10-year bonds can be marketed currently at an interest rate of only 10%. Under these circumstances it would be advantageous to retire the old issue with the proceeds from a new 10% issue because the future savings in interest will exceed by a considerable amount the premium to be paid on the call of the old issue.

通过新发行将原先发行的债券收回变现，这便是债券再融资，或称作再筹资。债券再融资可能在债券到期时或者在到期前、利率下降时发生，这时节约的新发行债券的利息金额能够更好地弥补收回原先发行债券的成本。

The desirability of refinancing may not be so obvious as in the preceding example. In determining whether refinancing is warranted in marginal cases, careful consideration must be given to factors such as the different maturity dates of the two issues, possible future changes in interest rates, changed loan requirements, different indenture provisions, income tax effects of refinancing, and legal fees, printing costs, and marketing costs involved in refinancing.

When refinancing takes place before the maturity date of the old issue, the call premium and unamortized discount and issue costs of the original bonds are considered in computing the gain or loss on bond retirement.[16]

Reporting Some Equity-Related Items As Liabilities

As discussed more fully in Chapter 13, the FASB has decided that certain equity-related items should actually be reported in the balance sheet as liabilities.[17] These items are as follows:

- Mandatorily redeemable preferred shares
- Financial instruments (such as written put options) that obligate a company to repurchase its own shares
- Financial instruments that obligate a company to issue a certain dollar value of its own shares

These items share the characteristic that, although related to equity shares, they each obligate the company to deliver items of a set value (either cash or equity shares) some time in the future. Again, each of these items will be illustrated in detail in Chapter 13.

---

[15] FASB ASC paragraphs 845-10-301 through 4.
[16] FASB ASC paragraph 470-50-40-2.
[17] FASB ASC Topic 480 (Distinguishing Liabilities from Equity).

Fair Value Option

 Discuss the use of the fair value option for financial assets and liabilities.

LO5 学习目标5
讨论公允价值在金融资产与金融负债中的应用。

For many assets and liabilities, the FASB and IASB have determined that fair value is the most relevant measurement attribute. Recall that fair value is defined as "the price that would be received to sell an asset or paid to transfer a liability in an orderly transaction between market participants at the measurement date."[18] Because accounting has long been founded on a backbone of historical cost, the FASB and IASB are transitioning cautiously, item by item, to fair value.

In 2007, with pre-Codification *SFAS No. 159*, the FASB took a bold step toward increased use of fair value by allowing companies a fair value option for the reporting of financial assets and liabilities.[19] Under the fair value option, a company has the option to report, at each balance sheet date, any or all of its financial assets and liabilities at their fair values on the balance sheet date. This is a very interesting accounting rule because a company can choose to report some financial assets and liabilities of a certain type at fair value while at the same time continuing to use another basis, such as historical cost, for other financial assets and liabilities of exactly the same type.

You should be asking yourself: Why did the FASB give companies this financial reporting flexibility? The FASB stated its reason as follows: "The objective is to improve financial reporting by providing entities with the opportunity to mitigate volatility in reported earnings caused by measuring related assets and liabilities differently without having to apply complex hedge accounting provisions." The best way to understand this rationale is through a simple example as given below.

Lily Kay Company has a very simple structure—the company has one asset, a Lusvardi Company bond that it purchased (on the day it was issued) as an investment, and one liability, one of its own bonds that Lily Kay issued to finance the purchase of the Lusvardi bond investment. Both bonds have the same terms: $1,000 face value, 20-year life, 10% coupon rate, and single interest payments made at the end of each year. Given the general level of interest rates in the economy and the riskiness of both Lily Kay Company and Lusvardi Company, both bonds were associated with a market interest rate of 10% when they were issued. Accordingly, both bonds were issued at par of $1,000. Lily Kay Company's balance sheet on the day it purchased the Lusvardi bond with the $1,000 cash raised by issuing its own bond is as follows:

Assets		Liabilities and Equity	
Lusvardi bond	$1,000	Bonds payable	$1,000
		Equity	0

As seen earlier, a risk associated with bonds is that their value fluctuates when market interest rates fluctuate. If, for example, the market interest rate associated with the Lusvardi bond asset were to increase to 12%, the value of the bond would decrease by $149 to $851.[20]

---

[18] FASB ASC Master Glossary, "Fair Value."
[19] Pre-Codification *Statement of Financial Accounting Standards No. 159*, "The Fair Value Option for Financial Assets and Financial Liabilities—Including an amendment of FASB Statement No. 115" (Norwalk, CT: Financial Accounting Standards Board, February 2007). This guidance is now found in the "Fair Value Option" subsections of FASB ASC Topic 825 (Financial Instruments).
[20] $N = 20, I = 12\%, PMT = \$100, FV = \$1,000 \rightarrow PV = \$851$.

This would represent an economic loss to Lily Kay Company. However, in the same way that the fair value of the bond asset is impacted by market interest rates, the fair value of the bond liability is also impacted by market interest rates. If the market interest rate associated with the Lily Kay Company bond were to also increase to 12%, the fair value of the bond would decrease to $851. This $149 decrease represents an economic gain because Lily Kay Company could pay a third party just $851 to take over its bond obligation, which is currently reported in its balance sheet at $1,000. The $149 loss on the bond asset is exactly offset by the $149 gain on the bond liability. Lily Kay Company's balance sheet would then appear as follows:

Assets		Liabilities and Equity	
Lusvardi bond	$851	Bonds payable	$851
		Equity	0

Under the FASB's fair value option, both the $149 loss and the $149 gain from the fair value fluctuations would be reported in Lily Kay Company's income statement. The net impact on income is $0, so retained earnings (and total equity in this case because there was no initial shareholder investment) stays at its initial balance of $0.

In this case, the bond liability serves as a hedge for fluctuations in the value of the bond asset. A hedge is an action taken to reduce the risk associated with a related investment or action. For example, if an airline company is worried about future fluctuations in the price of aviation fuel, the airline can enter into hedging arrangements whereby it enters into contracts to buy its fuel in the future at a price that is set now. Hedging is discussed in more detail in Chapter 19.

Now, assume that Lily Kay Company were required to report the Lusvardi bond asset at its fair value of $851 but were also required to report the bond liability at its historical issuance amount of $1,000. The resulting balance sheet would appear as follows:

Assets		Liabilities and Equity	
Lusvardi bond	$851	Bonds payable	$1,000
		Equity	(149)

The negative equity of $149 represents the recognized loss associated with the decline in fair value of the bond asset. And because the accounting requirement is that the bond liability be reported at its historical issuance amount of $1,000, the corresponding, and offsetting, economic gain is not recognized. Requiring one side of the balance sheet to include fair values but the other side to report historical amounts results in misleading reporting because the hedging effect of the related asset and liability is not reflected in the financial statements.

As explained more fully in Chapter 19, accounting rules and procedures exist that allow for the impact of hedging activities to be reflected in the financial statements. These accounting rules are found in FASB ASC Topic 815 (Derivatives and Hedging). However, the bookkeeping requirements underlying the accounting for hedges often prove to be extremely onerous. As shown in the simple Lily Kay example, for some cases the economic effect of hedging can be reflected quite nicely and simply in the financial statements by allowing companies the option of fair value reporting for both financial assets and financial liabilities. Thus, the intent of the fair value option is to simplify the accounting for economic hedges.

套期保值可以降低风险，但不能确保获利。

Please note that hedging reduces risk; it doesn't guarantee profits. In the example given above when the market interest rate increased to 12% for both the Lusvardi bond asset and the Lily Kay bond liability, the economic loss on the asset was offset by an economic gain on the liability. However, it could just as easily have been the case that the market interest rate decreased for both the bond asset and the bond liability. For example, assume that the market interest rate on both the Lusvardi bond asset and the Lily Kay bond liability decreased to 8%. The fair value of both the asset and the liability would then be $1,196.[21] In this case, an economic gain of $196 on the bond asset would be offset by an economic loss of $196 because of an increase in the fair value of the bond liability. The resulting balance sheet would appear as follows:

Assets		Liabilities and Equity	
Lusvardi bond	$1,196	Bonds payable	$1,196
		Equity	0

In retrospect, from a reporting standpoint, Lily Kay might wish it had not elected the fair value option for the bonds payable. Then the economic gain of $196 from the increase in the value of the asset would have been reported, but the offsetting loss would not have been reported. To prevent companies from using hindsight to selectively enhance reported results using the fair value option, a company must designate whether it is using the fair value option with respect to a financial asset or financial liability when the initial transaction to create the item occurs.[22] A company can't wait to see which way interest rates go and then cherry pick the economic gains while ignoring the economic losses.

In the examples given in this section, the gains and losses on the Lusvardi and Lily Kay bonds were exactly offsetting, meaning that the market interest rates for the two bonds moved together. This might be the case if the change in interest rates were caused by general economic factors that affected both companies equally. However, if the change in market interest rates is caused by firm-specific factors, there is no reason to think that they would move together. For example, assume that the financial condition of Lusvardi Company weakened, resulting in an increase in the market interest rate associated with the company's bonds from 10% to 12%. At the same time, assume that the financial condition of Lily Kay Company strengthened, resulting in a decrease in the market interest rate from 10% to 8%. The resulting balance sheet would appear as follows:

Assets		Liabilities and Equity	
Lusvardi bond	$851	Bonds payable	$1,196
		Equity	(345)

The $345 economic loss is a combination of the $149 loss from the weakening of Lusvardi Company and a $196 economic loss from the strengthening of Lily Kay Company as evidenced by the drop in the market interest rate from 10% to 8%. The $149 loss is easy to understand, but the $196 loss requires further explanation. How can an improvement in a company's economic circumstances result in a loss? Remember that losses and gains are reported from the standpoint of the shareholders. In this example, the shareholders of Lily Kay are now obligated to make 10% interest payments on the Lily Kay bonds for the next 20 years when in fact the circumstances of the company suggest that it need pay only 8%. In other words, Lily Kay Company is obligated to make above-market interest payments for the next 20 years. This represents a transfer of wealth from the shareholders,

---

[21] $N = 20, I = 8\%, PMT = \$100, FV = \$1,000 \rightarrow PV = \$1,196$.
[22] FASB ASC paragraph 825-10-25-4.

who are paying too much interest, to the bondholders, who are collecting too much interest. From an accounting standpoint, the important thing to note here is that use of the fair value option results in all of these interesting and relevant economic facts being reflected immediately in the financial statements.[23]

Off-Balance-Sheet Financing

LO6 Explain various types of off-balance-sheet financing, and understand the reasons for this type of financing.

A major issue facing the accounting profession today is how to deal with companies that do not disclose all their debt in order to make their financial position look stronger. This is often referred to as off-balance-sheet financing. Traditionally, leasing has been one of the most common forms of off-balance-sheet financing. The primary techniques that have been used to borrow money while keeping the debt off the balance sheet are:

1. Leases
2. Unconsolidated subsidiaries
3. Variable interest entities (VIEs)
4. Joint ventures
5. Research and development arrangements
6. Project financing arrangements

Leases

A lease is merely a seller-sponsored technique through which a buyer can finance the use of an asset. For accounting purposes, leases are considered to be either rentals (called *operating leases*) or asset purchases with borrowed money (called *capital leases*). A company using a leased asset tries to have the lease classified as an operating lease in order to keep the lease obligation off the balance sheet. The proper accounting treatment depends on whether the lease contract transfers effective ownership of the leased asset. Capital leases are accounted for as if the lease agreement transfers ownership of the leased asset from the lessor (the owner of a leased asset) to the lessee (the user of the leased asset). Operating leases are accounted for as rental agreements.

The four lease classification criteria are as follows:

1. Lease transfers ownership
2. Lease includes a bargain purchase option
3. Lease covers 75% or more of the economic life of the asset
4. Present value of lease payments is 90% or more of the asset value

If any one of these criteria is met, the lease is classified as a capital lease by the lessee; if none of the criteria are met, the lease is accounted for as an operating lease. An operating lease is accounted for as a rental, with neither the leased asset nor (more importantly to the lessee) the lease liability appearing on the lessee's balance sheet. The vast majority of leases, probably in excess of 90%, are accounted for as operating leases, with the obligation to make

---

[23] In August 2012, the FASB announced a proposed change in the fair value option for liabilities. The proposed change would classify unrealized gains and losses from fair value fluctuations of debt instruments that are driven by changes in the issuing company's own credit risk as part of other comprehensive income (OCI) rather than part of net income.

the future lease payments excluded from balance sheet recognition. Accounting for leases is discussed in great detail in Chapter 15.

Unconsolidated Subsidiaries

In 1987, the FASB issued pre-Codification *Statement No. 94* requiring all majority-owned subsidiaries to be consolidated.[24] Prior to the issuance of FASB *Statement No. 94*, subsidiaries involved in operations unrelated to the parent company's primary focus were not required to be consolidated. For example, IBM Credit LLC and GE Capital Services are each financing subsidiaries of their respective parent companies. The tremendous debt associated with these financing subsidiaries was not recognized on the balance sheets of their parent companies prior to 1987 because the subsidiaries were involved in nonhomogeneous operations. However, with the issuance of *Statement No. 94*, even these subsidiaries are now consolidated. Thus, the FASB eliminated one opportunity that companies have used for off-balance-sheet financing.

The objective of consolidated financial statements is to show the net assets that are owned *or* controlled by a company and its subsidiaries. For accounting purposes, a controlling interest in a subsidiary's net assets is presumed to exist when ownership by the parent company exceeds 50%. Of course, there are some instances when control can be achieved with less than 50% ownership, such as when a parent owns a large portion of a subsidiary, say 40%, and also controls access to important inputs to and outputs from the subsidiary's production process. This difficult issue of defining "control" is something that the FASB, now in conjunction with the IASB, continues to reevaluate from time to time.

Under current accounting rules, companies are able to avoid recognizing debt associated with subsidiaries that are less than 50% owned by the company. As described in Chapter 14, unconsolidated subsidiaries using the equity method are those subsidiaries for which the parent company owns between 20% and 50% of the outstanding shares. With this level of ownership, the presumption is that the parent influences but does not control the subsidiary. The equity method of accounting dictated for these subsidiaries provides that the parent reports, as an asset, its share of the net assets (assets minus liabilities) of the subsidiary; none of the individual liabilities of the subsidiary are reported in the parent company's balance sheet. Even with less than 50% ownership, a parent can often effectively control a subsidiary. For example, for many years Coca-Cola owned less than 50% of its major U.S. bottler but still effectively controlled the operations of this bottler. Because Coca-Cola owned less than 50%, however, the parent company was not required to report the liabilities of the bottler in its balance sheet. To illustrate the potential impact of unconsolidated subsidiaries on the reported amount of a company's debt, consider that Coca-Cola's reported liabilities as of December 31, 2009, were $23.325 billion, whereas the actual liabilities of Coca-Cola and its unconsolidated bottlers totaled $58.382 billion.[25] The topic of consolidation is briefly introduced in Chapter 14 and is covered extensively in advanced accounting courses.

Variable Interest Entities (VIEs)

An important category of unconsolidated subsidiaries is variable interest entities (VIEs). Much of the dissatisfaction about Enron's accounting leading up to its 2001 accounting

---

[24] Pre-Codification *Statement of Financial Accounting Standards No. 94*, "Consolidation of All Majority-Owned Subsidiaries" (Stamford, CT: Financial Accounting Standards Board, 1987).

[25] In February 2010, Coca-Cola announced that it intended to purchase the North American operations of its largest bottler. Apart from the operational reasons for making this acquisition, this transaction brought over $10 billion of liabilities onto Coca-Cola's balance sheet that had previously been hidden in its unconsolidated subsidiary.

scandal and bankruptcy centered around its use of so-called "special-purpose entities" (SPEs). A post-Enron revision of the accounting rules has changed the practice and terminology associated with these entities; they are now called *variable interest entities*. However, the fundamental concept of a variable interest entity is the same as a special-purpose entity. To illustrate how a VIE can serve as a form of off-balance-sheet financing, consider the following example. Sponsor Company requires the use of a building costing $100,000. Rather than buy the building (with borrowed money), Sponsor facilitates the establishment of VIE Company. VIE Company is started with a $10,000 investment from a private investor (who is not associated with Sponsor Company), along with a $90,000 bank loan. VIE now has $100,000 in cash with which it purchases the $100,000 building needed by Sponsor. VIE then leases the building to Sponsor, with the lease terms carefully crafted to allow for the lease to be accounted for as an operating lease. After this series of transactions, the building-related and lease-related items on the balance sheets of Sponsor and VIE are as follows:

Sponsor		VIE	
Assets:		Assets:	
....	$0	Building............................	$100,000
Liabilities:		Liabilities:	
....	0	Bank loan	90,000
		Equity:	
		Paid-in capital	10,000

As you can see, with the help of VIE, Sponsor now has use of the building but without any debt on its balance sheet. If VIE were classified as being "controlled" by Sponsor, then VIE's books would be consolidated with those of Sponsor, and both the building and the bank loan would appear on Sponsor's consolidated balance sheet. Thus, the creation of an "independent" VIE is another way to engage in off-balance-sheet financing.

From this simple example, you can see that the following issues are crucial in the accounting for a VIE:

- How much outside equity financing of the VIE is necessary for the VIE to be considered an independent entity? The 10% financing in this case ($10,000/$100,000) coincides with the general guideline contained in FASB ASC Topic 810 (Consolidation).[26]
- If the sponsor is contingently liable for the VIE's debt, is the VIE an independent entity? When the sponsor guarantees, or cosigns, the debt of the VIE, the VIE certainly is less like an entity independent of the sponsor. According to FASB rules, loan cosigning by the sponsor can be evidence that the risks of ownership are actually borne by the sponsor and not the VIE equity investor. If the risks of ownership are borne by the sponsor, then the sponsor would be required to report in its balance sheet both the assets and liabilities of the VIE.

The accounting rules that existed for special-purposes entities allowed sponsor companies to carefully design their SPEs so that they could be accounted for as separate companies. In the wake of the Enron scandal and the unwelcome focus on SPEs as a tool for financial statement manipulation, the FASB has not only changed the terminology (from SPE to VIE) but has also substantially tightened the accounting rules to prevent variable interest entities from serving as forms of off-balance-sheet financing. The focus of the current FASB rules is on the expected profits and losses of the special entity; the entity expected

[26] FASB ASC paragraph 810-10-25-45.

> **FYI**
>
> Enron used its SPEs to engage in strategically timed purchases of assets so that Enron could avoid reporting losses on declines in the values of the assets. Also, Enron used SPEs to take the other side of a number of hedging transactions, as discussed in Chapter 19. The provisions of FASB ASC Subtopic 810-10 are now designed to prevent, or at least reduce, all of these abuses.

to bear the majority of the expected losses or reap the majority of the expected gains should include the assets and liabilities of the VIE in its balance sheet, independent of technical voting control.

SIC 12 Consolidation—Special Purpose Entities was issued internationally in December 1998. *SIC 12* is a good example of a principles-based standard. The gist of *SIC 12* is contained in its paragraph 8, reproduced here in its entirety: "An SPE [special-purpose entity] shall be consolidated when the substance of the relationship between an entity and the SPE indicates that the SPE is controlled by that entity." If, in the judgment of the accountant, an entity "controls" an SPE, then the entity is required to consolidate the SPE, meaning that all of its assets and liabilities are included in the balance sheet of the controlling entity. In this context, "control" is not limited to voting control. For example, if a special-purpose entity has been set up with all of its operating decisions determined in advance by rigid policies, then the company that established the special-purpose entity and the "autopilot" operating policies effectively controls the SPE no matter what its ownership percentage is. This concept of "control" is an essential one, but further discussion is outside the scope of this text.

Joint Ventures

Companies will, on occasion, join forces with other companies to share the costs and benefits associated with specifically defined projects. These joint ventures are often developed to share the risks associated with high-risk projects. For example, following the identification of the human genome's complete structure, pharmaceutical companies have been forming joint ventures. These joint ventures are intended to perform research to identify the exact structure of proteins manufactured by specific genes associated with specific diseases. The ultimate objective is to use this detailed understanding of the biochemistry underlying specific diseases to be able to design chemical treatments, or, even better, cures. Start-up costs for this type of joint venture can easily exceed $100 million. By involving several pharmaceutical companies, the costs, risks, and results can be shared.

Because the benefits of these joint ventures are uncertain, companies could incur substantial liabilities with few, if any, assets resulting from their efforts. As a result (as is sometimes the case with unconsolidated subsidiaries), a joint venture is sometimes carefully structured to ensure that its liabilities are not disclosed in the balance sheets of the companies that are partners.

A common form of a joint venture is a 50/50 partnership between two companies. For example, before its merger with **Chevron** in 2001, **Texaco** had two 50/50 joint venture partnerships: one with Chevron and one with **Saudi Refining, Inc.** The Chevron joint venture was called **Caltex** and engaged in oil exploration, refining, and marketing in Africa, Asia, the Middle East, Australia, and New Zealand. The joint venture with Saudi Refining was called **Star** and marketed gasoline in the eastern United States. The advantage of a 50/50 joint venture is that both companies can account for their investment using the equity method. Thus,

> **FYI**
>
> Many U.S. automobile companies have formed joint ventures with foreign car companies to develop and manufacture cars. For example, **Ford Motor Co.** has teamed up with **Mazda** in joint ventures in both North America and Asia.

joint ventures are often just a special type of unconsolidated subsidiary. For example, the Caltex and Star joint ventures had total long-term liabilities in excess of $3 billion, none of which were reported in Texaco's balance sheet. The accounting for joint ventures is discussed in more detail in Chapter 14.

Research and Development Arrangements

Another way a company may obtain off-balance-sheet financing is with research and development arrangements. These involve situations in which an enterprise obtains the results of research and development activities funded partially or entirely by others. The main accounting issue is whether the arrangement is, in essence, a means of borrowing to fund research and development or if it is simply a contract to do research for others.[27] In deciding on the appropriate accounting treatment, a major consideration is whether the enterprise is obligated to repay the funds provided by the other parties regardless of the outcome of the research and development activities. If there is an obligation to repay, the enterprise should estimate and recognize that liability and record the research and development expenses in the current year in accordance with FASB ASC Topic 730 (Research and Development). If the financial risk associated with the research and development is transferred from the enterprise to other parties and there is no obligation to them, then a liability need not be reported by the enterprise.

Research and development arrangements may take a variety of forms, including a limited partnership. For example, assume that Kincher Company formed a limited partnership for the purpose of conducting research and development. Kincher is the general partner and manages the activities of the partnership. The limited partners are strictly investors. The question is this: Should Kincher record the research and development expenses and the obligation to the investors on its books? The answer depends on an assessment of who is at risk and whether Kincher is obligated to repay the limited partners regardless of the results of the research and development. If the limited partners are at risk and have no guarantee or claim against Kincher Company for any of the funds contributed, the debt and related expenses need not be reported on Kincher's books.

Project Financing Arrangements

At times, companies become involved in long-term commitments that are related to project financing arrangements. As an example, assume that Striker Corporation, a large construction company, has decided to establish a separate company, Paveway, in order to undertake a highway construction project. Paveway is to be organized as a separate legal entity, and all loans acquired by Paveway will specifically state that they are to be repaid from the cash flows of Paveway itself, with the assets of Paveway serving as collateral for the loans. It is likely that Striker would have a contingent obligation to satisfy the debt of Paveway even though the debt itself is intended to be repaid from Paveway cash flows. In this case, Striker would disclose this commitment in a note to the financial statements. This type of arrangement is another form of off-balance-sheet financing.[28]

Reasons for Off-Balance-Sheet Financing

表外融资可使公司不局限于信贷限制而借到更多的钱。同时，如果一家公司的财务状况看起来很好，就可以以更低的成本借款。

Companies might use one of the preceding or other techniques to avoid including debt on the balance sheet for several reasons. It may allow a company to borrow more than it

[27] FASB ASC Subtopic 730-20 (Research and Development—Research and Development Arrangements).
[28] FASB ASC Topic 440 (Commitments).

otherwise could due to debt-limit restrictions. Also, if a company's financial position looks stronger, it will usually be able to borrow at a lower cost.

Whatever the reasons, the problems of off-balance-sheet financing are serious. Many investors and lenders aren't sophisticated enough to see through the off-balance-sheet borrowing tactics and therefore make ill-informed decisions. For example, in periods of economic downturn, a company with hidden debt may find it is not able to meet its obligations and, as a result, may suffer severe financial distress or, in extreme cases, business failure. In turn, unsuspecting creditors and investors may sustain substantial losses that could have been avoided had they known the true extent of the company's debt.

Analyzing a Firm's Debt Position

LO7 学习目标7
利用各种比率分析企业的债务状况。

7 Analyze a firm's debt position using ratios.

Those parties considering investing in, or lending money to, a firm are particularly interested in that firm's obligations and capital structure. The term *leverage* refers to the relationship between a firm's debt and assets or its debt and stockholders' equity. A firm that is highly leveraged has a large amount of debt relative to its assets or equity. A common measure of a firm's leverage is the debt-to-equity ratio, calculated by dividing total liabilities by total stockholders' equity. As an example, consider the following information from the 2011 annual report of IBM.

(In millions)	2011	2010
Long-term debt	$22,857	$21,846
Total liabilities	96,197	90,279
Total stockholders' equity	20,236	23,172
Income before income taxes	21,003	19,723
Interest expense	411	368

IBM's debt-to-equity ratios for 2011 and 2010 are as follows:

$$2011: \$96{,}197/\$20{,}236 = 4.75$$
$$2010: \$90{,}279/\$23{,}172 = 3.90$$

A debt-to-equity ratio exceeding 1.0 indicates that the firm has more liabilities than stockholders' equity. For IBM, the debt-to-equity ratio has increased from 2010 to 2011. Investors generally prefer a higher debt-to-equity ratio to obtain the advantages of financial leverage, while creditors favor a lower ratio to increase the safety of their debt. Debt-to-equity ratios for a number of U.S. companies are presented in Exhibit 12-8.

产权比率的可接受度和一家公司在行业中的运营状况具有很强的联系。

As these data illustrate, what constitutes an acceptable debt-to-equity ratio depends to a great extent on the industry in which a company operates. For example, financial institutions, such as **Bank of America**, typically have very high debt-to-equity ratios because the financial assets held by such institutions provide very good collateral for loans. Note that **General Electric**, which has a large amount of financial assets and liabilities in its GE Capital Services subsidiary, has a debt-to-equity ratio indicative of a financial institution. At the other end of the spectrum, companies with few tangible assets to offer as loan collateral typically have lower debt-to-equity ratios. The extreme example of this is **Yahoo!** with a debt-to-equity ratio of just 0.19.

Because there is no hard and fast rule for what is included in the word *debt*, alternative definitions and interpretations of the debt-to-equity ratio have developed. For example,

Exhibit 12-8 | Debt-to-Equity Ratios for Selected U.S. Companies for Fiscal 2011 ($ in millions)

Company (Industry)	Total Liabilities	Total Equity	Debt-to-Equity Ratio
Bank of America (banking)	$1,898,945	$230,101	8.25
Disney (entertainment)	32,671	39,453	0.83
General Electric (diversified industrial and financing)	599,108	118,134	5.07
McDonald's (fast food)	18,600	14,390	1.29
Merck (pharmaceuticals)	48,185	56,943	0.85
Microsoft (software)	51,621	57,083	0.90
Yahoo! (Internet portal)	2,331	12,596	0.19

© Cengage Learning 2014

the ratio is often varied to include only long-term debt. If this definition were used for IBM, the debt-to-equity ratio for the two-year period would be:

$$2011: \$22,857/\$20,236 = 1.13$$
$$2010: \$21,846/\$23,172 = 0.94$$

Note that the debt-to-equity ratios differ dramatically depending on how "debt" is defined: The debt-to-equity ratio is 4.75 if debt is defined to include all liabilities but is only 1.13 if debt is defined to include just long-term debt. Because there is no requirement for companies or analysts to compute ratios in particular ways, you are certain to encounter different measures of the debt-to-equity ratio. The point to be remembered is this: Make sure you understand the inputs to a ratio before you try to interpret the output. Debt to one person may not mean the same thing to another. Another common variation of the leverage measure is to compare total liabilities to total assets. This measure, frequently called the *debt ratio*, was introduced in Chapter 3.

> **FYI**
>
> The sum of a company's income before income taxes and interest expense is often called *EBIT* (*earnings before interest and taxes*).

Another measure of a company's performance relating to debt is the number of times interest is earned. This measure compares a company's interest obligations with its earnings ability. Times interest earned is calculated by adding a company's income before income taxes and interest expense and then dividing by the interest expense for the period. In the case of IBM, times interest earned for 2011 and 2010 is computed as follows:

times interest earned
利息保障倍数

$$2011: (\$21,003 + \$411)/\$411 = 52.1$$
$$2010: (\$19,723 + \$368)/\$368 = 54.6$$

The number of times interest is earned reflects the company's ability to meet interest payments and the degree of safety afforded the creditors. Note that in both 2010 and 2011, IBM offered creditors a large margin of safety. In both years, IBM's operations generated over 50 times the amount needed to be able to pay the company's interest obligation for the year.

Disclosing Debt in the Financial Statements

LO8 学习目标8

回顾财务报表附注，理解与债务融资相关的财务信息披露要求。

在财务报表附注中披露的关于负债融资的内容包括：负债的性质、到期日、利率、清算方式、转换权利、偿债基金要求、借款限制、抵押资产、股利限制和其他重大相关内容。当期到期的长期负债的比重也应在财务报表附注中披露。

8 Review the notes to financial statements, and understand the disclosure associated with debt financing.

In disclosing details about long-term debt in the notes to the financial statements, the nature of the liabilities, maturity dates, interest rates, methods of liquidation, conversion privileges, sinking fund requirements, borrowing restrictions, assets pledged, dividend limitations, and other significant matters should be indicated. The portion of long-term debt coming due in the current period should also be disclosed.

Bond liabilities are often combined with other long-term debt for balance sheet presentation, with supporting details disclosed in a note. An example of such a note taken from the 2011 annual report of IBM is presented in Exhibit 12-9. Note that IBM enters

Exhibit 12-9 | IBM—Disclosure of Long-Term Debt

IBM—Disclosure of Long-Term Debt			
At December 31:	**Maturities**	**2011**	**2010**
U.S. Dollar Notes and Debentures (average interest rate at December 31, 2011):			
3.72%	2012–2013	$ 8,615*	$ 6,326
1.02%	2014–2015	2,414*	5,019
4.94%	2016–2020	8,600	6,359
2.90%	2021	500	—
7.00%	2025	600	600
6.22%	2027	469	469
6.50%	2028	313	313
5.875%	2032	600	600
8.00%	2038	187	187
5.60%	2039	1,545	1,545
7.00%	2045	27	27
7.125%	2096	322	322
		24,192	21,766
Other currencies (average interest rate at December 31, 2011, in parentheses):			
Euros (6.6%)	2012–2016	1,037	1,897
Japanese yen (0.8%)	2013–2014	1,123	1,162
Swiss francs (3.8%)	2012–2020	173	540
Other (5.1%)	2012–2014	177	240
		26,702	25,606
Less: Net unamortized discount		533	531
Add: Fair value adjustment**		994	788
		27,161	25,863
Less: Current maturities		4,306	4,017
Total		$22,857	$21,846

* $1.6 billion in debt securities issued by IBM International Group Capital LLC, which is an indirect, 100 percent owned finance subsidiary of the company, is included in 2012–2015. Debt securities issued by IBM International Group Capital LLC are fully and unconditionally guaranteed by the company.

** The portion of the company's fixed rate debt obligations that is hedged is reflected in the Consolidated Statement of Financial Position as an amount equal to the sum of the debt's carrying value plus a fair value adjustment representing changes in the fair value of the hedged debt obligations attributable to movements in benchmark interest rates.

IBM, 2011, 10K Report

into long-term borrowing arrangements using a variety of different instruments and in a variety of different currencies. In U.S. dollars, IBM has both long-term debentures (unsecured bonds) and notes. The 7.125% debenture issue is interesting because it doesn't mature until 2096. IBM obtains loans denominated in foreign currencies for a variety of reasons. First, some countries are reluctant to allow large multinational corporations such as IBM to do business in their countries without using local financing. It helps IBM establish good local relations if it uses local financial institutions as much as possible. Also, some of IBM's foreign subsidiaries are relatively self-contained, meaning that almost all operating, investing, and financing activities are handled locally. Sometimes IBM gets foreign currency financing because the interest rate is low. (Look at the 0.8% average rate on the Japanese yen loans.) Finally, foreign currency financing is a way for IBM to hedge, or protect itself, against fluctuations in the value of foreign currencies. For example, if IBM has assets denominated in Thai baht and the baht decreases in value, IBM will have lost money. However, if IBM has an equal amount of loans denominated in Thai baht, the loss from the decrease in the value of the Thai baht assets will be offset by the gain from the decrease in value of the Thai baht liabilities. This is called a *hedge* and results in IBM being immune from the effects of exchange rate changes, up or down.

EXPANDED MATERIAL

To this point in the chapter, we have covered the most common issues associated with debt: issuance, the payment of interest, and its retirement. In this Expanded Material, we will introduce and discuss an issue that does not occur frequently but, when it does occur, has a significant impact. The issue to be discussed is troubled debt restructuring: how to account for concessions made on the debt of firms in poor financial condition.

Accounting for Troubled Debt Restructuring

LO9 学习目标9
理解债务重组发生的条件，并且能够对债务重组进行会计处理。

⑨ Understand the conditions under which troubled debt restructuring occurs, and be able to account for troubled debt restructuring.

A significant accounting problem is created when economic conditions make it difficult for an issuer of long-term debt to make the cash payments required under the terms of the debt instrument. These payments include interest payments, principal payments on installment obligations, periodic payments to bond retirement funds, or even payments to retire debt at maturity. To avoid bankruptcy proceedings or foreclosure on the debt, investors may agree to make concessions and revise the original terms of the debt to permit the issuer to recover from financial problems. The revision of debt terms in such situations, referred to as troubled debt restructuring, can take many different forms. For example, there may be a suspension of interest payments for a period of time, a reduction in the interest rate, an extension of the maturity date of the debt, or even an exchange of assets or equity securities for the debt. The primary accounting question in these cases, on both the books of the issuer and the investor, is whether a gain or loss should be recognized upon the restructuring of the debt.

In FASB ASC Subtopic 470-60 (Debt—Troubled Debt Restructurings by Debtors), the FASB defined *troubled debt restructuring* as a situation in which "the creditor for economic or legal reasons related to the debtor's financial difficulties grants a concession to the debtor that it would not otherwise consider.... That concession either stems from an agreement between the creditor and the debtor or is imposed by law or a court."[29] The key word in this definition is *concession*. If a concession is not made by creditors, accounting for the restructuring follows the procedures discussed for extinguishment of debt prior to maturity.

The major issue addressed by the FASB in Subtopic 470-60 is whether a troubled debt restructuring agreement should be viewed as a significant economic transaction. It was decided that if it is considered to be a significant economic transaction, entries should be made on the issuer's books to reflect any gain or loss. If the restructuring is not considered to be a significant economic transaction, no entries are required. The accounting treatment thus depends on the nature of the restructuring. The FASB conclusions are summarized in the table below.

For the issuer, each type of restructuring is discussed and illustrated in the following sections. For the investor, the procedures associated with an asset swap and an equity swap are discussed in this chapter. The complexities associated with a modification of terms from the point of view of the investor (or creditor) are discussed in Chapter 14 where we discuss the accounting for the impairment of a loan, which is addressed in FASB ASC Subtopic 310-40 (Receivables—Troubled Debt Restructurings by Creditors).

Type	Restructuring Considered Significant Economic Transaction: Gain or Loss Recognized	Restructuring Not Considered Significant Economic Transaction: No Gain or Loss Recognized
Transfer of assets in full settlement (asset swap)	XXX	
Grant of equity interest in full settlement (equity swap)	XXX	
Modification of terms: Total payment under new structure exceeds debt carrying value		XXX
Modification of terms: Total payment under new structure is less than debt carrying value	XXX	

Transfer of Assets in Full Settlement (Asset Swap)

债务人以资产（如不动产、存货、应收账款或投资）方式转让给债权人以偿还全部债务。这种情况通常存在两种利得或损失：（1）转让资产产生的利得或损失；（2）在债务重组中因让步而取得的利得。

A debtor that transfers assets, such as real estate, inventories, receivables, or investments, to a creditor to fully settle a payable usually will recognize two types of gains or losses: (1) a gain or loss on disposal of the asset and (2) a gain arising from the concession granted in the restructuring of the debt. The computation of these gains and/or losses is made as follows:

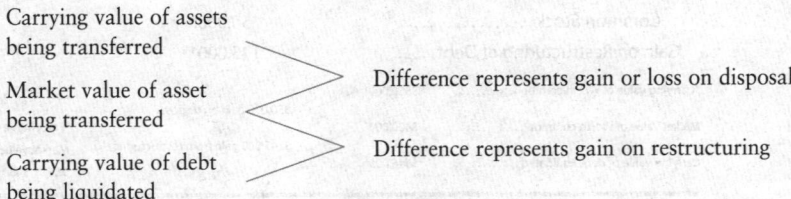

The gain or loss on disposal of an asset is usually reported as an ordinary income item unless it meets criteria for reporting it as an unusual or irregular item. Similarly, the gain on restructuring is typically considered to be part of ordinary income.

[29] FASB ASC paragraphs 470-60-15-5 and 6.

An investor always recognizes a loss on the restructuring due to the concession granted unless the investment has already been written down in anticipation of the loss. The computation of the loss is made as follows:

Carrying value of investment liquidated
Market value of asset being transferred
} Difference represents loss on restructuring

The classification of this loss depends on the criteria being used to recognize irregular or extraordinary items. However, usually the loss is anticipated as market values of the investment decline, and it is recognized as an ordinary loss, either prior to the restructuring or as part of the restructuring.

To illustrate these points, assume that Stanton Industries is behind in its interest payments on outstanding bonds of $500,000 and is threatened with bankruptcy proceedings. The carrying value of the bonds on Stanton's books is $545,000 after deducting the unamortized discount of $5,000 and adding unpaid interest of $50,000. To settle the debt, Stanton transfers long-term investments it holds in Worth common stock with a carrying value of $350,000 and a fair value of $400,000 to all investors on a pro rata basis.

Assume that Realty Inc. holds $40,000 face value of Stanton's bonds. Because of the troubled financial condition of Stanton Industries, Realty Inc. has previously recognized as a loss a $5,000 decline in the value of the debt and is carrying the investment at $35,000 on its books plus interest receivable of $4,000. The entry on Stanton's books to record the asset transfer would be as follows:

> **Stop & Think**
>
> From the standpoint of the debtor, which ONE of the following is NOT possible on an asset swap done as part of a debt restructuring?
>
> a) Loss on disposal of the asset and loss on the debt restructuring
> b) Gain on disposal of the asset and gain on the debt restructuring
> c) Loss on disposal of the asset and gain on the debt restructuring

Stanton Industries (Issuer)		Realty Inc. (Investor)	
Interest Payable............. 50,000		Long-Term Investments—	
Bonds Payable............. 500,000		Worth Common Stock.............	32,000†
Discount on Bonds Payable.......	5,000	Loss on Restructuring of Debt...........	7,000
Long-Term Investments—		Bond Investment—Stanton Industries	35,000
Worth Common Stock..........	350,000	Interest Receivable.....................	4,000
Gain on Disposal of Worth			
Common Stock.................	50,000*		
Gain on Restructuring of Debt.....	145,000*		

*Carrying value of Worth common........... $350,000
Market value of Worth common............. $400,000 } $50,000 gain on disposal
Carrying value of debt liquidated........... $545,000 } $145,000 gain from restructuring

†Percentage of debt held by Realty Inc.: $40,000/$500,000 = 8%
Market value of long-term investment received in settlement of debt:
0.08 × $400,000 = $32,000

Grant of Equity Interest (Equity Swap)

A debtor that grants an equity interest to the investor as a substitute for a liability must recognize a gain equal to the difference between the fair value of the equity interest and the carrying value of the liquidated liability. A creditor (investor) must recognize a loss equal to the difference between the same fair value of the equity interest and the carrying value of the debt as an investment. For example, assume that Stanton Industries transferred 20,000 shares of common stock to satisfy the $500,000 face value of bonds. The par value of the common stock per share is $1, and the market value at the date of the restructuring is $20 per share. Assume that the other facts described in the preceding illustration of an asset swap are unchanged. The entry on Stanton's books to record the grant of the equity interest is as follows:

Stanton Industries (Issuer)			Realty Inc. (Investor)		
Interest Payable	50,000		Long-Term Investments—Stanton		
Bonds Payable	500,000		Common Stock	32,000	
Discount on Bonds Payable		5,000	Loss on Restructuring of Debt	7,000	
Common Stock		20,000	Bond Investment—Stanton Industries		35,000
Paid-In Capital in Excess of Par		380,000	Interest Receivable		4,000
Gain on Restructuring of Debt		145,000*			

*Market value of common stock $400,000
Carrying value of debt liquidated $545,000
$145,000 gain from restructuring

The entry on Stanton's books for an equity swap differs from that made for the asset swap because there can be no gain or loss on exchange of a company's own stock.

Modification of Debt Terms

There are many ways debt terms may be modified to aid a troubled debtor. Modification may involve either the interest or the maturity value or both. Interest concessions may involve a reduction of the interest rate, forgiveness of unpaid interest, or a moratorium on interest payments for a period of time. Maturity value concessions may involve an extension of the maturity date or a reduction in the amount to be repaid at maturity. Basically, the FASB decided that most modifications of debt did not result in a significant economic transaction for the issuer of the debt and thus did not give rise to a gain or loss at the date of restructuring. It argued that the new terms were merely an extension of an existing debt and that the modifications should be reflected in future periods through modified interest charges based on computed implicit interest rates. The only exception to this general rule occurs if the total payments to be made under the new structure, including all future interest payments, are less than the carrying value of the debt at the time of restructuring. Under this exception, the difference between the total future cash payments required and the carrying value of the debt is recognized immediately as a gain on the debtor's books. These provisions are summarized here:

基本上，FASB认定大多数的债务变更并没有导致债务发行方产生重大经济交易，所以并没有给债务重组带来得失。该委员会认为新的条款仅仅是对现有债务的延续，修改后内容应通过变更利息收费在未来一段时间得到体现，而变更利息收费应基于计算后的隐含利率。

Description of the Restructuring	Accounting Treatment
Substantially modify the loan terms. The sum of the future payments (undiscounted) does **not** exceed the carrying value of the loan.	Make a journal entry. New carrying value of the loan equals the undiscounted future payments. **No** interest expense in subsequent periods.
Slightly modify the loan terms. The sum of the future payments (undiscounted) still exceeds the carrying value of the loan.	**No** journal entry. However, a new "implicit" interest rate is computed and used to compute interest expense in subsequent periods.

To illustrate the accounting for a "substantial" restructuring, assume the interest rate on the Stanton Industries bonds (see page 12-49) is reduced from 10% to 7%, the maturity date is extended from three to five years from the restructuring date, and the past interest due of $50,000 is forgiven. The total future payments to be made after this restructuring are as follows:

Maturity value of bonds	$500,000
Interest—0.07 × $500,000 × 5 years	175,000
Total payments to be made after restructuring	$675,000

Because the $675,000 exceeds the carrying value of $545,000 [($500,000 − $5,000) + $50,000], no gain is recognized on the books of Stanton Industries at the time of restructuring.

However, if, in addition to the preceding changes, $200,000 of maturity value is forgiven, the future payments would be reduced as follows:

Maturity value of bonds ($500,000 − $200,000)	$300,000
Interest—0.07 × $300,000 × 5 years	105,000
Total payments to be made after restructuring	$405,000

Now the carrying value exceeds the future payments by $140,000, and this gain would be recognized by Stanton as follows:

Interest Payable	50,000	
Bonds Payable	500,000	
Discount on Bonds Payable		5,000
Restructured Debt		405,000
Gain on Restructuring of Debt		140,000

In this case, the total future cash flows to be repaid are less than the amount that is owed, meaning that the implicit interest rate is negative. In order to raise the rate to zero, the carrying value must be reduced to the cash to be realized and a gain recognized for the difference. All interest payments in the future are offset directly to the debt account. No interest expense will be recognized in the future because of the extreme concessions made in the restructuring. By charging all interest payments to the debt account, the balance remaining at the maturity date will be the maturity value of the debt.

When terms are modified just "slightly," the total carrying value of the restructured debt is not changed, and no gain is recognized. The amount recognized as interest expense in the remaining periods of the debt instrument's life is based on a computed implicit interest rate. The implicit interest rate is the rate that equates the present value of all future debt payments to the present carrying value of the debt. The interest expense for each period is equal to the carrying value of the debt for the period involved times the implicit interest rate. The computation of the implicit interest rate can be complex and usually requires the use of a business calculator. Computing implicit interest rates (internal rates of return) is explained in the Time Value of Money Review module.

To illustrate the computation of an implicit interest rate, the initial restructuring of Stanton Industries described above will be used. The question to be answered is what rate of interest will equate the total future payments of $675,000 to the present carrying value of $545,000. Interest is paid and compounded semiannually.

Business Calculator Keystrokes

PV = − $545,000 (this is the carrying value of the loan; enter as a negative number)

PMT = $17,500 ($500,000 × 0.07 × 6/12)

FV = $500,000 (amount to be paid in a lump sum at the loan maturity date)

N = 10 (the total loan term is five years; interest payments are semiannual)

I = ???

The solution returned by the calculator is 2.47% for each six-month period.

Using the Excel RATE Function

Excel Label	Your Input
Nper	10
Pmt	17,500
Pv	−545,000
Fv	500,000
Type	0

Press "Enter" to see the answer of 2.47%.

Using this rate, the recorded interest expense for the first six months would be $13,462, or 2.47% of $545,000. Because the actual cash payment for interest is $17,500, the carrying value of the debt will decline by $4,038 ($17,500 − $13,462). The interest expense for the second semiannual period will be less than for the first period because of the decrease in the carrying value of the debt [($545,000 − $4,038) × 0.0247 = $13,362 interest expense]. These computations are the same as those required in applying the effective-interest method of amortization described earlier. Continuation of the procedure for the 10 periods would leave a balance of $500,000, the maturity value, in the liability account of Stanton Industries. The entries to record the restructuring on Stanton's books and the first two interest payments would be as follows:

Bonds Payable	500,000	
Interest Payable	50,000	
Discount on Bonds Payable		5,000
Restructured Debt		545,000
Interest Expense	13,462	
Restructured Debt	4,038	
Cash		17,500
Interest Expense	13,362	
Restructured Debt	4,138	
Cash		17,500

Any combination of these methods of bond restructuring may be employed. Accounting for these multiple restructurings can become very complex and must be carefully evaluated. As stated previously, the accounting for a modification of terms by the creditor is discussed in Chapter 14.

SOLUTIONS TO OPENING SCENARIO QUESTIONS

1. A bond rating downgrade indicates that a company's riskiness has increased. Accordingly, the downgrades increased the market interest rate on IBM's debt. Prior to the downgrades, the market interest rate on IBM's debt was approximately 0.5% above the interest rate on comparable U.S. Treasury bonds. After the downgrades, this spread grew to 0.7%.

2. The interest rate that investors must be paid to get them to purchase a bond is related to the riskiness of the bond issuer. Historically, investors have viewed U.S. Treasury bonds as being essentially riskless. As a result, the market interest rate on U.S. Treasury bonds is sometimes called the "risk-free rate." Because there is some risk associated with the bonds of all issuing corporations, the market interest rate associated with corporate bonds is higher than the rate on comparable U.S. Treasury bonds.

3. The long-term debt obligation is fixed, in monetary terms, by a variety of contracts. IBM has virtually no uncertainty about the amounts it owes under these contracts. In contrast, the retirement obligation is an estimate based on expected employee life spans, future healthcare cost trends, and so forth. IBM has great uncertainty about the amounts it will ultimately pay for these retirement obligations.

Stop & Think SOLUTIONS

1. (Page 12-6) The correct answer is D. The current ratio is just one indicator of a company's ability to meet its current obligations. Another indicator is the ability of the company to generate operating cash flow. In fact, from a practical standpoint, current obligations are satisfied with normal ongoing operating cash flow rather than through the liquidation of a company's existing current assets. Because Wal-Mart has the ability to generate a stable stream of operating cash flow, the company is still able to meet its current obligations even though its current ratio is just 0.88.

2. (Page 12-21) The correct answer is A. Do not confuse the market and the stated rates. The stated rate is only used for computing the amount of the interest payments. The market rate is used for computing the present value amounts of the principal and interest payments.

3. (Page 12-26) The correct answer is B. The periodic interest payment is the same each period and is equal to the bond maturity value multiplied by the coupon rate.

4. (Page 12-48) The correct answer is A. The gain or loss on disposal of an asset is computed by comparing the carrying value with its market value. The market value could be greater than or less than book value. Regarding the restructuring, there can only be a gain for the debtor. Remember what we are doing here—getting the creditor to forgive the debt. That means the debtor will be able to retire debt at less than its carrying value. The debtor is getting a good deal—and this good deal is classified as a gain.

SOLUTION TO USING THE FASB'S CODIFICATION

The "Debt—Overall" subtopic (470-10) includes a section (S99) on SEC material. Under the heading "SEC Staff Guidance," you can see a reference to "Staff Accounting Bulletins." One of the topics under that heading is "SAB Topic 4.A, Subordinated Debt." The authoritative GAAP reference is FASB ASC paragraph 470-10-S99-2, and the guidance is as follows: "Subordinated debt may not be included in the stockholders' equity section of the balance sheet. Any presentation describing such debt as a component of stockholders' equity must be eliminated. Furthermore, any caption representing the combination of stockholders' equity and only subordinated debts must be deleted."

Note that this classification restriction is imposed on those who prepare financial statements. In contrast, users of financial statements, such as banks and financial analysts, are free to reclassify balance sheet items in any way they choose. Thus, for purposes of debt covenant calculations, banks often exclude goodwill from the balance sheet assets and reclassify subordinated debt from a liability to equity.

Review Chapter 12 Learning Objectives

1 Understand the various classification and measurement issues associated with debt.

Debt can be classified as either current or noncurrent. Debt is considered current if it will be paid within one year or the current operating cycle, whichever period is longer. Theoretically, all debt should be recorded at its present value. However, most current obligations arising in the normal course of business are not discounted. Some obligations cannot be measured with certainty. These obligations are estimated and recorded at an approximate amount.

2 Account for short-term debt obligations, including those expected to be refinanced, and describe the purpose of lines of credit.

Short-term debt obligations can result from operations or from nonoperating activities. The most common example of a short-term obligation resulting from operations is accounts payable. Other short-term operating liabilities include wages payable, interest payable, and taxes payable. Notes payable involve a more formal credit arrangement. These notes typically specify an interest rate and a payment date. Notes payable can be classified as trade or nontrade. Short-term obligations expected to be refinanced on a long-term basis should be classified as noncurrent if certain criteria are met.

Negotiating a line of credit allows a company to arrange the source of its financing in advance of the time that the funds are actually needed.

3 Apply present value concepts to the accounting for long-term debts such as mortgages.

The present value of a long-term obligation is the amount of cash it would take today to completely satisfy the obligation. Mortgages and secured loans are loans that are backed by specific assets as collateral. These types of loans reduce the risk to the lender because the securing assets can be seized if the loan payments are not made. In accounting for the repayment of a mortgage obligation, each payment amount must be divided between the amount paid for interest and the amount paid for principal.

4 Understand the various types of bonds; compute the price of a bond issue; and account for the issuance, interest, and redemption of bonds.

Bonds come in various shapes and sizes. They are issued by governments and corporations; they can be secured or unsecured, term or serial, registered or coupon—to name a few of the variations. All bonds share one feature: the borrowing of money now with some form of repayment in the future.

Most bonds also involve periodic interest payments. The market price of a bond is determined using present value techniques that incorporate the market rate of interest and the stated rate of the bond. The difference between the market and stated rates will result in a premium or discount. This premium or discount is amortized over time.

When bonds are retired, the debt is removed from the books of the debtor when cash is paid. Bonds can be refinanced at or prior to maturity. Any gain on the early retirement of debt is reported as an ordinary item on the income statement.

5 Discuss the use of the fair value option for financial assets and liabilities.

Under the fair value option, a company has the option to report, at each balance sheet date, any or all of its financial assets and liabilities at their fair values on the balance sheet date. The resulting unrealized gains and losses are reported in the income statement. This simple procedure allows companies to include the economic effects of hedging activities in the financial statements.

6 Explain various types of off-balance-sheet financing, and understand the reasons for this type of financing.

Off-balance-sheet financing is a method companies employ to avoid disclosing obligations in the financial statements. Common examples of off-balance-sheet financing include leasing, unconsolidated subsidiaries, variable interest entities, joint ventures, research and development arrangements, and project financing arrangements. Most areas involving off-balance-sheet financing have been addressed by the FASB, and disclosure associated with the financing arrangement is often required in the notes to the financial statements.

7 Analyze a firm's debt position using ratios.

Ratios can be used to compare a firm's debt position over time or at the same time across companies. The most common measure of a firm's debt position is the debt-to-equity ratio. This ratio compares a firm's liabilities and its stockholders' equity. A common variation on this ratio is to include only long-term debt in the numerator. Times interest earned is another ratio often used to evaluate a company's debt position. This ratio is computed by dividing a firm's income before interest expense and taxes by interest expense for the period.

8 Review the notes to financial statements, and understand the disclosure associated with debt financing.

Common disclosure associated with long-term debt includes information relating to maturities, interest rates, conversion privileges, and debt covenants. The portion of long-term debt coming due in the current period is also disclosed.

EXPANDED MATERIAL

9 Understand the conditions under which troubled debt restructuring occurs, and be able to account for troubled debt restructuring.

When a firm finds itself in financial trouble, options used to alleviate some of the distress are to retire the debt at a reduced amount or to restructure the terms of its debt. Debt can be retired immediately at a reduced value with assets or by trading the debt for stock ownership. Another option for restructuring debt is to modify the terms of the debt. These modifications might include forgoing interest payments, reducing the interest rate on the debt, reducing the amount of the principal, or a combination of these options. If these modifications result in the total payments under the new structure being greater than the carrying value of the debt, no gain is recognized. A gain is recognized, however, if the total payments are less than the debt's current carrying value.

FASB-IASB CODIFICATION SUMMARY

Topic	FASB Accounting Standards Codification	Original FASB Standard	Corresponding IASB Standard	Differences between U.S. GAAP and IFRS
Short-term obligations expected to be refinanced	Section 470-10-45 par. 14	SFAS No. 6 par. 10-11	IAS 1 par. 72	Under IFRS, for a short-term obligation to be classified as long term, the refinancing must take place by the balance sheet date.
Splitting convertible debt proceeds into debt and equity	Subtopic 470-20	APB Opinion No. 14	IAS 32 par. 28-32	Under IFRS, ALL convertible debt issues are divided into their debt and equity components. This separation is only done in certain circumstances under U.S. GAAP.
Consolidation of variable interest entities (VIE)	Section 810-10-25 par. 20 through 59	FIN 46R	SIC 12	Under IFRS, a VIE is consolidated when the economic substance of the relationship indicates that the VIE is controlled. Compared to U.S. GAAP, this is very much a principles-based approach.
Fair value option	Topic 825, "Fair Value Option" subsections	SFAS No. 159	IFRS 9	U.S. GAAP and IFRS are generally consistent.
Troubled debt restructuring	Subtopic 470-60	SFAS No. 15	IAS 39 par. 39 through 41	No substantial differences

KEY TERMS

Account payable 12-8
Amortization 12-23
Bearer (coupon) bonds 12-17
Bond certificates 12-15
Bond discount 12-19
Bond indenture 12-16
Bond issuance costs 12-23
Bond premium 12-19
Bond refinancing 12-34
Callable bonds 12-18
Collateral trust bond 12-17
Commodity-backed bonds 12-18
Convertible bonds 12-18

Convertible debt securities 12-30
Debenture bonds, or debentures 12-17
Debt-to-equity ratio 12-43
Effective-interest method 12-25
Face value, par value, or maturity value 12-16
Hedge 12-36
Joint venture 12-41
Junk bonds 12-17
Liabilities 12-4
Line of credit 12-11
Loan (mortgage) amortization 12-13

Long-term debt 12-14
Market, yield, or effective interest rate 12-19
Mortgage 12-13
Municipal debt 12-16
Nontrade notes payable 12-9
Notes payable 12-9
Off-balance-sheet financing 12-38
Promissory note 12-9
Registered bonds 12-17
Secured bonds 12-16
Secured loan 12-14
Serial bonds 12-16

Stated (contract) rate 12-19
Straight-line method 12-24
Term bonds 12-16
Times interest earned 12-44
Trade notes payable 12-9
Trust indenture 12-15
Unsecured bonds 12-17
Variable interest entity (VIE) 12-39
Zero-interest (deep-discount) bonds 12-17

EXPANDED MATERIAL
Troubled debt restructuring 12-46

Tutorial Activities

Tutorial Activities with author-written, content-specific feedback, available on *CengageNOW* for Stice & Stice.

QUESTIONS

1. Identify the major components included in the definition of *liabilities* established by the FASB.
2. (a) What is meant by *executory contract*?
   (b) Do these contracts fit the definition of liabilities included in this chapter?
3. Distinguish between current and noncurrent liabilities.
4. At what amount should liabilities generally be reported?
5. Under what circumstances is a short-term loan classified among the long-term liabilities on the balance sheet?
6. How does the international standard for classification of short-term obligations to be refinanced differ from U.S. GAAP?
7. What is a line of credit?
8. Why is it important to use present value concepts in properly valuing long-term liabilities?
9. When money is borrowed and monthly payments are made, how does one determine the portion of the payment that is interest and the portion that is principal?
10. Distinguish between (a) secured and unsecured bonds, (b) collateral trust and debenture bonds, (c) convertible and callable bonds, (d) coupon and registered bonds, (e) municipal and corporate bonds, and (f) term and serial bonds.
11. What is meant by *market rate of interest*, *stated or contract rate*, and *effective rate*? Which one of these rates changes during the lifetime of the bond issue?
12. What amortization method for premiums and discounts on bonds is recommended in FASB ASC Section 835-30-35 (Interest—Imputation of Interest—Subsequent Measurement)? Why? When can the alternative method be used?
13. List three ways that bonds are commonly retired prior to maturity. How should the early extinguishment of debt be presented on the income statement?
14. What purpose is served by issuing callable bonds?
15. What are the distinguishing features of convertible debt securities? What questions relate to the nature of this type of security?
16. How does the accounting for convertible debt under *IAS 32* differ from the accounting prescribed by U.S. GAAP?
17. The conversion of convertible bonds to common stock may be viewed as an exchange involving no gain or loss or as a transaction for which market values should be recognized and a gain or loss reported. What arguments support each of these views for the issuer?
18. What is meant by *refinancing* or *refunding* a bond issue? When may refinancing be advisable?
19. Briefly explain the "fair value option."
20. Why did the FASB decide to allow the fair value option?
21. What provision of the fair value option prevents companies from using hindsight to selectively enhance reported results using the fair value option?
22. Why is off-balance-sheet financing popular with many companies? What problems are associated with the use of this method of financing?
23. How can a variable interest entity (VIE) be used as a vehicle for off-balance-sheet financing?
24. What is a joint venture, and how can a joint venture be a form of off-balance-sheet financing?

EXPANDED MATERIAL

25. What distinguishes a troubled debt restructuring from other debt restructurings?
26. What is the recommended accounting treatment for bond restructurings effected as
    (a) An asset swap?
    (b) An equity swap?
    (c) A modification of terms?

PRACTICE EXERCISES

Practice 12-1

Working Capital
Use the following information to compute working capital.

Deferred sales revenue	$ 900
Accounts payable	1,100
Accounts receivable	1,750
Cash	400
Sales	10,000
Accrued wages payable	375
Sales returns and allowances	700
Bonds payable (to be repaid in six months)	1,000
Bonds payable (to be repaid in five years)	4,000

Practice 12-2
Current Ratio
Refer to the data in Practice 12-1. Compute current ratio.

Practice 12-3
Short-Term Obligations Expected to Be Refinanced
The company has the following three loans payable scheduled to be repaid in February of next year. As of December 31 of this year, compute (1) total current liabilities and (2) total noncurrent liabilities.

(a) The company intends to repay Loan A, for $10,000, when it comes due in February. In the following September, the company intends to get a new loan for $8,000 from the same bank.

(b) The company intends to refinance Loan B for $15,000 when it comes due in February. The refinancing contract, for $18,000, will be signed in May, *after* the financial statements for this year have been released.

(c) The company intends to refinance Loan C for $20,000 before it comes due in February. The actual refinancing, for $17,500, took place in January, *before* the financial statements for this year have been released.

Practice 12-4
Total Cost of Line of Credit
The company arranged a line of credit for $500,000 on January 1. The commitment fee is 0.05% (five one-hundredths of 1%) of the total credit line. In addition, the company must pay interest of 5.9% (compounded annually) on any actual loans acquired under the credit line arrangement. This year, the company borrowed $260,000 under the agreement on May 1; this loan was still outstanding at the end of the year. Compute the total cost of the credit line (including interest) for the year.

Practice 12-5
Computation of Monthly Payments
Florence Clark purchased a house for $300,000. She paid cash of 10% of the purchase price and signed a mortgage for the remainder. She will repay the mortgage in monthly payments for 30 years, with the first payment to occur in one month. The interest rate is 7.5% compounded monthly. What is the amount of her monthly payment?

Practice 12-6
Present Value of Future Payments
Refer to Practice 12-5. What is the present value of Florence's monthly mortgage payments after 12 payments have been made?

Practice 12-7
Market Price of a Bond
The company intends to issue 20-year bonds with a face value of $1,000. The bonds carry a coupon rate of 9%, and interest is paid semiannually. On the issue date, the market interest rate for bonds issued by companies with similar risk is 12% compounded semiannually. Compute the market price of one bond on the date of issue.

Practice 12-8
Market Price of a Bond
The company intends to issue 10-year bonds with a face value of $1,000. The bonds carry a coupon rate of 13%, and interest is paid semiannually. On the issue date, the market interest rate for bonds issued by companies with similar risk is 8% compounded semiannually. Compute the market price of one bond on the date of issue.

Practice 12-9
Accounting for Issuance of Bonds
Bonds with a face value of $1,000 were issued for $1,025. Make the necessary journal entry on the books of the issuer.

Practice 12-10
Accounting for Issuance of Bonds
Bonds with a face value of $1,000 were issued for $920. Make the necessary journal entry on the books of the issuer.

Practice 12-11
Bond Issuance between Interest Dates
The company had planned to issue bonds with a face value of $100,000 on January 1. Because of regulatory delays, the bonds were not issued until February 1. The bonds have a coupon rate of 9%, which is equal to

the market rate of interest (for companies of similar risk) on the issue date of February 1. Interest is to be paid semiannually; the first interest payment of $4,500 ($100,000 × 0.09 × 6/12) will be made on July 1, as originally scheduled. Make the journal entry necessary on the books of the issuer on February 1 to record the issuance of these bonds.

Practice 12-12
Straight-Line Amortization
On January 1, the company issued 10-year bonds with a face value of $200,000. The bonds carry a coupon rate of 10%, and interest is paid semiannually. On the issue date, the market interest rate for bonds issued by companies with similar risk was 12% compounded semiannually. The issuance price of the bonds was $177,060. Make the journal entries needed on the books of the issuer to record the first two interest payments on June 30 and December 31. Use straight-line amortization of the bond discount.

Practice 12-13
Effective-Interest Amortization
On January 1, the company issued 10-year bonds with a face value of $200,000. The bonds carry a coupon rate of 10%, and interest is paid semiannually. On the issue date, the market interest rate for bonds issued by companies with similar risk was 12% compounded semiannually. The issuance price of the bonds was $177,060. Make the journal entries needed on the books of the issuer to record the first two interest payments on June 30 and December 31. Use effective-interest amortization of the bond discount.

Practice 12-14
Bond Premiums and Discounts on the Cash Flow Statement
The company has bonds outstanding with a face value of $50,000 and an unamortized premium of $2,350 at the beginning of the year and $2,000 as of the end of the year. Sales (all for cash) were $42,000 for the year. Total interest expense of $4,650 was reported for the year. Because interest expense is the only expense for this company, net income for the year was $37,350 ($42,000 − $4,650). Prepare the Operating Activities section of the cash flow statement using both (1) the direct method and (2) the indirect method.

Practice 12-15
Market Redemption of Bonds
The company has outstanding bonds payable with a total face value of $100,000. On July 1, the company redeemed the bonds by purchasing them on the open market for a total of $102,700. Make the necessary journal entry on the issuer's books to record the redemption of the bonds assuming that (1) the bonds have an unamortized discount of $2,000 and (2) the bonds have an unamortized premium of $2,000.

Practice 12-16
Accounting for Issuance of Convertible Bonds
The company issued convertible bonds with a total face value of $100,000 for $111,000. If the bonds had been issued without the conversion feature, their issuance price would have been $101,000. Make the journal entry necessary to record the issuance of the bonds.

Practice 12-17
Accounting for Conversion of Convertible Bonds
The company has convertible bonds with a total face amount of $100,000 and a carrying value of $98,500. The bonds are converted into 2,000 shares of $1 par common stock. Each share of stock had a market value of $55 on the date of conversion. Make the journal entry to record the conversion. (*Note:* On the bond issuance date, it had been less than reasonably possible that the bonds would eventually be converted. In other words, ultimate conversion had been viewed as an unlikely event.)

Practice 12-18
Fair Value Option
The company has one asset, a bond (called Bond B) that it purchased (on the day it was issued) as an investment, and one liability, one of its own bonds (called Bond X) that the company issued to finance the purchase of the Bond B investment. The company had no initial shareholder investment. Both bonds have the same terms: $1,000 face value, 30-year life, 8% coupon rate, and single interest payments made at the end of each year. On their issuance dates, both bonds were associated with a market interest rate of 8%. The company has determined to account for both the bond asset and the bond liability using the fair value option. (1) Prepare a balance sheet for the company as of the issuance date of investment Bond B and the company's own Bond Payable X. (2) On the very next day, the market interest rate with respect to Bond B had risen to 13% and the market interest rate with respect to Bond Payable X had risen to 11%. Prepare the company's balance sheet.

Practice 12-19

Debt-to-Equity Ratio
Consider the following information:

Short-term debt.	$ 12,000
Interest expense	8,200
Total current liabilities.	27,000
Long-term debt.	93,000
Cash	6,200
Total liabilities.	130,000
Total stockholders' equity	85,000
Income before income taxes	19,000

Compute the debt-to-equity ratio assuming that (1) *debt* is defined to include all liabilities, (2) *debt* is defined to include just interest-bearing debt, and (3) *debt* is defined to include just long-term, interest-bearing debt.

Practice 12-20

Times Interest Earned Ratio
Refer to Practice 12-19. Compute the times interest earned ratio.

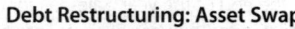

Practice 12-21

Debt Restructuring: Asset Swap
The company has bonds payable with a total face value of $100,000 and a carrying value of $103,000. In addition, unpaid interest on the bonds has been accrued in the amount of $6,000. The lender has agreed to the settlement of the bonds in exchange for land worth $90,000. The land has a historical cost of $64,000. Make the journal entry necessary on the books of the borrower to record this settlement of the bonds payable.

Practice 12-22

Debt Restructuring: Equity Swap
The company has bonds payable with a total face value of $150,000 and a carrying value of $142,000. In addition, unpaid interest on the bonds has been accrued in the amount of $8,000. The lender has agreed to the settlement of the bonds in exchange for 20,000 shares of $1 par common stock. The shares have a current market value of $140,000. Make the journal entry necessary on the books of the borrower to record this settlement of the bonds payable.

Practice 12-23

Debt Restructuring: Substantial Modification
On January 1, the company obtained a $10,000, 8% loan. The $800 interest is payable at the end of each year, with the principal amount to be repaid in five years. As of the end of the year, the first year's interest of $800 is not yet paid because the company is experiencing financial difficulties. The company negotiated a restructuring of the loan. The payment of all of the interest ($4,000 = $800 × 5 years) will be delayed until the end of the loan term. In addition, the amount of principal repayment will be dropped from $10,000 to $5,000. (1) Make the journal entry necessary on the company's books to record this debt restructuring. (2) Compute the amount of interest expense that will be recognized *next* year.

Practice 12-24

Debt Restructuring: Slight Modification
Refer to Practice 12-23. Assume all of the same facts except that the principal repayment amount will be dropped to $8,000 (from $10,000) instead of to $5,000. (1) Make the journal entry necessary on the company's books to record this debt restructuring. (2) Compute the amount of interest expense that will be recognized *next* year.

EXERCISES

Exercise 12-25

Accounting for Mortgages
On January 1, 2015, Lily Company purchased a building for $1,000,000. The company made a 25% down payment and took out a mortgage payable over 30 years with monthly payments of $5,503.23. The first payment is due February 1, 2015. The mortgage interest rate is 8%.

1. Determine how much of the first two mortgage payments would be applied to interest expense and how much would be applied to reducing the principal. (*Note:* The 8% interest rate is compounded monthly.)
2. Make the journal entry necessary to record the first mortgage payment on February 1, 2015.

Exercise 12-26

Mortgage Amortization Schedule
On July 1, 2015, Ketchikan Inc. borrowed $90,000 to finance the purchase of machinery. The terms of the mortgage require payments to be made at the end of every month with the first payment of $1,589 being due on July 31, 2015. The length of the mortgage is seven years, and the mortgage carries an interest rate of 12% compounded monthly.

1. Prepare a mortgage amortization schedule for the last six months of 2015.
2. How much interest expense will be reported in 2015 in connection with this mortgage?
3. What amount will be reported in Ketchikan's balance sheet as mortgage liability at the end of 2015?

Exercise 12-27

Computation of Market Values of Bond Issues
What is the market value of each of the following bond issues? (*Note:* Round to the nearest dollar.)

(a) 10% bonds of $1,000,000 sold on bond issue date; 10-year life; interest payable semiannually; effective rate, 12%
(b) 9% bonds of $200,000 sold on bond issue date; five-year life; interest payable semiannually; effective rate, 8%
(c) 8% bonds of $150,000 sold 30 months after bond issue date; 15-year life; interest payable semiannually; effective rate, 10%

Exercise 12-28

Selling Bonds at Par, Premium, or Discount
In each of the following independent cases, state whether the bonds were issued at par, a premium, or a discount. Explain your answers.

(a) Pop-up Manufacturing sold 1,500 of its $1,000, 8% stated-rate bonds when the market rate was 7%.
(b) Splendor, Inc., sold 500 of its $2,000, 8 3/4% bonds to yield 9%.
(c) Cards Corporation issued 1,000 of its 9%, $100 face value bonds at an effective rate of 9 1/2%.
(d) Floppy, Inc., sold 3,000 of its 10% bonds with a face value of $2,500 at a time when the market rate was 9%.
(e) Cintron Co. sold 5,000 of its 12% contract-rate bonds with a stated value of $1,000 at an effective rate of 12%.

Exercise 12-29

Zero-Coupon Bonds
George's Inc. is considering issuing bonds to finance the acquisition of a nationwide chain of distributors of George's products. George's is contemplating two different types of bonds to raise the required $90 million purchase price. The first is a traditional 10-year, 14% bond with semiannual interest payments. The second is a 10-year, zero-coupon bond.

Assuming the market rate of interest is 14%, compute the face value of the bond issuance and make the journal entries necessary to record the issuance if (a) a traditional bond is issued and (b) a zero-coupon bond is issued.

Exercise 12-30

Issuance and Reacquisition of Bonds
On January 1, 2014, Housen Company issued 10-year bonds of $500,000 at 102. Interest is payable on January 1 and July 1 at 10%. On April 1, 2015, Housen Company reacquires and retires 50 of its own $1,000 bonds at 98 plus accrued interest. The fiscal period for Housen Company is the calendar year.

Prepare entries to record (1) the issuance of the bonds, (2) the interest payments and adjustments relating to the debt in 2014, (3) the reacquisition and retirement of bonds in 2015, and (4) the interest payments and adjustments relating to the debt in 2015. Assume the premium or discount is amortized on a straight-line basis. (*Note:* Round to the nearest dollar.)

Exercise 12-31

Amortization of Bond Premium or Discount
On January 1, 2014, Terrel Company sold $100,000 of 10-year, 8% bonds at 93.5, an effective rate of 9%. Interest is to be paid on July 1 and December 31. Compute the amount of premium or discount amortization in 2014 and 2015 using (1) the straight-line method and (2) the effective-interest method. Make the journal entries to record the amortization when the effective-interest method is used.

Exercise 12-32

Bond Interest and Premium or Discount Amortization
Assume that $140,000 of Denham Springs School District 8% bonds are sold on the bond issue date for $128,598. Interest is payable semiannually, and the bonds mature in 15 years. The purchase price provides a return of 9% on the investment.

1. What entries would be made on the investor's books for the receipt of the first two interest payments, assuming premium or discount amortization on each interest date by (a) the straight-line method and (b) the effective-interest method? (*Note:* Round to the nearest dollar.)
2. What entries would be made on Denham Springs School District's books to record the first two interest payments, assuming premium or discount amortization on each interest date by (a) the straight-line method and (b) the effective-interest method? (*Note:* Round to the nearest dollar.)

Exercise 12-33

Discount and Premium Amortization
Tanzanite Corporation issued $500,000 of 7% debentures to yield 11%, receiving $424,624. Interest is payable semiannually, and the bonds mature in five years.

1. What entries would be made by Tanzanite for the first two interest payments, assuming premium or discount amortization on interest dates by (a) the straight-line method and (b) the effective-interest method? (*Note:* Round to the nearest dollar.)
2. What entries would be made on the books of the investor for the first two interest receipts, assuming premium or discount amortization on interest dates and that one party obtained all the bonds and used the straight-line method of amortization? (*Note:* Round to the nearest dollar.)
3. If the sale is made to yield 5%, $543,760 being received, what entries would be made by Tanzanite for the first two interest payments, assuming premium or discount amortization on interest dates by (a) the straight-line method and (b) the effective-interest method? (*Note:* Round to the nearest dollar.)

Exercise 12-34

Sale of Bond Investment
Jennifer Stack acquired $50,000 of Oldtown Corp. 9% bonds on July 1, 2012. The bonds were acquired at 92; interest is paid semiannually on March 1 and September 1. The bonds mature September 1, 2019. Stack's books are kept on a calendar-year basis. On February 1, 2015, Stack sold the bonds for 97 plus accrued interest. Assuming straight-line amortization and no reversing entry at January 1, 2015, give the entry to record the sale of the bonds on February 1. (*Note:* Round to the nearest dollar.)

Exercise 12-35

Retirement of Debt before Maturity
The Long-Term Debt section of Rodman Company's balance sheet as of December 31, 2014, included 8% bonds payable of $300,000 less unamortized discount of $22,000. Further examination revealed that these bonds were issued to yield 11%. The amortization of the bond discount was recorded using the effective-interest method. Interest was paid on January 1 and July 1 of each year. On July 1, 2015, Rodman retired the bonds at 104 before maturity.
    Prepare the journal entries to record the July 1, 2015, payment of interest, including the amortization of the discount since December 31, 2014, and the early retirement on the books of Rodman Company.

Exercise 12-36

Retirement of Bonds
The December 31, 2014, balance sheet of Spring Company includes the following items:

8% bonds payable due December 31, 2021	$200,000
Premium on bonds payable	8,750

The bonds were issued on December 31, 2013, at 105, with interest payable on June 30 and December 31 of each year. The straight-line method is used for premium amortization.

On April 1, 2015, Spring retired $100,000 of these bonds at 99 plus accrued interest. Prepare the journal entries to record retirement of the bonds, including accrual of interest since the last payment and amortization of the premium.

Exercise 12-37

Retirement and Refinancing of Bonds

Chiam Corporation has $300,000 of 12% bonds, callable at 102, with a remaining 10-year term, and interest payable semiannually. The bonds are currently valued on the books at $290,000, and the company has just made the interest payment and adjustments for amortization of any premium or discount. Similar bonds can be marketed currently at 10% and would sell at par.

1. Give the journal entries to retire the old debt and issue $300,000 of new 10% bonds at par.
2. In what year will the reduction in interest offset the cost of refinancing the bond issue?

Exercise 12-38

Issuance of Convertible Bonds

Joy Insurance decides to finance expansion of its physical facilities by issuing convertible debenture bonds. The terms of the bonds follow: maturity date 10 years after May 1, 2014, the date of issuance; conversion at option of holder after two years; 20 shares of $1 par value stock for each $1,000 bond held; interest rate of 12% and call provision on the bonds of 102. The bonds were sold at 101.

1. Give the entry on Joy's books to record the sale of $900,000 of bonds on July 1, 2014; interest payment dates are May 1 and November 1.
2. Assume the same condition as in (1) except that the sale of the bonds is to be recorded in a manner that will recognize a value related to the conversion feature. The estimated sales price of the bonds without the conversion feature is 98.

Exercise 12-39

Convertible Bonds

Clarkston Inc. issued $1,000,000 of convertible 10-year, 11% bonds on July 1, 2014. The interest is payable semiannually on January 1 and July 1. The discount in connection with the issue was $9,500, which is amortized monthly using the straight-line basis. The debentures are convertible after one year into five shares of the company's $1 par common stock for each $1,000 of bonds.

On August 1, 2015, $100,000 of the bonds were converted. Interest has been accrued monthly and paid as due. Any interest accrued at the time of conversion of the bonds is paid in cash.

Prepare the journal entries on Clarkston's books to record the conversion, amortization, and interest on the bonds as of August 1 and August 31, 2015. (*Note:* Round to the nearest dollar. On the bond issuance date, it had been at least reasonably possible that the bonds would eventually be converted.)

Exercise 12-40

Fair Value Option

Ryan Marie Company has one asset, a bond issued by Miles Company that Ryan Marie purchased (on the day it was issued) as an investment. Ryan Marie also has only one liability, one of its own bonds that was to finance the purchase of the Miles bond investment. The company had no initial shareholder investment. Both bonds have the same terms: $1,000 face value, 10-year life, 11% coupon rate, and single interest payments made at the end of each year. On their issuance dates, both bonds were associated with a market interest rate of 8%. The company has determined to account for both the bond asset and the bond liability using the fair value option.

1. Prepare a balance sheet for Ryan Marie Company as of the date it both purchased the Miles bond investment and issued its own bonds payable.
2. On the very next day, the market interest rate with respect to the Miles bond investment had risen to 13%, and the market interest rate with respect to Ryan Marie's bond had risen to 11%. Prepare the company's balance sheet.
3. Repeat (2) but this time assume that the market interest rate for the Miles bond had gone down to 6%, and the market interest rate of the Ryan Marie bond had increased to 14%.
4. Repeat (2) but this time assume that the market interest rate for the Miles bond had increased to 14%, and the market interest rate of the Ryan Marie bond had gone down to 6%.

EXPANDED MATERIAL

Exercise 12-41

Troubled Debt Restructuring—Asset Swap

McKeon Machine Company has outstanding a $210,000 note payable to Tejon Investment Corporation. Because of financial difficulties, McKeon negotiates with Tejon to exchange inventory of machine parts to satisfy the debt. The cost of the inventory transferred is carried on McKeon's books at $160,000. The estimated retail value of the inventory is $195,000. McKeon uses a perpetual inventory system. Prepare journal entries for the exchange on the books of McKeon Machine Company according to the requirements of ASC Subtopic 470-60.

Exercise 12-42

Troubled Debt Restructuring—Equity Swap

MedQuest Enterprises is threatened with bankruptcy due to its inability to meet interest payments and fund requirements to retire $5,000,000 of long-term notes. The notes are all held by Dynasty Insurance Company. In order to prevent bankruptcy, MedQuest has entered into an agreement with Dynasty to exchange equity securities for the debt. The terms of the exchange are as follows: 300,000 shares of $1 par common stock, current market value $10 per share, and 24,000 shares of $10 par preferred stock, current market value $65 per share. Prepare journal entries for the exchange on the books of MedQuest Enterprises according to the requirements of ASC Subtopic 470-60.

Exercise 12-43

Modification of Debt Terms

Moriarty Co. is experiencing financial difficulties. Income has exhibited a downward trend, and the company reported its first loss in company history this past year. The firm has been unable to service its debt and, as a result, has missed two semiannual interest payments. In an attempt to turn the company around, management has negotiated a modification of its debt terms with bondholders. These modified terms are effective January 1, 2015. The bonds are $10,000,000, 10-year, 10% bonds that were issued on January 2, 2010, and currently have an unamortized premium of $210,000. Prepare the necessary journal entries on Moriarty's books for each of the following independent situations.

(a) Bondholders agree to forgive past-due interest and reduce the interest rate on the debt from 10% to 5%.

(b) Bondholders agree to forgive past-due interest and forgive $3,000,000 of the face amount of the debt.

(c) Bondholders agree to forgive past-due interest, reduce the interest rate on the debt from 10% to 6%, and forgive $2,000,000 of the face value of the debt.

P3
Additional Activities of a Business

CHAPTER 13

Equity Financing

Learning Objectives

1. Identify the rights associated with ownership of common and preferred stock.
2. Record the issuance of stock for cash, on a subscription basis, and in exchange for noncash assets or for services.
3. Use both the cost and par value methods to account for stock repurchases.
4. Account for the issuance of stock rights and stock warrants.
5. Compute the compensation expense associated with the granting of employee stock options.
6. Determine which equity-related items should be reported in the balance sheet as liabilities.
7. Distinguish between stock conversions that require a reduction in retained earnings and those that do not.
8. List the factors that impact the Retained Earnings balance.
9. Properly record cash dividends, property dividends, small and large stock dividends, and stock splits.
10. Prepare a statement of comprehensive incomes, explain the background of unrealized gains and losses recorded as part of accumulated other comprehensive income, and list the major types of equity reserves found in foreign balance sheets.
11. Prepare a statement of changes in stockholders' equity.

Bill Gates is one of the two richest people in the United States. (The other one is mentioned further down—keep reading.) Microsoft, the company Bill Gates founded with partner Paul Allen in 1975, was originally best known for developing the first-generation DOS operating system used with IBM personal computers and their clones. Microsoft subsequently came to dominate (some would say monopolize) the software market with popular software packages such as Word,® Excel,® and PowerPoint,® based on its Windows® operating system.

In 1985, Microsoft decided to issue its stock publicly for the first time. Before this time, Microsoft had stock outstanding, but the stock was held by company officials and employees and was not publicly traded. A key consideration, of course, was what price to charge

Exhibit 13-1 | Microsoft's Price per Share of Stock

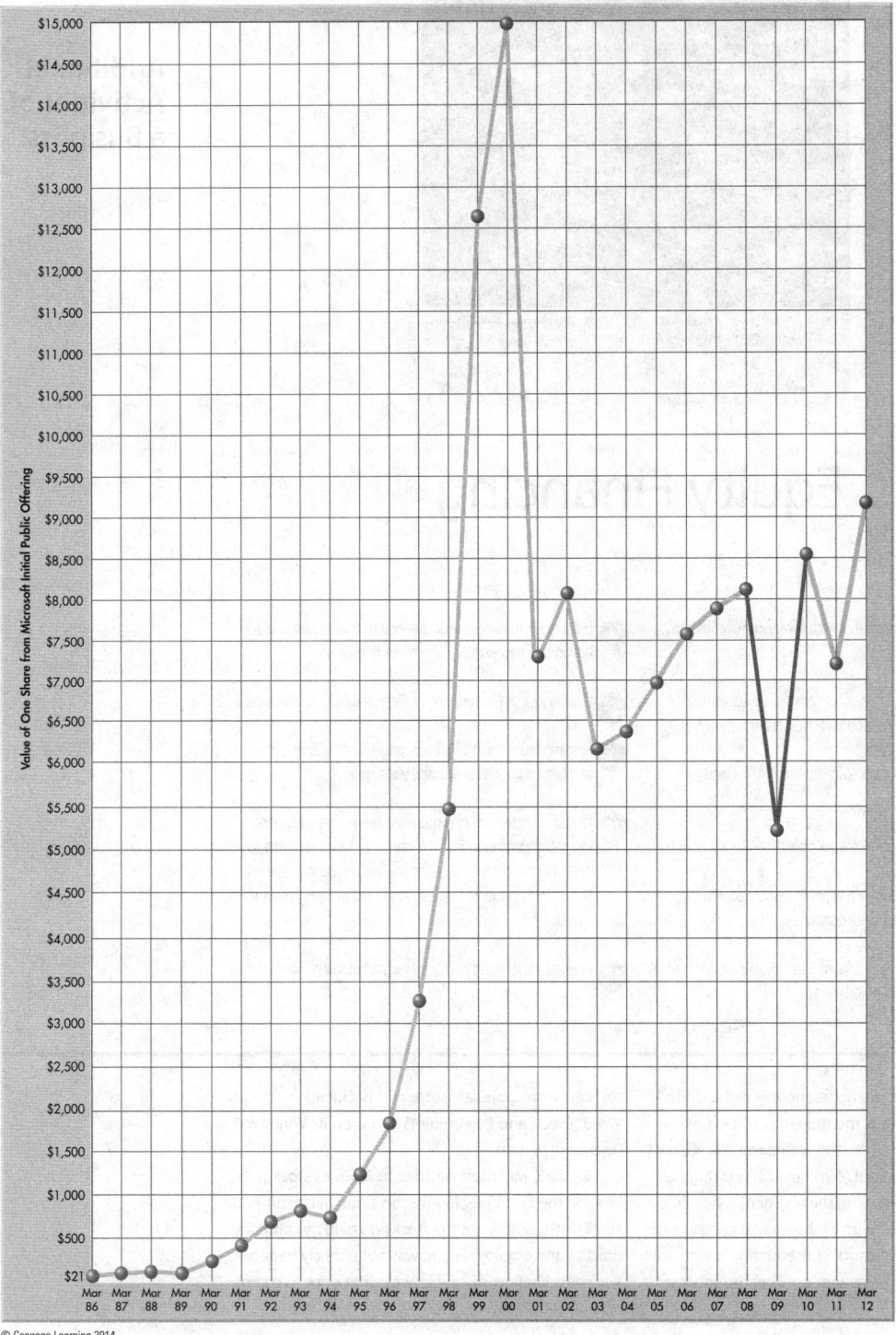

when issuing the shares. An initial price range of $16 to $19 per share was set, based on Microsoft's earnings per share and the price-earnings (P/E) ratios for similar firms that already had publicly traded stock. The large amount of interest in the Microsoft stock issue resulted in the final offering price being raised to $21 per share. On March 13, 1986, Microsoft shares were first publicly traded, and by the end of the first day of trading, the shares were at $27.75.[1] If you had purchased one of those initial shares for $21 in 1986, by December 1999 it would have been worth almost $15,000. (See Exhibit 13-1.) By December 2000, that same share of stock would have declined in value to $5,489 as a result of both the bursting of the dot.com bubble and the continued uncertainty about Microsoft's future caused by the antitrust lawsuits against the company. In June 2012, Microsoft had recovered some of its lost value, with one of the initial shares being worth $8,390.

A share of Microsoft stock does not trade for $8,390 because, since 1986, Microsoft has split its stock several times. A split is like cutting a pie into more pieces—the number of shares is increased and the price of each share is reduced proportionately. Most firms use stock splits to maintain their per-share price in the range that is considered normal, usually between $20 and $80 per share in the United States.

A glaring exception to this price-per-share range is stock of Berkshire Hathaway, which is headed by Warren Buffett, who annually vies with Bill Gates for the title of richest person in the United States. Buffett's company is involved in a number of diverse lines of business. Its largest operations are in property and casualty insurance; Geico is owned by Berkshire Hathaway. However, it also produces and sells Kirby vacuums, See's Candies, and World Book encyclopedias. In addition, Berkshire Hathaway has a substantial investment portfolio: It owns 13.0% of American Express, 8.8% of Coca-Cola, 5.5% of IBM, and 7.6% of Wells Fargo.[2] In fact, a whole industry has built up around financial analysts who interpret the investment choices made by Warren Buffett.

Because Berkshire Hathaway has been very profitable and has never split its stock, its price per share has risen higher than any other stock on the New York Stock Exchange. On June 13, 2012, Berkshire Hathaway shares closed at $120,855 each.[3]

By the way, in the 2011 annual *Forbes* survey of America's richest people, Bill Gates ($59 billion) beat out Warren Buffett ($39 billion) as the richest person in the United States for the 18th straight year.[4]

---

1. If you had purchased Microsoft stock in December 1999 and sold it in June 2012, what percentage return on your investment would you have earned during that time interval?

2. What is Berkshire Hathaway's relationship with Coca-Cola?

3. In the year 2012, Microsoft's price per share was around $29, whereas the price per share for Berkshire Hathaway was about $120,855. What additional information would you need to determine which company had a higher total market value?

Answers to these questions can be found on page 13-52.

Owner investments are reported in the Equity section of the balance sheet. For example, when a corporation issues new shares of stock to the public, the proceeds are recorded in the Equity section. These invested funds are called *contributed*, or *paid-in, capital*. Owners also contribute funds to a company by allowing profits to be reinvested. In a corporation, these reinvested profits are called *retained earnings*. In sole proprietorships and partnerships, paid-in capital and retained earnings are lumped

---

[1] Bro Uttal, "Inside the Deal That Made Bill Gates $350,000,000," *Fortune*, July 21, 1986, p. 23.
[2] From the 2011 Annual Report of Berkshire Hathaway.
[3] In May 1996, the shareholders of Berkshire Hathaway approved the creation of a new class of shares, called *Class B shares*. Originally, each of these shares had 1/30 the value of the original Class A shares. A 50-for-1 stock split of these shares in January 2010 now makes each B share worth 1/1,500 the value of the A shares. These actions were taken to head off some investment companies that had started buying Berkshire Hathaway shares, carving them up, and selling shares of the shares.
[4] In the 2011 *Forbes* survey, Warren Buffett was ahead of Paul Allen ($13.2 billion), who was Bill Gates' partner in the founding of Microsoft. Also, the five heirs to Sam Walton's Wal-Mart fortune had a combined net worth of $90 billion, making them the wealthiest family in America.

together into a single capital account. This chapter emphasizes the accounting for equity of corporations.

In a simple world, the Equity section of a corporation's balance sheet would include only the two sections just mentioned, paid-in capital and retained earnings. However, the increasing complexity of worldwide business necessitates a number of other equity items. For example, some equity-related items must be reported as liabilities in the balance sheet. In addition, unrealized gains or losses on some investment securities are shown in a separate equity category, as is the impact of foreign currency fluctuations on the equity of foreign subsidiaries. The items that can appear in the Equity section are summarized in Exhibit 13-2 and are discussed in the remainder of the chapter.

Although many items affect owners' equity, the major decisions associated with owner investment are illustrated in the time line in Exhibit 13-3. Note that many of the issues associated with transactions involving owners may or may not occur during

Exhibit 13-2 | Equity Items

Stockholders' Equity
Contributed capital:
Preferred stock
Common stock
Additional paid-in capital
Retained earnings
Less: Treasury stock
Accumulated other comprehensive income:
Foreign currency translation adjustment
Unrealized gains and losses on available-for-sale securities
Unrealized gains and losses on some derivatives
Noncontrolling interest
Total stockholders' equity

© Cengage Learning 2014

Exhibit 13-3 | Time Line of Issues Associated with Owners' Equity

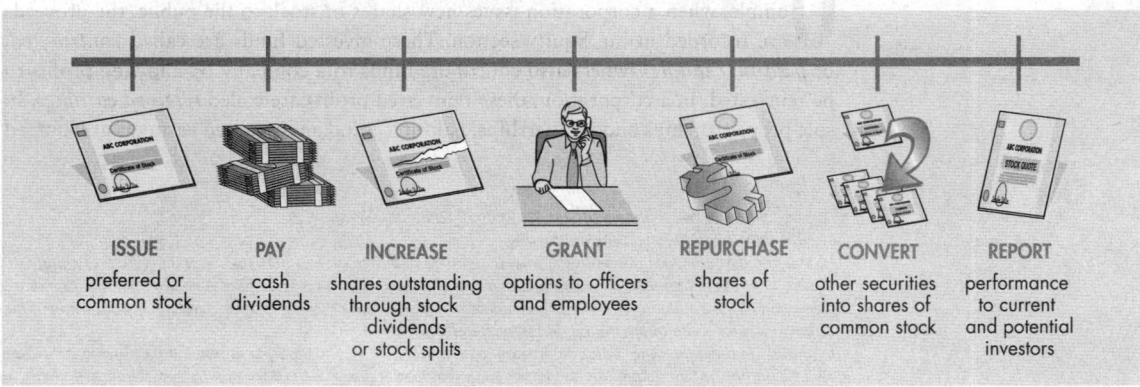

ISSUE preferred or common stock | PAY cash dividends | INCREASE shares outstanding through stock dividends or stock splits | GRANT options to officers and employees | REPURCHASE shares of stock | CONVERT other securities into shares of common stock | REPORT performance to current and potential investors

© Cengage Learning 2014

any given period. Dividends may or may not be paid, and options may or may not be granted. This chapter discusses many of the possible actions that may be taken by management that will affect owners' equity.

Nature and Classifications of Paid-In Capital

LO1 学习目标1
区别普通股与优先股的相关权利。

① Identify the rights associated with ownership of common and preferred stock.

A corporation is a legal, artificial entity that has an existence separate from its owners and may engage in business within prescribed limits just as if it were a real person. The modern corporation makes it possible for large amounts of resources to be assembled under one management. These resources are transferred to the corporation by individual owners, and in exchange for these resources, the corporation issues stock certificates evidencing ownership interests.[5] Stockholders elect a board of directors whose members oversee the strategic and long-run planning for the corporation. The directors select managers who supervise the day-to-day operations of the corporation.

Corporations are typically created under the incorporating laws of one of the 50 states. Because the states do not follow a uniform incorporating act, the conditions under which corporations may be created and under which they may operate are somewhat varied. Many businesses are incorporated in Delaware because constraints on cash dividends are loose, and Delaware laws governing corporations are generally seen as being "pro-business." In fact, of the 1,471 publicly traded companies in the United States with market values greater than $1 billion as of the end of the first quarter of 2004, more than 50% (752 of 1,471) were incorporated in Delaware.

In theory, regulation of corporations is strictly a state matter falling outside the jurisdiction of federal authorities. However, in practice almost all issues of stock to the public fall under the jurisdiction of the federal Securities and Exchange Commission (SEC). Exceptions are made when an issue is small (less than $1 million in any 12-month period), is made only to "accredited" investors (informed investors such as banks, investment companies, issuing company officers, and individuals with net worth exceeding $1 million), or is made only to residents of a single state.

When a corporation is formed, a single class of stock, known as *common stock*, is usually issued. Corporations may later find that there are advantages to issuing one or more additional classes of stock with varying rights and priorities. Stock with certain preferences (rights) over common stock is called *preferred stock*.

FYI

Boards of directors are composed of top managers of the company, top executives from other companies, prominent civic officials, and major shareholders. For example, the 2012 board of The Coca-Cola Company included Peter Ueberroth, former head of the Los Angeles Olympics Committee (1984) and former commissioner of Major League Baseball, and Alexis Herman, former U.S. Secretary of Labor and former director of Public Liaison for the White House.

---

[5] Briefly, the advantages of organizing a business as a corporation instead of as a sole proprietorship or partnership are that the investors in a corporation have limited liability (they can lose only what they put in; their other personal assets are safe), and ownership interest is easily transferable (there is no need to get approval from the other shareholders before selling your shares). The primary disadvantage is that corporate income is taxed twice: once at the corporate level and again at the individual level when shareholders receive cash dividends.

Common Stock

common stock
普通股

The owners of the common stock of a corporation can be thought of as the true owners of the business. If the corporation does poorly, the common stockholders are likely to lose some or all of their investment because they can receive cash from the corporation only after the claims of all other parties (i.e., lenders, employees, government, preferred stockholders) are satisfied. On the other hand, if the corporation does well, the common stockholders reap the benefit because they own all assets in excess of those needed to satisfy the fixed claims of others. In summary, the common stockholders bear the greatest risk, but they also stand to receive the highest return on their investment.

Unless restricted by terms of the articles of incorporation, certain basic rights are held by each common stockholder. These rights are as follows:

1. To vote in the election of directors and in the determination of certain corporate policies such as the management compensation plan or major corporate acquisitions.
2. To maintain one's proportional interest in the corporation through purchase of additional common stock if and when it is issued. This right is known as the *preemptive right* and ensures that a common stockholder's ownership percentage cannot be diluted against his or her will. In recent years, some states have eliminated the preemptive right.

Usually, each corporation has only one class of common stock. However, a recent phenomenon is the creation of multiple classes of common stock, each with slightly different ownership privileges. For example, **Google** has two classes of common stock. Google Class B common is held almost exclusively by insiders and is not publicly traded. Each share of Class B common has 10 votes in board elections, compared to one vote for each share of the publicly traded Class A common. With this share structure, Google is able to raise equity funding through issuance of Class A shares without seriously diluting voting control. Berkshire Hathaway, discussed in the opening scenario of this chapter, has created some Class B common shares that have 1/1,500 the value of the Class A shares—for those investors (such as you and the authors) who might not have the $120,855 necessary to buy one share of Berkshire's Class A shares. However, to repeat, most corporations have only one class of common stock.

> **FYI**
>
> Outside the United States, corporations sometimes have different classes of shares for local investors and for foreign investors. For example, Chinese corporations can have two classes of shares that trade on the Shanghai and Shenzhen stock exchanges: A shares, which only Chinese citizens (and selected foreign institutional investors) can own, and B shares, which can be purchased by foreigners. In February 2001, regulations were loosened, allowing Chinese citizens with approved foreign currency accounts to trade in B shares. Chinese B shares traded on The Stock Exchange of Hong Kong are called *H shares*. Shares of Chinese companies that trade on a U.S. exchange are called *N shares* (for "New York").

Par or Stated Value of Stock

The journal entry to record the issuance of common stock in exchange for cash frequently looks something like this:

Cash	XXX
Common Stock (at par value)..	XXX
Additional Paid-In Capital	XXX

Historically, par value was equal to the market value of the shares at issuance. Par value was also sometimes viewed by the courts as the minimum contribution by investors.[6] Accordingly, when corporate assets were insufficient to cover corporate liabilities, investors who had contributed less than par value were required to cover the shortfall. As a consequence, corporations began to issue shares with lower par values in order to protect investors. In addition, state incorporation laws were written to prevent payment of cash dividends whenever operating losses reduced corporate equity below total par value of shares issued. Lower par values allowed corporations more flexibility in their cash dividend policy.

> **FYI**
>
> Legal capital constraints are not usually a limiting factor for payment of cash dividends. More frequently, payment of dividends is restricted by debt covenants imposed by lenders. A typical debt covenant might require maintenance of a debt-to-equity ratio below a certain amount.

Today, most stocks have either a nominal par value or no par value at all. No-par stock sometimes has a stated value that, for financial reporting purposes, functions exactly like a par value. As can be seen from Exhibit 13-4, 84.6% of publicly traded stocks in the United States have par values of $1 or less.

Preferred Stock

The term *preferred stock* is somewhat misleading because it gives the impression that preferred stock is better than common stock. Preferred stock isn't better—it's different. In fact, a useful way to think of preferred stock is that preferred stockholders give up many of the rights of ownership in exchange for some of the protection enjoyed by creditors.

The rights of ownership given up by preferred stockholders are:

- *Voting.* In most cases, preferred stockholders are not allowed to vote for the board of directors. Voting rights can exist under circumstances specific to each preferred stock issue. For example, some preferred stockholders are granted corporate voting rights if the company fails to pay them cash dividends for, say, two consecutive quarters. When a company fails to pay preferred dividends, those dividends are said to have been "passed."

Exhibit 13-4 | Par Values of Publicly Traded Stocks

Par or Stated Values Publicly Traded Stocks in the United States For the Year 2003		
	All Firms	Only Firms with Market Value Greater Than $1 Billion
Less than $0.01	24.4%	9.9%
Exactly $0.01	36.7	38.0
Between $0.01 and $1.00	15.3	18.8
Exactly $1.00	8.2	13.2
Greater than $1.00	15.4	20.1

Source: Standard and Poor's *COMPUSTAT*. The database includes firms traded on the New York, American, and NASDAQ exchanges.

---

[6] For a more complete discussion of the legal significance of par value, see Philip McGough, "The Legal Significance of the Par Value of Common Stock: What Accounting Educators Should Know," *Issues in Accounting Education*, Fall 1988, pp. 330–350.

- *Sharing in success.* The cash dividends received by preferred stockholders are usually fixed in amount. Therefore, if the company does exceptionally well, preferred stockholders do not get to share in the success. As a result of this cap on dividends, the market value of preferred stock does not typically vary with the success of the company as does the price of common stock. Instead, the market value of preferred stock varies with changes in interest rates, in much the same way as bond prices change.

The protections enjoyed by preferred stockholders, relative to common stockholders, are:

- *Cash dividend preference.* Preferred stockholders are entitled to receive their full cash dividend before any cash dividends are paid to common stockholders.
- *Liquidation preference.* If the company goes bankrupt, preferred stockholders are entitled to have their investment repaid, in full, before common stockholders receive anything.

A later section in the chapter discusses in more detail the securities, such as preferred stock, that share the characteristics of both debt and equity. As financial markets become more sophisticated, the line between debt and equity continues to blur and disclosure issues associated with these hybrid securities become even more important.

Preferred stock is generally issued with a par value. When preferred stock has a par value, the dividend is stated in terms of a percentage of par value. When preferred stock is no par, the dividend must be stated in terms of dollars and cents. Thus, holders of 5% preferred stock with a $50 par value are entitled to an annual dividend of $2.50 per share before any distribution is made to common stockholders; holders of $5 no-par preferred stock are entitled to an annual dividend of $5 per share before dividends are paid to common stockholders.

A corporation may issue more than one class of preferred stock. For example, Citigroup described 14 classes of preferred stock in the notes to its 2008 financial statements; only four classes remained outstanding at the end of 2009. The classes vary in terms of dividend rates, redemption requirements, convertibility, and other features.

Cumulative and Noncumulative Preferred Stock When a corporation fails to declare dividends on cumulative preferred stock, such dividends accumulate and require payment in the future before any dividends may be paid to common stockholders.

For example, assume that Good Time Corporation has outstanding 100,000 shares of 9% cumulative preferred stock, $10 par. Dividends were last paid in 2012. Total dividends of $300,000 are declared in 2015 by the board of directors. The majority of this amount will be paid to the preferred shareholders as follows:

	Dividends to Preferred Shareholders	Dividends to Common Shareholders	Total Dividends
Cumulative dividend for 2013	$ 90,000	—	$ 90,000
Cumulative dividend for 2014	90,000	—	90,000
Dividends for 2015	90,000	$30,000	120,000
Total	$270,000	$30,000	$300,000

Dividends on cumulative preferred stock that are passed are referred to as dividends in arrears. Although these dividends are not a liability until declared by the board of directors, this information is important to stockholders and other users of the financial statements. The amount of dividends in arrears is disclosed in the notes to the financial statements. For example, Harrah's Entertainment, Inc., a large U.S. corporation that owns several casinos, hotels, and golf courses, disclosed in the notes to its 2009 financial statements that it had $652.6 million of dividends in arrears.[7]

With noncumulative preferred stock, it is not necessary to provide for passed dividends. A dividend omission on preferred stock in any one year means it is irretrievably lost. Dividends may be declared on common stock as long as the preferred stock receives the preferred rate for the current period. Thus, in the previous example, if the preferred stock were noncumulative, the 2015 dividends would be distributed as follows:

	Dividends to Preferred Shareholders	Dividends to Common Shareholders	Total Dividends
Dividend passed in 2013	—	—	—
Dividend passed in 2014	—	—	—
Dividends for 2015	$90,000	$210,000	$300,000
Total	$90,000	$210,000	$300,000

Preferred stock contracts normally provide for cumulative dividends. Also, courts have generally held that dividend rights on preferred stock are cumulative in the absence of specific provisions to the contrary.

Participating Preferred Stock Dividends on preferred stock are generally of a fixed amount. However, participating preferred stock issues provide for additional dividends to be paid to preferred stockholders after dividends of a specified amount are paid to the common stockholders. A participative provision makes preferred stock more like common stock. Although once quite common, participating preferred stocks are now relatively rare.

Convertible Preferred Stock Preferred stock is convertible when it can be exchanged by its owner for some other security of the issuing corporation. Conversion rights generally provide for the exchange of preferred stock into common stock. Conversion of preferred stock into common stock would be attractive when the company has done well, allowing the preferred shareholders to escape from the preferred dividend limits. In some instances, preferred stock may be convertible into bonds, thus allowing investors the option of changing their positions from stockholders to creditors. The journal entries required for stock conversions are illustrated later in the chapter. Consideration of convertible preferred stock is important in the calculation of diluted earnings per share; this is discussed in Chapter 18.

Callable Preferred Stock Many preferred issues are callable, meaning they may be called and cancelled at the option of the corporation. The call price is usually specified in the original agreement and provides for payment of dividends in arrears as part of the repurchase price.

Redeemable Preferred Stock Redeemable preferred stock is preferred stock that is redeemable at the option of the stockholder or upon other conditions not within the control of the issuer (e.g., redemption on a specific date or upon reaching a certain level of earnings). This feature makes redeemable preferred stock somewhat like a loan in that

---

[7] Harrah's Entertainment is no longer publicly traded and now goes under the name **Caesars Entertainment Corporation**. In 2010, the former holders of the cumulative preferred shares converted those shares, and the associated dividends in arrears, into common stock.

the issuing corporation may be forced to repay the stock proceeds. The FASB currently requires disclosure of the extent of redemption requirements for all issues of preferred stock that are callable or redeemable.[8] As described in a later section in this chapter, preferred stock that *must* be redeemed, called mandatorily redeemable preferred stock, is reported as a liability in the balance sheet instead of as equity.

Current Developments in the Accounting for Preferred Stock Since 1990 the FASB has been wrestling with the sticky issue of separating debt financing from equity financing. Their most current attempt is a *Preliminary Views* document, "Financial Instruments with Characteristics of Equity," released on November 30, 2007. This document explains that many provisions of existing U.S. GAAP conflict with the conceptual framework definition of a liability, so a substantial reworking of the liability/equity distinction, with perhaps an accompanying change in the conceptual framework, is necessary.

In the *Preliminary Views* document, the FASB recommended the "basic ownership approach" to identifying equity. This approach hinges on the idea that equity claims are those that remain when all other claims have been satisfied. Thus, the only elements of financing that should be identified as "equity" are the most basic elements that are left when all claims with a higher priority have been satisfied.[9]

Application of this basic ownership approach would result in a very restrictive definition of equity. In fact, *all* preferred stock, whether redeemable or not, would be reported as a liability under this approach. User comments to both the FASB and the IASB have been overwhelmingly against this "basic ownership approach." Instead, users prefer a "perpetual approach," which describes an equity instrument as one for which there is no requirement to repay the invested funds, and the holder of the instrument is entitled to some assets if the company is liquidated. Preferred shares would be classified as equity under this "perpetual approach." Both the FASB and the IASB are leaning toward the "perpetual approach." However, remember that no final decision has been made, so stay tuned. For the time being, most preferred stock is classified as equity.

Issuance of Capital Stock

LO2 学习目标2
掌握为现金、认购股票或进行非货币性资产或服务的交换而发行股票的会计处理。

2 Record the issuance of stock for cash, on a subscription basis, and in exchange for noncash assets or for services.

Stock can be issued in exchange for cash, on a subscription basis, in exchange for noncash consideration, or as part of a business combination. The accounting for each of these possibilities is described on the following pages.

Capital Stock Issued for Cash

The issuance of stock for cash is recorded by a debit to Cash and a credit to Capital Stock for the par or stated value.[10] When the amount of cash received from the sale of stock is more than the par or stated value, the excess is recorded separately as a credit to an

---
[8] FASB ASC paragraphs 505-10-50-4 and 5.
[9] *Preliminary Views,* "Financial Instruments with Characteristics of Equity" (Norwalk, CT: Financial Accounting Standards Board, November 2007), par. D11.
[10] *Capital stock* is a general term; when it is used in account titles in the text, it represents either preferred stock or common stock. When an illustration is meant to apply specifically to preferred or common stock, the appropriate term is used in the account title.

additional paid-in capital account. This account is carried on the books as long as the stock to which it relates is outstanding. When stock is retired, the Capital Stock balance as well as any related Additional Paid-In Capital balance is generally cancelled.

> additional paid-in capital
> 资本溢价

To illustrate, assume that Goode Corporation issued 4,000 shares of $1 par common stock on April 1, 2013, for $45,000 cash. The entry to record the transaction is as follows:

2013
Apr. 1   Cash 45,000
           Common Stock 4,000
           Paid-In Capital in Excess of Par 41,000

If, in the example, the common stock were no-par stock but with a $1 stated value, the entry would be the same except that the $41,000 would be designated Paid-In Capital in Excess of Stated Value. Generally, stock is assigned a par or a stated value. However, if there is no such value assigned, the entire amount of cash received on the sale of stock is credited to the capital stock account, and no additional paid-in capital account is associated with the stock. Assuming Goode Corporation's stock was no-par common without a stated value, the entry to record the sale of 4,000 shares for $45,000 would be as follows:

2013
Apr. 1   Cash 45,000
           Common Stock 45,000

Capital Stock Sold on Subscription

Capital stock may be issued on a subscription basis. A subscription is a legally binding contract between the subscriber (purchaser of stock) and the corporation (issuer of stock). The contract states the number of shares subscribed, the subscription price, the terms of payment, and other conditions of the transaction. A subscription gives the corporation a legal claim for the contract price and gives the subscriber the legal status of a stockholder unless certain rights as a stockholder are specifically withheld by law or by terms of the contract. Ordinarily, stock certificates evidencing share ownership are not issued until the full subscription price has been received by the corporation.

The following entries illustrate the recording and issuance of capital stock sold on subscription.

November 1–30: Received subscriptions for 5,000 shares of $1 par common at $12.50 per share with 50% down, balance due in 60 days.

    Common Stock Subscriptions Receivable 62,500
        Common Stock Subscribed 5,000
        Paid-In Capital in Excess of Par 57,500
    Cash 31,250
        Common Stock Subscriptions Receivable 31,250

December 1–31: Received balance due on one-half of subscriptions and issued stock to the fully paid subscribers, 2,500 shares.

    Cash 15,625
        Common Stock Subscriptions Receivable 15,625
    Common Stock Subscribed 2,500
        Common Stock 2,500

Contributed capital would be reported in the Stockholders' Equity section of the December 31 balance sheet as follows:

Stockholders' Equity	
Contributed capital:	
Common stock, $1 par, 2,500 shares issued and outstanding	$ 2,500
Common stock subscribed, 2,500 shares	2,500
Paid-in capital in excess of par	57,500
	$62,500
Less: Common stock subscriptions receivable	15,625
Total contributed capital	$46,875

Capital Stock Subscriptions Receivable should normally not be shown as an asset but as an offset to equity.[11] This treatment is deemed appropriate because the legal penalty against subscribers who don't fully pay the contract price is often minimal, increasing the probability that the issuer of the stock may not fully collect on the subscriptions receivable. SEC rules allow subscription amounts receivable as of the balance sheet date to be shown as a current asset if the full contract price is collected prior to the date the financial statements are actually issued. For example, **Nebo Products**, a Draper, Utah-based importer of hand tools and camping gear (manufactured in Taiwan, China, and India), reported stock subscriptions receivable totaling $1,302,586 in its December 31, 2001, balance sheet. Of this amount, $201,664 was reported as a current asset, and $1,100,922 was reported as a subtraction from stockholders' equity. By way of explanation, Nebo reported the following in its 2001 annual report: "From January 2002 to March 25, 2002 [the date on the audit opinion], the company collected a total of $201,664 of stock subscriptions receivable."[12]

Subscription Defaults If a subscriber defaults on a subscription by failing to make a payment when it is due, a corporation may (1) return to the subscriber the amount paid, (2) return to the subscriber the amount paid less any reduction in price or expense incurred on the resale of the stock, (3) declare the amount paid by the subscriber as forfeited, or (4) issue to the subscriber shares equal to the number paid for in full. The practice followed will depend on the policy adopted by the corporation within the legal limitations set by the state in which it is incorporated.

Capital Stock Issued for Consideration Other Than Cash

When capital stock is issued for consideration in the form of property other than cash or for services received, the fair market value of the stock or the fair market value of the property or services, whichever is more objectively determinable, is used to record the transaction. If a quoted market price for the stock is available, that amount should be used as a basis for recording the exchange. Otherwise, it may be possible to determine the fair market value of the property or services received, for example, through appraisal by a competent outside party.

[11] FASB ASC paragraph 505-10-45-2.
[12] Nebo Products, 2001, 10K Report.

To illustrate, assume that AC Company issues 200 shares of $0.50 par value common stock in return for land. The company's stock is currently selling for $50 per share. The entry on AC Company's books would be as follows:

Land	10,000	
Common Stock		100
Paid-In Capital in Excess of Par		9,900

If, on the other hand, the land has a readily determinable market price of $12,000 but AC Company's common stock has no established fair market value, the transaction would be recorded as follows:

Land	12,000	
Common Stock		100
Paid-In Capital in Excess of Par		11,900

If no readily determinable value is available for either the stock or the property or services received, the accepted procedure is to have the value of the property or services independently appraised. If the transaction is material, the source of the appraisal should be disclosed in the financial statements.

When stock is issued in exchange for services, the journal entry is similar to that just illustrated. Assume that AC Company decides not to pay a key employee in cash but instead grants the employee 100 shares of $0.50 par common stock, with a market value of $50 per share, as payment of salary. The transaction would be recorded as follows:

Salary Expense	5,000	
Common Stock		50
Paid-In Capital in Excess of Par		4,950

This entry is interesting because it is so noncontroversial. However, if AC Company were to pay the employee with stock options instead of with actual shares of stock, the accounting would be highly controversial. Accounting for stock options given as employee compensation is discussed later in the chapter.

Issuance of Capital Stock in a Business Combination

Corporations often merge; the combination of **Mars** and **Wrigley** in a $22 billion deal in 2008 is one recent example. The union of two corporations is called a business combination. The combination can be accomplished by one corporation paying cash to buy out the shareholders of the other, by an exchange of stock whereby all the shareholders of the two separate corporations become joint shareholders of the new combined company, or by a mixture of a cash buyout and a stock swap.

The accounting for a business combination assumes that one of the companies is dominant and is acquiring the other company. The assets of the company being acquired are revalued to their fair value. In addition, the acquiring company records goodwill if the value of the cash and stock given in the acquisition exceeds the fair value of the net assets acquired. Accounting for business combinations is discussed in detail in advanced accounting texts. Accounting for the acquisition of a business and any resulting goodwill was covered in Chapters 10 and 11.

Stock Repurchases

 Use both the cost and par value methods to account for stock repurchases.

For a variety of reasons, a company may find it desirable to reacquire shares of its own stock. **ExxonMobil**, for example, has been the most aggressive company in buying back its own stock. As of December 31, 2011, ExxonMobil had spent a cumulative net amount of $176.9 billion in buying back its own shares. Coca-Cola, another company well known for stock repurchasing, had spent more than $31.3 billion as of December 31, 2011, in buying back its own stock. In general, companies acquire their own stock to:

1. Provide shares for incentive compensation and employee savings plans.
2. Obtain shares needed to satisfy requests by holders of convertible securities (bonds and preferred stock).
3. Reduce the amount of equity relative to the amount of debt.
4. Invest excess cash temporarily.
5. Remove some shares from the open market in order to protect against a hostile takeover.
6. Improve per-share earnings by reducing the number of shares outstanding and returning inefficiently used assets to shareholders.
7. Display confidence that the stock is currently undervalued by the market.

Whatever the reason, a company's stock may be reacquired by exercise of call or redemption provisions or by repurchase of the stock in the open market. State laws normally prohibit the repurchase of stock if the repurchase would impair the ability of creditors to be repaid. In many states, the total amount spent to repurchase shares cannot exceed the sum of additional paid-in capital and retained earnings. In addition, share repurchases at exorbitant prices are banned because they dilute the stock value for the remaining shareholders.

In accounting for the reacquisition of stock, remember that reacquisitions do not give rise to income or loss. A company issues stock to raise capital. In reacquiring shares of its stock, the company is merely reducing its invested capital. Gains or losses arise from the operating and investing activities of the business, not from transactions with shareholders.

A company's stock may be reacquired for immediate retirement or be reacquired and held as treasury stock for subsequent disposition, either eventual retirement or reissuance. There are two methods of accounting for treasury stock transactions: the cost method and the par value method. After a short discussion of treasury stock, these methods will be discussed in detail.

Treasury Stock

When a company's own stock is reacquired and held in the name of the company, it is referred to as treasury stock. Treasury shares may subsequently be reissued or formally retired. Before discussing how to account for treasury stock, three important features should be noted:

- Treasury stock should not be viewed as an asset; instead, it should be reported as a reduction in total owners' equity.
- There is no income or loss on the reacquisition, reissuance, or retirement of treasury stock.

- Retained earnings can be decreased by treasury stock transactions but is never increased by such transactions.

> **Caution**
> Reacquisition of shares may reduce retained earnings, but it can *never* increase retained earnings.

Two methods for recording treasury stock transactions are generally accepted: (1) the cost method, which records the treasury stock in a special equity account until the shares are reissued or retired; and (2) the par (or stated) value method, which accounts for the purchase of treasury stock as if the shares were being retired.

Cost Method of Accounting for Treasury Stock Under the cost method, the purchase of treasury stock is recorded by debiting a treasury stock account for the total amount paid to repurchase the shares. The treasury stock account is reported as a deduction from total stockholders' equity on the balance sheet.

The cost method of accounting for treasury stock transactions is illustrated in the following example:

2014—*Newly organized corporation issued 10,000 shares of common stock, $1 par, at $15:*

Cash	150,000	
Common Stock		10,000
Paid-In Capital in Excess of Par		140,000

Net income for the first year of business was $30,000.

2015—*Reacquired 1,000 shares of common stock at $40 per share:*

Treasury Stock	40,000	
Cash		40,000

2015—*Sold 200 shares of treasury stock at $50 per share:*

Cash	10,000	
Treasury Stock (200 × $40)		8,000
Paid-In Capital from Treasury Stock		2,000

Because the treasury stock is reissued at a price greater than the $40 repurchase price, the excess is recorded in an additional paid-in capital account. (*Note:* No gain is recorded.)

2015—*Sold 500 shares of treasury stock at $34 per share:*

Cash	17,000	
Paid-In Capital from Treasury Stock	2,000	
Retained Earnings	1,000	
Treasury Stock (500 × $40)		20,000

Because the treasury stock is reissued at a price less than the $40 repurchase price, Retained Earnings is debited for the difference, or as in this example, any paid-in capital from prior treasury stock reissuances may first be debited.

2015—*Retired remaining 300 shares of treasury stock (3% of original issue of 10,000 shares):*

Common Stock	300	
Paid-In Capital in Excess of Par	4,200	
Retained Earnings [300 × ($40 − $15)]	7,500	
Treasury Stock (300 × $40)		12,000

由于库存股再发行价低于回购价（40美元），留存收益被记在借方以示区别。在这个例子中，任何因先前库存股的再发行而产生的实收资本都应先记入借方。

> **FYI**
>
> In the 1980s, a large number of "greenmail" treasury stock transactions occurred. A firm repurchased its shares from a troublesome shareholder at a price significantly greater than the market value. In many cases, the "greenmail" in excess of the market value of the repurchased shares had to be expensed.

Alternatively, the entire $11,700 difference between Common Stock and the cost to acquire the treasury stock may be debited to Retained Earnings.

It should be noted that in the example, all treasury stock was acquired at $40 per share. If several acquisitions of treasury stock are made at different prices, the resale or retirement of treasury shares must be recorded using the actual cost to reacquire the shares being sold or retired (specific identification) or using the basis of a cost flow assumption, such as FIFO or average cost.

Par (or Stated) Value Method of Accounting for Treasury Stock If the par (or stated) value method is used, the purchase of treasury stock is regarded as a withdrawal of a group of stockholders. Similarly, the sale or reissuance of treasury stock, under this approach, is viewed as the admission of a new group of stockholders, requiring entries giving effect to the investment by this group. Thus, the purchase and sale are viewed as two separate and unrelated transactions.

Using the data given for the cost method illustration, the following entries would be made for 2015 under the par value method:

2015—Reacquired 1,000 shares of common stock at $40 per share:

Treasury Stock	1,000	
Paid-In Capital in Excess of Par	14,000	
Retained Earnings [1,000 × ($40 − $15)]	25,000	
Cash		40,000

Sold 200 shares of treasury stock at $50 per share:

Cash	10,000	
Treasury Stock		200
Paid-In Capital in Excess of Par		9,800

Sold 500 shares of treasury stock at $34 per share:

Cash	17,000	
Treasury Stock		500
Paid-In Capital in Excess of Par		16,500

Retired remaining 300 shares of treasury stock:

Common Stock	300	
Treasury Stock		300

Evaluating the Cost and Par Value Methods Less than 10% of large U.S. companies use the par value method. Using the numbers from the example just given, the following comparison shows the impact on stockholders' equity of the two approaches after the original stock repurchases have occurred but prior to the reissuance or retirement of the treasury shares.

Comparison of Stockholders' Equity

	Cost Method	Par Value Method
Contributed capital:		
Common stock	$ 10,000	$ 10,000
Paid-in capital in excess of par	140,000	126,000
Total contributed capital	$150,000	$136,000
Retained earnings	30,000	5,000
Total contributed capital and retained earnings	$180,000	$141,000
Less: Treasury stock	40,000	1,000
Total stockholders' equity	$140,000	$140,000

Note that total stockholders' equity is the same regardless of which method is used. As the example shows, however, there may be differences in the relative amounts of contributed capital and retained earnings reported. Note again that retained earnings may be decreased by treasury stock transactions but can never be increased by buying or selling treasury stock. Exhibit 13-5 lists the 10 largest companies in the United States (in terms of their April 2012 market value) and their stock repurchases, according to reported information. It is interesting to note that two of these 10 companies—Microsoft and **Wal-Mart**—use the par value method of accounting for their treasury stock purchases. Note also that Google and **Apple** do not repurchase shares of their own stock.

> ## Stop & Think
>
> After looking at this comparison, why do you think so few companies use the par value method?
>
> a) Use of the cost method usually increases reported earnings.
> b) Use of the par value method usually involves reducing retained earnings.
> c) Use of the par value method requires the company to pay more for the repurchased shares.
> d) Use of the par value method increases long-term debt.

Exhibit 13-5 | Treasury Stock Purchases for the 10 Largest U.S. Companies

Rank	Market Value (in billions)	Repurchases during the Year	Balance Sheet Amount	Accounting Method
1. Apple	$546.0	$ 0	$ 0	?
2. ExxonMobil	407.4	22,055	176,932	Cost
3. Microsoft	273.5	3,738	0	Par Value
4. IBM	238.7	15,034	110,963	Cost
5. Chevron	218.0	4,250	29,685	Cost
6. General Electric	213.7	2,067	31,769	Cost
7. Wal-Mart	208.4	6,299	0	Par Value
8. Google	203.2	0	0	?
9. Berkshire Hathaway	202.2	67	67	Cost
10. AT&T	187.3	0	20,750	Cost

© Cengage Learning 2014

Retirement of Repurchased Shares If shares of stock are reacquired at par (or stated) value and then retired, the capital stock account is debited, and the cash account is credited. However, if the purchase price of the stock exceeds the par value, the excess amount may be (1) charged to any paid-in capital balances applicable to that class of stock, (2) allocated between Paid-In Capital and Retained Earnings, or (3) charged entirely to Retained Earnings.[13] The alternative used depends on the existence of previously established paid-in capital amounts and on management's preference.

Stock Rights, Warrants, and Options

 Account for the issuance of stock rights and stock warrants.

LO4 学习目标4
掌握认股权和认股权证发行的会计处理。

A corporation may issue rights, warrants, or options that permit the purchase of the company's stock for a specified period (the exercise period) at a certain price (the exercise price). Although the terms *rights, warrants,* and *options* are sometimes used interchangeably, a distinction may be made as follows:

stock rights
认股权

- Stock rights—issued to existing shareholders to permit them to maintain their proportionate ownership interests when new shares are to be issued. (Some state laws require this preemptive right.)

stock warrants
认股权证

- Stock warrants—sold by the corporation for cash, generally in conjunction with the issuance of another security.

stock options
股票期权

- Stock options—granted to officers or employees, usually as part of a compensation plan.

A company may offer rights, warrants, or options to raise additional capital, to encourage the sale of a particular class of securities, or as compensation for services received. The exercise period is generally longer for warrants and options than for rights. Warrants and rights may be traded independently among investors, whereas options generally are restricted to a particular person or specified group to whom the options are granted. The accounting considerations relating to stock rights, warrants, and options are described in the following sections.

Stock Rights

When announcing rights to purchase additional shares of stock, the directors of a corporation specify a date on which the rights will be issued. All stockholders of record on the issue date are entitled to receive the rights. Thus, between the announcement date and the issue date, the stock is said to sell *rights-on*. After the rights are issued, the stock sells *ex-rights*, and the rights may be sold separately by those receiving them from the corporation. An expiration date is also designated when the rights are announced, and rights not exercised by this date are worthless.

FYI

A company would include warrants to encourage investors to purchase the company's bonds. Of course, another way to encourage investors to purchase the bonds is to increase the interest rate paid on the bonds. Therefore, warrants can be viewed as decreasing the interest rate that must be paid.

When rights are issued to stockholders, only a memorandum entry is made on the issuing company's books stating the number of shares that may be claimed under the outstanding rights. This information is required so the corporation may retain

[13] FASB ASC paragraph 505-30-30-8.

sufficient unissued or reacquired stock to meet the exercise of the rights. Upon surrender of the rights and the receipt of payments as specified by the rights, the stock is issued. At this time, a memorandum entry is made to record the decrease in the number of rights outstanding accompanied by an entry to record the stock sale. The entry for the sale is recorded the same as any other issue of stock, with appropriate recognition of the cash received, the par, or stated, value of the stock issued, and any additional paid-in capital. Information concerning outstanding rights should be reported with the corporation's balance sheet so that the effects of the future exercise of remaining rights may be determined.

Stock Warrants

Warrants may be sold in conjunction with other securities as a "sweetener" to make the purchase of the securities more attractive. For example, warrants to purchase shares of a corporation's common stock may be issued with bonds to encourage investors to purchase the bonds. A warrant has value when the exercise price is less than the market value, either present or potential, of the security that can be purchased with the warrants. Warrants issued with other securities may be detachable or nondetachable. Detachable warrants are similar to stock rights because they can be traded separately from the security with which they were originally issued. Nondetachable warrants cannot be separated from the security with which they were issued.

Part of the issuance price of debt securities is assigned to any detachable stock warrants and classified as part of owners' equity.[14] The value assigned to the warrants is determined by the relative fair value method which is illustrated in the following equation:

$$\text{Value assigned to warrants} = \text{Total issue price} \times \frac{\text{Market value of warrants}}{\text{Market value of security without warrants} + \text{Market value of warrants}}$$

Although the FASB's standards are directed only to warrants attached to debt, it appears logical to extend the conclusions of that opinion to warrants attached to preferred stock. Thus, if a market value exists for the warrants at the issuance date, a separate equity account is credited with that portion of the issuance price assigned to the warrants. If the warrants are exercised, the value assigned to the common stock is the value allocated to the warrants plus the cash proceeds from the issuance of the common stock. If the warrants are allowed to expire, the value assigned to the warrants may be transferred to a permanent paid-in capital account.

> **FYI**
> From an investor standpoint, both the preferred shares and the detachable warrants are recorded at their fair values.

Accounting for detachable warrants attached to a preferred stock issue is illustrated as follows. Assume that Stewart Co. sells 1,000 shares of $50 par preferred stock for $58 per share. As an incentive to purchase the stock, Stewart Co. gives the purchaser detachable warrants enabling holders to subscribe to 1,000 shares of $2 par common stock for $25 per share. The warrants expire after one year. Immediately following the issuance of the preferred stock, the warrants are selling at $3, and the fair market value

---
[14] FASB ASC paragraph 470-20-25-2.

of the preferred stock without the warrant attached is $57. The proceeds of $58,000 should be allocated by Stewart Co. as follows:

$$\text{Value assigned to the warrants} = \$58,000 \times \frac{\$3}{\$57 + \$3} = \$2,900$$

The entry on Stewart's books to record the sale of the preferred stock with detachable warrants is as follows:

Cash	58,000	
Preferred Stock, $50 par		50,000
Paid-In Capital in Excess of Par—Preferred Stock		5,100
Common Stock Warrants		2,900

If the warrants are exercised, the entry to record the issuance of common stock would be as follows:

Common Stock Warrants	2,900	
Cash	25,000	
Common Stock, $2 par		2,000
Paid-In Capital in Excess of Par—Common Stock		25,900

This entry would be the same regardless of the market price of the common stock at the issuance date.

If the warrants in the example were allowed to expire, the following entry would be made:

Common Stock Warrants	2,900	
Paid-In Capital from Expired Warrants		2,900

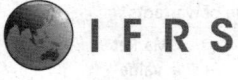

Under current U.S. GAAP, if warrants are nondetachable, the securities are considered inseparable, and no allocation is made to recognize the value of the warrant. The entire proceeds are assigned to the security to which the warrant is attached. Thus, for nondetachable warrants, the accounting treatment is similar to that for convertible securities, such as convertible bonds. Clearly, from a conceptual standpoint this inconsistency is not justified because the economic value of a warrant exists, even if the warrant cannot be traded separately or "detached." This is essentially the same argument made for recognizing the conversion feature of a convertible security. Notwithstanding this argument, a separate instrument does not exist for a nondetachable warrant, and current practice in the United States does not require a separate value to be assigned to these warrants. In its October 2000 *Exposure Draft*, "Accounting for Financial Instruments with Characteristics of Liabilities, Equity, or Both," the FASB recommended the relative fair value method for allocating the proceeds for all securities that combine different elements of debt, preferred stock, and common stock. But so far no such comprehensive standard has been adopted in the United States. In contrast, *IAS 32* requires all compound financial instruments to be recorded as separate debt and equity components.

Accounting for Share-Based Compensation

LO5 Compute the compensation expense associated with the granting of employee stock options.

学习目标5
计算与员工股票期权激励相关的奖励费用。

During 1994, debate over the proper accounting for employee stock options escalated into a full-scale war, with the FASB pitted against the business community and, ultimately, the Congress of the United States. The subject of all the controversy was this: Should the fair value of stock options granted to employees be estimated and recognized as part of compensation expense? In his letter to the shareholders in Berkshire Hathaway's 1993 annual report, Warren Buffett approvingly summarized the position of the FASB:

> If options aren't a form of compensation, what are they? If compensation isn't an expense, what is it? And if expenses shouldn't go into the calculation of earnings, where in the world should they go?[15]

In spite of this logic, the FASB surrendered to the pressure and did not require the recognition of a stock option expense because "the debate threatened the future of accounting standard-setting in the private sector,"[16] meaning that Congress had suggested the possibility of abolishing the FASB if it didn't toe the line on stock option accounting. The FASB's compromise was to encourage companies to recognize a stock option expense or, if they didn't, then to disclose an estimate of this expense in the notes to the financial statements. Almost all companies chose the disclosure route.

In 2002, stock option accounting again became a hot issue in the wake of the financial accounting scandals that began to bubble to the surface in 2001. Many financial statement users pointed to stock option accounting as another example of poor accounting rules that allowed companies to hide their activities from investors and creditors. In this case, the activity being hidden was the granting of stock options to top corporate executives.

> **FYI**
>
> Employee stock options are *not* the same as the call and put stock options traded on major exchanges. Traded option contracts can exist between any two parties. Call options entitle the owner to buy shares of a certain stock at a set "exercise" price. Put options entitle the owner to sell shares at a set price.

So, in 2003 the FASB again added stock option accounting to its agenda but quickly found that the strong feelings against expensing the cost of stock options had not died down. When the FASB issued an Exposure Draft in March 2004 that basically repeated its position from back in 1994, yet another firestorm of protest arose. The FASB received 14,239 comment letters in response to this Exposure Draft; by comparison, issuance of a typical Exposure Draft rarely elicits more than 100 comment letters, and usually the FASB receives just 20 or 30 comment letters. Business lobbying of Congress against the FASB's Exposure Draft prompted passage of a House Resolution mandating alternative accounting that would have greatly reduced companies' reported stock option compensation expense; mercifully, this bill died in the Senate.

In opposing the FASB's proposal to require expensing the fair value of stock options granted to employees, businesses concocted a marvelous array of pseudo-theoretical arguments that we, the authors, would rather not repeat here. Theoretical arguments aside, the vast majority of corporations in the United States opposed the FASB's attempt to require recognition of a stock option compensation expense for a simple reason: Recognition of a stock option compensation expense would reduce reported earnings. The area of stock option accounting is a perfect illustration of why we need an independent financial accounting standard setter such as the FASB—financial statement users need informative and unbiased information about companies, which those companies would sometimes prefer not to include in the financial statements. In December 2004, the FASB adopted pre-Codification *Statement No. 123* (revised 2004), "Share-Based Payment," which requires the expensing of the fair value of stock options granted as compensation. This standard is now found in FASB ASC Topic 718 (Compensation—Stock Compensation).

[15] Berkshire Hathaway, 1993, 10K Report.
[16] Pre-Codification *Statement of Financial Accounting Standards No. 123*, "Accounting for Stock-Based Compensation" (Norwalk, CT: Financial Accounting Standards Board, 1995), par. 60.

The recognition and disclosure requirements for stock option compensation plans are illustrated in the following example. A simple plan is illustrated first, followed by some exposure to the accounting for more complex plans.

Basic Stock Option Compensation Plan

On January 1, 2013, the board of directors of Neff Company authorized the grant of 10,000 stock options to supplement the salaries of certain employees. Each stock option permits the purchase of one share of Neff common stock at a price of $50 per share; the market price of the stock on January 1, 2013, is also $50 per share. (This is typical of many actual stock option plans for real companies. For example, in its 2011 annual report, Toys "R" Us states that options granted under its 2010 Incentive Plan have an exercise price equal to the fair value of the shares on the date of the grant.) The options vest, or become exercisable, beginning on January 1, 2016, and only if the employees stay with the company for the entire three-year vesting period. The options expire on December 31, 2016.

Neff is required to estimate the fair value of the options as of the grant date. Clearly, each option has value because the stock price could increase above $50 during the three-year period and the options give the employees the right to buy the stock at the fixed exercise price of $50. Computation of the fair value of the options involves consideration of factors such as the expected volatility of the stock price and the length of time the options are valid. For example, the higher the volatility of the stock price, the higher the value of the option, because there is a better chance that the stock price will increase significantly. Of course, increased volatility also means that there is an increased probability that the stock price will decrease. However, this doesn't negatively impact the option value because the employees can choose not to exercise the option if the share price drops below the option price of $50. Also, an option with a longer term has increased value because there is a better chance of a significant stock price increase over a long time period than there is over a short one. Exact computation of option values involves formulas derived using stochastic calculus (the famous Black-Scholes model) or discrete probability lattice models (such as the binomial model). Unfortunately, we don't have time to cover stochastic calculus in this text. However, commercially available software packages make option valuation no more difficult than using a spreadsheet.

For the Neff Company example, assume that an option-pricing formula is used to estimate a grant date value of $10 for each of the employee stock options. Thus, the total fair value of the options granted is $100,000 (10,000 × $10) as of the grant date. Once the options granted have been valued, the remaining accounting problem is determining when the compensation expense should be recognized. The compensation should be charged to the periods in which the employees perform the services for which the options are granted. In the Neff example, no specific service period is mentioned, so compensation cost is allocated over the three-year period between the January 1, 2013, grant date and the January 1, 2016, vesting date. The journal entry to record the recognition of compensation expense for 2013 is as follows:

> **FYI**
>
> In general, an employee has taxable income in the amount of the difference between the option exercise price and the stock price on the date the options are exercised. The worst-case scenario occurs when an employee exercises options, holds the stock, and the stock subsequently declines drastically in value. If the stock price has declined enough, selling the stock might not generate enough cash even to pay the tax.

Neff公司被要求估计期权授予日的公允价值。显然，每份期权会因为股票价格可能在三年时间里超过50美元及给予员工按50美元固定行权价购买股票的权利而具有价值。计算期权的公允价格涉及一些因素，如预期的股价波动率和期权有效期的长度。

2013
Dec. 31   Compensation Expense ($100,000/3 years)....................... 33,333
                Paid-In Capital from Stock Options   33,333

Note that this paid-in capital is *not* from the investment of cash in the business but instead represents an investment of work by the employees covered under the stock option plan.

Similar entries would be made in 2014 and 2015. At the end of the three-year service period, the balance in the additional paid-in capital from stock options account is $100,000, which is equal to the grant date value of the options.

The journal entry to record the exercise of all 10,000 of the options on December 31, 2016, to purchase shares of Neff's no-par common stock would be as follows:

2016
Dec. 31 Cash (10,000 × $50) 500,000
          Paid-In Capital from Stock Options............................. 100,000
              Common Stock (no par)..................................... 600,000

If the options had been allowed to expire unexercised, the following journal entry could be made on December 31, 2016, the end of the exercise period, to reclassify the paid-in capital from the stock options:

2016
Dec. 31 Paid-In Capital from Stock Options............................. 100,000
              Paid-In Capital from Expired Options 100,000

Required Disclosure The following note disclosure (illustrated for 2013) is required each year:

Employee Stock Options	Shares	Exercise Price
Outstanding at January 1, 2013	0	—
Granted during 2013	10,000	$50
Exercised during 2013	0	—
Forfeited during 2013	0	—
Outstanding at December 31, 2013	10,000	$50
Options exercisable at December 31, 2013	0	
Weighted-average fair value of options granted during 2013	$10	
Compensation expense associated with the stock option plan in 2013	$33,333	

The note should also include a general description of the employee stock option plan as well as a description of the techniques used in estimating the fair value of the options.

IASB Standard The release of pre-Codification FASB *Statement No. 123* (revised 2004) is an excellent example of how the convergence between FASB and IASB standards is improving the quality of both sets of standards. In February 2004, the IASB adopted *International Financial Reporting Standard (IFRS) 2*, "Share-Based Payment." This standard requires essentially the same expensing of stock options as initially proposed by the FASB back in 1994. Because the granting of employee stock options is much less common outside the United States, the IASB did not experience nearly as much opposition to its stock option expensing proposal as did the FASB. And once the IASB had adopted its standard, the FASB could wave the flag of "international harmonization" to aid in promulgating the U.S. stock option expensing standard over the protests of the U.S. business community and Congress.

Accounting for Performance-Based Plans

The simple example above is based on a simple stock option plan. In such a plan, the plan terms (i.e., the option exercise price and the number of options granted) are fixed as of the date the options are granted. In a performance-based stock option plan, the plan terms are dependent on how well the individual or company performs after the date the options are granted. In the simple stock option plan of Neff Company that is illustrated above, Neff's employees needed only to stay with the company for the entire three-year vesting period in order to receive the full value of the options. With a performance-based plan, the terms of the option depend on how well an employee performs or how well the company performs during the vesting period. To illustrate, assume that the terms of the Neff Company stock-based compensation plan are as follows:

- On January 1, 2013, the board of directors of Neff Company authorized the grant of stock options to supplement the salaries of certain employees.
- Each stock option permits the purchase of one share of Neff common stock at a price of $50 per share; the market price of the stock on January 1, 2013, is also $50 per share.
- The options vest, or become exercisable, beginning on January 1, 2016, and only if the employees stay with the company for the entire three-year vesting period. The options expire on December 31, 2016.
- The number of options granted, instead of being fixed at 10,000 as in the earlier example, is contingent on Neff's level of sales for 2015. If Neff's sales for 2015 are less than $50 million, only the 10,000 options will vest. If Neff's 2015 sales are between $50 million and $80 million, an additional 2,000 options will vest, making a total of 12,000. Finally, if Neff's 2015 sales exceed $80 million, a total of 15,000 options will vest.

> **Caution**
> Stock price and option fair value changes after the grant date do not impact compensation expense.

For the Neff performance-based stock option plan, the computation of compensation expense is done by combining the value of the options on the grant date with the number of options that are probable to vest. As in the earlier example, application of an option valuation method results in a computed value for each option of $10 as of the grant date. The number of options probable to vest depends, of course, on the probable level of 2015 sales. As of December 31, 2013, when compensation expense for the first year must be recorded, Neff forecasts that 2015 sales will be around $60 million, indicating that 12,000 options will vest. Recognition of compensation expense for 2013 involves recognizing one-third of the $120,000 (12,000 × $10) total estimated expense for the three-year service period. Note that the change in Neff's stock price during the year (from $50 to $56) does not affect the calculation. The options are valued once, at the grant date, and that value is used for the life of the options. The journal entry to recognize compensation expense is as follows:

2013
Dec. 31 Compensation Expense ($120,000/3 years)....................... 40,000
          Paid-In Capital from Stock Options 40,000

对于Neff的附市场业绩条件的股票期权计划，激励费用的计量可以通过组合授予日的期权数量和可能行权的期权数额来完成。在早先的案例中，运用期权价格的估价方法，得出授予日每份期权的价格为10美元。期权可能行权的数额当然取决于2015年可能的销售水平。在2013年12月31日，第一年的激励费用必须被记录下来。Neff预测2015年的销售会在6 000万美元左右，预计会有12 000份期权行权。2013年应确认的激励费用等于三年服务期内估计总共应确认的120 000美元（12 000×10）激励费用的1/3。

Events in 2014 lead Neff to lower its forecast of 2015 sales. As of December 31, 2014, Neff expects 2015 sales to be only $40 million. Accordingly, it is probable that only 10,000 options will vest on January 1, 2016. The new estimate for total compensation expense for the three-year service period is $100,000 (10,000 × $10). Because two-thirds of the service period has elapsed, aggregate compensation expense recognized should be $66,667 ($100,000 × 2/3). Because compensation expense of $40,000 was recognized in 2013, the necessary journal entry in 2014 is as follows:

2014
Dec. 31 Compensation Expense ($66,667 − $40,000)   26,667
             Paid-In Capital from Stock Options   26,667

Upon close examination, it can be seen that this computation of compensation expense differs from that typically encountered in situations with changing accounting estimates. Usually, the effects of changes in estimates are spread over current and future periods. In this case, such a procedure would result in 2014 compensation expense of $30,000, an allocation of the remaining compensation expense of $60,000 ($100,000 − $40,000) evenly over the remaining two years of the service period, 2014 and 2015. However, a so-called "catch-up adjustment" is required when recognizing compensation expense related to performance-based option plans. The catch-up adjustment makes the cumulative expense recognized equal to the amount it would have been had the updated estimate for 2015 sales been used all along.

Actual sales for 2015 are $85 million (Neff had a pretty good year). As a result, according to the terms of the performance-based plan, 15,000 options will vest as of January 1, 2016. Because the entire service period has elapsed, aggregate compensation expense recognized should be $150,000 (15,000 × $10). Because compensation expense of $66,667 ($40,000 + $26,667) has already been recognized in 2013 and 2014, the necessary journal entry in 2015 is as follows:

2015
Dec. 31 Compensation Expense ($150,000 − $66,667)   83,333
             Paid-In Capital from Stock Options   83,333

The journal entry to record the exercise of all 15,000 of the options on December 31, 2016, to purchase shares of Neff's no-par common stock would be as follows:

2016
Dec. 31 Cash (15,000 × $50)   750,000
             Paid-In Capital from Stock Options   150,000
                Common Stock (no par)   900,000

Accounting for Awards That Call for Cash Settlement

Neff Company's stock-based compensation plans discussed above stipulated that the compensation would be paid in the form of stock options. Because settlement of these stock options requires Neff to issue its own stock and does not require any transfer of assets, the stock options are considered to be equity instruments. When a stock-based compensation plan calls for a cash settlement or gives the employee the option of choosing a cash settlement instead of receiving stock options, work by employees during the service period creates a liability for the firm because the firm is obligated to transfer assets (cash) in the future.

To illustrate the accounting for share-based compensation plans that call for settlement in cash, assume that Neff Company, the company used in the earlier example on stock option plans, has decided that instead of granting its employees 10,000 stock options, it will grant an equal number of cash stock appreciation rights (SARs). A cash SAR awards an employee a cash amount equal to the market value of the issuing firm's shares above a specified threshold price. Neff Company promises that after January 1, 2016, it will pay the exerciser

> **Stop & Think**
>
> Assume that Neff's managers are greedy, unscrupulous scoundrels. Which ONE of the following might Neff's performance-based stock option plan cause Neff's management (the ones who are receiving the stock options) to do?
>
> a) Delay the recognition of 2014 sales into 2015, and accelerate the recognition of 2016 sales into 2015.
> b) Accelerate the recognition of 2015 sales into 2014, and delay the recognition of 2015 sales into 2016.
> c) Accelerate the recognition of 2015 sales into 2014, and delay the recognition of 2013 sales into 2014.
> d) Accelerate the recognition of 2014 sales into 2013, and delay the recognition of 2012 sales into 2013.

of each cash SAR an amount equal to the excess of the share price on the exercise date over the $50 threshold price. The cash SARs vest beginning on January 1, 2016, only for the employees who stay with the company for the entire three-year vesting period. The cash SARs expire on December 31, 2016. From an employee's standpoint, this cash SAR plan is economically equivalent to the basic stock option plan illustrated earlier in the chapter.

From the standpoint of Neff's accounting treatment, the cash SAR plan is different from the stock option plan discussed previously because the cash SAR plan creates a liability to transfer cash. All journal entries to record compensation expense for 2013, 2014, and 2015 and for the redemption of the cash SARs on December 31, 2016, are given below.

Assume the following information:

Fair value of one SAR:

January 1, 2013	$10
December 31, 2013	6
December 31, 2014	7
December 31, 2015	9

The forecast of the cash settlement amount is updated at the end of each period using current data to estimate the fair value of each SAR. This fair value is impacted by the existing stock price, the amount of time remaining until the award settlement date, and the volatility of the underlying stock price. As of December 31, 2013, because the estimated fair value of each SAR is $6, the best estimate of the amount of cash that will be transferred when the cash SARs are exercised is $60,000 (10,000 × $6). The journal entry to recognize 2013 compensation expense is as follows:

2013
Dec. 31   Compensation Expense ($60,000/3 years)..................   20,000
                Share-Based Compensation Liability..........................   20,000

As of December 31, 2014, the estimated fair value of each SAR is $7. The new estimate for total compensation expense for the three-year service period is $70,000 (10,000 × $7). Because two-thirds of the service period has elapsed, aggregate compensation expense recognized should be $46,667 ($70,000 × 2/3). Because compensation expense of $20,000 was recognized in 2013, the necessary journal entry in 2014 is as follows:

2014
Dec. 31   Compensation Expense ($46,667 − $20,000)..................   26,667
                Share-Based Compensation Liability..........................   26,667

Except for the account titles, this catch-up adjustment is exactly like those illustrated previously.

The estimated fair value of each SAR is $9 on December 31, 2015. Aggregate compensation expense for the three-year service period is $90,000 (10,000 × $9). Because compensation expense of $46,667 ($20,000 + $26,667) has already been recognized in 2013 and 2014, the necessary journal entry in 2015 is as follows:

2015
Dec. 31 Compensation Expense ($90,000 − $46,667)..................... 43,333
          Share-Based Compensation Liability........................... 43,333

Between the time the cash SARs vest and the time they are exercised, the company's stock price can still move, affecting the ultimate amount of cash paid out for the cash SARs. The impact of these post-vesting price movements on the cash SAR payable account are recognized as compensation expense in the year the price movements occur. The share price on December 31, 2016, is $61, meaning that Neff will pay $11 ($61 − $50) for each SAR. The required entry in 2016 to reflect this information is:

2016
Dec. 31 Compensation Expense {[10,000 × ($61 − $50)] − $90,000}....... 20,000
          Share-Based Compensation Liability........................... 20,000

The entry to record the cash payments made to holders of the 10,000 cash SARs that vested on January 1, 2016, and were exercised on December 31, 2016, is shown below.

2016
Dec. 31 Share-Based Compensation Liability............................ 110,000
          Cash [10,000 × ($61 − $50)].................................. 110,000

If the exercise period extended beyond 2016 and if cash SARs remained outstanding, an entry would be made at the end of each year to revise the estimated amount of the cash SAR liability. These revisions are recognized as part of compensation expense for the period.

Broad-Based Plans

Some employers grant employee stock options and employee stock purchase rights to substantially all employees. Under FASB ASC Topic 718 (Compensation—Stock Compensation), compensation expense is recognized if employees are allowed to purchase shares for more than a 5% discount from the market price.[17] The rationale is that allowing employees to purchase stock for an excessive discount is just an alternative way to grant compensation.

Reporting Some Equity-Related Items as Liabilities

LO6 学习目标6
判断哪些权益相关项目应在资产负债表中作为负债进行列报。

6 Determine which equity-related items should be reported in the balance sheet as liabilities.

In the field of finance, a *debt claim* is one that entitles the debt holders to a fixed payment when company assets are sufficient to meet that payment; if company assets are below that amount, the debt holders get all of the assets. An *equity claim* is one that entitles the equity holders to all company assets in excess of the debt holders' portion. The definitions of liabilities and equities given by the FASB in its *Statement of Accounting Concepts No. 6* embody similar notions: Equity is defined as the residual amount of assets left after deducting the liability claims.

[17] FASB ASC paragraph 718-50-25-1a(2).

Although examples of pure equity (common stock) and pure debt (a bank loan) are easy to distinguish, many securities are in a middle ground and have characteristics of both debt and equity. For example, preferred stock is like debt in that the payments (both dividend and liquidation amounts) are capped, but it is also like equity because the payments aren't guaranteed and have lower priority than debt claims. As another example, convertible debt may be exchanged for equity if the issuing firm performs well; as the performance of the issuing firm improves, the convertible debt gradually changes in nature from debt to equity.

These examples illustrate that the line between a liability and an equity can be very unclear. As mentioned several times earlier in the chapter, for several years the FASB has been performing a fundamental review of the accounting distinction between debt and equity. As a result of this review, the FASB has decided that certain equity-related items should actually be reported in the balance sheet as liabilities.[18] These items are as follows:

- Mandatorily redeemable preferred shares
- Financial instruments (such as written put options) that obligate a company to repurchase its own shares
- Financial instruments that obligate a company to issue a certain dollar value of its own shares

These items share the characteristic that, although related to equity shares, they each obligate the company to deliver items of a set value (either cash or equity shares) some time in the future. Each of these items is illustrated below.

In addition, this section includes a brief description of noncontrolling interest which has historically been called *minority interest*. Noncontrolling interest is an item that has often in the past been classified as a liability but that should now be classified as equity.

Mandatorily Redeemable Preferred Shares

As mentioned above, preferred stock embodies some of the characteristics of a debt instrument because preferred shareholders are typically not entitled to additional payments based on the success of the issuing company. In some cases, the ownership contract associated with preferred shares stipulates that those shares must be redeemed by the issuing company at a specified future date. For example, consider preferred shares that are issued now in exchange for $1,000 cash but the issuing company agrees that in 10 years it will redeem those shares for, say, $1,100 cash. In this case, you can call these financial instruments "shares" if you like, but the more you consider them, the more they resemble a liability. In fact, mandatorily redeemable preferred shares are a textbook example of a financial instrument that fits the conceptual framework definition of a liability: ". . . present obligation to transfer assets . . . in the future as a result of past transactions or events."

Historically, the SEC required that firms not include mandatorily redeemable preferred stock under the Stockholders' Equity heading. Instead, mandatorily redeemable preferred stock was listed above the Equity section in a gray area between the liabilities and equities; this reporting of mandatorily redeemable preferred stock as neither debt nor equity was referred to as "mezzanine" treatment. The FASB now requires mandatorily redeemable preferred shares to be reported as liabilities in the balance sheet. For example, in 2004, **Critical Path**, a seller of messaging technology, reported the following in its balance sheet (in thousands of U.S. dollars):

Total liabilities	$ 59,011
Mandatorily redeemable preferred stock	122,377
Total shareholders' deficit	(112,189)
Total liabilities, mandatorily redeemable preferred stock and shareholders' deficit	$ 69,199

[18] FASB ASC Topic 480 (Distinguishing Liabilities from Equity).

Under FASB ASC Topic 480, Critical Path, and all other U.S. companies, are now required to include mandatorily redeemable preferred stock in the computation of total liabilities.

An example of the new presentation required under FASB ASC Topic 480 (pre-Codification *Statement No. 150)* can be found in the financial statements of **American Physicians Service Group**, an insurance and financial services company. The Liabilities section of the company's 2009 balance sheet is as follows (in thousands of U.S. dollars):

Reserve for loss and loss adjustment expense	$ 88,668
Unearned premiums	36,341
Reinsurance premiums payable	30
Funds held under reinsurance treaties	2,379
Accrued expenses and other liabilities	6,465
Mandatorily redeemable preferred stock	6,679
Total liabilities	$140,562

To understand the journal entries associated with mandatorily redeemable preferred shares, consider the following simple example. On January 1, 2013, Tarazi Company issued mandatorily redeemable preferred shares in exchange for $100 cash. No dividends are to be paid on these shares, and they must be redeemed in exactly one year, on January 1, 2014, for $110. You can see that the interest rate implicit in this agreement is 10%; Tarazi is agreeing to pay $10 in interest in order to use the $100 issuance proceeds for one year. The journal entries to record the issuance, accrual of interest, and redemption of these preferred shares are as follows:

2013
Jan.	1	Cash	100	
		Mandatorily Redeemable Preferred Shares (liability)		100
Dec.	31	Interest Expense ($100 × 0.10)	10	
		Mandatorily Redeemable Preferred Shares (liability)		10

2014
Jan.	1	Mandatorily Redeemable Preferred Shares (liability)	110	
		Cash		110

A related class of shares is called "temporary equity." Shares classified as "temporary equity" are shares, either common or preferred, that can be redeemed at the option of the shareholders. According to SEC *Accounting Series Release (ASR) No. 268*, "Presentation in Financial Statements of 'Redeemable Preferred Stocks,'" such securities are to be reported in the balance sheet outside of the Stockholders' Equity section, similar to the "mezzanine" treatment described above.[19]

Written Put Options

As discussed in a previous section, most successful companies have approved extensive programs of share repurchases. One such company is **Dell Computer**. In the past, as part of this effort Dell wrote put options allowing other parties to sell Dell's shares back to Dell at set prices on specific dates. For example, on February 2, 2001, Dell had obligated itself to repurchase 122 million shares of its own stock at an average repurchase price of $44 per share. Because this obligation was in the form of a put option, Dell was not certain that it would have to repurchase the shares. In fact, Dell was hoping that its share price would stay above $44 per share so that the options would never be exercised. In the extreme, if Dell's share price were to drop to $0, the company would have had to buy back 122

---

[19] This standard can be found in FASB ASC paragraph 480-10-S99-1.

million worthless shares for a total of $5.4 billion ($44 per share × 122 million shares). Of course, it was unlikely that Dell's share price would drop all the way to $0, and if that were to actually happen, the company would have more pressing things to worry about than honoring its obligation under these put contracts. Accordingly, the fair value of Dell's obligation was somewhere between $0 (if the share price stayed above $44) and $5.4 billion (if the share price dropped all the way to $0). Precise estimation of the fair value of the put options involves the use of option-pricing formulas, as discussed earlier.

Why would Dell write these put options in the first place? The reason is that when Dell writes the put options, the party buying the options (usually a large financial institution) pays Dell some cash up front (equal to the fair value of the options on that date) for the right to be able to sell Dell shares to Dell at a set price in the future. Dell takes the cash and hopes that its share price stays high. The financial institution pays the cash and hopes that Dell's share price will go down.

为什么戴尔公司首先发行看跌期权？理由是，当戴尔公司发行这些看跌期权时，期权购买方（通常是大型金融机构）预先会支付给戴尔公司一笔现金（等同于当天期权的公允价值），以获得在未来按特定价格出售戴尔股票的权利。戴尔公司获得现金且希望股价保持在高位，但金融机构支付现金并希望戴尔股价会下跌。

Historically, companies have often recorded these put options as part of equity. However, the FASB now instructs companies to record the fair value of the obligation under written put options on a company's own shares as a liability.[20]

To understand the journal entries associated with written put options, consider the following simple example. On January 1, 2013, Kamili Company wrote a put option agreeing to purchase one share of its own stock for $100 on December 31, 2014, at the option of the purchaser of the put option. The market price of Kamili's shares on January 1, 2013, was $100. Given the past volatility in Kamili's share price and the two-year period until the option expiration date, there is some chance that Kamili's shares will actually be trading for less than $100 on December 31, 2014. If this is the case, the put option holder will exercise the option to sell a share of Kamili stock to Kamili for $100 at a time when the shares are worth less than $100. Assume that the use of an option-pricing formula indicates that, as of January 1, 2013, this put option has a fair value of $20. The journal entry that Kamili would make to record the writing of the put option is as follows:

```
2013
Jan.   1    Cash ................................................................   20
                Put Option (liability).........................................        20
```

By December 31, 2013, Kamili's share price has declined to $88 per share. Accordingly, the odds that the share price will be less than $100 on December 31, 2014, have increased, making it more likely that the put option holder will find it attractive to exercise the option and require Kamili to repurchase one of its own shares at an amount greater than its market value. Assume that an option-pricing formula suggests that the fair value of the put option on December 31, 2013, is $30, up from $20 at the beginning of the year. The necessary adjusting entry is as follows:

```
2013
Dec.  31    Loss on Put Option ..............................................   10
                Put Option (liability) ($30 − $20 already recognized)...........   10
```

On December 31, 2014, the put option expiration date, the market price of Kamili stock is $82 per share. At this price, the put option holder of course decides to exercise the option and sell one share of Kamili stock to Kamili for $100. One way to think of this transaction is that the put option holder can go out into the market, buy a share of Kamili stock for $82, and then exercise the put option to require Kamili to buy that same share of stock for $100. Accordingly, the option holder will net a gain of $18 on the option exercise date. In this case, this is less than the option holder expected to gain, as evidenced by the fact that the option holder paid $20 to purchase this option back on January 1, 2013.

[20] FASB ASC paragraph 480-10-25-8.

The journal entry that Kamili would make to record the purchase of one share of its stock in conjunction with the exercise of the put option is as follows:

2014
Dec. 31 Treasury Stock (the fair value of the share repurchased) 82
              Put Option (liability).. 30
                  Gain on Put Option   12
                  Cash..   100

The $12 gain on the put option reflects the fact that Kamili's estimated obligation under the put option decreased from $30 at the beginning of the year to just $18 ($100 − $82) at the option exercise date.

Obligation to Issue Shares of a Certain Dollar Value

Companies occasionally agree to satisfy their obligations by delivering shares of their own stock rather than by paying cash. This is especially true for startup companies that are trying to conserve their limited cash supply. Depending on how the contract is written, this promise to deliver shares of one's stock to satisfy an obligation can be recorded as equity or as a liability. The two following examples illustrate this distinction.

Example 1: On October 1, 2013, Lily Company, a software startup firm, experienced trouble with its office air conditioning system. The repair bill is $5,000. Rather than pay this amount in cash, Lily has agreed to deliver 200 shares of its no-par common stock to the repairperson on February 1, 2014. On October 1, 2013, Lily's shares have a market value of $25 per share. The journal entries that Lily would make to record the repairs and the delivery of the shares are as follows:

2013
Oct. 1 Maintenance Expense (200 shares × $25)............................ 5,000
             Common Stock Issuance Obligation (equity).......................   5,000

2014
Feb. 1 Common Stock Issuance Obligation (equity) 5,000
             Common Stock   5,000

The account "Common Stock Issuance Obligation (equity)" is similar to the common stock subscribed account introduced earlier in the chapter; both are included in the Equity section of the balance sheet. An obligation that requires a company to deliver a fixed number of its shares should be classified as equity because the party to whom the shares must be delivered is at risk to the same extent as are the existing shareholders. If Lily's shares go down in value between October 1, 2013, and February 1, 2014, the repairperson suffers in that the value of the shares received will be less than $5,000. Similarly, if Lily's shares go up in value, the repairperson benefits. In short, once Lily has made the promise to deliver a fixed number of shares to the repairperson, he or she experiences the same ups and downs in economic circumstances as do the existing shareholders of Lily Company. Accordingly, on the December 31, 2013, balance sheet, Lily Company will report this obligation to deliver a fixed number of its shares as part of equity.

Example 2: As in Example 1, on October 1, 2013, Lily Company received air conditioning repair services costing $5,000. Again, the company, wishing to conserve cash, promises to pay the repair bill with shares of its own stock on February 1, 2014. However, in this example, Lily doesn't fix the number of shares to be handed over on February 1 but instead promises to deliver shares with a market value of $5,000 on February 1. On October 1, 2013, Lily's shares have a market value of $25 per share, and on February 1,

2014, the shares have a market value of $20 per share. The journal entries that Lily would make to record the repairs and the delivery of the shares are as follows:

2013
Oct. 1 Maintenance Expense... 5,000
             Common Stock Issuance Obligation (liability)...................... 5,000
2014
Feb. 1 Common Stock Issuance Obligation (liability)......................... 5,000
             Common Stock (250 shares × $20)................................. 5,000

The account "Common Stock Issuance Obligation (liability)" would be reported as a liability on Lily's December 31, 2013, balance sheet. Because Lily has an obligation to deliver shares with a fixed monetary amount, the repairperson really doesn't care whether Lily's shares increase or decrease in value between October 1, 2013, and February 1, 2014. No matter what happens to the value of Lily's shares, the repairperson gets $5,000 worth of shares. Between October 1, 2013, and February 1, 2014, the repairperson does not share in the risks and rewards of ownership in Lily Company, so the obligation to deliver the shares is reported as a liability rather than as equity.

By the way, this provision will ultimately require a change in the conceptual framework. Currently, the conceptual framework definition of a liability includes only obligations to "transfer assets or provide services." The FASB may revise this definition to include obligations to transfer shares without transferring the risks and rewards of ownership. However, as mentioned several times earlier in the chapter, the FASB is currently undertaking a comprehensive review of the definitions of liability and equity items that probably will require more extensive changes in the conceptual definitions of those items.

Noncontrolling Interest

A consolidated balance sheet is the combined balance sheet for both a parent company and all of the subsidiaries that it controls. A consolidated balance sheet includes *all* assets and liabilities of the parent and the subsidiaries it controls. Thus, even though the parent owns only, say, 80% of a subsidiary, *all* of that subsidiary's assets and liabilities are included in the consolidated total. The intuition here is that the parent, with its 80% ownership, completely controls the assets of the subsidiary even though it doesn't own them completely.

那些母公司持股比例低于100%但其控制子公司的所有资产和负债被计入合并总数的情况，意味着取得合并资产负债表中资产的资金既不是来自合并负债也不是来自母公司，而是来自上述案例中持有子公司20%股权比例的股东。他们被称为少数股东，其提供的融资被称作少数股股东权益。

The fact that all of the assets and liabilities of a subsidiary owned less than 100% by the parent are in the consolidated total means that the consolidated balance sheet includes assets for which the acquisition was financed by funds coming not from consolidated liabilities and not from parent equity but instead from the shareholders who, in the example given above, own the other 20% of the subsidiary. These are called minority shareholders, and the financing provided by them is called minority interest. Minority interest is the amount of equity investment made by outside shareholders to consolidated subsidiaries that are not 100% owned by the parent.

The FASB uses the term noncontrolling interest to replace "minority interest" and directs that this item be classified in the consolidated balance sheet as part of equity.[21] This treatment brings U.S. GAAP in line with the IFRS contained in *IAS 27*.

Other than bringing consistent treatment within the set of U.S. companies and consistency with international standards, no one is really pleased with the classification of noncontrolling interest as part of equity. Everyone realizes that the claims of the noncontrolling, or minority, shareholders are fundamentally different from the claims of the shareholders who directly control the parent and indirectly control the subsidiaries in the consolidated group. However, the claim of the noncontrolling shareholders also isn't a liability. If it isn't equity and it isn't a liability, what is it? Historically, noncontrolling, or minority, interest has been reported as a liability, an equity, and as an in-between item in the "mezzanine" that was

[21] FASB ASC paragraph 810-10-45-16.

mentioned earlier. Given the existing conceptual framework, classifying noncontrolling interest as equity is the best the FASB can do. As part of the FASB's general reexamination of the difference between liability and equity items, the conceptual framework definitions may be revised to clarify the status of noncontrolling interest.

Stock Conversions

7 Distinguish between stock conversions that require a reduction in retained earnings and those that do not.

As noted earlier, stockholders may be permitted by the terms of their stock agreement or by special action of the corporation to exchange their holdings for stock of other classes. No gain or loss is recognized by the issuer on these conversions because it is an exchange of one form of equity for another. In certain instances, the exchanges may affect only corporate contributed capital accounts; in other instances, the exchanges may affect both capital and retained earnings accounts.

To illustrate the different conditions, assume that the capital of Sorensen Corporation on December 31, 2015, is as follows:

Preferred stock, $50 par, 10,000 shares	$ 500,000
Paid-in capital in excess of par—preferred	100,000
Common stock, $1 par, 100,000 shares	100,000
Paid-in capital in excess of par—common	2,900,000
Retained earnings	1,000,000

Each preferred share is convertible into four common shares at any time at the option of the shareholder.

Case 1: One Preferred Share for Four Common Shares ($1 par)

On December 31, 2015, 1,000 shares of preferred stock are exchanged for 4,000 shares of common. The amount originally paid for the 1,000 preferred shares, $60,000, is now the consideration identified with 4,000 shares of common stock with a total par value of $4,000. The conversion is recorded as shown below.

Preferred Stock, $50 par	50,000	
Paid-In Capital in Excess of Par—Preferred	10,000	
Common Stock, $1 par		4,000
Paid-In Capital in Excess of Par—Common		56,000

Case 1 is the usual case because par values for preferred stocks are typically high relative to par values of common stocks. This is so because preferred stock par values are still approximately equal to the market value of the preferred stock at the issue date, whereas the par value of common stocks is usually set at some very low value (as discussed earlier in the chapter).

Case 2: One Preferred Share for Four Common Shares ($20 par)

In Case 2, assume that the par value of the common shares is $20. In converting 1,000 shares of preferred for 4,000 shares of common, an increase in common stock at par of $80,000 (4,000 × $20) must be recognized, although it is accompanied by a decrease in the preferred equity of only $60,000. This type of conversion is generally recorded as follows:

Preferred Stock, $50 par	50,000	
Paid-In Capital in Excess of Par—Preferred	10,000	
Retained Earnings	20,000	
Common Stock, $20 par		80,000

The problems relating to the conversion of bonds for capital stock were described in Chapter 12.

For an investor, conversion of preferred stock for common stock often requires only retitling the investment account because both types of investment are carried at fair market value in the books of the investor. A special journal entry may be required if the conversion is also associated with a change in the investor's classification of the investment (e.g., from trading security to available-for-sale security). Investment reclassification is discussed in Chapter 14.

Factors Affecting Retained Earnings

LO8 学习目标8
列出影响留存收益余额的因素。

8 List the factors that impact the Retained Earnings balance.

The retained earnings account is essentially the meeting place of balance sheet and income statement accounts. In successive periods, retained earnings are increased by income and decreased by losses and dividends. As a result, the Retained Earnings balance represents the net accumulated earnings of a corporation.

A number of other factors can affect retained earnings in addition to net income, losses, and dividends. These factors include prior-period adjustments for corrections of errors, quasi-reorganizations, stock dividends, and treasury stock transactions. The transactions and events that increase or decrease retained earnings may be summarized as follows:

Retained Earnings

Decreases	*Increases*
Error corrections	Error corrections
Some changes in accounting principle	Some changes in accounting principle
Net loss	Net income
Cash dividends	Quasi-reorganizations
Stock dividends	
Treasury stock transactions	
Stock conversions	

Net Income and Dividends

The primary source of retained earnings is the net income generated by a business. The retained earnings account is increased by net income and is reduced by net losses from business activities. When operating losses or other debits to Retained Earnings produce a debit balance in this account, the debit balance is referred to as a *deficit*.

Dividends are distributions to the stockholders of a corporation in proportion to the number of shares held by the respective owners. Distributions may take the form of cash, other assets, notes (in essence, these are deferred cash dividends), and stock dividends. Most dividends involve reductions in retained earnings. Exceptions include some large stock dividends, which involve a reduction in additional paid-in capital, and liquidating dividends, which represent a return of invested capital to stockholders and call for reductions in contributed capital.

Use of the term *dividend* without qualification normally implies the distribution of cash. Dividends in a form other than cash, such as property or stock dividends, should be designated by their special form. Distributions from a capital source other than retained earnings should carry a description of their special origin, for example, liquidating dividend or dividend distribution of paid-in capital.

Prior-Period Adjustments

在某些情形下，过去几年出现的错误通常需要在调整当年调整留存收益账户时予以更正，被归类为前期调整。

In some situations, errors made in past years are discovered and corrected in the current year by an adjustment to the retained earnings account, referred to as a *prior-period adjustment*. Several types of errors can occur in measuring the results of operations and the financial status of an enterprise. Accounting errors can result from mathematical mistakes, a failure to apply appropriate accounting procedures, or a misstatement or omission of certain information. In addition, a change from an accounting principle that is not generally accepted to one that is accepted is considered a correction of an error.[22]

Fortunately, most errors are discovered during the accounting period, prior to closing the books. When this is the case, corrections can be made by making correcting entries directly to the accounts. This is much better than error correction by prior-period adjustment because the error is fixed immediately and it isn't advertised to the world through disclosure of a retained earnings adjustment.

Sometimes errors go undetected during the current period, but they are offset by an equal misstatement in the subsequent period. When this happens, the under- or overstatement of income in one period is counterbalanced by an equal over- or understatement of income in the next period. After the closing process is completed for the second year, the retained earnings account is correctly stated. If a counterbalancing error is discovered during the second year, however, it should be corrected at that time.

When errors of past periods are not counterbalancing, retained earnings will be misstated until a correction is made in the accounting records. If the error is material, a prior-period adjustment should be made directly to the retained earnings account. If an error resulted in an understatement of income in previous periods, a correcting entry would be needed to increase Retained Earnings; if an error overstated income in prior periods, then Retained Earnings would have to be decreased. These adjustments for corrections in net income of prior periods typically would be shown as a part of the total change in retained earnings as follows:

Retained earnings, unadjusted beginning balance	$XXX
Add or deduct prior-period adjustments	XX
Retained earnings, adjusted beginning balance	$XXX
Add current year's net income or deduct current year's net loss	XX
	$XXX
Deduct dividends	XX
Retained earnings, ending balance	$XXX

An example of a prior-period adjustment made to correct an error is in the August 2006 financial statements of **Apollo Group**, an education provider and parent company of the University of Phoenix. In 2006, Apollo made prior-period adjustments to reflect errors in the accounting for share-based compensation and the allowance for doubtful accounts. The adjustment also reflected corrections needed to change the accounting for cash, revenue, property and equipment, leases, and other investments to be in accordance with GAAP. The company corrected these errors by reducing its beginning Retained Earnings balance by $72.7 million.

[22] FASB ASC Topic 250 (Accounting Changes and Error Corrections).

FYI

The provisions of *IAS 8* regarding prior-period adjustments are the same as those under U.S. GAAP.

Another type of prior-period adjustment occurs when a company changes an accounting method or principle. When there is a change in accounting principle or method, a company is required to determine how the income statement would have been different in past years if the new accounting method had been used all along. To improve comparability, income statements for all years presented (for example, for all three years if three years of comparative data are provided) must be restated using the new accounting method. The beginning balance of Retained Earnings for the oldest year presented reflects an adjustment for the cumulative income effect of the accounting change on the net incomes of all preceding years for which a detailed income statement is not presented.

Techniques for analyzing and correcting errors are covered in detail in Chapter 20. Chapter 20 also covers prior-period adjustments associated with changes in accounting principle.

Other Changes in Retained Earnings

The most common changes in retained earnings result from earnings (or losses) and dividends. Other changes may result from treasury stock transactions (explained earlier in the chapter) or from a quasi-reorganization, which is performed only under special circumstances in which a business seeks a "fresh start." Quasi-reorganizations are covered in the Web Material (see www.cengagebrain.com) associated with this chapter.

Retained Earnings Restrictions

A company's Retained Earnings balance has historically served as a constraint on the payment of cash dividends and on the repurchase of treasury shares. For example, the General Corporation Law of the state of California states that:

> Neither a corporation nor any of its subsidiaries shall make any distribution to the corporation's shareholders [unless] . . . the amount of the retained earnings of the corporation immediately prior thereto equals or exceeds the amount of the proposed distribution. (Division 1, Chapter 5, Section 500)

However, in most states this constraint is no longer absolute. California law allows the payment of cash dividends even if the preceding retained earnings provision is not satisfied, as long as the total equity and working capital of the corporation are at specified levels. Other states, with Delaware often being viewed as the leader, have even less restrictive laws.

This flexibility in state laws doesn't mean that the level of retained earnings is not important. Banks and other lenders often place retained earnings restrictions in their loan contracts. For example, **Coinmach Service Corp.**, a Plainview, New York-based company that provides outsourced laundry equipment services for multifamily housing properties, disclosed the following in its 2007 financial statements:

> The covenant described above in the indenture governing the 11% Senior Secured Notes relating to restrictions on our ability to pay dividends permits quarterly dividend payments for the life of the notes in an amount equal to the difference between our distributable cash flow and our consolidated interest expense, so long as we satisfy an interest coverage test for the preceding fiscal quarter and no default is continuing.[23]

[23] Coinmach Service Corp., 2007, 10K Report.

In addition, industry regulations, such as banking codes, can also restrict the amount of retained earnings that can be used to support dividend payments. This is illustrated in a note from the 2009 financial statements of **Dimeco Inc.**, a bank that has been based in Pennsylvania since 1905.

> The Pennsylvania Banking Code restricts the availability of capital funds for payment of dividends by all state-chartered banks to the surplus of the Bank. Accordingly, at December 31, 2009, the balance in the capital surplus account totaling approximately $1,756,000 is unavailable for dividends.[24]

Retained earnings may also be restricted at the discretion of the board of directors. For example, the board may designate a portion of retained earnings as restricted for a particular purpose, such as expansion of plant facilities.

If restrictions on retained earnings are material, they are generally disclosed in a note to the financial statements. Occasionally, the restricted portion of retained earnings is reported on the balance sheet separately from the unrestricted amount that is available for dividends. The restricted portion may be designated as appropriated retained earnings and the unrestricted portion as unappropriated (or free) retained earnings. Whatever the form of disclosure, the main idea behind restrictions on retained earnings is to notify stockholders that some of the assets that might otherwise be available for dividend distribution are being retained within the business for specific purposes.

FASB CODIFICATION

The Issue: You have been working as a part-time accountant for a small electronics company. Your company makes remote control devices for home entertainment systems. The company has suffered five very tough years and has a large negative retained earnings balance to show for it. However, recent successes suggest that profits will be substantially improved in the future.

Unfortunately, the large negative retained earnings balance makes your company's reported financial statements look terrible. The company's CEO has come to you to see if you have any ideas about removing this accumulated deficit from the company's books. The CEO knows that the company's financial statements can be "refreshed" by going through a formal legal reorganization, but she is hoping that you can come up with a less costly process that will directly address the accumulated deficit on the balance sheet.

The Question: Is there a way to eliminate a negative retained earnings balance without going through a formal legal reorganization of the company?

Searching the Codification: Here are two hints. First, you are looking for "reorganizations," which are transactions that have a broad impact on the financial statements. Hence, you should look under the collection of topics labeled "Broad Transactions." Second, you don't want a "real" reorganization. You are looking for an imitation or informal reorganization. Another way to say this is "quasi-reorganization."

The Answer: The accounting technique for eliminating a large negative retained earnings balance is described on page 13-52.

[24] Dimeco, Inc., 2009, 10K Report.

Accounting for Dividends

LO9 学习目标9
正确记录现金股利、财产股利、小额和大额股票股利及股票分割。

9 Properly record cash dividends, property dividends, small and large stock dividends, and stock splits.

Among the powers delegated by the stockholders to the board of directors is the power to control the dividend policy. Whether dividends will or will not be paid, as well as the nature and the amount of dividends, are matters that the board determines. In setting dividend policy, the board of directors must answer two questions:

1. Do we have the legal right to declare a dividend?
2. Is a dividend distribution financially advisable?

In answering the first question, the board of directors must observe the state incorporation laws governing the payment of dividends. The availability of capital as a basis for dividends is a determination to be made by the legal counsel, not by the accountant. The accountant must report accurately the sources of each capital increase or decrease; the legal counsel investigates the availability of such sources as bases for dividend distributions.

> **FYI**
> It has been recommended that the format of the Stockholders' Equity section in the balance sheet be changed to give emphasis to the specific legal restrictions on cash distributions to shareholders. See Michael L. Roberts, William D. Samson, and Michael T. Dugan, "The Stockholders' Equity Section: Form without Substance?" *Accounting Horizons*, December 1990, p. 35.

The board of directors must also consider the second question (i.e., does the payment of a dividend make financial sense?). Literally thousands of research papers by finance professors have examined the issue of the "best" corporate dividend policy. Full discussion of this issue is a topic for a corporate finance class. Three general observations are made here:

- Old stable companies pay out a large portion of their income as cash dividends.
- Young growing companies pay out a small portion of their income as cash dividends. They keep the funds inside the company for expansion.
- Once a company has established a certain level of cash dividends, any subsequent reduction is seen as very bad news by investors. Accordingly, companies are quite cautious about raising their dividends, waiting until they are sure they can maintain the increased level permanently.

When a dividend is legally declared and announced, it cannot be revoked. The amount of the dividend is thereafter reported as a dividends payable liability until it is paid to the shareholders.

> **FYI**
> After the record date, stock no longer carries a right to dividends, and it sells at a lower price. Stock on the New York Stock Exchange is normally quoted ex-dividend several trading days prior to the record date because of the time required to deliver the stock and to record the stock transfers.

Recognition and Payment of Dividends

Three dates are essential in the recognition and payment of dividends: (1) date of declaration, (2) date of record, and (3) date of payment. Dividends are made payable to stockholders of record as of a date following the date of declaration and preceding the date of payment. The liability for dividends payable is recorded on the declaration date and is cancelled on the payment date. No entry is required on the record date, but a list of the stockholders is made as of the close of business on this date. These are the persons who receive dividends on the payment date. For example, on August 10, 2012, American Express paid a quarterly cash dividend of $0.20, or 20 cents, per share to shareholders of record as of July 6, 2012. These dividends were declared on May 1, 2012.

Cash Dividends

The most common type of dividend is a cash dividend. For the corporation, these dividends involve a reduction in Retained Earnings and in Cash. For the investor, a cash dividend generates cash and is recognized as dividend revenue. Entries to record the declaration and payment of a $100,000 cash dividend by a corporation follow:

Declaration of Dividend:

Dividends (or Retained Earnings)	100,000	
Dividends Payable		100,000

Payment of Dividend:

Dividends Payable	100,000	
Cash		100,000

In most circumstances, the declaration of a dividend is viewed as a noncancellable, legal obligation to pay the dividend to the shareholders. However, this is not always true, as demonstrated by this December 11, 2001, press release from Enron:

> HOUSTON—Enron Corp. (NYSE: ENE) announced today that previously declared dividends will not be paid on the corporation's common stock, the Cumulative Second Preferred Convertible Stock, the Enron Capital LLC 8% Cumulative Guaranteed Monthly Income Preferred Shares, and the Enron Capital Resources, L.P. 9% Cumulative Preferred Securities, Series A.

This press release was made about a week after Enron filed for Chapter 11 bankruptcy, probably to head off an additional landslide of lawsuits. Obviously, if the dividends had been paid to the shareholders, the creditors, who were resigned to recovering just pennies on the dollar for the amounts owed to them, would have sued to reclaim the assets paid out as dividends.

Property Dividends

property dividend
财产股利

A distribution to stockholders that is payable in some asset other than cash is generally referred to as a property dividend. Frequently, the assets to be distributed are securities of other companies owned by the corporation. The corporation thus transfers to its stockholders the ownership interest in such securities. Property dividends occur most frequently in closely held corporations.

This type of transfer is sometimes referred to as a nonreciprocal transfer to owners inasmuch as nothing is received by the company in return for its distribution to the stockholders. These transfers should be recorded using the fair value (as of the day of declaration) of the assets distributed and a gain or loss recognized for the difference between the carrying value on the books of the issuing company and the fair value of the assets.[25] Property dividends are valued at carrying value if the fair value is not determinable.

To illustrate the entries for a property dividend, assume that Bigler Corporation owns 100,000 shares in Tri-State Oil Co., carrying value $2,700,000, current fair market value $3,000,000, or $30 per share, which it wishes to distribute to its stockholders. There are 1,000,000 shares of Bigler Corporation stock outstanding. Accordingly, a dividend of 1/10 of a share of Tri-State Oil Co. stock is declared on each share of Bigler Corporation stock outstanding. The entries for Bigler for the dividend declaration and payment are as follows:

Declaration of Dividend:

Dividends (or Retained Earnings)	3,000,000	
Property Dividends Payable		2,700,000
Gain on Distribution of Property Dividends		300,000

Payment of Dividend:

Property Dividends Payable	2,700,000	
Investment in Tri-State Oil Co. Stock		2,700,000

Stock Dividends

A corporation may distribute to stockholders additional shares of the company's own stock as a stock dividend. A stock dividend involves no transfer of cash or any other asset to shareholders. In essence, a stock dividend results in the same pie (the company) being cut up into more pieces (shares outstanding), with each shareholder owning the same proportion of the pieces as before the stock dividend. From a shareholder's standpoint, receipt of a stock dividend is an economic nonevent.

Fear that investors were being deceived into thinking that receipt of a stock dividend actually represented income led to development of the rules governing how the issuing company must account for stock dividends. As described by Professor James Tucker, stock dividends acquired a shady reputation in the late 1800s because they were viewed as being similar to "stock watering."[26] *Stock watering* is the practice of issuing stock without receiving adequate compensation in return, thus diluting the value of the shares. In addition, in the 1920s and 1930s, accountants and regulatory authorities became concerned that companies issuing stock dividends were wrongly leading investors to believe that receiving a stock dividend was equivalent to receiving a cash dividend. This impression was particularly easy to convey when a company had a practice of issuing small, regular stock dividends (e.g., a 2.5% annual stock dividend). Also, from the issuing company's standpoint, a stock dividend involved no cash outlay, and the standard accounting treatment required only a small reduction in Retained Earnings equal to the par value of the newly issued shares.

The Committee on Accounting Procedure (CAP) issued *Accounting Research Bulletin (ARB) No. 11* in September 1941, which made it considerably more difficult for firms to issue small stock dividends by requiring a reduction in Retained Earnings equal to the market value of the newly issued shares. To see what a difference this makes, recall that par values are typically around $1 per share, whereas market values usually range between $20 and $80 per share. Professor Stephen Zeff cites *ARB No. 11* as one of the earliest examples of the economic consequences of accounting standards, in this case, the use of an accounting standard to reduce the incidence of small, regular stock dividends.[27]

---

[25] FASB ASC paragraph 845-10-30-1.
[26] James J. Tucker III, "The Role of Stock Dividends in Defining Income, Developing Capital Market Research and Exploring the Economic Consequences of Accounting Policy Decisions," *The Accounting Historians Journal*, Fall 1985, pp. 73–94.
[27] Stephen A. Zeff, "Towards a Fundamental Rethinking of the Role of the 'Intermediate' Course in the Accounting Curriculum," in *The Impact of Rule-Making on Intermediate Financial Accounting Textbooks*, Daniel J. Jensen, ed. (Columbus, OH: 1982), pp. 33–51.

Small versus Large Stock Dividends In accounting for stock dividends, a distinction is made between a small and a large stock dividend.[28] Recall that the specific objective of the Committee on Accounting Procedures was to discourage regularly recurring small stock dividends. As a general guideline, a stock dividend of less than 20%–25% of the number of shares previously outstanding is considered a small stock dividend. Stock dividends involving the issuance of more than 20%–25% are considered large stock dividends.[29]

With a small stock dividend, companies must transfer from Retained Earnings to Capital Stock and Additional Paid-In Capital an amount equal to the fair market value of the additional shares issued. Such a transfer is consistent with the general public's view of a stock dividend as a distribution of corporate earnings at an amount equivalent to the fair market value of the shares received. The following example illustrates the entries for the declaration and issuance of a small stock dividend.

Assume that stockholders' equity for the Fuji Company on July 1 is as follows:

Common stock, $1 par, 100,000 shares outstanding	$ 100,000
Paid-in capital in excess of par	1,100,000
Retained earnings	750,000

The company declares a 10% stock dividend, or a dividend of 1 share of common for every 10 shares held. Before the stock dividend, the stock is selling for $22 per share. After the 10% stock dividend, each original share worth $22 will become 1.1 shares, each with a value of $20 ($22/1.1). The stock dividend is to be recorded at the market value of the new shares issued, or $200,000 (10,000 new shares at the postdividend price of $20). The entries to record the declaration of the dividend and the issuance of stock by Fuji Company are as follows:

Declaration of Dividend:

Retained Earnings	200,000	
Stock Dividends Distributable		10,000
Paid-In Capital in Excess of Par		190,000

Issuance of Dividend:

Stock Dividends Distributable	10,000	
Common Stock, $1 par		10,000

If a balance sheet is prepared after the declaration of a stock dividend but before issue of the shares, Stock Dividends Distributable is reported in the Stockholders' Equity section as an addition to capital stock outstanding.

Because the focus of the CAP was on reducing the number of small stock dividends, the accounting requirements governing large stock dividends are less specific than those for small stock dividends. Accordingly, the existing standard is quite general, as follows:

> . . . there is no need to capitalize retained earnings, other than to the extent occasioned by legal requirements. (FASB ASC 505-20-30-6)

In practice, this standard results in the par or stated value of the newly issued shares being transferred to the capital stock account from either the retained earnings or paid-in capital in excess of par accounts.[30] To illustrate, assume that Fuji Company declares a large stock dividend of 50%, or a dividend of one share for every two held. Legal requirements call for the transfer to Capital Stock of an amount equal to the par value of the

---

[28] FASB ASC paragraph 505-20-25-3.

[29] In *Accounting Series Release No. 124*, the SEC specified that for publicly traded companies, stock dividends of 25% or more should be accounted for as large stock dividends and those of less than 25% as small stock dividends.

[30] Some large stock dividends are effected by reducing both paid-in capital in excess of par and retained earnings by a total of the par value of the newly issued shares.

shares issued. Entries for the declaration of the dividend and the issuance of the 50,000 new shares (100,000 × 0.50) are as follows:

Declaration of Dividend:

Retained Earnings	50,000	
Stock Dividends Distributable		50,000
OR		
Paid-In Capital in Excess of Par	50,000	
Stock Dividends Distributable		50,000

Issuance of Dividend:

Stock Dividends Distributable	50,000	
Common Stock, $1 par		50,000

Stop & Think

You are hired as an accounting consultant by a company that is considering issuing either a 20% stock dividend or a 25% stock dividend. From an accounting standpoint, which would you recommend?

a) If the company wishes to minimize the impact of the stock dividend on reported profits for the current year, declare a 20% stock dividend.

b) If the company wishes to minimize the impact of the stock dividend on reported profits for the current year, declare a 25% stock dividend.

c) If the company is confident about its future ability to generate profits and pay cash dividends, declare a 20% stock dividend as a way to proclaim this confidence in a public way.

d) If the company is confident about its future ability to generate profits and pay cash dividends, declare a 25% stock dividend as a way to proclaim this confidence in a public way.

虽然从投资者角度来看，股票股利与股票分割类似，但股票股利对公司资本成本的影响不同于股票分割。股票股利表现为已发行股票数量的增加，而且由于票面价格或者设定股价未变，股本账户余额应相应增加。作为对比，股票分割只不过将股本余额分割为更多的部分，伴随着票面价格或者设定股价的减少。

FYI

A *reverse stock split* is the consolidation of shares outstanding into a smaller number of shares. Conventional wisdom is that shares trading for less than $10 are viewed with some skepticism, and a reverse split can make the stock look more respectable. Whatever the conventional wisdom, a reverse stock split is almost always viewed as bad news by investors.

Stock Dividends versus Stock Splits

A corporation may effect a stock split by reducing the par or stated value of each share of capital stock and proportionately increasing the number of shares outstanding. For example, a corporation with 1,000,000 shares of $3 par stock outstanding may split the stock on a 3-for-1 basis. After the split, the corporation will have 3,000,000 shares of $1 par stock outstanding, and each stockholder will have three shares for every one previously held. However, each share now represents only one-third of the capital interest it previously represented; furthermore, each share of stock can be expected to sell for approximately one-third of its previous market price. From an investor's perspective, therefore, a stock split can be viewed the same as a stock dividend.

Although a stock dividend can be compared to a stock split from the investor's point of view, its effects on corporate capital differ from those of a stock split. A stock dividend results in an increase in the number of shares outstanding, and because the par or stated value of each share is unchanged, the Capital Stock balance also increases. In contrast, a stock split merely divides the existing Capital Stock balance into more parts, with a reduction in the par or stated value of each share. Because a stock split does not involve any transfers among the capital accounts, no journal entry is necessary. Instead, the change in the number of shares outstanding, as well as the change in the par or stated value, may be recorded by means of a memorandum entry.

Exhibit 13-6 provides a comparative example of the effects of a 100% stock dividend and a 2-for-1 stock split. The simple example in Exhibit 13-6 illustrates that, from an accounting perspective, the effects of a large stock dividend can be very different from the effects of a stock split even though both result in the creation of the same number of new shares. The required

Exhibit 13-6 | Comparative Example—Stock Dividend versus Stock Split

Stockholders' Equity*	
Common stock, $5 par, 50,000 shares outstanding	$250,000
Paid-in capital in excess of par	400,000
Retained earnings	300,000
Total stockholders' equity	$950,000

*Prior to stock dividend or stock split.

Stockholders' Equity After 100% Stock Dividend		Stockholders' Equity After 2-for-1 Stock Split	
Common stock, $5 par, 100,000 shares outstanding	$500,000	Common stock, $2.50 par, 100,000 shares outstanding	$250,000
Paid-in capital in excess of par*	400,000	Paid-in capital in excess of par	400,000
Retained earnings	50,000	Retained earnings	300,000
Total stockholders' equity	$950,000	Total stockholders' equity	$950,000

*Some or all of the $250,000 transfer to common stock at par could have been made from paid-in capital in excess of par.

© Cengage Learning 2014

transfer from Retained Earnings (or Paid-In Capital in Excess of Par) can significantly impact the Stockholders' Equity section of the balance sheet. For example, in the illustration in Exhibit 13-6, the 100% stock dividend may hinder the issuing firm's ability to pay future cash dividends because the Retained Earnings balance is so drastically reduced; no such constraint arises when the issuance of the new shares is accounted for as a 2-for-1 stock split.

Although stock splits and stock dividends are distinctly different in an accounting sense, the terms "stock split" and "stock dividend" are used interchangeably in the financial press and sometimes even in the issuing company's annual report. For example, *The Wall Street Journal*'s description of a distribution as a split or dividend agrees with the actual accounting for the distribution only about 25% of the time.[31]

Liquidating Dividends

A liquidating dividend is a distribution representing a return to stockholders of a portion of contributed capital. Whereas a normal cash dividend provides a return on investment and is accounted for by reducing Retained Earnings, a liquidating dividend provides a return of investment. A liquidating dividend is accounted for by reducing Paid-In Capital.

To illustrate, assume that Stubbs Corporation declared and paid a cash dividend and a partial liquidating dividend amounting to $150,000. Of this amount, $100,000 represents a regular $10 cash dividend on 10,000 shares of common stock. The remaining $50,000

---

[31] See Graeme Rankine and Earl K. Stice, "The Market Reaction to the Choice of Accounting Method for Stock Splits and Large Stock Dividends," *Journal of Financial and Quantitative Analysis*, 1997.

represents a $5-per-share liquidating dividend, which is recorded as a reduction to Paid-In Capital in Excess of Par. The entries would be as follows:

Declaration of Dividend:

Dividends (or Retained Earnings)	100,000	
Paid-In Capital in Excess of Par	50,000	
Dividends Payable		150,000

Payment of Dividend:

Dividends Payable	150,000	
Cash		150,000

USING STOCK DIVIDENDS AS SIGNALS

The accounting treatment of stock dividends makes their declaration an interesting way to send a good news signal to the market. The reasoning goes like this: Because cash dividend payments are often restricted to the amount of retained earnings, the reduction in Retained Earnings required in accounting for a stock dividend might make it more difficult to declare cash dividends in the future. Accordingly, only firms with favorable future prospects would be likely to declare stock dividends. These firms would be confident that future earnings would bolster the Retained Earnings balance, making up for the reduction required by the stock dividend declaration.

So, according to this reasoning, if you see a firm declaring a stock dividend, you can conclude that the management of that firm must be confident that future earnings will be adequate to cover future cash dividends. This signaling view of stock dividends is supported by the fact that stock prices of companies instantly go up when they announce plans to issue a stock dividend. The accompanying graph shows the size of the positive market reaction to a stock dividend announcement, based on the size of the stock dividend.

Questions:

1. Assume that there is validity to this signaling theory of stock dividends. Which would be a stronger signal, a 20% stock dividend or a 25% stock dividend?
2. Again, assuming validity to the signaling theory, which would be a stronger signal, a 100% stock dividend or a 2-for-1 stock split?

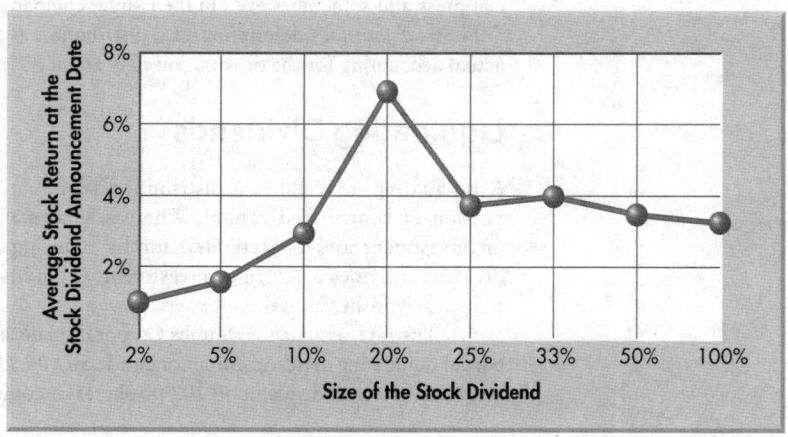

Sources: Graeme Rankine and Earl K. Stice, "Accounting Rules and the Signaling Properties of 20% Stock Dividends," *The Accounting Review*, January 1997; Graeme Rankine and Earl K. Stice, "The Market Reaction to the Choice of Accounting Method for Stock Splits and Large Stock Dividends," *Journal of Financial and Quantitative Analysis*, 1997.

Stockholders should be notified as to the allocation of the total dividend payment, so they can determine the amount that represents revenue and the amount that represents a return of investment.

Statement of Comprehensive Income and Other Equity Items

LO10 学习目标10
编制综合收益表，解释未实现损益作为累计其他综合收益的一部分进行记录的背景，列举国外资产负债表中权益储备的主要类型。

10 Prepare a statement of comprehensive incomes, explain the background of unrealized gains and losses recorded as part of accumulated other comprehensive income, and list the major types of equity reserves found in foreign balance sheets.

In addition to the two major categories of contributed capital and retained earnings, the Equity section of a U.S. balance sheet often includes a number of miscellaneous items. These items are gains or losses that bypass the income statement when they are recognized and are reported as part of accumulated other comprehensive income. A further discussion of these items follows. In addition, the following section includes a discussion of equity reserves, which are common in the balance sheets of foreign companies that do not use U.S. accounting principles.

Statement of Comprehensive Income

FASB ASC Topic 220 requires that all companies provide a statement of comprehensive income. An example of Microsoft's 2011 statement of comprehensive income is included in Exhibit 13-7.

Comprehensive income is the number used to reflect an overall measure of the change in a company's wealth during the period. In addition to including net income, comprehensive income also includes items that, in general, arise from changes in market conditions unrelated to the business operations of a company. These items are excluded from net income because they are viewed as yielding little information about the economic performance of a company's business operations. However, they are reported as part of comprehensive income because they do impact the value of assets and liabilities reported in the balance sheet.

Exhibit 13-7 | Microsoft's Statement of Comprehensive Income

Microsoft Statement of Comprehensive Income For the Year Ended June 30, 2011			
(In millions)	2011	2010	2009
Net income	23,150	18,760	14,569
Other comprehensive income:			
Net unrealized gains on derivatives	(627)	27	302
Net unrealized gains/(losses) on investments	1,054	265	(233)
Translation adjustments and other	381	(206)	(240)
Comprehensive income	23,958	18,846	14,398

Microsoft, 2012, 10K Report

The FASB discussed the concept of comprehensive income in its conceptual framework. However, it wasn't until 1998 that the concept was placed into practice with the issuance of pre-Codification *Statement No. 130*. This standard is now found in FASB ASC Topic 220 (Comprehensive Income). Comprehensive income is reported either as part of one continuous net income/comprehensive income statement or in a separate statement shown immediately after the income statement. The FASB encourages companies to provide one continuous net income/comprehensive income statement. However, most companies report comprehensive income in a separate statement placed immediately after the income statement. A discussion of the most common elements affecting comprehensive income follows.

Equity Items That Bypass the Income Statement and Are Reported As Part of Accumulated Other Comprehensive Income

Since 1980, the Equity sections of U.S. balance sheets have begun to fill up with a strange collection of items, each the result of an accounting controversy. These items are summarized in the following sections.

Foreign Currency Translation Adjustment The foreign currency translation adjustment arises from the change in the equity of foreign subsidiaries (as measured in terms of U.S. dollars) that occurs as a result of changes in foreign currency exchange rates. For example, if the Japanese yen weakens relative to the U.S. dollar, the equity of Japanese subsidiaries of U.S. firms will decrease, in dollar terms. Before 1981, these changes were recognized as losses or gains in the income statement. Multinational firms disliked this treatment because it added volatility to reported earnings. The FASB changed the accounting rule, and now these changes are reported as direct adjustments to equity, insulating the income statement from this aspect of foreign currency fluctuations.[32] Computation of this foreign currency translation adjustment is explained in Chapter 22.

Unrealized Gains and Losses on Available-for-Sale Securities Available-for-sale securities are those that were not purchased with the immediate intention to resell but that a company also doesn't necessarily plan to hold forever. These securities, along with trading securities (those purchased as part of an active buying and selling program), are reported on the balance sheet at their current market values. The unrealized gains and losses from market value fluctuations in trading securities are included in the income statement, but the unrealized gains and losses from market value fluctuations in available-for-sale securities are shown as a direct adjustment to equity. When the FASB was considering requiring securities to be reported at their market values, companies complained about the income volatility that would be caused by recognition of changes in the market value of securities. The FASB made the standard more acceptable to businesses by allowing unrealized gains and losses on available-for-sale securities to bypass the income statement and go straight to the Equity section.[33] Accounting for securities is covered in Chapter 14.

Unrealized Gains and Losses on Derivatives A derivative is a financial instrument, such as an option or a future, that derives its value from the movement of a price, an exchange rate, or an interest rate associated with some other item. For example, as discussed earlier in the chapter, an option to purchase a stock becomes more valuable

---

[32] FASB ASC Subtopic 830-30 (Foreign Currency Matters—Translation of Financial Statements).
[33] FASB ASC paragraph 320-10-35-1b.

as the price of the stock increases. Similarly, the right to purchase foreign currency at a fixed exchange rate becomes more valuable as that foreign currency becomes more expensive. As will be discussed in Chapter 19, companies often use derivatives to manage their exposure to risk stemming from changes in prices and rates. Frequently, derivatives are used to manage risk associated with sales or purchases that will not occur until a future period. In these cases, in order to ensure proper matching of gains and losses, derivative gains and losses are sometimes deferred and reported as part of accumulated other comprehensive income.

To illustrate the computation and reporting of comprehensive income, consider the following example. The last few lines of Kendall Company's income statement were as follows:

Income before income taxes	$2,000
Income tax expense	(800)
Income from continuing operations	$1,200
Income from discontinued operations:	
Income from operations (including loss on disposal of $200)	$ 250
Income tax expense	(100)
Income from discontinued operations	150
Net income	$1,350

In addition, Kendall had the following items impacting comprehensive income:

	Amount This Year (Before Taxes)
Unrealized gain (loss) on available-for-sale securities	$100
Unrealized gain (loss) on derivative instruments	(20)
Foreign currency translation adjustment, increase (decrease) in stockholders' equity	300

Assume that the income tax rate for all items is 40%. Kendall Company would report its comprehensive income for the year as follows:

Net income	$1,350
Other comprehensive income:	
Unrealized gain on available-for-sale securities [$100 × (1 − 0.40)]	60
Unrealized loss on derivative instruments [−$20 × (1 − 0.40)]	(12)
Foreign currency translation adjustment [$300 × (1 − 0.40)]	180
Comprehensive income	$1,578

In this illustration, each of the other comprehensive income items is shown net of income taxes. An alternative approach is to report all of the items before tax and then show the total income tax effect of the other comprehensive income items as a single separate line in the computation of comprehensive income.

In this case, comprehensive income is composed of three primary components:

- Income from continuing operations
- Income from discontinued operations
- Other comprehensive income

The most important source of income is income from continuing operations because this income not only arises from the core business of the company but also represents the

最重要的收入来源是持续经营收入，因为这项收入不仅源自公司的核心业务，还显示公司未来产生持续现金流的能力。其他综合收益来自不属于公司核心经营活动的一部分（如股价变动、外币价格的变动及其他），同时在各个年度间正负波动。综合收益的报告不但使得财务报表使用者能够了解各年度影响公司的所有财富变化，而且能够识别哪些财富是未来预期持续产生的，哪些是暂时性、一年期的。

potential for a continuing stream of income in the future. Other comprehensive income arises from events (such as changes in security values, changes in foreign exchange rates, and so forth) that are not part of a company's core operations and that also fluctuate, almost randomly, from positive to negative from year to year. The reporting of comprehensive income allows the financial statement user to see all of the wealth changes that impacted the company during the year but to also distinguish between those wealth changes that are expected to persist in the future and those that are transitory, one-year items.

Balance Sheet Reporting The accumulated amount of comprehensive income is reflected in the Equity section of the balance sheet in two ways:

- Net income (less dividends) is cumulated in retained earnings.
- Other comprehensive income is cumulated in accumulated other comprehensive income.

> **FYI**
>
> The income tax effects of other comprehensive income items are usually deferred and don't impact the amount of current income taxes payable. Deferred income taxes are discussed in Chapter 16.

In essence, you can think of the accumulated other comprehensive income account as the "retained earnings" of other comprehensive income items. To illustrate, refer back to the Kendall Company example. Assume that the beginning balance in Retained Earnings was $5,000, the beginning balance in Accumulated Other Comprehensive Income was an equity reduction of $500, and the dividends paid for the year were $400. The Equity section of Kendall's balance sheet at the end of the year would include the following two items:

Retained earnings ($5,000 + $1,350 − $400) $5,950
Accumulated other comprehensive income (−$500 + $60 − $12 + $180). . . . .   (272)

International Accounting: Equity Reserves

As discussed earlier in this chapter, state incorporation laws link the ability of a firm to pay cash dividends to the Retained Earnings balance. In other words, total equity is divided into two parts: the equity that is available to be distributed to shareholders and the equity that is not available for distribution. Restriction of the distribution of equity ensures that an equity "cushion" exists for the absorption of operating losses, thus increasing the chances of creditors to be fully repaid.

Laws in foreign countries are often more explicit than U.S. state incorporation laws in linking the payment of cash dividends to the amount of distributable equity. Equity is divided among various equity reserve accounts, each with legal restrictions dictating whether it can be distributed to shareholders. In that type of legal environment, the accounting for equity accounts directly influences a firm's ability to pay dividends and thus becomes an important part of corporate financing policy.

A brief summary of accounting for equity reserves is given in the following sections. The discussion is based on equity accounting practice in the United Kingdom. Because of the worldwide British influence left from the days of the British Empire, the U.K. model is widely used.

The major types of equity reserve accounts are illustrated in Exhibit 13-8. Remember that the most important distinction is whether the reserve is part of distributable or non-distributable equity.

Exhibit 13-8 | Equity Reserves

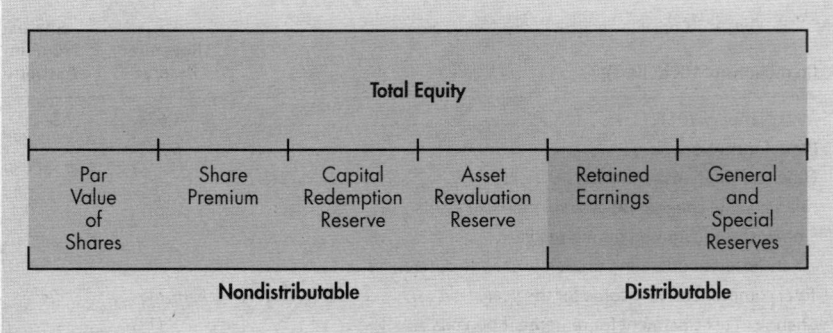

© Cengage Learning 2014

Par Value and Share Premium These accounts correspond closely with U.S. practice, with the share premium account being the same as the paid-in capital in excess of par account. Usually, a country's laws restrict the ability of a firm to "refund" any of this paid-in capital, so these two accounts are part of nondistributable equity.

Capital Redemption Reserve When shares are reacquired, total equity is reduced. To protect the ability of creditors to be fully repaid, these reductions are usually considered to be reductions in distributable equity. To reflect this fact in the accounts, an amount equal to the par value of the shares reacquired is transferred from Retained Earnings (part of distributable equity) to Capital Redemption Reserve (part of nondistributable equity).

Asset Revaluation Reserve In many countries, property, plant, and equipment can be written up to its current market value. The recognition of this unrealized gain increases equity. The question is whether the additional equity can be used to support additional cash dividend payments. The answer is no. A revaluation reserve is established as part of nondistributable equity, and unrealized gains from increases in fixed asset market values are credited to the revaluation reserve.

General and Special Reserves As discussed earlier, the board of directors can voluntarily restrict the use of retained earnings for the payment of cash dividends. These restrictions can later be rescinded. In the United States, these restrictions can be disclosed in a financial statement note or recognized as a formal appropriation of a portion of retained earnings. In many foreign countries, these restrictions are acknowledged by transferring part of retained earnings to a general or a special reserve account. Note that these reserves are still part of distributable equity; the board of directors can remove the restrictions at any time.

Some of the reserves mentioned are illustrated with the accounts of **Swire Pacific Limited** shown in Exhibit 13-9. Swire Pacific Limited is based in Hong Kong and is one of the largest companies in the world. The primary operations of the company are in the regions of Hong Kong, China, and Taiwan, where it has operated for more than 125 years. Swire operates **Cathay Pacific Airways** and has extensive real estate holdings in Hong Kong.

As you can see from the amounts included in its calculation, the "revenue reserve" is generally equivalent to what we call "retained earnings." The "investment revaluation reserve" is equivalent to the accumulated unrealized gain or loss on available-for-sale securities. Thus, the legal limit on dividend payments by Swire Pacific is HK$18.399 billion.

Exhibit 13-9 | Equity Section for Swire Pacific Limited

(In millions of HK dollars)	Revenue Reserve	Share Premium Account	Capital Redemption Reserve	Investment Revaluation Reserve
At 1st January 2011	11,673	342	49	24
Profit for the year	16,745	—	—	—
Other comprehensive income				
Net fair value changes on available-for-sale assets				
– net losses recognised during the year	—	—	—	(45)
– transferred to operating profit—exchange differences	—	—	—	(3)
Total comprehensive income for the year	16,745	—	—	(48)
Change in tax treatment for retirement benefits	(14)	—	—	—
2010 final dividend	(3,761)	—	—	—
2011 first interim dividend	(1,730)	—	—	—
2011 special interim dividend	(4,514)	—	—	—
At 31st December 2011	18,399	342	49	(24)

Source: Swire Pacific Limited, 10K Report

Disclosures Related to the Equity Section

LO11 Prepare a statement of changes in stockholders' equity.

In accounting for capital stock, it should be recognized that stock may be:

- Authorized but unissued
- Subscribed for and held for issuance pending receipt of cash for the full amount of the subscription price
- Outstanding in the hands of stockholders
- Reacquired and held by the corporation for subsequent reissuance
- Cancelled by appropriate corporation action

Thus, a corporation must maintain an accurate record of all transactions involving capital stock. Separate general ledger accounts are required for each source of capital including each class of stock. In addition, subsidiary records are needed to keep track of individual stockholders and stock certificates.

Contributed capital and its components should be disclosed separately from retained earnings on the balance sheet. Within the Contributed Capital section, it is important to identify the major classes of stock and the additional paid-in capital. Although it is common practice to report a single amount for additional paid-in capital, separate accounts should be provided in the ledger to identify the individual sources of additional paid-in capital, for example, Paid-In Capital in Excess of Par or Stated Value, Paid-In Capital from Treasury Stock, or Paid-In Capital from Stock Options.

For each class of stock, a description of the major features should be disclosed, such as par or stated value, dividend preference, or conversion terms. The number of shares authorized, issued, and outstanding should also be disclosed.

As an illustration, the Stockholders' Equity section from the balance sheet of IBM as of December 31, 2011, is presented in Exhibit 13-10. Many companies do not provide as much detail on the balance sheet as is illustrated for IBM.

Exhibit 13-10 | IBM's Stockholders' Equity Section

(Dollars in millions)	2011	2010
Stockholders' equity		
Common stock, par value $0.20 per share and additional paid-in capital.	48,129	45,418
Shares authorized: 4,687,500,000		
Shares issued (2011—2,182,469,838; 2010—2,161,800,054)		
Retained earnings	104,857	92,532
Treasury stock, at cost (shares: 2011—1,019,287,274; 2010—933,806,510)	(110,963)	(96,161)
Accumulated other comprehensive income/(loss)	(21,885)	(18,743)
Total IBM Stockholders' equity	20,138	23,046
Noncontrolling interests	97	126
Total equity	20,236	23,172

IBM, 2011, 10K Report

Readers of financial statements should be provided with an explanation of the changes in individual equity balances during the period. When stockholders' equity is composed of numerous accounts, as in the following example, a statement of changes in stockholders' equity is usually presented. The statement of changes in stockholders' equity for IBM for 2011 is illustrated in Exhibit 13-11.

Exhibit 13-11 | Statement of Changes in Stockholder's Equity for IBM

(Dollars in millions)	Common Stock and Additional Paid-In Capital	Retained Earnings	Treasury Stock	Accumulated Other Comprehensive Income/(Loss)	Total IBM Stockholders' Equity	Non-controlling Interests	Total Equity
2011							
Equity, January 1, 2011	$45,418	$ 92,532	$ (96,161)	$(18,743)	$23,046	$126	$23,172
Net income plus other comprehensive income/(loss):							
Net income		15,855			$15,855		$15,855
Other comprehensive income/(loss)				(3,142)	(3,142)		(3,142)
Total comprehensive income/(loss)					$12,713		$12,713
Cash dividends declared—common stock		(3,473)			(3,473)		(3,473)
Common stock issued under employee plans (20,669,785 shares)	2,394				2,394		2,394
Purchases (1,717,246 shares) and sales (4,920,198 shares) of treasury stock under employee plans—net		(56)	231		175		175
Other treasury shares purchased, not retired (88,683,716 shares)			(15,034)		(15,034)		(15,034)
Changes in other equity	317				317		317
Changes in noncontrolling interests						(29)	(29)
Equity, December 31, 2011	$48,129	$104,857	$(110,963)	$(21,885)	$20,138	$ 97	$20,236

IBM, 2011, 10K Report

SOLUTIONS TO OPENING SCENARIO QUESTIONS

1. Your return would have been a negative 44.1% = ($8,390 − $15,000)/$15,000.
2. In 2011, Berkshire Hathaway owned 8.8% of the shares of The Coca-Cola Company.
3. You would also need to know how many shares of stock of each company were outstanding. In June 2012, Microsoft had about 8.45 billion shares outstanding and the total market value of the company was $245 billion. Also in June 2012, Berkshire Hathaway had just 1.7 million shares outstanding, and the total market value of the company was $200 billion.

Stop & Think SOLUTIONS

1. (Page 13-17) The answer is B. When a company's stock price has increased since the time the stock was originally issued (as is true for most companies), the par value method reduces retained earnings when shares are repurchased. Reduced retained earnings can hinder a firm's ability to pay cash dividends. The cost method does not involve a reduction in retained earnings until the repurchased shares are actually retired.
2. (Page 13-26) The answer is A. Because the number of options granted depends on reported sales in 2015, the greedy, unscrupulous managers of Neff will do their best to boost the reported sales for 2015. They can do this by delaying the recognition of some 2014 sales and reporting them in 2015, and by accelerating the recognition of some 2016 sales and reporting them in 2015.
3. (Page 13-42) The answer is C. The surprising answer to this question is discussed in the boxed item "Using Stock Dividends as Signals" in this chapter. A 20% stock dividend, because it requires the transfer of the market value of the new shares from retained earnings, causes a much larger decrease in retained earnings than does a 25% stock dividend that only requires the transfer of the par value. If a firm is nervous about the size of its dividend pool, it should not declare a 20% stock dividend, as this could drastically reduce retained earnings. However, if a company is confident about its future ability to generate profits and pay cash dividends and it wants to proclaim this confidence in a public way, then it should declare a 20% stock dividend. This blatant reduction in the retained earnings safety net shows management's optimism about the future.

SOLUTION TO USING THE FASB'S CODIFICATION

Under Topic 852 (Reorganizations), you should have seen Subtopic 852-20 (Quasi-Reorganizations). Section 852-20-05 contains the following: "This Subtopic addresses the accounting applicable to a corporate readjustment procedure in which, without the creation of a new corporate entity and without the intervention of formal court proceedings, an entity restates its balance sheet to fair value. This corporate readjustment procedure may eliminate an accumulated deficit." Well, this sounds like what we are looking for.

The quasi-reorganization process is described in Section 852-20-25 as follows: "If a corporation elects to restate its assets, capital stock, additional paid-in capital, and retained earnings or accumulated deficit through a readjustment and therefore avail itself of permission to relieve its future income account or retained earnings account of charges that would otherwise be made against it, it shall make a clear report to its shareholders of the restatements proposed to be made, and obtain their formal consent. It shall present a fair balance sheet as at the date of the readjustment, in which the adjustment of carrying amounts is reasonably complete, in order that there may be no continuation of the circumstances that justify charges to additional paid-in capital. When the amounts to be written off in a readjustment have been determined, they shall be charged first against retained earnings to the full extent of such retained earnings; any balance may then be charged against additional paid-in capital." In other words, in a quasi-reorganization, assets are revalued to reflect their fair values. This may require significant write-downs of assets against retained earnings, thus initially increasing the accumulated deficit. The total deficit is then written off (retained earnings is adjusted to a zero balance) against paid-in capital balances, giving the company's balance sheet a substantially restructured equity section with, as of the quasi-reorganization date, a fresh start with respect to retained earnings.

Review Chapter 13 Learning Objectives

1 **Identify the rights associated with ownership of common and preferred stock.**

Common stockholders are the true owners of the business. They are the first to lose their investment when a business does poorly, and they are the ones who get rich when a business does well. Common stockholders vote in the election of members of the board of directors.

Preferred stockholders usually cannot vote in director elections. Preferred stock dividends must be paid in full before any common stock dividends can be paid. Preferred stock can be cumulative, participating, convertible, callable, redeemable, or some combination of these.

Par values of common stocks are usually very low (less than $1). Par values of preferred stocks often approximate the issuance price.

2 **Record the issuance of stock for cash, on a subscription basis, and in exchange for noncash assets or for services.**

When stock is sold for cash, the amount of the proceeds is usually divided between par value (or stated value) and additional paid-in capital.

When stock is sold on a subscription basis, any unpaid subscription amount (Stock Subscriptions Receivable) is reported as a subtraction from stockholders' equity.

When stock is issued in exchange for noncash assets or for services, the transaction is recorded using the fair market value of the assets or services or the fair market value of the stock, whichever is more objectively determinable.

3 **Use both the cost and par value methods to account for stock repurchases.**

When capital stock is acquired and retired, the capital stock account is reduced, and Retained Earnings can be reduced for all or part of the excess over par value paid to reacquire the stock. Additional paid-in capital created at the issuance of the stock can also be reduced or eliminated when the stock is reacquired.

Treasury stock is stock reacquired but not immediately retired. When the par value method is used, the treasury shares are accounted for in a manner similar to a stock retirement. When the cost method is used, the entire cost to reacquire the treasury shares is shown in a contra equity account until the shares are reissued or retired.

4 **Account for the issuance of stock rights and stock warrants.**

Stock rights are issued to existing shareholders to allow them to purchase sufficient shares to maintain their proportionate interest when new shares are issued. Only memorandum entries are needed to record the issuance of stock rights.

Stock warrants are issued in conjunction with other securities to make those other securities more attractive to investors. The proceeds of the security issuance are allocated between the security and a detachable stock warrant. No allocation is done for nondetachable warrants.

5 **Compute the compensation expense associated with the granting of employee stock options.**

With a simple stock-based compensation plan, total compensation expense is the number of options granted multiplied by the fair value of each option as of the grant date. This expense is allocated over the service period.

With a performance-based stock option plan, total compensation expense is equal to the fair value of each option as of the grant date multiplied by the number of options that are probable to be awarded. This amount is reevaluated at the end of each year, and a catch-up adjustment is made to compensation expense.

Some stock-based compensation plans call for payment in cash such as with cash stock appreciation rights (SARs). These obligations are remeasured at the end of each year, and a catch-up adjustment is made to compensation expense.

6 **Determine which equity-related items should be reported in the balance sheet as liabilities.**

Certain equity-related items are reported in the balance sheet as liabilities. These items are as follows:

- Mandatorily redeemable preferred shares
- Financial instruments (such as written put options) that obligate a company to repurchase its own shares
- Financial instruments that obligate a company to issue a certain dollar value of its own shares

In addition, the FASB has clarified that noncontrolling interest should be classified as equity in the consolidated balance sheet.

7 **Distinguish between stock conversions that require a reduction in retained earnings and those that do not.**

When total paid-in capital (par value plus additional paid-in capital) associated with stock that is to be converted is less than the total par value of the postconversion shares, the retained earnings account is debited for the difference.

8 **List the factors that impact the Retained Earnings balance.**

Retained earnings is reduced by the following:
- Some error corrections
- Some changes in accounting principle
- Net losses
- Cash dividends
- Stock dividends
- Treasury stock transactions
- Preferred stock conversions

Retained earnings is increased by the following:
- Some error corrections
- Some changes in accounting principle
- Net income
- Quasi-reorganizations

The Retained Earnings balance is often a constraint on the amount of cash dividends a firm can pay because of state incorporation law restrictions. In addition, a firm may voluntarily restrict the use of retained earnings.

9 **Properly record cash dividends, property dividends, small and large stock dividends, and stock splits.**

A dividend payable is recorded on the dividend declaration date and is removed from the books when the dividend is distributed. When a property dividend is paid, a gain or loss is recorded on the declaration date to recognize the difference between the book value and fair value of the asset to be distributed as the property dividend.

A stock dividend is a distribution of additional shares to stockholders without receiving any cash in return. In essence, a stock dividend results in company ownership being divided into more pieces, with each stockholder owning a proportionately increased number of shares.

Stock dividends and stock splits are accounted for as follows:

- *Small stock dividend (less than 20%–25%):* Retained Earnings is reduced by the market value of the new shares created.
- *Large stock dividend (more than 20%–25%):* Retained Earnings and/or Additional Paid-In Capital is reduced by the par value of the new shares created.
- *Stock split:* No journal entry is made. A memorandum entry records the facts that the par value of each share is reduced and the number of outstanding shares is increased.

10 **Prepare a statement of comprehensive incomes, explain the background of unrealized gains and losses recorded as part of accumulated other comprehensive income, and list the major types of equity reserves found in foreign balance sheets.**

The FASB encourages companies to provide one continuous net income/comprehensive income statement. However, most companies report comprehensive income in a separate statement placed immediately after the income statement. Unrealized gains and losses that bypass the income statement and are recognized as direct equity adjustments as part of accumulated other comprehensive income are as follows:

- *Foreign currency translation adjustment.* Changes in the equity of foreign subsidiaries resulting from foreign currency exchange rate fluctuations.
- *Unrealized gains and losses on available-for-sale securities.* Unrealized gains and losses from market value fluctuations of available-for-sale securities.
- *Unrealized gains and losses on derivatives.* Unrealized gains and losses from market value fluctuations of derivative instruments that are intended to manage risks associated with future sales or purchases.

The Equity sections of foreign balance sheets often include a number of equity reserves. These reserves are designed to carefully divide equity into the portion that is available for distribution to shareholders and the portion that is nondistributable. Some of these equity reserves are the capital redemption reserve, the asset revaluation reserve, and general and special reserves.

11 **Prepare a statement of changes in stockholders' equity.**

A statement of changes in stockholders' equity outlines the changes during a given period in the different equity categories.

FASB-IASB CODIFICATION SUMMARY

Topic	FASB Accounting Standards Codification	Original FASB Standard	Corresponding IASB Standard	Differences between U.S. GAAP and IFRS
Stock warrants	Section 470-20-25 par. 2	APB Opinion No. 14 par. 16	IAS 32 par. 28	Under IFRS, all compound financial instruments, such as stock warrants, are to be separated into separate debt and equity components. Under U.S. GAAP, this is required only if the stock warrants are "detachable."
Stock-based compensation	Topic 718	SFAS No. 123R	IFRS 2	No substantial differences
Reporting equity-related items as liabilities	Topic 480	SFAS No. 150	IAS 32	No substantial differences
Noncontrolling interest	Section 810-10-45 par. 16	SFAS No. 160 par. 5	IAS 27 par. 27	No substantial differences

KEY TERMS

Additional paid-in capital 13-11
Appropriated retained earnings 13-37
Available-for-sale securities 13-46
Board of directors 13-5
Business combination 13-13
Callable 13-9
Cash dividend 13-39
Convertible 13-9
Cost method 13-15
Cumulative preferred stock 13-8
Derivative 13-46
Detachable warrants 13-19
Dividends in arrears 13-8
Equity reserve 13-48
Foreign currency translation adjustment 13-46
Large stock dividend 13-41
Liquidating dividend 13-43
Minority interest 13-32
Noncontrolling interest 13-32
Noncumulative preferred stock 13-9
Nondetachable warrants 13-19
Nonreciprocal transfer to owners 13-39
Par value 13-6
Par (or stated) value method 13-15
Participating preferred stock 13-9
Performance-based stock option plan 13-24
Property dividend 13-39
Redeemable preferred stock 13-9
Small stock dividend 13-41
Stated value 13-7
Statement of changes in stockholders' equity 13-51
Stock appreciation rights (SARs) 13-25
Stock options 13-18
Stock rights 13-18
Stock split 13-42
Stock warrants 13-18
Subscription 13-11
Treasury stock 13-14

Tutorial Activities

Tutorial Activities with author-written, content-specific feedback, available on *CengageNOW for Stice & Stice*.

QUESTIONS

1. What basic rights are held by each common stockholder?
2. What is the historical significance of par value?
3. What rights of ownership are given up by preferred shareholders? What additional protections are enjoyed by preferred shareholders?
4. What was the user response to the FASB proposal, in its November 2007 *Preliminary Views* document, that preferred stock be classified in the balance sheet as a liability?
5. How is stock valued when it is issued in exchange for non-cash assets or for services?
6. Why might a company repurchase its own stock?
7. (a) What is the basic difference between the cost method and the par value method of accounting for treasury stock? (b) How will total stockholders' equity differ, if at all, under the two methods?
8. There is frequently a difference between the purchase price and the selling price of treasury stock. Why isn't this difference shown as a gain or a loss on the income statement?
9. Explain the difference in the accounting for detachable and nondetachable warrants.
10. What option value is used in the computation of compensation expense associated with a basic stock-based compensation plan?
11. With a performance-based stock option plan, a catch-up adjustment is necessary when the probable number of options that will vest changes from one year to the next. Describe this catch-up adjustment.
12. When a stock-based award calls for settlement in cash, how is the obligation accounted for?
13. How should mandatorily redeemable preferred shares be reported in the balance sheet?
14. When a corporation writes a put option on its own shares, what does the corporation receive? What does the corporation agree to do?
15. What distinguishes a situation in which an obligation to issue shares is recorded as equity from a situation in which an obligation to issue shares is recorded as a liability?
16. What is noncontrolling interest?
17. How are errors corrected when they are discovered in the current year? in a subsequent year?
18. How can retained earnings be restricted by law? In what other ways can retained earnings be restricted?
19. The following announcement appeared on the financial page of a newspaper: The board of directors of Benton Co., at its meeting on June 15, 2015, declared the regular quarterly dividend on outstanding common stock of $1.40 per share, payable on July 10, 2015, to the stockholders of record at the close of business June 30, 2015.
    (a) What is the purpose of each of the three dates given in the announcement?
    (b) When would the common stock of Benton Co. normally trade "ex-dividend"?
20. The directors of The Dress Shoppe are considering declaring either a stock dividend or a stock split. They have asked you to explain the difference between a stock dividend and a stock split and the accounting for a small stock dividend versus a large stock dividend.
21. (a) What is a liquidating dividend? (b) Under what circumstances are such distributions made?
22. What three types of unrealized gains and losses are shown as direct equity adjustments (part of accumulated other comprehensive income), bypassing the income statement? Briefly explain each.
23. In accounting for the equity of foreign companies, what is the primary purpose of equity reserves?

PRACTICE EXERCISES

Practice 13-1

Computation of Dividends, Common and Noncumulative Preferred
The company has 10,000 shares of 6%, $100 par preferred stock outstanding. In addition, the company has 100,000 shares of common stock outstanding. The company started business on January 1, 2014. Total cash dividends paid during 2014 and 2015 were $45,000 and $100,000, respectively. Compute the total dividends paid to preferred shareholders and to common shareholders in both years, assuming that the preferred stock is noncumulative.

Practice 13-2

Computation of Dividends, Common and Cumulative Preferred
Refer to the data in Practice 13-1. Compute the total dividends paid to preferred shareholders and to common shareholders in both years, assuming that the preferred stock is cumulative.

Practice 13-3 ② **Issuance of Common Stock**
The company issued 10,000 shares of $1 par common stock for cash of $40 per share. Make the necessary journal entry.

Practice 13-4 ② **Accounting for Stock Subscriptions**
The company received subscriptions for 20,000 shares of $1 par common stock for $25 per share. The company received 40% of the subscription amount immediately and the remainder two months later. Make the journal entries necessary to record the initial subscriptions (and cash receipt) and the subsequent receipt of the remaining cash.

Practice 13-5 ② **Issuing Stock in Exchange for Services**
The company is experiencing a cash flow shortfall and has asked certain key employees to accept shares of common stock (instead of cash) in payment of salaries. The employees accepted 35,000 shares of $0.50 par common stock in place of salaries of $575,000. Make the necessary journal entry.

Practice 13-6 ③ **Accounting for Treasury Stock: Cost Method**
The company repurchased 10,000 shares of $1 par common stock for a total of $300,000. None of the shares were retired. A month later, the company sold 4,000 of these shares for $144,000. The shares were initially issued for $20 per share. Make the necessary journal entries to record the repurchase of the 10,000 shares and the subsequent sale of the 4,000 shares.

Practice 13-7 ③ **Accounting for Treasury Stock: Par Value Method**
Refer to Practice 13-6. Make the necessary journal entries using the par value method.

Practice 13-8 ④ **Accounting for Stock Warrants**
The company issued 20,000 shares of 7%, $50 par preferred stock. Associated with each share of stock was a detachable common stock warrant. Each warrant entitles the holder to purchase one share of the company's $1 par common stock for $20 per share. Each unit (one share of preferred stock and one warrant) was issued for $55. It is estimated that each warrant could have been issued for $3 if issued alone, and the preferred stock could have been issued for $52 if issued alone. Some time after the issuance, all of the warrants were exercised. Make the journal entries necessary to record both the issuance of the preferred stock-warrant units and the subsequent exercise of the warrants.

Practice 13-9 ⑤ **Accounting for a Basic Stock-Based Compensation Plan**
On January 1, the company granted 150,000 stock options to key employees. Each option allows an employee to buy one share of $1 par common stock for $25, which was the market price of the shares on the grant date of January 1. In order to be able to exercise the options, the employees must remain with the company for three entire years. It is estimated that the fair value of each option on the date of grant was $4. At the end of three years, all of the options were exercised when the market price of the shares was $38 per share. Make all of the journal entries necessary with respect to these options in the first year. Also make the journal entry that would be made at the end of three years to record the exercise of the options.

Practice 13-10 ⑤ **Accounting for a Performance-Based Stock Option Plan**
Refer to Practice 13-9. Assume that the stock-based compensation plan is performance based. As of the end of the first year, the number of options that are probable to vest is 150,000. At the end of the second year, the number of options that are probable to vest is 120,000. As in Practice 13-9, the options have a three-year service period. Make the journal entries necessary at the end of the first year and the second year to recognize the compensation expense associated with this performance-based plan.

Practice 13-11 ⑤ **Accounting for Cash Stock Appreciation Rights**
Refer to Practice 13-9. Assume that the stock-based compensation plan involves stock appreciation rights (SARs). At the end of three years, the employees are given a cash award equal to the excess of the fair value at that time of 150,000 shares of stock above the threshold price of $25. The estimated fair value of each SAR is $8 at the end of the first year and $5 at the end of the second year. The service period is three years. Make the journal entries necessary at the end of the first year and the second year to recognize the compensation expense associated with these stock appreciation rights.

Practice 13-12
Accounting for Mandatorily Redeemable Preferred Shares
On January 1, Year 1, the company issued mandatorily redeemable preferred shares in exchange for $1,000 cash. No dividends are to be paid on these shares, and they must be redeemed in exactly two years, on January 1, Year 3, for $1,166.40. The interest rate implicit in this agreement is 8%. Make the journal entries to record the issuance, accrual of interest in Year 1 and Year 2, and redemption of these preferred shares on January 1, Year 3.

Practice 13-13
Accounting for a Written Put Option
On January 1, Year 1, the company wrote a put option agreeing to purchase 100 shares of its own stock for $50 per share on December 31, Year 2, at the option of the purchaser of the put option. The market price of the company's shares on January 1, Year 1, was $50 per share. As of January 1, Year 1, this put option has a fair value of $1,200. Because the company's shares increased in value during Year 1, the put option has a fair value of just $350 on December 31, Year 1. On December 31, Year 2, the company's shares have a market price of $46 per share, so the purchaser of the put option exercised the option on that date. The company uses the cost method for treasury stock. Make the journal entries necessary on January 1, Year 1, on December 31, Year 1, and on December 31, Year 2 on the books of the company that wrote the put option.

Practice 13-14
Accounting for Stock Conversion
Stockholders of the company converted 12,000 shares of $40 par preferred stock into 60,000 shares of $1 par common stock. The preferred shares were originally issued for $44 per share. Make the journal entry necessary to record the conversion.

Practice 13-15
Prior-Period Adjustments
The Retained Earnings balance at the end of last year was $50,000. In June of this year, well after last year's books were closed, it was found that a mistake had been made in computing depreciation expense last year. The mistake resulted in reported depreciation expense that was $4,000 too high last year. Net income for this year was $12,000; cash dividends declared and paid this year totaled $4,500. Show the computation of the correct ending balance in Retained Earnings for this year. Ignore income taxes.

Practice 13-16
Accounting for Declaration and Payment of Dividends
On August 17, the company declared cash dividends of $35,000. The dividends were paid on September 16. Make the journal entries necessary to record both events.

Practice 13-17
Accounting for Property Dividends
On January 1, the company purchased 10,000 shares of Wilsonville Company stock for $20 per share as an available-for-sale investment. In March, the company decided to distribute the Wilsonville shares as a property dividend to its stockholders. The Wilsonville shares had a market price of $27 per share on March 23, the date the property dividend was declared. The Wilsonville property dividend was distributed on April 15. Make the journal entries necessary to record the declaration and distribution of this property dividend.

Practice 13-18
Accounting for Small Stock Dividends
The company had 20,000 shares of $1 par common stock outstanding. When each share of stock had a market value of $44, the company declared and distributed a 10% stock dividend. After the distribution of the dividend shares, each share of stock had a market value of $40. Make the journal entries necessary to record the declaration and distribution of this stock dividend.

Practice 13-19
Large Stock Dividends and Stock Splits
The company had 10,000 shares of $1 par common stock outstanding. When each share of stock had a market value of $130, the company decided to reduce the price per share of stock to $65 by doubling the number of shares outstanding. Make the journal entries necessary to record the declaration of the decision to double the number of shares and to distribute the shares assuming that (1) the distribution is accounted for as a large stock dividend and (2) the distribution is accounted for as a stock split.

C13 | Equity Financing

Practice 13-20
Accounting for Liquidating Dividends
The board of directors of the company has decided that the interests of the shareholders will be best served if the company is liquidated in an orderly fashion, with the proceeds to be distributed to the shareholders. As the first installment in this liquidation, a total dividend of $500,000 was distributed to the shareholders. Of this amount, $30,000 is a regular dividend, and $470,000 is a liquidating dividend. Make the journal entries necessary to record the declaration and payment of this combined dividend.

Practice 13-21
Comprehensive Income
The company started business on January 1, 2013. Net income and dividends for the first three years of the company's existence are as follows:

	Net Income (Loss)	Dividends
2013	$(1,500)	$ 0
2014	600	150
2015	2,100	550

The company has some foreign subsidiaries and also maintains a portfolio of available-for-sale securities. During 2013, 2014, and 2015, the U.S. dollar value of the equity of the foreign subsidiaries and the market value of the securities in the available-for-sale portfolio fluctuated as shown below.

	Change in U.S. Dollar Value	Change in Value of Portfolio
2013	Increase of $275	Decrease of $900
2014	Decrease of $725	Decrease of $400
2015	Decrease of $195	Increase of $560

Compute comprehensive income for each of the three years: 2013, 2014, and 2015.

Practice 13-22
Accumulated Other Comprehensive Income
Refer to Practice 13-21. Compute the balance in (1) Retained Earnings and (2) Accumulated Other Comprehensive Income as of the end of each year: 2013, 2014, 2015.

Practice 13-23
International Equity Reserves
The company, based in the United Kingdom, has the following equity accounts:

Retained earnings	$1,000
Asset revaluation reserve	3,200
Par value of shares	100
Special reserve	400
Share premium	1,700
Total equity	$6,400

Compute the amount of (1) nondistributable and (2) distributable equity.

Practice 13-24
Statement of Changes in Stockholders' Equity
Beginning balances in the equity accounts were as follows:

Common stock, at par	$ 2,000
Paid-in capital in excess of par	14,000
Accumulated other comprehensive income	(3,500)
Retained earnings	18,000
Treasury stock	(6,000)
Total stockholders' equity	$24,500

The following is true for the year:

(a) Net income was $6,300.
(b) Equity increased $200 from an increase in value of available-for-sale securities.
(c) Dividends were $2,000.
(d) Treasury stock of $1,600 was purchased. Assume the cost method.
(e) Shares of stock for $800 were issued. Par value was $50.

Prepare a statement of changes in stockholders' equity for the year.

EXERCISES

Exercise 13-25

Issuance of Common Stock

Verdero Company is authorized to issue 100,000 shares of $2 par value common stock. Verdero has the following transactions:

(a) Issued 20,000 shares at $30 per share; received cash.
(b) Issued 250 shares to attorneys for services in securing the corporate charter and for preliminary legal costs of organizing the corporation. The value of the services was $9,000.
(c) Issued 300 shares, valued objectively at $10,000, to the employees instead of paying them cash wages.
(d) Issued 12,500 shares of stock in exchange for a building valued at $295,000 and land valued at $80,000. (The building was originally acquired by the investor for $250,000 and has $100,000 of accumulated depreciation; the land was originally acquired for $30,000.)
(e) Received cash for 6,500 shares of stock sold at $38 per share.
(f) Issued 4,000 shares at $45 per share; received cash.

Make the journal entries necessary for Verdero Company to record each transaction.

Exercise 13-26

Dividends—Different Classes of Stock

Solar Storm Inc. began operations on June 30, 2013, and issued 60,000 shares of $1 par common stock on that date. On December 31, 2013, Solar Storm declared and paid $24,200 in dividends. After a vote of the board of directors, Solar Storm issued 25,000 shares of 7% cumulative, $10 par, preferred stock on January 1, 2015. On December 31, 2015, Solar Storm declared and paid $16,500 in dividends, and on December 31, 2016, Solar Storm declared and paid $34,800 in dividends. Determine the amount of dividends to be distributed to each class of stock for each of Solar Storm's dividend payments.

Exercise 13-27

Preferred Stock—Cumulative and Noncumulative

Anderson Company paid dividends at the end of each year as follows: 2013, $150,000; 2014, $240,000; and 2015, $560,000. Determine the amount of dividends per share paid on common and preferred stock for each year, assuming independent capital structures as follows:

(a) 300,000 shares of no-par common; 10,000 shares of $100 par, 9% noncumulative preferred.
(b) 250,000 shares of no-par common; 20,000 shares of $100 par, 9% noncumulative preferred.
(c) 250,000 shares of no-par common; 20,000 shares of $100 par, 9% cumulative preferred.
(d) 250,000 shares of $1 par common; 30,000 shares of $100 par, 9% cumulative preferred.

Exercise 13-28

Issuance of Capital Stock with Subscriptions

Palo Verde Company was incorporated on January 1, 2015, with the following authorized capitalization:

- 25,000 shares of common stock, stated value $6 per share
- 8,000 shares of 8% cumulative preferred stock, par value $20 per share

Make the entries required for each of the following transactions:

(a) Issued 14,000 shares of common stock for a total of $518,000 and 5,000 shares of preferred stock at $25 per share.
(b) Subscriptions were received for 3,000 shares of common stock at a price of $41. A 25% down payment is received.

(c) Collected the remaining amount owed on the stock subscriptions and issued the stock.
(d) Sold the remaining authorized shares of common stock at $53 per share.

Exercise 13-29

Acquisition and Retirement of Stock

Holanna Company reported the following balances related to common stock as of December 31, 2014:

Common stock, $1 par, 200,000 shares issued and outstanding .... $ 200,000
Paid-in capital in excess of par 2,400,000

The company purchased and immediately retired 18,000 shares at $19 on August 1, 2015, and 32,000 shares at $9 on December 31, 2015. Make the entries to record the acquisition and retirement of the common stock. (Assume all shares were originally sold at the same price.)

Exercise 13-30

Treasury Stock: Par Value and Cost Methods

The stockholders' equity of Thomas Company as of December 31, 2014, was as follows:

Common stock, $1 par, authorized 275,000 shares; 240,000 shares issued
 and outstanding.. $ 240,000
Paid-in capital in excess of par 3,840,000
Retained earnings.. 900,000

On June 1, 2015, Thomas reacquired 15,000 shares of its common stock at $16. The following transactions occurred in 2015 with regard to these shares.

July 1 Sold 5,000 shares at $20.
Aug. 1 Sold 7,000 shares at $14.
Sept. 1 Retired 1,000 shares.

1. Using the cost method to account for treasury stock:
   (a) Prepare the journal entries to record all treasury stock transactions in 2015.
   (b) Prepare the Stockholders' Equity section of the balance sheet at December 31, 2015, assuming Retained Earnings of $1,005,000 (before the effects of treasury stock transactions).
2. Using the par value method to account for treasury stock:
   (a) Prepare the journal entries to record all treasury stock transactions in 2015.
   (b) Prepare the Stockholders' Equity section of the balance sheet at December 31, 2015, assuming Retained Earnings of $1,005,000 (before the effects of treasury stock transactions).

Exercise 13-31

Stock Rights

In 2015, Calton Inc. had 100,000 shares of $1.50 par value common stock outstanding. Calton issued 100,000 stock rights. Five rights, plus $50 in cash, are required to purchase one new share of Calton common stock. On the date the rights were issued, Calton common stock was selling for $55 per share. What entries must Calton make to record the issuance of the stock rights?

Exercise 13-32

Accounting for Stock Warrants

Western Company wants to raise additional equity capital. After analysis of the available options, the company decides to issue 1,000 shares of $20 par preferred stock with detachable warrants. The package of the stock and warrants sells for $90. The warrants enable the holder to purchase 1,000 shares of $2 par common stock at $30 per share. Immediately following the issuance of the stock, the stock warrants are selling at $9 per share. The market value of the preferred stock without the warrants is $85.

1. Prepare a journal entry for Western Company to record the issuance of the preferred stock and the attached warrants.
2. Assuming that all the warrants are exercised, prepare a journal entry for Western to record the exercise of the warrants.
3. Assuming that only 70% of the warrants are exercised (and the remaining 30% lapse), prepare the journal entries for Western to record the exercise and expiration of the warrants.

Exercise 13-33

Accounting for a Basic Stock-Based Compensation Plan

On January 1, 2014, Obregon Supply Company established a stock-based compensation plan for its senior employees. A total of 45,000 options was granted that permit employees to purchase 45,000 shares of $2 par common stock at $29 per share. Each option had a fair value of $7 on the grant date. Options are exercisable beginning on January 1, 2017, and can be exercised anytime during 2017. The market price for Obregon common stock on January 1, 2014, was $32.

Assume that all options were exercised on December 31, 2017. Prepare all entries required for the years 2014–2017.

Exercise 13-34

Accounting for a Performance-Based Stock Option Plan

Rhiener Corporation initiated a performance-based employee stock option plan on January 1, 2014. The performance base for the plan is net sales in the year 2016. The plan provides for stock options to be awarded to the employees as a group on the following basis:

Level	Net Sales Range	Options Granted
1	<$250,000	10,000
2	$250,000–$499,999	20,000
3	$500,000–$1,000,000	30,000
4	>$1,000,000	40,000

The options become exercisable on January 1, 2017. The option exercise price is $20 per share. On January 1, 2014, each option had a fair value of $9. The market prices of Rhiener stock on selected dates in 2014–2016 were as follows:

January 1, 2014	$25
December 31, 2014	30
December 31, 2015	35
December 31, 2016	32

Year 2016 sales estimates as of selected dates were as follows:

January 1, 2014	$400,000
December 31, 2014	450,000
December 31, 2015	550,000

Actual sales for 2016 were $700,000. Calculate the compensation expense Rhiener should report for the years 2014, 2015, and 2016 related to this performance-based stock option plan.

Exercise 13-35

Stock Appreciation Rights

San Juan Corporation established a stock option plan that provides for cash payments to employees based on the appreciation of stock prices from an established threshold price. The plan was instituted on January 1, 2015, and provides benefits to employees who work for the succeeding three years. Cash payments to employees will be made on January 1, 2018, and will equal the excess of the stock price over the threshold price on that date. In total, 10,000 of these cash stock appreciation rights (SARs) were granted to employees.

The threshold price established for the SARs is $10 per share. The estimated fair value of each SAR on selected dates in 2015–2017 was as follows:

December 31, 2015	$ 6
December 31, 2016	10
December 31, 2017	8

Prepare the journal entries on San Juan's books for the years 2015, 2016, 2017, and 2018 related to this plan.

Exercise 13-36

Convertible Preferred Stock

Stockholders' equity for Channa Co. on December 31 was as follows:

Preferred stock, $14 par, 25,000 shares issued and outstanding	$ 350,000
Paid-in capital in excess of par—preferred stock	100,000
Common stock, $9 par, 125,000 shares issued and outstanding	1,125,000
Paid-in capital in excess of par—common stock	875,000
Retained earnings	1,600,000

Preferred stock is convertible into common stock.

Provide the entry made on Channa Co.'s books assuming that 6,000 shares of preferred are converted under each assumption listed:

1. Preferred shares are convertible into common on a share-for-share basis.
2. Each share of preferred stock is convertible into 4.0 shares of common.
3. Each share of preferred stock is convertible into 1.5 shares of common.

Exercise 13-37

Reporting Errors from Previous Periods

Endicott Company's December 31, 2014, balance sheet reported retained earnings of $86,500, and net income of $124,000 was reported in the 2014 income statement. While preparing financial statements for the year ended December 31, 2015, Tom Dryden, accountant for Endicott Company, discovered that net income for 2014 had been overstated by $36,000 due to an error in recording depreciation expense for 2014. Net income for 2015 was $106,000, and dividends of $30,000 were declared and paid in 2015.

1. What effect, if any, would the $36,000 error made in 2014 have on the company's 2015 financial statements?
2. Compute the amount of retained earnings to be reported in Endicott Company's December 31, 2015, balance sheet.

Exercise 13-38

Cash Dividend Computations

Consistent Company has been paying regular quarterly dividends of $1.50 and wants to pay the same amount in the third quarter of 2015. Given the following information, (1) what is the total amount that Consistent will have to pay in dividends in the third quarter in order to pay $1.50 per share, and (2) what is the total amount of dividends to be distributed during the year assuming no equity transactions occur after June 30?

2015

Jan.	1	Shares outstanding, 800,000; $2 par (1,500,000 shares authorized).
Feb.	15	Issued 50,000 new shares at $10.50.
Mar.	31	Paid quarterly dividends of $1.50 per share.
May	12	Converted $1,000,000 of $1,000 bonds to common stock at the rate of 100 shares of stock per $1,000 bond.
June	15	Issued an 11% stock dividend.
	30	Paid quarterly dividends of $1.50 per share.

Exercise 13-39

Property Dividends

Phelps Company distributed the following dividends to its stockholders:

(a) 450,000 shares of Bedrock Corporation stock, carrying value of investment, $975,000; fair market value, $1,350,000.

(b) 220,000 shares of Great Basin Company stock, a closely held corporation. The shares were purchased by Phelps three years ago at $6.25 per share, but no current market price is available.

Indicate the journal entries to account for the declaration and the payment of the dividends.

Exercise 13-40

Stock Dividends

The balance sheet of Carmen Corporation shows the following:

Common stock, $1 stated value, 80,000 shares issued and outstanding...............	$ 80,000
Paid-in capital in excess of stated value	1,120,000
Retained earnings	350,000

A 25% stock dividend is declared, with the board of directors authorizing a transfer from Retained Earnings to Common Stock at the stated value of the shares.

1. Provide entries to record the declaration and issuance of the stock dividend.
2. What was the effect of the issuance of the stock dividend on the ownership equity of each stockholder in the corporation?
3. Provide entries to record the declaration and issuance of the dividend if the board of directors had elected to declare a 15% stock dividend instead of 25%. The market value of the stock is $10 per share after the 15% stock dividend is issued.

Exercise 13-41

Stock Dividends and Stock Splits

The capital accounts for Alston Market on June 30, 2015, are as follows:

Common stock, $6 par, 50,000 shares issued and outstanding.........................	$ 300,000
Paid-in capital in excess of par	600,000
Retained earnings...	1,840,000

Shares of the company's stock are selling at this time at $44. What entries would you make in each of the following cases?

(a) A 10% stock dividend is declared and issued.
(b) A 50% stock dividend is declared and issued.
(c) A 2-for-1 stock split is declared and issued.

Exercise 13-42

Small Stock Dividend

Zenon Company has 450,000 shares of $1 par value common stock outstanding. In declaring and distributing a 10% stock dividend, Zenon initially issued only 40,000 new shares; the other stock dividend shares have not yet been issued as of the end of the year. Prepare all journal entries necessary to record the declaration and distribution of the stock dividend. The market price of the shares is $21 per share after the 10% stock dividend is issued.

Exercise 13-43

Liquidating Dividend

Van Etten Company declared and paid a cash dividend of $3.25 per share on its $1 par common stock. Van Etten has 100,000 shares of common stock outstanding and total paid-in capital from common stock of $800,000. As part of the dividend announcement, Van Etten stated that retained earnings served as the basis for only $0.50 per share of the dividend; investors should consider the remainder to be a return of investment. Prepare the journal entries necessary on Van Etten's books to record the declaration and distribution of this dividend.

Exercise 13-44

Correcting the Retained Earnings Account

The retained earnings account for Carlitos Inc. shows the following debits and credits. Indicate all entries required to correct the account. What is the corrected amount of retained earnings?

Account: Retained Earnings

				Balance	
Date	Item	Debit	Credit	Debit	Credit
Jan. 1	Balance				291,700
(a)	Loss from fire	3,175			288,525
(b)	Goodwill impairment	32,200			256,325
(c)	Stock dividend	50,000			206,325
(d)	Loss on sale of equipment	17,550			188,775
(e)	Officers' compensation related to income of prior periods—accrual overlooked	210,400		21,625	
(f)	Loss on retirement of preferred shares at more than issuance price	28,000		49,625	
(g)	Paid-in capital in excess of par		79,500		29,875
(h)	Stock subscription defaults		3,725		33,600
(i)	Gain on retirement of preferred stock at less than issuance price		14,700		48,300
(j)	Gain on early retirement of bonds at less than book value		8,100		56,400
(k)	Gain on life insurance policy settlement		7,800		64,200
(l)	Correction of prior-period error		31,050		95,250

Exercise 13-45

Equity Adjustments
The following data are for Radial Company:

Contributed capital and retained earnings	$875,000
Foreign currency translation adjustment	72,000
Unrealized gain on available-for-sale securities	95,000

(*Note:* The currencies in the countries where Radial has foreign subsidiaries have strengthened relative to the U.S. dollar.)
    Compute total stockholders' equity for Radial Company.

Exercise 13-46

Analysis of Owners' Equity
From the following information, reconstruct the journal entries that were made by Rivers Corporation during 2015.

	Dec. 31, 2015		Dec. 31, 2014	
	Amount	Shares	Amount	Shares
Common stock	$175,000	7,000	$150,000	6,000
Paid-in capital in excess of par	54,250	—	36,000	—
Paid-in capital from treasury stock	1,000	200	—	—
Retained earnings	76,500*	—	49,000	—
Treasury stock	15,000	300	—	—

*Includes net income of $40,000 for 2015. There were no dividends. Assume that revenues and expenses were closed to a temporary account, Income Summary. Use this account to complete the closing process. At the beginning of 2015, 2,500 shares of common stock (issued when the company was formed) were purchased for $90,000; these were retired later in the year. The cost method is used to record treasury stock transactions. Treasury stock purchased during the year was purchased at a cost of $50 per share.

Exercise 13-47

Reporting Stockholders' Equity

Kenny Co. began operations on January 1, 2014, by issuing at $15 per share one-half of the 950,000 shares of $1 par value common stock that had been authorized for sale. In addition, Kenny has 500,000 shares of $5 par value, 6% preferred shares authorized. During 2014, Kenny had $1,025,000 of net income and declared $237,500 of dividends.

During 2015, Kenny had the following transactions:

Jan.	10	Issued an additional 100,000 shares of common stock for $17 per share.
Apr.	1	Issued 150,000 shares of the preferred stock for $8 per share.
July	19	Authorized the purchase of a custom-made machine to be delivered in January 2016. Kenny restricted $295,000 of retained earnings for the purchase of the machine.
Oct.	23	Sold an additional 50,000 shares of the preferred stock for $9 per share.
Dec.	31	Reported $1,215,000 of net income and declared a dividend of $635,000 to stockholders of record on January 15, 2016, to be paid on February 1, 2016.

1. Prepare the Stockholders' Equity section of Kenny's balance sheet for December 31, 2014.
2. Prepare a statement of changes in stockholders' equity for 2015.
3. Prepare the Stockholders' Equity section of Kenny's balance sheet for December 31, 2015.

P3

Additional Activities of a Business

CHAPTER 14

Investments in Debt and Equity Securities

Learning Objectives

1. Determine why companies invest in other companies.
2. Understand the varying classifications associated with investment securities.
3. Account for the purchase of debt and equity securities.
4. Account for the recognition of revenue from investment securities.
5. Account for the change in fair value of investment securities.
6. Account for the sale of investment securities.
7. Record the transfer of investment securities between categories.
8. Properly report purchases, sales, and changes in fair value of investment securities in the statement of cash flows.
9. Explain the proper classification and disclosure of investments in securities.

EM EXPANDED MATERIAL

10. Account for the impairment of a loan receivable.

Many companies invest in other companies. In some cases, the investor may own another company in its entirety; for example, The Walt Disney Company owns 100% of the American Broadcasting Company (ABC). In other cases, the investor may own just a portion of another company as is the case with Berkshire Hathaway, which owns more than 8% of The Coca-Cola Company, 13% of American Express, and more than 7% of Wells Fargo. In

FYI

Citigroup is the first company in history to exceed $1 trillion in total assets. As of December 31, 2009, the company reported total assets of $1.857 trillion and total liabilities of $1.702 trillion.

Exhibit 14-1 | Investment in Debt and Equity Securities—2011

Company	Total Investments (in billions)	Percentage of Total Assets
Berkshire Hathaway	$125.2	31.9%
Coca-Cola	9.5	11.8%
Microsoft	54.0	49.7%
Citigroup	861.0	45.9%
Verizon	4.0	1.8%

© Cengage Learning 2014

other instances, investors may purchase debt rather than equity interests. Exhibit 14-1 lists selected U.S. companies with investment account balances.

As the exhibit illustrates, company investment in other companies can be quite substantial. Berkshire Hathaway, a company whose major stockholder, Warren Buffett, is the second richest person in America, is a holding company that basically buys ownership in other companies. Microsoft, whose major stockholder, Bill Gates, is the richest person in America, makes more money than it can reinvest in its own company. As a result, it invests in other companies, sometimes in order to exercise strategic influence on companies that are developing new technologies. College Retirement Equities Fund (CREF) is a company established to assist in the retirement plans for employees of nonprofit educational and research organizations. College professors and others have money withheld from their salaries and forwarded to CREF, which invests that money. As of December 31, 2011, CREF had more than $100 billion, or 99.5% of the company's total assets, invested in the debt and equity securities of other companies. Exhibit 14-2 displays the asset portion of CREF's balance sheet as of December 31, 2011. How do companies like CREF, Berkshire Hathaway, and Microsoft account for their huge investments in securities? That topic is the focus of this chapter.

Exhibit 14-2 | College Retirement Equities Fund Partial Balance Sheet

(In millions)—2011	
Investments	
Portfolio investments	$101,429
Cash	162
Dividends and interest receivable	161
Receivable from securities sold	232
Other	3
TOTAL ASSETS	$101,987

© Cengage Learning 2014

1. What is the important difference between Disney's investment in ABC and Berkshire Hathaway's investment in Coca-Cola?
2. What is the important difference between the investing operations of Berkshire Hathaway and the investing operations of Microsoft?
3. Whose money does CREF invest?

Answers to these questions can be found on page 14-46.

Accounting for investments in debt and equity securities has generated a great deal of interest for many years. The primary area of concern is the recognition and disclosure of changes in fair value. Because the value of investment securities can change dramatically in a short period of time, accounting information that reflects this change in value is useful to businesses and financial statement users. To address the issue of valuation, the FASB issued pre-Codification *Statement of Financial Accounting Standards No. 115*, "Accounting for Certain Investments in Debt and Equity Securities." The major effect of this standard, issued in 1993, was to require businesses to record many of their investment securities at fair value. This position differs from previous standards in that increases, as well as decreases, in the value of certain securities are reported in the financial statements. The fair value requirements of pre-Codification *SFAS No. 115* were augmented in 2006 by the refined definition of fair value and the increased disclosure requirements included in pre-Codification *Statement of Financial Accounting Standards No. 157*, "Fair Value Measurements." The provisions of both of these standards are now contained in FASB ASC Topic 320 (Investments—Debt and Equity Securities).

In this chapter, we discuss why and how companies invest in other companies. We will also address the accounting issues associated with investments in both debt and equity securities. Accounting for these investments involves several activities. These activities are summarized in Exhibit 14-3. Each of the issues presented in Exhibit 14-3 will be addressed in turn. Following the discussion of these issues, the Expanded Material section of the chapter discusses the accounting for the impairment of a loan receivable.

Exhibit 14-3 | Time Line of Business Issues Involved with Investment Securities

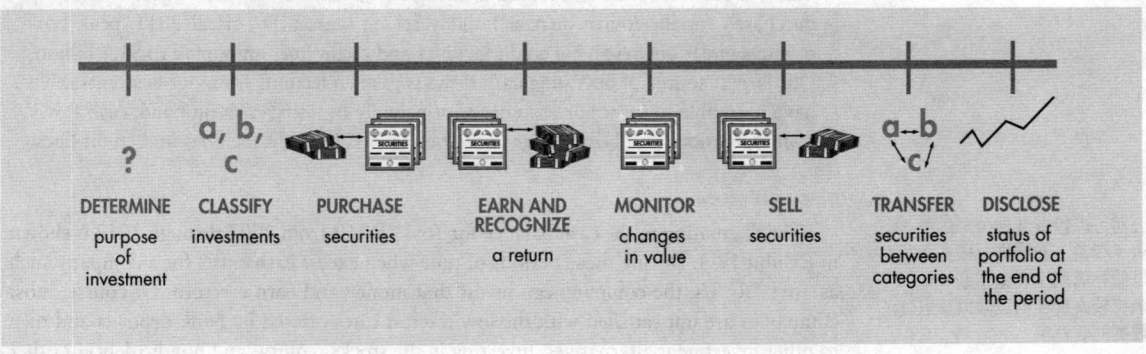

Why Companies Invest in Other Companies

LO1 学习目标1
确定一家公司为什么向其他公司投资。

① Determine why companies invest in other companies.

Companies invest in the debt and equity securities of other companies for a host of reasons. Five of the more common reasons are discussed in this section.

Safety Cushion

微软公司贷款给银行、政府和其他公司，并以有息证券的形式储存了大量的现金。

Microsoft holds more cash and short-term investments than just about any company. As of June 30, 2011, Microsoft reported holding $52.8 billion in cash and short-term investments. Of this amount, only $9.610 billion was actually composed of cash; the remainder was a mixture of certificates of deposit, U.S. Treasury securities, corporate notes and bonds, and other short-term interest-earning securities. In essence, Microsoft has stored a substantial amount of cash in the form of interest-earning loans to banks, governments, and other corporations. In *Time* magazine (January 13, 1997), it was reported that Bill Gates has a rule that Microsoft must always have a large enough liquid investment balance to operate for a year without any revenue. Thus, this large investment balance is a safety cushion to ensure that Microsoft can continue to operate even in the face of extreme adversity. Other companies have much smaller safety cushions, but the general principle is that investments are sometimes made to give a company a ready source of funds on which it can draw when needed.

Cyclical Cash Needs

Some companies operate in seasonal business environments that need cyclical inventory buildups requiring large amounts of cash, followed by lots of sales and cash collections. For example, the following is an excerpt from the January 28, 2012, 10-K filing of Toys "R" Us, the large retail toy chain:

> In general, our primary uses of cash are providing for working capital purposes (which principally represents the purchase of inventory), servicing debt, remodeling existing stores (including conversions), financing construction of new stores and paying expenses, such as payroll costs, to operate our stores. Our working capital needs follow a seasonal pattern, peaking in the third quarter of the year when inventory is purchased for the fourth quarter holiday selling season. For fiscal 2011, peak borrowings under our revolving credit facilities and credit lines amounted to $1.1 billion. Our largest source of operating cash flows is cash collections from our customers. We have been able to meet our cash needs principally by using cash on hand, cash flows from operations and borrowings under our revolving credit facilities and credit lines.

Toys "R" Us, 2012, 10K Report

公司可以投资其他公司的股票（权益）和债券（债务）以储存周期性现金结余，并承担较高程度的风险以赚取较高的收益率。

The fluctuation in the cash balance for Toys "R" Us from 2007 through 2012 is shown in Exhibit 14-4. During those periods of time when excess cash exists for a company such as Toys "R" Us, the company can invest that money and earn a return. Of course, most companies are not satisfied with the low interest rates offered by bank deposits and turn to other investment alternatives. Investing in the stocks (equity) and bonds (debt) of other

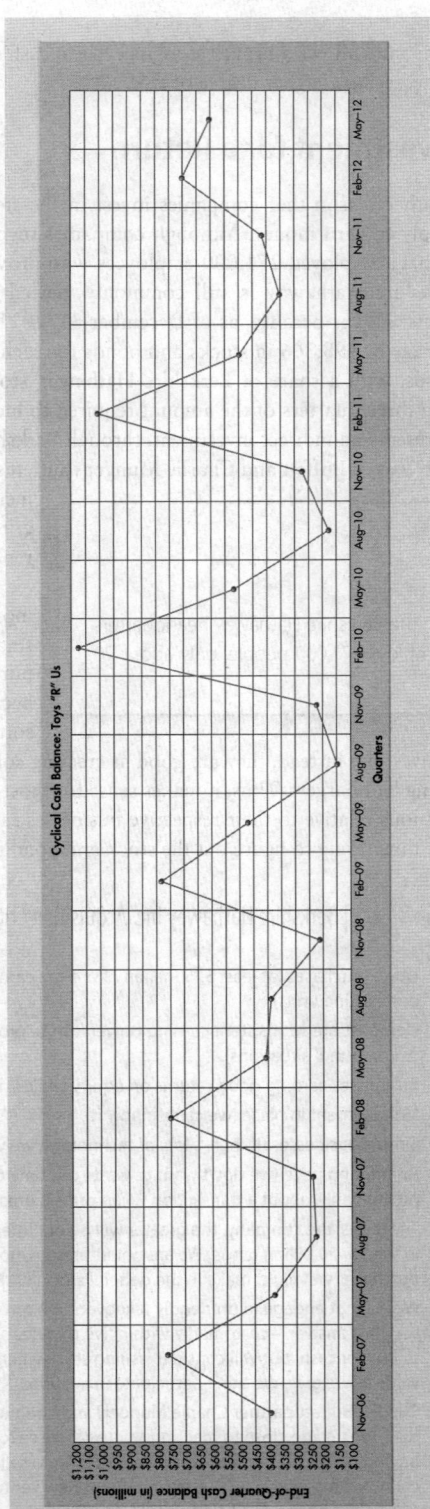

Exhibit 14-4 | Cyclical Cash Balance: Toys "R" Us

Toys "R" Us, 2012, 10K Report

companies allows a firm to store its cyclical cash surplus and earn a higher rate of return by accepting a higher degree of risk.

Investment for a Return

Another reason that companies invest in the stocks and bonds of other companies is simply to earn money. Although companies owned by Berkshire Hathaway at the end of 2011 employed 271,000 employees who provide a variety of products and services, Berkshire Hathaway is still commonly viewed as making its money through investments. This is because, as of December 31, 2011, Berkshire Hathaway had invested an average of $98,366 in stocks and bonds for each ownership share outstanding. In other words, with a share of Berkshire Hathaway stock selling for around $120,000, more than three-quarters of the amount required to buy a share of Berkshire Hathaway stock represents an indirect investment, through Berkshire Hathaway, in the stocks and bonds that Warren Buffett and Charlie Munger (Buffett's partner) have decided are good investments. Berkshire Hathaway's investment criteria, reprinted from the 2011 annual report, are listed in Exhibit 14-5.

Berkshire Hathaway is the exception; most U.S. corporations engage in only a small amount of investment solely for the purpose of earning a return. This is so because those companies, such as Microsoft, Intel, and McDonald's, are not experts in investing. Instead, they are good at creating software, developing computer chips, and selling hamburgers. Thus, it makes sense for those companies to concentrate on operating decisions relative to their respective businesses rather than to spend management's valuable time trying to figure out the stock and bond markets.

> **FYI**
>
> Warren Buffett is proud that although the Berkshire Hathaway headquarters staff must oversee an empire that employs 271,000 people, only about 20 people work in the corporate offices.

Exhibit 14-5 | Berkshire Hathaway Inc. Acquisition Criteria

1. Large purchases (at least $75 million of pre-tax earnings unless the business will fit into one of our existing units),
2. Demonstrated consistent earning power (future projections are of *no* interest to us, nor are "turnaround" situations),
3. Businesses earning good returns on equity while employing little or no debt,
4. Management in place (we can't supply it),
5. Simple businesses (if there's lots of technology, we won't understand it),
6. An offering price (we don't want to waste our time or that of the seller by talking, even preliminarily, about a transaction when price is unknown).

The larger the company, the greater will be our interest: We would like to make an acquisition in the $5–20 billion range. We are not interested, however, in receiving suggestions about purchases we might make in the general stock market.

We will not engage in unfriendly takeovers. We can promise complete confidentiality and a very fast answer—customarily within five minutes—as to whether we're interested. We prefer to buy for cash, but will consider issuing stock when we receive as much in intrinsic business value as we give. We don't participate in auctions.

Charlie [Buffett partner Charlie Munger] and I frequently get approached about acquisitions that don't come close to meeting our tests: We've found that if you advertise an interest in buying collies, a lot of people will call hoping to sell you their cocker spaniels. A line from a country song expresses our feeling about new ventures, turnarounds, or auction-like sales: "When the phone don't ring, you'll know it's me."

Berkshire Hathaway, Inc., 2011, 10K Report

Exhibit 14-6 | The Coca-Cola Company's Ownership Percentage of Major Bottlers of Its Products—2009

Bottler	Location	Coca-Cola's Ownership Percentage
Coca-Cola Enterprises	United States, Canada, and Great Britain (largest bottler of Coca-Cola products in the world)	34%
Coca-Cola Amatil	Australia, New Zealand, and Pacific Islands	30
Coca-Cola FEMSA	Mexico, Central and South America	32
Coca-Cola Hellenic Bottling Company	Europe (primarily eastern)	23

Source: Coca-Cola

Investment for Influence

For companies in which Berkshire Hathaway is a large shareholder, Warren Buffett is not content to be a passive investor. For example, he has been on the board of directors of The Coca-Cola Company, **The Gillette Company**, and **The Washington Post Company**. In general, companies can invest in other companies for many reasons other than to earn a return. Some reasons are to ensure a supply of raw materials, to influence the board of directors, or to diversify product offerings. For example, Coca-Cola historically has not bottled its own soft drinks; those bottling franchises are owned by independent bottlers all over the world. However, to ensure that the bottling segment of the soft drink supply chain remains predictably open to Coca-Cola, Coca-Cola owns sizable portions of a number of the major bottlers of its soft drinks. Some of these bottlers, their location, and Coca-Cola's ownership percentage are listed in Exhibit 14-6.[1]

To summarize, large investments in other companies are often made for business reasons such as to be able to exercise influence over the conduct of that company's operations.

Stop & Think

As of December 31, 2011, **Ford Motor** owned 3.5% of **Mazda**. Which ONE of the following possible motivations do you think is the primary motivation for this investment by Ford?

a) Safety cushion
b) Cyclical cash needs
c) Investment for a return
d) Investment for influence

Purchase for Control

Warren Buffett first invested in GEICO insurance in 1951, soon after graduating from Columbia. He describes the company as his "first business love," partly stemming from his admiration of its basic strategy of being the low-cost provider of a necessary product. In 1976, Buffett decided that Berkshire Hathaway should buy a large number of GEICO shares. At the beginning of 1995, Berkshire Hathaway owned almost 50% of GEICO and obviously exercised significant influence over the operation of the company. In 1995, Buffett decided to buy the remaining shares of GEICO, making GEICO a wholly owned subsidiary of Berkshire Hathaway.

[1] In February 2010, Coca-Cola announced that it intended to purchase the North American operations of its largest bottler, Coca-Cola Enterprises. Coca-Cola's announced intention for the acquisition is to create operational efficiencies and to increase its control of its product's bottling in the key North American market. Coca-Cola completed this acquisition in October 2010.

When a company purchases enough of another company to be able to control operating, investing, and financing decisions, different accounting treatment is required for that acquisition. For accounting purposes, a parent company is required to report the results of all of its subsidiaries of which it owns more than 50% as if the parent and subsidiaries were one company. For example, Berkshire Hathaway has a controlling interest in a host of different subsidiaries incorporated in many different states and countries scattered from Omaha, Nebraska, to Cologne, Germany. The financial performances of these subsidiaries are included in the financial statements of Berkshire Hathaway. This is the reason the financial statements of most large corporations are called *consolidated financial statements*: They include aggregated, or consolidated, results for both the parent and all of its majority-owned subsidiaries.

Classification of Investment Securities

LO2 学习目标2
理解与投资证券相关的多种分类。

2 Understand the varying classifications associated with investment securities.

As mentioned previously, FASB ASC Topic 320 addresses the valuation of securities. The statement applies to all debt securities and to equity securities for which a readily determinable fair value is available.[2] If, however, the investment in equity securities of a company is large enough, a different method of accounting (called the "equity method") for equity securities is applied.

Before we discuss the various classifications of securities under the provisions of Topic 320, let's first review what debt and equity securities are.

Debt Securities

From Chapter 12 you will recall that debt securities are financial instruments issued by a company that typically have the following characteristics: (1) a maturity value representing the amount to be repaid to the debt holder at maturity, (2) an interest rate (either fixed or variable) that specifies the periodic interest payments, and (3) a maturity date indicating when the debt obligation will be redeemed.

Equity Securities

Equity securities represent ownership in a company. These shares of stock typically carry with them the right to collect dividends and to vote on corporate matters. In addition, equity securities are an attractive investment because of the potential for significant increases in the price of the security. Features of equity securities were covered in detail in Chapter 13. Sophisticated trading markets for both debt and equity securities have developed over time, with the New York Stock Exchange, the New York Bond Exchange, and NASDAQ being the premier trading exchanges for stocks and bonds.

For accounting purposes, debt and equity securities falling under the scope of FASB ASC Topic 320 can be classified into one of four categories: held to maturity, available for sale, trading, and equity method. Exhibit 14-7 illustrates the major classifications of debt and equity securities.

---

[2] FASB ASC paragraph 320-10-15-5.

Exhibit 14-7 | Classifications of Debt and Equity Securities

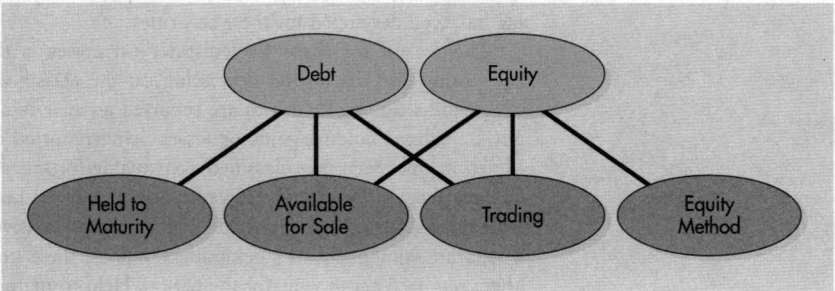

© Cengage Learning 2014

Held-to-Maturity Securities

Held-to-maturity securities are debt securities purchased by a company with the intent and ability to hold those securities until they mature.[3] Note that this category includes only debt securities because equity securities typically do not mature. Note also that the company must have the intention of holding the security until it matures. Simply intending to hold a security for a long period of time does not qualify for inclusion in this category.

Available-for-Sale Securities

Debt securities that are not being held until maturity and are not classified as trading securities are considered, by default, to be "available-for-sale" securities.[4] Available-for-sale securities are also equity securities that are not considered trading securities and are not accounted for using the equity method. Most of the typical company's investment securities are classified as available for sale. This is because the typical company uses its investment securities as a store of excess cash and is not actively managing the investment portfolio to make profits on stock trading.[5]

Trading Securities

Trading securities are debt and equity securities purchased with the intent of selling them in the near future. Trading involves frequent buying and selling of securities, generally for the purpose of "generating profits on short-term differences in price."[6]

Equity Method Securities

equity method security
以权益法核算的证券

Equity method securities are equity securities purchased with the intent of being able to control or significantly influence the operations of the investee. As a result, a large block of stock (presumed to be at least 20% of the outstanding stock unless there exists evidence to the contrary) must be owned to be classified as an equity method security.[7] Because the

---

[3] FASB ASC paragraph 320-10-25-1c.
[4] FASB ASC paragraph 320-10-25-1b.
[5] The FASB and the IASB are currently considering a revision to the system of classifying securities. The Boards have tentatively decided that more investment securities will be classified as "FVNI" (fair value with unrealized gains and losses reported in net income; this is the current "trading security" treatment). All, or almost all, equity security investments (stocks) would be classified as "FVNI." Any change in the classification system will almost certainly not take effect until 2015. See FASB Summary of Decisions Reached to Date During Redeliberations, "Accounting for Financial Instruments," as of August 9, 2012.
[6] FASB ASC paragraph 320-10-25-1a.
[7] FASB ASC paragraph 323-10-15-8.

intent associated with these securities is not simply to earn a return on an investment but includes being able to affect the operations of the investee, a different method of accounting has been developed for these securities.

The reason for these four distinct categories is that the FASB requires different accounting and disclosure, depending on the classification of the securities. Securities classified as trading securities are reported at their fair value on the balance sheet with any unrealized holding gains or losses being reported on the income statement as part of net income. Securities classified as available-for-sale securities are also reported on the balance sheet at fair value. However, any unrealized holding gains and losses associated with these securities are reported as other comprehensive income and are accumulated as a separate component of stockholders' equity; these unrealized gains and losses do not affect reported net income for the period. Held-to-maturity securities are reported on the balance sheet at their amortized cost and are not reported at fair value. The accounting for held-to-maturity securities is generally the mirror image of the accounting by an issuer of long-term debt as discussed in Chapter 12. Equity method securities are not reported at their fair value on the balance sheet. Instead, the investment account is increased or decreased as the net assets of the investee increase and decrease. Exhibit 14-8 summarizes the accounting treatment for debt and equity securities.

Why the Different Categories?

Why does the FASB have these different categories for classifying securities? Why didn't they just make the rule that all increases and decreases in fair value go on the income statement? If you think about the classification scheme, it makes a lot of sense. Take, for example, held-to-maturity securities. Companies plan on holding these securities until they mature (hence the name). The company has no intention of realizing any changes in fair value on these securities between the purchase date and the maturity date, so there is no reason to recognize any changes in fair value prior to the maturity date. Similarly, companies hold equity method securities not to realize changes in the fair value of those securities but to maintain some level of influence over the investee. Thus, the fair value of the investment is not of primary importance to the investor. In summary, because appreciation in price is not a major reason for holding held-to-maturity and equity method securities, adjustments for temporary changes in fair value are not required.

Trading securities are purchased with the intent of realizing profits in the short term. Thus, changes in fair value are recorded in the period in which they occur, whether that change has been realized through an arm's-length transaction or not. Because an unrealized gain (or loss) can be turned into a realized gain (or loss) with a simple phone

Exhibit 14-8 | The Different Accounting Treatments for Debt and Equity Securities

Classification of Securities	Types of Securities	Disclosure on the Balance Sheet	Treatment of Temporary Changes in Fair Value
Held to maturity	Debt	Amortized cost	Not recognized
Available for sale	Debt and equity	Fair value	Reported in stockholders' equity
Trading	Debt and equity	Fair value	Reported on the income statement
Equity method	Equity	Historical cost adjusted for changes in the net assets of the investee	Not recognized

© Cengage Learning 2014

> **FYI**
>
> Who decides how a security is to be classified? Management does. Management's intent is the key factor in determining the reasons for holding certain securities. As you can guess, judgment plays a significant role in this classification.

为什么不把可供出售金融资产公允价值变动视同交易性金融资产进行处理呢？答案在于这些公允价值变动的可能性，即可供出售金融资产实现公允价值变动的可能性不那么明确。

call to a portfolio manager, it makes sense to include the change in fair value on the income statement of the period in which the change occurs.

What about available-for-sale securities? Why not treat increases and decreases in fair value on this type of security similar to the treatment for trading securities? The answer lies in the probability of realizing those changes in fair value. With trading securities, it is likely that those changes in fair value will be realized sooner rather than later; that is the reason they are called *trading securities*. The same likelihood of realization is not as certain with available-for-sale securities. Because it is less certain that the changes in fair value of available-for-sale securities will actually be realized in the current period, the FASB elected to bypass the income statement and require these increases in value to be reported directly in the Stockholders' Equity section of the balance sheet as part of Accumulated Other Comprehensive Income. In addition, although these unrealized gains and losses are excluded from net income, they are included in the computation of comprehensive income. Because available-for-sale securities are not purchased with the primary intent of making money on short-term price fluctuations, it seems reasonable to exclude unrealized gains and losses on these securities from the computation of the periodic net income.

The Fair Value Option

As explained in Chapter 12, in 2007 the FASB took a bold step toward increased use of fair value by allowing companies a fair value option for the reporting of financial assets and liabilities.[8] Under the fair value option, a company has the option to report, at each balance sheet date, any or all of its financial assets and liabilities at their fair values on the balance sheet date. The unrealized gains and losses from changes in the fair values of financial assets and liabilities accounted for using the fair value option are reported in the income statement. As illustrated in Chapter 12, this fair value option allows companies to reflect in the income statement, without complicated hedge accounting procedures, the offsetting economic effects of the hedging of corresponding financial assets and liabilities.

The election of this fair value option for an investment security trumps the classification of the security as described above (trading, available for sale, held to maturity, and equity method). Accordingly, even though a security is classified as available for sale, if the company elects the fair value option for that security then the unrealized gains and losses are included in earnings in the income statement rather than in other comprehensive income as is typically required for available-for-sale securities. Similarly, equity method or held-to-maturity securities, which typically are NOT reported in the balance sheet at fair value, are reported at fair value if the company has elected the fair value option with respect to those particular securities. In essence, all investment securities for which the fair value option is elected are accounted for in the same way as the trading security accounting illustrated later in the chapter.[9]

---

[8] *Pre-Codification Statement of Financial Accounting Standards No. 159,* "The Fair Value Option for Financial Assets and Financial Liabilities—Including an Amendment of FASB Statement No. 115" (Norwalk, CT: Financial Accounting Standards Board, February 2007). This guidance is now found in the "Fair Value Option" subsections of FASB ASC Topic 825 (Financial Instruments).
[9] The FASB and the IASB are considering eliminating the possibility of using the fair value option with equity method securities. See *FASB Summary of Decisions Reached to Date During Redeliberations,* "Accounting for Financial Instruments," as of August 9, 2012.

Classification of Investment Securities According to IFRS

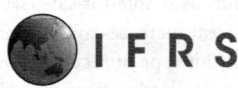

The classification of investment securities under IFRS, specifically *IFRS 9*, is very similar to the classification categories under U.S. GAAP. In fact, it is apparent that *IFRS* has been heavily influenced by pre-Codification *SFAS No. 115* (adopted in 1993 and now included in Topic 320). The same categories of trading, available-for-sale, and held-to-maturity investments exist. Under IFRS, the available-for-sale category exists but is typically referred to by a description rather than a label.[10]

The fair value option for financial assets, as described above, also exists in IFRS under the provisions of *IFRS 9*.[11] In fact, Sir David Tweedie, the chairman of the IASB, has stated several times that he thinks that the perfect accounting standard for the accounting for all investment securities would consist of just two paragraphs. The first paragraph would say that *all* investment securities should be reported on the balance sheet at fair value, with unrealized gains and losses from changes in fair value to be reported through "profit and loss" (the income statement); this is the fair value option comprehensively applied to all investment securities. The second paragraph of this perfect accounting standard would say: "Reread Paragraph 1."

Purchase of Securities

 Account for the purchase of debt and equity securities.

The purchase of debt and equity securities is recorded at cost just like the purchase of any other asset. But because debt securities are bought and sold between interest payment dates, accounting for the amount of accrued interest since the last payment date adds a minor complexity.

Purchase of Debt Securities

The purchase of debt securities is recorded at cost, which includes brokerage fees, taxes, and other charges incurred in their acquisition. When debt securities are acquired between interest payment dates, the amount paid for the securities is increased by a charge for accrued interest to the date of purchase. This charge should not be reported as part of the investment cost. Two assets have been acquired—the security and the accrued interest receivable—and should be reported in two separate asset accounts. Upon receipt of the interest, Interest Receivable is closed and Interest Revenue is credited for the amount of interest earned since the purchase date. Instead of recording the interest as a receivable (asset approach), Interest Revenue may be debited for the accrued interest paid at the time of purchase. The subsequent collection of interest would then be credited in full to Interest Revenue. The latter procedure (revenue approach) is usually more convenient.

To illustrate the entries for the acquisition of debt securities, assume that $100,000 in U.S. Treasury notes are purchased at 104¼ (debt securities are normally quoted at a price per $100 face value) on May 1. Interest is 9% payable semiannually on January 1

---

[10] The existing provisions of *IFRS 9* suggest that the available-for-sale classification should be relatively rare under IFRS. Implementation of *IFRS 9* has been delayed until 2015 while the FASB and the IASB jointly consider the differences between their respective standards.
[11] Initially, the fair value option under IFRS has applied only to financial assets. In May 2010, the IASB extended the fair value option to financial liabilities.

and July 1. Accrued interest of $3,000 would thus be added to the purchase price. The debt securities are classified by the purchaser as trading securities because management will sell the securities if a change in the price will result in a profit. The entries to record the purchase of the notes and the subsequent collection of interest under the alternate procedures would be as follows:

Asset Approach

May 1	Investment in Trading Securities		104,250	
	Interest Receivable		3,000	
	Cash			107,250
July 1	Cash		4,500	
	Interest Receivable			3,000
	Interest Revenue			1,500

Revenue Approach

May 1	Investment in Trading Securities		104,250	
	Interest Revenue		3,000	
	Cash			107,250
July 1	Cash		4,500	
	Interest Revenue			4,500

The important point is that under either approach, the interest revenue recognized for the period is equal to the interest earned, not the amount received. In this case, the company earned $1,500, representing interest for the period May 1 to June 30.

Purchase of Equity Securities

Shares of stock are usually purchased for cash through stock exchanges (e.g., New York, NASDAQ, or regional exchanges) and from individuals and institutional investors rather than from the corporations themselves. The investment is recorded at the amount paid, including brokers' commissions, taxes, and other fees incidental to the purchase price. Even when part of the purchase price is deferred, the full cost should be recorded as the investment in stock, with a liability account established for the amount yet to be paid. If stock is acquired in exchange for properties or services instead of cash, the fair value of the consideration given or the value at which the stock is currently selling, whichever is more clearly determinable, should be used as the basis for recording the investment. If two or more securities are acquired for a lump-sum price, the cost should be allocated to each security in an equitable manner, as illustrated in Chapter 10 with the basket purchase of long-term operating assets.

To illustrate the accounting for the purchase of equity securities, assume that Gondor Enterprises purchased 300 shares of Boromir Co. stock at $75 per share and 500 shares of Faramir Inc. stock at $50 per share. Gondor classifies the Boromir stock as a trading security because management has

Stock purchased for cash through stock exchanges is recorded at the amount paid, including brokers' commissions, taxes, and other fees at the amount paid.

no intention of holding these securities for a long period of time and will sell them as soon as it is economically advantageous for the company. The Faramir stock is classified as available for sale.[12] The journal entry to record the purchases would be as follows:

Investment in Trading Securities—Boromir Co.	22,500*	
Investment in Available-for-Sale Securities—Faramir Inc.	25,000†	
Cash		47,500

Computations:
*300 × $75 = $22,500
†500 × $50 = $25,000

Recognition of Revenue from Investment Securities

4 Account for the recognition of revenue from investment securities.

A primary reason that companies invest in the debt or equity securities of other companies is to earn a return in the form of either interest or dividends. In the case of debt securities, the computation of that return is complicated because a difference often exists between the purchase price and the maturity value of the debt instrument. The resulting premium or discount can affect the amount of interest revenue recognized in each future period—depending on how the securities are classified when purchased. For equity securities, the recognition of revenue from an investment depends on the level of ownership in the investee. Each of these issues is discussed in the following sections.

Recognition of Revenue from Debt Securities

Recall from Chapter 12 that debt securities carry with them a stated rate of interest that when multiplied by the maturity value of the securities indicates the amount of cash to be received in interest each year. Often, interest is received on a semiannual basis. When interest is received, Cash is debited and Interest Revenue is credited. However, when debt securities are acquired at a higher or lower price than their maturity value and the debt securities are classified as held to maturity, periodic amortization of the premium or accumulation of the discount with corresponding adjustments to interest revenue is required. One could amortize a premium or discount associated with trading or available-for-sale securities. But recall that one of the primary reasons for this amortization process is to ensure that the carrying value of held-to-maturity securities is equal to its maturity value on the maturity date. If securities are not classified as being held to maturity, the amortization process becomes less relevant.[13]

As explained in Chapter 12, a premium or discount results when the stated rate of interest and the market rate of interest on the date of acquisition of the debt security are different. If the stated rate of interest is higher than the prevailing market rate, investors

---

[12] Historically, brokerage fees and other costs involved with purchasing investment securities have been included in the initial recorded cost of the securities. However, for securities accounted for using the fair value option, brokerage fees and other upfront costs are to be expensed when incurred; see FASB ASC paragraph 825-10-25-3. This immediate expensing of upfront fees also applies to trading securities. The historical approach of including upfront fees as part of the initial recorded amount for the securities still applies to available-for-sale and held-to-maturity securities; see FASB ASC paragraphs 310-20-15-2 through 4.

[13] In all examples that follow as well as in the end-of-chapter material, we will assume that premiums and discounts associated only with held-to-maturity securities are amortized.

> **FYI**
>
> You will need to be comfortable with present value computations if you are to understand the calculations that follow. The Time Value of Money Review module contains an overview of the time value of money.

will pay a higher price for the debt security (a premium) to receive the higher interest payments. When the market rate of interest is higher than the stated rate, investors will pay less than the face amount of the debt security, resulting in a discount.

The present value computations associated with computing the value of a debt security were illustrated in Chapter 12 and an example is included here. Assume that on January 1, 2014, Silmaril Technologies purchased five-year, 10% bonds with a face value of $100,000 and interest payable semiannually on January 1 and July 1. The market rate on bonds of similar quality and maturity is 8%. Silmaril computes the market price of the bonds as follows:

Present value of principal:
  Maturity value of bonds after five years $100,000
  Present value of $100,000: $FV = \$100{,}000$; $N = 10$; $I = 4\%$ .... $ 67,556
Present value of interest payments:
  Semiannual payment, 5% of $100,000 .... $ 5,000
  Present value of 10 payments of $5,000: $PMT = \$5{,}000$; $N = 10$; $I = 4\%$ 40,554
Total present value (market price) of the bonds (rounded) $108,110

We will use two examples to illustrate the accounting for interest revenue. First, we will assume that Silmaril intends to take advantage of short-term price fluctuations (thereby making them trading securities), and second, we will assume that Silmaril intends, and has the ability, to hold the bonds until they mature (making them held-to-maturity securities).

Interest Revenue for Debt Securities Classified as Trading Recall from Chapter 12 that the investor typically does not use a premium or discount account but instead records the investment at cost and nets the face value and any premium or discount. Silmaril would make the following journal entry to record the initial purchase of the bonds:[14]

interest revenue for debt securities classified as trading
划分为交易性金融资产的债券利息收入

Investment in Trading Securities 108,110
  Cash 108,110

When interest payments are received, the journal entry to record their receipt would be

Cash 5,000
  Interest Revenue 5,000

Interest Revenue for Debt Securities Classified as Held to Maturity The entry to record the initial purchase of the bonds had they been originally classified as held to maturity would be

interest revenue for debt securities classified as held to maturity
划分为持有至到期的债券利息收入

Investment in Held-to-Maturity Securities 108,110
  Cash 108,110

To determine the amount of premium to amortize each period, Silmaril would prepare an amortization table, as illustrated. This table is based on the effective-interest method of amortization.[15]

---

[14] The journal entries would be similar had the security been classified as available for sale. The only difference would be in the account title.
[15] As explained in Chapter 12, the straight-line method of interest amortization can be used when the results do not differ materially from effective-interest amortization. However, in all the examples that follow as well as in the end-of-chapter material, we will use the effective-interest method.

Amortization of Bond Premium—Effective-Interest Method
$100,000, Five-Year Bonds, Interest at 10% Payable Semiannually,
Sold at $108,110 to Yield 8% Compounded Semiannually

Interest Payment	A Interest Received (0.05 × $100,000)	B Interest Revenue (0.04 × Bond Carrying Value)	C Premium Amortization (A − B)	D Unamortized Premium (D − C)	Bond Carrying Value ($100,000 + D)
				$8,110	$108,110
1	$5,000	$4,324	$676	7,434	107,434
2	5,000	4,297	703	6,731	106,731
3	5,000	4,269	731	6,000	106,000
4	5,000	4,240	760	5,240	105,240
5	5,000	4,210	790	4,450	104,450
6	5,000	4,178	822	3,628	103,628
7	5,000	4,145	855	2,773	102,773
8	5,000	4,111	889	1,884	101,884
9	5,000	4,075	925	959	100,959
10	5,000	4,041*	959	0	100,000

*Rounding differences are adjusted with last entry.

Stop & Think

Theoretically, we should amortize the discount or premium associated with trading and available-for-sale debt securities just as we do with held-to-maturity securities. In this simple example, why don't we?

a) Both trading and available-for-sale debt securities are adjusted to fair value at the end of each reporting period.
b) Most U.S. companies don't hold any trading or available-for-sale debt securities.
c) Neither trading nor available-for-sale debt securities are ever sold at premiums or discounts to face value.
d) Companies avoid amortizing discounts and premiums on trading and available-for-sale debt securities for income tax reasons.

When the first interest payment of $5,000 is received from the bond issuer, Silmaril would make the following journal entry:

Cash	5,000	
Interest Revenue		4,324
Investment in Held-to- Maturity Securities		676

Subsequent receipts of interest would be recorded with a similar journal entry, the only difference being that the amount amortized would differ, depending on which interest payment was received.

Recognition of Revenue from Equity Securities

Once an equity security is purchased, one of two basic methods must be used to account for the revenue earned on that investment depending on the control or degree of influence exercised by the acquiring company (investor) over the acquired company (investee). In those instances where the level of ownership in the investee is such that the investor is able to control or significantly influence decisions made by the investee, the use of the equity method is appropriate. The accounting procedures associated with the equity method are outlined in FASB ASC Topic 323 (Investments—Equity Method and Joint Ventures). When the acquiring company does not exercise significant influence over the investee, the equity securities are classified as trading or available-for-sale securities.

The ability of the investor to exercise significant influence over such decisions as dividend distribution and operational and financial administration may be indicated in several ways: representation on the investee's board of directors, participation in policy-making processes, material intercompany transactions, interchange of managerial personnel, or technological dependency of investee on investor. Another important consideration is the extent of ownership by an investor in relation to the concentration of other stockholdings. While it is clear that ownership of more than 50% of common stock virtually assures control by the acquiring company, ownership of 50% or less may give effective control if the remaining shares of the stock are widely held and no significant blocks of stockholders are consistently united in their ownership. The FASB recognizes that the degree of influence and control will not always be clear and that judgment will be required in assessing the status of each investment. To achieve a reasonable degree of uniformity in the application of its position, the FASB has set 20% as an ownership standard; the ownership of 20% or more of the voting stock of the company carries the presumption, in the absence of evidence to the contrary, that an investor has the ability to exercise significant influence over that company. Conversely, ownership of less than 20% leads to the presumption that the investor does not have the ability to exercise significant influence unless such ability can be demonstrated.[16] Again, the 20% criterion is only a guideline, and judgment is required in determining the appropriate accounting method in cases where ownership is 50% or less.[17]

Both the FASB and the IASB are currently deliberating the issue of control in the context of whether a sizable equity investment should be accounted for using the equity method (which is illustrated in this chapter) or consolidation (which is outside the scope of this book). In their discussions of control, the FASB and IASB have described control as the power to direct the affairs of another company to the extent that profits or returns of that company are significantly affected. The current thinking of the FASB and the IASB is that one company has control over another when it has more than half of the voting rights, when it possesses substantive contractual control of key activities, or when it has a large minority voting interest in the election of the Board of Directors and no other party or organized group of parties has a significant voting interest. Thus, one company could be classified as "controlling" another with less than 50% ownership. For example, Coca-Cola might be classified as controlling the bottling subsidiaries listed in Exhibit 14-6. As of 2012, the FASB and IASB were still considering this area. The existing standard is that control exists when one company owns more than 50% of another.

Until the FASB provides a definitive standard addressing the issue of control, the percentage-of-ownership criterion is widely accepted as the basis for determining the appropriate method of accounting for long-term investments in equity securities when the investor does not possess absolute voting control. If it is determined that control exists, the combined financial results are reported in consolidated financial statements. If significant influence exists, the equity method of accounting is applied to the investment. If not, then the securities are classified as either trading or available for sale. Note that because preferred stock is generally nonvoting stock and does not provide for significant influence, it is always classified as either trading or available for sale.

In the case of consolidation, the investor and investee are referred to respectively as the parent company and the subsidiary company. Where control exists, preparation of consolidated financial statements is required. This means that the financial statement balances of the parent and subsidiary companies are combined, or consolidated, for financial reporting purposes even though

> **FYI**
>
> Remember, consolidation is not an alternative to the equity method. It constitutes procedures employed in addition to those used with the equity method.

---

[16] FASB ASC paragraphs 322-10-15-6 through 8.
[17] FASB ASC paragraph 323-10-15-10.

the companies continue to operate as separate entities. In the consolidation process, any intercompany transactions are eliminated, for example, any sales and purchases between the parent and subsidiary companies. By eliminating all intercompany transactions, the combined balances or consolidated totals appropriately reflect the financial position and results of operation of the total economic unit. This treatment reflects the fact that majority ownership of common stock assures control by the parent over the decision-making processes of the subsidiary. The important point is this: The process of consolidation builds on the journal entries made when the equity method is applied. In fact, the equity method of accounting is often referred to as a "one-line consolidation." Coca-Cola provides an example of an instance where the company owned a greater than 50% interest in a subsidiary and yet did not prepare consolidated financial statements for the subsidiary. Recall from our previous discussion of acquiring companies for influence that Coca-Cola owned 30% of Coca-Cola Amatil, an Australian-based bottler. In past years, Coca-Cola's ownership interest in Coca-Cola Amatil exceeded 50%, yet the company did not consolidate. The reason Coca-Cola did not consolidate was that, as the company indicated in the notes to its financial statements, its control was considered temporary.

Previous accounting standards allowed separate reporting for certain majority-owned subsidiaries if those subsidiaries had "nonhomogeneous" operations, a large minority interest, or a foreign location. Separate reporting by subsidiaries occurred most often when the operations of the subsidiary and parent were significantly different (i.e., nonhomogeneous). Typically, the subsidiary was engaged in finance, insurance, leasing, or real estate, while the parent company was a manufacturer or merchandiser. Examples include **General Electric Capital Services (GECS)** and **IBM Credit Corporation**, which are finance companies that are wholly owned by **General Electric** and **IBM**, respectively. Traditionally, the financial statements of these subsidiaries were not consolidated with those of their respective parent companies.

Since the issuance of pre-Codification *Statement of Financial Accounting Standards No. 94*, the FASB has required the consolidation of all majority-owned subsidiaries unless control is temporary or does not rest with the majority owner (as, for instance, when the subsidiary is in legal reorganization or in bankruptcy) and is considering expanding the concept of control to encourage the consolidation of subsidiaries for which a parent company has control even with a less-than-majority ownership interest.[18] Thus, even though a subsidiary has nonhomogeneous operations, a large minority interest, or a foreign location, it should be consolidated. The reporting entity is to be the total economic unit consisting of the parent and all of its subsidiaries.

To summarize, in the absence of persuasive evidence to the contrary, equity securities are classified as trading or available for sale when ownership is less than 20%; the equity method is used when ownership is such that the investor has the ability to significantly influence or control the investee's operations; in those instances where control is deemed to exist, the equity method, along with additional consolidation procedures, is used. These relationships dealing with the effect of ownership interest and control or influence and the proper accounting method to be used are summarized in Exhibit 14-9. Note that the percentages are given only as guidelines. Subjective assessment of the ability of an investor to influence or control an investee should also be considered when determining the appropriate accounting for the investment.

We will first discuss and illustrate the accounting and reporting issues associated with the recognition of revenue on trading and available-for-sale equity securities. The more complex equity method will then be discussed.

---

[18] *Pre-Codification Statement of Financial Accounting Standards No. 94*, "Consolidation of All Majority-Owned Subsidiaries" (Stamford, CT: Financial Accounting Standards Board, 1987).

Exhibit 14-9 | Effect of Ownership Interest and Control or Influence on Accounting for Long-Term Investments in Common Stocks

Ownership Interest	Control or Degree of Influence	Accounting Method	Applicable Standard
More than 50%	Control	Equity method and consolidation procedures	FASB ASC Topic 810
20 to 50%	Significant influence	Equity method	FASB ASC Topic 323
Less than 20%	No significant influence	Account for as trading or available for sale	FASB ASC Topic 320

© Cengage Learning 2014

Revenue for Equity Securities Classified As Trading and Available for Sale When an investment in another company's stock does not involve either a controlling interest or significant influence, it is classified as either trading or available for sale. Recall that equity securities cannot be classified as held to maturity. Revenue is recognized when dividends are declared (if the investor knows about the declaration) or when the dividends are received from the investee. Continuing a previous example, assume that Gondor Enterprises receives the following dividends from its investees:

Company	Classification	Number of Shares Held	Dividends Received per Share
Boromir Co.	Trading securities	300	$2.00
Faramir Inc.	Available-for-sale securities	500	3.75

The journal entry to record receipt of the dividends would be:

Cash	2,475*	
Dividend Revenue		2,475

*[(300 × $2.00) + (500 × $3.75) = $2,475]

Revenue for Securities Classified As Equity Method Securities The equity method of accounting for long-term investments in common stock reflects the economic substance of the relationship between the investor and investee rather than the legal distinction of the separate entities. The objective of this method is to reflect the underlying claim by the investor on the net assets of the investee company.

Under the equity method, the investment is initially recorded at cost, just as any other investment. However, with the equity method, the investment account is periodically adjusted to reflect changes in the underlying net assets of the investee. The investment balance is increased to reflect a proportionate share of the earnings of the investee company or decreased to reflect a share of any losses reported. If preferred stock dividends have been declared by the investee, they must be deducted from income reported by the investee before computing the investor's share of investee earnings or losses. When dividends are received by the investor, the investment account is reduced. Thus, the equity method results in an increase in the investment account when the investee's net assets increase; similarly, the investment account decreases when the investee records a loss or pays out dividends.

We will illustrate the equity method with a simple example. Assume that BioTech Inc. purchased 40% of the outstanding stock of Medco Enterprises on January 1 of the current year by paying $200,000. During the year, Medco reported net income of

在权益法下，最初以成本记录投资，就如其他投资一样。然而，由于权益法的使用，投资的账面价值应予以周期性调整，从而反映被投资者标的资产的变动。投资账面余额的增加反映了投资者对被投资公司所拥有的相应收益份额，投资账面余额的减少则反映了相应份额的损失。在计算投资者所享有或承担的投资收益及损失前，如果被投资公司宣告了优先股股利，就应将它们从被投资公司所报告的利润中减去。

$50,000 and paid dividends of $10,000. BioTech would make the following journal entries during the year:

Investment in Medco Enterprises Stock	200,000	
Cash		200,000
To record the purchase of 40% of Medco stock.		
Investment in Medco Enterprises Stock	20,000	
Income from Investment in Medco Enterprises Stock ($50,000 × 0.40)		20,000
To record the recognition of revenue from investment in Medco.		
Cash ($10,000 × 0.40)	4,000	
Investment in Medco Enterprises Stock		4,000
To record the receipt of a dividend on Medco stock.		

Notice that Medco Enterprises' book value increased by $40,000 during the year ($50,000 in income less $10,000 dividend). BioTech's investment in Medco increased by 40% of this amount ($16,000 = $20,000 − $4,000). The equity method of accounting maintains a relationship between the book value of the investee and the investment account on the books of the investor. As the subsidiary's book value changes, so does the investment account on the books of the parent company.

Comparing the Provisions of FASB ASC Topics 320 and 323 To contrast and illustrate the accounting entries under various methods, assume that Powell Corporation purchases 5,000 shares of San Juan Company common stock on January 2 at $20 per share, including commissions and other costs. San Juan has a total of 25,000 shares outstanding; thus, the 5,000 shares represent a 20% ownership interest. We will illustrate the accounting differences in revenue recognition for equity securities by assuming that (1) the securities are classified as available for sale and (2) the securities are classified as equity method securities and accounted for using the equity method. The appropriate entries under both assumptions are shown in Exhibit 14-10. The actual method used would depend

Exhibit 14-10 | Journal Entries to Record Revenue Recognition Using FASB ASC Topics 320 and 323

Available for Sale (Topic 320)			Equity Method (Topic 323)		
Jan. 2 Purchased 5,000 shares of San Juan Company common stock at $20 per share:					
Investment in Available-for-Sale Securities	100,000		Investment in San Juan Company Stock	100,000	
Cash		100,000	Cash		100,000
Oct. 31 Received dividend of $0.80 per share from San Juan Company ($0.80 × 5,000 shares):					
Cash	4,000		Cash	4,000	
Dividend Revenue		4,000	Investment in San Juan Company Stock		4,000
Dec. 31 San Juan Company announced earnings for the year of $60,000:					
No entry			Investment in San Juan Company Stock	12,000	
			Income from Investment in San Juan Company Stock (0.20 × $60,000)		12,000

© Cengage Learning 2014

on the degree of influence exercised by the investor as indicated by a consideration of all relevant factors, as well as the percentage owned. Exhibit 14-10 highlights the basic differences in accounting for investments using FASB ASC Topics 320 (on standard investments in debt and equity securities) and 323 (on the equity method used when an investment is made in order to create significant influence). Under both methods, the investment is originally recorded at cost. Dividends received are recognized as dividend revenue for the available-for-sale securities and as a reduction in the investment account under the equity method.

The investor's percentage of the earnings of the investee company are recorded as income and as an increase to the investment account under the equity method, whereas no entry is required for this event when the securities are classified as available for sale. If the securities had been classified as trading, the journal entries to recognize revenue would have been identical to those made for the available-for-sale securities.

Equity Method: Purchase for More than Book Value When a company is purchased by another company, the purchase price usually differs from the recorded book value of the underlying net assets of the acquired company. For example, assume that Snowbird Company purchased 100% of the common stock of Ski Resorts International for $8 million, although the book value of Ski Resorts' net assets is only $6.5 million. In effect, Snowbird is purchasing some undervalued assets, above-normal earnings potential, or both.

As explained in Chapter 10, if the purchase price of an ongoing business exceeds the recorded value, the acquiring company must allocate this purchase price among the assets acquired using their current market values as opposed to the amounts carried on the books of the acquired company. If part of the purchase price cannot be allocated to specific assets, either tangible or intangible, that amount is recorded as goodwill. If the fair values of the acquired assets have decreased, the assets acquired might be recorded at an amount less than their carrying value on the books of the acquired company. Whether assets are increased or decreased as a result of the purchase, future income determination will use the new (adjusted) values to determine the depreciation and amortization charges.

When only a portion of a company's stock is purchased and the equity method is used to reflect the income of the partially owned company, an adjustment to the investee's reported income, similar to that just described, may be required. To determine whether such an adjustment is necessary, the acquiring company must compare the purchase price of the common stock with the recorded net asset value of the acquired company at the date of purchase. If the purchase price exceeds the investor's share of book value, the computed excess must be analyzed in the same way as described above for a 100% purchase. Although no entries to adjust asset values are made on the books of either company, an adjustment to the investee's reported income is required under the equity method for the investor to reflect the economic reality of paying more for the investment than the underlying net book value. If depreciable assets had been adjusted to higher market values on the books of the investee to reflect the price paid by the investor, additional depreciation would have been taken by the investee company. Similarly, if the purchase price reflected amortizable intangibles, additional amortization would have been required. These adjustments would have reduced the reported income of the investee. To reflect this condition, an adjustment is made by the investor to the income reported by the investee in applying the equity method. This adjustment serves to meet the objective of computing the income reported using the equity method in the same manner as would be done if the company were 100% purchased and consolidated financial statements were prepared.

To illustrate, assume that the book value of common stockholders' equity (net assets) of Stewart Inc. was $500,000 at the time Phillips Manufacturing Co. purchased 40% of its common shares for $250,000. Based on a 40% ownership interest, the market value of the net assets of Stewart Inc. would be $625,000 ($250,000/0.40), or $125,000 more than the book value. Assume that a review of the asset values discloses that the market value of depreciable properties exceeds the carrying value of these assets by $50,000. The remaining $75,000 difference ($125,000 − $50,000) is attributed to a special operating license. Assume further that the average remaining life of the depreciable assets is 10 years and that the license is to be amortized over 20 years. Phillips Manufacturing Co. would adjust its share of the annual income reported by Stewart Inc. to reflect the additional depreciation and the amortization of the license as follows:

Additional depreciation ($50,000 × 0.40)/10 years	$2,000
License amortization ($75,000 × 0.40)/20 years	1,500
	$3,500

Each year for the first 10 years, Phillips would make the following entry in addition to entries made to recognize its share of Stewart Inc.'s income and dividends:

Income from Investment in Stewart Inc. Stock	3,500	
Investment in Stewart Inc. Stock		3,500

To adjust share of income on Stewart Inc. common stock for proportionate depreciation on excess market value of depreciable property, $2,000, and for amortization of the unrecorded license, $1,500.

After the tenth year, the adjustment would be for $1,500 until the license amount is fully amortized.

To complete the illustration, assume that the purchase was made on January 2, 2015; Stewart Inc. declared and paid dividends of $70,000 to common stockholders during 2015, and it reported net income of $150,000 for the year ended December 31, 2015. At the end of 2015, the investment in Stewart Inc. common stock would be reported on the balance sheet of Phillips Manufacturing Co. at $278,500, computed as follows:

Investment in Stewart Inc. Common Stock		
Acquisition cost	$250,000	
Add: Share of 2015 earnings of investee company ($150,000 × 0.40)	60,000	$310,000
Less: Dividends received from investee ($70,000 × 0.40)	$ 28,000	
Additional depreciation of undervalued assets	2,000	
Amortization of unrecorded license	1,500	31,500
Year-end carrying value of investment (equity in investee company)		$278,500

This illustration assumes that the fiscal years of the two companies coincide and that the purchase of the stock is made at the beginning of the year. If a purchase is made at a time other than the beginning of the year, the income earned up to the date of the purchase is assumed to be included in the cost of purchase. Only income earned by the investee subsequent to acquisition should be recognized by the investor.

The adjustments for additional depreciation and intangible asset amortization are needed only when the purchase price is greater than the underlying book value at the date of acquisition. If the purchase price is less than the underlying book value at the time of acquisition, it is assumed

额外折旧和无形资产摊销的调整仅在购买日的购买价格大于账面价值之时才需要。如果购买价格小于相应的账面价值，则假设被投资公司的特定资产被高估了。为了减少包括在被投资公司利润中的折旧，进行适当的调整是必要的。这里的会计分录调整与上述例子相反。除高估资产加上（不是减去）被投资公司账面价值的调整外，其余的计算均相似。

FYI

Goodwill associated with an equity method investment is not tested for impairment using the techniques described in Chapter 11. Instead, as described later in the chapter, the entire equity method investment is considered to see whether any declines in value are permanent.

that specific assets of the investee are overvalued. An adjustment is necessary to reduce the depreciation included in the reported income of the investee. The journal entry to reflect this adjustment is the reverse of the one illustrated previously. The computations would also be similar except that the adjustments for overvalued assets would be added to (instead of subtracted from) the carrying value of the investment.

If the excess of the investment cost over the share of the book value of the net assets of the investee is attributable to goodwill, the computation of investment income is simplified. This is so because this goodwill, just like goodwill recorded in connection with the acquisition of an entire business, is not amortized. Accordingly, in the Phillips Manufacturing example if the $75,000 excess had been attributed to goodwill instead of to the operating license, income for the investment in the first year would have been $58,000 ($60,000 − $2,000) rather than $56,500 ($60,000 − $2,000 − $1,500).

Equity Method: Joint Ventures As explained in Chapter 12, a *joint venture* is a form of off-balance-sheet financing. What was not mentioned in Chapter 12 is that joint ventures are accounted for using the equity method. The manner in which joint ventures serve as a form of off-balance-sheet financing is illustrated in the following example. Owner A Company and Owner B Company each own 50% of Ryan Julius Company, which does research and marketing for the products of both Owner A and Owner B. Ryan Julius has assets of $10,000 and liabilities of $9,000. Because neither Owner A nor Owner B owns more than 50% of Ryan Julius, both companies would account for their investment using the equity method. The balance sheets of both companies would include the following with respect to their investment in Ryan Julius:

Owner A Balance Sheet
Investment in Ryan Julius [($10,000 − $9,000) × 0.50] $500

Owner B Balance Sheet
Investment in Ryan Julius [($10,000 − $9,000) × 0.50] $500

The off-balance-sheet financing aspect of joint ventures can be seen in that the $9,000 in liabilities of Ryan Julius are not reported in the balance sheet of either of the companies that own Ryan Julius. In this way, Owner A and Owner B have used the Ryan Julius joint venture to jointly borrow $9,000 without either one of them being required to report the liability in its balance sheet. As mentioned in Chapter 12, before their merger, **Chevron** and **Texaco** had a 50-50 joint venture partnership, **Caltex**. The Caltex joint venture had total liabilities in excess of $6 billion, none of which were reported in either Chevron's or Texaco's balance sheet.

Not all joint ventures have the 50-50 ownership structure illustrated here. If the owner of a joint venture is, say, 70-30, the minority owner will still account for the joint venture using the equity method, but the majority owner will be required to consolidate the joint venture and list all of the assets and liabilities of the joint venture in its (the majority owner's) balance sheet.

Equity Method Accounting According to IFRS

Equity method accounting under IFRS is the same, in all important respects, as under U.S. GAAP. The relevant standard is *IAS 28*. Under IFRS, the term "associate" is used for what is called an "equity method investee" under U.S. GAAP. If this were an advanced accounting text, we would probably discuss the proportionate consolidation for joint ventures that is allowed under *IAS 31*; proportionate consolidation is allowed only in specialized industries under U.S. GAAP. However, because this is not an advanced accounting text, we will leave the very interesting proportionate consolidation discussion to another day.

Accounting for the Change in Value of Securities

LO5 学习目标5
解释投资类证券公允价值变动的会计处理。

⑤ Account for the change in fair value of investment securities.

The fair value of debt and equity securities can rise and fall on a daily basis. Some of these changes in fair value can be considered temporary while others might be of a more permanent nature. Prior to 1993, when pre-Codification FASB *Statement No. 115* was issued, if temporary price changes occurred, only declines (and their subsequent recovery) in value of securities were recognized in the financial statements. The existing standard requires, for many types of debt and equity securities, both increases and decreases in fair value to be reflected in the financial statements. This section of the chapter deals with accounting for temporary changes in a security's fair value. We also briefly discuss the accounting for permanent declines in fair value.

Accounting for Temporary Changes in the Fair Value of Securities

Recall from our previous discussion that all publicly traded debt securities and those publicly traded equity securities not being held with the intent to influence the investee are to be classified into one of three categories. Those categories and their required disclosures were summarized in Exhibit 14-8.

The following example will be used throughout this section to illustrate accounting for changes in fair value. Eastwood Incorporated purchased five different securities on March 23, 2015. A schedule showing the type and cost of each security, along with its fair value on December 31, 2015, is as follows:

Security	Classification	Cost	Fair Value, Dec. 31, 2015
1	Trading	$ 8,000	$ 7,000
2	Trading	3,000	3,500
3	Available for sale	5,000	6,100
4	Available for sale	12,000	11,500
5	Held to maturity	20,000*	19,000

*Security 5 was purchased at face value. If the security were purchased at a price other than face value, the amortization procedures described previously would be employed.

The entry to record the initial purchase would be as follows:

Investment in Trading Securities	11,000	
Investment in Available-for-Sale Securities	17,000	
Investment in Held-to-Maturity Securities	20,000	
Cash		48,000

Securities 1 and 2 are classified by management as trading securities because management has no intention of holding these securities for a long period of time and will sell them as soon as it is economically advantageous for the company. Securities 3 and 4 are deemed by management to be available-for-sale securities. Management purchased security 5 at face value and intends to hold it until it matures.

During an accounting period, the fair value of securities will rise and fall. Only at the end of the period, when financial statements are prepared, is a company required to account for any change in fair value. At the end of the accounting period, the fair value of the portfolio of securities for certain categories is compared with the historical cost and an adjustment is made for the difference.

Trading Securities At the end of 2015, the fair value of the trading securities portfolio has decreased by $500 ($11,000 cost less $10,500 fair value). As a result, the following journal entry would be made:

Unrealized Loss on Trading Securities 500
    Market Adjustment—Trading Securities 500

The loss of $500 reflects the fact that the fair value of the trading securities portfolio has declined during the period. The loss is classified as unrealized because these securities have not been sold. This entry introduces a valuation account, *Market Adjustment—Trading Securities*. This account is combined with Investment in Trading Securities and is reported on the balance sheet. The use of a valuation account allows the company to maintain a record of historical cost. To determine realized and unrealized holding gains and losses, a record of historical cost is necessary. The unrealized loss on the trading securities account would be reported on the income statement under Other Expenses and Losses or would be combined with dividend and interest revenue in one item called Net Investment Income.

> **FYI**
>
> Once the adjusting entry is made, the trading securities account and the market adjustment account should always sum to the fair value of the trading securities. The same is true for available-for-sale securities.

Available-for-Sale Securities For available-for-sale securities, adjustments similar to those illustrated for trading securities would be made; the only difference would be that instead of any unrealized gain or loss being disclosed on the income statement, it would be reported as part of other comprehensive income and then accumulated directly in stockholders' equity as part of Accumulated Other Comprehensive Income. Continuing the Eastwood example, at the end of 2015, its available-for-sale portfolio had increased from $17,000 to $17,600. This $600 increase in fair value of the securities above their cost would be recorded with the following journal entry:

Market Adjustment—Available-for-Sale Securities 600
    Unrealized Increase/Decrease in Value of Available-for-Sale Securities 600

Note that the unrealized increase/decrease in value of the available-for-sale securities account would serve to increase the amount of stockholders' equity, which is consistent with the fact that an asset has increased in value. The $600 increase would *not* be included in the computation of net income, but it would be in Other Comprehensive Income and added to net income when computing comprehensive income for the year.

Held-to-Maturity Securities Security 5 has decreased in value from $20,000 to $19,000. However, because this security is classified as held to maturity, no adjustment is made for the difference between carrying value and fair value. Exhibit 14-11 summarizes how the securities and the resulting increases and decreases in fair value would be reported in the financial statements of Eastwood Inc. for 2015.

Exhibit 14-11 | Financial Statement Disclosure of Securities

Eastwood Inc.
Balance Sheet (Partial)
December 31, 2015

Assets:			
Investment in trading securities, at cost...	$11,000		
Less: Market adjustment—trading securities.....................................	(500)	$10,500	
Investment in available-for-sale securities, at cost...........................	$17,000		
Add: Market adjustment—available-for-sale securities	600	17,600	
Investment in held-to-maturity securities, at amortized cost		20,000	$48,100
Stockholders' Equity:			
Add: Unrealized increase in fair value of available-for-sale securities.....................		$ 600	

Eastwood Inc.
Income Statement (Partial)
For the Year Ended December 31, 2015

Other expenses and losses:	
Unrealized loss on trading securities	$ 500

© Cengage Learning 2014

At the end of 2016, similar adjustments must be made to reflect changes in fair value. Assume the following fair values at the end of 2016:

Security	Classification	Cost	Fair Value, Dec. 31, 2016
1	Trading	$ 8,000	$ 7,700
2	Trading	3,000	3,600
3	Available for sale	5,000	6,500
4	Available for sale	12,000	10,700
5	Held to maturity	20,000	20,700

By the end of 2016, the trading securities portfolio had increased to a fair value of $11,300 ($7,700 + $3,600). Comparing this amount to the historical cost of $11,000 indicates that Market Adjustment—Trading Securities should have a debit balance of $300. Because its current balance is a $500 credit (carried over from 2015), an adjusting entry must be made. The adjusting entry is as follows:

Market Adjustment—Trading Securities	800	
Unrealized Gain on Trading Securities		800

The balance in Market Adjustment—Trading Securities, which appears here in T-account form, would be added to Investment in Trading Securities and reported on the balance sheet. The $800 unrealized gain would be included in the computation of net income for 2016.

Market Adjustment—Trading Securities

		12/31/2015 Balance	500
12/31/2016 Adjustment	800		
12/31/2016 Balance	300		

At the end of 2016, the fair value of the available-for-sale securities has decreased from $17,600 to $17,200. Because fair value now exceeds historical cost by $200, the market adjustment account should have a $200 debit balance. Its current balance, carried over from 2015, is $600 (debit). The journal entry made at the end of 2016 to adjust the account is as follows:

Unrealized Increase/Decrease in Value of Available-for-Sale Securities..............	400	
Market Adjustment—Available-for-Sale Securities		400

The effect on the market adjustment—available-for-sale securities account is reflected in the following T-account. Again, no adjustment is made for changes in the fair value of held-to-maturity securities. The $400 unrealized decrease would be subtracted from net income in computing comprehensive income for 2016.

Market Adjustment—Available-for-Sale Securities

12/31/2015 Balance	600		
		12/31/2016 Adjustment	400
12/31/2016 Balance	200		

The financial statements for Eastwood Inc. at the end of 2016 would include the effects of each of the above adjusting entries as shown in Exhibit 14-12.

Equity Method Securities   Assume that security 5 is an equity method security rather than a held-to-maturity security. As with held-to-maturity securities, no journal entries are made to reflect changes in fair value of equity method securities. Thus, the $20,700 fair value of the securities on December 31, 2016, would not be used to adjust the reported balance sheet amount of the equity method securities. However, the $20,700 fair value would be disclosed in the notes to the financial statements. For

Exhibit 14-12 | Financial Statement Disclosure of Securities

Eastwood Inc.
Balance Sheet (Partial)
December 31, 2016

Assets:			
Investment in trading securities, at cost	$11,000		
Add: Market adjustment—trading securities...	300	$11,300	
Investment in available-for-sale securities, at cost	$17,000		
Add: Market adjustment—available-for-sale securities	200	17,200	
Investment in held-to-maturity securities, at amortized cost.............................		20,000	$48,500
Stockholders' Equity:			
Add: Unrealized increase in fair value of available-for-sale securities		$ 200	

Eastwood Inc.
Income Statement (Partial)
For the Year Ended December 31, 2016

Other expenses and losses:	
Unrealized gain on trading securities...	$ 800

example, in the notes to its 2009 financial statements, Coca-Cola disclosed that its investment in its bottler **Coca-Cola Enterprises** was recorded in the Coca-Cola balance sheet at just $25 million but that the current market value of the investment was $3.4 billion.

Accounting for "Other-than-Temporary" Declines in the Fair Value of Securities

Sometimes the fair value of investments declines due to economic circumstances that are unlikely to improve. For example, in 2001 the value of numerous Internet stocks decreased significantly without much expectation that they would ever recover. If a decline in the fair value of an individual security is judged to be other than temporary, regardless of whether the security is debt or equity and regardless of whether it is being accounted for as a trading, available-for-sale, held-to-maturity, or equity method security, the cost basis of that security should be reduced by crediting the investment account rather than a market adjustment account. In addition, the write-down should be recognized as a loss and charged against current income. The new cost basis for the security may not be adjusted upward to its original cost for any subsequent increases in fair value. If, however, the security is classified as a trading security or an available-for-sale security, a market adjustment account may be used to record future increases and decreases in fair value.

如果一项证券公允价值的下降被判定为非暂时性的，那么无论该证券是债务证券还是权益证券，也无论是按交易性、可供出售、持有至到期还是按权益法进行核算，该项证券都应该贷记投资账户而非市场调整账户，不反映其成本基础。此外，减值金额被确认为损失并影响当期损益。

Determining whether a decline in fair value is other than temporary may sound like an impossible task because no one can predict which way market prices will move in the future. Also, investors are always confident that their carefully chosen investments that have declined in value will recover soon. In *Staff Accounting Bulletin (SAB) No. 59*,[19] the SEC staff suggests that one consider the following in determining whether a decline in fair value is other than temporary:

- How long has the fair value of the security been below its original cost? A rule of thumb (*not* in the official GAAP provisions) is that securities that have had fair values less than their costs for over six months have probably experienced an "other-than-temporary" decline in fair value.

> **FYI**
> Because of the permanent change in the operations of some industries (e.g., travel and tourism-related industries) in the wake of the September 11, 2001, attack on the World Trade Center, accountants and auditors were particularly careful in determining whether investments in companies in these industries had suffered "other-than-temporary" declines in value.

- What is the current financial condition of the investee and its industry? If the investee has experienced losses for several years, and if the investee's entire industry has performed poorly, the decline in fair value is probably other than temporary.

- Will the investor's plans involve holding the security long enough for it to recover its value? For example, if a security has declined in fair value by 40% and the investor plans to sell the security in five months, it is unlikely that the security will recover its fair value in that time.

[19] This SEC guidance is contained in the formal U.S. GAAP provisions in FASB ASC paragraph 320-10-S99-1.

FASB CODIFICATION

The Issue: You are the accounting expert in a mid-sized technology company that has a substantial investment portfolio. The company maintains this portfolio in order to have sufficient liquidity to take advantage of any favorable acquisition opportunities in your volatile industry. In recent years, the balance sheet value of your portfolio has fluctuated substantially because of the ups and downs in the market. Your CEO hates this "mark-to-market" accounting. She has heard that if you were to classify your debt securities as held to maturity, you wouldn't be required to report these balance sheet fluctuations.

You have been trying to convince the CEO that the held-to-maturity classification is extremely restrictive, but she has not been persuaded by your arguments. What you need is some authoritative support showing that very few debt security investments can be classified as held to maturity.

The Question: Under what circumstances can debt securities NOT be classified as held to maturity?

Searching the Codification: The location of the authoritative guidance on the accounting for investment securities is Topic 320 (Investments—Debt and Equity Securities). The relevant section is 320-10-25 on "Recognition."

The Answer: The authoritative guidance for classifying debt securities as held to maturity is given on page 14-46.

Sale of Securities

 Account for the sale of investment securities.

LO6 学习目标6
投资证券出售的会计处理。

When securities are sold, an entry must be made to remove the carrying value of the security from the investor's books and to record the receipt of cash. The difference between the carrying value and the cash received is a realized gain or loss. For trading and available-for-sale securities, the carrying value will be equal to the security's original cost. The carrying value of held-to-maturity and equity method securities will change as any premium or discount is amortized (in the case of held-to-maturity securities) or when the book value of the investee changes (in the case of equity method securities).

How does the market adjustment account come into play when a security is sold? Simply put, it does not. The market adjustment account is adjusted only at the end of each accounting period prior to the issuance of financial statements. The market adjustment account is used to reflect the fair value of the securities portfolio as of the end of the period; it is not to be associated with transactions that are measuring the amount of realized gains or losses. This approach makes practical sense if you think of a large company with an investment portfolio containing several hundred different securities. The significant effort required to associate a specific portion of the market adjustment account with each individual security (and to maintain this identification as hundreds or even thousands of securities are traded during the year) would not result in any improvement in the reported financial result.

在公平交易中，证券一经售出就会产生已实现损益。在出售时，证券的账面价值与销售价格的差额均在利润表中予以确认。当公允价值发生变动但证券仍被投资者持有时，就会产生未实现损益。

At this point, it is important to distinguish between a realized and an unrealized gain or loss. A realized gain or loss occurs when an arm's-length transaction has occurred and a security has actually been sold. When the sale occurs, any difference between the carrying value of the security and the selling price is recognized on the income statement. An unrealized gain or loss arises when the fair value of a security changes, yet the security is still being held by the investor. As discussed previously, these unrealized gains and losses may or may not be recognized, depending upon the security's classification or whether the company has elected the fair value option with respect to that security.

In the case of a debt security, an entry must be made prior to recording the sale to record any interest earned to the date of the sale and to amortize any premium or discount. For example, continuing the Silmaril Technologies example from page 14-15, assume that the debt securities are sold on April 1, 2016, for $103,000, which includes accrued interest of $2,500. The carrying value of the debt securities on January 1, 2016, is $105,240. Interest revenue of $2,105 ($105,240 × 0.08 × 3/12) would be recorded, and a receivable relating to interest of $2,500 would be established. The investment account would be reduced by $395 to reflect the amortization of the premium for the three-month period between January 1 and April 1.

Interest Receivable	2,500	
Investment in Held-to-Maturity Securities		395
Interest Revenue		2,105

A second entry would remove the book value of the investment from Silmaril's books, record the receipt of cash of $103,000, eliminate the Interest Receivable balance, and record a loss equal to the difference between the investment's carrying value and the amount of cash received (net of interest).

Cash	103,000	
Realized Loss on Sale of Securities	4,345	
Interest Receivable		2,500
Investment in Held-to-Maturity Securities		104,845

These two entries could easily be combined into a single journal entry:

Cash	103,000	
Realized Loss on Sale of Securities	4,345	
Investment in Held-to-Maturity Securities		105,240
Interest Revenue		2,105

Impact of Sale of Securities on Unrealized Gains and Losses

The sale of a portion of an investment securities portfolio during the year complicates the computation and interpretation of the unrealized increases and decreases in the fair value of trading and available-for-sale securities. To illustrate, consider the following simple example. At the beginning of Year 1, Levi Company purchased a portfolio of

---

Stop & Think

What is the difference between *realized* and *recognized*?

a) *Realized* relates to the past, whereas *recognized* relates to the future.
b) *Realized* relates to trading securities, whereas *recognized* relates to available-for-sale securities.
c) *Realized* relates to the collection of cash, whereas *recognized* relates to the recording of an accounting journal entry.
d) *Realized* relates to financial statements, whereas *recognized* relates to income taxes.

trading securities for $10. At the end of Year 1, the portfolio had a value of $12. At the end of Year 2, the entire portfolio is sold for $9. The surprisingly difficult question is this: What is the amount of the unrealized gain or loss on the portfolio for Year 2? If you quickly answered "$3 unrealized loss," you need to read the following discussion carefully.

At the end of Year 1, the market adjustment account has a $2 debit balance to reflect the $2 increase ($10 ↑ to $12) in the fair value of the trading portfolio during Year 1. In addition, at the end of Year 2, the market adjustment account must have a $0 balance because the cost of the remaining trading securities ($0) is exactly equal to the fair value of those securities ($0). The necessary adjustment to the market adjustment account during Year 2 can be identified using the following T-account:

Market Adjustment—Trading

End of Year 1	2		
		Nec. Adj. in Year 2	2
End of Year 2	0		

The required journal entry is as follows:

Unrealized Loss—Trading 2
    Market Adjustment—Trading 2

The reason that the unrealized loss for Year 2 is not equal to the $3 decline ($12 − $9) in the portfolio for the year is that a portion of that decline is included in the *realized* loss recorded when the trading securities are sold. The realized loss is the $1 difference between the original cost of the securities ($10) and their selling price ($9). The realized loss is recorded with the following entry:

Cash 9
Realized Loss—Trading 1
    Investment Securities—Trading 10

The realized and unrealized losses in Year 2 in this case can be thought of as follows:

- *Realized loss* is the difference between the selling price and the original cost of the securities.
- *Unrealized loss* is the amount needed to adjust the end-of-year market adjustment account to its appropriate balance. More intuitively, in this simple example, it represents the reversal of the cumulative unrealized gains and losses recognized in past years on securities that were sold during this year. This reversal is needed to avoid double counting because those cumulative unrealized gains and losses from past years will impact the computation of the gain or loss realized this year.

- 已实现损失是证券销售价格与初始成本的差额。
- 未实现损失是指需要把年末市场调整账户调整为正确余额的数额。

As you can see, the interpretation of the unrealized loss is quite difficult. In a more complicated example, in which only a portion of the securities portfolio is sold, the unrealized gain or loss becomes a mixture of unrealized gains and losses for the year for securities still held at the end of this year and a reversal of unrealized gains and losses from past years for securities sold this year. What you should remember is that with an active securities portfolio, for which many purchases and sales of securities occur throughout the year, the computed amount of unrealized gain or loss for the year has no easy interpretation.

Lest you be discouraged by the unwelcome news contained in the previous paragraph, rest assured that the accounting system for investment securities actually does yield meaningful information. This can be seen by computing the total of the realized and unrealized gains and losses for the year. In this case, the sum of the $1 realized loss and the $2 unrealized loss is a total loss of $3 for the year. This total is exactly equal to the economic performance of the portfolio during the year; the portfolio decreased from a fair value of $12 at the beginning of the year to $9 at the end of the year. So, even though the interpretation of the unrealized gain or loss by itself is somewhat difficult, the sum of the realized and unrealized gains and losses is always easy to interpret in that the sum is equal to the total economic return on the portfolio for the year.

The preceding discussion dealt with trading securities. The concept is exactly the same for available-for-sale securities. The only difference is that the unrealized "gains" and "losses" are not included in the income statement. However, it is still true that the sum of the realized gains and losses and the unrealized increases and decreases for an available-for-sale portfolio is equal to the economic return on the portfolio during the year. For example, in 2007 Berkshire Hathaway reported a net realized gain of $5,598 million and a net unrealized loss of $2,981 million on its available-for-sale portfolio. The combination of these two numbers reveals that the total economic return for the portfolio during 2007 was a gain of $2,617 million ($5,598 million gain − $2,981 million loss).

Derecognition

On July 17, 2008, two large financial industry trade groups implored the FASB to rethink an accounting rule change that would hurt the financial ratios of financial institutions, cause some of them to violate loan covenants, "force some banks to tighten their lending requirements," and "make it more cumbersome for [the financial institutions] to raise capital."[20] These consequences would arise, it was claimed, from an FASB rule that would require financial institutions to change the accounting for $10.5 trillion in asset-backed securities. The financial institutions had accounted for the transfer of these securities as sales, removing them from their books as illustrated in the previous section. The new FASB rule would require that these transfers instead be accounted for as loans (with the securities serving as collateral), with the security assets returned to the balance sheets of the financial institutions, balanced by a $10.5 trillion liability for the loans. There is a HUGE difference between accounting for a security transfer as a sale and accounting for it as a collateralized loan. This is another example of the practice of off-balance-sheet financing that was introduced in Chapter 12. By the way, on July 30, 2008, the FASB decided to delay the rule change until 2010, giving the financial institutions some time to figure out how to explain to the users of their financial statements what had been going on with the missing $10.5 trillion.

As explained in Chapter 7 and according to FASB ASC Topic 860 (Transfers and Servicing), a transfer of a financial asset is accounted for as a sale (resulting in derecognition) when the transfer satisfies each of the following three conditions.[21]

- Legal control—The transferor has given up legal claim to the assets, meaning that even if it declares bankruptcy its creditors cannot go after the transferred assets.
- Actual control—The transferor cannot prevent the transferee from using the transferred assets however desired, such as selling them or pledging them as collateral for a loan.
- Effective control—The transferor does not have the right to force the transferee to return the assets, such as with a repurchase agreement.

[20] Marine Cole, "Securities Groups to FASB: Push Back Deadline for FAS 140," *Financial Week*, July 17, 2008.
[21] FASB ASC paragraph 860-10-40-5.

The international standard governing derecognition is in *IAS 39*. Whereas Topic 860 focuses on the transfer of control, *IAS 39* focuses on the transfer of risks and rewards. Under the provisions of *IAS 39*, the transfer of a financial asset is recorded as a sale "if the entity transfers substantially all the risks and rewards of ownership of the financial asset."[22]

Transferring Securities between Categories

 Record the transfer of investment securities between categories.

LO7 学习目标7
记录不同类别投资证券之间的转换。

On occasion, management will change its intentions with respect to holding certain securities. For example, a company may originally purchase securities for the purpose of making effective use of excess cash; subsequently, the company may decide to pursue a long-term business relationship with the investee. As a result, the company may reclassify the security from a trading security to an available-for-sale security. In addition, a company may initially purchase an equity security as a short-term investment and subsequently elect to increase its ownership interest to the point where the equity method is appropriate. This section of the chapter discusses the procedures employed when a security is transferred between investment security categories. Transitions to and from the equity method are covered in the Web Material (see www.cengagebrain.com) associated with this chapter. By the way, investment securities for which the fair value option has been elected must always be accounted for according to that choice; the fair value election is irrevocable.[23]

Transferring Debt and Equity Securities between Categories

If a company reclassifies a security, the security is accounted for at the fair value at the time of the transfer.[24] Because these securities are maintained on the books at their historical cost, the historical cost of the securities must be removed from the "old" category, and the securities are recorded in the "new" category at their current fair value. The change in value that has occurred is accounted for differently, depending on the category being transferred to and the category being transferred from. Exhibit 14-13 summarizes how these unrealized gains and losses are accounted for in each category.

To illustrate each type of transfer, we will use the data from the Eastwood Inc. example as of December 31, 2016 (page 14-26). Recall that on that date Eastwood Inc. had the following securities:

Security	Classification	Cost	Fair Value, Dec. 31, 2016
1	Trading	$ 8,000	$ 7,700
2	Trading	3,000	3,600
3	Available for sale	5,000	6,500
4	Available for sale	12,000	10,700
5	Held to maturity	20,000	20,700

---
[22] *International Accounting Standard 39*, "Financial Instruments: Recognition and Measurement" (London: International Accounting Standards Board, August 18, 2005), par. 20.
[23] The FASB is considering banning *all* investment security "reclassifications." The IASB is not necessarily in agreement. See *FASB Summary of Decisions Reached to Date During Redeliberations*, "Accounting for Financial Instruments," as of August 9, 2012.
[24] FASB ASC paragraph 320-10-35-10.

Exhibit 14-13 | Accounting for Transfers of Securities between Categories

Transferred	Treatment of the Change in Value
From trading	Any unrealized change in value not previously recognized will be recognized in net income in the current period. Previously recognized changes in value are not to be reversed.
To trading	Any unrealized change in value not previously recognized will be recognized in net income in the current period.
From held to maturity to available for sale	Recognize any unrealized change in value in a stockholders' equity account.
From available for sale to held to maturity	Any unrealized change in value recorded in a stockholders' equity account is to be amortized over the security's remaining life using the effective-interest method.*

* FASB ASC paragraph 320-10-35-10d.

© Cengage Learning 2014

During 2017, Eastwood Inc. elects to reclassify certain of its securities. The category being transferred from and to, along with the fair value for each security on the date of the transfer, is as follows:

Security	Transferring from	Transferring to	Fair Value, Date of Transfer
2	Trading	Available for sale	$ 3,800
3	Available for sale	Held to maturity	5,900
4	Available for sale	Trading	10,300
5	Held to maturity	Available for sale	20,400

The different types of reclassifications are illustrated in the following sections.

From the Trading Security Category Assume that Eastwood elects to reclassify security 2 from a trading security to an available-for-sale security. The security's historical cost is removed from the trading security classification, along with the associated $600 market adjustment (as of December 31, 2016), and the security is recorded at its current fair value as an available-for-sale security. The $200 difference between the fair value as of December 31, 2016, and the fair value at the date of transfer is recorded as an unrealized gain. The following journal entry illustrates this procedure:

Investment in Available-for-Sale Securities	3,800	
Market Adjustment—Trading Securities		600
Unrealized Gain on Transfer of Securities		200
Investment in Trading Securities		3,000

Alternatively, Eastwood could have recognized the $800 difference between fair value and historical cost as an unrealized gain at the time of the transfer and made an adjustment to the market adjustment—trading securities account at the end of the period. The net result of either approach would be the same. In the remainder of the examples that follow, we will adjust the market adjustment account on the date of the transfer.

Into the Trading Security Category Suppose Eastwood Inc. elects to reclassify security 4 from an available-for-sale security to a trading security. Recall that unrealized holding gains and losses associated with available-for-sale securities are recorded in the stockholders' equity account, Unrealized Increase/Decrease in Value of Available-for-Sale Securities. The amount in this account associated with security 4 is removed, and the security is recorded as a trading security at its current fair value.

Investment in Trading Securities	10,300	
Market Adjustment—Available-for-Sale Securities	1,300	
Unrealized Loss on Transfer of Securities	1,700	
Unrealized Increase/Decrease in Value of Available-for-Sale Securities		1,300
Investment in Available-for-Sale Securities		12,000

With this journal entry, security 4 is recorded as a trading security at its current fair value of $10,300. The carrying value of security 4 (historical cost less market adjustment) as an available-for-sale security is eliminated from the company's books. Because the security is now classified as a trading security, all changes in fair value should be reflected in the income statement. Thus, this journal entry transfers the unrealized changes in value from the stockholders' equity account to the income statement and recognizes the additional $400 decline in value since the last balance sheet date. The amount of the unrealized increase/decrease is determined by comparing the security's historical cost, obtained from subsidiary records, with its carrying value as of December 31, 2016. In this example, the unrealized decrease is $1,300 ($12,000 less $10,700). The final result of this journal entry is to reclassify the security and to record on the income statement the decline in fair value since the purchase of the security.

From the Held-to-Maturity to the Available-for-Sale Category

Although transfers of debt securities from the held-to-maturity category should not occur often, they will happen on occasion. FASB ASC Topic 320 lists a number of circumstances that might lead a firm to reclassify a held-to-maturity security.[25] In this instance, Eastwood Inc. has elected to reclassify security 5 from a security being held until maturity to one that is available to be sold. Recall that security 5's fair value on the date of the transfer is $20,400. The security is recorded as an available-for-sale security at its current fair value with any difference between its carrying cost and its fair value being recorded as an unrealized increase/decrease in value of available-for-sale securities. The following journal entry will accomplish these objectives:

Investment in Available-for-Sale Securities	20,400	
Unrealized Increase/Decrease in Value of Available-for-Sale Securities		400
Investment in Held-to-Maturity Securities		20,000

Because security 5 was originally classified as held to maturity, no adjustment has been made in prior periods to record any changes in value. Thus, there is no market adjustment account related to this transfer.

From the Available-for-Sale to the Held-to-Maturity Category

Eastwood Inc. elects to reclassify security 3 from one that is available to be sold to a security that will be held until maturity. Recall that security 3 was originally purchased for $5,000, had a fair value on December 31, 2016, of $6,500, and has a fair value on the date of the transfer of $5,900. The following entry should be made:

Investment in Held-to-Maturity Securities	5,900	
Unrealized Increase/Decrease in Value of Available-for-Sale Securities	600	
Investment in Available-for-Sale Securities		5,000
Market Adjustment—Available-for-Sale Securities		1,500

The debit to Unrealized Increase/Decrease in Value of Available-for-Sale Securities reflects the fact that the security has declined in value by $600 since the last balance sheet date. The $1,500 credit to the market adjustment account removes the previously recorded

可供出售金融资产未实现价值增减的借方表示从上一个资产负债表日到即日价值减少了600美元。它在被划分为可供出售金融资产时，贷记市场调整账户1 500美元（6 500–5 000），以注销之前记录的证券价值的增值。这些金额的合计数说明3号证券价值增加了900美元（5 900–5 000）。

[25] FASB ASC paragraph 320-10-25-6.

Stop & Think

Which ONE of the following statements is correct with respect to ALL transfers of investment securities from one category to another?

a) All unrealized losses as of the date of transfer are recognized immediately as part of income.
b) All unrealized gains as of the date of transfer are recognized immediately as part of income.
c) All unrealized losses as of the date of transfer are recognized immediately as part of other comprehensive income.
d) All transferred securities are recorded at their fair value on the date of transfer.

increase in value for this security ($6,500 − $5,000) while it was classified as available for sale. The combination of these amounts illustrates that security 3 has increased in value by $900 ($5,900 − $5,000) since its acquisition.

Once the security is classified as held to maturity, increases and decreases in its value will not be reflected in the financial statements. The treatment of the $900 unrealized increase in value (gain) existing at the transfer date is a bit of a problem because, on the one hand, the gain can't be ignored because it occurred while the security was classified as available for sale, but on the other hand, the gain would never have been recognized if the security had always been classified as held to maturity. Any unrealized increases and decreases in value that have been recorded to date (while the security has been available to be sold) must be amortized over the remaining life of the security using the effective-interest method and offset against (or added to) any interest revenue received on the debt security. The unamortized balance of an unrealized gain or loss continues to be reported as part of Accumulated Other Comprehensive Income in the Equity section of the balance sheet.[26] In addition, because the security is now classified as held to maturity, the company must also begin amortizing it down to its eventual maturity value. For example, if security 3 has a maturity value of $4,500, Eastwood Inc. must amortize, as a premium, the $1,400 difference between the security's carrying value and its maturity value ($5,900 less $4,500), as discussed previously. Thus, the interest revenue from security 3 will be adjusted for two types of amortization: the unrealized gain (increasing interest revenue) that existed at the transfer date and the carrying value to the maturity value (reducing interest revenue).

Investment Securities and the Statement of Cash Flows

LO8 学习目标8
在现金流量表中恰当地报告投资证券的购买、出售及公允价值变动。

8 Properly report purchases, sales, and changes in fair value of investment securities in the statement of cash flows.

The purchase and sale of available-for-sale, held-to-maturity, and equity method securities are reported in the Investing Activities section of the statement of cash flows. In contrast, the cash flows associated with the purchase and sale of trading securities (and fair value option securities) are shown in the Operating or Investing Activities depending on the reason the securities were acquired.[27] This difference stems from the fact that a company that maintains a trading securities portfolio or that chooses to account for certain investment securities using the fair value option often considers as part of its business operations the attempt to make money through the correct timing of purchases and sales of these securities.

The difficulties in reporting the cash flows associated with investment securities are associated with the proper treatment of both realized and unrealized gains and losses. In addition, a special adjustment must be made to operating cash flow associated with

[26] FASB ASC paragraph 320-10-35-10d.
[27] FASB ASC paragraph 320-10-45-11.

equity method securities because the cash received in the form of dividends is not equal to the income reported from the investment. These issues are discussed in the following sections.

Cash Flows from Gains and Losses on Available-for-Sale Securities

Caesh Company came into existence with a $1,000 cash investment by owners on January 1, 2015, and entered into the following transactions during 2015:

Cash sales	$ 1,700
Cash expenses	(1,400)
Purchase of investment securities	(600)
Sale of investment securities (costing $200)	170

The investment securities are classified as available for sale. In addition, the market value of the remaining securities was $500 on December 31, 2015. Given these transactions, Caesh Company's net income for 2015 can be computed as follows:

Sales	$ 1,700
Expenses	(1,400)
Operating income	$ 300
Realized loss on sale of securities ($200 − $170)	(30)
Net income	$ 270

> Caesh公司会披露其可供出售金融资产组合的未实现公允价值增值100美元，这100美元是由该组合期末公允价值500美元减去成本400美元得来的，它不应包括在净利润中，而应该在累计其他综合收益中列示。

In addition, Caesh Company will report a $100 unrealized increase in the fair value of its available-for-sale portfolio. This $100 increase is the difference between the $500 ending fair value of the portfolio and the $400 cost ($600 − $200 sold) of the portfolio. This $100 unrealized increase is not included in the computation of net income but is reported as an increase in the Accumulated Other Comprehensive Income portion of equity.

Recall from Chapter 5 that the general treatment of gains and losses in the Operating Activities section of the statement of cash flows is that gains are subtracted and losses are added when the indirect method is used. This approach stems from the fact that the cash flow effects of the transactions creating the gains and losses will be reported in the Investing Activities section, so the impact of those gains and losses must be removed from the Operating Activities section. With this in mind, the statement of cash flows for Caesh Company for 2015 can be prepared as follows:

Operating activities:		
Net income	$ 270	
Plus: Realized loss on sale of securities	30	$ 300
Investing activities:		
Purchase of investment securities	$(600)	
Sale of investment securities	170	(430)
Financing activities:		
Initial investment by owners		1,000
Net increase in cash		$ 870

As you can see, the realized gains and losses from the sale of available-for-sale securities are treated in exactly the same way, and for exactly the same reasons, as the gains and losses from the sale of property, plant, and equipment that were discussed in Chapter 5.

Cash Flows from Gains and Losses on Trading Securities

If the investment securities purchased by Caesh Company are classified as trading securities and are deemed to have been acquired for operating purposes, the cash flows associated with the purchase and sale of the securities are reported in the Operating Activities section of the statement of cash flows. In addition, net income is $370 instead of $270 because the $100 unrealized increase in the fair value of the portfolio is reported as an unrealized gain in the income statement. The statement of cash flows appears as follows:

Operating activities:		
Net income		$ 370
Purchase of investment securities		(600)
Sale of investment securities		170
Plus: Realized loss on sale of securities		30
Less: Unrealized gain on trading securities	(100)	$ (130)
Investing activities		0
Financing activities:		
Initial investment by owners		1,000
Net increase in cash		$ 870

未实现利得应该从经营现金流中扣减，但并不是因为要避免重复计算。相反，这100美元未实现利得要从经营现金流的中扣减，因为该收益虽然增加了利润但在这个会计期间并未产生任何现金流。

The realized loss on the sale of the securities is added back because all of the cash flow effects of the sale are reflected in the $170 cash proceeds, which are reported separately; to fail to adjust for the realized loss, which is included in net income, would double count this $30. The unrealized gain is subtracted in the computation of operating cash flow, but the subtraction occurs for a different reason than to avoid double counting. Instead, the $100 unrealized gain is subtracted in the computation of operating cash flow because the gain increases income but does not result in any cash flow this period. The increased cash flow will come in the future when the securities are sold for a higher price, at which time the cash proceeds will be reported as a separate item. Similarly, the amount of an unrealized loss on trading securities would be added back in the computation of cash from operating activities.

> **FYI**
>
> Alternatively, the $600 cash outflow for the purchase of investment securities, the $170 cash inflow from the sale of trading securities, and the $30 realized loss can all be netted together and reported as a net cash outflow from the $400 increase in the cost of the trading securities portfolio. If this is done, the fact that securities are sold for more or less than their cost is reflected in the amount of the realized gain or loss, which is already imbedded in net income.

Equity Method Securities and Operating Cash Flow

When a company owns equity method securities, an adjustment to operating cash flow must be made to reflect the fact that the cash received from the securities in the form of dividends is not equal to the income from the securities included in the computation of net income. To illustrate, assume that Daltone Company owns 30% of the outstanding shares of Chase Company. Chase Company's net income for the year was $100,000, and cash dividends paid were $40,000. Daltone would include $30,000 ($100,000 × 0.30) in its income statement as income from the investment. However, Daltone received only $12,000 ($40,000 × 0.30) in cash dividends from its investment in Chase. Accordingly, Daltone would report a subtraction in the

Operating Activities section of its statement of cash flows for the $18,000 ($30,000 − $12,000) difference between the income reported and the cash dividends received.

Classification and Disclosure

LO9 学习目标9
如何合理分类并披露投资证券。

9 Explain the proper classification and disclosure of investments in securities.

We have discussed the treatment of the gains and losses (both realized and unrealized) associated with selling, valuing, and/or reclassifying securities. Gains and losses from the sale of securities and unrealized gains and losses from changes in fair value while holding trading securities are reported in the income statement as Other Revenues and Expenses, or are combined with dividend and interest revenue and reported as Net Investment Income. Unrealized gains and losses on available-for-sale securities are reported in the Accumulated Other Comprehensive Income section of stockholders' equity and are included as Other Comprehensive Income in the computation of comprehensive income. As with any asset, significant permanent declines in the value of investments are recognized as a loss in the year they occur. Berkshire Hathaway, for example, includes a one-line summary of all of its realized gains and losses for the year in its income statement and discloses further details in the notes. The relevant note disclosure for Berkshire Hathaway for 2011 is included in Exhibit 14-14. Note that Berkshire Hathaway has cumulative unrealized gains on its debt and equity investments totaling almost $33 billion. How is it possible that none of this unrealized amount shows up on Berkshire Hathaway's income statement? The company classifies its securities as either held to maturity (for some debt securities), available for sale (for most debt and equity securities), or equity method (for some large investments).

Although the unrealized increases associated with the available-for-sale securities are not reported on the income statement, they are included in the computation of comprehensive income. Berkshire Hathaway's statement of comprehensive income is included in Exhibit 14-15.

The total unrealized increase reported for the available-for-sale portfolio is $29,521 million ($27,381 million + $2,140 million). The "reclassification" item reported in the

Exhibit 14-14 | Berkshire Hathaway—Note Disclosure Relating to Investments (partial)

3)	Investments in fixed maturity securities			
Investments in securities with fixed maturities as of December 31, 2011 are summarized below (in millions).				
	Amortized Cost	Unrealized Gains	Unrealized Losses*	Fair Value
December 31, 2011				
U.S. Treasury, U.S. government corporations and agencies................	$ 2,894	$ 41	$ —	$ 2,935
States, municipalities and political subdivisions..........................	2,862	208	—	3,070
Foreign governments	10,608	283	(48)	10,843
Corporate bonds...	11,120	1,483	(155)	12,448
Mortgage-backed securities...	2,564	343	(15)	2,892
	$30,048	$2,358	$(218)	$32,188

*Fixed maturity investments that were in a continuous unrealized loss position for more than 12 months had unrealized losses of $20 million as of December 31, 2011.

Exhibit 14-14 | Berkshire Hathaway—Note Disclosure Relating to Investments (partial) (*Continued*)

(4) Investments in equity securities

Investments in equity securities as of December 31, 2011 are summarized below (in millions).

	Cost Basis	Unrealized Gains	Unrealized Losses	Fair Value
December 31, 2011				
Banks, insurance and finance	$16,697	$9,480	$(1,269)	$24,908
Consumer products	12,390	14,320	—	26,710
Commercial, industrial and other	20,523	4,973	(123)	25,373
	$49,610	$28,773	$(1,392)	$76,991

As of December 31, 2011, there were no equity security investments that were in a continuous unrealized loss position for more than twelve months where other-than-temporary impairment losses were not recorded. As of December 31, 2011, we believed that the impairment of each of the individual securities that had been in an unrealized loss position was temporary. Our belief was based on: (a) our ability and intent to hold securities to recovery; (b) our assessment that the underlying business and financial condition of the issuers improved over the past year and that such conditions were currently favorable; (c) our opinion that the relative price declines were not significant; (d) the fact that the market prices of these issuers had increased over the past year; and (e) our belief that it was reasonably possible that market prices will increase to and exceed our cost in a relatively short period of time.

(5) Other Investments

A summary of other investments follows (in millions).

	Cost	Net Unrealized Gains	Fair Value	Carrying Value
December 31, 2011				
Other fixed maturity and equity securities:				
Insurance and other	$13,051	$1,055	$14,106	$13,111
Finance and financial products	3,198	623	3,821	3,810
	$16,249	$1,678	$17,927	$16,921

Fixed maturity and equity investments in the preceding table include our investments in The Goldman Sachs Group, Inc. ("GS"), General Electric Company ("GE"), Wm Wrigley Jr. Company ("Wrigley"), The Dow Chemical Company ("Dow") and Bank of America Corporation ("BAC").

(6) Investment gains/losses and other-than-temporary investment losses

Investment gains/losses are summarized below (in millions).

	2011	2010	2009
Fixed maturity securities —			
Gross gains from sales and other disposals	$310	$720	$357
Gross losses from sales and other disposals	(10)	(16)	(54)
Equity securities —			
Gross gains from sales and other disposals	1,889	2,603	701
Gross losses from sales and other disposals	(36)	(266)	(617)
Other	29	1,017	(69)
	$2,182	$4,058	$318
Net investment gains/losses are reflected in the Consolidated Statements of Earnings as follows.			
Insurance and other	$1,973	$4,044	$358
Finance and financial products	209	14	(40)
	$2,182	$4,058	$318

Berkshire Hathaway, Inc., 2011, 10K Report

Exhibit 14-15 | Berkshire Hathaway—Statement of Comprehensive Income for 2011

	2011	2010	2009
Comprehensive income attributable to Berkshire:			
Net earnings	$10,254	$12,967	$ 8,055
Other comprehensive income:			
Net change in unrealized appreciation of investments	(2,146)	5,398	17,607
Applicable income taxes	811	(1,866)	(6,263)
Reclassification of investment appreciation in net earnings	(1,245)	(1,068)	2,768
Applicable income taxes	436	374	(969)
Foreign currency translation	(126)	(172)	851
Applicable income taxes	(18)	(21)	(17)
Prior service cost and actuarial gains/losses of defined benefit plans	(1,121)	(76)	(41)
Applicable income taxes	401	25	(1)
Other	3	195	(206)
Other comprehensive income, net	(3,005)	2,789	13,729
Comprehensive income attributable to Berkshire	$ 7,249	$15,756	$21,784

Berkshire Hathaway, Inc., 2011, 10K Report

资产负债表中个别证券的恰当列示取决于管理者的意图。如果管理者打算或希望在一年内或一个经营周期内卖掉证券，就应该把这项证券划分为流动资产。因为交易性金融资产被定义为短期的，应划分为流动资产。持有至到期投资往往被划分为非流动资产，除非它们一年到期。可供出售金融资产是划分为流动的还是非流动的，一般取决于管理者的意图。

statement of comprehensive income includes the reversal of prior-year unrealized gains or losses on securities that were sold during the year.

Appropriate presentation of individual securities on the balance sheet depends on the intent of management. If management intends or is willing to sell the securities within one year or the current operating cycle, whichever is longer, the security is classified as a current asset. Because trading securities are short term by definition, they are always classified as current. Held-to-maturity securities are always classified as noncurrent unless they mature within a year. Available-for-sale securities are classified as current or noncurrent, depending on the intentions of management.

In addition to the reporting required in the income statement, balance sheet, and statement of cash flows, the following additional disclosures are required in the financial statement notes:

1. Trading securities:
   - The change in net unrealized holding gain or loss that is included in the income statement.
2. Available-for-sale securities:
   - Aggregate fair value, gross unrealized holding gains and gross unrealized holding losses, and amortized cost basis by major security type. For debt securities, the company should disclose information about contractual maturities.
   - The proceeds from sales of available-for-sale securities and the gross realized gains and losses on those sales and the basis on which cost was determined in computing realized gains and losses.
   - The change in net unrealized holding gain or loss on available-for-sale securities that has been included in stockholders' equity during the period.
3. Held-to-maturity securities:
   - Aggregate fair value, gross unrealized holding gains and gross unrealized holding losses, and amortized cost basis by major security type. In addition, the company should disclose information about contractual maturities.

4. Transfers of securities between categories:
   - Gross gains and losses included in earnings from transfers of securities from available-for-sale into the trading category.
   - For securities transferred from held-to-maturity, the company should disclose the amortized cost amount transferred, the related realized or unrealized gain or loss, and the reason for transferring the security.

In Exhibit 14-16, an excerpt from the note on the fair value of investment securities is taken from the 2011 annual report of Wells Fargo & Company, a major company in the banking industry. The actual note is much more complicated with much more detail.

With its adoption of *IFRS 13* in May 2011, the IASB has a fair value measurement and disclosure standard comparable to U.S. GAAP.

Exhibit 14-16 | Wells Fargo—Note Disclosure for Investment Securities (partial)

Assets and Liabilities Recorded at Fair Value on a Recurring Basis
The table below presents the balances of assets and liabilities measured at fair value on a recurring basis.

(in millions)	Level 1	Level 2	Level 3	Netting	Total
Balance at December 31, 2011					
Trading assets (excluding derivatives)	$ 6,871	$ 48,847	$ 2,149	—	$ 57,867
Total securities available for sale					
Securities of U.S. Treasury and federal agencies	$ 869	$ 6,099	$ —	—	6,968
Securities of U.S. states and political subdivisions	—	21,077	11,516	—	32,593
Mortgage-backed securities	—	132,447	293	—	132,740
Corporate debt securities	317	17,792	295	—	18,404
Collateralized debt obligations	—	—	8,599	—	8,599
Asset-backed securities	—	9,062	9,786	—	18,848
Other debt securities	—	1,044	—	—	1,044
Marketable equity securities	1,366	684	1,367	—	3,417
Total securities available for sale	$ 2,552	$ 188,205	$31,856	—	$222,613
Total derivative assets	$ 506	$ 105,202	$ 2,988	$(81,143)	$ 27,553
Mortgages held for sale	—	41,381	3,410	—	44,791
Loans held for sale	—	1,176	—	—	1,176
Loans	—	5,893	23	—	5,916
Mortgage servicing rights (residential)	—	—	12,603	—	12,603
Other assets	88	135	244	—	467
Total assets recorded at fair value	$10,017	$ 390,839	$53,273	$(81,143)	$372,986
Derivative liabilities	$ (264)	$(100,618)	$ (4,576)	$ 89,990	$ (15,468)
Short sale liabilities	(4,764)	(6,068)	—	—	(10,832)
Other liabilities	—	(98)	(44)	—	(142)
Total liabilities recorded at fair value	$ (5,028)	$(106,784)	$ (4,620)	$ 89,990	$ (26,442)

Wells Fargo, 2011, 10K Report

EXPANDED MATERIAL

To this point in the chapter, we have talked about securities for which there is a tradable market. In some instances, a company may invest in another firm in the form of a nonmarketable security. The most common example of this type of security would be a loan. In this Expanded Material, we deal with the most complex issue associated with these nonmarketable securities: impairment.

Accounting for the Impairment of a Loan

LO10 学习目标10
应收贷款减值的会计处理。

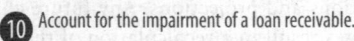 Account for the impairment of a loan receivable.

A common example of an investment for which there might be no market value would be a loan receivable. Accounting for loans receivable is straightforward except for impairment.[28] Loans may arise by a company lending money to a borrower or by selling inventory and assets in return for a receivable. An entry to Loans Receivable is thus offset by a credit to Sales, Cash, or a surrendered asset. Financial institutions engage in such loans on a regular basis. A critical issue with these loans is when cost should be abandoned as the valuation basis. In other words, when should the loan be written down, or written off?

Because it is assumed that no ready market exists for these loans, the market valuations prescribed by FASB ASC Topic 320 cannot apply.

Loans receivable are thus carried at a cost valuation unless evidence exists of a probable impairment. FASB ASC Topic 310 (Receivables) defines impairment as follows:

> A loan is impaired when, based on current information and events, it is probable that a creditor will be unable to collect all amounts due according to the contractual terms of the loan agreement.[29]

All amounts due according to contractual terms include both interest and principal payments. Troubled debt restructuring is direct evidence of impairment; however, impairment may occur even though a formal restructuring has not occurred. If sufficient writedown has not previously been made, the restructuring will give rise to an additional decrease in the value of the loan receivable.[30]

Measurement of Impairment

A creditor shall measure impairment for loans with no market value at the present value of expected future cash flows discounted at the loan's effective interest rate, that is, the rate implicit in the original loan contract. The impairment is recorded by creating a valuation

---

[28] See Chapter 7 for discussion of notes receivable.
[29] FASB ASC paragraph 310-10-35-16.
[30] The FASB is considering a "three-bucket" credit deterioration model for loan impairment. Bucket 1 would contain the good loans. Bucket 2 would contain those loans that, statistically and as a group, have deteriorated to the point that credit losses are reasonably possible. Bucket 3 would contain those loans that have individually and specifically been evaluated as being reasonably possible of experiencing credit losses. See *FASB Summary of Decisions Reached to Date During Redeliberations*, "Accounting for Financial Instruments," as of August 9, 2012.

如果在陷入困境的债务重组中重构贷款协议，那么新的修正合同条款中的贴现利率应该以初始合同利率为基础，而不是在重组协议中特别规定的利率。贴现率的选择在FASB的规定中是一个难点。

> **FYI**
>
> Again, you will need to be comfortable with present values if you are to understand the computations in this section. See the Time Value of Money Review module if you need a review.

allowance account and charging the estimated loss to Bad Debt Expense. Thus, accounting for loans receivable is similar to accounting for accounts receivable except that the measurement method is more specifically defined by the FASB.

If a loan agreement is restructured in a troubled debt restructuring, the interest rate to be used to discount the new modified contract terms is based on the original contract rate, not the rate specified in the restructuring agreement. The selection of the discount rate to use was one of the difficult issues addressed by the FASB. The continued use of the original loan rate is consistent with the historic cost principle. The estimate of future cash flows is derived from the creditor's best estimate based on reasonable and supportable assumptions and projections. Any future changes in the estimates or timing of future cash flows result in a recalculation of the impairment and an adjustment of the receivable and valuation allowance accounts with a charge or credit to Bad Debt Expense. Income arising from the passage of time will be recognized as part of interest revenue in each respective reporting period.

Example of Accounting for Loan Impairment

Assume that Malone Enterprises reports a loan receivable from Stockton Co. in the amount of $500,000. The initial loan's repayment terms include a 10% interest rate plus annual principal payments of $100,000 on January 1 each year. The loan was made on January 1, 2013. Stockton made the $50,000 interest payment in 2013 but did not make the $100,000 principal payment nor the $50,000 interest payment for 2014. Malone is preparing its annual financial statements on December 31, 2014. The loan receivable has a carrying value of $550,000 including the $50,000 interest receivable for 2014, Stockton is having financial difficulty, and Malone has concluded that the loan is impaired. Analysis of Stockton's financial conditions indicates the principal and interest currently due can probably be collected, but it is probable that no further interest can be collected. The probable amount and timing of the collections is determined to be as follows:

December 31, 2015	$175,000
December 31, 2016	200,000
December 31, 2017	175,000
	$550,000

The present value at December 31, 2014, of the expected future cash flows discounted at 10% is $455,860, calculated as follows:

Date	Payment	Time of Discount	Present Value @ 10%
Dec. 31, 2015	$175,000	1 year	$159,091
Dec. 31, 2016	200,000	2 years	165,289
Dec. 31, 2017	175,000	3 years	131,480
Present value at December 31, 2014			$455,860

The impairment loss to be reported for 2014 is $94,140, or the $550,000 carrying value less the present value of $455,860. The journal entry to record the impairment is as follows:

2014
Dec. 31 Bad Debt
           Expense 94,140
             Allowance
               for Loan
               Impairment 94,140

> **FYI**
>
> If you look closely, you will realize that the computations being made in this table are conceptually identical to those done in the bond amortization table on page 14-16.

The allowance would be reported as an offset to the loan receivable account.

If Stockton makes the payments as projected, the accounting for the cash received and the recognition of interest revenue is computed by constructing an amortization schedule similar to that illustrated here.

Interest Revenue from Loan Impairment

Date	(1) Loan Receivable before Current Payment	(2) Allowance for Loan Impairment	(3) Net Receivable (1) − (2)	(4) Interest Revenue 10% × (3)	(5) Payment Received
Dec. 31, 2015	$550,000	$94,140	$455,860	$45,586	$175,000
Dec. 31, 2016	375,000	48,554*	326,446	32,645	200,000
Dec. 31, 2017	175,000	15,909†	159,091	15,909	175,000
				$94,140	$550,000

*$94,140 − $45,586 = $48,554
†$48,554 − $32,645 = $15,909

The entries on December 31, 2015, to record the receipt of the 2015 loan payment and to recognize interest revenue for the year are as follows:

2015
Dec. 31 Cash 175,000
             Loan Receivable 175,000
         Allowance for Loan Impairment................................. 45,586
             Interest Revenue*... 45,586

*Alternatively, a company may show all changes in present value as an adjustment to Bad Debt Expense in the same manner in which impairment initially was recognized.[31]

The T-accounts for the loan receivable and allowance accounts for 2014 and 2015 are as follows:

Loan Receivable				Allowance for Loan Impairment			
Beg. Bal.	550,000					12/31/2014	94,140
		12/31/2015	175,000	12/31/2015	45,586		
Bal.	375,000					Bal.	48,554

Similar entries would be made at the end of 2016 and 2017 using the amounts included in the preceding amortization schedule. Note that computation of the amortization of the allowance for loan impairment account is identical to the computation for the amortization of Discount on Notes Receivable used in Chapter 7. If all payments are made as scheduled, the loan receivable and allowance accounts will both be closed out as of December 31, 2017.

[31] FASB ASC paragraph 310-10-35-40.

SOLUTIONS TO OPENING SCENARIO QUESTIONS

1. Disney owns 100% of ABC. As a result, the shareholders of Disney, through their board of directors, control the strategic decisions of ABC. In contrast, Berkshire Hathaway owns a little more than 8% of Coca-Cola. Berkshire Hathaway may be able to influence the actions of Coca-Cola but certainly not control them.
2. The primary business activity of Berkshire Hathaway is to invest in other companies and earn a return from those investments. In contrast, Microsoft's primary business activity is the development and sale of software. Microsoft's investments serve as both a temporary storage place for excess cash as well as strategic investments in order to exercise influence on the operations of other companies.
3. CREF invests the retirement funds of educators. Many college professors have their retirement funds invested through CREF.

Stop & Think SOLUTIONS

1. (Page 14-7) The correct answer is D. The investment by Ford in Mazda is part of a broader strategic alliance. Ford and Mazda are partners in a joint venture in Thailand, have joint plans for production and sales in China, and are partners in production facilities in the United States. In addition, this investment by Ford gives the company a presence in Japan, the homeland of the company's primary foreign competitors, Toyota and Honda. Before the fourth quarter of 2010, Ford's ownership of Mazda was 33%. As discussed in this chapter, for accounting purposes the ownership threshold for "significant influence" is assumed to be 20%. However, it is clear that Ford's 3.5% ownership of Mazda exists to give Ford significant influence.
2. (Page 14-16) The correct answer is A. Recall that both trading and available-for-sale debt securities are reported in the balance sheet at fair value. Accordingly, after carefully amortizing a discount or premium on these debt securities, the securities would then just be adjusted to current fair value anyway. However, in a more comprehensive example, achieving a proper split between interest revenue and unrealized holding gains and losses would require that the discount or premium first be amortized before adjusting the security to fair value.
3. (Page 14-30) The correct answer is C. Recognized is an accounting term, which indicates that a transaction has been recorded using a journal entry. In the context of investment securities, realized means that a gain or loss amount has actually been confirmed through the sale of the securities.
4. (Page 14-36) The correct answer is D. As seen in the examples, all transferred securities are recorded at their fair value on the date of transfer. Depending on the type of transfer, unrealized gains and losses will be treated in a variety of ways.

SOLUTION TO USING THE FASB'S CODIFICATION

Under FASB ASC Section 320-10-25, you can see material labeled "Restrictions on Classification of a Debt Security as Held-to-Maturity." Paragraph 320-10-25-3 confirms what you have been telling your CEO: "Use of the held-to-maturity category is restrictive because the use of amortized cost must be justified for each investment in a debt security."

This section also lists circumstances when the held-to-maturity classification is definitely NOT appropriate. For example, paragraph 320-10-25-4b identifies potential "needs for liquidity" as a circumstance in which a debt security must NOT be classified as held to maturity. Because the securities in your company's investment portfolio are held to provide liquidity for potential business acquisitions, the held-to-maturity classification is NOT appropriate.

Review Chapter 14 Learning Objectives

① Determine why companies invest in other companies.

Companies invest in the debt and equity securities of other businesses for a variety of reasons. The most common reason is to earn a return on idle cash. Other reasons for investing in other companies include establishing a business relationship through ownership, diversifying seasonal or industry risk, and gaining access to a company's research or technology. The intended outcome of investing in other companies is to enhance the overall return to shareholders.

② Understand the varying classifications associated with investment securities.

Securities are classified based on management's intent in holding the securities. If a firm invests in the equity securities of another company with the intent of influencing or controlling the decisions and activities of that company, the investment is accounted for using the equity method. Investments in debt and equity securities where the intent is to sell those securities should the need for cash arise or to take advantage of increases in value are classified as trading securities. Debt securities that are intended to be held until they mature are classified as held-to-maturity securities. All remaining investment securities are classified as available for sale.

③ Account for the purchase of debt and equity securities.

Debt and equity securities are accounted for at cost, which includes brokerage fees, taxes, and other charges incurred at acquisition. In the case of debt securities, accrued interest presents an additional complexity. The amount of interest accrued prior to the purchase date must be accounted for separately from the cost of the investment.

④ Account for the recognition of revenue from investment securities.

The method for recognizing revenue from investments depends on how the investment was originally classified. For debt securities, the revenue recognized is termed *interest revenue*. For trading and available-for-sale debt securities, the amount of interest revenue is a function of the stated rate of interest associated with the debt interest. In the case of held-to-maturity securities, any premium or discount associated with the initial purchase must be amortized and offset against interest revenue. For equity securities classified as trading or available for sale, dividends declared by the investee are recorded as revenue. If an investment is accounted for using the equity method, then the amount of revenue recognized is a function of the percentage of ownership. The net income of the investee is multiplied by the ownership interest and recorded as revenue.

⑤ Account for the change in fair value of investment securities.

Temporary changes in the fair value of debt and equity securities classified as trading or available for sale are accounted for through the use of a market adjustment account. The use of this account results in securities being valued at fair value on the balance sheet. For trading securities, the increase or decrease in fair value is reported on the income statement. In the case of available-for-sale securities, the change in fair value is disclosed as a separate component of stockholders' equity. Temporary changes in fair value for held-to-maturity securities and equity method securities are not recognized. If a decline in the fair value of an investment is judged to be permanent, the amount of the decline is recorded in the current period's income, and the investment's cost basis is adjusted.

⑥ Account for the sale of investment securities.

When an investment is sold, its carrying value is removed from the books, and the difference between carrying value and the cash received is recorded as a realized gain or loss. In the case of debt securities, an adjustment may be required to record interest revenue earned but not received prior to the sale and to amortize any premium or discount.

⑦ Record the transfer of investment securities between categories.

On occasion, management may elect to reclassify certain of its investment securities. If the reclassification involves a movement to or from the trading classification, any change in fair value not previously recognized in income is recorded in the current period. If the reclassification is from held to maturity to available for sale, changes in fair value since the investment's acquisition are recorded as a separate component of stockholders' equity. If an available-for-sale security is reclassified as a held-to-maturity security, all previously recorded changes in fair value are amortized over the remaining life of the investment.

⑧ Properly report purchases, sales, and changes in fair value of investment securities in the statement of cash flows.

The purchase and sale of available-for-sale, held-to-maturity, and equity method securities are reported in the Investing Activities section of the statement of cash flows. The cash flows associated with the purchase and sale of trading securities and securities accounted for using the fair value options are shown in the Operating or Investing Activities section depending on the reason the securities were acquired. For available-for-sale securities, realized losses are added and realized gains are subtracted when computing cash from operating activities. With trading securities, unrealized gains are also subtracted, and unrealized losses are also added even if those trading securities are considered to be part of operating activities. With equity method securities, an adjustment to operating cash flow must be made to reflect the fact that the cash received from the securities in the form of dividends is not equal to the income from the securities included in the computation of net income.

9 **Explain the proper classification and disclosure of investments in securities.**

Realized gains and losses on the sale of investment securities are disclosed on the income statement in the period of the sale. Unrealized gains and losses on trading securities are also disclosed on the income statement. Unrealized increases and decreases on securities being classified as available for sale are disclosed in the Stockholders' Equity section of the balance sheet. Additional note disclosure relating to investment securities is required, and the appropriate disclosure varies, depending on the classification of the security. For investment securities reported at fair value, the magnitude of the fair values determined using Level 1, Level 2, and Level 3 inputs is disclosed.

EXPANDED MATERIAL

10 **Account for the impairment of a loan receivable.**

On some occasions, particularly in the case of loans made to other companies, a market value may not exist for the investment. In these instances, the investor must regularly assess the collectibility of the investment, and if it is determined that an "impairment" exists, an adjustment to the value of the receivable must be made. Impairment is measured by comparing the present value of expected future cash flows with the carrying value of the investment.

FASB-IASB CODIFICATION SUMMARY

Topic	FASB Accounting Standards Codification	Original FASB Standard	Corresponding IASB Standard	Differences between U.S. GAAP and IFRS
Classification as trading, available for sale, or held to maturity	Section 320-10-25 par. 1	SFAS No. 115 par. 6-12	IFRS 9 par 4.1, B4	Some differences, but application of *IFRS 9* has been delayed until 2015.
Equity method	Topic 323	APB Opinion No. 18	IAS 28	No substantial differences
Fair value option	Topic 825, "Fair Value Option" subsections	SFAS No. 159	IFRS 9	Interesting differences in terms of when the fair value option is acceptable, but application of *IFRS 9* has been delayed until 2015.
Derecognition of investment securities	Topic 860	SFAS No. 140	IAS 39 par. 20	Under U.S. GAAP, the transfer of a financial asset is recorded as a sale if control of the asset passes from the transferor to the transferee. Under IFRS, the transfer is recorded as a sale if the risks and rewards associated with the cash flows from the financial assets pass from the transferor to the transferee.
Classification of cash flows from the purchase and sale of investment securities	Section 320-10-45 par. 11	SFAS No. 115 par. 18	IAS 7 par. 15-16	Under IFRS, cash flows from the purchase and sale of trading securities are classified under operating activities; for other security categories, the cash flows are investing activities. Under U.S. GAAP, trading security cash flows may be operating or investing, depending on management intent.
Loan impairment	Section 310-10-35	SFAS No. 114	IAS 39 par. 58 through 65	No substantial differences

KEY TERMS

Available-for-sale securities 14-9
Control 14-17
Debt securities 14-8
Derecognition 14-32
Equity method 14-16
Equity method securities 14-9
Equity securities 14-8
Held-to-maturity securities 14-9
Parent company 14-17
Significant influence 14-16
Subsidiary company 14-17

Tutorial Activities

Tutorial Activities with author-written, content-specific feedback, available on *CengageNOW for Stice & Stice*.

QUESTIONS

1. Why might a company invest in the securities of another company?
2. What securities fall under the scope of FASB ASC Topic 320?
3. What criteria must be met for a security to be classified as held to maturity?
4. What criteria must be met for a security to be classified as a trading security?
5. What is "the fair value option"?
6. How does the classification of investment securities under International Financial Reporting Standards (trading, available for sale, and held to maturity) differ from the classification under U.S. GAAP?
7. (a) When computing the price to be paid for a debt security, the stated rate of interest is used to determine what value?
   (b) How does the market or effective rate affect a debt security's value?
8. How does one compute the interest revenue to be recognized on a debt security if the effective-interest method is being used?
9. What other factors are considered when determining whether effective control exists when the investor does not possess absolute voting control?
10. (a) What factors may indicate the ability of an investor owning less than a majority voting interest to exercise significant influence on the investee's operating and financial policies?
    (b) What factors may indicate the investor's inability to exercise significant influence?
11. How is a joint venture a form of off-balance-sheet financing?
12. In the United States, we use the term "equity method investee" to describe a company in which another company has purchased between 20% and 50% of the shares and is thus able to exert significant influence. What term is used for an "equity method investee" in IFRS?
13. How are changes in value reported in the financial statements for trading securities? Available-for-sale securities? Held-to-maturity securities?
14. What type of account is Market Adjustment? How is it disclosed on the financial statements?
15. How is an "other-than-temporary" decline in the value of investments recorded?
16. What impact does the sale of investment securities during the year have on the computation of unrealized gains and losses on trading securities? On unrealized increases and decreases on available-for-sale securities?
17. When transferring securities between categories, how is the transfer accounted for? At what value are the securities recorded?
18. How are realized gains and losses on trading securities handled in the statement of cash flows? How are unrealized gains and losses on trading securities handled?
19. Are trading, available-for-sale, and held-to-maturity securities disclosed on the balance sheet as current or long-term assets?
20. Where are the cash flow effects of purchases and sales of equity securities reported?
21. What additional disclosures are required for trading, available-for-sale, and held-to-maturity securities?

EXPANDED MATERIAL

22. Why is the impairment of a loan accounted for differently from the decline in value of a debt security?

PRACTICE EXERCISES

Practice 14-1

Purchasing Debt Securities: Asset Approach
On January 1, Issuing Company issued $50,000 in debt securities. The stated interest rate on the debt securities is 8%, with interest payable semiannually, on June 30 and December 31. On February 1, Purchasing Company purchased the bonds from the private investor who acquired them when they were originally issued. Purchasing Company paid the private investor an amount equal to the face value of the securities plus accrued interest. The securities were purchased as trading securities. Make the journal entries necessary on Purchasing Company's books to record the security purchase and the receipt of interest on June 30 using the asset approach.

Practice 14-2

Purchasing Debt Securities: Revenue Approach
Refer to the data in Practice 14-1. Make the journal entries necessary on Purchasing Company's books to record the security purchase and the receipt of interest on June 30 using the revenue approach.

Practice 14-3

Purchasing Equity Securities
The company purchased 2,000 shares of equity securities for $27 per share. The shares were purchased as an available-for-sale investment. Make the journal entry necessary to record the purchase.

Practice 14-4

Computing the Value of Debt Securities
On January 1, the company purchased debt securities with a face value of $100,000. The securities mature in seven years. The securities have a stated interest rate of 8%, and interest is paid semiannually. The prevailing market interest rate on these debt securities is 12% compounded semiannually. Compute the fair value of the securities.

Practice 14-5

Interest Revenue for Held-to-Maturity Securities
On January 1, the company purchased debt securities for cash of $25,518. The securities have a face value of $20,000, and they mature in 15 years. The securities have a stated interest rate of 10%, and interest is paid semiannually, on June 30 and December 31. The prevailing market interest rate on these debt securities is 7% compounded semiannually. The securities were purchased as a held-to-maturity investment. Make the journal entries to record (1) the purchase of the securities, (2) the June 30 receipt of interest, and (3) the December 31 receipt of interest.

Practice 14-6

Cost Method, Equity Method, and Consolidation
Identify how each of the following investments in equity securities should be classified by the investor company:

	Number of Shares Owned by Investor Company	Total Shares of Investee Company Outstanding
1	1,200	10,000
2	6,000	8,000
3	20,000	55,000

Practice 14-7

Revenue for Trading and Available-for-Sale Securities
The company owns 1,000 shares of Stock A and 3,000 shares of Stock B. The company received dividends of $1.75 per share from Stock A and $0.97 per share from Stock B. The company classifies Stock A as a trading security and Stock B as an available-for-sale security. Make the journal entry or entries necessary to record the receipt of the cash dividends.

Practice 14-8

Revenue for Equity Method Securities
On January 1 of Year 1, Burton Company purchased 2,000 shares of the 8,000 outstanding shares of Company A for a total of $27,000. The purchase price was equal to 25% of the book value of Company A's equity. Company A's net income in Year 1 was $20,000; net income in Year 2 was $25,000. Dividends per share paid by Company A were $0.80 in Year 1 and $1.00 in Year 2. Make all journal entries necessary on Burton's book to record its investment in Company A in Year 1 and Year 2.

Practice 14-9

Equity Method: Excess Depreciation
On January 1 of Year 1, Stratton Company purchased 5,000 shares of the 15,000 outstanding shares of Company B for a total of $82,000. At the time of the purchase, the book value of Company B's equity was $202,000. Any excess of investment purchase price over the book value of Company B's equity is attributable to a building owned by Company B. The building has a remaining useful life of 11 years. Company B's net income in Year 1 was $72,000. Dividends per share paid by Company B were $1.65 in Year 1. (1) Make all journal entries necessary on Stratton's books to record its investment in Company B in Year 1. (2) Compute the Year 1 ending balance in Stratton Company's investment in Company B account.

Practice 14-10

Equity Method: Cost Greater than Book Value
On January 1 of Year 1, Dridge Company purchased 2,500 shares of the 10,000 outstanding shares of Company C for a total of $100,000. At the time of the purchase, the book value of Company C's equity was $300,000. Company C assets having a fair value greater than book value at the time of the acquisition were as follows:

Asset	Book Value	Fair Value	Remaining Life
Inventory	$ 40,000	$ 50,000	less than one year
Building	200,000	250,000	10 years
Goodwill	0	40,000	indefinite

Company C's net income in Year 1 was $70,000. Dividends per share paid by Company C were $2.00 in Year 1. (1) Make all journal entries necessary on Dridge's books to record its investment in Company C in Year 1. Assume that the goodwill is not impaired. (2) Compute the Year 1 ending balance in Dridge Company's investment in Company C account.

Practice 14-11

Changes in Value: Trading Securities
On December 1, the company purchased securities for $4,000. On December 31, the company still held the securities. Make the necessary adjusting journal entry to record a change in value of the securities assuming that their December 31 fair value was (a) $5,200 and (b) $2,600. In addition, before considering the impact of the change in value of the securities, the net income for the company was $3,000. Compute net income assuming that the December 31 fair value of the securities was (c) $5,200 and (d) $2,600. Ignore income taxes. Assume that the securities are classified as trading.

Practice 14-12

Changes in Value: Available-for-Sale Securities
Refer to Practice 14-11. Make the adjusting journal entries for (a) and (b) and the computations for (c) and (d), assuming that the securities are classified as available for sale.

Practice 14-13

Changes in Value: Held-to-Maturity Securities
Refer to Practice 14-11. Make the adjusting journal entries for (a) and (b) and the computations for (c) and (d), assuming that the securities are classified as held to maturity. The changes in value are not deemed to be "other than temporary."

Practice 14-14

Changes in Value: Equity Method
Refer to Practice 14-11. Make the adjusting journal entries for (a) and (b) and the computations for (c) and (d), assuming that the securities are accounted for using the equity method. Ignore the impact of the investee company income and dividends. The changes in value are not deemed to be "other than temporary."

Practice 14-15

Sale of Securities
During Year 1, the company purchased 1,000 shares of stock for $23 per share. Near the end of Year 1, the company sold 400 shares. Make the journal entry to record the sale, assuming that the shares were sold for (1) $27 per share and (2) $20 per share. The shares were classified as trading securities.

Practice 14-16

Sale of Securities and the Market Adjustment Account

The company purchased the following securities during Year 1:

Security	Classification	Cost	Fair Value (Dec. 31, Year 1)
A	Trading	$ 9,000	$10,000
B	Trading	10,000	16,000

On July 23, Year 2, the company sold all of the shares of security B for a total of $9,500. As of December 31, Year 2, the shares of security A had a fair value of $5,800. No other activity occurred during Year 2 in relation to the trading security portfolio. (1) What amount should the company report as *realized gain or loss* in the Year 2 income statement? Clearly indicate whether the amount is a gain or a loss. (2) What amount should the company report as *unrealized gain or loss* in the Year 2 income statement? Clearly indicate whether the amount is a gain or a loss.

Practice 14-17

Transfer between Categories: To and from Trading

The company purchased the following securities during Year 1:

Security	Classification	Cost	Fair Value (Dec. 31, Year 1)
A	Trading	$5,000	$4,000
B	Available for sale	6,000	8,000

In Year 2, the company reclassified both of these securities. Security A was reclassified as available for sale; the fair value of security A at the time of the reclassification was $5,500. Security B was reclassified as trading; the fair value of security B at the time of the reclassification was $4,100. Make the journal entries necessary to record both of these reclassifications.

Practice 14-18

Transfer between Categories: Available for Sale

The company purchased the following securities during Year 1:

Security	Classification	Cost	Fair Value (Dec. 31, Year 1)
A	Available for sale	$ 8,200	$ 7,100
B	Held to maturity	10,000	13,500

In Year 2, the company reclassified both of these securities. Security A was reclassified as held to maturity; the fair value of security A at the time of the reclassification was $9,000. Security B was reclassified as available for sale; the fair value of security B at the time of the reclassification was $9,600. Make the journal entries necessary to record both of these reclassifications. (*Note:* The held-to-maturity securities were acquired at their face value, so there has been no amortization.)

Practice 14-19

Cash Flow and Available-for-Sale Securities

The company entered into the following transactions during the year:

Purchase of investment securities	$400
Sale of investment securities	470

The company had no investment securities at the beginning of the year. The cost of the investment securities sold was $350. The fair value of the remaining securities was $65 on December 31. The net income for the year was $880. Assume that net income does not include any noncash items and does not reflect gains or losses related to investment securities.

Assume that the securities are classified as available for sale. Compute (1) cash flow from operating activities and (2) cash flow from investing activities.

Practice 14-20
Cash Flow and Trading Securities
Refer to Practice 14-19. Assume that the securities are classified as trading and that they were purchased for operating purposes. Compute (1) cash flow from operating activities and (2) cash flow from investing activities.

Practice 14-21
Disclosure: Computation of Total Economic Gain
During Year 1, Walters Company purchased 6,000 shares of Company A common stock for $25 per share and 10,000 shares of Company B common stock for $32 per share. These investments are classified as available-for-sale securities. At December 31, Year 1, Walters Company appropriately recorded a $95,000 debit to Market Adjustment—Available-for-Sale Securities. On March 23, Year 2, the 6,000 shares of Company A common stock were sold for $41 per share. The fair value of the Company B shares on December 31, Year 2, was $38 per share. (1) Prepare *all* journal entries *needed in Year 2* related to these securities. (2) Compute the total increase in economic value generated by Walters' stock portfolio during Year 2.

E X P A N D E D   M A T E R I A L

Practice 14-22
Loan Impairment: Initial Measurement
On January 1 of Year 1, the lending company made a $10,000, 8% loan. The $800 interest is receivable at the end of each year, with the principal amount to be received at the end of five years. As of the end of Year 1, the first year's interest of $800 has not yet been received because the borrower is experiencing financial difficulties. The lending company negotiated a restructuring of the loan. The payment of all of the interest ($4,000 = $800 × 5 years) will be delayed until the end of the five-year loan term. In addition, the amount of principal repayment will be dropped from $10,000 to $5,000. Make the journal entry necessary on the lending company's books to record this loan impairment on December 31 of Year 1. (*Note: No* interest revenue has been recognized in Year 1 in connection with the loan.)

Practice 14-23
Loan Impairment: Subsequent Interest Revenue
Refer to Practice 14-22. Make all journal entries necessary on the lending company's books in connection with the loan during Year 2, Year 3, Year 4, and Year 5. Assume that all cash payments are received according to the renegotiated schedule.

EXERCISES

Exercise 14-24
Recording Securities Transactions
The following transactions of Kelsey, Inc., occurred within the same accounting period:

(a) Purchased $55,000 U.S. Treasury 6% bonds, paying 102 plus accrued interest of $1,400. Kelsey uses the revenue approach to record accrued interest on purchased bonds. Kelsey classified this security as a trading security.

(b) Purchased 2,100 shares of Dulce Co. common stock at $67 per share. Kelsey classifies this stock as an available-for-sale security.

(c) Received semiannual interest on the U.S. Treasury bonds.

(d) Sold 400 shares of Dulce at $81 per share.

(e) Sold $20,000 of U.S. Treasury 6% bonds at 101 plus accrued interest of $180.

(f) Purchased an $18,000, six-month certificate of deposit. The certificate is classified as a trading security.

Prepare the entries necessary to record these transactions.

Exercise 14-25

Accounting for the Purchase and Sale of Securities
During January 2015, Aragorn Inc. purchased the following securities:

Security	Classification	No. of Shares	Total Cost
Gimli Corporation stock	Trading	500	$ 9,000
Legolas International Inc. stock	Available for sale	1,000	22,000
Glorfindel Enterprises stock	Available for sale	2,500	42,500
Mirkwood Co. bonds	Held to maturity	—	24,000
U.S. Treasury bonds	Trading	—	11,000

During 2015, Aragorn received interest from Mirkwood and the U.S. Treasury totaling $3,630. Dividends received on the stock held amounted to $1,760. During November 2015, Aragorn sold 200 shares of the Gimli stock at $17 per share and 250 shares of the Glorfindel stock at $19 per share.

Give the journal entries required by Aragorn to record the (1) purchase of the debt and equity securities; (2) receipt of interest and dividends during 2015; and (3) sale of the equity securities during November.

Exercise 14-26

Accounting Methods for Equity Securities
For each of the following independent situations, determine the appropriate accounting method to be used: cost or equity. For cost method situations, determine whether the security should be classified as trading or available for sale. For equity method situations, determine whether consolidated financial statements would be required. Explain the rationale for your decision.

(a) ATV Company manufactures and sells four-wheel recreational vehicles. It also provides insurance on its products through its wholly owned subsidiary, RV Insurance Company.

(b) Buy Right Inc. purchased 20,000 shares of Big Supply Company common stock to be held as a long-term investment. Big Supply has 200,000 shares of common stock outstanding.

(c) Super Tire Manufacturing Co. holds 5,000 shares of the 10,000 outstanding shares of nonvoting preferred stock of Valley Corporation. Super Tire considers the investment as being long-term in nature.

(d) Takeover Company owns 15,000 of the 50,000 shares of common stock of Western Supply Company. Takeover has tried and failed to obtain representation on Western's board of directors. Takeover intends to sell the securities if it cannot obtain board representation at the next stockholders' meeting, scheduled in three weeks.

(e) Espino Inc. purchased 50,000 shares of Independent Mining Company common stock. Independent has a total of 125,000 common shares outstanding. Espino has no intention to sell the securities in the foreseeable future.

Exercise 14-27

Investment in Equity Securities
On January 10, 2015, Delta Corporation acquired 12,000 shares of the outstanding common stock of Kennedy Company for $600,000. At the time of purchase, Kennedy Company had outstanding 48,000 shares with a book value of $2.4 million. On December 31, 2015, the following events took place:

(a) Kennedy reported net income of $160,000 for the calendar year 2015.

(b) Delta received from Kennedy a dividend of $0.55 per share of common stock.

(c) The fair value of Kennedy Company stock had temporarily declined to $44 per share.

Give the entries that would be required to reflect the purchase and subsequent events on the books of Delta Corporation, assuming that (1) the security is classified as available for sale and (2) the equity method is appropriate.

Exercise 14-28

Investment in Equity Securities—Unrecorded Intangible
Alpha Co. acquired 20,000 shares of Beta Co. on January 1, 2014, at $12 per share. Beta Co. had 80,000 shares outstanding with a book value of $800,000. The difference between the book value and fair value of Beta Co. on January 1, 2014, is attributable to a broadcast license intangible asset. Beta Co. recorded

earnings of $360,000 and $390,000 for 2014 and 2015, respectively, and paid per-share dividends of $1.60 in 2014 and $2.00 in 2015. Assuming a 20-year straight-line amortization policy for the broadcast license, give the entries to record the purchase in 2014 and to reflect Alpha's share of Beta's earnings and the receipt of the dividends for 2014 and 2015.

Exercise 14-29

Investment in Equity Securities—Fair Value Different from Book Value
On January 3, 2015, McDonald Inc. purchased 40% of the outstanding common stock of Old Farms Co., paying $128,000 when the book value of the net assets of Old Farms equaled $250,000. The difference was attributed to equipment, which had a book value of $60,000 and a fair value of $100,000, and to buildings, with a book value of $50,000 and a fair value of $80,000. The remaining useful life of the equipment and buildings was 4 years and 12 years, respectively. During 2015, Old Farms reported net income of $80,000 and paid dividends of $50,000.

Prepare the journal entries made by McDonald Inc. during 2015 related to its investment in Old Farms.

Exercise 14-30

Amortization of a Premium on a Debt Security
On January 1, 2015, Randy Incorporated purchased $500,000 of 20-year, 10% bonds when the market rate of interest was 8%. Interest is to be paid on June 30 and December 31 of each year.

1. Prepare the journal entry to record the purchase of the debt security classified as held to maturity.
2. Prepare the journal entry to record the receipt of the first two interest payments, assuming that Randy accounts for the debt security as held to maturity and uses the effective-interest method.

Exercise 14-31

Amortization of a Discount on a Debt Security
On January 1, 2015, Cougar Creations Inc. purchased $100,000 of five-year, 8% bonds when the effective rate of interest was 10%, paying $92,277. Interest is to be paid on July 1 and December 31.

1. Prepare an interest amortization schedule for the bonds.
2. Prepare the journal entries made by Cougar Creations on July 1 and December 31 of 2015 to recognize the receipt of interest and to amortize the discount.

Exercise 14-32

Valuation of a Debt Security
Using the information from Exercise 14-31, provide the journal entry that would be necessary to properly value the debt security if, on December 31, 2015, the bond's fair value was $96,500. Assume the security was initially classified as follows:

1. A trading security
2. An available-for-sale security
3. A held-to-maturity security

Exercise 14-33

Trading Securities
During 2015, Litten Company purchased trading securities as a short-term investment. The costs of the securities and their fair values on December 31, 2015, follow:

Security	Cost	Fair Value, Dec. 31, 2015
A	$ 65,000	$ 75,000
B	100,000	54,000
C	220,000	226,000

At the beginning of 2015, Litten had a zero balance in the market adjustment—trading securities account. Before any adjustments related to these trading securities, Litten had net income of $300,000.

1. What is net income after making any necessary trading security adjustments? (Ignore income taxes.)
2. What would net income be if the fair value of security B were $95,000?

Exercise 14-34

Accounting for Trading Securities

During 2014, Spelling Inc. purchased the following trading securities:

Security	Cost	Fair Value, Dec. 31, 2014
Bizarre Corp. common	$31,000	$33,000
8% U.S. Treasury notes	16,000	9,000
PhalCo bonds	22,000	25,000

At the beginning of 2014, Spelling had a zero balance in Market Adjustment—Trading Securities.

1. What entry would be made at year-end, assuming the preceding values?
2. What entry would be made during 2015, assuming one-half of the Bizarre Corp. common stock is sold for $17,000?
3. Give the entry that would be made at the end of 2015, assuming the following situations:
   (a) The fair value of remaining securities is $50,000.
   (b) The fair value of remaining securities is $52,500.
   (c) The fair value of remaining securities is $56,000.

Exercise 14-35

Debt and Equity Securities

American Steel Corp. acquired the following securities in 2015:

Security	Classification	Cost	Fair Value, Dec. 31, 2015
A	Trading	$10,000	$12,000
B	Trading	16,000	10,000
C	Available for sale	12,000	15,000
D	Available for sale	20,000	15,000
E	Held to maturity	20,000	22,000

At the beginning of 2015, American Steel had a zero balance in each of its market adjustment accounts.

1. What entry or entries would be made at the end of 2015, assuming the preceding fair values?
2. If net income before any adjustments related to investment securities was $100,000, what would reported income be after adjustments? (Ignore income taxes.)

Exercise 14-36

Temporary and "Other-than-Temporary" Changes in Value

The securities portfolio for Malibu Industries contained the following trading securities:

Securities (common stock)	Initial Cost	Fair Value, Dec. 31, 2014	Fair Value, Dec. 31, 2015
Brooks Co.	$15,000	$18,000	$22,000
Sonoma Co.	12,000	8,000	5,000
Taylor Co.	24,000	20,000	25,000

1. Assuming that all changes in fair value are considered temporary, what is the effect of the changes in value on the 2014 and 2015 financial statements? Give the valuation entries for these years, assuming that the market adjustment account has a $0 balance at the beginning of 2014.
2. Assume that at December 31, 2015, management believed that the fair value of the Sonoma Co. common stock reflected an "other-than-temporary" decline in the value of that stock. Give the entries to be made on December 31, 2015, under this assumption.

Exercise 14-37

Reclassification of Securities

Kyoto Inc. had the following portfolio of securities at the end of its first year of operations:

Security	Classification	Cost	Year-End Fair Value
A	Trading	$ 8,000	$13,000
B	Trading	15,000	18,000

1. Provide the entry necessary to adjust the portfolio of securities to its fair value.
2. In the following year, Kyoto elects to reclassify security B as an available-for-sale security. On the date of the transfer, security B's fair value is $16,500. Provide the journal entry to reclassify security B.

Exercise 14-38

Reclassification of Securities

Bicknel Technologies Inc. purchased the following securities during 2014:

Security	Classification	Cost	Fair Value, Dec. 31, 2014
A	Trading	$ 2,000	$ 4,000
B	Trading	7,000	6,000
C	Available for sale	18,000	16,000
D	Available for sale	5,000	4,000
E	Held to maturity	14,000	15,000

At the beginning of 2014, Bicknel Technologies had a zero balance in each of its market adjustment accounts. During 2015, after the 2014 financial statements had been issued, Bicknel determined that security B should be reclassified as an available-for-sale security and security C should be reclassified as a trading security. The fair values on the date of the transfer are $5,500 for security B and $17,000 for security C.

Prepare the journal entries to do the following:

1. Adjust the portfolio of securities to its fair value at December 31, 2014.
2. Reclassify security B as an available-for-sale security in 2015.
3. Reclassify security C as a trading security in 2015.

Exercise 14-39

Valuation of Securities

Truss Builders Co. reported the following selected balances on its financial statements for each of the four years 2013–2016:

	2013	2014	2015	2016
Market adjustment—Available-for-sale securities	$0	$ 6,200	$4,600	$ (800)
Market adjustment—Trading securities	0	(1,800)	300	1,550

Based on these balances, reconstruct the valuation entries that must have been made each year.

Exercise 14-40
Accounting for Securities

During 2014, the first year of its operations, Profit Industries purchased the following securities:

Security	Classification	Cost	Fair Value, Dec. 31, 2014	Fair Value, Dec. 31, 2015
A	Trading	$18,000	$13,000	$ 9,000
B	Trading	8,000	9,000	10,000
C	Available for sale	17,000	15,000	17,000
D	Available for sale	24,000	28,000	13,000

During 2015, Profit sold one-half of security A for $8,000 and one-half of security D for $15,000. Provide the journal entries required to do the following:

1. Adjust the portfolio of securities to its fair value at the end of 2014.
2. Record the sale of security A and security D.
3. Adjust the portfolio of securities to its fair value at the end of 2015.

Exercise 14-41
Investment Securities and the Statement of Cash Flows

Indicate how each of the following transactions or events would be reflected in a statement of cash flows prepared using the indirect method. Each transaction or event is independent of the others. For items (a) and (d), assume that the balance in the market adjustment account was zero at the beginning of the year. In all cases, assume that trading securities were acquired for operating purposes.

(a) At year-end, the trading securities portfolio has an aggregate cost of $185,000 and an aggregate fair value of $150,000.

(b) During the year, trading securities and available-for-sale securities were purchased for $50,000 and $70,000, respectively. The securities were paid for in cash.

(c) Trading securities on hand at the beginning of the period (cost $40,000) were sold for $62,000 cash.

(d) At year-end, the trading securities portfolio has an aggregate cost of $170,000 and an aggregate fair value of $190,000.

Exercise 14-42
Gain and Losses and the Statement of Cash Flows

Miss Maggie Company entered into the following transactions during the year:

Purchase of trading securities	$500
Sale of trading securities	220
Purchase of available-for-sale securities	900
Sale of available-for-sale securities	470

Miss Maggie had no investment securities at the beginning of the year. The cost of the trading securities sold was $300; the cost of the available-for-sale securities sold was $150. The fair value of the remaining securities on December 31 was as follows: trading securities, $310; available-for-sale securities, $460. The net income for the year was $1,000. Assume that net income does not include any noncash items except for those related to investment securities. In all cases, assume that trading securities were acquired for operating purposes.

Compute (1) cash flow from operating activities and (2) cash flow from investing activities.

E X P A N D E D   M A T E R I A L

Exercise 14-43
Accounting for the Impairment of a Loan

Tortuga Enterprises loaned $350,000 to Turner Inc. on January 1, 2014. The terms of the loan require principal payments of $70,000 each year for five years plus interest at the market rate of interest of 6%. The first principal and interest payment is due on January 1, 2015. Turner made the required payments during 2015 and 2016. However, during 2016 Turner began to experience financial difficulties, requiring Tortuga to reassess the collectibility of the loan. On December 31, 2016, Tortuga determines that the remaining principal payments will be collected, but the collection of interest is unlikely.

1. Compute the present value of the expected future cash flows as of December 31, 2016.
2. Provide the journal entry to record the loan impairment as of December 31, 2016.
3. Provide the journal entries for 2017 to record the receipt of the principal payment on January 1 and the recognition of interest revenue as of December 31, assuming that Tortuga's assessment of the collectibility of the loan has not changed.

P3

Additional Activities of a Business

CHAPTER 15

Leases

Learning Objectives

1. Describe the circumstances in which leasing makes more business sense than does an outright sale and purchase.

2. Understand the accounting issues faced by the asset owner (lessor) and the asset user (lessee) in recording a lease transaction.

3. Outline the types of contractual provisions typically included in lease agreements.

4. Apply the lease classification criteria in order to distinguish between capital and operating leases.

5. Properly account for both capital and operating leases from the standpoint of the lessee (asset user).

6. Properly account for both capital and operating leases from the standpoint of the lessor (asset owner).

7. Prepare and interpret the lease disclosures required of both lessors and lessees.

8. Compare the treatment of accounting for leases in the United States with the requirements of International Accounting Standards.

EM EXPANDED MATERIAL

9. Record a sale-leaseback transaction for both a seller-lessee and a purchaser-lessor.

Which company owns the largest number of commercial jets in the world? Did you guess Delta, United, or American? Those are good guesses. As of December 31, 2011, those three airlines, which are the three largest in the United States, owned the following number of aircraft:

	Number of Aircraft Owned on December 31, 2011
Delta	574
American	608
United	361

The company that owns the most commercial jets, however, is General Electric. Through its GE Capital Aviation Services subsidiary, General Electric owns over 1,800 aircraft that it leases to more than 245 customer airlines in over 75 countries. Aircraft leasing companies own about 40% of the passenger jets flying today. The leasing companies buy the jets from Boeing or Airbus and in turn lease them to an airline. Not one to let a good business opportunity slip away, Boeing is also in the leasing business. In a move that was seen by many as putting itself in close competition with companies that already buy its planes and lease them to airlines, Boeing restructured Boeing Capital Corporation in 1999 in an effort to become a major player in the airplane financing business.[1]

Airlines use these leasing arrangements as an alternative to obtaining loans to buy the planes themselves. Large stable airlines typically sign long-term leases of 15 to 20 years. Smaller airlines trying to establish a market toehold are likely to sign more expensive short-term leases of four to eight years.[2] The flexibility that lease financing gives to airlines was illustrated in the wake of the September 11, 2001, World Trade Center attack when the business of most airlines suffered substantially. Airlines were able to cancel or renegotiate their leases to adapt to this lower passenger traffic. Of course, the leasing companies were also impacted; they began to scrutinize the financial condition of their potential customer airlines more carefully. In fact, in October 2001, International Lease Finance Corporation (ILFC) (which leases 927 aircraft worldwide, mostly outside the United States) shipped 30 pilots to Zurich to snatch 19 of ILFC's planes that had been leased to Swissair. Like auto repossession specialists, the pilots boarded the planes and flew them to France. The reason for the repossession was that ILFC's planes appeared to be in danger of being dragged into the bankruptcy proceedings of Swissair.[3]

As an accountant, a question you might ask yourself while flying at 35,000 feet is whether your airline reports its leased planes as assets on its balance sheet. The answer is sometimes yes but often no. In the case of Delta, a company that leased 201 airplanes (or 26% of its fleet) as of December 31, 2011, only 111 of those leased aircraft were reported on the company's balance sheet. The remaining 90 planes, for which Delta had made contractual promises to pay billions of dollars in the future, were not reported on the balance sheet as assets, nor were the future lease payments reported as a liability. The only financial statement indication that these planes even exist is buried in the lease note to Delta's financial statements.

So, when is a leased airplane an asset? Keep reading; that question is what this chapter is all about.

1. How is it that General Electric owns so many more airplanes than does American Airlines?
2. Why do airlines find it attractive to lease rather than buy their airplanes?
3. Do leased airplanes appear as assets in the balance sheets of the airlines that are using the planes? Explain.

Answers to these questions can be found on page 15-41.

A lease is a contract specifying the terms under which the owner of property, the lessor, transfers the right to use the property to a lessee. In this chapter, we will focus on how leases are accounted for from both the lessor's and the lessee's perspectives. We will discuss the issues associated with classifying a lease as a debt-financed purchase of property (capital lease) or as a rental (operating lease) and the disclosure issues associated with that classification. In addition, we will illustrate how businesses can have definite obligations to pay significant amounts of money in the future relating to operating lease obligations yet not recognize those obligations as liabilities on the balance sheet.

Historically, a major challenge for the accounting profession has been to establish accounting standards that prevent companies from using the legal form of a lease to avoid

---

[1] Jeff Cole, "Boeing Overhauls Financing Operation, Heightening Rivalry with Its Lessors," *The Wall Street Journal*, October 4, 1999, p. A3.
[2] John H. Taylor, "Fasten Seat Belts, Please," *Forbes*, April 2, 1990, p. 84.
[3] J. Lynn Lunsford, "With Airlines in a Dive, Secretive Leasing Firm Plays a Crucial Role," *The Wall Street Journal*, February 12, 2002, p. A1.

C15 | Leases

> **FYI**
>
> The Committee on Accounting Procedure (CAP) addressed the issue of leasing in 1949 with *ARB No. 38*. The APB, formed in 1959, issued four opinions on the subject. The FASB issued pre-Codification *Statement No. 13* on leases in 1976 and has subsequently issued over a dozen amendments and interpretations of the lease accounting rules.

recognizing future payment obligations as a liability. "Off-balance-sheet financing" continues to be a perplexing problem for the accounting profession, and leasing is probably the oldest and most widely used means of keeping debt off the balance sheet. This chapter will discuss in detail and analyze the criteria established by the FASB in an attempt to bring more long-term leases onto the balance sheet as well as specific accounting procedures used for leased assets. In addition, we will discuss how International Financial Reporting Standards differ from those in the United States.

Economic Advantages of Leasing

LO1 学习目标1
描述租赁比直接销售和购买更具商业意义的环境。

① Describe the circumstances in which leasing makes more business sense than does an outright sale and purchase.

Before discussing the accounting treatment of leases, it is important first to consider the valid business reasons for entering into a lease agreement. It would be unfair and incorrect to imply that the only reason companies lease property is to avoid reporting the lease obligation in the financial statements. Although the accounting ramifications are an important consideration in structuring a deal as a lease, other financial and tax considerations also play an important role in the leasing decision.

Every situation is different, but there are three primary advantages to the lessee of leasing over purchasing.

no down payment
无首付

1. *No down payment.* Most debt-financed purchases of property require a portion of the purchase price to be paid immediately by the borrower. This provides added protection to the lender in the event of default and repossession. Lease agreements, in contrast, frequently are structured so that 100% of the value of the property is financed through the lease. This aspect of leasing makes it an attractive alternative to a company that does not have sufficient cash for a down payment or wishes to use available capital for other operating or investing purposes. Of course, many leases also require a down payment; as an example, look carefully at the fine print the next time you see a car lease advertisement on television.

2. *Avoid risks of ownership.* There are many risks accompanying the ownership of property. These risks include casualty loss, obsolescence, changing economic conditions, and physical deterioration. If the market value of a leased asset decreases dramatically, the lessee may terminate the lease, although usually with some penalty. On the other hand, if you own the asset, you are stuck with it when the market value declines.

Car leasing provides increased sales for automakers while making payments more affordable for car owners.

3. *Flexibility*. Business conditions and requirements change over time. If assets are leased, a company can more easily replace assets in response to these changes. This flexibility is especially important in businesses where innovation and technological change make the future usefulness of particular equipment or facilities highly uncertain. A prime example of this condition in recent years has been in high-tech industries with rapid change in areas such as computer technology, robotics, and telecommunications. Flexibility is a primary reason for the popularity of automobile leasing. Car buyers like the flexibility of choosing a brand-new car every two or three years as their leases run out.

The lessor also may find benefits to leasing its property rather than selling it. Advantages of the lease to the lessor include the following:

1. *Increased sales*. For the reasons suggested in the preceding paragraphs, customers may be unwilling or unable to purchase property. By offering potential customers the option of leasing its products, a manufacturer or dealer may significantly increase its sales volume.
2. *Ongoing business relationship with lessee*. When property is sold, the purchaser frequently has no more dealings with the seller of the property. In leasing situations, however, the lessor and lessee maintain contact over a period of time, and long-term business relationships often can be established through leasing.
3. *Residual value retained*. In many lease arrangements, title to the leased property never passes to the lessee. The lessor benefits from economic conditions that may result in a significant residual value at the end of the lease term. The lessor may lease the asset to another lessee or sell the property and realize an immediate gain. For example, new car leasing provides auto dealers with a supply of two- to three-year-old used cars, which can then be sold or leased again.

> **Caution**
> The sooner you get comfortable with the terms *lessee* and *lessor*, the better. The *lessor* is the legal owner of the leased asset; the *lessee* is the party that will use the leased asset.

In summary, a leasing arrangement is often a sound business practice for both the lessee and the lessor. The remainder of the chapter discusses the intricate and interesting accounting implications of leases.

Simple Example

❷ Understand the accounting issues faced by the asset owner (lessor) and the asset user (lessee) in recording a lease transaction.

A simple example will be used to introduce the accounting issues associated with leases. Owner Company owns a piece of equipment with a market value of $10,000 and an estimated useful life of five years. User Company wishes to acquire the equipment for use in its operations. One option for User Company is to purchase the equipment from Owner by borrowing $10,000 from a bank at an interest rate of 10%. User can use the $10,000 to buy the equipment from Owner and can repay the principal and interest on the bank loan in five equal annual installments of $2,638.

Alternatively, User Company can lease the asset from Owner for five years, making five annual "rental" payments of $2,638. From User's standpoint, the lease is equivalent to purchasing the asset, the only difference being the legal form of the transaction. User will still use the equipment for five years and will still make payments of $2,638 per year. From Owner's standpoint, the primary difference in the transaction is that now Owner is not just selling the equipment but is also substituting for the bank in providing financing.

With this lease arrangement, the key accounting issue for Owner Company is as follows:

- On the date the lease is signed, should Owner Company recognize an equipment sale?

The correct answer to this question hinges on factors that have been discussed in previous chapters in connection with inventory sales and revenue recognition.

- Has effective ownership of the equipment been passed from Owner to User?
- Is the transaction complete, meaning does Owner have any significant responsibilities remaining in regard to the equipment?
- Is Owner reasonably certain that the five annual payments of $2,638 can be collected from User?

The key accounting issue for User Company is as follows:

- On the date the lease is signed, should User recognize the leased equipment as an asset and the obligation to make the lease payments as a liability?

The correct answer to this question also hinges on whether effective ownership, as opposed to legal ownership, of the equipment changes hands when Owner and User sign the lease agreement.

Accounting for leases is a classic illustration of the accounting aphorism "substance over form." The legal form of the lease is that Owner Company maintains ownership of the equipment, but whether the lease transfers economic ownership of the asset from Owner to User depends on the specifics of the lease agreement. Consider the following four independent scenarios:

- The lease agreement stipulates that Owner is to maintain legal title to the equipment for the five-year lease period, but title is to pass to User at the end of the lease.
- The lease agreement stipulates that Owner is to maintain legal title to the equipment for the five-year lease period, but at the end of the lease period User has the option to buy the equipment for $1.
- The useful life of the equipment is just five years. Accordingly, when the lease term is over, the equipment can no longer be used by anyone else.
- Present value calculations suggest that payment of the five annual $2,638 lease payments is equivalent to paying $10,000 for the equipment on the lease-signing date.

In each of these four scenarios, the economic substance of the lease is that the lease signing is equivalent to the transfer of effective ownership, and the fact that Owner retains legal title of the equipment during the lease period is a mere technicality. On the other hand, if the lease agreement does not provide for the transfer of the legal title at the end of the lease, if the lease covers only a fraction of the useful life of the equipment, and if the lease payments are not large enough to "pay" for the equipment, then economically the lease is just a rental, not a transfer of ownership.

For accounting purposes, leases are separated into two groups, capital leases and operating leases. Capital leases are accounted for as if the lease agreement transfers ownership of the asset from the lessor to the lessee. In the preceding example, if the lease is accounted for as a capital lease, Owner Company would recognize the sale of the equipment on the lease-signing date and would recognize earned interest revenue as the five annual lease payments are collected. On the lease-signing date, User Company would recognize the leased asset, as well as the liability for the future lease payments, on its balance sheet.

Operating leases are accounted for as rental agreements, with no transfer of effective ownership associated with the lease. In the foregoing example, if the lease is accounted for as an operating lease, Owner Company recognizes no sale on the lease-signing date. Instead, lease rental revenue is recognized each year when the lease payment is collected. User Company recognizes no leased asset and no lease liability but reports only a periodic lease rental expense equal to the annual lease payments.

From this simple introduction, you may receive the misleading impression that accounting for leases is straightforward and noncontroversial. In fact, most companies using assets under lease agreements go to great lengths to ensure that they can account for the bulk of their leases as operating leases because it allows them to keep both the asset and the associated liability off the balance sheet. Keeping the asset off the balance sheet improves financial ratio measures of efficiency, and keeping the liability off the balance sheet improves measures of leverage. For companies that lease a large portion of the assets that they use, the accounting standards associated with leasing are the most critical accounting standards that they apply.

The following sections contain a more detailed description of the kinds of provisions found in lease agreements. In addition, the specific accounting rules used to distinguish between operating leases and capital leases will be explained.

Nature of Leases

LO3 学习目标3
概述租赁协议中典型合同条款的类型。

③ Outline the types of contractual provisions typically included in lease agreements.

Leases vary widely in their contractual provisions. Reasons for this variability include cancellation provisions and penalties, bargain renewal and purchase options, lease term, economic life of assets, residual asset values, minimum lease payments, interest rates implicit in the lease agreement, and the degree of risk assumed by the lessee, including payments of certain costs such as maintenance, insurance, and taxes. These and other relevant facts must be considered in determining the appropriate accounting treatment of a lease.

The many variables affecting lease capitalization have been given precise definitions that must be understood in order to account for the various types of leases found in practice. Each of these variables is defined and briefly discussed in the following sections.

cancellation provisions
撤销条款

Cancellation Provisions

Some leases are noncancellable, meaning that these lease contracts are cancellable only on the outcome of some remote contingency or that the cancellation provisions and penalties of these leases are so costly to the lessee that, in all likelihood, cancellation will not occur. All cancellable leases are accounted for as operating leases; some, but not all, noncancellable leases are accounted for as capital leases.

> **Caution**
> To determine whether a bargain purchase option exists, the parties to the lease must be able to make a reasonable estimate as to what the fair value of the leased asset will be at the end of the lease.

Bargain Purchase Option

Leases often include a provision giving the lessee the right to purchase leased property at some future date. If the specified purchase option price is expected to be considerably less than the fair value at the date the purchase option may be exercised, the option is called a bargain purchase option. By definition, a bargain purchase option is one that is expected to be exercised. Accordingly, a lease agreement including a bargain purchase option is likely to result in the transfer of asset ownership from the lessor to the lessee. Noncancellable leases with bargain purchase options are accounted for as capital leases.

> **FYI**
> The lease term is an important concept in capital lease accounting for lessees because it can determine the period over which the leased asset is depreciated.

Lease Term

An important variable in lease agreements is the lease term, that is, the time period from the beginning to the end of the lease. The beginning of the lease term occurs when the leased property is transferred to the lessee. The end of the lease term is more flexible because many leases include provisions allowing the lessee to extend the lease period. For accounting purposes, the end of the lease term is defined as the end of the fixed noncancellable lease period plus all renewal option periods that are likely to be exercised. A bargain renewal option is one with such an attractive lease rate, or other favorable provision, that at the inception of the lease, it is likely that the lease will be renewed beyond the fixed lease period. If a bargain purchase option is included in the lease contract, the lease term includes any renewal periods preceding the date of the bargain purchase option but does not extend beyond the date of the bargain purchase option.

Residual Value

The market value of the leased property at the end of the lease term is referred to as its *residual value*. In some leases, the lease term extends over the entire economic life of the asset or the period in which the asset continues to be productive, and there is little, if any, residual value. In other leases, the lease term is shorter, and a significant residual value does exist. If the lessee can purchase the asset at the end of the lease term at a materially reduced price from its residual value, a bargain purchase option is present, and it can be assumed that the lessee would exercise the option and purchase the asset.

> **Caution**
> The residual value risk for unguaranteed residual values is borne by the lessor; the residual value risk for guaranteed residual values is borne by the lessee.

Some lease contracts require the lessee to guarantee a minimum residual value. If the market value at the end of the lease term falls below the guaranteed residual value, the lessee must pay the difference. This provision protects the lessor from loss due to unexpected declines in the market value of the asset. For example, assume that the car you lease is expected to have a $15,000 residual value at the end of the lease term and that you guarantee that amount to the car dealership. However, at the end of the lease term, the residual value of the car is only $10,000. You are then obligated to pay the dealership the $5,000 difference because the dealership is, in effect, guaranteed the full amount of the residual value that was estimated at the beginning of the lease. You

如果承租人在租赁期期末能够以大大低于剩余价值的价格购买资产，那么就存在一项廉价购买选择权，可以假设承租人会实施选择权并购买该项资产。

may buy the car for the $15,000 guaranteed amount, but the lease terms do not require the purchase.

If there is no bargain purchase option or guarantee of the residual value, the lessor reacquires the property at the end of the lease term and may offer to renew the lease, lease the asset to another lessee, or sell the property. The actual amount of the residual value is unknown until the end of the lease term; however, it must be estimated at the inception of the lease. The residual value under these circumstances is referred to as the unguaranteed residual value.

Minimum Lease Payments

The rental payments required over the lease term plus any amount to be paid for the residual value either through a bargain purchase option or a guarantee of the residual value are referred to as the minimum lease payments. Lease payments sometimes include charges for items such as insurance, maintenance, and taxes incurred for the leased property. These are referred to as executory costs, and they are not included as part of the minimum lease payments. In addition, building lease payments are often composed of a fixed minimum amount with additional payments made based on sales by the lessee. The additional payments are not considered part of the minimum lease payment.

To illustrate the computation of minimum lease payments, assume that Dorney Leasing Co. owns and leases road equipment for three years at $3,000 per month. Included in the lease payment is $500 per month for executory costs to insure and maintain the equipment. At the end of the three-year period, Dorney is guaranteed a residual value of $10,000 by the lessee.

Minimum lease payments:

Rental payments exclusive of executory costs ($2,500 × 36)............................	$ 90,000
Guaranteed residual value...	10,000
Total minimum lease payments	$100,000

How did Dorney decide that a $2,500 monthly lease payment would be sufficient? Calculation of the appropriate lease payment involves consideration of the fair value of the leased equipment, the guaranteed residual value, the lease term, and the appropriate interest rate. Dorney computed the $2,500 monthly lease payment by using an interest rate of 12% compounded monthly (1% per month) and a fair value of the road equipment of $82,258. The computation is as follows:

Present value of 36 monthly payments of $2,500 ($3,000 less executory costs of $500) at 1% interest (12% compounded monthly) paid at the end of each month:

$PMT = \$2,500; N = 36; I = 1\%; PV$	$75,269

Present value of $10,000 guaranteed residual value at the end of three years at 12% compounded monthly:

$FV = \$10,000; N = 36; I = 1\%; PV$	6,989
Present value of minimum lease payments...	$82,258

Of course, this computation is backwards; in actuality, Dorney would use the $82,258 fair value and the interest rate of 12% compounded monthly to compute the desired monthly lease payment of $2,500. The interest rate used is called the implicit interest rate: the rate used by the lessor in calculating the desired lease payment.

> **FYI**
>
> If the lessee cannot ascertain the lessor's implicit rate, the incremental borrowing rate is used in the lessee's present value calculations. Two reasons the lessee would not be able to compute the implicit rate are if the asset being leased does not have a readily determinable fair value or if a reliable estimate of residual value cannot be obtained.

As discussed later in the chapter, the present value of the minimum lease payments is also an important quantity for the lessee. A complication arises because the implicit interest rate used by the lessor in calculating the lease payments may not be the appropriate discount rate for the lessee. For purposes of computing the present value of the minimum lease payments, the lessee uses the *lower* of the implicit interest rate used by the lessor and the lessee's own incremental borrowing rate. The lessee's incremental borrowing rate is the rate at which the lessee could borrow the amount of money necessary to purchase the leased asset, taking into consideration the lessee's financial situation and the current conditions in the marketplace.

The use of present value formulas and tables in discounting minimum lease payments is illustrated later in the chapter.

Lease Classification Criteria

 Apply the lease classification criteria in order to distinguish between capital and operating leases.

LO4 学习目标4
运用租赁分类标准区分融资性租赁和经营性租赁。

Leasing was one of the topics on the original agenda of the FASB, and in 1976 the Board issued pre-Codification *Statement No. 13*, "Accounting for Leases." The objective of the FASB in issuing *Statement No. 13* was to reflect the economic reality of leasing by requiring that some long-term leases be accounted for as capital acquisitions by the lessee and sales by the lessor. To accomplish this objective, the FASB identified criteria to determine whether a lease is merely a rental contract (an operating lease) or is, in substance, a purchase of property (a capital lease). The lease classification criteria and their applicability to lessees and lessors are summarized in Exhibit 15-1. These criteria are now found in FASB ASC Topic 840.

General Classification Criteria—Lessee and Lessor

应用于承租人和出租人之间所有租赁的四个一般分类标准为：所有权转移、廉价购买权、经济寿命和公允价值。

The four general criteria that apply to all leases for both the lessee and lessor relate to transfer of ownership, bargain purchase options, economic life, and fair value. The transfer of ownership criterion is met if the lease agreement includes a clause that transfers full ownership of the property to the lessee by the end of the lease term. Of all the classification criteria, transfer of ownership is the most objective and therefore the easiest to apply.

The second general criterion is met if the lease contains a bargain purchase option that makes it reasonably assured that the property will be purchased by the lessee at some future date. This criterion is more difficult to apply than the first criterion because the future fair value of

> **FYI**
>
> The FASB's intent was that these general criteria would require most long-term leases to be accounted for as capital leases. However, companies have been clever in how they construct lease agreements, so most leases are accounted for as operating leases.

Exhibit 15-1 | Lease Classification Criteria

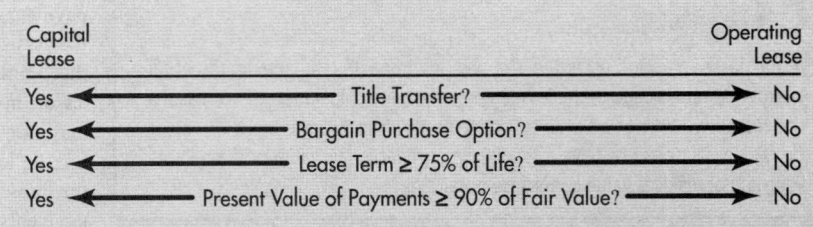

Additional *revenue recognition* criteria applicable to lessors:
1. Collectibility of the minimum lease payments is reasonably predictable.
2. No important uncertainties surround the amount of unreimbursable costs yet to be incurred by the lessor.

- **Lessee:** Capital lease if any one of general criteria is met.
- **Lessor:** Capital lease if any one of general criteria is met and both revenue recognition criteria are met.

© Cengage Learning 2014

the leased property must be estimated at the inception of the lease and compared with the purchase option price to determine whether a bargain purchase is indeed indicated.

The third criterion relates to the economic life of the asset. This criterion is met if the lease term is equal to 75% or more of the estimated economic life of the leased property. As defined earlier, the lease term includes renewal periods if renewal seems assured. The economic life criterion is somewhat subjective because of the uncertainty of an asset's economic life. This criterion does not apply to land leases because land has an unlimited life.

如果在租赁初期，最低租赁付款额现值超过了租赁资产公允价值的90%，租赁实质上就是财产购买。

The fourth general criterion focuses on the fair value of the property in relation to the provisions of the lease. This criterion is met if, at the beginning of the lease term, the present value of the minimum lease payments equals or exceeds 90% of the fair value of the leased asset. If the lessee is obligated to pay, in present value terms, almost all the fair value of the leased property, the lease is in substance a purchase of the property. The key variable in this criterion is the discounted minimum lease payments.

The rate used to discount the future minimum lease payments is critical in determining whether the fair value criterion is met. The lower the discount rate used, the higher the present value of the minimum lease payments and the greater the likelihood that the fair value criterion of 90% will be met. As explained earlier, the FASB specified that the lessor should use the implicit interest rate of the lease agreement. The lessee also uses the lessor's implicit interest rate if it is known and if it is lower than the lessee's incremental borrowing rate. If the lessee cannot determine the lessor's

Stop & Think

How exactly does using a higher incremental borrowing rate reduce the likelihood that a lessee will be required to account for a lease as a capital lease?

a) A higher incremental borrowing rate increases the incidence of bargain purchase options.
b) A higher incremental borrowing rate increases the expected useful life of the leased asset.
c) The use of a higher discount rate increases the likelihood that the lease will be canceled.
d) The use of a higher discount rate lowers the computed present value of the minimum payments.

During World War II, the United Kingdom was in dire need of warships. The problem was that the United Kingdom had no money, and U.S. law prohibited the United States from loaning money to another country for purchasing ships. The solution: An 1892 statute that allowed the secretary of war to lease U.S. military property. Thus was born the famous Lend-Lease Bill, which allowed the United States to provide warships to the United Kingdom.

implicit interest rate, the lessee must use its incremental borrowing rate.

Because incremental borrowing rates are often higher than the implicit interest rates and because lessees generally do not want to capitalize leases, many lessees use the borrowing rate and do not attempt to estimate the implicit rate. In the 1980s, the FASB proposed tightening the capital lease criteria by requiring lessees to estimate the implicit interest rate in all cases. The FASB dropped the proposal when criticism of this proposed provision became widespread.

The four criteria outlined represent the FASB's attempt to precisely delineate the difference between operating and capital leases. In practice, companies have become very skilled at structuring lease agreements according to whether they want to account for the lease as an operating or a capital lease. In essence, the precise nature of the FASB's four criteria provides a legalistic framework that firms easily circumvent through clever structuring of the lease. As a result, the goal of lease accounting that represents substance over form is not entirely met.

An alternative to the FASB's precise framework is the IASB approach, which relies more on accounting judgment. The International Accounting Standard on leases (*IAS 17*, "Accounting for Leases") states simply: "A lease is classified as a finance (i.e., capital) lease if it transfers substantially all the risks and rewards incident to ownership."[4] This type of standard places the responsibility of distinguishing between operating and capital/finance leases on the accountant. Paragraph 10 in *IAS 17* does provide some guidance on distinguishing between operating and finance leases. The paragraph gives the following examples of situations that "would normally lead to a lease being classified as a finance lease:"

通常，一项租赁被划分为融资性租赁的例子如下：
- 在租赁期期末将租赁资产所有权转移给承租人；
- 承租人有权在租赁期满时，以显著低于公允价值的价格购买资产，在租赁日即合理估计承租人会行使该项选择权；
- 尽管所有权未发生转移，但租赁期是资产经济寿命的大部分；
- 在租赁期期初，最低租赁付款额的现值至少等于租赁资产的公允价值。

(a) the lease transfers ownership of the asset to the lessee by the end of the lease term;

(b) the lessee has the option to purchase the asset at a price that is expected to be sufficiently lower than the fair value at the date the option becomes exercisable for it to be reasonably certain, at the inception of the lease, that the option will be exercised;

(c) the lease term is for the major part of the economic life of the asset even if title is not transferred;

(d) at the inception of the lease the present value of the minimum lease payments amounts to at least substantially all of the fair value of the leased asset

As you can recognize as you read the *IAS 17* list, the IASB guidance is exactly the same, in spirit, to the FASB guidance. However, the "75% of economic life" criterion of the FASB becomes a "major part of the economic life" in IFRS. Similarly, the "90% of fair value" criterion of the FASB becomes "substantially all of the fair value" under IFRS. The international standard on lease accounting is a classic example of the principles-based approach in IFRS compared to the rules-based approach in U.S. GAAP.

Revenue Recognition Criteria—Lessor

In addition to meeting one of the four general criteria, a lease must meet two additional revenue recognition criteria to be classified by the lessor as a capital lease.[5] As indicated

---

[4] *International Accounting Standard No. 17*, "Accounting for Leases" (London: International Accounting Standards Board, revised December 2003).
[5] FASB ASC paragraph 840-10-25-42. If the lease involves real estate, these revenue recognition criteria are more complex and depend on whether the lease involves just land, land and buildings, or just part of a building. See FASB ASC paragraphs 840-10-25-54 through 69.

in Exhibit 15-1, the first of the two revenue recognition criteria relates to collectibility. Collection of the minimum lease payments must be reasonably predictable.

The second additional criterion requires substantial completion of performance by the lessor. This means that any unreimbursable costs yet to be incurred by the lessor under the terms of the lease are known or can be reasonably estimated at the lease inception date. If the leased asset is constructed by the lessor, this criterion is applied at the later of the lease inception date or the date construction is completed.

Application of General Lease Classification Criteria

To illustrate the application of the lease classification criteria, four different leasing situations are presented in Exhibit 15-2. A summary analysis of each lease also is presented in the exhibit. Following is a brief explanation of the analysis for each of the four leases.

Lease 1 will be treated as an operating lease by the lessee but as a capital lease by the lessor. The lease does not meet any of the first three general criteria. Because the lessee does not know the implicit interest rate of the lessor, the incremental borrowing rate is used to test for the present value criterion. The present value of the minimum lease payments using the incremental borrowing rate is less than 90% of the fair value of the property; thus, the present value criterion is not met for the lessee. Because the lessor uses the implicit interest rate, the present value criterion is met. The two additional criteria applicable to the lessor are also met.

Lease 2 will be treated as a capital lease by both the lessee and the lessor because title passes to the lessee at the end of the lease term and the additional lessor criteria are both met. Because of the difference in the present value calculations, if the title had not passed, Lease 2 would be treated as an operating lease by the lessee but as a capital lease by the lessor.

Exhibit 15-2 | Application of Lease Classification Criteria to Lease Situations

Lease Provisions	Lease 1	Lease 2	Lease 3	Lease 4
Cancellable	No	No	No	Yes
Title passes to lessee	No	Yes	No	Yes
Bargain purchase option	No	No	Yes	No
Lease term	10 years	10 years	8 years	10 years
Economic life of asset	14 years	15 years	13 years	12 years
Present value of minimum lease payments as a percentage of fair value—incremental borrowing rate	80%	79%	95%	76%
Present value of minimum lease payments as a percentage of fair value—implicit interest rate	92%	91%	92%	82%
Lessee knows implicit interest rate	No	No	Yes	Yes
Rental payments collectible and lessor costs certain	Yes	Yes	No	Yes
Analysis of Leases:				
Lessee				
Treat as capital lease	No	Yes	Yes	No
Criteria met	None	Title	Bargain purchase, present value	Must be noncancellable
Lessor				
Treat as capital lease	Yes	Yes	No	No
First four criteria met	Present value	Title, present value	Bargain purchase, present value	Must be noncancellable
Lessor criteria met	Yes	Yes	No	n/a

© Cengage Learning 2014

Lease 3 will be treated as a capital lease by the lessee but as an operating lease by the lessor. The bargain purchase option criterion is met as is the present value criterion. However, because there is some uncertainty as to the collectibility of the rental payments and the amount of lessor costs to be incurred, the lease fails to meet the revenue recognition criteria applicable to the lessor.

Lease 4 will be treated as an operating lease by both the lessee and the lessor. The lease is a cancellable lease, and even though title passes to the lessee at the end of the lease, it would be classified as a rental agreement.

Accounting for Leases—Lessee

LO5 学习目标5
从承租人（资产使用者）角度恰当地核算融资性租赁和经营性租赁。

 Properly account for both capital and operating leases from the standpoint of the lessee (asset user).

All leases as viewed by the lessee may be divided into two types: operating leases and capital leases. If a lease meets any one of the four general classification criteria discussed previously, it is treated as a capital lease. Otherwise, it is accounted for as an operating lease.

Accounting for operating leases involves the recognition of rent expense over the term of the lease. The leased property is not reported as an asset on the lessee's balance sheet, nor is a liability recognized for the obligation to make future payments for use of the property. Information concerning the lease is limited to disclosure in notes to the financial statements. Accounting for a capital lease essentially requires the lessee to report on the balance sheet the present value of the future lease payments, both as an asset and a liability. The asset is amortized as though it had been purchased by the lessee. The liability is accounted for in the same manner as would be a mortgage on the property. The difference in the impact of these two treatments on the financial statements of the lessee often can be significant, as illustrated here.

Accounting for Operating Leases—Lessee

Operating leases are considered to be simple rental agreements with debits being made to an expense account as the payments are made. For example, assume the lease terms for manufacturing equipment are $40,000 a year on a year-to-year basis. The entry to record the lease payment for a year would be as follows:

Rent Expense..	40,000	
Cash..		40,000

Lease payments frequently are made in advance. If the lease period does not coincide with the lessee's fiscal year or if the lessee prepares interim reports, a prepaid rent account would be required to record the unexpired portion of the lease payment at the end of the accounting period involved. The prepaid rent account would be adjusted at the end of each period.

Operating Leases with Varying Lease Payments Some operating leases specify lease terms that provide for varying lease payments over the lease term. Most commonly, these types of agreements call for lower initial payments and scheduled increases later in the life of the lease. They may even provide an inducement to prospective lessees in the form of a "rent holiday" (free rent). In some cases, however, the lease may provide for higher initial payments. In cases with varying lease payments, periodic expense should be recognized on a straight-line basis.[6]

When recording lease payments under these agreements, differences between the actual payments and the debit to expense would be reported as Rent Payable or Prepaid Rent, depending on whether the payments were accelerating or declining. For example, assume the terms of the lease for an aircraft by International Airlines provide for payments of $150,000 a year for the first two years of the lease and $250,000 for each of the next three years. The total lease payments for the five years would be $1,050,000, or $210,000 a year on a straight-line basis. The required entries in the first two years would be as follows:

Rent Expense...	210,000	
Cash..		150,000
Rent Payable..		60,000

The entries for each of the last three years are as follows:

Rent Expense...	210,000	
Rent Payable...	40,000	
Cash..		250,000

The portion of Rent Payable due in the subsequent year would be classified as a current liability.

This process of making appropriate accrual adjustments to report rent expense of an equal amount each period seems simple. However, in February 2005 the chief accountant of the SEC wrote a letter to the AICPA explaining that many U.S. companies had been improperly reporting lease-related rent expense because of a failure to make these simple accrual adjustments.[7]

As explained later in the chapter, a large amount of detail concerning operating leases is disclosed in the notes to the financial statements. This disclosure includes summary information about lease provisions and a schedule of future minimum lease payments associated with operating leases.

Accounting for Capital Leases—Lessee

Capital leases are considered to be more like a purchase of property than a rental. Consequently, accounting for capital leases by lessees requires entries similar to those required for the purchase of an asset with long-term credit terms. The amounts to be recorded as an asset and as a liability are the present values of the future minimum lease payments as previously defined. The discount rates used by lessees to record capital leases are the same as those used to apply the classification criteria previously discussed, that is, the lower of the implicit interest rate (if known) and the incremental borrowing rate. The minimum lease payments consist of the total rental payments, bargain purchase options, and lessee-guaranteed residual values.[8]

---

[6] Periodic lease expense is recognized on a straight-line basis "unless another systematic and rational basis is more representative of the time pattern in which use benefit is derived from the leased property, in which case that basis shall be used." FASB ASC paragraph 840-20-25-1.

[7] Letter from Donald T. Nicolaisen, chief accountant of the SEC, to Robert J. Kueppers, chairman of the Center for Public Company Audit Firms at the American Institute of Certified Public Accountants, February 7, 2005, available at **http://www.sec.gov/info/accountants/staffletters/cpcaf020705.htm**.

[8] An important exception to the use of the present value of future minimum lease payments as a basis for recording a capital lease is included in FASB ASC paragraph 840-30-30-3, as follows: "If the present value of the minimum lease payments exceeds the fair value of the leased property at lease inception, the amount measured initially as the asset and obligation shall be the fair value." In this case, an implicit interest rate would have to be computed using the fair value of the asset.

FASB CODIFICATION

The Issue: You are part of the management team of a start-up company. Your company has outgrown its existing facility and has decided to move to a larger building. You have agreed with a real estate management company to lease a building that the real estate management company will build to your specifications. This is called a "build-to-suit" lease. You personally have carefully negotiated the lease terms so that your company will account for the lease as an operating lease.

During the three-month construction period, and before you have moved in and started using the building, the lease contract requires you to make monthly lease payments. Note that these payments are made BEFORE you start using the building.

The Question: What is the proper accounting treatment for these lease payments made BEFORE you start using the building under the operating lease agreement?

Searching the Codification: This is a question we would love to address using the "Search" box in the top right corner of the FASB ASC home page. However, the search facility doesn't work when you are using the "Basic View" version; this is one of the things you get when you pay your $800+ to upgrade to the "Professional View." But we can still answer this question using the menus and our knowledge of the transaction. Let's proceed step by step.

- Of course, we'll start by going to Topic 840, Leases.
- Because the lease we are talking about is an operating lease, let's choose Subtopic 840-20, Operating Leases.
- Now things get tough. However, we can narrow our search by realizing that we are talking about how to account for something that happens at the beginning of the lease agreement. So, we want to look in either Recognition or Initial Measurement.
- Under both of the options, we have to remember that we are talking about the accounting rules from the standpoint of the lessee.
- You are close—go ahead and find out how the lessee in an operating lease arrangement is to account for early lease payments made under a build-to-suit lease.

The Answer: The correct treatment is described on page 15-42.

Illustrative Entries for Capital Leases Assume that Marshall Corporation leases equipment from Universal Leasing Company with the following terms:

- Lease period: Five years, beginning January 1, 2015. Noncancellable.
- Rental amount: $65,000 per year payable annually in advance; includes $5,000 to cover executory costs.
- Estimated economic life of equipment: Five years.
- Expected residual value of equipment at end of lease period: None.

Because the lease payments are payable in advance, one way to compute the present value of the lease is to add the amount of the first payment (made on the lease-signing date) to the present value of the annuity of the four remaining payments.[9] Assuming that Marshall Corporation's incremental borrowing rate and the implicit interest rate on the lease are both 10%, the present value for the lease would be $250,192 computed as follows using a business calculator:

Toggle so that the payments are assumed to occur at the beginning (BEG) of the period.
$PMT = \$60,000; N = 5; I = 10\% \rightarrow PV = \$250,192$

The journal entries to record the lease at the beginning of the lease term would be

2015
Jan. 1 Leased Equipment 250,192
            Obligations under Capital Leases 250,192
            To record the lease.
      1 Lease Expense 5,000
         Obligations under Capital Leases 60,000
            Cash 65,000
            To record the first lease payment (including executory costs of $5,000).

> **FYI**
>
> When a lease is capitalized, the asset is included on the balance sheet and written off over time. The word *amortization*, instead of *depreciation*, is typically used when describing the systematic expensing of the cost of a leased asset.

一旦确认了租赁资产和租赁负债，就必须定期编制租赁资产的折旧及租赁负债（包括利息）的支付分录。资产价值的摊销应与承租人所拥有资产的折旧使用相同的方法。

The term *lease expense* is used to record the executory costs related to the leased equipment, such as insurance and taxes. It is possible to record the lease liability at the gross amount of the payments ($300,000 = 5 × $60,000) and offset it with a discount account—Discount on Lease Contract. The net method is more common in accounting for leases by the lessee and will be used in this chapter.

Once the leased asset and the lease liability are recorded, periodic entries must be made to recognize the gradual depreciation of the leased asset and the payment (with interest) of the lease liability. The asset value is amortized in accordance with the lessee's normal method of depreciation for owned assets. The amortization period to be used depends on which of the criteria is used to qualify the lease as a capital lease. If the lease qualifies under the ownership transfer or bargain purchase option criteria, the economic life of the asset should be used because it is assumed that the lessee will take ownership of the asset for the remainder of its useful life at the end of the lease term. If the lease fails to satisfy the ownership transfer or bargain purchase option criteria but does qualify under either the lease term or present value of minimum lease payments criteria, the length of the lease term should be used for amortization purposes. In the Marshall Corporation example, the equipment lease qualifies for capitalization under the lease term criterion because the lease period is equal to the economic life of the equipment. Accordingly, the equipment is amortized over the economic life of five years.

租赁负债的记录金额应随着租赁费的支付而逐渐减少，计算和确认未偿付的利息费用。以承租人新增借款利率和出租人内含利率中较低者作为计算利息费用的利率。

The recorded amount of the lease liability should be reduced each period as the lease payments are made. Interest expense on the unpaid balance is computed and recognized. The lessee's incremental borrowing rate, or the lessor's implicit interest rate if lower, is the

---

[9] The annuity present value tables assume that the payments occur at the end of the period. To compute the present value of an annuity when the payments occur at the beginning of the period, split the annuity into a payment now plus the remaining payments. For example:
$PVn = \$60,000 + [\$60,000\ PVAF_{4|10\%}]$
$PVn = \$60,000 + [\$60,000(3.1699)]$
$PVn = \$250,194$ (differs from $250,192 because of rounding in the tables)

Exhibit 15-3 | Schedule of Lease Payments [Five-Year Lease, $60,000 Annual Payments (Net of Executory Costs), 10% Interest]

Date	Description	Amount	Interest Expense*	Principal	Lease Obligation
1/1/2015	Initial balance				$250,192
1/1/2015	Payment	$ 60,000		$ 60,000	190,192
12/31/2015	Payment	60,000	$19,019	40,981	149,211
12/31/2016	Payment	60,000	14,921	45,079	104,132
12/31/2017	Payment	60,000	10,413	49,587	54,545
12/31/2018	Payment	60,000	5,455	54,545	0
		$300,000	$49,808	$250,192	

*Preceding lease obligation × 10%.

© Cengage Learning 2014

interest rate that should be used in computing interest expense. Exhibit 15-3 shows how the $60,000 payments (excluding executory costs) would be allocated between payment on the obligation and interest expense. To simplify the schedule, it is assumed that all lease payments after the first payment are made on December 31 of each year. If the payments were made in January, an accrual of interest at December 31 would be required.

If the normal company depreciation policy for this type of equipment is straight line, the required entry at December 31, 2015, for amortization of the leased asset would be as follows:

2015

Dec. 31 Amortization Expense on Leased Equipment........................ 50,038*
              Accumulated Amortization on Leased Equipment 50,038

*Computation: $250,192/5 = $50,038

Similar entries would be made for each of the remaining four years. Although the credit could be made directly to the asset account, the use of a contra asset account provides the necessary disclosure information about the original lease value and accumulated amortization to date.

In addition to the entry recording amortization, another entry is required at December 31, 2015, to record the second lease payment, including a prepayment of 2016's executory costs. As indicated in Exhibit 15-3, the interest expense for 2015 would be computed by multiplying the incremental borrowing rate of 10% by the initial present value of the obligation less the immediate $60,000 first payment, or ($250,192 − $60,000) × 0.10 = $19,019.

2015

Dec. 31 Prepaid Executory Costs.. 5,000
              Obligations under Capital Leases 40,981
              Interest Expense... 19,019
                  Cash... 65,000

Because of the assumption that all lease payments after the first payment are made on December 31, the portion of each payment that represents executory costs must be recorded as a prepayment and charged to lease expense in the following year.

Based on the preceding journal entries and using information contained in Exhibit 15-3, the December 31, 2015, balance sheet of Marshall Corporation would include information concerning the leased equipment and related obligation as illustrated here:

Marshall Corporation
Balance Sheet (Partial)
December 31, 2015

Assets		Liabilities	
Current assets:		Current liabilities:	
Prepaid executory costs—		Obligations under capital	
leased equipment	$ 5,000	leases, current portion	$ 45,079
Land, buildings, and equipment:		Noncurrent liabilities:	
Leased equipment	$250,192	Obligations under capital	
Less: Accumulated amortization	50,038	leases, exclusive of $45,079	
Net value	$200,154	included in current liabilities ...	$104,132

Note that the principal portion of the payment due December 31, 2016, is reported as a current liability on the December 31, 2015, balance sheet.[10]

The income statement would include the amortization on leased property of $50,038, interest expense of $19,019, and executory costs of $5,000 as expenses for the period. The total expense of $74,057 exceeds the $65,000 rental payment made in the first year. As the amount of interest expense declines each period, the total expense will be reduced and, for the last two years, will be less than the $65,000 payments (Exhibit 15-4). The total amount debited to expense over the life of the lease will be the same regardless of whether the lease is accounted for as an operating lease or as a capital lease. If an accelerated depreciation method of amortization is used, the difference in the early years between the expense and the payment would be even larger.

In addition to the amounts recognized in the capital lease journal entries previously given, a note to the financial statements would be necessary to explain the terms of the lease and future minimum lease payments in more detail.

Accounting for Leases with a Bargain Purchase Option
Frequently, the lessee is given the option of purchasing the property at some future date at a bargain price. As discussed previously, the present value of the bargain purchase option is part of the minimum lease payments and should be included in the capitalized value of the lease. Assume in the preceding example that there is a bargain purchase option of $75,000 exercisable after five years, and the economic life of the equipment is expected to be 10 years. The other lease terms remain the same. The present value of the minimum lease payments would be increased by the present value of the bargain purchase amount of $75,000, or $46,569, computed as follows:

Toggle back so that the payments are assumed to occur at the end (END) of the period.
$FV = \$75,000; N = 5; I = 10\%$ → $PV = \$46,569$

---

[10] There have been some theoretical arguments advanced against this method of allocating lease obligations between current and noncurrent liabilities. See Robert J. Swieringa, "When Current Is Noncurrent and Vice Versa," *The Accounting Review*, January 1984, pp. 123–130. Professor Swieringa identifies two methods of making the allocation: the "change in present value" (CPV) approach that is used in the example and the "present value of the next year's payment" (PVNYP) approach that allocates a larger portion of the liability to the current category. A later study shows that the CPV method is followed almost universally in practice. See A. W. Richardson, "The Measurement of the Current Portion of Long-Term Lease Obligations—Some Evidence from Practice," *The Accounting Review*, October 1985, pp. 744–752. While there is theoretical support for both positions, this text uses the CPV method in chapter examples and problem materials.

Exhibit 15-4 | Schedule of Expenses Recognized—Capital and Operating Leases Compared

Year	Expenses Recognized—Capital Lease				Expenses Recognized—Operating Lease	Difference
	Interest	Executory Costs	Amortization	Total		
2015	$19,019	$ 5,000	$ 50,038	$ 74,057	$ 65,000	$ 9,057
2016	14,921	5,000	50,038	69,959	65,000	4,959
2017	10,413	5,000	50,038	65,451	65,000	451
2018	5,455	5,000	50,038	60,493	65,000	(4,507)
2019	0	5,000	50,040*	55,040	65,000	(9,960)
	$49,808	$25,000	$250,192	$325,000	$325,000	$ 0

*Rounded.

© Cengage Learning 2014

> **FYI**
>
> In FASB ASC paragraph 840-30-35-14, the FASB states that no gain or loss should be recognized when a leased asset is purchased. As with the exchange of similar assets, the fair value of the equipment on the purchase date is ignored unless evidence of significant impairment exists. See Chapter 11.

The total present value of the future minimum lease payments is $296,761 ($250,192 + $46,569). This amount will be used to record the initial asset and liability. The asset balance of $296,761 will be amortized over the asset life of 10 years because of the existence of the bargain purchase option; this makes the transaction, in reality, a sale. The liability balance will be reduced as shown in Exhibit 15-5.

At the date of exercising the option, the net balance in the leased equipment asset account and its related accumulated amortization account would be transferred to the regular equipment account. The entries at the exercise of the option would be as follows:

2019

Dec. 31 Obligations under Capital Leases 68,182
          Interest Expense.. 6,818
              Cash.. 75,000
          To record exercise of bargain purchase option.

          Equipment... 148,381
          Accumulated Amortization on Leased Equipment................. 148,380*
              Leased Equipment.. 296,761
          To transfer remaining balance in leased asset account to equipment account.

*Computation:
Accumulated amortization: $296,761/10 years = $29,676 per year; 5 years × $29,676 per year = $148,380.

If the equipment is not purchased and the lease is permitted to lapse, a loss equal to the $73,381 difference ($148,381 − $75,000) between the equipment's remaining book

Exhibit 15-5 | Schedule of Lease Payments [Five-Year Lease with Bargain Purchase Option of $75,000 after Five Years, $60,000 Annual Payments (Net of Executory Costs), 10% Interest]

Date	Description	Amount	Interest Expense	Principal	Lease Obligation
1/1/2015	Initial balance				$296,761
1/1/2015	Payment	$ 60,000		$ 60,000	236,761
12/31/2015	Payment	60,000	$23,676	36,324	200,437
12/31/2016	Payment	60,000	20,044	39,956	160,481
12/31/2017	Payment	60,000	16,048	43,952	116,529
12/31/2018	Payment	60,000	11,653	48,347	68,182
12/31/2019	Payment	75,000	6,818	68,182	0
		$375,000	$78,239	$296,761	

© Cengage Learning 2014

value and the remaining balance in the lease liability account (including accrued interest) would have to be recognized by the following entry:

2019

Dec. 31 Loss from Failure to Exercise Bargain Purchase Option............... 73,381
        Obligations under Capital Leases 68,182
        Interest Expense... 6,818
        Accumulated Amortization on Leased Equipment.................. 148,380
            Leased Equipment... 296,761

Accounting for Leases with a Lessee-Guaranteed Residual Value If the lease agreement requires the lessee to guarantee a residual value, the lessee treats the guarantee similar to a bargain purchase option and includes the present value of the guarantee as part of the capitalized value of the lease. At the expiration of the lease term, the amount of the guarantee will be reported as a liability under the lease. In addition, the remaining book value of the leased asset will be equal to the guaranteed residual value. If the fair value of the leased asset is less than the guaranteed residual value, a loss is reported for the difference, and the lessee must make up the difference with a cash payment.

Accounting for Purchase of Asset during Lease Term When a lease does not provide for a transfer of ownership or a purchase option, it is still possible that the lessee may purchase leased property during the term of the lease. Usually the purchase price will differ from the recorded lease obligation at the purchase date. No gain or loss should be recorded on the purchase, but the difference between the purchase price and the obligation still on the books should be charged or credited to the acquired asset's carrying value.[11]

To illustrate, assume that on December 31, 2017, rather than making the lease payment due, the lessee purchased the leased property in the Marshall Corporation example described on page 15-15 for $120,000. At that date, the remaining liability recorded on the lessee's books is $114,545 (lease obligation of $104,132 + interest payable of $10,413; see Exhibit 15-3) and the net book value of the recorded leased asset is $100,078, the

---
[11] FASB ASC paragraph 840-30-35-15.

original capitalized value of $250,192 less $150,114 amortization ($50,038 × 3). The entry to record the purchase on the lessee's books would be as follows:

2017
Dec. 31 Interest Expense.. 10,413
         Obligations under Capital Leases 104,132
         Equipment.. 105,533
         Accumulated Amortization on Leased Equipment..................... 150,114
             Leased Equipment... 250,192
             Cash... 120,000

The purchased equipment is capitalized at $105,533, which is the book value of the leased asset, $100,078, plus $5,455, the excess of the purchase price over the carrying value of the lease obligation ($120,000 − $114,545).

Treatment of Leases on Lessee's Statement of Cash Flows

Operating leases present no special problems to the lessee in preparing a statement of cash flows. The lease payments reduce, and thus require no adjustment to, net income under the indirect method except for accrued or prepaid rent expense. The cash payments would be reported as operating expense outlays under the direct method.

Adjustments for capital leases by the lessee, however, are more complex. The amortization of leased assets would be treated the same as depreciation, that is, added to net income under the indirect method and ignored under the direct method. The portion of the cash payment allocated to interest expense would require no adjustment under the indirect method and would be reported as part of the cash payment for interest expense under the direct method. The portion of the cash payment allocated to the lease liability would be reported as a financing outflow under either method. The signing of a capital lease would not be reported as either an investing or financing activity because it is a noncash transaction. The impact of a capital lease on the lessee's statement of cash flows is summarized in Exhibit 15-6.

To illustrate the impact of a capital lease on the lessee's statement of cash flows, refer back to the Marshall Corporation example starting on page 15-15. Assume that in 2015, Marshall

Exhibit 15-6 | Impact of a Capital Lease on the Lessee's Statement of Cash Flows

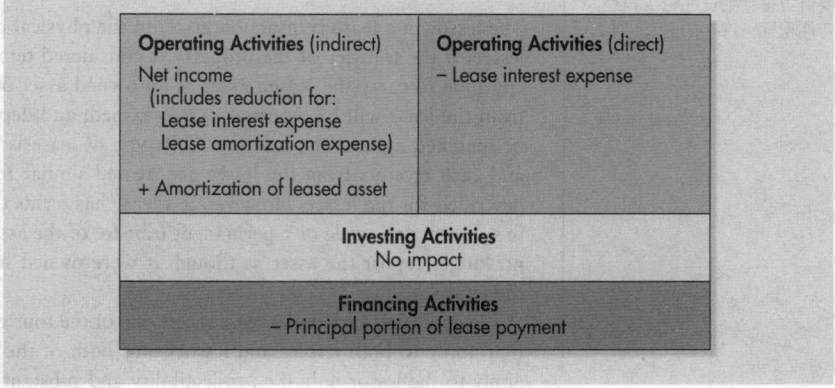

Corporation's income before any lease-related expenses is $200,000. For simplicity, ignore income taxes and executory costs. Net income for the year can be computed as follows:

Income before lease-related expenses	$200,000
Lease-related interest expense	(19,019)
Lease-related amortization expense	(50,038)
Net income	$130,943

The statement of cash flows for Marshall Corporation for 2015, displaying only the lease-related items and using the indirect method to report cash flow from operating activities, would appear as follows:

Operating activities:

Net income	$ 130,943
Add: Amortization of asset leased under capital lease	50,038
Net cash flow from operating activities	$ 180,981

Investing activities:

No lease-related items

Financing activities:

Repayment of lease liability ($60,000 + $40,981)	$(100,981)

In addition, the supplemental disclosure to the statement of cash flows would include the following two lease-related items:

- Significant noncash transaction: During 2015, the company leased equipment under a capital lease arrangement. The present value of the minimum future payments under the lease was $250,192 on the lease-signing date.
- Cash paid for interest was $19,019.

Accounting for Leases—Lessor

6 Properly account for both capital and operating leases from the standpoint of the lessor (asset owner).

The lessor in a lease transaction gives up the physical possession of the property to the lessee. If the transfer of the property is considered temporary in nature, the lessor will continue to carry the leased asset as an owned asset on the balance sheet; the revenue from the lease will be reported as it is earned; and depreciation of the leased asset will be matched against the revenue. This type of lease is described as an *operating lease*, and cash receipts from the lessee are treated similar to the operating lease procedures described for the lessee. However, if a lease has terms that make the transaction similar in substance to a sale or a permanent transfer of the asset to the lessee, the lessor should no longer report the asset as though it were owned but should reflect the transfer to the lessee.

As indicated earlier, if a lease meets one of the four general lease classification criteria that apply to both lessees and lessors plus both of the revenue recognition criteria that apply to the lessor only (i.e., collectibility and substantial completion), it is classified by

> **FYI**
>
> The sale of new cars provides a good example of a sales-type lease. **Ford Motor** has a financing subsidiary to handle leasing. When a car is leased from a dealership, the auto company earns a profit on the lease as well as interest from the lease contract.

the lessor as a capital lease and recorded as either a direct financing lease or a sales-type lease.

Direct financing leases involve a lessor who is primarily engaged in financing activities, such as a bank or finance company. The lessor views the lease as an investment. The revenue generated by this type of lease is interest revenue. Sales-type leases, on the other hand, involve manufacturers or dealers who use leases as a means of facilitating the marketing of their products. Thus, there are two different types of revenue generated by this type of lease: (1) an immediate profit or loss, which is the difference between the cost of the property being leased and its sales price, or fair value, at the inception of the lease and (2) interest revenue earned over time as the lessee makes the lease payments that pay off the lease obligation plus interest.

For either an operating, direct financing, or sales-type lease, a lessor may incur certain costs, referred to as initial direct costs, in connection with obtaining the lease. These costs include the costs to negotiate the lease, perform the credit check on the lessee, and prepare the lease documents.[12]

Initial direct costs are accounted for differently, depending on which of the three types of leases is involved. Exhibit 15-7 summarizes the accounting treatment for initial direct costs. These costs will be discussed further as each type of lease is presented.

direct financing leases
直接融资租赁
sales-types lease
销售型租赁

Exhibit 15-7 | Accounting for Initial Direct Costs

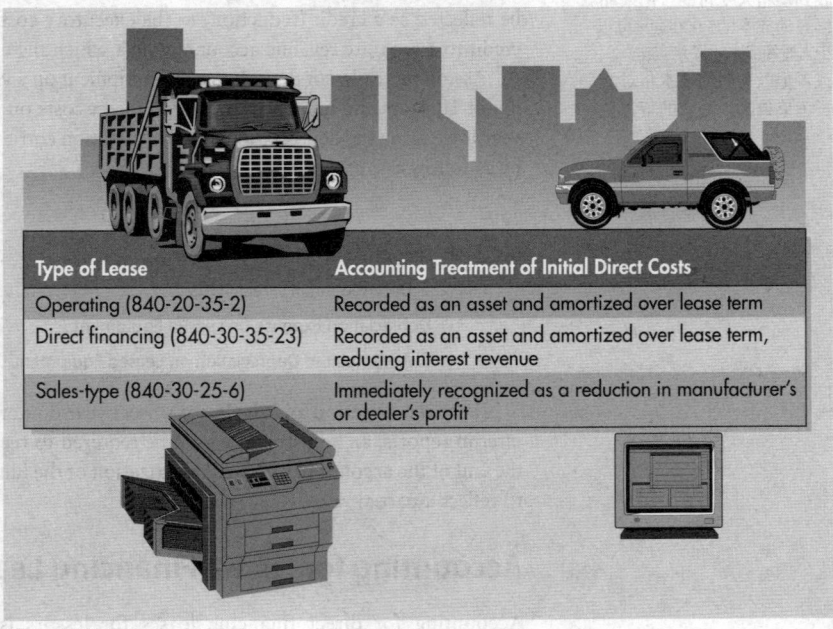

Type of Lease	Accounting Treatment of Initial Direct Costs
Operating (840-20-35-2)	Recorded as an asset and amortized over lease term
Direct financing (840-30-35-23)	Recorded as an asset and amortized over lease term, reducing interest revenue
Sales-type (840-30-25-6)	Immediately recognized as a reduction in manufacturer's or dealer's profit

© Cengage Learning 2014

[12] FASB ASC paragraph 840-20-25-17.

Accounting for Operating Leases—Lessor

Accounting for operating leases for the lessor is very similar to that described for the lessee. The lessor recognizes revenue as the payments are received. If there are significant variations in the payment terms, entries will be necessary to reflect a straight-line pattern of revenue recognition. Initial direct costs incurred in connection with an operating lease are deferred and amortized on a straight-line basis over the term of the lease, thus matching them against rent revenue.

To illustrate accounting for an operating lease on the lessor's books, assume that the equipment leased for five years by Universal Leasing Company to Marshall Corporation (page 15-15) on January 1, 2015, for $65,000 a year, including executory costs of $5,000 per year, had a cost of $400,000 to the lessor, Universal Leasing. Initial direct costs of $15,000 were incurred to obtain and finalize the lease. The equipment has an estimated life of 10 years, with no residual value. Assuming no purchase or renewal options or guarantees by the lessee, the lease does not meet any of the four general classification criteria and would be treated as an operating lease. The entries to record the payment of the initial direct costs and the receipt of the lease payments by Universal Leasing would be as follows:

2015

Jan.	1	Deferred Initial Direct Costs...	15,000	
		Cash..		15,000
	1	Cash..	65,000	
		Rent Revenue...		60,000
		Executory Costs..		5,000

The $5,000 payment received from the lessee to reimburse the executory costs may be reflected as a credit (reduction) to the executory costs account, as shown here, or as a credit to a separate revenue account against which the executory costs can be matched.

Assuming the lessor depreciates the equipment on a straight-line basis over its expected life of 10 years and amortizes the initial direct costs on a straight-line basis over the five-year lease term, the depreciation and amortization entries at the end of the first year would be as follows:

2015

Dec.	31	Amortization of Initial Direct Costs.................................	3,000	
		Deferred Initial Direct Costs...................................		3,000
	31	Depreciation Expense on Leased Equipment........................	40,000	
		Accumulated Depreciation on Leased Equipment...............		40,000

If the rental period and the lessor's fiscal year do not coincide or if the lessor prepares interim reports, an adjustment would be required to record the unearned rent revenue at the end of the accounting period. Amortization of the initial direct costs would be adjusted to reflect a partial year.

Accounting for Direct Financing Leases

Accounting for direct financing leases for lessors is very similar to that used for capital leases by lessees but with the entries reversed to provide for interest revenue rather than interest expense and reduction of a lease payment receivable rather than a lease liability. The lease payment receivable is reported at its present value; this is the standard practice followed with all long-term receivables, as explained in Chapter 7. The lease payment receivable is sometimes recorded by the lessor at the gross amount of the lease payments with an offsetting valuation account for the unearned interest, or aggregate amount of interest that will be earned by the lessor over the course of the lease. Unearned interest revenue is computed as the difference between the total expected lease payments and the fair value, or cost, of the leased asset. This approach is illustrated for the first year in the following example. Although the remainder of the journal entries in the chapter report the lease payment receivable at its net present value, note that in each case the receivable could be shown at its gross amount less an adjustment for unearned interest revenue.

Illustrative Entries for Direct Financing Leases Referring to the lessee example on page 15-15, assume that the cost of the equipment to the Universal Leasing Company was the same as its fair value, $250,192, and that the purchase by the lessor had been entered into Equipment Purchased for Lease. The entry to record the initial lease would be this:

2015

Jan.	1	Lease Payments Receivable...	250,192	
		Equipment Purchased for Lease		250,192

or if the lease payment receivable is recorded at its gross amount:

Jan.	1	Lease Payments Receivable...	300,000	
		Equipment Purchased for Lease		250,192
		Unearned Interest Revenue		49,808

The first payment would be recorded as follows:

Jan.	1	Cash	65,000	
		Lease Payments Receivable		60,000
		Executory Costs		5,000

出租人支付履约成本但向承租人索取该成本。出租人通过借记现金和贷记履约成本费用账户来记录收取的履约成本。当出租人支付时，则借记费用。出租人对承租人的这些费用起到一个中间人的作用，只有当承租人无法支付该项费用时，出租人才会支出。

The lessor is paying the executory costs but charging them to the lessee. The lessor can record the receipt of the executory costs by debiting Cash and crediting Executory Costs. As the lessor pays the costs, the expense account is debited. The lessor is serving as a conduit for these costs to the lessee and will have an expense only if the lessee fails to make the payments. Interest revenue will be recognized over the lease term as shown in Exhibit 15-8.

At the end of the first year, the following entries would be made to record the receipt of the second lease payment, to recognize the interest revenue for 2015, and to recognize the advance payment for next year's executory costs as a deferred credit.

2015

Dec.	31	Cash	65,000	
		Lease Payments Receivable		40,981
		Interest Revenue...		19,019
		Deferred Executory Costs (a liability).............................		5,000

Exhibit 15-8 | Schedule of Lease Receipts and Interest Revenue [Five-Year Lease, $60,000 Annual Payments (Exclusive of Executory Costs), 10% Interest]

Date	Description	Interest Revenue*	Payment Receipt	Reduction in Receivable	Lease Payments Receivable
1/1/2015	Initial balance				$250,192
1/1/2015	Receipt		$ 60,000	$ 60,000	190,192
12/31/2015	Receipt	$19,019	60,000	40,981	149,211
12/31/2016	Receipt	14,921	60,000	45,079	104,132
12/31/2017	Receipt	10,413	60,000	49,587	54,545
12/31/2018	Receipt	5,455	60,000	54,545	0
		$49,808	$300,000	$250,192	

*Preceding lease payment receivable × 10%.

© Cengage Learning 2014

or if the lease payment receivable is recorded at its gross amount:

Dec. 31	Cash	65,000	
	Lease Payments Receivable		60,000
	Deferred Executory Costs (a liability)		5,000
31	Unearned Interest Revenue	19,019	
	Interest Revenue		19,019

Notice that unlike the operating lease example, no annual depreciation expense is recorded by the lessor in association with an asset leased under a capital lease agreement. This is because the asset has been "sold" to the lessee and removed from the lessor's books.

Based on the journal entries, the asset portion of the balance sheet of the lessor at December 31, 2015, will report the lease receivable as follows:

Universal Leasing Company
Balance Sheet (Partial)
December 31, 2015

Assets

Current assets:
Lease payments receivable .... $ 45,079
Noncurrent assets:
Lease payments receivable (exclusive of $45,079 included in current assets) $104,132

If a direct financing lease contains a bargain purchase option, the present value of the option is added to the receivable. The periodic entries and computations are made as though the bargain purchase amount was an additional rental payment.

Lessor Accounting for Direct Financing Leases with Residual Value

If leased property is expected to have residual value, the present value of the expected residual value is added to the receivable account. It does not matter whether the residual value is guaranteed or unguaranteed. If guaranteed, it is treated in the accounts exactly like a bargain purchase option. If unguaranteed, the lessor is expected to have an asset equal in value to the residual amount at the end of the lease term.

> **Caution**
>
> The fair value in this example ($296,761) is different from the fair value in the previous example ($250,192) because, in the previous example, the asset was assumed to be worthless at the end of the lease term. In this example, the asset is estimated to have a residual value of $75,000. The present value of that $75,000 (i.e., $46,569) accounts for the difference.

To illustrate the recording of residual values, assume the same facts for the Universal Leasing Company as the example on pages 15-19–15-20 except that the asset has a residual value at the end of the five-year lease term of $75,000 (either guaranteed or unguaranteed) rather than a bargain purchase option. Assume the cost of the equipment to the Universal Leasing Company was again the same as its fair value, $296,761.

The entries to record this lease and the first payment follow:

2015				
Jan.	1	Lease Payments Receivable..	296,761	
		Equipment Purchased for Lease.................................		296,761
	1	Cash...	65,000	
		Lease Payments Receivable.....................................		60,000
		Executory Costs...		5,000

The computation of interest revenue would be identical to the interest expense computation illustrated in Exhibit 15-5 for the lessee.

At the end of the first year, the lessor would make the following entries:

2015				
Dec.	31	Cash...	65,000	
		Lease Payments Receivable.....................................		36,324
		Deferred Executory Costs...		5,000
		Interest Revenue..		23,676

At the end of the lease term, the lessor would make the following entry to record the recovery of the leased asset, assuming the residual value was the same as originally estimated:

2019				
Dec.	31	Equipment..	75,000	
		Lease Payments Receivable.....................................		68,182
		Interest Revenue..		6,818

Initial Direct Costs Related to Direct Financing Leases If the lessor incurs any initial direct costs in conjunction with a direct financing lease, those costs are recorded as a separate asset, increasing the net lease investment. Because the initial net lease investment is increased but the lease payments remain the same, the existence of initial direct costs results in a lower implicit interest rate earned by the lessor. Including initial direct costs as part of the initial net lease investment effectively spreads the initial costs over the lease term and reduces the amount of interest revenue that would otherwise be recognized.

如果出租人发生了与融资租赁相关的初始直接费用，那么这些费用应作为单独资产确认，增加租赁投资净额。因为初始租赁投资净额增加而租赁费仍是相同的，所以初始直接费用的存在会导致出租人赚取的内含利率较低。初始直接费用作为初始租赁投资净额的一部分在整个租赁期平摊初始成本，并减少未确认利息收入金额。

Accounting for Sales-Type Leases—Lessor

Accounting for sales-type leases adds one more dimension to the lessor's revenue, an immediate profit or loss arising from the difference between the sales price of the leased property and the lessor's cost to manufacture or purchase the asset. If there is no difference between the sales price and the lessor's cost, the lease is not a sales-type lease. The lessor also will recognize interest revenue over the lease term for the difference between the sales price and the gross amount of the minimum lease payments. The three values that must be identified to determine these income elements, therefore, can be summarized as follows:

1. The minimum lease payments as defined previously for the lessee, that is, rental payments over the lease term net of any executory costs plus the amount to be paid under a bargain purchase option or guarantee of the residual value
2. The fair value of the asset
3. The cost or carrying value of the asset to the lessor increased by any initial direct costs to lease the asset

The manufacturer's or dealer's profit is the difference between the fair value of the asset and the cost or carrying value of the asset to the lessor. If cost exceeds the fair value, a loss will be reported. The difference between the gross rentals and the fair value of the asset is interest revenue and arises because of the time delay in paying for the asset as described by the lease terms. The relationship between these three values can be demonstrated as follows:

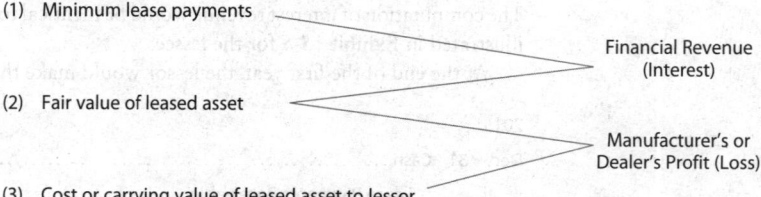

(1) Minimum lease payments

Financial Revenue (Interest)

(2) Fair value of leased asset

Manufacturer's or Dealer's Profit (Loss)

(3) Cost or carrying value of leased asset to lessor

To illustrate this type of lease, assume that the lessor for the equipment described on page 15-15 is American Manufacturing Company rather than Universal Leasing. The fair value of the equipment is equal to its present value (the future lease payments discounted at 10%), or $250,192. This computation is reversed from what would happen in practice; normally, the fair value is known, and the minimum lease payments are set at an amount that will yield the desired rate of return to the lessor.

Assume that the equipment cost American Manufacturing $160,000 and initial direct costs of $15,000 were incurred. The three values and the related revenue amounts would be as follows:

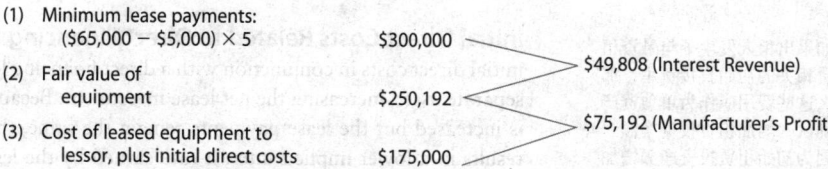

(1) Minimum lease payments:
($65,000 − $5,000) × 5 $300,000
                                                    $49,808 (Interest Revenue)
(2) Fair value of
    equipment $250,192
                                                    $75,192 (Manufacturer's Profit)
(3) Cost of leased equipment to
    lessor, plus initial direct costs $175,000

Illustrative Entries for Sales-Type Leases The interest revenue ($49,808) is the same as that illustrated for a direct financing lease on page 15-25, and it is recognized over the lease term by the same entries and according to Exhibit 15-8. The manufacturer's profit is recognized as revenue immediately in the current period by including the fair value of the asset as a sale and debiting the cost of the equipment carried in Finished Goods Inventory to Cost of Goods Sold. The initial direct costs previously deferred are recognized as an expense immediately by increasing Cost of Goods Sold by the amount expended for these costs. This reduces the amount of immediate profit to be recognized. The reimbursement of executory costs is treated in the same way as illustrated for direct financing leases.

The entries to record this information on American Manufacturing Company's books at the beginning of the lease term would be as follows:

2015
Jan. 1	Lease Payments Receivable..	250,192	
	Sales..		250,192
1	Cost of Goods Sold	175,000	
	Finished Goods Inventory		160,000
	Deferred Initial Direct Costs		15,000
1	Cash	65,000	
	Lease Payments Receivable		60,000
	Executory Costs...		5,000

> **Caution**
> The sales account is always credited for the present value of the minimum lease payments.

> **FYI**
> These journal entries to record a sales-type lease may seem complex, but look more carefully—these are exactly the entries one makes when reporting a credit sale and a subsequent partial payment.

The first journal entry records the sale and recognizes a receivable, reported at its present value. The second journal entry simply removes the inventory and deferred direct costs from the books of the lessor and recognizes the cost of goods sold. The final entry records the first payment. The example does not show the payment for the initial direct costs. The deferred initial direct costs account would have been charged at the time these costs were paid.

The 2015 income statement would include the sales and cost of goods sold amounts yielding the manufacturer's profit of $75,192 and interest revenue of $19,019. A note to the statements would describe in more detail the nature of the lease and its terms.

Accounting for Sales-Type Leases with a Bargain Purchase Option or Guarantee of Residual Value If the lease agreement provides for the lessor to receive a lump-sum payment at the end of the lease term in the form of a bargain purchase option or a guarantee of residual value, the minimum lease payments include these amounts. The receivable is thus increased by the present value of the future payment, and sales are increased by the present value of the additional amount.

To illustrate a sales-type lease with a bargain purchase option, assume that American Manufacturing was the lessor on the lease described on page 15-15 and in Exhibit 15-5.

The initial entries when either a bargain purchase option or a guarantee of residual value of $75,000 is payable at the end of the five-year lease term would be as follows:

2015
Jan.	1	Lease Payments Receivable....................................	296,761	
		Sales..		296,761
	1	Cost of Goods Sold...	175,000	
		Finished Goods Inventory		160,000
		Deferred Initial Direct Costs		15,000
	1	Cash...	65,000	
		Lease Payments Receivable		60,000
		Executory Costs..		5,000

Because the lease now includes a bargain purchase option, Sales increases by $46,569 (present value of the bargain purchase amount) over the amount recognized in the previous example. The manufacturer's profit is also increased by this amount.

Accounting for Sales-Type Leases with Unguaranteed Residual Value

When a sales-type lease does not contain a bargain purchase option or a guaranteed residual value but the economic life of the leased asset exceeds the lease term, the residual value of the property will remain with the lessor. As indicated earlier, this is called an *unguaranteed residual value*. Because the sales amount reflects the present value of the minimum lease payments, an unguaranteed residual value would not be included in the sales amount. However, the cost of goods sold would be reduced by the present value of the unguaranteed residual value to recognize the fact that the lessor will be receiving back the $75,000 leased asset (worth a present value of $46,569) at the end of the lease term. In essence, this $46,569 residual value is not "sold" but is merely loaned to the lessee for the period of the lease, after which it will be returned to the lessor. The entry to record the initial lease described earlier with an unguaranteed residual value follows:

2015
Jan.	1	Lease Payments Receivable....................................	250,192	
		Sales..		250,192
	1	Cost of Goods Sold ($175,000 − $46,569)............................	128,431	
		Finished Goods Inventory ($160,000 − $46,569)		113,431
		Deferred Initial Direct Costs		15,000
	1	Lease Payments Receivable....................................	46,569	
		Finished Goods Inventory		46,569

The only difference between accounting for an unguaranteed residual value and a guaranteed residual value or bargain purchase option is that rather than increasing Sales by the present value of the residual value, the present value of the unguaranteed residual value is deducted from the cost of the leased equipment sold. This reduction occurs because the portion of the leased asset represented by the unguaranteed residual value will be returned at the end of the lease term and, therefore, is not "sold" on the lease-signing date. The $46,569 in inventory represented by the present value of the unguaranteed residual value has not been sold but has been exchanged for a receivable of equal amount.

Note that the gross profit on the transaction is the same regardless of whether the residual value is guaranteed or unguaranteed, as follows:

	Guaranteed Residual Value	Unguaranteed Residual Value
Sales	$296,761	$250,192
Cost of goods sold	175,000	128,431
Gross profit	$121,761	$121,761

Third-Party Guarantees of Residual Value When a lease is used by the seller as a means to provide financing to the buyer and to increase sales, the seller wants to account for the lease as a sales-type lease, not as an operating lease, so that the revenue from the sale can be recognized immediately. On the other hand, the buyer would prefer to account for the lease as an operating lease to keep the lease obligation off the balance sheet. A third-party guarantee of residual value is a clever trick that companies have devised to get around the accounting rules and allow the desires of both the seller-lessor and the buyer-lessee to be satisfied.

Consider the example just given in which the guaranteed residual value is $75,000. In this case, the fair value of the equipment on the lease-signing date is $296,761. From the lessor's standpoint, the present value of the minimum lease payments, including the guaranteed residual value, is also $296,761. Accordingly, the lease meets the 90% of fair value criterion, and the lease is accounted for as a sales-type lease.

Here is where the fun begins. The lessee, instead of guaranteeing the residual value itself, can pay an insurance company or investment firm to guarantee the residual value. For a fee, the insurance company bears the risk that the residual value of the leased asset might fall below the guaranteed residual value. If this happens, the insurance company, not the lessee, will make up the difference. By the purchase of this "insurance policy," the lessee removes the guaranteed residual value from its calculation of the present value of the minimum lease payments. Without the guaranteed residual value, the present value of the minimum lease payments is only $250,192, just 84% ($250,192/$296,761) of the fair value of the leased asset. As a result, the lessee accounts for the lease as an operating lease.

In summary, a third-party guarantee of residual value allows the seller-lessor to recognize the entire profit from the lease transaction immediately but also permits the buyer-lessee to treat the lease as an operating lease and keep the lease liability off the balance sheet.

Obviously these "insurance policies" are designed to take advantage of the precision of the FASB 90% criterion. As U.S. companies transition to IFRS, it is likely that the number of these third-party guarantee arrangements will decrease because the principles-based nature of the IASB's lease classification standard will require accountants to be very skeptical of transactions designed to mask the economic substance of a lease.

Sale of Asset during Lease Term

If the lessor sells an asset to the lessee during the lease term, a gain or loss is recognized on the difference between the receivable balance and the selling price of the asset. Thus, if the leased asset described in Exhibit 15-8 is sold on December 31, 2017, for $140,000 before the $60,000 rental payment is made, a gain of $25,455 would be reported. The following journal entry would be made to record the sale:

2017
Dec. 31 Cash 140,000
              Interest Revenue 10,413
              Lease Payments Receivable 104,132
              Gain on Sale of Leased Asset 25,455

Although the lessor does recognize a gain or loss on the sale, as mentioned earlier, the lessee accounts for the transaction as an exchange of similar assets and defers any gain or loss through an adjustment in the value placed on the purchased asset.

Treatment of Leases on Lessor's Statement of Cash Flows

Operating leases present no special problems to the lessor in preparing a statement of cash flows except for initial direct costs. Because initial direct costs are recognized as an asset when the lease is an operating lease, the payment of these costs would be reported as an investing cash outflow. Under the indirect method, the amortization of initial direct costs would be added to net income in the same way income is adjusted for depreciation. Under the direct method, the amortization would be ignored. The lease payment receipts would be reported as part of net income and would require no adjustment under the indirect method and would be reported as part of the revenue receipts under the direct method.

Capital leases must be analyzed carefully to determine their impact on the statement of cash flows. Direct financing leases would require adjustments similar to those made by the lessee for capital leases except that for the lender (lessor), the transaction is viewed as an investing activity rather than a financing activity as was the case for the borrower (lessee). The portion of the receipt that represents interest will be included in net income and requires no adjustment under the indirect method. It would be part of cash inflows from interest under the direct method. The portion of the lease payment representing the principal would be reported as a cash inflow from investing activities.

Under sales-type leases, the manufacturer's profit, net of initial direct costs, is reported in net income, but the cash inflow comes as the lease payments are received. Under the indirect method, this requires a deduction from net income for the manufacturer's profit at the inception of the lease. This would automatically occur as the changes in inventory, deferred initial costs, and net lease payments receivable are reflected in the Operating section of the statement of cash flows. Because the transaction is being accounted for as a sale, all further receipts under the indirect method are reported as operating inflows either as interest revenue or as reductions in the net lease payments receivable. Under the direct method, the entire lease receipt would be included in cash flows from operating activities. A summary of the treatment of lease impact on the statement of cash flows is included in Exhibit 15-9.

To illustrate the impact of a lease on the lessor's statement of cash flows, refer back to the American Manufacturing Company sales-type lease example starting on page 15-19. Assume that in 2015, American Manufacturing's income before any lease-related items is $200,000. For simplicity, ignore income taxes and executory costs and assume that all of the nonlease items included in income are cash items. Net income for the year can be computed as follows:

Exhibit 15-9 | Summary of Lease Impact on Statement of Cash Flows

	Operating Activities		Investing Activities	Financing Activities
	Indirect Method	Direct Method		
Lessee:				
Operating lease payments	NI	– Cash		
Capital lease:				
Lease payments—interest	NI	– Cash		
Lease payments—principal				– Cash
Amortization of asset	+ NI	No impact		
Lessor:				
Operating lease:				
Initial direct costs (IDC)			– Cash	
Amortization of IDC	+ NI	No impact		
Lease receipts	NI	+ Cash		
Direct financing lease:				
Initial direct costs			– Cash	
Amortization of IDC	+ NI	No impact		
Lease receipts—interest	NI	+ Cash		
Lease receipts—principal			+ Cash	
Sales-type lease:				
Initial direct costs			– Cash	
Manufacturer's or dealer's profit (net of IDC)	– NI	No impact		
Lease receipts—interest	NI	+ Cash		
Lease receipts—principal	+ NI	+ Cash		

Key:
    NI = Included in net income
    + NI = Added as an adjustment to net income
    – NI = Deducted as an adjustment to net income
    + Cash = Reported as a receipt of cash
    – Cash = Reported as a payment of cash

© Cengage Learning 2014

Income before lease-related items	$ 200,000
Lease-related sales	250,192
Lease-related cost of goods sold	(175,000)
Lease-related interest revenue	19,019
Net income	$ 294,211

The computation of cash from operating activities for American Manufacturing Company for 2015, using the indirect method to report cash flow from operating activities, would appear as follows:

Operating activities:

Net income	$ 294,211
Less: Increase in lease payments receivable ($250,192 – $60,000 – $40,981)	(149,211)
Plus: Decrease in finished goods inventory	175,000
Net cash flow from operating activities	$ 320,000

Note that the total operating cash flow of $320,000 is equal to the $200,000 income before lease-related items (which were assumed to be all cash items) plus the two $60,000 lease payments received during the year. This illustrates again that a sales-type lease impacts the lessor's financial statements in the same way as any other long-term credit sale.

Disclosure Requirements for Leases

LO7 学习目标7
编制并解释出租人和承租人所要求的租赁披露。

 Prepare and interpret the lease disclosures required of both lessors and lessees.

The FASB has established specific disclosure requirements for all leases, regardless of whether they are classified as operating or capital leases. The required information supplements the amounts recognized in the financial statements and usually is included in a single note to the financial statements.

The following information is required for all leases that have initial or remaining noncancellable lease terms in excess of one year:

Lessee
1. Gross amount of assets recorded as capital leases, along with related accumulated amortization.
2. Future minimum rental payments required as of the date of the latest balance sheet presented in the aggregate and for each of the five succeeding fiscal years. These payments should be separated between operating and capital leases. For capital leases, executory costs should be excluded.
3. Rental expense for each period for which an income statement is presented. Additional information concerning minimum rentals, contingent rentals, and sublease rentals is required for the same periods.
4. A general description of the lease contracts, including information about restrictions on such items as dividends, additional debt, and further leasing.
5. For capital leases, the amount of imputed interest necessary to reduce the lease payments to present value.

Exhibit 15-10 presents a note accompanying the 2011 financial statements of Delta Air Lines, illustrating the required lessee disclosures for both operating and capital leases.

Several points should be highlighted relating to Delta's lease disclosure. First, compare the minimum lease payments for Delta's capital leases to the payments to be made for its operating leases. The expected payments for operating leases exceed those for capital leases by a factor of almost 12. Note also that Delta discloses the portion of the minimum lease payments on its capital leases that represents interest. With the information in this note, we can approximate the impact that the obligations related to Delta's operating leases would have on its balance sheet if those leases were capitalized.

To approximate the present value of these future operating lease payments, we can make some simplifying assumptions:

- The appropriate interest rate for discounting future cash flows is 10%.
- The uneven stream of future operating lease payments by Delta is roughly equivalent to $1,340 million per year for 11 years. This rough approximation stems from the fact that the payments in the first five years average $1,340 million per year and the total of the payments is $14,268 million, which is roughly equal to $1,340 million a year for 11 years.

Exhibit 15-10 | Delta Air Lines—Lessee Disclosure

NOTE 7. LEASE OBLIGATIONS

We lease aircraft, airport terminals, maintenance facilities, ticket offices and other property and equipment from third parties. Rental expense for operating leases, which is recorded on a straight-line basis over the life of the lease term, totaled $1.1 billion, $1.2 billion and $1.3 billion for the years ended December 31, 2011, 2010 and 2009, respectively. Amounts due under capital leases are recorded as liabilities, while assets acquired under capital leases are recorded as property and equipment. Amortization of assets recorded under capital leases is included in depreciation and amortization expense. Many of our aircraft, facility, and equipment leases include rental escalation clauses and/or renewal options. Our leases do not include residual value guarantees and we are not the primary beneficiary in or have other forms of variable interest with the lessor of the leased assets. As a result, we have not consolidated any of the entities that lease to us.

The following tables summarize, as of December 31, 2011, our minimum rental commitments under capital leases and noncancellable operating leases (including certain aircraft under Contract Carrier agreements) with initial or remaining terms in excess of one year:

Capital Leases

Years Ending December 31, (in millions)	Capital Leases
2012	$ 221
2013	196
2014	168
2015	155
2016	163
Thereafter	323
Total minimum lease payments	1,226
Less: amount of lease payments representing interest	(489)
Present value of future minimum capital lease payments	737
Plus: unamortized premium, net	(6)
Less: current obligations under capital leases	(117)
Long-term capital lease obligations	$ 614

Operating Leases

Years Ending December 31, (in millions)	Delta Lease Payments	Contract Carrier Aircraft Lease Payments[1]	Total
2012	$ 926	$ 536	$ 1,462
2013	912	529	1,441
2014	862	518	1,380
2015	765	506	1,271
2016	677	449	1,126
Thereafter	6,660	928	7,588
Total minimum lease payments	$10,802	$3,466	$14,268

[1] Represents the minimum lease obligations under our Contract Carrier agreements with ExpressJet Airlines, Inc. (formerly Atlantic Southeast Airlines, Inc.), Chautauqua Airlines, Inc. ("Chautauqua"), Compass, Mesaba, Pinnacle, Shuttle America Corporation ("Shuttle America") and SkyWest Airlines, Inc.

At December 31, 2011, we and our wholly-owned subsidiary Comair operated 111 aircraft under capital leases and 90 aircraft under operating leases. Our Contract Carriers under capacity purchase agreements (excluding Comair) operated 550 aircraft under operating leases.

© Delta Air Lines, 2011, 10K Report

Given these simplifying assumptions, it is easy to compute that the present value of an annuity of $1,340 million per year for 11 years is $8.7 billion if the interest rate is 10%. This $8.7 billion approximates the economic value of Delta's obligations under its operating leases.

If Delta were required to report these future obligations as liabilities, there would be a noticeable impact on the company's reported liabilities—long-term debt would increase from $11.8 billion to $20.5 billion. For this reason, companies go to great lengths to structure leases so that the leases can be classified as operating leases and the lease obligation can be excluded from the balance sheet.

Lessor
1. The following components of the net investment in sales-type and direct financing leases as of the date of each balance sheet presented:
   (a) Future minimum lease payments receivable with separate deductions for amounts representing executory costs and the accumulated allowance for uncollectible minimum lease payments receivable
   (b) Unguaranteed residual values accruing to the benefit of the lessor
   (c) Unearned revenue (the difference between the gross lease payments and the present value of the lease payments)
   (d) For direct financing leases only, initial direct costs
2. Future minimum lease payments to be received for each of the five succeeding fiscal years as of the date of the latest balance sheet presented, including information on contingent rentals
3. The amount of unearned revenue included in income to offset initial direct costs for each year for which an income statement is prepared
4. For operating leases, the cost of assets leased to others and the accumulated depreciation related to these assets
5. A general description of the lessor's leasing arrangements

An example of lessor disclosure of sales-type and direct financing leases for International Lease Finance Corporation, one of the major lessors of airplanes mentioned at the beginning of this chapter, is shown in Exhibit 15-11.

Exhibit 15-11 | International Lease Finance Corporation—Lessor Disclosure

Note J — Net Investment in Finance and Sales-type Leases
The following lists the components of the net investment in finance and sales-type leases:

	December 31, 2011	December 31, 2010
Total lease payments to be received	$ 86,592	$ 59,234
Estimated residual values of leased flight equipment (unguaranteed)	46,857	29,543
Less: Unearned income	(28,615)	(21,157)
Less: Allowance for credit losses	(23,088)	—
Net investment in finance and sales-type leases	$ 81,746	$ 67,620

At December 31, 2011, minimum future lease payments on finance and sales-type leases are as follows:

2012	$19,505
2013	17,442
2014	14,509
2015	12,375
2016	10,931
Thereafter	11,830
Total minimum lease payments to be received	$86,592

© Cengage Learning 2014

- 出租人应提供截至每个资产负债表日销售型及直接融资租赁净投资的各组成部分为：
（1）分别扣减履约成本金额以及未收回应收最低租赁额累计准备金后的未来最低租赁收款额；
（2）应计入出租人利益的未担保余值；
（3）未实现收入，即租赁付款总额与租赁费用现值的差额；
（4）初始直接费用，仅针对直接融资租赁。
- 截至最新提供的资产负债表日随后5个财政年度每年应收的未来最低租赁付款额，包括或有租金的信息。
- 收入中的预收款项数额，以抵销利润表编制当年的初始直接费用。
- 对于经营性租赁，出租给其他人的成本及有关这些资产的累计折旧。
- 出租人租赁安排的一般说明。

International Accounting of Leases

LO8 学习目标8
比较美国租赁会计的处理与国际会计准则要求的不同。

8 Compare the treatment of accounting for leases in the United States with the requirements of International Accounting Standards.

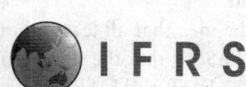

As mentioned earlier in the chapter, the International Accounting Standard on leases (*IAS 17*) relies on the exercise of accounting judgment to distinguish between operating and capital leases. *IAS 17* states that a finance lease, which is the same as our capital lease, is "a lease that transfers substantially all the risks and rewards incident to ownership of an asset." This standard has been criticized because it leaves the classification of a lease as either operating or capital almost exclusively up to the accountant (subject to the approval of an external auditor). However, before finding fault with *IAS 17*, remember that the four lease classification criteria adopted as part of pre-Codification *Statement No. 13* have not been successful in preventing U.S. companies from cleverly constructing most leases to be classified as operating.

In October 2002, the FASB circulated a proposal regarding principles-based accounting standards. As envisioned by their proponents, principles-based standards would involve fewer rigid thresholds and rules (such as the four lease classification criteria) and would rely more on accountants exercising professional judgment in the interpretation and execution of the standards.[13] *IAS 17* is just such a principles-based standard. The entire idea of principles-based standards is still being debated, but the area of lease accounting provides a good illustration of the limitation of principles-based standards. Although *IAS 17* is indeed a principles-based standard, when the rule is actually applied in practice around the world, accountants often sneak a peek at the four lease classification criteria included in FASB ASC paragraph 840-10-25-1 in order to be able to use the *IAS 17* "principle" in the context of an actual lease contract. As U.S. companies switch to IFRS, it is likely that accountants and auditors will continue to reference the FASB's four lease classification criteria for help in applying the principles of *IAS 17*.

A very interesting lease accounting proposal has been circulating for a number of years among accounting standard setters around the world. The standard setters of the United States, the United Kingdom, Canada, Australia, and New Zealand sponsored a research project that resulted in a new lease accounting proposal in 1996. This proposal, titled "Accounting for Leases: A New Approach," notes that current lease accounting standards fail in their objective of requiring companies to recognize significant rights and obligations as assets and liabilities in the balance sheet. The proposal also suggests that the lease accounting rules be simplified as follows: All lease contracts are to be accounted for as capital leases.

To illustrate the dramatic impact that this "new approach" would have on the reporting of leases for lessees, consider the following table:

	Fair value of leased asset = $10,000	Present value of minimum lease payments = $8,999	Present value of minimum lease payments = $9,001
Lease obligation reported under current U.S. GAAP		$ 0	$9,001
Lease obligation that would be reported under the New Approach for lease accounting		$8,999	$9,001

[13] Proposal—"Principles-Based Approach to U.S. Standard Setting" (Norwalk, CT: Financial Accounting Standards Board, October 21, 2002).

In each of the two cases, the fair value of the leased asset is $10,000. In the first case, the present value of the minimum lease payments is $8,999, which is 89.9% of the fair value of the leased asset. The present value of the minimum payments is less than 90% of the fair value of the leased asset, and assuming that none of the other capital lease criteria are satisfied, the lease would be accounted for as an operating lease under U.S. GAAP. With the lease classified as an operating lease, the lessee would not report any obligation for the future lease payments. Under the new approach, an $8,999 obligation would be reported for the present value of the future minimum lease payments. In the second case, the present value of the lease payments is $9,001, which is more than 90% of the fair value of the leased asset. This lease would be classified as a capital lease under existing U.S. GAAP, and the $9,001 obligation would be reported under both U.S. GAAP and the new approach. Note that under the new approach, the small $2 change in the present value of the lease payments, from $8,999 to $9,001, is reflected in the correspondingly small increase in the recorded amount of the lease obligation. However, under U.S. GAAP, this small change in the present value of the payments results in a huge change in the reported liability. Whenever there is a knife-edge accounting rule such as this, one can be sure that companies will be very careful, and inventive, in making certain that the present value of their lease payments is just below the 90% threshold.

More recently, the FASB and IASB have both endorsed the idea that all leases should be capitalized. The terminology currently being used by the FASB is that the signing of a lease creates a "right-of-use asset" and a "lease obligation." The FASB and IASB circulated an exposure draft along these lines in 2010 and have since been holding public hearings, doing feasibility inquiries, and encouraging feedback from interested parties. A revised exposure draft was scheduled to be released in late 2012.

This proposal to capitalize all leases is still in the discussion stage. Given the great efforts that U.S. companies now expend to keep leases off the balance sheet, a proposal to capitalize all leases is sure to touch off one of the largest accounting debates of the past 30 years.

EXPANDED MATERIAL

Lease agreements can be very complicated. Some of these complications have been specifically designed to circumvent the accounting rules and allow for favorable classification of leases. One example is the third-party guarantee of residual values mentioned earlier in the chapter. Another example is the sale-leaseback transaction described in this section. It is a transaction that usually has the effect of sweeping assets and liabilities right off a company's balance sheet even as those assets continue to be used exactly as they were before.

Sale-Leaseback Transactions

 Record a sale-leaseback transaction for both a seller-lessee and a purchaser-lessor.

LO9 学习目标9

记录卖方（承租人）和买方（出租人）的售后回租交易。

售后回租交易的典型特征是一方将资产出售给另一方，然后第一方再租回该项资产。因此，出卖者成为承租人，而购买者成为出租人。

A common type of lease arrangement is referred to as a sale-leaseback transaction. Typical of this type of lease is an arrangement whereby one party sells the property to a second party, and then the first party leases the property back. Thus, the seller becomes a seller-lessee and the purchaser a purchaser-lessor.

The accounting problem raised by this transaction is whether the seller-lessee should recognize the profit from the original sale immediately or defer it over the lease term. The FASB rule is that if the initial sale produces a profit, it should be deferred and amortized in proportion to the amortization of the leased asset if it is a capital lease or in proportion to the rental payments if it is an operating lease. If the transaction produces a loss because the fair value of the asset is less than its carrying value, an immediate loss should be recognized.[14]

There are two exceptions to the profit deferral rule. First, if the seller-lessee's remaining ownership rights are "minor" after the sale-leaseback transaction, then the sale and leaseback are separate transactions, and any profit on the sale is recognized immediately. Second, if the profit on the sale is "large," defined as larger than the present value of the minimum payments on the leaseback, then the "excess" profit (the amount greater than the present value of the minimum leaseback payments) is recognized at the time of the sale with the remainder of the profit deferred and recognized according to the normal process.

> **Stop & Think**
>
> Why would a company sell an asset and then turn right around and lease that same asset back?
>
> a) To increase the reported amount of total liabilities
> b) To decrease the reported amount of total liabilities
> c) To increase the reported amount of total assets
> d) To increase the reported amount of current liabilities

To illustrate the accounting treatment for a sale at a gain, assume that on January 1, 2015, Hopkins Inc. sells equipment having a carrying value of $750,000 on its books to Ashcroft Co. for $950,000 and immediately leases back the equipment. The following conditions are established to govern the transaction:

1. The term of the lease is 10 years, noncancellable. A down payment of $200,000 is required plus equal lease payments of $107,107 at the beginning of each year. The implicit interest rate is 10%.

2. The equipment has a fair value of $950,000 on January 1, 2015, and an estimated economic life of 20 years. Straight-line depreciation is used on all owned assets.

3. Hopkins has an option to renew the lease for $10,000 per year for 10 years, the rest of its economic life. Title passes at the end of the lease term.

Analysis of this lease shows that it qualifies as a capital lease under both the lease term and present value of payments criteria. It meets the 75% of economic life criterion because of the bargain renewal option, which makes both the lease term and the economic life of the equipment 20 years. It meets the 90% of fair value criterion because the present value of the lease payments is equal to the fair value of the equipment ($950,000).[15]

---

[14] FASB ASC paragraphs 840-40-25-3 and 840-40-35-1.
[15] Computation of present value of lease:
   (a) Present value of 10 years' rentals:
      Payments at the beginning of the period (BEG): $PMT = \$107{,}107; N = 10; I = 10\% \rightarrow \$723{,}939$.
   (b) Present value of second 10 years' rentals:
      Payments at the beginning of the period (BEG): $PMT = \$10{,}000; N = 10; I = 10\% \rightarrow \$67{,}590$, present value at beginning of second 10 years' lease period. Present value at beginning of lease, 10 years earlier: $FV = \$67{,}590; N = 10; I = 10\% \rightarrow \$26{,}059$.
   (c) Total present value, $723,939 + $26,059 + $200,000 down payment = $950,000 (rounded).

The journal entries for the first year of the lease for Hopkins, the seller-lessee, and Ashcroft, the purchaser-lessor, follow:

Hopkins Inc. (Seller-Lessee)

2015				
Jan. 1	Cash		950,000	
	Equipment			750,000
	Unearned Profit on Sale-Leaseback			200,000
	To record original sale of equipment.			
1	Leased Equipment		950,000	
	Obligations under Capital Lease			642,893
	Cash ($200,000 + $107,107)			307,107
	To record lease of equipment, including down payment and first payment.			
Dec. 31	Amortization Expense on Leased Equipment		47,500	
	Accumulated Amortization on Leased Equipment			47,500
	To record amortization of equipment over 20-year period ($950,000/20).			
31	Interest Expense		64,289	
	Obligations under Capital Lease		42,818	
	Cash			107,107
	To record second lease payment (interest expense: $642,893 × 0.10 = $64,289).			
31	Unearned Profit on Sale-Leaseback		10,000	
	Revenue Earned on Sale-Leaseback			10,000
	To record recognition of revenue over 20-year life in proportion to the amortization of the leased asset.			

Ashcroft Co. (Purchaser-Lessor)

Jan. 1	Equipment		950,000	
	Cash			950,000
	To record purchase of equipment.			
1	Cash		307,107	
	Lease Payments Receivable		642,893	
	Equipment			950,000
	To record direct financing sale-leaseback to Hopkins Inc. Gross receivable = (10 × $107,107) + (10 × $10,000) = $1,171,070			
Dec. 31	Cash		107,107	
	Lease Payments Receivable			42,818
	Interest Revenue			64,289
	To record receipt of second lease payment (see computations for Hopkins Inc.).			

（SFAS No.28）如果售后回租交易形成了经营性租赁，那么之前的销售利润应该在租赁资产余下的使用年限内予以递延和确认。（IAS17）如果初始按公允价值销售，那么当期应确认收益，即使随后的租回形成了经营性租赁。

The amortization entries and recognition of the deferred gain on the sale for Hopkins Inc. would be the same each year for the 20-year lease term. The interest expense and interest revenue amounts would decline each year using the effective interest method of computation.

If the lease had not met the criteria, it would have been recorded as an operating lease. The gain on the sale would have been deferred and recognized in proportion to the lease payments. The yearly gain recognition amounts would closely parallel that just illustrated because both the amortization of a leased asset and the pattern of lease payments typically follow a straight-line process.

If the initial sale had been at a loss, an immediate recognition of the loss would have been recorded.

The provisions of *IAS 17* regarding the deferral of sale profits on a sale-leaseback are essentially the same as under U.S. GAAP. The wording in *IAS 17* is somewhat different (and, frankly, a bit more clear) than in FASB ASC Subtopic 840-40, but the international accounting is basically the same as that required under U.S. GAAP.

SOLUTIONS TO OPENING SCENARIO QUESTIONS

1. American Airlines leases many of the airplanes that it uses. It leases these planes from financing companies, such as GE Capital Aviation Services, that buy the airplanes from the manufacturer and then make money by leasing the planes to airlines.

2. By leasing many of their airplanes, the airlines give themselves financing flexibility. If they experience a decline in the need for aircraft, it is much easier to get out of a lease than it is to sell an unneeded plane in order to pay off the loan used to buy the plane in the first place.

3. As illustrated with data from Delta Air Lines, some leased airplanes are reported as an asset in the leasing airline's balance sheet and some are not. This chapter explains the accounting rules that determine when a leased asset is reported on the leasing company's balance sheet as an asset.

Stop & Think SOLUTIONS

1. (Page 15-10) The correct answer is D. The use of a higher discount rate results in a lower computed present value. A lower present value reduces the probability that a lease will satisfy the 90% of market value criterion and thus reduces the likelihood that the lease will be classified as a capital lease.

2. (Page 15-39) The correct answer is B. One reason for a firm to do a sale-leaseback is to remove an asset (and the associated payment obligation) from the balance sheet. A carefully constructed sale-leaseback deal results in the lease being classified as an operating lease—with the leased asset and the lease liability disclosed only in the financial statement notes.

Another reason to do a sale-leaseback is to put the property in the hands of a professional property management firm, allowing the company to concentrate on its core business. For example, imagine a large engineering consulting firm with an office building located on a prime piece of land in a large city. What does an engineering consulting firm know about maximizing the use of the property? Nothing. But it needs the office building. So, the firm sells the building and property to a property management firm and then leases them back. The engineering consulting firm is now concentrating on what it does best—engineering—and the property is being managed by a firm of professionals.

SOLUTION TO USING THE FASB'S CODIFICATION

You should have found the following in FASB ASC paragraph 840-20-25-8: "If a build-to-suit lease is classified as an operating lease, the lessee shall consider construction period lease payments made before the beginning of the lease term to be prepaid rent."

So, if these payments are prepaid rent, they should then be added in with all of the other lease/rent payments so that the total amount is recognized as expense in a straight-line fashion over the lease term.

Review Chapter 15 Learning Objectives

1 **Describe the circumstances in which leasing makes more business sense than does an outright sale and purchase.**

The three primary advantages to a lessee of leasing over purchasing are that a lease often involves no down payment, leasing avoids the risks of ownership, and leasing gives the lessee flexibility to change assets when technology or preferences change.

The economic advantages to a lessor include an increase in sales by providing financing to customers who might not otherwise be able to buy, establishment of an ongoing relationship with customers, and retention of the residual value of the leased asset after the lease term is over.

2 **Understand the accounting issues faced by the asset owner (lessor) and the asset user (lessee) in recording a lease transaction.**

For the lessor, the key accounting issue is whether or not a sale should be recognized on the date the lease is signed. The proper accounting hinges on whether the lease signing transfers effective ownership of the leased asset, whether the lessor has any significant additional responsibilities remaining after the lease is signed, and whether payment collectibility is reasonably assured.

For the lessee, the key accounting issue is whether the leased asset and the lease payment obligation should be recognized on the balance sheet. Again, the proper accounting treatment depends on whether the lease signing transfers effective ownership of the leased asset.

Capital leases are accounted for as if the lease agreement transfers ownership of the leased asset from the lessor to the lessee. Operating leases are accounted for as rental agreements.

3 **Outline the types of contractual provisions typically included in lease agreements.**

- *Cancellation provisions*. A noncancellable lease agreement is one that can be cancelled by the lessee only under very unusual circumstances. Only noncancellable leases can be classified as capital leases.
- *Bargain purchase option*. If the lessee has the option to purchase the leased asset in the future at an amount low enough such that exercise of the option is likely, a bargain purchase option exists.
- *Lease term*. The lease term includes the noncancellable lease period plus any periods covered by bargain renewal options that include favorable lease terms (e.g., low lease payments) that make it likely that the lessee will renew the lease.
- *Residual value*. The residual value is the value of the leased asset at the end of the lease term. Sometimes, the lease agreement requires that the lessee guarantee the residual value; if the residual value falls below the guaranteed amount, the lessee must pay the lessor the difference.
- *Minimum lease payments*. The minimum lease payments include the periodic lease payments plus any bargain purchase option amount or the amount of any guaranteed residual value. The lessor computes the present value of the minimum lease payments using the implicit interest rate. The lessee computes the present value using the lower of the implicit interest rate and the lessee's own incremental borrowing rate.

④ Apply the lease classification criteria in order to distinguish between capital and operating leases.

The four general lease classification criteria, applicable to both lessors and lessees, are as follows:

- *Transfer of ownership.* The lease includes a provision that title to the leased asset passes to the lessee by the end of the lease term.
- *Bargain purchase option.* A bargain purchase option exists that makes it reasonably assured that the lessee will acquire the asset.
- *75% of economic life.* The lease term is equal to 75% or more of the economic life of the leased asset.
- *90% of asset value.* The present value of the minimum lease payments is greater than or equal to 90% of the fair value of the leased asset on the lease-signing date.

If any one of these criteria is met, the lease is classified as a capital lease by the lessee. For the lessor, the lease is a capital lease if, in addition to one of the general criteria, both of the revenue recognition criteria are met:

- *Collection* of the minimum lease payments is reasonably assured.
- The *lessor* has substantially completed its obligations to the lessee as of the date of the lease signing; no significant work remains to be done.

⑤ Properly account for both capital and operating leases from the standpoint of the lessee (asset user).

An operating lease is accounted for as a rental, with the lease payment amount being recognized as rent expense. With a capital lease, an asset and a liability are recognized on the lease-signing date. The asset is subsequently amortized over the lease term or, if the ownership transfer or bargain purchase option criteria are met, over the economic life of the asset. The lease payments are recorded as reductions in the balance of the lease liability, with a part of the payment being classified as interest expense.

⑥ Properly account for both capital and operating leases from the standpoint of the lessor (asset owner).

An operating lease is accounted for as a rental, with the lease payment amount being recognized as rent revenue. The lessor continues to depreciate the leased asset.

For a lessor, there are two types of capital leases: direct financing leases and sales-type leases. With a direct financing lease, a lease receivable is recognized on the lease-signing date. Interest revenue on the receivable balance is recognized during the lease term. With a sales-type lease, in addition to interest revenue over the life of the lease, a profit is recognized on the lease-signing date equal to the difference between the fair value of the leased asset and its cost.

With operating leases and direct financing leases, initial direct costs are capitalized and amortized over the lease term. With a sales-type lease, initial direct costs are immediately recognized as a reduction in the sale profit.

⑦ Prepare and interpret the lease disclosures required of both lessors and lessees.

Required disclosures for lessees include the following:

- Gross amount and accumulated amortization associated with assets leased under capital leases
- Rental expense associated with operating leases
- Schedule of future minimum lease payments for both capital and operating leases

Required disclosures for lessors include the following:

- Schedule of future minimum lease payments to be received for both capital and operating leases
- Cost and accumulated depreciation of assets leased to others under operating leases

⑧ Compare the treatment of accounting for leases in the United States with the requirements of International Accounting Standards.

IAS 17 does not include specific lease classification criteria; instead, it states that a capital lease is "a lease that transfers substantially all the risks and rewards incident to ownership of an asset." A proposal is now circulating internationally that suggests that all leases longer than one year should be capitalized.

EXPANDED MATERIAL

⑨ Record a sale-leaseback transaction for both a seller-lessee and a purchaser-lessor.

A sale-leaseback is a transaction in which one party sells an asset to another, and then the first party immediately leases the asset back and continues to use it. Apart from a couple of exceptions, any gain realized on a sale-leaseback by the seller-lessee is deferred and amortized over the life of the lease. A loss on the sale is recognized immediately.

FASB-IASB CODIFICATION SUMMARY

Topic	FASB Accounting Standards Codification	Original FASB Standard	Corresponding IASB Standard	Differences between U.S. GAAP and IFRS
Lease classification criteria	Section 840-10-25 par. 1	SFAS No. 13 par. 7	IAS 17 par. 8-10	In substance, the standards are the same. IFRS provides less detail.
Lease discount rate (for lessees)	Section 840-10-25 par. 31	SFAS No. 13 par. 7	IAS 17 par. 20	In IFRS, no explicit mention is made of using the lower of the implicit rate or the incremental borrowing rate. Instead, the implicit rate is to be used if known.
Revenue recognition criteria (for lessor)	Section 840-10-25 par. 42	SFAS No. 13 par. 8	IAS 17 par. 42	Substantially the same. Rather than the two explicit criteria, IFRS merely says that a sale in a sales-type lease is recognized "in accordance with the policy followed by the entity for outright sales."
Initial direct costs (for lessors)	Section 840-20-35 par. 2 Section 840-30-35 par. 23 Section 840-30-25 par. 6	SFAS No. 13 par. 19 SFAS No. 13 par. 18 SFAS No. 13 par. 17	IAS 17 par. 38, 42	No apparent differences
Sale-leaseback accounting	Section 840-40-25 par. 3 Section 840-40-35 par. 1	SFAS No. 13 par. 7	IAS 17 par. 58-63	No apparent differences

KEY TERMS

Bargain purchase option 15-7
Bargain renewal option 15-7
Direct financing leases 15-23
Executory costs 15-8
Guaranteed residual value 15-7
Implicit interest rate 15-8
Incremental borrowing rate 15-9
Initial direct costs 15-23
Lease 15-2
Lease term 15-7
Lessee 15-2
Lessor 15-2
Minimum lease payments 15-8
Noncancellable 15-6
Sales-type leases 15-23
Unguaranteed residual value 15-8

EXPANDED MATERIAL

Sale-leaseback 15-38

Tutorial Activities

Tutorial Activities with author-written, content-specific feedback, available on *CengageNOW for Stice & Stice*.

QUESTIONS

1. What are the principal advantages to a lessee in leasing rather than purchasing property?
2. What are the principal advantages to a lessor in leasing rather than selling property?
3. Conceptually, what is the difference between a capital lease and an operating lease?
4. What is a bargain purchase option?
5. How is the lease term measured?
6. (a) What discount rate is used to determine the present value of a lease by the lessee?
   (b) By the lessor?

7. What criteria must be met before a lease can be properly accounted for as a capital lease on the books of the lessee?
8. In determining the classification of a lease, a lessor uses the criteria of the lessee plus two additional criteria. What are these additional criteria, and why are they included in the classification of leases by lessors?
9. What is the basic difference between an operating lease and a capital lease from the viewpoint of the lessee?
10. If an operating lease requires the payment of uneven rental amounts over its life, how should the lessee recognize rental expense?
11. What amount should be recorded as an asset and a liability for capital leases on the books of the lessee?
12. Why do asset and liability balances for capital leases usually differ after the first year?
13. A capitalized lease should be amortized in accordance with the lessee's normal depreciation policy. What time period should be used for lease amortization?
14. The use of the capital lease method for a given lease will always result in a lower net income than the operating lease method. Do you agree? Explain fully.
15. (a) How does a capital lease for equipment affect the lessee's statement of cash flows?
    (b) How would the treatment on the statement of cash flows differ if the contract was identified as a purchase of equipment with a down payment and a long-term note payable for the balance?
16. Distinguish a sales-type lease from a direct financing lease.
17. Unguaranteed residual values accrue to the lessor at the expiration of the lease. How are these values treated in a sales-type lease?
18. Under what circumstances are the minimum lease payments for the lessee different from those of the lessor?
19. Why is the principal portion of a lease receipt of a financing lease treated as an investment inflow on the lessor's books while the principal portion of a lease payment is treated as a financial cash outflow on the lessee's books?
20. Describe the specific lease disclosure requirements for lessees.
21. What disclosures are required by the FASB for lessors under sales-type and direct financing leases?
22. How does the lease classification standard in *IAS 17* differ from that in FASB ASC Topic 840?
23. What lease accounting proposal has been circulating among the members of the international accounting community?

EXPANDED MATERIAL

24. When should the profit or loss be recognized by the seller-lessee in a sale-leaseback arrangement?

PRACTICE EXERCISES

Practice 15-1
Present Value of Minimum Payments
A lease involves payments of $10,000 per year for 20 years. The payments are made at the end of each year. The lease does *not* involve a guaranteed residual value. The appropriate interest rate is 7% compounded annually. Compute the present value of the minimum payments.

Practice 15-2
Present Value of Minimum Payments
A lease involves payments of $1,000 per month for two years. The payments are made at the end of each month. The lease also involves a guaranteed residual value of $10,000 to be paid at the end of the two-year period. The appropriate interest rate is 12% compounded monthly. Compute the present value of the minimum payments.

Practice 15-3
Computation of Payments
The lessor is computing the appropriate monthly lease payment. The fair value of the leased asset is $75,000. The guaranteed residual value at the end of the lease term is $12,000. The appropriate interest rate is 12% compounded monthly. The lease term is 36 months, and the lease payments occur at the end of each month. What is the appropriate amount of the monthly payment?

Practice 15-4
Computation of Implicit Interest Rate
A lease involves payments of $1,000 per month for five years. The payments are made at the end of each month. The lease also involves a guaranteed residual value of $10,000 to be paid at the end of the five-year period. The fair value of the leased asset is $35,000. Compute the interest rate implicit in the lease.

Practice 15-5
Incremental Borrowing Rate and Implicit Interest Rate
A lease involves payments of $8,000 per month for four years. The payments are made at the end of each month. The lease also involves a guaranteed residual value of $25,000 to be paid at the end of the four-year period. Compute the present value of the minimum payments using (1) the rate implicit in the lease of 9% compounded monthly and (2) the lessee's incremental borrowing rate of 12% compounded monthly.

Practice 15-6
Lease Criteria
The lessor leased equipment to the lessee. The fair value of the equipment is $246,000. Lease payments are $35,000 per year, payable at the *end* of the year, for 10 years. The interest rate implicit in the lease is 9%. At the end of 10 years, the lessor will repossess the equipment. The lease does *not* include a bargain purchase option, and the equipment has a total estimated useful life of 15 years. Is the lease an operating lease or a capital lease? Explain.

Practice 15-7
Journal Entries for an Operating Lease—Lessee
On January 1, the lessee company signed an operating lease contract. The lease contract calls for $3,000 payments at the end of each year for 10 years. The rate implicit in the lease is 10%. Make the journal entries necessary on the books of the lessee company (1) on the lease-signing date and (2) to record the first lease payment.

Practice 15-8
Operating Lease with Varying Payments—Lessee
The company is a lessee and signed a three-year operating lease that calls for a payment of $10,000 at the end of the first year and payments of $40,000 at the end of each year for the second and third years. Make the journal entries necessary to record the lease payments at the end of each of the three years.

Practice 15-9
Journal Entries for a Capital Lease—Lessee
Refer to Practice 15-7. Assume that the lease is to be accounted for as a capital lease. Also assume that the leased asset is to be amortized over the 12-year asset life rather than the 10-year lease term. Make the journal entries necessary on the books of the lessee company (1) on the lease-signing date and (2) at the end of the first year, including the recording of the first lease payment.

Practice 15-10
Accounting for a Bargain Purchase Option—Lessee
A lease involves payments of $10,000 per year for six years. The payments are made at the end of each year. The lease involves a bargain purchase option of $6,000 to be exercised at the end of the six-year period. The total economic life of the leased asset is nine years. The interest rate implicit in the lease is 12% compounded annually. Make the journal entries necessary on the books of the lessee company (1) on the lease-signing date and (2) at the end of the first year, including the recording of the first lease payment.

Practice 15-11
Purchasing a Leased Asset during the Lease Term—Lessee
On December 31, the company, a lessee, purchased some machinery that it had been leasing under a capital lease arrangement. The leased asset and lease liability were originally recorded at $500,000. At the time of the purchase, the accumulated amortization on the leased asset was $200,000, and the remaining balance of the lease liability was $325,000. The leased asset was purchased for $360,000 cash. Make the necessary journal entry on the books of the lessee.

Practice 15-12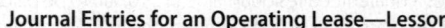
Leases on a Statement of Cash Flows—Lessee
Refer to Practice 15-7. Net income for the year was $10,000. Except for lease-related items, there were no changes in current operating assets or liabilities during the year; no purchases or sales of property, plant, or equipment; and no dividends paid, stock issued, or loans obtained or repaid. Prepare a complete statement of cash flows using the indirect method of reporting operating cash flow assuming that the lease is accounted for as (1) an operating lease (net income was $10,000) and (2) a capital lease (net income was $9,621). (*Note*: The capital lease entries for the year are made in Practice 15-9.)

Practice 15-13
Journal Entries for an Operating Lease—Lessor
On January 1, the lessor company purchased a piece of equipment for $24,000. The equipment has an expected life of four years with zero salvage value. The lessor company immediately leased the equipment

under an operating lease agreement. The lease calls for the lessor company to receive lease payments of $6,800 per year to be received at the beginning of the year. Make the journal entries necessary on the books of the lessor company to record (1) the purchase of the equipment for cash, (2) the lease signing (including receipt of the first lease payment), and (3) depreciation of the leased equipment.

Practice 15-14

Journal Entries for a Direct Financing Lease—Lessor

Refer to Practice 15-13. Assume that the lease is accounted for as a direct financing lease instead of as an operating lease. The interest rate implicit in the lease is 9%. Make the journal entries necessary on the lessor's books to record (1) the signing of the lease, (2) the receipt of the initial $6,800 lease payment on the lease-signing date, and (3) the recognition of interest revenue at the end of the first year.

Practice 15-15

Direct Financing Lease with a Residual Value

On January 1, the lessor company purchased a piece of equipment for $50,000. The equipment has an expected salvage value of $1,987; this amount is *not* guaranteed. The lessor company immediately leased the equipment under a direct financing lease agreement. The lease calls for the lessor company to receive annual lease payments of $7,800 per year for 10 years, to be received at the beginning of the year; at the end of 10 years, the equipment is returned to the lessor company. The interest rate implicit in the lease is 12%. Make the journal entries necessary on the lessor's books to record (1) the signing of the lease, (2) the receipt of the initial $7,800 lease payment on the lease-signing date, (3) the recognition of interest revenue at the end of the first year, and (4) the journal entry at the end of 10 years to record the final interest revenue accrual and the recovery of the equipment, assuming that the salvage value was equal to its estimated amount. (*Hint:* Interest revenue in the 10th year is $213.)

Practice 15-16

Journal Entries for a Sales-Type Lease—Lessor

On January 1, the lessor company purchased a piece of equipment for $7,000 as inventory. The lessor company immediately leased the equipment under a sales-type lease agreement; the cash selling price of the equipment is $10,000. The lease calls for the lessor company to receive five annual lease payments of $2,600 per year, to be received at the beginning of the year. The interest rate implicit in the lease is 15%. Make the journal entries necessary on the books of the lessor company to record (1) the lease signing (including receipt of the first lease payment) and (2) the recognition of interest revenue at the end of the first year.

Practice 15-17

Sales-Type Lease with a Bargain Purchase Option

On January 1, the lessor company purchased a piece of equipment for $6,000 as inventory. The lessor company immediately leased the equipment under a sales-type lease agreement. The lease calls for the lessor company to receive five annual lease payments of $2,500 per year, to be received at the beginning of the year. In addition to the five annual payments of $2,500 at the beginning of each year, the lessor is to receive a bargain purchase option amount of $500 at the end of five years. The interest rate implicit in the lease is 12%. Make the journal entries necessary on the books of the lessor company to record (1) the lease signing (including receipt of the first lease payment) and (2) the recognition of interest revenue at the end of the first year.

Practice 15-18

Sales-Type Lease with an Unguaranteed Residual Value

Refer to Practice 15-17. Assume the same facts except that the $500 bargain purchase option is instead a $500 *unguaranteed* residual value. Make the journal entries necessary on the books of the lessor company to record (1) the lease signing (including receipt of the first lease payment) and (2) the recognition of interest revenue at the end of the first year.

Practice 15-19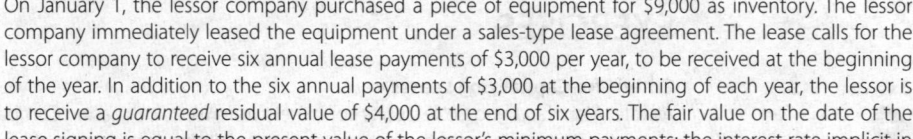

Third-Party Guarantees of Residual Value

On January 1, the lessor company purchased a piece of equipment for $9,000 as inventory. The lessor company immediately leased the equipment under a sales-type lease agreement. The lease calls for the lessor company to receive six annual lease payments of $3,000 per year, to be received at the beginning of the year. In addition to the six annual payments of $3,000 at the beginning of each year, the lessor is to receive a *guaranteed* residual value of $4,000 at the end of six years. The fair value on the date of the lease signing is equal to the present value of the lessor's minimum payments; the interest rate implicit in the lease is 11%. The equipment has a useful life of 10 years, there is no bargain purchase option, and the title does not transfer at the end of the lease term. Also, the residual value is guaranteed by a third-party insurance company, not by the lessee company. Make the journal entries necessary to record the lease signing, including the first lease payment, (1) on the books of the *lessor* company and (2) on the books of the *lessee* company.

Practice 15-20

Selling a Leased Asset During the Lease Term—Lessor

On December 31 of Year 1, the company, a lessor, sold some machinery that it had been leasing under a direct financing lease arrangement. On January 1 of Year 1 (after receipt of the lease payment for the year), the following account balances were associated with the lease:

Gross Lease Payments Receivable	$117,000
Unearned Interest Revenue	20,000
Present Value of Lease Payments Receivable	$ 97,000

The interest rate implicit in the lease is 10%. The leased machinery is sold for $65,000 cash. Make the journal entry or entries necessary on the books of the lessor to record this sale. (*Note*: Don't forget any necessary year-end adjustment.)

Practice 15-21

Leases on a Statement of Cash Flows—Lessor

On January 1, the lessor company purchased some equipment (for cash) that the company then immediately leased. The lease contract calls for the receipt of $5,000 payments at the end of each year for eight years. The residual value of the equipment at the end of the eight-year lease term is expected to be $6,500. The rate implicit in the lease is 13%. Except for lease-related items, there were no changes in current operating assets or liabilities during the year; no purchases or sales of property, plant, or equipment; and no dividends paid, stock issued, or loans obtained or repaid. The equipment has a total useful life of 12 years with no salvage value. Prepare a complete statement of cash flows for the lessor using the indirect method of reporting operating cash flow assuming that the lease is accounted for as (1) an operating lease (net income was $30,000) and (2) a direct financing lease (net income was $30,640).

Practice 15-22

Debt-to-Equity Ratio Adjusted for Operating Leases

As of December 31, the company has total assets of $10,000 and total liabilities of $4,000. Future minimum payments on operating leases for which the company is the lessee are $600 per year for the next 15 years. Assume that the lease payments occur at the end of the year. The appropriate discount rate is 8%. Calculate (1) the company's debt-to-equity ratio using its reported numbers and (2) the company's debt-to-equity ratio assuming that the operating leases were accounted for as capital leases.

E X P A N D E D   M A T E R I A L

Practice 15-23

Sale-Leaseback Transactions—Lessor and Lessee

On January 1, Seller-Lessee sold a building to Buyer-Lessor for $200,000. The building had originally cost Seller-Lessee $230,000 and had accumulated depreciation of $70,000 on the date of the sale. On the day of the sale, Seller-Lessee leased the building back from Buyer-Lessor. The lease calls for annual lease payments of $23,750 at the end of each year for the next 25 years. The interest rate implicit in the lease is 11%. On January 1, the building had a fair value of $200,000 and a remaining useful life of 25 years (with zero expected salvage value). Make all lease-related journal entries necessary for the year on the books of (1) Seller-Lessee and (2) Buyer-Lessor.

EXERCISES

Exercise 15-24

Criteria for Capitalizing Leases

Atwater Manufacturing Co. leases its equipment from Westside Leasing Company. In each of the following cases, assuming none of the other criteria for capitalizing leases are met, determine whether the lease would be a capital lease or an operating lease under FASB ASC Topic 840. Your decision is to be based only on the terms presented, considering each case independently of the others.

(a) At the end of the lease term, the market value of the equipment is expected to be $20,000. Atwater has the option of purchasing it for $5,000.

(b) The fair value of the equipment is $75,000. The present value of the lease payments is $67,000 (excluding any executory costs).

(c) Ownership of the property automatically passes to Atwater at the end of the lease term.

(d) The economic life of the equipment is 12 years. The lease term is eight years.

(e) The lease requires payments of $9,000 per year in advance plus executory costs of $500 per year. The lease period is three years, and Atwater's incremental borrowing rate is 12%. The fair value of the equipment is $28,000.

(f) The lease requires payments of $6,000 per year in advance, which includes executory costs of $500 per year. The lease period is three years, and Atwater's incremental borrowing rate is 10%. The fair value of the equipment is $16,650.

Exercise 15-25

Entries for Lease—Lessor and Lessee

Doxey Company purchased a machine on January 1, 2015, for $1,250,000 for the express purpose of leasing it. The machine was expected to have a nine-year life from January 1, 2015, to have no salvage value, and to be depreciated on a straight-line basis. On March 1, 2015, Doxey leased the machine to Mondale Company for $300,000 a year for a four-year period ending February 28, 2019. The appropriate interest rate is 12% compounded annually. Doxey paid a total of $15,000 for maintenance, insurance, and property taxes on the machine for the year ended December 31, 2015. Mondale paid $300,000 to Doxey on March 1, 2015. Doxey retains title to the property and plans to lease it to someone else after the four-year lease period. Give all the 2015 entries relating to the lease on (1) Doxey Company's books and (2) Mondale Company's books. Assume both sets of books are maintained on the calendar-year basis.

Exercise 15-26

Entries for Operating Lease—Lessee

Mighty Inc. leases some of the equipment it uses. The lease term is five years, and the lease payments are to be made in advance as shown in the following schedule.

January 1, 2015	$ 60,000
January 1, 2016	60,000
January 1, 2017	90,000
January 1, 2018	110,000
January 1, 2019	140,000
Total	$460,000

The equipment is to be used evenly over the five-year period. For each of the five years, give the entry that should be made at the time the lease payment is made to allocate the proper share of rent expense to each period. The lease is classified as an operating lease by Mighty Inc.

Exercise 15-27

Entries for Lease—Lessee

Bingham Smelting Company entered into a 15-year noncancellable lease beginning January 1, 2015, for equipment to use in its smelting operations. The term of the lease is the same as the expected economic life of the equipment. Bingham uses straight-line depreciation for all plant assets. The provisions of the lease call for annual payments of $290,000 in advance plus $20,000 per year to cover executory costs, such as taxes and insurance, for the 15-year period of the lease. At the end of the 15 years, the equipment is expected to be scrapped. The incremental borrowing rate of Bingham is 10%. The lessor's computed implicit interest rate is unknown to Bingham.

Record the lease on the books of Bingham and give all the entries necessary to record the lease for its first year plus the entry to record the second lease payment on December 31, 2015. (*Note:* Round to the nearest dollar.)

Exercise 15-28

Entries for Lease—Lessee

On January 2, 2015, Jacques Company entered into a noncancellable lease for new equipment. The equipment was built to Jacques Company's specifications and is in an area in which rental to another lessee would be difficult. Rental payments are $300,000 a year for 10 years, payable in advance. The equipment has an estimated economic life of 20 years. The taxes, maintenance, and insurance are to be paid directly by Jacques Company, and the title to the equipment is to be transferred to Jacques at the end of the lease term. Assume the cost of borrowing funds for this type of an asset by Jacques Company is 12%.

1. Give the entry on Jacques' books that should be made at the inception of the lease.
2. Give the entries for 2015 and 2016, assuming the second payment and subsequent payments are made on December 31 and assuming double-declining-balance amortization.

Exercise 15-29

Schedule of Lease Payments

Stagg Construction Co. is leasing equipment from Cloud Inc. The lease calls for payments of $50,000 a year plus $3,000 a year executory costs for five years. The first payment is due on January 1, 2015, when the lease is signed, with the other four payments coming due on December 31 of each year. Stagg has also been given the option of purchasing the equipment at the end of the lease at a bargain price of $95,000. Stagg has an incremental borrowing rate of 9%, the same as the implicit interest rate of Cloud. Stagg has hired you as an accountant and asks you to prepare a schedule showing how the lease payments will be split between principal and interest and the outstanding lease liability balance over the life of the lease.

Exercise 15-30

Entry for Purchase by Lessee

Cordon Enterprise Company leases many of its assets and capitalizes most of the leased assets. At December 31, the company had the following balances on its books in relation to a piece of specialized equipment:

Leased Equipment	$80,000
Accumulated Amortization—Leased Equipment	49,300
Obligations under Capital Leases	26,000

Amortization has been recorded up to the end of the year, and no accrued interest is involved. At December 31, Cordon decided to purchase the equipment for $32,000 and paid cash to complete the purchase. Give the entry required on Cordon's books to record the purchase.

Exercise 15-31

Entry for Sale by Lessor

Smithston Corporation leased equipment to Dayplanner Co. on January 1, 2015. The terms of the lease called for annual lease payments to be made at the first of each year. Smithston's implicit interest rate for the transaction is 12%. On July 1, 2017, Dayplanner purchased the equipment and paid $58,000 to complete the transaction. After the 2017 payment was made, the following balance relating to the leased equipment was on the books of Smithston as of January 1, 2017:

Lease Payments Receivable (net)	$75,750

Prepare the journal entry that should be made by Smithston to record the sale, including the accrual of interest through July 1.

Exercise 15-32
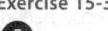

Computation of Implicit Interest Rate

Moor Leasing leases equipment to Wong Manufacturing. The fair value of the equipment is $527,169. Lease payments, excluding executory costs, are $60,000 per year, payable in advance, for 15 years. What is the implicit rate of interest Moor Leasing should use to record this capital lease on its books?

Exercise 15-33

Direct Financing Lease—Lessor

Deseret Finance Company purchased a printing press to lease to Quality Printing Company. The lease was structured so that at the end of the lease period of 15 years, Quality would own the printing press. Lease payments required in this lease were $190,000 (excluding executory costs) per year, payable in advance. The cost of the press to Deseret was $1,589,673, which is also its fair value at the time of the lease.

1. Why is this a direct financing lease?
2. Give the entry to record the lease transaction on the books of Deseret Finance Company.
3. Give the entry at the end of the first year on Deseret Finance Company's books to recognize interest revenue.

Exercise 15-34

Direct Financing Lease with Residual Value

Massachusetts Casualty Insurance Company decides to enter the leasing business. It acquires a specialized packaging machine for $300,000 cash and leases it for a period of six years, after which the machine is to be returned to the insurance company for disposition. The expected unguaranteed residual value of the machine is $20,000. The lease terms are arranged so that a return of 12% is earned by the insurance company.

1. Calculate the annual lease payment, payable in advance, required to yield the desired return.
2. Prepare entries for the lessor for the first year of the lease, assuming the machine is acquired and the lease is recorded on January 1, 2015. The first lease payment is made on January 1, 2015, and subsequent payments are made each December 31.
3. Assuming that the packaging machine is sold by Massachusetts to the lessee at the end of the six years for $29,000, give the required entry to record the sale.

Exercise 15-35

Table for Direct Financing Lease—Lessor

Wenville Savings and Loan Company acquires a piece of specialized manufacturing equipment for $2,000,000 that it leases on January 1, 2015, to a local factory for $466,646 per year, payable in advance. Because of rapid technological developments, the equipment is expected to be replaced after four years. It is expected that the machine will have a residual value of $450,000 to Wenville Savings at the end of the lease term. The implicit rate of interest in the lease is 8%.

1. Prepare a four-year table for Wenville Savings and Loan similar to Exhibit 15-8.
2. How would the table differ if the local factory guaranteed the residual value to Wenville?

Exercise 15-36

Capital Lease with Guaranteed Residual Value—Lessee

Mario Automobile Company leases automobiles under the following terms. A three-year lease agreement is signed in which the lessor receives annual rental of $4,000 (in advance). At the end of the three years, the lessee agrees to make up any deficiency in residual value below $3,500. The cash price of the automobile is $13,251. The implicit interest rate is 12%, which is known to the lessee, and the lessee's incremental borrowing rate is 14%. The lessee estimates the residual value at the end of three years to be $4,200 and depreciates its automobiles on a straight-line basis.

1. Give the entries on the lessee's books required in the first year of the lease, including the second payment on April 30, 2016. Assume the lease begins May 1, 2015, the beginning of the lessee's fiscal year.
2. What balances relative to the lease would appear on the lessee's balance sheet at the end of Year 3?
3. Assume that at the end of the three years, the automobile is sold by the lessee (with the permission of the lessor) for $3,800. Prepare the entries to record the sale and settlement with the lessor.

Exercise 15-37

Sales-Type Lease—Lessor

Salcedo Co. leased equipment to Erickson Inc. on April 1, 2015. The lease, appropriately recorded as a sale by Salcedo, is for an eight-year period ending March 31, 2023. The first of eight equal annual payments of $175,000 (excluding executory costs) was made on April 1, 2015. The cost of the equipment to Salcedo is $940,000. The equipment has an estimated useful life of eight years with no residual value expected. Salcedo uses straight-line depreciation and takes a full year's depreciation in the year of purchase. The cash selling price of the equipment is $1,026,900.

1. Give the entry required to record the lease on Salcedo's books.
2. How much interest revenue will Salcedo recognize in 2015?

Exercise 15-38

Sales-Type Lease—Lessor

Loco Leasing and Manufacturing Company uses leases as a means of financing sales of its equipment. Loco leased a machine to Potomac Construction for $15,000 per year, payable in advance, for a 10-year period. The cost of the machine to Loco was $86,000. The fair value at the date of the lease was $100,000. Assume a residual value of $0 at the end of the lease.

1. Give the entry required to record the lease on Loco's books.
2. How much profit will Loco recognize initially on the lease, excluding any interest revenue?
3. How much interest revenue would be recognized in the first year?

Exercise 15-39

Effect of Lease on Reported Income—Lessee and Lessor

On February 20, 2015, Hudson Inc. purchased a machine for $2,100,000 for the purpose of leasing it. The machine is expected to have a 12-year life, has no residual value, and is depreciated on the straight-line basis to the nearest month. The machine was leased to Donah Company on March 1, 2015, for a five-year period at a monthly rental of $34,000. Assume that the lease payments are made at the end of the month and that the appropriate interest rate is 11% compounded monthly. There is no provision for the renewal of the lease or purchase of the machine by the lessee at the expiration of the lease term. Hudson paid $72,000 of commissions associated with negotiating the lease in February 2015.

1. What expense should Donah record as a result of the lease transaction for the year ended December 31, 2015?
2. What income or loss before income taxes should Hudson record as a result of the lease transaction for the year ended December 31, 2015?

Exercise 15-40

Cash Flow Treatment of Capital Leases—Lessee

The following information relates to a capital lease between Glass Electric Co. (lessee) and Williams Manufacturing Inc. (lessor). The lease term began on January 1, 2015. Glass capitalized the 10-year lease and recorded $150,000 as an asset. The annual lease payment, made at the beginning of each year, is $22,193 at 10% interest. Glass uses the straight-line method to depreciate its owned assets. How will this lease be reported on Glass' statement of cash flows for 2015 if the second lease payment is made on December 31, 2015, and Glass uses the indirect method?

Exercise 15-41

Cash Flow Treatment of Capital Leases—Lessor

On January 1, 2015, Warr Delivery Company purchased some equipment for $64,768 in cash. Warr Delivery immediately leased the equipment; Warr Delivery is the lessor. The lease contract calls for the receipt of $14,000 payments at the end of each year for five years. The residual value of the equipment at the end of the five-year lease term is expected to be $15,868. The rate implicit in the lease is 9%. Except for lease-related items, there were no changes in current operating assets or liabilities during the year; no purchases or sales of property, plant, or equipment; and no dividends paid, stock issued, or loans obtained or repaid. The equipment has a total useful life of eight years with no salvage value. Prepare a complete statement of cash flows for Warr Delivery for 2015 using the indirect method of reporting operating cash flow assuming that the lease is accounted for as (1) an operating lease (net income was $70,000), (2) a direct financing lease (net income was $69,925), and (3) a sales-type lease (net income was $69,925; for comparability, make the unreasonable assumption that sales and cost of goods sold are the same amount).

Exercise 15-42

Lease Disclosures—Lessee

The following lease information was obtained by a staff auditor for a client, Kroller Inc., at December 31, 2015. Indicate how this information should be presented in Kroller's two-year comparative financial statements. Include any notes to the statements required to meet generally accepted accounting principles. Lease payments are made on December 31 of each year.

Leased building; minimum lease payments per year; 10 years remaining life on December 31, 2014........	$ 45,000
Executory costs per year	2,000
Capitalized lease value, 12% interest	343,269
Accumulated amortization of leased building at December 31, 2015	114,423
Amortization expense for 2015........	22,885
Obligations under capital leases; balance at December 31, 2015........	239,770
Obligations under capital leases; balance at December 31, 2014........	254,259

Exercise 15-43

Lease Disclosure on the Financial Statements

Acme Enterprises leased equipment from Monument Equipment Co. on January 1, 2015. The terms of the lease agreement require five annual payments of $20,000 with the first payment being made on January 1, 2015, and each subsequent payment being made on December 31 of each year. Because the equipment has an expected useful life of five years, the lease qualifies as a capital lease for Acme. Acme does not know Monument's implicit interest rate and therefore uses its own incremental borrowing rate of 12% to calculate the present value of the lease payments. Acme uses the sum-of-the-years'-digits method for amortizing leased assets. The expected salvage value of the leased asset is $0.

1. Prepare a schedule that shows the lease obligation balance in each year of the lease.
2. Prepare an asset amortization schedule for the leased asset.
3. Compare the amount shown on the year-end balance sheet for the leased asset with that of the lease obligation for the years 2015 through 2019 and explain why the amounts differ.

Exercise 15-44

Impact of Capitalizing the Value of Operating Leases

The following information comes from the 2015 financial statements of Jessica Hatch Company:

Total liabilities........	$250,000
Total stockholders' equity	110,000

In addition, Jessica Hatch has a large number of operating leases. The future payments on these operating leases are disclosed in the notes to the financial statements as follows:

Year	Payment
2016	$ 30,000
2017	30,000
2018	30,000
2019	30,000
2020	30,000
Thereafter........	330,000

All of these lease payments occur at the end of the year. The incremental borrowing rate of Jessica Hatch Company is 10%. This is also the implicit rate in all of the leases that Jessica Hatch signs.

1. Compute the debt-to-equity ratio (total liabilities/total equity).
2. Compute the debt ratio (total liabilities/total assets).
3. Assuming that Jessica Hatch's operating leases are accounted for as capital leases, compute the debt-to-equity ratio.
4. Assuming that Jessica Hatch's operating leases are accounted for as capital leases, compute the debt ratio.

EXPANDED MATERIAL

Exercise 15-45

Sale-Leaseback Accounting

On July 1, 2015, Flashlight Corporation sold equipment it had recently purchased to an unaffiliated company for $480,000. The equipment had a book value on Flashlight's books of $390,000 and a remaining life of six years. On that same day, Flashlight leased back the equipment at $95,000 per year, payable in advance, for a six-year period. Flashlight's incremental borrowing rate is 11%, and it does not know the lessor's implicit interest rate. What entries are required for Flashlight to record the transactions involving the equipment during the first full year, assuming the second lease payment is made on June 30, 2016? Ignore consideration of the lessee's fiscal year. The lessee uses the double-declining-balance method of depreciation for similar assets it owns outright.

Exercise 15-46

Sale-Leaseback Transaction

Smalltown Grocers sold its plant facilities to United Grocers, Inc., for $813,487. United immediately leased the building back to Smalltown for 20 annual payments of $96,000 with the first payment due immediately. The terms of the lease agreement provide a bargain purchase option wherein Smalltown has the option of purchasing the building at the end of the lease term for $100,000. If United's implicit interest rate is 12% (lower than Smalltown's incremental borrowing rate), prepare the entries that should be made by United to record the purchase of the building and the receipt of the first two payments from Smalltown Grocers, assuming this leasing arrangement qualifies as a capital lease for United.

P3

Additional Activities of a Business

CHAPTER 16

Income Taxes

Learning Objectives

1. Understand the concept of deferred taxes and the distinction between permanent and temporary differences.

2. Compute the amount of deferred tax liabilities and assets including the use of a valuation allowance and the uncertainty of tax positions.

3. Explain the provisions of tax loss carrybacks and carryforwards, and be able to account for these provisions.

4. Schedule future tax rates, and determine the effect on deferred tax assets and liabilities.

5. Determine appropriate financial statement presentation and disclosure associated with deferred tax assets and liabilities.

6. Comply with income tax disclosure requirements associated with the statement of cash flows.

7. Describe how, with respect to deferred income taxes, International Accounting Standards have converged toward the U.S. treatment.

Accounting for deferred taxes is both complicated and controversial. You will learn about a few of the complications in this chapter. The controversy has stemmed from the FASB's attempts to use accounting theory to define exactly what the phrase "income tax expense" means. Because of the idiosyncrasies of the income tax code, there are many cases in which income is earned this year but is not taxed until a future year; this gives rise to a deferred income tax liability equal to the amount of additional tax expected to be paid in the future based on business activities completed this year. Similarly, there are many cases in which a company can create a business expense this year but the tax code does not allow for the deduction of that expense until a future year; this gives rise to a deferred income tax asset equal to the expected future tax savings from business activities completed this year. "Income tax expense" for this year must reflect ALL of the tax consequences, both current and deferred, of business activities undertaken this year.

In February 1992, the FASB issued pre-Codification *Statement No. 109*, "Accounting for Income Taxes," in response to five years of complaints and controversy surrounding the standard it superseded, pre-Codification FASB *Statement No. 96*. *Statement No. 96* was so unpopular that some observers predicted it would result in an unraveling of public confidence in the FASB, with the possibility that the FASB would be replaced just as its two predecessor bodies, the Committee on Accounting Procedure (CAP) and the Accounting Principles Board (APB), had been. The two primary complaints against *Statement No. 96* were that it was overly complicated and that it severely restricted the recognition of deferred tax assets.

Issued in 1987, *Statement No. 96* mandated that the deferred tax amounts reported on the balance sheet should be valued using expected future tax rates. Previously, deferred tax items had been valued using tax rates in effect when the deferred taxes arose in past years. This accounting change, coupled with the fact that the Tax Reform Act of 1986 had lowered the maximum corporate tax rate from 46% to 34%, caused significant downward revisions in the reported amounts of deferred taxes. For a firm with a deferred tax liability, the combined result was a decrease in the reported liability (a debit) and the recognition of a corresponding one-time gain (a credit). The business press of the period was full of articles warning investors of the large cosmetic accounting gains that companies were expected to report.[1] General Electric adopted *Statement No. 96* in 1987; as a result, General Electric's finance subsidiary showed a gain of $518 million, increasing the subsidiary's net income by 106%. IBM adopted *Statement No. 96* in 1988 and showed a gain of $315 million. Exxon made the adoption in 1989 and increased net income by 18% with a $535 million gain.

In response to one of the major criticisms of *Statement No. 96*, *Statement No. 109*, as explained more fully in this chapter, allows the recognition of most deferred tax assets. Once again, the business press warned investors to beware of firms reporting one-time accounting gains because of the change in accounting for deferred taxes.[2] These gains come about because previously unrecorded deferred tax assets are recognized (a debit), along with a corresponding gain (a credit). For example, on September 30, 1992, IBM announced that it would report a $1.9 billion gain as a result of adopting *Statement No. 109*. Interestingly, this gain was used to partially offset a $2.1 billion write-off of buildings and equipment.[3]

1. Why was the release of pre-Codification FASB *Statement No. 96* in 1987 a dangerous event for the FASB?

2. Adoption of FASB *Statement No. 96* resulted in big one-time gains for many firms. What external event resulted in these gains?

3. How did adoption of pre-Codification *FASB Statement No. 109* result in big one-time gains for many firms?

Answers to these questions can be found on page 16-33.

This chapter begins with a discussion of the reasons for differences between financial reporting income and taxable income. This discussion leads into the topic of deferred taxes and how differences in the timing of the recognition of revenues and expenses for tax and financial reporting purposes cause differences between income tax payable and income tax expense for a period. Accounting for these deferred tax assets and liabilities comprises the bulk of this chapter. Additional topics covered include net operating loss carrybacks and carryforwards and their relationship to deferred taxes, the effect of deferred taxes on the statement of cash flows, common deferred tax items for large corporations, the accounting for uncertain tax positions, and the disclosure requirements associated with deferred taxes. We will also discuss how the international standards for deferred tax accounting have become more similar to U.S. GAAP over the past few years.

---

[1] For an example, see Lee Berton, "FASB Is Expected to Issue Rule Allowing Many Firms to Post Big, One-Time Gains," *The Wall Street Journal*, November 4, 1987, p. 4.
[2] See Mary Beth Grover, "Cosmetics," *Forbes*, March 30, 1992, p. 78.
[3] See Michael W. Miller and Laurence Hooper, "IBM Announces Write-Off for Total of $2.1 Billion," *The Wall Street Journal*, September 30, 1992, p. A3.

Deferred Income Taxes: An Overview

LO1 学习目标1
理解递延所得税的定义以及永久性差异与暂时性差异的区别。

taxable income
应税收入

 Understand the concept of deferred taxes and the distinction between permanent and temporary differences.

When taking introductory financial accounting courses, many students are surprised to learn that corporations in the United States compute two different income numbers: financial income for reporting to stockholders and taxable income for reporting to the Internal Revenue Service (IRS). The existence of these two "sets of books" seems unethical to some, illegal to others. However, the difference between the information needs of the stockholders and the efficient revenue collection needs of the government makes the computation of the two different income numbers essential. The different purposes of these reporting systems were summarized by the U.S. Supreme Court in the Thor Power Tool case (1979):

> The primary goal of financial accounting is to provide useful information to management, shareholders, creditors, and others properly interested; the major responsibility of the accountant is to protect these parties from being misled. The primary goal of the income tax system, in contrast, is the equitable collection of revenue.

In summary, U.S. corporations compute income in two different ways, and rightly so. The existence of these two different numbers that can each be called "income before taxes" makes it surprisingly difficult to define what is meant by "income tax expense" and to compute an appropriate balance sheet value for income tax liabilities and prepaid income tax assets. This accounting difficulty stems from two basic considerations:

1. How to account for revenues and expenses that have already been recognized and reported to shareholders in a company's financial statements but will not affect taxable income until subsequent years.
2. How to account for revenues and expenses that have already been reported to the IRS but will not be recognized in the financial statements until subsequent years.

Accounting for deferred income taxes focuses on temporary differences between financial accounting income and taxable income. For example, the income tax rules allow companies to deduct depreciation faster than is typically done for the financial accounting books. Over the life of the asset, the amount of depreciation is the same for both sets of books, but *temporarily*, there is a difference between the cumulative depreciation deduction reported in the tax books and the amount of cumulative depreciation expense recognized in the financial accounting books. It is this temporary difference that results in deferred income taxes. The accounting for deferred taxes is summarized in Exhibit 16-1.

Caution
Although the emphasis in this chapter is on accounting for federal income taxes, most states also assess a tax on income. The conceptual issues are applicable to both federal and state taxes. Often, state income tax laws are patterned after the federal law. Multinational companies are also often subject to foreign income taxation. Having multiple taxing jurisdictions complicates the establishment of income tax accounting standards and increases the materiality of income tax payments.

Stop & Think
This discussion mentions two sets of books, the financial accounting and the income tax records. Which ONE of the following is the most important third set of accounting records in a well-run business?

a) Managerial accounting records
b) State sales tax records
c) CEO astrological chart records
d) Corporate property tax records

Exhibit 16-1 | A Summary of Temporary Differences and Deferred Income Taxes

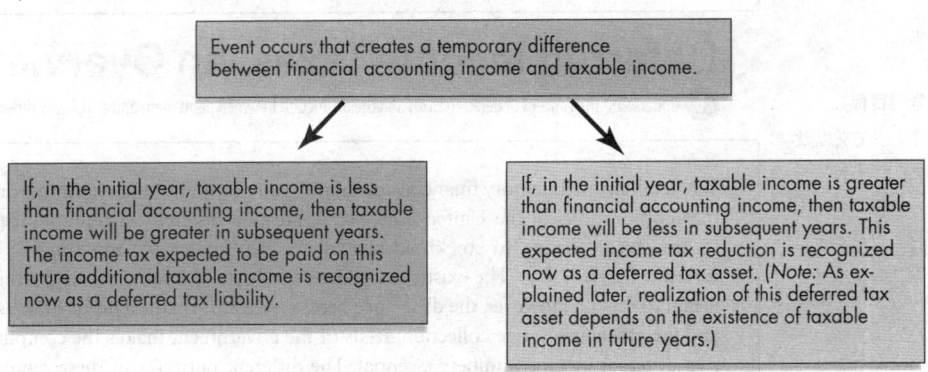

Event occurs that creates a temporary difference between financial accounting income and taxable income.

If, in the initial year, taxable income is less than financial accounting income, then taxable income will be greater in subsequent years. The income tax expected to be paid on this future additional taxable income is recognized now as a deferred tax liability.

If, in the initial year, taxable income is greater than financial accounting income, then taxable income will be less in subsequent years. This expected income tax reduction is recognized now as a deferred tax asset. (*Note:* As explained later, realization of this deferred tax asset depends on the existence of taxable income in future years.)

© Cengage Learning 2014

Two simple examples will be used to illustrate the accounting issues resulting from this difference between financial accounting income and taxable income.

Example 1. Simple Deferred Income Tax Liability

In 2015, Ibanez Company earned revenues of $30,000. Ibanez has no expenses other than income taxes. Assume that in this case, the income tax law specifies that income is taxed when received in cash and that Ibanez received $10,000 cash in 2015 and expects to receive $20,000 in 2016. The income tax rate is 40%, and we will assume for the moment that the tax rate is expected to remain the same into the foreseeable future.

The two amounts to be determined are total income tax liability at the end of the year and total income tax expense for the year. Obviously, the income tax liability is at least $4,000 because that is how much the IRS is expecting based on Ibanez's reported taxable income of $10,000. In addition, it would be misleading to the shareholders not to tell them of the expected tax to be paid on the additional $20,000 to be received in cash in 2016. Remember, this $20,000 in income has been reported to the shareholders because it was earned in 2015, but it has not yet been reported to the IRS. The expected tax on the $20,000 is $8,000 ($20,000 × 0.40) and is called a *deferred tax liability*. It is a liability because it requires a payment in the future (hence the word *deferred*) as a result of a past transaction (the past transaction is the earning of the income). This liability can be thought of as the expected income tax on income earned but not yet taxed. The journal entry to record all the tax-related information for Ibanez for 2015 is as follows:

很显然，与税务部门预期的一样，在应税收入10 000美元的基础上计算出的所得税负债至少是4 000美元。此外，不告知股东余下的20 000美元在2016年收到现金时需要支付的税金可能会形成误导。值得注意的是，20 000美元收入由于是2015年获取的，因此已经在财务报表中有所体现，但是未向税务部门报告。预期税费是8 000美元（20 000× 40%），称作递延所得税负债。

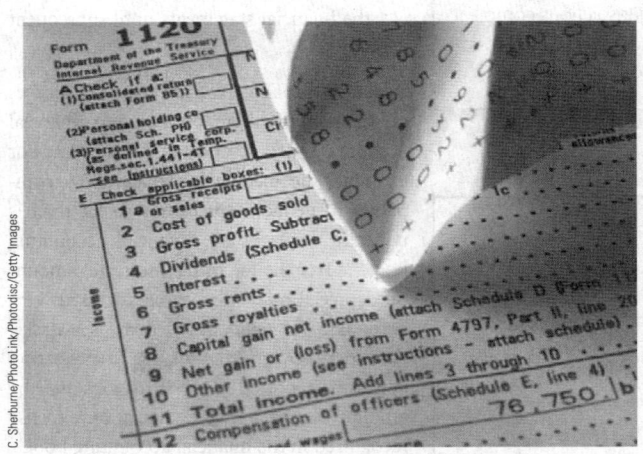

Corporations keep two "sets of books" to compute income—one for reporting financial income and the other for reporting taxable income to the IRS.

Income Tax Expense ($4,000 current year + $8,000 deferred)..............	12,000
Income Taxes Payable	4,000
Deferred Tax Liability	8,000

It is important to recognize the difference between the two recorded liabilities. Income taxes payable is an existing legal liability that the IRS fully expects to collect by March 15, 2016 (corporations pay

> **FYI**
>
> Although accounting standard-setting bodies have not expressed interest in abandoning deferred income tax accounting, many writers through the years have suggested that basing income tax expense on the actual tax payments is the most practical way of reporting income taxes. If this solution were to become the standard, there would be no need for a chapter on income taxes in an intermediate accounting text. This would undoubtedly please authors, faculty, and students alike.

taxes at different times than do individuals). Deferred tax liability is not an existing legal liability; as far as the IRS is concerned, it doesn't exist. However, because Ibanez knows that $20,000 of the revenues earned in 2015 will be taxed in 2016, recognition of the deferred tax liability is necessary to ensure that all expenses associated with 2015 revenues are reported in the 2015 income statement and that all obligations are reported on the December 31, 2015, balance sheet.

As can be seen from the income tax journal entries for 2015, total income tax expense of $12,000 is the sum of the current and deferred tax expenses. The 2015 income statement for Ibanez Company is as follows:

Revenues		$30,000
Income tax expense:		
Current	$4,000	
Deferred	8,000	12,000
Net income		$18,000

Some have argued that reported income tax expense should just be the amount currently payable according to IRS rules. This type of disclosure would lead to a rude surprise in 2016 for the Ibanez shareholders: Ibanez will owe $8,000 in income tax in 2016 even if no new revenues are generated in 2016.

Example 2. Simple Deferred Tax Asset

In 2015, its first year of operations, Gupta Company generated service revenues totaling $60,000, all taxable in 2015. Gupta Company offers a warranty on its service. No warranty claims were made in 2015, but Gupta estimates that in 2016 warranty costs of $10,000 will be incurred for claims relating to 2015 service revenues. The $10,000 estimated warranty expense is reported in the 2015 financial statements as required by GAAP. For tax purposes, however, assume that the IRS does not allow any tax deduction until the actual warranty services are performed. Also assume that the income tax rate is 40% and that Gupta Company had no expenses in 2015 other than warranty costs and income taxes.

Income taxes payable as of the end of 2015 is $24,000 ($60,000 × 0.40) because Gupta is required to report $60,000 in revenues to the IRS but is not allowed to take any warranty deduction until 2016. What about the $10,000 warranty deduction Gupta expects to take in 2016? Gupta can expect this deduction to lower the 2016 tax bill by $4,000 ($10,000 × 0.40). This $4,000 is called a *deferred tax asset* and represents the expected benefit of a tax deduction for an expense item that has already been incurred and reported to the shareholders but is not yet deductible according to IRS rules. In effect, Gupta is paying taxes this year in anticipation of lower taxes next year—a prepayment of taxes. The journal entry to record all the tax-related information for Gupta for 2015 is as follows:

Income Tax Expense ($24,000 current − $4,000 deferred benefit)	20,000	
Deferred Tax Asset	4,000	
Income Taxes Payable		24,000

Total income tax expense of $20,000 is the difference between the current tax expense and the deferred tax benefit. The 2015 income statement for Gupta Company is as follows:

Revenues		$60,000
Warranty expense		10,000
Income before taxes		$50,000
Income tax expense:		
Current	$24,000	
Deferred benefit	(4,000)	20,000
Net income		$30,000

As explained in detail later in the chapter, deferred tax assets can be much more complicated than this simple example indicates. The two most common complications revolve around (1) the likelihood that a company will be able to realize the deferred tax asset in the future (a company that experiences repeated operating losses, for example, may not be able to take full advantage of the deferred tax asset) and (2) changing tax rates (a change in future tax rates affects the amount of deferred tax assets and liabilities). As mentioned at the start of this chapter, dissatisfaction over the FASB's handling of these issues related to the accounting for deferred income tax assets contributed to the acrimonious demise of pre-Codification *Statement No. 96* in 1992.

Permanent and Temporary Differences

permanent and temporary differences
永久性差异和暂时性差异

Before more detailed deferred tax examples are presented, some of the specific differences between financial accounting standards and tax rules will be described.

Some differences between financial and taxable income are permanent differences. These differences are caused by specific provisions of the tax law that exempt certain types of revenues from taxation and prohibit the deduction of certain types of expenses. Nontaxable revenues and nondeductible expenses are never included in determining taxable income, but they are included in determining financial income under GAAP. Permanent differences are created by political and social pressures to favor certain segments of society or to promote certain industries or economic activities. Examples of nontaxable revenues include proceeds from life insurance policies, interest received on municipal bonds, and a portion of the dividend revenue received by one corporation from its investments in other corporations. Examples of nondeductible expenses include fines for violation of laws and payment of life insurance premiums. Permanent differences also arise because income tax rates are different in different jurisdictions. For example, the state of Texas has no state income tax while the corporate income tax rate for income generated in New York is 7.1%. Permanent differences do not create accounting problems. Because they are never included in the computation of taxable income, they have no impact on either current or future (deferred) tax obligations.

> **FYI**
>
> Although permanent differences do not create financial accounting problems, that doesn't mean that they aren't important. The dream of a tax accountant is to be able to structure a company's transactions so that all of the revenue differences are permanent ones, meaning that the revenue is never taxed.

More commonly, differences between pretax financial income and taxable income arise from business events that are recognized for both financial reporting and tax purposes but in different time periods. In some cases, income tax payments are deferred to a period later than when the effect of the event on financial income is recognized. In other cases, income tax payments are required before the effect of the event on financial income is recognized.

These differences are referred to as temporary differences because, over time, their impact on financial income and taxable income will be the same.

A common example of a temporary difference, and one that historically has been the most significant for U.S. companies, is the computation of depreciation. As indicated in Chapter 11, depreciation for federal income tax purposes is referred to as *cost recovery* and has varied over time as to the degree of acceleration in the recovery of asset costs. On the other hand, the most common depreciation method used to determine financial income is the straight-line method, which recognizes an even amount of depreciation expense each year the asset is in service. In the early years of an asset's life, straight-line depreciation reported on the income statement usually is less than the cost recovery deduction on the income tax return. In the latter portion of an asset's life, however, this pattern reverses; that is, the depreciation expense on the income statement exceeds the cost recovery deduction on the tax return.

There are many other temporary differences in addition to depreciation, and new income tax laws continue to create new ones as income taxes are used to meet changing economic and policy objectives. Some examples of temporary differences are given in Exhibit 16-2. This list is just a sample of the differences between financial accounting standards and income tax laws that can create temporary differences between financial and taxable income.

taxable temporary differences
应纳税暂时性差异

The examples in Exhibit 16-2 are presented in two major categories. The first category includes differences, called taxable temporary differences, that will result in taxable amounts

Exhibit 16-2 | Examples of Temporary Differences

1. Differences That Create Deferred Tax Liabilities for Future Taxable Amounts
   (a) Revenues or gains are taxable *after* they are recognized for financial reporting purposes.
       - Installment sales method or cash basis used for tax purposes, but accrual method of recognizing sales revenue used for financial reporting purposes.
       - Unrealized gain on trading securities recognized as a gain in the period in which the value increases for financial reporting purposes but becomes a taxable gain only when the securities are sold.
   (b) Expenses or losses are deductible for tax purposes *before* they are recognized for financial reporting purposes.
       - MACRS used for tax purposes, but straight-line method of depreciation used for financial reporting purposes.
       - Intangible drilling costs for extractive industry written off as incurred for tax purposes but capitalized for financial reporting purposes.
2. Differences That Create Deferred Tax Assets for Future Deductible Amounts
   (a) Revenues or gains are taxable *before* they are recognized for financial reporting purposes.
       - Rent revenue received in advance of period earned recognized as revenue for tax purposes but deferred to be recognized in future periods for financial reporting purposes.
       - Subscription revenue received in advance of period earned recognized as revenue for tax purposes but deferred to be recognized in future periods for financial reporting purposes.
   (b) Expenses or losses are deductible for tax purposes *after* they are recognized for financial reporting purposes.
       - Warranty expense or bad debt expense deductible for tax purposes only when actually incurred but accrued in the year of sale for financial reporting purposes.
       - Restructuring charge deductible for tax purposes only when expenses actually incurred or losses actually realized but accrued in the year of the restructuring for financial reporting purposes.
       - Unrealized loss on trading securities recognized as a loss in the period in which the value decreases for financial reporting purposes but becomes a tax deductible loss only when the securities are sold.

© Cengage Learning 2014

Stop & Think

How can a company have both deferred tax assets and deferred tax liabilities at the same time?

a) A company can have both deferred tax assets and deferred tax liabilities at the same time only if it has negative retained earnings.

b) A company can have both deferred tax assets and deferred tax liabilities at the same time only if the effective income tax rate is greater than 50%.

c) Deferred tax assets and deferred tax liabilities result from different transactions, so a company can have both at the same time.

d) Actually, a company *cannot* have both deferred tax assets and deferred tax liabilities at the same time.

deductible temporary differences
可抵扣暂时性差异

in future years. Income taxes expected to be paid on future taxable amounts are reported on the balance sheet as a deferred tax liability. The second category includes differences, called deductible temporary differences, that will result in deductible amounts in future years. Income tax benefits (savings) expected to be realized from future deductible amounts are reported on the balance sheet as a deferred tax asset. Exhibit 16-3 provides examples of deferred tax assets and deferred tax liabilities taken from the 2011 financial statements of several large U.S. companies. The large deferred tax liabilities of the capital-intensive companies listed in Exhibit 16-3 highlight the importance of deferred tax liabilities arising from depreciation. The $47,645 million deferred tax liability recognized by Berkshire Hathaway stems from its large investment portfolio. Increases in the value of investments are recognized for financial reporting purposes as they occur but are not taxed until the investments are sold; this gives rise to deferred tax liabilities.

Illustration of Permanent and Temporary Differences

To illustrate the effect of permanent and temporary differences on the computation of income taxes, assume that for the year ended December 31, 2015, Monroe Corporation reported income before taxes of $420,000. Assume that this amount includes $20,000 of nontaxable revenues and $5,000 of nondeductible expenses, both permanent differences. In addition, assume that Monroe has one temporary difference: The depreciation (cost recovery) deduction on the 2015 income tax return exceeds depreciation expense on the

Exhibit 16-3 | Selected Deferred Tax Assets and Deferred Tax Liabilities for 2011

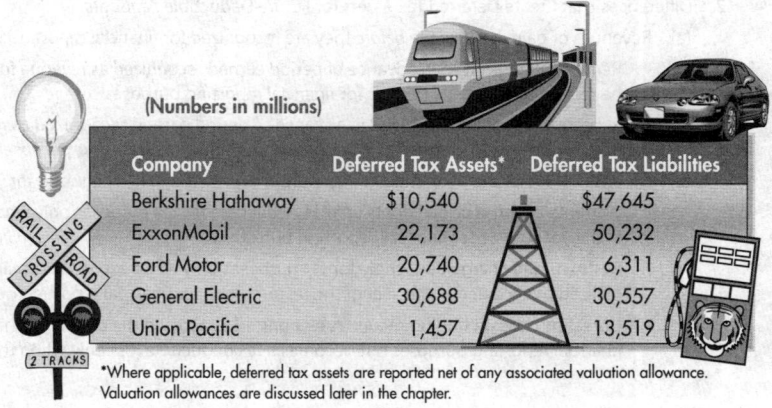

(Numbers in millions)

Company	Deferred Tax Assets*	Deferred Tax Liabilities
Berkshire Hathaway	$10,540	$47,645
ExxonMobil	22,173	50,232
Ford Motor	20,740	6,311
General Electric	30,688	30,557
Union Pacific	1,457	13,519

*Where applicable, deferred tax assets are reported net of any associated valuation allowance. Valuation allowances are discussed later in the chapter.

© Cengage Learning 2014

永久性差异既不包括在以税收为目的的会计收益中，也不包括在应税收益中。此外，由于永久性差异是不可逆的，不会对后续年度的应付所得税产生影响，不会与递延所得税的结果有关联；而暂时性差异会影响会计收益和应税收益，导致所得税的说明更加复杂和有争议。一般来说，暂时性差异会计也称作跨期税收分配。

income statement by $30,000. Assuming a corporate income tax rate of 35% for 2015, income taxes payable for the year would be computed as follows:

Pretax financial income (from income statement)		$420,000
Add (deduct) permanent differences:		
Nontaxable revenues	$(20,000)	
Nondeductible expenses	5,000	(15,000)
Financial income subject to tax		$405,000
Add (deduct) temporary differences:		
Excess of tax depreciation over book depreciation		(30,000)
Taxable income		$375,000
Tax on taxable income (income taxes payable): $375,000 × 0.35		$131,250

> **Caution**
>
> It is important that you be able to distinguish among the terms *pretax financial income*, *pretax financial income subject to tax*, and *taxable income*. This simple illustration highlights these terms and will make the later discussion clearer. Where there are no permanent differences, pretax financial income and pretax financial income subject to tax are the same. Unless otherwise noted, the shorter term is used in the remainder of the chapter.

As illustrated, the permanent differences are not included in either the financial income subject to tax or the taxable income. In addition, because these permanent differences never reverse, they have no impact on income taxes payable in subsequent periods and are thus not associated with any deferred tax consequences. Temporary differences are the cause of the complexity and controversy in accounting for income taxes because they impact financial income and taxable income in different periods. In general, the accounting for temporary differences is referred to as interperiod tax allocation.

Annual Computation of Deferred Tax Liabilities and Assets

② Compute the amount of deferred tax liabilities and assets including the use of a valuation allowance and the uncertainty of tax positions.

LO2 学习目标2
学会计算递延所得税负债和递延所得税资产，包括考虑估计备抵和不确定的税务状况。

As illustrated with the earlier examples, the basic concepts underlying deferred tax accounting are fairly simple. The examples that follow introduce some of the complexities associated with the specific provisions of FASB ASC Topic 740 (Income Taxes). Before launching into these examples, take a moment to reflect on how lucky you are not to have taken this class a few years ago. At that time, this chapter was based on pre-Codification *Statement No. 96*, which was much more difficult to understand and to implement and was hated by practitioners, financial statement users, students, and professors alike.

Topic 740 reflects the Board's preference for the asset and liability method of interperiod tax allocation, which emphasizes the measurement and reporting of balance sheet amounts. The major advantages of the asset and liability method of accounting for deferred taxes are as follows:

1. Because the assets and liabilities recorded under this method are in agreement with the FASB definitions of financial statement elements, the method is conceptually consistent with other standards.

2. The asset and liability method is a flexible method that recognizes changes in circumstances and adjusts the reported amounts accordingly. This flexibility may improve the predictive value of the financial statements.

One drawback of the asset and liability method is that in some ways, it is still too complicated (even after the significant simplification implemented in the wake of pre-Codification *Statement No. 96*). Many financial statement users claim that they ignore deferred tax assets and liabilities anyway, and thus, efforts devoted to deferred tax accounting are just a waste of time. For example, one financial statement analysis textbook reports that "because of the uncertainty over whether (and when) a deferred tax liability will be paid, some individuals elect to exclude deferred tax liabilities from liabilities when performing analysis."[4] On the other hand, research using stock market data suggests that investors compute values of companies as if the reported deferred tax liabilities are bona fide liabilities.[5]

The following list summarizes the procedure to be followed each year to compute the amount of deferred tax liabilities and assets to be included in the financial statements.[6]

1. Identify the types and amounts of existing temporary differences.
2. Measure the deferred tax liability for taxable temporary differences using applicable current and future tax rates.
3. Measure the deferred tax asset for deductible temporary differences using applicable current and future tax rates.
4. Reduce deferred tax assets by a valuation allowance if it is more likely than not (a likelihood of more than 50%) that some portion or all of the deferred tax assets will not be realized. The valuation allowance should reduce the deferred tax asset to the amount that is more likely than not to be realized.

Several examples will illustrate the computation of deferred tax assets and liabilities.

Example 3. Deferred Tax Liability

If a company has only deferred tax liabilities to consider, the accounting for deferred taxes is relatively straightforward. To illustrate, assume that Roland Inc. begins operations in 2015. For 2015, Roland computes pretax financial income of $75,000. The only difference between financial accounting income and taxable income is depreciation. Roland uses the straight-line method of depreciation for financial reporting purposes and an accelerated cost recovery method on its tax return. The depreciation amounts for existing plant assets for the years 2015 through 2018 are as follows:

Year	Financial Reporting	Income Tax Reporting
2015	$ 25,000	$ 40,000
2016	25,000	30,000
2017	25,000	25,000
2018	25,000	5,000
	$100,000	$100,000

[4] Charles H. Gibson, *Financial Statement Analysis: Using Financial Accounting Information*, 6th ed. (Cincinnati, OH: South-Western Publishing Co., 1995), p. 321.
[5] Dan Givoly and Carla Hayn, "The Valuation of the Deferred Tax Liability: Evidence from the Stock Market," *The Accounting Review*, April 1992, pp. 394–410.
[6] FASB ASC paragraph 740-10-30-5.

The enacted tax rate for 2015 and future years is 40%. Roland's taxable income for 2015 is $60,000, computed as follows:

Financial income subject to tax	$ 75,000
Deduct temporary difference:	
Excess of tax depreciation over book depreciation	(15,000)
Taxable income	$ 60,000
Tax ($60,000 × 0.40)	$ 24,000

Roland 公司记录的当期负债是24 000美元。2015年年末，依照税法累计的折旧超出账簿上的累计数15 000美元（40 000–25 000）。应税暂时性差异会引起未来需要冲回15 000美元应税额。在当期法定税率为40%的前提下，未来应纳所得税为6 000美元（15 000×40%），因此2015年12月31日的资产负债表上会列示6 000美元递延所得税负债。

Thus, Roland records a current liability of $24,000. At the end of 2015, aggregate tax depreciation exceeds aggregate book depreciation by $15,000 ($40,000 – $25,000). This taxable temporary difference will result in a taxable amount of $15,000 in future years as the difference reverses. With the currently enacted 40% tax rate, income tax on this future taxable amount will total $6,000 ($15,000 × 0.40). Accordingly, a deferred tax liability of $6,000 will be reported on the December 31, 2015, balance sheet. Because the depreciable asset is a noncurrent operating asset, the associated deferred tax liability is also classified as noncurrent.

The journal entry to record Roland's income taxes for 2015 would be as follows:

Income Tax Expense ($24,000 current + $6,000 deferred)	30,000	
Income Taxes Payable		24,000
Deferred Tax Liability—Noncurrent		6,000

Income taxes would be shown on Roland's 2015 income statement as follows:

Income before income taxes		$75,000
Current	$24,000	
Deferred	6,000	30,000
Net income		$45,000

Stop & Think

How might the current and deferred income tax numbers for 2015 change if the 2015 income tax rate were 40% but Roland expected tax rates in future periods to be 30% instead of 40%?

a) The numbers would be the same.
b) Both the current and deferred amounts would be multiplied by 30% instead of 40%.
c) The current amount would be multiplied by 30% instead of 40%.
d) The deferred amount would be multiplied by 30% instead of 40%.

The December 31, 2015, balance sheet would report a current liability of $24,000 for income taxes payable and, as noted above, a noncurrent deferred tax liability of $6,000.

So as to not unnecessarily complicate this example, we will assume that Roland earns financial income subject to tax of $75,000 in each of the years 2016 through 2018. In 2016, Roland reports taxable income of $70,000, computed as follows:

Financial income subject to tax	$75,000
Deduct temporary difference:	
Excess of tax depreciation over book depreciation	(5,000)
Taxable income	$70,000
Tax ($70,000 × 0.40)	$28,000

Roland's current taxes payable are $28,000. In each subsequent year following the initial deferral, the ending deferred tax liability is determined and compared with the beginning balance. The difference between the beginning and ending balances is recorded as an adjustment to the deferred tax liability account. At the end of 2016, aggregate tax depreciation exceeds aggregate book depreciation by $20,000 ($70,000 − $50,000). The deferred tax liability account, therefore, must be adjusted to a balance of $8,000 ($20,000 × 0.40). The amount of the adjustment is $2,000 ($8,000 less the beginning balance of $6,000). The following journal entry records the current payable and the adjustment to the deferred tax liability account:

Income Tax Expense ($28,000 current + $2,000 deferred)	30,000	
Income Taxes Payable		28,000
Deferred Tax Liability—Noncurrent		2,000

Because the depreciation expense for tax and financial reporting purposes is the same for 2017, no adjustment to the deferred tax liability account would be necessary for that year. Income for tax purposes would be equal to financial accounting income, and tax expense and taxes payable would be recorded with the journal entry shown below.

Income Tax Expense	30,000	
Income Taxes Payable ($75,000 × 0.40)		30,000

For 2018, income for tax purposes would be equal to $95,000, computed as follows:

Financial income subject to tax	$75,000
Add reversal of temporary difference:	
Excess of book depreciation over tax depreciation	20,000
Taxable income	$95,000
Tax ($95,000 × 0.40)	$38,000

Therefore, current taxes payable would be $38,000. The accumulated difference of $20,000 in the deferred tax account reverses, and aggregate tax depreciation and aggregate book depreciation are the same ($100,000). Thus, the journal entry to record the current year's payable as well as to reduce the deferred tax liability to zero would be as shown:

Income Tax Expense ($38,000 current − $8,000 deferred benefit)	30,000	
Deferred Tax Liability—Noncurrent	8,000	
Income Taxes Payable		38,000

The income tax benefit reduces the current income tax expense for 2018. The T-account summarizing the changes in the deferred tax liability account from 2015 to 2018 is as follows:

Deferred Tax Liability

		For 2015	6,000
		Balance, end of 2015	6,000
		for 2016	2,000
		Balance, end of 2016	8,000
		for 2017	0
		Balance, end of 2017	8,000
For 2018	8,000		
		Balance, end of 2018	0

Effect of Currently Enacted Changes in Future Tax Rates The example assumed a constant future tax rate of 40%. If changes in future tax rates have been enacted, the deferred tax liability (or asset) is measured using the enacted tax rate for the future years when the temporary difference is expected to reverse. To illustrate, assume that in 2015, Congress enacts legislation that reduces corporate tax rates for 2016 and subsequent years. In the Roland Inc. example, all of the temporary difference reverses in 2018, and the deferred tax liability should be measured using the tax rate enacted for that year. If the enacted tax rate for 2018 is 35%, the deferred tax liability at the end of 2015 would be $5,250 ($15,000 × 0.35), rather than $6,000 as computed earlier. At the end of 2016, the deferred tax liability would be $7,000 ($20,000 × 0.35), and the required adjustment would be $1,750 ($7,000 − $5,250).

IAS 12 is very similar to, but not exactly the same as, U.S. GAAP regarding the use of future tax rates. Under U.S. GAAP, as described in the previous paragraph, measurement of deferred tax liabilities and assets is done using the income tax rates that had been enacted as of the measurement date. This provision has the objective of measuring the deferred tax items at the tax rates that are expected to be in effect when the temporary items reverse, which will not be the same as the income tax rate for the current year if future tax rate changes have already been enacted into law. IFRS carries this concept one step further. Under *IAS 12*, deferred tax items are to be measured at income tax rates "that have been enacted or substantively enacted by the end of the reporting period." The "substantively enacted" part of this IFRS provision refers to cases in which governments in some jurisdictions announce an income tax rate change but the formal legal enactment of the change does not occur for several months. This is an example of the international standard taking a step back from legal literalism in order to capture the economic essence of a transaction or an event.

> **Caution**
>
> The entire effect of a change in rates is reflected in tax expense on income from continuing operations even if some of the deferred tax balances relate to "below-the-line" or accumulated other comprehensive income items. See FASB ASC paragraph 740-10-45-17.

Subsequent Changes in Enacted Tax Rates When rate changes are enacted after a deferred tax liability or asset has been recorded, Topic 740 requires that the beginning deferred account balance be adjusted to reflect the new tax rate. Again using the Roland Inc. example, assume that the enacted tax rate for 2018 changed from 40% to 35% during 2016. The balance in the deferred tax liability at the beginning of 2016 is $6,000 ($15,000 × 0.40). The following adjusting entry would be made to reflect the newly enacted 35% tax rate for 2018:

Deferred Tax Liability—Noncurrent 750*
   Income Tax Benefit—Rate Change (reduction in income tax expense) 750
*($15,000 × 0.05)

The income effect of the change is reflected in income tax expense. In this case, the effect is a tax benefit resulting from a lower tax rate and would be shown as a reduction in income tax expense on the 2016 income statement.

Example 4. Deferred Tax Asset

Assume that Sandusky Inc. begins operations in 2015. For 2015, Sandusky computes pretax financial income of $22,000. The only difference between financial and taxable income is the recognition of warranty expense. Sandusky accrues estimated warranty expense in the year of sale for financial reporting purposes but deducts only actual warranty expenditures for tax purposes. Accrued warranty expense for 2015 was $18,000; no actual warranty expenditures were made in 2015. Therefore, taxable income in 2015 is $40,000, computed as follows:

Financial income subject to tax	$22,000
Add temporary difference:	
Excess of warranty expense over warranty deductions	18,000
Taxable income	$40,000
Tax ($40,000 × 0.40)	$16,000

The difference in 2015 between warranty expense for financial reporting and tax purposes is a deductible temporary difference because it will result in future tax deductions of $18,000. The deferred tax asset implied by this difference is $7,200 ($18,000 × 0.40). Warranty expenditures for 2015 sales are expected to be $6,000 in each of the years 2016 through 2018. Because the underlying warranty obligation is assumed to be one-third current and two-thirds noncurrent, the associated deferred tax asset would be classified in the same ratio.

The future tax deduction of $18,000 will provide a tax benefit only if Sandusky has taxable income in future periods against which the deduction can be offset. Accordingly, to record a deferred tax asset, one must assume that sufficient taxable income will exist in future years. Conditions under which this assumption may or may not be reasonable are described later in the chapter in the section entitled "Valuation Allowance for Deferred Tax Assets."

Assuming that future taxable income will be sufficient to allow for full realization of the tax benefits of the $18,000 future tax deduction (and let's assume, just to keep things simple, that financial income subject to tax is $22,000 in each of the next three years), the journal entry to record Sandusky's income taxes for 2015 would be as follows:

Income Tax Expense ($16,000 current − $7,200 deferred benefit)	8,800	
Deferred Tax Asset—Current	2,400*	
Deferred Tax Asset—Noncurrent	4,800†	
Income Taxes Payable		16,000

*One-third of underlying warranty obligation is current (1/3 × $7,200).
†Two-thirds of underlying warranty obligation is noncurrent (2/3 × $7,200).

Sandusky's 2015 income statement would present income tax expense as follows:

Income before income taxes		$22,000
Income tax expense:		
Current	$16,000	
Deferred (benefit)	(7,200)	8,800
Net income		$13,200

Sandusky's December 31, 2015, balance sheet would report deferred tax assets of $2,400 under current assets and $4,800 under noncurrent assets. Income taxes payable for 2015 would be shown with current liabilities.

In subsequent periods, Sandusky's taxable income would be less than reported pretax financial income because the deductible temporary differences would begin to reverse. In the years 2016 through 2018, taxable income would be equal to $16,000, computed as follows:

Income subject to tax	$22,000
Reversal of temporary difference:	
Excess of warranty deductions over warranty expense	(6,000)
Taxable income	$16,000
Tax ($16,000 × 0.40)	$ 6,400

The amount of the deductible temporary difference would decline each year, affecting first the amount classified as noncurrent and finally eliminating the current portion of the deferred tax asset account. The following table illustrates the journal entries that would be made each year:

	2016	2017	2018
Income Tax Expense..........................	6,400	6,400	6,400
Income Taxes Payable.....................		6,400	6,400	6,400
Income Tax Expense..........................	2,400	2,400	2,400
Deferred Tax Asset—Current.............		2,400	2,400	2,400
Deferred Tax Asset—Current................	2,400	2,400	
Deferred Tax Asset—Noncurrent..........		2,400	2,400	

The first journal entry records the current period's tax liability. The second journal entry recognizes that the current portion of the deferred tax asset has expired. The final journal entry simply reclassifies the deferred tax asset from noncurrent to current, indicating that a portion of the deductible temporary difference will reverse in the upcoming period.

Example 5. Deferred Tax Liabilities and Assets

Hsieh Company began operation on January 1, 2015. For 2015, Hsieh reported pretax financial income of $38,000. As of December 31, 2015, the actual differences between Hsieh Company's financial accounting and income tax records for 2015 and the estimated differences for 2016 through 2018 are summarized as follows:

	Financial Reporting		Income Tax Reporting	
	Depreciation Expense	Warranty Expense	Depreciation Deduction	Warranty Deduction
2015 (actual)	$25,000	$18,000	$40,000	$ 0
2016 (estimated)	25,000	0	30,000	6,000
2017 (estimated)	25,000	0	25,000	6,000
2018 (estimated)	25,000	0	5,000	6,000

The enacted income tax rate for all years is 40% (note that Example 5 simply combines Examples 3 and 4). For 2015, taxable income would be computed as follows:

Financial income subject to tax	$ 38,000
Add (deduct) temporary differences:	
Excess of warranty expense over warranty deductions	18,000
Excess of tax depreciation over book depreciation	(15,000)
Taxable income	$ 41,000
Tax ($41,000 × 0.40)	$ 16,400

As of December 31, 2015, aggregate tax depreciation exceeds aggregate book depreciation by $15,000 ($40,000 − $25,000). As explained previously, this represents a future taxable amount. The income tax expected to be paid on this amount is $6,000 ($15,000 × 0.40). This $6,000 is a deferred tax liability as of December 31, 2015. Because the difference relates to a noncurrent item, the deferred tax liability is a noncurrent liability.

2015年12月31日，Hsieh 公司根据会计基础确认了18 000美元的保修费用，后续三年准备在税收基础上扣减。假设未来的应税收益足够确认抵扣形成的税收优惠，将形成递延所得税资产7 200美元（18 000×40%）。因为保修债务部分（6 000美元）是流动的，部分（12 000美元）是非流动的；同样递延所得税资产部分（2 400美元）是流动的，部分（4 800美元）是非流动的。

As of December 31, 2015, Hsieh has recognized an $18,000 warranty expense for financial accounting purposes, which it plans to deduct for tax purposes over the next three years. Assuming that future taxable income will be sufficient to allow the tax benefit of this deduction to be fully realized, this future deductible amount creates a deferred tax asset of $7,200 ($18,000 × 0.40). Because the underlying warranty liability is part current ($6,000) and part noncurrent ($12,000), the deferred tax asset would also be classified as part current ($2,400 = $6,000 × 0.40) and part noncurrent ($4,800 = $12,000 × 0.40). The journal entries to record Hsieh's current taxes payable as well as the deferred portion of its 2015 income tax expense are as follows:

Income Tax Expense..	16,400	
Income Taxes Payable...		16,400
Deferred Tax Asset—Current	2,400	
Deferred Tax Asset—Noncurrent..	4,800	
Income Tax Benefit (a subtraction from income tax expense)..................		1,200
Deferred Tax Liability—Noncurrent		6,000

Note that this journal entry is a combination of the journal entries associated with the deferred taxes from Examples 3 and 4. For reporting purposes, current deferred tax assets and current deferred tax liabilities are netted against one another and reported as a single amount. Similarly, noncurrent deferred tax assets and liabilities are netted and reported as a single amount.[7] In this example, the amounts to be reported on Hsieh's December 31, 2015, balance sheet are a $2,400 current deferred tax asset and a $1,200 noncurrent deferred tax liability ($6,000 liability − $4,800 asset). The income tax benefit would be shown as a $1,200 reduction of current income tax expense in the 2015 income statement.

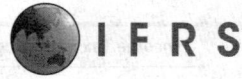

Deferred Tax Classification under IFRS Under IFRS, deferred tax assets and liabilities are to be classified as noncurrent assets and liabilities. As seen in the examples explained earlier, under U.S. GAAP, the deferred tax items are classified as current or noncurrent based on the classification of the underlying item that gives rise to the deferred income tax asset or liability. The IFRS classification provision is contained in *IAS 1*, which outlines, among other things, the basic structure of the financial statements.

Valuation Allowance for Deferred Tax Assets

A deferred tax asset represents future income tax benefits. But the tax benefits will be realized only if there is sufficient taxable income from which the deductible amount can be deducted. Topic 740 requires that the deferred tax asset be reduced by a valuation allowance if, based on all available evidence, it is "more likely than not" that some portion or all the deferred tax asset will not be realized. As applied to deferred tax assets, "more likely than not" means a likelihood of more than 50%.[8] The valuation allowance is a contra asset account that reduces the asset to its expected realizable value. Before we get into the details of the valuation allowance, it is important for you to realize that for most companies, and for profitable companies in particular, the valuation allowance is not an issue. The valuation allowance becomes an issue when future profitability is in doubt.

In the Hsieh Company example (Example 5 on page 16-15), it was assumed that there would be sufficient taxable income to allow for the full realization of the benefits from the $18,000 warranty deduction, and thus, no valuation allowance was established. Some

---
[7] FASB ASC paragraph 740-10-45-6.
[8] FASB ASC paragraph 740-10-30-5e.

possible sources of taxable income to be considered in evaluating the realizable value of a deferred tax asset are as follows:[9]

1. Future reversals of existing taxable temporary differences
2. Future taxable income exclusive of reversing temporary differences
3. Taxable income in prior (carryback) years

The first source of future taxable income, reversals of taxable temporary differences, can be identified without making assumptions about the profitability of future operations. In 2015, Hsieh Company has a $15,000 excess of aggregate tax depreciation over aggregate book depreciation, which will result in a future taxable amount. The reversal of this temporary difference will provide taxable income in the future against which the $18,000 warranty deduction can be offset. If it appears more likely than not that no other income will be available, then only $15,000 of the $18,000 warranty deduction is expected to be realized. Accordingly, the total deferred tax asset is $7,200 ($18,000 × 0.40), but the realizable amount is only $6,000 ($15,000 × 0.40). The $1,200 difference would be recorded as a valuation allowance, an offset to the reported deferred tax asset. Two journal entries can be used to record this deferred tax information. First, the deferred tax asset and liability are recognized, as follows.

Deferred Tax Asset—Current	2,400	
Deferred Tax Asset—Noncurrent	4,800	
Income Tax Benefit (a subtraction from income tax expense)		1,200
Deferred Tax Liability—Noncurrent		6,000

Note that this is the same as the deferred tax journal entry shown earlier. The second journal entry represents the fact that it is more likely than not that $1,200 of the deferred tax asset will not be realized.

Income Tax Expense	1,200	
Allowance to Reduce Deferred Tax Asset to Realizable Value—Current		400
Allowance to Reduce Deferred Tax Asset to Realizable Value—Noncurrent		800

For classification purposes, the valuation allowance is allocated proportionately between the current and noncurrent portions of the deferred tax asset.[10] In this example, because one-third of the deferred tax asset is current ($6,000/$18,000), one-third, or $400 ($1,200 × 1/3), of the valuation allowance is classified as current. Of course, these two journal entries can be combined into one. The net effect of the two entries is that there is no deferred tax component of income tax expense—the $6,000 income tax expense associated with the deferred tax liability is exactly offset by the $6,000 ($7,200 − $1,200) income tax benefit (net) associated with the realizable portion of the deferred tax asset.

In 2016 and subsequent years, the company should reconsider available evidence to determine whether the valuation account should be adjusted.

在评估递延所得税可实现价值时需要考虑应税收益的几个可能因素：
- 所得税暂时性差异在未来撤销的可能性；
- 排除可撤销暂时性差异之外的未来应税收益；
- 之前（递延）的应税收益。

Stop & Think

In what way do the data regarding deferred tax assets and liabilities provide valuable information to current and potential investors and creditors?

a) Data regarding deferred tax assets and liabilities allow investors and creditors to better compute cost of goods sold.
b) Data regarding deferred tax assets and liabilities allow investors and creditors to better estimate bad debt expense.
c) Data regarding deferred tax assets and liabilities allow investors and creditors to better estimate future tax-related cash flows.
d) Data regarding deferred tax assets and liabilities allow investors and creditors to better compute earnings before interest and taxes.

---

[9] FASB ASC paragraph 740-10-30-18.
[10] FASB ASC paragraph 740-10-45-5.

The other two sources through which the benefit of a deferred tax asset can be realized include taxable income expected from profitable operations in future years and taxable income in prior carryback years. This latter source relates to specific carryback provisions of the tax law, which are explained later in the chapter.

Topic 740 stipulates that both positive and negative evidence be considered when determining whether deferred tax assets will be fully realized.[11] Examples of negative evidence include cumulative losses in recent years, a history of the expiration of unused tax loss carryforwards, and unsettled circumstances that might cause a currently profitable company to report losses in future years. Positive evidence includes the existence of an order backlog sufficient to yield enough taxable income for the deferred tax asset to be realized, the existence of appreciated assets, and a strong earnings history.

The FASB was very reluctant to allow firms to consider possible future taxable income when evaluating the realizability of deferred tax assets because, as stated in pre-Codification FASB *Statement* No. 96:

> Incurring losses or generating profits in future years are future events that are not recognized in financial statements for the current year. Those future events shall not be anticipated, regardless of probability, for purposes of recognizing and measuring a deferred tax liability or asset in the current year. The tax consequences of those future events shall be recognized and reported in the financial statements in future years when the events occur.[12]

However, because many firms complained that it was unfair to require them to report deferred tax liabilities but not allow them to report deferred tax assets, the FASB reconsidered and revised its position. Topic 740 explicitly allows a firm to consider potential future income in evaluating the realizability of deferred tax assets.

Valuation Allowance under *IAS 12* Simply stated, under the provisions of *IAS 12*, there is no valuation allowance. Instead, deferred tax assets are recognized only "to the extent that it is probable that taxable profit will be available against which the deductible temporary difference can be utilised." Thus, under U.S. GAAP, all deferred tax assets are initially recognized and then are reduced by a valuation allowance if it is more likely than not that there will not be sufficient future taxable income to allow for the realization of the deferred tax asset. Under IFRS, deferred tax assets are only recognized in the first place if their realization is probable; there is no need for a valuation allowance. However, much more important than the procedural difference between U.S. GAAP and IFRS is the difference in probability thresholds for ultimate deferred tax asset recognition. Under U.S. GAAP, the realizability of the deferred tax asset must be more likely than not, interpreted as a probability of 50%. Under IFRS, the realizability must be "probable." Although no one has put a definitive probability percentage on "probable," everyone agrees that probable is more than 50%, usually substantially more. Thus, the international standard is stricter than is U.S. GAAP with respect to the recognition of deferred tax assets.

Accounting for Uncertain Tax Positions In spite of the voluminous nature of the tax code, there are still many areas in which the deductibility of certain expenses or losses and the claiming of some tax credits are in question. Professional tax preparers are constantly giving advice to clients regarding aggressive tax positions that may, upon close scrutiny, be rejected by the Internal Revenue Service. Tax preparers are not required to be absolutely certain that a position will be sustained by the IRS in order to be justified in

---

[11] FASB ASC paragraph 740-10-30-17.
[12] Pre-Codification FASB *Statement No. 96*, "Accounting for Income Taxes" (Stamford, CT: Financial Accounting Standards Board, 1987), par. 15.

recommending that tax position to a client. According to U.S. Treasury Department regulations, a tax preparer or a taxpayer can justifiably advocate an aggressive tax position, without fear of legal or professional censure, if there is "substantial authority" to support a position.[13] "Substantial authority" is generally defined in practice as being a greater than 40% probability of having the tax position sustained.

The existence of aggressive tax positions that are not certain to be sustained upon IRS scrutiny raises the financial accounting question of whether the tax benefit associated with these tax positions should be recognized as a reduction in income tax expense. Topic 740 states that the tax benefit associated with an uncertain tax benefit can be recognized only if it is *more likely than not* that the position will be sustained upon audit by the IRS. You can see that, under this interpretation, there will be some uncertain tax positions that might be taken by taxpayers but the tax benefits are not immediately recognized for financial accounting purposes because those benefits are not yet more likely than not.

Some examples of areas where tax benefits might be considered uncertain include the following:

- Classifying a revenue transaction as tax exempt (when it may not be)
- Electing not to file a tax return in a certain jurisdiction (when filing might be appropriate)
- Establishing a capitalization threshold for routine property and equipment purchases (when the tax law does not prescribe a threshold)

Topic 740 requires the use of a two-step process to determine the recognition of any tax benefit associated with an uncertain tax position. The two steps relating to recognition and measurement are as follows:

1. Step 1—Determine if it is more likely than not that a tax position would be sustained if it were examined, and it must be assumed that the tax position will be examined. Remember, more likely than not means a likelihood of greater than 50%. If a tax position meets this criterion, then the analysis moves to step 2.
2. Step 2—The measurement of the tax benefit is based on a probability assessment of the likelihood of specific outcomes and the amounts associated with those outcomes. The amount of the benefit is measured by taking the largest amount of tax benefit that is greater than 50% likely of being realized upon settlement.

An example is used to illustrate this two-step process. Company A has taken a tax position on an issue for which the tax law is subject to interpretation. For tax purposes, Company A has claimed a deduction in the current period that results in a $100 reduction in taxes to be paid this period. If this expenditure is reviewed, it is possible that the IRS may disallow all or part of the deduction. Company A must now determine how much should be reported as Income Tax Expense on the income statement and as Income Taxes Payable on the balance sheet.

Case 1: Highly Certain Tax Position In this example, if the probability were greater than 50% that the tax benefit of $100 would be achieved, this would be deemed a "highly certain" tax position. A "highly certain" tax position is one in which the position is based on clear and unambiguous tax law and where it is more likely than not (that is, a greater than 50% probability) that the position taken and the amount in question would be upheld if reviewed. In this instance, there would be no additional tax liability recognized because the amount of tax benefit claimed on the tax return and the amount of benefit expected to be received based on the tax position analysis are the same.

[13] *IRC Section 6662(d).*

Case 2: Uncertain Tax Position—More Likely Than Not Suppose instead that there is a range of possible outcomes associated with this tax position. The company is required to provide an assessment of both the probability of an outcome as well as the amount of allowable reduction in taxes associated with that probability. Assume the assessment of probabilities as shown below.

There is a xx% probability that	The allowable reduction in taxes payable will be	The cumulative probability of occurrence is
10%	$100	10%
20	80	30
25	60	55
20	40	75
15	20	90
10	0	100

If Company A determines that the technical merits of its position exceed the more-likely-than-not threshold (step 1), the amount of tax benefit to be recognized for financial statement purposes in this example is $60, the amount at which the cumulative probability exceeds 50% (step 2). What this means is that Company A would now need to record an additional tax liability, called an *unrecognized tax benefit*, for the $40 difference—the difference between the actual reduction in taxes (or tax benefit) on the income tax return filed this period and the expected amount of benefit based on this tax position analysis.[14]

The required journal entry is as follows:

Income Tax Expense...	40	
Unrecognized Tax Benefit..		40

The account, Unrecognized Tax Benefit, is a liability and would be classified as current if payment is anticipated within one year. It is important to note that liabilities relating to uncertain tax positions are not to be combined with deferred tax assets or liabilities for disclosure purposes.

Case 3: Uncertain Tax Position—NOT More Likely Than Not If the company completes step 1 of the analysis and determines that it is NOT more likely than not that the tax position will be sustained (that is, there is a less than 50% chance the position will be supported upon review), then the entire amount of the position must be recognized as a liability with the following journal entry:

Income Tax Expense...	100	
Unrecognized Tax Benefit..		100

Topic 740 also requires note disclosure relating to the beginning balance of unrecognized tax benefits, additions based on tax positions related to the current year, additions related to tax positions for prior years, reductions for tax positions of prior years, and adjustments related to any settlements made during the year.

Exhibit 16-4 includes a portion of the financial statement note disclosure about uncertain tax positions made by **General Mills** in its May 30, 2010, financial statements. Note that a $30.7 million tax benefit, and then a $52.6 million tax expense, were recorded in consecutive years with respect to the same uncertain tax position. Clearly, a substantial amount of complex judgment must be used in assessing the probabilities and amounts associated with these uncertain tax positions.

[14] FASB ASC paragraph 740-10-25-16.

Exhibit 16-4 | General Mills Disclosure about Uncertain Tax Positions—2010

NOTE 14. INCOME TAXES (in part)
The IRS has concluded its field examination of our 2006 and prior federal tax years, which resulted in payments of $17.6 million in fiscal 2009 and $56.5 million in fiscal 2008 to cover the additional U.S. income tax liability plus interest related to adjustments during these audit cycles. The IRS also proposed additional adjustments for the fiscal 2002 to 2006 audit cycles related to the amount of capital loss and depreciation and amortization we reported as a result of our sale of noncontrolling interest in our GMC subsidiary. The IRS has proposed adjustments that effectively eliminate most of the tax benefits associated with this transaction. We believe our positions are supported by substantial technical authority and are vigorously defending our positions. We are currently in negotiations with the IRS Appeals Division for fiscal 2002 to 2006. We have determined that a portion of this matter should be included as a tax liability and have accordingly included it in our total liabilities for uncertain tax positions. The IRS initiated its audit of our fiscal 2007 and 2008 tax years during fiscal 2009.

In the third quarter of fiscal 2008, we recorded an income tax benefit of $30.7 million as a result of a favorable U.S. district court decision on an uncertain tax matter. In the third quarter of fiscal 2009, the U.S. Court of Appeals for the Eighth Circuit issued an opinion reversing the district court decision. As a result, we recorded $52.6 million (including interest) of income tax expense related to the reversal of cumulative income tax benefits from this uncertain tax matter recognized in fiscal years 1992 through 2008. We expect to make cash tax and interest payments of approximately $31.7 million in connection with this matter. . . .

In Millions	Fiscal Year 2010	Fiscal Year 2009
Balance, beginning of year	$570.1	$534.6
Tax position related to current year:		
Additions	19.7	66.8
Tax positions related to prior years:		
Additions	7.1	48.9
Reductions	(37.6)	(63.7)
Settlements	(1.9)	(13.0)
Lapses in statutes of limitations	(4.5)	(3.5)
Balance, end of year	$552.9	$570.1

General Mills, 2010, 10K Report

FASB CODIFICATION

The Issue: Your brother-in-law is a bit of a know-it-all. He has heard that you are taking an accounting class. He thinks he is an accounting expert because he took, and passed (barely), an intermediate financial accounting class several years ago. He is now trying to embarrass you at a family gathering by showing how much more he knows about accounting than you do.

He has just thrown the following question at you: "What is INTRAperiod tax allocation?" Fortunately, he has been called away to a phone call. You have five minutes to go online and use the FASB's Codification to avoid the humiliation of being bested by your obnoxious brother-in-law.

The Question: What is INTRAperiod tax allocation?

Searching the Codification: Your initial thought is that your brother-in-law has made a mistake. The accounting for temporary differences and deferred income taxes is called INTERperiod tax allocation. But because of the wicked smile he gave you when he asked the question, you know there is a trick here. The best place to start your search is FASB ASC Topic 740. Good luck!

The Answer: A discussion of INTRAperiod tax allocation is given on page 16-35.

LO3 学习目标3

解释税收损失抵前和抵后的规定，并能对这些规定做出说明。

Carryback and Carryforward of Operating Losses

3 Explain the provisions of tax loss carrybacks and carryforwards, and be able to account for these provisions.

Because income tax is based on the amount of taxable income reported, no tax is payable if a company experiences an operating loss. As an incentive to those businesses that experience alternate periods of income and losses, U.S. tax laws provide a way to ease the risk of loss years. This is done through a carryback and carryforward provision that permits a company to apply a net operating loss occurring in one year against income of other years. Specifically, the Internal Revenue Code provides for a two-year carryback and a 20-year carryforward.[15]

Net Operating Loss (NOL) Carryback

If you were profitable in prior periods and, as a result, paid taxes, you can get a refund of some or all those tax payments in the period in which you incur an operating loss. A net operating loss (NOL) carryback is applied to the income of the two preceding years in reverse order, beginning with the second year and moving to the first year. If unused net operating losses are still available, they may be carried forward up to 20 years to offset any future income. Amended income tax returns must be filed for each year to which the carryback is applied to receive refunds of previously paid income taxes. Net operating loss carrybacks result in a journal entry establishing a current receivable for the tax refund claim. The benefit that arises from such refunds is used to reduce the loss in the current period. This treatment is supported in theory because it is the current year's operating loss that results in the tax refund.

To illustrate, assume that Prairie Company had the following pattern of income and losses for the years 2014 through 2016:

Year	Income (Loss)	Income Tax Rate	Income Tax
2014	$ 10,000	35%	$3,500
2015	14,000	30	4,200
2016	(19,000)	30	0

2016年19 000美元的净经营损失先抵转至2014年，再抵转至2015年。这两年共计6 200美元（3500+900×30%）的所得税可申请返还。

The $19,000 net operating loss in 2016 would be carried back to 2014 first and then to 2015. An income tax refund claim of $6,200 would be filed for the two years [$3,500 + 0.30($9,000)]. The entry to record the income tax receivable in 2016 would be as follows:

Income Tax Refund Receivable.. 6,200
    Income Tax Benefit from NOL Carryback... 6,200

[15] Before 1997, the carryback period was three years and the carryforward period was 15 years. Also, as an alternative, a taxpayer can elect to forgo the carryback and carry the entire loss forward for up to 20 years. This election is seldom made because carrybacks result in current refunds of taxes. In recognition of the economic damage caused by the September 11, 2001, World Trade Center attack, the Job Creation and Worker Assistance Act of 2002 extended the carryback period for NOLs created in 2001 or 2002 from two years to five years.

The refund will be reflected on the income statement as a reduction of the operating loss as follows:

Net operating loss before income tax benefit	$(19,000)
Income tax benefit from NOL carryback	6,200
Net loss	$(12,800)

The 2016 net operating loss reduces the 2014 taxable income to zero and the 2015 taxable income to $5,000 ($14,000 − $9,000). If another net operating loss occurs next year (in 2017), it may be carried back to the remaining $5,000 from 2015.

Net Operating Loss (NOL) Carryforward

If an operating loss exceeds income for the two preceding years, the remaining unused loss may be applied against income earned over the next 20 years as a net operating loss (NOL) carryforward. Under the provisions of Topic 740, a deferred tax asset is recognized for the potential future tax benefit from a loss carryforward. Full realization of the benefit, however, depends on the company having income equal to the carryforward in the next 20 years. As is true for other deferred tax assets, a valuation allowance is used to reduce the asset if it is more likely than not that some or all of the future benefit will not be realized.

To illustrate the carryforward provisions, let's continue the previous example and assume that in 2017 Prairie Company incurred an operating loss of $35,000. This loss would be carried back to the years 2015 and 2016 in that order. However, the only income remaining against which operating losses can be applied is $5,000 from 2015. After applying $5,000 to the 2015 income, $30,000 is left to carry forward against future income. The tax benefit from the carryback is $1,500 ($5,000 × 0.30). Assuming the enacted tax rate for future years is 30%, the potential tax benefit from the carryforward is $9,000 ($30,000 × 0.30). The entry in 2017 to record the tax benefits would be as follows:

Stop & Think

These net operating loss carrybacks sound like a great feature of the tax law. However, what did the company have to do to take advantage of this aspect of the law?

a) Experience a tax loss
b) Experience substantial taxable income
c) Experience a financial accounting loss
d) Experience substantial financial accounting income

Income Tax Refund Receivable	1,500	
Deferred Tax Asset—NOL Carryforward	9,000	
Income Tax Benefit from NOL Carryback		1,500
Income Tax Benefit from NOL Carryforward		9,000

The deferred tax asset of $9,000 would be reported on the balance sheet as a current asset if it is expected to be realized in 2018. Any portion that is expected to be realized after 2018 would be classified as noncurrent. The $10,500 in tax benefits would be shown on the 2017 income statement as a reduction of the operating loss.

Assuming that Prairie becomes profitable in future periods, the deferred tax asset associated with the NOL carryforward would be used to offset any taxes payable resulting from profitable operations. As an example, assume that Prairie reports taxable income of $50,000 in 2018. Rather than pay $15,000 ($50,000 × 0.30) in taxes, Prairie would be

The IRS provides a two-year carryback and a 20-year carryforward provision that allows a company to apply a net operating loss occurring in one year against income of other years.

allowed to offset the deferred tax asset against the liability. The journal entry made by Prairie associated with its tax liability would then be as follows:

Income Tax Expense....................	15,000	
Income Taxes Payable		6,000
Deferred Tax Asset—NOL		
Carryforward.......................		9,000

The journal entry recorded at the end of 2017 indicates that it is more likely than not that the carryforward benefit will be realized in full. If, however, it is more likely than not that some portion or all of the deferred tax asset will not be realized, a valuation allowance account is needed to reduce the asset to its estimated realizable value. For example, assume that Prairie Company's recent losses resulted from a declining market for its products and that the weight of available evidence indicates continuing losses in subsequent years. As a result, management believes it is more likely than not that none of the asset will be realized. In this case, the journal entry to record the carryback and carryforward would be as follows:

Income Tax Refund Receivable...	1,500	
Deferred Tax Asset—NOL Carryforward	9,000	
Income Tax Benefit from NOL Carryback..		1,500
Allowance to Reduce Deferred Tax Asset to		
Realizable Value—NOL Carryforward		9,000

As a result of this entry, the net deferred tax asset is zero—the expected realizable value. If market conditions improve and the company does have taxable income in subsequent years, the valuation allowance account would be decreased (debited) and an income tax benefit account would be credited.

Under pre-Codification *APB Opinion No. 11*, future tax benefits from an NOL carryforward could be reported as an asset only if future income were "assured beyond reasonable doubt." Although such a criterion is not easily met, there were cases in which NOL carryforward benefits were reported as an asset. In pre-Codification *Statement No. 96*, the FASB was even more restrictive and prohibited reporting income tax benefits from carryforwards as an asset under any circumstances. The adoption of the more-likely-than-not approach for deferred tax assets in pre-Codification *Statement No. 109* in 1992 led the Board to conclude that a similar approach should be used for net operating loss carryforwards. That is, NOL carryforwards are reported as assets if it is more likely than not that future income will be sufficient to allow for the realization of the tax benefit. This is a significant change in accounting for NOL carryforwards. Under *Statement No. 109*, millions of dollars of previously unreported income tax carryforwards are now included in the assets of companies. For example, IBM indicated in the notes to its 1990 financial statements that in addition to $110 million of unrecognized deferred tax assets under FASB *Statement No. 96*, it had $700 million of unrecognized tax credit carryforwards. As reported at the beginning of the

> **FYI**
>
> Under certain conditions, a company may acquire another company's NOL carryforwards as part of an acquisition or a merger. In some situations, these unused carryforwards are a company's most valuable "asset" to another company.

Exhibit 16-5 | Example of Deferred Tax Asset Valuation Allowances 2011

For the Year 2011 (in millions)	Deferred Tax Assets	Valuation Allowance	Reason Given for Need for Valuation Allowance
AT&T Inc.	$17,903	$ 917	Certain state NOL carryforwards may expire unused.
Verizon	19,465	2,376	Certain state and foreign NOL carryforwards may expire unused.
ExxonMobil	23,477	1,304	No reason given.
IBM	11,828	912	Certain local, state, and foreign NOL carryforwards may expire unused.

© Cengage Learning 2014

chapter, IBM announced in September 1992 that it would recognize a gain of $1.9 billion as a result of the deferred tax assets it would be able to recognize because of its adoption of *Statement No. 109*.

Deferred tax asset valuation allowances were discussed in the preceding section. Four U.S. companies with deferred tax asset valuation allowances are given in Exhibit 16-5. As the exhibit indicates, a very common reason for a company to have a deferred tax asset valuation allowance is that it has state, federal, or foreign NOL carryforwards that it doesn't think it will be able to use before they expire.

Scheduling for Enacted Future Tax Rates

 Schedule future tax rates, and determine the effect on deferred tax assets and liabilities.

LO4 学习目标4
解释未来所得税率，并确定其对递延所得税资产和递延所得税负债的影响。

Recall that the two major complaints about FASB *Statement No. 96* were that it did not allow for the recognition of most deferred tax assets and that it was too complicated. The complaints about nonrecognition of deferred tax assets came primarily from companies and users of financial statements who thought the inconsistent treatment of deferred tax assets and liabilities was misleading and unfair. Complaints about the complexities of pre-Codification *Statement No. 96* came primarily from preparers of financial statements. Those complaints focused on one topic: scheduling of the periods in which temporary differences are expected to reverse. Under the provisions of *Statement No. 96*, scheduling was required each year to determine which deferred tax assets could be realized because no future income could be assumed, and these assets were realizable only through the carryback and carryforward provisions of the tax law. In addition, under the provisions of *Statement No. 96*, scheduling was necessary to determine how deferred tax assets and liabilities should be classified based on the expected period of their reversal.

In 1992, the FASB eliminated much of the need for scheduling through the "more-likely-than-not" criterion for future income and because deferred tax assets and liabilities are classified according to the classification of the underlying items instead of according to the expected reversal period. However, scheduling is still required in a limited number of cases. One such case arises when differences in enacted future tax rates make it necessary to schedule the timing of a reversal in order to match that reversal with the tax rate expected to be in effect when it occurs.

Consider again the Hsieh Company example introduced on page 16-15. When that example was covered before, it was assumed that the enacted income tax rate was 40% for all periods. Assume now that the enacted tax rates are as follows: 2015, 40%; 2016, 35%; 2017, 30%; and 2018, 25%. As of December 31, 2015, using the 40% rate to value the deferred tax asset stemming from the future deductible amount of $18,000 and the deferred tax liability resulting from the future taxable amount of $15,000 would be misleading because it is known that the tax rate will not be 40% when those temporary differences reverse. A more accurate valuation can be obtained by applying tax rates expected to be in effect when the differences reverse, as follows:

	Enacted Tax Rate	Deductible Amount	Asset Valuation	Taxable Amount	Liability Valuation
2016	35%	$ 6,000	$2,100	$ 0	$ 0
2017	30	6,000	1,800	0	0
2018	25	6,000	1,500	15,000	3,750
Total		$18,000	$5,400	$15,000	$3,750

The noncurrent deferred tax liability is $3,750 ($15,000 × 0.25), which is the expected tax to be paid on the taxable amount when it is taxed in 2018. The current deferred tax asset is $2,100 ($6,000 × 0.35), and the noncurrent deferred tax asset is $3,300 [($6,000 × 0.30) + ($6,000 × 0.25)]. The journal entry to record the deferred portion of income tax expense for 2015 would be as follows:

Deferred Tax Asset—Current	2,100	
Deferred Tax Asset—Noncurrent	3,300	
Income Tax Benefit (a subtraction from income tax expense)		1,650
Deferred Tax Liability—Noncurrent		3,750

In this example, it was assumed that future income is more likely than not to be sufficient to allow for full deductibility of the $6,000 deductible amount each year. Accordingly, the tax benefit is computed as the deductible amount times the tax rate for that year. However, if the future income was not deemed sufficient to allow for offset of the deductible amounts and if the deferred tax asset could be realized only through the carryback provision of the tax law, the deferred tax asset would be valued using the tax rate in the carryback year. For example, if future income is unlikely but 2015 taxable income exceeds $18,000, then the deductible amounts will be realized only through carryback and offset against 2015 taxable income. If this is the case, the deferred tax asset would be valued using the tax rate in effect for 2015, the carryback year.

Financial Statement Presentation and Disclosure

5 Determine appropriate financial statement presentation and disclosure associated with deferred tax assets and liabilities.

On classified balance sheets, deferred tax assets and liabilities must be reported as either current or noncurrent. As discussed previously, FASB ASC Topic 740 provides for some offsetting of deferred assets and liabilities. For offsetting to be acceptable, the asset and liability must both be current or both be noncurrent. A current asset cannot be offset against a noncurrent liability. Most companies are subject to state and municipal income taxes as well as federal income taxes. If a business enterprise pays income taxes in more than one tax jurisdiction, no offsetting is permitted across jurisdictions.

The income statement must show, either in the body of the statement or in a note, the following selected components of income taxes related to continuing operations:[16]

利润表必须在报表中或者通过附注列示以下与持续经营相关的所得税部分：
- 期所得税费用或收益；
- 递延所得税费用或收益；
- 投资税贷方；
- 作为税项抵扣的政府拨款；
- 经营损失抵后的收益；
- 递延所得税负债或递延所得税资产因《税法》或税率的变化而产生的调整；
- 因环境变化而调整期初备抵账户余额。

1. Current tax expense or benefit
2. Deferred tax expense or benefit
3. Investment tax credits
4. Government grants recognized as tax reductions
5. Benefits of operating loss carryforwards
6. Adjustments of a deferred tax liability or asset for enacted changes in tax laws or rates or a change in the tax status of an enterprise
7. Adjustments in the beginning-of-the-year valuation allowance because of a change in circumstances

The kind of disclosure typically made for income taxes is illustrated by an excerpt from the notes to the 2011 financial statements of ExxonMobil, presented in Exhibit 16-6.

The current portion of income tax expense (with an $1.547 billion tax expense for U.S. federal and $28.849 billion tax expense for non-U.S. income taxes in the ExxonMobil example) can be viewed as the one place in the financial statements where the financial accounting records and the tax records coincide. Roughly speaking, the $1.547 billion

Exhibit 16-6 | ExxonMobil—Disclosure for Provision for Income Taxes

18. Income, Sales-Based and Other Taxes

(Millions of dollars)	2011 U.S.	2011 Non-U.S.	2011 Total	2010 U.S.	2010 Non-U.S.	2010 Total	2009 U.S.	2009 Non-U.S.	2009 Total
Income taxes									
Federal and non-U.S.									
Current	$ 1,547	$28,849	$ 30,396	$1,224	$21,093	$ 22,317	$ (838)	$15,830	$14,992
Deferred—net	1,577	(1,417)	160	49	(1,191)	(1,142)	650	(665)	(15)
U.S. tax on non-U.S. operations	15	—	15	46	—	46	32	—	32
Total federal and non-U.S.	3,139	27,432	30,571	1,319	19,902	21,221	(156)	15,165	15,009
State	480	—	480	340	—	340	110	—	110
Total income taxes	3,619	27,432	31,051	1,659	19,902	21,561	(46)	15,165	15,119
Sales-based taxes	5,652	27,851	33,503	6,182	22,365	28,547	6,271	19,665	25,936
All other taxes and duties									
Other taxes and duties	1,539	38,434	39,973	776	35,342	36,118	581	34,238	34,819
Included in production and manufacturing expenses	1,342	1,425	2,767	1,001	1,237	2,238	699	1,318	2,017
Included in SG&A expenses	181	623	804	201	570	771	197	538	735
Total other taxes and duties	3,062	40,482	43,544	1,978	37,149	39,127	1,477	36,094	37,571
Total	$12,333	$95,765	$108,098	$9,819	$79,416	$89,235	$7,702	$70,924	$78,626

ExxonMobil, 2011, 10K Report

[16] FASB ASC paragraph 740-10-50-9.

tax expense that ExxonMobil reports as the consolidated current portion of U.S. federal income tax for 2011 is the same number that would appear on a hypothetical ExxonMobil 2011 consolidated tax return for the U.S. federal jurisdiction under the heading of "Total Tax Refund" for the year. A careful look at Exhibit 16-6 reveals that this isn't all of the tax ExxonMobil paid during the year. First, additional income taxes of $15 million (extra income tax that must be paid to the U.S. government for income earned in a foreign country) and $480 million (state income taxes) were also payable for 2011. Also, note that because of the existence of deferred taxes, the amount of reported income tax expense (related to U.S. federal income taxes) is $1,577 million more than the amount of income tax actually owed for the year. In addition, to highlight the large taxes associated with its industry, ExxonMobil reports that in 2011 it owed a total of $77.047 billion ($33.503 + $43.544) worldwide for sales-based taxes, other taxes, and duties.

As another example of disclosure, see Exhibit 16-7, which is a portion of IBM's 2011 financial statement note related to income taxes. IBM reported in the notes to its 2011

Exhibit 16-7 | IBM—Disclosure for Deferred Tax Assets and Liabilities

The significant components of deferred tax assets and liabilities that are recorded in the Consolidated Statement of Financial Position were as follows:

Deferred Tax Assets
($ in millions)

At December 31:	2011	2010
Retirement benefits	$ 5,169	$ 4,131
Share-based and other compensation	1,598	1,570
Domestic tax loss/credit carryforwards	914	948
Deferred income	834	1,080
Foreign tax loss/credit carryforwards	752	758
Bad debt, inventory and warranty reserves	608	564
Capitalized research and development	70	291
Depreciation	474	470
Other	1,409	1,486
Gross deferred tax assets	11,828	11,298
Less: valuation allowance	912	795
Net deferred tax assets	$10,916	$10,503

Deferred Tax Liabilities
($ in millions)

At December 31:	2011	2010
Leases	$ 2,149	$ 1,950
Depreciation	1,421	1,223
Goodwill and intangible assets	796	909
Software development costs	466	638
Retirement benefits	551	338
Other	1,121	1,114
Gross deferred tax liabilities	$ 6,504	$ 6,172

The valuation allowance at December 31, 2011, principally applies to certain foreign, state and local loss carryforwards that, in the opinion of management, are more likely than not to expire unutilized. However, to the extent that tax benefits related to these carryforwards are realized in the future, the reduction in the valuation allowance will reduce income tax expense. The year-to-year change in the allowance balance was an increase of $117 million.

IBM, 2011, 10K Report

financial statements that it had a valuation allowance for its deferred tax assets of $912 million on December 31, 2011. The note also indicates that the valuation allowance is principally associated with foreign and state loss carryforwards and state credit carryforwards that IBM believes it is more likely than not that it won't be able to use.

Firms also disclose the specific accounting differences between the financial statements and the tax return that give rise to deferred tax assets and deferred tax liabilities. The most common source of deferred tax items is depreciation. As an illustration, IBM provides significant disclosure as to the specific makeup of its deferred tax assets and liabilities. This disclosure is reproduced in Exhibit 16-7. Overall, as of December 31, 2011, IBM had $10.916 billion in deferred tax assets (net of a $912 million valuation allowance) and $6.504 billion in deferred tax liabilities. In contrast, for ExxonMobil, the total deferred tax liability as of December 31, 2011 (not shown in Exhibit 16-6), was $50.232 billion; of this amount, 91.5%, or $45.951 billion, arose from accelerated tax depreciation and other income tax issues related to property, plant, and equipment.

In addition to the disclosures already described, the reported amount of income tax expense related to continuing operations must be reconciled with the amount of income tax expense that would result from applying federal tax rates to pretax financial income from continuing operations. This reconciliation provides information to readers of the financial statements regarding how the entity has been affected by special provisions of the tax code such as permanent differences, tax credits, and so forth. To illustrate, Exhibit 16-8 is the income tax rate reconciliation for Berkshire Hathaway for 2011. The company begins by reporting that its 2011 income tax expense would have been $5,360 million ($15,314 million × 0.35) if the federal tax rate of 35.0% had been applied to all of its earnings before income taxes. Berkshire Hathaway's effective tax rate for the year of 29.8% is computed by dividing reported income tax expense by earnings before income taxes ($4,568 million/$15,314 million). By looking at Exhibit 16-8, you can see that this difference between the 35.0% statutory rate and the 29.8% effective rate is *not* caused by temporary differences (except for the tax rate changes affecting these temporary differences). As illustrated in this chapter, temporary differences affect whether income tax is payable this year but do not affect whether the income tax expense is accrued this year. The items included in Exhibit 16-8 reflect permanent differences between the tax that Berkshire Hathaway must pay and the tax the company would pay if all income were taxed at the 35.0% rate. For example, Berkshire Hathaway owed an extra $289 million in income taxes for the year

Exhibit 16-8 | Berkshire Hathaway—Reconciliation of Effective Tax Rate to Federal Statutory Rate

Charges for income taxes are reconciled to hypothetical amounts computed at the U.S. federal statutory rate in the table shown below (in millions).

	2011	2010	2009
Earnings before income taxes..............................	$15,314	$19,051	$11,552
Hypothetical amounts applicable to above computed at the federal statutory rate	$ 5,360	$ 6,668	$ 4,043
Dividends received deduction and tax exempt interest...	(497)	(504)	(512)
State income taxes, less federal income tax benefit.......	289	219	81
Foreign tax rate differences...............................	(208)	(154)	(92)
U.S. income tax credits	(241)	(182)	(134)
BNSF holding gain..	—	(342)	—
Other differences, net	(135)	(98)	152
Total income taxes...	$ 4,568	$ 5,607	$ 3,538

Berkshire Hathaway, Inc., 2011, 10K Report

Stop & Think

What is the rationale behind excluding from a corporation's taxable income dividends received from another corporation?

a) The dividend exclusion increases the progressive nature of income tax rates.
b) The dividend exclusion is necessary to avoid the recognition of unrealizable deferred tax assets.
c) Without the exclusion, corporate income would be subject to triple taxation.
d) It is futile to search for any underlying rationale in income tax rules.

because state income taxes must be paid on top of the 35.0% federal income tax. In addition, lower income tax rates in foreign countries resulted in Berkshire Hathaway's saving $208 million in income tax for the year. Offsetting these extra taxes is the fact that some of Berkshire Hathaway's 2011 income will never be taxed. Berkshire Hathaway saved $497 million in income taxes because some of its interest income (on municipal securities) is not taxable and because dividends paid by one corporation to another are partially excluded from tax; this tax provision yielded a permanent $497 million tax savings to Berkshire Hathaway in 2011.

Deferred Taxes and the Statement of Cash Flows

LO6 Comply with income tax disclosure requirements associated with the statement of cash flows.

FASB ASC Topic 230 (Statement of Cash Flows) requires separate disclosure of the amount of cash paid for income taxes during a period. This separate disclosure is required for just two items: cash paid for income taxes and cash paid for interest. Financial statements are used to assess the amount and timing of future cash flows, and in the case of interest and income taxes, the FASB argued that this specific cash flow information should be readily available and easily disclosed by most firms.[17] As an example, **Disney** discloses in its financial statements that for the year ended October 1, 2011, it reported income tax expense of $2,785 million (on the income statement) and cash paid during the year for income taxes of $2,341 million (on the statement of cash flows).

Income taxes affect the Operating Activities section of the statement of cash flows.[18] When the direct method is used, cash paid for income taxes is shown as a separate line item. When the indirect method is used, the treatment of income taxes is a bit more complicated. Adjustments to convert net income into cash from operations are needed for changes in income taxes payable and receivable accounts and for changes in deferred tax asset and liability accounts. In addition, supplemental disclosure of the amount of cash paid for income taxes is required.

As an illustration of how income taxes are handled in the statement of cash flows, consider the following information for Collazo Company for 2015:

Revenue (all cash)		$30,000
Income tax expense:		
Current	$10,300	
Deferred	1,700	12,000
Net income		$18,000

---

[17] FASB ASC paragraph 230-10-50-2.
[18] The FASB considered allocating income taxes paid among the Operating, Investing, and Financing Activities sections of the statement of cash flows. For example, any income tax effects from the disposal of equipment could be disclosed in the Investing Activities section. However, it was concluded that this allocation would be unnecessarily complex, with the cost of doing it outweighing the benefit. See pre-Codification FASB *Statement No. 95*, par. 92.

In addition, Collazo had the balance sheet amounts shown below at the beginning and end of the year.

	December 31, 2015	December 31, 2014
Income tax refund receivable	$2,000	$ 0
Income taxes payable	0	1,000
Deferred tax liability	9,700	8,000

Using the format developed in Chapter 5, we will analyze the income statement and convert the accrual basis number to the cash basis, as demonstrated in the following table:

Income Statement		Adjustments	Statement of Cash Flows	
Revenue (all cash)	$ 30,000	—	$ 30,000	Cash collected from customers
Income tax expense—current	(10,300)	− $2,000—Increase in tax receivable	(13,300)	Cash paid for taxes
Income tax expense—deferred	(1,700)	− 1,000—Decrease in taxes payable + 1,700—Increase in deferred tax liability	0	
Net income	$ 18,000	− $1,300—Total adjustments	$ 16,700	Cash flow from operations

Using the resulting information, the Operating Activities section of Collazo's statement of cash flows is as follows if the direct method is used:

Cash collected from customers	$ 30,000
Income taxes paid	(13,300)
Cash provided by operating activities	$ 16,700

If the indirect method is used, the Operating Activities section is as follows:

Net income	$18,000
(Increase) decrease in income tax refund receivable	(2,000)
Increase (decrease) in income taxes payable	(1,000)
Increase (decrease) in deferred tax liability	1,700
Cash provided by operating activities	$16,700

In addition, if the indirect method is used, the amount of cash paid for income taxes, $13,300, must be separately disclosed either in the statement of cash flows or in the notes to the financial statements.

International Accounting for Deferred Taxes

LO7 学习目标7
描述《国际会计准则》如何在递延所得税处理方式上与美国准则趋同。

⑦ Describe how, with respect to deferred income taxes, International Accounting Standards have converged toward the U.S. treatment.

In the past, accounting standards around the world have differed substantially in the area of deferred taxes. However, over the past 15 years, the U.S. approach to deferred tax accounting has become used almost everywhere. This section discusses the different approaches that have been used around the world and recent developments in the international harmonization of deferred tax accounting.

The approach to deferred tax accounting used in the United States (and discussed in this chapter) is sometimes called the *comprehensive recognition approach* because it requires recognition of all temporary differences between financial accounting income and taxable income. At the other extreme, the *no-deferral approach* recognizes none of the differences. These two approaches are described in this section.

no-deferral approach
不可递延法
comprehensive recognition approach
综合认定法

No-Deferral Approach

The simplest approach to accounting for differences between financial accounting and taxable income is just to ignore the differences and report income tax expense equal to the amount of tax payable for the year. Historically, this no-deferral approach was quite common around the world. In countries where there is a close correspondence between financial accounting standards and tax rules, the no-deferral approach yields financial statement numbers that are not that much different from what would be generated using the full-blown deferred tax accounting practices used in the United States. The no-deferral approach has become almost extinct now (except in smaller, privately held companies) as companies seek to converge to the prevailing international practice; the no-deferral approach has been formally frowned upon since the original issuance of *IAS 12* in 1979.

Comprehensive Recognition Approach

The IASB has embraced the comprehensive recognition approach to deferred tax accounting that underlies FASB ASC Topic 740 in the United States. The original version of *IAS 12* required that deferred taxes be included in the computation of income tax expense and that deferred taxes be reported on the balance sheet, but it left open the method used to compute the deferred taxes. In 1996, the IASC (predecessor to the IASB) revised *IAS 12*; the accounting required in the revised version is very similar to the deferred tax accounting practices that have been described throughout this chapter. The good news for U.S. accountants and accounting students is that the world appears to have come around to the U.S. way of accounting for deferred taxes, so we don't have to learn very much in order to understand international accounting for deferred taxes.

Partial Recognition Approach

Historically, the United Kingdom employed an innovative technique for accounting for deferred taxes that results in a deferred tax liability being recorded only to the extent that the deferred taxes are actually expected to be paid in the future. To use the U.K. terminology, deferred income taxes are recognized only if they are expected to "crystallise." An equivalent concept in the United States might be "realized." For example, if a company is growing and continually purchasing new assets, as deferred taxes on the older assets reverse, they will be offset by taxes being deferred on the new assets. In such cases, if the firm is assumed to be a going concern, the tax deferral may continue indefinitely as new assets replace old ones. In the United Kingdom, it is said that this type of deferred tax liability will not crystallise, and so historically it was not recognized. Only if it is expected that deferrals on new assets will not offset older assets will crystallisation occur—and then a deferred tax liability would be recognized. The reasoning behind the U.K. approach to deferred tax liabilities is actually quite interesting: If a liability is deferred indefinitely, the present value of that liability is zero. This concept highlights a common criticism of U.S. deferred tax accounting—no accounting recognition is given to the fact that by deferring income tax payments, firms are decreasing the present value of their tax obligation. Despite its conceptual attractiveness, the U.K. partial recognition approach was dropped in the interest of international harmonization. In its description of its new standard (*FRS 19*), the Accounting Standards Board (ASB) of the United Kingdom gives this lukewarm evaluation of the comprehensive recognition approach:

> In recent years, the partial provision method of accounting for deferred tax . . . has lost favour internationally, primarily because it is subjective (relying heavily on management expectations about future events) and inconsistent with other areas of accounting. Other major standard-setters and *IAS 12* (revised 1996) now require deferred tax to be provided for in full. Whilst the ASB could see the merits of the partial provision method, it accepted some of the arguments against it and concluded that deferred tax was not an area where a good case could be made for taking a stand against the direction of international opinion.[19]

In summary, both the no-deferral and partial recognition approaches have been used around the world in the past, but *IAS 12* now requires the comprehensive recognition approach that is employed in the United States. It appears that the international differences in accounting for deferred income taxes will be relatively small in future years.

 SOLUTIONS TO OPENING SCENARIO QUESTIONS

1. Financial statement users and preparers complained about pre-Codification *Statement No. 96* on both practical and conceptual grounds. These complaints were so heated that the FASB's credibility was damaged. For a time, there were suggestions that, because of its "mishandling" of the accounting for deferred taxes, the FASB should be replaced with a different standard setter.

2. Pre-Codification *Statement No. 96* required that deferred tax liabilities be valued using current income tax rates instead of the tax rates that existed when the deferred tax liability was first recognized. Because the Tax Reform Act of 1986 had lowered corporate income tax rates, *Statement No. 96* resulted in recognition of a reduction in the recorded amount of deferred tax liabilities and a corresponding gain.

3. Under FASB Pre-Codification *Statement No. 96*, deferred tax assets were generally not recognized; in fact, this was one of the complaints about *Statement No. 96*. With the adoption of pre-Codification FASB *Statement No. 109*, these deferred tax assets were recognized on the balance sheet along with the recognition of a corresponding gain.

Stop & Think SOLUTIONS

1. (Page 16-3) The correct answer is A. An obvious third set of books for a well-run company, arguably the most important, is the managerial accounting system. Of course, the managerial records would be tailored to the needs of each company. Different aspects of the managerial records would emphasize CONTROL, EVALUATION, and PLANNING. A small business would combine the functions of all three sets of books—financial, tax, and managerial—into one set of reports. As a company's information needs become more sophisticated, there is increased divergence among these three sets of books.

2. (Page 16-8) The correct answer is C. Deferred tax assets and deferred tax liabilities result from different types of transactions. For example, a deferred tax asset can result from warranties, while a deferred tax liability can result from accelerated depreciation of a depreciable asset. The differences between GAAP and tax law provide numerous instances that can result in either deferred tax assets or deferred tax liabilities.

3. (Page 16-11) The correct answer is D. As will be pointed out in an upcoming section of the text, deferred tax assets and deferred tax liabilities are to be measured using tax rates expected to be applicable in the period of the reversal. Thus, if rates in the future are expected to be 30%, then the deferred amount would be multiplied by 30% instead of 40%.

4. (Page 16-17) The correct answer is C. One of the key purposes of financial statements, according to the conceptual framework, is to aid investors and creditors in assessing the amounts, timing, and uncertainty of future cash flows.

---

[19] **http://www.asb.org.uk**. *FRS 19*, "Deferred Tax," background to FRS requirements.

By reporting to financial statement users the existence of additional future cash flows (deferred tax liabilities) and additional future cash savings (deferred tax assets), deferred tax accounting helps users assess future cash flows.

5. (Page 16-23) The correct answer is A. Although carrybacks and carryforwards work to the benefit of the company in that it is able to either receive a refund of taxes previously paid or to reduce the amount of taxes to be paid in the future, one must remember that the company had to report a net operating loss in order to take advantage of this feature of the tax law. The carryback and carryforward provisions ease the pain of an operating loss.

6. (Page 16-30) The correct answer is C. Dividends paid to shareholders are already double taxed. The corporation must pay tax on the income, leaving less income to pay to shareholders as dividends. Then the shareholders must pay income tax when they receive the dividends. When a corporation is a shareholder and receives dividends, then that dividend income would be taxed for a third time without the special tax provision excluding the dividends from income taxation for the receiving corporation.

SOLUTION TO USING THE FASB'S CODIFICATION

You should have found Topic 740 in the "Expenses" collection of topics. And right there in the topic table of contents is Subtopic 740-20 (Income Taxes—Intraperiod Tax Allocation). A quick look at the "Overview and Background" section reveals the following in FASB ASC paragraph 740-20-05-2: "This Subtopic addresses the process of intraperiod tax allocation that allocates total income tax expense or benefit of an entity for a period to different components of comprehensive income and shareholders' equity. This includes allocating income tax expense or benefit for the year to: (a) continuing operations, (b) discontinued operations, (c) extraordinary items, (d) other comprehensive income, and (e) items charged or credited directly to shareholders' equity."

Ahh, this makes sense. The IRS doesn't care whether you classify a certain income-generating event as an extraordinary item or a discontinued operation—you still have to pay tax on any income generated. Intraperiod tax allocation is the process of assigning your total tax bill to the different categories of income. So, when your brother-in-law comes back in the room, try to be gracious in victory.

Review Chapter 16 Learning Objectives

① Understand the concept of deferred taxes and the distinction between permanent and temporary differences.

Deferred taxes result from the different objectives being used and applied for computing taxable income and income for financial reporting purposes. Because of differences between the tax code and GAAP, the accounting treatment for certain issues will differ. These differences can result in temporary timing differences that will eventually reverse or permanent differences that will not reverse. Temporary timing differences that result in taxable income in the future are termed *taxable temporary differences* and result in deferred tax liabilities. Those differences that result in expected deductible amounts in the future are termed *deductible temporary differences* and result in deferred tax assets.

② Compute the amount of deferred tax liabilities and assets including the use of a valuation allowance and the uncertainty of tax positions.

Computing the amount of deferred tax assets and liabilities involves four steps: (1) identify the types and amounts of temporary timing differences, (2) compute the deferred tax liability associated with taxable temporary differences using current and future tax rates, (3) compute the amount of deferred tax asset associated with deductible temporary differences using current and future tax rates, and (4) reduce the amount of deferred tax asset if it is more likely than not that some or all of the asset may not be realized, using a valuation allowance account. The claiming of uncertain tax deductions may require the recognition of an unrecognized tax benefit liability to the extent that the claimed deduction is in excess of the deduction that is more likely than not to be sustained upon taxing authority review.

③ Explain the provisions of tax loss carrybacks and carryforwards, and be able to account for these provisions.

Tax law requires corporations to pay taxes if they report taxable income. If a business reports a loss, the tax code allows that business to offset the loss against income in other years. The business is allowed to carry back its net operating losses up to two years to obtain a refund of taxes previously paid or to carry forward an operating loss up to 20 years in order to reduce the tax liability associated with future periods. A carryforward results in a deferred tax asset and may require the use of a valuation allowance account if it is more likely than not that the deferred asset may not be realized.

④ Schedule future tax rates, and determine the effect on deferred tax assets and liabilities.

Deferred tax assets and liabilities are recorded at the tax rates expected to be in effect in the periods of reversal. Thus, if Congress enacts rate changes or the corporation's taxable income level results in different expected future tax rates, these differing rates must be reflected in the valuation of deferred tax assets and liabilities.

⑤ Determine appropriate financial statement presentation and disclosure associated with deferred tax assets and liabilities.

Deferred tax assets and liabilities are disclosed on the balance sheet as either current or noncurrent, based on the classification of the underlying asset or obligation. Additional disclosure is required relating to the tax expense (or benefit) for the period, deferred tax expense (or benefit), benefits associated with tax loss carryforwards, the effect of changes in tax rates, and adjustments associated with the valuation allowance account.

⑥ Comply with income tax disclosure requirements associated with the statement of cash flows.

The amount of cash paid for income taxes must be disclosed using either the direct or indirect methods. With the direct method, the amount of cash paid for income taxes would be disclosed directly on the statement of cash flows. Under the indirect method, adjustments are made to net income for changes in receivable and payable balances associated with current and deferred tax assets and liabilities. Thus, with this method, the actual amount paid for taxes may not be disclosed in the body of the statement of cash flows. If this is the case, disclosure of cash paid for taxes is required in the notes to the financial statements or at the bottom of the statement of cash flows.

⑦ Describe how, with respect to deferred income taxes, International Accounting Standards have converged toward the U.S. treatment.

Historically, companies around the world have used the no-deferral, the partial recognition, and the comprehensive recognition approaches to deferred tax accounting. With the revision of *IAS 12* in 1996, it now appears that deferred tax accounting around the world is converging toward the comprehensive recognition approach employed in the United States.

FASB-IASB CODIFICATION SUMMARY

Topic	FASB Accounting Standards Codification	Original FASB Standard	Corresponding IASB Standard	Differences between U.S. GAAP and IFRS
Use of currently enacted tax rates	Section 740-10-10 par. 3	SFAS No. 109 par. 18	IAS 12 par. 46	Under U.S. GAAP, currently enacted tax rates for future years are used in valuing deferred tax assets and liabilities. Under IFRS, tax rates that have been "substantively enacted" are also used. Substantively enacted tax rates are future tax rates that have been announced by the government but that have not yet been formally enacted into law.
Current/noncurrent classification of deferred tax assets and liabilities	Section 740-10-45 par. 4	SFAS No. 109 par. 41	IAS 1 par. 56	Under U.S. GAAP, deferred tax assets and liabilities are classified current or noncurrent based on the classification of the associated asset or liability. Under IFRS, all deferred tax items are classified as noncurrent.
Recognition of deferred tax assets	Section 740-10-30 par. 5e	SFAS No. 109 par. 17e	IAS 12 par. 24	Under U.S. GAAP, deferred tax assets are recognized if it is "more likely than not" (50%+ probability) that the future tax benefits will be realized. Under IFRS, the probability threshold is "probable," which is generally seen to be higher than "more likely than not."
Uncertain tax positions	Topic 740	FASB FIN No. 48	No specific accounting standard in IAS	Under IFRS, there is no standard regarding the recognition of a tax liability related to an uncertain tax position.
Cash paid for income taxes	Section 230-10-50 par. 2	SFAS No. 95 par. 121	IFRS 7 par. 35	Both U.S. GAAP and IFRS require separate disclosure of the amount of cash paid for income taxes. Under IFRS, this amount may be allocated among operating, investing, and financing activities.

KEY TERMS

Asset and liability method of interperiod tax allocation 16-9
Deductible temporary differences 16-8
Effective tax rate 16-29
Financial income 16-3
Interperiod tax allocation 16-9
Net operating loss (NOL) carryback 16-22
Net operating loss (NOL) carryforward 16-23
Permanent differences 16-6
Taxable income 16-3
Taxable temporary differences 16-7
Temporary differences 16-7
Uncertain tax position 16-19
Valuation allowance 16-16

Tutorial Activities

Tutorial Activities with author-written, content-specific feedback, available on *CengageNOW* for *Stice & Stice*.

QUESTIONS

1. Accounting methods used by a company to determine income for financial reporting purposes frequently differ from those used to determine taxable income. What is the justification for these differences?
2. Distinguish between a nondeductible expense and a temporary difference that results in a taxable income greater than pretax financial income reported in the income statement.
3. Distinguish between taxable temporary differences and deductible temporary differences, and give at least two examples of each type.
4. One possibility for reporting income tax expense in the income statement for a given year is to merely report the amount of income tax payable in that year. What is wrong with this approach?
5. What are the major advantages of the asset and liability method?
6. What is a drawback of the asset and liability method?
7. Describe how a change in enacted future tax rates is accounted for under the asset and liability method.
8. When is a valuation allowance necessary?
9. How does the FASB define the probability term "more likely than not" in Topic 740?
10. What are the sources of income through which the tax benefit of a deferred tax asset can be realized?
11. In applying the net operating loss carryback and carryforward provisions, what order of application is followed for federal tax purposes?
12. How is the classification of assets (current or noncurrent) arising from NOL carryforwards determined under FASB ASC Topic 740?
13. Under what conditions would scheduling the temporary difference reversals be required under Topic 740?
14. How would you define "uncertain" tax position?
15. What are the two steps that are required in determining the amount of tax benefit to be recognized in association with an uncertain tax position?
16. "In practice, the provisions for accounting for uncertain tax positions are relatively easy to apply." Do you agree or disagree? Explain.
17. What was the most significant change in accounting for income tax carryforwards between pre-Codification *Statement No. 96* and pre-Codification *Statement No. 109*? (*Note:* Pre-Codification *Statement No. 109* is the source for most of the existing provisions in FASB ASC Topic 740.)
18. How do changes in the balances of deferred income taxes affect the amount of cash paid for income taxes?
19. If a company experiences a current operating loss, it may carry the loss backward and forward. What impact do these carrybacks and carryforwards have on the reported operating loss? on the statement of cash flows?
20. What rules govern the netting of deferred tax assets and deferred tax liabilities?
21. In the past, why was accounting for income taxes not as significant an issue in some foreign countries as it is in the United States?
22. In 1996, the IASB revised *IAS 12*. Did that revision make the international standard for deferred tax accounting more or less similar to the U.S. standard?
23. Briefly describe the partial recognition approach to accounting for deferred income taxes.

PRACTICE EXERCISES

Practice 16-1
Simple Deferred Tax Liability
The company had sales for the year of $100,000. Of these sales, only $70,000 was collected in cash. The other $30,000 is expected to be collected in cash next year. For this business, the tax rules stipulate that income is not taxed until it is collected in cash. The only expense is income tax expense, and the tax rate is 25% this year and in all future years. Make all journal entries necessary to record income tax expense for the year.

Practice 16-2
Reversal of a Simple Deferred Tax Liability
Refer to the data in Practice 16-1. Those data are for Year 1. In Year 2, the company had sales for the year of $100,000 but collected $130,000 in cash—all of the cash for the sales for Year 2 plus the unpaid $30,000 for sales made in Year 1. The tax rate in Year 2 is still 25%. Make all journal entries necessary to record income tax expense for Year 2.

Practice 16-3
Simple Deferred Tax Asset
The company had sales for the year of $200,000. Expenses (except for income taxes) for the year totaled $170,000. Of this $170,000 in expenses, $12,000 is bad debt expense. The tax rules applicable to this company stipulate that bad debts are not tax deductible until the accounts are actually written off. None of the accounts were written off this year but are expected to be written off next year or the following year. The tax rate is 30% this year and in all future years. Make all journal entries necessary to record income tax expense for the year. Assume that the company has been profitable and is expected to be profitable in the future.

Practice 16-4
Permanent and Temporary Differences
The company reported pretax financial income in its income statement of $50,000. Among the items included in the computation of pretax financial income were the following:

Interest revenue from municipal bonds	$10,000
Nondeductible expenses	17,000
Warranty expenses (not deductible until actually provided; none provided this year)	8,000

The income tax rate is 30%. Compute the following: (1) financial income subject to tax, (2) taxable income, (3) income tax expense, and (4) net income.

Practice 16-5
Deferred Tax Liability
On January 1, the company purchased investment securities for $1,000. The securities are classified as trading. By December 31, the securities had a fair value of $1,800 but had not yet been sold. Excluding the trading securities, income before taxes for the year was $10,000. Assume that there are no other book-tax differences. The income tax rate is 35% for the current year and all future years. Prepare the journal entry or entries necessary to record income tax expense for the year.

Practice 16-6
Deferred Tax Liability
On January 1, 2015, the company purchased a piece of equipment for $75,000. The equipment has a five-year useful life and $0 residual value. The company uses straight-line depreciation for financial accounting purposes. Assume that the depreciation deduction for income tax purposes is as follows: 2015 = $25,000; 2016 = $20,000; 2017 = $15,000; 2018 = $10,000; and 2019 = $5,000. Assume that revenue in each year 2015–2019 is $50,000, that the revenue is the same for both tax and financial reporting purposes, and that the only expenses are depreciation and income taxes. The income tax rate is 40% in all years. Prepare the journal entry or entries to record income tax expense in each year 2015–2019.

Practice 16-7
Variable Future Tax Rates
Refer to Practice 16-5. Assume that the income tax rate is 35% for the current year but that the enacted tax rate for all future years is 42%. Prepare the journal entry or entries necessary to record income tax expense for the year.

Practice 16-8

Change in Enacted Tax Rates
Refer to Practice 16-6. Assume that on January 1, 2017, Congress changes the enacted tax rate. Make the journal entry necessary to record this tax rate change on January 1, 2017, assuming that (1) the new tax rate is 30% and (2) the new tax rate is 43%.

Practice 16-9

Deferred Tax Asset
On January 1, the company purchased investment securities for $1,000. The securities are classified as trading. By December 31, the securities had a fair value of $100 but had not yet been sold. Excluding the trading securities, income before taxes for the year was $5,000. Assume that there are no other book-tax differences. The income tax rate is 45% for the current year and all future years. Assume that the company has been profitable in past years and is more likely than not to be profitable in future years. Prepare the journal entry or entries necessary to record income tax expense for the year.

Practice 16-10

Deferred Tax Asset
The company started business on January 1 and had revenues of $60,000 for the year. In addition to income tax expense, the company's only other expenses are as follows:

- *Bad debt expense of $10,000.* Tax rules do not allow any deduction until the bad debts are actually written off. During the year, bad debts totaling $2,000 were written off.
- *Postretirement health care benefit expense of $15,000.* Tax rules do not allow any deduction until the actual retiree health care expenditures are made. No expenditures were made during the year.

The income tax rate is 35% for the current year and all future years. Assume that the company is more likely than not to be profitable in future years. Prepare the journal entry or entries necessary to record income tax expense for the year.

Practice 16-11

Deferred Tax Liabilities and Assets
On January 1, the company purchased investment securities for $2,000. The securities are classified as trading. By December 31, the securities had a fair value of $4,200 but had not yet been sold. The company also recognized a $7,000 restructuring charge during the year. The restructuring charge is composed of an impairment write-down on a manufacturing facility. Tax rules do not allow a deduction for the write-down unless the facility is actually sold; the facility was not sold by the end of the year. Excluding the trading securities and the restructuring charge, income before taxes for the year was $25,000. Assume that there are no other book-tax differences. The income tax rate is 40% for the current year and all future years. Prepare the journal entry or entries necessary to record income tax expense for the year. State any assumptions you must make.

Practice 16-12

Deferred Tax Liabilities and Assets
On January 1, the company purchased investment securities for $1,000. The securities are classified as trading. By December 31, the securities had a fair value of $700 but had not yet been sold. On January 1, the company also purchased a piece of equipment for $10,000. The equipment has a four-year useful life and $0 residual value. The company uses straight-line depreciation for financial accounting purposes. Assume that the depreciation deduction for income tax purposes is $3,300 in the first year of the life of the equipment. Excluding the trading securities and the depreciation, income before taxes for the year was $4,000. Assume that there are no other book-tax differences. The income tax rate is 40% for the current year and all future years. Prepare the journal entry or entries necessary to record income tax expense for the year. State any assumptions you must make.

Practice 16-13

Valuation Allowance
Refer to Practice 16-9. The company had no taxable income in past years. Analysis of prospects for the future indicates that it is more likely than not that total taxable income in the foreseeable future will be no more than $400. Assume that the income tax expense journal entry required in Practice 16-9 has already been made. Make any necessary adjusting entry.

Practice 16-14

Valuation Allowance
Refer to Practice 16-10. The company had no taxable income in past years. Analysis of prospects for the future indicates that it is more likely than not that total taxable income in the foreseeable future will be no more than $20,000. Assume that the income tax expense journal entry required in Practice 16-10 has already been made. Make any necessary adjusting entry.

Practice 16-15

Uncertain Tax Position
The company has taken a tax position that is subject to review by the Internal Revenue Service. The company determines that there is a 40% probability that the position will not be sustained upon review. Is this a "highly certain" tax position? Why or why not?

Practice 16-16

Uncertain Tax Position
The company has determined that there is an 80% likelihood that its position on a tax issue will be upheld upon review by taxing authorities and that the entire amount of the position, $100,000, will be allowed. Is this a "highly certain" tax position? Why or why not?

Practice 16-17

Uncertain Tax Position
The company is evaluating its tax position on a certain issue and has determined that although it is more likely than not that its position will be sustained, it is less certain about the amount that will be sustained. It has provided the following probability estimates and amounts:

There is a xx% probability that	The allowable reduction in taxes payable will be	The cumulative probability of occurrence is
15%	$100	15%
20	80	35
10	60	45
15	40	60
20	20	80
20	0	100

Determine the amount of the unrecognized tax benefit liability and provide the journal entry required to recognize the liability associated with the unrecognized tax benefit.

Practice 16-18

NOL Carryback
Taxable income and income tax rates for 2013–2015 for the company have been as follows:

Year	Taxable Income	Income Tax Rate	Total Tax Paid
2013	$ 75,000	25%	$18,750
2014	50,000	30	15,000
2015	(80,000)	35	0

Make the journal entry necessary to record any NOL carryback in 2015.

Practice 16-19

NOL Carryforward
Refer to Practice 16-18. Assume that the net operating loss in 2015 was $150,000 instead of $80,000. Make the journal entry necessary to record (1) any NOL carryback in 2015 and (2) any NOL carryforward created in 2015. The enacted tax rate for future years is 35%. State any assumptions you must make.

Practice 16-20

NOL Carryforward

Taxable income and income tax rates for 2013–2018 for the company are shown below.

Year	Taxable Income	Income Tax Rate	Total Tax Paid
2013	$ 30,000	30%	$9,000
2014	15,000	35	5,250
2015	20,000	35	7,000
2016	(100,000)	40	?
2017	50,000	35	?
2018	(200,000)	30	?

Make the journal entry necessary to record any NOL carryforward created in 2018. The enacted tax rate for future years is 40%.

Practice 16-21

Scheduling for Enacted Future Tax Rates

Refer to Practice 16-6. Assume that the enacted tax rates are as follows:

2015	40%
2016	37
2017	37
2018	37
2019	34

For simplicity, assume that temporary differences reverse in a FIFO pattern; that is, assume that the first temporary difference created is the first to reverse. Prepare the journal entry or entries to record income tax expense in 2015.

Practice 16-22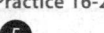

Reporting Deferred Tax Assets and Liabilities

Refer to Practice 16-12. (1) What deferred tax amount or amounts would appear on the balance sheet? (2) Prepare the financial statement note disclosure needed to identify the sources of the deferred tax amounts. Refer to Exhibit 16-7.

Practice 16-23

Computation of Effective Tax Rate

Refer to Practice 16-4. Compute the effective tax rate.

Practice 16-24

Reconciliation of Statutory Rate and Effective Rate

The company reported sales of $60,000. Other income statement items for the year were as follows:

Interest revenue from municipal bonds	$ 7,000
Depreciation expense (tax depreciation was $36,000)	25,000
Expenses not deductible for tax purposes	18,000
Warranty expenses (not deductible until actually provided; $2,000 provided this year)	10,000

The income tax rate is 40%. (1) Compute the effective tax rate and (2) provide a reconciliation of the statutory tax rate of 40% to the effective tax rate.

Practice 16-25

Deferred Taxes and Operating Cash Flow
The company assembled the following information with respect to operating cash flow for the year:

Net income	$10,000
Depreciation	2,000
Increase in accounts receivable	1,200
Decrease in inventory	850
Decrease in accounts payable	300
Increase in income taxes payable	40
Increase in deferred tax liability	1,430

Compute cash flow from operating activities.

Practice 16-26

Cash Paid for Income Taxes
The company reported the following balance sheet information:

	2015	2014
Income taxes payable	$ 17,000	$22,000
Deferred income tax liability	130,000	90,000

Total income tax expense for 2015 was $60,000. Compute the amount of cash paid for income taxes in 2015.

EXERCISES

Exercise 16-27

Identification of Temporary Differences
Indicate which of the following items are temporary differences and which are nontaxable or nondeductible. For each temporary difference, indicate whether the item considered alone would create a deferred tax asset or a deferred tax liability.

(a) Tax depreciation in excess of book depreciation, $150,000
(b) Excess of income on installment sales over income reportable for tax purposes, $130,000
(c) Premium payment for life insurance policy on president, $95,000
(d) Rent collected in advance of period earned, $75,000
(e) Warranty provision accrued in advance of period paid, $40,000
(f) Interest revenue received on municipal bonds, $30,000

Exercise 16-28

Calculation of Taxable Income
Using the information given in Exercise 16-27 and assuming pretax financial income of $3,100,000, calculate taxable income.

Exercise 16-29

Deferred Tax Liability
Faro Inc. began operating on January 1, 2015. At the end of the first year of operations, Faro reported $400,000 income before income taxes on its income statement but only $320,000 taxable income on its tax return. Analysis of the $80,000 difference revealed that $45,000 was a permanent difference and $35,000 was a temporary tax liability difference related to a current asset. The enacted tax rate for 2015 and future years is 35%.

1. Prepare the journal entries to record income taxes for 2015.
2. Assume that at the end of 2016, the accumulated temporary tax liability difference related to future years is $70,000. Prepare the journal entry to record any adjustment to deferred tax liabilities at the end of 2016.

Exercise 16-30

Deferred Tax Asset

Lofthouse Machinery Co. includes a two-year warranty on its machinery sales. At the end of 2015, an analysis of the warranty records reveals an accumulated temporary difference of $120,000 for warranty expenses; book expenses related to warranties have exceeded tax deductions allowed. The enacted income tax rate for 2015 and future years is 40%. Management concludes that it is more likely than not that Lofthouse will have future income to realize the future tax benefit from this temporary difference. They also conclude that 20% of the warranty liability is current and 80% is noncurrent.

1. How would the deferred tax information be reported on the Lofthouse balance sheet at December 31, 2015?
2. If management assumed that only 70% of the tax benefit from the temporary difference could be realized, how would the deferred tax information be reported on the balance sheet at December 31, 2015? (Recall that the valuation allowance is allocated proportionately between the current and noncurrent portions of the deferred tax asset.)

Exercise 16-31

Determinants of "More Likely than Not"

Fulton Company computed a pretax financial loss of $15,000 for the first year of its operations ended December 31, 2015. This loss did not include $25,000 in unearned rent revenue that was recognized as taxable income in 2015 when the cash was received.

1. Prepare the journal entries necessary to record income tax for the year. The income tax rate is 40%. Assume it is more likely than not that future taxable income will be sufficient to allow for the full realization of any deferred tax assets and that unearned rent revenue is a current liability.
2. If future taxable income from operations was not expected to be sufficient to allow for the full realization of any deferred tax assets, what other sources of income may be considered to determine the need for a valuation allowance?

Exercise 16-32

Deferred Tax Asset Valuation Allowance

Relevan Company computed a pretax financial loss of $15,000 for the first year of its operations ended December 31, 2015. Included in the loss was $42,000 in uncollectible accounts expense that was accrued on the books in 2015 using an allowance system based on a percentage of sales. For income tax purposes, deductions for uncollectible accounts are allowed when specific accounts receivable are determined to be uncollectible and written off. No accounts receivable have been written off as uncollectible in 2015.

1. Prepare the journal entries necessary to record income taxes for the year. The enacted income tax rate is 35% for 2015 and all future years. Assume that it is more likely than not that future taxable income will be sufficient to allow for the full realization of any deferred tax assets. Accounts Receivable and the related allowance account are reported under current assets on the balance sheet.
2. Repeat (1), assuming that it is more likely than not that future taxable income will be zero before considering the actual bad debt losses in future years.

Exercise 16-33

Changing Tax Rates

Goshute Company computed pretax financial income of $50,000 for the year ended December 31, 2015. Taxable income for the year was $15,000. Accumulated temporary differences as of December 31, 2014, were $120,000. A deferred tax liability of $48,000 was included on the December 31, 2014, balance sheet. Accumulated temporary differences as of December 31, 2015, are $155,000. The differences are related to noncurrent items.

1. Prepare the journal entries necessary to record income tax for 2015. The enacted income tax rate is assumed to be 40% for 2015 and future years.
2. On January 1, 2016, the income tax rate is changed to 32% for 2016 and all future years. Prepare the necessary journal entry, if any.

Exercise 16-34

Deferred Tax Liability

Hinton Exploration Company reported pretax financial income of $621,000 for the calendar year 2015. Included in the Other Income section of the income statement was $98,000 of interest revenue from municipal bonds held by the company. The income statement also included depreciation expense of $580,000 for a machine that cost $3,250,000. The income tax return reported $650,000 as MACRS depreciation on the machine.

The enacted tax rate is 40% for 2015 and future years. Prepare the journal entry or entries necessary to record income taxes for 2015.

Exercise 16-35

Deferred Tax Asset

Pro-Tech-Tronics Company computed pretax financial income of $35,000 for the first year of its operations ended December 31, 2015. Unearned rent revenue of $55,000 had been recognized as taxable income in 2015 when the cash was received but had not yet been recognized in the financial accounting records.

The unearned rent is expected to be recognized on the books in the following pattern.

2016	$15,000
2017	20,000
2018	12,000
2019	8,000
Total	$55,000

The enacted tax rates for this year and the next four years are as follows:

2015	34%
2016	34
2017	30
2018	30
2019	37

Prepare the journal entries necessary to record income taxes for 2015. Assume that there will be sufficient income in each future year to realize any deductible amounts.

Exercise 16-36

Deferred Tax Assets and Liabilities

Fibertek, Inc., computed a pretax financial income of $40,000 for the first year of its operations ended December 31, 2015. Included in financial income was $25,000 of nondeductible expenses, $22,000 gross profit on installment sales that was deferred for tax purposes until the installments were collected, and $18,000 in bad debt expense that had been accrued on the books in 2015.

The temporary differences are expected to reverse in the following patterns:

Year	Gross Profit on Collections	Bad Debt Write-Offs
2016	$ 5,000	$ 6,000
2017	7,000	12,000
2018	4,000	
2019	6,000	
Totals	$22,000	$18,000

The enacted tax rates for this year and the next four years are as follows:

2015	40%
2016	35
2017	32
2018	30
2019	32

Prepare the journal entries necessary to record income taxes for 2015. Assume that there will be sufficient income in each future year to realize any deductible amounts. For classification purposes, the bad debt write-offs are considered to be associated with a current asset, and the receivable for installment sales is classified as both current and noncurrent, depending on the expected timing of the receipt.

Exercise 16-37

Deferred Tax Assets and Liabilities
Flatworld Shipping Company reports taxable income of $972,000 on its income tax return for the year ended December 31, 2015, its first year of operations. Temporary differences between financial income and taxable income for the year are as follows:

Tax depreciation in excess of book depreciation	$ 95,000
Accrual for product liability claims in excess of actual claims (estimated product claims payable is a current liability)	180,000
Reported installment sales income in excess of taxable installment sales income (installments receivable is a current asset)	315,000

The enacted income tax rate is 35% for 2015 and all future years. Prepare the journal entries necessary to record income taxes for 2015.

Exercise 16-38

Computation of Deferred Asset and Liability Balances
Friedman Construction reported taxable income of $50,000 for 2015, its first fiscal year. The enacted tax rate for 2015 is 40%. Enacted tax rates and deductible amounts for 2016–2018 are as follows:

	Enacted Tax Rate	Deductible Amount
2016	38%	$12,000
2017	35	15,000
2018	36	18,000

1. Prepare the journal entries necessary to record income taxes for 2015. Assume that there will be sufficient income in each future year to realize any deductible amounts. For classification purposes, assume that all deductible amounts relate to noncurrent items.
2. Repeat (1), assuming that it is more likely than not that taxable income for all future periods will be zero or less.

Exercise 16-39

Computation of Deferred Asset and Liability Balances
Dixon Type and Supply Company reported taxable income of $75,000 for 2015, its first fiscal year. The enacted tax rate for 2015 is 40%. Enacted tax rates and deductible amounts for 2016–2019 are as follows:

	Enacted Tax Rate	Deductible Amount
2016	35%	$14,000
2017	32	24,000
2018	30	16,000
2019	32	40,000

1. Prepare the journal entries necessary to record income taxes for 2015. Assume that there will be sufficient income in each future year to realize any deductible amounts. For classification purposes, assume that all deductible amounts relate to noncurrent items.
2. Repeat (1), assuming it is more likely than not that taxable income for all future periods will be zero or less.

Exercise 16-40

NOL Carryback and Carryforward

The historical financial data shown below are available for the Bradshaw Manufacturing Company.

Year	Income	Tax Rate	Tax Paid
2012	$175,000	40%	$ 70,000
2013	230,000	42	96,600
2014	310,000	35	108,500

In 2015, Bradshaw suffered an $820,000 net operating loss due to an economic recession. The company elects to use the carryback provision in the tax law.

1. Using the information given, calculate the refund due arising from the loss carryback and the amount of the loss available to carry forward to future periods. Assume that the enacted tax rate is 34% for 2015 and all future years.
2. Prepare the entry necessary to record the loss carryback and carryforward. Assume that there will be sufficient taxable income in the carryforward period to realize all benefits from NOL carryforwards.
3. Using the answers from (1) and (2), prepare the bottom portion of the 2015 income statement reflecting the effect of the loss carryback and carryforward.

Exercise 16-41

NOL Carryback and Carryforward

The following historical financial data are available for Lexis Company.

Year	Income	Tax Rate	Tax Paid
2012	$500,000	35%	$175,000
2013	150,000	30	45,000
2014	30,000	30	9,000

In 2015, Lexis Company suffered a $1 million net operating loss. The company will use the carryback provision of the tax law.

1. Using the information given, calculate the refund due for the loss carryback and the amount of the loss available to carry forward to future periods. Assume that the enacted tax rate for 2015 and all future years is 40%.
2. Prepare journal entries to record the loss carryback and carryforward. Assume that it is more likely than not that future taxable income will be sufficient to allow for the full realization of any deferred tax assets.
3. Evaluate the reasonableness of the assumption in (2).

Exercise 16-42

Cash Flow and Income Taxes

Joyce Smithers Inc. reported the following amounts related to income taxes on its 2015 income statement.

Income tax expense—current $32,000
Income tax expense—deferred .... (8,000)

Smithers also reported the following amounts on its December 31, 2014 and 2015, balance sheets:

	2015	2014
Deferred tax liability	$26,000	$34,000
Income taxes payable	10,000	4,000

If Smithers uses the indirect method of reporting cash flows, what information concerning income taxes would it include in its statement of cash flows and related disclosure?

Exercise 16-43

Cash Flow and Income Taxes

Victoria Clothing reported the following amounts related to income taxes on its 2015 income statement.

Income tax benefit from NOL carryback	$12,000
Income tax benefit from NOL carryforward	28,000

Victoria also reported the following on its December 31, 2014 and 2015, balance sheets.

	2015	2014
Deferred tax asset—NOL carryforward	$28,000	$ 0
Income tax refund receivable	12,000	4,000

1. If Victoria uses the indirect method of reporting cash flows, what information concerning income taxes would Victoria include in its statement of cash flows and related disclosure?
2. If Victoria uses the direct method of reporting cash flows, what information concerning income taxes would Victoria include in its statement of cash flows and related disclosure?

P3
Additional Activities of a Business

CHAPTER 17
Employee Compensation—Payroll, Pensions, and Other Compensation Issues

Learning Objectives

1. Account for payroll and payroll taxes, and understand the criteria for recognizing a liability associated with compensated absences.

2. Compute performance bonuses, and recognize the issues associated with postemployment benefits.

3. Understand the nature and characteristics of employer pension plans, including the details of defined benefit plans.

4. Use the components of the pension-related asset/liability and changes in the components to compute the periodic expense associated with pensions and to compute the impact on other comprehensive income.

5. Prepare required disclosures associated with pensions, and understand the accounting treatment for pension settlements and curtailments.

6. Explain the differences in accounting for pensions and postretirement benefits other than pensions.

Press reports in the United States often talk about the rising "national debt." As of September 30, 2011, borrowing from the public by the U.S. Treasury totaled $10.174 trillion. This obligation is the most publicized liability of the U.S. government, but it is not the only large one. As of the same date, the present value of the government liability under military and civilian pension plans and for veterans' benefits was $5.792 trillion.[1] These liabilities are certainly large (a trillion dollar bills laid end to end would stretch from the earth to the moon and back 197 times), but all other U.S. government liabilities are surpassed by the Social Security and Medicare obligations. Of course, in one sense it is not correct to view Social Security as a pension plan or Medicare as a company retiree healthcare plan; those plans are a social insurance arrangement in which current workers

[1] *Financial Report of the United States Government—2011* (Washington, D.C.: Department of the Treasury).

pay for the benefits of past workers in the hopes that they (the current workers) will be supported by the contributions of future workers. With that qualification, it is still interesting to evaluate the funding status of Social Security and Medicare as if they were private company plans. As of September 30, 2011, the U.S. Treasury estimated that the present value of future Social Security benefits to current and future participants in the plan (over an infinite horizon) exceeded the present value of expected future contributions from those workers and their employers by $12.4 trillion. And the present value of the Medicare obligation to those same people (in excess of their expected contributions) is $38.8 trillion!

A widely recognized phenomenon of the past 100 years has been the increasing life expectancy of people in almost all countries of the world. For example, in 1900 the average life expectancy of people in the United States was 47.3 years; by 2009 it had increased to 78.5 years.[2] As people live longer, they must deal with the problem of financing their extended retirement years. The magnitude of the problem in the United States will increase in the next 10 to 15 years as the "baby boomer" population of the 1940s and 1950s moves into retirement. It is estimated that the proportion of the U.S. population that is over 65 will increase from the current 13% to 20% by the year 2030.

As a country's population ages, an increasingly large share of the country's resources must be used to honor obligations to retired people. This is also true of a business enterprise. For example, it has been reported that at one time approximately $1,100 of the sales price of each General Motors vehicle was required to be used to satisfy the pension and healthcare claims of retired workers who no longer worked at General Motors.

Complex accounting issues associated with employee compensation do not begin, however, when an employee retires. As introduced in Chapter 13, stock compensation has become an increasingly complex and controversial issue. In addition, companies must address issues associated with the computation of performance bonuses and liabilities associated with sick and vacation pay. Finally, the compensation issues associated with payroll, such as the differing employee and employer payroll taxes, introduce added complexity to the topic of employee compensation.

The event line displayed in Exhibit 17-1 outlines the various issues associated with employee compensation. Naturally, immediate compensation for services provided is the issue with which we all are most familiar. The next issue on the event line relates to accruing an obligation for sick days, vacation days, and other types of compensated absences. These obligations are accrued in the current period and are often related to the amount of time an employee has been employed. Stock options and other types of performance bonuses, which often are accounted for at the end of an accounting period, constitute the next event. In some instances, employees may leave an employer prior to retirement yet still be entitled to certain benefits. These benefits are known as *postemployment benefits* and are different from the final event listed—pensions and other postretirement benefits.

Exhibit 17-1 | Employee Compensation Event Line

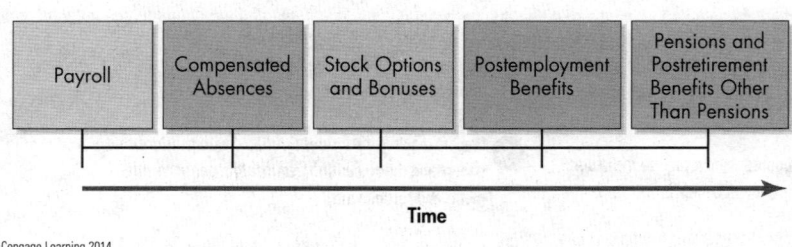

© Cengage Learning 2014

1. The U.S. federal government has two obligations that each total over $5 trillion. One of these obligations is the "national debt." What is the other?

2. How will the changing age mix of the U.S. population over the next 30 years make the satisfaction of retired workers' Social Security claims more difficult?

3. In addition to the pension costs associated with retired workers, what other substantial cost must General Motors bear with respect to retired workers?

Answers to these questions can be found on page 17-43.

---

[2] *Health, United States, 2011*, National Center for Health Statistics, Centers for Disease Control and Prevention, U.S. Department of Health and Human Services (Table 22. Life expectancy at birth, at 65 years of age, and at 75 years of age, by sex, race, and Hispanic origin: United States, selected years 1900–2009).

C17 | Employee Compensation—Payroll, Pensions, and Other Compensation Issues

This chapter will proceed in the order of the employee compensation event line. We first focus on payroll, followed by issues related to compensated absences. Stock options and bonuses are then briefly discussed. Issues related to postemployment benefits are then reviewed, followed by a detailed discussion of pensions, including a discussion of the international standards for pension accounting. Postretirement benefits other than pensions are discussed in the final section of this chapter.

Routine Employee Compensation Issues

1 Account for payroll and payroll taxes, and understand the criteria for recognizing a liability associated with compensated absences.

LO1 学习目标1
了解工资和工资税的会计处理，理解与带薪缺勤有关的负债确认标准。

In the area of employee compensation, the complexities associated with pensions have received a great deal of attention in recent years. Before we turn our attention to pensions, we will first discuss employee compensation issues associated with the current pay period. Along with accounting for current payroll issues, we will discuss issues associated with compensated absences: sick pay, vacation pay, and so on.

Payroll and Payroll Taxes

payroll and payroll taxes
工资与工资税

In an ongoing entity, salaries and wages of officers and other employees accrue daily. Normally, no entry is made for these expenses until payment is made. A liability for unpaid salaries and wages is recorded, however, at the end of an accounting period when a more precise matching of revenues and expenses is desired. An estimate of the amount of unpaid wages and salaries is made, and an adjusting entry is prepared to recognize the amount due. Usually, the entire accrued amount is identified as salaries payable with no attempt to identify the withholdings associated with the accrual. When payment is made in the subsequent period, the amount is allocated between the employee and other entities such as government taxing units, unions, and insurance companies.

For example, assume that a company has 15 employees who are paid every two weeks. At December 31, four days of unpaid wages have accrued. Analysis reveals that the 15 employees earn a total of $1,000 a day. Thus, the adjusting entry at December 31 would be as follows:

Salaries and Wages Expense	4,000
Salaries and Wages Payable	4,000

When payment is made, Salaries and Wages Payable will be debited for $4,000.

Social Security and income tax legislation impose five taxes based on payrolls:

1. Federal old-age, survivors', and disability (tax to both employer and employee)
2. Federal hospital insurance (tax to both employer and employee)
3. Federal unemployment insurance (tax to employer only)
4. State unemployment insurance (tax to employer only)
5. Individual income tax (tax to employee only but withheld and paid by employer)

Federal old-age, survivors, and disability tax
联邦年迈、幸存者和残疾税

Federal Old-Age, Survivors', and Disability Tax The Federal Insurance Contributions Act (FICA), generally referred to as Social Security legislation, provides for FICA taxes from both employers and employees to provide funds for federal old-age, survivors', and disability benefits for certain individuals and members of their families. At one time, only employees were covered by this legislation; however, coverage now includes most individuals who are self-employed.

Provisions of the legislation require an employer of one or more employees, with certain exceptions, to withhold FICA taxes from each employee's wages. The amount of the tax is based on a tax rate and wage base as currently specified in the law. The tax rate and wage base both have increased dramatically since the inception of the Social Security program in the 1930s. The initial rate of FICA tax was 1% in 1937; the rate in effect for 2012 was 6.20%. During that same period, the annual wages subject to FICA tax increased from $3,000 to $110,100. The taxable wage base is subject to yearly increases based on cost-of-living adjustments in Social Security benefits.

The employer remits the amount of FICA tax withheld for all employees, along with a matching amount, to the federal government. The employer is required to maintain complete records and submit detailed support for the tax remittance. The employer is responsible for the full amount of the tax even if employee contributions are not withheld. (*Note:* For 2011 and 2012, a special tax break was given to individuals, lowering the FICA tax rate to 4.20%; the rate remained at 6.20% for employers.)

Federal Hospital Insurance The Federal Insurance Contributions Act (FICA) also includes a provision for Medicare tax. This tax differs from the tax previously discussed in that the tax is applied to all wages earned; there is no upper limit. The tax rate for 2012 was 1.45% for both the employer and the employee.[3]

Federal Unemployment Insurance The Federal Social Security Act and the Federal Unemployment Tax Act (FUTA) provide for the establishment of unemployment insurance plans. Employers with insured workers employed in each of 20 weeks during a calendar year or who pay $1,500 or more in wages during any calendar quarter are affected.

Under present provisions of the law, the federal government taxes eligible employers on the first $7,000 paid to every employee during the calendar year. The rate of tax in effect since 1985 has been 6.2%, but the employer is allowed a tax credit limited to 5.4% for taxes paid under state unemployment compensation laws. No tax is levied on the employee. When an employer is subject to a tax of 5.4% or more as a result of state unemployment legislation, the federal unemployment tax is 0.8% of the qualifying wages.

Payment to the federal government is required quarterly. Unemployment benefits are paid by the individual states. Revenues collected by the federal government under the acts are used to meet the cost of administering state and federal unemployment plans as well as to provide supplemental unemployment benefits.

State Unemployment Insurance State unemployment compensation laws are not the same in all states. In most states, laws call for tax only on employers, but in a few states, taxes are applicable to both employers and employees. Each state law specifies the classes of exempt employees, the number of employees required or the amount of wages paid before the tax is applicable, and the contributions that are to be made by employers and employees. Exemptions are frequently similar to those under the federal act. Tax payment is generally required on or before the last day of the month following each calendar quarter.

Although the normal tax on employers may be 5.4%, states have merit rating or experience plans providing for lower rates based on employers' individual employment experiences. Employers with stable employment records are taxed at a rate in keeping with the limited amount of benefits required for their former employees; employers with less satisfactory employment records contribute at a rate more nearly approaching 5.4% in view of the higher amount of benefits paid to their former employees. Savings under state

---

[3] For illustrative purposes and end-of-chapter exercises and problems, a combined FICA rate of 7.65% will be used.

merit systems are allowed as credits in the calculation of the federal contribution, so the federal tax does not exceed 0.8% even though an employer entitled to a lower rate under the merit rating system makes payment of less than 5.4%.

Income Tax Federal income taxes on the wages of individuals are collected in the period in which the wages are paid. The "pay-as-you-go" plan requires employers to withhold income tax from wages paid to their employees. Most states and many local governments also impose income taxes on the earnings of employees that the employer must withhold and remit. Withholding is required not only of employers engaged in a trade or business but also of religious and charitable organizations, educational institutions, social organizations, and governments of the United States, the states, the territories, and their agencies, instrumentalities, and political subdivisions. Certain classes of wage payments are exempt from withholding although they are still subject to income tax.

An employer must meet withholding requirements under the law even if wages of only one employee are subject to such withholdings. The amounts to be withheld by the employer are developed from formulas provided by the law or from tax withholding tables made available by the government. Withholding is based on the length of the payroll period, the amount earned, and the number of withholding exemptions claimed by the employee. Taxes required under FICA (both employee and employer portions) and income tax that has been withheld by the employer are paid to the federal government at the same time. These combined taxes are deposited in an authorized bank quarterly, monthly, or several times each month, depending on the amount of the liability. Quarterly and annual statements providing a summary of all wages paid by the employer must also be filed.

> **FYI**
>
> Not all countries require employers to withhold income tax from employees. For example, in Hong Kong an employee is entirely responsible to accumulate sufficient funds to pay the 15% flat income tax due at the end of the year. Financial institutions are happy to arrange "tax loans" for those who forget to set aside the money to pay their taxes.

Accounting for Payroll Taxes To illustrate the accounting procedures for payroll taxes, assume that salaries for the month of January for a retail store with 15 employees are $16,000. The state unemployment compensation law provides for a tax on employers of 5.4%. Income tax withholdings for the month are $1,600. Assume that FICA rates are 7.65% for employer and employee. Entries for the payroll and the employer's payroll taxes follow:

Salaries Expense	16,000	
FICA Taxes Payable		1,224
Employees Income Taxes Payable		1,600
Cash		13,176
To record payment of payroll and related employee withholdings.		
Payroll Tax Expense	2,216*	
FICA Taxes Payable		1,224
State Unemployment Taxes Payable		864
Federal Unemployment Taxes Payable		128
To record the payroll tax liability of the employer.		

*Computation:

Tax under FICA (0.0765 × $16,000)	$1,224
Tax under state unemployment insurance legislation (0.054 × $16,000)	864
Tax under FUTA [0.008 (0.062 − credit of 0.054) × $16,000]	128
Total payroll tax expense	$2,216

When tax payments are made to the proper agencies, the tax liability accounts are debited and Cash is credited.

The employer's payroll taxes, as well as the taxes withheld from employees, are based on amounts paid to employees during the period regardless of the basis employed for reporting income. When financial reports are prepared on the accrual basis, the employer will have to recognize both accrued payroll and the employer's payroll taxes relating thereto by adjustments at the end of the accounting period.

For example, assume that the salaries and wages accrued at December 31 were $9,500. Of this amount, $2,000 was subject to unemployment tax and $6,000 to FICA tax. Although the salaries and wages will not be paid until January of the following year, the concept of matching requires these costs to be allocated in the period in which they were incurred. This allocation is accomplished with an adjusting entry. The adjusting entry for the employer's payroll taxes would be as follows:

> **Caution**
> Don't forget that to ensure that the financial statements are properly stated, an adjusting entry is required at the end of an accounting period if salaries and wages are owed.

Payroll Tax Expense	583*	
FICA Taxes Payable		459
State Unemployment Taxes Payable		108
Federal Unemployment Taxes Payable		16
To accrue the payroll tax liability of the employer.		
*Computation:		
Tax under FICA (0.0765 × $6,000)	$459	
Tax under state unemployment insurance legislation (0.054 × $2,000)	108	
Tax under FUTA (0.008 × $2,000)	16	
Total payroll tax expense	$583	

Agreements with employees may provide for payroll deductions and employer contributions for other items, such as group insurance plans, pension plans, savings bond purchases, or union dues. Such agreements call for accounting procedures similar to those described for payroll taxes.

Compensated Absences

Compensated absences include payments by employers for vacation, holiday, illness, or other personal activities. Employees often earn paid absences based on the time employed. Generally, the longer an employee works for a company, the longer the vacation allowed or the more liberal the time allowed for illnesses. At the end of any given accounting period, a company has a liability for earned but unused compensated absences. The matching principle requires that the estimated amounts earned be charged against current revenue and a liability established for that amount.[4] The difficult part of this accounting treatment is estimating how much should be accrued. The FASB requires a liability to be recognized for compensated absences that (1) have been earned through services already rendered, (2) vest or can be carried forward to subsequent years, and (3) are estimable and probable.

---

[4] FASB ASC paragraphs 710-10-25-1 through 3, Compensated Absences.

For example, assume that a company has a vacation pay policy for all employees. If all employees had the same anniversary date for computing time in service, the computations would not be too difficult. However, most plans provide for a flexible employee starting date. To compute the liability, a careful inventory of all employees must be made to include the number of years of service, rate of pay, carryover of unused vacation from prior periods, turnover, and the probability of taking the vacation.

To illustrate the accounting for compensated absences, assume that S&N Corporation has 20 employees who are paid an average of $700 per week. During 2014, employees earned a total of 40 vacation weeks but took only 30 weeks of vacation that year. They took the remaining 10 weeks of vacation in 2015 when the average rate of pay was $800 per week. The entry to record the accrued vacation pay on December 31, 2014, follows:

Wages Expense...	7,000	
Vacation Wages Payable		7,000
To record accrued vacation wages ($700 × 10 weeks).		

This entry assumes that wages expense has already been recorded for the 30 weeks of vacation taken during 2014. Therefore, the income statement would reflect the total wages expense for the entire 40 weeks of vacation earned during the period. On its December 31, 2014, balance sheet, S&N would report a current liability of $7,000 to reflect the obligation for the 10 weeks of vacation pay that are owed. In 2015, when the additional vacation weeks are taken and the payroll is paid, S&N would make the following entry:

Wages Expense...	1,000	
Vacation Wages Payable...	7,000	
Cash...		8,000
To record payment at current rates of previously earned vacation time ($800 × 10 weeks).		

Because the vacation weeks have now been used, this entry eliminates the liability. An adjustment to Wages Expense is required because the liability was recorded at the rates of pay in effect during the time the compensation (vacation pay) was earned. However, the cash is being paid at the current rate, which requires an adjustment to Wages Expense. If the rate of pay for the 10 weeks of vacation taken in 2015 had remained the same as the rate used to record the accrual on December 31, 2014, there would not have been an adjustment to Wages Expense. The entry to record payment in 2015 would simply be a debit to the payable and a credit to Cash for $7,000.

An exception to the requirement for accrual of compensated absences, such as vacation pay, is made for sick pay. The FASB decided that sick pay should be accrued only if it vests with the employee, that is, the employee is entitled to compensation for a certain number of "sick days" regardless of whether the employee is actually absent for that period. Upon leaving the firm, the employee would be compensated for any unused sick time. If the sick pay does not vest, it is recorded as an expense only when actually paid.[5]

Although compensated absences are not deductible for income tax purposes until the vacation, holiday, or illness occurs and the payment is made, GAAP requires them to be recognized as liabilities on the financial statements.

---

[5] FASB ASC paragraphs 710-10-25-6 through 8, Sick Pay Benefits.

FASB CODIFICATION

The Issue: You are an accounting student and are generally acknowledged to be the best accounting student on campus. Your organic chemistry professor (you are taking a broad set of elective courses to enhance your accounting training), Harold Pearl, has come to you with an accounting question. Professor Pearl reports that he had a very unpleasant conversation with the university accountant the day before. The accountant says that because Professor Pearl receives a university "sabbatical" once every seven years, the cost of that "sabbatical" must be partially accrued (whatever that means; Professor Pearl is not sure) in each of the six years leading up to the "sabbatical" year. The result is that the university compensation cost related to Professor Pearl in each year is one-sixth higher than Professor Pearl's actual annual cash compensation. As a result, Professor Pearl's cash compensation must be reduced by 17% … immediately.

Professor Pearl is dismayed. To him, this seems unfair. He reports to you that this "sabbatical" year is not a year in which he relaxes on the beach. Sure, he has no classes that year. However, during that year he is required to appear at the organic chemistry lab each day and mentor chemistry graduate students. He enjoys the work, but it is not as if he were really taking the year off. He wants you to help him convince the university accountant that it is not right to "accrue," in advance, the cost of his "sabbatical" year salary.

The Question: Should a university accrue an expense, in advance, for faculty who receive a periodic sabbatical year?

Searching the Codification: There are two ways to find the answer to Professor Pearl's question. First, the brute force approach is to just type "sabbatical" into the search bar at the top right of the FASB ASC home page. Unfortunately, this doesn't work when using the Basic View (free) version of the Codification. So, the second approach is to look through the menu of the 71X (Compensation) family of topics. Here are some hints. This looks like a general compensation issue not related to pensions, stock compensation, or severance benefits (euphemistically called "nonretirement postemployment benefits"). Next, this is an overall issue, not one related to airlines or regulated industries. Final hint: This is an issue of when the sabbatical year cost should be recognized (accrued now or recognized in the sabbatical year itself).

The Answer: The correct treatment is described on page 17-44.

Nonroutine Employee Compensation Issues

LO2 学习目标2
学习计算绩效奖金，确认与雇用后福利有关的事项。

② Compute performance bonuses, and recognize the issues associated with postemployment benefits.

In addition to routine compensation issues that are addressed on a regular basis, several other compensation issues arise, often at the end of the period. These issues, performance-based incentive plans either in the form of stock or bonus, are discussed in this section. We conclude this section with a discussion of the compensation issues that may arise following employment but prior to retirement.

Stock-Based Compensation and Bonuses

As discussed in Chapter 13, stock options are often a part of an employee's compensation package. While stock option compensation (particularly performance based) is more common for upper management and directors, many companies have stock option plans available for all employees. The amount of compensation expense reported related to stock-based compensation is a function of the fair value of the options on the date they are granted and the type of stock-based compensation plan. With a simple stock-based compensation plan, total compensation expense is the number of options granted multiplied by the fair value of each option as of the grant date. This expense is allocated over the period of time that the employees have to stay with the company in order to earn the options. With a performance-based stock option plan, total compensation expense is equal to the fair value of each option as of the grant date multiplied by the number of options that are probable to be awarded. This amount is reevaluated at the end of each year. Some stock-based compensation plans call for payment in cash such as with cash stock appreciation rights (SARs). These liability amounts are remeasured at the end of each year, and a catch-up adjustment is made to compensation expense. Refer back to Chapter 13 for a discussion of the details associated with stock-based compensation.

> **FYI**
>
> The existence of an earnings-based bonus plan is intended to encourage managers to work harder and smarter to improve the company's performance. However, such a plan also increases managers' incentive to manipulate reported earnings. In fact, one of the factors looked at by auditors in evaluating the risk of financial statement fraud in a company is whether the company has an earnings-based management bonus plan.

In addition to stock options, employees often earn bonuses based on a company's performance over a given period of time. This additional compensation should be recognized in the period in which it is earned. Bonuses are often based on some measure of the employer's income. For example, assume that Photo Graphics, Inc., gives its store managers a 10% bonus based on individual store earnings. The bonus is to be based on income after deduction for the bonus but before deduction for income taxes. Assume furthermore that income for a particular store is $100,000 before charging any bonus or income taxes. The bonus would be calculated as follows:

$$B = 0.10(\$100{,}000 - B)$$
$$B = \$10{,}000 - 0.10B$$
$$B + 0.10B = \$10{,}000$$
$$1.10B = \$10{,}000$$
$$B = \$9{,}091 \text{ (rounded)}$$

The bonus would be reported on the income statement as an operating expense, and the bonus payable would be shown as a current liability on the balance sheet unless the bonus was paid immediately in cash. As an example of a bonus plan, **ExxonMobil** disclosed in its 2012 proxy statement filed with the SEC that it has a management bonus plan targeted at its top managers. The plan grants a certain number of "earnings bonus units" to the managers; a manager is entitled to receive cash equal to ExxonMobil's cumulative reported net earnings per share for the next three years up to a cap amount of $6.00 for each award unit granted in 2011. ExxonMobil's CEO, Rex W. Tillerson, received $4,368,000 in earnings-based bonus in 2011; his salary for the year was $2,387,000.

Postemployment Benefits

In a business world where downsizing has become commonplace, an employee cannot count on remaining with one employer for his or her entire career. In addition, employees

Exhibit 17-2 | Note Disclosure for Postemployment Benefits—NCR

Employee Severance Costs

In the first quarter of 2007, the Company initiated the manufacturing realignment related to its ATM products, which included outsourcing of certain manufacturing activities in the Americas region and shifting other manufacturing activities from high cost to low cost geographies primarily in the EMEA [Europe, Middle East, and Africa] and APJ [Asia Pacific Japan] regions. As a result of this realignment, the Company recorded $46 million for employee severance and other termination benefits in cost of products in the Condensed Consolidated Statements of Operations in the first quarter of 2007.

© Cengage Learning 2014

Stop & Think

Which ONE of the following is NOT a criterion used in identifying a postemployment benefit obligation?
a) The employer's obligation is proportional to the amount of the employee's salary or wage.
b) The employer's obligation relates to rights that vest.
c) The payment of the liability is probable, and the amount can be reasonably estimated.
d) The employer's obligation in the future relates to services already provided by the employee.

---

are making job changes for reasons such as to facilitate career advancement and to enhance their family's quality of life. For these reasons and others, compensation issues following employment but preceding retirement have increased in magnitude. The most common situation in which this issue arises is when an employee is terminated. Examples of the types of benefits typically granted to terminated employees include supplemental unemployment benefits, severance benefits, disability-related benefits, job training and counseling, and continuation of benefits such as healthcare benefits and life insurance coverage.[6] These are exactly the type of benefits that are often granted to employees as part of a restructuring. Thus, a postemployment benefit obligation would often comprise part of a restructuring charge. In a restructuring, the postemployment benefit obligation is recognized only when the termination is approved by management, the details of the termination are set, and the employees have been notified.[7]

The same criteria used in accounting for compensated absences are applied to postemployment benefits. Those criteria are (1) the employer's obligation in the future relates to services already provided by the employee, (2) the employer's obligation relates to rights that vest, and (3) the payment of the liability is probable and the amount can be reasonably estimated.[8] If these criteria are met, then entries made are similar to those illustrated previously for compensated absences. To illustrate the magnitude of postemployment benefits, consider the disclosure provided by **NCR** in the notes to its 2007 first quarter report, shown in Exhibit 17-2.

Accounting for Pensions

Understand the nature and characteristics of employer pension plans, including the details of defined benefit plans.

Financing retirement years is accomplished by establishing some type of pension plan that sets aside funds during an employee's working years so that at retirement the funds and

---

[6] FASB ASC paragraphs 712-10-25-1 through 5, Other Postemployment Benefits.
[7] FASB ASC paragraphs 420-10-25-4 through 10, One-time Employee Termination Benefits.
[8] FASB ASC paragraph 712-10-25-4.

earnings from investment of the funds may be returned to the employee in lieu of earned wages. In the United States, three major categories of pension plans have emerged:

1. Government plans, primarily Social Security
2. Individual plans, such as individual retirement accounts (IRAs)
3. Employer plans

The third category, employer pension plans, involves several difficult and controversial accounting and reporting issues.

A related accounting issue is the employer's accounting for postretirement benefits other than pensions. These benefits extend beyond the active years of employment and include such items as health care, life insurance, legal services, special discounts on items produced or sold by the employer, and tuition assistance. For both pensions and for other postretirement benefits, the accounting objective is to properly measure both the balance sheet obligation and the current year earnings impact of the value of these promises.

Nature and Characteristics of Employer Pension Plans

The subject of employers' accounting for pensions is very complex, partly because of the many variations in plans that have been developed. Most pension plans are specifically designed for one employer and are known as single-employer pension plans. If several companies contribute to the same plan, it is called a *multiemployer pension plan*. This chapter, like the accounting standards, focuses on accounting for single-employer pension plans.

Funding of Employer Pension Plans The basic purpose of all employer pension plans is the same: to provide retirement benefits to employees. A principal issue concerning pension plans is how to provide sufficient funds to meet the needs of retirees. The Social Security system of the federal government has frequently been criticized because it is not a "funded" plan. FICA taxes (contributions) paid by employers and employees in the current year are used to pay benefits to individuals who are currently retired. This means that the current employees must have faith that a future generation will do the same for them. Such a system creates much doubt and uncertainty.

Private plans are not permitted to operate in this way. Federal law, such as the Employee Retirement Income Security Act (ERISA) of 1974, requires companies to fund their pension plans in an orderly manner so that the employee is protected at retirement. Some pension plans are funded entirely by the employer and are referred to as noncontributory pension plans. In other cases, the employee also contributes to the cost of the pension plan, referred to as a contributory pension plan.[9] The amounts and timing of contributions depend on the particular circumstances and plan provisions. While the provisions of pension plans vary widely and in many cases are very complex, there are two basic classifications of pension plans: (1) defined contribution plans and (2) defined benefit plans.

Defined Contribution Pension Plans Defined contribution pension plans are relatively simple in their construction and raise very few accounting issues for employers. Under these plans, the employer pays a periodic contribution amount into a separate trust fund, which is administered by an independent third-party trustee. The contribution may be defined as a fixed amount each period, a percentage of the employer's income, a percentage of employee earnings, or a combination of these or other factors. As contributions to the fund are made, they are invested by the fund administrator. When an employee retires, the accumulated value in the fund is used to determine the pension

[9] Employee contributions are not considered in subsequent discussions and examples because the chapter is concerned with employers' accounting for pensions.

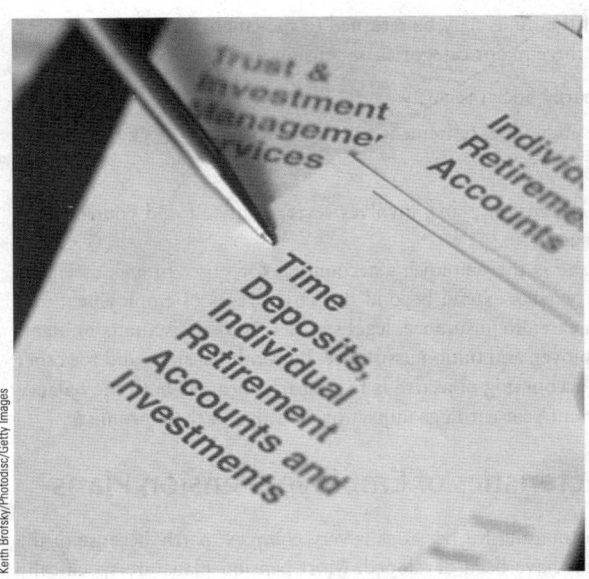

Pensions represent a substantial liability for many companies.

payout to the employee. The employee's retirement income therefore depends on how the fund has been managed. If investments have been made wisely, the employee will fare better than if the investments have been managed poorly. In effect, the investment risk is borne by the employee. The employer's obligation extends only to making the specified periodic contribution. This amount is charged to pension expense, and no further accounting is required for the plan. As an example of this type of plan, many college professors belong to a defined contribution plan called TIAA/CREF. The college or university makes contributions on behalf of the professor, who then must rely on the good judgment of the TIAA/CREF fund managers to ensure his or her retirement security. As of March 2012, TIAA/CREF was the largest private pension plan in the world with assets in excess of $487 billion held on behalf of 3.7 million active and retired employees.

Defined Benefit Pension Plans Defined benefit pension plans are much more complex than defined contribution plans. Under defined benefit plans, the employee is guaranteed a specified retirement income often related to his or her number of years of employment and average salary over a certain number of years. The periodic amount of the employer's contribution is based on the expected future benefits to be paid to employees and is affected by a number of variables. Because the benefits are defined, the contributions (funding) must vary as conditions change. Exhibit 17-3 illustrates the basic nature of a defined benefit plan. A defined contribution plan could be illustrated in the same manner except that the contributions (rather than the benefits) would be defined. This difference, however, is significant and accounts for the complexity of defined benefit plans.

在固定收益养老金计划下，员工特定的退休收入与其被雇用年限和特定年限的平均工资相关。

> **FYI**
>
> In a sense, all pension plans are funded completely by the employee. When considering an acceptable level of compensation, both the firm and the employee should consider total compensation: current salary, fringe benefits, and deferred compensation. A higher employer pension contribution presumably means lower current compensation.

Under defined benefit plans, the investment risk is, in substance, borne by the employer. While a separate trust fund usually is maintained for contributions and investment earnings, the employer ultimately is responsible to ensure that employees receive the defined benefits provided by the plan. A pension fund may be viewed essentially as funds set aside to meet the employer's future pension obligation just as funds may be set aside for other purposes, for example, to retire bonds at maturity. One major difference, however, is that a future obligation to retire bonds is a definite amount, while the employer's future obligation for retirement benefits is based on many estimates and assumptions. In addition, U.S. federal law requires minimum pension plan funding, whereas sinking fund requirements are privately negotiated between the borrower and the bondholders.

在固定收益计划下，投资的风险实质上是由雇主承担的。当为了提存和投资的需要维持独立的信托基金时，雇主需要对最终确保雇员收到计划下的设定收益承担责任。

Defined Benefits Defined benefit pension plans provide for an increase in future retirement benefits as additional services are rendered by an employee. In effect, the employee's total compensation for a period consists of current wages or salaries plus deferred compensation represented by the right to receive a defined amount of future benefits. The amount of future benefits earned by employees for a particular period is

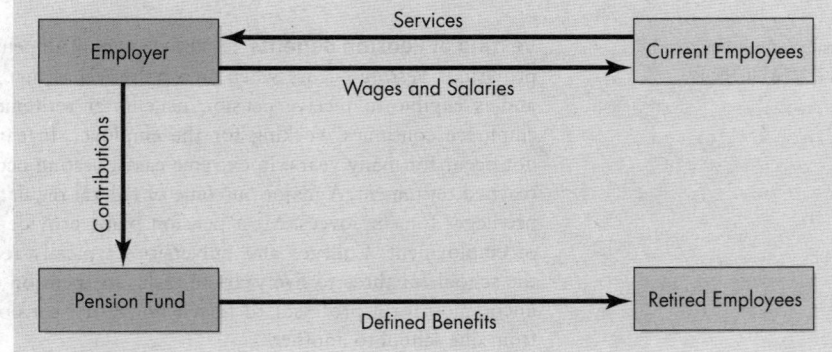

Exhibit 17-3 | Defined Benefit Pension Plans

例如，雇员每服务1年将获得100美元/月的养老金福利。因此，一名工作了30年的退休员工将获得3 000美元/月（100×30）的福利，即年服务回报乘以退休后预计剩余的月份数。一部分计划把部分福利分摊到不同的服务年限。例如，每服务1年将获得100美元/月的福利，大于20年时每增加1年将获得120美元/月。大多数计划包括基于当前或未来员工收入的福利公式。例如，计划可能会提供员工退休前5年平均年收入的2%作为每月的福利。

determined by actuaries, not accountants. However, an understanding of the basic concepts used in measuring future retirement benefits is necessary for understanding the accounting issues relating to pensions.

The amount of future benefits earned for a period is based on the plan's benefit formula, which specifies how benefits are attributed (assigned) to years of employee service. Some plans attribute equal benefits to each year of service rendered, for example, a pension benefit of $100 per month for each year of employee service rendered. Thus, an employee who retires after 30 years of service would be entitled to a monthly benefit of $3,000 ($100 per month × 30 years of service). The benefit attributed to each year of service would be $100 multiplied by the number of months of life expectancy after retirement. Some plans attribute different benefits to different years of service, for example, a pension benefit of $100 per month for each year of service up to 20 years and $120 per month for each additional year of service. Many plans include a benefit formula based on current or future employee earnings. For example, a plan might provide monthly benefits of 2% of an employee's average annual earnings for the five years preceding retirement.

The measurement of future benefits is highly subjective. The amount of benefits earned by employees for a period is based on many variables, including the average age of employees, length of service, expected turnover, vesting provisions, and life expectancy. Thus, one must estimate how many of the current employees will retire and when they will retire, the number of employees who

FYI

The issue of risk and who bears it is very important. With a defined benefit plan, the employee is not completely free of risk; receipt of the benefit payments might be in jeopardy if the employing firm goes bankrupt. To mitigate this risk, Congress created the **Pension Benefit Guaranty Corporation (PBGC)**, a federally supported pension plan insurer. The PBGC collects insurance premiums from participating companies and is given a high-priority claim against company assets in case of bankruptcy.

Stop & Think

Many companies are changing their plans from defined benefit to defined contribution. Why would employers do this?

a) The total cost of a defined contribution plan is always lower.
b) The U.S. government has mandated a gradual switch from defined benefit to defined contribution plans.
c) A defined contribution pension plan is an attractive form of off-balance-sheet financing.
d) A shift from a defined benefit to a defined contribution plan shifts the investment risk from the company to the employee.

vesting of pension benefits
养老金福利的授予

Vesting of Pension Benefits   A key element in all pension plans is the vested benefits provision. *Vesting* occurs when an employee has met certain specified requirements and is eligible to receive pension benefits at retirement regardless of whether the employee continues working for the employer. In early pension plans, vesting did not occur for many years. In extreme cases, vesting occurred only when an employee reached retirement. A major outcome of federal regulation is the much earlier vesting privileges for employees. Most pension plans provide for full vesting after 10 years of employment. Colleges and universities typically require professors to remain at the school for three to five years in order for pension contributions to vest. It is not uncommon for a professor to forfeit nonvested pension contributions when moving from one school to another.

funding of defined benefit plans
固定收益计划的缴存

Funding of Defined Benefit Plans   The periodic amounts to be contributed to a defined benefit plan by the employer are directly related to the future benefits expected to be paid to current employees. The methods of funding pension plans vary widely. Most defined benefit plans require periodic contributions that accumulate to the balance needed to pay the promised retirement benefits to employees. Some plans specify an even amount for each year of employee service. Others require a lower amount in the early years of employee service, with an accelerating schedule over the years. Still other plans provide for a higher amount at first and then a declining pattern of funding. The contribution amounts are determined by actuarial formulas and must be adjusted as estimates and assumptions are revised to reflect changing conditions.

All funding methods are based on present values. The additional future benefits earned by employees each year must be discounted to their present value, referred to as the actuarial present value, using an assumed rate of return on pension fund investments. In many cases, employers contribute an amount equal to the present value of future benefits attributed to current services. As noted, however, funding patterns vary, and the amount contributed for a particular period may be less than or greater than the present value of the additional benefits earned for the period. Assume, for example, that the present value of future benefits earned in the current period is determined to be $30,000, using a discount rate of 10%. If the funding method requires a contribution of only $25,000 for the period, the employer has an unfunded obligation of $5,000. At the end of the following year, this obligation will have increased to $5,500 to reflect the interest cost of 10%. When contributions exceed the present value of the future benefits, lower contributions will be required in subsequent periods as a result of earnings on the "overfunded" amount.

The Pension Benefit Guaranty Corporation is charged with monitoring the funding status of defined benefit pension plans in the United States. As of December 31, 2011, the PBGC protects the retirement incomes of about 44 million working Americans in 26,500 defined benefit pension plans. The PBGC provides federal insurance for participants in U.S. pension plans much as the FDIC provides insurance for bank depositors. The PBGC is not funded by general tax revenues; instead, it collects insurance premiums from employers, receives income on investments, and receives funds from pension plans that it takes over. In 2011, the PBGC was directly responsible for the future benefits of 1.5 million active and retired workers whose pension plans had failed. The PBGC Web site lists an interesting rogue's gallery of companies that have declared bankruptcy and passed responsibility for their employees' pensions to the PBGC. The list includes **Circuit City**, **Polaroid**, **Lehman Brothers**… and many more.

Issues in Accounting for Defined Benefit Plans

Although the provisions of defined benefit pension plans can be extremely complex and the application of accounting standards to a specific plan can be highly technical, the accounting issues themselves are identified easily. Following is a list of these issues, all of which relate to accounting and reporting by employers.

1. The amount of net periodic pension expense to be recognized on the income statement
2. The amount of pension liability or asset to be reported on the balance sheet
3. Accounting for pension settlements, curtailments, and terminations
4. Disclosures needed to supplement the amounts reported in the financial statements

The issue of funding pension plans is purposely omitted from the list. Funding decisions are affected by tax laws, governmental regulations, actuarial computations, and contractual terms, not by accounting standards. They should not directly affect the amount that is reported as net periodic pension expense under the accrual concept.

The next section of the chapter illustrates the basic computational and accounting issues related to pensions in the context of a simple illustration. The simple example is then followed by a more complex illustration that introduces the intricacies for which pension accounting is famous.

Simple Illustration of Pension Accounting

Thakkar Company has established a defined benefit pension plan. As of January 1, 2015, only one employee, Lorien Bach, is enrolled in the plan. Some characteristics of the plan and of Bach as of January 1, 2015, are outlined as follows:

- Bach is 35 years old and has worked for Thakkar for 10 years.
- Bach's salary for 2014 was $40,000.
- Thakkar's pension plan pays a benefit based on an employee's highest salary. Pension payments begin after an employee turns 65, and payments are made at the end of the year. The annual payment is equal to 2% of the highest salary times number of years with the company.
- Bach is an unusually predictable person; it is known with certainty that she will not quit, be fired, or die before age 65. Also, it is known with certainty that she will live exactly 75 years and will therefore collect 10 annual pension payments after she retires. Bach's benefits are already fully vested.
- In valuing pension fund liabilities, Thakkar uses a discount rate of 10%.
- As of January 1, 2015, Thakkar Company has a pension fund containing $10,000. During 2015, Thakkar made additional contributions to the fund totaling $1,500. Also, the fund earned a return of $1,200 during the year. Over the long run, Thakkar expects to earn an average return of 12% on pension fund assets.

Estimation of Pension Obligation The first step in estimating Thakkar Company's pension obligation is to compute the amount of the annual pension payment to be made to Bach when she retires. The amount of the payment depends on Bach's years of service and highest salary. As of January 1, 2015, Bach has put in 10 years of service and, assuming that her most recent salary of $40,000 is her highest salary to date, the forecasted amount of her annual pension payment can be computed as follows:

$$(2\% \times 10 \text{ years}) \times \$40{,}000 = \$8{,}000$$

It is known that Bach will live long enough after retirement at age 65 to collect 10 annual pension payments; thus, the total amount of pension benefits that Thakkar expects to pay to Bach is $80,000 (10 years × $8,000). However, $80,000 is an overstatement of the value of Thakkar's pension obligation because the payments won't begin for another 30 years. To properly compute the present value of the payments to Bach, allowance must be made for the fact that the first payment won't be made until Bach is 66 years old (recall that pension payments are made at the end of the year), the payments are spread over 10 years, and Thakkar Company's discount rate is 10%. This discount rate can be thought of as the rate of interest Thakkar could earn on a portfolio of high-quality fixed-income investments (such as highly rated corporate bonds).[10] In *IAS 19*, the IASB recognizes that not all countries have an active market in high-quality corporate bonds. In such markets, the IASB requires the use of the rate on government bonds. In the Web Material (www.cengagebrain.com) associated with this chapter, it is shown that, using the 10% discount rate, the present value of the expected pension payments to Bach is equal to $2,817.

The $2,817 amount can be thought of as follows: If Thakkar Company deposited $2,817 on January 1, 2015, in a bank account yielding 10%, by the end of 30 years when Bach retires, that $2,817 will have accumulated to an amount large enough to support payments of $8,000 per year to Bach for the succeeding 10 years. The $2,817 is the actuarial present value of Thakkar's pension obligation. An actuarial present value takes into account both time value of money considerations and actuarial assumptions (i.e., how long until Bach retires, how long Bach will live after retirement). In practice, such calculations are performed by professionals called *actuaries*. Financial accountants do not need to know how to perform the detailed actuarial present value calculations, but they should understand the general concepts underlying the calculations.

The $2,817 pension obligation just computed is called the accumulated benefit obligation (ABO). The ABO is the actuarial present value of the expected future pension payments, using the current salary as the basis for forecasting the amount of the pension benefit payments. The ABO approach ignores the impact of expected future salary increases on the amount of the benefit payments. An alternative measure of the pension obligation that does consider the impact of future salary increases is called the projected benefit obligation (PBO).

> **FYI**
>
> Over the past 10 years, *Job Rated Almanac* has rated being an actuary as one of the top jobs in America based on income, outlook, physical demands, stress, and security. How much do actuaries make? Starting salaries are around $54,000, with top salaries exceeding $130,000. Training in math, computers, communication, and business are needed to become a successful actuary.

To illustrate the difference between the PBO and the ABO, assume that Thakkar Company expects Bach's 2014 salary of $40,000 to increase 5% every year until retirement. As a result, Bach's salary is expected to increase to $172,877 by the year 2044, Bach's last year of employment.[11] The pension benefit payment based on this salary is as follows:

$$(2\% \times 10 \text{ years}) \times \$172,877 = \$34,575 \text{ (rounded)}$$

The PBO at January 1, 2015, is $12,176 (see the Web Material associated with this chapter for details of the computation). This is the present value of the 10 future annual payments of $34,575 that Bach is expected to receive. The diagram in Exhibit 17-4 illustrates the relationship between the future payments and the PBO.

Both the PBO and the ABO computations are based on the amount of pension benefits that have already been earned—in this case, on the 10 years of service Bach has provided

---
[10] FASB ASC paragraph 715-30-35-43.
[11] PV = $40,000, N = 30, I = 5% → FV = $172,877.

Exhibit 17-4 | Thakkar Company—Projected Benefit Obligation, January 1, 2015

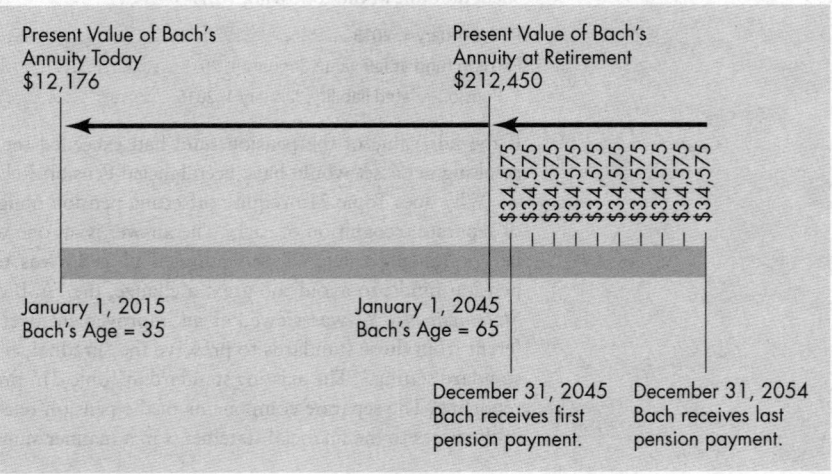

to Thakkar. The difference between the PBO and the ABO comes in the estimate of Bach's highest salary. The ABO computations ignore likely future salary increases; the PBO computations include estimates of those increases. The quantitative difference between these two approaches can be substantial. For Thakkar, the $2,817 ABO is substantially lower than the $12,176 value computed for the PBO.

The numerical relationship between the ABO and the PBO can be presented as follows:

Accumulated benefit obligation, January 1, 2015	$ 2,817
Additional amounts related to projected pay increases	9,359
Projected benefit obligation, January 1, 2015	$12,176

So which is a better measure of a firm's pension obligation, the PBO or the ABO? FASB ASC Topic 715 identifies the PBO as the measure appropriate for use in the financial statements. The ABO is not involved in any of the pension-related recognition provisions, but it is disclosed in the notes to the financial statements. This choice of the PBO as the primary measure of a firm's pension obligation was not without some controversy.[12] It was argued that use of the PBO is not appropriate because it embodies future salary increases and that the historical cost accounting model does not include recognition of future events. This argument was countered with the observation that the use of a discount rate also results in recognition of future events because the discount rate includes a premium for expected future inflation. It was argued that to allow recognition of the impact of expected future inflation but not to allow consideration of expected salary increases would result in a gross understatement of the pension obligation in some cases. Hence, the PBO is the primary measure of a firm's pension obligation.

As of January 1, 2015, the pension obligation for Thakkar, as measured by the PBO, is $12,176, and from the information given at the beginning of the illustration, the total fair value of the pension fund is $10,000. One possible way to present this information on a balance sheet is to list the pension fund among the noncurrent assets and the pension obligation as a noncurrent liability. However, FASB standards stipulate that these two items be offset against one another and requires that a single net amount be shown as either a net

---

[12] Adoption of FASB *Statement No. 87* (the source of the standards in FASB ASC Topic 715) was opposed by three of the seven members of the Board. A description of the dissenting views is included at the end of the primary text of this pre-Codification *Statement* (following paragraph 77).

pension asset or a net pension liability.[13] Thakkar would calculate the appropriate balance sheet amount in the following way:

PBO, January 1, 2015	$12,176
Pension fund at fair value, January 1, 2015	10,000
Pension-related liability, January 1, 2015	$ 2,176

If the fair value of the pension fund had exceeded the projected benefit obligation, the resulting net asset would have been labeled Pension-Related Asset.

Why does Topic 715 require offsetting pension obligations and pension funds instead of separate recognition of each? The answer is, in one word, tradition. Accepted practice before *Statement No. 87* was adopted in 1985 was to offset pension obligations and pension funds; to avoid too great a change, the FASB decided to maintain that method. *Statement No. 87* was viewed as an improvement over prior standards but not too different from those standards to preserve the "gradual, evolutionary" nature of accounting standard setting.[14] The existing standard in Topic 715 preserves that traditional method of reporting. The separate components of the pension-related liability or asset are disclosed in the notes to the financial statements in a manner similar to the table shown previously.

Computation of Pension Expense for 2015 In the simple Thakkar Company example, measurement of pension expense[15] for the year involves consideration of three factors:

1. Implied interest on the beginning-of-the-period pension obligation (which increases the PBO)
2. New pension benefits earned by employees through service during the year (which increase the PBO)
3. Investment return on the pension fund (which increases the fair value of the pension fund)

These three factors will be considered in turn.

Interest Cost The projected benefit obligation on January 1, 2015, is $12,176. This represents an amount owed by Thakkar to its employee, Bach. The 10% discount rate used in the computation of the PBO is called the obligation discount rate and can be viewed as the implied interest rate on this debt. In a sense, employees have agreed to loan the company money (by deferring the receipt of some of their compensation) to be repaid when they retire. As is the case with all loans, there is a charge for interest for the time period for which the money is loaned. Accordingly, one aspect of annual pension expense is the increase in the PBO resulting from implicit interest on this pension obligation, computed as follows:

PBO, Beginning of Period	×	Discount Rate	=	Interest Cost
$12,176	×	0.10	=	$1,218 (rounded)

Service Cost Bach's work for Thakkar Company during the year results in an increase in the forecasted annual pension benefit payments from Thakkar to Bach because those payments are now computed based on 11 years of service instead of 10 years. The impact of this extra year of service is to increase the December 31, 2015, projected benefit obligation by $1,339 over what it would have been if Bach had just vacationed for the entire year. (See the

---

[13] FASB ASC paragraph 715-30-25-1. In a more complicated example, additional pension-related items would also be included in the balance sheet; these items are reported in the accumulated other comprehensive income portion of equity. These items are discussed later in the chapter.
[14] Pre-Codification *Statement of Financial Accounting Standards No. 87*, par. 107.
[15] To avoid confusion, the text discussion refers to *pension expense* instead of *pension cost*. Periodic pension cost may be expensed immediately or it may be capitalized as part of an asset such as inventory. In all of our examples, we will assume that pension costs are expensed immediately.

Web Material associated with this chapter for the detailed present value computations.) Therefore, the service cost element of pension expense for the year is $1,339. In practice, of course, service cost computations are very complex and are done by actuaries.

Return on the Pension Fund Pension expense is reduced by the return on the pension fund for the year. Just as liabilities and assets are offset to arrive at a net measure of accrued pension liability or prepaid pension cost, the return on the pension fund is offset against interest and service costs to compute a single net pension expense number. FASB ASC paragraphs 715-30-35-22 and 23 indicate that instead of using the actual return, the expected long-term return should be used; more about why this number is used will be discussed shortly. This return is typically computed by multiplying the fair value of the pension fund as of the beginning of the year by some estimate of the average rate of return the pension fund is expected to earn over the long run. For Thakkar Company, this long-term expected rate of return has been estimated to be 12%, and for this introductory example, we will assume that expected return and actual return are equal. Accordingly, for 2015, Thakkar's net pension expense is reduced by $1,200 ($10,000 × 0.12).

In addition to these changes in the PBO and the pension fund, two additional events are common when dealing with pension plans: contributions to the plan and benefits paid from the plan. Contributions increase the amount in the pension fund; in this example, contributions of $1,500 were made during the year. Benefits paid from the plan have two effects: They reduce the amount in the pension fund, and they reduce the PBO. The reason the PBO is reduced is that if the benefits have been paid, they are no longer projected to be paid. In this simplified example, no benefits were paid during the year.

To review, the PBO is a present value measure of the future benefits expected to be paid to employees based on their employment to date but taking into consideration, if applicable, expected increases in wages that would affect their retirement benefits. The measurement is based on actuarial estimation of such factors as life expectancy, employee turnover, and interest rates. The projected benefit obligation increases each year as additional benefits are earned by employees through another year of service (service cost) and by the passage of time that brings employees one year closer to receiving their benefits (interest cost). The PBO decreases each year by the pension payments to retired employees. In addition, the obligation may increase or decrease by changes in any of the actuarial assumptions enumerated previously. These changes can be summarized as shown below.

| Project benefit obligation, beginning of year | + | Service cost and interest cost | − | Retirement benefits paid | ± | Change in actuarial assumptions | = | Projected benefit obligation, end of year |

The fair value of the pension fund is based on its market value at a given measurement date. The fair value of the pension fund increases each year by employer contributions to the fund and decreases by the retirement benefits paid. The fair value also changes by the amount of earnings on the pension fund, including changes in the market value of the fund. These changes can be summarized as follows:

| Fair value of pension fund, beginning of year | + | Employer contributions | − | Retirement benefits paid | ± | Actual return on pension fund | = | Fair value of pension fund, end of year |

Exhibit 17-5 illustrates how service costs, interest costs, and return on the pension fund change the PBO and the fair value of the pension fund (FVPF) and how those changes are combined to be reflected on the income statement.

Exhibit 17-5 | Analysis of Pension Components

Components Pension	Fair Value of Pension Fund		Projected Benefit Obligation		Balance Sheet: Pension-Related Liability	Income Statement: Pension Expense
January 1 balance	$10,000	+	$(12,176)	=	$(2,176)	
Service costs			(1,339)			
Interest costs			(1,218)			$1,357
Expected* return	1,200					
Contributions	1,500					
Benefits paid	0		0			
December 31 balance	$12,700	+	$(14,733)	=	$(2,033)	

*In this example, expected return and actual return are equal.

© Cengage Learning 2014

Net pension expense for 2015 for Thakkar is computed as follows:

Interest cost	$ 1,218
Service cost	1,339
Less: Expected return on the pension fund	(1,200)
Net pension expense	$ 1,357

Note that benefits paid have no effect on the net pension liability as they reduce the FVPF and the PBO by the same amount. Also note that the amount of contributions to the pension fund is not reflected on the income statement. That amount would be disclosed as a cash outflow on the statement of cash flows.

The Thakkar Company illustration contains only the most basic elements of accounting for pensions. In more complex cases, pension expense is affected by amortization of deferred gains and losses from prior periods, amortization of the impact of a change in the terms of the pension plan, and amortization of the impact of changes in the actuarial assumptions. The accounting for these components of pension expense is illustrated in a subsequent example.

Computation of Pension-Related Liability As of December 31, 2015, the PBO for Thakkar is $14,733 (see the Web Material associated with this chapter for the detailed calculations), and the total FVPF is $12,700 ($10,000 + $1,200 return + $1,500 new contributions). As illustrated previously, the PBO and the FVPF are offset to arrive at a single balance sheet amount. As of December 31, 2015, Thakkar Company would perform the following calculation:

PBO, December 31, 2015	$ 14,733
Pension fund at fair value, December 31, 2015	(12,700)
Pension-related liability, December 31, 2015	$ 2,033

The net accrued pension liability of $2,033 would typically be shown in the Noncurrent Liability section of Thakkar's balance sheet.[16] The preceding table would be included in the notes to the financial statements.

Basic Pension Journal Entries The basic accounting entries for pensions are straightforward. An entry is made to accrue the pension expense, and another entry is made

---

[16] FASB ASC paragraph 715-20-45-3. A portion of the pension-related liability is reported as current to the extent that the present value of benefits to be paid in the next 12 months exceeds the fair value of the plan assets.

to record the contribution to the pension fund. For convenience, a single account, the pension-related asset/liability account, is used to reflect changes in the net pension asset or liability. Because Thakkar started the year with a credit balance of $2,176 in this account, it is a liability account in this example. Thakkar Company would make the following journal entries for 2015:

Pension Expense	1,357	
Pension-Related Asset/Liability		1,357
To record 2015 pension expense.		
Pension-Related Asset/Liability	1,500	
Cash		1,500
To record 2015 contribution to pension plan.		

As a result of these entries, pension expense of $1,357 would be reported as an expense on the income statement. The combined effect of the two entries is to decrease the Pension-Related Liability account by $143 ($1,500 − $1,357); the balance in Pension-Related Liability is $2,033 ($2,176 beginning balance − $143 decrease). In a more complicated example, the summary journal entry to recognize pension expense can also involve either a debit or credit to other comprehensive income and/or accumulated other comprehensive income. This is illustrated in the following examples.

Key Points from the Thakkar Company Example Before considering a more complicated example, take a moment now to review some important points illustrated with the Thakkar Company example.

- The actuarial computations are complicated, even in the simplest possible example. For proof, see the Web Material associated with this chapter. The good news is that in real life these computations are done by actuaries.
- The balance sheet and income statement amounts related to pensions are sensitive to the actuarial assumptions made.
- The balance sheet amount is a combination of two items: the projected benefit obligation and the fair value of the pension fund. The details of the computation are disclosed in the notes to the financial statements.
- Net pension expense is also a conglomeration of several items. The three main items are interest cost, service cost, and expected return on the pension fund.

In the next section, the discussion of pension accounting continues with a more complex example. That example provides detailed coverage of the treatment of deferred items and illustrates the impact of pension accounting on the Accumulated Other Comprehensive Income section of stockholders' equity. A work sheet approach that greatly simplifies the handling of complex pension situations is introduced.

Comprehensive Pension Illustration

❹ Use the components of the pension-related asset/liability and changes in the components to compute the periodic expense associated with pensions and to compute the impact on other comprehensive income.

The Thakkar Company example included only three factors in the computation of pension expense. In a more general case, a company could recognize as many as five different components of net periodic pension expense. The five components are as follows:

1. Service cost
2. Interest cost

3. Actual return on the pension fund (if any)
4. Amortization of prior service cost (if any)
5. Deferral of current period gain or loss and amortization of deferred net gain or loss

The PBO and the FVPF are used extensively in computing pension cost. Because the FASB (in Topic 715) requires the pension fund (FVPF) and the obligation (PBO) to be offset against each other, they are not reported separately on the employer's balance sheet. However, detailed records of these and other pension-related balances must be maintained to compute pension cost. These detailed records include accounts for the following three items:

1. Projected Benefit Obligation
2. Fair Value of Pension Fund
3. Accumulated Other Comprehensive Income (AOCI)
   (a) Deferred pension gains and losses
   (b) Prior service cost

Exhibit 17-6 contains a summary of the important elements that impact the reported amounts of these pension-related balance sheet items. These different elements will be discussed in the following example. Throughout the discussion of the components of pension expense, an illustration for a hypothetical company, Thornton Electronics, Inc., will be used.

Exhibit 17-6 | Overview of Work Sheet Format

	Pension-Related Asset/Liability		Accumulated Other Comprehensive Income	
	Projected Benefit Obligation (−)	Fair Value of Pension Fund (+)	Deferred Gain/Loss (+/−)	Prior Service Cost (+)
Dec. 1 Balance Sheet				
Income Statement	− Service Cost	+ Actual Return on Pension Fund	+/− Difference between Actuarial Estimates with Actual Experience	− Amortization of Prior Service Cost
	− Interest Cost		+/− Amortization of Gain/Loss	
	+ Benefits Paid	− Benefits Paid		
Statement of Cash Flows		+ Contributions		
Dec. 31 Balance Sheet	Projected Benefit Obligation (−)	Fair Value of Pension Fund (+)	Deferred Gain/Loss (+/−)	Prior Service Cost (+)

Note: All signs are relative to the balance sheet. Positive amounts are debits; negative amounts are credits.

© Cengage Learning 2014

Thornton Electronics—2015

Thornton's pension-related balances as of January 1, 2015, are as follows:

Item	Where Reported	Amount
Projected benefit obligation	Notes	$1,500,000
Fair value of pension fund	Notes	1,385,000
Pension-related liability	Balance Sheet	115,000
Prior service cost (Accumulated other comprehensive income; subtraction from equity)	Balance Sheet	75,000

The PBO, the FVPF, and the net pension liability have been explained previously. Prior service cost is described below.

Prior Service Cost When a pension plan is initially adopted or amended to provide increased benefits, employees are granted additional benefits for services performed in years prior to the plan's adoption or amendment. The cost of these additional benefits to the employer is called *prior service cost*. The amount of prior service cost is determined by actuaries and represents the increase in the PBO arising from the adoption or amendment of the plan. Although prior service cost initially arises from a plan adoption or amendment made in the current period, the accounting profession has been in general agreement that the cost should not be recognized as part of expense at the plan's adoption or amendment date but should be amortized over future periods. This treatment assumes that an adoption or amendment is not part of the normal, ongoing cost of the pension plan and so should not be included in its entirety in the computation of net pension expense for the current period. Instead, the cost represented by a plan adoption or amendment is recognized in the current period as a reduction in other comprehensive income. The prior service cost amount is then amortized in subsequent years, increasing net pension expense in those years. Assuming that the plan adoption occurred on December 31, 2014, the journal entry to record the plan adoption is as follows:

当初始设立或者为了增加福利而修改养老金计划时，雇员因为计划设立或修改之前的服务年限被授予额外的福利，这些额外的成本对于雇主来说是前期服务成本。前期服务成本金额是由精算师和增加的计划收益义务确定的，而计划收益义务的增大是因计划的设立和修改而造成的。

Stop & Think

What is the relationship between prior service cost and the measurement of the PBO?

a) There is no relationship between prior service cost and the PBO.
b) The projected benefit obligation includes some amount related to prior service cost.
c) Prior service cost includes some amount related to the projected benefit obligation.
d) The projected benefit obligation and prior service cost are always equal to each other.

Other Comprehensive Income	75,000	
Projected Benefit Obligation		75,000

To record December 31, 2014, prior service cost arising from plan amendment.

As shown in Exhibit 17-6, prior service cost is an element of the Accumulated Other Comprehensive Income section of equity; the other comprehensive income amount of $75,000 recognized in the journal entry above was closed, at 2014 year-end, to the prior service cost portion of accumulated other comprehensive income. The projection benefit obligation amount is used in computing the net pension-related asset or liability that is reported in the balance sheet.

Exhibit 17-7 | Thornton Electronics, Inc.—Pension Work Sheet, January 1, 2015

	Financial Statement Accounts			Detailed Accounts		
				Pension Asset/Liability		AOCI
	Net Pension Expense	Cash	Pension-Related Asset/(Liability)	Accumulated Other Comprehensive Income	Projected Benefit Obligation	Fair Value of Pension Fund	Prior Service Cost
Balance, January 1, 2015			(115,000)	75,000	(1,500,000)	1,385,000	75,000

Note: Positive amounts are debits; negative amounts are credits.

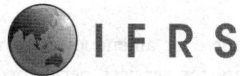

Under *IAS 19*, "Employee Benefits," prior service cost is accounted for differently from that explained above. According to paragraph 103 of *IAS 19*, past service cost (equivalent to prior service cost) is recognized as an expense immediately. In contrast, the approach under U.S. GAAP is to spread the expensing of prior service cost over some future time period. The rationale under U.S. GAAP is that granting employees retroactive benefits when a plan is adopted or changed will create "employee goodwill" that will benefit future periods. The rationale under IFRS is that the cost of the retroactive benefits is a result of the decision to grant those benefits and should be expensed in the period in which that decision is made.

The January 1, 2015, pension information for Thornton Electronics would appear in a pension work sheet as shown in Exhibit 17-7. The work sheet is divided into two sections: the Financial Statement Accounts section, which shows the net effect of pension-related items on the balance sheet and income statement, and the Detailed Accounts section, which lists detailed pension information, to be disclosed in the notes to the financial statements. The formal balance sheet account, Pension-Related Asset/(Liability), summarizes in one number the projected benefit obligation and the fair value of pension fund information contained in the detailed records. The equity account Accumulated Other Comprehensive Income includes deferred gains and losses associated with pension-related items such as the pension plan adoption mentioned earlier. In the work sheet, a credit amount is indicated by parentheses, and the numbers without parentheses are debits.

FYI

Many different interest rates are used throughout the accounting standards. The obligation discount rate can vary over time; thus, the computation of the benefit obligation may vary from one year to another as a result of the change in interest rates. An increase in the rate lowers the present value of the liability; a decrease in the rate increases it. In formulating *Concepts Statement No. 7*, the FASB studied the different ways in which accountants use interest rates.

Information summarizing the 2015 pension activity of Thornton Electronics follows:

Service cost as reported by actuaries	$75,000
Contributions to pension plan	$115,000
Benefits paid to retirees	$125,000
Fair value of pension fund at December 31, 2015	$1,513,500
Obligation discount rate	11.0%
Long-term expected rate of return on the pension fund	10.0%

The 2015 pension information has been entered in the pension work sheet shown in Exhibit 17-8. An explanation for each entry follows.

Exhibit 17-8 | Thornton Electronics, Inc.—Pension Work Sheet for 2015

	Financial Statement Accounts				Detailed Accounts		
					Pension Asset/Liability		AOCI
	Net Pension Expense	Cash	Pension-Related Asset/ (Liability)	Accumulated Other Comprehensive Income	Projected Benefit Obligation	Fair Value of Pension Fund	Prior Service Cost
Balance, January 1, 2015			(115,000)	75,000	(1,500,000)	1,385,000	75,000
(a) Service cost	75,000				(75,000)		
(b) Interest cost	165,000				(165,000)		
(c) Actual return	(138,500)					138,500	
(d) Benefits paid					125,000	(125,000)	
(e) PSC amortization	13,636						(13,636)
(f) Pension contribution		(115,000)				115,000	
Balance, December 31, 2015	115,136	(115,000)	(101,500)	61,364	(1,615,000)	1,513,500	61,364

Notes: Positive amounts are debits; negative amounts are credits.
The shaded area indicates that no changes are made directly to these accounts. These accounts simply reflect changes that are made to the detailed accounts.

© Cengage Learning 2014

服务成本是雇员在当期获取额外收益的现值。服务成本是由精算师根据养老金计划福利公式计算求得的。

Service Cost Recall that service cost is the present value of additional benefits earned by employees during the period. As explained earlier, service cost for the period is determined by actuaries based on the pension plan's benefit formula. Thornton Electronics' actuaries reported 2015 service cost of $75,000. This $75,000 is recorded in work sheet entry (a) as an increase in net periodic pension expense (a debit which ultimately reduces the retained earnings portion of equity when the expense is closed to Retained Earnings) and an increase to the PBO (a credit).

a. Pension Expense 75,000
    Projected Benefit Obligation 75,000
    To record 2015 service cost.

Interest Cost The interest cost represents the fact that the present value of Thornton's pension obligation is increased by the interest on the beginning PBO. The obligation discount rate is used to discount the PBO and to compute the interest cost. The interest cost for 2015 is $1,500,000 × 0.11, or $165,000. The interest cost is shown in entry (b) as a debit to the net periodic pension expense and a credit to the PBO.

b. Pension Expense 165,000
    Projected Benefit Obligation 165,000
    To record 2015 interest cost.

Actual Return on the Pension Fund The assets created by employer contributions to a pension plan usually earn a return that reduces the reported amount of annual pension expense. The return is composed of elements such as interest revenue, dividends, rentals, and changes in the market value of the assets. If a decline in the market value of the pension fund exceeds the earnings on the assets, the actual return will be a negative figure that would increase the pension expense rather than decrease it. The actual return can be computed by comparing the fair value of the pension fund at the beginning and end of the year. After adjusting for current-year contributions and benefits paid to retirees, any change is the actual return on the pension fund. The actual return on the pension fund for Thornton Electronics in 2015 is $138,500, computed as follows:

Fair value of pension fund, December 31, 2015	$1,513,500
Fair value of pension fund, January 1, 2015	1,385,000
Increase in fair value	$ 128,500
Add benefits paid	125,000
Deduct contributions made	(115,000)
Actual return on the pension fund	$ 138,500

The actual return on the pension fund assets is always computed in determining net periodic pension expense. However, as illustrated later, the actual return may be adjusted to the expected return when there is a difference between the two amounts. In this case, the actual return of $138,500 is equal to the expected return ($1,385,000 × 0.10).

The actual return of $138,500 is shown in entry (c) as a credit to the net periodic pension expense (representing a decrease in the expense and, ultimately, an increase in retained earnings) and a debit to the fair value of pension assets (representing an increase in the asset).

c. Pension Fund	138,500	
Pension Expense		138,500

To record 2015 actual return on pension fund.

Note that benefits paid from fund assets do not reduce the account Cash; benefit payments are shown in entry (d) as a decrease in both the pension fund and the remaining PBO. The benefit payments are made by the pension plan trustee to the retired employees using the assets in the pension fund, so the company itself does not make those direct cash payments. Instead, the entry to reduce cash because of company contributions to the pension fund is shown later.

d. Projected Benefit Obligation	125,000	
Pension Fund		125,000

To record 2015 benefits paid.

Amortization of Prior Service Cost Prior service cost (PSC) is the cost of benefits granted to employees for past service when a pension plan is adopted or amended. As illustrated in Exhibit 17-7, the prior service cost amount is initially recorded as a credit (increase) to the PBO and a debit (reduction) to Other Comprehensive Income. This other comprehensive income reduction is eventually closed to Accumulated Other Comprehensive Income, reducing this equity account. This deferred loss is then spread out, or amortized to pension expense, over future periods.

The FASB states that prior service cost should be amortized by "assigning an equal amount to each future period of service of each employee active at the date of the amendment who is expected to receive benefits under the plan."[17] The future period of service is referred to as the expected service period. Because employees will have varying years of remaining service, this amortization method will result in a declining amortization charge.

When a company has many employees retiring or terminating in a systematic pattern, a method similar to the sum-of-the-years'-digits depreciation method can be used. The FASB has provided an illustration of how this computation can be made.[18] Assume that Thornton Electronics, Inc., has 150 employees who are expected to receive benefits for

前期服务成本是当养老金计划设立或修改时，员工因过去的服务而被授予的福利成本。前期服务成本金额贷记计划收益义务，借记其他综合收益。其他综合收益减少并最终接近累计其他综合收益，减少权益账户；递延损失会延续或者在未来期间摊销到养老金费用中。

---

[17] FASB ASC paragraph 715-30-35-11.
[18] Ibid., Appendix B, illustration 3. FASB ASC paragraphs 715-30-55-93 through 100.

prior services under an amendment adopted at the end of 2014. Ten percent of the employees (15 employees) are expected to leave (either retire or quit with vesting privileges) in each of the next 10 years. Employees hired after the plan's amendment date do not affect the amortization. The formula for the sum-of-the-years'-digits depreciation method illustrated in Chapter 11 can be used with a slight modification to reflect the decreased number of employees each period. Thus, the total service years for Thornton Electronics, Inc., could be computed with the following formula:

$$\frac{N(N+1)}{2} \times D = \text{Total future years of service}$$

where

N = Number of remaining years of service
D = Decrease in number of employees working each year

Therefore

$$\frac{10(11)}{2} \times 15 = 825$$

The numerator would begin with the total employees at the time of the plan's amendment and decline by D each period. Under these assumptions, 825 service years will be rendered by the affected employees. The fraction used to determine the amortization has a numerator that declines by 15 employees each year and a denominator that is the sum of the service years, or 825. If the increase in the projected benefit obligation, or prior service cost, arising from the plan's amendment at the end of 2014 was $75,000, the amortization for 2015 would be 150/825 × $75,000, or $13,636. In the following two years, the amount amortized would be 135/825 × $75,000, or $12,273, and 120/825 × $75,000, or $10,909, respectively.

Although the FASB has indicated a preference for this sum-of-the-years'-digits–type method of amortization, the consistent use of an alternative amortization approach that more rapidly reduces the prior service cost is acceptable. An example of such an alternative is the straight-line amortization of prior service cost over the average remaining service period of the employees. To illustrate the straight-line approach using the Thornton Electronics example, the average remaining service life would be 5.5 years (825/150 employees), and $13,636 ($75,000/5.5) would be amortized for each full year.

A separate amortization schedule is necessary for each amendment of the plan. There is no need to alter the schedule for new employees because they would not receive benefits from prior services. If the planned termination or retirement pattern does not occur, adjustments may be necessary later to completely amortize the prior service cost.

For the Thornton Electronics example, the amortization amount based on the number of service years remaining is used. For 2015, this amount is $13,636. In entry (e) of Exhibit 17-8, the $13,636 is shown as an increase in net periodic pension expense (with a debit) and an increase in accumulated other comprehensive income (with a credit).

e. Pension Expense	13,636	
Accumulated Other Comprehensive Income		13,636
To record 2015 amortization of prior service cost.		

Recall that prior service cost is a subcategory of Accumulated Other Comprehensive Income, an equity account. Thus, a credit to Accumulated Other Comprehensive Income reduces the amount of unamortized prior service cost, but this then means that the subtraction from equity is smaller; equity is increased. The prior service cost amount is systematically amortized until the entire equity subtraction has been transferred from accumulated other comprehensive, through pension expense and net income, and into retained earnings. The amortization process increases pension expense each year, but there is no net annual effect on equity (or on annual comprehensive income); instead, the net annual equity effect is that a portion of the equity reduction is transferred from accumulated other comprehensive income to retained earnings each year. The entire reduction in equity, and in comprehensive income, caused by the granting of retroactive benefits upon the plan adoption was recognized immediately when the plan adoption journal entry was initially made, as illustrated earlier.

Plan Contributions Federal government pension funding rules in the United States make U.S. companies with defined benefit pension plans contribute minimum amounts to their pension funds each year. Under the Pension Protection Act of 2006, companies are required to contribute an amount equal to their service cost and interest cost each year plus an additional contribution designed to eliminate any remaining shortfall within seven years. These shortfalls could arise, for example, if the investment performance of the pension plan is worse than expected. Of course, if past superior pension fund performance has created a surplus in the pension fund, subsequent contributions can be cut back or even eliminated for a time.

In the Thornton example, the cash contribution to the pension fund is $115,000. The necessary journal entry is shown as entry (f) in the work sheet in Exhibit 17-8 and is as follows:

f. Pension Fund	115,000	
Cash		115,000

To record 2015 contribution to the pension plan.

Note the large shaded area on the left side, the Financial Statement Accounts side, of the work sheet. This shaded area represents the fact that the detailed factors that impact the pension-related asset/liability and the pension-related portion of accumulated other comprehensive income during the year are not recorded directly in those accounts but are instead recorded in the detailed accounts contained on the right side of the work sheet. The year-end balance sheet balances in the work sheet ($101,500 for the pension-related liability and $61,364 for accumulated other comprehensive income) reflect the totals from the detailed accounts. The pension-related liability balance is the combination of the end-of-year projected benefit obligation and the fair value of the pension fund ($1,615,000 liability and $1,513,500 asset). In this simple example, the accumulated other comprehensive income balance includes only the unamortized prior service cost.

Summary Journal Entries The six detailed journal entries described above and illustrated in the pension work sheet in Exhibit 17-8 can be summarized in two summary journal entries, as follows:

Pension Expense	115,136	
Pension-Related Asset/Liability		101,500
Accumulated Other Comprehensive Income		13,636

Summary journal entry to recognize pension expense for 2015.

Pension-Related Asset/Liability	115,000	
Cash		115,000

Summary journal to record pension fund contribution for 2015.

In the first journal entry, the amount credited to Pension-Related Asset/Liability is calculated strictly by reference to the three primary components of pension expense: service cost, interest cost, and the actual return on the pension fund. In this case, that total is $101,500 ($75,000 + $165,000 − $138,500). The remaining amount of pension expense in this example, prior service cost amortization of $13,636, represents a reclassification from accumulated other comprehensive income to pension expense (which is then closed to Retained Earnings). Additional components of pension expense and their impact on this summary journal entry are illustrated in later examples.

Financial Statement Reporting The four numbers on the Financial Statement Accounts side of the work sheet are reported in Thornton's financial statements, as follows:

- *Net pension expense.* The $115,136 expense is reported as part of compensation expense in Thornton's income statement.
- *Cash.* The $115,000 negative cash amount associated with Thornton's defined benefit pension plan is reported as a cash outflow from operating activities in Thornton's statement of cash flows.
- *Pension-related liability.* The $101,500 pension-related liability is reported in Thornton's balance sheet.
- *Accumulated other comprehensive income.* The $61,364 debit balance in Accumulated Other Comprehensive Income is reported as a subtraction from equity in Thornton's balance sheet.

Note again that the left side of the work sheet includes the items to be reported in Thornton's financial statements and the right side of the work sheet represents the underlying detail that is used to construct the necessary financial statement note disclosure.

IFRS and Net Interest Cost The computation of pension expense under U.S. GAAP involves a net interest calculation, with pension expense increased by the implied interest cost on the PBO and pension expense decreased by the expected return on the pension fund. In the computation of this "net interest cost," it is typically the case that two different interest rates are used: the discount rate on the PBO and the expected return on the pension fund. Under IFRS, a single interest rate is applied to the net pension asset or liability. In essence, this approach constrains the PBO discount rate and the pension fund expected return to be the same number. The practical effect of this constraint is that net pension expense is increased because historically companies have assumed a higher expected pension fund return than the rate on high-quality corporate bonds used with the PBO.

Thornton Electronics—2016

The Thornton Electronics example continues with the following information for 2016:

Service cost as reported by actuaries.	$87,000
Contributions to pension plan	$75,000
Benefits paid to retirees	$132,000
Actual return on pension fund	$26,350
Actuarial change increasing projected benefit obligation	$80,000
Obligation discount rate	11.0%
Long-term expected rate of return on pension fund	10.0%

The pension work sheet to record the 2016 pension information is shown in Exhibit 17-9. Entries (a) through (e) are similar to those shown previously for 2015. Note that the amount of prior service cost (PSC) amortization has decreased because the remaining service years of the employees in place at the time of the plan amendment have declined; referring back to the earlier discussion, the amount is computed

Exhibit 17-9 | Thornton Electronics, Inc.—Pension Work Sheet for 2016

	Financial Statement Accounts				Detailed Accounts			
					Pension Asset/Liability		AOCI	
	Net Pension Expense	Cash	Pension-Related Asset/ (Liability)	Accumulated Other Comprehensive Income	Projected Benefit Obligation	Fair Value of Pension Fund	Prior Service Cost	Deferred Pension (Gain)/ Loss
Balance, January 1, 2015			(101,500)	61,364	(1,615,000)	1,513,500	61,364	
(a) Service cost	87,000				(87,000)			
(b) Interest cost	177,650				(177,650)			
(c) Actual return	(26,350)					26,350		
(d) Benefits paid					132,000	(132,000)		
(e) PSC amortization	12,273						(12,273)	
(f) Deferred loss	(125,000)							125,000
(g) PBO change					(80,000)			80,000
(h) Pension contribution		(75,000)				75,000		
Balance, December 31, 2016	125,573	(75,000)	(344,800)	254,091	(1,827,650)	1,482,850	49,091	205,000

Notes: Positive amounts are debits; negative amounts are credits.
The shaded area indicates that no changes are made directly to these accounts. These accounts simply reflected changes that are made to the detailed accounts.

© Cengage Learning 2014

as follows: 135/825 × $75,000 = $12,273. Entries (f) and (g) relate to deferred gains and losses and are explained below.

Deferral of Gains and Losses Because pension costs include many assumptions and estimates, frequent adjustments must be made for variations between the actual results and the estimates or projections that were used in determining net periodic pension expense for previous periods. For example, the market value of the pension fund may increase at a much higher or lower rate than anticipated, the employee turnover rate may differ from that projected in earlier periods, or the interest rate may differ significantly from expectations. Such differences between expected results and actual experience give rise to a deferred pension gain or loss.

Treatment of these pension gains and losses has been a subject of controversy throughout the FASB's long study of pension accounting. Immediate recognition as part of annual pension expense is opposed by many accountants who are concerned about the volatility of pension expense. However, these pension gains and losses do represent economic events that should be reflected in the financial statements. The FASB decided to minimize the volatility of net periodic pension expense by allowing deferral of some gains and losses and amortization over future periods rather than requiring recognition of gains and losses in the period they arise.[19] These pension gains and losses are recognized in other comprehensive income instead of in the computation of net pension expense. The cumulative amount of these deferred gains and losses is included in the accumulated other comprehensive income portion of equity in the balance sheet.

---

[19] Alternatively, a company may elect to recognize all gains or losses immediately. If this election is made, the company must (1) apply the immediate recognition method consistently, (2) recognize all gains or losses immediately, and (3) disclose the fact that immediate recognition is being followed. FASB ASC paragraph 715-30-35-20. For purposes of this chapter, all illustrations and end-of-chapter material will assume that the deferred recognition method is used.

Although actuarial estimates may change for several reasons, only two will be considered in this illustration: (1) the current-year difference between the actual and expected return on the pension fund and (2) actuarial changes in determining the PBO.

Deferral of Current-Year Difference between Actual and Expected Return on the Pension Fund

As mentioned earlier, in estimating the return on the pension fund, the expected long-term rate of return on assets should be used rather than a more volatile short-term rate. Thus, in the short run, the actual return on the pension fund usually will differ from the expected return. By deferring the difference between the expected return and the actual return, pension expense will tend to be reduced by the expected long-term rate of return rather than by the more volatile short-term return rates. If the actual return on the pension fund exceeds the expected return, the difference is a deferred gain; if the expected return exceeds the actual return, the difference is a deferred loss. The deferred gain or loss is recognized as part of other comprehensive income in the current period; the cumulative amount is reported as accumulated other comprehensive income in the Equity section of the balance sheet. The financial statement impact of deferred pension gains and losses can be summarized as shown below.

	Income Statement	Balance Sheet
Deferred gain	**Increases** pension expense	**Increases** AOCI
Debit net pension expense		
Credit other comprehensive income (OCI)		
Deferred loss	**Decreases** pension expense	**Decreases** AOCI
Credit net pension expense		
Debit other comprehensive income (OCI)		

Now, look at this chart in terms of computing comprehensive income, which is the sum of two things: net income and other comprehensive income. When a gain is deferred, pension expense is increased (reducing net income), but the "other comprehensive income" portion of comprehensive income is increased. The net effect is that there is no overall impact on the amount of comprehensive income, but merely in the mix between net income and other comprehensive income. The same is true, in the opposite direction, with a deferred loss. So, the deferred gain and the deferred loss amount are actually included in the computation of comprehensive income but are excluded in the computation of the "net income" portion of comprehensive income.

The expected return on the pension fund is computed by multiplying the market-related value of the pension fund by the expected long-term rate of return. The FASB defines *market-related value of the pension fund* as either (1) the fair market value of the pension fund at the beginning of the current year or (2) a weighted-average value based on market values of the pension fund over a period not to exceed five years.[20] If asset values have been increasing, the weighted-average value will be lower than the beginning fair market value, resulting in a lower expected return.

When the actual return on the pension fund exceeds the expected return, the excess is called a *deferred gain*. This amount is added in the computation of pension expense. The reason the deferred gain increases pension expense is because the "gain" (actually it is better-than-expected pension fund performance) is not allowed to reduce pension expense this period. The result is to increase pension expense and to report the deferred

[20] Different methods of calculating market-related value may be used for different classes of assets. However, a company must apply the methods consistently from year to year.

当养老金的实际回报大于预期回报时，超出部分叫作递延收益，这个金额会加到养老金费用的计算中。递延收益之所以会增加养老金费用，是因为该"收益"（养老金基金实际业绩好于预期）不允许在当期减少养老金费用，结果是增加了养老金费用，把递延收益作为其他综合收益的增加项。当养老金的实际回报小于预期回报时，所产生差异叫作递延损失，这个金额需要从养老金费用的计算中剔除，因为该"损失"（养老金基金实际业绩劣于预期）不允许在当期增加养老金费用，递延损失作为其他综合收益的减少项。

gain as an increase in other comprehensive income. When the actual return is less than the expected return, the difference is called a *deferred loss*. This amount is subtracted in the computation of pension expense because the "loss" (worse-than-expected pension fund performance) is not allowed to increase pension expense this period. The deferred loss is reported as a reduction in other comprehensive income. Because the actual return on the pension fund is deducted in computing pension expense, the net effect of the deferred pension gain or loss adjustment is that the expected return, rather than the actual return, is used to reduce pension expense, thus achieving a smoothing of pension expense over time.

> **FYI**
>
> The net result of using the expected return on the pension fund instead of the actual return is that reported pension expense equals what it would be if the pension fund were to perform exactly as expected, with any large differences amortized to expense in future years, as illustrated later in the chapter.

To illustrate the computation of the deferred pension gain or loss arising from differences between the actual and expected return, assume that Thornton Electronics computes the expected return on the pension fund using the fair market value of the pension fund at the beginning of the year. The expected return on the pension fund for 2016 is $151,350 ($1,513,500 × 0.10). Because the actual return for the year of only $26,350 is much less than the expected return, the $125,000 difference is treated as a deferred pension loss and results in a reduction in pension expense.

As mentioned, combining the effects of the actual return and the deferred loss results in a net reduction in pension expense equal to the expected return of $151,350 (actual return of $26,350 + deferred loss of $125,000). The deferred loss is recorded in entry (f) in the 2016 pension work sheet as a credit (decrease) to annual Pension Expense and a debit to Other Comprehensive Income. Once this debit to Other Comprehensive Income is closed at year-end to Accumulated Other Comprehensive Income, the cumulative amount is called Deferred Net Pension Gain/Loss and is part of accumulated other comprehensive income in the Equity section of the balance sheet.

f. Other Comprehensive Income 125,000
        Pension Expense 125,000
    To record 2016 deferred loss stemming from the actual return on the pension fund being less than expected.

Differences in Actuarial Estimates of PBO

As indicated earlier, the actuarial computation of the projected benefit obligation involves many estimates, including future interest rates, life expectancy rates, and future salary rates. The effects of changing these estimates are deferred and accumulated for possible amortization to pension expense over future periods. During 2016, Thornton's actuaries reevaluated their actuarial assumptions in light of experience with Thornton's employees and calculated that the projected benefit obligation should be increased by $80,000. This increase is identified as a loss and is deferred to future periods. The deferred loss arising from the adjustment to the PBO becomes part of the deferred net pension gain or loss for possible future amortization. This adjustment is shown as entry (g) in the 2016 work sheet, as follows.

g. Other Comprehensive Income 80,000
        Projected Benefit Obligation 80,000
    To record 2016 impact of a revision in actuarial estimates associated with the projected benefit obligation.

This change in actuarial estimate is recorded in work sheet entry (g) as a credit (increase) to the PBO and a debit to Other Comprehensive Income. Note that the change has no impact on pension expense for 2016: the reduction in equity bypasses expense and net income and retained earnings and is instead eventually reflected in accumulated other comprehensive income. However, the change will impact future years in two ways. First, because the PBO is higher, interest cost in future years will be higher. Second, depending on future developments, the deferred loss may be amortized to pension expense in future years. Circumstances under which deferred losses and gains are amortized are described later in the chapter.

From the work sheet in Exhibit 17-9, it can be seen that a $75,000 contribution to the pension fund is recorded in entry (h) as illustrated previously.

Summary Journal Entries The eight detailed journal entries described above and illustrated in the pension work sheet in Exhibit 17-9 can be summarized in three summary journal entries, as shown below.

Pension Expense	125,573	
Other Comprehensive Income	125,000	
Pension-Related Asset/Liability		238,300
Accumulated Other Comprehensive Income		12,273
Summary journal entry to recognize pension expense for 2016.		
Pension-Related Asset/Liability	115,000	
Cash		115,000
Summary journal to record pension fund contribution for 2016.		
Other Comprehensive Income	80,000	
Pension-Related Asset/Liability		80,000
To record 2016 impact of a revision in actuarial estimates associated with the projected benefit obligation.		

在第一个分录中，与养老金有关的资产/负债的贷记金额涉及养老金费用的三个主要部分：服务成本、利息成本和养老金基金的实际回报。在本例中，总额是238 300美元（87 000+177 650−26 350）。此外，前期服务成本的摊销额12 273美元代表从累计其他综合收益到养老金费用的重分类。最后，由养老金基金不良业绩引起的递延损失减少了当期的养老金费用，应确认为当年负的其他综合收益，并作为账户常规结转的一部分结转至累计其他综合收益。

In the first journal entry, the amount credited to Pension-Related Asset/Liability is calculated strictly by reference to the three primary components of pension expense: service cost, interest cost, and the actual return on the pension fund. In this case, that total is $238,300 ($87,000 + $177,650 − $26,350). In addition, as illustrated previously, prior service cost amortization of $12,273 represents a reclassification from accumulated other comprehensive income to pension expense. Finally, the deferred loss resulting from the underperformance of the pension fund reduces pension expense in the current period and instead is recognized as negative other comprehensive income for the year which is then closed to Accumulated Other Comprehensive Income as part of the regular closing of the accounts.

The pension fund contribution journal entry is recorded as illustrated previously. Also, in this year, one additional summary entry is needed to reflect the $80,000 increase in the projected benefit obligation from the change in actuarial assumptions. This change does not impact pension expense in the current year but does reduce comprehensive income by $80,000.

Financial Statement Reporting The four numbers on the Financial Statement Accounts side of the work sheet are reported in Thornton's financial statements, as follows:

- *Net pension expense*. The $125,573 expense is reported as part of compensation expense in Thornton's income statement. Note that the combination of $26,350 actual return plus the $125,000 deferred loss means that the total amount subtracted in the computation of pension expense is $151,350 ($26,350 + $125,000), which is the expected return on the pension fund for the year.

- *Cash*. The $75,000 negative cash amount associated with Thornton's defined benefit pension plan is reported as a cash outflow from operating activities in Thornton's statement of cash flows.

- *Pension-related liability.* The $344,800 pension-related liability is reported in Thornton's balance sheet.
- *Accumulated other comprehensive income.* The $254,091 debit balance in Accumulated Other Comprehensive Income is reported as a subtraction from equity in Thornton's balance sheet.

Note again that the left side of the work sheet includes the items to be reported in Thornton's financial statements, and the right side of the work sheet represents the underlying detail that is used to construct the necessary financial statement note disclosure.

Under old U.S. GAAP rules that were superseded in 2006, the cumulative portion of the deferred gains and losses was combined with the net pension-related asset or liability in the balance sheet. As a result, the reported balance sheet pension item was an unsavory conglomeration of asset, liability, and equity items, all rolled into one number. The resulting mysterious, and often misleading, nature of this number was a primary motivation behind the change in the rules in 2006. In addition, the old rules were viewed as deficient because the most basic facts about a defined benefit pension plan—is the plan overfunded or underfunded, and by how much—were not reflected in the balance sheet. This old, confusing method of accounting has now been eliminated from both U.S. GAAP and, in 2011, from IFRS.

Thornton Electronics—2017

The Thornton Electronics pension information for 2017 follows:

Service cost as reported by actuaries	$115,000
Contributions to pension plan	$80,000
Benefits paid to retirees	$140,000
Actual return on pension fund	$175,500
Obligation discount rate	11.0%
Long-term expected rate of return on the pension fund	10.0%
Accumulated benefit obligation, December 31, 2017	$1,795,150

This information is recorded in the 2017 pension work sheet shown in Exhibit 17-10. Entries (a) through (f) are similar to those made in 2016. Again, note that the prior service cost amortization amount is lower than in prior years, reflecting the continuing decline in the expected remaining service lives of those employees who were in place when the plan's amendment was initiated; the amount, as computed earlier, is 120/825 × $75,000 = $10,909. Entry (f) reflects the fact that the actual return on the pension fund of $175,500 for the year exceeded the expected return of $148,285 ($1,482,850 × 0.10). The excess of $27,215 is considered an unexpected gain and is credited to Other Comprehensive Income. The same amount is debited to the net periodic pension expense. Entry (g) relates to amortization of deferred pension gains and losses and will now be explained.

Amortization of Deferred Net Pension Gain or Loss from Prior Years Under certain conditions, an employer's net periodic pension expense will include the amortization of deferred net pension gain or loss. The deferred pension gain or loss from prior years (recognized in accumulated other comprehensive income) is amortized over future years if it accumulates to more than an amount defined by the FASB as a corridor amount. Amortization is only required for a deferred net gain or loss that exceeds 10% of the greater of the PBO or the market-related value of the pension fund as of the beginning of the year. The rationale behind this approach is that the deferred gains and losses are not a concern as long as they are small, indicating that the estimates are close to being correct.

Exhibit 17-10 | Thornton Electronics, Inc.—Pension Work Sheet for 2017

	Financial Statement Accounts				Detailed Accounts			
					Pension Asset/Liability		AOCI	
	Net Pension Expense	Cash	Pension-Related Asset/ (Liability)	Accumulated Other Comprehensive Income	Projected Benefit Obligation	Fair Value of Pension Fund	Prior Service Cost	Deferred Pension (Gain)/ Loss
Balance, January 1, 2017			(344,800)	254,091	(1,827,650)	1,482,850	49,091	205,000
(a) Service cost	115,000				(115,000)			
(b) Interest cost	201,042				(201,042)			
(c) Actual return	(175,500)					175,500		
(d) Benefits paid					140,000	(140,000)		
(e) PSC amortization	10,909						(10,909)	
(f) Deferred gain	27,215							(27,215)
(g) Amortization of deferred loss	4,447							(4,447)
(h) Pension contribution		(80,000)				80,000		
Balance, December 31, 2017	183,113	(80,000)	(405,342)	211,520	(2,003,692)	1,598,350	38,182	173,338

Notes: Positive amounts are debits; negative amounts are credits.
The shaded area indicates that no changes are made directly to these accounts. These accounts simply reflected changes that are made to the detailed accounts.

© Cengage Learning 2014

The 10% rule used in defining the corridor amount is just an arbitrary attempt to define "small." Over time, if the estimates are not systematically bad, one would expect the total deferred net gain or loss to fluctuate randomly around zero.

If the deferred net gain or loss does exceed the corridor amount, that is an indication that the estimates have been systematically incorrect and the cumulative deferred amounts should begin to be recognized. The FASB indicated that any systematic method of amortizing the deferred net gain or loss that equaled or exceeded the straight-line amortization over the remaining expected service years of the employees would be acceptable as long as the procedure is applied consistently to both gains and losses. The amortization of a deferred gain reduces the net periodic pension expense, and the amortization of a deferred loss increases the net periodic pension expense. It is important to remember that only deferred gains and losses from prior years are subject to amortization. Accordingly, the corridor comparison applies only to the beginning balances in Projected Benefit Obligation, Fair Value of Pension Fund, and the deferred net pension gain/loss accounts.

This corridor amortization is a compromise between immediate recognition of gains and losses (which is viewed as causing too much volatility in earnings) and permanent deferral. Permanent deferral makes sense as long as the gains and losses tend to cancel out, but it becomes less reasonable when a "large" deferred gain or loss accumulates. The corridor amount is simply an arbitrary definition of what amount of deferred gain or loss is considered "large."

Stop & Think

When would a company find itself exceeding the corridor amount?

a) Only when the company has pension fund assets in excess of total stockholders' equity
b) Only when the company is off in its pension estimates by a significant amount or by smaller regular amounts over a long period of time
c) Only when the company has pension fund assets in excess of 10% of total assets
d) Only when the company has a projected benefit obligation in excess of 10% of total liabilities

To illustrate the computation of the corridor amount, Thornton would apply the 10% corridor threshold to the projected benefit obligation at the beginning of the year because the PBO exceeds the market value of the pension fund at the beginning of the year.[21] Thus, the corridor amount is $182,765 ($1,827,650 × 0.10). Because the deferred loss at January 1, 2017, is $205,000, only the excess of $22,235 ($205,000 − $182,765) is subject to amortization. The average remaining employee service life on January 1, 2017, is assumed to be five years, so the 2017 amortization is $4,447 ($22,235/5). This amount represents amortization of a deferred loss and is an addition to the other components in computing pension expense. The loss amortization is recorded in entry (g) in the 2017 pension work sheet as a debit to the net periodic pension expense and a credit to Accumulated Other Comprehensive Income, resulting in a reclassification out of Accumulated Other Comprehensive Income and into pension expense. Note the size of the loss amortization amount ($4,447) in relation to the size of the deferred loss itself ($205,000). Clearly, this deferral of gains and losses and subsequent corridor amortization accomplishes the goal of reducing volatility in annual pension expense.

Pension Expense	4,447	
Accumulated Other Comprehensive Income		4,447
To record 2017 amortization of deferred net pension loss in excess of the corridor amount.		

Summary Journal Entries The eight detailed journal entries described above and illustrated in the pension work sheet in Exhibit 17-10 can be summarized in two summary journal entries, as follows:

Pension Expense	183,113	
Other Comprehensive Income		27,215
Pension-Related Asset/Liability		140,542
Accumulated Other Comprehensive Income		15,356
Summary journal entry to recognize pension expense for 2017.		
Pension-Related Asset/Liability	80,000	
Cash		80,000
Summary journal to record pension fund contribution for 2017.		

In the first journal entry, the amount credited to Pension-Related Asset/Liability is calculated strictly by reference to the three primary components of pension expense: service cost, interest cost, and the actual return on the pension fund. In this case, that total is $140,542 ($115,000 + $201,042 − $175,500). In addition, in this year, there are two types of amortization—prior service cost amortization of $10,909 and deferred loss amortization of $4,447. Both of these amortization amounts, totaling $15,356, represent a reclassification from accumulated other comprehensive income to pension expense. Finally, the deferred gain of $27,215 resulting from the overperformance of the pension fund increases pension expense (and reduces net income) in the current period but is also recognized as an increase in other comprehensive income for the year. From this final aspect of the summary journal entry, it can be seen that ultimately NET income is impacted by the expected return on the pension fund but COMPREHENSIVE income is impacted by the actual return.

Financial Statement Reporting The four numbers on the Financial Statement Accounts side of the work sheet are reported in Thornton's financial statements, as shown on page 17-37.

---

[21] For simplicity, the fair market value of pension assets is used as the market-related value. Recall that an alternative measure is the weighted average of the fair market value of pension assets from prior years.

> **FYI**
>
> Sir David Tweedie, former chairman of the IASB, is known for his witty, concise, and controversial statements about accounting standards. In a televised interview, he said the following about the usefulness of the numbers generated under the corridor approach: "You may as well take the [cumulative deferred gain or loss], divide it by the cube root of the number of miles to the moon, and multiply it by your shoe size. I mean, it doesn't mean a thing."

- *Net pension expense.* The $183,113 expense is reported as part of compensation expense in Thornton's income statement. Note that the combination of $175,500 actual return less the $27,215 deferred gain means that the net amount subtracted in the computation of pension expense is $148,285 ($175,500 − $27,215), which is the expected return on the pension fund for the year.

- *Cash.* The $80,000 negative cash amount associated with Thornton's defined benefit pension plan is reported as a cash outflow from operating activities in Thornton's statement of cash flows.

- *Pension-related liability.* The $405,342 pension-related liability is reported in Thornton's balance sheet. This liability represents substantial underfunding of Thornton's pension plan. It is likely that if this were a real company the federal pension regulations would require substantial increases in the pension contribution amount to alleviate this underfunding.

- *Accumulated other comprehensive income.* The $211,520 debit balance in Accumulated Other Comprehensive Income is reported as a subtraction from equity in Thornton's balance sheet.

IFRS and Deferred Pension Gains and Losses The accounting for deferred pension gains and losses under IFRS is both similar to and different from the treatment under U.S. GAAP. The initial deferral is exactly the same as has been illustrated above: Pension gains and losses stemming from differences between estimates of pension fund returns, employee postretirement life spans, and so forth are recognized immediately as part of Other Comprehensive Income (OCI). OCI is then closed to Accumulated Other Comprehensive Income (AOCI), which is reported in the Equity section of the balance sheet. The difference between U.S. GAAP and IFRS is in the subsequent treatment of this AOCI. As explained above, under U.S. GAAP some of this accumulated deferred gain or loss is amortized to expense to the extent that it exceeds the 10% corridor amount. Under IFRS, there is no corridor amount; the deferred net pension gain or loss just stays in AOCI forever. Of course, the expectation is that if the AOCI balance gets large, either as an equity reduction or an equity increase, this will be a signal to adjust actuarial estimates for future years.

Disclosure of Pension Plans

LO5 Prepare required disclosures associated with pensions, and understand the accounting treatment for pension settlements and curtailments.

学习目标5
编制与养老金相关的披露，理解养老金结算和削减的会计处理。

The disclosure requirements relating to pensions are discussed in FASB ASC Topic 715. The FASB requires information similar to that presented in the work sheet that was used throughout the chapter for calculating pension costs. Specifically, the major disclosure requirements for most publicly traded companies are as follows:

1. A reconciliation between the beginning and ending balances for the projected benefit obligation

2. A reconciliation between the beginning and ending balances in the fair value of the pension fund
3. A disclosure of the accumulated benefit obligation
4. The funded status of the plans and the amounts recognized in the balance sheet
5. The components of pension expense for the period
6. Any effects on other comprehensive income for the period and the details of the existing balances in accumulated other comprehensive income
7. The assumptions used relating to the following items:
   (a) Discount rate
   (b) Rate of compensation increase
   (c) Expected long-term rate of return on the pension fund
8. Disclosure of the percentage of the different types of investments held in the pension fund along with a narrative description of investment strategy; because of recent volatility in investment returns, especially for real estate investments, the FASB has substantially increased the amount of disclosure required with respect to pension fund assets.[22]
9. For each of the next five years, disclose an estimate of the amount of cash to be paid in benefits (from the pension fund assets) and the amount of cash to be contributed by the company to the pension fund
10. For postretirement benefits (discussed later in this chapter): assumed healthcare cost trend rates and their effect on service and interest costs and the ABO if the assumed healthcare cost trend rates were one percentage point higher

As you can see, the work sheet used in this chapter provides much of the information required for disclosure. In addition to the disclosure requirement for defined benefit pension plans, *there are* also disclosure requirements for defined contribution plans. Specifically, an employer must disclose the amount of pension expense recognized for defined contribution plans separately from the amount of expense recognized for defined benefit plans. In addition, the nature and effect of any significant changes during the period should be disclosed.

For Thornton Electronics, most of the information needed for the disclosure of the details of the computation of annual pension expense and reconciliation of the funded status of the pension plan can be obtained from the 2017 pension work sheet in Exhibit 17-10. In addition, the accumulated benefit obligation (ABO) of $1,795,150 is disclosed.

Companies with more than one pension plan may combine the amounts of all pension plans. However, in those cases when the ABO exceeds the FVPF, that information must be disclosed separately in the notes. In addition, companies may combine the disclosure relating to their U.S. and non-U.S. plans unless the obligation associated with the non-U.S. plans is significant or the terms of the non-U.S. plans differ substantially from those of the U.S. plans. *In addition,* companies must separate the disclosures relating to pensions and postretirement benefits other than pensions (these benefits are discussed in the next section). This type of disclosure is illustrated in Exhibit 17-11 using an excerpt from the notes to the 2011 financial statements of General Motors. Note that General Motors reports information for its U.S. and non-U.S. pension plans separately.

---

[22] FASB ASC paragraph 715-20-50-1(d).

Exhibit 17-11 | Note Disclosure for U.S. and Non-U.S. Pension Plans—General Motors

	Successor			
	U.S. Plans Pension Benefits	Non-U.S. Plans Pension Benefits(a)	U.S. Plans Other Benefits	Non-U.S. Plans Other Benefits
	Year ended December 31, 2011			
Change in benefit obligations				
Beginning benefit obligation	$103,395	$ 24,762	$5,667	$ 4,252
Service cost	494	399	23	30
Interest cost	4,915	1,215	265	186
Plan participants' contributions	—	7	13	9
Amendments	(6)	(10)	(284)	(2)
Actuarial losses	8,494	1,530	548	343
Benefits paid	(8,730)	(1,561)	(439)	(180)
Early retirement reinsurance program receipts	—	—	29	—
Foreign currency translation adjustments	—	(508)	—	(128)
Canadian healthcare trust settlement	—	—	—	(3,051)
Curtailments, settlements, and other	—	(69)	—	31
Ending benefit obligation	108,562	25,765	5,822	1,490
Change in plan assets				
Beginning fair value of plan assets	91,007	14,903	—	—
Actual return on plan assets	10,087	686	—	—
Employer contributions	1,962	836	426	171
Plan participants' contributions	—	7	13	9
Benefits paid	(8,730)	(1,561)	(439)	(180)
Foreign currency translation adjustments	—	(258)	—	—
Settlements	—	(34)	—	—
Other	23	(38)	—	—
Ending fair value of plan assets	94,349	14,541	—	—
Ending funded status	$ (14,213)	$(11,224)	$(5,822)	$(1,490)
Amounts recorded in the consolidated balance sheet are comprised of:				
Noncurrent asset	$ —	$ 61	$ —	—
Current liability	(99)	(324)	(411)	(65)
Noncurrent liability	(14,114)	(10,961)	(5,411)	(1,425)
Net amount recorded	$ (14,213)	$(11,224)	$(5,822)	$(1,490)
Amounts recorded in Accumulated other comprehensive income (loss) are comprised of:				
Net actuarial loss	$ (1,352)	$ (2,498)	$(1,003)	$ (177)
Net prior service credit	15	19	251	76
Total recorded in Accumulated other comprehensive income (loss)	$ (1,337)	$ (2,479)	$ (752)	$ (101)

General Motors, 2011, 10K Report

pension settlements and curtailments
养老金计划的处理与削减

Pension Settlements and Curtailments

If a pension plan is settled or the benefits are curtailed, a question arises as to how the employer should treat a resulting gain or loss. Settlement of a pension plan occurs when an employer takes an irrevocable action that relieves the employer of primary responsibility for all or part of the obligation. Examples of a settlement transaction include the employer's purchase of an annuity from an insurance company that would cover employees' vested benefits or a lump-sum cash payment to the employees in exchange for their rights to receive specified pension benefits. A curtailment of a pension plan arises from an event that significantly reduces the benefits that will be provided for present employees' future services. Curtailments include (1) the termination of employees' services earlier than expected, for example, as a result of closing a plant or discontinuing a segment of the business and (2) the termination or suspension of a pension plan so that employees do not earn additional benefits for future services.[23]

As discussed throughout this chapter, in Topic 715 the FASB provides for delayed recognition of pension gains and losses arising from the ordinary operations of the pension plan. In addition, the statement provides for delayed recognition of prior service cost. Thus, at any given time, deferred gains, losses, and prior service cost usually exist.

The FASB felt it was clear that if a pension plan is completely terminated and all pension obligations are settled and pension funds are disbursed, previously deferred pension amounts should be recognized. What wasn't clear, however, is what happens when partial settlements or curtailments take place. The rules are discussed below.

Settlements Pension plans occasionally become overfunded because a rising stock market causes the value of the pension fund to exceed the pension obligation. To take advantage of this situation, companies sometimes settle their pension plans by purchasing annuity contracts from insurance companies for less than the amount in the pension fund. Subject to regulations such as ERISA, the excess funds can then be used for other corporate purposes.

The accounting issue surrounding settlements centers on whether the gain should be recognized immediately or deferred and recognized in future periods. The FASB decided that if the settlement (1) was an irrevocable action, (2) relieved the employer of primary responsibility for the pension benefit obligation, and (3) eliminated significant risks related to the obligation and the assets used to effect the settlement, the previously deferred net gain or loss should be recognized in the current period. If only part of the projected benefit obligation (PBO) is settled, a pro rata portion of the gain should be recognized currently.[24]

Curtailments As indicated previously, a pension plan curtailment is an event that significantly reduces the expected years of future service of present employees or eliminates for a significant number of employees the accrual of defined benefits for their future services. Examples include termination of employees' services earlier than expected, such as occurs when a segment of the business is discontinued, or termination or suspension of a plan so that it earns no further benefits for future services.

Any prior service cost associated with years of service no longer expected to be rendered as a result of the curtailment is recognized as a loss. In addition, the projected benefit obligation of the pension plan may be changed as a result of the curtailment, giving rise to an additional gain or loss. The FASB provided for offsetting previously deferred pension gains and losses against the gain or loss from changes in the projected benefit obligation and called the difference *curtailment gains or losses*. If the sum of all gains and losses attributed to the curtailment, including the write-off of prior service cost, is a loss, it is recognized in the period when it is probable that the curtailment will occur and the effects are estimable. If the sum of all gains and losses attributed to the curtailment is a gain, it is recognized when the related employees are terminated or when the plan's suspension or amendment is adopted.[25]

---

[23] FASB ASC paragraph 715-30-15-6.
[24] FASB ASC paragraph 715-30-35-79.
[25] FASB ASC paragraphs 7-15-30-35-92 through 94.

Postretirement Benefits Other than Pensions

LO6 学习目标6
解释养老金会计和非养老金退休后福利会计的区别。

⑥ Explain the differences in accounting for pensions and postretirement benefits other than pensions.

FASB ASC Section 715-60-05 includes an overview of the accounting standards for postretirement benefits other than pensions. Although the primary focus is on healthcare benefits, the rules also apply to other postretirement benefits, such as the cost of life insurance contracts, legal assistance benefits, and tuition assistance. The rules relate only to single-employer–defined benefit postretirement plans. The benefits are defined either in monetary amounts, such as a designated amount of life insurance, or as benefit coverage, such as specified coverage for hospital or doctor care. In general, the costs of these benefits are accounted for by employers in the same way as pension costs, that is, on an accrual basis. However, as noted later, there are some important differences between pensions and other postretirement benefits.

Nature of Postretirement Healthcare Plans

There are a number of unique features of postretirement healthcare benefits as compared with pension benefits. Because the details of the accounting rules are reflected in these features, they will be considered first before the differences between accounting for pensions and other postretirement benefits are discussed.

Informal Rather than Formal Plans Many company postretirement benefit plans are not written into formal contracts. Companies often begin paying for postretirement healthcare benefits as a continuation of healthcare coverage for active employees. In some cases, the practice becomes part of union contract bargaining, and informal plans are changed to formal, union-negotiated contractual plans. Even though a plan may be informal, and thus not legally binding, the courts have sometimes interpreted the informal plan as a contract and have required companies to honor the plan. Historically, General Motors has had the largest postretirement benefit plan in the United States, with that nonpension postretirement obligation peaking at $81.5 billion on December 31, 2005. Interestingly, in the past, General Motors has clearly indicated in its financial statement notes that although it is reporting a liability for these postretirement benefits, it does not recognize these benefits as a legal obligation. In the notes to the 1998 financial statements, the management of General Motors stated the following:

> GM has disclosed in the consolidated financial statements certain amounts associated with estimated future postretirement benefits other than pensions and characterized such amounts as "accumulated postretirement benefit obligations," "liabilities," or "obligations." Notwithstanding the recording of such amounts and the use of these terms, GM does not admit or otherwise acknowledge that such amounts or existing postretirement benefit plans of GM (other than pensions) represent legally enforceable liabilities of GM.

This note is especially interesting in light of what occurred between General Motors (GM) and the United Auto Workers (UAW) since 2005. Because of continued large operating losses, GM sought concessions from the UAW to reduce benefits costs. Under an agreement worked out in 2005 and approved in court in 2006, GM retirees were required to begin to pay deductibles, premiums, and copayments for the first time. It was estimated that the changes would save GM about $1 billion per year and reduce GM's recognized liability for retiree medical care by $17.4 billion. Subsequently, in the final negotiations over the General Motors bankruptcy, these retiree healthcare benefits were sacrificed by GM employees in an effort to help save the restructured company. As seen in Exhibit 17-11, employee concessions had reduced the obligation to $5.8 billion by the end of 2011. (*Note:* GM's retiree healthcare obligation is also discussed at the beginning of Chapter 20.)

Nonfunded Rather than Funded Plans Most company plans for postretirement benefits are not funded. Thus, companies rely on current revenues to meet current costs of the plan. Unlike pension contributions, postretirement benefit plan contributions usually are not deductible for income tax purposes. As discussed earlier, ERISA, a federal law, requires companies to fund their pension liability during an employee's working years. There has been no similar federal legislation to encourage funding of postretirement benefit costs. In some instances, a separate insurance carrier is used to cover the risk. In many cases, especially for larger companies, a form of self-insurance has developed.

pay-as-you-go accounting rather than accrual accounting
现金收付实现制而非权责发生制

Pay-as-You-Go Accounting Rather than Accrual Accounting Because postretirement benefit plans usually are not funded, almost all companies previously charged these costs against revenue in the period the benefit costs were incurred rather than in the period when the employee service was rendered. This policy results in uneven charges against revenue and does not recognize a liability for unfunded postretirement benefits. Before the adoption of pre-Codification *SFAS No. 106* in 1990, the total of unfunded postretirement benefits for all companies was estimated to amount to more than $1 trillion.[26]

Uncertainty of Future Benefits Rather than Clearly Defined Benefits Defined benefit pension plans establish terms that make the amount of their future pension obligation measurable with reasonably high reliability. Salary trends, mortality tables, and discount rates are reasonably objective and have been used in accounting for defined benefit pension plans. Healthcare costs, however, involve many variables that make accrual accounting difficult to implement. Over the years, factors such as longer life expectancy, improved medical treatment facilities, and early retirements have combined to cause healthcare costs for retired employees to increase dramatically. The amount of these costs absorbed by government Medicare programs has varied over time and will continue to vary as Congress works to bring government finances under control. As the Medicare plans cover fewer of these costs, employers and individuals are required to absorb higher costs.

Other variables that must be considered before an accrual entry can be made for postretirement benefits include age of retirees, geographic location of retirement, geographic differences in health costs, dependent coverage, gender of retiree, costs of new medical technology, emergence of new diseases, retirement dates, and so forth. Estimating future benefit costs based on these variables can be costly and time consuming for companies. However, the alternative is to throw up your hands in despair and record nothing at all. This unacceptable alternative was what existed before 1990.

Nonpay-Related Rather than Pay-Related Benefits Most postretirement benefits are granted to employees after a certain number of service years or when an employee reaches a specified preretirement age. The amount of benefits to be received is usually

[26] Lee Berton, "FASB Plan Would Make Firms Deduct Billions for Potential Retiree Benefits," *The Wall Street Journal*, August 17, 1988, p. 3.

unrelated to the level of compensation. The date when an employee becomes eligible for these benefits is known as the full eligibility date. No postretirement benefits are granted unless the employee meets this service or age requirement. After that date is reached, the employee is eligible to receive 100% of the postretirement benefits regardless of any future service or regardless of pay level reached. Thus, the period over which an employee earns postretirement benefits extends from the hire date to the full eligibility date.

In contrast, because most pension plans increase an employee's benefits for each additional year of service rendered and for salary increases, the employee continues to earn pension benefits until retirement. Accordingly, the period over which postretirement benefits are earned differs from that over which pension benefits are earned. There are, of course, many exceptions to this description of pensions and postretirement benefits. Some pension plans are nonpay related, and some healthcare postretirement benefit plans are pay related.

Overview of the Accounting for Postretirement Benefits Other than Pensions

Most companies adopted accrual accounting for postretirement benefits beginning with their 1993 financial statements. The same five components for net periodic pension expense listed on pages 17-21–17-22 are required for net periodic postretirement benefit expense. Service cost and prior service cost are charged (attributed) to the years from the hire date to the full eligibility date rather than from the hire date to the retirement date as is true for pension expenses.[27] Any retirement benefit fund assets may be offset against retirement benefit obligations if the assets are clearly restricted for the payment of postretirement benefits.

The disclosure required for postretirement benefit plans includes all requirements for pension plans plus information about health cost trend assumptions and sensitivity analysis of how postretirement expenses and the postretirement obligation would vary if the healthcare costs trend rate were increased by 1%. The details of accounting for postretirement benefits other than pensions are included in the Web Material associated with this chapter.

SOLUTIONS TO OPENING SCENARIO QUESTIONS

1. The "national debt," which represents the total amount borrowed by the U.S. federal government in the form of U.S. Treasury notes, bills, bonds, and so forth, totaled $10.2 trillion on September 30, 2011. At that same time, the federal government's pension obligation to its employees totaled $5.8 trillion. Note that this $5.8 trillion is NOT the Social Security obligation; instead, this is the amount of pension benefits owed to U.S. federal employees.

2. By the year 2030, it is estimated that 20% of the U.S. population will be over 65 years old. With this high proportion of older people in the population, the Social Security payroll taxes of each working person will be required to cover the Social Security benefits of more retired people.

In 1950, each retired person was supported by 16 workers. In 2004, the ratio was 3.3 workers per retiree. In 2025, the ratio will reach two workers per retiree and remain at that level for the foreseeable future. Social Security reform is a political football that neither major political party has mustered the will to attack.

3. General Motors must cover both the pension and the healthcare costs of its retired workers. In fact, in recent years at General Motors the cost of covering the healthcare costs of retired workers has exceeded the pension costs. Exhibit 20-1 in Chapter 20 illustrates how the bankruptcy and reorganization of General Motors in 2009 drastically reduced the company's obligation for retiree health care.

---

[27] If the period of service needed to earn the postretirement benefits does not include previous years, the attribution period will be from a later date, referred to as the *beginning of the credited service period*. FASB ASC paragraph 715-60-35-66.

Stop & Think SOLUTIONS

1. (Page 17-10) The correct answer is A. Notice that the definition of a liability closely parallels the criteria used in accounting for postemployment benefits. The benefits are probable future sacrifices of economic benefit resulting from past transactions. The definitions provided in the conceptual framework have been used extensively by the FASB in addressing complex accounting issues.

2. (Page 17-13) The correct answer is D. With a defined benefit plan, the employer bears the majority of the investment risk. With a defined contribution plan, the risk shifts to the employee. Companies would prefer that, where possible, employees bear the investment risk.

3. (Page 17-23) The correct answer is B. Prior service cost is the present value of pension benefits granted to existing employees on the date a plan is initiated. As a result, this amount is included in the computation of the projected benefit obligation (PBO).

4. (Page 17-35) The correct answer is B. A company would exceed the corridor amount only when it was off in its estimates by a significant amount over a long period of time. Because the corridor amount is 10% of a very large number (either plan assets or PBO), a company would have to have made a series of bad estimates. Typically, a company will monitor the amount of its unrealized gains and losses and adjust its estimates to compensate.

SOLUTION TO USING THE FASB'S CODIFICATION

The accounting for sabbatical leaves is discussed in FASB ASC paragraph 710-10-25-4: "The appropriate accounting for a sabbatical leave depends on the purpose of the leave. If a sabbatical leave is granted only to perform research or public service to enhance the reputation of or otherwise benefit the employer, the compensation is not attributable to services already rendered [see paragraph 710-10-25-1(a)]; a liability shall not be accrued in advance of the employee's services during such leave. If the leave is granted to provide compensated unrestricted time off for past service and the other conditions for accrual are met, a liability for sabbatical leave shall be accrued."

So, because Professor Pearl will be required to stay on campus and conduct research, at the direction of the university, during the "sabbatical" leave, the anticipated compensation cost for Professor Pearl is NOT judged to be incurred during the six years leading up to the "sabbatical" year, but instead is a cost to be recognized during the "sabbatical" year itself. The university accountant who is using Professor Pearl's future "sabbatical" as a reason to cut his compensation this year is twisting the accounting rules. In fact, it is more accurate to state that the university accountant doesn't understand the accounting rules. He or she needs to get more familiar with the use of the FASB's Codification.

Review Chapter 17 Learning Objectives

① Account for payroll and payroll taxes, and understand the criteria for recognizing a liability associated with compensated absences.

Accounting for payroll and payroll taxes is a routine event that occurs at the end of every pay period. In addition to accounting for the taxes withheld from employees, care must be taken to ensure that employer payroll taxes are considered. Employers are responsible for FICA as well as state and federal unemployment taxes. As employees work, they often earn the right to receive, in the future, time off for sickness or vacation. These days are referred to as *compensated absences* and must be accounted for as expenses in the period in which the employee earns those rights.

② Compute performance bonuses, and recognize the issues associated with postemployment benefits.

In addition to regular payroll, employees may have the opportunity to receive additional compensation based on the achievement of performance goals. This additional compensation often takes the form of bonuses or stock options. The accounting for stock options requires estimates as to future value and can become quite complex. In some cases, employees will leave a firm, either voluntarily or involuntarily. Benefits promised to these employees following employment but prior to retirement must be accounted for in a fashion similar to the accounting for compensated absences.

③ Understand the nature and characteristics of employer pension plans, including the details of defined benefit plans.

Pension plans can be structured as either defined benefit plans or defined contribution plans. With *defined contribution plans*, the employee receives, upon retirement, the funds that have accumulated over time. Accounting for defined contribution plans is straightforward. *Defined benefit plans* are more challenging in that the value of the benefits is often difficult to measure. These benefits are often a function of years of service, future salary levels, and life expectancy. Actuaries are employed to provide estimates as to projected future benefits.

④ Use the components of the pension-related asset/liability and changes in the components to compute the periodic expense associated with pensions and to compute the impact on other comprehensive income.

The prepaid/accrued pension account reflects the difference between the present value of the amount expected to be paid in the future (PBO) and the fair value of the pension fund (FVPF) set aside to meet that obligation. Additional pension-related factors are reported as part of accumulated other comprehensive income. These additional factors include prior service costs and deferred gains/losses related to differences between expected and actual returns on the pension fund.

Each year, an assessment is made as to the additional benefits owed as a result of another year of service, the effects of being a year closer to paying out benefits, and the return received as a result of setting aside funds to meet these future obligations. The additional factors mentioned in the previous paragraph also affect the amount reported on the income statement in that they each may require adjustment over time.

⑤ Prepare required disclosures associated with pensions, and understand the accounting treatment for pension settlements and curtailments.

Detailed disclosure relating to pensions is required. The assumptions made by actuaries relating to expected return on assets, discount rates, and projected increases in salaries are required to be disclosed. In addition, firms are required to disclose the components of the pension-related asset or liability from the balance sheet as well as the periodic pension expense amount disclosed on the income statement. Most of the required disclosures can be provided through presentation of a work sheet such as those illustrated in the chapter.

In the event that the benefits associated with a pension plan are curtailed, any prior service cost associated with the curtailment is recognized as a loss and offset against adjustments required to the PBO. Pension settlements often give rise to gains or losses. The FASB determined that those gains and losses resulting from irrevocable actions by the company that relieve the company of future obligations are to be recognized immediately.

⑥ Explain the differences in accounting for pensions and postretirement benefits other than pensions.

Although many of the concepts used in accounting for pensions are similar to those used in accounting for postretirement benefits other than pensions, there are some important differences. A common difference, unrelated to the accounting for these benefits, relates to other postretirement benefits being largely unfunded by companies. Other differences relate to other postretirement benefits often not being a function of salary levels and to the difficulty of measuring these other benefits.

FASB-IASB CODIFICATION SUMMARY

Topic	FASB Accounting Standards Codification	Original FASB Standard	Corresponding IASB Standard	Differences between U.S. GAAP and IFRS
Compensated absences	Section 710-10-25 par. 1-8	SFAS No. 43 par. 6-16	IAS 19 par. 13-18	No substantial differences
Postemployment benefits	Section 712-10-05 par. 2-6 Section 712-10-15 par. 3-5 Section 712-10-25 par. 1-5	SFAS No. 112 par. 1-6 SFAS No. 88 par. 15	IAS 19 par. 159-171	No substantial differences
Discount rate for projected benefit obligation	Section 715-30-35 par. 43	SFAS No. 87 par. 44	IAS 19 par. 83	IFRS allows use of the interest rate on government bonds in countries lacking a developed corporate bond market.
Computation of net interest cost	Section 715-30-35 par. 43, 47	SFAS No. 87 par. 44, 45	IAS 19 par. 83, 123	A single interest rate is applied to the *net* pension asset or liability; there is no separate interest cost from the PBO and expected return from the pension fund
Prior service cost	Section 715-30-35 par. 10-11	SFAS No. 87 par. 24-25	IAS 19 par. 103	Under IFRS, the "past" service cost amount is recognized as an expense immediately.
Balance sheet numbers: one net number for the difference between PBO and the pension fund, with AOCI shown separately	Section 715-30-25 par. 1, 4	SFAS No. 87 par. 35, 38	IAS 19 par. 63	No substantial differences
Corridor amortization	Section 715-30-35 par. 24	SFAS No. 87 par. 32	IAS 19 par. 120(c)	Under IFRS there is no corridor amortization.
Settlements and curtailments	Various sections in Subtopics 715-30 and 715-60; illustrations in Section 715-30-55	SFAS No. 88	IAS 19 par. 109-112	No substantial differences
Disclosure	Sections 715-29-50 715-30-50 715-60-50	SFAS No. 132(R)	IAS 19 par. 135-152	No substantial differences
Postretirement benefits other than pensions	Subtopic 715-60	SFAS No. 106	In general, no distinction between pensions and other postretirement benefits. Guidance on medical benefits found in IAS 19 par. 96-98	Differences similar to the differences in accounting for pensions.

KEY TERMS

Accumulated benefit obligation (ABO) 17-16
Actual return on the pension fund 17-26
Actuarial present value 17-14
Compensated absences 17-6
Contributory pension plan 17-11
Corridor amount 17-34
Curtailment of a pension plan 17-40
Deferred net pension gain or loss 17-32
Deferred pension gain or loss 17-30
Defined benefit pension plans 17-12
Defined contribution pension plans 17-11
Expected return on the pension fund 17-31
Expected service period 17-26
Fair value of the pension fund 17-19
Full eligibility date 17-43
Market-related value of the pension fund 17-31
Net periodic pension expense 17-15
Noncontributory pension plans 17-11
Obligation discount rate 17-18
Pension fund 17-12
Pension plan 17-10
Pension-related asset/liability 17-21
Postretirement benefits other than pensions 17-11
Prior service cost 17-23
Projected benefit obligation (PBO) 17-16
Service cost 17-19
Settlement of a pension plan 17-39
Single-employer pension plans 17-11
Vested benefits 17-14

Tutorial Activities

Tutorial Activities with author-written, content-specific feedback, available on *CengageNOW for Stice & Stice*.

QUESTIONS

1. Gross payroll is taxed by both federal and state governments. Identify these taxes and indicate who bears the cost of the tax, the employer or the employee.
2. How should compensated absences be accounted for?
3. The sales manager for Off-Road Enterprises is entitled to a bonus equal to 12% of profits. What difficulties may arise in the interpretation of this profit-sharing agreement?
4. Distinguish between (a) a defined benefit pension plan and a defined contribution pension plan, (b) a contributory pension plan and a noncontributory pension plan, and (c) a multiemployer pension plan and a single-employer pension plan.
5. What is meant by the word *vesting*?
6. What factors must actuaries consider in determining the amount of future benefits under a defined benefit pension plan?
7. What four accounting issues were addressed by the FASB in relation to defined benefit pension plans?
8. Distinguish between the accumulated benefit approach and the projected benefit approach in determining the amount of future benefits earned by employees under a defined benefit pension plan.
9. List and briefly describe the five basic components of net periodic pension expense.
10. Explain how prior service costs arise (a) at the inception of a pension plan and (b) at the time of a plan's amendment.
11. How is the service cost portion of net periodic pension expense to be measured?
12. Does pension expense include the actual return on plan assets or the expected return? Explain.
13. Is prior service cost recognized as an expense in the period in which it initially arises?
14. The FASB permits the use of an average market value of plan assets for some pension computations. In other cases, the fair market value at a specific measurement date must be used. Under what circumstances is the average market value permissible?
15. Which pension-related items impact the reported amount of accumulated other comprehensive income?
16. Why is a corridor amount identified in recognizing gain or loss from pension plans?
17. What is the function of the pension disclosure requirement included in the pension standards?

18. Distinguish between a pension settlement and a pension curtailment.
19. What is meant by *postretirement benefits*, and what is the primary issue in accounting for their costs?
20. Describe the differences between pension plans and other postretirement benefit plans.
21. What is the *full eligibility date*, and why is it an important date in accounting for postretirement benefits?
22. Describe the major differences between the accounting for pensions and other postretirement benefits.

PRACTICE EXERCISES

Practice 17-1

Wages and Wages Payable
The company pays its employees each Monday for the work performed during the preceding five-day work week. Total payroll for one week is $25,000. December 31 fell on a Wednesday. (1) Make the journal entry necessary to record wages payable as of December 31. (2) Make the journal entry necessary on the following January 5 to record payment of wages for the preceding week. Assume that this is a very strict company and that there were no holidays during the week.

Practice 17-2

Accounting for Payroll Taxes
Total wages and salaries for the month of January were $50,000. Because it is January, no employee has yet reached the FICA tax cap amount, so the full FICA tax percentage is applicable to the entire amount of wages and salaries. The same is true of the federal unemployment tax amount. The state requires a 5.4% employer tax on all wages and salaries. Income taxes withheld from employees' pay during the month totaled $7,000. Make the summary journal entries to record payment of wages and salaries and recognition of total salary and wage expense (including payroll tax expense) for the month.

Practice 17-3

Compensated Absences
During Year 1 (the first year of the company's existence), employees of the company earned vacation days as follows:

Employee	Average Wage per Day	Vacation Days Earned This Year	Vacation Days Taken This Year
1	$160	10	10
2	200	15	10
3	250	20	5

(1) Make the journal entry necessary at the end of Year 1 to record the unused vacation days earned during the year and (2) make the journal entry necessary in Year 2 to record the use of all of these vacation days. Assume that all employees received a 10% pay raise in Year 2.

Practice 17-4

Earnings-Based Bonus
The manager is entitled to a bonus equal to 5% of her store's earnings. The difficult part is that calculation of the store's earnings includes a subtraction for the amount of the bonus. The store's earnings before the bonus total $200,000. Calculate the store manager's bonus.

Practice 17-5

Postemployment Benefits
The company has decided to restructure operations at one of its stores. As part of this restructuring, the company has determined that the store facility is impaired. The store originally cost $3,000,000 and has accumulated depreciation of $1,300,000. The fair value of the store is determined to be $800,000. In addition, 32 employees at the store are being terminated. As part of the severance package, each employee is entitled to job training benefits (costing $500 per employee), supplemental healthcare and life insurance benefits for six months (costing $3,300 per employee), and two months' salary (averaging $5,000 per employee). Make the journal entry or entries necessary to record this restructuring.

Practice 17-6

Computing the Accumulated Benefit Obligation (ABO)
Wu Company has established a defined benefit pension plan for its lone employee, Ronald Dalton. Annual payments under the pension plan are equal to Ronald's highest lifetime salary multiplied by (2% × number of years with the company). As of the beginning of 2015, Ronald had worked for Wu Company for 10 years. His salary in 2014 was $50,000. Ronald is expected to retire in 25 years, and his salary increases are expected to average 3% per year during that period. Ronald is expected to live for 15 years after retiring and will receive the first annual pension payment one year after he retires. Compute Wu Company's accumulated benefit obligation (ABO) as of January 1, 2015, assuming (1) an 8% discount rate and (2) a 12% discount rate.

Practice 17-7

Computing the Projected Benefit Obligation (PBO)
Refer to Practice 17-6. Compute Wu Company's projected benefit obligation (PBO) as of January 1, 2015, assuming (1) an 8% discount rate and (2) a 12% discount rate.

Practice 17-8

Pensions in the Balance Sheet and in the Income Statement
The company reports the following balances in its pension-related accounts as of January 1 of Year 1.

Fair value of plan assets	$870,000
Projected benefit obligation (PBO)	925,000

At December 31 of Year 1, the company estimates service costs for the year of $101,000 and interest costs equal to 10% of the beginning PBO balance. In addition, plan assets earned a return of $117,300. Over the long run, the company expects to earn 12% per year on its pension fund assets. (1) What pension amount would the company have reported in its balance sheet as of January 1 of Year 1? Clearly state whether the amount is an asset or a liability. (2) Compute the amount to be reported on the income statement as pension expense for Year 1.

Practice 17-9

Simple Computation of the Net Pension Asset or Liability
On January 1 of Year 1, the company had a projected benefit obligation (PBO) of $10,000 and a pension fund with a fair value of $9,200. There was no prior service cost, nor were there deferred pension gains or losses. The following information relates to the pension plan during the year:

Service cost	$1,200
Actual return on the pension fund	$250
Benefits paid to retirees	$100
Contribution to the pension fund	$1,050
Discount rate for PBO	9%
Expected return on pension fund	10%

Compute (1) the pension-related amount that should be reported on the company's balance sheet on January 1 of Year 1, (2) the PBO as of December 31, and (3) the fair value of the pension fund as of December 31.

Practice 17-10

Simple Computation of Pension Expense
Refer to Practice 17-9. Compute pension expense for the year.

Practice 17-11

Basic Pension Journal Entries
Refer to Practice 17-9. Make two *summary* journal entries necessary with respect to the pension plan for the year.

Practice 17-12

Simple Pension Work Sheet
Refer to Practice 17-9. Enter all of the pension information, including the beginning balances, in a pension work sheet. Use the pension work sheet to display the computation of pension expense for the year as well as the ending balances for all pension-related items.

Practice 17-13

Amortization of Prior Service Cost
On January 1, the company adopted a new defined benefit pension plan. Existing employees were given credit in the new plan for their past service to the company. This created an immediate projected benefit obligation of $1,000,000. The company has 30 employees; three of these employees are expected to leave the company per year for the next 10 years. Using the amortization method that is similar to sum-of-the-years'-digits depreciation, compute the amount of prior service cost that should be amortized for the year.

Practice 17-14

Difference between Actual and Expected Return on Pension Fund
As of January 1, the company had the following pension-related balances:

Projected benefit obligation (PBO)	$(15,000)
Fair value of pension fund	$17,000
Deferred net pension (gain)/loss	$(1,100)
Discount rate for the PBO	8%

During the year, service cost was $1,500. The actual return on the pension fund was $700. Compute pension expense for the year and the ending balance in deferred net pension (gain)/loss assuming that (1) the expected return on the pension fund is 10% and (2) the expected return on the pension fund is 12%.

Practice 17-15

Impact of Changes in Actuarial Estimates
Refer to Practice 17-6 and Practice 17-7. Assume that as of January 1, 2015, Wu Company changed the discount rate it uses to compute the PBO from 8% to 12%. Assume that before this change, Wu Company had the following pension-related balances:

Projected benefit obligation (PBO)	$(26,169)
Fair value of pension fund	23,000
Deferred net pension (gain)/loss	1,100
Prior service cost	2,000

Compute (1) the pension-related asset/liability balance and accumulated other comprehensive income balance that would be reported in the balance sheet *before* the change to 12%, (2) the PBO balance after the change to 12%, (3) interest cost for 2015, and (4) the pension-related asset/liability balance and accumulated other comprehensive income balance that would be reported in the balance sheet immediately *after* the change to 12% (before the impact of any other 2015 transactions).

Practice 17-16

Pension Work Sheet
On January 1 of Year 1, the company had a projected benefit obligation (PBO) of $10,000 and a pension fund with a fair value of $9,200. Prior service cost was $2,000; it was being amortized on a straight-line basis over the five-year average remaining life of the affected employees. The balance in the deferred pension gain was $700. The following information relates to the pension plan during the year:

Service cost	$1,200
Actual return on the pension fund	$1,550
Benefits paid to retirees	$300
Contribution to the pension fund	$1,050
Discount rate for PBO	8%
Expected return on pension fund	11%

Enter all of the pension information, including the beginning balances, in a pension work sheet. Use the work sheet to display the computation of pension expense for the year as well as the ending balances for all pension-related items.

Practice 17-17

The Corridor Amount
The company had the following pension-related balances as of January 1:

Projected benefit obligation (PBO)	$(20,000)
Fair value of pension fund	23,000
Deferred net pension loss	3,100
Prior service cost	1,000

The average remaining service life of employees working on January 1 is six years. Compute the amount of the deferred net pension loss that should be amortized during the year.

Practice 17-18

Reconciliation of Beginning and Ending PBO Balances

On January 1 of Year 1, the company had a projected benefit obligation (PBO) of $10,000 and a pension fund with a fair value of $9,200. Prior service cost was $2,000; it was being amortized on a straight-line basis over the five-year average remaining life of the affected employees. The balance in the deferred pension gain was $700. The following information relates to the pension plan during the year:

Service cost	$1,200
Actual return on the pension fund	$1,550
Benefits paid to retirees	$300
Contribution to the pension fund	$1,050
Discount rate for PBO	8%
Expected return on pension fund	11%

Prepare the note disclosure necessary to reconcile the beginning balance in the PBO and the ending balance in the PBO.

Practice 17-19

Reconciliation of Beginning and Ending Pension Fund Balances

Refer to Practice 17-18. Prepare the note disclosure necessary to reconcile the beginning balance in the pension fund and the ending balance in the pension fund.

EXERCISES

Exercise 17-20

Recording Payroll and Payroll Taxes

Express Company paid one week's wages of $21,200 in cash (net pay after all withholdings and deductions) to its employees. Income tax withholdings were equal to 17% of the gross payroll, and the only other deductions were 7.65% for FICA tax and $160 for union dues. Give the entries that should be made on the company's books to record the payroll and the tax accruals to be recognized by the employer, assuming that the company is subject to unemployment taxes of 5.4% (state) and 0.8% (federal). Assume that all wages for the week are subject to FICA and unemployment taxes.

Exercise 17-21

Monthly Payroll Entries

Aggie Co. sells agricultural products. Aggie pays its salespeople a salary plus a commission. The salary is the same for each salesperson, $1,000 per month. The commission varies by length of employment and is a percentage of the company's total gross sales. Each salesperson starts with a commission of 1.0%, which is increased an additional 0.5% for each full year of employment with Aggie, to a maximum of 5.0%. The total gross sales for the month of January were $120,000.

Aggie has six salespeople as follows:

	Number of Years Employment
Frank	10
Sally	9
Tina	8
Barry	6
Mark	3
Lisa	0.75

Assume that the FICA rate is 7.65%, the FUTA rate is 6.2%, and the state unemployment rate is 5.4%. (Assume that the federal government allows the maximum credit for state unemployment tax paid.) The federal income tax withholding rate is 30%. Compute the January salaries and commissions expense, and make any necessary entries to record the payroll transactions including cash payment of all the taxes payable.

Exercise 17-22

Compensated Absence—Vacation Pay

General Aviation Company employs six people. Each employee is entitled to three weeks' paid vacation every year the employee works for the company. The conditions of the paid vacation are (a) for each full year of work, an employee will receive three weeks of paid vacation (no vacation accrues for a portion of a year), (b) each employee will receive the same pay for vacation time as the regular pay in the year taken, and (c) unused vacation pay can be carried forward. Based on the following data, compute the liability for vacation pay as of December 31, 2015.

Employee	Starting Date	Cumulative Vacation Taken as of December 31, 2015	Weekly Salary
Marci Clark	December 21, 2008	14 weeks	$850
Bradford Sayer	July 17, 2012	5 weeks	725
Sorena Williams	April 8, 2014	None	650
Jonathan Beecher	December 17, 2007	18 weeks	800
Brian Giles	July 17, 2013	1 week	450
Dale Murphy	May 31, 2015	None	500

Exercise 17-23

Calculation of Bonus

Illinois Wholesale Company has an agreement with its sales manager entitling that individual to 7% of company earnings as a bonus. Company income for the calendar year before bonus and income tax is $350,000. Income tax is 30% of income after bonus.

1. Compute the amount of bonus if the bonus is calculated on income before deductions for bonus and income tax.
2. Compute the amount of bonus if the bonus is calculated on income after deduction for bonus but before deduction for income tax.

Exercise 17-24

Computing Defined Benefit Pension Payments

Francisco Company has established a defined benefit pension plan for its lone employee, Derrald Ryan. Annual payments under the pension plan are equal to 3% of Derrald's highest lifetime salary multiplied by the number of years with the company. Derrald's salary in 2014 was $75,000. Derrald is expected to retire in 20 years, and his salary increases are expected to average 4% per year during that period. As of the beginning of 2015, Derrald had worked for Francisco Company for 12 years.

1. What is the amount of the annual pension payment that should be used in computing Francisco's accumulated benefit obligation (ABO) as of January 1, 2015?
2. What is the amount of the annual pension payment that should be used in computing Francisco's projected benefit obligation (PBO) as of January 1, 2015?

Exercise 17-25

Computation of Pension Service Cost

Pension plan information for Naperville Window Company is as follows:

January 1, 2015	PBO	$4,780,000
	ABO	$3,950,000
During 2015	Pension benefits paid to retired employees	$315,000
December 31, 2015	PBO	$5,425,000
	ABO	$4,245,000
Obligation discount rate		10%

Assuming no change in actuarial assumptions, what is the pension service cost for 2015?

Exercise 17-26

Computing the Amount of Pension-Related Asset/Liability

Using the information given for the following three independent cases, compute the amount of pension-related asset/liability that would be reported on the balance sheet. Clearly indicate whether the amount would be shown as an asset or as a liability. Also compute the amount of pension-related accumulated other comprehensive income that would be reported on the balance sheet.

	Case 1	Case 2	Case 3
Prior service cost	$ 310	$ 190	$ 50
PBO	1,000	900	1,000
Deferred net pension gain	70	120	200
ABO	750	800	850
FVPF	700	1,300	900

Exercise 17-27

Amortization of Prior Service Cost—Plan Amendment
Queensland Company has five employees belonging to its pension plan. One employee per year is expected to retire over the next five years.
On January 1, 2015, Queensland initiated an amendment to its pension plan that increased the PBO for the plan by $620,000. If Queensland amortizes the prior service cost of the pension plan using the sum-of-the-years'-digits method, determine the amortization for the each of the next five years.

Exercise 17-28

Amount of Funding and Amortization of Prior Service Cost
Da Vinci Inc. has a workforce of 400 employees. A new pension plan is negotiated on January 1, 2015, with the labor union. Based on the provisions of the pension agreement, prior service cost related to the new plan amounts to $4,823,000. The cost is to be funded evenly with annual contributions over a 10-year period, with the first payment due at the end of 2015. The cost is to be amortized over the average remaining service life of the covered employees. The interest rate for funding purposes is 12%. It is anticipated that, on the average, 10 employees will retire per year over the next 40 years.

1. Compute the annual amount Da Vinci will pay to fund its prior service cost.
2. Compute the amount of amortization of prior service cost for 2015, 2017, and 2022.

Exercise 17-29

Amortization of Prior Service Cost—Straight-Line Method
Osvaldo Awning Co. has prior service cost of $1,262,000 arising from a pension plan amendment. The board of directors decided to amortize this cost over the average remaining service period for its 45 employees on a straight-line basis. It is assumed that employees will retire at the rate of three employees per year over a 15-year period.

1. Compute the average remaining service life and the annual amortization of prior service cost for Osvaldo.
2. Assume that pension expense other than amortization of prior service cost was $460,000 for the year and also assume that all of this amount is associated with service cost, interest cost, and actual return on plan assets (meaning that actual return equaled expected return this year). Also assume that $520,000 was contributed by the employer to the pension fund. Prepare the summary journal entries to record pension expense and the pension contribution for the current year.

Exercise 17-30

Computation of Actual Return on the Pension Fund
Longlee Electrical Company maintains a fund to cover its pension plan. The following data relate to the fund for 2015:

January 1	FVPF	$875,000
	Market-related value of the pension fund (five-year weighted average)	715,000
During year	Pension benefits paid	62,000
	Contributions made to the fund	70,000
December 31	FVPF	980,000
	Market-related value of the pension fund (five-year weighted average)	730,000

Compute the 2015 actual return on the pension fund for Longlee Electrical.

Exercise 17-31

Return on the Pension Fund—Expected and Actual
Rasband Photography has a pension plan covering its 100 employees. Rasband anticipates an 11% return on its pension fund. The fund trustee furnishes Rasband with the following information relating to the pension fund for 2015:

January 1	FVPF	$1,500,000
	Market-related value of the pension fund (five-year weighted average)	1,350,000
During year	Actual return on the pension fund	110,000
December 31	FVPF	1,620,000
	Market-related value of the pension fund (five-year weighted average)	1,480,000

Compute the difference between the actual and expected return on the pension fund. How should the difference be treated in determining pension expense for 2015? Rasband bases expected return on the market-related value of the pension fund.

Exercise 17-32

Amortization of Deferred Gain on the Pension Fund
Melba Enterprises has a deferred gain of $425,000 relating to its pension plan as of January 1, 2015. Management has chosen to amortize this deferral on a straight-line basis over the 10-year average remaining service life of its employees, subject to the limitation of the corridor amount. Additional facts about the pension plan as of January 1, 2015, are as follows:

PBO	$2,050,000
ABO	1,900,000
Fair value of the pension fund	1,500,000
Market-related value of the pension fund (five-year weighted average)	1,350,000

Compute the minimum amortization of deferred gain to be recognized by Melba in 2015.

Exercise 17-33

Computations Associated with Deferred Gains and Losses
The computation of pension expense includes (1) a deferral of the difference between actual and expected return on the pension fund and (2) amortization of deferred pension gains and losses. Determine the proper addition (deduction) to pension expense related to deferred gains and losses and their amortization under each of the following independent conditions.

	A	B	C	D
(1) Actual return on the pension fund	$200,000	$200,000	$500,000	$500,000
(2) Expected return on the pension fund	$180,000	$230,000	$400,000	$550,000
(3) Deferred (gain) loss at beginning of year	$200,000	$275,000	$(100,000)	$(175,000)
(4) Average service life of employees used for amortization	10 years	5 years	8 years	12 years
(5) Corridor amount	$100,000	$150,000	$50,000	$175,000

Exercise 17-34

Computation of Pension Expense and Summary Journal Entries
The accountants for Eden Financial Services provide you with the following detailed information at December 31, 2015. Based on these data, prepare the summary journal entries related to the recognition of pension expense and the pension contribution for 2015.

Service cost	$ 52,000
Actual return on pension plan assets	81,000
Interest cost	59,000
Excess of expected return over actual return on pension plan assets	15,000
Amortization of deferred pension loss from prior years	24,000
Amortization of prior service cost	36,000
Contribution to pension fund	100,000

Exercise 17-35

Pension Expense Computation

Fredco's defined benefit pension plan had a PBO of $10,000,000 at the beginning of the year. This was based on a 10% discount rate (obligation discount rate). The fair value of pension plan assets at the beginning of the year was $10,400,000. These assets were expected to earn a long-term rate of return on the fair value of 8%. During the year, service cost was $750,000. At the beginning of the year, prior service cost was $25,000; this entire remaining amount will be amortized this period. There was no deferred net pension gain (loss) at the beginning of the year. The actual return on pension plan assets for the year was $900,000. The ABO was $9,500,000 at the beginning of the year. Compute Fredco's net periodic pension expense for the year.

Exercise 17-36

Preparing a Pension Work Sheet

The following information relates to the defined benefit pension plan of Mascare Company.

January 1, 2015:
- PBO $9,000
- FVPF $11,000
- Expected return on plan assets 8%
- Obligation discount rate 10%

For the year ended December 31, 2015:
- Service cost $1,200
- Benefit payments to retirees 500
- Contributions to pension fund 100
- Actual return on plan assets 1,500

Prepare a pension work sheet for Mascare Company for 2015.

Exercise 17-37

Pension-Related Balance Sheet Items

From the following information for each of three independent cases, prepare the pension note disclosure that outlines the items that go into the computation of the pension-related asset or liability reported in the balance sheet as well as the pension-related accumulated other comprehensive income reported in the balance sheet.

	(in thousands)		
	Case 1	Case 2	Case 3
Projected benefit obligation	$12,500	$6,290	$890
Accumulated benefit obligation	9,700	4,100	750
Fair value of the pension fund	15,300	4,200	650
Market-related value of the pension fund	12,800	5,000	560
Deferred net (gain) or loss from prior years	(200)	(850)	100
Prior service cost	800	2,300	125

P4
Other Dimensions of Financial Reporting

CHAPTER 19

Derivatives, Contingencies, Business Segments, and Interim Reports

Learning Objectives

DERIVATIVES

1. Understand the business and accounting concepts connected with derivatives and hedging activities.
2. Identify the different types of risk faced by a business.
3. Describe the characteristics of the following types of derivatives: swaps, forwards, futures, and options.
4. Define *hedging*, and outline the difference between a fair value hedge and a cash flow hedge.
5. Account for a variety of different derivatives and for hedging relationships.

CONTINGENCIES

6. Apply the accounting rules for contingent items to the areas of lawsuits and environmental liabilities.

SEGMENT REPORTING

7. Prepare the necessary supplemental disclosures of financial information by product line and by geographic area.

INTERIM REPORTING

8. Recognize the importance of interim reports, and outline the difficulties encountered when preparing those reports.

This chapter is a little different from the other chapters in the text. The chapter is comprised of four modules: derivatives, contingencies, segment reporting, and interim reporting. Each of the modules is self-contained and can be studied independently. So do as much or as little of this chapter as your instructor thinks best. Of course, you are free to sneak a look at any of the modules that your instructor does not assign.

DERIVATIVES

Procter & Gamble (P&G) is a sophisticated marketer of consumer products such as Tide®, Pampers®, Folgers®, and Crest®. Apparently this sophistication hasn't always extended to P&G's understanding of derivative financial instruments. In November 1993,

FYI

The largest part of Enron's business before its bankruptcy in 2001 was the trading of derivative contracts. When the scandals swirling around Enron caused the company to lose credibility with its customers, its derivative trading activity plummeted literally overnight.

P&G agreed to buy a complex derivative that would give the company lower current interest payments in exchange for an agreement to make higher payments in the future depending on the future level of interest rates.[1] When interest rates increased after the derivative was purchased, P&G learned a rough lesson relative to the risk associated with speculative derivatives. After the smoke had cleared, the increased interest payments from the derivative arrangement had cost P&G $195.5 million. A note written by former P&G chairman Edwin Artzt after this fiasco said that the officials who bought the derivative were like "farm boys at a country carnival."[2]

Procter & Gamble is just one in a long list of organizations that lost large amounts of money by trading in derivatives: **JP Morgan** ($3.0 billion in 2012), **Orange County** ($1.7 billion in 1994), **Morgan Stanley** ($9.0 billion in 2008), **Société Générale** ($7.2 billion in 2008), and on and on. The combination of the complexity of derivatives, which are frequently misunderstood even by corporate treasurers and portfolio managers, and the lack of disclosure about derivatives created a dangerous environment in which users of financial statements could be completely unaware of huge company risks. This is exactly the type of situation the SEC was created to address. Accordingly, in recent years the FASB, with the blessing and prodding of the SEC, has significantly improved the accounting for and disclosure of derivative financial instruments. However, don't get the impression that improved accounting disclosure has led to complete understanding of derivatives. Even with this improved accounting, overly aggressive use of derivatives contributed to the worldwide financial institution meltdown in the second half of 2008.

The first module in this chapter explains the general nature of derivatives, the types of risk companies face and how different types of derivatives can be used to hedge those risks, and the standards governing the accounting for derivatives.

Simple Example of a Derivative

LO1 学习目标1

理解关于衍生工具和套期活动的交易与会计概念。

① Understand the business and accounting concepts connected with derivatives and hedging activities.

Assume that you are an employee of Nauvoo Software Solutions. On October 1, 2015, you purchase 100 shares of stock in the company at the market price of $50 per share, making the total purchase price $5,000. If you were to prepare a personal balance sheet, how would you report these shares? Obviously, the 100 shares of Nauvoo stock would be reported as a $5,000 asset.

Now assume that you are nervous about possible price fluctuations in the stock. On January 1, 2016, you need to make a college tuition payment of $5,000 on behalf of your daughter, and you must make certain that you have $5,000 on that date. You can't

---

[1] Kelley Holland, Linda Himelstein, and Zachary Schiller, "The Bankers Trust Tapes," *Business Week*, October 16, 1995, p. 106.
[2] Carol J. Loomis, "Like Farm Boys at a Country Carnival," *Fortune*, November 27, 1995, p. 34.

sell the Nauvoo shares now (and put the $5,000 cash under your mattress) because your employment contract states that any shares you purchase from the company must be held for at least three months before you can sell them. Your risk management dilemma is as follows: You must hold the Nauvoo shares as an asset for the next three months, but a downward movement in the stock price between now and January 1 would be disastrous for you.

The answer to your problem is the following agreement: If the price of Nauvoo stock is above $50 per share on January 1, you agree to pay a cash amount equal to that excess (multiplied by 100 shares) to John Bennett, a local stock speculator. If the price of Nauvoo stock goes below $50, John Bennett agrees to pay you a cash amount equal to the deficit (multiplied by 100 shares). As detailed later in the chapter, the broad name given to agreements such as this is a *derivative*. A derivative is a financial instrument or other contract that derives its value from the movement of the price, foreign exchange rate, or interest rate on some other underlying asset or financial instrument.

衍生工具是一种金融工具或者其他契约，其价值源于价格的波动、外汇汇率的波动或者其他资产或金融工具的利率波动。

How does this derivative agreement solve your risk management dilemma? Look at the following chart:

	Stock Price on January 1		
	$45	$50	$55
Value of shares	$4,500	$5,000	$5,500
Receipt from (payment to) Bennett	500	0	(500)
Net amount	$5,000	$5,000	$5,000

Because of the structure of the agreement, you wind up with $5,000 on January 1 no matter what happens to the price of Nauvoo stock between now and then. After the fact, a derivative contract is sometimes a good deal and sometimes a bad one. If the price actually increases to $55, it would have been better had you not entered into the agreement. Because of the absolute necessity of having $5,000 on January 1, however, you are willing to trade off any stock profits you might make for the right to receive payments that will reimburse your stock losses.[3]

FYI

In the past, a derivative instrument such as this was said to have "off-balance-sheet risk" because it could fluctuate in value after the initial agreement date, but these fluctuations would not be reflected in the balance sheet. As explained later, the accounting standards have been changed to bring these fluctuations onto the balance sheet.

How much money will change hands between you and John Bennett on October 1, the day you enter into the derivative contract? In other words, do you have to pay John Bennett anything up front to get him to sign the agreement, or does he have to pay you? The valuation of derivatives is way beyond the scope of this book, but two of the factors that would be considered are the expected return on Nauvoo stock over the three-month period (on average, stock prices move up 3% or 4% per quarter) and the difference in the way you and John Bennett view risk. If you are very nervous about risk and John Bennett is not, he has the advantage in the bargaining and may be able to extract an up-front payment from you. For simplicity, the valuation assumptions made

---

[3] Another question is why John Bennett, the speculator, would be willing to enter into this agreement. An arrangement such as this is one way for a speculator to make money if a price or rate moves in the direction he or she thinks it will. In this case, John Bennett's valuation analysis has led him to believe that the price of Nauvoo stock will move up in the next three months, and the derivative is a way for Bennett to make money if his analysis is correct.

in this chapter will be very basic; for more advanced treatment, you will need to talk to your finance professor. The simplest assumptions are that you and John Bennett have the same risk preferences and that the $50 price of the stock on October 1 is equal to the expected price on January 1. If these two assumptions hold, the money exchanged at the signing of the agreement on October 1 is $0 because the probability of your being required to make a payment to Bennett on January 1 is equal to the probability that he will have to make a payment to you.

Another way to describe the arrangement between you and John Bennett is as follows: You have agreed, three months in advance, to sell 100 shares of Nauvoo stock to John Bennett at a price of $50 per share. A forward sale such as this is similar to what the finance people call a *short sale*. To demonstrate that a forward sale is equivalent to the original exchange of cash payments you and John Bennett agreed to, consider the following:

> If the shares are worth, say, $5,500 on January 1, John Bennett will pay you $5,000 for the shares and then be able to immediately sell them for $5,500, netting a cash increase of $500. At the same time, you will have received $5,000, which is $500 less than you would have received if you had simply sold the shares in the market. In place of executing the forward sale, the same cash flow effects are achieved if you simply give John Bennett $500 in cash.

The same analysis could be done to show that requiring John Bennett to buy the shares for $5,000 when they are worth just $4,500 is equivalent to a simple cash transfer of $500 from John Bennett to you. A general characteristic of derivative arrangements is that although they are phrased in terms of the exchange of some underlying item (shares of stock, interest payments, pounds of orange juice concentrate, Japanese yen), they are often settled by a simple exchange of cash.

Now, let's talk about some accounting. What journal entry would you be required to make to recognize the signing of the agreement on October 1? The answer is that you make no journal entry. No cash changes hands; you and John Bennett have merely exchanged promises about some future action. This type of contract is called an executory contract and is very common in business. Another example of an executory contract is an operating lease, a promise to make payments in the future in exchange for the promise to receive the use of an asset in the future. Like an operating lease, the derivative contract is "off balance sheet" on the day it is signed.

On December 31, 2015, the price of Nauvoo stock is $47 per share, making your investment in Nauvoo shares worth $4,700 ($47 × 100). The payment exchange with John Bennett is to be made on the following day. With the price per share at $47, it appears that you will receive a payment from Bennett of $300 [($50 − $47) × 100]. How should this information be reflected in the Assets section of your December 31, 2015, balance sheet? Four possibilities are outlined below.

	Option 1	Option 2	Option 3	Option 4
Nauvoo stock	$5,000	$4,700	$5,000	$4,700
Derivative payment receivable	$0	$0	$300	$300
Valuation of stock	Cost	Fair value	Cost	Fair value
Recognition of derivative receivable?	No	No	Yes	Yes

Option 4 provides the best information because it reports the fair value of both the stock investment and the derivative payment receivable. Historically, the generally accepted treatment in the United States was Option 2, with some added disclosure about the derivative agreement.[4] The FASB has now adopted a standard that results in Option 4, the recognition of the fair value of derivatives in the financial statements.[5]

The remainder of this module details how derivatives are used to hedge risk and how information about derivatives should be reported in the financial statements.

Types of Risk

LO2 学习目标2
区分在交易中面对的不同类型的风险。

❷ Identify the different types of risk faced by a business.

Most firms use derivatives as a tool for managing risk. Accordingly, before discussing the different types of derivatives, we will briefly outline the various types of risk.

Price Risk

Price risk is the uncertainty about the future price of an asset. It was uncertainty about the future price of Nauvoo Software Solutions stock that prompted the derivative contract in the preceding example. Firms can be exposed to price risk with existing assets, such as financial securities or inventory, or with assets to be acquired in the future, such as equipment to be purchased next month.

Credit Risk

Credit risk is the uncertainty that the party on the other side of an agreement will abide by the terms of the agreement. The most common example of credit risk is the uncertainty over whether a credit customer will ultimately pay his or her account. Banks are in the business of properly evaluating credit risk, and the success or failure of a bank depends largely on how good the bank's credit analysts are at identifying who will repay a loan and who won't. Credit risk analysis is a specialized skill, and many retail companies, through the acceptance of credit card purchases, have contracted their credit risk analysis to **Visa**, **MasterCard**, **Discover**, or **American Express**. In the Nauvoo stock and derivative contract example, the credit risk is the possibility that John Bennett, the party on the other side of the agreement, will not make the payments required under the agreement.

Interest Rate Risk

Interest rate risk is the uncertainty about future interest rates and their impact on future cash flows as well as on the fair value of existing assets and liabilities. A variable-rate mortgage is a good illustration of one type of interest rate risk. The periodic interest payments on the variable-rate mortgage will fluctuate in the future, depending on the level of future interest rates. A fixed-rate mortgage is a good example of another type of interest rate risk. If interest rates decrease, the present value of future fixed payments to be made under a fixed-rate mortgage will increase. Thus, the fair value of the mortgage liability increases; this is the downside of obligating yourself to a fixed stream of interest payments when there is a possibility that interest rates may go down in the future. In summary, interest rate risk exposes a firm to uncertainty about future cash flows as well

---

[4] Pre-Codification *Statement of Financial Accounting Standards No. 119*, "Disclosure about Derivative Financial Instruments and Fair Value of Financial Instruments" (Norwalk, CT: Financial Accounting Standards Board, 1994).
[5] FASB ASC Topic 815 (Derivatives and Hedging).

as uncertainty about the fair value of assets and liabilities that have values tied to the level of interest rates.

Exchange Rate Risk

Exchange rate risk is the uncertainty about future U.S. dollar cash flows arising when assets and liabilities are denominated in a foreign currency. For example, many compensation packages for U.S. citizens working in foreign countries include an end-of-contract bonus payment if the employee sticks it out and stays on the foreign assignment for the entire length of the contract. If this bonus is denominated in the currency of the foreign country, the employee knows with certainty the future amount of his or her foreign currency bonus, but the U.S. dollar value bonus depends on the exchange rate prevailing when the bonus is received. U.S. multinational firms face the same risk when sales, purchases, loans, and investments are denominated in foreign currencies.

> **FYI**
>
> Other types of risk include liquidity risk, theft risk, competitive risk, and business cycle risk. See Johnson and Swieringa, "Derivatives, Hedging and Comprehensive Income," *Accounting Horizons*, December 1996, p. 109.

Some degree of risk is an unwanted but common side effect of doing business. For example, the variation in the cost of jet fuel is a nuisance and a worry to the major airlines. Similarly, fluctuations in the U.S. dollar/Japanese yen exchange rate wreak havoc on the competitive plans of both U.S. and Japanese car manufacturers. On the other hand, managing risk is the very reason for the existence of some businesses. Much of the revenue generated by a bank arises because the bank has expertise in evaluating and managing credit, interest rate, and exchange rate risk. The following sections discuss derivatives and hedging from the standpoint of a manufacturing, retailing, or service firm that is trying to use these techniques to reduce the risks that arise as part of doing business. Coverage of the more complicated risk management strategies of banks and financial institutions is outside the scope of this text.

Types of Derivatives

 学习目标3
描述互换、远期、期货与期权衍生工具的特征。

❸ Describe the characteristics of the following types of derivatives: swaps, forwards, futures, and options.

Recall that a derivative is a financial instrument or other contract that derives its value from the movement of the price, exchange rate, or interest rate on some other underlying asset or financial instrument. In addition, a derivative does not require a firm to take delivery or make delivery of the underlying asset or financial instrument; in situations in which actual delivery is required, the underlying item can easily be converted into cash.[6] For example, you may have heard about the buying and selling of pork belly futures. These contracts (futures contracts are explained later) can qualify as derivatives because, fortunately, they do not require the holder to either deliver or take delivery of a truckload of pork bellies. Instead, these contracts are settled by cash payments, much as the Nauvoo stock derivative contract was settled, not with the delivery of any shares of stock, but by a cash payment.

The most common types of derivatives are swaps, forwards, futures, and options. Each type is explained.

[6] FASB ASC paragraph 815-10-15-83.

Swap

A swap is a contract in which two parties agree to exchange payments in the future based on the movement of some agreed-upon price or rate. A common type of swap is an interest rate swap. In an interest rate swap, two parties agree to exchange future interest payments on a given loan amount; usually, one set of interest payments is based on a fixed interest rate and the other is based on a variable interest rate. To illustrate, assume that Pratt Company has a good working relationship with a bank that issues only variable-rate loans. Pratt takes advantage of its relationship at the bank and on January 1, 2015, receives a two-year, $100,000 loan, with interest payments occurring at the end of each year. The interest rate for the first year is the prevailing market rate of 10%, and the rate in the second year will be equal to the market interest rate on January 1 of that year. Pratt is reluctant to bear the risk associated with the uncertainty about what the interest payment in the second year will be. So Pratt enters into an interest rate swap agreement with another party (not the bank) whereby Pratt agrees to pay a fixed interest rate of 10% on the $100,000 loan amount to that party in exchange for receiving from that party a variable amount based on the prevailing market rate multiplied by $100,000. This is called a *pay-fixed, receive-variable swap*.

Instead of exchanging the entire amount of the interest payments called for under the swap contract, Pratt would probably settle the agreement by exchanging a small cash payment, depending on what has happened to interest rates. Accordingly, Pratt will receive an amount equal to [$100,000 × (Jan. 1, 2016, interest rate − 10%)] if the January 1, 2016, interest rate is more than 10% and will pay the same amount if the rate is less than 10%. The interest swap payment will be made in 2016. To see the impact of this interest rate swap, consider the following table:

	Interest Rate on January 1, 2016		
	7%	10%	13%
Variable-rate interest payment in 2016.....................	$ (7,000)	$(10,000)	$(13,000)
Receipt (payment) for interest rate swap..................	(3,000)	0	3,000
Net interest payment in 2016............................	$(10,000)	$(10,000)	$(10,000)

The interest rate swap agreement has changed Pratt's uncertain future interest payment into a payment of $10,000 no matter what the prevailing interest rates are in 2016. Why didn't Pratt just go out and get a fixed-rate loan in the first place? Sometimes, in this case because of Pratt's special relationship with the bank, it is easier to get one type of loan or investment security than another. A derivative instrument can effectively change the loan that you got into the loan that you want.

Forwards

A forward contract is an agreement between two parties to exchange a specified amount of a commodity, security, or foreign currency at a specified date in the future with the price or exchange rate being set now. To illustrate, assume that on November 1, 2015, Clayton Company sold machine parts

> **Caution**
> Don't forget that one of the characteristics of a derivative, whether it relates to yen, wheat, pork bellies, or stock index levels, is that it can be, and usually is, settled in the end with a cash payment instead of with actual delivery of the underlying item.

Stop & Think

What type of credit risk is associated with a forward contract?
a) The risk that the party required to make the settlement payment will refuse to pay
b) The risk that the price, interest rate, or exchange rate will increase
c) The risk that the price, interest rate, or exchange rate will decrease
d) The risk that overall company net income will decrease between now and the contract settlement date

to Maruta Company for ¥30,000,000 to be received on January 1, 2016. The current exchange rate is ¥120 = $1. To ensure the dollar amount that will be received, Clayton enters into a forward contract with a large bank, agreeing that on January 1 Clayton will deliver ¥30,000,000 to the bank and the bank will give U.S. dollars in exchange at the rate of ¥120 = $1, or $250,000 (¥30,000,000/¥120 per $1). This forward contract guarantees the U.S. dollar amount that Clayton will receive from the receivable denominated in Japanese yen.

Operationally, this forward contract would usually be settled as follows. Given the exchange rate on January 1, 2016, if ¥30,000,000 is worth less than $250,000, the bank will pay Clayton the difference in cash (U.S. dollars). If ¥30,000,000 is worth more than $250,000, Clayton pays the difference to the bank in cash. Therefore, no yen need be delivered as part of the contract; the contract is settled with a U.S. dollar cash payment.

The impact of the forward exchange contract is shown in the following table:

	Exchange Rate on January 1		
	¥118 = $1	¥120 = $1	¥122 = $1
Value of ¥30,000,000	$254,237	$250,000	$245,902
Clayton receipt (payment) to settle forward contract	(4,237)	0	4,098
Net U.S. dollar receipt by Clayton	$250,000	$250,000	$250,000

If Clayton is nervous about exchange rate changes, why agree to denominating the transaction in Japanese yen in the first place? The answer is that some types of transactions and some products are routinely negotiated in terms of a certain currency. For example, almost all crude oil sales are denominated in U.S. dollars, regardless of the countries of the companies conducting the transaction. In addition, if denominating a sale in a certain currency will make the customer feel more comfortable, companies are likely to follow the policy that "the customer is always right."

In this simple example, the forward exchange rate of ¥120 = $1 is equal to the prevailing exchange rate, called the spot rate, on the date the forward contract is signed. Usually, the forward rate would differ from the spot rate in order to compensate the bank for providing this risk-reduction service to Clayton. For example, a forward rate of ¥121 = $1 means that the

A wheat futures contract can protect the farmer from wide fluctuations in wheat prices.

bank would receive cash payments from Clayton when the dollar value of ¥30,000,000 was higher than $247,934 (¥30,000,000/¥121 per $1). With this lower threshold (instead of $250,000), it would be more likely that the bank would receive cash from Clayton to settle the forward contract. In this chapter, we will make the simplifying assumption that spot rates and forward rates are equal to one another.

Futures

A futures contract is a contract, traded on an exchange, that allows a company to buy or sell a specified quantity of a commodity or a financial security at a specified price on a specified future date. A futures contract is very similar to a forward contract with the difference being that a forward contract is a private contract negotiated between two parties, whereas a futures contract is a standardized contract that is sponsored by a trading exchange and can be traded among different parties many times in a single day. So, with a forward contract, you know the party with whom you will be exchanging cash to settle the contract; with a futures contract, all these cash settlements are handled through the exchange and you never know, or care, who is on the other side of the contract.

> **FYI**
>
> The difference between a *forward contract* and a *futures contract* is similar to the difference between investing as a partner in a company and buying stock in a company. When you invest, you personally negotiate the amount you will invest and your percentage ownership, and you know who sold you the investment. When you buy stock, you buy a standardized chunk of a company and because the shares are purchased through an exchange, you have no idea who owned the shares before you bought them.

> **FYI**
>
> Hedging future purchases is where derivative use sometimes is abused. The people in the corporate finance office start to think that they can forecast changes in wheat prices, so they buy forward contracts far in excess of that needed to hedge future wheat purchases. These extra contracts are speculations on the movement of wheat prices, and they expose the company to substantial speculative risk.

As an example of the use of a futures contract, assume that Hyrum Bakery uses 1,000 bushels of wheat every month. On December 1, 2015, Hyrum decides to protect itself against price movements for its January 1, 2016, wheat purchase because long-term spring weather forecasts often come out in December, causing wide fluctuations in wheat prices. To protect against these fluctuations, Hyrum buys a futures contract on December 1 that obligates it to purchase 1,000 bushels of wheat on January 1, 2016, at a price of $4 per bushel (which is also the prevailing price of wheat on December 1). This is a standardized exchange-traded futures contract, so Hyrum has no idea who is on the other side of the agreement; that is, Hyrum doesn't know who is promising to deliver the wheat.

As with other derivatives, a wheat futures contract is usually settled by a cash payment at the end of the contract instead of by actual delivery of the wheat. Settlement of Hyrum's futures contract would be as follows. If the price of wheat is less than $4 per bushel on January 1, Hyrum will make a cash payment of that difference, multiplied by 1,000 bushels. If the price of wheat is more than $4 per bushel on January 1, Hyrum will receive a cash payment equal to that difference multiplied by 1,000 bushels.[7] The effect of the futures contract is illustrated in the table shown on page 19-10.

---

[7] For exchange-traded futures contracts, cash settlements usually are not deferred until the end of the contract but occur at the end of every day based on price movements during that day.

	Wheat Price on January 1		
	$3.80	$4.00	$4.20
Cost to purchase 1,000 bushels	$(3,800)	$(4,000)	$(4,200)
Hyrum receipt (payment) to settle futures contract	(200)	0	200
Net cost of January wheat	$(4,000)	$(4,000)	$(4,000)

Option

An option is a contract giving the owner the right, but not the obligation, to buy or sell an asset at a specified price any time during a specified period in the future. Options come in two general types: call options and put options. A call option gives the owner the right to buy an asset at a specified price, and a put option gives the owner the right to sell an asset at a specified price. In exchange for the rights inherent in the option, the owner of the option pays an amount in advance to the party on the other side of the transaction, who is called the *writer of the option*. Like a futures contract, many options are standardized contracts that are traded on organized exchanges.

An option differs from the derivative instruments discussed previously because it protects the owner against unfavorable movements in prices or rates while allowing the owner to benefit from favorable movements. With the swaps, forwards, and futures discussed earlier, the protection from unfavorable movements was "paid for" by sacrificing the benefits from favorable movements. With an option, the protection is "paid for" with an up-front cash payment when the option is purchased.

Because of the asymmetrical nature of options, the owner of an option and the writer of an option are in very different positions. With a call option, for example, the owner of the option can buy the designated asset at a fixed price no matter how high the market price of the asset goes. If the market price of the asset decreases, the option owner can just throw the option away because it is cheaper to buy the asset at the low market price. So, the maximum amount that the owner of an option can lose is the price paid to buy the option. On the other side of the transaction, the writer of the option has no such downside protection. No matter how high market prices increase, the writer of a call option must sell the asset at the fixed option price. So, there is no limit to the amount that a call option writer can lose.[8] Because this discussion of derivative instruments focuses on the use of derivatives for risk management and risk reduction, only buyers of options will be considered.

To illustrate the use of options in managing risk, assume that, on October 1, 2015, Woodruff Company decides that it will need to purchase 1,000 ounces of gold for use in its computer chip manufacturing process in January 2016. Gold is selling for $1,100 per ounce on October 1, 2015. For cash flow reasons, Woodruff plans to delay the purchase of the gold until January 1, 2016, and is concerned about potential increases in the market price of gold between October 1, 2015, and January 1, 2016.

To reduce the price risk associated with the gold, Woodruff enters into a call option contract on October 1. The contract gives Woodruff the right, but not the obligation, to purchase 1,000 ounces of gold at a price of $1,100 per ounce. The option period extends to January 1, 2016, and Woodruff has to pay $20,000 to buy this option.[9] In exchange

---

[8] The losses of the writer of a put option are limited to the full amount of the option price. Even if the asset becomes completely worthless, the put option writer must buy it at the option price.

[9] Computation of option values was outlined in Chapter 13, but a detailed treatment is beyond the scope of this text. Briefly, the price that must be paid to purchase a call option is higher when the option exercise price is lower, when the length of the option is longer, and when the movement of the price of the underlying asset (gold in this example) is more volatile.

for this $20,000 payment, the option arrangement protects Woodruff from unfavorable movements in the price of gold but also allows Woodruff to benefit from favorable movements. This can be seen from the following table:

	Gold Price (per ounce) on January 1		
	$1,000	$1,100	$1,200
Cost of 1,000 ounces of gold if			
• Buy gold at January 1 price..................	$1,000,000	$1,100,000	$1,200,000
• Exercise option	$1,100,000	$1,100,000	$1,100,000
Will option be exercised?........................	No	Same either way	Yes
Cost of gold.....................................	$1,000,000	$1,100,000	$1,100,000

> **Caution**
> Remember that an option is a right, not an obligation. The owner of the option can always throw it away and forget the whole deal.

The existence of the option contract means that Woodruff will pay no more than $1,100,000 for the gold. Because the option is a right and not an obligation, Woodruff can ignore it, as in the preceding case in which the January 1 price of gold is $1,000 per ounce, and just buy gold at the market price prevailing on January 1. Remember that this ability to enjoy protection from unfavorable price changes but to benefit from favorable price changes was not free; it cost Woodruff $20,000 at the beginning of the option period. As with the other derivative instruments, this option can be settled on January 1 by a direct cash payment from the option writer to Woodruff in place of the actual delivery of the gold. If the cost of 1,000 ounces of gold is more than $1,100,000 on January 1, the option writer pays Woodruff the difference.

Types of Hedging Activities

LO4 学习目标4
定义套期并概括说明公允价值套期与现金流量套期的差别。

④ Define *hedging*, and outline the difference between a fair value hedge and a cash flow hedge.

The preceding illustrations of the different types of derivatives—swaps, forwards, futures, and options—also illustrated how these derivatives are used in hedging activities. Broadly defined, hedging is the structuring of transactions to reduce risk. Hedging occurs naturally as part of many business activities, examples of which follow.

- In the retail sale of gasoline, one risk to the gasoline retailer is that movement in worldwide oil prices will cause variation in the cost to purchase gasoline. This "cost of goods sold" risk is partially offset by the fact that the retail selling price of gasoline also goes up when oil prices rise. So, the increase in the cost is offset by the increase in the selling price.
- Banks are vulnerable to interest rate increases because this increases the amount they must pay to get the use of depositors' money. However, this risk is hedged because an interest rate increase also allows a bank to raise the rates it charges on its loans.
- Multinational companies can be impacted by changes in exchange rates. If a U.S. multinational has a subsidiary in France, a decline in the value of the euro will cause

the dollar value of the subsidiary's euro-denominated assets to decline. This loss is partially offset, however, because the dollar value of the subsidiary's euro-denominated liabilities will also decline.

Derivatives can be used in hedging activities through the acquisition of a derivative with the characteristic that changes in the value of the derivative are expected to offset changes in the value of the item being hedged. Let's review how derivatives were used as hedges in each of the derivative illustrations given in the preceding section.

- *Pratt swap*. The interest rate swap was structured to offset changes in the variable-rate interest payments.
- *Clayton forward*. The forward currency contract was entered into to offset changes in the dollar value of the receivable denominated in Japanese yen.
- *Hyrum future*. The wheat futures contract was acquired to offset movements in the expected purchase price of the following month's supply of wheat.
- *Woodruff option*. The gold call option was purchased to offset the negative impact of changes in the market price of gold on the cost of gold for production purposes.

> **FYI**
> Historically, cash flow hedges have been very controversial. Firms have claimed to be using derivatives to hedge forecasted transactions when in fact the dollar value of supposed hedging activity has been far greater than any possible future transactions. Using a derivative in this way transforms the derivative from a hedging tool into a speculative investment.

The FASB has defined two of the broad categories of hedging activities as follows:[10]

- *Fair value hedges*. A fair value hedge is a derivative that offsets, at least partially, the change in the fair value of an asset or a liability. A derivative can also serve as a hedge of the fair value of firm commitments even though the assets and liabilities associated with a firm commitment are not recognized until the actual transaction date.
- *Cash flow hedges*. A cash flow hedge is a derivative that offsets, at least partially, the variability in cash flows from forecasted transactions that are probable.

公允价值套期是一种衍生工具，其作用是至少部分补偿资产或负债公允价值的变动。

现金流量套期是一种衍生工具，其作用是至少部分补偿由可能的预测性交易带来的现金流变动。

The FASB has identified a third category of hedges related to foreign currency risk. Some of these hedges are fair value hedges, and some are cash flow hedges. In addition, some of these hedges relate to the foreign currency risk associated with the net investment in foreign subsidiaries. This category of hedges is covered in more detail in advanced accounting courses.

The next section illustrates the proper accounting for derivatives, particularly those designated as hedges.

Accounting for Derivatives and for Hedging Activities

LO5 学习目标5
多种不同的衍生工具和套期关系的会计处理。

5 Account for a variety of different derivatives and for hedging relationships.

Several factors combined in 1993 and 1994 to move the accounting for derivatives to the top of the FASB's agenda. First was the tremendous proliferation in the use of derivatives by U.S. businesses. Second was the derivative-related catastrophes experienced by

[10] FASB ASC paragraph 815-20-35-1.

companies such as Procter & Gamble. And third was the SEC's urging for improvement in the accounting for derivatives. In October 1994, the FASB released pre-Codification *Statement No. 119* with the main focus being on improved disclosure (not recognition) for the 1994 fiscal year. *Statement No. 119* was viewed as a temporary stopgap standard.

A more comprehensive recognition standard for derivatives, FASB pre-Codification *Statement No. 133*, was adopted in June 1998; its effective date was subsequently delayed to fiscal years beginning after June 15, 2000. The delay was motivated by two reasons: Companies wanted more time to figure out how to implement the standard and they did not want to implement the standard before January 1, 2000, because of "Y2K" concerns with their computer systems. The adoption of FASB *Statement No. 133* was not the end of the quest for better derivative accounting. A special Derivatives Implementation Group (DIG) was established by the FASB with the sole purpose of handling derivative accounting issues. Until it stopped meeting in June 2009, the DIG had commented on 190 different issues relative to accounting for derivatives. So keep in mind that the brief treatment of derivative accounting in this chapter is just an overview. However, this overview does cover the key elements of accounting for derivatives.

Overview of Accounting for Derivatives and Hedging Activities

The accounting difficulty caused by derivatives is illustrated in this simple matrix:

	Historical Cost	Subsequent Changes in Value
Traditional assets and liabilities	Focus	Frequently ignored
Derivatives	Small or zero	Everything

As the matrix shows, the historical cost focus of traditional accounting is misplaced with derivatives because derivatives often have little or no up-front historical cost. With derivatives, the subsequent changes in prices or rates are critical to determining the value of the derivative, yet these changes are frequently ignored in traditional accounting.

Because derivatives do not mesh well with the traditional accounting model, the FASB has endorsed a different approach, based on two simple notions:

1. *Balance sheet.* Derivatives should be reported in the balance sheet at their fair value as of the balance sheet date. No other measure of value is relevant for derivatives.
2. *Income statement.* When a derivative is used to hedge risk, the gains and losses on the derivative should be reported in the same income statement in which the income effects on the hedged item are reported. This sometimes requires unrealized gains and losses being temporarily deferred in an accumulated other comprehensive income account that is reported as part of equity.

A consequence of this approach is that the appropriate treatment of changes in the fair value of a derivative depends on whether the derivative serves as a hedge and, if so, the type of hedge, as follows:

- *No hedge.* All changes in the fair value of derivatives that are not designated as hedges are recognized as gains or losses in the income statement in the period in which the value changes. In a sense, a derivative that does not serve as a hedge can be thought of as a speculation about the direction of movement of some price or rate.

- *Fair value hedge.* Changes in the fair value of derivatives designated as fair value hedges are recognized as gains or losses in the period of the value change. These derivative gains or losses are offset (either in whole or in part) by the recognition of gains or losses on the change in fair value of the item being hedged. The net effect is that when gains or losses on derivatives designated as fair value hedges exceed the gains or losses on the item being hedged, the excess affects reported net income.
- *Cash flow hedge.* Changes in the fair value of derivatives designated as cash flow hedges are recognized as part of the accumulated other comprehensive income account. In effect, this treatment defers recognition of the gain or loss and classifies the deferred item as an equity adjustment. These deferred derivative gains and losses are recognized in net income in the period in which the hedged cash flow transaction was forecasted to occur.

> **FYI**
>
> Assessing hedge effectiveness when the critical elements of the hedged item and the hedging derivative are not the same involves statistical procedures and can be quite difficult. For a discussion, see John D. Finnerty and Dwight Grant, "Alternative Approaches to Testing Hedge Effectiveness under SFAS No. 133," *Accounting Horizons*, June 2002, p. 95.

An important aspect of this approach is that derivatives must be identified as hedges of specific items at the beginning of the hedging relationship. Firms cannot wait until after they see the results for the period to decide whether they want to designate certain derivatives as hedges. The designation of a derivative as a hedge should be supported with formal documentation.

To account for a derivative as a hedge, a company must define, in advance, how it will determine whether the derivative is functioning as an effective hedge. For the simple examples given in this chapter, hedge effectiveness is easy to assess because the terms of the derivatives have been constructed to exactly match the amount and timing of the underlying hedged item. Partial hedge ineffectiveness would occur if, for example, the derivative maturity date did not exactly match the date of a forecasted purchase. Similarly, hedge ineffectiveness occurs when the amount in the derivative agreement (such as the number of units of foreign currency or of pounds of a commodity) is either more or less than the amount of the underlying hedged item. Derivative gains or losses associated with hedge ineffectiveness are recognized in income immediately in the period in which they occur.

Disclosure Companies are required to provide a description of their risk management strategy and how derivatives fit into that strategy. For both fair value and cash flow hedges, companies also must disclose the amount of derivative gains or losses that are included in income because of hedge ineffectiveness. Finally, for cash flow hedges, a company must describe the transactions that will cause deferred derivative gains and losses to be recognized in net income and disclose the amount of deferred gains or losses that are expected to be recognized in net income in the next 12 months.[11]

> **FYI**
>
> A favorite ploy of financial reporters is to report the notional amount of derivatives in order to exaggerate their importance.

Another item that is often referred to in the business press is the *notional amount* of the derivative instrument. The notional amount is the total face amount of the asset or liability that underlies the derivative contract. For example, with a forward contract, the notional amount is the U.S. dollar value of the commodity or currency

---

[11] FASB ASC paragraph 815-30-50-1.

to be exchanged. The notional amount of derivative instruments is often reported and is frequently misleading. For example, the Clayton forward contract described earlier in the chapter has a notional amount of $250,000 (¥30,000,000/¥120 per $1) but has a fair value of $0 on the day the forward agreement is signed, and in the example, the total cash payment stemming from the derivative does not exceed $4,237. In summary, notional amounts grossly overstate both the fair value and the potential cash flows of derivatives.

The accounting for derivatives will be illustrated using the information from the previous four derivative examples.

Illustrations of Accounting for Derivatives and Hedging Activities

Pratt Swap On January 1, 2015, Pratt Company received a two-year, $100,000, variable-rate loan and entered into an interest rate swap agreement. The journal entry to record this information follows:

2015
Jan. 1   Cash 100,000
                Loan Payable... 100,000

No entry is made to record the swap agreement because as of January 1, 2015, the swap has a fair value of $0. The value is zero because the interest rate on January 1, 2015, is 10%, and if it is assumed that the best forecast of the future interest rate is the current rate of 10%, it is expected that, on average, no payments will be exchanged under the swap agreement.[12]

Assume now that the actual market interest rate on December 31, 2015, is 11%. With this rate, Pratt will receive a $1,000 payment [$100,000 × (0.11 − 0.10)] at the end of 2016 under the swap agreement. Accordingly, on December 31, 2015, Pratt has a $1,000 receivable under the swap agreement, and the receivable has a present value of $901 (FV = $1,000, N = 1, I = 11%, PV = $901). The impact of the change in interest rates on the interest rate swap and on reported interest expense is accounted for as follows:

	2015 Balance Sheet	2015 Income Statement
Underlying item	No change in the reported loan balance	No impact on 2015 interest expense; the impact will show up in 2016 interest expense
Derivative	Creation of a $901 receivable under the interest rate swap	Deferred gain of $901 on the interest rate swap; gain recognized in 2016 to offset increased interest expense

The interest rate swap asset is reported at its present value of $901 in the December 31, 2015, balance sheet. However, the $901 gain from the increase in the value of the swap is not included in the 2015 income statement. The swap is intended to offset changes in interest expense in 2016. Accordingly, the gain on the swap is deferred so that it can be offset against the increased interest expense to be reported in 2016. The deferral of the gain merely means that it is temporarily reported as an increase in equity under Accumulated Other Comprehensive Income. The deferred gain would also be included as an addition in the statement of comprehensive income (but not in the normal income statement) for 2015.

---

[12] As mentioned earlier, detailed treatment of the valuation of derivatives is outside the scope of this text. Remember that the valuation assumptions used here represent a simplification.

The journal entry to record Pratt's 2015 interest payment, along with the adjusting entry to recognize the change in the fair value of the swap, is as follows:

2015
Dec. 31 Interest Expense.. 10,000
              Cash ($100,000 × 0.10).. 10,000
         Interest Rate Swap (asset)....................................... 901
              Other Comprehensive Income.............................. 901

The journal entries necessary in Pratt's books at the end of 2016 are as follows:

2016
Dec. 31 Interest Expense.. 11,000
              Cash ($100,000 × 0.11).. 11,000
         Cash (from swap agreement) 1,000
              Interest Rate Swap (asset) 901
              Other Comprehensive Income ($901 × 0.11; rounded).......... 99
         Accumulated Other Comprehensive Income 1,000
              Interest Expense 1,000
         Loan Payable... 100,000
              Cash... 100,000

The $99 credit to Other Comprehensive Income represents the increase in the value of the swap payment receivable stemming from the passage of time. Also, recall that Other Comprehensive Income is closed to the equity account Accumulated Other Comprehensive Income at the end of each year. The debit to Accumulated Other Comprehensive Income of $1,000 removes this amount from the Accumulated Other Comprehensive Income portion of equity and transfers it, after the accounts are closed, to Retained Earnings.

An important thing to notice in these journal entries is that net interest expense is $10,000 because of the hedging effect of the swap. Also notice that the value changes in a derivative designated as a cash flow hedge are deferred in comprehensive income and then reflected in earnings in the period when the hedged cash flow occurs.

Clayton Forward On November 1, 2015, Clayton Company sold machine parts to Maruta Company for ¥30,000,000 to be received on January 1, 2016. On the same date, Clayton also entered a yen forward contract. The journal entry to record this information is as follows:

2015
Nov. 1 Yen Receivable (¥30,000,000/¥120 per $1) 250,000
             Sales... 250,000

No entry is made to record the forward contract because as of November 1, 2015, the forward has a fair value of $0. The value is zero because settlement payments are made under the contract only if the exchange rate on January 1, 2016, differs from ¥120 = $1. If the current exchange rate of ¥120 = $1 is assumed to be the best forecast of the future rate, it is expected that, on average, no payments will be exchanged under the forward contract.

Assume now that the actual exchange rate on December 31, 2015, is ¥119 = $1. At this exchange rate, Clayton will have a loss on the forward contract and be required to make a $2,101 payment [(¥30,000,000/¥119 per $1) − $250,000] on January 1, 2016, to settle the forward contract. Accordingly, on December 31, 2015, Clayton has a $2,101 loss and payable under the forward contract. However, there is also an increase in the yen receivable and a corresponding gain on foreign exchange due to the change in yen value relative to the U.S. dollar. The impact of the change in the yen exchange rate on both the yen receivable and the value of the forward contract is accounted for as follows:

	2015 Balance Sheet	2015 Income Statement
Underlying item	Increase of $2,101 in the value of the yen receivable	Exchange gain of $2,101
Derivative	Creation of a $2,101 liability	Loss on forward contract of $2,101 under the forward contract

The forward contract liability is reported at its fair value of $2,101 in the December 31, 2015, balance sheet. In addition, the $2,101 loss on the forward contract is included in the 2015 income statement, thus offsetting the gain reported from the increase in dollar value of the yen receivable. This accounting treatment accurately reflects the intent of the forward contract hedge; that is, unrealized gains and losses from changes in value of the forward contract are meant to offset similar changes in value in the item of concern, the yen receivable.

The adjusting entries to recognize the change in the fair value of the forward contract and in the U.S. dollar value of the yen receivable are as follows:

FYI

These journal entries illustrate that, after the fact, hedging is not always a good idea. In the Clayton example, the forward contract hedge wipes out the gain on the increase in the value of the yen receivable. The advantage of a hedge is that it reduces volatility, but that sometimes means canceling out gains.

在2015年12月31日的资产负债表中，远期合同负债以公允价值2 101美元列报。此外，由远期合同造成的2 101美元亏损将纳入2015年利润表，这样就抵销了所收日元的美元价值的增长。

2015
Dec. 31 Loss on Forward Contract.. 2,101
                Forward Contract (liability).. 2,101
          Yen Receivable... 2,101
                Gain on Foreign Currency... 2,101

The increase in the yen receivable reflects the $2,101 increased dollar value of the receivable after the change in the exchange rate to ¥119 = $1. This gain is offset by the loss from the change in value of the forward contract. The forward contract is a fair value hedge of the value of the receivable, so both changes in value are recognized in earnings.

The journal entries necessary in Clayton's books on January 1, 2016, to record receipt of the yen payment and settlement of the yen forward contract are as follows:

2016
Jan. 1 Cash (¥30,000,000/¥119 per $1).. 252,101
                Yen Receivable... 252,101
          Forward Contract (liability)... 2,101
                Cash (forward contract settlement)........................ 2,101

It should be noted that the Clayton forward contract does not qualify for hedge accounting under FASB ASC Topic 815. The FASB explicitly excluded foreign currency–denominated assets and liabilities from the set of items that can be considered as items underlying a hedge.[13] Thus, derivatives that serve as economic hedges of foreign currency assets and liabilities are accounted for as speculations, with all gains and losses recognized as part of income immediately. However, because the accounting standards [in Topic 830 (Foreign Currency Matters)] already require that foreign currency assets and liabilities be revalued at current exchange rates at the end of each period, with the resulting exchange gains and losses recognized in income, the net effect is the same as if the foreign currency derivatives were accounted for as fair value hedges after all. This fact can be seen by reviewing the Clayton forward example: The gains and losses from both the foreign currency receivable and the yen forward contract are recognized in income immediately, effectively offsetting one another.[14]

By excluding derivatives associated with foreign currency assets and liabilities from the hedge accounting rules of Topic 815, the FASB has reduced the disclosure burden of companies that use such derivatives as hedges. The fair value option of Section 825-10-25, which was discussed in detail in Chapter 12, is another effort by the FASB to allow companies to report the economic effects of hedging activity without the elaborate documentation that is required under Topic 815.

Hyrum Future On December 1, 2015, Hyrum Company decided to hedge against potential fluctuations in the price of wheat for its forecasted January 2016 purchases and bought a futures contract entitling and obligating Hyrum to purchase 1,000 bushels of wheat on January 1, 2016, for $4.00 per bushel. No entry is made to record the futures contract because, as of December 1, 2015, the future has a fair value of $0. The value is zero because settlement payments are made under the contract only if the price of wheat on January 1, 2016, differs from $4.00 per bushel. If the current price of $4.00 per bushel is assumed to be the best forecast of the future price, it is expected that, on average, no payments will be exchanged under the futures contract.

Assume that the actual price of wheat on December 31, 2015, is $4.40 per bushel. At this price, Hyrum will receive a $400 payment [1,000 bushels × ($4.40 − $4.00)] on January 1, 2016, to settle the futures contract. Accordingly, on December 31, 2015, Hyrum has a $400 receivable under the futures contract. The impact of the change in wheat prices on the wheat futures contract and on the anticipated cost of wheat purchases in January 2016 is accounted for as follows:

	2015 Balance Sheet	2015 Income Statement
Underlying item	No impact; the higher-priced wheat won't be purchased until January 2016	No impact on 2015 cost of goods sold; the impact will show up in 2016 cost of goods sold
Derivative	Creation of a $400 receivable under the wheat futures contract	Deferred gain of $400 on the wheat futures contract; gain recognized in 2016 to offset increased cost of goods sold

The wheat futures asset is reported at its fair value of $400 in the December 31, 2015, balance sheet. However, the $400 gain from the increase in the value of the futures

---

[13] FASB ASC paragraph 815-20-25-43.
[14] As mentioned earlier, in this chapter we make the simplifying assumption that spot rates and forward rates are equal to one another. When this is not true, the foreign currency and derivative gains and losses will not exactly offset because foreign currency assets and liabilities are valued using the spot rate and derivative instruments are valued using the forward rate.

> **Caution**
>
> It is *not* the case that derivative losses are reported immediately and derivative gains are deferred. If wheat prices had declined, Hyrum would have experienced a loss on the wheat futures contract, which would have been deferred until 2016.

contract is not included in the 2015 income statement. The futures contract is intended to offset changes in the purchase price of wheat in January 2016. Accordingly, the gain on the futures contract is deferred so that it can be offset against the increased cost of goods sold to be reported in 2016. As with the interest rate swap discussed earlier, the deferral of the gain means that it is temporarily reported as an increase in equity under Accumulated Other Comprehensive Income.

The adjusting entry to recognize the change in the fair value of the futures contract is as follows:

2015

Dec.	31	Wheat Futures Contract (asset)	400	
		Other Comprehensive Income...		400

The gain from the increase in the value of Hyrum's futures contract is deferred as part of other comprehensive income. The wheat futures contract is a cash flow hedge, with the futures contract payment intended to offset the increased amount that Hyrum will have to pay to make its forecasted purchase of 1,000 bushels of wheat on January 1, 2016.

The journal entries necessary in Hyrum's books on January 1, 2016, to record the purchase of 1,000 bushels of wheat in the open market and cash settlement of the wheat futures contract are as follows:

2016

Jan.	1	Wheat Inventory	4,400	
		Cash (1,000 bushels × $4.40).......................................		4,400
		Cash (futures contract settlement)	400	
		Wheat Futures Contract (asset)		400
		Accumulated Other Comprehensive Income	400	
		Gain on Futures Contract..		400

The gain on the futures contract is recognized in earnings on January 1, 2016, the forecasted date of the transaction that was hedged. To the extent that the wheat inventory is used to make bread and that bread is sold in 2016, the gain on the futures contract will offset the increased cost of goods sold arising from the increase in the price of wheat to $4.40 per bushel.

Woodruff Option On October 1, 2015, Woodruff Company paid $20,000 to purchase a call option to buy 1,000 ounces of gold at a price of $1,100 per ounce some time before January 1, 2016. This option is intended to protect Woodruff against increases in the price of the gold that it needs for 2016. Because Woodruff paid cash for the gold call option, the following journal entry is made on October 1:

2015

Oct.	1	Gold Call Option (asset)...	20,000	
		Cash...		20,000

Assume that the actual price of gold on December 31, 2015, is $1,128 per ounce. At this gold price, Woodruff will receive a $28,000 payment [($1,128 × 1,000 ounces) − ($1,100 × 1,000 ounces)] on January 1, 2016, to settle the call option. Accordingly, on December 31, 2015, the call option is worth $28,000. The impact of the change in the price of gold on the gold call option and on the anticipated cost of gold purchases in January 2016 is accounted for as follows:

	2015 Balance Sheet	2015 Income Statement
Underlying item	No impact; the higher-priced gold won't be purchased until January 2016	No impact on 2015 cost of goods sold; the impact will show up in 2016 cost of goods sold
Derivative	Increase from $20,000 to $28,000 of the recorded value of the gold call option	Deferred gain of $8,000 on the gold call option; gain recognized in 2016 to offset increased cost of goods sold

The gold call option is reported at its fair value of $28,000 in the December 31, 2015, balance sheet. This represents an $8,000 increase ($28,000 − $20,000) over the amount originally paid for the option. However, the $8,000 gain from the increase in the value of the call option is not included in the 2015 income statement. The call option is intended to offset changes in the purchase price of gold in January 2016. Accordingly, the gain on the call option is deferred so that it can be offset against the increased production costs to be reported in 2016.

The adjusting entry to recognize the change in the fair value of the option is as follows:

2015

Dec. 31 Gold Call Option ($28,000 − $20,000).................................. 8,000
  Other Comprehensive Income.....................................   8,000

The journal entries necessary in Woodruff's books on January 1, 2016, to record the purchase of 1,000 ounces of gold and the cash settlement of the option contract are as follows:

2016

Jan. 1 Gold Inventory 1,128,000
  Cash (1,000 ounces × $1,128)...............................   1,128,000

  Cash (gold call option settlement) 28,000
  Gold Call Option (asset)   28,000

  Accumulated Other Comprehensive Income 8,000
  Gain on Gold Call Option....................................   8,000

As mentioned previously, the gain from the increase in the value of the gold call option would be offset against the increased production costs in January 2016 resulting from the increase in the price of gold. The $8,000 gain does not completely offset the $28,000 increase in production costs because Woodruff had to pay $20,000 to purchase the gold call option in the first place.

FASB CODIFICATION

The Issue: You have been doing some part-time bookkeeping for a local ski resort. Because of your accounting background, the general manager of the resort has come to rely on your understanding of business transactions. A salesperson for a local brokerage firm has just visited the general manager. The salesperson was trying to sell the general manager on the idea of a "weather derivative" to help manage the risk the ski resort faces from low or late snowfall. The general manager had never heard of such a thing. The general manager has asked you to find out if there is such a thing as a "weather derivative."

The Question: Is there such a thing as a "weather derivative"?

Searching the Codification: Of course, the quickest way to find out the answer to this question is to just do a general search online. However, that wouldn't be nearly as sophisticated, or fun, as searching the FASB Codification. In addition, if you can find some coverage of "weather derivatives" in the Codification, you will know that this is a mainstream transaction, common enough to be addressed by the FASB. This is a good opportunity to just relax and scan through Topic 815 (Derivatives and Hedging—Broad Transactions).

The Answer: The existence of weather derivatives is discussed on page 19–36.

Summary

The centerpiece of accounting for derivatives and hedging activities is that derivatives are recognized as assets and liabilities and reported on the balance sheet at their fair values. For a derivative designated as a fair value hedge, changes in fair value are included in earnings and offset against changes in fair value of the hedged item. For a cash flow hedge, gains and losses are deferred in accumulated other comprehensive income and recognized in earnings on the forecasted date of the hedged transaction. In formulating an International Financial Reporting Standard for derivatives, the IASB drew heavily on the work done by the FASB. The general provisions of *IAS 39* are very similar to the provisions of FASB ASC Topic 815.

CONTINGENCIES

During 1983, Pennzoil initiated negotiations for the acquisition of Getty Oil. Before the Pennzoil-Getty deal could be closed, Texaco swooped in and bought Getty right out from underneath Pennzoil's nose for $10.2 billion. Pennzoil immediately sued Texaco for $14 billion in damages caused by Texaco's interference in Pennzoil's attempted acquisition of Getty. In December 1985, a Houston jury awarded $10.5 billion to Pennzoil. The case was appealed in both 1986 and 1987, with judgment in each instance against Texaco. With the uncertainty of a multibillion-dollar judgment hanging over its head, Texaco found it increasingly difficult to calm the fears of its suppliers and creditors. Texaco played its trump card in April 1987 and declared Chapter 11 bankruptcy. This action forced Pennzoil to the bargaining table, and in December 1987 the two companies negotiated a $3 billion payment to settle the case. Texaco made the payment on April 7, 1988.[15]

---

[15] Edward B. Deakin, "Accounting for Contingencies: The Pennzoil-Texaco Case," *Accounting Horizons*, March 1989, p. 21.

In addition to illustrating the strategic use of Chapter 11 bankruptcy, the Texaco-Pennzoil case serves as a classic example of the difficulties surrounding the accounting for contingencies. Among the interesting accounting questions here are the following:

- During the 4.5-year life of this lawsuit, when should Texaco have recognized a liability, and for what amount?
- At the same time, when should Pennzoil have recognized an asset for the receivable from Texaco?

As the Texaco-Pennzoil case suggests, uncertainty about the future sometimes makes it difficult to identify a company's assets and liabilities. The definitions of assets and liabilities given in the conceptual framework discussed in Chapter 1 use the word "probable"; an asset is a probable future economic benefit, and a liability is a probable future economic sacrifice. In this module, the specific accounting rules governing the accounting for contingent items will be discussed. These rules will be illustrated with coverage of the accounting for lawsuits and for environmental liabilities.

Accounting for Contingencies: Probable, Possible, and Remote

LO6 Apply the accounting rules for contingent items to the areas of lawsuits and environmental liabilities.

A contingency is defined in FASB ASC Topic 450 (Contingencies) as follows:

> ... an existing condition, situation, or set of circumstances involving uncertainty as to possible gain ... or loss ... to an entity that will ultimately be resolved when one or more future events occur or fail to occur.[16]

As defined, contingencies may relate to either assets or liabilities and to either a gain or loss. The primary focus of this module is on contingent losses that might give rise to a liability, but the accounting for contingent gains is also discussed briefly.

Historically, when the existence of an obligation depended on the occurrence of a future event, recognition of the liability was deferred until the event occurred. This approach can fail to reflect the existence of significant obligations that are highly likely to materialize and that exist because of past transactions or events. For example, Texaco's contingent obligation to Pennzoil arose because of Texaco's interference in Pennzoil's attempted acquisition of Getty Oil, a past event. The future events determining whether Texaco would have to make payments to Pennzoil were the court verdicts. For Texaco to fail to record its liability until the day the $3 billion was actually paid to Pennzoil would be grossly misleading to users of the financial statements.

FASB ASC Topic 450 specifies different accounting for contingent items based on the probability of the occurrence of the resolving future event. The likelihood of the event and the accounting actions recommended are shown in Exhibit 19-1.

If the occurrence of an event that would create a liability is probable and if the amount of the obligation can be reasonably estimated, the contingency should be recognized as a liability. Many estimated liabilities are in reality probable contingent liabilities because the existence of the obligation depends on some future event occurring. For example, the

---

[16] FASB ASC Section 450-10-20—Glossary.

Exhibit 19-1 | Accounting for Contingencies

Contingent Losses:

Likelihood	Accounting Action
Probable	Recognize a probable liability if the amount can be reasonably estimated. If not estimable, disclose facts in a note. FASB ASC paragraph 450-20-25-2.
Reasonably possible	Disclose a possible liability in a note. FASB ASC paragraph 450-20-50-3.
Remote	Make no recognition or disclosure unless contingency represents a guarantee. Then note disclosure is required. FASB ASC paragraph 460-10-50-2.

Contingent Gains:

Likelihood	Accounting Action
Probable plus	Recognize a contingent asset if the probability of its occurrence is very high (more than probable) and if the amount can be reasonably estimated. Otherwise, disclose the facts in a note. FASB ASC paragraph 450-30-25-1.
Reasonably possible	Disclose a possible asset in a note, but be careful to avoid misleading implications. In practice, possible contingent gains are often not disclosed. FASB ASC paragraph 450-30-50-1.
Remote	Make no recognition or disclosure.

© Cengage Learning 2014

estimated amount of warranty liability is a probable contingent liability because warranties depend on the need to provide future repairs or service. In addition, a pension obligation depends on employees staying with the company long enough to earn full pension benefits, and frequent-flier trips are contingent on whether customers accumulate enough miles for free trips and whether they actually claim their free trips.

The rules governing accounting for contingent assets are somewhat confused. The wording in FASB ASC Topic 450 about contingent gains goes back to *ARB No. 50*, which was originally adopted in 1958. *ARB No. 50* says that contingent gains (and, by extension, contingent assets) are not to be recognized before they are "realized." This appears to be in conflict with the asset definition in *Concepts Statement No. 6*, which says that an asset is a "probable future economic benefit." The international rules add another view. In *IAS 37*, paragraph 33, we read that a contingent asset should be recognized when it "is virtually certain." The only thing we can conclude with certainty from all of this is that the probability threshold for the recognition of a contingent asset is higher than that for a contingent liability. This reflects the conservatism that has been at the roots of accounting for years.

If a contingent liability is *reasonably possible*, defined as more than remote but less than likely, it should be disclosed in a note to the financial statements. Possible gains are often not disclosed to avoid any misleading implications about the likelihood that the gain will eventually be realized. If a contingent item is *remote*, that is, the chance of occurrence is slight, there is no requirement that it be disclosed unless it is a contingent liability under a guarantee arrangement such as guaranteeing, or cosigning, the loan of another party. The requirement to disclose certain contingencies that have a remote probability of occurrence does NOT exist in *IAS 37*.

The timing of the disclosures made in the Texaco-Pennzoil case illustrates the different treatment of contingent losses and contingent gains. As seen in Exhibit 19-2, the initial lawsuit was filed in early 1984, and Texaco was careful to mention the possibility of a loss in its 1984 and 1985 financial statements. Pennzoil made no mention of the contingent gain in its 1984 or its 1985 financial statements. In the body of the 1986 annual report,

如果一项或有负债是适度可能的——可能性大于微弱可能而小于非常可能，那么它应当在财务报表附注中予以披露。可能盈利经常不予披露，以避免对最终实现利润产生误导性暗示。如果一个或有项目是微弱可能的——发生的可能性很小，那么除非这是一项担保性质的或有负债（如担保人，或者联名签署、借款的另一方），否则不予披露。

Exhibit 19-2 | Accounting Treatment in the Texaco-Pennzoil Case

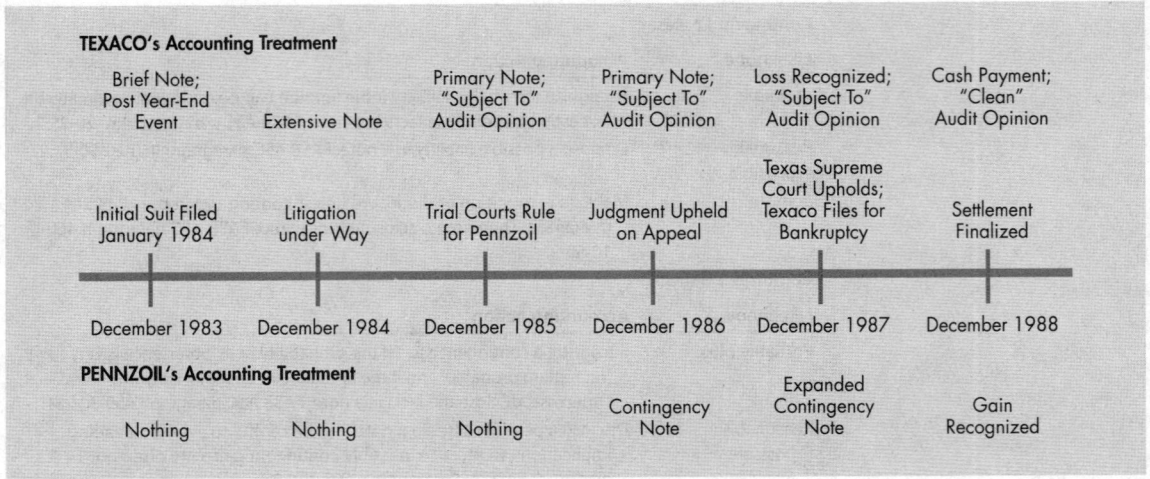

Texaco management took two pages to discuss the Pennzoil litigation. In addition, the financial statements included another page in the notes discussing the case. Texaco's management concluded the discussion by stating that the Pennzoil litigation could materially affect Texaco. At the same time, the uncertainty surrounding Texaco's future, given the large judgment hanging over its head, caused Texaco's auditor to render a qualified audit opinion. While Texaco's financial statements were being drastically impacted by this contingent loss, Pennzoil's financial statements included just a brief note about the contingent gain. In 1987, Texaco formally recognized the $3 billion liability and filed for Chapter 11 bankruptcy. Pennzoil did not recognize the gain until 1988 when the payment was actually received. This case nicely illustrates the asymmetry between the treatment of contingent losses and the treatment of contingent gains.

As described here, the accounting for contingent liabilities and contingent assets is inconsistent with fair value measurement.[17] Even a contingent liability with remote probability of realization has a fair value which would be reflected if, for example, another company were to accept responsibility for that contingency. As FASB standards move increasingly to a fair value measurement standard, it is likely that the area of accounting for contingencies will be revisited.

FASB ASC Topic 450 does not provide specific guidelines as to how the words *probable*, *possible*, and *remote* should be interpreted in terms of probability percentages. For example, is a 60% likelihood "probable" or just "possible"? Surveys of statement preparers and users reveal a great diversity in the numerical interpretations of these probability terms as used in the accounting standards. Thus, the contingency standard that

> **FYI**
>
> In the area of deferred taxes, the FASB has introduced a fourth probability term, "more likely than not," defined as a probability level of 50%. Use of the more-likely-than-not criterion is discussed in Chapter 16.

---

[17] See FASB ASC paragraphs 450-20-05-4 through 7.

seems fairly easy to apply given the straightforward guidelines outlined in Exhibit 19-1 is actually very difficult to apply consistently in practice. This is illustrated below with a discussion of the accounting for lawsuits and environmental liabilities.

Accounting for Lawsuits

The United States is the land of the lawsuit. Companies are sued by customers who claim they were injured by defective products, auditors are sued by stockholders who claim they were injured by defective financial statements, and parents are sued by children who claim they were injured by defective upbringing. Typically, a lawsuit takes a long time to wind its way through the courts. Even after a decision has been handed down by a lower court, many appeal opportunities are available. Thus, both the amount and timing of a loss arising from litigation are generally highly uncertain. Some companies carry insurance to protect themselves against these losses, so the impact of the losses on the financial statements is minimized. For uninsured risks, however, a decision must be made as to when the liability for litigation becomes probable, and thus, a recorded loss. In ASC Topic 450, the FASB identifies several key factors to consider in making the decision. These include the following:[18]

诉讼可能变为负债需考虑的因素包括：
• 诉讼的性质；
• 案件进程，包括在财务报表日和发布日期间的进程；
• 按照损失可能性考虑法律建议；
• 以前类似案件的经验；
• 管理层打算如何应对诉讼。

1. The nature of the lawsuit
2. Progress of the case in court, including progress between date of the financial statements and their issuance date
3. Views of legal counsel as to the probability of loss
4. Prior experience with similar cases
5. Management's intended response to the lawsuit

If analysis of these and similar factors results in the judgment that a loss is probable and the amount of the loss can be reasonably estimated, the liability should be recorded. A settlement after the balance sheet date but before the statements are issued would be evidence that the loss was probable at year-end, and it would result in reporting the loss in the current financial statements.

Another area of potential liability involves unasserted claims; that is, a cause of action has occurred but no claim has yet been asserted. For example, a person may be injured on a company's property, but as of the date the financial statements are issued, no legal action has been taken. As another example, a violation of a government regulation may have occurred, but no federal action has yet been taken. If it is probable that a substantiated claim will be filed and upheld and the amount of the claim can be reasonably estimated, accrual of the liability should be made. If the amount cannot be reasonably estimated, note disclosure is required. If assertion of the claim is judged not to be at least reasonably possible, no accrual or disclosure is necessary.

As a practical matter, it should be noted that a company would be very unlikely to record a loss from unasserted claims or from pending litigation unless negotiations for a settlement had been substantially completed. When that is the case, the loss is no longer a contingency but an estimated loss.

Once a company has determined that the facts and circumstances require that it recognize a liability, the company must then generate a reasonable estimate of the amount of the liability. Even though the company doesn't know the exact amount of the future payout, it can usually specify a range of possible payouts. Under U.S. GAAP, the company should choose the amount within the range that is the best estimate. If no amount in the range is

---

[18] Ibid., par. 36. FASB ASC paragraph 450-20-55-12.

any better than any other amount, the company should recognize the lowest amount in the range and then disclose the potential additional loss exposure.[19]

Under IFRS, the estimation process for recognizing an amount associated with a probable future payout differs substantially from U.S. GAAP. The focus in *IAS 37* is on recognizing the fair value of the obligation. Accordingly, the company is expected to estimate the amount that would have to be paid right now in order to settle the obligation or to transfer the obligation to a third party.[20] This estimate involves consideration of the possible payouts, the probabilities of each, and the time value of money if the payout is expected to stretch over a long time period. As you can see, this process results in a recognized liability with much more economic meaning than does the U.S. GAAP process of picking either the single most likely outcome or the lowest in a range of equally probable outcomes.

Disclosure Some companies do not disclose any information regarding potential liabilities from lawsuits. Others provide a brief, general description of pending lawsuits. Sometimes companies provide fairly specific information about pending actions and claims. However, companies must be careful not to increase their chances of losing pending lawsuits, and they generally do not disclose dollar amounts of potential losses, which might be interpreted as an admission of guilt and a willingness to pay a certain amount. As an illustration, **ExxonMobil** disclosed the information in Exhibit 19-3 in its 1991, 1997, 2007, and 2009 annual reports in connection with lawsuits filed as a result of the *Valdez* oil spill. Note that, in 1991, Exxon sounds quite optimistic that it has settled the bulk of the claims related to the oil spill and that any further claims "will not have a materially adverse effect" upon the company. This optimistic disclosure is particularly interesting in light of the $5 billion adverse judgment discussed in the 1997 disclosure (although the amount of this judgment was later reduced by order of the U.S. Supreme Court).

Another example of disclosure relating to contingent liabilities can be found in the financial statements of **Altria**, maker of Marlboro cigarettes. The company's 2011 financial statements contain more than 20 pages of disclosure relating to thousands of lawsuits (in various stages of litigation) against the company involving billions of dollars in damage awards. In Item 3. *Legal Proceedings*, the company gives the following statement:

> Altria Group, Inc. and its subsidiaries record provisions in the consolidated financial statements for pending litigation when they determine that an unfavorable outcome is probable and the amount of the loss can be reasonably estimated. At the present time, while it is reasonably possible that an unfavorable outcome in a case may occur, except as discussed elsewhere in this Item 3. *Legal Proceedings*: (i) management has concluded that it is not probable that a loss has been incurred in any of the pending tobacco-related cases; (ii) management is unable to estimate the possible loss or range of loss that could result from an unfavorable outcome in any of the pending tobacco-related cases; and (iii) accordingly, management has not provided any amounts in the consolidated financial statements for unfavorable outcomes, if any. Legal defense costs are expensed as incurred.
>
> Altria Group, Inc. and its subsidiaries have achieved substantial success in managing litigation. Nevertheless, litigation is subject to uncertainty and significant challenges remain. It is possible that the consolidated results of operations, cash flows or financial position of Altria Group, Inc., or one or more of its subsidiaries, could be materially affected in a particular fiscal quarter or fiscal year by an unfavorable outcome or settlement of certain pending litigation.

---

[19] FASB ASC paragraph 450-20-30-1.
[20] *IAS 37* paragraphs 36 through 47.

Exhibit 19-3 | Exxon—1991, 1997, 2007, and 2009 Disclosure Concerning *Exxon Valdez* Oil Spill

Disclosure in 1991 (in part)

On March 24, 1989, the Exxon Valdez, a tanker owned by Exxon Shipping Company, a subsidiary of Exxon Corporation, ran aground on Bligh Reef in Prince William Sound off the port of Valdez, Alaska, and released approximately 260,000 barrels of crude oil. More than 315 lawsuits, including class actions, have been brought in various courts against Exxon Corporation and certain of its subsidiaries.

On October 8, 1991, the United States District Court for the District of Alaska approved a civil agreement and consent decree. . . . These agreements provided for guilty pleas to certain misdemeanors, the dismissal of all felony charges and the remaining misdemeanor charges by the United States, and the release of all civil claims against Exxon . . . by the United States and the state of Alaska. The agreements also released all claims related to or arising from the oil spill by Exxon. . . .

Payments under the plea agreement totaled $125 million—$25 million in fines and $100 million in payments to the United States and Alaska for restoration projects in Alaska. Payments under the civil agreement and consent decree will total $900 million over a ten-year period. The civil agreement also provides for the possible payment, between September 1, 2002, and September 1, 2006, of up to $100 million for substantial loss or decline in populations, habitats, or species in areas affected by the oil spill which could not have been reasonably anticipated on September 25, 1991.

The remaining cost to the corporation from the Valdez accident is difficult to predict and cannot be determined at this time. It is believed the final outcome, net of reserves already provided, will not have a materially adverse effect upon the corporation's operations or financial condition.

Disclosure in 1997 (in part)

On September 24, 1996, the United States District Court for the District of Alaska entered a judgment in the amount of $5.058 billion in the Exxon Valdez civil trial that began in May 1994. The District Court awarded approximately $19.6 million in compensatory damages to fisher plaintiffs, $38 million in prejudgment interest on the compensatory damages and $5 billion in punitive damages to a class composed of all persons and entities who asserted claims for punitive damages from the corporation as a result of the Exxon Valdez grounding. The District Court also ordered that these awards shall bear interest from and after entry of the judgment. The District Court stayed execution on the judgment pending appeal based on a $6.75 billion letter of credit posted by the corporation. Exxon has appealed the judgment. The corporation continues to believe that the punitive damages in this case are unwarranted and that the judgment should be set aside or substantially reduced by the appellate courts. Since it is impossible to estimate what the ultimate earnings impact will be, no charge was taken in 1996 or 1997 related to these verdicts.

Disclosure in 2007 (in part)

A number of lawsuits, including class actions, were brought in various courts against Exxon Mobil Corporation and certain of its subsidiaries relating to the accidental release of crude oil from the tanker Exxon Valdez in 1989. All the compensatory claims have been resolved and paid. All of the punitive damage claims were consolidated in the civil trial that began in 1994. The first judgment from the United States District Court for the District of Alaska in the amount of $5 billion was vacated by the United States Court of Appeals for the Ninth Circuit as being excessive under the Constitution. The second judgment in the amount of $4 billion was vacated by the Ninth Circuit panel without argument and sent back for the District Court to reconsider in light of the recent U.S. Supreme Court decision in Campbell v. State Farm. The most recent District Court judgment for punitive damages was for $4.5 billion plus interest and was entered in January 2004. The Corporation posted a $5.4 billion letter of credit. ExxonMobil and the plaintiffs appealed this decision to the Ninth Circuit, which ruled on December 22, 2006, that the award be reduced to $2.5 billion. On January 12, 2007, ExxonMobil petitioned the Ninth Circuit Court of Appeals for a rehearing en banc of its appeal. On May 23, 2007, with two dissenting opinions, the Ninth Circuit determined not to re-hear ExxonMobil's appeal before the full court. ExxonMobil filed a petition for writ of certiorari to the U.S. Supreme Court on August 20, 2007. On October 29, 2007, the U.S. Supreme Court granted ExxonMobil's petition for a writ of certiorari. Oral argument was held on February 27, 2008. While it is reasonably possible that a liability for punitive damages may have been incurred from the Exxon Valdez grounding, it is not possible to predict the ultimate outcome or to reasonably estimate any such potential liability.

Disclosure in 2009 (in part)

A number of lawsuits, including class actions, were brought in various courts against Exxon Mobil Corporation and certain of its subsidiaries relating to the accidental release of crude oil from the tanker Exxon Valdez in 1989. All the compensatory claims and the punitive damage award have been paid.

Exxon Mobil; 1991, 1997, 2007, and 2009; 10K Report

From 2007 through 2012, the FASB circulated a proposal that would have increased the amount of disclosure related to companies' loss contingencies. Among other things, the FASB proposal would have required companies to provide more detailed, systematic loss contingency disclosure, including a table summarizing the reasons for any increases or decreases in a company's recognized losses relative to contingencies. The FASB received substantial business community pushback to this proposal. Companies expressed concern that increased loss contingency disclosures would prove to be a fishing ground for opposing attorneys looking for negative information. The FASB dropped the proposal in July 2012.

Accounting for Environmental Liabilities

An area that is receiving increasing attention in our society, both politically and from an accounting perspective, is the environment. Most citizens recognize the need to protect our environment and, in many instances, to recover from past environmental abuses. What is not so obvious are the staggering costs associated with environmental liabilities. As but one example, current legislation in the United States mandates the cleanup of existing toxic waste sites. The Environmental Protection Agency (EPA) is empowered to clean up waste sites and then can charge the cleanup costs to those parties the EPA deems responsible. This can cost companies $25 to $100 million or more for each polluted site. The total environmental cleanup obligation in the United States has been estimated to be at least $750 billion and may perhaps exceed $1 trillion.[21]

Even though environmental costs represent one of the critical issues facing businesses today, many, if not most, companies do not fully reflect those costs in their financial statements. The primary reason is that these loss contingencies often cannot be reasonably estimated. As discussed earlier in this chapter, if a liability cannot be reasonably estimated, no amount can be recognized.

In recent years, accounting standard setters have issued several statements and Exposure Drafts designed to improve the environmental liability information reported in the financial statements and notes. The SEC staff has issued *Staff Accounting Bulletin (SAB) No. 92*, which sets forth the SEC's interpretation of GAAP regarding contingent liabilities, with particular applicability to companies having environmental liabilities. In 1996, the AICPA issued *Statement of Position (SOP) 96-1*, "Environmental Remediation Liabilities (Including Auditing Guidance)." *SOP 96-1* outlines key events that can be used to determine whether an environmental liability is probable. For example, if a company acknowledges that it has some responsibility for environmental damage and if an initial cleanup feasibility study has been completed, it is reasonable to assume that the contingent liability is probable and the firm should recognize its share of the total cost. In addition, because a big part of dealing with the cleanup of an environmental site involves legal recovery of cleanup costs from other firms that initially refused to pay for their share of the cleanup, firms are allowed to recognize these potential recoveries as assets if they are probable.

The FASB has codified the accounting standards related to environmental remediation costs in FASB ASC Subtopic 410-30 (Environmental Obligations). Accounting standards related to asset retirement obligations (costs associated with cleaning up after retiring a long-term asset) are included in FASB ASC Subtopic 410-20 (Asset Retirement Obligations) and are discussed in Chapters 10 and 11.

---

[21] American Society of Civil Engineers, **http://www.asce.org/pressroom/publicpolicy/vgwaste.cfm**, July 8, 2002.

SEGMENT REPORTING

Who sells more soft drinks, Coca-Cola or PepsiCo? Coke sells more soft drinks in the United States, with a 2011 market share of 41.9%, compared to 28.5% for Pepsi.[22] So how is it that PepsiCo employs 297,000 people, whereas Coke employs just 146,200? The answer is that PepsiCo does much more than sell soft drinks. PepsiCo's revenue is split 50–50 between its food (Frito-Lay and Quaker Oats) and soft drink (Pepsi-Cola) segments. Which business strategy is more successful, the concentrated strategy of Coke or the diversified strategy of Pepsi? In recent years, the focused approach of Coke has been the winner; the July 2012 market value of The Coca-Cola Company was $176 billion, which is greater than the $109 billion of PepsiCo. An attempt at increased focus was behind the October 1997 strategic change of direction at PepsiCo involving the spinoff of its restaurant businesses (Pizza Hut, Taco Bell, and KFC) to focus more attention on soft drinks and snack foods.[23]

Like PepsiCo, many businesses today are large, complex organizations engaged in a variety of activities that bear little relationship to each other. For example, a company might manufacture airplane engines, operate a real estate business, and manage a professional hockey team. Such companies, referred to as diversified companies, or conglomerates, operate in multiple industries and do not fit into any one specific industry category. The different segments of a diversified company often operate in distinct and separate markets, involve different management teams, and experience different growth patterns, profit potentials, and degrees of risk. In effect, the segments of the company behave almost like, and in some cases are, separate companies within an overall corporate structure. Yet, if only total company information is presented for a highly diversified company, the different degrees of risk, profitability, and growth potential for major segments of the company cannot be analyzed and compared.

Business Segments

LO7 学习目标7
按生产线和地理区域编制必要的追加财务信息披露。

 Prepare the necessary supplemental disclosures of financial information by product line and by geographic area.

Historically, the United States has led the world in the quality and quantity of financial information required to be disclosed about business segments. In 1939, U.S. companies were encouraged to make separate disclosures concerning operations of foreign business segments because of the "disturbed conditions abroad"—polite language for World War II.[24] Increased creation of firms with many diverse lines of business in the 1960s caused the APB to issue a nonbinding statement encouraging diversified companies to provide summary business segment information to financial statement users. The segment disclosure rules were refined and made mandatory in 1976 with the issuance of pre-Codification *Statement No. 14* by the FASB.

Information to be disclosed in the financial statement notes under the provisions of FASB *Statement No. 14* included revenues, operating profit, and identifiable assets for each significant industry segment of a company. Other provisions of *Statement No. 14* required disclosure of revenues from major customers and information about foreign operations and export sales.

---

[22] "Top-10 CSD [Carbonated Soft-Drinks] for 2011," *Beverage Digest*, March 20, 2012.
[23] Lori Bongiorno, "Fiddling with the Formula at Pepsi?" *Business Week*, October 14, 1996, p. 42; and Nikhil Deogun, "Pepsi Has Had Its Fill of Pizza, Tacos, Chicken," *The Wall Street Journal*, January 24, 1997, p. B1.
[24] The information in this historical review is adapted from the following source: *Research Report* (prepared by Paul Pacter), "Reporting Disaggregated Information" (Norwalk, CT: Financial Accounting Standards Board, February 1993).

Although the disclosure required of U.S. companies under pre-Codification *Statement No. 14* was more extensive than the segment disclosure required by the accounting standards of any other country in the world, financial statement users have consistently requested that firms be required to disclose more. In 1994, the AICPA Special Committee on Financial Reporting (often called the *Jenkins Committee*) made the improvement of segment reporting its first recommendation. In response to this push for even better segment reporting, the FASB issued pre-Codification *Statement No. 131* in June 1997. In an early example of international cooperation in creating accounting standards, the FASB worked closely with the Accounting Standards Board in Canada and with the International Accounting Standards Board in developing the segment reporting standard. The provisions of pre-Codification *Statement No. 131* are now contained in FASB ASC Topic 280 (Segment Reporting).

According to the provisions of FASB ASC Topic 280, companies are required to disclose the following information concerning business segments:

1. Total segment operating profit or loss
2. Amounts of certain income statement items such as operating revenues, depreciation, interest revenue, interest expense, tax expense, and significant noncash expenses
3. Total segment assets
4. Total capital expenditures
5. Reconciliation of the sum of segment totals to the company total for each of the following items:
   - Revenues
   - Operating profit
   - Assets

In addition to these five items, companies must also disclose how operating segments are identified. Segments are to be identified using the same criteria, whatever they might be, used by management to distinguish business segments for internal reporting purposes. The objective of this requirement is to provide external users with the same type of information about business segments that is used internally. Some companies were concerned about this definition of reportable business segments because they have dozens or even hundreds of internally reportable segments. The FASB responded to this concern by specifying how large a segment must be for separate disclosure to be required. Specifically, a segment is reportable if it meets any one of the following three criteria:

- *Revenue test.* A segment should be reported if its total revenue (both to external customers and to other internal segments) is 10% or more of the company's total revenue (external and internal).
- *Profit test.* A segment should be reported if the absolute value of its operating profit (or loss) is more than 10% of the total of the operating profit for all segments that reported profits (or the total of the losses for all segments that reported losses).
- *Asset test.* A segment should be reported if it contains 10% or more of the combined assets of all operating segments.

The FASB also decided that segments can be combined for reporting purposes, even if they are treated as separate segments internally, if the segments have similar products or services, similar processes, similar customers, similar distribution methods, and are subject to similar regulations.

Companies typically define their business segments in terms of product lines or geographic areas. For those firms defining their segments along product lines, the FASB

如果一个业务分部满足以下三个标准中的任何一个，就要进行单独披露：
- 收入测试。如果一个分部的总收入（包括出售给外部顾客和出售给内部其他分部的收入）大于或等于公司（外部和内部）总收入的10%，那么该分部应当单独报告；
- 利润测试。如果一个分部的营业利润（或者亏损）的绝对值大于或等于所有报告营业利润的分部的利润总额（或者所有报告营业亏损的分部的亏损总额）的10%，那么该分部应当单独报告。
- 资产测试。如果一个经营分部的资产大于或等于所有经营分部总资产的10%，那么该分部应当单独报告。

> **FYI**
>
> The FASB received more than 200 comment letters in response to its June 1996 Exposure Draft for pre-Codification *Statement No. 131*. A key concern of businesses was that the Exposure Draft required them to disclose information that might be used by competitors. In response to these concerns, the FASB dropped the original proposal that firms be required to report research and development expenditures and liabilities by segment.

requires additional disclosure of revenues and long-lived assets for the company's home country and for all foreign operations combined. If one foreign country comprises a material portion of operations, separate revenue and long-lived asset disclosure should be made for that country. A company may consider also showing revenue and long-lived asset subtotals for "groups" of countries, such as for Europe or Asia.

For companies defining their business segments geographically, additional revenue information must be disclosed by product line. This product line information is provided on a companywide basis, however, not by geographic segment.

Companies are also required to disclose supplemental information about major customers. If revenues from any one customer are more than 10% of total revenue, this fact must be disclosed (although the name of the customer isn't disclosed) along with the amount of the revenue and the names of the operating segments in which the revenue is reported.

To illustrate the type of business segment disclosure provided under FASB ASC Topic 280, the segment information given in the 2011 annual report of PepsiCo will be used. PepsiCo discloses that it has six reportable segments, as follows:

- Frito-Lay North America (PepsiCo defines North America to be the United States and Canada.)
- Quaker Foods North America
- Latin America Foods
- PepsiCo Americas Beverages
- Europe
- Asia, Middle East & Africa

Exhibit 19-4 contains information on PepsiCo's sales and operating profit by segment.

Notice that the bulk of PepsiCo's sales and operating profit occur in North America. In addition to this sales, operating profit, and total asset disclosure, PepsiCo gives information, by segment, on amortization of intangibles, depreciation, and capital spending.

Application of accounting principles to individual segments of a business presents some unique problems. For example, if a firm uses LIFO and all of the inventory is part of one LIFO pool for financial reporting purposes, how is LIFO to be applied in calculating cost of goods sold for individual segments? Another example is the allocation of income tax expense to different segments when the income tax return is prepared for the entire company as a whole. Because of difficulties such as these, the FASB states in Topic 280 that, for segment reporting purposes, firms are to report to external users following the same accounting practices that are used for internal purposes. What this means is that the financial data reported in the segment disclosures won't always conform

> **Stop & Think**
>
> How could The Coca-Cola Company use PepsiCo's reported segment information to aid it in formulating its competitive strategy?
> a) To compute total company sales
> b) To compute total company return on equity
> c) To compute segment profit margins
> d) To determine segment advertising strategies

Exhibit 19-4 | Net Sales, Operating Profit, and Total Assets by Reportable Segment, for PepsiCo

BUSINESS SEGMENTS Net Revenue: (In millions of dollars)	2011	2010	2009
Frito-Lay North America	$13,322	$12,573	$12,421
Quaker Foods North America	2,656	2,656	2,687
Latin America Foods	7,156	6,315	5,703
PepsiCo Americas Beverages	22,418	20,401	10,116
Europe	13,560	9,602	7,028
Asia, Middle East & Africa	7,392	6,291	5,277
Total division	$66,504	$57,838	$43,232

Operating Profit: (In millions of dollars)	2011	2010	2009
Frito-Lay North America	$ 3,621	$ 3,376	$ 3,105
Quaker Foods North America	797	741	781
Latin America Foods	1,078	1,004	904
PepsiCo Americas Beverages	3,273	2,776	2,172
Europe	1,210	1,054	948
Asia, Middle East & Africa	887	708	700
Total division	$10,866	$ 9,659	$ 8,610

Total Assets: (In millions of dollars)	2011	2010	2009
Frito-Lay North America	$ 6,120	$ 6,027	$ 6,093
Quaker Foods North America	1,174	1,217	1,241
Latin America Foods	4,731	4,053	3,575
PepsiCo Americas Beverages	31,187	31,622	7,670
Europe	18,479	13,032	9,471
Asia, Middle East & Africa	6,048	5,569	4,787
Total division	$67,739	$61,520	$32,837

© Cengage Learning 2014

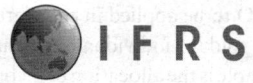

with GAAP. The FASB views this as part of the price to be paid to reduce the incremental bookkeeping cost required for firms to provide segment information. With the release of *IFRS 8* in November 2006, the IASB adopted this same method of identifying reportable segments.

In summary, consider the question of how much segment information is enough. Of course, when asked whether they want more information or less, financial statement users will always reply that they want more. Ultimately, every user would like unlimited access to the accounting records of all companies. Understandably, companies are reluctant to disclose everything to everyone. The FASB must set segment reporting standards to balance users' desire for relevant data against firms' legitimate concern about disclosing proprietary information.

INTERIM REPORTING

The Business Roundtable is an organization of approximately 160 CEOs of top U.S. corporations. On August 20, 1990, The Business Roundtable sent a letter to one of the commissioners of the SEC.[25] The letter was critical of the work of the FASB and suggested that FASB rules were burdening U.S. business "with a costly reporting infrastructure that overloads the user with data but provides very little insight into the economic condition or results of the enterprise." The Roundtable also complained that FASB rules were putting U.S. firms at a competitive disadvantage overseas where foreign accounting standard setters are more sympathetic to business concerns.

One of the specific problem areas identified by The Business Roundtable was quarterly reporting. The Roundtable described quarterly reports as being very costly in terms of preparation and counterproductive because they cause management to focus on short-term earnings rather than long-term growth.

The Roundtable pointed out that many foreign companies (such as those in the United Kingdom) are required to report only semiannually.

This concern about the counterproductivity of quarterly reporting was echoed by Peter A. Magowan, then-CEO of Safeway, the large supermarket chain based in Oakland, California. In November 1986, Safeway was taken private in a $5.3 billion leveraged buyout (LBO). In looking back on the success of the restructuring that followed the LBO, Magowan reported that one of the key advantages enjoyed by Safeway was that as a private company, it was no longer locked into the cycle of fixation on reported quarterly earnings. According to Magowan, this freedom from pressure to report ever-increasing quarterly profits made it possible for Safeway to institute aggressive pricing, store expansion, and increased spending for training and technology—all actions that would hurt reported profits in the short run but were for the long-term good of the company.[26]

In spite of concerns that quarterly reports lead to a myopic focus on short-term profits by management, they are still required disclosure in the United States. Publicly traded firms must file quarterly financial statements with the SEC in a 10-Q filing within 40 days of the end of the quarter for large firms and 45 days for smaller firms. An outline of the special problems associated with the preparation of interim reports is given in this module.

Interim Reports

 Recognize the importance of interim reports, and outline the difficulties encountered when preparing those reports.

LO8 学习目标8
认识中期报告的重要性，并概括编制这些报告时遇到的困难。

Statements showing financial position and operating results for intervals of less than a year are referred to as interim financial statements. Interim reports are considered essential in providing investors and others with timely information as to the position and progress of an enterprise. Notwithstanding the need for interim reports, significant difficulties are associated with them. One problem is caused by the seasonal factors of certain businesses. For example, in some companies, revenues fluctuate widely among interim periods; in other businesses, significant fixed costs are incurred during a single period but are to benefit several periods. Not only must costs be allocated to appropriate periods of benefit but also they must be matched against the realized revenues for the interim period to determine a reasonable income measurement.

---

[25] John S. Reed, Chairman, Accounting Principles Task Force of The Business Roundtable; letter dated August 20, 1990, addressed to Philip R. Lochner, Jr., Commissioner, Securities and Exchange Commission.
[26] Peter A. Magowan, "The Case for LBOs: The Safeway Experience," *California Management Review*, Fall 1989, p. 9. In April 1990, Safeway again issued shares to the public.

In preparing interim reports, adjustments for accrued items, generally required only at year-end, must be considered at the end of each interim period. Because of the additional time and extra costs involved to develop complete information, many estimates of expenses are made for interim reports. The increased number of estimates adds an element of subjectivity to these reports. Another problem is that extraordinary items or the disposal of a business segment will have a greater impact on an interim period's earnings than on the results of operations for an entire year. In analyzing interim financial statements, special attention should be given to these and similar considerations.

Two prominent viewpoints exist in relation to the reporting of interim results. One viewpoint is that each reporting interval is to be recognized as a separate accounting period. Thus, the results of operations for each interim period are determined in essentially the same manner as for the annual accounting period. Under this approach, the same judgments, estimations, accruals, and deferrals are recognized at the end of each interim period as for the annual period. This is the approach followed in *IAS 34*.

The other viewpoint, and the one accepted by the FASB, is that the interim period is an integral part of the annual period.[27] Essentially, the revenues and expenses for the total period are allocated among interim periods on some reasonable basis, for example, time, sales volume, or productive activity. Under the integral part of annual period concept, the same general accounting principles and reporting practices employed for annual reports are to be utilized for interim statements, but modifications may be required so the interim results will better relate to the total results of operations for the annual period. As an example of the type of modification that may be required, assume that a company uses the LIFO method of inventory valuation and encounters a situation where liquidation of the base period inventory occurs at an interim date but the inventory is expected to be replaced by the end of the annual period. Under these circumstances, the inventory reported at the interim date should not reflect the LIFO liquidation, and the cost of goods sold for the interim period should include the expected cost of replacing the liquidated LIFO base.

integral part of annual period concept
年度报告的重要组成部分

Another example of a required modification deals with a change in accounting principle during an interim period. As explained in Chapter 20, these changes should follow the provisions of FASB ASC Topic 250 (Accounting Changes and Error Corrections). Those provisions state that the change should be applied retroactively to all of the results reported.[28]

Stop & Think

What is the biggest barrier to the release of *daily* financial statements by publicly traded companies?
a) Generation of daily stock price data
b) Generation of daily accounting estimates
c) Generation of daily sales data
d) Generation of daily cost of goods sold data

To illustrate the added insight that quarterly information can provide, quarterly data for **Toys "R" Us** from its 2011 annual report are provided in Exhibit 19-5. The retail toy business is very seasonal, and this fact is reflected in the quarterly numbers for Toys "R" Us. Reported revenue is at its maximum in the quarter that concludes at the end of January (the fourth quarter), which encompasses the Christmas selling season. Anyone reading only the annual net income numbers of Toys "R" Us misses the potentially valuable information contained in the wide variation in net income from quarter to quarter.

---

[27] FASB ASC paragraphs 270-10-45-1 and 2.
[28] FASB ASC paragraphs 250-10-45-14 through 16.

Exhibit 19-5 | Summary Quarterly Data for Toys "R" Us

Quarterly Financial Data
(In millions)

The following table sets forth certain unaudited quarterly financial information:

	First Quarter	Second Quarter	Third Quarter	Fourth Quarter
2011 Net Sales	$2,636	$2,648	$2,700	$5,925
2011 Gross Margin	978	1,025	986	1,981
2011 Net Earnings/(Loss)	(67)	(34)	(93)	343
2010 Net Sales	2,608	2,565	2,719	5,972
2010 Gross Margin	945	959	987	2,034
2010 Net Earnings/(Loss)	(56)	(14)	(93)	330

Toys "R" Us, 2011, 10K Report

Notice that Toys "R" Us' quarterly results are labeled "unaudited." Obviously, the small amount of information provided about each quarter does not "present fairly" the results of Toys "R" Us' operations for that quarter. Accordingly, quarterly reports are almost always labeled "unaudited" because they do not fairly present a firm's operations, cash flows, and financial position in the same way as do the annual financial statements that are audited. Quarterly reports submitted to the SEC in the 10-Q filing are not required to be audited although they are to be prepared in accordance with GAAP.

Stop & Think SOLUTIONS

1. (Page 19-8) The correct answer is A. Credit risk is the uncertainty over whether the party on the other side of an agreement will abide by the terms of the agreement. A forward contract is a private agreement negotiated between two parties. There is always the possibility that the party required to make the settlement payment at the end of the forward contract will refuse to pay. Accordingly, there is credit risk associated with a forward contract.

2. (Page 19-31) The correct answer is C. PepsiCo's segment information can tell Coke where Pepsi is enjoying the most soft drink success, where PepsiCo is weak, and what PepsiCo's profit margins are. The profit margin information is probably the most useful to Coca-Cola. Without any disclosure by Pepsi, market research can probably tell Coca-Cola where Pepsi's strengths and weaknesses are with regard to sales. However, the information about Pepsi's costs and profits is hard to find out unless Pepsi discloses it.

3. (Page 19-34) The correct answer is B. Technically, it is possible right now for most large firms to prepare daily financial statements. And many firms actually do compile daily sales and gross profit reports. However, it isn't clear whether making the estimates necessary to prepare full financial statements would provide useful information. As discussed in the chapter, even the preparation of quarterly reports requires more estimates and approximations than does the preparation of the annual report. The cost of the timeliness of daily reports very likely exceeds any associated benefit.

SOLUTION TO USING THE FASB'S CODIFICATION

In FASB ASC Topic 815 (Derivatives and Hedging), you can see listed Subtopic 815-45 (Weather Derivatives). This is a good indication that "weather derivatives" actually exist. Clicking on the Glossary yields the following definition of a "weather derivative": "A forward-based or option-based contract for which settlement is based on a climatic or geological variable. One example of such a variable is the occurrence or nonoccurrence of a specified amount of snow at a specified location within a specified period of time."

Section 815-45-55 provides some illustrations of accounting for a weather derivative. The weather derivative used in the illustration is based on daily temperature. The firms involved in the weather derivative arrangement are described as follows: "Entity A is a construction materials entity that has its sales decrease during cold winters or a chemical manufacturer that has its natural gas consumption costs increase during cold winters. Entity B is a natural gas distribution entity that experiences lower revenues during warm winters." Whether the company receives cash or pays cash under the weather derivative contract depends on the average temperature for a specified period.

Review Chapter 19 Learning Objectives

DERIVATIVES

❶ Understand the business and accounting concepts connected with derivatives and hedging activities.

Uncertainty about the future fair value of assets and liabilities or about future cash flows exposes firms to risk. One way to manage this risk is through the use of derivatives. A *derivative* is a financial instrument or other contract that derives its value from the movement of prices, interest rates, or exchange rates associated with an underlying item. Many derivatives are executory contracts, meaning that they are not a transaction but are an exchange of promises about future actions.

❷ Identify the different types of risk faced by a business.

Of the many types of risk faced by a firm, four important types are as follows:

- *Price risk*. Uncertainty about the future price of an asset
- *Credit risk*. Uncertainty over whether the party on the other side of a transaction will abide by the terms of the agreement
- *Interest rate risk*. Uncertainty about future interest rates and their impact on cash flows and the fair value of financial instruments
- *Exchange rate risk*. Uncertainty about the future U.S. dollar cash flows stemming from assets and liabilities denominated in foreign currencies

❸ Describe the characteristics of the following types of derivatives: swaps, forwards, futures, and options.

- *Swap*. Contract in which two parties agree to exchange payments in the future based upon some price or rate. A good example is the exchange of a stream of variable-rate interest payments for a stream of fixed-rate payments. A swap can transform the stream of future cash flows that you have into the cash flow stream that you want.
- *Forwards*. Agreement between two parties to exchange a specified amount of a commodity, security, or foreign currency at a specified date with the price or rate being set now. Forward contracts are usually settled with cash payments instead of by actual delivery of the underlying asset.
- *Futures*. Very similar to a forward contract, with the difference being that a futures contract is a standardized instrument that is sponsored by and traded on an organized exchange.
- *Option*. Contract giving the owner the right, but not the obligation, to buy or sell an asset at a specified exercise price. A *call option* gives the owner the right to buy an asset; a *put option* gives the owner the right to sell an asset. The buyer of an option must pay cash in advance for the option; in exchange, the buyer is protected against unfavorable price or rate movements but can still benefit from favorable movements.

4 **Define *hedging*, and outline the difference between a fair value hedge and a cash flow hedge.**

Hedging is the structuring of transactions to reduce risk. Much hedging occurs naturally in business as increases in costs or in the value of liabilities are offset by related increases in revenues or in the value of assets. Derivatives are also used for hedging. The FASB has identified two general types of hedges for which derivatives can be used:

- *Fair value hedge.* The change in the fair value of the derivative offsets changes in fair values of assets or liabilities
- *Cash flow hedge.* Cash flows from the derivative offset variability in the cash flows from forecasted transactions

5 **Account for a variety of different derivatives and for hedging relationships.**

The fair value of all derivatives is to be recognized and reported in the balance sheet. Changes in fair value are reported as follows:

- *Derivative is not a hedge.* Changes in fair value are reported as gains or losses in the income statement.
- *Derivative is a fair value hedge.* Changes in fair value are reported as gains or losses in the income statement and are offset by gains or losses on changes in the fair value of the asset or liability being hedged.
- *Derivative is a cash flow hedge.* Changes in fair value are deferred and reported in comprehensive income (an equity adjustment). These deferred gains and losses are recognized in income on the forecasted date of the cash flows being hedged.

CONTINGENCIES

6 **Apply the accounting rules for contingent items to the areas of lawsuits and environmental liabilities.**

If a contingent liability is probable and can be reasonably estimated, it should be recognized in the financial statements. If a contingent liability is only possible, it should be disclosed in the financial statement notes. Contingent liabilities that are remote should not, in general, be disclosed. Contingent assets are generally not recognized until any remaining uncertainty is very small.

In accounting for lawsuits, firms are usually reluctant to disclose specific amounts or to overestimate the likelihood of losing the suit because they don't want to increase their chances of losing the lawsuit or of paying a large judgment amount.

Accounting for environmental remediation liabilities is complicated by the fact that the future cost of the cleanup is very difficult to estimate. In addition, each cleanup project is surrounded by suits and countersuits between government agencies and the responsible firms and among the responsible firms themselves. The SEC requires substantial disclosure of the details of a firm's environmental cleanup projects.

SEGMENT REPORTING

7 **Prepare the necessary supplemental disclosures of financial information by product line and by geographic area.**

Historically, segment reporting in the United States has been more extensive than in any other country. The FASB worked with the AcSB in Canada and with the IASB to improve segment reporting worldwide.

Under the provisions of FASB ASC Topic 280, companies are required to disclose the following information for each business segment: revenues, operating profit, assets, capital expenditures, and certain income statement items such as depreciation and interest revenue and expense.

Companies are to define their reportable business segments using the same practice that is used internally. The objective of this requirement is to provide external users the same type of segment information used inside the company.

INTERIM REPORTING

8 **Recognize the importance of interim reports, and outline the difficulties encountered when preparing those reports.**

In the United States, publicly traded firms are required to file quarterly summary financial statements with the SEC in a filing called a *10-Q*. These interim financial statements are prepared using the "integral part of annual period" concept. Using this concept, each quarter is not viewed as a separate period but as an integral part of the year, and estimates are used to appropriately allocate a share of the annual results to each quarter. Quarterly reports are typically not audited, but they still are to be prepared in accordance with GAAP.

FASB-IASB CODIFICATION SUMMARY

Topic	FASB Accounting Standards Codification	Original FASB Standard	Corresponding IASB Standard	Differences between U.S. GAAP and IFRS
Accounting for derivatives	Topic 815	SFAS No. 133	IAS 39	No substantial differences at the conceptual level, but numerous technical differences that are beyond the scope of this book.
Recognition of contingent liabilities and contingent assets	Contingent liabilities: Section 450-20-25 Contingent assets: Section 450-30-25	SFAS No. 5 par. 3 and 17	IAS 37 par. 10, 27-28, 31, 34	Generally the same. Under IFRS, there is no requirement to disclose contingent guarantee obligations when their likelihood is remote.
Measurement of contingent liabilities	Section 450-20-30 par. 1	FIN No. 14 par. 3	IAS 37 par. 36-47	Under U.S. GAAP, the estimated liability is the low end of the estimated range if each estimate in the range is equally likely. Under IFRS, the estimated liability is the amount required to settle the obligation.
Segment reporting	Topic 280	SFAS No. 131	IFRS 8	No substantial differences
Relation between interim reporting and annual reporting	Section 270-10-45 par. 1-2	APB Opinion No. 28 par. 9	IAS 34 par. 28	Under U.S. GAAP, an interim period is viewed as a subcomponent of the annual period. Under IFRS, accounting principles are applied to an interim period in the same way they are applied to an annual period.

KEY TERMS

Call option 19-10
Cash flow hedge 19-12
Conglomerates 19-29
Contingent gains 19-22
Contingent losses 19-22
Credit risk 19-5
Derivative 19-3
Exchange rate risk 19-6
Executory contract 19-4
Fair value hedge 19-12
Forward contract 19-7
Futures contract 19-9
Hedging 19-11
Integral part of annual period concept 19-34
Interest rate risk 19-5
Interest rate swap 19-7
Interim financial statements 19-33
Notional amount 19-14
Option 19-10
Price risk 19-5
Put option 19-10
Swap 19-7

Tutorial Activities

Tutorial Activities with author-written, content-specific feedback, available on *CengageNOW for Stice & Stice*.

QUESTIONS

DERIVATIVES

1. How does a derivative differ from other financial instruments and contracts?
2. Why is a derivative often an executory contract? Give another example of an executory contract.
3. Briefly describe the four types of risk discussed in the chapter.
4. Why would a company enter into an interest rate swap?
5. What is the difference between a forward contract and a futures contract?
6. How does an option differ from the other types of derivatives discussed in the chapter?
7. Describe the purpose of a cash flow hedge, and give an example of a cash flow hedge.
8. Why is traditional historical cost accounting inappropriate when accounting for derivative contracts?
9. When does partial hedge ineffectiveness occur?
10. Derivatives are to be reported in the balance sheet at their fair value on the balance sheet date. How are unrealized gains and losses on derivatives recognized in the financial statements?
11. What is the notional amount of a derivative? How can the notional amount be misleading?
12. A derivative used as an economic hedge of foreign currency risk associated with a foreign currency–denominated asset or liability is not accounted for as a hedge under the provisions of FASB ASC Topic 815 (Derivatives and Hedging). How are these derivatives accounted for?
13. How does the accounting for a speculative derivative investment differ from that for a derivative that serves as a hedge?
14. What international standard governs the accounting for derivatives? How does this standard differ from U.S. GAAP?

CONTINGENCIES

15. How should contingent liabilities that are reasonably possible of becoming liabilities be reported in the financial statements?
16. Describe the appropriate treatment of contingent gains.
17. What factors are important in deciding whether a pending lawsuit should be reported as a liability on the balance sheet?
18. What factors must a company consider in estimating the amount to recognize for a probable contingent liability?
19. Under what circumstances should the existence of an environmental liability be considered "probable"?

SEGMENT REPORTING

20. In what ways can segment information assist in the analysis of a company's financial statements?
21. How is a business segment to be identified under the provisions of FASB ASC Topic 280 (Segment Reporting)?
22. How large must an internally defined segment be for separate financial statement disclosure to be required?
23. Is segment information prepared according to GAAP? Explain.

INTERIM REPORTING

24. Distinguish between the two primary viewpoints concerning the preparation of interim financial statements.
25. Why should investors be careful in interpreting interim reports?

PRACTICE EXERCISES

Practice 19-1

The Mechanics of a Derivative Contract

Skull Valley Airlines is a passenger airline. One of Skull Valley's primary expenses is the cost of aviation fuel. Of course, the cost of aviation fuel is heavily influenced by the worldwide price of oil which is known to fluctuate dramatically from year to year or even from month to month. It is February of Year 1. Skull Valley wishes to enter into a forward contract that will hedge the cost of the aviation fuel it will purchase in November of Year 1. Skull Valley plans to use 700,000 gallons of aviation fuel in November. On February 1, Skull Valley entered into a forward contract with Speculator A to purchase 700,000 gallons of aviation fuel from Speculator A for delivery on November 1 at a price of $5.50 per gallon As you know, derivative contracts, such as this forward contract, are rarely settled through actual delivery of the underlying item (700,000 gallons of aviation fuel in this example). Instead, a net cash payment is made from one of the parties in the contract to the other party. What net cash payment will be made on November 1 in each of the following circumstances: (1) Price of aviation fuel is $4.50 per gallon? (2) Price of aviation fuel is $5.00 per gallon? (3) Price of aviation fuel is $5.50 per gallon? (4) Price of aviation fuel is $6.00 per gallon? [Note:

Make sure to state both the amount of the net cash payment and the direction of the payment (from Skull Valley to Speculator A or from Speculator A to Skull Valley)].

Practice 19-2

Understanding the Terms of an Interest Rate Swap
On January 1 of Year 1, the company entered into a two-year $100,000 variable interest rate loan. In the first year of the loan, the interest rate is 10%. In its second year, the interest rate is equal to the prime lending rate on January 1 of Year 2. The company does not want to bear the risk associated with the uncertain interest rate in the second year. Accordingly, on January 1 of Year 1, the company enters into a pay-fixed, receive-variable interest rate swap with a speculator. This swap obligates the company to pay the speculator a fixed amount of $10,000 ($100,000 × 0.10) on December 31 of Year 2. In return, the company will receive from the speculator on December 31 of Year 2 a variable amount equal to $100,000 multiplied by the prime lending rate on January 1 of Year 2. This amount received from the speculator is exactly enough to pay the interest due on the variable-rate loan in Year 2. Typically, interest rate swaps such as this are settled with a single net cash payment rather than the actual payment of $10,000 and receipt of the variable amount. What net amount will the company pay or receive on December 31 of Year 2 if the prime lending rate on January 1 of Year 2 is (1) 7%, (2) 15%, and (3) 10%?

Practice 19-3

Understanding the Impact of an Interest Rate Swap
Refer to Practice 19-2 and complete the following:

1. Compute the total amount (including all swap-related cash flows) that the company will pay in interest in Year 2, assuming that the prime lending rate on January 1 of Year 2 is (a) 7%, (b) 15%, and (c) 10%. Comment on your computations.
2. When the speculator entered into the interest rate swap agreement on January 1 of Year 1, which direction did the speculator think that interest rates were going to go—up or down? Explain.

Practice 19-4

Understanding the Terms of a Forward Contract
The company is a golf course developer that constructs approximately 15 courses per year. Next year, the company will buy 5,000 trees to install in the courses it builds. In recent years, the price of trees has fluctuated wildly. To eliminate this uncertainty, the company has found a reputable financial institution that will enter into a forward contract for 5,000 trees. On January 1 of Year 1, the company agrees to buy 5,000 trees on January 1 of Year 2 from the financial institution. The price is set at $400 per tree. Of course, the financial institution doesn't own any trees. As with most derivative contracts, this agreement will be settled by an exchange of cash on January 1 of Year 2 based on the price of trees on that date. What net amount will the golf course developer pay or receive on January 1 of Year 2 under the forward contract if the price of each tree on that date is (1) $250, (2) $600, and (3) $400? Remember that the forward contract was for 5,000 trees.

Practice 19-5

Understanding the Impact of a Forward Contract
Refer to Practice 19-4 and complete the following:

1. Compute the total amount (including all forward-related cash flows) that the golf course developer will pay to buy 5,000 trees in Year 2, assuming that the price of a tree on January 1 of Year 2 is (a) $250, (b) $600, and (c) $400. Comment on your computations.
2. When the financial institution entered into the tree forward contract on January 1 of Year 1, which direction did the financial institution think that tree prices were going to go—up or down? Explain.

Practice 19-6

Understanding the Terms of a Futures Contract
The mining company produces 25,000 pounds of copper each month in its mining operations. To eliminate the price risk associated with copper sales, on December 1 of Year 1, the mining company entered into a futures contract to sell 25,000 pounds of copper on January 1 of Year 2. The futures price is $0.77 per pound. The futures contract is managed through an exchange, so the mining company does not know the party on the other side of the contract. As with most derivative contracts, this futures contract will be settled by an exchange of cash on January 1 of Year 2 based on the price of copper on that date. What net amount will the mining company pay or receive on January 1 of Year 2 under the futures contract if the price of copper per pound on that date is (1) $0.62, (2) $0.88, and (3) $0.77? Remember that the futures contract is for 25,000 pounds and that the mining company is selling the copper.

Practice 19-7
Understanding the Impact of a Futures Contract
Refer to Practice 19-6 and complete the following:

1. Compute the total amount (including all futures-related cash flows) that the mining company will receive to sell 25,000 pounds of copper in January of Year 2, assuming that the price of copper per pound on January 1 of Year 2 is (a) $0.62, (b) $0.88, and (c) $0.77. Comment on your computations.
2. Assume that the party on the other side of the futures contract was a speculator. When that speculator entered into the copper futures contract on December 1 of Year 1, which direction did the speculator think that copper prices were going to go—up or down? Explain.

Practice 19-8
Understanding the Terms of an Option Contract
The company makes colorful 100% cotton shirts that are very popular among sophisticated business executives. The company uses 100,000 pounds of cotton each month in its production process. On December 1 of Year 1, the company purchased a call option to buy 100,000 pounds of cotton on January 1 of Year 2. The option exercise price is $0.39 per pound. It cost the company $2,500 to buy this option. As with most derivative contracts, this option contract will be settled by an exchange of cash on January 1 of Year 2 based on the price of cotton on that date. What net amount will the shirt company pay or receive on January 1 of Year 2 under the option contract if the price of cotton per pound on that date is (1) $0.52, (2) $0.30, and (3) $0.39? Remember that the option contract is for 100,000 pounds and that the shirt company has the option to buy the cotton.

Practice 19-9
Understanding the Impact of an Option Contract
Refer to Practice 19-8 and complete the following:

1. Compute the total amount (including all option-related cash flows) that the shirt company will pay to buy 100,000 pounds of cotton in January of Year 2, assuming that the price of cotton per pound on January 1 of Year 2 is (a) $0.52, (b) $0.30, and (c) $0.39. Comment on your computations.
2. Assume that the party who wrote the cotton call option contract was a speculator. When that speculator wrote the cotton call option on December 1 of Year 1, which direction did the speculator think that cotton prices were going to go—up or down? Explain.

Practice 19-10
Understanding the Impact of Overhedging: Interest Rate Swap
Refer to Practice 19-2 and Practice 19-3. What would be the impact on the company's total cash payment in Year 2 if the pay-fixed, receive-variable interest rate swap had been based on a loan amount of $300,000 instead of $100,000? In other words, what would be the company's total cash payment in Year 2 if the variable-rate loan is $100,000 but the interest rate swap is for a $300,000 loan and the January 1 of Year 2 prime lending rate is (1) 7%, (2) 15%, and (3) 10%? Comment on your computations.

Practice 19-11
Understanding the Impact of Partial Hedging: Forward Contract
Refer to Practice 19-4 and Practice 19-5. What would be the impact on the golf course developer's total cash payment to purchase trees in Year 2 if the forward contract had been for just 1,500 trees rather than the full 5,000 trees expected to be purchased in Year 2? In other words, what would be the golf course developer's total cash payment in Year 2 if it purchases 5,000 trees but the forward contract is for 1,500 trees and the January 1 of Year 2 tree price is (1) $250, (2) $600, and (3) $400? Comment on your computations.

Practice 19-12
Overview of Accounting for Derivatives: Fair Value Hedge
On December 1 of Year 1, the company made a $100,000 investment in a highly risky Internet stock. The investment is classified as a trading security. Part of the investment agreement prevents the company from selling the investment before January 1 of Year 2. To remove uncertainty about fluctuations in the value of the investment, the company entered into a forward contract with a speculator. Under the forward contract, the company will sell the investment to the speculator on January 1 of Year 2 for $100,000. (*Note*: For simplicity, ignore the inconsistency in the fact that the securities are classified as trading yet the forward contract guarantees that the company will not earn any return when the securities are sold.) Make all journal entries necessary on December 31 of Year 1 in connection with both the investment securities and the forward contract, assuming that the market value of the securities on December 31 is (1) $130,000, (2) $75,000, and (3) $100,000.

Practice 19-13

Overview of Accounting for Derivatives: Cash Flow Hedge
A farmer expects to sell 5,000 bushels of corn on January 1 of Year 2. On December 1 of Year 1, the farmer enters into a futures contract to sell the corn on January 1 of Year 2 at $2.30 per bushel. The market price of corn on December 1 was also $2.30 per bushel. Make all journal entries necessary on December 31 of Year 1 in connection with the futures contract, assuming that the market price of corn per bushel on December 31 is (1) $2.50, (2) $2.15, and (3) $2.30.

Practice 19-14

Computing the Notional Amount
Compute the notional amount of the derivative contract for each of the following:

1. The interest rate swap contract. See Practice 19-2.
2. The tree forward contract. See Practice 19-4.
3. The copper futures contract. See Practice 19-6.
4. The corn futures contract. See Practice 19-13.

Practice 19-15

Accounting for an Interest Rate Swap
Refer to Practice 19-2. Make any necessary journal entry on the borrowing company's books on December 31 of Year 1 in connection with the interest rate swap, assuming that the prime lending rate on December 31 is (1) 7%, (2) 15%, and (3) 10%. Even though the swap payment is not made until December 31 of Year 2, for simplicity ignore the time value of money.

Practice 19-16

Accounting for a Forward Contract
Refer to Practice 19-4. Make any necessary journal entry on the golf course developer's books on December 31 of Year 1 in connection with the tree forward contract, assuming that the price per tree on that date is (1) $250, (2) $600, and (3) $400.

Practice 19-17

Accounting for a Futures Contract
Refer to Practice 19-6. Make any necessary journal entry on the mining company's books on December 31 of Year 1 in connection with the copper futures contract, assuming that the price of copper per pound on that date is (1) $0.62, (2) $0.88, and (3) $0.77.

Practice 19-18

Accounting for an Option Contract
Refer to Practice 19-8. Make any necessary journal entry on the shirt company's books on December 31 of Year 1 in connection with the cotton option contract, assuming that the price of cotton per pound on that date is (1) $0.52, (2) $0.30, and (3) $0.39. Remember that the cotton option was purchased for $2,500.

Practice 19-19

Accounting for a Foreign Currency Futures Contract
On December 1 of Year 1, Lorien Company made a credit sale to a Thai company. The amount of the sale was 100,000 Thai baht. Lorien will collect the account on January 1 of Year 2. On December 1, the exchange rate was 40 Thai baht for 1 U.S. dollar. On December 1, Lorien entered into a futures contract to sell 100,000 Thai baht on January 1 of Year 2 at an exchange rate of 40 Thai baht for 1 U.S. dollar. Make all journal entries necessary on December 31 of Year 1 in connection with both the account receivable and the futures contract, assuming that the exchange rate for 1 U.S. dollar on December 31 is (1) 50 Thai baht, (2) 37 Thai baht, and (3) 40 Thai baht.

Practice 19-20

Accounting for a Derivative Speculation
The company specializes in speculating on the direction of movements in the price of gold. On December 1 of Year 1, the company entered into a futures contract to sell 100 ounces of gold at $1,119 per ounce on January 1 of Year 2. The company expected the price of gold to decline between December 1 and January 1. The market price of gold on December 1 of Year 1 was $1,119 per ounce. Make all journal entries necessary on December 31 of Year 1 in connection with the futures contract, assuming that the price per ounce of gold on December 31 is (1) $1,050, (2) $1,213, and (3) $1,119.

Practice 19-21

Contingent Liabilities
The company has the following three potential obligations. Describe how each will be reported in the financial statements.

1. The company has guaranteed a loan for one of its suppliers. If the supplier fails to repay the loan, the company will be required to repay it. Currently, the probability of the supplier defaulting on the loan is considered remote.
2. The company has been sued by a group of shareholders who claim that they were deceived by the company's financial reporting practices. It is possible that the company will lose this lawsuit.
3. The company is involved in litigation over who must clean up a toxic waste site near one of the company's factories. It is probable, but not certain, that the company will be required to pay for the cleanup.

Practice 19-22

Accounting for Contingent Losses and Contingent Gains

In each of the following cases, make the necessary journal entry, if any. If no journal entry is necessary, describe how the item would be reported in the financial statements.

1. The company has sued another company for patent infringement and won a preliminary judgment of $800,000 in the case. This judgment is under appeal. The company's attorneys agree that it is possible (not probable) that the sued company will win this appeal.
2. The company has long owned a manufacturing site that has now been discovered to be contaminated with toxic waste. The company has acknowledged its responsibility for the contamination. An initial cleanup feasibility study has shown that it will cost at least $450,000 to clean up the toxic waste.
3. The company has been sued for patent infringement and lost the case. A preliminary judgment of $290,000 was issued and is under appeal. The company's attorneys agree that it is possible (not probable) that the company will lose this appeal.

Practice 19-23

Segment Reporting

Rainbow Company has internally organized itself into the following seven segments:

	Total Revenues	Operating Profit	Total Assets
Segment 1	$1,000	$150	$ 600
Segment 2	600	30	100
Segment 3	500	80	200
Segment 4	700	100	300
Segment 5	200	20	800
Segment 6	100	10	110
Segment 7	80	15	100
Total	$3,180	$405	$2,210

Segments 3 and 4 have similar products, use similar processes, and distribute their products through similar channels.

Rainbow Company is concerned about reporting segment information for each segment. According to FASB ASC Topic 280 (Segment Reporting), which of the segments should be separately reported?

Practice 19-24

Interim Reporting

The company has historically reported bad debt expense of 1% of sales in each quarter. For the current year, the company followed the same procedure in the first three quarters of the year. However, in the fourth quarter, the company, in consultation with its auditor, determined that bad debt expense for the year should be $140. Sales in each quarter of the year were as follows: first quarter, $1,000; second quarter, $800; third quarter, $1,100; fourth quarter, $1,500. Make the adjusting journal entry necessary to record bad debt expense in the fourth quarter.

EXERCISES

Exercise 19-25

Derivatives: Identifying a Hedge
Shank Company manufactures candy. On September 1, Shank purchased a futures contract that obligates it to sell 150,000 pounds of sugar on September 30 at $0.41 per pound. Shank typically purchases 150,000 pounds of sugar per month to use as a raw material in the candy production process. It purchased the futures contract to hedge against movements in the price of sugar during the month of September.

In Shank's case, the sugar futures contract does not hedge against movements in the price of sugar. Demonstrate this by computing the net cost of the 150,000 pounds of sugar purchased in September under three sets of circumstances, at the price per pound of $0.38, $0.41, and $0.44.

Exercise 19-26

Derivatives: Accounting for Swaps
On January 1, 2015, Slidell Company received a two-year, $500,000 loan, with interest payments occurring at the end of each year and the principal to be repaid on December 31, 2016. The interest rate for the first year is the prevailing market rate of 7%, and the rate in 2016 will be equal to the market interest rate on January 1, 2016. In conjunction with this loan, Slidell enters into an interest rate swap agreement to receive a swap payment (based on $500,000) if the January 1, 2016, interest rate is greater than 7% and will make a swap payment if the rate is less than 7%. The interest swap payment will be made on December 31, 2016.

Make all journal entries necessary on Slidell's books in 2015 and 2016 to record this loan and the interest rate swap. On January 1, 2016, the interest rate is 6%.

Exercise 19-27

Derivatives: Accounting for Forward Contracts
On September 1, 2015, Ramus Company purchased machine parts from Ho Man Tin Company for 6,000,000 Hong Kong dollars to be paid on January 1, 2016. The exchange rate on September 1 is HK$7.7 = $1. On the same date, Ramus enters into a forward contract and agrees to purchase HK$6,000,000 on January 1, 2016, at the rate of HK$7.7 = $1.

Make all journal entries necessary on Ramus' books on three dates—September 1, 2015, December 31, 2015, and January 1, 2016—to record this purchase and the forward contract. On December 31, 2015, and on January 1, 2016, the exchange rate is HK$8.0 = $1. Ramus uses a perpetual inventory system.

Exercise 19-28

Derivatives: Accounting for Futures Contracts
Shelby Organics produces bottled orange juice. Orange juice concentrate is typically bought and sold by the pound, and Shelby uses 50,000 pounds of orange juice concentrate each month. On December 1, 2015, Shelby entered into an orange juice concentrate futures contract to buy 50,000 pounds of concentrate on January 1 at a price of $0.95 per pound, which is also the market price of concentrate on December 1. Shelby designates the futures contract as a hedge of the forecasted purchase of orange juice concentrate in January.

Make all journal entries necessary on Shelby's books on December 1, 2015, December 31, 2015, and January 1, 2016, to record this futures contract and to record the purchase of 50,000 pounds of orange juice concentrate on January 1. On December 31, 2015, and on January 1, 2016, the market price of concentrate is $0.85 per pound.

Exercise 19-29

Derivatives: Accounting for Options
Far West Clothing Mills uses approximately 250,000 pounds of cotton each month to make the cotton fabric used in its patented no-wrinkle, long-sleeved white shirts. On December 1, 2015, Far West purchased an option to buy 250,000 pounds of cotton on January 1, 2016, at a price of $0.50 per pound. The market price on December 1 is $0.50 per pound. Far West had to pay $2,000 to purchase the cotton option. Far West designated the option as a hedge against price fluctuations for its January purchases of cotton.

Make all journal entries necessary on Far West's books on December 1, 2015, December 31, 2015, and January 1, 2016, to record this option and to record the purchase of 250,000 pounds of cotton on January 1. On December 31, 2015, and on January 1, 2016, the market price of cotton is $0.42 per pound.

Exercise 19-30

Derivatives: Notional Amounts
Refer back to Exercises 19-27 and 19-28.

1. What is the notional value of the Hong Kong dollar forward contract described in Exercise 19-27? What is the fair value of the forward contract on December 31, 2015?
2. What is the notional value of the orange juice concentrate futures contract described in Exercise 19-28? What is the fair value of the futures contract on December 31, 2015?

Exercise 19-31

Derivatives: Accounting for a Speculation

Warsaw Signal Company specializes in predicting price movements in the soybean market. On November 1, 2015, it was convinced that soybean prices were too low. Accordingly, Warsaw entered into futures contracts to purchase 50,000 bushels of soybeans at $5.00 per bushel on January 1, 2016. The market price of soybeans on November 1, 2015, was $5.00 per bushel.

1. Make the adjusting journal entry necessary on December 31, 2015, if the market price of soybeans is $4.75 per bushel on that date.
2. Make the adjusting journal entry necessary on December 31, 2015, if the market price of soybeans is $5.20 per bushel on that date.

Exercise 19-32

Contingencies: Types of Liabilities

For each of the following scenarios, identify whether the event described is an actual liability, a contingent liability, or not a liability.

(a) Apple Inc. has used the toxic substance, iocaine powder, in its production process. Recently adopted federal regulations require companies to clean up any factory sites contaminated with iocaine. Apple has begun a preliminary investigation into the iocaine contamination at its factory sites.
(b) Banana Corp. financed its warehouse facilities with a long-term mortgage that calls for semiannual payments of $7,000. The mortgage's current outstanding balance is $98,000.
(c) Orange Company sells computer systems and supplies. It offers its customers a one-year, money-back guarantee. In the past, approximately 10% of customers have exercised this return privilege.
(d) Kiwi Industries manufactures and distributes outdoor recreational equipment. An individual recently filed a lawsuit as a result of injuries sustained while using Kiwi equipment. Attorneys for Kiwi believe the chance of losing the case is minimal.
(e) Berry Incorporated, a newly formed company, has an unfunded pension plan that calls for retirement benefits to be paid to employees who retire after a minimum of 10 years of employment with the company.
(f) John Townson, a successful entrepreneur, has expressed a desire to establish university scholarships for disadvantaged youth in his community. He has been contacted by numerous universities, but as of yet, nothing firm has been established.

Exercise 19-33

Contingencies: Disclosure of Contingencies

A lawsuit has been filed against See-Me-Here, Inc., a manufacturer of video postcards, by See-Me-Wherever, another manufacturer of video postcards. The suit alleges patent right infringements by See-Me-Here and asks for compensatory damages. For the following possible situations, determine whether See-Me-Here should report the information concerning the lawsuit as a liability on the balance sheet, and if so, how much; disclose it in a note; or do nothing. Give reasons for your answers.

(a) The suit hasn't been filed, but See-Me-Here's legal counsel has informed management that an unintentional patent infringement has occurred.
(b) See-Me-Here's legal counsel believes an out-of-court settlement is probable and will cost See-Me-Here approximately $700,000.
(c) See-Me-Here's legal counsel believes it is probable that the case will result in an undeterminable loss to See-Me-Here.
(d) See-Me-Here's legal counsel is convinced that the suit will result in a loss to See-Me-Here but isn't sure of the dollar damages.
(e) See-Me-Here's legal counsel believes there is a remote chance for a loss to occur.
(f) See-Me-Here's legal counsel believes it is reasonably possible that the case will result in a $2,800,000 loss to See-Me-Here.

Exercise 19-34

Contingencies: Contingent Losses

Conrad Corporation sells motorcycle helmets. In 2015, Conrad sold 4 million helmets before discovering a significant defect in their construction. By December 31, 2015, two lawsuits had been filed against Conrad. The first lawsuit, which Conrad has little chance of winning, is expected to settle out of court for $750,000 in January 2016. Conrad's attorneys think the company has a 50–50 chance of winning the second lawsuit, which is for $400,000. What accounting treatment should Conrad give the pending lawsuits in the 2015 year-end financial statements? (Include any necessary journal entries.)

Exercise 19-35

Contingencies: Contingent Liabilities

Bell Industries is a multinational company. In preparing the annual financial statements, the auditors met with Bell's attorneys to discuss various legal matters facing the firm. For each of the following independent items, determine the appropriate disclosure:

(a) Bell is being sued by a distributor for breach of contract. The attorneys believe there is a 30% chance Bell will lose the suit.
(b) One of Bell's subsidiaries has been accused by a federal agency of violating numerous environmental laws. The company faces significant fines if found guilty. The attorneys believe that the subsidiary has complied with all applicable laws, and they therefore place the probability of incurring the fines at less than 10%.
(c) A subsidiary operating in a foreign country whose government is unstable was recently taken over by the government and nationalized. Bell is negotiating with representatives of that government, but company attorneys believe the probability of the company losing possession of its assets is approximately 90%.

Exercise 19-36

Segment Reporting: Reporting Segment Information

Multitasking Industries sells five different types of products. Internally, Multitasking is divided into five different divisions based on these five different product lines. Multitasking has prepared the following information to disclose to external users in the notes to its 2015 financial statements:

	Multitasking Industries Business Segment Information For the Year Ended December 31, 2015 (in millions of dollars)					
	Division 1	Division 2	Division 3	Division 4	Division 5	Total
Revenues	$320	$750	$94	$290	$105	$1,559
Operating profit	51	104	14	20	7	196
Total assets	530	2,110	372	415	280	3,707

According to the provisions of FASB ASC Topic 280 (Segment Reporting), what additional information must Multitasking provide?

Exercise 19-37

Segment Reporting: Types of Information Disclosed by Business Segment

Companies are required to disclose selected results in the financial statements for significant business segments. This information often takes the form of industry segment reporting by diversified companies, but it also can be by geographic areas.

Locate the annual report of **The Walt Disney Company** on the Internet at **http://www.disney.com** and identify the kind of segment disclosure Disney provides. Is this information useful to prospective investors? Why or why not?

Exercise 19-38

Interim Reporting: Interim Income Statements

The income statement of Heifer Technology Inc. for the year ended December 31, 2015, is given on the following page. Using the yearly income statement and the supplemental information, reconstruct the third-quarter interim statement for Heifer.

Supplemental information:

(a) Assume a 35% tax rate.
(b) Third-quarter sales were 30% of total sales.
(c) For interim reporting purposes, a gross profit rate of 41% can be justified.
(d) Variable operating expenses are allocated in the same proportion as sales. Fixed operating expenses are allocated based on the expiration of time. Of the total operating expenses, $70,000 relate to variable expenses.
(e) The equipment was sold June 1, 2015.
(f) The extraordinary loss occurred September 1, 2015.

Heifer Technology Inc.
Income Statement
For the Year Ended December 31, 2015

Sales	$1,200,000
Cost of goods sold	710,000
Gross profit on sales	$ 490,000
Operating expenses	104,000
Operating income	$ 386,000
Gain on sale of equipment	22,000
Income from continuing operations before income taxes	$ 408,000
Income taxes	142,800
Income from continuing operations	$ 265,200
Extraordinary loss (net of income tax savings of $45,000)	(80,000)
Net income	$ 185,200

Exercise 19-39

Interim Reporting: Interim LIFO Liquidation
On December 31, 2014, Courtney Company had LIFO ending inventory consisting of 800 units with a LIFO cost of $15 per unit. During the first quarter of 2015, Courtney sold 1,400 units. As of March 31, 2015, the inventory of Courtney is 650 units, and the current purchase price of inventory is $38 per unit. The reduction in the level of inventory is temporary, and Courtney fully expects inventory levels to be at or above 800 units by December 31, 2015. The recorded cost of goods sold for Courtney for the first quarter of 2015 is $49,750 [(1,250 × $38) + (150 × $15)]. What adjusting entry, if any, should Courtney make on March 31, 2015, to correctly apply LIFO to the reporting of quarterly results?

P4

Other Dimensions of Financial Reporting

CHAPTER 20

Accounting Changes and Error Corrections

Learning Objectives

① Understand the two different types of accounting changes that have been identified by accounting standard setters.

② Recognize the difference between a change in accounting estimate and a change in accounting principle, and know how a change in accounting estimate is reflected in the financial statements.

③ Prepare the retrospective adjustment of prior periods' financial statements, and any necessary cumulative adjustment, associated with a change in accounting principle.

④ Report pro forma results for prior years following a business combination.

⑤ Recognize the various types of errors that can occur in the accounting process, understand when errors counterbalance, and be able to correct errors when necessary.

Statement of Financial Accounting Standards No. 106, "Employers' Accounting for Postretirement Benefits Other Than Pensions," was issued in 1992 (and is now included in the FASB Codification as Section 715-60). These "postretirement benefits other than pensions" are primarily retiree healthcare costs. The overall impact of this standard on corporate profits established a record for a new accounting rule and was estimated to result in a decrease in the reported profits of major U.S. companies by as much as $1 trillion.[1] As an example of the effect, the standard required General Motors to recognize a liability relating to retiree healthcare benefits of $33 billion.

The amazing thing about the accounting change mandated by the FASB back in 1992 is that before the rule change, the liability amount recorded by all U.S. companies for their retiree healthcare obligations totaled exactly zero. Nil. Nada. Zilch. Let's be honest: This wasn't very informative accounting for these obligations. The economic obligations certainly existed before 1992, but the accounting rules did not require companies to report the obligations in their balance sheets.

For General Motors (GM), the after-tax income effect of the adoption of *Statement No. 106* was to decrease earnings by $21 billion and decrease

---

[1] Lee Berton and Robert J. Brennan, "New Medical-Benefits Accounting Rule Seen Wounding Profits, Hurting Shares," *The Wall Street Journal*, April 22, 1992, p. C1.

earnings per share (EPS) by $33.38. Because this retiree healthcare obligation had been built up over many years preceding the mandated accounting change in 1992, it makes sense to ask whether the entire estimated after-tax cost of $21 billion should have been reported by GM as an expense in the year of adoption, or whether there was a more informative way to recognize this cost. This issue, the proper reporting of accounting changes, is discussed in this chapter.

The retiree healthcare obligation created by GM through the company's promises to its employees over the years, and finally recognized in the financial statements starting in 1992, has had an extremely interesting and controversial history. The controversy swirls around the claim that these healthcare promises contributed to the eventual bankruptcy of GM. And part of the blame is placed at the feet of the accounting profession. The fact that, before 1992, the true cost of these healthcare promises was not included in the financial statements may have led pre-1992 GM decision makers to have the mistaken impression that the promises were "free." The cost of these "free" benefits eventually helped kill the company.

In the negotiations over the GM bankruptcy, these retiree healthcare benefits were sacrificed by GM employees in an effort to help save the restructured company. Exhibit 20-1 shows that the recorded obligation went from $0 in 1991 (because of the flaw in the accounting rules described above), to a high of over $80 billion in 2005, and then back to almost $0 in 2009 (because GM's employees agreed to release the financially ruined company from its previous promises).

Exhibit 20-1 | History of General Motors' Reported Retiree Healthcare Obligation (in millions)

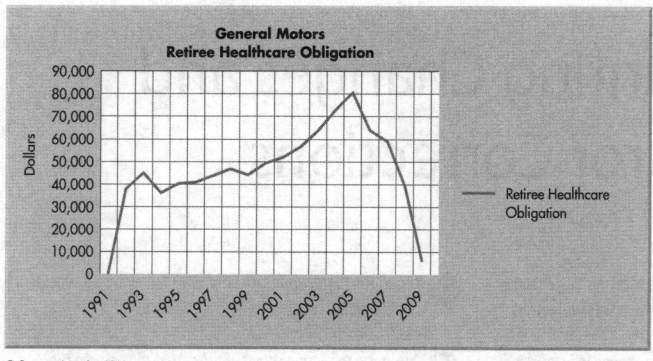

© Cengage Learning 2014

1. Before FASB *Statement No. 106*, companies typically recognized no cost and no liability for their retiree healthcare benefit plans. List several reasons for a firm to reduce its retiree health benefits in response to the FASB's requirement that companies recognize the cost and obligation associated with such plans.

2. FASB *Statement No. 106* resulted in firms reporting lower earnings and higher liabilities. Would you expect stock prices to decline for companies with large retiree healthcare plans? Would you expect it to be harder for these firms to obtain loans?

3. General Motors was required to recognize a one-time $21 billion expense upon its adoption of FASB *Statement No. 106*. This $21 billion represented the cumulative after-tax cost of GM's retiree healthcare plan for all years preceding 1992. How else might GM have recorded this $21 billion?

Answers to these questions can be found on page 20-27.

A company's financial statements sometimes report significantly different results from year to year. This may be due to changes in economic circumstances, but it also may be due to changes in accounting methods or corrections of errors in recording past transactions.

Changing the accounting methods used can have a dramatic impact on a company's financial statements. Because of this impact, one can argue that accounting changes detract from the informational characteristics of comparability and consistency discussed in Chapter 1. So why are these accounting changes made? The main reasons for such changes can be summarized as follows:

1. A company, as a result of experience or new information, may change its estimates of revenues or expenses—for example, the estimate of uncollectible accounts receivable or the estimated service lives of depreciable assets.
2. Due to changes in economic conditions, companies may need to change methods of accounting to more clearly reflect the current economic situation.
3. Accounting standard-setting bodies may require the use of a new accounting method or principle, such as new reporting requirements for postretirement benefits.
4. Management may be pressured to report profitable performance. Clever accounting changes can result in higher net income, thereby reflecting favorably on management.

Whatever the reason, accountants must keep the primary qualitative characteristic of usefulness in mind. They must determine whether the reasons for accounting changes are appropriate and then how best to report the changes to facilitate understanding of the financial statements.

The detection of errors in accounting for past transactions presents a similar problem. The errors must be corrected and appropriate disclosures made so that readers of the financial statements will clearly understand what has happened. The purpose of this chapter is to discuss the different types of accounting changes and error corrections and the related accounting procedures that should be used.

Accounting Changes

LO1 学习目标1

理解被会计准则制定机构确认的两种会计变更类型。

会计变更的类型包括：
- 会计估计变更；
- 会计原则变更。

① Understand the two different types of accounting changes that have been identified by accounting standard setters.

The accounting profession has identified two main categories of accounting changes:[2]

1. Change in accounting estimate
2. Change in accounting principle

As pointed out in Chapter 1, a major objective of published financial statements is to provide users information to help them predict, compare, and evaluate future earning power and cash flows of the reporting entity. When a reporting entity adjusts its past estimates of revenues earned or costs incurred or changes its accounting principles from one method to another, it becomes more difficult for a user to predict the future from past historical statements. The basic accounting issue is whether accounting changes should be reported as adjustments of the prior periods' statements (thus increasing their

---

[2] FASB ASC Section 250-10-20, Presentation—Accounting Changes and Error Corrections—Overall—Glossary. *(SFAS No. 154, "Accounting Changes and Error Corrections: A Replacement of APB Opinion No. 20 and FASB Statement No. 3," May 2005, par. 2.)* A third category of accounting changes, changes in reporting entity, is much less common and is not covered in any detail in this chapter.

comparability with current and future statements) or whether the changes should affect only the current and future years.

Several alternatives have been suggested for reporting accounting changes.

1. Restate the financial statements presented for prior periods to reflect the effect of the change. Adjust the beginning retained earnings balance of the earliest period reported for the cumulative effect of the change in all preceding years.
2. Make no adjustment to statements presented for prior periods. Report the cumulative effect of the change in the current year as a direct entry to Retained Earnings.
3. Same as (2), except report the cumulative effect of the change as a special item in the income statement instead of directly to Retained Earnings.
4. Report the cumulative effect in the current year as in (3) but also present limited pro forma information for all prior periods included in the financial statements reporting "what might have been" if the change had been made in the prior years.
5. Make the change effective only for current and future periods with no catch-up adjustment.

Each of these methods for reporting an accounting change has been used by companies in the past, and arguments can be made for each of the approaches. For example, some accountants argue that accounting principles should be applied consistently for all reported periods. Therefore, if a new accounting principle is used in the current period, the financial statements presented for prior periods should be restated so that the results shown for all reported periods are based on the same accounting principles. Other accountants contend that restating financial statements may dilute public confidence in those statements. Principles applied in earlier periods were presumably appropriate at that time and should be considered final. In addition, restating financial statements is costly, requires considerable effort, and is sometimes impossible due to lack of data.

Consider the GM example at the beginning of this chapter. How should the liability and the effect on earnings have been reported? Specifically, what would have been the appropriate journal entry? Obviously, GM would recognize a liability of $33 billion. Because GM will not receive a tax deduction for the other postretirement benefits until those expenses are actually paid, GM would also recognize a deferred tax asset of $12 billion. This deferred tax asset would be recognized because GM expensed the cost of the benefits now for financial accounting purposes but does not expect to receive the tax deduction for those expenses until they are paid in the future: Recall from Chapter 16 that this would result in taxable income being higher than financial income in the current period, resulting in a deferred tax asset. As a result, the journal entry would appear as follows:

Deferred Tax Asset...	12 billion
????	21 billion
Other Postretirement Benefits Liability.............................	33 billion

What account should replace the question marks? Should it be an income statement account, a balance sheet account, or some other type of account? In accordance with the accounting rules in existence at the time, GM debited an expense called "Cumulative Effect of an Accounting Change" and reported the $21 billion reduction in earnings as a below-the-line item on the income statement. International practice is different with respect to the handling of this type of accounting change. Under the provisions of *International Accounting Standard (IAS) 8*, companies would debit the beginning balance in the retained earnings account, reasoning that the adjustment was related to prior periods

FYI

Cumulative effects of changes in accounting principles used to be shown as below-the-line items on the income statement.

and the income from those prior periods had been previously closed to the retained earnings account. In addition, all income statements presented for prior years would be retrospectively restated as if the new standard had always been in effect; this is alternative (1) described previously.

As part of its continuing effort to harmonize U.S. GAAP with International Accounting Standards, the FASB adopted *Statement No. 154* in May 2005. This statement changed the U.S. approach to accounting for accounting changes and error corrections to be in conformity with *IAS 8*. The coverage in this chapter reflects this new standard which now forms the basis of FASB Codification Topic 250, "Accounting Changes and Error Corrections."

Change in Accounting Estimate

 Recognize the difference between a change in accounting estimate and a change in accounting principle, and know how a change in accounting estimate is reflected in the financial statements.

LO2 学习目标2

认识会计估计变更和会计原则变更的不同，并且知道会计估计变更在财务报表中是如何反映的。

Contrary to what many people believe, accounting information cannot always be measured and reported precisely. Also, to be reported on a timely basis for decision making, accounting data often must be based on estimates of future events. The financial statements incorporate these estimates, which are based on the best professional judgment given the information available at that time. At a later date, however, additional experience or new facts sometimes make it clear that the estimates need to be revised to more accurately reflect the existing business circumstances. When this happens, a change in accounting estimate occurs.

会计估计变更的例子包括：
- 无法收回的应收账款；
- 折旧或无形资产的使用年限；
- 折旧资产的剩余价值；
- 保修义务；
- 将耗尽的矿产储备量；
- 养老金或其他雇用后福利的精算假设；
- 递延成本收益期数。

Examples of areas for which changes in accounting estimates often are needed include the following:

1. Uncollectible receivables
2. Useful lives of depreciable or intangible assets
3. Residual values for depreciable assets
4. Warranty obligations
5. Quantities of mineral reserves to be depleted
6. Actuarial assumptions for pensions or other postemployment benefits
7. Number of periods benefited by deferred costs

Exhibit 20-2 provides examples of disclosure relating to estimates contained in the 2011 annual reports of two companies: H. J. Heinz Company and McDonald's. Even though the companies had different auditors (PricewaterhouseCoopers and Ernst & Young, respectively), it is surprising how similar the note disclosures are.

Accounting for a change in estimate has already been discussed in Chapter 4 and throughout the text in areas for which changes in estimates are common. By way of review, all changes in estimates should be reflected either in the current period or in current and future periods. No retroactive adjustments or pro forma (as-if) statements are to be prepared for a change in accounting estimate. Changes in estimates are considered to be part of the normal accounting process, not corrections or changes of past periods. However, disclosures such as the ones in Exhibit 20-3, reported by

> **Stop & Think**
>
> Why aren't changes in estimates accounted for by restating prior years' financial statements?
>
> a) The data necessary to perform restatements typically are not available.
> b) Restating prior years' financial statements would force most companies to make a large penalty payment to the Internal Revenue Service.
> c) With most restatements, the deferred tax consequences would cause an unusually large reduction in retained earnings.
> d) With restatements, prior-period financial statements would be constantly revised, reducing the reliance placed on them by investors and creditors.

United Airlines, are useful in helping readers of financial statements understand the impact of changes in estimates.

Some changes in accounting principle are actually just another form of a change in estimate. For example, if a company changes its depreciation method, it is really making a statement about a change in the expected usage pattern with respect to that asset. As required by the Accounting Changes and Error Corrections Topic (250) of the FASB ASC, a change in depreciation method is accounted for as a change in estimate and is called "a change in accounting estimate effected by a change in accounting principle."

Exhibit 20-2 | H. J. Heinz Company and McDonald's—Disclosure Relating to Estimates

NOTES TO CONSOLIDATED FINANCIAL STATEMENTS
H. J. Heinz Company and Subsidiaries
I. Significant Accounting Policies

Use of Estimates: The preparation of financial statements, in conformity with accounting principles generally accepted in the United States of America, requires management to make estimates and assumptions that affect the reported amounts of assets and liabilities, the disclosure of contingent assets and liabilities at the date of the financial statements, and the reported amounts of revenues and expenses during the reporting period. Actual results could differ from these estimates.

McDonald's Corporation
Summary of Significant Accounting Policies

Estimates in financial statements
The preparation of financial statements in conformity with accounting principles generally accepted in the U.S. requires management to make estimates and assumptions that affect the amounts reported in the financial statements and accompanying notes. Actual results could differ from those estimates.

H. J. Heinz, 2011, 10K Report; McDonald's, 2011, 10K Report

Exhibit 20-3 | United Airlines—Disclosure of Change in Estimate

UAL Corporation (the "Company") follows a deferred revenue accounting policy to record the fair value of its Mileage Plus frequent flyer obligation. The Company defers the portion of the sales proceeds of ticketed revenue on United and our alliance partners, as well as revenue associated with mileage sales to third parties, that represents the estimated air transportation fair value of the miles awarded. This deferred revenue is then recognized when the miles are redeemed.

Some of these miles will never be redeemed by Mileage Plus members, and the Company recognizes an estimate of revenue from the expected expired miles, which is referred to as breakage, over an estimated redemption period. The Company reviews its breakage estimates annually based upon the latest available information regarding mileage redemption and expiration patterns.

During the first quarter of 2010 the Company obtained additional historical data, previously unavailable, which has enabled the Company to refine its breakage estimates. This new data indicates that a larger number of miles than previously estimated are expected to expire. As a result, the Company has changed its estimate of Mileage Plus breakage on a prospective basis, effective beginning in the first quarter of 2010. In addition to this change in estimate, the Company is making an improvement to the accounting model for Mileage Plus breakage that is inseparable from the change in estimate.

These changes will result in the recognition of approximately $64 million of incremental passenger revenue in the first quarter of 2010, reducing the net amount of revenue that we otherwise would have deferred to future periods.

United Airlines, 10K Report

To illustrate a change in accounting estimate effected by a change in accounting principle, assume that Telstar Company, a high-power telescope sales and manufacturing firm, elected in 2015 to change from the double-declining-balance method of depreciation to the straight-line method to make its financial reporting more consistent with the majority of its competitors. Telstar's depreciable assets have a cost of $500,000 and, to keep things simple, assume that they were all acquired on January 1, 2012, have an expected useful life of 10 years, and have an expected salvage value of zero. For tax purposes, assume that Telstar had elected to use the straight-line method and will continue to do so. Assume further that Telstar presents comparative income statements for three years and that the past difference in book and tax depreciation is the only difference in accounting treatment impacting Telstar's financial and taxable income.

These and other assumptions are necessary because, in most instances, a change in accounting principle involves temporary differences between book and tax income, creating the need for interperiod tax allocation. The exact amounts of any deferred income tax liabilities or potential deferred income tax assets are dependent on several factors, such as current tax laws and current and future tax rates. Therefore, in this chapter, including the end-of-chapter material, the impact of income tax either is ignored or the assumed amounts are provided to simplify the illustrations and focus on the effects of accounting changes and error corrections.

For Telstar, the greater accelerated depreciation charged on the books in prior years, as compared to the straight-line tax depreciation taken, resulted in a previously recorded deferred tax asset. The income tax rate is assumed to be 30%. This and other relevant information for Telstar is presented below.

Year	Double-Declining-Balance Depreciation (used for books)	Straight-Line Depreciation (used for taxes)	Depreciation Difference	Deferred Tax Effects	Effects on Income (net of taxes)
2012	$100,000	$ 50,000	$50,000	$15,000	$35,000
2013	80,000	50,000	30,000	9,000	21,000
2014	64,000	50,000	14,000	4,200	9,800
Cumulative before 2015	$244,000	$150,000	$94,000	$28,200	$65,800

The data indicate that cumulative depreciation expense for the years prior to 2015 would have been $94,000 ($244,000 − $150,000) less if the straight-line method had been used. Thus, income would have been $94,000 higher, less the applicable income taxes of $28,200, leaving a net income difference of $65,800. The total impact on Telstar's balance sheet as of January 1, 2015, is as follows:

ASSETS
Gross Property, Plant, and Equipment — No impact
Accumulated Depreciation — $94,000 higher with double declining balance
Net Property, Plant, and Equipment — $94,000 lower with double declining balance
Deferred Tax Asset — $28,200 higher with double declining balance
Total Assets — $65,800 lower with double declining balance

LIABILITIES
No impact

EQUITIES
Retained Earnings — $65,800 lower with double declining balance

Because a change in depreciation method is to be accounted for as "a change in accounting estimate effected by a change in accounting principle," no attempt is made to go back and change the depreciation and deferred tax information reported in 2012, 2013, and 2014. Instead, the change is accounted for in the current and future periods as illustrated in Chapter 11 in the discussion of changes in depreciation lives. The remaining depreciable book value as of January 1, 2015, is depreciated over the remaining life of seven years using the new straight-line method. Depreciation expense for 2015 is computed as follows:

$$[(\$500,000 - \$244,000) - \$0 \text{ salvage value}]/7 \text{ years} = \$36,571$$

The table below shows the depreciation amount that would be reported in the books and for income tax purposes after the accounting change. You can see that the lower depreciation expense reported under the straight-line method applied on the books results in the gradual reversal of the deferred tax asset that had been recognized previously. By the end of seven years (in 2021), the deferred tax effects will have completely reversed.

下表显示了将在账面价值中报告的折旧金额和所得税目下的会计变更后折旧数额。从中可以看到，直线法下报告的较低折旧费用导致了以前被确认的递延所得税资产逐步转回。截至第7年（2021年）年末，递延所得税的影响完全转回。

Year	First Double-Declining-Balance and then Straight-Line Depreciation (used for books)	Straight-Line Depreciation (used for taxes)	Depreciation Difference	Deferred Tax Effects	Effects on Income (net of taxes)
Cumulative before 2015	$244,000	$150,000	$ 94,000	$28,200	$65,800
2015	36,571	50,000	(13,429)	(4,029)	(9,400)
2016	36,571	50,000	(13,429)	(4,029)	(9,400)
.					
.					
.					
2021 (adjusted for rounding)	36,574	50,000	(13,426)	(4,026)	(9,400)
Cumulative through 2021.	$500,000	$500,000	$ 0	$ 0	$ 0

Change in Accounting Principle

LO3 学习目标3

③ Prepare the retrospective adjustment of prior periods' financial statements, and any necessary cumulative adjustment, associated with a change in accounting principle.

编制前期财务报表的追溯调整，以及任何必要的与会计原则变更相关的累计调整。

A *change in accounting principle* involves a change from one generally accepted principle or method to another.[3] A change in principle does not include the initial adoption of an accounting principle as a result of transactions or events that had not occurred (or were immaterial) in previous periods. A change from a principle that is not generally accepted to one that is generally accepted is considered to be an error correction rather than a change in accounting principle.

As indicated in previous chapters, companies may select among alternative accounting principles to account for business transactions. For example, for financial reporting purposes, inventory may be accounted for using FIFO, LIFO, or other acceptable methods. These

---
[3] The classification "change in accounting principle" includes changes in methods used to account for transactions. No attempt is made in FASB ASC Topic 250 to distinguish between a principle and a method.

alternative methods are often equally available to a given company, but in most instances, criteria for selection among the methods are inadequate. As a result, companies have found it rather easy to justify changing from one accounting principle or method to another.

从一种可接受的会计原则变为另一种会计原则的影响，通过追溯调整各年报告的财务报表和报告中所有以前年度对利润的变更累积影响，作为对最早期报告留存收益的期初余额的调整予以反映。

The effect of a change from one accepted accounting principle to another is reflected by retrospectively adjusting the financial statements for all years reported, and reporting the cumulative effect of the change in the income for all preceding years as an adjustment to the beginning balance in retained earnings for the earliest year reported. For example, in a standard set of financial statements presenting balance sheets for two years and income statements and statements of cash flows for three years, all of the statements would be redone using the new accounting principle. In addition, the statement of stockholders' equity that is typically included with the financial statements would reflect the cumulative effect on income in prior years with an adjustment to beginning retained earnings in the first of the three years reported.

To illustrate the general treatment of a change in accounting principle, assume that as of January 1, 2015, Forester Company changed from the LIFO inventory costing method to the FIFO method for both financial reporting and income tax purposes. There are no deferred tax consequences because both the old and new methods apply to both financial and tax reporting. However, additional taxes will be payable for prior years as a result of the change in inventory method used for tax purposes. The income tax rate is 30%. The following balance sheet and income statement data are based on LIFO as shown below.

	If Continued Using LIFO	As Originally Reported Using LIFO	
Balance Sheet	2015	2014	2013
Cash	$ 150	$ 120	$ 100
Inventory	3,800	3,000	2,500
Total assets	$3,950	$3,120	$2,600
Income taxes payable	$ 165	$ 105	$ 90
Paid-in capital	1,645	1,260	1,000
Retained earnings	2,140	1,755	1,510
Total liabilities and equities	$3,950	$3,120	$2,600
Income Statement	2015	2014	2013
Sales	$1,500	$1,200	$1,000
Cost of goods sold	950	850	700
Gross profit	$ 550	$ 350	$ 300
Income tax expense	165	105	90
Net income	$ 385	$ 245	$ 210

The data for 2013 and 2014 are the actual financial statements that were released for those years. The LIFO data for 2015 are the financial statements that would have been released had Forester decided to continue using LIFO.

The following LIFO and FIFO inventory valuation data have been assembled:

	LIFO	FIFO	Difference
January 1, 2013, inventory	$2,100	$2,350	$250
December 31, 2013, inventory	2,500	2,900	400
December 31, 2014, inventory	3,000	3,600	600
December 31, 2015, inventory	3,800	4,500	700

As discussed in Chapter 9, the excess of FIFO inventory valuation over LIFO inventory valuation is called the LIFO reserve and can be thought of as inventory holding gains (during times of inflation) that are recognized when FIFO is used (reducing reported cost of goods sold) but that are not recognized when LIFO is used. The LIFO financial statement data and the inventory valuation differences can be used to construct the FIFO financial statements for 2013–2015, as follows:

	After Changing to FIFO	If Originally Used FIFO	
Balance Sheet	2015	2014	2013
Cash	$ 150	$ 120	$ 100
Inventory	4,500	3,600	2,900
Total assets	$4,650	$3,720	$3,000
Income taxes payable	$ 195	$ 105	$ 90
FIFO taxes payable	180	180	120
Paid-in capital	1,645	1,260	1,000
Retained earnings	2,630	2,175	1,790
Total liabilities and equities	$4,650	$3,720	$3,000
Income Statement	2015	2014	2013
Sales	$1,500	$1,200	$1,000
Cost of goods sold	850	650	550
Gross profit	$ 650	$ 550	$ 450
Income tax expense	195	165	135
Net income	$ 455	$ 385	$ 315

Details of the computations of retained earnings and the FIFO taxes payable amounts are given below.

Retained Earnings As of January 1, 2013, a retrospective switch to FIFO means that cumulative before-tax profits from the years before 2013 are increased by $250, corresponding to the amount of the LIFO reserve on that date. The increase in cumulative after-tax profits is $175 ($250 × [1 − 0.30]). Accordingly, retained earnings as of January 1, 2013, is increased by $175. The computation of the ending balance in retained earnings for 2013 would be shown as follows in the 2015 three-year comparative statement of stockholders' equity for Forester.

Retained earnings, January 1, 2013, as originally reported	$1,300
Add adjustment for cumulative effect on prior years of retrospectively applying the FIFO method of inventory valuation	175
Adjusted retained earnings, January 1, 2013	$1,475
Add net income for 2013 (under FIFO)	315
Retained earnings, December 31, 2013	$1,790

FIFO taxes payable
先进先出应交税费

FIFO Taxes Payable Because the switch is being made for both book and tax purposes, the increase in taxable profits of $250 creates a "FIFO taxes payable" of $75 ($250 × 0.30) corresponding to the tax that is now owed on excess FIFO profits from the years before 2013. In addition, the $45 increased tax expense for 2013 ($135 FIFO − $90 LIFO) represents additional FIFO taxes payable as of the end of 2013. The total of $120 ($75 + $45) is reported in the revised December 31, 2013, balance sheet. This amount increases by $60 ($165 FIFO taxes in 2014 − $105 LIFO taxes in 2014), to $180, by the end of 2014 to reflect the additional FIFO taxes payable created in 2014.

The primary financial statements reported in 2015 are the three years of retrospectively prepared FIFO-based financial statements. The disadvantage of this retrospective approach is that the comparative balance sheet and income statement for 2014 that are included in the 2015 financial statements are different from the balance sheet and income statement for 2014 that were originally released the year before. Some financial statement users may be confused by the fact that, for example, Forester's 2014 net income of $245 as originally reported has been retrospectively changed to $385 in the financial statements released in 2015. This disadvantage is outweighed by the fact that the comparative financial statements released in 2015 all reflect the FIFO method of inventory valuation, and so those financial statements can be meaningfully compared from one year to the next.

2015年报告的主要财务报表是在三年追溯性地、以先进先出法为基础编制的财务报表。这种追溯方法的缺点是，包含在2015年财务报表里的2014年比较资产负债表和利润表不同于2014年资产负债表和利润表。例如，Forester 2014年最初报告的245美元净利润在2015年公布的财务报表中变成了385美元，这可能使得一些报表使用者感到很迷惑。这个缺点可以通过以下方式加以改变：2015年公布的比较财务报表反映先进先出法下的存货计价，所以这些财务报表可以一年一年地进行有意义的比较。

In addition to the preparation of retrospectively adjusted primary financial statements, the change in accounting principle from LIFO to FIFO also necessitates note disclosure that shows the impact of the change on each financial statement item in each year reported. The following information would be reported in the financial statements notes in 2015, the year of the change. Note that because balance sheet data are typically reported only for two years, disclosure of the balance sheet comparisons for 2013 is not needed.

For 2015	Computed Using LIFO	As Reported Using FIFO	Effect of Change
Balance Sheet			
Cash	$ 150	$ 150	$ 0
Inventory	3,800	4,500	700
Total assets	$3,950	$4,650	$ 700
Income taxes payable	$ 165	$ 195	$ 30
FIFO taxes payable	0	180	180
Paid-in capital	1,645	1,645	0
Retained earnings	2,140	2,630	490
Total liabilities and equities	$3,950	$4,650	$ 700
Income Statement			
Sales	$1,500	$1,500	$ 0
Cost of goods sold	950	850	(100)
Gross profit	$ 550	$ 650	$ 100
Income tax expense	165	195	30
Net income	$ 385	$ 455	$ 70

For 2014	As Originally Reported	Using FIFO	Effect of Change
Balance Sheet			
Cash	$ 120	$ 120	$ 0
Inventory	3,000	3,600	600
Total assets	$3,120	$3,720	$ 600
Income taxes payable	$ 105	$ 105	$ 0
FIFO taxes payable	0	180	180
Paid-in capital	1,260	1,260	0
Retained earnings	1,755	2,175	420
Total liabilities and equities	$3,120	$3,720	$ 600
Income Statement			
Sales	$1,200	$1,200	$ 0
Cost of goods sold	850	650	(200)
Gross profit	$ 350	$ 550	$ 200
Income tax expense	105	165	60
Net income	$ 245	$ 385	$ 140

For 2013	As Originally Reported	Using FIFO	Effect of Change
Income Statement			
Sales	$1,000	$1,000	$ 0
Cost of goods sold	700	550	(150)
Gross profit	$ 300	$ 450	$ 150
Income tax expense	90	135	45
Net income	$ 210	$ 315	$ 105

Impractical to Determine Period-Specific Effects Sometimes the cumulative effect of a change in accounting principle can be determined, but it is impractical to determine the precise periods when past differences arose. For example, it is possible that in a case such as the Forester example just given, the company may be able to determine the LIFO and FIFO inventory valuations on January 1, 2015, when the accounting change is made, but not be able to determine differences in prior years. In such a case, the beginning balance sheet accounts, including beginning retained earnings, are adjusted for the earliest year in which the necessary data are available. If Forester were only able to determine the January 1, 2015, inventory balances under LIFO ($3,000) and FIFO ($3,600), the following retained earnings computation would be presented for 2015:

Retained earnings, January 1, 2015, as originally reported	$1,755
Add adjustment for cumulative effect on prior years of retrospectively applying the FIFO method of inventory valuation	420
Adjusted retained earnings, January 1, 2015	$2,175
Add net income for 2015 (under FIFO)	455
Retained earnings, December 31, 2015	$2,630

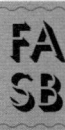

FASB CODIFICATION

The Issue: You are the newly hired accountant for Deedle Development, a real estate company that develops time share units in beautiful but out-of-the-way places. One of your company's current projects is a multistage development on the hillside overlooking picturesque South Willow Lake located in the Stansbury Mountains southwest of Grantsville, Utah. In past years, for financial reporting purposes Deedle has accounted for this development as a three-phase project, even though one of the phases involves the construction of two separate buildings. Legal fees and development costs have been appropriately allocated among the three phases. Starting this year, Deedle has decided to account for the South Willow development as a four-phase project. This change was not prompted by any changes in the project design or timeline; instead, Deedle's management has merely decided that separation of the costs (and revenues) of the development into four phases will more accurately reflect the economics of the project.

The Question: Is this change from three phases to four phases to be accounted for as a change in estimate (prospectively), or a change in principle (retrospectively)?

Searching the Codification: There are three ways to search for the answer to this question.

- Scan the table of contents for Topic 250, Accounting Changes and Error Corrections. Because this question appears to be specific to a particular industry (real estate), Topic 250 might list guidance on industry-specific issues.
- Scan the table of contents for the collection of industry topics in the Codification; these have topic numbers in the 900s. You will find a number of industry topics specific to real estate.
- Use the "Search" box in the top right corner of the Codification home page. Try the search term "time share."

The Answer: The correct treatment is described on page 20-27.

Prospective Application In other cases, it is simply impossible to determine the past impact of an accounting change. For example, a change to the LIFO method of inventory valuation is usually made effective with the beginning inventory in the year of change rather than with some prior year because of the difficulty in identifying prior-year LIFO layers or dollar-value pools. Thus, the beginning inventory in the year of change becomes the same as the previous inventory valued using another costing method, such as FIFO, and this becomes the base LIFO layer. The LIFO assumption is then applied prospectively, meaning that it is used from that time forward.

Accounting Change Mandated by a Change in Accounting Standards Most changes in accounting principle are recognized in connection with a company's adoption of a mandated new accounting principle. For example, the opening scenario of this chapter describes the large impact on companies when they adopted *SFAS No. 106* and were required to recognize a large liability for their previously unrecognized obligation for retirees' health care. Almost all standards include specific instructions about how to account for the necessary change in accounting principle. In the unlikely event that a new standard does not include specific instructions on how to report the impact of the change, FASB ASC 250-10-45 (paragraphs 3 and 5) states that the presumption is that the change is to be accounted for retrospectively, as illustrated earlier.

Pro Forma Disclosures after a Business Combination

LO4 学习目标4
报告企业合并前几年的预测表结果。

4 Report pro forma results for prior years following a business combination.

A business combination can substantially alter the size and mix of the operations reported in a single set of financial statements. For example, on January 11, 2001, **America Online** merged with **Time Warner** to form **AOL Time Warner**. This merger was accounted for as the acquisition of Time Warner by America Online. A comparison of the financial statements for AOL before and after this acquisition is quite startling. For example, AOL revenues in 2000 were $6.886 billion. Revenues in 2001, the year after the merger, were $38.234 billion. Assets in 2000 were $10.673 billion; assets in 2001 were $208.559 billion. Clearly, investors are not able to decipher this drastic change in the make-up of an economic entity without substantial supplemental disclosure. (*Note:* Setting the accounting aside, this merger was a disaster from a business standpoint. In 2003, after recognizing a record-breaking loss of $99 billion in 2002, the merger company dropped the "AOL" from the name and reverted to the name "Time Warner.")

FASB ASC 805解释了企业合并所需的补充披露。如同合并在当年年初发生的，合并后企业必须披露合并年度的预测表结果。此外，前期需要披露同样的预测表，如同企业合并发生在该年年初。在预测表中，企业必须披露至少包括各期间的收入和净利润。

The supplemental disclosure required following a business combination is explained in FASB ASC Section 805-10-50.[4] The combined company is required to disclose pro forma results for the year of the combination as if the combination had occurred at the beginning of the year. In addition, the same pro forma disclosure is required for the preceding year, as if the business combination had occurred at the beginning of that year. At a minimum, a company must include revenue and net income for the respective periods in this pro forma disclosure.[5] Preparing these pro forma disclosures involves more than simply adding together the sales and net income amounts from the financial statement prepared by the separate companies before they combined. For example, depreciation expense must be recomputed using the fair value amounts recorded for the depreciable assets of the acquired company when the purchase was recorded.

To illustrate the adjustments that must be made in preparing these pro forma disclosures, assume that on December 31, 2015, Sump Pump Company acquired Rock Wall Company for $500,000. This amount exceeded the recorded value of Rock Wall Company's net assets by $100,000 on the acquisition date. The entire excess was attributable to a piece of Rock Wall's equipment that had a remaining useful life of five years as of the

---

[4] FASB ASC paragraphs 805-10-50-1,2.
[5] Companies sometimes change their structures or report their operations in such a way that the financial statements are, in effect, those of a different reporting entity. Specifically, a change in reporting entity includes: (1) presenting consolidated or combined statements in place of statements of individual companies; (2) changing specific subsidiaries composing the group of companies for which consolidated statements are presented; and (3) changing the companies included in combined financial statements. In these cases, the financial statements must be adjusted retroactively to disclose what the statements would have looked like if the current entity had been in existence in the prior years. Thus, previous years' financial statements presented for comparison with the current year (the year of change) must be restated to reflect results of operations, financial condition, and cash flows as if the current reporting entity had been in existence in those years.

acquisition date. Information reported for the two companies for 2014 and 2015 was as follows:

	2015	2014
Sump Pump Company:		
Revenue	$3,500,000	$3,000,000
Net income	250,000	200,000
Rock Wall Company:		
Revenue	$ 250,000	$ 400,000
Net income	40,000	75,000

The necessary pro forma information that would be included in the notes to Sump Pump Company's 2015 financial statements is as follows:

	2015 Reported Results	2015 Results for Combined Companies	2014 Reported Results	2014 Results for Combined Companies
Revenue	$3,500,000	$3,750,000	$3,000,000	$3,400,000
Net income	250,000	270,000	200,000	255,000

2015 combined income computation:

$$\$250{,}000 + \$40{,}000 - \text{extra depreciation } (\$100{,}000/5 \text{ years}) = \$270{,}000$$

2014 combined income computation:

$$\$200{,}000 + \$75{,}000 - \text{extra depreciation } (\$100{,}000/5 \text{ years}) = \$255{,}000$$

Error Corrections

LO5 学习目标5
识别在会计处理过程中可能发生的不同类型差错，理解差错自动抵销的情形并能在必要时更正差错。

5. Recognize the various types of errors that can occur in the accounting process, understand when errors counterbalance, and be able to correct errors when necessary.

Error corrections are not considered accounting changes, but their treatment is specified in FASB ASC Topic 250. Accounting errors made in prior years are corrected from a reporting standpoint by restating the financial statements for all years presented and, if needed, by reporting an adjustment to the beginning retained earnings for the earliest year reported. Basically, errors in the financial statements are fixed in subsequent years by releasing corrected financial statements and providing note disclosure of the line-by-line impact of the errors. This reporting is essentially the same as the reporting required for a change in accounting principle, as discussed in the preceding section.

From a bookkeeping standpoint, errors that have not already been "counterbalanced" or reversed are reported as prior-period adjustments and debited or credited directly to Retained Earnings for the current year. Examples of errors include mathematical mistakes, improper application of accounting principles, omissions of material facts, or fraudulent financial reporting. These bookkeeping corrections will be illustrated in this section. As you will soon see, the bookkeeping correction of accounting errors is a good test of how well you understand your debits and credits.

Types of Errors

There are a number of different kinds of errors. Some errors are discovered in the period in which they are made and are easily corrected. Others may not be discovered currently and are reflected on the financial statements until discovered. Some errors are never discovered; however, the effects of these errors may be counterbalanced in subsequent periods, and after this takes place, account balances are again accurately stated. Errors may be classified as follows:

1. *Errors discovered currently in the course of normal accounting procedures.* Examples of this type of error are clerical errors, such as an addition error, posting to the wrong account, misstating an account, or omitting an account from the trial balance. These types of errors usually are detected during the regular summarizing process of the accounting cycle and are readily corrected.

2. *Errors limited to balance sheet accounts.* Examples include debiting Accounts Receivable instead of Notes Receivable, crediting Interest Payable instead of Notes Payable, or crediting Interest Payable instead of Salaries Payable. Another example is not recording the exchange of convertible bonds for stock. Such errors are frequently discovered and corrected in the period in which they are made. When such errors are not found until a subsequent period, corrections must be made at that time and balance sheet data subsequently restated for comparative reporting purposes.

3. *Errors limited to income statement accounts.* The examples and correcting procedures for this type of error are similar to those in (2). For example, Office Salaries may be debited instead of Sales Salaries. This type of error should be corrected as soon as it is discovered. Even though the error would not affect net income, the misstated accounts should be restated for analysis purposes and comparative reporting.

4. *Errors affecting both income statement accounts and balance sheet accounts.* Certain errors, when not discovered currently, result in the misstatement of net income and thus affect both the income statement accounts and the balance sheet accounts. The balance sheet accounts are carried into the succeeding period; hence, an error made currently and not detected will affect future earnings. Such errors may be classified into two groups:

    (a) *Errors in net income that, when not detected, are automatically counterbalanced in the following fiscal period.* Net income amounts on the income statements for two successive periods are inaccurately stated; certain account balances on the balance sheet at the end of the first period are inaccurately stated, but the account balances in the balance sheet at the end of the succeeding period will be accurately stated. In this class are errors such as the misstatement of inventories and the omission of adjustments for prepaid and accrued items at the end of the period.

(b) *Errors in net income that, when not detected, are not automatically counterbalanced in the following fiscal period.* Account balances on successive balance sheets will be inaccurately stated until such time as entries are made compensating for or correcting the errors. In this class are errors such as the recognition of capital expenditures as expenses and the omission of charges for depreciation and amortization.

When errors affecting income are discovered, careful analysis is necessary to determine the required action to correct the account balances. As indicated, most errors will be caught and corrected prior to closing the books. The few material errors not detected until subsequent periods and those that have not already been counterbalanced must be treated as prior-period adjustments.

The following sections describe and illustrate the procedures to be applied when error corrections require prior-period adjustments. It is assumed that each of the errors is material. Errors that are discovered usually affect the income tax liability for a prior period. Amended tax returns are usually prepared either to claim a refund or to pay any additional tax assessment. For simplicity, the examples on the following pages and in the exercises and problems at the end of the chapter ignore the income tax effects of errors.

Illustrative Example of Error Correction

Assume that Supply Master, Inc., began operations at the beginning of 2013. An auditing firm is engaged for the first time in 2015. Before the accounts are adjusted and closed for 2015, the auditor reviews the books and accounts and discovers the errors summarized on pages 20-18 and 20-19. Effects of these errors on the financial statements, before any correcting entries, are indicated as follows: A plus sign (+) indicates an overstatement and a minus sign (−) indicates an understatement. Each error correction is discussed in the following paragraphs.

(1) Understatement of Merchandise Inventory It is discovered that the merchandise inventory as of December 31, 2013, was understated by $1,000. The effects of the misstatement were as shown below.

	Income Statement	Balance Sheet
2013	Cost of goods sold overstated (ending inventory too low)	Assets understated (inventory too low)
	Net income understated	Retained earnings understated
2014	Cost of goods sold understated (beginning inventory too low)	Balance sheet items not affected, retained earnings understatement for 2013 being corrected by net income overstatement for 2014
	Net income overstated	

Because this type of error counterbalances after two years, no correcting entry is required in 2015.

Analysis Sheet to Show Effects

	At End of 2013			
	Income Statement		Balance Sheet	
	Section	Net Income	Section	Retained Earnings
(1) Understatement of merchandise inventory of $1,000 on December 31, 2013.	Cost of Goods Sold +	−	Current Assets −	−
(2) Failure to record merchandise purchases on account of $850 in 2013; purchases were recorded in 2014.	Cost of Goods Sold −	+	Current Liabilities −	+
(3) Failure to record merchandise sales on account of $1,800 in 2014. (It is assumed that the sales for 2014 were recognized as revenue in 2015.)				
(4) Failure to record accrued sales salaries of $450 on December 31, 2013; expense was recognized when payment was made.	Selling Expense −	+	Current Liabilities −	+
(5) Failure to record prepaid taxes of $275 on December 31, 2013; amount was included in Miscellaneous General Expense.	General Expense +	−	Current Assets −	−
(6) Failure to record accrued interest on notes receivable of $150 on December 31, 2013; revenue was recognized when collected in 2014.	Other Revenue −	−	Current Assets −	−
(7) Failure to record unearned service fees of $225 on December 31, 2014; amount received was included in Miscellaneous Revenue.				
(8) Failure to record depreciation of delivery equipment. On December 31, 2013, $1,200.	Selling Expense −	+	Noncurrent Assets +	+
On December 31, 2014, $1,200.				
(9) Incorrectly capitalizing an expenditure for operating expenses on January 1, 2013; depreciation expense of $400 was incorrectly recognized in 2013 and 2014.	Operating Expense −	+	Noncurrent Assets +	+

> **Caution**
>
> Errors (1) through (6) provide examples of errors that will counterbalance over two periods. However, errors that will "fix themselves" still result in misstated financial statements for each year of the two-year period. Investors and creditors may make ill-advised decisions based on those misstated financial statements.

If the error had been discovered in 2014 instead of 2015, an entry would have been made to correct the account balances so that operations for 2014 would be reported accurately. The beginning inventory for 2014 would have been increased by $1,000, the amount of the asset understatement, and Retained Earnings would have been credited for this amount, representing the income understatement in 2013. The correcting entry in 2014 would have been as follows:

Merchandise Inventory	1,000	
Retained Earnings		1,000

of Errors on Financial Statements

At End of 2014				At End of 2015			
Income Statement		Balance Sheet		Income Statement		Balance Sheet	
Section	Net Income	Section	Retained Earnings	Section	Net Income	Section	Retained Earnings
Cost of Goods Sold −	+						
Cost of Goods Sold +	−						
Sales −	−	Accounts Receivable −	−	Sales +	+		
Selling Expense +	−						
General Expense −	+						
Other Revenue +	+						
Other Revenue +	+	Current Liabilities −	+	Other Revenue −			
		Noncurrent Assets +	+			Noncurrent Assets +	+
Selling Expense −	+	Noncurrent Assets +	+			Noncurrent Assets +	+
Operating Expense +	−	Noncurrent Assets +	+			Noncurrent Assets +	+

无论企业是采用定期盘存制还是采用永续盘存制，纠错分录都是一样的。如差错（2）一样，纠错分录有时是不同的，这主要取决于企业使用的存货制度。

Caution
This entry is made only if the error is identified at the end of 2014.

This correcting entry is the same whether the company uses a periodic or a perpetual inventory system. As seen with error (2), the correcting entry is sometimes different, depending on what type of inventory system the company uses.

(2) Failure to Record Merchandise Purchases It is discovered that purchase invoices as of December 28, 2013, for $850 had not been recorded until 2014. The goods had been included in the inventory at the end of 2013. The effects of failure to record the purchases were as shown on page 20-20.

	Income Statement	Balance Sheet
2013	Cost of goods sold understated (purchases too low)	Liabilities understated (accounts payable too low)
	Net income overstated	Retained earnings overstated
2014	Cost of goods sold overstated (purchases too high) Net income understated	Balance sheet items not affected, retained earnings overstatement for 2013 being corrected by net income understatement for 2014

Because this is a counterbalancing error, no correcting entry is required in 2015.

If the error had been discovered in 2014 instead of 2015, a correcting entry would have been necessary. In 2014, Purchases was debited and Accounts Payable was credited for $850 for merchandise acquired in 2013 and included in the ending inventory of 2013. Retained Earnings would have to be debited for $850, representing the net income overstatement for 2013, and Purchases would have to be credited for the same amount to reduce the balance in 2014. The correcting entry in 2014, assuming the company uses a periodic inventory system, would have been as follows:

Retained Earnings 850
    Purchases 850

If the company had used a perpetual system, the incorrect purchase would have been debited directly to Inventory. Accordingly, the correcting entry would have been made in 2014:

Retained Earnings 850
    Inventory 850

(3) Failure to Record Merchandise Sales It is discovered that sales on account of $1,800 for the last week of December 2014 had not been recorded until 2015. The goods sold were not included in the inventory at the end of 2014. The effects of the failure to report the revenue in 2014 follow:

	Income Statement	Balance Sheet
2014	Revenue understated (sales too low)	Assets understated (accounts receivable too low)
	Net income understated	Retained earnings understated

When the error is discovered in 2015, Sales is debited for $1,800 and Retained Earnings is credited for this amount, representing the net income understatement for 2014. The following entry is made:

Sales 1,800
    Retained Earnings 1,800

(4) Failure to Record Accrued Expense Accrued sales salaries of $450 as of December 31, 2013, were overlooked in adjusting the accounts. Sales Salaries is debited for salary payments. The effects of the failure to record the accrued expense of $450 as of December 31, 2013, were as shown on page 20-21.

	Income Statement	Balance Sheet
2013	Expenses understated (sales salaries too low)	Liabilities understated (accrued salaries not reported)
	Net income overstated	Retained earnings overstated
2014	Expenses overstated (sales salaries too high) Net income understated	Balance sheet items not affected, retained earnings overstatement for 2013 being corrected by net income understatement for 2014

No entry is required in 2015 to correct the accounts for the failure to record the accrued expense at the end of 2013, the misstatement in 2013 having been counterbalanced by the misstatement in 2014. However, if comparative income statements were presented in 2015, then the amounts reported for sales salaries in 2013 and 2014 would be corrected. If the error had been discovered in 2014, an entry would have been required to correct the accounts for the failure to record the accrued expense at the end of 2013 if the net income for 2014 is not to be misstated. If accrued expenses are to be properly recorded at the end of 2014, Retained Earnings would be debited for $450, representing the net income overstatement for 2013, and Sales Salaries would be credited for the same amount, representing the amount to be subtracted from salary expenses in 2014. The correcting entry made in 2014 follows:

Retained Earnings.. 450
    Sales Salaries.. 450

(5) Failure to Record Prepaid Expense It is discovered that Miscellaneous General Expense for 2013 included taxes of $275 that should have been deferred in adjusting the accounts on December 31, 2013. The effects of the failure to record the prepaid expense were as follows:

	Income Statement	Balance Sheet
2013	Expenses overstated (miscellaneous general expense too high)	Assets understated (prepaid taxes not reported)
	Net income understated	Retained earnings understated
2014	Expenses understated (miscellaneous general expense too low) Net income overstated	Balance sheet items not affected, retained earnings understatement for 2013 being corrected by net income overstatement for 2014

Because this is a counterbalancing error, no entry to correct the accounts is required in 2015.

If the error had been discovered in 2014 instead of 2015, a correcting entry would have been necessary. If prepaid taxes had been properly recorded at the end of 2014, Miscellaneous General Expense would have to be debited for $275, the expense relating to operations of 2014, and Retained Earnings would have to be credited for the same amount, representing the net income understatement for 2013. The following correcting entry would have been made in 2014:

Miscellaneous General Expense.. 275
    Retained Earnings.. 275

(6) Failure to Record Accrued Revenue Accrued interest on notes receivable of $150 was overlooked in adjusting the accounts on December 31, 2013. The revenue was recognized when the interest was collected in 2014. The effects of the failure to record the accrued revenue follow:

	Income Statement	Balance Sheet
2013	Revenue understated (interest revenue too low)	Assets understated (interest receivable not reported)
	Net income understated	Retained earnings understated
2014	Revenue overstated (interest revenue too high)	Balance sheet items not affected, retained earnings understatement for 2013 being corrected by net income overstatement for 2014
	Net income overstated	

Because the balance sheet items at the end of 2014 were correctly stated, no entry to correct the accounts is required in 2015.

If the error had been discovered in 2014 instead of 2015, an entry would have been necessary to correct the account balances. If accrued interest on notes receivable had been properly recorded at the end of 2014, Interest Revenue would have to be debited for $150, the amount to be subtracted from receipts of 2014, and Retained Earnings would have to be credited for the same amount, representing the net income understatement for 2013. The correcting entry in 2014 would have been as follows:

Interest Revenue	150
Retained Earnings...	150

(7) Failure to Record Unearned Revenue Fees of $225 received in advance for miscellaneous services as of December 31, 2014, were overlooked in adjusting the accounts. Miscellaneous Revenue had been credited when fees were received. The effects of the failure to recognize the unearned revenue of $225 at the end of 2014 were as follows:

	Income Statement	Balance Sheet
2014	Revenue overstated (miscellaneous revenue too high)	Liabilities understated (unearned service fees not reported)
	Net income overstated	Retained earnings overstated

An entry is required to correct the accounts for the failure to record the unearned revenue at the end of 2014 if the net income for 2015 is not to be misstated. If the unearned revenue was properly recorded at the end of 2015, Retained Earnings would be debited for $225, representing the net income overstatement for 2014, and Miscellaneous Revenue would be credited for the same amount, representing the revenue that is to be identified with 2015. The correcting entry follows:

Retained Earnings...	225
Miscellaneous Revenue	225

(8) Failure to Record Depreciation Delivery equipment was acquired at the beginning of 2013 at a cost of $6,000. The equipment has an estimated five-year life. Its depreciation of $1,200 was overlooked at the end of 2013 and 2014. The effects of the failure to record depreciation for 2013 were as follows:

> **Caution**
> Error (8) does not counterbalance in the following year. Thus, financial statements have the potential to be misstated for several years. In this example, the error could continue until the delivery equipment is removed from the books.

	Income Statement	Balance Sheet
2013	Expenses understated (depreciation of delivery equipment too low)	Assets overstated (accumulated depreciation of delivery equipment too low)
	Net income overstated	Retained earnings overstated
2014	Expenses not affected	Assets overstated (accumulated depreciation of delivery equipment too low)
	Net income not affected	Retained earnings overstated

It should be observed that the misstatements arising from the failure to record depreciation are not counterbalanced in the succeeding year.

Failure to record depreciation for 2014 affected the statements as follows:

	Income Statement	Balance Sheet
2014	Expenses understated (depreciation of delivery equipment too low)	Assets overstated (accumulated depreciation of delivery equipment too low)
	Net income overstated	Retained earnings overstated

When the omission is recognized, Retained Earnings must be decreased by the net income overstatements of prior years and Accumulated Depreciation must be increased by the depreciation that should have been recorded. The correcting entry in 2015 for depreciation that should have been recognized for 2013 and 2014 is as follows:

Retained Earnings 2,400
    Accumulated Depreciation—Delivery Equipment 2,400

(9) Incorrectly Capitalizing an Expenditure Operating expenses of $2,000 were paid in cash at the beginning of 2013. However, the payment was incorrectly recorded as the purchase of equipment. The "equipment" was assumed to have an estimated five-year life with $0 residual value, and depreciation of $400 was recognized at the end of 2013 and 2014. The effects of this incorrect capitalization of an expenditure were as follows:

	Income Statement	Balance Sheet
2013	Expenses understated (operating expenses too low, partially offset by depreciation expense)	Assets overstated (asset, net of accumulated depreciation, is recorded when there should not be any asset)
	Net income overstated	Retained earnings overstated
2014	Expenses overstated (depreciation too high)	Assets overstated (asset is still incorrectly recorded, though the net amount is less)
	Net income understated	Retained earnings overstated

When the error is discovered, Retained Earnings must be decreased by the net income overstatement of 2013 (partially offset by the net income understatement in 2014) and the accounts related to the "equipment" (Equipment and Accumulated Depreciation) must be eliminated. The correcting entry in 2015 is as follows:

Retained Earnings 1,200
Accumulated Depreciation—Equipment 800
    Equipment. 2,000

Required Disclosure for Error Restatements

If an error (either accidental or intentional in nature) is subsequently discovered that affected a prior period, the nature of the error, its effect on previously issued financial statements, and the effect of its correction on current period's net income and EPS should be disclosed in the period in which the error is corrected.[6] In addition, any comparative financial statements provided must be corrected.

An example of the disclosure provided when an error correction is made through a prior-period adjustment is given in Exhibit 20-4; the error correction (intentional errors in this instance) was made in 2000 by Xerox Corporation. Xerox provides extensive disclosure as to the effect of the errors on the income statement and the balance sheet for each year affected. Recall that Xerox's accounting difficulties were discussed in Chapter 6. As you read over the businesslike description of the accounting errors uncovered at Xerox, keep in mind that underlying this dry verbiage lie the destroyed careers of many accountants and managers at Xerox who stepped over the earnings management line into the area of earnings misstatement (see Chapter 6). Between the lines of this note one can also sense the lost trust of Xerox shareholders, customers, suppliers, and regulators.

Summary of Accounting Changes and Error Corrections

The summary listed below presents the appropriate accounting procedures applicable to each of the four main categories covered in FASB ASC Topic 250, Accounting Changes and Error Corrections. Naturally, accountants must apply these guidelines with judgment and should seek to provide the most relevant and reliable information possible.

Summary of Procedures for Reporting Accounting Changes and Error Corrections

Category	Accounting Procedures
I. Change in estimate	1. Adjust either current-period results or current- and future-period results.
	2. No separate cumulative adjustment or restated financial statements.
II. Change in accounting principle	1. Direct cumulative adjustment to beginning retained earnings balance of earliest year presented in the financial statements.
	2. Restate financial statements to reflect new principle for comparative purposes.
III. Pro forma disclosures after a business combination	1. Supplemental disclosure for the year of the combination and the preceding year of revenues and net income as if the combination had occurred at the beginning of the preceding year.
IV. Error corrections	1. If detected in period error occurred, correct accounts through normal accounting cycle adjustments.
	2. If detected in a subsequent period, adjust for effect of material errors by making prior-period adjustments directly to Retained Earnings balance for the years affected by those errors. If the error relates to a year that is not presented in the financial statements, the Retained Earnings balance for the earliest year presented is adjusted. Also correct each item presented in comparative financial statements.
	3. Once an error is discovered in previously issued financial statements, the nature of the error, its effect on the financial statements, and its effect on the current period's income and EPS should be disclosed.

[6] FASB ASC paragraph 250-10-50-7.

Exhibit 20-4 | Xerox Corporation—Disclosure of Error Correction

2. Restatement

We have restated our Consolidated Financial Statements for the fiscal years ended December 31, 1999 and 1998 as a result of two separate investigations conducted by the Audit Committee of the Board of Directors. These investigations involved previously disclosed issues in our Mexico operations and a review of our accounting policies and procedures and application thereof. As a result of these investigations, it was determined that certain accounting practices and the application thereof misapplied GAAP and certain accounting errors and irregularities were identified. The Company has corrected the accounting errors and irregularities in its Consolidated Financial Statements. The Consolidated Financial Statements have been adjusted as follows:

In fiscal 2000 the Company had initially recorded charges totaling $170 ($120 after taxes) which arose from imprudent and improper business practices in Mexico that resulted in certain accounting errors and irregularities. Over a period of years, several senior managers in Mexico had collaborated to circumvent certain of Xerox's accounting policies and administrative procedures. The charges related to provisions for uncollectible long-term receivables, the recording of liabilities for amounts due to concessionaires and, to a lesser extent, for contracts that did not fully meet the requirements to be recorded as sales-type leases. The investigation of the accounting issues discovered in Mexico has been completed. The Company has restated its prior year Consolidated Financial Statements to reflect reductions to pre-tax income of $53 and $13 in 1999 and 1998, respectively. It is not practical to determine what portion, if any, of the approximate remaining $101 of the Mexican charge reflected in adjusted 2000 results of operations relates to prior years.

In connection with our acquisition of the remaining 20 percent of Xerox Limited from Rank Group, Plc in 1997, we recorded a liability of $100 for contingencies identified at the date of acquisition. During 1998, we determined that the liability was no longer required. During 1998 and 1999, we charged to the liability certain expenses incurred as part of the consolidation of our European back-office operations. This reversal should have been recorded as a reduction of Goodwill and Deferred tax assets. Therefore, we have restated our previously reported Consolidated Financial Statements to reflect decreases of $67 to Goodwill and $33 of Deferred tax assets and increases in Selling, administrative and general expenses of $76 in 1999 and $24 in 1998.

In addition to the above items, we have made adjustments in connection with certain misapplications of GAAP under SFAS No. 13, "Accounting for Leases." These adjustments primarily relate to the accounting for lease modifications and residual values as well as certain other items. The following table presents the effects of all of the aforementioned adjustments on pre-tax income (loss).

	Year Ended December 31,		
	2000	1999	1998
Increase (decrease) to pre-tax income (loss):			
Mexico	$ 69	$ (53)	$ (13)
Rank Group acquisition	6	(76)	(24)
Lease issues, net	87	83	(165)
Other, net	10	(82)	18
Total	$172	$(128)	$(184)

These adjustments resulted in the cumulative net reduction of Common shareholders' equity and Consolidated Tangible Net Worth (as defined in our $7 Billion Revolving Credit Agreement) of $137 and $76, respectively, as of December 31, 2000.

Retained earnings at December 31, 1997 was restated from $3,960 to $3,852 as a result of the effect of these aforementioned adjustments on years prior to 1998.

The following tables present the impact of the adjustments and restatements on a condensed basis.

(Continued)

Exhibit 20-4 | Xerox Corporation—Disclosure of Error Correction (continued)

	Amount Previously Reported	As Adjusted
(in millions, except per share amounts)		
Year ended December 31, 2000:*		
Statement of operations:		
Revenues	$18,632	$18,701
Costs and expenses	19,188	19,085
Income (loss) from continuing operations	(384)	(257)
Basic loss per share	$ (0.63)	$ (0.44)
Diluted loss per share	$ (0.63)	$ (0.44)
Balance Sheet:		
Current finance receivables, net	$ 5,141	$ 5,097
Inventories, net	1,930	1,932
Equipment and operating leases, net	717	724
Deferred taxes and other current assets	1,284	1,247
Finance receivables due after one year, net	8,035	7,957
Intangible and other assets, net	3,062	3,061
Goodwill, net	1,639	1,578
Other current liabilities	1,648	1,630
Deferred taxes and other liabilities	1,933	1,876
Common shareholders' equity	3,630	3,493

	Amount Previously Reported	As Adjusted
(in millions, except per share amounts)		
Year ended December 31, 1999:**		
Statement of operations:		
Revenues	$19,548	$19,567
Costs and expenses	17,512	17,659
Income (loss) from continuing operations	1,424	1,339
Basic earnings per share	$ 2.09	$ 1.96
Diluted earnings per share	$ 1.96	$ 1.85
Balance Sheet:		
Accounts receivable, net	$ 2,622	$ 2,633
Current finance receivables, net	5,115	4,961
Inventories, net	2,285	2,290
Equipment and operating leases, net	676	695
Finance receivables due after one year, net	8,203	8,058
Intangible and other assets, net	2,831	2,810
Goodwill, net	1,724	1,657
Other current liabilities	2,163	2,176
Deferred taxes and other liabilities	2,623	2,521
Common shareholders' equity	4,911	4,648
Year ended December 31, 1998:**		
Statement of operations:		
Revenues	$19,747	$19,593
Costs and expenses	18,984	19,014
Income (loss) from continuing operations	585	463
Basic earnings per share	$ 0.82	$ 0.63
Diluted earnings per share	$ 0.80	$ 0.62

*As reported in the Company's unaudited financial statements included in its report on Form 8-K dated April 19, 2001.
**Revenues and costs and expenses have been reclassified to reflect the Change in classification of shipping and handling costs as discussed in Note 1.

United Airlines, 10K Report

SOLUTIONS TO OPENING SCENARIO QUESTIONS

1. Reducing retiree health benefits would reduce the earning impact and the size of the liability to be reported under FASB *Statement No. 106*. Without the changes, firms might fear that the adverse financial statement effects would lower their stock price, reduce their ability to maintain management bonuses, or make it more difficult to obtain loans. In one sense, the existence of such consequences is counterintuitive, because FASB *Statement No. 106* mandated only a change in accounting for retiree benefit plans—plans that have been in existence for years. However, the fact that firms seemed to be willing to change their retiree plans in response to a change in accounting again supports the belief that the way something is accounted for has real economic consequences.

   Another reason that a company might have reduced its retiree health benefits in response to the adoption of FASB *Statement No. 106* is that, in the absence of the accounting requirement, the company had never before quantified the cost of the promises it was making to its workers. FASB *Statement No. 106* forced some companies to face economic reality and acknowledge that they could no longer make these costly promises to employees.

2. In a perfect world, one would expect no impact on stock prices or on the ability to get loans. This is because the impact of retiree healthcare plans on the financial condition of a company would have already been taken into account by sophisticated investors and bankers who are known to use all sorts of data not found in financial statements when doing their financial analyses. However, the world is not perfect, and it is possible that the financial effects of retiree healthcare plans either were not fully factored into investment decisions, or the estimates of those effects were systematically in error. There is some evidence that firms found that they had been underestimating the cost of their retiree healthcare plans. If this is true, FASB *Statement No. 106* could have impacted stock prices and creditworthiness of firms with large retiree healthcare plans.

3. GM could have recognized this $21 billion after-tax cost as correction of a past error with a restatement of past income statements to reflect the cost in the years in which it occurred. As explained in this chapter, this approach, the restatement approach, is the approach now required by the FASB.

Stop & Think SOLUTION

1. (Page 20-6) The correct answer is D. Changes in estimates are made on an ongoing basis and are a routine part of the accounting process. Each year, estimates as to the percentage of accounts receivable that will be uncollected, the amount of warranty claims that will be serviced, and percentage of costs incurred on long-term contracts, to name a few, must be reassessed. If previously issued financial statements were required to be restated in every case where an estimate was changed, then prior-period statements would continually be reissued. Investors and creditors would be unable to rely on the information provided by companies because they would know that the information would be changing. It is a good thing that accounting standards do not require financial statements to be restated for every change in estimate.

SOLUTION TO USING THE FASB'S CODIFICATION

Your search of the Codification will lead you to Topic 978, Real Estate—Time-Sharing Activities. The table of contents for this topic reveals that there is material specific to Topic 250, Accounting Changes and Error Corrections. Paragraph 978-250-35-2 says the following (in part): "A change in the delineation of a project or its phases without a significant change in facts and circumstances related to the project's development shall be accounted for as a change in the method of applying an accounting principle under Subtopic 250-10. An example of this latter change would be a decision to divide the same development of a project into more or fewer phases, which would be a change only in how the project is accounted for rather than a change in the nature (that is, the facts and circumstances) of the project itself."

So, Deedle Development's change in accounting for the South Willow project from three phases to four phases would be accounted for as a change in accounting principle and thus would be applied retrospectively.

Review Chapter 20 Learning Objectives

① Understand the two different types of accounting changes that have been identified by accounting standard setters.

The accounting profession has identified two different types of accounting changes: change in accounting estimate and change in accounting principle. The distinction between the two is important because different accounting treatment and disclosure are required for each type of accounting change.

② Recognize the difference between a change in accounting estimate and a change in accounting principle, and know how a change in accounting estimate is reflected in the financial statements.

A change in accounting estimate does not involve a restatement of prior periods' financial statements. Instead, the effects of these types of changes are reflected in the current and future periods. Previous chapters discussed the accounting for common areas involving changing estimates. Examples include bad debt expense (Chapter 7), depreciation (Chapter 10), and actuarial assumptions (Chapter 17). A change in depreciation method is accounted for as a change in estimate and is called "a change in accounting estimate effected by a change in accounting principle."

③ Prepare the retrospective adjustment of prior periods' financial statements, and any necessary cumulative adjustment, associated with a change in accounting principle.

A change in accounting principle is implemented by recomputing all financial statement amounts for the preceding years (at least those that will be included in the current year's comparative financial statements). These recomputed amounts are included in the comparative financial statements reported this year. Any income effect in even earlier years is shown as an adjustment to the beginning balance in Retained Earnings for the earliest year reported. Note disclosure gives a line-by-line comparison between these retrospectively adjusted financial statements and the financial statements (using the former accounting principles) that were originally reported.

④ Report pro forma results for prior years following a business combination.

After a business combination, supplemental disclosure for the year of the combination and the preceding year is required. Pro forma disclosure of revenues and net income must be made as if the combination had occurred at the beginning of the preceding year.

⑤ Recognize the various types of errors that can occur in the accounting process, understand when errors counterbalance, and be able to correct errors when necessary.

Numerous errors can occur during the accounting process. Many of those errors will be discovered and corrected in the normal course of business. Some errors will be detected after the books have been closed for an accounting period, thereby requiring an adjustment to the Retained Earnings balance. Most errors that go undetected counterbalance over a two-year period, but those that do not often require a cumulative adjustment once they have been detected. When an error is detected, all financial statements presented for comparative purposes are corrected and restated.

FASB-IASB CODIFICATION SUMMARY

Topic	FASB Accounting Standards Codification	Original FASB Standard	Corresponding IASB Standard	Differences between U.S. GAAP and IFRS
Disclosure after a business combination	Section 805-10-50 par. 1-2	SFAS No. 141(R) par. 68	IFRS 3 par. 59-63 and B64-B67	No substantial differences
Change in accounting principle	Section 250-10-45 par. 1-16 Section 250-10-50 par. 1-3	SFAS No. 154 par. 4-18 APB No. 28 par. 28	IAS 8 par. 14-31	No substantial differences
Change in accounting estimate	Section 250-10-45 par. 17-20 Section 250-10-50 par. 4-5	SFAS No. 154 par. 19-22 SFAS No. 157 par. 20	IAS 8 par. 32-40	No substantial differences
Correction of an error	Section 250-10-45 par. 22-28 Section 250-10-50 par. 7-11	SFAS No. 154 par. 25-26 SFAS No. 16 par. 10-15 APB No. 9 par. 17-18 APB No. 9 par. 26-27 APB No. 28 par. 29	IAS 8 par. 41-49	No substantial differences

KEY TERMS

Accounting changes 20-3

Accounting errors 20-15

Change in accounting estimate 20-5

Change in accounting principle 20-8

Tutorial Activities

Tutorial Activities with author-written, content-specific feedback, available on *CengageNOW* for *Stice & Stice*.

QUESTIONS

1. How do accounting changes detract from the informational characteristics of comparability and consistency as described in FASB *Concepts Statement No. 2*?
2. What are the two categories of accounting changes? Explain briefly why such changes are made.
3. What alternative procedures have been suggested as solutions for reporting accounting changes?
4. (a) List several examples of areas for which changes in accounting estimates are often made. (b) Explain briefly the proper accounting treatment for a change in estimate. (c) Why is this procedure considered proper for recording changes in accounting estimates?
5. What is the proper way to account for a change in depreciation method?
6. (a) List several examples of changes in accounting principle that a company may make. (b) Explain briefly the proper accounting treatment for recognizing currently a change in accounting principle.
7. Why does a change in accounting principle require justification?
8. (a) When should the effects of a change in accounting principle be reported only as a direct adjustment to the current year's beginning Retained Earnings balance? (b) When should the effects of a change in accounting principle be reported only prospectively?
9. Dallas Company purchased a delivery van in 2012. At the time of purchase, the van's service life was estimated to be seven years with a salvage value of $500. The company has been using the straight-line method of depreciation. During 2015, the company determined that because of extensive use, the van's service life would be only five years with no salvage value. Also, the company has decided to change the depreciation method used from straight-line to the sum-of-the-years'-digits method. How would these changes be treated?
10. Describe the required disclosures following a business combination.
11. Describe the effect of each of the following:
    a. Depreciation is changed from the straight-line method to an accelerated method.
    b. Depreciation is changed from an accelerated method to the straight-line method.
    c. Income on construction contracts that had been reported on a completed-contract basis is now reported on the percentage-of-completion basis.
    d. The valuation of inventories is changed from a FIFO to a LIFO basis.
    e. It is determined that warranty expenses in prior years should have been 5% of sales instead of 4%.
    f. The valuation of inventories is changed from a LIFO to a FIFO basis.
    g. Your accounts receivable clerk has learned that a major customer has declared bankruptcy.
    h. Your patent lawyer informs you that your rival has perfected and patented a new invention making your product obsolete.
12. (a) How are accounting errors to be treated?
    (b) What are counterbalancing errors?
13. Mendez Manufacturing Company failed to record accrued interest for 2012, $800; 2013, $700; and 2014, $950. What is the amount of overstatement or understatement of the retained earnings account at December 31, 2015?
14. Goods purchased FOB shipping point were shipped to Merkley & Co. on December 31, 2015. The purchase was recorded in 2015, but the goods were not included in ending inventory. (a) What effect would this error have had on reported income for 2015 had it not been discovered? (b) What entry should be made on the books to correct this error, assuming that the books have not yet been closed for 2015?

PRACTICE EXERCISES

Practice 20-1
Change in Depreciation Life
On January 1, 2011, the company purchased equipment for $100,000. Originally, the equipment had a 15-year expected useful life and $13,000 residual value. The company uses straight-line depreciation. On January 1, 2015, the company realized that the equipment would have a total useful life of 12 years instead of 15 years and that the residual value would be $4,000 instead of $15,000. Compute depreciation expense for 2015. (*Note:* If you need some hints on how to do this exercise, look back at Chapter 11.)

Practice 20-2
Change in Depreciation Life
On January 1, 2011, the company purchased equipment for $100,000. Originally, the equipment had a 12-year expected useful life and $4,000 residual value. The company uses straight-line depreciation. On January 1, 2015, the company realized that the equipment would have a total useful life of 15 years instead of 12 years and that the residual value would be $15,000 instead of $4,000. Compute depreciation expense for 2015. (*Note:* If you need some hints on how to do this exercise, look back at Chapter 11.)

Practice 20-3
Change from Double-Declining-Balance to Straight-Line Depreciation
On January 1, 2012, the company purchased equipment for $600,000. The equipment has a 20-year expected useful life and $0 residual value. Initially, the company used double-declining-balance depreciation. On January 1, 2015, the company changed to straight-line depreciation. The expected useful life and residual value are unchanged. Compute depreciation expense for 2015. Ignore income taxes.

Practice 20-4
Deferred Tax Impact of a Change in Depreciation Method
Refer to Practice 20-3. Assume that before 2015 the company used straight-line depreciation for tax purposes while using double-declining-balance depreciation for book purposes. The change to straight-line depreciation in 2015 is made for book purposes; the company continues to use straight-line depreciation for tax purposes. The income tax rate is 40%. (1) Compute the amount of the deferred tax asset or liability that would be included in the December 31, 2014, balance sheet and (2) compute the amount of the deferred tax asset or liability that would be included in the December 31, 2015, balance sheet.

Practice 20-5
Change from Straight-Line to Double-Declining-Balance Depreciation
On January 1, 2012, the company purchased equipment for $400,000. The equipment has an eight-year expected useful life and $0 residual value. Initially, the company used straight-line depreciation. On January 1, 2015, the company changed to double-declining-balance depreciation. Compute depreciation expense for 2015. Ignore income taxes.

Practice 20-6
Change from LIFO to FIFO: First Year Retained Earnings
As of January 1, 2015, the company decided to change from the LIFO method of inventory valuation to the FIFO method. The change is being made for both book and tax purposes. Data for the past four years (including 2015) are as follows:

	2015	2014	2013	2012
Sales	$2,000	$1,500	$1,200	$1,000
Cost of goods sold—LIFO	1,200	900	720	600
Ending inventory—LIFO	200	150	120	100
Ending income taxes payable—LIFO	n/a	240	192	160
Ending retained earnings—LIFO	1,668	1,188	828	540
Cost of goods sold—FIFO	1,170	880	710	595
Ending inventory—FIFO	300	220	170	140

The ending income taxes payable—LIFO amount is not given because, in 2015, income taxes payable will be computed using the newly adopted FIFO numbers. As you can see from the prior years, it is the practice of the company to pay all income taxes in the subsequent year.

The company's income tax rate is 40%, and the company has no expenses except for cost of goods sold and income tax expense. Compute the retrospectively recalculated Retained Earnings balance as of January 1, 2013, after the change to FIFO is made.

Practice 20-7

Change from LIFO to FIFO: Year-by-Year Retained Earnings Calculations
Refer to Practice 20-6. Compute (1) the retrospectively recalculated Retained Earnings balances as of December 31, 2013, and December 31, 2014, and (2) the Retained Earnings balance as of December 31, 2015, after the change to FIFO is made. Note that the company does not pay dividends.

Practice 20-8

Change from LIFO to FIFO: Year-by-Year Income Taxes Payable Calculations
Refer to Practice 20-6. Compute TOTAL income taxes payable, after the change to FIFO is made, as of December 31, 2013, December 31, 2014, and December 31, 2015. Recall that the change to FIFO will necessitate the payment of any tax savings that had been created by the use of LIFO.

Practice 20-9

Change from LIFO to FIFO: Income Statement Comparative Disclosure
Refer to Practice 20-6. Prepare the comparative note disclosure that would be provided in the notes to the 2015 financial statements with respect to the income statements for 2013, 2014, and 2015.

Practice 20-10

Change from LIFO to FIFO: Impractical to Identify Yearly Differences
Refer to Practice 20-6. Assume that the detailed information listed in Practice 20-6 is not available. Instead, the company only knows that the beginning inventory for 2015 is $150 using LIFO and $220 using FIFO. Show the retained earnings computation for 2015 that would be included in the statement of stockholders' equity for the year.

Practice 20-11

Disclosures Following a Business Combination
On December 31, 2015, Big Company acquired Tiny Company for $150,000. This amount exceeded the recorded value of Tiny Company's net assets by $30,000 on the acquisition date. The entire excess was attributable to a Tiny Company building that had a remaining useful life of 15 years as of the acquisition date. Information reported for the two companies for 2014 and 2015 was as follows:

	2015	2014
Big Company:		
Revenue	$500,000	$400,000
Net income	60,000	50,000
Tiny Company:		
Revenue	$ 75,000	$ 90,000
Net income	12,000	20,000

Prepare the necessary pro forma information that would be included in the notes to Big Company's 2015 financial statements. For simplicity, ignore income taxes.

Practice 20-12

Misstatement of Inventory
The company miscounted its inventory at the end of the year. The correct amount of inventory was $100,000. The error was not discovered until the following May when the books for the preceding year were already closed. Make the correcting entry necessary the following May, assuming that the incorrectly reported amount of inventory at the end of the preceding year was (1) $75,000 and (2) $110,000. Ignore income taxes.

Practice 20-13

Failure to Record Inventory Purchases

The company purchased inventory for $10,000 on December 28. The inventory purchase was not recorded until the following January 5. However, the inventory was appropriately included in the inventory count on December 31. The error was not discovered until the following May when the books for the preceding year had already been closed. Make the correcting entry necessary the following May, assuming that the company uses (1) the periodic inventory method and (2) the perpetual inventory method. Ignore income taxes.

Practice 20-14

Failure to Record Inventory Purchases and Inventory

Refer to Practice 20-13. Assume that in addition to failing to record the purchase, the company also failed to include the inventory in the ending inventory count. Make the correcting entry necessary the following May, assuming that the company uses (1) the periodic inventory method and (2) the perpetual inventory method. Ignore income taxes.

Practice 20-15

Misstatement of Sales

The company miscounted its total credit sales in the last two weeks of the year. The correct amount of credit sales for this period was $300,000. The error was not discovered until the following year when the books for the preceding year were already closed. Make the correcting entry necessary the following year, assuming the facts that follow. Ignore income taxes and assume (perhaps unreasonably) that no errors occurred in recording expenses associated with the sales.

(a) The incorrectly reported amount of credit sales was $260,000, and the error was found when the accounts were collected in cash.
(b) The incorrectly reported amount of credit sales was $260,000, and *none* of these credit sales had been collected in cash by the time the error was discovered.
(c) The incorrectly reported amount of credit sales was $325,000, and the error was found when the accounts were collected in cash.
(d) The incorrectly reported amount of credit sales was $325,000, and *none* of these credit sales had been collected in cash by the time the error was discovered.

Practice 20-16

Failure to Record Accrued Expense

In December 2014, the company neglected to accrue a $1,000 expense for rent. The expense was recognized in January 2015 when the rent was paid in cash. Make the necessary correcting entry, assuming that (1) the error was found in May 2015 after the 2014 books had been closed and (2) the error was found in May 2016 after the 2015 books had been closed. Ignore income taxes.

Practice 20-17

Failure to Record Prepaid Expense

In December 2014, the company paid $1,800 for insurance for the first six months of 2015. This payment was mistakenly recorded as insurance expense in 2014. Make the necessary correcting entry, assuming that (1) the error was found in August 2015 after the 2014 books had been closed and (2) the error was found in August 2016 after the 2015 books had been closed. Ignore income taxes.

Practice 20-18

Failure to Record Accrued Revenue

In December 2014, the company failed to recognize $4,000 in consulting revenue earned during 2014. This revenue was recognized when the cash was received in January 2015. Make the necessary correcting entry, assuming that (1) the error was found in May 2015 after the 2014 books had been closed and (2) the error was found in May 2016 after the 2015 books had been closed. Ignore income taxes.

Practice 20-19

Failure to Record Unearned Revenue

In December 2014, the company received $6,000 for services to be provided in early 2015. This payment was mistakenly recorded as service revenue in 2014. Make the necessary correcting entry, assuming that (1) the error was found in May 2015 after the 2014 books had been closed and (2) the error was found in May 2016 after the 2015 books had been closed. Ignore income taxes.

Practice 20-20

Failure to Record Depreciation

In January 2013, the company purchased equipment for $10,000. The equipment has a useful life of 10 years with $0 expected salvage value. The company uses straight-line depreciation. The company mistakenly failed to record depreciation expense on this equipment. Make the necessary correcting entry, assuming that (1) the error was found in May 2015 after the 2014 books had been closed and (2) the error was found in May 2016 after the 2015 books had been closed. Ignore income taxes.

Practice 20-21

Immediately Expensing Equipment that Is Subsequently Sold
On January 1, 2012, equipment was purchased for $10,000. The entire purchase price was expensed immediately. The equipment has a useful life of 10 years with $0 expected salvage value. The company uses straight-line depreciation. On January 1, 2015, the equipment was sold for $5,500 cash. The incorrect expensing of the purchase price, along with the subsequent failure to recognize depreciation, was discovered in May 2015 after the books for 2014 had been closed. (1) Make the necessary correcting entry in 2015 and (2) describe any necessary corrections to the 2015 comparative income statement (which includes 2013 and 2014).

Practice 20-22

Incorrect Capitalization
In January 2013, the company made $24,000 in expenditures. These expenditures should have been expensed immediately. Instead, the company recorded this $24,000 payment as a purchase of equipment with a useful life of 12 years and $0 expected salvage value. The company uses straight-line depreciation. The company proceeded to depreciate this "equipment." Make the necessary correcting entry, assuming that (1) the error was found in May 2015 after the 2014 books had been closed and (2) the error was found in May 2016 after the 2015 books had been closed. Ignore income taxes.

Practice 20-23

Disclosure of a Prior-Period Adjustment
Refer to Practice 20-22. Assume that the error was found in May 2015. Net income for 2015 (correctly stated) was $50,000. Dividends for 2015 were $15,000. The Retained Earnings balance as originally reported at the end of 2014 was $130,000. Prepare a statement of retained earnings for 2015.

EXERCISES

Exercise 20-24

Change in Accounting Estimate and in Depreciation Method
Manchester Manufacturing purchased a machine on January 1, 2011, for $50,000. At the time, it was determined that the machine had an estimated useful life of 10 years and an estimated residual value of $2,000. The company used the double-declining-balance method of depreciation. On January 1, 2015, the company decided to change its depreciation method from double declining balance to straight line. The machine's remaining useful life was estimated to be five years with a residual value of $500.

Give the entry required to record the company's depreciation expense for 2015.

Exercise 20-25

Change in Accounting Estimate
Danje Corporation purchased a machine on January 1, 2012, for $3,600,000. At the date of acquisition, the machine had an estimated useful life of 10 years with no residual value. The machine is being depreciated on a straight-line basis. On January 1, 2015, Danje determined, as a result of additional information, that the machine had an estimated useful life of 15 years from the date of acquisition with no residual value.

What is the amount of depreciation expense on the machine that should be charged to Danje Corporation's income statement for the year ended December 31, 2015?

Exercise 20-26

Change in Accounting Estimate
Albrecht Inc. began business in 2012. An examination of the company's allowance for bad debts account reveals the following.

	Estimated Bad Debts	Actual Bad Debts
2012	$11,000	$4,500
2013	13,000	6,800
2014	16,500	8,950
2015	No adjustment yet	9,500

In the past, the company has estimated that 3% of credit sales would be uncollectible. The accountant for Albrecht has determined that the percentage used in estimating bad debts has been inappropriate. She would like to revise the estimate downward to 1.5%. The company president has stated that if the previous estimates of bad debt expense were incorrect, the financial statements should be restated using the more accurate estimate.

1. Assuming that credit sales for 2015 are $650,000, provide the adjusting entry to record bad debt expense for the year.
2. What catch-up entry, if any, would be made to correct the inaccurate estimates for previous years?
3. How would you respond to the president's request to restate the prior years' financial statements?

Exercise 20-27

Change in Accounting Estimate

On January 1, 2015, management of Micro Storage Inc. determined that a revision in the estimates associated with the depreciation of storage facilities was appropriate. These facilities, purchased on January 5, 2013, for $600,000, had been depreciated using the straight-line method with an estimated salvage value of $60,000 and an estimated useful life of 20 years. Management has determined that the storage facilities' expected remaining useful life is 10 years and that they have an estimated salvage value of $80,000.

1. How much depreciation was recognized by Micro Storage in 2013 and 2014?
2. How much depreciation will be recognized by Micro Storage in 2015 as a result of the changes in estimates?
3. What journal entry is required to account for the changes in estimates at the beginning of 2015?

Exercise 20-28

Change in Estimate of Natural Resources

Hollow Mining Company purchased a tract of land with estimated copper ore deposits totaling 1,500,000 tons. The purchase price for the land was $4.8 million. During the first year of operation, Hollow mined and sold 160,000 tons of ore. During the second year, Hollow mined and sold 210,000 tons of ore. At the beginning of the third year, new geological engineering estimates determined that a total of 790,000 tons of copper ore remained. During Year 3, 245,000 tons of ore were mined and sold.

1. What was the original depletion rate used by Hollow in Years 1 and 2?
2. Make the accounting entries for depletion expense for Hollow Mining Company at the end of Years 1 and 2.
3. What is the depletion rate, carried to four decimals, for Year 3, and what accounting entry should be made to reflect the change in accounting estimate in Year 3? (*Note:* Round to four decimal places.)

Exercise 20-29

Change in Depreciation Method

Modern Lighting Inc. has in the past depreciated its computer hardware using the straight-line method, assuming a 10% salvage value and an expected useful life of five years. As a result of the rapid obsolescence associated with the computer industry, Modern Lighting has determined that it receives most of the benefit from its computer systems in the first few years of ownership. Therefore, as of January 1, 2015, Modern Lighting proposes changing to the sum-of-the-years'-digits method for depreciating its computer hardware. The following information is available regarding all of Modern Lighting's computer purchases:

	Cost
2012	$45,000
2013	25,000
2014	30,000

1. Compute the depreciation taken by Modern Lighting during 2012, 2013, and 2014. Assume that all purchases were made at the beginning of the year.
2. Compute the amount of depreciation expense for 2012–2014, assuming the sum-of-the-years'-digits method had been used.
3. Compute the amount of depreciation expense for 2015.

Exercise 20-30

Change in Accounting Principle
Keairnes Supplies decided to change from LIFO to FIFO as of January 1, 2015. The change is being made for both book and tax purposes.

Year	Net Income Computed Using LIFO	Excess of LIFO Cost of Goods Sold over FIFO Cost of Goods Sold	Income Effect (Net of Tax)
Prior to 2013		$14,000	$ 9,000
2013	$68,000	7,200	4,800
2014	61,500	8,750	5,250
2015	86,000	10,500	7,500
		$40,450	$26,550

1. Using LIFO, the beginning retained earnings as of January 1, 2013, was $182,000. Compute adjusted beginning retained earnings, using FIFO, as of January 1, 2013.
2. The three-year comparative income statement for 2015 includes net income for 2013, 2014, and 2015. In that comparative income statement, prepared after the change for FIFO has been adopted, what amount of net income will be reported for each year?

Exercise 20-31

Change in Accounting Principle without Detailed Prior-Year Information
Refer to Exercise 20-30. Assume that the detailed information for 2013 and 2014 is not available. During 2015, dividends of $20,000 were paid (compared to dividends of $16,500 in both 2013 and 2014). Based on this information, prepare the retained earnings statement for 2015. (*Note*: Do NOT prepare the comparative retained earnings statements for 2013 and 2014.) The December 31, 2014, Retained Earnings balance as reported using LIFO was $290,000.

Exercise 20-32

Changes in Accounting Estimates and Accounting Principles
Due to changing economic conditions and to making its financial statements more comparable to those of other companies in its industry, the management of Kelsea Inc. decided on January 1, 2015, to review its accounting practices.

Kelsea decided to change its allowance for bad debts from 2% to 3.5% of its outstanding receivables balance.

Kelsea decided to begin using the straight-line method of depreciation on its building instead of the sum-of-the-years'-digits method. The change will be effective as of January 1, 2015. Based on further information, it also was decided that the building has 10 more years of useful life as of January 2, 2015. Kelsea bought the building on January 1, 2005, at a cost of $550,000. At that time, Kelsea estimated it would have a 15-year useful life. The building has no expected salvage value. Prior years' depreciation is as follows:

2005	$68,750	2010	$45,833
2006	64,167	2011	41,250
2007	59,583	2012	36,667
2008	55,000	2013	32,083
2009	50,417	2014	27,500

Kelsea determined that starting with the current year, it would depreciate the company's printing press using hours of use as the depreciation base. The press, which had been purchased on January 1, 2000, at a cost of $930,000, was being depreciated for 25 years using the straight-line method. No salvage value was anticipated. It is estimated that this type of press provides 200,000 total hours of use and, as of January 1, 2015, it had been used 76,000 hours. At the end of 2015, the plant manager determined that the press had been run 6,250 hours during the year. Ignore income taxes relating to this change.

1. Evaluate each of the foregoing changes and determine whether it is a change in estimate or a change in accounting principle.
2. Give the journal entries required at December 31, 2015, to account for bad debt expense and depreciation expense given the preceding changes. Kelsea's receivable balance at December 31, 2015, was $345,000. Allowance for Bad Debts carried a $1,000 debit balance before adjustment.

Exercise 20-33

Accounting Errors

The following errors in the accounting records of the Chipp & Simon Partnership were discovered on January 10, 2015.

REVERSE SOLVABLE

Year of Error	Ending Inventories Overstated	Accrued Rent Depreciation Understated	Accrued Interest Revenue Not Recorded	Expense Not Recorded
2012	$42,000		$11,000	
2013		$18,000	31,000	
2014	34,000			$7,000

The partners share net income and losses as follows: 65%, Chipp; 35%, Simon.

1. Prepare a correcting journal entry on January 10, 2015, assuming that the books were closed for 2014.
2. Prepare a correcting journal entry on January 10, 2015, assuming that the books are still open for 2014 and that the partnership uses the perpetual inventory system.

Exercise 20-34

Analysis of Errors

State the effect of each of the following errors made in 2014 on the balance sheets and the income statements prepared in 2014 and 2015.

REVERSE SOLVABLE

(a) The ending inventory is understated as a result of an error in the count of goods on hand.

(b) The ending inventory is overstated as a result of the inclusion of goods acquired and held on a consignment basis. No purchase was recorded on the books.

(c) A purchase of merchandise at the end of 2014 is not recorded until payment is made for the goods in 2015; the goods purchased were included in the inventory at the end of 2014.

(d) A sale of merchandise at the end of 2014 is not recorded until cash is received for the goods in 2015; the goods sold were excluded from the inventory at the end of 2014.

(e) Goods shipped to consignees in 2014 were reported as sales; goods in the hands of consignees at the end of 2014 were not recognized for inventory purposes; sale of such goods in 2015 and collections on such sales were recorded as credits to the receivables established with consignees in 2014.

(f) The total of one week's sales during 2014 was credited to Gain on Sale—Machinery.

(g) No depreciation is taken in 2014 for equipment sold in April 2014. The company reports on a calendar-year basis and computes depreciation to the nearest month.

(h) No depreciation is taken in 2014 for equipment purchased in October 2014. The company reports on a calendar-year basis and computes depreciation to the nearest month.

(i) Customer notes receivable are debited to the accounts receivable account.

Exercise 20-35

Error Disclosure

Comparative statements for Bodie Corporation are as follows:

Bodie Corporation
Income Statements and Statement of Retained Earnings
For the Years Ended December 31

	2014	2013
Sales	$4,600,000	$4,350,000
Cost of goods sold	2,346,000	2,305,500
Gross profit	$2,254,000	$2,044,500
Expenses	1,598,000	1,533,000
Net income	$ 656,000	$ 511,500
Beginning retained earnings	$1,441,000	$1,077,500
Net income	656,000	511,500
Dividends	(157,000)	(148,000)
Ending retained earnings	$1,940,000	$1,441,000

In 2014, Bodie Corporation discovers that ending inventory for 2013 was understated by $11,000.

Prepare comparative income and retained earnings statements for 2013 and 2014. Ignore income tax effects, and assume that the 2014 books have not been closed.

Exercise 20-36

Journal Entries to Correct Accounts

The first audit of the books for Ringer Company was made for the year ended December 31, 2015. In reviewing the books, the auditor discovered that certain adjustments had been overlooked at the end of 2014 and 2015 and that other items had been improperly recorded. Omissions and other failures for each year are summarized as follows:

	2014	2015
Sales Salaries Payable	$1,800	$1,400
Interest Receivable	700	550
Prepaid Insurance	450	250
Advances from Customers	1,900	2,200
(Collections from customers had been included in sales but should have been recognized as advances from customers because goods were not shipped until the following year.)		
Equipment	1,600	1,300
(Expenditures had been recognized as repairs but should have been recognized as cost of equipment; the depreciation rate on such equipment is 10% per year, but depreciation in the year of the expenditure is to be recognized at 5%.)		

Prepare journal entries to correct revenue and expense accounts for 2015, and record assets and liabilities that require recognition on the balance sheet as of December 31, 2015. Assume that the nominal accounts for 2015 have not yet been closed into the income summary account.

Exercise 20-37

Error Analysis

In early 2014, while reviewing Huffman Inc.'s 2013 financial records, the accountant discovered several errors. For each of the following errors, indicate the effect on net income (i.e., understatement, overstatement, or no effect) for both 2013 and 2014, assuming that no correction had been made and the company uses a periodic system for inventory.

(a) Certain items of ending inventory were accidentally not counted at the end of 2013.

(b) Machinery was sold in May 2013, but the company continued to deduct depreciation for the remainder of 2013, although the asset was removed from the books in May.

(c) The 2013 year-end purchases of inventory were not recorded until the beginning of 2014, although the inventory was correctly counted at the end of 2013.

(d) Goods sold on account in 2013 were not recorded as sales until 2014.

(e) Insurance costs incurred but unpaid in 2013 were not recorded until paid in 2014.

(f) Interest revenue in 2013 was not recorded until 2014.

(g) The 2013 year-end purchases were not recorded until the beginning of 2014. The inventory associated with these purchases was omitted from the ending inventory count in 2013.

(h) A check for January 2014 rent was received and recorded as revenue at the end of 2013.

(i) Interest accrued in 2013 on a note payable was not recorded until it was paid in 2014.

P4
Other Dimensions of Financial Reporting

CHAPTER 23
Analysis of Financial Statements

Learning Objectives

1. Organize a systematic financial ratio analysis using common-size financial statements and the DuPont framework.

2. Recognize the potential impact that differing accounting methods can have on the financial ratios of otherwise essentially identical companies.

3. Perform a simple valuation of a company using financial statement data.

Home Depot is the leading retailer in the do-it-yourself home improvement market. As of January 29, 2012, Home Depot had 2,252 stores throughout the United States, Canada, China, and Mexico. With each store averaging 104,000 square feet (and an additional 24,000 square feet in the outside garden center), that is a lot of shelf space filled with paint, lumber, hardware, and plumbing fixtures. If plumbing fixtures don't seem very exciting to you, consider this: Home Depot is the 144th largest company in the United States (in terms of market value), with a 2012 market value of $76 billion.[1] In fiscal 2012, Home Depot's sales reached $70.4 billion.[2]

Home Depot's prospects weren't always so rosy. Back in 1985, when sales were only $700 million, Home Depot experienced severe profitability problems that threatened to terminate the company's expansion in its infancy. For example, Home Depot's gross profit percentage (gross profit/sales) had decreased from 27.3% to 25.9%. This decrease of 1.4 percentage points doesn't seem like much until you calculate that this decrease, with sales of $700 million, caused a gross profit reduction of $9.8 million ($700 million × 0.014) and reduced total operating profit by 34%. Overall, Home Depot's net income in 1985 was only $8.2 million, down 42% from the year before.

Home Depot also experienced cash flow problems, in large part due to rapid increases in the level of inventory. Part of this inventory increase was the natural result of Home Depot's expansion. But Home Depot stores were also starting to fill up with

[1] 2012 Forbes Global 2000 listing. This list can be viewed by accessing Forbes' Web site at **http://www.forbes.com**.
[2] 2012 10-K filing of The Home Depot, Inc.

excess inventory because of lax inventory management. In 1983, the average Home Depot store contained enough inventory to support average sales for 75 days. By 1985, the number of days' sales in inventory had increased to 83 days. Combined with Home Depot's rapid growth, this inventory inefficiency caused total inventory to increase by $69 million in 1985, and this increase in inventory was instrumental in Home Depot's negative cash from operations of $43 million. Driven by this declining profitability and negative cash flow, Home Depot's stock value took a dive in 1985, and the beginning of 1986 found Home Depot wondering where it would find the investors and creditors to finance its aggressive expansion plans.

In 1986, however, Home Depot pulled off an incredible turnaround. Gross profit percentage went back up to 27.5%, operating income almost tripled compared to 1985, and net income increased from $8.2 million to $23.9 million. A computerized inventory management program was instituted, and the number of days' sales in inventory dropped to 80 days. Improved profitability and more efficient management of inventory combined to transform the negative $43 million operating cash flow in 1985 into positive cash from operations of $66 million in 1986. Home Depot even used a clever sale-leaseback arrangement to get $32 million of debt off its balance sheet.[3]

1. Company A had sales of $1,000 and a gross profit percentage of 20%. By how many dollars would total gross profit increase if the gross profit percentage were to increase from 20% to 23%?

2. What was the primary cause of Home Depot's negative operating cash flow of $43 million in 1985?

3. By how much did Home Depot's operating cash flow increase from 1985 to 1986?

Answers to these questions can be found on page 23-26.

The Home Depot example illustrates how financial statement information can be used to evaluate the health of a business and identify specific areas that need improvement. This final chapter in the textbook covers financial statement analysis and reinforces the principle that the entire purpose of preparing financial statements is so that the statements can be used. This chapter summarizes the discussions of financial ratios that have appeared throughout the text and presents a coherent framework in which ratios can be systematically analyzed. The chapter also illustrates how differing accounting assumptions impact the values of financial ratios. The chapter concludes with a brief introduction to the use of financial statement data in valuing a company.

Framework for Financial Statement Analysis

LO1 学习目标1
运用百分比财务报表和杜邦分析框架进行系统性的财务比率分析。

① Organize a systematic financial ratio analysis using common-size financial statements and the DuPont framework.

Financial statement analysis is the examination of both the relationships among financial statement numbers and the trends in those numbers over time. One purpose of financial statement analysis is to use the past performance of a company to predict its future

---

[3] The troubles of Home Depot in 1985 are the subject of a popular Harvard Business School case: Professor Krishna Palepu, "The Home Depot, Inc.," Harvard Business School, 9-188-148.

profitability and cash flows. Another purpose of financial statement analysis is to evaluate the performance of a company with an eye toward identifying problem areas. For example, the Home Depot numbers from 1985 indicated that the company had an inventory management problem that was severely reducing cash from operations. Home Depot's management used this information to spur inventory management improvements, and Home Depot's investors and creditors used the information in forecasting cash from operations for subsequent years. In summary, financial statement analysis is both diagnostic, identifying where a firm has problems, and prognostic, predicting how a firm will perform in the future.

Most pieces of information are meaningful only when they can be compared to some benchmark. For example, if you ask your friend how she feels and she says, "38," you will have some difficulty interpreting the information. If you know, however, that she felt 32 yesterday and that the happiest people you know are between 39 and 41, you can reasonably infer that your friend was unhappy yesterday but is feeling much better today. Similarly, the informativeness of financial ratios is greatly enhanced when they are compared with past values and with values for other firms in the same industry.

To enhance users' ability to do time-series comparisons, the SEC requires comparative financial reporting. Annual statements, for example, must include income and cash flow statements for three years and balance sheets for two years. These are minimum standards. Many companies include comparative statistics for 10 years in their annual reports.

Industry comparisons can be made by comparing financial statements for specific companies in an industry and by comparing a company's ratios with overall industry averages. The *COMPUSTAT* database from which the information in many of the exhibits in this text has been extracted is one source of industry data. Other well-known commercial sources for industry benchmark ratios include **Value Line** and **Dun & Bradstreet**.

> **FYI**
>
> Financial information is almost always compared to what was reported the previous year. For example, when Home Depot publicly announced on November 29, 2011, that its third-quarter sales were $17.3 billion, the press release also stated that this amount represented a 4.4% increase from the prior year.

The Accounting Principles Board stated that comparisons between financial statements are most informative and useful under the following conditions:[4]

1. The presentations are in good form; that is, the arrangement within the statements is identical.
2. The content of the statements is identical; that is, the same items from the underlying accounting records are classified under the same captions.
3. Accounting principles are not changed, or if they are changed, the financial effects of the changes are disclosed.
4. Changes in circumstances or in the nature of the underlying transactions are disclosed.

To the extent that the foregoing criteria are not met, comparisons may be misleading. Consistent practices and

> **Caution**
>
> This chapter presents only an introduction to financial statement analysis. A good source for further information is Palepu and Healy, *Business Analysis and Valuation: Using Financial Statements, Text and Cases*, 5th ed. (South-Western: Mason, Ohio, 2012).

---

[4] *Statement of the Accounting Principles Board No. 4*, "Basic Concepts and Accounting Principles Underlying Financial Statements of Business Enterprises" (New York: American Institute of Certified Public Accountants, 1970), pars. 95–99.

procedures are also important, especially when comparisons are made for a single enterprise. The potential impact of accounting differences on financial ratio comparisons is illustrated in a later section in this chapter.

Financial statement analysis is sometimes wrongly viewed as just the computation of a bunch of financial ratios: Take every financial statement number and divide it by every other number. This is a very inefficient and ineffective approach to analyzing a set of financial statements. This shotgun approach usually fails to lead to any concrete conclusions. This section of the chapter introduces the DuPont framework, which is one useful way to structure the analysis of financial ratios. In addition, this section explains the use of common-size financial statements, which are easy to prepare, easy to use, and should be the first step in any comprehensive financial statement analysis.

Common-Size Financial Statements

The first problem encountered when using comparative data to analyze financial statements is that the scale, or size, of the numbers is usually different. If a firm has more sales this year than last year, it is now a larger company, and the levels of expenses and assets this year can't be meaningfully compared to the levels last year. In addition, if a company is of medium size in its industry, how can its financial statements be compared to those of the larger firms? The quickest and easiest solution to this comparability problem is to divide all financial statement numbers for a given year by sales for the year. The resulting financial statements are called common-size financial statements, with all amounts for a given year being shown as a percentage of sales for that year.

common-size financial statements
百分比财务报表分析法

Exhibit 23-1 is a common-size income statement for Colesville Corporation, a hypothetical example. To illustrate the usefulness of a common-size income statement, consider the question of whether Colesville's gross profit in 2015 is too low. In comparison to the gross profit of $1,280,000 in 2013, the $1,700,000 gross profit for 2015 looks pretty good. Sales in 2015 are higher than sales in 2013, however, so the absolute levels

Exhibit 23-1 | Common-Size Income Statement

Colesville Corporation Comparative Income Statements For the Years Ended December 31						
	2015	%	2014	%	2013	%
Net sales	$5,700,000	100.0	$6,600,000	100.0	$3,800,000	100.0
Cost of goods sold	4,000,000	70.2	4,800,000	72.7	2,520,000	66.3
Gross profit on sales	$1,700,000	29.8	$1,800,000	27.3	$1,280,000	33.7
Selling expenses	$1,120,000	19.6	$1,200,000	18.2	$ 960,000	25.3
General expense	400,000	7.0	440,000	6.7	400,000	10.5
Total operating expenses	$1,520,000	26.6	$1,640,000	24.9	$1,360,000	35.8
Operating income (loss)	$ 180,000	3.2	$ 160,000	2.4	$ (80,000)	(2.1)
Other revenue (expense)	80,000	1.4	130,000	2.0	160,000	4.2
Income before taxes	$ 260,000	4.6	$ 290,000	4.4	$ 80,000	2.1
Income taxes	80,000	1.4	85,000	1.3	20,000	0.5
Net income	$ 180,000	3.2	$ 205,000	3.1	$ 60,000	1.6

Minor adjustments to percentage computations have been made to counteract the cumulative effect of rounding.

of gross profit in the two years cannot be compared. But looking at the common-size information it is seen that gross profit is 33.7% of sales in 2013, compared to 29.8% in 2015. The common-size information reveals something that was not apparent in the raw numbers: In 2013, an item selling for $1 yielded an average gross profit of 33.7 cents; in 2015, an item selling for $1 yielded an average gross profit of 29.8 cents. Is this good or bad? Well, in 2015, Colesville made less gross profit from each dollar of sales than in 2013, so this is bad news. The good news is that gross profit as a percentage of sales is improved in 2015 relative to 2014 (27.3%).

Each item in the income statement can be analyzed in the same way. In 2015, bottom-line net income was 3.2% of sales, compared to just 1.6% in 2013. How can the gross profit percentage be better in 2013 while the net income percentage is worse? The answer lies in an examination of the remaining income statement items. Total operating expenses were 35.8% of sales in 2013, compared to just 26.6% in 2015. With a common-size income statement, each of the income statement items can be examined in this way, yielding much more information value than just looking at the raw income statement numbers.

A full analysis of Colesville's common-size income statement requires a comparison to industry averages. Assume that for companies in Colesville's industry, gross profit averages 31.5% of sales. Combined with the information previously discussed, this suggests that Colesville was outperforming its industry in 2013, suffered serious gross profit problems in 2014, and has started a slow comeback in 2015.

At this point, you should be saying to yourself: Yes, but what is the exact explanation for Colesville's drop in gross profit percentage from 2013? And how was Colesville able to reduce operating expenses? These questions illustrate the usefulness and the limitation of financial statement analysis. Our analysis of Colesville's income statement has pointed out two areas in which Colesville has experienced significant income statement change in the past two years, but the only way to find out why these financial statement numbers changed is to gather information from outside the financial statements: Ask management, read press releases, talk to financial analysts who follow the firm, and/or read industry newsletters. In short, financial statement analysis may not give you all the final answers, but it can guide you toward the questions you should be asking.

A common-size balance sheet also expresses each amount as a percentage of sales for the year. As an illustration, a comparative balance sheet for Colesville Corporation with each item expressed in both dollar amounts and percentages is shown in Exhibit 23-2.

> **FYI**
>
> A common-size balance sheet can also be prepared using total assets to standardize each amount instead of using total sales. If this is done, the asset percentages are good indications of the company's asset mix.

The most informative section of the common-size balance sheet is the Assets section, which can be used to determine how efficiently a company is using its assets. For example, compare total assets for Colesville in 2014 and 2015. Colesville has total assets of $2,278,000 in 2015. Is Colesville managing its assets more efficiently than in 2014 when total assets were $2,191,000? Comparing the raw numbers cannot give a clear answer because Colesville's level of sales is different in the two years. The common-size balance sheet indicates that each dollar of sales in 2014 required assets of 33.2 cents, whereas each dollar of sales in 2015 required assets of 40.0 cents. So, in which of the two years is Colesville more efficient at using its assets to generate sales? In 2014, when each dollar of sales required a lower level of assets. Examination of the individual asset accounts suggests that the primary reason for less efficient total asset usage in 2015 is land, building, and equipment: A dollar of sales in 2014 required only 16.3 cents of land, building, and equipment, compared to 22.4 cents in 2015.

Exhibit 23-2 | Common-Size Balance Sheet

Colesville Corporation
Comparative Balance Sheets
December 31

	2015	%	2014	%	2013	%
Assets						
Current assets	$ 855,000	15.0	$ 955,500	14.5	$ 673,500	17.7
Land, building, and equipment (net)	1,275,000	22.4	1,075,000	16.3	925,000	24.4
Intangible assets	100,000	1.8	100,000	1.5	100,000	2.6
Other assets	48,000	0.8	60,500	0.9	61,500	1.6
Total assets	$2,278,000	40.0	$2,191,000	33.2	$1,760,000	46.3
Liabilities and Stockholders' Equity						
Current liabilities	$ 410,000	7.2	$ 501,000	7.6	$ 130,000	3.4
Noncurrent liabilities	400,000	7.0	600,000	9.1	400,000	10.5
Total liabilities	$ 810,000	14.2	$1,101,000	16.7	$ 530,000	13.9
Paid-in capital	$1,100,000	19.3	$ 800,000	12.1	$1,000,000	26.3
Retained earnings	368,000	6.5	290,000	4.4	230,000	6.1
Total stockholders' equity	$1,468,000	25.8	$1,090,000	16.5	$1,230,000	32.4
Total liabilities and stockholders' equity	$2,278,000	40.0	$2,191,000	33.2	$1,760,000	46.3

Minor adjustments to the percentage computations have been made to counteract the cumulative effect of rounding.

© Cengage Learning 2014

DuPont framework
杜邦分析框架

DuPont Framework

As discussed in Chapter 3, return on equity (net income/equity) is the single measure that summarizes the financial health of a company. Return on equity can be interpreted as the number of cents of net income an investor earns in one year by investing one dollar in the company. As a very rough rule of thumb, return on equity (ROE) consistently above 15% is a sign of a company in good health; ROE consistently below 15% is a sign of trouble. Return on equity for Colesville Corporation for the years 2015 and 2014 is computed as follows:

	2015	2014
Net income	$ 180,000	$ 205,000
Stockholders' equity	$1,468,000	$1,090,000
Return on equity	12.3%	18.8%

So, what can we say about Colesville's overall performance in 2015? It was bad relative to the rough ROE benchmark of 15%, and it was bad relative to ROE in 2014 of 18.8%. How do we pin down the exact reason(s) for the poor performance in 2015? That's what this section is about.

The DuPont framework (named after a system of ratio analysis developed internally at DuPont around 1920) provides a systematic approach to identifying general factors causing ROE to deviate from normal. The DuPont system also provides a framework for computing financial ratios to yield more in-depth analysis of a company's areas of strength and weakness. The insight behind the DuPont framework is that ROE can be decomposed into three components as shown in Exhibit 23-3.

Exhibit 23-3 | Analysis of ROE Using the DuPont Framework

Return on Equity	=	Profitability	×	Efficiency	×	Leverage
	=	Return on Sales	×	Asset Turnover	×	Assets-to-Equity Ratio
	=	$\dfrac{\text{Net Income}}{\text{Sales}}$	×	$\dfrac{\text{Sales}}{\text{Assets}}$	×	$\dfrac{\text{Assets}}{\text{Equity}}$

© Cengage Learning 2014

For each of the three ROE components—profitability, efficiency, and leverage—one ratio summarizes a company's performance in that area. These ratios are as follows:

- *Return on sales* is computed as net income divided by sales and is interpreted as the number of pennies in profit generated from each dollar of sales.
- *Asset turnover* is computed as sales divided by assets and is interpreted as the number of dollars in sales generated by each dollar of assets.
- *Assets-to-equity ratio* is computed as assets divided by stockholders' equity and is interpreted as the number of dollars of assets a company is able to acquire using each dollar invested by stockholders.

The DuPont analysis of Colesville's ROE for 2015 and 2014 is as follows:

Return on Equity		=	$\dfrac{\text{Net Income}}{\text{Sales}}$	×	$\dfrac{\text{Sales}}{\text{Assets}}$	×	$\dfrac{\text{Assets}}{\text{Equity}}$
2015	12.3%	=	$\dfrac{\$180,000}{\$5,700,000}$	×	$\dfrac{\$5,700,000}{\$2,278,000}$	×	$\dfrac{\$2,278,000}{\$1,468,000}$
		=	3.16%	×	2.50	×	1.55
2014	18.8%	=	$\dfrac{\$205,000}{\$6,600,000}$	×	$\dfrac{\$6,600,000}{\$2,191,000}$	×	$\dfrac{\$2,191,000}{\$1,090,000}$
		=	3.11%	×	3.01	×	2.01

The results of the DuPont analysis suggest that Colesville's ROE is lower in 2015, not because of a decrease in profitability of sales but because of the following.

1. In 2015, assets are used less efficiently to generate sales. Each $1 of assets generated $3.01 in sales in 2014 but only $2.50 in sales in 2015.
2. In 2015, Colesville is less effective at leveraging stockholders' investment. By use of borrowing, Colesville was able to turn each $1 of invested funds in 2014 into $2.01 of assets, which is more than the $1.55 in assets in 2015.

This preliminary DuPont analysis is only the beginning of a proper ratio analysis. If a DuPont analysis suggests problems in any of the three ROE components, there are further ratios in each area that can shed more light on the exact nature of the problem. A sampling of those ratios is discussed next. Many of these ratios were introduced in prior chapters.

Profitability Ratios If the DuPont calculations had shown that Colesville had a profitability problem in 2015, a common-size income statement could have been used to identify which expenses were causing the problem. Referring back to the common-size income statement in Exhibit 23-1, cost of goods sold as a percentage of sales is lower in 2015 than in 2014 (70.2% versus 72.7%). This positive development is partially offset by higher 2015 selling expenses (19.6% versus 18.2%) and higher general expenses (7.0% versus 6.7%). To summarize, the return on sales gives an overall indication of whether a firm has a problem with the profitability of each dollar of sales; the common-size income statement can be used to pinpoint exactly which expenses are causing the problem.

Efficiency Ratios The asset turnover ratio suggests that Colesville is less efficient at using its assets to generate sales in 2015 than it was in 2014. Which assets are causing this problem? One way to get a quick indication is to review the common-size balance sheet in Exhibit 23-2. The common-size balance sheet numbers indicate that in 2015, Colesville has a much larger amount of land, buildings, and equipment as a percentage of sales (22.4%) than in 2014 (16.3%), suggesting that Colesville is using its land, buildings, and equipment less efficiently in 2015. If the individual current assets were listed on the balance sheets (only total current assets are reported on the balance sheets in Exhibit 23-2), a similar analysis could be done with each individual current asset account.

In addition to the common-size balance sheet, specific financial ratios have been developed to indicate whether a firm is holding too much or too little of a particular asset. A selection of the most common of these ratios is discussed next. Many of the detailed asset balances used in the following calculations are not listed in Colesville's summary balance sheets contained in Exhibit 23-2.

Accounts Receivable Turnover The amount of receivables usually bears a close relationship to the volume of credit sales. The appropriateness of the level of receivables may be evaluated by computing the accounts receivable turnover. This ratio is computed by dividing sales by the average accounts receivable for the year. The sales amount is used because companies typically don't separately disclose the amount of credit sales. The computations for Colesville Corporation for 2014 and 2015 follow.

	2015	2014
Sales	$5,700,000	$6,600,000
Net receivables:		
Beginning of year	$375,000	$333,500
End of year	$420,000	$375,000
Average receivables		
[(beginning balance + ending balance)/2]	$397,500	$354,250
Accounts receivable turnover	14.3 times	18.6 times

Receivables turnover represents the average number of sales/collection cycles completed by the firm during the year. The higher the turnover, the more rapid is a firm's average collection period for receivables. The numbers indicate that Colesville collected its receivables more rapidly in 2014 (18.6 times) than in 2015 (14.3 times).

The average accounts receivable balance is used in the calculation because of the desire to compare sales, which were made throughout the year, with the average level of receivables outstanding throughout the year. The ending balance in receivables may not be a good reflection of the normal receivable balance prevailing during the year. For example, if a business grows significantly during the year, the ending balance in the receivables account is

在计算时，我们通常使用平均应收账款余额，需要将全年销售额和全年未偿付应收账款平均水平进行对比分析，因为年末应收账款余额并不能很好地反映企业全年的应收账款水平。

> **Caution**
>
> If sales occur seasonally, the ending balance in receivables may be unusually large (if many sales occur near the end of the year) or small (if the year-end occurs during a natural business lull). Averaging the beginning and ending balance will not correct for seasonality because the same thing happens each year. If quarterly data are available, the average of the quarterly balances can be used to correct for seasonality.

greater than the average prevailing balance during the year. The opposite is true if the business shrinks during the year. Using the average receivables balance is a way to adjust for changes in the size of a business during the year. Similar adjustments are made with other ratios that compare end-of-year balance sheet amounts to sales made or expenses incurred throughout the year.

Average Collection Period Average receivables are sometimes expressed in terms of the average collection period, which shows the average time required to collect receivables. Average receivables outstanding divided by average daily sales gives the average collection period. This measure is computed for Colesville as illustrated here.

	2015	2014
Average receivables.	$397,500	$354,250
Sales.	$5,700,000	$6,600,000
Average daily sales (sales/365)	$15,616	$18,082
Average collection period (average receivables/average daily sales)	25.5 days	19.6 days

This same measurement can be obtained by dividing the number of days in a year by the receivables turnover.

What constitutes a reasonable average collection period varies with individual businesses. For example, if the credit sale contract gives customers 60 days to pay, a 40-day average collection period would be reasonable. If customers are supposed to pay in 30 days, however, a 40-day average collection period would indicate slow collections.

Inventory Turnover The amount of inventory carried relates closely to sales volume. The inventory position and the appropriateness of its size may be evaluated by computing the inventory turnover. The inventory turnover is computed by dividing cost of goods sold by average inventory. Inventory turnover for Colesville is computed as follows:

	2015	2014
Cost of goods sold.	$4,000,000	$4,800,000
Inventory:		
Beginning of year.	$330,000	$125,000
End of year.	$225,000	$330,000
Average receivables		
[(beginning balance + ending balance)/2]	$277,500	$227,500
Inventory turnover.	14.4 times	21.1 times

在计算存货周转率时，我们通常用销售额替代销货成本。这样计算并不是完全准确的，因为销售额是一个零售数额，而销货成本和存货是批发数额。

Inventory turnover sometimes is computed using sales instead of cost of goods sold. This is not entirely correct because sales is a retail number and both cost of goods sold and inventory are wholesale numbers. However, when it comes to ratios, people are free to perform the calculations any way they wish. The most important thing is that the

> **Caution**
> Be careful when using ratios computed by someone else or extracted from a published source. Make sure you know exactly what formula was used to compute the ratio.

computation is made the same way and is compared with other values computed in the same way.

Number of Days' Sales in Inventory Average inventories are sometimes expressed as the number of days' sales in inventory. Information is thus afforded concerning the average time it takes to turn over the inventory. The number of days' sales in inventory is calculated by dividing average inventory by average daily cost of goods sold. The number of days' sales also can be obtained by dividing the number of days in the year by the inventory turnover rate. The latter procedure for Colesville is illustrated here.

	2015	2014
Inventory turnover for year	14.4 times	21.1 times
Number of days' sales in inventory (365/inventory turnover)	25.3 days	17.3 days

Colesville is holding a 25-day supply of inventory in 2015 compared to a 17-day supply in 2014. Is the 2015 level too high? The important thing with inventory, receivables, cash, and all other assets is for a company to hold just enough but not too much. For example, the 17-day supply of inventory in 2014 might be too low, exposing Colesville to the risk of running out of inventory. As mentioned earlier, drawing meaningful conclusions requires that the ratio values be compared to an industry benchmark to find out what level of inventory is normal for Colesville's industry.

> **Stop & Think**
> You have probably heard of just-in-time inventory systems. What would a just-in-time system do to a company's number of days' sales in inventory?
> a) Increase it
> b) Reduce it
> c) Leave it unchanged

Fixed Asset Turnover In addition to analyzing the level of the individual current assets, ratios can be used to determine whether the level of long-term assets is appropriate. As mentioned previously, the common-size balance sheet indicates that in 2015 Colesville has a much larger amount of land, buildings, and equipment, as a percentage of sales (22.4%), than in 2014 (16.3%). An alternate way to represent this same information is to compute the fixed asset turnover. Fixed asset turnover is computed as sales divided by average long-term assets and is interpreted as the number of dollars in sales generated by each dollar invested in fixed assets. The computation for Colesville follows.

	2015	2014
Sales	$5,700,000	$6,600,000
Land, building, and equipment:		
Beginning of year	$1,075,000	$ 925,000
End of year	$1,275,000	$1,075,000
Average fixed assets		
[(beginning balance + ending balance)/2]	$1,175,000	$1,000,000
Fixed asset turnover	4.85 times	6.60 times

As suggested by the common-size balance sheet, Colesville is less efficient at using its fixed assets to generate sales in 2015 than it was in 2014.

Other Measures of Activity The efficiency ratios just outlined are not the only ratios that can be used to evaluate how efficiently a company is using its resources. For example, in its 2012 annual report, Home Depot reports that its average weekly sales per store is $601,000 and its annual sales per square foot of store space is $299. The key thing to remember with ratios is that there are no rules limiting the ratios that can be computed; users and managers are free to calculate and use any ratios they think will aid their understanding of the company.

Margin versus Turnover Profitability and efficiency combine to determine a company's return on assets. Return on assets is computed as net income divided by total assets and is the cents amount of net income generated by each dollar of assets. The return on assets is impacted by both the profitability of each dollar of sales and the efficiency of using assets to generate sales. Return on assets for Colesville is computed as follows:

	2015	2014
Net income	$180,000	$205,000
Total assets:		
Beginning of year	$2,191,000	$1,760,000
End of year	$2,278,000	$2,191,000
Average total assets		
[(beginning balance + ending balance)/2]	$2,234,500	$1,975,500
Return on assets	8.1%	10.4%

Even though profitability, as measured by return on sales, is approximately the same in 2015 and 2014, the return on assets is higher in 2014 because in that year Colesville was more efficient at using assets to generate sales.

> **FYI**
>
> Thomas Selling and Clyde Stickney have documented the trade-off between margin and turnover described in this section. They report that industries with high levels of fixed costs and other barriers to entry are characterized by a low asset turnover and high profit margins. Industries with low fixed costs and commodity-like products have a high asset turnover and low profit margins. See *Financial Analysts Journal*, January–February 1989, p. 43.

The profitability of each dollar in sales is sometimes called a company's margin. The degree to which assets are used to generate sales is called turnover. The nature of business is that some industries, such as the supermarket industry, are characterized by low margin but high turnover. Other industries, such as the jewelry store business, are characterized by high margin but low turnover. The important point to remember is that companies with a low margin can still earn an acceptable level of return on assets if they have a high turnover. This is illustrated with the information for selected U.S. companies given in Exhibit 23-4. Notice the wide variation in return on sales, ranging from 1.2% for **Safeway** to 33.1% for **Microsoft**. Notice also that the variation in return on assets is less. The companies with a high return on sales (Microsoft and McDonald's) have a low asset turnover, whereas those with a low return on sales (Safeway and Wal-Mart) have a high turnover. Margin isn't everything and neither is turnover—the important thing is how they combine to generate return on assets.

Leverage Ratios Leverage ratios are an indication of the extent to which a company is using other people's money to purchase assets. Leverage is borrowing so that a company can purchase more assets than the stockholders are able to pay for through their own

Exhibit 23-4 | Return on Sales and Asset Turnover for Selected U.S. Companies in 2011

Company	Return on Sales	Asset Turnover	Return on Assets
Microsoft	33.1%	0.64	21.3%
Home Depot	5.5%	1.74	9.6%
McDonald's	20.4%	0.82	16.7%
Safeway	1.2%	2.89	3.4%
Wal-Mart	3.5%	2.29	8.1%

© Cengage Learning 2014

investment. The assets-to-equity ratios for Colesville for 2014 and 2015 indicate that leverage was higher in 2014. Higher leverage increases return on equity through the following chain of events.

- More borrowing means that more assets can be purchased without any additional equity investment by stockholders.
- More assets means that more sales can be generated.
- More sales means that net income should increase.

高杠杆提高权益收益率的途径为：
- 更多的贷款意味着在不需要股东增加投资的情形下购买更多的资产；
- 更多的资产意味着能获得更多的销售收入；
- 更多的收入意味着净利润的增加。

Investors generally prefer high leverage to increase the size of their company without increasing their investment, but lenders prefer low leverage to increase the safety of their loans. The field of corporate finance deals with how to optimally balance these opposing tendencies and choose the perfect capital structure for a firm. As a general rule of thumb, most large U.S. companies borrow about half the funds they use to purchase assets.

Two common leverage ratios, debt ratio and debt-to-equity ratio, are explained here.

Debt Ratio Debt ratio is computed as total liabilities divided by total assets and can be interpreted as the percentage of total funds, both borrowed and invested, that a company acquires through borrowing. Debt ratios for Colesville for 2014 and 2015 are computed here.

	2015	2014
Total liabilities	$810,000	$1,101,000
Total assets	$2,278,000	$2,191,000
Debt ratio	35.6%	50.3%

Debt-to-Equity Ratio Another common way to measure the level of leverage is the debt-to-equity ratio, computed as total liabilities divided by total equity. This ratio is computed for Colesville as follows:

	2015	2014
Total liabilities	$810,000	$1,101,000
Stockholders' equity	$1,468,000	$1,090,000
Debt-to-equity ratio	0.55	1.01

> **Stop & Think**
>
> Company Z has an assets-to-equity ratio of 2.5. What are its debt and debt-to-equity ratios?
>
> a) Debt ratio = 0.60; debt-to-equity ratio = 1.50
> b) Debt ratio = 0.40; debt-to-equity ratio = 0.60
> c) Debt ratio = 0.60; debt-to-equity ratio = 1.00
> d) Debt ratio = 1.50; debt-to-equity ratio = 0.60

The assets-to-equity ratio used in the DuPont framework, the debt ratio, and the debt-to-equity ratio measure the same thing: the level of borrowing relative to funds (borrowing and investment) used to finance the company. The most important thing to remember, as stated before, is that you use comparable ratios when analyzing a company. It doesn't matter whether you use the debt ratio or the debt-to-equity ratio, but make sure you don't compare one company's debt ratio to another company's debt-to-equity ratio.

To illustrate the impact of financial leverage on stockholders, assume that Company A has stockholders' equity of $500,000 and has no liabilities. The company estimates that its income before income taxes will be $80,000 without any borrowed capital. Income taxes are estimated to be 30% of income; therefore, net income is estimated to be $56,000 [$80,000 − (0.30 × $80,000)]. This would result in a return on equity of 11.2% ($56,000/$500,000).

Exhibit 23-5 illustrates the effects of borrowing an extra $1 million at 12% interest under the assumptions (1) that the $1,000,000 in additional assets earns a before-tax return on assets of 15%, more than the cost of the borrowed funds, and (2) that the additional assets earn a before-tax return of 5%, less than the cost of the borrowed funds. In the first case, because the company can earn a higher return from the new $1,000,000 in assets than it must pay to use the borrowed money, return on equity increases from 11.2% to 15.4%. In essence, the stockholders get to keep the difference between what they can earn from the assets and what they must pay the lender to borrow the money. On the other hand, the risk of financial leverage can be seen under the second assumption as the return on equity decreases from 11.2% to 1.4%.

times interest earned
利息保障倍数

Times Interest Earned A measure of the debt position of a company in relation to its earnings ability is the number of times interest is earned. The times interest earned calculation is made by dividing income before any charges for interest or income taxes by the interest requirements for the period. The resulting figure reflects the company's

Exhibit 23-5 | The Positive and Negative Aspects of Financial Leverage

	Assumption 1: Borrowed Capital Earns 15%	Assumption 2: Borrowed Capital Earns 5%
Income before interest and taxes:		
Without borrowed funds.................	$ 80,000	$ 80,000
On $1,000,000 borrowed.................	150,000	50,000
	$230,000	$130,000
Interest (12% × $1,000,000)..............	120,000	120,000
Income before taxes	$110,000	$ 10,000
Income taxes (30%)......................	33,000	3,000
Net income.............................	$ 77,000	$ 7,000
Stockholders' equity	$500,000	$500,000
Return on equity.........................	15.4%	1.4%

© Cengage Learning 2014

ability to meet interest payments and the degree of safety afforded the creditors. The times interest earned ratio for Colesville is computed as follows:

	2015	2014
Income before income taxes	$260,000	$290,000
Add interest: 10% of long-term debt		
$400,000 × 0.10	40,000	
$600,000 × 0.10		60,000
Earnings before interest and taxes	$300,000	$350,000
Times interest earned	7.5 times	5.8 times

Pretax income was used in the computation because income tax applies only after interest is deducted, and it is pretax income that protects creditors. The times interest earned ratio indicates that Colesville's creditors are happier in 2015 because their interest requirements are covered 7.5 times, offering a larger margin of safety than in 2014. However, this high times interest earned value might also indicate that Colesville has not properly leveraged its investment capital in 2015. Again, the appropriate level of times interest earned represents a balancing of the desire of investors to leverage their investment with the desire of creditors for safety concerning the collection of their loans.

A computation similar to times interest earned, but more inclusive, is the fixed charge coverage. Fixed charges include such obligations as interest on bonds and notes, lease obligations, and any other recurring financial commitments. The number of times that fixed charges are covered is calculated by adding the fixed charges to pretax income and then dividing the total by the fixed charges.

Other Common Ratios

Not all commonly used ratios fit into the DuPont framework. Ratios for measuring liquidity, cash flow, dividend payments, and stock price performance are outlined in this section.

Current Ratio An important concern about any company is its liquidity, or the ability to meet its current obligations. If a firm cannot meet its obligations in the short run, it may not be around to enjoy the long run. The most commonly used measure of liquidity is the current ratio. Current ratio is computed by dividing total current assets by total current liabilities. For Colesville, current ratios for December 31, 2014, and December 31, 2015, are computed as follows:

	2015	2014
Current assets	$855,000	$955,500
Current liabilities	$410,000	$501,000
Debt ratio	2.09	1.91

Historically, the rule of thumb has been that a current ratio below 2.0 suggests the possibility of liquidity problems. However, advances in information technology have enabled companies to be much more effective in minimizing the need to hold cash, inventories, and other current assets. As a result, current ratios for successful companies these days are frequently less than 1.0. As mentioned previously in relation to other ratios, the best way to interpret a current ratio is to compare the value to the current ratio for the same firm in previous years and to different companies in the same industry. Current ratios for selected U.S. companies are given in Exhibit 23-6.

Exhibit 23-6 | Current Ratios for Selected U.S. Companies in 2011

Company	Current Ratio
Coca-Cola	1.05
Delta Air Lines	0.61
Home Depot	1.55
McDonald's	1.25
Wal-Mart	0.88

cash flow adequacy ratio
现金充足率

Cash Flow Adequacy Ratio The current ratio is an indirect measure of a company's ability to meet its upcoming obligations. Ratios based on cash flow from operations give a more direct indication of a company's ability to generate sufficient cash to satisfy predictable cash requirements. One overall indicator of cash flow sufficiency is the cash flow adequacy ratio.[5] This ratio is computed by dividing cash flow from operating activities by the total primary cash requirements, defined as the sum of dividend payments, long-term asset purchases, and long-term debt repayments. The following information for Colesville Corporation is needed to compute this ratio.

	2015	2014
Net income	$180,000	$205,000
Depreciation expense	100,000	80,000
(Increase) Decrease in noncash current assets	60,000	(231,500)
Increase (Decrease) in current liabilities	(91,000)	371,000
Cash from operating activities	$249,000	$424,500
Long-term asset purchases	$300,000	$230,000
Long-term debt repayments	200,000	0
Dividends paid	102,000	145,000
Total primary cash requirements	$602,000	$375,000

Note that long-term asset purchases in 2015 and 2014 were enough to offset the depreciation of assets for the year and increase the level of net land, buildings, and equipment.

The computation of the cash flow adequacy ratio is as follows:

	2015	2014
Cash from operating activities	$249,000	$424,500
Total primary cash requirements	$602,000	$375,000
Cash flow adequacy ratio	0.41	1.13

Because the cash flow adequacy ratio in 2015 is less than 1.0, Colesville was not able to satisfy its primary cash requirements with cash generated by operations. A look at

[5] See Chapter 5 for a summary of other cash flow ratios.

Colesville's balance sheets in Exhibit 23-2 indicates that the shortfall has been partially compensated for by the issuance of additional stock in 2015. One study has shown that for a sample of Fortune 500 companies, the cash flow adequacy ratio averaged 0.88.[6]

Earnings per Share Earnings per share (EPS) is such a fundamental number that we usually forget that it is a financial ratio. The necessary adjustments for dilutive securities and so forth were covered fully in Chapter 18 and are not repeated here. For Colesville, EPS for 2015 and 2014 is computed as follows:

	2015	2014
Net income	$180,000	$205,000
Weighted shares outstanding	90,000	75,000
Earnings per share	$2.00	$2.73

Dividend Payout Ratio All net income belongs to the stockholders. Cash dividends are the portion of net income paid to the stockholders in the form of cash. An important ratio in analyzing a firm's dividend policy is the dividend payout ratio, computed as dividends divided by net income. Colesville's dividend payout ratios for 2015 and 2014 are computed as follows:

	2015	2014
Dividends	$102,000	$145,000
Net income	$180,000	$205,000
Dividend payout ratio	56.7%	70.7%

FYI

Finance and accounting professors often prefer to compute the inverse of the P/E ratio, called the *earnings-price (EP) ratio*. There are some interesting econometric reasons that EP is better than P/E, but so far the business press and most businesspeople have stuck with the P/E ratio.

In general, high-growth firms have low dividend payout ratios (Microsoft didn't begin paying cash dividends to its common stockholders until 2003), and low-growth stable firms have higher dividend payout ratios.

Price-Earnings Ratio The market price of a share of stock is often expressed as a multiple of earnings to indicate how attractive the market views the stock as an investment. This ratio is called the *price-earnings ratio*, or *P/E ratio*, and is computed by dividing the market price per share of stock by the EPS. In the United States, P/E ratios typically range between 10.0 and 30.0. Assuming market values per share of Colesville stock at the end of 2015 of $29 and at the end of 2014 of $60, P/E ratios would be computed as follows:

	2015	2014
Market value per share	$29.00	$60.00
Earnings per share	$2.00	$2.73
Price-earnings ratio	14.5	22.0

High P/E ratios are generally associated with firms for which strong future growth is predicted.

[6] Don E. Giacomino and David E. Mielke, "Cash Flows: Another Approach to Ratio Analysis," *Journal of Accountancy*, March 1993, pp. 55–58.

Book-to-Market Ratio   The ratio of book value to market value, called the *book-to-market ratio*, is frequently used in investment analysis. The book-to-market ratio reflects the difference between a company's balance sheet value and the company's actual market value. A company's book-to-market ratio is almost always less than 1.0. This is so because many assets are reported at historical cost, which is usually less than market value, and other assets are not included in the balance sheet at all. Research has shown that firms with high book-to-market ratios tend to have high stock returns in future years.[7] One possible reason for this is that the accounting book value reflects fundamental underlying value and a high book-to-market ratio indicates that the market is currently undervaluing a company. For Colesville Corporation, the book-to-market ratio is computed as follows:

	2015	2014
Book value of stockholders' equity	$1,468,000	$1,090,000
Year-end shares outstanding	100,000	70,000
Market value per share	× $29	× $60
Total market value of equity	$2,900,000	$4,200,000
Book-to-market ratio	0.51	0.26

A summary of the financial ratios discussed in this section is presented in Exhibit 23-7. This overview of financial ratios is intended to emphasize the point that the preparation of

FASB CODIFICATION

The Issue: To you, it seems to create a lot of extra work to have to provide financial statements for several past years instead of just one year. You wonder who made up this requirement and do companies really have to provide several years of data?

The Question: Where is the authoritative guidance saying that comparative financial statements are to be presented?

Searching the Codification: Well, we aren't going to use the Codification for this one. If we did, we would find this generic statement in FASB ASC paragraph 205-10-45-1: "The presentation of comparative financial statements in annual and other reports enhances the usefulness of such reports and brings out more clearly the nature and trends of current changes affecting the entity. Such presentation emphasizes the fact that statements for a series of periods are far more significant than those for a single period and that the accounts for one period are but an installment of what is essentially a continuous history."

Somewhere we read (actually, it was in Chapter 3 of this book) that the detailed comparative financial statement requirements come from the SEC. U.S. federal regulations are contained in the Code of Federal Regulations (CFR). The regulations related to the public trading of securities are contained in Title 17, Commodity and Securities Exchanges. So, get your favorite search engine and type in the following search string:

"CFR Title 17 consolidated balance sheet"

Have fun!

The Answer: The correct treatment is described on page 23-26.

[7] See Eugene F. Fama and Kenneth R. French, "The Cross-Section of Expected Stock Returns," *The Journal of Finance*, June 1992, p. 427.

Exhibit 23-7 | Summary of Selected Financial Ratios

(1)	Return on equity	$\dfrac{\text{Net income}}{\text{Stockholders' equity}}$	Number of pennies earned during the year on each dollar invested

DuPont Framework

(2)	Return on sales	$\dfrac{\text{Net income}}{\text{Sales}}$	Number of pennies earned during the year on each dollar of sales
(3)	Asset turnover	$\dfrac{\text{Sales}}{\text{Total assets}}$	Number of dollars of sales during the year generated by each dollar of assets
(4)	Assets-to-equity ratio	$\dfrac{\text{Total assets}}{\text{Stockholders' equity}}$	Number of dollars of assets acquired for each dollar of funds invested by stockholders

Efficiency:

(5)	Accounts receivable turnover	$\dfrac{\text{Sales}}{\text{Average accounts receivable}}$	Number of sales/collection cycles completed during the year
(6)	Average collection period	$\dfrac{\text{Average accounts receivable}}{\text{Average daily sales}}$	Average number of days that elapse between sale and cash collection
(7)	Inventory turnover	$\dfrac{\text{Cost of goods sold}}{\text{Average inventory}}$	Number of purchase/sale cycles completed during the year
(8)	Number of days' sales in inventory	$\dfrac{\text{Average inventory}}{\text{Average daily cost of goods sold}}$	Average number of days of sales that can be made using only the supply of inventory on hand
(9)	Fixed asset turnover	$\dfrac{\text{Sales}}{\text{Average fixed assets}}$	Number of dollars of sales during the year generated by each dollar of fixed assets

Leverage:

(10)	Debt ratio	$\dfrac{\text{Total liabilities}}{\text{Total assets}}$	Percentage of funds needed to purchase assets that were obtained through borrowing
(11)	Debt-to-equity ratio	$\dfrac{\text{Total liabilities}}{\text{Stockholders' equity}}$	Number of dollars of borrowing for each dollar of equity investment
(12)	Times interest earned	$\dfrac{\text{Earnings before interest and taxes}}{\text{Interest expense}}$	Number of times that interest payments could be covered by operating earnings

Other Financial Ratios

(13)	Return on assets	$\dfrac{\text{Net income}}{\text{Total assets}}$	Number of pennies of income generated by each dollar of assets
(14)	Current ratio	$\dfrac{\text{Current assets}}{\text{Current liabilities}}$	Measure of liquidity; number of times current assets could cover current liabilities
(15)	Cash flow adequacy ratio	$\dfrac{\text{Cash flow from operations}}{(\text{Purchases of long-term assets} + \text{Repayments of long-term debt} + \text{Cash dividend payments})}$	Number of times that cash from operations can cover predictable cash requirements
(16)	Earnings per share	$\dfrac{\text{Net income}}{\text{Weighted number of shares outstanding}}$	Dollars of net income attributable to each share of common stock
(17)	Dividend payout ratio	$\dfrac{\text{Cash dividends}}{\text{Net income}}$	Percentage of net income paid out to the stockholders as dividends
(18)	Price-earnings ratio	$\dfrac{\text{Market price per share}}{\text{Earnings per share}}$	Amount investors are willing to pay for each dollar of earnings; indication of growth potential
(19)	Book-to-market ratio	$\dfrac{\text{Stockholders' equity}}{\text{Market value of shares outstanding}}$	Number of dollars of book equity for each dollar of market value

© Cengage Learning 2014

the financial statements by the accountant is not the end of the process but just the beginning. Those financial statements are then analyzed by investors, creditors, and management to detect signs of existing deficiencies in performance and to predict how the firm will perform in the future. As repeated throughout this section, proper interpretation of a ratio depends on comparing the ratio value to the value for the same firm in previous years and to values for other firms in the same industry. In addition, diversity or inconsistency in accounting practice can harm the comparability of ratio values. This point is illustrated in the next section.

Impact of Alternative Accounting Methods

LO2 学习目标2
确认不同会计处理方法对实质上完全相同的公司财务比率的潜在影响。

② Recognize the potential impact that differing accounting methods can have on the financial ratios of otherwise essentially identical companies.

This section illustrates the impact of accounting method differences on reported financial statement numbers and the resulting financial ratios. The balance sheets and income statements for 2015 for two hypothetical companies, Sai Kung Company and Tuen Mun Limited, both of which started business on January 1, 2015, are shown below. To keep things simple, there are no income taxes in the example.

The following additional information relates to Sai Kung and Tuen Mun.

1. Sai Kung and Tuen Mun both purchased investment securities for $275. In both cases, the fair value of the securities dropped to $200. Sai Kung classifies the securities as trading; Tuen Mun classifies them as available for sale.

2. Sai Kung uses LIFO, and Tuen Mun uses FIFO. If Sai Kung had used FIFO, ending inventory would have been $1,000.

3. Both companies purchased similar buildings and equipment for $3,000 at the start of the year. Sai Kung assumes a 10-year useful life; Tuen Mun uses a 30-year life.

4. Both companies leased additional buildings and equipment at the beginning of the year. The annual lease payment is $150. The present value of the lease obligation on the lease signing date was $1,000. The terms of the leases are very similar. Sai Kung classifies its lease as a capital lease; Tuen Mun classifies its lease as an operating lease.

	Sai Kung	Tuen Mun
Cash	$ 100	$ 100
Investment securities	200	200
Accounts receivable	500	500
Inventory	700	1,000
Total current assets	$ 1,500	$ 1,800
Buildings and equipment (net)	2,700	2,900
Capital lease assets	900	0
Total assets	$ 5,100	$ 4,700

(Continued)

	Sai Kung	Tuen Mun
Current liabilities	$ 1,000	$ 1,000
Long-term debt	1,500	1,500
Capital lease obligations	950	0
Total liabilities	$ 3,450	$ 2,500
Paid-in capital	$ 1,500	$ 1,500
Retained earnings	150	775
Other equity	0	(75)
Total equities	$ 1,650	$ 2,200
Total liabilities and equities	$ 5,100	$ 4,700
Sales	$ 6,000	$ 6,000
Cost of goods sold	4,000	3,700
Gross profit	$ 2,000	$ 2,300
Depreciation expense	(400)	(100)
Lease expense	0	(150)
Other operating expenses	(1,125)	(1,125)
Operating income	$ 475	$ 925
Interest expense:		
Long-term debt ($1,500 × 0.10)	(150)	(150)
Capital lease ($1,000 × 0.10)	(100)	0
Loss on investment securities	(75)	0
Net income	$ 150	$ 775

A careful comparison of the financial statements for Sai Kung and Tuen Mun reveals that the companies are economically identical. The differences between the two sets of financial statements are caused by differences in accounting treatment. Consider the following:

1. Both companies have a $75 economic loss on investment securities. Sai Kung recognizes this loss in its income statement; Tuen Mun recognizes the loss as an equity adjustment.
2. If both companies had used FIFO, ending inventory, cost of goods sold, and gross profit would have been the same for both.
3. The purchased buildings and equipment are similar; the difference is that Sai Kung recognized $300 ($3,000/10) of depreciation in 2015, whereas Tuen Mun assumed a longer life and recognized depreciation of $100 ($3,000/30).
4. The leased buildings and equipment are also similar, as are the terms of the lease contracts. Because Sai Kung accounts for the lease as a capital lease, it recognizes depreciation expense of $100 ($1,000/10 years) and interest expense of $100 ($1,000 × 0.10). Tuen Mun accounts for the lease as an operating lease and reports lease expense equal to the annual lease payment of $150.

In this example, these four accounting differences cause significant differences between the financial statements of two otherwise essentially identical companies. To illustrate the impact of these accounting differences on the financial ratios of the two companies, ratios (1) through (14) in Exhibit 23-7 are computed and compared for Sai Kung and Tuen Mun. When required, end-of-year amounts are used in place of average balances.

两家公司租赁的建筑物和设备是相同的，租赁条款也是相同的。由于Saikung公司在会计上将其确认为融资性租赁，计提的折旧费用是100美元（1 000/10），利息费用是100美元（1 000 × 0.1）。Tuen Mun公司在会计上将其按经营性租赁处理，从而将租赁费用等同于年租金支出150美元。

	Sai Kung	Tuen Mun
(1) Return on equity	9.1%	35.2%
(2) Return on sales	2.5%	12.9%
(3) Asset turnover	1.18	1.28
(4) Assets-to-equity ratio	3.09	2.14
(5) Accounts receivable turnover	12.0	12.0
(6) Average collection period	30.4	30.4
(7) Inventory turnover	5.71	3.7
(8) Number of days' sales in inventory	63.9	98.6
(9) Fixed asset turnover	1.67	2.07
(10) Debt ratio	67.6%	53.2%
(11) Debt-to-equity ratio	2.09	1.14
(12) Times interest earned	1.90	6.17
(13) Return on assets	2.9%	16.5%
(14) Current ratio	1.5	1.8

The differences in accounting method have made Tuen Mun appear to be a superior company on almost every dimension. Tuen Mun has better return on equity, better profitability, and better overall efficiency. In addition, Tuen Mun appears to be a less risky company because its leverage is lower and its liquidity, as indicated by the current ratio, is higher.

The point of this example is that ratio comparisons can yield misleading implications if the ratios come from companies with differing accounting practices. Frequently, financial ratios from companies are compared without adjusting for underlying accounting differences. Be careful.

Introduction to Equity Valuation

 Perform a simple valuation of a company using financial statement data.

LO3 学习目标3
利用财务报表数据进行简单的公司估值。

In Chapter 12, we discussed the valuation of bonds. You saw that once you are given the appropriate market interest rate to use in valuing bonds, the calculation of the current value of the bond is quite straightforward. The ease of this process stems from the fact that the future cash flows associated with the bonds are certain because they are set as part of the original bond contract. Thus, the art of bond trading really boils down to being able to determine what the correct market interest rate is, given the riskiness of the bond being valued; after that is done, the actual calculation of the bond value is simple arithmetic.

Valuing stocks is much more difficult than valuing bonds. When valuing stocks, not only does one need to determine the appropriate interest rate to use, but also one must estimate uncertain future cash flows. Because accounting numbers are frequently used in equity valuation models, we introduce the topic of equity valuation here. Realize that this is a basic introduction. The experts in equity valuation are the finance professors, and this topic is covered at length in finance courses.

To illustrate several simple equity valuation models, we use the following information for McDonald's as of the end of 2011.

	2011	2010	2009	2008
Diluted earnings per share	$5.27	$4.58	$4.11	$3.76
Dividends per share	2.53	2.26	2.05	1.625

For simplicity, we will assume that the required rate of return on equity capital for McDonald's is 15%. Don't be deceived by the seemingly casual manner in which we are assuming a 15% rate of return—in any valuation exercise, determining the correct required rate of return, given the riskiness of the company being valued, is crucial to arriving at a reasonable valuation. Entire courses in finance are devoted to learning how to properly compute required rates of return on equity investments.

constant future dividends
固定未来股利模型

Constant Future Dividends In this simple model, the equity shares are valued as if the current cash dividend amount is a guaranteed fixed payment to be received each year forever. Valuation in this case is easy; the future dividend stream is a perpetuity (an annuity of infinite length). The appropriate valuation formula is as follows:

$$\text{Price} = \frac{\text{Dividends}}{r}$$

where r is the required rate of return on equity capital. Using this simple model, the implied price per share for McDonald's is computed as follows:

$$\text{Price} = \$2.53 \div 0.15 = \$16.87$$

constant dividend growth
固定股利增长模型

Constant Dividend Growth In this simple model (sometimes called the Gordon growth model), dividends are assumed to grow at a constant rate forever. The valuation formula is as follows:

$$\text{Price} = \frac{\text{Forecasted dividend next year}}{r - g}$$

where g is the expected future dividend growth rate. For McDonald's, the dividend growth rate from 2009 to 2011 averaged 11% per year. Using this value, the implied price per share is computed as follows:

$$\text{Price} = [\$2.53 \times (1 + 0.11)] \div (0.15 - 0.11) = \$70.21$$

price-earnings multiple
价格—盈利乘数模型

Price-Earnings Multiple Market prices incorporate all kinds of information. For example, the market prices for firms in a given industry include average investor expectations about future earnings growth in that industry and required rates of return for firms in that industry. This information is summarized in the price-earnings (P/E) ratio, computed as (price per share ÷ earnings per share). Rather than directly estimating growth rates and required rates of return, an investor can value a company's shares by using the information in the P/E ratio as follows:

$$\text{Price} = \text{Earnings} \times \text{P/E Ratio}$$

P/E ratios for a selection of restaurant chains as of the end of 2011 are as follows:

Brinker International.	16.4
Darden Restaurants	14.7
Starbucks	27.6
Yum! Brands	21.5

These companies are considered to be competitors of McDonald's. **Brinker International** operates restaurants all over world under the names Chili's, Macaroni Grill, and others. **Darden Restaurants** operates under the names Red Lobster and Olive Garden, among others. **Starbucks** sells coffee in more than 17,000 locations worldwide. **Yum! Brands** operates over 37,000 fast-food locations worldwide under the names KFC, Pizza Hut, Taco Bell, A&W, and more. Using the average of these ratios (20.1), the implied price per share for McDonald's is computed as follows:

$$\text{Price} = \$5.27 \times 20.1 = \$105.93$$

Discounted Free Cash Flow In theory, a company should be worth the discounted value of the future cash flows to be generated by the company. A way to look at this directly is to compute the discounted present value of free cash flow. In this context, free cash flow is defined as:

Cash from operating activities
− Cash paid for capital expenditures
= Free cash flow

Free cash flow for McDonald's for 2009, 2010, and 2011 is computed as follows:

(millions of dollars)	2011	2010	2009
Cash from operating activities	$7,150.1	$6,341.6	$5,751.0
− Capital expenditures	2,729.8	2,135.5	1,952.1
Free cash flow	$4,420.3	$4,206.1	$3,798.9

In order to use this discounted free cash flow model, we need to make forecasts about the following:

- Future growth rates in free cash flow
- Forecasting horizon
- What happens in the "terminal year"

Future Growth Rates Free cash flow increased by 10.7% from 2009 to 2010 and 5.1% from 2010 to 2011. For our analysis, we will use the 7.9% average for these two years.

Forecasting Horizon We should extend our free cash flow growth rate forecasts for as many years in the future for which we have reliable data. Also, as shown in the next section, our forecasts only need to extend for as long as we think the firm can generate above-normal cash flows from new investments. We will choose a three-year forecasting horizon to keep the illustration simple; in this case, the choice is arbitrary.

Terminal Year Bill Gates of Microsoft may be the smartest person in the United States—he is certainly the richest. If you were to go into partnership with Bill and give him $1 billion, he probably would have enough great business ideas in his head that he could take that $1 billion and start an innovative business that would generate cash flows with a present value far in excess of $1 billion. Now, what if you were to give him another $10 billion? Does he have enough good ideas to be able to use that additional $10 billion to generate excess profits? What if you next gave him another $100 billion? The point is this: Eventually, even Bill Gates is going to run out of innovative ideas. At that time, any additional investment funds you give him will be used in just an average way, earn an average return, and the present value of the cash flows from the investment will exactly equal the amount of the investment. To use a phrase often used in finance, all that will be left will be "zero net present value" projects—projects that return exactly the average required rate of return.

The key thing to remember: You don't increase the value of your business by engaging in average, "zero net present value" projects. With such projects, the discounted value of future cash flows is completely offset by the initial cost of the project. Instead, you increase the value of your business by using investment funds in innovative ways that earn above-normal returns. Once a business has run out of innovative ideas, growth via new projects will not increase its value because the discounted present value of new projects is exactly offset by the initial cost of the projects. So, once the terminal year is reached, when it is expected that the company will have no new above-average ideas, the valuation impact of any additional growth can be ignored. For illustration purposes, we will assume that McDonald's will run out of innovative ideas after three years (from 2011), at the end of 2014. After that, free cash flow will be assumed to be constant forever.

The forecasted free cash flow for McDonald's, given our assumptions, is given in Exhibit 23-8. Remember, in this example we are picturing ourselves as standing at the end of 2011 looking into

> **FYI**
>
> Remember that this is merely an introduction to equity valuation using discounted cash flow analysis. In this example, we have used a short forecasting horizon and an unsophisticated cost of capital number, and we have assumed (without stating it) that McDonald's has no debt. In your finance and financial statement analysis courses, you will learn how to enhance this simple model.

Exhibit 23-8 | Forecasted Free Cash Flow for McDonald's

Present Value of Forecasted Free Cash Flow for McDonald's
2011 Free Cash Flow Value — $4,420.3 million
3 Years of 7.9% Growth; Constant Free Cash Flow Thereafter
15% Required Rate of Return

(millions of dollars)	2012	2013	2014	2015	2016
Free cash flow	$4,770	$5,146	$5,553	$5,553	$5,553
Present value as of the end of 2011; using 15% rate of return	$4,147	$3,891	$3,651	$24,341*	
Total present value	$36,030				

Note: All numbers shown are rounded.

*This is the present value of the cash flows to occur after it is assumed that McDonald's runs out of new ideas (at the end of 2014). The present value of this perpetuity (an annuity of infinite length) extending from 2015 into the future is computed in two steps:

1. As of the end of 2014, the perpetuity of $5,553 per year forever has a present value of $37,020, computed as $5,553/0.15.

2. In order to add the $37,020 value of the perpetuity to the present value of the other free cash flows, it must be discounted back as a lump sum three more years to the end of 2011, resulting in the $24,341 shown above.

© Cengage Learning 2014

McDonald's future. The exhibit also illustrates the calculation of the present value of these forecasted free cash flows.

At the end of 2011, McDonald's had 1,021 million shares outstanding. Thus, the estimated price per share is computed as follows:

Price = $36,030 million ÷ 1,021 million shares = $35.29

Comparison of the Valuation Models The computed prices for McDonald's shares at the end of 2011, using each of the four models, are as follows:

	Estimated Price
Model 1 (constant future dividends)	$ 16.87
Model 2 (constant dividend growth)	70.21
Model 3 (price-earnings multiple)	105.93
Model 4 (discounted free cash flow)	35.29

The actual market price of a share of McDonald's stock at the end of 2011 was $98.86.

This valuation exercise should leave you feeling dissatisfied for two reasons. First, our estimates are all over the map, ranging from $16.87 per share to $105.93 per share. Second, except for the price-earnings multiple model, our estimated values are not even close to the actual $98.86 value of McDonald's shares at the end of 2011. You should come away from this simple valuation exercise with the following three lessons.

Equity Valuation Is Difficult Proper use of the price-earnings multiple model would involve considering which of the four benchmark companies we used in computing an average P/E ratio might be the best match with McDonald's. Also, we would probably look at the accounting practices of each of the benchmark companies to determine if their net incomes were reflecting their underlying business performance in the same way as McDonald's. To fully implement the discounted free cash flow model, we would be required to gather information on McDonald's expansion plans in order to give more sophisticated estimates of future growth rates. In addition, we would have to make a more informed decision rather than just assuming that McDonald's will run out of innovative ideas in three years. And we would put a lot more work into calculating the cost of capital.

Price-Earnings Valuation Is Simple and Often Relatively Accurate, but It Begs the Question of Identifying the Underlying Determinants of Value The price-earnings multiple model frequently yields a price that is not far off the actual market price because, with this model, we are allowing the market to do most of the work for us in terms of forecasting industry growth rates, setting an appropriate rate of return, and so forth. This model is often used in getting a ballpark estimate for the appropriate price of a company's shares, especially when a company is issuing shares for the first time. However, this model is a black box that avoids consideration of the fundamental operating performance forecasts for a company.

The Most Useful Part of Equity Valuation Is Often What It Reveals about What Investors Must Believe about a Stock in Order to Give It Its Current Market Price One thing we learn from the McDonald's discounted free cash flow valuation is that investors must believe that McDonald's free cash flow is going to grow faster than 7.9%, or McDonald's is not going to run out of innovative ideas in three years, or both. In fact, it would require assumptions more like 13.6% growth for the next 20 years to yield an estimated price close to McDonald's actual market price. Thus, this valuation analysis can yield interesting insights into how a company is currently viewed by market participants.

SOLUTIONS TO OPENING SCENARIO QUESTIONS

1. Total gross profit would increase by $30, from $200 ($1,000 × 0.20) to $230 ($1,000 × 0.23).
2. The primary cause of Home Depot's negative operating cash flow of $43 million in 1985 was an increase in inventory during the year of $69 million.
3. Home Depot's operating cash flow increased by $109 million, from a negative $43 million in 1985 to a positive $66 million in 1986.

Stop & Think SOLUTIONS

1. (Page 23-10) The correct answer is B. The objective of a just-in-time inventory system is to reduce the level of inventory as far as possible. Reduced inventory means a lower number of days' sales in inventory.
2. (Page 23-13) The correct answer is A. With an assets-to-equity ratio of 2.5, hypothetical Company Z has the following simplified balance sheet:

Assets	2.5
Liabilities	1.5
Equities	1.0

Assets-to-equity ratio: 2.5 ÷ 1.0 = 2.5
Debt ratio: 1.5 ÷ 2.5 = 0.60
Debt-to-equity ratio: 1.5 ÷ 1.0 = 1.5

It is always true (prove it to yourself using algebra) that the debt-to-equity ratio is equal to the assets-to-equity ratio minus 1.

SOLUTION TO USING THE FASB'S CODIFICATION

Hopefully you found the following.

Title 17 CFR Section 210.3-01: "There shall be filed, for the registrant and its subsidiaries consolidated, audited balance sheets as of the end of each of the two most recent fiscal years."

With the clue that the balance sheet requirement is in Section 210.3-01, you may then have been able to find the requirements for the income statement and statement of cash flows as well.

Title 17 CFR Section 210.3-02: "There shall be filed, for the registrant and its subsidiaries consolidated and for its predecessors, audited statements of income and cash flows for each of the three fiscal years preceding the date of the most recent audited balance sheet being filed."

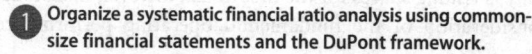

Review Chapter 23 Learning Objectives

① Organize a systematic financial ratio analysis using common-size financial statements and the DuPont framework.

Financial statement analysis is used to predict a company's future profitability and cash flows from its past performance and to evaluate the performance of a company with an eye toward identifying problem areas. The informativeness of financial ratios is greatly enhanced when they are compared with past values and with values for other firms in the same industry.

Common-size financial statements are computed by dividing all financial statement amounts for a given year by sales for that year. A common-size income statement reveals the number of pennies of each expense for each dollar of sales. The Assets section of a common-size balance sheet tells how many pennies of each asset are needed to generate each dollar of sales.

The DuPont framework decomposes return on equity (ROE) into three areas:

- *Profitability.* Return on sales is computed as net income divided by sales and is interpreted as the number of pennies in profit generated from each dollar of sales.

- *Efficiency.* Asset turnover is computed as sales divided by assets and is interpreted as the number of dollars in sales generated by each dollar of assets.
- *Leverage.* Assets-to-equity ratio is computed as assets divided by equity and is interpreted as the number of dollars of assets a company is able to acquire using each dollar invested by stockholders.

If a company has a profitability problem, the common-size income statement is the best tool for detecting which expenses are responsible. Financial ratios for detailed analysis of a company's efficiency and leverage have been developed; a number of them are summarized in Exhibit 23-7.

Margin is the profitability of each dollar in sales, and turnover is the degree to which assets are used to generate sales. Companies with a low margin can still earn an acceptable level of return on assets if they have a high turnover.

② Recognize the potential impact that differing accounting methods can have on the financial ratios of otherwise essentially identical companies.

Ratio comparisons can yield misleading implications if the ratios come from companies with differing accounting practices. Adjustments for accounting differences should be made before financial ratios are compared.

③ Perform a simple valuation of a company using financial statement data.

Four models used in estimating values of equity securities are as follows:

- Constant future dividends
- Constant dividend growth
- Price-earnings multiple
- Discounted free cash flow

Three lessons to be learned from simple equity valuation are as follows:

- Equity valuation is difficult.
- Price-earnings valuation is simple and often relatively accurate, but it begs the question of identifying the underlying determinants of value.
- The most useful part of equity valuation is often what it reveals about what investors must believe about a stock in order to give it its current market price.

KEY TERMS

Common-size financial statements 23-4
DuPont framework 23-6
Financial statement analysis 23-2
Margin 23-11
Perpetuity 23-22
Turnover 23-11

Tutorial Activities

Tutorial Activities with author-written, content-specific feedback, available on *CengageNOW for Stice & Stice.*

QUESTIONS

1. Financial statement analysis can be used to identify a company's weak areas so that management can work for improvement. Can financial statement analysis be used for any other purpose? Explain.
2. Why are comparative financial statements considered more meaningful than statements prepared for a single period? What conditions increase the usefulness of comparative statements?
3. An analysis of a company's financial ratios reveals the underlying reasons for profitability and efficiency problems. Do you agree or disagree? Explain.
4. What is a *common-size financial statement?* What are its advantages?
5. What is the purpose of the DuPont framework?
6. (a) How is the inventory turnover computed? (b) What precautions are necessary in arriving at the inventory number to be used in the turnover calculation? (c) How would you interpret a rising inventory turnover rate?
7. Indicate how each of the following measurements is calculated, and appraise its significance.
   (a) Times interest earned
   (b) Return on equity
   (c) Earnings per share
   (d) Price-earnings ratio
   (e) Dividend payout ratio
   (f) Book-to-market ratio
8. Explain how the turnover of assets can affect return on assets.
9. Under what conditions is the return on assets equal to the ROE?
10. How do accounting differences impact the usefulness of financial ratio comparisons?
11. What variables are used to determine a share price when using the constant dividend growth model?
12. In using the discounted free cash flow valuation model, what is the significance of the terminal year?
13. What are three lessons one can learn by studying basic equity valuation models?

PRACTICE EXERCISES

Practice 23-1

Common-Size Income Statement

Comparative income statements for South Drive Company for Year 2 and Year 1 are given below.

	Year 2	Year 1
Sales	$ 900,000	$ 500,000
Cost of goods sold	(432,000)	(240,000)
Gross profit on sales	$ 468,000	$ 260,000
Wage expense	(54,000)	(30,000)
Rent expense	(90,000)	(50,000)
Operating income	$ 324,000	$ 180,000
Interest expense	(80,000)	(30,000)
Net income	$ 244,000	$ 150,000

1. Prepare a common-size income statement for Year 1 and Year 2.
2. Return on sales for South Drive is lower in Year 2 than in Year 1. What expense is causing this lower profitability?

Practice 23-2

Balance Sheet

The following data are taken from the comparative balance sheet prepared for Route 13 Company.

	Year 2	Year 1
Cash	$ 39,063	$ 25,000
Accounts receivable	62,500	40,000
Inventories	67,000	30,000
Property, plant, and equipment	156,250	100,000
Total assets	$324,813	$195,000

Sales for Year 2 were $1,250,000. Sales for Year 1 were $800,000.

1. Prepare a common-size balance sheet for Year 1 and Year 2.
2. Overall, Route 13 Company is less efficient at using its assets to generate sales in Year 2 than in Year 1. What asset is responsible for this decreased efficiency?

Practice 23-3

Preparing a Common-Size Income Statement

Company A reported the following income statement data for the most recent three years:

	Year 3	Year 2	Year 1
Sales	$ 330,000	$ 260,000	$ 300,000
Cost of goods sold	(163,000)	(144,000)	(156,000)
Operating expenses:			
Marketing expense	(21,000)	(21,000)	(22,000)
R&D expense	(27,000)	(6,000)	(14,000)
Administrative expense	(45,000)	(50,000)	(48,000)
Operating income	$ 74,000	$ 39,000	$ 60,000
Interest expense	(6,000)	(11,000)	(7,000)
Income before income taxes	$ 68,000	$ 28,000	$ 53,000
Income tax expense	(25,000)	(8,000)	(20,000)
Net income	$ 43,000	$ 20,000	$ 33,000

Prepare a common-size income statement for each year.

Practice 23-4

Interpreting a Common-Size Income Statement

Refer to Practice 23-3. Briefly explain why overall profitability declined in Year 2 and then went back up in Year 3.

Practice 23-5

Preparing a Common-Size Balance Sheet

Company A reported the following balance sheet data for the most recent three years:

	Year 3	Year 2	Year 1
Cash	$ 8,000	$ 8,000	$ 6,000
Accounts receivable	18,000	37,000	18,000
Inventory	36,000	47,000	36,000
Current assets	$ 62,000	$ 92,000	$ 60,000
Property, plant, and equipment (net)	138,000	126,000	123,000
Total assets	$200,000	$218,000	$183,000
Accounts payable	$ 28,000	$ 39,000	$ 21,000
Short-term debt	15,000	20,000	15,000
Current liabilities	$ 43,000	$ 59,000	$ 36,000
Long-term debt	52,000	65,000	58,000
Total liabilities	$ 95,000	$124,000	$ 94,000
Paid-in capital	19,000	19,000	19,000
Retained earnings	86,000	75,000	70,000
Total liabilities and equities	$200,000	$218,000	$183,000

Prepare the Assets section of a common-size balance sheet for each year. (*Note:* Refer to Practice 23-3 for sales data.)

Practice 23-6
Interpreting a Common-Size Balance Sheet
Refer to Practice 23-5. Briefly explain why overall efficiency declined in Year 2 and then went back up in Year 3.

Practice 23-7
Computing the DuPont Framework Ratios
Refer to Practices 23-3 and 23-5. Compute the following ratios for Year 1, Year 2, and Year 3 for Company A:

1. Return on equity
2. Return on sales
3. Asset turnover
4. Assets-to-equity ratio

Practice 23-8
Interpreting the DuPont Framework Ratios
Refer to Practice 23-7. Interpret the changes in the DuPont framework ratios from Year 1 to Year 2 and from Year 2 to Year 3.

Practice 23-9
Accounts Receivable Ratios
Refer to Practices 23-3 and 23-5. Compute the following ratios for Year 2 and Year 3 for Company A:

1. Accounts receivable turnover
2. Average collection period

Practice 23-10
Inventory Ratios
Refer to Practices 23-3 and 23-5. Compute the following ratios for Year 2 and Year 3 for Company A:

1. Inventory turnover
2. Number of days' sales in inventory

Practice 23-11
Fixed Asset Turnover
Refer to Practices 23-3 and 23-5. Compute fixed asset turnover for Year 2 and Year 3 for Company A.

Practice 23-12
Margin and Turnover
Refer to Practice 23-7. Company B and Company C had the following DuPont framework ratio values for Year 3:

	Company B	Company C
Return on sales	7.8%	24.7%
Asset turnover	2.75	0.87
Assets-to-equity ratio	1.90	1.90

Which company—A, B, or C—had the highest ROE in Year 3? Comment on your results.

Practice 23-13
Debt Ratio and Debt-to-Equity Ratio
Refer to Practices 23-3 and 23-5. Compute the following ratios for Year 1, Year 2, and Year 3 for Company A:

1. Debt ratio
2. Debt-to-equity ratio

Practice 23-14
Times Interest Earned
Refer to Practices 23-3 and 23-5. Compute times interest earned for Year 1, Year 2, and Year 3 for Company A.

Practice 23-15

Current Ratio

Refer to Practices 23-3 and 23-5. Compute the current ratio for Year 1, Year 2, and Year 3 for Company A.

Practice 23-16

Cash Flow Adequacy Ratio

The company reported the following information with respect to its statement of cash flows:

Cash from issuance of additional shares of stock	$1,000
Decrease in inventory	75
Cash used to purchase property, plant, and equipment	400
Net income	780
Cash used to repay long-term loans	600
Increase in accounts payable	100
Depreciation	300
Cash dividends paid	200
Increase in accounts receivable	150

Compute the company's cash flow adequacy ratio.

Practice 23-17

Earnings per Share and Dividend Payout Ratio

	Company S	Company T
Net income	$1,000	$15,000
Dividends	50	6,000
Weighted shares outstanding	200	10,000

Compute (1) earnings per share and (2) dividend payout ratio for Companies S and T. Indicate which of the two companies is more likely to be an older company in a low-growth industry.

Practice 23-18

Price-Earnings Ratio and Book-to-Market Ratio

	Company M	Company N
Net income	$5,000	$75,000
Stock price per share	$64.00	$30.00
Weighted shares outstanding	625	125,000
Total stockholders' equity	$56,000	$600,000

Compute (1) the price-earnings ratio and (2) the book-to-market ratio for Companies M and N. Indicate which of the two companies is more likely to be in a high-growth industry.

Practice 23-19

Equity Valuation Using Dividends and P/E Ratio

The following information has been collected regarding John Scott Company:

Most recent annual cash dividend per share	$0.65
Dividend growth rate over the past five years	7%
Most recent earnings per share	$1.53
Average P/E ratio of similar firms	18
Required rate of return on equity capital	12%

Practice 23-20

Equity Valuation Using Discounted Free Cash Flow
The following information has been collected regarding Burton Dee Company:

Free cash flow	$3,500
Annual growth rate in free cash flow over the past five years	25%
Number of shares outstanding	3,000
Required rate of return on equity capital	12%
Length of time until terminal year	4 years

Estimate a price per share for Burton Dee's stock using the discounted free cash flow model.

Estimate a price per share for John Scott's stock using the following equity valuation models.
1. Constant future dividends
2. Constant dividend growth
3. Price-earnings multiple

EXERCISES

Exercise 23-21

Common-Size Income Statements
Comparative income statements for Xenon Corporation for 2015 and 2014 follow.

	2015	2014
Sales	$950,000	$600,000
Cost of goods sold	595,000	325,000
Gross profit	$355,000	$275,000
Selling and general expenses	115,000	94,000
Operating income	$240,000	$181,000
Interest expense	45,000	35,000
Income before income taxes	$195,000	$146,000
Income taxes	72,000	57,000
Net income	$123,000	$ 89,000

1. Prepare common-size income statements for Xenon Corporation for 2015 and 2014.
2. Return on sales for Xenon is lower in 2015 than in 2014. What expense or expenses are causing this lower profitability?

Exercise 23-22

Common-Size Balance Sheets
The following data are taken from the comparative balance sheets prepared for Gubler Wholesale Company.

	2015	2014
Cash	$ 43,000	$ 22,000
Accounts receivable (net)	31,000	42,000
Inventories	71,000	33,000
Property, plant, and equipment (net)	106,000	59,000
Total assets	$251,000	$156,000

Sales for 2015 were $1,200,000. Sales for 2014 were $1,000,000.

1. Prepare the Assets section of common-size balance sheets for Gubler Wholesale Company for 2015 and 2014.
2. Overall, Gubler Wholesale is less efficient at using its assets to generate sales in 2015 than in 2014. What asset or assets are responsible for this decreased efficiency?

Exercise 23-23

DuPont Framework
Using the following data, estimate the return on equity (ROE) for the following industries.

	Assets-to-Equity Ratio	Asset Turnover	Return on Sales
Retail jewelry stores	1.6	1.5	0.040
Retail grocery stores	1.8	5.6	0.014
Electric service companies	2.6	0.5	0.069
Legal services firms	1.7	3.5	0.073

Exercise 23-24

Ratios for Receivables and Fixed Assets
The following financial statement data are for Moonbeam Inc.

	2015	2014	2013
Sales	$265,000	$220,000	$180,000
Accounts receivable (net)	75,000	65,000	30,000
Property, plant, and equipment (net)	190,000	155,000	160,000

For 2014 and 2015, compute:

(a) Accounts receivable turnover
(b) Average collection period
(c) Fixed asset turnover

Use the average of the beginning and ending asset balances in computing the ratios.

Exercise 23-25

Analysis of Inventory
Income statements for Eldermon Sales Company follow. Analyze the inventory position at the end of each year as well as the profitability of inventory sales in each year. What conclusions would you make concerning the inventory trend?

	2015	2014	2013
Sales	$125,000	$100,000	$75,000
Cost of goods sold:			
Beginning inventory	$ 30,000	$ 25,000	$ 5,000
Purchases	105,000	80,000	85,000
	$135,000	$105,000	$90,000
Ending inventory	45,000	30,000	25,000
	$ 90,000	$ 75,000	$65,000
Gross profit	$ 35,000	$ 25,000	$10,000

Exercise 23-26

Effect of Leverage

Trunks Company estimates that pretax earnings for the year ended December 31, 2015, will be $230,000 if it operates without borrowed capital. Income tax is 40% of earnings. Average stockholders' equity for 2015 is $740,000. Assuming that the company is able to borrow $800,000 at 12% interest, indicate the effects on net income and return on equity if borrowed capital earns (1) 15% and (2) 8%. Explain the cause of the variations.

Exercise 23-27

Margin and Turnover

The following information is obtained from the primary financial statements of two retail companies. One company markets its gift merchandise in a resort area; the other company is a discount household goods store. Neither company has any debt. By analyzing these data, indicate which company is more likely to be the gift shop and which is the discount household goods store. Support your answer.

	Company A	Company B
Revenue	$6,000,000	$6,000,000
Average total assets	1,200,000	6,000,000
Net income	125,000	600,000

Exercise 23-28

Equity Ratios

Montpelier Lumber Corp. reported the following information.

	2015	2014	2013
8% bonds payable	$ 800,000	$ 800,000	$ 800,000
Common stock, $1 par	250,000	220,000	220,000
Additional paid-in capital	2,000,000	1,430,000	1,430,000
Retained earnings	200,000	150,000	100,000
Net income	190,000	110,000	90,000
Dividends	90,000	60,000	40,000
Year-end stock price per share	22	25	12

Compute the following for each year, 2013–2015.

1. Return on equity
2. Times interest earned (ignore income taxes)
3. Earnings per share
4. Dividend payout ratio
5. Price-earnings ratio
6. Book-to-market ratio

Exercise 23-29

Debt Covenants and Financing Alternatives

Cubicle Company is in need of another factory building. The building will cost $500,000. Cubicle is considering the following possible financing alternatives to acquire the building.

(a) Lease the building under an operating lease.
(b) Issue common stock in the amount of $500,000.
(c) Negotiate a long-term bank loan for $500,000.
(d) Negotiate a long-term bank loan for $350,000 and increase short-term borrowing by $150,000.

Currently, Cubicle has current assets of $600,000, noncurrent assets of $975,000, current liabilities of $280,000, and noncurrent liabilities of $410,000. Under existing loan covenants, Cubicle must maintain a current ratio of 2.0 or more and a debt-to-equity ratio of less than 0.80. Which, if any, of the financing alternatives will allow Cubicle to avoid violating the loan covenants?

Exercise 23-30

Analysis of Financial Data

The December 31, 2015, balance sheet of Copepper's Inc. and additional information follow. These are the only accounts on Copepper's balance sheet.

Amounts indicated by a question mark (?) can be calculated from the additional information given.

Assets		Liabilities and Stockholders' Equity	
Cash	$ 25,000	Accounts payable	$?
Accounts receivable (net)	?	Income taxes payable (current)	25,000
Inventory	?	Long-term debt	?
Property, plant, and equipment (net)	294,000	Common stock	300,000
		Retained earnings	?
	$432,000		$?

Additional information follows:

Current ratio (at year-end)	1.5 to 1
Total liabilities divided by total stockholders' equity	0.8
Inventory turnover based on sales and ending inventory	15 times
Inventory turnover based on cost of goods sold and ending inventory	10.5 times
Gross margin for 2015	$315,000

1. What was Copepper's December 31, 2015, balance in Accounts Payable?
2. What was Copepper's December 31, 2015, balance in Retained Earnings?
3. What was Copepper's December 31, 2015, balance in Inventory?

Exercise 23-31

Equity Valuation

The following information has been collected about DeeAnn Company:

Most recent annual cash dividend per share	$0.35
Dividend growth rate over the past five years	5%
Most recent earnings per share	$2.80
Average P/E ratio of similar firms	19
Required rate of return on equity capital	14%
Free cash flow for most recent year	$12,800
Annual growth rate in free cash flow over past five years	25%
Number of shares outstanding	4,000
Length of time until terminal year	4 years

Estimate a price per share for DeeAnn's stock using the following equity valuation models.

1. Constant future dividends
2. Constant dividend growth
3. Price-earnings multiple
4. Discounted free cash flow
5. Which of the four estimates do you think is most reliable? Why?

APPENDIX A

 I F R S Summary of U.S. GAAP/IFRS Differences

Topic	U.S. GAAP	IASB Standard
Chapter 1: Financial Reporting		
Accounting standard setter	Financial Accounting Standards Board (FASB)	International Accounting Standards Board (IASB)
Financial accounting standards	FASB Accounting Standards Codification (ASC)	• International Financial Reporting Standards (IFRS) • International Accounting Standards (IAS)
Group to address issues of interpretation or for which no formal standard currently exists	Emerging Issues Task Force (EITF)	• International Financial Reporting Interpretations Committee (IFRIC) • Standing Interpretations Committee (SIC) before 2002

Topic	FASB Accounting Standards Codification	Original FASB Standard	Corresponding IASB Standard	Differences Between U.S. GAAP and IFRS
Chapter 3: The Balance Sheet and Notes to the Financial Statements				
Classified balance sheet	Section 210-10-05 par. 4 Section 210-10-45 par. 1 through 12	ARB 43 Ch., 3A par. 4-8	IAS 1 par. 60-61	No substantial differences in the descriptions and definitions of current assets and current liabilities
Classification of short-term obligations to be refinanced	Section 470-10-45 par. 14	SFAS No. 6 par. 10-11	IAS 1 par. 72	Under IFRS, for a short-term obligation to be classified as long term, the refinancing must take place by the balance sheet date
Subsequent events	Topic 855	SFAS No. 165	IAS 10	No substantial differences
Chapter 4: The Income Statement				
Discontinued operations	Subtopic 205-20	SFAS No. 144	IFRS 5	Under IFRS, a discontinued operation must be a major line of business or geographic segment. Also, under IFRS, separate disclosure must be made of the cash flows of the discontinued operations.

A-1

Topic	FASB Accounting Standards Codification	Original FASB Standard	Corresponding IASB Standard	Differences Between U.S. GAAP and IFRS
Extraordinary items	Subtopic 225-20	APB Opinion No. 30	IAS 1 par. 87	Under IFRS, no income or expense items are allowed to be classified as "extraordinary."
Change in accounting principle	Section 250-10-45 par. 1-16 Section 250-10-50 par. 1-3	SFAS No. 154 par. 4-18 APB No. 28 par. 28	IAS 8 par. 14-31	No substantial differences.
Chapter 5: Statement of Cash Flows and Articulation				
Definition of cash equivalents	Section 230-10-20 (Glossary)—Cash equivalents	SFAS No. 95 par. 8	IAS 7 par. 7	No substantial differences
Noncash investing and financing activities	Section 230-10-50 par. 3	SFAS No. 95 par. 32	IAS 7 par. 43	No substantial differences
Direct and indirect methods	Section 230-10-45 par. 25, 28	SFAS No. 95 par. 27-28	IAS 7 par. 18-19	No substantial differences
Classification of interest paid	Section 230-10-45 par. 17(d)	SFAS No. 95 par. 23(d)	IAS 7 par. 33	U.S. GAAP—operating IFRS—operating or financing
Classification of income taxes paid	Section 230-10-45 par. 17(c)	SFAS No. 95 par. 23(c)	IAS 7 par. 35	U.S. GAAP—operating IFRS—operating, investing, or financing
Classification of interest received	Section 230-10-45 par. 16(b)	SFAS No. 95 par. 22(b)	IAS 7 par. 33	U.S. GAAP—operating IFRS—operating or investing
Classification of dividends received	Section 230-10-45 par. 16(b)	SFAS No. 95 par. 22(b)	IAS 7 par. 33	U.S. GAAP—operating IFRS—operating or investing
Classification of dividends paid	Section 230-10-45 par. 15(a)	SFAS No. 95 par. 20(a)	IAS 7 par. 34	U.S. GAAP—financing IFRS—operating or financing

Topic	U.S. GAAP	IASB Standard
Chapter 6: Earnings Management		
General characterization of the standards	Rules oriented. U.S. GAAP contains about 25,000 pages with lots of detailed guidance.	Principles oriented. IFRS contains just 2,500 pages with many detailed accounting decisions left up to the professional judgment of the accountant.

Topic	FASB Accounting Standards Codification	Original FASB Standard	Corresponding IASB Standard	Differences between U.S. GAAP and IFRS
Fair Value Module				
Fair values in financial reporting	Topic 820	SFAS No. 157	Exposure Draft: Fair Value Measurement, May 2009	No substantial differences.

Topic	FASB Accounting Standards Codification	Original FASB Standard	Corresponding IASB Standard	Differences Between U.S. GAAP and IFRS
Chapter 7: The Revenue/Receivables/Cash Cycle				
Bad debts	Section 310-10-35 par. 7-9	SFAS No. 5 par. 22	No explicit standard	No apparent differences
Warranties	Section 460-10-25 par. 5-7	SFAS No. 5 par. 24	IAS 37 par. 14, 39	No substantial differences
Compensating balances	Section 210-10-S99 par. 1	SEC Regulation S-X, Rule 5-02, Caption 1	IAS 7 par. 48	No substantial differences

Topic	FASB Accounting Standards Codification	Original FASB Standard	Corresponding IASB Standard	Differences Between U.S. GAAP and IFRS
Imputation of interest on receivables	Section 835-30-25 par. 2, 12	APB No. 21 par. 9, 13	No explicit standard	No apparent differences
Derecognition of receivables	Section 860-10-40 par. 5	SFAS No. 140 par. 9	IAS 39 par. 20	U.S. GAAP includes a list of three criteria that must be satisfied for derecognition. IFRS has a conceptual two-step test based on risks and rewards and control. In practice, the derecognition result is almost always the same.
Chapter 8: Revenue Recognition				
Revenue recognition	Topic 605	Contained in a large number of different standards	IAS 18, IAS 11	U.S. GAAP and IFRS are generally consistent, but many detailed differences exist. The FASB and IASB are currently working on a joint revenue recognition project.
Completed-contract method	Subtopic 605-35	ARB 45 and SOP 81-1	IAS 11	Under IFRS, the completed contract method is not allowed.
Pre-sale revenue recognition for biological assets	Section 905-330-35	SOP 85-3	IAS 41	Under IFRS, changes in the fair value of biological assets are recognized as gains and losses. Under U.S. GAAP, a similar procedure is acceptable under some circumstances, but not required.
Multiple-element arrangements	Subtopic 605-25	EITF 08-1	IAS 18	IFRS does not contain any specific provisions related to multiple-element arrangements.
Chapter 9: Inventory and Cost of Goods Sold				
LIFO	Section 330-10-30 par. 9-11	ARB 43, Chapter 4	IAS 2 par. 23-27	LIFO is not allowable under IFRS.
Lower of cost or market	Section 330-10-35 par. 1-12	ARB 43, Chapter 4	IAS 2 par. 28-33	Under IFRS, inventory is recorded at lower of cost or net realizable value, and inventory write-down losses can be reversed if the selling price subsequently recovers.
Foreign currency transactions	Section 830-20-35 par. 2	SFAS No. 52 par. 16b	IAS 21 par. 23a, 28	No substantial differences
Chapter 10: Investments in Noncurrent Operating Assets—Acquisition				
Interest capitalization	Subtopic 835-20	SFAS No. 34	IAS 23	Under IFRS, net "borrowing costs" are capitalized. The net amount is the gross interest paid less interest received on investment of idle funds.
Asset retirement obligation	Subtopic 410-20	SFAS No. 143	IAS 16 and IAS 37	No substantial differences
Business combinations	Topic 805	SFAS No. 141R	IFRS 3	No substantial differences

Topic	FASB Accounting Standards Codification	Original FASB Standard	Corresponding IASB Standard	Differences Between U.S. GAAP and IFRS
Intangible assets	Topic 350	SFAS No. 142	IAS 38	No substantial differences
Research and development	Topic 730	SFAS No. 2 SFAS No. 86	IAS 38	Under IFRS, development costs, which are costs incurred after technological feasibility, are capitalized. This matches U.S. GAAP for software development costs, but not for ordinary R&D.
Chapter 11: Investments in Noncurrent Operating Assets—Utilization and Retirement				
Impairment of tangible assets	Subtopic 360-10 various subsections on "Impairment"	SFAS No. 144	IAS 36	Under U.S. GAAP, the impairment test is a two-step test. Under IFRS, the impairment test involves just one step, a comparison of the book value to the "recoverable amount" of the asset.
Impairment of intangible assets	Topic 350	SFAS No. 142	IAS 36	U.S. GAAP includes three different impairment tests for intangibles. Under IFRS, there is just one test, which is the same as is used for tangible assets.
Upward revaluation	Not part of U.S. GAAP	Not part of U.S. GAAP	IAS 16	Upward revaluations of property, plant, and equipment are generally not allowable under U.S. GAAP.
Asset retirement obligations	Subtopic 410-20	SFAS No. 143	IAS 16 and IAS 37	No substantial differences
Assets classified as held for sale	Section 360-10-45	SFAS No. 144	IFRS 5	No substantial differences
Chapter 12: Debt Financing				
Short-term obligations expected to be refinanced	Section 470-10-45 par. 14	SFAS No. 6 par. 10-11	IAS 1 par. 72	Under IFRS, for a short-term obligation to be classified as long term, the refinancing must take place by the balance sheet date.
Splitting convertible debt proceeds into debt and equity	Subtopic 470-20	APB Opinion No. 14	IAS 32 par. 28-32	Under IFRS, ALL convertible debt issues are divided into their debt and equity components. This separation is only done in certain circumstances under U.S. GAAP.
Consolidation of variable interest entities (VIE)	Section 810-10-25 par. 20 through 59	FIN 46R	SIC 12	Under IFRS, a VIE is consolidated when the economic substance of the relationship indicates that the VIE is controlled. Compared to U.S. GAAP, this is very much a principles-based approach.
Fair value option	Topic 825, "Fair Value Option" subsections	SFAS No. 159	IFRS 9	U.S. GAAP and IFRS are generally consistent.
Troubled debt restructuring	Subtopic 470-60	SFAS No. 15	IAS 39 par. 39 through 41	No substantial differences

Topic	FASB Accounting Standards Codification	Original FASB Standard	Corresponding IASB Standard	Differences Between U.S. GAAP and IFRS
Chapter 13: Equity Financing				
Stock warrants	Section 470-20-25 par. 2	APB Opinion No. 14 par. 16	IAS 32 par. 28	Under IFRS, all compound financial instruments, such as stock warrants, are to be separated into separate debt and equity components. Under U.S. GAAP, this is required only if the stock warrants are "detachable."
Stock-based compensation	Topic 718	SFAS No. 123R	IFRS 2	No substantial differences
Reporting equity-related items as liabilities	Topic 480	SFAS No. 150	IAS 32	No substantial differences
Noncontrolling interest	Section 810-10-45 par. 16	SFAS No. 160 par. 5	IAS 27 par. 27	No substantial differences
Chapter 14: Investments in Debt and Equity Securities				
Classification as trading, available for sale, or held to maturity	Section 320-10-25 par. 1	SFAS No. 115 par. 6-12	IFRS 9 par 4.1, B4	Some differences, but application of *IFRS 9* has been delayed until 2015.
Equity method	Topic 323	APB Opinion No. 18	IAS 28	No substantial differences
Fair value option	Topic 825, "Fair Value Option" subsections	SFAS No. 159	IFRS 9	Interesting differences in terms of when the fair value option is acceptable, but application of *IFRS 9* has been delayed until 2015.
Derecognition of investment securities	Topic 860	SFAS No. 140	IAS 39 par. 20	Under U.S. GAAP, the transfer of a financial asset is recorded as a sale if control of the asset passes from the transferor to the transferee. Under IFRS, the transfer is recorded as a sale if the risks and rewards associated with the cash flows from the financial assets pass from the transferor to the transferee.
Classification of cash flows from the purchase and sale of investment securities	Section 320-10-45 par. 11	SFAS No. 115 par. 18	IAS 7 par. 15-16	Under IFRS, cash flows from the purchase and sale of trading securities are classified under operating activities; for other security categories, the cash flows are investing activities. Under U.S. GAAP, trading security cash flows may be operating or investing, depending on management intent.
Loan impairment	Section 310-10-35	SFAS No. 114	IAS 39 par. 58 through 65	No substantial differences
Chapter 15: Leases				
Lease classification criteria	Section 840-10-25 par. 1	SFAS No. 13 par. 7	IAS 17 par. 8-10	In substance, the standards are the same. IFRS provides less detail.
Lease discount rate (for lessees)	Section 840-10-25 par. 31	SFAS No. 13 par. 7	IAS 17 par. 20	In IFRS, no explicit mention is made of using the lower of the implicit rate or the incremental borrowing rate. Instead, the implicit rate is to be used if known.

Topic	FASB Accounting Standards Codification	Original FASB Standard	Corresponding IASB Standard	Differences Between U.S. GAAP and IFRS
Revenue recognition criteria (for lessor)	Section 840-10-25 par. 42	SFAS No. 13 par. 8	IAS 17 par. 42	Substantially the same. Rather than the two explicit criteria, IFRS merely says that a sale in a sales-type lease is recognized "in accordance with the policy followed by the entity for outright sales."
Initial direct costs (for lessors)	Section 840-20-35 par. 2 Section 840-30-35 par. 23 Section 840-30-25 par. 6	SFAS No. 13 par. 19 SFAS No. 13 par. 18 SFAS No. 13 par. 17	IAS 17 par. 38, 42	No apparent differences
Sale-leaseback accounting	Section 840-40-25 par. 3 Section 840-40-35 par. 1	SFAS No. 13 par. 7	IAS 17 par. 58-63	No apparent differences
Chapter 16: Income Taxes				
Use of currently enacted tax rates	Section 740-10-10 par. 3	SFAS No. 109 par. 18	IAS 12 par. 46	Under U.S. GAAP, currently enacted tax rates for future years are used in valuing deferred tax assets and liabilities. Under IFRS, tax rates that have been "substantively enacted" are also used. Substantively enacted tax rates are future tax rates that have been announced by the government but that have not yet been formally enacted into law.
Current/noncurrent classification of deferred tax assets and liabilities	Section 740-10-45 par. 4	SFAS No. 109 par. 41	IAS 1 par. 56	Under U.S. GAAP, deferred tax assets and liabilities are classified current or noncurrent based on the classification of the associated asset or liability. Under IFRS, all deferred tax items are classified as noncurrent.
Recognition of deferred tax assets	Section 740-10-30 par. 5e	SFAS No. 109 par. 17e	IAS 12 par. 24	Under U.S. GAAP, deferred tax assets are recognized if it is "more likely than not" (50%+ probability) that the future tax benefits will be realized. Under IFRS, the probability threshold is "probable," which is generally seen to be higher than "more likely than not."
Uncertain tax positions	Topic 740	FASB FIN No. 48	No specific accounting standard in IAS	Under IFRS, there is no standard regarding the recognition of a tax liability related to an uncertain tax position.
Cash paid for income taxes	Section 230-10-50 par. 2	SFAS No. 95 par. 121	IFRS 7 par. 35	Both U.S. GAAP and IFRS require separate disclosure of the amount of cash paid for income taxes. Under IFRS, this amount may be allocated among operating, investing, and financing activities.

Topic	FASB Accounting Standards Codification	Original FASB Standard	Corresponding IASB Standard	Differences Between U.S. GAAP and IFRS
Chapter 17: Employee Compensation—Payroll, Pensions, and Other Compensation Issues				
Compensated absences	Section 710-10-25 par. 1-8	SFAS No. 43 par. 6-16	IAS 19 par. 13-18	No substantial differences
Postemployment benefits	Section 712-10-05 par. 2-6 Section 712-10-15 par. 3-5 Section 712-10-25 par. 1-5	SFAS No. 112 par. 1-6 SFAS No. 88 par. 15	IAS 19 par. 159-171	No substantial differences
Discount rate for projected benefit obligation	Section 715-30-35 par. 43	SFAS No. 87 par. 44	IAS 19 par. 83	IFRS allows use of the interest rate on government bonds in countries lacking a developed corporate bond market.
Computation of net interest cost	Section 715-30-35 par. 43, 47	SFAS No. 87 par. 44, 45	IAS 19 par. 83, 123	A single interest rate is applied to the *net* pension asset or liability; there is no separate interest cost from the PBO and expected return from the pension fund
Prior service cost	Section 715-30-35 par. 10-11	SFAS No. 87 par. 24-25	IAS 19 par. 103	Under IFRS, the "past" service cost amount is recognized as an expense immediately.
Balance sheet numbers: one net number for the difference between PBO and the pension fund, with AOCI shown separately	Section 715-30-25 par. 1, 4	SFAS No. 87 par. 35, 38	IAS 19 par. 63	No substantial differences
Corridor amortization	Section 715-30-35 par. 24	SFAS No. 87 par. 32	IAS 19 par. 120(c)	Under IFRS there is no corridor amortization.
Settlements and curtailments	Various sections in Subtopics 715-30 and 715-60; illustrations in Section 715-30-55	SFAS No. 88	IAS 19 par. 109-112	No substantial differences
Disclosure	Sections 715-29-50 715-30-50 715-60-50	SFAS No. 132(R)	IAS 19 par. 135-152	No substantial differences
Postretirement benefits other than pensions	Subtopic 715-60	SFAS No. 106	In general, no distinction between pensions and other postretirement benefits. Guidance on medical benefits found in IAS 19 par. 96-98	Differences similar to the differences in accounting for pensions.

Topic	FASB Accounting Standards Codification	Original FASB Standard	Corresponding IASB Standard	Differences Between U.S. GAAP and IFRS
Chapter 19: Derivatives, Contingencies, Business Segments, and Interim Reports				
Accounting for derivatives	Topic 815	SFAS No. 133	IAS 39	No substantial differences at the conceptual level, but numerous technical differences that are beyond the scope of this book.
Recognition of contingent liabilities and contingent assets	Contingent liabilities: Section 450-20-25 Contingent assets: Section 450-30-25	SFAS No. 5 par. 3 and 17	IAS 37 par. 10, 27-28, 31, 34	Generally the same. Under IFRS, there is no requirement to disclose contingent guarantee obligations when their likelihood is remote.
Measurement of contingent liabilities	Section 450-20-30 par. 1	FIN No. 14 par. 3	IAS 37 par. 36-47	Under U.S. GAAP, the estimated liability is the low end of the estimated range if each estimate in the range is equally likely. Under IFRS, the estimated liability is the amount required to settle the obligation.
Segment reporting	Topic 280	SFAS No. 131	IFRS 8	No substantial differences
Relation between interim reporting and annual reporting	Section 270-10-45 par. 1-2	APB Opinion No. 28 par. 9	IAS 34 par. 28	Under U.S. GAAP, an interim period is viewed as a subcomponent of the annual period. Under IFRS, accounting principles are applied to an interim period in the same way they are applied to an annual period.
Chapter 20: Accounting Changes and Error Corrections				
Disclosure after a business combination	Section 805-10-50 par. 1-2	SFAS No. 141(R) par. 68	IFRS 3 par. 59-63 and B64-B67	No substantial differences
Change in accounting principle	Section 250-10-45 par. 1-16 Section 250-10-50 par. 1-3	SFAS No. 154 par. 4-18 APB No. 28 par. 28	IAS 8 par. 14-31	No substantial differences
Change in accounting estimate	Section 250-10-45 par. 17-20 Section 250-10-50 par. 4-5	SFAS No. 154 par. 19-22 SFAS No. 157 par. 20	IAS 8 par. 32-40	No substantial differences
Correction of an error	Section 250-10-45 par. 22-28 Section 250-10-50 par. 7-11	SFAS No. 154 par. 25-26 SFAS No. 16 par. 10-15 APB No. 9 par. 17-18 APB No. 9 par. 26-27 APB No. 28 par. 29	IAS 8 par. 41-49	No substantial differences